SELECTED SOLUTIONS MANUAL

Noel George, *Ryerson University*

Susan Morante, *Mount Royal University*

Alicia Paterno Parsi, *Duquesne University*

Arash Parsi, *Duquesne University*

Kathleen Thrush Shaginaw, *Community College of Philadelphia and Particular Solutions, Inc.*

Mary Beth Kramer, *University of Delaware*

CHEMISTRY
A Molecular Approach
Canadian Edition

Nivaldo J. Tro

Travis Fridgen

Lawton E. Shaw

With Special Contributions by
Robert S. Boikess

PEARSON

Toronto

Vice-President, Editorial Director: Gary Bennett
Marketing Manager: Jenna Wulff
Developmental Editor: Toni Chahley
Project Manager: Rachel Thompson
Production Editor: Leanne Rancourt
Copy Editor/Proofreader: Leanne Rancourt

10 9 8 7 6 5 4 3 2 1 [CP]

ISBN 978-0-13-306048-5

Contents

Preface

The *Selected Solutions Manual* to accompany the Canadian edition of *Chemistry: A Molecular Approach* contains complete solutions to the odd-numbered questions and problems in the textbook:

- Review Questions
- Problems by Topic
- Cumulative Problems
- Challenge Problems
- Conceptual Problems

Solutions for all textbook questions are found in the *Complete Solutions Manual* (978-0-13-306372-1).

The vision of this Selected Solutions Manual is to give guidance that is useful for both the struggling student and the advanced student. The key to success in chemistry is problem solving. This extensively revised **Solutions Manual** can be a valuable tool when used correctly and can help you improve your performance in this course. Practice is imperative in problem solving, as it is with any skill. Work through problems step-by-step and develop your problem-solving strategy. First check your work based upon your own knowledge. Look at your answer. Is it reasonable? Are the units correct? Use this manual to compare your results with that of the authors. If you have made a mistake, examine the steps outlined within the **Solutions Manual** to determine where you went astray.

An important feature of this *Selected Solutions Manual* is that answers for the review questions are given. This will help you review the major concepts in the chapter.

The format of the solutions very closely follows the format seen in the textbook. Each mathematical problem includes **Given, Find, Conceptual Plan, Solution,** and **Check** sections.

Given and Find: Many students struggle with taking the written problem, parsing the information into categories, and determining the goal of the problem. It is also important to know which pieces of information in the problem are not necessary to solve the problem and if additional information needs to be gathered from sources, such as tables in the textbook.

Conceptual Plan: The conceptual plan shows a step-by-step method to solve the problem. In many cases, the given quantities need to be converted to a different unit. Under each of the arrows is the equation, constant, or conversion factor needed to complete this portion of the problem. In the "Problems by Topic" section of the end-of-chapter exercises, the odd-numbered and even-numbered problems are paired. This will allow you to use a conceptual plan from an odd-numbered problem in this manual as a starting point to solve the following even-numbered problem. Students should keep in mind that the examples shown are one way to solve the problems. Other mathematically equivalent solutions may be possible.

5.49 **Given:** m (CO_2) = 28.8 g, P = 742 mmHg, and T = 22 °C **Find:** V

Conceptual Plan: °C $\rightarrow$ K and mmHg $\rightarrow$ atm and g $\rightarrow$ mol then $n, P, T \rightarrow V$

$$K = °C + 273.15 \qquad \frac{1\ atm}{760\ mm\ Hg} \qquad \frac{1\ mol}{44.01\ g} \qquad PV = nRT$$

Solution: T_1 = 22 °C + 273.15 = 295 K, $P = 742\ \overline{mmHg} \times \dfrac{1\ atm}{760\ \overline{mmHg}}$ = 0.976316 atm,

$n = 28.8\ \overline{g} \times \dfrac{1\ mol}{44.01\ \overline{g}}$ = 0.654397 mol $PV = nRT$ Rearrange to solve for V.

$$V = \frac{nRT}{P} = \frac{0.654397\ \overline{mol} \times 0.08206\ \dfrac{L \cdot \overline{atm}}{\overline{mol} \cdot K} \times 295\ K}{0.976316\ \overline{atm}} = 16.2\ L$$

Check: The units (L) are correct. The magnitude of the answer (16 L) makes sense because one mole of an ideal gas under standard conditions (273 K and 1 atm) occupies 22.4 L. Although these are not standard conditions, they are close enough for a ballpark check of the answer. Since this gas sample contains 0.65 moles, a volume of 16 L is reasonable.

Solution: The solution section will walk you through solving the problem following the conceptual plan. Equations are rearranged to solve for the appropriate quantity. Intermediate results are shown with additional digits to minimize round-off error. The units are cancelled in each appropriate step.

Check: The check section confirms that the units in the answer are correct. This section also challenges the student to think about whether the magnitude of the answer makes sense. Thinking about what is a reasonable answer can help to uncover errors, such as calculation errors.

About the Authors

Noel George, Ph.D., is an Associate Professor in the Department of Chemistry and Biology at Ryerson University in Toronto, Ontario. He received his B.Sc. in Chemistry from Queen's University in 1992 and his Ph.D. in 1998 from the University of Guelph. Since starting at Ryerson he has focused his research on Chemical Education. He has a particular interest in the use of technology in education, concept inventories, and the assessment of knowledge gains in chemistry; applying those interests to the teaching of large enrollment general chemistry courses is a significant component of his research. Noel is passionate about teaching and engaging his students; his efforts have been recognized through multiple nominations for teaching awards, including one for TVO's Best Lecturer competition.

Susan Morante, M.Sc., is an Associate Professor and the Chair of the Department of Chemistry at Mount Royal University. She has also taught at the University of Calgary. She currently teaches organic chemistry but has taught most first- and second-year courses at one time or another. Before beginning her career in postsecondary education, Susan worked in various research and industrial labs. During that time she did research on the red blood cells of premature infants; set up protocols for intact, isolated cell membranes known as "ghosts"; and worked as a quality control chemist in an ink factory where she helped develop the formula for the first fluorescent highlighter pen to be patented in Canada. Susan is currently working on a project with her students to identify the pigments in bee hair.

Alicia Paterno Parsi, Ph.D., is an Assistant Professor in the Department of Chemistry and Biochemistry at Duquesne University. She earned her Ph.D. in Chemistry at the University of Illinois Urbana-Champaign on synthesis of novel bis-porphyrin electron transfer complexes. At Duquesne she directs the general Chemistry program, where she teaches in a large classroom setting and coordinates the recitations and laboratories. Alicia also leads training workshops for new graduate student teaching assistants.

Arash Parsi, Ph.D., is a Principal Research Chemist at the Westinghouse Electric Company in Pittsburgh, Pennsylvania. He earned his Ph.D. in Chemistry at the University of Illinois Urbana-Champaign on sonochemical synthesis and characterization of nanophasic catalysts. At Westinghouse, his work focuses on understanding corrosion product formation and transport of austenitic alloys. He also teaches general chemistry recitation.

1 Units of Measurement for Physical and Chemical Change

Review Questions

1.1 The main goal of chemistry is to seek to understand the behaviour of matter by studying the behaviour of atoms and molecules.

1.3 A physical property is one that a substance displays without changing its composition, whereas a chemical property is one that a substance displays only by changing its composition via a chemical change.

1.5 In chemical and physical changes, matter often exchanges energy with its surroundings. In these exchanges, the total energy is always conserved; energy is neither created nor destroyed. Systems with high potential energy tend to change in the direction of lower potential energy, releasing energy into the surroundings.

1.7 The SI base units include the metre (m) for length, the kilogram (kg) for mass, the second (s) for time, and the Kelvin (K) for temperature.

1.9 Prefix multipliers are used with the standard units of measurement to change the value of the unit by powers of 10.

For example, the kilometre has the prefix "kilo," meaning 1000 or 10^3. Therefore:

1 kilometre = 1000 metres = 10^3 metre

Similarly, the millimetre has the prefix "milli," meaning 0.001 or 10^{-3}.

1 millimetre = 0.001 metres = 10^{-3} metres

1.11 The density (d) of a substance is the ratio of its mass (m) to its volume (V):

$$\text{Density} = \frac{\text{mass}}{\text{Volume}} \text{ or } d = \frac{m}{V}$$

The density of a substance is an example of an intensive property, one that is independent of the amount of the substance. Mass is one of the properties used to calculate the density of a substance. Mass, in contrast, is an extensive property, one that depends on the amount of the substance.

1.13 Measured quantities are reported so that the number of digits reflects the uncertainty in the measurement. The nonplaceholding digits in a reported number are called significant figures.

1.15 In addition or subtraction, the result carries the same number of decimal places as the quantity with the fewest decimal places.

1.17   When taking an antilogarithm of a number, the mantissa of the number whose antilogarithm is being calculated determines the final significant figures in the answer. For example, $10^{1.236} = 17.2$

1.19   Random error is error that has equal probability of being too high or too low. Almost all measurements have some degree of random error. Random error can, with enough trials, average itself out. Systematic error is error that tends toward being either too high or too low. Systematic error does not average out with repeated trials.

Problems By Topic

1.21   (a)   physical property (colour can be observed without making or breaking chemical bonds)

        (b)   chemical property (combustion requires making and breaking of chemical bonds)

        (c)   physical property (the phase can be observed without making or breaking chemical bonds)

        (d)   physical property (density can be observed without making or breaking chemical bonds)

        (e)   physical property (mixing does not involve making or breaking chemical bonds, so this can be observed without making or breaking chemical bonds)

1.23   (a)   chemical property (burning involves breaking and making bonds, so bonds must be broken and made to observe this property)

        (b)   physical property (shininess is a physical property and so can be observed without making or breaking chemical bonds)

        (c)   physical property (odour can be observed without making or breaking chemical bonds)

        (d)   chemical property (burning involves breaking and making bonds, so bonds must be broken and made to observe this property)

1.25   (a)   chemical change (new compounds are formed as methane and oxygen react to form carbon dioxide and water)

        (b)   physical change (vaporization is a phase change and does not involve the making or breaking of chemical bonds)

        (c)   chemical change (new compounds are formed as propane and oxygen react to form carbon dioxide and water)

        (d)   chemical change (new compounds are formed as the metal in the frame is converted to oxides)

1.27   (a)   physical change (vaporization is a phase change and does not involve the making or breaking of chemical bonds)

        (b)   chemical change (new compounds are formed)

        (c)   physical change (vaporization is a phase change and does not involve the making or breaking of chemical bonds)

Units in Measurement

1.29   (a)   **Given:** T = 0.00 °C **Find:** T in kelvins

               Conceptual Plan: Use the relationship $\dfrac{T}{K} = \dfrac{T_C}{°C} + 273.15$

               Solution: $\dfrac{T}{K} = \dfrac{0.00\ °C}{°C} + 273.15; T = 273.15\ K$

               Check: Temperature in kelvins is 273.15 units larger than °C. The answer has two decimal places.

    (b)   **Given:** T = 77 K **Find:** T in °C

          Conceptual Plan: $\dfrac{T_C}{°C} = \dfrac{T}{K} - 273.15$

          Solution: $\dfrac{T_C}{°C} = \dfrac{77\ K}{K} - 273.15;\ T = -196\ °C$

          Check: Temperature in °C is 273.15 units smaller than in kelvins. The answer has no decimal places.

    (c)   **Given:** T = 37.0 °C **Find:** T in kelvins

          Conceptual Plan: $\dfrac{T}{K} = \dfrac{T_C}{°C} + 273.15$

          Solution: $\dfrac{T}{K} = \dfrac{37.0\ °C}{°C} + 273.15;\ T = 310.2\ K$

          Check: Temperature in kelvins is 273.15 units larger than °C. The answer has one decimal place.

1.31   **Given:** T = –77.5 °C **Find:** T in K

       Conceptual Plan: $\dfrac{T}{K} = \dfrac{T_C}{°C} + 273.15$

       Solution: $\dfrac{T}{K} = \dfrac{-77.5\ °C}{°C} + 273.15;\ T = 195.7\ K$

       Check: Temperature in kelvins is 273.15 units larger than °C. The answer has one decimal place.

1.33   Use Table 1.2 to determine the appropriate prefix multiplier and substitute the meaning into the expressions.

    (a) 10^{-9} is equivalent to "nano" so 1.2×10^{-9} m = 1.2 nanometres = 1.2 nm

    (b) 10^{-15} is equivalent to "femto" so 22×10^{-15} s = 22 femtoseconds = 22 fs

    (c) 10^{9} is equivalent to "giga" so 1.5×10^{9} g = 1.5 gigagrams = 1.5 Gg

    (d) 10^{6} is equivalent to "mega" so 3.5×10^{6} L = 3.5 megalitres = 3.5 ML

1.35   Use Table 1.2 to determine the appropriate prefix multiplier and substitute the meaning into the expressions.

    (a) 10^{-9} is equivalent to "nano" so 4.5 ns = 4.5 nanoseconds = 4.5×10^{-9} s

    (b) 10^{-15} is equivalent to "femto" so 18 fs = 18 femtoseconds = 18×10^{-15} s = 1.8×10^{-14} s
          Remember that in scientific notation the first number should be smaller than 10.

    (c) 10^{-12} is equivalent to "pico" so 128 pm = 128×10^{-12} m = 1.28×10^{-10} m
          Remember that in scientific notation the first number should be smaller than 10.

    (d) 10^{-6} is equivalent to "micro" so 35 μm = 35 micrograms = 35×10^{-6} g = 3.5×10^{-5} m
          Remember that in scientific notation the first number should be smaller than 10.

1.37   (b)   **Given:** 515 km **Find:** dm

          Conceptual Plan: km $\rightarrow$ m $\rightarrow$ dm
                    $\dfrac{1000\ m}{1 km}$ $\dfrac{10\ dm}{1 m}$

          Solution: 515 k̶m̶ x $\dfrac{1000\ m̶}{1 k̶m̶}$ x $\dfrac{10\ dm}{1 m̶}$ = 5.15×10^{6} dm

          Check: The units (dm) are correct. The magnitude of the answer (10^{6}) makes physical sense because a decimetre is a much smaller unit than a kilometre.

          Given: 515 km **Find:** cm

          Conceptual Plan: km $\rightarrow$ m $\rightarrow$ cm
                    $\dfrac{1000\ m}{1 km}$ $\dfrac{100\ cm}{1 m}$

          Solution: 515 k̶m̶ x $\dfrac{1000\ m̶}{1 k̶m̶}$ x $\dfrac{100\ cm}{1 m̶}$ = 5.15×10^{7} cm

          Check: The units (cm) are correct. The magnitude of the answer (10^{7}) makes physical sense because a centimetre is a much smaller unit than either a kilometre or a decimetre.

(c)   **Given:** 122.355 s **Find:** ms

Conceptual Plan: s → ms

$$\frac{1000 \text{ ms}}{1\text{s}}$$

Solution: $122.355 \text{ s} \times \dfrac{1000 \text{ ms}}{1 \text{ s}} = 1.22355 \times 10^5 \text{ ms}$

Check: The units (ms) are correct. The magnitude of the answer (10^5) makes physical sense because a millisecond is a much smaller unit than a second.

Given: 122.355 s **Find:** ks

Conceptual Plan: s → ks

$$\frac{1 \text{ ks}}{1000 \text{ s}}$$

Solution: $122.355 \text{ s} \times \dfrac{1 \text{ ks}}{1000 \text{ s}} = 1.22355 \times 10^{-1} \text{ ks} = 0.122355 \text{ ks}$

Check: The units (ks) are correct. The magnitude of the answer (10^{-1}) makes physical sense because a kilosecond is a much larger unit than a second.

(d)   **Given:** 3.345 kJ **Find:** J

Conceptual Plan: kJ → J

$$\frac{1000 \text{ J}}{1\text{kJ}}$$

Solution: $3.345 \text{ kJ} \times \dfrac{1000 \text{ J}}{1 \text{ kJ}} = 3.345 \times 10^3 \text{ J}$

Check: The units (J) are correct. The magnitude of the answer (10^3) makes physical sense because a joule is a much smaller unit than a kilojoule.

Given: 3.345×10^3 J (from above) **Find:** mJ

Conceptual Plan: J → mJ

$$\frac{1000 \text{ mJ}}{1\text{ J}}$$

Solution: $3.345 \times 10^3 \text{ J} \times \dfrac{1000 \text{ mJ}}{1 \text{ J}} = 3.345 \times 10^6 \text{ mJ}$

Check: The units (mJ) are correct. The magnitude of the answer (10^6) makes physical sense because a millijoule is a much smaller unit than a joule.

1.39   (a)   **Given:** 254 998 m **Find:** km

Conceptual Plan: m → km

$$\frac{1 \text{ km}}{1000 \text{ m}}$$

Solution: $254 \text{ 998 m} \times \dfrac{1 \text{ km}}{1000 \text{ m}} = 2.54998 \times 10^2 \text{ km} = 254.998 \text{ km}$

Check: The units (km) are correct. The magnitude of the answer (10^2) makes physical sense because a kilometre is a much larger unit than a metre.

(b)   **Given:** 254 998 m **Find:** Mm

Conceptual Plan: m → Mm

$$\frac{1 \text{ Mm}}{10^6 \text{ m}}$$

Solution: $254 \text{ 998 m} \times \dfrac{1 \text{ Mm}}{10^6 \text{ m}} = 2.54998 \times 10^{-1} \text{ Mm} = 0.254998 \text{ Mm}$

Check: The units (Mm) are correct. The magnitude of the answer (10^{-1}) makes physical sense because a megametre is a much larger unit than a metre or kilometre.

(c)   **Given:** 254 998 m **Find:** mm

Conceptual Plan: m → mm

$$\frac{1000 \text{ mm}}{1 \text{ m}}$$

Solution: $254 \text{ 998 m} \times \dfrac{1000 \text{ mm}}{1 \text{ m}} = 2.54998 \times 10^8 \text{ mm}$

Check: The units (mm) are correct. The magnitude of the answer (10^8) makes physical sense because a millimetre is a much smaller unit than a metre.

(d) **Given:** 254 998 m **Find:** cm

Conceptual Plan: m $\rightarrow$ **cm**

$$\frac{100\ cm}{1\ m}$$

Solution: $254\ 998\ m \times \dfrac{100\ cm}{1\ m} = 2.54998 \times 10^7\ cm$

Check: The units (cm) are correct. The magnitude of the answer (10^7) makes physical sense because a centimetre is a much smaller unit than a metre, but larger than a millimetre.

1.41 **Given:** 1 m square 1 m^2 **Find:** cm^2

Conceptual Plan: 1 m^2 $\rightarrow$ **cm^2**

$$\frac{100\ cm}{1\ m}$$

Notice that for squared units, the conversion factors must be squared.

Solution: $1\ m^2 \times \dfrac{(100\ cm)^2}{(1 m)^2} = 1 \times 10^4\ cm^2$

Check: The units of the answer are correct and the magnitude makes sense. The unit centimetre is smaller than a metre, so the value in square centimetres should be larger than in square metres.

Density

1.43 **Given:** mass and volume of penny, 2.35 g and 0.413 cm^3 respectively.

Find: Density of penny.

Conceptual Plan: $d_{penny} = m/V$, **compare to** d_{Cu}

Solution: $d_{penny} = \dfrac{m}{V} = \dfrac{2.35\ g}{0.413\ cm^3} = 5.69\ g\ cm^{-3}$

The density of pure copper is $8.96\ g\ cm^{-3}$. Therefore, this penny is not pure copper (and more likely, it is simply copper plated).

Check: The answer makes sense because the coin would have to be heavier to be copper. No pennies have been made of pure copper in several decades. A copper coin weighing 2.35 g contains roughly 2.5 ¢ of Cu. This penny is more likely copper plated.

1.45 **Given:** $m = 4.10 \times 10^3$ g, $V = 3.25$ L **Find:** d in $g\ cm^{-3}$

Conceptual Plan: $m, V \rightarrow d$ **then** $L \rightarrow cm^3$

$$d = m/V \qquad \frac{1000\ cm^3}{1\ L}$$

Solution: $d = \dfrac{4.10 \times 10^3\ g}{3.25\ L} \times \dfrac{1\ L}{1000\ cm^3} = 1.26\ g\ cm^{-3}$

Check: The units ($g\ cm^{-3}$) are correct. The magnitude of the answer seems correct.

1.47 (a) **Given:** $d = 1.11\ g\ cm^{-3}$, $V = 417$ mL **Find:** m

Conceptual Plan: $d, V \rightarrow m$ **then** $cm^3 \rightarrow$ **mL**

$$d = m/V \qquad \frac{1\ mL}{1\ cm^3}$$

Solution: $d = m/V$ Rearrange by multiplying both sides of equation by V. $\quad m = d \times V$

$$m = 1.11\ \frac{g}{cm^3} \times \frac{1\ cm^3}{1\ mL} \times 417\ mL = 4.63 \times 10^2\ g$$

Check: The units (g) are correct. The magnitude of the answer seems correct considering the value of the density is about $1\ g\ cm^{-3}$.

(b) **Given:** $d = 1.11\ g\ cm^{-3}$, $m = 4.1$ kg **Find:** V in L

Conceptual Plan: $d, V \rightarrow m$ **then** $kg \rightarrow$ **g and** $cm^3 \rightarrow$ **L**

$$d = m/V \qquad \frac{1000\ g}{1\ kg} \qquad \frac{1\ L}{1000\ cm^3}$$

Solution: $d = m/V$ Rearrange by multiplying both sides of equation by V and dividing both sides of the equation by d.

$$V = \frac{m}{d} = \frac{4.1\ kg}{1.11\ g\ cm^{-3}} \times \frac{1000\ g}{1\ kg} = 3.7 \times 10^3\ cm^3 \times \frac{1\ L}{1000\ cm^3} = 3.7\ L$$

Check: The units (L) are correct. The magnitude of the answer seems correct considering the value of the density is about 1 g cm^{-3}.

1.49   **Given:** $V = 245$ L $d = 0.803$ g mL^{-1} **Find:** m

Conceptual Plan: g mL^{-1} $\rightarrow$ g L^{-1} then d, $V \rightarrow m$

$$\frac{1000 \text{ mL}}{1 \text{ L}} \qquad d = m/V$$

Solution: $d = m/V$ Rearrange by multiplying both sides of equation by V. $m = d \times V$

$$m = 245 \text{ L} \times \frac{1000 \text{ mL}}{1 \text{ L}} \times (0.803 \text{ g mL}^{-1}) = 1.97 \times 10^5 \text{ g} = 1.97 \times 10^2 \text{ kg}$$

Check: The units (g) are correct. The magnitude of the answer seems correct considering the value of the density is less than 1 g mL^{-1} and the volume is very large.

1.51   The product of mass and acceleration is Force, F. Work (W) is when force is multiplied by distance

$W = m(kg) \times a(m\,s^{-2}) \times d(m)$

The unit for Work, therefore, is kg m^2 s^{-2}, or Joules (J)

The Reliability of a Measurement and Significant Figures

1.53   In order to obtain the readings, look to see where the bottom of the meniscus lies. Estimate the distance between two markings on the device.

(a)   73.5 mL – the meniscus appears to be sitting between the 73 mL mark and the 74 mL mark.

(b)   88.2 °C – the mercury is between the 88 °C mark and the 89 °C mark, but it is closer to the lower number.

(c)   645 mL – the meniscus appears to be just above the 640 mL mark.

1.55   Remember that

1.   interior zeroes (zeroes between two numbers) are significant.

2.   leading zeroes (zeroes to the left of the first nonzero number) are not significant. They only serve to locate the decimal point.

3.   trailing zeroes (zeroes at the end of a number) are categorized as follows:

- Trailing zeroes after a decimal point are always significant.

- Trailing zeroes before an implied decimal point are ambiguous and should be avoided by using scientific notation or by inserting a decimal point at the end of the number.

(a)   1 050 501 km

(b)   0.0020 m

(c)   0.0000000000000002 s

(d)   0.001090 cm

1.57   Remember all of the rules from Section 1.7.

(a)   Three significant figures. The 3, 1, and the 2 are significant (rule 1). The leading zeroes only mark the decimal place and are therefore not significant (rule 3).

(b)   Ambiguous. The 3, 1, and the 2 are significant (rule 1). The trailing zeroes occur before an implied decimal point and are therefore ambiguous (rule 4). Without more information, we would assume 3 significant figures. It is better to write this as 3.12×10^5 to indicate three significant figures or as 3.12000×10^5 to indicate six (rule 4).

(c)   Three significant figures. The 3, 1, and the 2 are significant (rule 1).

(d)   Five significant figures. The 1s, 3, 2, and 7 are significant (rule 1).

(e)   Ambiguous. The 2 is significant (rule 1). The trailing zeroes occur before an implied decimal point and are therefore ambiguous (rule 4). Without more information, we would assume one significant figure. It is better to write this as 2×10^3 to indicate one significant figure or as 2.000×10^3 to indicate four (rule 4).

1.59   (a) $\pi = 3.14$: 3 significant figures

        (b) $1 \text{ m}^3 = 1000 \text{ dm}^3$: exact number (by definition), unlimited number of significant figures

        (c) 5683.91 km^2: 6 significant figures

        (d) $3.0 \times 10^8 \text{ m s}^{-1}$: 2 significant figures

1.61   (a)   156.9 – The 8 is rounded up since the next digit is a 5.

        (b)   156.8 – The last two digits are dropped since 4 is less than 5.

        (c)   156.8 – The last two digits are dropped since 4 is less than 5.

        (d)   156.9 – The 8 is rounded up since the next digit is a 9, which is greater than 5.

Significant Figures in Calculations

1.63   (a) $9.15 \div 4.970 = 1.84$ – Three significant figures are allowed to reflect the three significant figures in the least precisely known quantity (9.15).

        (b) $1.54 \times 0.03060 \times 0.69 = 0.033$ – Two significant figures are allowed to reflect the two significant figures in the least precisely known quantity (0.69). The intermediate answer (0.03251556) is rounded up since the first nonsignificant digit is a 5.

        (c) $27.5 \times 1.82 \div 100.04 = 0.500$ – Three significant figures are allowed to reflect the three significant figures in the least precisely known quantity (27.5 and 1.82). The intermediate answer (0.50029988) is truncated since the first nonsignificant digit is a 2, which is less than 5.

        (d) $(2.290 \times 10^6) \div (6.7 \times 10^4) = 34$ – Two significant figures are allowed to reflect the two significant figures in the least precisely known quantity (6.7×10^4). The intermediate answer (34.17910448) is truncated since the first nonsignificant digit is a 1, which is less than 5.

1.65   (a)   43.7
                  − 2.341
                  41.359 = 41.4

Round the intermediate answer to one decimal place to reflect the quantity with the fewest decimal places (43.7). Round the last digit up since the first nonsignificant digit is 5.

        (b)   17.6
               + 2.838
               + 2.3
           + 110.77
              133.508 = 133.5

Round the intermediate answer to one decimal place to reflect the quantity with the fewest decimal places (2.3). Truncate nonsignificant digits since the first nonsignificant digit is 0.

        (c)   19.6
             + 58.33
             − 4.974
            72.956 = 73.0

Round the intermediate answer to one decimal place to reflect the quantity with the fewest decimal places (19.6). Round the last digit up since the first nonsignificant digit is 5.

(d)   5.99
       − 5.572
         0.418 = 0.42

Round the intermediate answer to two decimal places to reflect the quantity with the fewest decimal places (5.99). Round the last digit up since the first nonsignificant digit is 8.

1.67   Perform operations in parentheses first. Keep track of significant figures in each step by noting which is the last significant digit in an intermediate result.

(a)   (24.6681 x 2.38) + 332.58 = 58.$\underline{7}$10078
                        + 332.58
                        391.290078 = 391.3

The first intermediate answer has one significant digit to the right of the decimal, because it is allowed three significant figures (reflecting the quantity with the fewest significant figures (2.38)). Underline the most significant digit in this answer. Round the next intermediate answer to one decimal place to reflect the quantity with the fewest decimal places (58.7). Round the last digit up since the first nonsignificant digit is 9.

(b) $\dfrac{(85.3 - 21.489)}{0.0059} = \dfrac{63.\underline{8}11}{0.0059} = 1.\underline{0}81542 \times 10^4 = 1.1 \times 10^4$

The first intermediate answer has one significant digit to the right of the decimal, to reflect the quantity with the fewest decimal places (85.3). Underline the most significant digit in this answer. Round the next intermediate answer to two significant figures to reflect the quantity with the fewest significant figures (0.0059). Round the last digit up since the first nonsignificant digit is 8.

(c)   (512 ÷ 986.7) + 5.44 = 0.51$\underline{8}$9014
                        + 5.44
                        5.9589014 = 5.96

The first intermediate answer has three significant figures and three significant digits to the right of the decimal, reflecting the quantity with the fewest significant figures (512). Underline the most significant digit in this answer. Round the next intermediate answer to two decimal places to reflect the quantity with the fewest decimal places (5.44). Round the last digit up since the first nonsignificant digit is 8.

(d)   [(28.7 x 10^5) ÷ 48.533] + 144.99 = 59$\underline{1}$35.01
                        +   144.99
                        59280.01 = 59300 = 5.93 x 10^4

The first intermediate answer has three significant figures, reflecting the quantity with the fewest significant figures (28.7 x 10^5). Underline the most significant digit in this answer. Since the number is so large this means that when the addition is performed, the most significant digit is the 100's place. Round the next intermediate answer to the 100's places and put in scientific notation to remove any ambiguity. Note that the last digit is rounded up since the first nonsignificant digit is 8.

Unit Conversions

1.69   (a)   **Given:** 3.25 kg **Find:** g
                Conceptual Plan: kg → g
                Solution: $3.25 \text{ kg} \times \dfrac{1000 \text{ g}}{1 \text{ kg}} = 3.25 \times 10^3 \text{ g}$
                Check: Unit of g is correct, and the magnitude makes sense because g is much smaller than kg.

(b)   **Given:** 250 μs **Find:** s
       Conceptual Plan: μs $\rightarrow$ s

       Solution: $250\mu s \times \dfrac{1\ s}{1 \times 10^6 \mu s} = 2.5 \times 10^{-4}\ s$

       Check: Unit of s is correct, and the magnitude makes sense because μs is much smaller than s.

(c)   **Given:** 0.345 L **Find:** cm^3
       Conceptual Plan: L $\rightarrow$ cm^3

       Solution: $0.345\ \cancel{L} \times \dfrac{1000\ cm^3}{1\ \cancel{L}} = 345\ cm^3$

       Check: Unit of cm^3 is correct, and the magnitude makes sense because cm^3 is a thousand-fold smaller than L.

(d)   **Given:** 257 dm **Find:** km
       Conceptual Plan: 257 dm $\rightarrow$ m $\rightarrow$ km

       Solution: $257\ dm \times \dfrac{1\ m}{10\ dm} \times \dfrac{1\ km}{1000\ m} = 0.0257\ km$

       Check: The unit of km is correct. Consulting Table 1.2 of the text, deci is five orders of magnitude smaller than kilo, so the magnitude of the answer also makes sense.

1.71   **Given:** d = 10.0 km, v = 3.5 m s^{-1} **Find:** time in minutes
        Conceptual Plan: (1) km $\rightarrow$ m, (2) Find time using $t = d/v$, (3) t(s) $\rightarrow$ t(min).

        Solution: $d = 10.0\ km \times \dfrac{1000\ m}{1\ km} = 10\ 000\ m$ (two significant figures)

        $t = \dfrac{d}{v} = \dfrac{10000\ m}{3.5\ m\ s^{-1}} = 2857.14\ s$

        $t = 2857.14\ s \times \dfrac{1\ min}{60\ s} = 48\ min$

        Check: The unit is correct. A speed of 3.5 m s^{-1} is 210 m min^{-1}. To travel 10 000 m, the runner has to run roughly 50 minutes, which is very close to the answer. The final answer has two significant figures because the speed has two significant figures also.

1.73   (a)   **Given:** 195 m^2 **Find:** km^2
               Conceptual Plan: m^2 $\rightarrow$ km^2
               $$\dfrac{(1\ km)^2}{(1000\ m)^2}$$
               Notice that for squared units, the conversion factors must be squared.

               Solution: $195\ \cancel{m^2} \times \dfrac{(1\ km)^2}{(1000\ \cancel{m})^2} = 1.95 \times 10^{-4}\ km^2$

               Check: The units (km^2) are correct. The magnitude of the answer (10^{-4}) makes physical sense because a kilometre is a much larger unit than a metre.

        (b)   **Given:** 195 m^2 **Find:** dm^2
               Conceptual Plan: m^2 $\rightarrow$ dm^2
               $$\dfrac{(10\ dm)^2}{(1\ m)^2}$$
               Notice that for squared units, the conversion factors must be squared.

               Solution: $195\ \cancel{m^2} \times \dfrac{(10\ dm)^2}{(1\ \cancel{m})^2} = 1.95 \times 10^4\ dm^2$

               Check: The units (dm^2) are correct. The magnitude of the answer (10^4) makes physical sense because a decimetre is a much smaller unit than a metre.

        (c)   **Given:** 195 m^2 **Find:** cm^2
               Conceptual Plan: m^2 $\rightarrow$ cm^2
               $$\dfrac{(100\ cm)^2}{(1\ m)^2}$$

Notice that for squared units, the conversion factors must be squared.

Solution: $195 \text{ m}^2 \times \dfrac{(100 \text{ cm})^2}{(1 \text{ m})^2} = 1.95 \times 10^6 \text{ cm}^2$

Check: The units (cm^2) are correct. The magnitude of the answer (10^6) makes physical sense because a centimetre is a much smaller unit than a metre.

1.75   **Given:** Area = $2.5 \times 10^6 \text{ hm}^2$ **Find:** m^2 and km^2
Conceptual Plan: $\text{hm}^2 \rightarrow \text{m}^2 \rightarrow \text{km}^2$

Solution: $2.5 \times 10^6 \text{ hm}^2 \times \left(\dfrac{100 \text{ m}}{1 \text{ hm}}\right)^2 = 2.5 \times 10^{10} \text{ m}^2$

$2.5 \times 10^{10} \text{ m}^2 \times \left(\dfrac{1 \text{ km}}{1000 \text{ m}}\right)^2 = 2.5 \times 10^4 \text{ km}^2$

Check: The units (m^2 and km^2) are correct. A hectametre is 100 times larger than a metre, so a hm^2 is 10^4 times larger, so the magnitude of the first answer makes sense. Similarly, a km^2 is 10^6 fold larger than m^2, which is what is expected for the second part of the answer.

1.77   **Given:** 6.5 kg   **Find:** mL **Other:** 80 mg/0.80 mL and 15 mg kg^{-1} body
Conceptual Plan: $\text{kg body} \rightarrow \text{mg} \rightarrow \text{mL}$

$\dfrac{15 \text{ mg}}{1 \text{ kg body}} \quad \dfrac{0.80 \text{ mL}}{80 \text{ mg}}$

Solution: $6.5 \text{ kg} \times \dfrac{15 \text{ mg}}{1 \text{ kg body}} \times \dfrac{0.80 \text{ mL}}{80 \text{ mg}} = 0.9523809524 \text{ mL} = 0.95 \text{ mL}$

Check: The units are correct. The magnitude of the answer (1 mL) makes physical sense because it is reasonable amount of liquid to give to a baby. Two significant figures are allowed because of the statement in the problem. Truncate the last digit because the first nonsignificant digit is a 2.

Cumulative Problems

1.79   **Given:** solar year   **Find:** seconds
Other: 60 seconds/minute; 60 minutes/ hour; 24 hours/solar day; and 365.24 solar days/solar year
Conceptual Plan: $\text{yr} \rightarrow \text{day} \rightarrow \text{hr} \rightarrow \text{min} \rightarrow \text{sec}$

$\dfrac{365.24 \text{ day}}{1 \text{ solar yr}} \quad \dfrac{24 \text{ hr}}{1 \text{ day}} \quad \dfrac{60 \text{ min}}{1 \text{ hr}} \quad \dfrac{60 \text{ sec}}{1 \text{ min}}$

Solution: $1 \text{ solar yr} \times \dfrac{365.24 \text{ day}}{1 \text{ solar yr}} \times \dfrac{24 \text{ hr}}{1 \text{ day}} \times \dfrac{60 \text{ min}}{1 \text{ hr}} \times \dfrac{60 \text{ sec}}{1 \text{ min}} = 3.1556736 \times 10^7 \text{ sec} = 3.1557 \times 10^7 \text{ sec}$

Check: The units (seconds) are correct. The magnitude of the answer (10^7) makes physical sense because each conversion factor increases the value of the answer—a second is many orders of magnitude smaller than a year. Five significant figures are allowed because all conversion factors are assumed to be exact, except for the 365.24 days/solar year (five significant figures). Round up the last digit because the first nonsignificant digit is a 7.

1.81   (a)   Extensive – The volume of a material depends on how much there is present.

         (b)   Intensive – The boiling point of a material is independent of how much material you have, so these values can be published in reference tables.

         (c)   Intensive – The temperature of a material does not depend on how much there is present.

         (d)   Intensive – The electrical conductivity of a material is independent of how much material you have, so these values can be published in reference tables.

         (e)   Extensive – The energy contained in material depends on how much there is present. Many times energy is expressed in terms of Joules/mole, which then turns this quantity into an intensive property.

1.83   (a) $1.76 \times 10^{-3}/8.0 \times 10^2 = 2.2 \times 10^{-6}$. Two significant figures are allowed to reflect the quantity with the fewest significant figures (8.0×10^2).

(b)   Write all figures so that the decimal points can be aligned:

        0.0187
  + 0.0002 All quantities are known to four places to the right of the decimal place,
  − 0.0030 so the answer should be reported to four places to the right of the
      0.0159 decimal place or three significant figures.

(c) $[(136000)(0.000322)/0.082)](129.2) = 6.899910244 \times 10^4 = 6.9 \times 10^4$. Round the intermediate answer to two significant figures to reflect the quantity with the fewest significant figures (0.082). Round up the last digit since the first nonsignificant digit is 9.

1.85   **Given:** $r_{Au} = 3.8$ cm^2, $h_{Au} = 22$ cm, $d_{Au} = 19.3$ g cm^{-3}, $d_{sand} = 3.00$ g cm^{-3} **Find:** V_{sand}
     Conceptual Plan: (1) V_{Au} **bar, (2)** $m_{Au} = d_{Au} \times V_{Au} = m_{sand}$, **(3)** $V_{sand} = d_{sand}/m_{sand}$
     Solution: $V_{cyl} = (\pi r^2) \times h = (\pi \times (3.8 \text{ cm})^2) \times 22$ cm $= 998.0211$ cm^3 (two significant figures)

$$m_{Au} = d \times V = 19.3 \text{ g cm}^{-3} \times 998.021 \text{ cm}^3 = 19261.808 \text{ g}$$

Therefore, the volume of sand is:
$$V_{sand} = \frac{m}{d} = \frac{19261.808 \text{ g}}{3.00 \text{ g cm}^{-3}} = 6.4 \times 10^3 \text{ cm}^3$$

Check: The answer is in the correct units. Since density of gold is over six times greater than sand, the volume of sand needed would be six times larger than gold.

1.87   **Given:** $d_{Ti} = 4.51$ g cm^{-3}, $m_{Ti} = 3.5$ kg **Find:** V_{Ti} in litres
     Conceptual Plan: d(g cm^{-3}) $\rightarrow$ **d(kg L^{-1}), V = m/d**
     Solution: $\dfrac{4.51 \text{ g}}{\text{cm}^3} \times \dfrac{1 \text{kg}}{1000 \text{ g}} \times \dfrac{1000 \text{ cm}^3}{1 \text{ L}} = 4.51$ kg L^{-1}

$$V = \frac{m}{d} = \frac{3.5 \text{ kg}}{4.51 \text{ kg L}^{-1}} = 0.78 \text{ L}$$

Check: The units are L. Since the density of Ti is 4.51, the calculated volume has to be approximately ~4.5 times smaller than the mass

1.89   **Given:** $r_{steel} = 0.56$ cm^2, $h_{steel} = 5.49$ cm, $m_{steel} = 41$ g **Find:** d_{steel}
     Conceptual Plan: (1) V_{steel}, **(2) d = m/V**
     Solution: $V_{steel} = (\pi r^2) \times h = (\pi \times [0.56 \text{cm}]^2) \times 5.49$ cm $= 5.40877$ cm^3
$$d_{steel} = \frac{m}{V} = \frac{41 \text{ g}}{5.40877 \text{ cm}^3} = 7.6 \text{ g cm}^{-3}$$

Check: The answer is in the correct units (cm^3) and is very close to the density of pure iron, which makes physical sense.

1.91   **Given:** 185 m^3 of H$_2$O **Find:** mass of water in kg
     Other: d(H$_2$O) = 1.00 g cm^{-3}
     Conceptual Plan: m^3 $\rightarrow$ **cm^3, m = d $\times$ V, g** $\rightarrow$ **kg**
     Solution: $V = 185 \text{ m}^3 \times \dfrac{(100 \text{ cm})^3}{(1 \text{ m})^3} = 1.85 \times 10^8$ cm^3

$$m = d \times V = (1 \text{ g cm}^{-3}) \times (1.85 \times 10^8 \text{ cm}^3) = 1.85 \times 10^8 \text{ g}$$

$$1.85 \times 10^8 \text{ g} \times \frac{1 \text{ kg}}{1000 \text{ g}} = 1.85 \times 10^5 \text{ kg}$$

Check: The answer is in the correct unit. Density of water in SI units is 1000 kg m^{-3}, so the magnitude of the answer is correct.

1.93   **Given:** Usage = 3.8 L/100 km, $V_{gas} = 15$ L **Find:** distance (D)
     Conceptual Plan: D = V$_{gas}$/Usage
     Solution: Distance $= 15 \text{ L} \times \dfrac{100 \text{ km}}{3.8 \text{ L}} = 390$ km

Check: The answer is in the correct unit (km). The amount of gas available is roughly four times the consumption per 100 km, so the distance travelled should be close to 400 km.

1.95　**Given:** radius of nucleus of the hydrogen atom $= 1.0 \times 10^{-13}$ cm; radius of the hydrogen atom $= 52.9$ pm
Find: percent of volume occupied by nucleus (%)
Conceptual Plan: cm $\rightarrow$ m then pm $\rightarrow$ m then $r \rightarrow V$ then $V_{atom}, V_{nucleus} \rightarrow$ % $V_{nucleus}$

$$\frac{1\,m}{100\,cm} \qquad \frac{1\,m}{10^{12}\,pm} \qquad V = (4/3)\pi r^3 \qquad \% \, V_{nucleus} = \frac{V_{nucleus}}{V_{atom}} \times 100\%$$

Solution: 1.0×10^{-13} c̶m̶ $\times \dfrac{1\,m}{100\,\text{c̶m̶}} = 1.0 \times 10^{-15}$ m　and　52.9 p̶m̶ $\times \dfrac{1\,m}{10^{12}\,\text{p̶m̶}} = 5.29 \times 10^{-11}$ m

$V = (4/3)\pi r^3$　Substitute into %V equation.

$$\% \, V_{nucleus} = \frac{V_{nucleus}}{V_{atom}} \times 100\% \qquad \rightarrow \% \, V_{nucleus} = \frac{(4/3)\,\pi r^3_{nucleus}}{(4/3)\,\pi r^3_{atom}} \times 100\% \qquad \text{Simplify equation.}$$

$$\% \, V_{nucleus} = \frac{r^3_{nucleus}}{r^3_{atom}} \times 100\% \quad \text{Substitute numbers and calculate result.}$$

$$\% \, V_{nucleus} = \frac{(1.0 \times 10^{-15}\,m)^3}{(5.29 \times 10^{-11}\,m)^3} \times 100\% = (1.890359168 \times 10^{-5})^3 \times 100\% = 6.\underline{7}55118685 \times 10^{-13}\% = 6.8 \times 10^{-13}\%$$

Check: The units (none) are correct. The magnitude of the answer seems correct (10^{-15}), since a proton is so small. Converting fractions to percent is more common: $6.8 \times 10^{-13}\%$ of the atom is occupied by the proton. Two significant figures are allowed to reflect the significant figures in 1.0×10^{-13} cm. Round up the last digits because the first nonsignificant digit is a 5.

1.97　**Given:** radius of hydrogen $= 212$ pm; radius of ping pong ball $= 4.0$ cm, 6.02×10^{23} atoms and balls in a row
Find: row length (km)
Conceptual Plan: molecules $\rightarrow$ pm $\rightarrow$ m $\rightarrow$ km and ball $\rightarrow$ cm $\rightarrow$ m $\rightarrow$ km

$$\frac{212\,pm}{1\,molecule} \quad \frac{1\,m}{10^{12}\,pm} \quad \frac{1\,km}{1000\,m} \qquad\qquad \frac{4.0\,cm}{1\,ball} \quad \frac{100\,cm}{1\,m} \quad \frac{1\,km}{1000\,m}$$

Solution: 6.02×10^{23} m̶o̶l̶e̶c̶u̶l̶e̶ $\times \dfrac{212\,\text{p̶m̶}}{1\,\text{m̶o̶l̶e̶c̶u̶l̶e̶}} \times \dfrac{1\,\text{m̶}}{10^{12}\,\text{p̶m̶}} \times \dfrac{1\,km}{1000\,\text{m̶}} = 1.28 \times 10^{11}$ km

6.02×10^{23} b̶a̶l̶l̶s̶ $\times \dfrac{4.0\,\text{c̶m̶}}{1\,\text{b̶a̶l̶l̶}} \times \dfrac{1\,\text{m̶}}{100\,\text{c̶m̶}} \times \dfrac{1\,km}{1000\,\text{m̶}} = 2.4 \times 10^{19}$ km

Check: The units (km) are correct. The magnitude of the answers seem correct (10^{11} and 10^{19}). The answers are driven by the large number of atoms or balls. The ping pong ball row is 10^8 times longer. Three significant figures are allowed to reflect the significant figures in 212 pm. Two significant figures are allowed to reflect the significant figures in 4.0 cm.

1.99　**Given:** 39.33 g sodium/100 g salt; 1.25 g salt/100 g snack mix; Health Canada maximum 2.40 g sodium/day
Find: g snack mix
Conceptual Plan: g sodium $\rightarrow$ g salt $\rightarrow$ g snack mix

$$\frac{100\,g\,salt}{39.33\,g\,sodium} \quad \frac{100\,g\,snack\,mix}{1.25\,g\,salt}$$

Solution: $\dfrac{2.40\,\text{g̶ s̶o̶d̶i̶u̶m̶}}{1\,day} \times \dfrac{100\,\text{g̶ s̶a̶l̶t̶}}{39.33\,\text{g̶ s̶o̶d̶i̶u̶m̶}} \times \dfrac{100\,g\,snack\,mix}{1.25\,\text{g̶ s̶a̶l̶t̶}} = 488.\underline{1}770$ g snack mix/day

$= 488$ g snack mix/day

Check: The units (g) are correct. The magnitude of the answer seems correct (500) since salt is less than half sodium and there is a little over a gram of salt per 100 grams of snack mix. Three significant figures are allowed to reflect the significant figures in the Health Canada maximum and in the amount of salt in the snack mix.

1.101　**Given:** d(liquid nitrogen) $= 0.808$ g mL^{-1}; d(gaseous nitrogen) $= 1.15$ g L^{-1}; 175 L liquid nitrogen; 10.00 m x 10.00 m x 2.50 m room　**Find:** fraction of room displaced by nitrogen gas
Conceptual Plan: L $\rightarrow$ mL then $V_{liquid}, d_{liquid} \rightarrow m_{liquid}$ then set $m_{liquid} = m_{gas}$ then $m_{gas}, d_{gas} \rightarrow V_{gas}$ then

$$\frac{1000\,mL}{1\,L} \qquad\qquad d = m/V \qquad\qquad\qquad\qquad\qquad d = m/V$$

Calculate the $V_{room} \rightarrow cm^3 \rightarrow L$ **then calculate the fraction displaced**

$$V = l \times w \times h \quad \frac{(100 \text{ cm})^3}{(1 \text{ m})^3} \quad \frac{1 \text{ L}}{1000 \text{ cm}^3} \qquad\qquad \frac{V_{gas}}{V_{room}}$$

Solution: $175 \cancel{L} \times \dfrac{1000 \text{ mL}}{1 \cancel{L}} = 1.75 \times 10^5$ mL. Solve for m by multiplying both sides of the equation by V.

$$m = V \times d = 1.75 \times 10^5 \cancel{mL} \times \frac{0.808 \text{ g}}{1 \cancel{mL}} = 1.4\underline{1}4 \times 10^5 \text{ g nitrogen liquid} = 1.4\underline{1}4 \times 10^5 \text{ g nitrogen gas}$$

$d = m/V$. Rearrange by multiplying both sides of the equation by V and dividing both sides of the equation by d.

$$V = \frac{m}{d} = \frac{1.4\underline{1}4 \times 10^5 \cancel{g}}{1.15 \dfrac{\cancel{g}}{L}} = 1.22956\underline{5} \times 10^5 \text{ L nitrogen gas}$$

$$V_{room} = l \times w \times h = 10.00 \cancel{m} \times 10.00 \cancel{m} \times 2.50 \cancel{m} \times \frac{(100 \cancel{cm})^3}{(1 \cancel{m})^3} \times \frac{1 \text{ L}}{1000 \cancel{cm}^3} = 2.50 \times 10^5 \text{ L}$$

$$\frac{V_{gas}}{V_{room}} = \frac{1.22956\underline{5} \times 10^5 \cancel{L}}{2.50 \times 10^5 \cancel{L}} = 0.491\underline{8}272 = 0.492$$

Check: The units (none) are correct. The magnitude of the answer seems correct (0.5) since there is a large volume of liquid and the density of the gas is about a factor of 1000 less than the density of the liquid. Three significant figures are allowed to reflect the significant figures in the densities and the volume of the liquid given.

Challenge Problems

1.103   **Given:** F = 2.31 × 10^4 N, A = 125 cm^2 **Find:** pressure

Conceptual Plan: A (cm^2) $\rightarrow$ **A (m^2)**, $P = \dfrac{F}{A}$

Solution: $A = 125 \text{ cm}^2 \times \dfrac{1 \text{ m}^2}{(100 \text{ cm})^2} = 0.0125 \text{ m}^2$

$$P = \frac{F}{A} = \frac{2.31 \times 10^4 \text{ N}}{0.0125 \text{ m}^2} = 1.85 \times 10^6 \text{ Pa}$$

$$1.85 \times 10^6 \text{ Pa} \times \frac{1 \text{ bar}}{1 \times 10^5 \text{ Pa}} = 18.5 \text{ bar}$$

Check: The answer is in units of barr. Barr is a convenient unit for atmospheric pressure, and normal atmospheric pressure is 1.01 × 10^5 Pa. The pressure experienced by the diver's mask is more than 20 times that of atmospheric pressure.

1.105   Referring to the definition of energy in Chapter 6, 1 Joule = 1J = kg m^2 s^{-2}. For kinetic energy, if the units of mass are the kilogram (kg) and the units of the velocity are metres/second (m s^{-1}) then

$$\text{kinetic energy units} = mv^2 = \text{kg} \left(\frac{\text{m}}{\text{s}} \right)^2 = \frac{\text{kg} \cdot \text{m}^2}{\text{s}^2} = \text{J. Since a Newton (N) is a unit of force and has units}$$

of kg m s^{-2}, pressure = force / area and has units of N m^{-2}, and force = (mass) x (acceleration) or $F = ma$, then

$$\text{3/2 PV units} = \frac{\text{N}}{\cancel{\text{m}^2}} \cdot \cancel{\text{m}^3} = \frac{\text{kg} \cdot \text{m}}{\text{s}^2} \cdot \text{m} = \frac{\text{kg} \cdot \text{m}^2}{\text{s}^2} = \text{J.}$$

1.107   **Given:** cubic nanocontainers with an edge length = 25 nanometres
Find: a) volume of one nanocontainer; b) grams of oxygen that could be contained by each nanocontainer; c) grams of oxygen inhaled per hour; d) minimum number of nanocontainers per hour; and e) minimum volume of nanocontainers
Other: (pressurized oxygen) = 85 g L^{-1}; 0.28 g of oxygen per litre; average human inhales about 0.50 L of air per breath and takes about 20 breaths per minute; adult total blood volume = ~5 L
Conceptual Plan:

(a)   nm $\rightarrow$ m $\rightarrow$ cm then l $\rightarrow$ V then cm^3 $\rightarrow$ L

$$\frac{1 \text{ m}}{10^9 \text{ nm}} \quad \frac{100 \text{ cm}}{1 \text{ m}} \qquad V = l^3 \qquad \frac{1 \text{ L}}{1000 \text{ cm}^3}$$

(b)   L $\rightarrow$ g pressurized oxygen

$$\frac{85 \text{ g oxygen}}{1 \text{ L nanocontainers}}$$

(c)   hr $\rightarrow$ min $\rightarrow$ breaths $\rightarrow$ L$_{air}$ $\rightarrow$ g$_{O2}$

$$\frac{60 \text{ min}}{1 \text{ hr}} \quad \frac{20 \text{ breath}}{1 \text{ min}} \quad \frac{0.50 \text{ L}_{air}}{1 \text{ breath}} \quad \frac{0.28 \text{ g}_{CO}}{1 \text{ L}_{air}}$$

(d)   grams oxygen $\rightarrow$ number nanocontainers

$$\frac{1 \text{ nanocontainer}}{\text{part (b) grams of oxygen}}$$

(e)   number nanocontainers $\rightarrow$ volume nanocontainers

$$\frac{\text{part (a) volume}}{\text{of 1 nanocontainer}}$$

Solution:

(a) $25 \text{ nm} \times \dfrac{1 \text{ m}}{10^9 \text{ nm}} \times \dfrac{100 \text{ cm}}{1 \text{ m}} = 2.5 \times 10^{-6} \text{ cm}$

$V = l^3 = (2.5 \times 10^{-6} \text{ cm})^3 = 1.5625 \times 10^{-17} \text{ cm}^3 \times \dfrac{1 \text{ L}}{1000 \text{ cm}^3} = 1.5625 \times 10^{-20} \text{ L} = 1.6 \times 10^{-20} \text{ L}$

(b) $1.5625 \times 10^{-20} \text{ L} \times \dfrac{85 \text{ g oxygen}}{1 \text{ L nanocontainers}} = 1.328125 \times 10^{-18} \dfrac{\text{g pressurized O}_2}{\text{nanocontainer}}$

$= 1.3 \times 10^{-18} \dfrac{\text{g pressurized O}_2}{\text{nanocontainer}}$

(c) $1 \text{ hr} \times \dfrac{60 \text{ min}}{1 \text{ hr}} \times \dfrac{20 \text{ breath}}{1 \text{ min}} \times \dfrac{0.50 \text{ L}_{air}}{1 \text{ breath}} \times \dfrac{0.28 \text{ gO}_2}{1 \text{ L}_{air}} = 1.68 \times 10^2 \text{ g oxygen} = 1.7 \times 10^2 \text{ g oxygen}$

(d) $1.68 \times 10^2 \text{ g oxygen} \times \dfrac{1 \text{ nanocontainer}}{1.3 \times 10^{-18} \text{ g of oxygen}} = 1.292307692 \times 10^{20} \text{ nanocontainers}$

$= 1.3 \times 10^{20} \text{ nanocontainers}$

(e) $1.292307692 \times 10^{20} \text{ nanocontainers} \times \dfrac{1.5625 \times 10^{-20} \text{ L}}{\text{nanocontainer}} = 2.019230769 \text{ L} = 2.0 \text{ L}$

This volume is much too large to be feasible, since the volume of blood in the average human is 5 L.

Check:

(a)   The units (L) are correct. The magnitude of the answer $(10 - 20)$ makes physical sense because these are very, very tiny containers. Two significant figures are allowed, reflecting the significant figures in the starting dimension (25 nm – 2 significant figures). Round up the last digit because the first non-significant digit is a 6.

(b)   The units (g) are correct. The magnitude of the answer (10^{-18}) makes physical sense because these are very, very tiny containers and very few molecules can fit inside. Two significant figures are allowed, reflecting the significant figures in the starting dimension (25 nm) and the given concentration (85 g L^{-1}) – 2 significant figures in each. Truncate the nonsignificant digits because the first nonsignificant digit is a 2.

(c)   The units (g oxygen) are correct. The magnitude of the answer (10^2) makes physical sense because of the conversion factors involved and the fact that air is not very dense. Two significant figures are allowed because it is stated in the problem. Round up the last digit because the first nonsignificant digit is an 8.

(d) The units (nanocontainers) are correct. The magnitude of the answer (10^{20}) makes physical sense because these are very, very tiny containers and we need a macroscopic quantity of oxygen in these containers. Two significant figures are allowed, reflecting the significant figures in both of the quantities in the calculation – 2 significant figures. Round up the last digit because the first nonsignificant digit is a 9.

(e) The units (L) are correct. The magnitude of the answer (2) makes physical sense because of the magnitudes of the numbers in this step. Two significant figures are allowed reflecting the significant figures in both of the quantities in the calculation – 2 significant figures. Truncate the nonsignificant digits because the first nonsignificant digit is a 1.

Conceptual Problems

1.109 No. Since the container is sealed the atoms and molecules can move around, but they cannot leave. If no atoms or molecules can leave, the mass must be constant.

1.111 This problem is similar to Problem 42, only the dimension is changed to 7 cm on each edge.
Given: 7 cm on each edge cube   **Find:** cm^3
Conceptual plan: Read the information given carefully. The cube is 7 cm on each side.
$l, w, h \rightarrow V$

$V = l\,w\,h$

$in\ a\ cube\ l = w = h$

Solution: 7 cm x 7 cm x 7 cm = $(7\ cm)^3$ = 343 cm^3 or 343 cubes

1.113 Remember that density = mass/volume.

(a) The darker-coloured box has a heavier mass, but a smaller volume, so it is denser than the lighter-coloured box.

(b) The lighter-coloured box is heavier than the darker-coloured box and both boxes have the same volume, so the lighter-coloured box is denser.

(c) The larger box is the heavier box, so it cannot be determined with this information which box is denser.

2 Atoms and Elements

Review Questions

2.1   Scanning tunnelling microscopy is a technique that can image, and even move, individual atoms and molecules. A scanning tunnelling microscope works by moving an extremely sharp electrode over a surface and measuring the resulting tunnelling current, the electrical current that flows between the tip of the electrode, and the surface even though the two are not in physical contact.

2.3   The law of conservation of mass states the following: In a chemical reaction, matter is neither created nor destroyed. In other words, when you carry out any chemical reaction, the total mass of the substances involved in the reaction does not change.

2.5   The law of multiple proportions states the following: When two elements (call them A and B) form two different compounds, the masses of element B that combine with 1 g of element A can be expressed as a ratio of small whole numbers. This means that when two atoms (A and B) combine to form more than one compound, the ratio of B in one compound to B in the second compound will be a small whole number.

2.7   In the late 1800s, an English physicist named J.J. Thomson performed experiments to probe the properties of cathode rays. Thomson found that these rays were actually streams of particles with the following properties: They travelled in straight lines, they were independent of the composition of the material from which they originated, and they carried a negative electrical charge. He measured the charge to mass ratio of the particles and found that the cathode ray particle was about 2000 times lighter than hydrogen.

2.9   Rutherford's gold foil experiment directed positively charged α particles at an ultrathin sheet of gold foil. These particles were to act as probes of the gold atoms' structures. If the gold atoms were indeed like plum pudding—with their mass and charge spread throughout the entire volume of the atom—these speeding probes should pass right through the gold foil with minimum deflection. A majority of the particles did pass directly through the foil, but some particles were deflected, and some even bounced back. He realized that to account for the deflections, the mass and positive charge of an atom must all be concentrated in a space much smaller than the size of the atom itself.

2.11   Matter appears solid because the variation in its density is on such a small scale that our eyes cannot see it.

2.13   The number of protons in the nucleus defines the identity of an element.

2.15   Isotopes are atoms with the same number of protons but different numbers of neutrons. The percent natural abundance is the relative amount of each different isotope in a naturally occurring sample of a given element.

2.17   An ion is a charged particle. Positively charged ions are called cations. Negatively charged ions are called anions.

2.19   In a mass spectrometer, the sample is injected into the instrument and vaporized. The vaporized atoms are
        then ionized by an electron beam. The electrons in the beam collide with the vaporized atoms, removing
        electrons from the atoms and creating positively charged ions. Charged plates with slits in them accelerate
        the positively charged ions into a magnetic field, which deflects them. The amount of deflection depends on
        the mass of the ions—lighter ions are deflected more than heavier ones. Finally, the ions strike a detector
        and produce an electrical signal that is recorded.

2.21   A mole is an amount of material. It is defined as the amount of material containing 6.0221421×10^{23} particles
        (Avogadro's number). The numerical value of the mole is defined as being equal to the number of atoms in
        exactly 12 grams of pure carbon-12. It is useful for converting number of atoms to moles of atoms and moles
        of atoms to number of atoms.

2.23   The periodic law states the following: When elements are arranged in order of increasing mass, certain sets
        of properties recur periodically. Mendeleev organized all the known elements in a table consisting of a series
        of rows in which mass increased from left to right. The rows were arranged so that elements with similar
        properties were aligned in the same vertical column.

2.25   (a)   Noble gases are in group 18 and are mostly unreactive. As the name implies, they are all gases in their
               natural state.

        (b)   Alkali metals are in group 1 and are all reactive metals.

        (c)   Alkaline earth metals are in group 2 and are also fairly reactive.

        (d)   Halogens are in group 17 and are very reactive nonmetals.

Problems by Topic

The Laws of Conservation of Mass, Definite Proportions, and Multiple Proportions

2.27   **Given:** 1.50 g hydrogen; 11.9 g oxygen **Find:** grams water vapour
        Conceptual Plan: total mass reactants = total mass products
        Solution: Mass of reactants = 1.50 g hydrogen + 11.9 g oxygen = 13.4 grams
                 Mass of products = mass of reactants = 13.4 grams water vapour.
        Check: According to the law of conservation of mass, matter is not created or destroyed in a chemical reac-
        tion, so, since water vapour is the only product, the masses of hydrogen and oxygen must combine to form
        the mass of water vapour.

2.29   **Given:** sample 1: 38.9 g carbon, 448 g chlorine; sample 2: 14.8 g carbon, 134 g chlorine
        Find: are results consistent with definite proportions?
        Conceptual Plan: determine mass ratio of sample 1 and 2 and compare

$$\frac{\text{mass of chlorine}}{\text{mass of carbon}}$$

        Solution: Sample 1: $\dfrac{448 \text{ g chorine}}{38.9 \text{ g carbon}} = 11.5$ Sample 2: $\dfrac{134 \text{ g chlorine}}{14.8 \text{ g carbon}} = 9.05$

               Results are not consistent with the law of definite proportions because the ratio of chlorine to
               carbon is not the same.
        Check: According to the law of definite proportions, the mass ratio of one element to another is the same
        for all samples of the compound.

2.31   **Given:** mass ratio sodium to fluorine = 1.21:1; sample = 28.8 g sodium **Find:** g fluorine
        Conceptual Plan: g sodium $\rightarrow$ g fluorine

$$\frac{\text{mass of fluorine}}{\text{mass of sodium}}$$

        Solution: $28.8 \, \cancel{\text{g sodium}} \times \dfrac{1 \text{ g fluorine}}{1.21 \, \cancel{\text{g sodium}}} = 23.8 \text{ g fluorine}$

Check: The units of the answer (g fluorine) are correct. The magnitude of the answer is reasonable since it is less than the grams of sodium.

2.33   **Given:** 1 gram osmium: sample 1 = 0.168 g oxygen; sample 2 = 0.3369 g oxygen
         Find: are results consistent with multiple proportions?
         Conceptual Plan: determine mass ratio of oxygen
         $$\frac{mass\,of\,oxygen\,sample\,2}{mass\,of\,oxygen\,sample\,1}$$

         Solution: $\frac{0.3369\,g\,oxygen}{0.168\,g\,oxygen} = 2.00$ Ratio is a small whole number. Results are consistent with multiple proportions
         Check: According to the law of multiple proportions, when two elements form two different compounds, the masses of element B that combine with 1 g of element A can be expressed as a ratio of small whole numbers.

2.35   **Given:** sulfur dioxide = 3.49 g oxygen and 3.50 g sulfur; sulfur trioxide = 6.75 g oxygen and 4.50 g sulfur
         Find: mass oxygen per g S for each compound and then determine the mass ratio of oxygen
         $$\frac{mass\,of\,oxygen\,in\,sulfur\,dioxide}{mass\,of\,sulfur\,in\,sulfur\,dioxide}\quad\frac{mass\,of\,oxygen\,in\,sulfur\,trioxide}{mass\,of\,sulfur\,in\,sulfur\,trioxide}\quad\frac{mass\,of\,oxyen\,in\,sulfur\,trioxide}{mass\,of\,oxyen\,in\,sulfur\,dioxide}$$

         Solution: sulfur dioxide $= \dfrac{3.49\,g\,oxygen}{3.50\,g\,sulfur} = \dfrac{0.997\,g\,oxygen}{1\,g\,sulfur}$

         sulfur trioxide $= \dfrac{6.75\,g\,oxygen}{4.50\,g\,sulfur} = \dfrac{1.50\,g\,oxygen}{1\,g\,sulfur}$

         $$\frac{1.50\,g\,oxygen\,in\,sulfur\,trioxide}{0.997\,g\,oxygen\,in\,sulfur\,dioxide} = \frac{1.50}{1} = \frac{3}{2}$$

         Ratio is in small whole numbers and is consistent with multiple proportions.
         Check: According to the law of multiple proportions, when two elements form two different compounds, the masses of element B that combine with 1 g of element A can be expressed as a ratio of small whole numbers.

Atomic Theory, Nuclear Theory, and Subatomic Particles

2.37   **Given:** drop A $= -6.9 \times 10^{-19}$ C; drop B $= -9.2 \times 10^{-19}$ C; drop C $= -11.5 \times 10^{-19}$ C; drop D $= -4.6 \times 10^{-19}$ C
         Find: the charge on a single electron
         Conceptual Plan: determine the ratio of charge for each set of drops
         $$\frac{charge\,on\,drop\,1}{charge\,on\,drop\,2}$$

         Solution: $\dfrac{-6.9 \times 10^{-19}\,C\,drop\,A}{-4.6 \times 10^{-19}\,C\,drop\,D} = 1.5$ $\dfrac{-9.2 \times 10^{-19}\,C\,drop\,B}{-4.6 \times 10^{-19}\,C\,drop\,D} = 2$ $\dfrac{-11.5 \times 10^{-19}\,C\,drop\,C}{-4.6 \times 10^{-19}\,C\,drop\,D} = 2.5$

         The ratios obtained are not whole numbers, but can be converted to whole numbers by multiplying by 2.

         Therefore, the charge on the electron has to be 1/2 the smallest value experimentally obtained. The charge on the electron $= -2.3 \times 10^{-19}$ C.
         Check: The units of the answer (Coulombs) are correct. The magnitude of the answer is reasonable since all the values experimentally obtained are integer multiples of -2.3×10^{-19}.

2.39   **Given:** charge on body $= -15\ \mu$C **Find:** number of electrons, mass of the electrons
         Conceptual Plan: μC $\rightarrow$ C $\rightarrow$ **number of electrons** $\rightarrow$ **mass of electrons**
         $$\frac{1\,C}{10^6\,\mu C}\quad\frac{1\,electron}{-1.60 \times 10^{-19}C}\qquad\frac{9.10 \times 10^{-28}\,g}{1\,electron}$$

         Solution: $-15\ \cancel{\mu C} \times \dfrac{1\ \cancel{C}}{10^6\ \cancel{\mu C}} \times \dfrac{1\,electron}{-1.60 \times 10^{-19}\cancel{C}} = 9.375 \times 10^{13}$ electrons $= 9.4 \times 10^{13}$ electrons

         $9.375 \times 10^{13}\ \cancel{electrons} \times \dfrac{9.10 \times 10^{-28}\,g}{1\ \cancel{electron}} = 8.5 \times 10^{-14}\,g = 8.5 \times 10^{-17}$ kg

         Check: The units of the answers (number of electrons and grams) are correct. The magnitude of the answers is reasonable since the charge on an electron and the mass of an electron are very small.

2.41   **Given:** mass of proton **Find:** number of electron in equal mass
              Conceptual Plan: mass of protons $\rightarrow$ number of electrons

$$\frac{1.67262 \times 10^{-27} \text{ kg}}{1 \text{ proton}} \qquad \frac{1 \text{ electron}}{9.10938 \times 10^{-31} \text{ kg}}$$

Solution: $1.67262 \times 10^{-27} \text{ kg} \times \dfrac{1 \text{ electron}}{9.10938 \times 10^{-31} \text{ kg}} = 1.83615 \times 10^3 \text{ electrons} = 1836 \text{ electrons}$

Check: The units of the answer (electrons) are correct. The magnitude of the answer is reasonable since the mass of the electron is much less than the mass of the proton.

Isotopes and Ions

2.43   For each of the isotopes determine Z (the number of protons) from the periodic table and determine A (protons + neutrons). Then, write the symbol in the form $_Z^A X$.

   (a)   The copper isotope with 34 neutrons: Z = 29; A = 29 + 34 = 63; $_{29}^{63}\text{Cu}$

   (b)   The copper isotope with 36 neutrons: Z = 29; A = 29 + 36 = 65; $_{29}^{65}\text{Cu}$

   (c)   The potassium isotope with 21 neutrons: Z = 19; A = 19 + 21 = 40; $_{19}^{40}\text{K}$

   (d)   The argon isotope with 22 neutrons: Z = 18; A = 18 + 22 = 40; $_{18}^{40}\text{Ar}$

2.45   (a) $_7^{14}\text{N}$: Z = 7 ; A = 14; protons = Z = 7; neutrons = A – Z = 14 – 7 = 7

       (b) $_{11}^{23}\text{Na}$: Z = 11; A = 23; protons = Z = 11; neutrons = A – Z = 23 – 11 = 12

       (c) $_{86}^{222}\text{Rn}$: Z = 86; A = 222; protons = Z = 86; neutrons = A – Z = 222 – 86 = 136

       (d) $_{82}^{208}\text{Pb}$: Z = 82; A = 208; protons = Z = 82; neutrons = A – Z = 208 – 82 = 126

2.47   Carbon – 14: A = 14, Z = 6: $_6^{14}\text{C}$ # protons = Z = 6   # neutrons = A – Z = 14 – 6 = 8

2.49   In a neutral atom the number of protons = the number of electrons = Z. For an ion, electrons are lost (cations) or gained (anions).

       (a) Ni^{2+}: Z = 28 = protons; Z – 2 = 26 = electrons

       (b) S^{2-}: Z = 16 = protons; Z + 2 = 18 = electrons

       (c) Br^-: Z = 35 = protons; Z + 1 = 36 = electrons

       (d) Cr^{3+}: Z = 24 = protons; Z – 3 = 21 = electrons

2.51   Main group metal atoms will lose electrons to form a cation with the same number of electrons as the nearest, previous noble gas. Atoms in period 4 and higher lose electrons to form the same ion as the element at the top of the group.

       Nonmetal atoms will gain electrons to form an anion with the same number of electrons as the nearest noble gas.

Symbol	Ion Formed	Number of Electrons in Ion	Number of Protons in Ion
Ca	Ca^{2+}	18	20
Be	Be^{2+}	2	**4**
Se	Se^{2-}	36	34
In	In^{3+}	46	**49**

Atomic Mass

2.53 **Given:** Ga-69; mass = 68.92558 amu; 60.108%: Ga-71; mass = 70.92470 amu; 39.892 % **Find:** atomic mass Ga
Conceptual Plan: % abundance → **fraction and then find atomic mass**

$$\frac{\%\,abundance}{100} \qquad \text{Atomic mass} = \sum_{n}(\text{fraction of isotope } n) \times (\text{mass of isotope } n)$$

Solution: Fraction Ga-69 $= \dfrac{60.108}{100} = 0.60108$ Fraction Ga-71 $= \dfrac{39.892}{100} = 0.39892$

$$\text{Atomic mass} = \sum_{n}(\text{fraction of isotope } n) \times (\text{mass of isotope } n)$$

$$= 0.60108(68.92588 \text{ amu}) + 0.39892(70.92470 \text{ amu}) = 69.723 \text{ amu}$$

Check: Units of the answer (amu) are correct. The magnitude of the answer is reasonable because it lies between 68.92588 amu and 70.92470 amu and is closer to 68.92588, which has the higher % abundance. The mass spectrum is reasonable because it has two mass lines corresponding to the two isotopes, and the line at 68.92588 is about 1.5 times larger than the line at 70.92470.

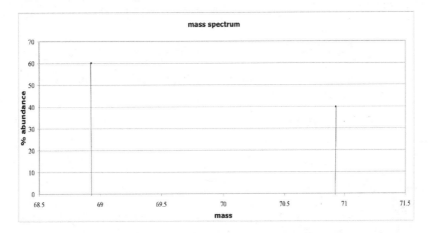

2.55 Fluorine has an isotope F-19 with a very large abundance so that the mass of fluorine is very close to the mass of the isotope and the line in the mass spectrum reflects the abundance of F-19. Chlorine has two isotopes, Cl-35 and Cl-37, and the mass of 35.45 amu is the weighted average of these two isotopes, so there is no line at 35.45 amu.

2.57 **Given:** isotope – 1 mass = 120.9038 amu, 57.4%; isotope – 2 mass = 122.9042 amu
Find: atomic mass of the element and identify the element
Conceptual Plan:
% abundance isotope 2 → **and then % abundance** → **fraction and then find atomic mass**

$$100\% - \%\,abundance\,isotope\,1 \qquad \frac{\%\,abundance}{100} \qquad \text{Atomic mass} = \sum_{n}(\text{fraction of isotope } n) \times (\text{mass of isotope } n)$$

Solution: 100.0% – 57.4% isotope 1 = 42.6% isotope 2

$$\text{Fraction isotope 1} = \frac{57.4}{100} = 0.574 \qquad \text{Fraction isotope 2} = \frac{42.6}{100} = 0.426$$

$$\text{Atomic mass} = \sum_{n}(\text{fraction of isotope } n) \times (\text{mass of isotope } n)$$

$$= 0.574(120.9038 \text{ amu}) + 0.426(122.9042 \text{ amu}) = 121.8 \text{ amu}$$

From the periodic table, Sb has a mass of 121.757 amu, so it is the closest mass and the element is antimony.
Check: The units of the answer (amu) are correct. The magnitude of the answer is reasonable because it lies between 120.9038 and 122.9042 and is slightly less than halfway between the two values because the lower value has a slightly greater abundance.

2.59 **Given:** Br-81; mass = 80.9163 amu; 49.31%: atomic mass Br = 79.904 amu **Find:** mass and abundance
Conceptual Plan: % abundance Br-79 → **then % abundance** → **fraction** → **mass Br-79**

$$100\% - \%\,Br\text{-}81 \qquad \frac{\%\,abundance}{100} \qquad \text{Atomic mass} = \sum_{n}(\text{fraction of isotope } n) \times (\text{mass of isotope } n)$$

Solution: $100.00\% - 49.31\% = 50.69\%$

$$\text{Fraction Br-79} = \frac{50.69}{100} = 0.5069 \qquad \text{Fraction Br-81} = \frac{49.31}{100} = 0.4931$$

Let X be the mass of Br-79

$$\text{Atomic mass} = \sum_{n}(\text{fraction of isotope } n) \times (\text{mass of isotope } n)$$

$$79.904 \text{ amu} = 0.5069(X \text{ amu}) + 0.4931(80.9163 \text{ amu})$$

$$X = 78.92 \text{ amu} = \text{mass Br-79}$$

Check: The units of the answer (amu) are correct. The magnitude of the answer is reasonable because it is less than the mass of the atom, and the second isotope (Br-81) has a mass greater than the mass of the atom.

The Mole Concept

2.61   **Given:** 3.8 mol sulfur **Find:** atoms of sulfur
    Conceptual Plan: mol S → atoms S

$$\frac{6.022 \times 10^{23}\,\text{atoms}}{\text{mol}}$$

Solution: $3.8 \,\overline{\text{mol S}} \times \dfrac{6.022 \times 10^{23}\,\text{atoms S}}{\overline{\text{mol S}}} = 2.3 \times 10^{24}$ atoms S

Check: The units of the answer (atoms S) are correct. The magnitude of the answer is reasonable since there is more than 1 mole of material present.

2.63   (a)   **Given:** 11.8 g Ar **Find:** mol Ar
        Conceptual Plan: g Ar → mol Ar

$$\frac{1\,\text{mol Ar}}{39.95\,\text{g Ar}}$$

Solution: $11.8 \,\overline{\text{g Ar}} \times \dfrac{1\,\text{mol Ar}}{39.95\,\overline{\text{g Ar}}} = 0.295$ mol Ar

Check: The units of the answer (mol Ar) are correct. The magnitude of the answer is reasonable since there is less than the mass of 1 mol present.

(b)   **Given:** 3.55 g Zn **Find:** mol Zn
        Conceptual Plan: g Zn → mol Zn

$$\frac{1\,\text{mol Zn}}{65.41\,\text{g Zn}}$$

Solution: $3.55 \,\overline{\text{g Zn}} \times \dfrac{1\,\text{mol Zn}}{65.41\,\overline{\text{g Zn}}} = 0.0543$ mol Zn

Check: The units of the answer (mol Zn) are correct. The magnitude of the answer is reasonable since there is less than the mass of 1 mol present.

(c)   **Given:** 26.1 g Ta **Find:** mol Ta
        Conceptual Plan: g Ta → mol Ta

$$\frac{1\,\text{mol Ta}}{180.95\,\text{g Ta}}$$

Solution: $26.1 \,\overline{\text{g Ta}} \times \dfrac{1\,\text{mol Ta}}{180.95\,\overline{\text{g Ta}}} = 0.144$ mol Ta

Check: The units of the answer (mol Ta) are correct. The magnitude of the answer is reasonable since there is less than the mass of 1 mol present.

(d)   **Given:** 0.211 g Li **Find:** mol Li
        Conceptual Plan: g Li → mol Li

$$\frac{1\,\text{mol Li}}{6.941\,\text{g Li}}$$

Solution: $0.211 \,\overline{\text{g Li}} \times \dfrac{1\,\text{mol Li}}{6.941\,\overline{\text{g Li}}} = 0.0304$ mol Li

Check: The units of the answer (mol Li) are correct. The magnitude of the answer is reasonable since there is less than the mass of 1 mol present.

2.65   **Given:** 3.78 g silver   **Find:** atoms Ag

         Conceptual Plan: g Ag $\rightarrow$ mol Ag $\rightarrow$ atoms Ag

$$\frac{1 \text{ mol Ag}}{107.87 \text{ g Ag}} \qquad \frac{6.022 \times 10^{23} \text{ atoms}}{\text{mol}}$$

         Solution: $3.78 \text{ g Ag} \times \dfrac{1 \text{ mol Ag}}{107.87 \text{ g Ag}} \times \dfrac{6.022 \times 10^{23} \text{ atoms Ag}}{1 \text{ mol Ag}} = 2.11 \times 10^{22}$ atoms Ag

         Check: The units of the answer (atoms Ag) are correct. The magnitude of the answer is reasonable since there is less than the mass of 1 mol of Ag present.

2.67   (a)   **Given:** 5.18 g P   **Find:** atoms P

         Conceptual Plan: g P $\rightarrow$ mol P $\rightarrow$ atoms P

$$\frac{1 \text{ mol P}}{30.97 \text{ g P}} \qquad \frac{6.022 \times 10^{23} \text{ atoms}}{\text{mol}}$$

         Solution: $5.18 \text{ g P} \times \dfrac{1 \text{ mol P}}{30.97 \text{ g P}} \times \dfrac{6.022 \times 10^{23} \text{ atoms P}}{1 \text{ mol P}} = 1.01 \times 10^{23}$ atoms P

         Check: The units of the answer (atoms P) are correct. The magnitude of the answer is reasonable since there is less than the mass of 1 mol of P present.

   (b)   **Given:** 2.26 g Hg   **Find:** atoms Hg

         Conceptual Plan: g Hg $\rightarrow$ mol Hg $\rightarrow$ atoms Hg

$$\frac{1 \text{ mol Hg}}{200.59 \text{ g Hg}} \qquad \frac{6.022 \times 10^{23} \text{ atoms}}{\text{mol}}$$

         Solution: $2.26 \text{ g Hg} \times \dfrac{1 \text{ mol Hg}}{200.59 \text{ g Hg}} \times \dfrac{6.022 \times 10^{23} \text{ atoms Hg}}{1 \text{ mol Hg}} = 6.78 \times 10^{21}$ atoms Hg

         Check: The units of the answer (atoms Hg) are correct. The magnitude of the answer is reasonable since there is much less than the mass of 1 mol of Hg present.

   (c)   **Given:** 1.87 g Bi   **Find:** atoms Bi

         Conceptual Plan: g Bi $\rightarrow$ mol Bi $\rightarrow$ atoms Bi

$$\frac{1 \text{ mol Bi}}{208.98 \text{ g Bi}} \qquad \frac{6.022 \times 10^{23} \text{ atoms}}{\text{mol}}$$

         Solution: $1.87 \text{ g Bi} \times \dfrac{1 \text{ mol Bi}}{208.98 \text{ g Bi}} \times \dfrac{6.022 \times 10^{23} \text{ atoms Bi}}{1 \text{ mol Bi}} = 5.39 \times 10^{21}$ atoms Bi

         Check: The units of the answer (atoms Bi) are correct. The magnitude of the answer is reasonable since there is less than the mass of 1 mol of Bi present.

   (d)   **Given:** 0.082 g Sr   **Find:** atoms Sr

         Conceptual Plan: g Sr $\rightarrow$ mol Sr $\rightarrow$ atoms Sr

$$\frac{1 \text{ mol Sr}}{87.62 \text{ g Sr}} \qquad \frac{6.022 \times 10^{23} \text{ atoms}}{\text{mol}}$$

         Solution: $0.082 \text{ g Sr} \times \dfrac{1 \text{ mol Sr}}{87.62 \text{ g Sr}} \times \dfrac{6.022 \times 10^{23} \text{ atoms Sr}}{1 \text{ mol Sr}} = 5.6 \times 10^{20}$ atoms Sr

         Check: The units of the answer (atoms Sr) are correct. The magnitude of the answer is reasonable since there is less than the mass of 1 mol of Sr present.

2.69   (a)   **Given:** 1.1×10^{23} gold atoms   **Find:** grams Au

         Conceptual Plan: atoms Au $\rightarrow$ mol Au $\rightarrow$ g Au

$$\frac{1 \text{ mol}}{6.022 \times 10^{23} \text{ atoms}} \qquad \frac{196.97 \text{ g Au}}{1 \text{ mol Au}}$$

         Solution: $1.1 \times 10^{23} \text{ atoms Au} \times \dfrac{1 \text{ mol Au}}{6.022 \times 10^{23} \text{ atoms Au}} \times \dfrac{196.97 \text{ g Au}}{1 \text{ mol Au}} = 36$ g Au

         Check: The units of the answer (g Au) are correct. The magnitude of the answer is reasonable since there are fewer than Avogadro's number of atoms in the sample.

   (b)   **Given:** 2.82×10^{22} helium atoms   **Find:** grams He

         Conceptual Plan: atoms He $\rightarrow$ mol He $\rightarrow$ g He

$$\frac{1 \text{ mol}}{6.022 \times 10^{23} \text{ atoms}} \qquad \frac{4.002 \text{ g He}}{1 \text{ mol He}}$$

Solution: 2.82×10^{22} atoms He $\times \dfrac{1\text{ mol He}}{6.022 \times 10^{23}\text{ atoms He}} \times \dfrac{4.002\text{ g He}}{1\text{ mol He}} = 0.187$ g He

Check: The units of the answer (g He) are correct. The magnitude of the answer is reasonable since there are fewer than Avogadro's number of atoms in the sample.

(c) **Given:** 1.8×10^{23} lead atoms **Find:** grams Pb
   Conceptual Plan: atoms Pb $\rightarrow$ **mol Pb** $\rightarrow$ **g Pb**

$$\dfrac{1\text{ mol}}{6.022 \times 10^{23}\text{ atoms}} \quad \dfrac{207.2\text{ g Pb}}{1\text{ mol Pb}}$$

   Solution: 1.8×10^{23} atoms Pb $\times \dfrac{1\text{ mol Pb}}{6.022 \times 10^{23}\text{ atoms Pb}} \times \dfrac{207.2\text{ g Pb}}{1\text{ mol Pb}} = 62$ g Pb

   Check: The units of the answer (g Pb) are correct. The magnitude of the answer is reasonable since there are fewer than Avogadro's number of atoms in the sample.

(d) **Given:** 7.9×10^{21} uranium atoms **Find:** grams U
   Conceptual Plan: atoms U $\rightarrow$ **mol U** $\rightarrow$ **g U**

$$\dfrac{1\text{ mol}}{6.022 \times 10^{23}\text{ atoms}} \quad \dfrac{238.029\text{ g U}}{1\text{ mol U}}$$

   Solution: 7.9×10^{21} atoms U $\times \dfrac{1\text{ mol U}}{6.022 \times 10^{23}\text{ atoms U}} \times \dfrac{238.029\text{ g U}}{1\text{ mol U}} = 3.1$ g U

   Check: The units of the answer (g U) are correct. The magnitude of the answer is reasonable since there are fewer than Avogadro's number of atoms in the sample.

2.71 **Given:** 52 mg diamond (carbon) **Find:** atoms C
   Conceptual Plan: mg C $\rightarrow$ **g C** $\rightarrow$ **mol C** $\rightarrow$ **atoms C**

$$\dfrac{1\text{ g C}}{1000\text{ mg C}} \quad \dfrac{1\text{ mol C}}{12.011\text{ g C}} \quad \dfrac{6.022 \times 10^{23}\text{ atoms}}{\text{mol}}$$

   Solution: 52 mg C $\times \dfrac{1\text{ g C}}{1000\text{ mg C}} \times \dfrac{1\text{ mol C}}{12.011\text{ g C}} \times \dfrac{6.022 \times 10^{23}\text{ atoms C}}{1\text{ mol C}} = 2.6 \times 10^{21}$ atoms C

   Check: The units of the answer (atoms C) are correct. The magnitude of the answer is reasonable since there is less than the mass of 1 mol of C present.

2.73 **Given:** 1 atom platinum **Find:** g Pt
   Conceptual Plan: atoms Pt $\rightarrow$ **mol Pt** $\rightarrow$ **g Pt**

$$\dfrac{1\text{ mol}}{6.022 \times 10^{23}\text{ atoms}} \quad \dfrac{195.08\text{ g Pt}}{1\text{ mol Pt}}$$

   Solution: 1 atom Pt $\times \dfrac{1\text{ mol Pt}}{6.022 \times 10^{23}\text{ atoms Pt}} \times \dfrac{195.08\text{ g Pt}}{1\text{ mol Pt}} = 3.239 \times 10^{-22}$ g Pt

   Check: The units of the answer (g Pt) are correct. The magnitude of the answer is reasonable since there is only 1 atom in the sample.

The Periodic Table and Atomic Mass

2.75 (a) K   Potassium is a metal

   (b) Ba   Barium is a metal

   (c) I   Iodine is a nonmetal

   (d) O   Oxygen is a nonmetal

   (e) Sb   Antimony is a metalloid

2.77 (a) tellurium   Te is in group 16 and is a main group element

   (b) potassium   K is in group 1 and is a main group element

   (c) vanadium   V is in group 5 and is a transition element

   (d) manganese   Mn is in group 7 and is a transition element

2.79　(a)　sodium　　　　　Na is in group 1 and is an alkali metal

　　　(b)　iodine　　　　　I is in group 17 and is a halogen

　　　(c)　calcium　　　　Ca is in group 2 and is an alkaline earth metal

　　　(d)　barium　　　　Ba is in group 2 and is an alkaline earth metal

　　　(e)　krypton　　　　Kr is in group 18 and is a noble gas

2.81　(a)　N and Ni would not be similar. Nitrogen is a nonmetal, nickel is a metal.

　　　(b)　Mo and Sn would not be similar. Although both are metals, molybdenum is a transition metal and tin is a main group metal.

　　　(c)　Na and Mg would not be similar. Although both are main group metals, sodium is in group 1 and magnesium is in group 2.

　　　(d)　Cl and F would be most similar. Chlorine and fluorine are both in group 17. Elements in the same group have similar chemical properties.

　　　(e)　Si and P would not be similar. Silicon is a metalloid and phosphorus is a nonmetal.

2.83　Main group metal atoms will lose electrons to form a cation with the same number of electrons as the nearest, previous noble gas.

Nonmetal atoms will gain electrons to form an anion with the same number of electrons as the nearest noble gas.

　　　(a)　O^{2-}　O is a nonmetal and has 8 electrons. It will gain electrons to form an anion. The nearest noble gas is neon with 10 electrons, so O will gain 2 electrons.

　　　(b)　K^+　K is a main group metal and has 19 electrons. It will lose electrons to form a cation. The nearest noble gas is argon with 18 electrons, so K will lose 1 electron.

　　　(c)　Al^{3+}　Al is a main group metal and has 13 electrons. It will lose electrons to form a cation. The nearest noble gas is neon with 10 electrons, so Al will lose 3 electrons.

　　　(d)　Rb^+　Rb is a main group metal and has 37 electrons. It will lose electrons to form a cation. The nearest noble gas is krypton with 36 electrons, so Rb will lose 1 electron.

Cumulative Problems

2.85　**Given:** 7.83 g HCN sample 1: 0.290 g H; 4.06 g N. 3.37 g HCN sample 2　**Find:** g C in sample 2
Conceptual Plan: g HCN sample 1 $\rightarrow$ g C in HCN sample 1 $\rightarrow$ ratio g C to g HCN $\rightarrow$ g C in HCN sample 2

$$g\,HCN - g\,H - g\,N \qquad \frac{g\,C}{g\,HCN} \qquad g\,HCN \times \frac{g\,C}{g\,HCN}$$

Solution: 7.83 g HCN $-$ 0.290 g H $-$ 4.06 g N $=$ 3.48 g C

$$3.37\ \overline{g\,HCN} \times \frac{3.48\,g\,C}{7.83\ \overline{g\,HCN}} = 1.50\,g\,C$$

Check: The units of the answer (g C) are correct. The magnitude of the answer is reasonable since the sample size is about half the original sample size, the g C are about half the original g C.

2.87　**Given:** in CO mass ratio O:C = 1.33:1; in compound X, mass ratio O:C = 2:1.　**Find:** formula of X
Conceptual Plan: determine the mass ratio of O:O in the two compounds
Solution: For 1 gram of C $\dfrac{2\,g\,O\ in\ compound\ X}{1.33\,g\,O\ in\ CO} = 1.5$

So, the ratio of O to C in compound X has to be 1.5:1 and the formula is C_2O_3.
Check: The answer is reasonable since it fulfills the criteria of multiple proportions and the mass ratio of O:C is 2:1.

2.89   **Given:** $^4\text{He}^{2+} = 4.00151$ amu **Find:** charge to mass ratio C/kg
        Conceptual Plan: determine total charge on $^4\text{He}^{2+}$ and then amu $^4\text{He}^{2+} \rightarrow$ g $^4\text{He}^{2+} \rightarrow$ kg $^4\text{He}^{2+}$

$$\frac{+\ 1.60218 \times 10^{-19}\text{C}}{\text{proton}} \qquad\qquad \frac{1\,\text{g}}{1.66054 \times 10^{-24}\,\text{amu}} \quad \frac{1\,\text{kg}}{1000\,\text{g}}$$

Solution: $\dfrac{2\ \cancel{\text{protons}}}{1\,\text{atom}\,^4\text{He}^{2+}} \times \dfrac{+\ 1.60218 \times 10^{-19}\,\text{C}}{\cancel{\text{proton}}} = \dfrac{3.20436 \times 10^{-19}\,\text{C}}{\text{atom}\,^4\text{He}^{2+}}$

$$\frac{4.00151\ \cancel{\text{amu}}}{1\,\text{atom}\,^4\text{He}^{2+}} \times \frac{1.66054 \times 10^{-24}\ \cancel{\text{g}}}{1\ \cancel{\text{amu}}} \times \frac{1\,\text{kg}}{1000\ \cancel{\text{g}}} = \frac{6.64466742 \times 10^{-27}\,\text{kg}}{1\,\text{atom}\,^4\text{He}^{2+}}$$

$$\frac{3.20436 \times 10^{-19}\,\text{C}}{\cancel{\text{atom}\,^4\text{He}^{2+}}} \times \frac{1\ \cancel{\text{atom}\,^4\text{He}^{2+}}}{6.64466742 \times 10^{-27}\,\text{kg}} = 4.82245 \times 10^7\ \text{C kg}^{-1}$$

Check: The units of the answer (C kg^{-1}) are correct. The magnitude of the answer is reasonable when compared to the charge to mass ratio of the electron.

2.91 $^{236}_{90}\text{Th}$ A $-$ Z = number of neutrons. $236 - 90 = 146$ neutrons. So, any nucleus with 146 neutrons is an isotone of $^{236}_{90}\text{Th}$.

Some would be $^{237}_{91}\text{Pa}$; $^{238}_{92}\text{U}$; $^{239}_{93}\text{Np}$; $^{240}_{94}\text{Pu}$; $^{235}_{89}\text{Ac}$; $^{234}_{88}\text{Ra}$; $^{241}_{95}\text{Am}$; $^{244}_{98}\text{Cf}$; etc.

2.93

Symbol	Z	A	Number protons	Number electrons	Number neutrons	Charge
O^{2-}	8	16	8	10	8	2 $-$
Ca^{2+}	20	40	20	18	20	2+
Mg^{2+}	12	25	12	10	13	2+
N^{3-}	7	14	7	10	7	3 $-$

2.95   **Given:** r(nucleus) = 2.7 fm; r(atom) = 70 pm (assume two significant figures)
        Find: vol(nucleus); vol(atom); % vol(nucleus)
        Conceptual Plan:

r(nucleus)(fm) $\rightarrow$ r(nucleus)(pm) $\rightarrow$ vol(nucleus) and then r(atom) $\rightarrow$ vol(atom) and then % vol

$$\frac{10^{-15}\text{m}}{1\,\text{fm}} \quad \frac{1\,\text{pm}}{10^{-12}\text{m}} \qquad V = \frac{4}{3}\pi r^3 \qquad\qquad V = \frac{4}{3}\pi r^3 \qquad \frac{\text{vol(nucleus)}}{\text{vol(atom)}} \times 100$$

Solution:

$$2.7\ \cancel{\text{fm}} \times \frac{10^{-15}\ \cancel{\text{m}}}{\cancel{\text{fm}}} \times \frac{1\,\text{pm}}{10^{-12}\ \cancel{\text{m}}} = 2.7 \times 10^{-3}\,\text{pm} \qquad V_{\text{nucleus}} = \frac{4}{3}\pi\,(2.7 \times 10^{-3}\,\text{pm})^3 = 8.2 \times 10^{-8}\ \text{pm}^3$$

$$V_{\text{atom}} = \frac{4}{3}\pi\,(70\,\text{pm})^3 = 1.4 \times 10^6\ \text{pm}^3 \qquad \frac{8.2 \times 10^{-8}\ \cancel{\text{pm}^3}}{1.4 \times 10^6\ \cancel{\text{pm}^3}} \times 100\% = 5.9 \times 10^{-12}\%$$

Check: The units of the answer (% vol) are correct. The magnitude of the answer is reasonable because the nucleus only occupies a very small % of the vol of the atom.

2.97   **Given:** mass of $^{12}\text{C} = 12$ exactly by definition **Find:** atomic mass of O if atomic mass of C was used instead of mass of ^{12}C

Other: atomic mass of C = 12.0107 amu, atomic mass of O = 15.9994 amu
Conceptual Plan: atomic mass of O/atomic mass of C $\rightarrow$ q. 12.000, q $\rightarrow$ atomic mass of O (using the new scale)

Solution: Mass of an isotope is determined in relationship to mass of ^{12}C. The mass ratio between the isotope of interest and ^{12}C is multiplied by 12 to determine the atomic mass of that isotope. For the sake of this problem, we are assuming that oxygen is a single isotope and its mass = 15.9994 amu. Since we are using atomic mass of C as the benchmark:

$$\frac{\text{mass O}}{\text{mass C}} = \frac{15.9994\ \text{amu}}{12.0107\ \text{amu}} = 1.332095548$$

Now, as the problem requested, we will arbitrarily assign the mass of 12.0107 as 12.0000. But this does not change the true ratio between atomic mass of C and that of O. But as before, mass of O is determined relative to mass of C. Therefore,

$$\text{mass O} = \text{mass C} \times q = 12.000 \text{ amu} \times 1.332095548 = 15.985 \text{ amu}$$

Check: Since the atomic mass of carbon, 12.0107, is closer to that of O, their ratio would be smaller than between ^{12}C and O. Therefore, the calculated mass would be smaller than the actual atomic mass of O.

2.99   **Given:** Cu sphere: r = 0.935 cm; d = 8.94 g cm⁻³ **Find:** number of Cu atoms
Conceptual Plan: r in inch → r in cm → vol sphere → g Cu → mol Cu → atoms Cu

$$V = \frac{4}{3}\pi r^3 \qquad \frac{8.96\,\text{g}}{\text{cm}^3} \qquad \frac{1\,\text{mol Cu}}{63.546\,\text{g}} \qquad \frac{6.022 \times 10^{23}\,\text{atoms}}{\text{mol}}$$

Solution:

$$\frac{4}{3}\pi(0.935)^3 \times \frac{8.94\,\cancel{\text{g}}}{\cancel{\text{cm}^3}} \times \frac{1\,\cancel{\text{mol Cu}}}{63.546\,\cancel{\text{g}}} \times \frac{6.022 \times 10^{23}\,\text{atoms Cu}}{1\,\cancel{\text{mol Cu}}} = 2.90 \times 10^{23}\,\text{atoms Cu}$$

Check: The units of the answer (atoms Cu) are correct. The magnitude of the answer is reasonable because there are about 8 mol Cu present.

2.101   **Given:** Li-6 = 6.01512 amu; Li-7 = 7.01601 amu; B = 6.941 amu **Find:** % abundance Li-6 and Li-7
Conceptual Plan: Let x = fraction Li-6 then $1 - x$ = fraction Li-7 → abundances

$$\text{Atomic mass} = \sum_n (\text{fraction of isotope } n) \times (\text{mass of isotope } n)$$

Solution: Atomic mass $= \sum_n (\text{fraction of isotope } n) \times (\text{mass of isotope } n)$

$$6.941 = (x)(6.01512\,\text{amu}) + (1 - x)(7.01601\,\text{amu})$$
$$0.07501 = 1.00089\,x$$
$$x = 0.07494 \qquad 1 - x = 0.92506$$
$$\text{Li-6} = 0.07494 \times 100 = 7.494\,\% \text{ and Li-7} = 0.92506 \times 100 = 92.506\,\%$$

Check: The units of the answer (%, which gives the relative abundance of each isotope) are correct. The relative abundances are reasonable because Li has an atomic mass closer to the mass of Li-7 than to Li-6.

2.103   **Given:** alloy of Au and Pd = 67.2 g; 2.49 × 10²³ atoms **Find:** % composition by mass
Conceptual Plan: atoms Au and Pd → mol Au and Pd → g Au and Pd → g Au

$$\frac{1\,\text{mol}}{6.022 \times 10^{23}\,\text{atoms}} \qquad \frac{196.97\,\text{g Au}}{1\,\text{mol Au}}, \frac{106.42\,\text{g Pd}}{1\,\text{mol Pd}}$$

Solution: Let X = atoms Au and Y = atoms Pd, develop expressions that will permit atoms to be related to moles and then to grams.

$$(\text{X}\,\cancel{\text{atoms Au}})\left(\frac{1\,\text{mol Au}}{6.022 \times 10^{23}\,\cancel{\text{atoms Au}}}\right) = \frac{X}{6.022 \times 10^{23}}\,\text{mol Au}$$

$$(\text{Y}\,\cancel{\text{atoms Pd}})\left(\frac{1\,\text{mol Pd}}{6.022 \times 10^{23}\,\cancel{\text{atoms Pd}}}\right) = \frac{Y}{6.022 \times 10^{23}}\,\text{mol Pd}$$

$$\text{X} + \text{Y} = 2.49 \times 10^{23}\,\text{atoms}; \text{ Y} = 2.49 \times 10^{23} - \text{X}$$

$$\left(\frac{X}{6.022 \times 10^{23}}\,\cancel{\text{mol Au}}\right)\left(\frac{196.97\,\text{g Au}}{\cancel{\text{mol Au}}}\right) = \frac{196.97\text{X}}{6.022 \times 10^{23}}\,\text{g Au}$$

$$\left(\frac{2.49 \times 10^{23} - \text{X}}{6.022 \times 10^{23}}\,\cancel{\text{mol Pd}}\right)\left(\frac{106.42\,\text{g Pd}}{\cancel{\text{mol Pd}}}\right) = \frac{106.42(2.49 \times 10^{23} - \text{X})}{6.022 \times 10^{23}}\,\text{g Pd}$$

g Au + g Pd = 67.2 g total

$$\frac{196.97\text{X}}{6.022 \times 10^{23}}\,\text{g Au} + \frac{106.42(2.49 \times 10^{23} - \text{X})}{6.022 \times 10^{23}}\,\text{g Pd} = 67.2\,\text{g}$$

$$\text{X} = 1.5426 \times 10^{23}\,\text{atoms Au}$$

$$(1.54 \times 10^{23}\,\cancel{\text{atoms Au}})\left(\frac{1\,\cancel{\text{mol Au}}}{6.022 \times 10^{23}\,\cancel{\text{atoms Au}}}\right)\left(\frac{196.97\,\text{g Au}}{\cancel{\text{mol Au}}}\right) = 50.37\,\text{g Au}$$

$$\left(\frac{50.37 \text{ g Au}}{67.2 \text{ g sample}}\right) \times 100 = 74.\underline{9}5\% \text{ Au} = 75.0\% \text{ Au}$$

% Pd = 100.0% − 75.0% Au = 25.0% Pd

Check: Units of the answer (% composition) are correct.

2.105 **Given:** Ag-107, 51.839%, Ag-109, $\dfrac{\text{mass Ag-109}}{\text{mass Ag-107}} = 1.0187$ **Find:** mass Ag-107

Conceptual Plan: % abundance Ag-107 → % abundance Ag-109 → fraction → mass Ag-107

$$100\% - (\% \text{Ag-107}) \qquad \frac{\%\,\text{abundance}}{100}$$

$$\text{Atomic mass} = \sum_n (\text{fraction of isotope } n) \times (\text{mass of isotope } n)$$

Solution: 100.00% − 51.839 % = 48.161% Ag − 109

$$\text{Fraction Ag-107} = \frac{51.839}{100.00} = 0.51839 \qquad \text{Fraction Ag-109} = \frac{48.161}{100.00} = 0.48161$$

Let X be the mass of Ag-107 then mass Ag-109 = 1.0187X

$$\text{Atomic mass} = \sum_n (\text{fraction of isotope } n) \times (\text{mass of isotope } n)$$

107.87 amu = 0.51839(X amu) + 0.48161(1.0187X amu)

X = 106.9\underline{0}7 amu = 106.91 amu mass Ag-107

Check: The units of the answer (amu) are correct. The answer is reasonable since it is close to the atomic mass number of Ag-107.

Challenge Problems

2.107 **Given:** $\dfrac{\text{mass 2 O}}{\text{mass 1 N}} = \dfrac{2.29}{1.00}; \dfrac{\text{mass 3 F}}{\text{mass 1 N}} = \dfrac{4.07}{1.00}$ **Find:** $\dfrac{\text{mass O}}{\text{mass 2 F}}$

Conceptual Plan: mass O/N and mass F/N → mass O/F → mass O/2F

$$\frac{\text{mass 2 O}}{\text{mass 1 N}} \quad \frac{\text{mass 3 F}}{\text{mass 1 N}} \quad \frac{\text{mass 2 O}}{\text{mass 3 F}}$$

Solution: $\dfrac{\text{mass 2 O}}{\text{mass 1 N}} = \dfrac{2.29}{1.00}; \dfrac{\text{mass 3 F}}{\text{mass 1 N}} = \dfrac{4.07}{1.00}$ $\left(\dfrac{2.29 \text{ mass 2O}}{4.07 \text{ mass 3F}}\right)\left(\dfrac{1O}{2O}\right)\left(\dfrac{3F}{2F}\right) = \dfrac{0.422 \text{ mass O}}{\text{mass 2 F}}$

Check: Mass ratio of O to F is reasonable since the mass of O is slightly less than the mass of fluorine.

2.109 **Given:** 7.36 g Cu, 0.51 g Zn **Find:** atomic mass of sample
Conceptual Plan: fraction Cu and Zn → atomic mass

$$\text{Atomic mass} = \sum_n (\text{fraction of atom } n) \times (\text{mass of atom } n)$$

Solution: 7.36 g Cu + 0.51 g Zn = 7.87 g sample

$$\left(\frac{7.36 \text{ g Cu}}{7.87 \text{ g sample}}\right)\left(\frac{63.55 \text{ g Cu}}{\text{mol Cu}}\right) + \left(\frac{0.51 \text{ g Zn}}{7.87 \text{ g sample}}\right)\left(\frac{65.41 \text{ g Zn}}{\text{mol Zn}}\right) = 63.67 \text{ g mol}^{-1}$$

Check: Units of the answer (g mol^{-1}) are correct. The magnitude of the answer is reasonable since it is between the mass of Cu (63.55 g mol^{-1}) and Zn (65.41 g mol^{-1}) and is closer to the mass of Cu.

2.111 **Given:** Mg = 24.312 amu, ^{24}Mg = 23.98504, 78.99%, ^{26}Mg = 25.98259 amu, $\dfrac{\text{abundance } ^{25}\text{Mg}}{\text{abundance } ^{26}\text{Mg}} = \dfrac{0.9083}{1}$
Find: mass ^{25}Mg
Conceptual Plan: abundance of ^{24}Mg and ratio ^{25}Mg /^{26}Mg → abundance ^{25}Mg and ^{26}Mg → mass ^{25}Mg

$$\text{Atomic mass} = \sum_n (\text{fraction of isotope } n) \times (\text{mass of isotope } n)$$

Solution: 100.00% − % abundance ^{24} = % abundance ^{25}Mg and ^{26}Mg

100.00% − 78 99% = 21.01% ^{25}Mg and ^{26}Mg

$$\text{fraction } ^{25}\text{Mg and } ^{26}\text{Mg} = \frac{21.01}{100.0} = 0.2101$$

$$\frac{\text{abundance } ^{25}\text{Mg}}{\text{abundance } ^{26}\text{Mg}} = \frac{0.9083}{1}$$

Let X = fraction ^{26}Mg, 0.9083X = fraction ^{25}Mg

fraction ^{25}Mg and ^{26}Mg = X + 0.9083X = 0.2101

X = ^{26}Mg = 0.1101, 0.9083X = ^{25}Mg = 0.1000

Atomic mass $= \sum_{n}$ (fraction of isotope n) x (mass of isotope n)

24.312 = (0.7899)(23.98504 amu) + (0.1000)(mass ^{25}Mg) + (0.1101)(25.98259 amu)

mass ^{25}Mg = 25.0$\underline{5}$6 amu = 25.06 amu

Check: The units of the answer (amu) are correct. The magnitude of the answer is reasonable since it is between the masses of ^{24}Mg and ^{26}Mg.

Conceptual Problems

2.113   If the amu and mole were not based on the same isotope, the numerical values obtained for an atom of material and a mole of material would not be the same. If, for example, the mole was based on the number of particles in C – 12 but the amu was changed to a fraction of the mass of an atom of Ne – 20 the number of particles and the number of amu that make up one mole of material would no longer be the same. We would no longer have the relationship where the mass of an atom in amu is numerically equal to the mass of a mole of those atoms in grams.

2.115   The different isotopes of the same element have the same number of protons and electrons, so the attractive forces between the nucleus and the electrons is constant and there is no difference in the radii of the isotopes. Ions, on the other hand, have a different number of electrons than the parent atom from which they are derived. Cations have fewer electrons than the parent atom. The attractive forces are greater because there is a larger positive charge in the nucleus than the negative charge in the electron cloud. So, cations are smaller than the parent atom from which they are derived. Anions have more electrons than the parent. The electron cloud has a greater negative charge than the nucleus, so the anions have larger radii than the parent.

3 Molecules, Compounds, and Nomenclature

Review Questions

3.1 The properties of compounds are generally very different from the properties of the elements that compose them. When two elements combine to form a compound, an entirely new substance results.

3.3 Chemical compounds can be represented by chemical formulas and molecular models. The type of formula or model you use depends on how much information you have about the compound and how much you want to communicate. An empirical formula gives the relative number of atoms of each element in the compound. It contains the smallest whole number ratio of the elements in the compound. A molecular formula gives the actual number of atoms of each element in a molecule of the compound. A structural formula shows how the atoms are connected. A ball and stick model shows the geometry of the compound. A space-filling model shows the relative sizes of the atoms and how they merge together.

3.5 Atomic elements are those that exist in nature with single atoms as their base units. Neon (Ne), gold (Au), and potassium (K) are a few examples of atomic elements.

Molecular elements do not normally exist in nature with single atoms as their base unit; rather, they exist as molecules, two or more atoms of the same element bonded together. Most exist as diatomic molecules, for example hydrogen (H_2), nitrogen (N_2), and oxygen (O_2). Some exist as polyatomic molecules: phosphorus (P_4) and sulfur (S_8).

Ionic compounds are generally composed of one or more metal cations (usually one type of metal) and one or more nonmetal anions bound together by ionic bonds. Sodium chloride (NaCl) and potassium sulfate (Na_2SO_4) would be examples of ionic compounds.

Molecular compounds are composed of two or more covalently bonded nonmetals. Examples would be water (H_2O), sulfur dioxide (SO_2), and nitrogen dioxide (NO_2).

3.7 Binary ionic compounds are named by using the name of the cation (metal) and the base name of the anion (nonmetal) + the suffix -ide. Ionic compounds that contain a polyatomic anion are named by using the name of the cation (metal) and the name of the polyatomic anion.

3.9 To name a binary molecular inorganic compound, list the name of the first element with a prefix to indicate the number of atoms in the compound if there is more than one, followed by the base name of the second element with a prefix to indicate the number of atoms in the compound if there is more than one, followed by the suffix -ide.

3.11 Binary acids are composed of hydrogen and a nonmetal. The names for binary acids have the following form: hydro plus the base name of the nonmetal + ic acid. Oxyacids contain hydrogen and an oxyanion. The names of oxyacids depend on the ending of the oxyanion and have the following forms: oxyanions ending with -ate: base name of the oxyanion + ic acid; oxyanions ending with -ite: base name of the oxyanion + ous acid.

3.13   An alkane is a hydrocarbon containing only single C to C bonds. An alkene contains at least one double C to C bond and an alkyne contains at least one triple C to C bond.

3.15   (a)   alcohol: R —— O —— H

    (b)   ethers: R —— O —— R'

    (c)   aldehyde:

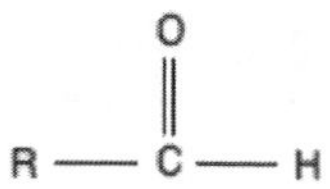

$$R - \overset{\overset{\textstyle O}{\|}}{C} - H$$

    (d)   ketone:

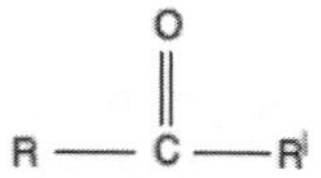

$$R - \overset{\overset{\textstyle O}{\|}}{C} - R'$$

    (e)   carboxylic acid:

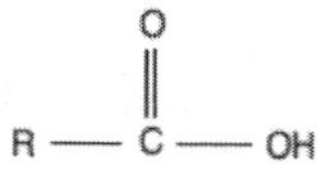

$$R - \overset{\overset{\textstyle O}{\|}}{C} - OH$$

    (f)   ester:

$$R - \overset{\overset{\textstyle O}{\|}}{C} - OR'$$

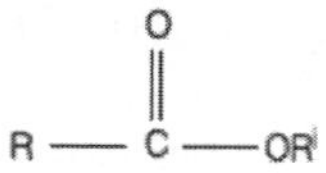

    (g)   amines: RNH_2

3.17   The chemical formula indicates the elements present in the compound and the relative number of atoms of each type. The chemical formula gives the conversion factor between the kind of element and the formula; it also allows the determination of mass percent composition.

3.19   Chemical formulas contain within them inherent relationships between atoms (or moles of atoms) and molecules (or moles of molecules). For example, the formula CCl_2F_2 tells us that one mole of CCl_2F_2 contains one mole of C atoms, two moles of Cl atoms, and two moles of F atoms.

3.21   The molecular formula is a whole-number multiple of the empirical formula. To find the molecular formula the molar mass of the compound must be known. The molecular molar mass divided by the empirical molar mass gives the whole number multiple used to convert the empirical formula to the molecular formula.

Problems by Topic

Chemical Formulas and Molecular View of Elements and Compounds

3.23   The chemical formula gives you the kind of atom and the number of each atom in the compound.

    (a) $Mg_3(PO_4)_2$ contains: 3 magnesium atoms, 2 phosphorus atoms, and 8 oxygen atoms

    (b) $BaCl_2$ contains: 1 barium atom and 2 chlorine atoms

    (c) $Fe(NO_2)_2$ contains: 1 iron atom, 2 nitrogen atoms, and 4 oxygen atoms

    (d) $Ca(OH)_2$ contains: 1 calcium atom, 2 oxygen atoms, and 2 hydrogen atoms

3.25   (a)   1 blue = nitrogen, 3 white = hydrogen: NH_3

    (b)   2 black = carbon, 6 white = hydrogen: C_2H_6

    (c)   1 yellow – green = sulfur, 3 red = oxygen: SO_3

3.27   (a)   Neon is an atomic element.

    (b)   Fluorine is one of the elements that exist as diatomic molecules, therefore it is a molecular element.

(c)   Potassium is a metal and therefore an atomic element.

(d)   Nitrogen is one of the elements that exist as diatomic molecules, therefore it is a molecular element.

3.29   (a) CO_2 is a compound composed of a nonmetal and a nonmetal, therefore it is a molecular compound.

(b) $NiCl_2$ is a compound composed of a metal and a nonmetal, therefore it is an ionic compound.

(c)   NaI is a compound composed of a metal and a nonmetal, therefore it is an ionic compound.

(d) PCl_3 is a compound composed of a nonmetal and a nonmetal, therefore it is a molecular compound.

3.31   (a)   white – hydrogen: a molecule composed of two of the same element, therefore it is a molecular element.

(b)   blue – nitrogen, white – hydrogen: a molecule composed of a nonmetal and a nonmetal, therefore it is a molecular compound.

(c)   purple – sodium: a substance composed of all the same atoms, therefore it is an atomic element.

Formulas and Names for Ionic Compounds

3.33   To write the formula for an ionic compound do the following: 1) Write the symbol for the metal cation and its charge and the symbol for the nonmetal anion and its charge. 2) Adjust the subscript on each cation and anion to balance the overall charge. 3) Check that the sum of the charges of the cations equals the sum of the charges of the anions.

(a)   calcium and oxygen: Ca^{2-} O^{2-} CaO   cations 2+, anions 2–

(b)   zinc and sulfur: Zn^{2+} S^{2-} ZnS   cations 2+, anions 2–

(c)   rubidium and bromine: Rb^+ Br^- RbBr   cation +, anions –

(d)   aluminum and oxygen: Al^{3+} O^{2-} Al_2O_3 cation 2(3+) = 6+, anions 3(2–) = 6–

3.35   To write the formula for an ionic compound do the following: 1) Write the symbol for the metal cation and its charge and the symbol for the polyatomic anion and its charge. 2) Adjust the subscript on each cation and anion to balance the overall charge. 3) Check that the sum of the charges of the cations equals the sum of the charges of the anions.

Cation = calcium: Ca^{2+}

(a)   hydroxide: OH^- $Ca(OH)_2$ cation 2+, anion 2(1–) = 2–

(b)   chromate: CrO_4^{2-} $CaCrO_4$ cation 2+, anion 2–

(c)   phosphate: PO_4^{3-} $Ca_3(PO_4)_2$ cation 3(2+) = 6+, anion 2(3–) = 6–

(d)   cyanide: CN^- $Ca(CN)_2$ cation 2+, anion 2(1–) = 2–

3.37   To name a binary ionic compound, name the metal cation followed by the base name of the anion + *-ide*.

(a) Mg_3N_2: The cation is magnesium; the anion is from nitrogen, which becomes nitride: magnesium nitride.

(b)   KF: The cation is potassium; the anion is from fluorine, which becomes fluoride: potassium fluoride.

(c) Na_2O: The cation is sodium; the anion is from oxygen, which becomes oxide: sodium oxide.

(d) Li_2S: The cation is lithium; the anion is from sulfur, which becomes sulfide: lithium sulfide.

(e)   CsF: The cation is cesium; the anion is fluorine, which becomes fluoride: cesium fluoride.

(f)   KI: The cation is potassium; the anion is iodine, which becomes iodide: potassium iodide.

(g)   SrCl$_2$:   The cation is strontium; the anion is chlorine, which becomes chloride: strontium chloride.

(h)   BaCl$_2$:   The cation is barium; the anion is chlorine, which becomes chloride: barium chloride.

3.39   To name these compounds you must first decide if the metal cation is invariant or can have more than one charge. Then, name the metal cation followed by the base name of the anion + -ide.

(a)   SnO: Sn can have more than one charge. The charge on Sn must be 2+ for the compound to be charge neutral: The cation is tin(II); the anion is from oxygen, which becomes oxide: tin(II) oxide.

(b)   Cr$_2$S$_3$:   Cr can have more than one charge. The charge on Cr must be 3+ for the compound to be charge neutral: The cation is chromium(III); the anion is from sulfur, which becomes sulfide: chromium(III) sulfide.

(c)   RbI: Rb is invariant: The cation is rubidium; the anion is from iodine, which becomes iodide: rubidium iodide.

(d)   BaBr$_2$:   Ba is invariant: The cation is barium; the anion is from bromine, which becomes bromide: barium bromide.

3.41   To name these compounds you must first decide if the metal cation is invariant or can have more than one charge. Then, name the metal cation followed by the name of the polyatomic anion.

(a)   CuNO$_2$:   Cu can have more than one charge. The charge on Cu must be 1+ for the compound to be charge neutral: The cation is copper(I); the anion is nitrite: copper(I) nitrite.

(b)   Mg(C$_2$H$_3$O$_2$)$_2$:   Mg is invariant: The cation is magnesium; the anion is acetate: magnesium acetate.

(c)   Ba(NO$_3$)$_2$:   Ba is invariant: The cation is barium; the anion is nitrate: barium nitrate.

(d)   Pb(C$_2$H$_3$O$_2$)$_2$:   Pb can have more than one charge. The charge on Pb must be 2+ for the compound to be charge neutral: The cation is lead(II); the anion is acetate: lead(II) acetate.

(e)   KClO$_3$:   K is invariant: The cation is potassium; the anion is chlorate: potassium chlorate.

(f)   PbSO$_4$:   Pb can have more than one charge. The charge on Pb must be 2+ for the compound to be charge neutral: The cation is lead(II); the anion is sulfate: lead(II) sulfate.

3.43   To write the formula for an ionic compound do the following: 1) Write the symbol for the metal cation and its charge and the symbol for the nonmetal anion or polyatomic anion and its charge. 2) Adjust the subscript on each cation and anion to balance the overall charge. 3) Check that the sum of the charges of the cations equals the sum of the charges of the anions.

(a)   sodium hydrogen sulfite: Na$^+$ HSO$_3^-$ NaHSO$_3$ cation 1+, anion 1−

(b)   calcium permanganate: Ca^{2+} MnO$_4^-$ Ca(MnO$_4$)$_2$ cation 1+, anion 2(1−)

(c)   silver nitrate: Ag$^+$ NO$_3^-$ AgNO$_3$ cation 1+, anion 1−

(d)   potassium sulfate: K$^+$ SO$_4^{2-}$ K$_2$SO$_4$ cation 2(1+) = 2+, anion 2−

(e)   rubidium hydrogen sulfate: Rb$^+$ HSO$_4^-$ RbHSO$_4$ cation 1+, anion 1−

(f)   potassium hydrogen carbonate: K$^+$ HCO$_3^-$ KHCO$_3$ cation 1+, anion 1−

3.45   Hydrates are named the same way as other ionic compounds with the addition of the term *prefix*hydrate, where the prefix is the number of water molecules associated with each formula unit.

(a)   CoSO$_4$ · 7H$_2$O   cobalt(II) sulfate heptahydrate

(b)   iridium(III) bromide tetrahydrate   IrBr$_3$ · 4H$_2$O

(c) $Mg(BrO_3)_2 \cdot 6H_2O$ magnesium bromate hexahydrate

(d)   potassium carbonate dihydrate $K_2CO_3 \cdot 2H_2O$

Formulas and Names for Molecular Compounds and Acids

3.47   (a)   CO   The name of the compound is the name of the first element, *carbon*, followed by the base name of the second element, *ox*, prefixed by *mono-* to indicate one and given the suffix *-ide*: carbon monoxide.

(b) NI_3 The name of the compound is the name of the first element, *nitrogen*, followed by the base name of the second element, *iod*, prefixed by *tri-* to indicate three and given the suffix *-ide*: nitrogen triiodide.

(c) $SiCl_4$ The name of the compound is the name of the first element, *silicon*, followed by the base name of the second element, *chlor*, prefixed by *tetra-* to indicate four and given the suffix *-ide*: silicon tetrachloride.

(d) N_4Se_4 The name of the compound is the name of the first element, *nitrogen*, prefixed by *tetra-* to indicate four followed by the base name of the second element, *selen*, prefixed by *tetra-* to indicate four and given the suffix *-ide*: tetranitrogen tetraselenide.

(e) I_2O_5 The name of the compound is the name of the first element, *iodine*, prefixed by *di-* to indicate two followed by the base name of the second element, *ox*, prefixed by *penta-* to indicate five and given the suffix *-ide*: diiodine pentaoxide.

3.49   (a)   phosphorus trichloride: PCl_3

(b)   chlorine monoxide: ClO

(c)   disulfur tetrafluoride: S_2F_4

(d)   phosphorus pentafluoride: PF_5

(e)   diphosphorus pentasulfide: P_2S_5

3.51   (a)   HI: The base name of I is *iod* so the name is hydroiodic acid.

(b) HNO_3:   The oxyanion is *nitrate*, which ends in *-ate*; therefore, the name of the acid is nitric acid.

(c) H_2CO_3:   The oxyanion is *carbonate*, which ends in *-ate*; therefore, the name of the acid is carbonic acid.

(d) H_3PO_4:   The oxyanion is *phosphate*, which ends in *-ate*; therefore, the name of the acid is phosphoric acid.

3.53   (a)   hydrofluoric acid: HF

(b)   hydrobromic acid: HBr

(c)   sulfurous acid: H_2SO_3

Organic Compounds

3.55   (a)   composed of metal cation and polyatomic anion – inorganic compound

(b)   composed of carbon and hydrogen – organic compound

(c)   composed of carbon, hydrogen, and oxygen – organic compound

(d)   composed of metal cation and nonmetal anion – inorganic compound

3.57   (a)   contains double bond – alkene

        (b)   contains only single bonds – alkane

        (c)   contains triple bond – alkyne

        (d)   contains only single bonds – alkane

3.59   (a)   but = 4 C, ane = single bonds: $CH_3CH_2CH_2CH_3$

        (b)   3 C = prop, single bonds = ane: propane

        (c)   oct = 8 C, ane = single bonds: $CH_3CH_2CH_2CH_2CH_2CH_2CH_2CH_3$

        (d)   5 C = pent, single bonds = ane: pentane

3.61   (a)   contains O: functionalized hydrocarbon: alcohol

        (b)   contains only C and H: hydrocarbon

        (c)   contains O: functionalized hydrocarbon: ketone

        (d)   contains N: functionalized hydrocarbon: amine

Formula Mass and the Mole Concept for Compounds

3.63   (a)   Pentane

        (b)   2-methylbutane

        (c)   2-methyl-4-(1-methylethyl)heptane

        (d)   4-ethyl-2-methylhexane

3.65   (a) $H_3C-CH_2-CH-CH_2-CH_2-CH_3$
                              |
                              CH_2
                              |
                              CH_3

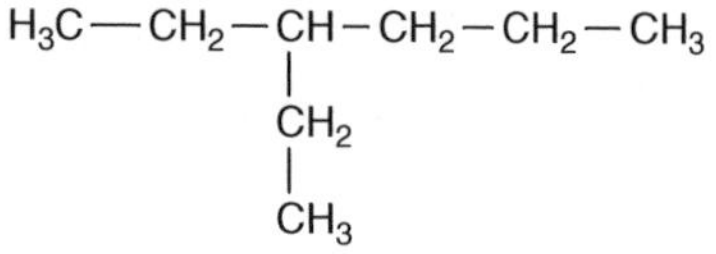

        (b) $H_3C-CH_2-\underset{\underset{CH_3}{|}}{\overset{\overset{CH_3}{|}}{C}}-CH_2-CH_3$

        (c) $H_3C-\underset{\overset{|}{CH_3}}{CH}-\underset{\overset{|}{CH_3}}{CH}-CH_3$

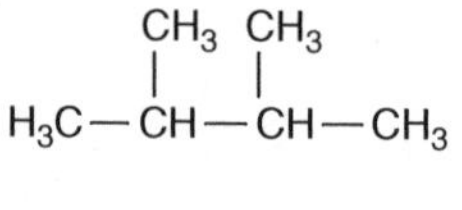

        (d) $CH_3-\underset{\overset{|}{CH_3}}{\overset{\overset{CH_3}{|}}{C}}-CH_2-\underset{\overset{|}{CH_3}}{CH}-CH_2-CH_2-\underset{\overset{|}{CH_2}}{CH}-CH_2-CH_3$

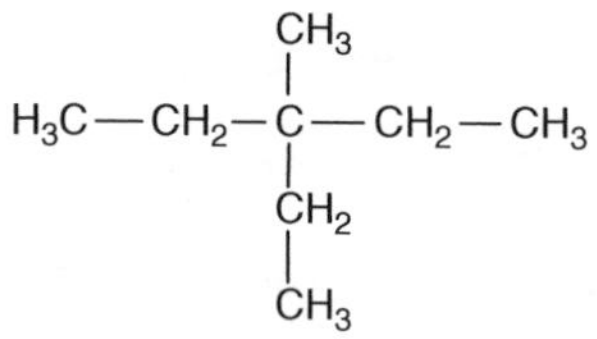

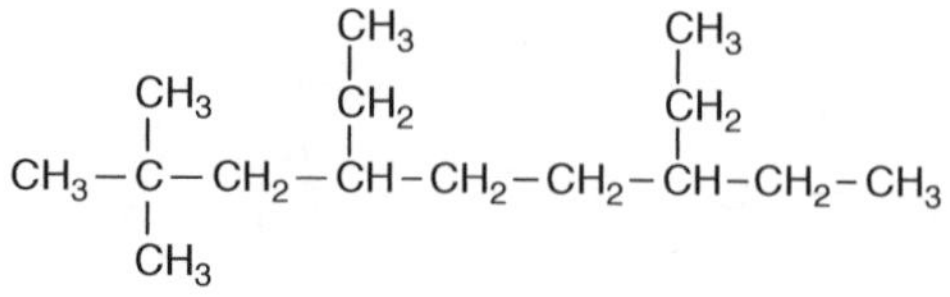

3.67   (a)   But-1-ene or butene

        (b)   3,4-dimethylpent-2-ene

        (c)   3-(1-methylethyl)hex-1-yne or 3-isopropylhexyne

        (d)   3,6-dimethylnon-4-yne

3.69   (a) $H_3C-CH_2-CH_2-C\equiv C-CH_2-CH_2-CH_3$

        (b) $H_3C-CH_2-CH=CH-CH_2-CH_2-CH_2-CH_2-CH_3$

(c)

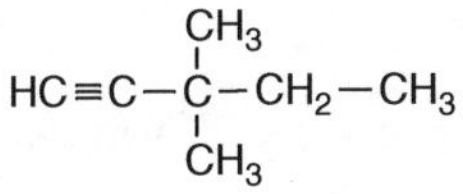

$$HC \equiv C - \overset{\overset{\displaystyle CH_3}{|}}{\underset{\underset{\displaystyle CH_3}{|}}{C}} - CH_2 - CH_3$$

(d)

$$H_3C - CH = \overset{}{\underset{\underset{\displaystyle CH_3}{|}}{C}} - CH_2 - \overset{\overset{\displaystyle CH_3}{|}}{\overset{\overset{\displaystyle CH_2}{|}}{}} \overset{\displaystyle CH_3}{} \\ \qquad\qquad CH_2 - \overset{}{\underset{}{CH}} - CH_3$$

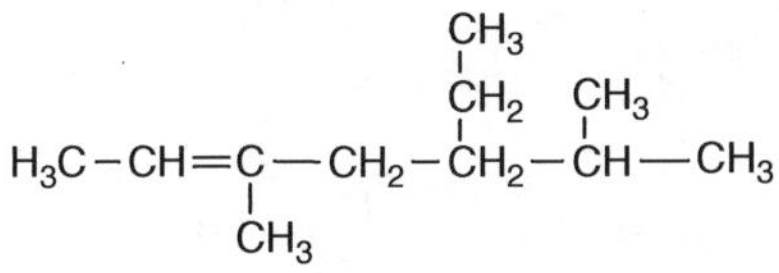

3.71   (a)   methylbenzene

        (b)   bromobenzene

        (c)   chlorobenzene

3.73   (a)   1,4-dibromobenzene

        (b)   1,3-diethylbenzene

        (c)   1-chloro-2-fluorobenzene

3.75   (a) 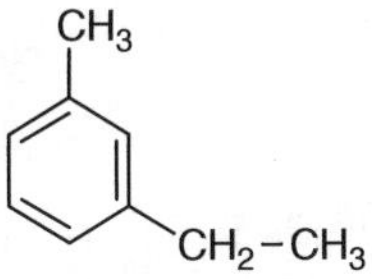   (b) 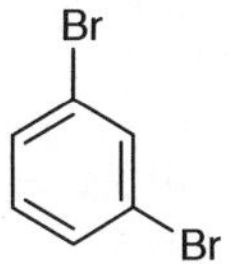   (c)

3.77   (a)   Propanol or Propan-1-ol

        (b)   4-methylhexan-2-ol

        (c)   2,6-dimethylheptan-4-ol

        (d)   3-methylpentan-3-ol

3.79   (a)   methyl butanoate

        (b)   propanoic acid

        (c)   5-methylhexanoic acid

        (d)   ethyl pentanoate

3.81   (a)   propoxyethane, or ethyl propyl ether

        (b)   pentoxyethane, or ethyl pentyl ether

        (c)   propoxypropane, or dipropyl ether

        (d)   butoxyethane, or butyl ethyl ether

3.83   (a)   diethylamine

        (b)   methylpropylamine

        (c)   butylmethylpropylamine

Formula Mass and the Mole Concept for Compounds

3.85   To find the formula mass, we sum the atomic masses of each atom in the chemical formula.

   (a) NO_2 formula mass $= 1 \times (\text{atomic mass N}) + 2 \times (\text{atomic mass O})$
                                                   $= 1 \times (14.01 \text{ amu}) + 2 \times (16.00 \text{ amu})$
                                                   $= 46.01 \text{ amu}$

   (b) C_4H_{10} formula mass $= 4 \times (\text{atomic mass C}) + 10 \times (\text{atomic mass H})$
                                                   $= 4 \times (12.01 \text{ amu}) + 10 \times (1.008 \text{ amu})$
                                                   $= 58.12 \text{ amu}$

   (c) $C_6H_{12}O_6$ formula mass $= 6 \times (\text{atomic mass C}) + 12 \times (\text{atomic mass H}) + 6 \times (\text{atomic mass O})$
                                                   $= 6 \times (12.01 \text{ amu}) + 12 \times (1.008 \text{ amu}) + 6 \times (16.00 \text{ amu})$
                                                   $= 180.16 \text{ amu}$

   (d) $Cr(NO_3)_3$ formula mass $= 1 \times (\text{atomic mass Cr}) + 3 \times (\text{atomic mass N}) + 9 \times (\text{atomic mass O})$
                                                   $= 1 \times (52.00 \text{ amu}) + 3 \times (14.01 \text{ amu}) + 9 \times (16.00 \text{ amu})$
                                                   $= 238.03 \text{ amu}$

3.87   (a)   **Given:** 25.5 g NO_2 **Find:** number of moles
                 Conceptual Plan: g NO_2 → mole NO_2
                                                     $\frac{1 \text{ mol}}{46.01 \text{ g } NO_2}$
                 Solution: $25.5 \text{ g } NO_2 \times \dfrac{1 \text{ mol } NO_2}{46.01 \text{ g } NO_2} = 0.554 \text{ mol } NO_2$
                 Check: The units of the answer (mole NO_2) are correct. The magnitude is appropriate because it is
                 less than 1 mole of NO_2.

         (b)   **Given:** 1.25 kg CO_2 **Find:** number of moles
                 Conceptual Plan: kg CO_2 → g CO_2 → mole CO_2
                                                     $\frac{1000 \text{ g } CO_2}{\text{kg } CO_2}$ $\frac{1 \text{ mol}}{44.01 \text{ g } CO_2}$
                 Solution: $1.25 \text{ kg } CO_2 \times \dfrac{1000 \text{ g } CO_2}{\text{kg } CO_2} \times \dfrac{1 \text{ mol } CO_2}{44.01 \text{ g } CO_2} = 28.4 \text{ mol } CO_2$
                 Check: The units of the answer (mole CO_2) are correct. The magnitude is appropriate because there
                 is over a kg of CO_2 present.

         (c)   **Given:** 38.2 g KNO_3 **Find:** number of moles
                 Conceptual Plan: g KNO_3 → mole KNO_3
                                                     $\frac{1 \text{ mol}}{101.11 \text{ g } KNO_3}$
                 Solution: $38.2 \text{ g } KNO_3 \times \dfrac{1 \text{ mol } KNO_3}{101.11 \text{ g } KNO_3} = 0.378 \text{ mol } KNO_3$
                 Check: The units of the answer (mole KNO_3) are correct. The magnitude is appropriate because there
                 is less than 1 mole of KNO_3.

         (d)   **Given:** 155.2 kg Na_2SO_4 **Find:** number of moles
                 Conceptual Plan: kg Na_2SO_4 → g Na_2SO_4 → mole Na_2SO_4
                                                     $\frac{1000 \text{ g } Na_2SO_4}{\text{kg } Na_2SO_4}$ $\frac{1 \text{ mol}}{142.05 \text{ g } Na_2SO_4}$
                 Solution: $155.2 \text{ kg } Na_2SO_4 \times \dfrac{1000 \text{ g } Na_2SO_4}{\text{kg } Na_2SO_4} \times \dfrac{1 \text{ mol } Na_2SO_4}{142.05 \text{ g } Na_2SO_4} = 1092 \text{ mol } Na_2SO_4$
                 Check: The units of the answer (mole Na_2SO_4) are correct. The magnitude is appropriate because
                 there is over 100 kg of Na_2SO_4 present.

3.89   (a)   **Given:** 6.5 g H_2O **Find:** number of molecules
                 Conceptual Plan: g H_2O → mole H_2O → number H_2O molecules
                                                     $\frac{1 \text{ mol}}{18.02 \text{ g } H_2O}$ $\frac{6.022 \times 10^{23} \text{ } H_2O \text{ molecules}}{\text{mol } H_2O}$

Solution: $6.5 \ \overline{g \ H_2O} \times \dfrac{1 \ \overline{mol \ H_2O}}{18.02 \ \overline{g \ H_2O}} \times \dfrac{6.022 \times 10^{23} \ H_2O \ molecules}{\overline{mol \ H_2O}} = 2.2 \times 10^{23} \ H_2O \ molecules$

Check: The units of the answer (H_2O molecules) are correct. The magnitude is appropriate: it is smaller than Avogadro's number, as expected, since we have less than 1 mole of H_2O.

(b)　**Given:** 389 g CBr_4 **Find:** number of molecules
Conceptual Plan: g CBr_4 → mole CBr_4 → number CBr_4 molecules

$$\dfrac{1 \ mol}{331.6 \ g \ CBr_4} \qquad \dfrac{6.022 \times 10^{23} \ CBr_4 \ molecules}{mol \ CBr_4}$$

Solution: $389 \ \overline{g \ CBr_4} \times \dfrac{1 \ \overline{mol \ CBr_4}}{331.6 \ \overline{g \ CBr_4}} \times \dfrac{6.022 \times 10^{23} \ CBr_4 \ molecules}{\overline{mol \ CBr_4}} = 7.06 \times 10^{23} \ CBr_4 \ molecules$

Check: The units of the answer (CBr_4 molecules) are correct. The magnitude is appropriate: it is larger than Avogadro's number, as expected, since we have more than 1 mole of CBr_4.

(c)　**Given:** 22.1 g O_2 **Find:** number of molecules
Conceptual Plan: g O_2 → mole O_2 → number O_2 molecules

$$\dfrac{1 \ mol}{32.00 \ g \ O_2} \qquad \dfrac{6.022 \times 10^{23} \ O_2 \ molecules}{mol \ O_2}$$

Solution: $22.1 \ \overline{g \ O_2} \times \dfrac{1 \ \overline{mol \ O_2}}{32.00 \ \overline{g \ O_2}} \times \dfrac{6.022 \times 10^{23} \ O_2 \ molecules}{\overline{mol \ O_2}} = 4.16 \times 10^{23} \ O_2 \ molecules$

Check: The units of the answer (O_2 molecules) are correct. The magnitude is appropriate: it is smaller than Avogadro's number, as expected, since we have less than 1 mole of O_2.

(d)　**Given:** 19.3 g C_8H_{10} **Find:** number of molecules
Conceptual Plan: g C_8H_{10} → mole C_8H_{10} → number C_8H_{10} molecules

$$\dfrac{1 \ mol}{106.16 \ g \ C_8H_{10}} \qquad \dfrac{6.022 \times 10^{23} \ C_8H_{10} \ molecules}{mol \ C_8H_{10}}$$

Solution:

$19.3 \ \overline{g \ C_8H_{10}} \times \dfrac{1 \ \overline{mol \ C_8H_{10}}}{106.16 \ \overline{g \ C_8H_{10}}} \times \dfrac{6.022 \times 10^{23} \ \overline{C_8H_{10} \ molecules}}{mol \ C_8H_{10}} = 1.09 \times 10^{23} \ C_8H_{10} \ molecules$

Check: The units of the answer (C_8H_{10} molecules) are correct. The magnitude is appropriate: it is smaller than Avogadro's number, as expected, since we have less than 1 mole of C_8H_{10}.

3.91　(a)　**Given:** 5.94×10^{20} SO_3 molecules **Find:** mass in g
Conceptual Plan: number SO_3 molecules → mole SO_3 → g SO_3

$$\dfrac{1 \ mol \ SO_3}{6.022 \times 10^{23} \ SO_3 \ molecules} \qquad \dfrac{80.07 \ g \ SO_3}{1 \ mol \ SO_3}$$

Solution: $5.94 \times 10^{20} \ \overline{SO_3 \ molecules} \times \dfrac{1 \ \overline{mol \ SO_3}}{6.022 \times 10^{23} \ \overline{SO_3 \ molecules}} \times \dfrac{80.07 \ g \ SO_3}{1 \ \overline{mol \ SO_3}} = 0.0790 \ g \ SO_3$

Check: The units of the answer (grams SO_3) are correct. The magnitude is appropriate: there is less than Avogadro's number of molecules so we have less than 1 mole of SO_3.

(b)　**Given:** 2.8×10^{22} H_2O molecules **Find:** mass in g
Conceptual Plan: number H_2O molecules → mole H_2O → g H_2O

$$\dfrac{1 \ mol \ H_2O}{6.022 \times 10^{23} \ H_2O \ molecules} \qquad \dfrac{18.02 \ g \ H_2O}{1 \ mol \ H_2O}$$

Solution: $2.8 \times 10^{22} \ \overline{H_2O \ molecules} \times \dfrac{1 \ \overline{mol \ H_2O}}{6.022 \times 10^{23} \ \overline{H_2O \ molecules}} \times \dfrac{18.02 \ g \ H_2O}{1 \ \overline{mol \ H_2O}} = 0.84 \ g \ H_2O$

Check: The units of the answer (grams H_2O) are correct. The magnitude is appropriate: there is less than Avogadro's number of molecules so we have less than 1 mole of H_2O.

(c)　**Given:** 1 $C_6H_{12}O_6$ molecule **Find:** mass in g
Conceptual Plan: number $C_6H_{12}O_6$ molecules → mole $C_6H_{12}O_6$ → g $C_6H_{12}O_6$

$$\dfrac{1 \ mol \ C_6H_{12}O_6}{6.022 \times 10^{23} \ C_6H_{12}O_6 \ molecules} \qquad \dfrac{180.16 \ g \ C_6H_{12}O_6}{1 \ mol \ C_6H_{12}O_6}$$

Solution:

$$1 \text{ C}_6\text{H}_{12}\text{O}_6 \text{ molecule} \times \frac{1 \text{ mol C}_6\text{H}_{12}\text{O}_6}{6.022 \times 10^{23} \text{ C}_6\text{H}_{12}\text{O}_6 \text{ molecules}} \times \frac{180.16 \text{ g C}_6\text{H}_{12}\text{O}_6}{1 \text{ mol C}_6\text{H}_{12}\text{O}_6} = 2.992 \times 10^{-22} \text{ g C}_6\text{H}_{12}\text{O}_6$$

Check: The units of the answer (grams $C_6H_{12}O_6$) are correct. The magnitude is appropriate: there is much less than Avogadro's number of molecules so we have much less than 1 mole of $C_6H_{12}O_6$.

3.93   **Given:** 1.8×10^{17} $C_{12}H_{22}O_{11}$ molecule **Find:** mass in mg
Conceptual Plan: number $C_{12}H_{22}O_{11}$ molecules $\rightarrow$ mole $C_{12}H_{22}O_{11}$ $\rightarrow$ g $C_{12}H_{22}O_{11}$ $\rightarrow$ mg $C_{12}H_{22}O_{11}$

$$\frac{1 \text{ mol C}_{12}\text{H}_{22}\text{O}_{11}}{6.022 \times 10^{23} \text{ C}_{12}\text{H}_{22}\text{O}_{11} \text{ molecules}} \quad \frac{342.3 \text{ g C}_{12}\text{H}_{22}\text{O}_{11}}{1 \text{ mol C}_{12}\text{H}_{22}\text{O}_{11}} \quad \frac{1 \times 10^3 \text{ mg C}_{12}\text{H}_{22}\text{O}_{11}}{1 \text{ g C}_{12}\text{H}_{22}\text{O}_{11}}$$

Solution:

$$1.8 \times 10^{17} \text{ C}_{12}\text{H}_{22}\text{O}_{11} \text{ molecules} \times \frac{1 \text{ mol C}_{12}\text{H}_{22}\text{O}_{11}}{6.022 \times 10^{23} \text{ C}_{12}\text{H}_{22}\text{O}_{11} \text{ molecules}} \times \frac{342.3 \text{ g C}_{12}\text{H}_{22}\text{O}_{11}}{1 \text{ mol C}_{12}\text{H}_{22}\text{O}_{11}} \times \frac{1 \times 10^3 \text{ mg C}_{12}\text{H}_{22}\text{O}_{11}}{1 \text{ g C}_{12}\text{H}_{22}\text{O}_{11}}$$

$$= 0.10 \text{ mg C}_{12}\text{H}_{22}\text{O}_{11}$$

Check: The units of the answer (milligrams $C_{12}H_{22}O_{11}$) are correct. The magnitude is appropriate: there is much less than Avogadro's number of molecules so we have much less than 1 mole of $C_{12}H_{22}O_{11}$.

Composition of Compounds

3.95   (a)   **Given:** CH_4 **Find:** mass percent C

Conceptual Plan: mass $\%\,C = \dfrac{1 \times \text{molar mass C}}{\text{molar mass CH}_4} \times 100$

Solution:

$$1 \times \text{molar mass C} = 1(12.01 \text{g mol}^{-1}) = 12.01 \text{ g C}$$

$$\text{molar mass CH}_4 = 1(12.01 \text{ g mol}^{-1}) + 4(1.008 \text{ g mol}^{-1}) = 16.04 \text{ g mol}^{-1}$$

$$\text{mass } \% \text{ C} = \frac{1 \times \text{molar mass C}}{\text{molar mass CH}_4} \times 100\%$$

$$= \frac{12.01 \text{ g mol}^{-1}}{16.04 \text{ g mol}^{-1}} \times 100\%$$

$$= 74.87\%$$

Check: The units of the answer (%) are correct. The magnitude is reasonable because it is between 0 and 100% and carbon is the heaviest element.

(b)   **Given:** C_2H_6 **Find:** mass percent C

Conceptual Plan: mass $\%\,C = \dfrac{2 \times \text{molar mass C}}{\text{molar mass C}_2\text{H}_6} \times 100$

Solution:

$$2 \times \text{molar mass C} = 2(12.01 \text{g mol}^{-1}) = 24.02 \text{ g C}$$

$$\text{molar mass C}_2\text{H}_6 = 2(12.01 \text{ g mol}^{-1}) + 6(1.008 \text{ g mol}^{-1}) = 30.07 \text{ g mol}^{-1}$$

$$\text{mass } \% \text{ C} = \frac{2 \times \text{molar mass C}}{\text{molar mass C}_2\text{H}_6} \times 100\%$$

$$= \frac{24.02 \text{ g mol}^{-1}}{30.07 \text{ g mol}^{-1}} \times 100\%$$

$$= 79.89\%$$

Check: The units of the answer (%) are correct. The magnitude is reasonable because it is between 0 and 100% and carbon is the heaviest element.

(c)   **Given:** C_2H_2 **Find:** mass percent C

Conceptual Plan: mass $\%\,C = \dfrac{2 \times \text{molar mass C}}{\text{molar mass C}_2\text{H}_2} \times 100$

Solution:

$$2 \times \text{molar mass C} = 2(12.01 \text{g mol}^{-1}) = 24.02 \text{ g C}$$

$$\text{molar mass } C_2H_2 = 2(12.01 \text{ g mol}^{-1}) + 2(1.008 \text{ g mol}^{-1}) = 26.04 \text{ g mol}^{-1}$$

$$\text{mass } \% \, C = \frac{2 \times \text{molar mass C}}{\text{molar mass } C_2H_2} \times 100\%$$

$$= \frac{24.02 \, \cancel{\text{g mol}^{-1}}}{26.04 \, \cancel{\text{g mol}^{-1}}} \times 100\%$$

$$= 92.26\%$$

Check: The units of the answer (%) are correct. The magnitude is reasonable because it is between 0 and 100% and carbon is the heaviest element.

(d)   **Given:** C_2H_5Cl **Find:** mass percent C

Conceptual Plan: $\text{mass } \% \, C = \dfrac{2 \times \text{molar mass C}}{\text{molar mass } C_2H_5Cl} \times 100$

Solution:

$$2 \times \text{molar mass C} = 2(12.01 \text{ g mol}^{-1}) = 24.02 \text{ g C}$$

$$\text{molar mass } C_2H_5Cl = 2(12.01 \text{ g mol}^{-1}) + 5(1.008 \text{ g mol}^{-1}) + 1(35.45 \text{ g mol}^{-1}) = 64.51 \text{ g mol}^{-1}$$

$$\text{mass } \% \, C = \frac{2 \times \text{molar mass C}}{\text{molar mass } C_2H_5Cl} \times 100\%$$

$$= \frac{24.02 \, \cancel{\text{g mol}^{-1}}}{64.51 \, \cancel{\text{g mol}^{-1}}} \times 100\%$$

$$= 37.23\%$$

Check: The units of the answer (%) are correct. The magnitude is reasonable because it is between 0 and 100% and chlorine is heavier than carbon.

3.97   **Given:** NH_3 **Find:** mass percent N

Conceptual Plan: $\text{mass } \% \, N = \dfrac{1 \times \text{molar mass N}}{\text{molar mass } NH_3} \times 100$

Solution:

$$1 \times \text{molar mass N} = 1(14.01 \text{ g mol}^{-1}) = 14.01 \text{ g N}$$

$$\text{molar mass } NH_3 = 3(1.008 \text{ g mol}^{-1}) + (14.01 \text{ g mol}^{-1}) = 17.03 \text{ g mol}^{-1}$$

$$\text{mass } \% \, N = \frac{1 \times \text{molar mass N}}{\text{molar mass } NH_3} \times 100\%$$

$$= \frac{14.01 \, \cancel{\text{g mol}^{-1}}}{17.03 \, \cancel{\text{g mol}^{-1}}} \times 100\%$$

$$= 82.27\%$$

Check: The units of the answer (%) are correct. The magnitude is reasonable because it is between 0 and 100% and nitrogen is the heaviest atom present.

Given: $CO(NH_2)_2$ **Find:** mass percent N

Conceptual Plan: $\text{mass } \% \, N = \dfrac{2 \times \text{molar mass N}}{\text{molar mass } CO(NH_2)_2} \times 100$

Solution:

$$2 \times \text{molar mass N} = 1(14.01 \text{ g mol}^{-1}) = 28.02 \text{ g N}$$

$$\text{molar mass } CO(NH_2)_2 = (12.01 \text{ g mol}^{-1}) + (16.00 \text{ g mol}^{-1}) + 2(14.01 \text{ g mol}^{-1}) + 4(1.008 \text{ g mol}^{-1})$$

$$= 60.06 \text{ g mol}^{-1}$$

$$\text{mass } \% \, N = \frac{2 \times \text{molar mass N}}{\text{molar mass } CO(NH_2)_2} \times 100\%$$

$$= \frac{28.02 \, \cancel{\text{g mol}^{-1}}}{60.06 \, \cancel{\text{g mol}^{-1}}} \times 100\%$$

$$= 46.65\%$$

Check: The units of the answer (%) are correct. The magnitude is reasonable. It is between 0 and 100% and there are two nitrogens and only one carbon and one oxygen per molecule.

Given: NH_4NO_3 **Find:** mass percent N

Conceptual Plan: mass % N $= \dfrac{2 \times \text{molar mass N}}{\text{molar mass } NH_4NO_3} \times 100$

Solution:

$2 \times$ molar mass N $= 2(14.01\text{g mol}^{-1}) = 28.02$ g N

molar mass $NH_4NO_3 = 2(14.01 \text{ g mol}^{-1}) + 4(1.008 \text{ g mol}^{-1}) + 3(16.00 \text{ g mol}^{-1}) = 80.05 \text{ g mol}^{-1}$

mass % N $= \dfrac{2 \times \text{molar mass N}}{\text{molar mass } NH_4NO_3} \times 100\%$

$= \dfrac{28.02 \text{ g mol}^{-1}}{80.05 \text{ g mol}^{-1}} \times 100\%$

$= 35.00\%$

Check: The units of the answer (%) are correct. The magnitude is reasonable because it is between 0 and 100%. The mass of nitrogen is less than the mass of oxygen and there are two nitrogens and three oxygens per molecule.

Given: $(NH_4)_2SO_4$ **Find:** mass percent N

Conceptual Plan: mass % N $= \dfrac{2 \times \text{molar mass N}}{\text{molar mass } (NH_4)_2SO_4} \times 100$

Solution:

$2 \times$ molar mass N $= 2(14.01\text{g mol}^{-1}) = 28.02$ g N

molar mass $(NH_4)_2SO_4 = 2(14.01 \text{ g mol}^{-1}) + 8(1.008 \text{ g mol}^{-1}) + (32.07 \text{ g mol}^{-1}) + 4(16.00 \text{ g mol}^{-1})$

$= 132.15 \text{ g mol}^{-1}$

mass % N $= \dfrac{2 \times \text{molar mass N}}{\text{molar mass } (NH_4)_2SO_4} \times 100\%$

$= \dfrac{28.02 \text{ g mol}^{-1}}{132.15 \text{ g mol}^{-1}} \times 100\%$

$= 21.20\%$

Check: The units of the answer (%) are correct. The magnitude is reasonable because it is between 0 and 100% and the mass of nitrogen is less than the mass of oxygen and sulfur.

The fertilizer with the highest nitrogen content is NH_3 with a N content of 82.27% N.

3.99   **Given:** 55.5 g CuF_2: 37.42 % F **Find:** g F in CuF_2
Conceptual Plan: g CuF_2 $\rightarrow$ g F

$\dfrac{37.42 \text{ g F}}{100.0 \text{ g } CuF_2}$

Solution: $55.5 \text{ g } CuF_2 \times \dfrac{37.42 \text{ g F}}{100.0 \text{ g } CuF_2} = 20.77 = 20.8$ g F

Check: The units of the answer (g F) are correct. The magnitude is reasonable because it is less than the original mass.

3.101   **Given:** 150 μg I; 76.45% I in KI **Find:** μg KI
Conceptual Plan: μg I $\rightarrow$ g I $\rightarrow$ g KI $\rightarrow$ μg KI

$\dfrac{1 \text{ g I}}{1 \times 10^6 \text{ } \mu\text{g I}}$ $\dfrac{100.0 \text{ g KI}}{76.45 \text{ g I}}$ $\dfrac{1 \times 10^6 \text{ } \mu\text{g KI}}{1 \text{ g KI}}$

Solution: $150 \text{ } \mu\text{g I} \times \dfrac{1 \text{ g I}}{1 \times 10^6 \text{ } \mu\text{g I}} \times \dfrac{100.0 \text{ g KI}}{76.45 \text{ g I}} \times \dfrac{1 \times 10^6 \text{ } \mu\text{g KI}}{1 \text{ g KI}} = 196 \text{ } \mu\text{g KI}$

Check: The units of the answer (μg KI) are correct. The magnitude is reasonable because it is greater than the original mass.

3.103   (a)   red – oxygen, white – hydrogen: 2H:O H_2O

(b)   black – carbon, white – hydrogen: 4H:C CH_4

(c)   black – carbon, white – hydrogen, red – oxygen: 2C:O:6H CH_3CH_2OH or C_2H_6O

3.105   (a)   **Given:** 0.0885 mol C_4H_{10} **Find:** mol H atoms

Conceptual Plan: mol C_4H_{10} → mole H atom

$$\frac{10 \text{ mol H}}{1 \text{ mol C}_4\text{H}_{10}}$$

Solution: 0.0885 mol C₄H₁₀ x $\dfrac{10 \text{ mol H}}{1 \text{ mol C}_4\text{H}_{10}}$ = 0.885 mol H atoms

Check: The units of the answer (mol H atoms) are correct. The magnitude is reasonable because it is greater than the original mol C_4H_{10}.

  (b)   **Given:** 1.3 mol CH_4 **Find:** mol H atoms

Conceptual Plan: mol CH_4 → mole H atom

$$\frac{4 \text{ mol H}}{1 \text{ mol CH}_4}$$

Solution: 1.3 mol CH₄ x $\dfrac{4 \text{ mol H}}{1 \text{ mol CH}_4}$ = 5.2 mol H atoms

Check: The units of the answer (mol H atoms) are correct. The magnitude is reasonable because it is greater than the original mol CH_4.

  (c)   **Given:** 2.4 mol C_6H_{12} **Find:** mol H atoms

Conceptual Plan: mol C_6H_{12} → mole H atom

$$\frac{12 \text{ mol H}}{1 \text{ mol C}_6\text{H}_{12}}$$

Solution: 2.4 mol C₆H₁₂ x $\dfrac{12 \text{ mol H}}{1 \text{ mol C}_6\text{H}_{12}}$ = 29 mol H atoms

Check: The units of the answer (mol H atoms) are correct. The magnitude is reasonable because it is greater than the original mol C_6H_{12}.

  (d)   **Given:** 1.87 mol C_8H_{18} **Find:** mol H atoms

Conceptual Plan: mol C_8H_{18} → mole H atom

$$\frac{18 \text{ mol H}}{1 \text{ mol C}_8\text{H}_{18}}$$

Solution: 1.87 mol C₈H₁₈ x $\dfrac{18 \text{ mol H}}{1 \text{ mol C}_8\text{H}_{18}}$ = 33.7 mol H atoms

Check: The units of the answer (mol H atoms) are correct. The magnitude is reasonable because it is greater than the original mol C_8H_{18}.

3.107   (a)   **Given:** 8.5 g NaCl **Find:** g Na

Conceptual Plan: g NaCl → mole NaCl → mol Na → g Na

$$\frac{1 \text{ mol NaCl}}{58.44 \text{ g NaCl}} \qquad \frac{1 \text{ mol Na}}{1 \text{ mol NaCl}} \qquad \frac{22.99 \text{ g Na}}{1 \text{ mol Na}}$$

Solution: 8.5 g NaCl x $\dfrac{1 \text{ mol NaCl}}{58.44 \text{ g NaCl}}$ x $\dfrac{1 \text{ mol Na}}{1 \text{ mol NaCl}}$ x $\dfrac{22.99 \text{ g Na}}{1 \text{ mol Na}}$ = 3.3 g Na

Check: The units of the answer (g Na) are correct. The magnitude is reasonable because it is less than the original g NaCl.

  (b)   **Given:** 8.5 g Na_3PO_4 **Find:** g Na

Conceptual Plan: g Na_3PO_4 → mole Na_3PO_4 → mol Na → g Na

$$\frac{1 \text{ mol Na}_3\text{PO}_4}{163.94 \text{ g Na}_3\text{PO}_4} \qquad \frac{3 \text{ mol Na}}{1 \text{ mol Na}_3\text{PO}_4} \qquad \frac{22.99 \text{ g Na}}{1 \text{ mol Na}}$$

Solution: 8.5 g Na₃PO₄ x $\dfrac{1 \text{ mol Na}_3\text{PO}_4}{163.94 \text{ g Na}_3\text{PO}_4}$ x $\dfrac{3 \text{ mol Na}}{1 \text{ mol Na}_3\text{PO}_4}$ x $\dfrac{22.99 \text{ g Na}}{1 \text{ mol Na}}$ = 3.6 g Na

Check: The units of the answer (g Na) are correct. The magnitude is reasonable because it is less than the original g Na_3PO_4.

  (c)   **Given:** 8.5 g $NaC_7H_5O_2$ **Find:** g Na

Conceptual Plan: g $NaC_7H_5O_2$ → mole $NaC_7H_5O_2$ → mol Na → g Na

$$\frac{1 \text{ mol NaC}_7\text{H}_5\text{O}_2}{144.10 \text{ g NaC}_7\text{H}_5\text{O}_2} \qquad \frac{1 \text{ mol Na}}{1 \text{ mol NaC}_7\text{H}_5\text{O}_2} \qquad \frac{22.99 \text{ g Na}}{1 \text{ mol Na}}$$

Solution: 8.5 g NaC₇H₅O₂ x $\dfrac{1 \text{ mol NaC}_7\text{H}_5\text{O}_2}{144.10 \text{ g NaC}_7\text{H}_5\text{O}_2}$ x $\dfrac{1 \text{ mol Na}}{1 \text{ mol NaC}_7\text{H}_5\text{O}_2}$ x $\dfrac{22.99 \text{ g Na}}{1 \text{ mol Na}}$ = 1.4 g Na

Check: The units of the answer (g Na) are correct. The magnitude is reasonable because it is less than the original g $NaC_7H_5O_2$.

(d)   **Given:** 8.5 g $Na_2C_6H_6O_7$ **Find:** g Na

     Conceptual Plan: g $Na_2C_6H_6O_7$ → mole $Na_2C_6H_6O_7$ → mol Na → g Na

$$\frac{1 \text{ mol } Na_2C_6H_6O_7}{236.1 \text{ g } Na_2C_6H_6O_7} \qquad \frac{2 \text{ mol Na}}{1 \text{ mol } Na_2C_6H_6O_7} \quad \frac{22.99 \text{ g Na}}{1 \text{ mol Na}}$$

     Solution:

$$8.5 \text{ g } Na_2C_6H_6O_7 \times \frac{1 \text{ mol } Na_2C_6H_6O_7}{236.1 \text{ g } Na_2C_6H_6O_7} \times \frac{2 \text{ mol Na}}{1 \text{ mol } Na_2C_6H_6O_7} \times \frac{22.99 \text{ g Na}}{1 \text{ mol Na}} = 1.7 \text{ g Na}$$

     Check: The units of the answer (g Na) are correct. The magnitude is reasonable because it is less than the original g $Na_2C_6H_6O_7$.

Chemical Formulas from Experimental Data

3.109   (a)   **Given:** 1.651 g Ag; 0.1224 g O   **Find:** empirical formula

     Conceptual Plan:

     convert mass to mol of each element → write pseudoformula → write empirical formula

$$\frac{1 \text{ mol Ag}}{107.9 \text{ g Ag}} \qquad \frac{1 \text{ mol O}}{16.00 \text{ g O}} \qquad\qquad \text{divide by smallest number}$$

     Solution: $1.651 \text{ g Ag} \times \dfrac{1 \text{ mol Ag}}{107.9 \text{ g Ag}} = 0.01530 \text{ mol Ag}$

$$0.1224 \text{ g O} \times \frac{1 \text{ mol O}}{16.00 \text{ g O}} = 0.007650 \text{ mol O}$$

$$Ag_{0.01530} O_{0.007650}$$

$$Ag_{\frac{0.01530}{0.007650}} O_{\frac{0.007650}{0.007650}} \rightarrow Ag_2O$$

     The correct empirical formula is Ag_2O.

(b)   **Given:** 0.672 g Co; 0.569 g As; 0.486 g O   **Find:** empirical formula

     Conceptual Plan:

     convert mass to mol of each element → write pseudoformula → write empirical formula

$$\frac{1 \text{ mol Co}}{58.93 \text{ g Co}} \quad \frac{1 \text{ mol As}}{74.92 \text{ g As}} \quad \frac{1 \text{ mol O}}{16.00 \text{ g O}} \qquad \text{divide by smallest number}$$

     Solution: $0.672 \text{ g Co} \times \dfrac{1 \text{ mol Co}}{58.93 \text{ g Co}} = 0.0114 \text{ mol Co}$

$$0.569 \text{ g As} \times \frac{1 \text{ mol As}}{74.92 \text{ g As}} = 0.00759 \text{ mol O}$$

$$0.486 \text{ g O} \times \frac{1 \text{ mol O}}{16.00 \text{ g O}} = 0.0304 \text{ mol O}$$

$$Co_{0.0114} As_{0.00759} O_{0.0304}$$

$$Co_{\frac{0.0114}{0.00759}} As_{\frac{0.00759}{0.00759}} O_{\frac{0.0304}{0.00759}} \rightarrow Co_{1.5}As_1O_4$$

$$Co_{1.5}As_1O_4 \times 2 \rightarrow Co_3As_2O_8$$

     The correct empirical formula is $Co_3As_2O_8$.

(c)   **Given:** 1.443 g Se; 5.841 g Br   **Find:** empirical formula

     Conceptual Plan:

     convert mass to mol of each element → write pseudoformula → write empirical formula

$$\frac{1 \text{ mol Se}}{78.96 \text{ g Se}} \qquad \frac{1 \text{ mol Br}}{79.90 \text{ g Br}} \qquad \text{divide by smallest number}$$

     Solution: $1.443 \text{ g Se} \times \dfrac{1 \text{ mol Se}}{78.96 \text{ g Se}} = 0.01828 \text{ mol Se}$

$$5.841 \text{ g Br} \times \frac{1 \text{ mol Br}}{79.90 \text{ g Br}} = 0.07310 \text{ mol Br}$$

$$Se_{0.01828}Br_{0.07310}$$

$$Se_{\frac{0.01828}{0.01828}}Br_{\frac{0.07310}{0.01828}} \rightarrow SeBr_4$$

     The correct empirical formula is $SeBr_4$.

3.111 (a) **Given:** in a 100 g sample: 74.03 g C, 8.70 g H, 17.27 g N **Find:** empirical formula
Conceptual Plan:
convert mass to mol of each element $\rightarrow$ **write pseudoformula** $\rightarrow$ **write empirical formula**

$$\frac{1 \text{ mol C}}{12.01 \text{ g C}} \quad \frac{1 \text{ mol H}}{1.008 \text{ g H}} \quad \frac{1 \text{ mol N}}{14.01 \text{ g N}} \qquad \text{divide by smallest number}$$

Solution: $74.03 \text{ g C} \times \dfrac{1 \text{ mol C}}{12.01 \text{ g C}} = 6.164 \text{ mol C}$

$8.70 \text{ g H} \times \dfrac{1 \text{ mol H}}{1.008 \text{ g H}} = 8.63 \text{ mol H}$

$17.27 \text{ g N} \times \dfrac{1 \text{ mol N}}{14.01 \text{ g N}} = 1.233 \text{ mol N}$

$C_{6.164}H_{8.63}N_{1.233}$

$C_{\frac{6.164}{1.233}} H_{\frac{8.63}{1.233}} N_{\frac{1.233}{1.233}} \rightarrow C_5H_7N$

The correct empirical formula is C_5H_7N.

(b) **Given:** in a 100 g sample: 49.48 g C, 5.19 g H, 28.85 g N, 16.48 g O **Find:** empirical formula
Conceptual Plan:
convert mass to mol of each element $\rightarrow$ **write pseudoformula** $\rightarrow$ **write empirical formula**

$$\frac{1 \text{ mol C}}{12.01 \text{ g C}} \quad \frac{1 \text{ mol H}}{1.008 \text{ g H}} \quad \frac{1 \text{ mol N}}{14.01 \text{ g N}} \quad \frac{1 \text{ mol O}}{16.00 \text{ g O}} \qquad \text{divide by smallest number}$$

Solution: $49.48 \text{ g C} \times \dfrac{1 \text{ mol C}}{12.01 \text{ g C}} = 4.120 \text{ mol C}$

$5.19 \text{ g H} \times \dfrac{1 \text{ mol H}}{1.008 \text{ g H}} = 5.15 \text{ mol H}$

$28.85 \text{ g N} \times \dfrac{1 \text{ mol N}}{14.01 \text{ g N}} = 2.059 \text{ mol N}$

$16.48 \text{ g O} \times \dfrac{1 \text{ mol O}}{16.00 \text{ g O}} = 1.030 \text{ mol O}$

$C_{4.120} H_{5.15} N_{2.059} O_{1.030}$

$C_{\frac{4.120}{1.030}} H_{\frac{5.15}{1.030}} N_{\frac{2.059}{1.030}} O_{\frac{1.030}{1.030}} \rightarrow C_4H_5N_2O$

The correct empirical formula is $C_4H_5N_2O$.

3.113 **Given:** in a 100 g sample: 75.69 g C, 8.80 g H, 15.51 g O **Find:** empirical formula
Conceptual Plan:
convert mass to mol of each element $\rightarrow$ **write pseudoformula** $\rightarrow$ **write empirical formula**

$$\frac{1 \text{ mol C}}{12.01 \text{ g C}} \quad \frac{1 \text{ mol H}}{1.008 \text{ g H}} \quad \frac{1 \text{ mol O}}{16.00 \text{ g O}} \qquad \text{divide by smallest number}$$

Solution: $75.69 \text{ g C} \times \dfrac{1 \text{ mol C}}{12.01 \text{ g C}} = 6.302 \text{ mol C}$

$8.80 \text{ g H} \times \dfrac{1 \text{ mol H}}{1.008 \text{ g H}} = 8.73 \text{ mol H}$

$15.51 \text{ g O} \times \dfrac{1 \text{ mol O}}{16.00 \text{ g O}} = 0.9694 \text{ mol O}$

$C_{6.302}H_{8.73}O_{0.9694}$

$C_{\frac{6.302}{0.9694}} H_{\frac{8.73}{0.9694}} O_{\frac{0.9694}{0.9694}} \rightarrow C_{6.50}H_{9.01}O$

$C_{6.50}H_{9.01}O \times 2 = C_{13}H_{18}O_2$

The correct empirical formula is $C_{13}H_{18}O_2$.

3.115 **Given:** 0.77 mg N, 6.61 mg N_xCl_y **Find:** empirical formula
Conceptual Plan:
find mg Cl $\rightarrow$ **convert mg to g for each element** $\rightarrow$ **convert mass to mol of each element** $\rightarrow$

$$\text{mg } N_xCl_y - \text{mg N} \qquad \frac{1 \text{ g}}{1000 \text{ mg}} \qquad \frac{1 \text{ mol N}}{14.01 \text{ g N}} \qquad \frac{1 \text{ mol Cl}}{35.45 \text{ g Cl}}$$

write pseudoformula $\rightarrow$ **write empirical formula**

$$\text{divide by smallest number}$$

Solution: 6.61 mg N_xCl_y – 0.77 mg N = 5.84 mg Cl

$$0.77 \text{ mg N} \times \frac{1 \text{ g N}}{1000 \text{ mg N}} \times \frac{1 \text{ mol N}}{14.01 \text{ g N}} = 5.5 \times 10^{-5} \text{ mol N}$$

$$5.84 \text{ mg Cl} \times \frac{1 \text{ g Cl}}{1000 \text{ mg Cl}} \times \frac{1 \text{ mol Cl}}{35.45 \text{ g Cl}} = 1.6 \times 10^{-4} \text{ mol Cl}$$

$$N_{5.5 \times 10^{-5}} Cl_{1.6 \times 10^{-4}}$$

$$N_{\frac{5.5 \times 10^{-5}}{5.5 \times 10^{-5}}} Cl_{\frac{1.6 \times 10^{-4}}{5.5 \times 10^{-5}}} \rightarrow NCl_3$$

The correct empirical formula is NCl_3.

3.117   (a)   **Given:** empirical formula = C_6H_7N, molar mass = 186.24 g mol^{-1} **Find:** molecular formula

Conceptual Plan: molecular formula = empirical formula x n $n = \dfrac{\text{molar mass}}{\text{empirical formula mass}}$

Solution: empirical formula mass = $6(12.01 \text{ g mol}^{-1}) + 7(1.008 \text{ g mol}^{-1}) + 1(14.01 \text{ g mol}^{-1}) = 93.13 \text{ g mol}^{-1}$

$$n = \frac{\text{molar mass}}{\text{formula molar mass}} = \frac{186.24 \text{ g mol}^{-1}}{93.13 \text{ g mol}^{-1}} = 1.998 = 2$$

$$\text{molecular formula} \quad = C_6H_7N \times 2$$
$$= C_{12}H_{14}N_2$$

(b)   **Given:** empirical formula = C_2HCl, molar mass = 181.44 g mol^{-1} **Find:** molecular formula

Conceptual Plan: molecular formula = empirical formula x n $n = \dfrac{\text{molar mass}}{\text{empirical formula mass}}$

Solution: empirical formula mass = $2(12.01 \text{ g mol}^{-1}) + 1(1.008 \text{ g mol}^{-1}) + 1(35.45 \text{ g mol}^{-1}) = 60.48 \text{ g mol}^{-1}$

$$n = \frac{\text{molar mass}}{\text{formula molar mass}} = \frac{181.44 \text{ g mol}^{-1}}{60.48 \text{ g mol}^{-1}} = 3$$

$$\text{molecular formula} \quad = C_2HCl \times 3$$
$$= C_6H_3Cl_3$$

(c)   **Given:** empirical formula = $C_5H_{10}NS_2$, molar mass = 296.54 g mol^{-1} **Find:** molecular formula

Conceptual Plan: molecular formula = empirical formula x n $n = \dfrac{\text{molar mass}}{\text{empirical formula mass}}$

Solution: empirical formula mass = $5(12.01 \text{ g mol}^{-1}) + 10(1.008 \text{ g mol}^{-1})$
$$+ 1(14.01 \text{ g mol}^{-1}) + 2(32.07) = \quad 148.28 \text{ g mol}^{-1}$$

$$n = \frac{\text{molar mass}}{\text{formula molar mass}} = \frac{296.54 \text{ g mol}^{-1}}{148.28 \text{ g mol}^{-1}} = 2$$

$$\text{molecular formula} \quad = C_5H_{10}NS_2 \times 2$$
$$= C_{10}H_{20}N_2S_4$$

3.119   **Given:** 33.01 g CO_2, 13.51 g H_2O **Find:** empirical formula
Conceptual Plan:
$$\textbf{mass } CO_2, H_2O \rightarrow \textbf{mol } CO_2, H_2O \rightarrow \textbf{mol C, mol H} \rightarrow \textbf{pseudoformula} \rightarrow \textbf{empirical formula}$$

$$\frac{1 \text{ mol } CO_2}{44.01 \text{ g } CO_2} \quad \frac{1 \text{ mol } H_2O}{18.02 \text{ g } H_2O} \quad \frac{1 \text{ mol C}}{1 \text{ mol } CO_2} \quad \frac{2 \text{ mol H}}{1 \text{ mol } H_2O} \qquad \text{divide by smallest number}$$

Solution:

$$33.01 \text{ g } CO_2 \times \frac{1 \text{ mol } CO_2}{44.01 \text{ g } CO_2} = 0.7500 \text{ mol } CO_2$$

$$13.51 \text{ g } H_2O \times \frac{1 \text{ mol } H_2O}{18.02 \text{ g } H_2O} = 0.7497 \text{ mol } H_2O$$

$$0.7500 \text{ mol } CO_2 \times \frac{1 \text{ mol C}}{1 \text{ mol } CO_2} = 0.7500 \text{ mol C}$$

$$0.7497 \, \overline{\text{mol H}_2\text{O}} \times \frac{2 \text{ mol H}}{1 \, \overline{\text{mol H}_2\text{O}}} = 1.499 \text{ mol H}$$

$$C_{0.7500} H_{1.499}$$

$$C_{\frac{0.7500}{0.7500}} H_{\frac{1.499}{0.7500}} \rightarrow CH_2$$

The correct empirical formula is CH_2.

3.121   **Given:** 4.30 g sample, 8.59 g CO_2, 3.52 g H_2O **Find:** empirical formula

Conceptual Plan:

mass CO_2, H_2O $\rightarrow$ mol CO_2, H_2O $\rightarrow$ mol C, mol H $\rightarrow$ mass C, mass H, mass O $\rightarrow$ mol O $\rightarrow$

$$\frac{1 \text{ mol } CO_2}{44.01 \text{ g } CO_2} \quad \frac{1 \text{ mol } H_2O}{18.02 \text{ g } H_2O} \quad \frac{1 \text{ mol C}}{1 \text{ mol } CO_2} \quad \frac{2 \text{ mol H}}{1 \text{ mol } H_2O} \quad \frac{12.01 \text{ g C}}{1 \text{ mol C}} \quad \frac{1.008 \text{ g H}}{1 \text{ mol H}} \quad \text{g sample} - \text{gC} - \text{g H} \quad \frac{1 \text{ mol O}}{16.00 \text{ g O}}$$

pseudoformula $\rightarrow$ empirical formula

　　　　divide by smallest number

Solution:

$$8.59 \, \overline{\text{g } CO_2} \times \frac{1 \text{ mol } CO_2}{44.01 \, \overline{\text{g } CO_2}} = 0.195 \text{ mol } CO_2$$

$$3.52 \, \overline{\text{g } H_2O} \times \frac{1 \text{ mol } H_2O}{18.02 \, \overline{\text{g } H_2O}} = 0.195 \text{ mol } H_2O$$

$$0.195 \, \overline{\text{mol } CO_2} \times \frac{1 \text{ mol C}}{1 \, \overline{\text{mol } CO_2}} = 0.195 \text{ mol C}$$

$$0.195 \, \overline{\text{mol } H_2O} \times \frac{2 \text{ mol H}}{1 \, \overline{\text{mol } H_2O}} = 0.390 \text{ mol H}$$

$$0.195 \, \overline{\text{mol } CO} \times \frac{12.01 \text{ mol C}}{1 \, \overline{\text{mol } CO}} = 2.34 \text{ g C}$$

$$0.390 \, \overline{\text{mol } H_2O} \times \frac{1.008 \text{ g H}}{1 \, \overline{\text{mol H}}} = 0.393 \text{ g H}$$

$$4.30 \text{ g} - 2.34 \text{ g} - 0.393 \text{ g} = 1.57 \text{ g O}$$

$$1.57 \, \overline{\text{g O}} \times \frac{1 \text{ mol O}}{16.00 \, \overline{\text{g O}}} = 0.0979 \text{ mol O}$$

$$C_{0.195} H_{0.390} O_{0.0979}$$

$$C_{\frac{0.195}{0.0979}} H_{\frac{0.390}{0.0979}} O_{\frac{0.0979}{0.0979}} \rightarrow C_2H_4O$$

The correct empirical formula is C_2H_4O.

Cumulative Problems

3.123   (a)   alkene; 2,3,4-trimethylpent-2-ene

　　　　(b)   alkane; 2,2,4-trimethylhexane

　　　　(c)   carboxylic acid; 3-methylpentanoic acid

　　　　(d)   amine; butyl(1-methylethyl)amine

　　　　(e)   alcohol; 2,4-dimethylhexan-1-ol

3.125   **Given:** 145 mL C_2H_5OH, d = 0.789 g cm^{-3} **Find:** number of molecules

Conceptual Plan: cm^3 $\rightarrow$ mL: mL C_2H_5OH $\rightarrow$ g C_2H_5OH $\rightarrow$ mol C_2H_5OH $\rightarrow$ molecules C_2H_5OH

$$\frac{1 \text{ cm}^3}{1 \text{ mL}} \qquad \frac{1 \text{ mL } C_2H_5OH}{0.789 \text{ g } C_2H_5OH} \quad \frac{1 \text{ mol } C_2H_5OH}{46.07 \text{ g } C_2H_5OH} \quad \frac{6.022 \times 10^{23} \text{ molecules } C_2H_5OH}{1 \text{ mol } C_2H_5OH}$$

Solution:

$$145 \, \overline{\text{mL } C_2H_5OH} \times \frac{0.789 \, \overline{\text{g } C_2H_5OH}}{\overline{\text{cm}^3}} \times \frac{1 \, \overline{\text{cm}^3}}{1 \, \overline{\text{mL}}} \times \frac{1 \text{ mol } C_2H_5OH}{46.07 \, \overline{\text{g } C_2H_5OH}} \times \frac{6.022 \times 10^{23} \text{ molecules } C_2H_5OH}{1 \, \overline{\text{mol } C_2H_5OH}}$$

$$= 1.50 \times 10^{24} \text{ molecules } C_2H_5OH$$

Check: The units of the answer (molecules C_2H_5OH) are correct. The magnitude is reasonable because we had more than two moles of C_2H_5OH and we have more than two times Avogadro's number of molecules.

3.127   (a)   To write the formula for an ionic compound do the following: 1) Write the symbol for the metal cation and its charge and the symbol for the nonmetal anion or polyatomic anion and its charge. 2) Adjust the subscript on each cation and anion to balance the overall charge. 3) Check that the sum of the charges of the cations equals the sum of the charges of the anions.

potassium chromate: K^+ CrO_4^{2-}; K_2CrO_4 cation $2(1+) = 2+$; anion $2-$

Given: K_2CrO_4 **Find:** mass percent of each element

Conceptual Plan: %K, then %Cr, then %O

mass %K $= \dfrac{2 \times \text{molar mass K}}{\text{molar mass K}_2\text{CrO}_4} \times 100$ mass %Cr $= \dfrac{1 \times \text{molar mass Cr}}{\text{molar mass K}_2\text{CrO}_4} \times 100$ mass %O $= \dfrac{4 \times \text{molar mass O}}{\text{molar mass K}_2\text{CrO}_4} \times 100$

molar mass of K = 39.10 g mol^{-1}, molar mass Cr = 52.00 g mol^{-1}, molar mass O = 16.00 g mol^{-1}

Solution: molar mass K_2CrO_4 = $2(39.10$ g mol$^{-1}) + 1(52.00$ g mol$^{-1}) + 4(16.00$ g mol$^{-1}) = 194.20$ g mol^{-1}

2 x molar mass K = $2(39.10$ g mol$^{-1}) = 78.20$ g K   1 x molar mass Cr = $1(52.00$ g mol$^{-1}) = 52.00$ g Cr

$$\text{mass \% K} = \frac{2 \times \text{molar mass K}}{\text{molar mass K}_2\text{CrO}_4} \times 100\% \qquad \text{mass \% Cr} = \frac{1 \times \text{molar mass Cr}}{\text{molar mass K}_2\text{CrO}_4} \times 100\%$$

$$= \frac{78.20 \; \text{g mol}^{-1}}{194.20 \; \text{g mol}^{-1}} \times 100\% \qquad\qquad = \frac{52.00 \; \text{g mol}^{-1}}{194.20 \; \text{g mol}^{-1}} \times 100\%$$

$$= 40.27\% \qquad\qquad\qquad = 26.78\%$$

$$4 \times \text{molar mass O} = 4(16.00 \text{ g mol}^{-1}) = 64.00 \text{ g O}$$

$$\text{mass \% O} = \frac{4 \times \text{molar mass O}}{\text{molar mass K}_2\text{CrO}_4} \times 100\%$$

$$= \frac{64.00 \; \text{g mol}^{-1}}{194.20 \; \text{g mol}^{-1}} \times 100\%$$

$$= 32.96\%$$

Check: The units of the answer (%) are correct. The magnitude is reasonable because each is between 0 and 100% and the total is 100%.

(b)   To write the formula for an ionic compound do the following: 1) Write the symbol for the metal cation and its charge and the symbol for the nonmetal anion or polyatomic anion and its charge. 2) Adjust the subscript on each cation and anion to balance the overall charge. 3) Check that the sum of the charges of the cations equals the sum of the charges of the anions.

Lead(II)phosphate: Pb^{2+} PO_4^{3-}; $Pb_3(PO_4)_2$ cation $3(2+) = 6+$; anion $2(3-) = 6-$

Given: $Pb_3(PO_4)_2$ **Find:** mass percent of each element

Conceptual Plan: %Pb, then % P, then %O

mass %PB $= \dfrac{3 \times \text{molar mass Pb}}{\text{molar mass Pb}_3(\text{PO}_4)_2} \times 100$ mass %P $= \dfrac{2 \times \text{molar mass P}}{\text{molar mass Pb}_3(\text{PO}_4)_2} \times 100$ mass %O $= \dfrac{8 \times \text{molar mass O}}{\text{molar mass Pb}_3(\text{PO}_4)_2} \times 100$

Solution: molar mass $Pb_3(PO_4)_2$ = $3(207.2$ g mol$^{-1}) + 2(30.97$ g mol$^{-1}) + 8(16.00$ g mol$^{-1}) = 811.5$ g mol^{-1}

3 x molar mass Pb = $3(207.2$ g mol$^{-1}) = 621.6$ g Pb   2 x molar mass P = $2(30.97$ g mol$^{-1}) = 61.94$ g P

$$\text{mass \% Pb} = \frac{3 \times \text{molar mass Pb}}{\text{molar mass Pb}_3(\text{PO}_4)_2} \times 100\% \qquad \text{mass \% P} = \frac{2 \times \text{molar mass P}}{\text{molar mass Pb}_3(\text{PO}_4)_2} \times 100\%$$

$$= \frac{621.6 \; \text{g mol}^{-1}}{811.5 \; \text{g mol}^{-1}} \times 100\% \qquad\qquad = \frac{61.94 \; \text{g mol}^{-1}}{811.5 \; \text{g mol}^{-1}} \times 100\%$$

$$= 76.60\% \qquad\qquad\qquad = 7.632\%$$

$$4 \times \text{molar mass O} = 8(16.00 \text{ g mol}^{-1}) = 128.0 \text{ g O}$$

$$\text{mass \% O} = \frac{8 \times \text{molar mass O}}{\text{molar mass Pb}_3(\text{PO}_4)_2} \times 100\%$$

$$= \frac{128.0 \; \text{g mol}^{-1}}{811.5 \; \text{g mol}^{-1}} \times 100\%$$

$$= 15.77\%$$

Check: The units of the answer (%) are correct. The magnitude is reasonable because each is between 0 and 100% and the total is 100%.

(c) sulfurous acid: H_2SO_3
Given: H_2SO_3 **Find:** mass percent of each element
Conceptual Plan: %H, then %S, then %O

$$\text{mass \%H} = \frac{\text{2 x molar mass H}}{\text{molar mass } H_2SO_3} \times 100 \quad \text{mass \%S} = \frac{\text{1 x molar mass S}}{\text{molar mass } H_2SO_3} \times 100 \quad \text{mass \%O} = \frac{\text{3 x molar mass O}}{\text{molar mass } H_2SO_3} \times 100$$

Solution: molar mass $H_2SO_3 = 2(1.008 \text{ g mol}^{-1}) + 1(32.07 \text{ g mol}^{-1}) + 3(16.00 \text{ g mol}^{-1}) = 82.086 \text{ g mol}^{-1}$
2 x molar mass H $= 1(1.008 \text{ g mol}^{-1}) = 2.016$ g H   1 x molar mass S $= 1(32.07 \text{ g mol}^{-1}) = 32.07$ g S

$$\text{mass \%H} = \frac{\text{2 x molar mass H}}{\text{molar mass } H_2SO_3} \times 100\% \qquad\qquad \text{mass \% S} = \frac{\text{1 x molar mass S}}{\text{molar mass } H_2SO_3} \times 100\%$$

$$= \frac{2.016 \text{ g mol}^{-1}}{82.086 \text{ g mol}^{-1}} \times 100\% \qquad\qquad\qquad = \frac{32.07 \text{ g mol}^{-1}}{82.086 \text{ g mol}^{-1}} \times 100\%$$

$$= 2.456\% \qquad\qquad\qquad\qquad\qquad = 39.07\%$$

3 x molar mass O $= 3(16.00 \text{ g mol}^{-1}) = 48.00$ g O

$$\text{mass \% O} = \frac{\text{3 x molar mass O}}{\text{molar mass } H_2SO_3} \times 100\%$$

$$= \frac{48.00 \text{ g mol}^{-1}}{82.086 \text{ g mol}^{-1}} \times 100\%$$

$$= 58.48\%$$

Check: The units of the answer (%) are correct. The magnitude is reasonable because each is between 0 and 100% and the total is 100%.

(d) To write the formula for an ionic compound do the following: 1) Write the symbol for the metal cation and its charge and the symbol for the nonmetal anion or polyatomic anion and its charge. 2) Adjust the subscript on each cation and anion to balance the overall charge. 3) Check that the sum of the charges of the cations equals the sum of the charges of the anions.
cobalt(II)bromide: Co^{2+} Br^-; $CoBr_2$ cation 2+ = 2+; anion 2(1–) = 2–
Given: $CoBr_2$ **Find:** mass percent of each element
Conceptual Plan: %Co, then %Br

$$\text{mass \%Co} = \frac{\text{1 x molar mass Co}}{\text{molar mass } CoBr_2} \times 100 \quad \text{mass \%Br} = \frac{\text{2 x molar mass Br}}{\text{molar mass } CoBr_2} \times 100$$

Solution: molar mass $CoBr_2 = (58.93 \text{ g mol}^{-1}) + 2(79.90 \text{ g mol}^{-1}) = 218.73 \text{ g mol}^{-1}$
2 x molar mass Co $= 1(58.93 \text{ g mol}^{-1}) = 58.93$ g Co   1 x molar mass Br $= 2(79.90 \text{ g mol}^{-1}) = 159.80$ g Br

$$\text{mass \% Co} = \frac{\text{1 x molar mass Co}}{\text{molar mass } CoBr_2} \times 100\% \qquad\qquad \text{mass \% Br} = \frac{\text{2 x molar mass Br}}{\text{molar mass } CoBr_2} \times 100\%$$

$$= \frac{58.93 \text{ g mol}^{-1}}{218.73 \text{ g mol}^{-1}} \times 100\% \qquad\qquad\qquad = \frac{159.80 \text{ g mol}^{-1}}{218.73 \text{ g mol}^{-1}} \times 100\%$$

$$= 26.94\% \qquad\qquad\qquad\qquad\qquad = 73.058\%$$

Check: The units of the answer (%) are correct. The magnitude is reasonable because each is between 0 and 100% and the total is 100%.

3.129   **Given:** 25 g CF_2Cl_2/mo. **Find:** g Cl/yr.
Conceptual Plan: g CF_2Cl_2/mo $\rightarrow$ g Cl/mo $\rightarrow$ g Cl/yr.

$$\frac{70.90 \text{ g Cl}}{120.91 \text{ g } CF_2Cl_2} \qquad \frac{12 \text{ mo.}}{1 \text{ yr.}}$$

Solution: $\dfrac{25 \text{ g } CF_2Cl_2}{\text{mo.}} \times \dfrac{70.90 \text{ g Cl}}{120.91 \text{ g } CF_2Cl_2} \times \dfrac{12 \text{ mo.}}{1 \text{ yr.}} = 1.8 \times 10^2$ g Cl/yr.

Check: The units of the answer (g Cl) is correct. The magnitude is reasonable because it is less than the total CF_2Cl_2/yr.

3.131   **Given:** MCl_3, 65.57% Cl **Find:** identify M
Conceptual Plan: g Cl $\rightarrow$ mol Cl $\rightarrow$ mol M $\rightarrow$ atomic mass M

$$\frac{1 \text{ mol Cl}}{35.45 \text{ g Cl}} \qquad \frac{1 \text{ mol M}}{3 \text{ mol Cl}} \qquad \frac{\text{g M}}{\text{mol M}}$$

Solution: in 100 g sample: 65.57 g Cl, 34.43 g M

$$65.57 \text{ g Cl} \times \frac{1 \text{ mol Cl}}{35.45 \text{ g Cl}} \times \frac{1 \text{ mol M}}{3 \text{ mol Cl}} = 0.6165 \text{ mol M} \qquad \frac{34.43 \text{ g M}}{0.6165 \text{ mol M}} = 55.84 \text{ g mol}^{-1} \text{ M}$$

molar mass of 55.84 = Fe
The identity of M = Fe.

3.133   **Given:** in a 100 g sample: 79.37 g C, 8.88 g H, 11.75 g O, molar mass = 272.37 g mol^{-1}
Find: molecular formula
Conceptual Plan:
convert mass to mol of each element $\rightarrow$ **pseudoformula** $\rightarrow$ **empirical formula** $\rightarrow$ **molecular formula**

$\frac{1 \text{ mol C}}{12.01 \text{ g C}}$ $\qquad$ $\frac{1 \text{ mol H}}{1.008 \text{ g H}}$ $\qquad$ $\frac{1 \text{ mol O}}{16.00 \text{ g O}}$ $\qquad$ divide by smallest number $\qquad$ empirical formula x n

Solution: $79.37 \text{ g C} \times \dfrac{1 \text{ mol C}}{12.01 \text{ g C}} = 6.609 \text{ mol C}$

$8.88 \text{ g H} \times \dfrac{1 \text{ mol H}}{1.008 \text{ g H}} = 8.81 \text{ mol H}$

$11.75 \text{ g O} \times \dfrac{1 \text{ mol O}}{16.00 \text{ g O}} = 0.7344 \text{ mol O}$

$C_{6.609}H_{8.81}O_{0.7344}$

$C_{\frac{6.609}{0.7344}} H_{\frac{8.81}{0.7344}} O_{\frac{0.7344}{0.7344}} \rightarrow C_9H_{12}O$

The correct empirical formula is $C_9H_{12}O$.
empirical formula mass = $9(12.01 \text{ g mol}^{-1}) + 12(1.008 \text{ g mol}^{-1}) + 1(16.00 \text{ g mol}^{-1}) = 136.19 \text{ g mol}^{-1}$

$$n = \frac{\text{molar mass}}{\text{formula molar mass}} = \frac{272.37 \text{ g mol}^{-1}}{136.19 \text{ g mol}^{-1}} = 2$$

molecular formula $= C_9H_{12}O \times 2 = C_{18}H_{24}O_2$

3.135   **Given:** 13.42 g sample, 39.61 g CO_2, 9.01 g H_2O, molar mass = 268.34 g mol^{-1}
Find: molecular formula
Conceptual Plan:
mass CO_2, H_2O $\rightarrow$ **mol CO_2, H_2O** $\rightarrow$ **mol C, mol H** $\rightarrow$ **mass C, mass H, mass O** $\rightarrow$ **mol O** $\rightarrow$

$\frac{1 \text{ mol CO}_2}{44.01 \text{ g CO}_2}$ $\frac{1 \text{ mol H}_2O}{18.02 \text{ g H}_2O}$ $\frac{1 \text{ mol C}}{1 \text{ mol CO}_2}$ $\frac{2 \text{ mol H}}{1 \text{ mol H}_2O}$ $\frac{12.01 \text{ g C}}{1 \text{ mol C}}$ $\frac{1.008 \text{ g H}}{1 \text{ mol H}}$ g sample – gC – g H $\frac{1 \text{ mol O}}{16.00 \text{ g O}}$

pseudoformula $\rightarrow$ **empirical formula** $\rightarrow$ **molecular formula**

divide by smallest number $\qquad$ empirical formula x n

$39.61 \text{ g CO}_2 \times \dfrac{1 \text{ mol CO}_2}{44.01 \text{ g CO}_2} = 0.9000 \text{ mol CO}_2$

$9.01 \text{ g H}_2O \times \dfrac{1 \text{ mol H}_2O}{18.02 \text{ g H}_2O} = 0.5000 \text{ mol H}_2O$

$0.9000 \text{ mol CO}_2 \times \dfrac{1 \text{ mol C}}{1 \text{ mol CO}_2} = 0.9000 \text{ mol C}$

$0.5000 \text{ mol H}_2O \times \dfrac{2 \text{ mol H}}{1 \text{ mol H}_2O} = 1.000 \text{ mol H}$

$0.9000 \text{ mol C} \times \dfrac{12.01 \text{ g C}}{1 \text{ mol C}} = 10.81 \text{ g C}$

$1.000 \text{ mol H} \times \dfrac{1.008 \text{ g H}}{1 \text{ mol H}} = 1.008 \text{ g H}$

$13.42 \text{ g} - 10.81 \text{ g} - 1.008 \text{ g} = 1.60 \text{ g O}$

$1.60 \text{ g O} \times \dfrac{1 \text{ mol O}}{16.00 \text{ g O}} = 0.100 \text{ mol O}$

$C_{0.9000}H_{1.000}O_{0.100}$

$C_{\frac{0.9000}{0.100}} H_{\frac{1.000}{0.100}} O_{\frac{0.100}{0.100}} \rightarrow C_9H_{10}O$

The correct empirical formula is $C_9H_{10}O$.

empirical formula mass = $9(12.01 \text{ g mol}^{-1}) + 10(1.008 \text{ g mol}^{-1}) + 1(16.00 \text{ g mol}^{-1}) = 134.2 \text{ g mol}^{-1}$

$$n = \frac{\text{molar mass}}{\text{formula molar mass}} = \frac{268.34 \text{ g mol}^{-1}}{134.2 \text{ g mol}^{-1}} = 2$$

$$\text{molecular formula} = C_9H_{10}O \times 2 = C_{18}H_{20}O_2$$

3.137 **Given:** 4.93 g $MgSO_4 \cdot xH_2O$, 2.41 g $MgSO_4$ **Find:** value of x
Conceptual Plan: g $MgSO_4$ → mol $MgSO_4$ g H_2O → mol H_2O Determine mole ratio

$$\frac{1 \text{ mol } MgSO_4}{120.38 \text{ g } MgSO_4} \qquad \frac{1 \text{ mol } H_2O}{18.02 \text{ g } H_2O} \qquad \frac{\text{mol } H_2O}{\text{mol } MgSO_4}$$

Solution:

$$2.41 \text{ g } MgSO_4 \times \frac{1 \text{ mol } MgSO_4}{120.38 \text{ g } MgSO_4} = 0.0200 \text{ mol } MgSO_4$$

Determine g H_2O: 4.93 g $MgSO_4 \cdot xH_2O$ – 2.41 g $MgSO_4$ = 2.52 g H_2O

$$2.52 \text{ g } H_2O \times \frac{1 \text{ mol } H_2O}{18.02 \text{ g } H_2O} = 0.140 \text{ mol } H_2O$$

$$\frac{0.140 \text{ mol } H_2O}{0.0200 \text{ mol } MgSO_4} = 7$$

$$x = 7$$

3.139 **Given:** molar mass = 177 g mol^{-1}, g C 8(g H) **Find:** molecular formula
Conceptual Plan: C_xH_yBrO
Solution: in 1 mol compound, let x = mol C and y = mol H, assume mol Br = 1, assume mol O = 1
$$177 \text{ g mol}^{-1} = x(12.01 \text{ g mol}^{-1}) + y(1.008 \text{ g mol}^{-1}) + 1(79.90 \text{ g mol}^{-1}) + 1(16.00 \text{ g mol}^{-1})$$
$$x(12.01 \text{ g mol}^{-1}) = 8 \{y(1.008 \text{ g mol}^{-1})\}$$
$$177 \text{ g mol}^{-1} = 8y(1.008 \text{ g mol}^{-1}) + y(1.008 \text{ g mol}^{-1}) + 79.90 \text{ g mol}^{-1} + 16.00 \text{ g mol}^{-1}$$
$$81 = 9y(1.008)$$
$$y = 9 = \text{mol H}$$
$$x(12.01) = 8 \times 9(1.008)$$
$$x = 6 = \text{mol C}$$
molecular formula = C_6H_9BrO
Check: molar mass = $6(12.01 \text{ g mol}^{-1}) + 9(1.008 \text{ g mol}^{-1}) + 1(79.90 \text{ g mol}^{-1}) + 1(16.00 \text{ g mol}^{-1}) = 177.0 \text{ g mol}^{-1}$

3.141 **Given:** 23.5 mg $C_{17}H_{22}ClNO_4$ **Find:** total number of atoms
Conceptual Plan: mg compound → g compound → mol compound → mol atoms → number of atoms

$$\frac{1 \text{ g}}{1000 \text{ mg}} \qquad \frac{1 \text{ mol}}{339.8 \text{ g}} \qquad \frac{45 \text{ mol atoms}}{1 \text{ mol compound}} \qquad \frac{6.022 \times 10^{23} \text{ atoms}}{1 \text{ mol atoms}}$$

Solution: $23.5 \text{ mg} \times \frac{1 \text{ g}}{1000 \text{ mg}} \times \frac{1 \text{ mol cpd}}{339.8 \text{ g}} \times \frac{45 \text{ mol atoms}}{1 \text{ mol cpd}} \times \frac{6.022 \times 10^{23} \text{ atoms}}{\text{mol}} = 1.87 \times 10^{21}$ atoms

Check: The units of the answer (number of atoms) is correct. The magnitude of the answer is reasonable since the molecule is so complex.

3.143 **Given:** MCl_3, 2.395 g sample, 3.606×10^{-2} mol Cl **Find:** atomic mass M
Conceptual Plan: mol Cl → g Cl → g X

$$\frac{35.45 \text{ g Cl}}{1 \text{ mol Cl}} \qquad \text{g sample} - \text{g Cl} = \text{g M}$$

mol Cl → mol M → atomic mass M

$$\frac{1 \text{ mol M}}{3 \text{ mol Cl}} \qquad \frac{\text{g M}}{\text{mol M}}$$

Solution:

$$3.606 \times 10^{-2} \text{ mol Cl} \times \frac{35.45 \text{ g}}{1 \text{ mol Cl}} = 1.278327 \text{ g Cl}$$

$$2.395 \text{ g} - 1.278327 \text{ g M} = 1.116673 \text{ g M}$$

$$3.606 \times 10^{-2} \text{ mol Cl} \times \frac{1 \text{ mol M}}{3 \text{ mol Cl}} = 1.116673 \times 10^{-2} \text{ mol M}$$

$$\frac{1.116673 \text{ g M}}{0.01116673 \text{ mol M}} = 92.90 \text{ g mol}^{-1} \text{ M (the metal is niobium)}$$

atomic mass = 92.90 amu

3.145   **Given:** $Fe_xCr_yO_4$; 28.59% O **Find:** x and y
Conceptual Plan: %O → **molar mass $Fe_xCr_yO_4$** → **mass Fe + Cr**

$$\frac{mass\ O}{molar\ mass\ compound} \times 100 = \%O \qquad mass\ cpd - mass\ O = mass\ Fe + Cr$$

Solution: $\dfrac{28.59\ g\ O}{100.0} = \dfrac{64.00\ g\ O}{molar\ mass\ cpd}$ molar mass = 223.8 g mol^{-1}

Mass Fe + Cr = molar mass − (4x molar mass O) = 223.8 − 64.00 = 159.8 g
Molar mass Fe = 55.85, molar mass Cr = 52.00
Since the mass of the two metals is close, the average mass can be used to determine the total moles of

Fe and Cr present in the compound. Average mass of Fe and Cr = 53.5. $\dfrac{159.8g}{53.5g\ mol^{-1}} = 2.96 = 3\ mol$
metal.
Let x = mol Fe and y = mol Cr
x mol Fe + y mol Cr = 3 mol total
x mol Fe(55.85 g Fe/mol) + y mol Cr(52.00 g mol^{-1}) = 159.8
y mol Cr = 3 − x mol Fe
$x(55.85) + (3 − x)(52.00) = 159.8$
So $x = 1$ and $y = 2$.
Check: Formula = $FeCr_2O_4$ would have a molar mass of Fe + 2Cr + 4O = 55.85 + 2(52.00) + 4(16.00) = 223.85
and the molar mass of the compound is 223.8.

3.147   **Given:** 0.0552% $NaNO_2$; 255 g bag **Find:** mass Na in bag
Conceptual Plan: g bag → **g NaNO2** → **g Na**

$$\frac{0.0552\ g\ NaNO_2}{100.0\ g\ bag} \qquad \frac{22.99\ g\ Na}{69.00\ g\ NaNO_2}$$

Solution: $225\ \cancel{g\ bag} \times \dfrac{0.0552\ \cancel{g\ NaNO_2}}{100.0\ \cancel{g\ bag}} \times \dfrac{22.99\ \cancel{g\ Na}}{69.00\ \cancel{g\ NaNO_2}} \times \dfrac{1000\ mg\ Na}{\cancel{g\ Na}} = 41.4\ mg\ Na$

Check: The units of the answer (mg Na) are correct. The magnitude of the answer is reasonable because only
a small % of the total mass is Na.

Challenge Problems

3.149   **Given:** g NaCl + g NaBr = 2.00 g, g Na = 0.75 g **Find:** g NaBr
Conceptual Plan:
      Let x = mol NaCl, y = mol NaBr, then x(molar mass NaCl) = g NaCl, y(molar mass NaBr) = g NaBr
Solution: $x(58.4) + y(102.9) = 2.00$
            $x(23.0) + y(23.0) = 0.75$ $y = 0.0326 − x$
            $58.4x + 102.9(0.0326 − x) = 2.00$
            $58.4x + 3.354 − 102.9x = 2.00$
            $44.5x \qquad = 1.354$
            $x = 0.03043$ mol NaCl
            $y = 0.0326 − 0.03043 = 0.00217$ mol NaBr
        g NaBr = (0.00217)(102.9 g mol^{-1}) = 0.22 g NaBr

Check: The units of the answer (g NaBr) are correct. The magnitude is reasonable since it is less than the
total mass.

3.151   **Given:** sample of $CaCO_3$ and $(NH_4)_2CO_3$ is 61.9% CO_3^{2-} **Find:** % $CaCO_3$
Conceptual Plan: Let x = $CaCO_3$, y = $(NH_4)_2CO_3$, then x(molar mass $CaCO_3$) = g $CaCO_3$,
      y(molar mass $(NH_4)_2CO_3$) = g $(NH_4)_2CO_3$
      then, a 100.0 g sample contains: x(100.0) g $CaCO_3$; y(96.1) g $(NH_4)_2CO_3$; and 61.9 g CO_3^{2-}
Solution: $x(100.0) + y(96.1) = 100.0$
            $x(60.0) + y(60.0) = 61.9$ $y = 1.03167 − x$
            $100.0x + 96.1(1.032 − x) = 100$
            $100.0x + 99.14 − 96.1x = 100$
            $3.9x \qquad = 0.96$

$$x = 0.22 \text{ mol CaCO}_3$$
$$y = 1.032 - 0.22 = 0.81 \text{ mol (NH}_4)_2\text{CO}_3$$
$$\text{g CaCO}_3 = (0.22 \text{ mol})(100.0 \text{ g mol}^{-1}) = 22.0 \text{ g CaCO}_3 \text{ in a 100 g sample:}$$
$$\text{mass \% CaCO}_3 = 22.0\%$$

Check: The units of the answer (mass % $CaCO_3$) are correct. The magnitude is reasonable since it is between 0 and 100%.

3.153   **Given:** rock contains: 38.0% PbS, 25.0% $PbCO_3$, 17.4% $PbSO_4$ **Find:** kg rock needed for 5.0 metric tonne Pb
Conceptual Plan: determine kg Pb/ 100 kg rock then tonne Pb → kg Pb → kg rock

$$\frac{1000 \text{ kg}}{\text{metric tonne}} \quad \frac{100 \text{ kg rock}}{64.2 \text{ kg rock}}$$

Solution: in 100 kg rock:

$$(38.0 \text{ kg PbS} \times \frac{207.2 \text{ kg Pb}}{239.3 \text{ kg PbS}}) + (25.0 \text{ kg PbCO}_3 \times \frac{207.2 \text{ kg Pb}}{267.2 \text{ kg PbCO}_3}) + (17.4 \text{ kg PbSO}_4 \times \frac{207.2 \text{ kg Pb}}{303.1 \text{ kg PbSO}_4})$$

$$= 64.2 \text{ kg Pb}$$

$$5.0 \text{ metric tonne Pb} \times \frac{1000 \text{ kg Pb}}{\text{metric tonne Pb}} \times \frac{100 \text{ kg rock}}{64.2 \text{ kg Pb}} = 7.8 \times 10^3 \text{ kg rock}$$

Check: The units of the answer (kg rock) are correct. The magnitude is reasonable since it is greater than the amount of Pb needed.

3.155   **Given:** molar mass = 229 g mol^{-1}, six times mass C as H, **Find:** molecular formula
Conceptual Plan: Let x = mass of C, then $6x$ = mass of C
Solution: in 1 mol of the compound: g C + g H + g S + g I = 229 g
Since the molar mass of I = 127, there can not be more than 1 mol of I in the compound, so
$$x + 6x + g S + 127 = 229$$
$$x + 6x + g S = 102$$
If the compound contains 1 mol S, then $7x = 102 - 32 = 70$ and $x = 10$ g H and $6x = 60$ g C

$$10 \text{ g H} \times \frac{1 \text{ mol H}}{1.0 \text{ g H}} = 10 \text{ mol H}$$

$$60 \text{ g C} \times \frac{1 \text{ mol C}}{12 \text{ g C}} = 5 \text{ mol C}$$

1 mol I and 1 mol S, so empirical formula is $C_5H_{10}SI$
Check: Molar mass of $C_5H_{10}SI$ = 5(12) + 10(1.0) + 32 + 127 = 229 g mol^{-1}, which is the mass given.

3.157   **Given:** compound is 1/3 X by mass, atomic mass X is 3/4 atomic mass Y **Find:** empirical formula
Conceptual Plan: mass X and Y → mass ratio X:Y and then g X → mol X and g Y → mol Y and then

$$\frac{\text{g X}}{\text{atomic mass X}} \quad \frac{\text{g Y}}{\text{atomic mass Y}}$$

mole ratio

Solution: $\dfrac{\text{mass X}}{\text{mass Y}} = \dfrac{\frac{1}{3}}{\frac{2}{3}} = \dfrac{1}{2}$ $\text{mol X} = \dfrac{1 \text{ g}}{\text{atomic mass X}}$ and $\text{mol Y} = \dfrac{2 \text{ g}}{\text{atomic mass Y}}$

But atomic mass X = 3/4 atomic mass Y so:

$$\text{mol X} = \frac{1 \text{ g}}{3/4(\text{atomic mass Y})} \quad \text{and} \quad \text{mol Y} = \frac{2 \text{ g}}{\text{atomic mass Y}}$$

$$\frac{\text{mol X}}{\text{mol Y}} = \frac{\dfrac{1 \text{ g}}{3/4(\text{atomic mass Y})}}{\dfrac{2 \text{ g}}{\text{atomic mass Y}}} = \frac{2}{3} \qquad \text{Empirical Formula} = X_2Y_3$$

Conceptual Problems

3.159   The sphere in the molecular models represents the electron cloud of the atom. On this scale, the nucleus would be too small to see.

3.161   The statement is incorrect because a chemical formula is based on the ratio of atoms combined, not the ratio of grams combined. The statement should read the following: The chemical formula for ammonia (NH_3) indicates that ammonia contains three hydrogen atoms to each nitrogen atom.

3.163 H_2SO_4: Atomic mass S is approximately twice atomic mass O, both are much greater than atomic mass H. The order of % mass is % O > % S > % H.

4 Chemical Reactions and Stoichiometry

Review Questions

4.1   Reaction stoichiometry is the numerical relationships between chemical amounts in a balanced chemical equation. The coefficients in a chemical reaction specify the relative amounts in moles of each of the substances involved in the reaction.

4.3   No, the percent yield would not be different if the actual yield and theoretical yield were calculated in moles. The relationship between grams and moles is the molar mass. This would be the same value for the actual yield and the theoretical yield.

4.5   Molarity is a concentration term. It is the amount of solute (in moles) divided by the volume of solution (in litres). The molarity of a solution can be used as a conversion factor between moles of the solute and litres of the solution.

4.7   Acids are molecular compounds that ionize—form ions—when they dissolve in water. A strong acid is one that completely ionizes in solution. A weak acid is one that does not completely ionize in water. A solution of a weak acid is composed mostly of the nonionized acid.

4.9   The solubility rules are a set of empirical rules that have been inferred from observations on many ionic compounds. The solubility rules allow us to predict if a compound is soluble or insoluble.

4.11   A precipitation reaction is one in which a solid or precipitate forms upon mixing two solutions. An example is $2 \, KI(aq) + Pb(NO_3)_2(aq) \rightarrow PbI_2(s) + 2 \, KNO_3(aq)$.

4.13   A molecular equation is an equation showing the complete neutral formulas for each compound in the reaction as if they existed as molecules. Equations that list individually all of the ions present as either reactants or products in a chemical reaction are complete ionic equations. Equations that show only the species that actually change during the reaction are net ionic equations.

4.15   When an Arrhenius acid and an Arrhenius base are mixed, the $H^+(aq)$ from the acid combines with the OH^- from the base to form $H_2O(l)$. An example is $HCl(aq) + NaOH(aq) \rightarrow H_2O(l) + NaCl(aq)$.

4.17   Aqueous reactions that form a gas upon mixing two solutions are called gas-evolution reactions. An example is $H_2SO_4(aq) + Li_2S(aq) \rightarrow H_2S(g) + Li_2SO_4(aq)$.

4.19   Oxidation–reduction reactions, or redox reactions, are reactions in which electrons are transferred from one reactant to the other. An example is $4 \, Fe(s) + 3 \, O_2(g) \rightarrow 2 \, Fe_2O_3(s)$.

4.21   To identify redox reactions by using oxidation states, begin by assigning oxidation states to each atom in the reaction. A change in oxidation state for the atoms indicates a redox reaction.

4.23   A substance that causes the oxidation of another substance is called an oxidizing agent. A substance that causes the reduction of another substance is called a reducing agent.

Problems by Topic

Writing and Balancing Chemical Equations

4.25   **Conceptual Plan:** write a skeletal reaction → balance atoms in more complex compounds → balance elements that occur as free elements → clear fractions

      Solution: Skeletal reaction: $SO_2(g) + O_2(g) + H_2O(l) \rightarrow H_2SO_4(aq)$

                     Balance O: $SO_2(g) + 1/2O_2(g) + H_2O(l) \rightarrow H_2SO_4(aq)$

                     Clear fraction: $2SO_2(g) + O_2(g) + 2H_2O(l) \rightarrow 2H_2SO_4(aq)$

      Check:

	left side	right side
	2 S atoms	2 S atoms
	8 O atoms	8 O atoms
	4 H atoms	4 H atoms

4.27   **Conceptual Plan:** write a skeletal reaction → balance atoms in more complex compounds → balance elements that occur as free elements → clear fractions

      Solution: Skeletal reaction: $Na(s) + H_2O(l) \rightarrow H_2(g) + NaOH(aq)$

                     Balance H: $Na(s) + H_2O(l) \rightarrow 1/2H_2(g) + NaOH(aq)$

                     Clear fraction: $2Na(s) + 2H_2O(l) \rightarrow H_2(g) + 2NaOH(aq)$

      Check:

	left side	right side
	2 Na atoms	2 Na atoms
	4 H atoms	4 H atoms
	2 O atoms	2 O atoms

4.29   **Conceptual Plan:** write a skeletal reaction → balance atoms in more complex compounds → balance elements that occur as free elements → clear fractions

      Solution: Skeletal reaction: $C_{12}H_{22}O_{11}(aq) + H_2O(l) \rightarrow C_2H_5OH(aq) + CO_2(g)$

                     Balance H: $C_{12}H_{22}O_{11}(aq) + H_2O(l) \rightarrow 4C_2H_5OH(aq) + CO_2(g)$

                     Balance C: $C_{12}H_{22}O_{11}(aq) + H_2O(l) \rightarrow 4C_2H_5OH(aq) + 4CO_2(g)$

      Check:

	left side	right side
	12 C atoms	12 C atoms
	24 H atoms	24 H atoms
	12 O atoms	12 O atoms

4.31   (a)   **Conceptual Plan:** write a skeletal reaction → balance atoms in more complex compounds → balance elements that occur as free elements → clear fractions

           Solution: Skeletal reaction: $PbS(s) + HBr(aq) \rightarrow PbBr_2(s) + H_2S(g)$

                           Balance Br: $PbS(s) + 2HBr(aq) \rightarrow PbBr_2(s) + H_2S(g)$

          Check:

	left side	right side
	1 Pb atom	1 Pb atom
	1 S atom	1 S atom
	2 H atoms	2 H atoms
	2 Br atoms	2 Br atoms

      (b)   **Conceptual Plan:** write a skeletal reaction → balance atoms in more complex compounds → balance elements that occur as free elements → clear fractions

           Solution: Skeletal reaction: $CO(g) + H_2(g) \rightarrow CH_4(g) + H_2O(l)$

                           Balance H: $CO(g) + 3H_2(g) \rightarrow CH_4(g) + H_2O(l)$

         Check:

	left side	right side
	1 C atom	1 C atom
	1 O atom	1 O atom
	6 H atoms	6 H atoms

      (c)   **Conceptual Plan:** write a skeletal reaction → balance atoms in more complex compounds → balance elements that occur as free elements → clear fractions

           Solution: Skeletal reaction: $HCl(aq) + MnO_2(s) \rightarrow MnCl_2(aq) + H_2O(l) + Cl_2(g)$

                           Balance Cl: $4HCl(aq) + MnO_2(s) \rightarrow MnCl_2(aq) + H_2O(l) + Cl_2(g)$

                           Balance O: $4HCl(aq) + MnO_2(s) \rightarrow MnCl_2(aq) + 2H_2O(l) + Cl_2(g)$

	Check:	left side	right side
		4 H atoms	4 H atoms
		4 Cl atoms	4 Cl atoms
		1 Mn atom	1 Mn atom
		2 O atoms	2 O atoms

(d) **Conceptual Plan: write a skeletal reaction $\rightarrow$ balance atoms in more complex compounds $\rightarrow$ balance elements that occur as free elements $\rightarrow$ clear fractions**

Solution: Skeletal reaction: $C_5H_{12}(l) + O_2(g) \rightarrow CO_2(g) + H_2O(l)$

Balance C: $C_5H_{12}(l) + O_2(g) \rightarrow 5CO_2(g) + H_2O(l)$

Balance H: $C_5H_{12}(l) + O_2(g) \rightarrow 5CO_2(g) + 6H_2O(l)$

Balance O: $C_5H_{12}(l) + 8O_2(g) \rightarrow 5CO_2(g) + 6H_2O(l)$

Check:

left side	right side
5 C atoms	5 C atoms
12 H atoms	12 H atoms
16 O atoms	16 O atoms

4.33 (a) **Conceptual Plan: balance atoms in more complex compounds $\rightarrow$ balance elements that occur as free elements $\rightarrow$ clear fractions**

Solution: Skeletal reaction: $CO_2(g) + CaSiO_3(s) + H_2O(l) \rightarrow SiO_2(s) + Ca(HCO_3)_2(aq)$

Balance C: $2CO_2(g) + CaSiO_3(s) + H_2O(l) \rightarrow SiO_2(s) + Ca(HCO_3)_2(aq)$

Check:

left side	right side
2 C atoms	2 C atoms
8 O atoms	8 O atoms
1 Ca atom	1 Ca atom
1 Si atom	1 Si atom
2 H atoms	2 H atoms

(b) **Conceptual Plan: balance atoms in more complex compounds $\rightarrow$ balance elements that occur as free elements $\rightarrow$ clear fractions**

Solution: Skeletal reaction: $Co(NO_3)_3(aq) + (NH_4)_2S(aq) \rightarrow Co_2S_3(s) + NH_4NO_3(aq)$

Balance S: $Co(NO_3)_3(aq) + 3(NH_4)_2S(aq) \rightarrow Co_2S_3(s) + NH_4NO_3(aq)$

Balance Co: $2Co(NO_3)_3(aq) + 3(NH_4)_2S(aq) \rightarrow Co_2S_3(s) + NH_4NO_3(aq)$

Balance N: $2Co(NO_3)_3(aq) + 3(NH_4)_2S(aq) \rightarrow Co_2S_3(s) + 6NH_4NO_3(aq)$

Check:

left side	right side
2 Co atoms	2 Co atoms
12 N atoms	12 N atoms
18 O atoms	18 O atoms
24 H atoms	24 H atoms
3 S atoms	3 S atoms

(c) **Conceptual Plan: balance atoms in more complex compounds $\rightarrow$ balance elements that occur as free elements $\rightarrow$ clear fractions**

Solution: Skeletal reaction: $Cu_2O(s) + C(s) \rightarrow Cu(s) + CO(g)$

Balance Cu: $Cu_2O(s) + C(s) \rightarrow 2Cu(s) + CO(g)$

Check:

left side	right side
2 Cu atoms	2 Cu atoms
1 O atom	1 O atom
1 C atom	1 C atom

(d) **Conceptual Plan: balance atoms in more complex compounds $\rightarrow$ balance elements that occur as free elements $\rightarrow$ clear fractions**

Solution: Skeletal reaction: $H_2(g) + Cl_2(g) \rightarrow HCl(g)$

Balance Cl: $H_2(g) + Cl_2(g) \rightarrow 2HCl(g)$

Check:

left side	right side
2 H atoms	2 H atoms
2 Cl atoms	2 Cl atoms

Types of Aqueous Solutions and Solubility

4.35   (a)   Yes. CsCl is an ionic compound. An aqueous solution is an electrolyte solution, so it conducts electricity.

      (b)   No. CH_3OH is a molecular compound that does not dissociate. An aqueous solution is a nonelectrolyte solution, so it does not conduct electricity.

      (c)   Yes. $Ca(NO_3)_2$ is an ionic compound. An aqueous solution is an electrolyte solution, so it conducts electricity.

      (d)   No. $C_6H_{12}O_6$ is a molecular compound that does not dissociate. An aqueous solution is a nonelectrolyte solution, so it does not conduct electricity.

4.37   (a) $AgNO_3$ is soluble. Compounds containing NO_3^- are always soluble with no exceptions. The ions in the solution are $Ag^+(aq)$ and $NO_3^-(aq)$.

      (b) $Pb(C_2H_3O_2)_2$ is soluble. Compounds containing $C_2H_3O_2^-$ are always soluble with no exceptions. The ions in the solution are $Pb^{2+}(aq)$ and $C_2H_3O_2^-(aq)$.

      (c) KNO_3 is soluble. Compounds containing K^+ are always soluble with no exceptions. The ions in solution are $K^+(aq)$ and $NO_3^-(aq)$.

      (d) $(NH_4)_2S$ is soluble. Compounds containing NH_4^+ are always soluble with no exceptions. The ions in solution are $NH_4^+(aq)$ and $S^{2-}(aq)$.

Precipitation Reactions

4.39   (a) $LiI(aq) + BaS(aq) \rightarrow$ Possible products: Li_2S and BaI_2. Li_2S is soluble. Compounds containing S^{2-} are normally insoluble but Li^+ is an exception. BaI_2 is soluble. Compounds containing I^- are normally soluble and Ba^{2+} is not an exception. $LiI(aq) + BaS(aq) \rightarrow$ No Reaction

      (b) $KCl(aq) + CaS(aq) \rightarrow$ Possible products: K_2S and $CaCl_2$. K_2S is soluble. Compounds containing S^{2-} are normally insoluble but K^+ is an exception. $CaCl_2$ is soluble. Compounds containing Cl^- are normally soluble and Ca^{2+} is not an exception. $KCl(aq) + CaS(aq) \rightarrow$ No Reaction

      (c) $CrBr_2(aq) + Na_2CO_3(aq) \rightarrow$ Possible products: $CrCO_3$ and $NaBr$. $CrCO_3$ is insoluble. Compounds containing CO_3^{2-} are normally insoluble and Cr^{2+} is not an exception. $NaBr$ is soluble. Compounds containing Br^- are normally soluble and Na^+ is not an exception.
$CrBr_2(aq) + Na_2CO_3(aq) \rightarrow CrCO_3(s) + 2\,NaBr(aq)$

      (d) $NaOH(aq) + FeCl_3(aq) \rightarrow$ Possible products: $NaCl$ and $Fe(OH)_3$. $NaCl$ is soluble. Compounds containing Na^+ are normally soluble, no exceptions. $Fe(OH)_3$ is insoluble. Compounds containing OH^- are normally insoluble and Fe^{3+} is not an exception.
$3\,NaOH(aq) + FeCl_3(aq) \rightarrow 3\,NaCl(aq) + Fe(OH)_3(s)$

4.41   (a) $K_2CO_3(aq) + Pb(NO_3)_2(aq) \rightarrow$ Possible products: KNO_3 and $PbCO_3$. KNO_3 is soluble. Compounds containing K^+ are always soluble, no exceptions. $PbCO_3$ is insoluble. Compounds containing CO_3^{2-} are normally insoluble and Pb^{2+} is not an exception.
$K_2CO_3(aq) + Pb(NO_3)_2(aq) \rightarrow 2\,KNO_3(aq) + PbCO_3(s)$

      (b) $Li_2SO_4(aq) + Pb(C_2H_3O_2)_2(aq) \rightarrow$ Possible products: $LiC_2H_3O_2$ and $PbSO_4$. $LiC_2H_3O_2$ is soluble. Compounds containing Li^+ are always soluble, no exceptions. $PbSO_4$ is insoluble. Compounds containing SO_4^{2-} are normally soluble but Pb^{2+} is an exception.
$Li_2SO_4(aq) + Pb(C_2H_3O_2)_2(aq) \rightarrow 2\,LiC_2H_3O_2(aq) + PbSO_4(s)$

      (c) $Cu(NO_3)_2(aq) + MgS(s) \rightarrow$ Possible products: CuS and $Mg(NO_3)_2$. CuS is insoluble. Compounds containing S^{2-} are normally insoluble and Cu^{2+} is not an exception. $Mg(NO_3)_2$ is soluble. Compounds containing NO_3^- are always soluble, no exceptions. $Cu(NO_3)_2(aq) + MgS(s) \rightarrow CuS(s) + Mg(NO_3)_2(aq)$

(d) $Sr(NO_3)_2(aq) + KI(aq) \rightarrow$ Possible products: SrI_2 and KNO_3. SrI_2 is soluble. Compounds containing I^- are normally soluble and Sr^{2+} is not an exception. KNO_3 is soluble. Compounds containing K^+ are always soluble, no exceptions. $Sr(NO_3)_2(aq) + KI(aq) \rightarrow$ No Reaction

Ionic and Net Ionic Equations

4.43   (a) $H^+(aq) + \cancel{Cl^-}(aq) + \cancel{Li^+}(aq) + OH^-(aq) \rightarrow H_2O(l) + \cancel{Li^+}(aq) + \cancel{Cl^-}(aq)$
$H^+(aq) + OH^-(aq) \rightarrow H_2O(l)$

(b) $\cancel{Mg^{2+}}(aq) + S^{2-}(aq) + Cu^{2+}(aq) + 2\,\cancel{Cl^-}(aq) \rightarrow CuS(s) + \cancel{Mg^{2+}}(aq) + 2\,\cancel{Cl^-}(aq)$
$Cu^{2+}(aq) + S^{2-}(aq) \rightarrow CuS(s)$

(c) $\cancel{Na^+}(aq) + OH^-(aq) + H^+(aq) + \cancel{NO_3^-}(aq) \rightarrow H_2O(l) + \cancel{Na^+}(aq) + \cancel{NO_3^-}(aq)$
$H^+(aq) + OH^-(aq) + \rightarrow H_2O(l)$

(d) $6\,\cancel{Na^+}(aq) + 2\,PO_4^{3-}(aq) + 3\,Ni^{2+}(aq) + 6\,\cancel{Cl^-}(aq) \rightarrow Ni_3(PO_4)_2(s) + 6\,\cancel{Na^+}(aq) + 6\,\cancel{Cl^-}(aq)$
$3\,Ni^{2+}(aq) + 2\,PO_4^{3-}(aq) \rightarrow Ni_3(PO_4)_2(s)$

4.45 $Hg_2^{2+}(aq) + \cancel{2NO_3^-}(aq) + \cancel{2Na^+}(aq) + 2\,Cl^-(aq) \rightarrow Hg_2Cl_2(s) + \cancel{2Na^+}(aq) + \cancel{2NO_3^-}(aq)$
$Hg_2^{2+}(aq) + 2\,Cl^-(aq) \rightarrow Hg_2Cl_2(s)$

4.47   Skeletal reaction: $HBr(aq) + KOH(aq) \rightarrow H_2O(l) + KBr(aq)$
                          acid   base   water   salt
Net ionic equation: $H^+(aq) + OH^-(aq) \rightarrow H_2O(l)$

4.49   (a)   Skeletal reaction: $H_2SO_4(aq) + Ca(OH)_2(aq) \rightarrow H_2O(l) + CaSO_4(s)$
                          acid   base   water   salt
Balanced reaction: $H_2SO_4(aq) + Ca(OH)_2(aq) \rightarrow 2\,H_2O(l) + CaSO_4(s)$

(b)   Skeletal reaction: $HClO_4(aq) + KOH(aq) \rightarrow H_2O(l) + KClO_4(aq)$
                          acid   base   water   salt
Balanced reaction: $HClO_4(aq) + KOH(aq) \rightarrow H_2O(l) + KClO_4(aq)$

(c)   Skeletal reaction: $H_2SO_4(aq) + NaOH(aq) \rightarrow H_2O(l) + Na_2SO_4(aq)$
                          acid   base   water   salt
Balanced reaction: $H_2SO_4(aq) + 2\,NaOH(aq) \rightarrow 2\,H_2O(l) + Na_2SO_4(aq)$

4.51   (a)   Skeletal reaction: $2\,HBr(aq) + NiS(s) \rightarrow NiBr_2(aq) + H_2S(g)$
                                                          gas
Balanced reaction: $2\,HBr(aq) + NiS(s) \rightarrow NiBr_2(aq) + H_2S(g)$

(b)   Skeletal reaction: $NH_4I(aq) + NaOH(aq) \rightarrow NH_4OH(aq) + NaI(aq) \rightarrow H_2O(l) + NH_3(g) + NaI(aq)$
                                                          decomposes   gas
Balanced reaction: $NH_4I(aq) + NaOH(aq) \rightarrow H_2O(l) + NH_3(g) + NaI(aq)$

(c)   Skeletal reaction: $HBr(aq) + Na_2S(aq) \rightarrow NaBr(aq) + H_2S(g)$
                                                          gas
Balanced reaction: $2\,HBr(aq) + Na_2S(aq) \rightarrow 2\,NaBr(aq) + H_2S(g)$

(d)   Skeletal reaction:
$HClO_4(aq) + Li_2CO_3(aq) \rightarrow H_2CO_3(aq) + LiClO_4(aq) \rightarrow H_2O(l) + CO_2(g) + LiClO_4(aq)$
                          decomposes   gas
Balanced reaction: $2\,HClO_4(aq) + Li_2CO_3(aq) \rightarrow H_2O(l) + CO_2(g) + 2\,LiClO_4(aq)$

Oxidation–Reduction and Combustion

4.53   (a)   Ag. The oxidation state of Ag = 0. The oxidation state of an atom in a free element is 0.

(b) Ag^+. The oxidation state of Ag^+ = +1. The oxidation state of a monatomic ion is equal to its charge.

(c) CaF_2. The oxidation state of Ca = +2, and the oxidation state of F = − 1. The oxidation state of a group 2 metal always has an oxidation state of +2, the oxidation of F is − 1 since the sum of the oxidation states in a neutral formula unit = 0.

(d) H_2S. The oxidation state of H = +1, and the oxidation state of S = − 2. The oxidation state of H when listed first is +1, the oxidation state of S is − 2 since S is in group 16 and the sum of the oxidation states in a neutral molecular unit = 0.

(e) $CO_3{}^{2-}$. The oxidation state of C = +4, and the oxidation state of O = − 2. The oxidation state of O is normally − 2, and the oxidation state of C is deduced from the formula since the sum of the oxidation states must equal the charge on the ion. (C ox state) + 3(O ox state) = − 2; (C ox state) + 3(− 2) = − 2, so C ox state = + 4.

(f) $CrO_4{}^{2-}$. The oxidation state of Cr = +6, and the oxidation state of O = − 2. The oxidation state of O is normally −2, and the oxidation state of Cr is deduced from the formula since the sum of the oxidation states must equal the charge on the ion. (Cr ox state) + 4(O ox state) = − 2; (Cr ox state) + 4(− 2) = − 2, so Cr ox state = + 6.

4.55   (a)   CrO. The oxidation state of Cr = +2, and the oxidation state of O = − 2. The oxidation state of O is normally − 2, and the oxidation state of Cr is deduced from the formula since the sum of the oxidation states must = 0.
(Cr ox state) + (O ox state) = 0; (Cr ox state) + (− 2) = 0, so Cr = +2.

(b) CrO_3. The oxidation state of Cr = +6, and the oxidation state of O = − 2. The oxidation state of O is normally − 2, and the oxidation state of Cr is deduced from the formula since the sum of the oxidation states must = 0.
(Cr ox state) + 3(O ox state) = 0; (Cr ox state) +3 (− 2) = 0, so Cr = +6.

(c) Cr_2O_3. The oxidation state of Cr = +3, and the oxidation state of O = − 2. The oxidation state of O is normally − 2, and the oxidation state of Cr is deduced from the formula since the sum of the oxidation states must = 0.
2(Cr ox state) + 3(O ox state) = 0; 2(Cr ox state) + 3(− 2) = 0, so Cr = +3.

4.57   (a) $$4\,Li(s) + O_2(g) \rightarrow 2\,Li_2O(s)$$
Oxidation states: 0   0   +1   − 2
This is a redox reaction since Li increases in oxidation number (oxidation) and O decreases in number (reduction). O_2 is the oxidizing agent, and Li is the reducing agent.

(b) $$Mg(s) + Fe^{2+}(aq) \rightarrow Mg^{2+}(aq) + Fe(s)$$
Oxidation states: 0   +2   +2   0
This is a redox reaction since Mg increases in oxidation number (oxidation) and Fe decreases in number (reduction). Fe^{2+} is the oxidizing agent, and Mg is the reducing agent.

(c) $$Pb(NO_3)_2(aq) + Na_2SO_4(aq) \rightarrow PbSO_4(s) + 2\,NaNO_3(aq)$$
Oxidation states: +2 +5 − 2   +1 +6 − 2   +2 +6 −2   +1 +5 −2
This is a not a redox reaction since none of the atoms undergoes a change in oxidation number.

(d) $$HBr(aq) + KOH(aq) \rightarrow H_2O(l) + KBr(aq)$$
Oxidation states: +1 − 1   +1 − 2 +1   +1 −2   +1 −2
This is a not a redox reaction since none of the atoms undergoes a change in oxidation number.

4.59   (a)   Skeletal reaction: $S(s) + O_2(g) \rightarrow SO_2(g)$
Balanced reaction: $S(s) + O_2(g) \rightarrow SO_2(g)$

(b)   Skeletal reaction: $C_3H_6(g) + O_2(g) \rightarrow CO_2(g) + H_2O(g)$
Balance C: $C_3H_6(g) + O_2(g) \rightarrow 3CO_2(g) + H_2O(g)$
Balance H: $C_3H_6(g) + O_2(g) \rightarrow 3CO_2(g) + 3H_2O(g)$
Balance O: $C_3H_6(g) + 9/2\,O_2(g) \rightarrow 3CO_2(g) + 3H_2O(g)$
Clear fraction: $2C_3H_6(g) + 9O_2(g) \rightarrow 6CO_2(g) + 6H_2O(g)$

(c) Skeletal reaction: $Ca(s) + O_2(g) \rightarrow CaO(s)$

Balance O: $Ca(s) + O_2(g) \rightarrow 2CaO(s)$

Balance Ca: $2Ca(s) + O_2(g) \rightarrow 2CaO(s)$

(d) Skeletal reaction: $C_5H_{12}S(l) + O_2(g) \rightarrow CO_2(g) + H_2O(g) + SO_2(g)$

Balance C: $C_5H_{12}S(l) + O_2(g) \rightarrow 5CO_2(g) + H_2O(g) + SO_2(g)$

Balance H: $C_5H_{12}S(l) + O_2(g) \rightarrow 5CO_2(g) + 6H_2O(g) + SO_2(g)$

Balance S: $C_5H_{12}S(l) + O_2(g) \rightarrow 5CO_2(g) + 6H_2O(g) + SO_2(g)$

Balance O: $C_5H_{12}S(l) + 9O_2(g) \rightarrow 5CO_2(g) + 6H_2O(g) + SO_2(g)$

Reaction Stoichiometry

4.61   **Given:** 7.2 moles C_6H_{14} **Find:** balanced reaction, moles O_2 required
Conceptual Plan: balance the equation then mol $C_6H_{14} \rightarrow$ mol O_2

$2 C_6H_{14}(g) + 19 O_2(g) \rightarrow 12 CO_2(g) + 14 H_2O(g)$ $\dfrac{19 \text{ mol } O_2}{2 \text{ mol } C_6H_{14}}$

Solution: $7.2 \text{ mol } C_6H_{14} \times \dfrac{19 \text{ mol } O_2}{2 \text{ mol } C_6H_{14}} = 68.4 \text{ mol } O_2 = 68 \text{ mol } O_2$

Check: The units of the answer (mol O_2) are correct. The magnitude is reasonable because much more O_2 is needed than C_6H_{14}.

4.63   (a) **Given:** 2.5 mol N_2O_5 **Find:** mol NO_2
Conceptual Plan: mol $N_2O_5 \rightarrow$ mol NO_2

$\dfrac{4 \text{ } NO_2}{2 \text{ } N_2O_5}$

Solution: $2.5 \text{ mol } N_2O_5 \times \dfrac{4 \text{ mol } NO_2}{2 \text{ mol } N_2O_5} = 5.0 \text{ mol } NO_2$
Check: The units of the answer (mol NO_2) are correct. The magnitude is reasonable since it is greater than mol N_2O_5.

(b) **Given:** 6.8 mol N_2O_5 **Find:** mol NO_2
Conceptual Plan: mol $N_2O_5 \rightarrow$ mol NO_2

$\dfrac{4 \text{ } NO_2}{2 \text{ } N_2O_5}$

Solution: $6.8 \text{ mol } N_2O_5 \times \dfrac{4 \text{ mol } NO_2}{2 \text{ mol } N_2O_5} = 13.6 \text{ mol } NO_2 = 14 \text{ mol } NO_2$
Check: The units of the answer (mol NO_2) are correct. The magnitude is reasonable since it is greater than mol N_2O_5.

(c) **Given:** 15.2 g N_2O_5 **Find:** mol NO_2
Conceptual Plan: g $N_2O_5 \rightarrow$ mol $N_2O_5 \rightarrow$ mol NO_2

$\dfrac{1 \text{ mol } N_2O_5}{108.02 \text{ g } N_2O_5}$ $\dfrac{4 \text{ } NO_2}{2 \text{ } N_2O_5}$

Solution: $15.2 \text{ g } N_2O_5 \times \dfrac{1 \text{ mol } N_2O_5}{108.02 \text{ g } N_2O_5} \times \dfrac{4 \text{ mol } NO_2}{2 \text{ mol } N_2O_5} = 0.2814 \text{ mol } NO_2 = 0.281 \text{ mol } NO_2$
Check: The units of the answer (mol NO_2) are correct. The magnitude is reasonable since 15 g is about 0.13 mol N_2O_5 and the answer is greater than mol N_2O_5.

(d) **Given:** 2.87 kg N_2O_5 **Find:** mol NO_2
Conceptual Plan: kg $N_2O_5 \rightarrow$ g $N_2O_5 \rightarrow$ mol $N_2O_5 \rightarrow$ mol NO_2

$\dfrac{1000 \text{ g } N_2O_5}{\text{kg } N_2O_5}$ $\dfrac{1 \text{ mol } N_2O_5}{108.02 \text{ g } N_2O_5}$ $\dfrac{4 \text{ } NO_2}{2 \text{ } N_2O_5}$

Solution:
$2.87 \text{ kg } N_2O_5 \times \dfrac{1000 \text{ g } N_2O_5}{\text{kg } N_2O_5} \times \dfrac{1 \text{ mol } N_2O_5}{108.02 \text{ g } N_2O_5} \times \dfrac{4 \text{ mol } NO_2}{2 \text{ mol } N_2O_5} = 53.14 \text{ mol } NO_2 = 53.1 \text{ mol } NO_2$
Check: The units of the answer (mol NO_2) are correct. The magnitude is reasonable since 2.87 kg is about 27 mol N_2O_5 and the answer is greater than mol N_2O_5.

4.65 **Given:** 3 mol SiO_2 **Find:** mol C, mol SiC, mol CO

Conceptual Plan: mol SiO_2 → mol C → mol SiC → mol CO

$$\frac{3\,C}{SiO_2} \qquad \frac{SiC}{SiO_2} \qquad \frac{2\,CO}{SiO_2}$$

Solution: $3\ \overline{\text{mol } SiO_2} \times \dfrac{3 \text{ mol C}}{\overline{\text{mol } SiO_2}} = 9 \text{ mol C}$ $\qquad$ $3\ \overline{\text{mol } SiO_2} \times \dfrac{\text{mol SiC}}{\overline{\text{mol } SiO_2}} = 3 \text{ mol SiC}$

$$3\ \overline{\text{mol } SiO_2} \times \frac{2 \text{ mol CO}}{\overline{\text{mol } SiO_2}} = 6 \text{ mol CO}$$

Given: 6 mol C **Find:** mol SiO_2, mol SiC, mol CO

Conceptual Plan: mol C → mol SiO_2 → mol SiC → mol CO

$$\frac{SiO_2}{3\,C} \qquad \frac{SiC}{3\,C} \qquad \frac{2\,CO}{3\,C}$$

Solution: $6\ \overline{\text{mol C}} \times \dfrac{\text{mol } SiO_2}{3\ \overline{\text{mol C}}} = 2 \text{ mol } SiO_2$ $\qquad$ $6\ \overline{\text{mol C}} \times \dfrac{\text{mol SiC}}{3\ \overline{\text{mol C}}} = 2 \text{ mol SiC}$

$$6\ \overline{\text{mol C}} \times \frac{2 \text{ mol CO}}{3\ \overline{\text{mol C}}} = 4 \text{ mol CO}$$

Given: 10 mol CO **Find:** mol SiO_2, mol C, mol SiC

Conceptual Plan: mol CO → mol SiO_2 → mol C → mol SiC

$$\frac{SiO_2}{2\,CO} \qquad \frac{3\,C}{2\,CO} \qquad \frac{SiC}{2\,CO}$$

Solution: $10\ \overline{\text{mol CO}} \times \dfrac{\text{mol } SiO_2}{2\ \overline{\text{mol CO}}} = 5.0 \text{ mol } SiO_2$ $\qquad$ $10\ \overline{\text{mol C}} \times \dfrac{3 \text{ mol C}}{2\ \overline{\text{mol CO}}} = 15 \text{ mol C}$

$$10\ \overline{\text{mol CO}} \times \frac{\text{mol SiC}}{2\ \overline{\text{mol CO}}} = 5.0 \text{ mol SiC}$$

Given: 2.8 mol SiO_2 **Find:** mol C, mol SiC, mol CO

Conceptual Plan: mol SiO_2 → mol C → mol SiC → mol CO

$$\frac{3\,C}{SiO_2} \qquad \frac{SiC}{SiO_2} \qquad \frac{2\,CO}{SiO_2}$$

Solution: $2.8\ \overline{\text{mol } SiO_2} \times \dfrac{3 \text{ mol C}}{\overline{\text{mol } SiO_2}} = 8.4 \text{ mol C}$ $\qquad$ $2.8\ \overline{\text{mol } SiO_2} \times \dfrac{\text{mol SiC}}{\overline{\text{mol } SiO_2}} = 2.8 \text{ mol SiC}$

$$2.8\ \overline{\text{mol } SiO_2} \times \frac{2 \text{ mol CO}}{\overline{\text{mol } SiO_2}} = 5.6 \text{ mol CO}$$

Given: 1.55 mol C **Find:** mol SiO_2, mol SiC, mol CO

Conceptual Plan: mol C → mol SiO_2 → mol SiC → mol CO

$$\frac{SiO_2}{3\,C} \qquad \frac{SiC}{3\,C} \qquad \frac{2\,CO}{3\,C}$$

Solution: $1.55\ \overline{\text{mol C}} \times \dfrac{1 \text{ mol } SiO_2}{3\ \overline{\text{mol C}}} = 0.517 \text{ mol } SiO_2$ $\qquad$ $1.55\ \overline{\text{mol C}} \times \dfrac{\text{mol SiC}}{3\ \overline{\text{mol C}}} = 0.517 \text{ mol SiC}$

$$1.55\ \overline{\text{mol C}} \times \frac{2 \text{ mol CO}}{3\ \overline{\text{mol C}}} = 1.03 \text{ mol CO}$$

SiO_2	C	SiC	CO
3	9	3	6
2	**6**	2	4
5.0	15	5.0	**10**
2.8	8.4	2.8	5.6
0.517	**1.55**	0.517	1.03

4.67 **Given:** 3.2 g Fe **Find:** g HBr; g H_2

Conceptual Plan: g Fe → mol Fe → mol HBr → g HBr

$$\frac{\text{mol Fe}}{55.8 \text{ g Fe}} \qquad \frac{2 \text{ mol HBr}}{\text{mol Fe}} \qquad \frac{80.9 \text{ g HBr}}{\text{mol HBr}}$$

g Fe → mol Fe → mol H_2 → g H_2

$$\frac{\text{mol Fe}}{55.8 \text{ g Fe}} \qquad \frac{1 \text{ mol } H_2}{\text{mol Fe}} \qquad \frac{2.02 \text{ g } H_2}{\text{mol } H_2}$$

Solution: $3.2 \; \bar{g} \, \overline{Fe} \times \dfrac{1 \; \overline{mol \; Fe}}{55.8 \; \bar{g} \, \overline{Fe}} \times \dfrac{2 \; \overline{mol \; HBr}}{1 \; \overline{mol \; Fe}} \times \dfrac{80.9 \; g \; HBr}{1 \; \overline{mol \; HBr}} = 9.3 \; g \; HBr$

$3.2 \; \bar{g} \, \overline{Fe} \times \dfrac{1 \; \overline{mol \; Fe}}{55.8 \; \bar{g} \, \overline{Fe}} \times \dfrac{1 \; \overline{mol \; H_2}}{1 \; \overline{mol \; Fe}} \times \dfrac{2.02 \; g \; H_2}{1 \; \overline{mol \; H_2}} = 0.12 \; g \; H_2$

Check: The units of the answers (g HBr, g H_2) are correct. The magnitude of the answers is reasonable because molar mass HBr is greater than Fe and molar mass H_2 is much less than Fe.

4.69 (a) **Given:** 3.67 g Ba **Find:** g $BaCl_2$
  Conceptual Plan: g Ba $\rightarrow$ **mol Ba** $\rightarrow$ **mol $BaCl_2$** $\rightarrow$ **g $BaCl_2$**

  $\dfrac{mol \; Ba}{137.33 \; g \; Ba} \qquad \dfrac{1 \; mol \; BaCl_2}{1 \; mol \; Ba} \qquad \dfrac{208.23 \; g \; BaCl_2}{1 \; mol \; BaCl_2}$

  Solution: $3.67 \; \bar{g} \, \overline{Ba} \times \dfrac{1 \; \overline{mol \; Ba}}{137.33 \; \bar{g} \, \overline{Ba}} \times \dfrac{1 \; \overline{mol \; BaCl_2}}{1 \; \overline{mol \; Ba}} \times \dfrac{208.23 \; g \; BaCl_2}{1 \; \overline{mol \; BaCl_2}} = 5.5647 \; g \; BaCl_2 = 5.56 \; g \; BaCl_2$

  Check: The units of the answer (g $BaCl_2$) are correct. The magnitude of the answer is reasonable because it is larger than grams Ba.

  (b) **Given:** 3.67 g CaO **Find:** g $CaCO_3$
  Conceptual Plan: g CaO $\rightarrow$ **mol CaO** $\rightarrow$ **mol $CaCO_3$** $\rightarrow$ **g $CaCO_3$**

  $\dfrac{mol \; CaO}{56.08 \; g \; CaO} \qquad \dfrac{mol \; CaCO_3}{1 \; mol \; CaO} \qquad \dfrac{100.09 \; g \; CaCO_3}{mol \; CaCO_3}$

  Solution:

  $3.67 \; \bar{g} \, \overline{CaO} \times \dfrac{1 \; \overline{mol \; CaO}}{56.08 \; \bar{g} \, \overline{CaO}} \times \dfrac{1 \; \overline{mol \; CaCO_3}}{1 \; \overline{mol \; CaO}} \times \dfrac{100.09 \; g \; CaCO_3}{1 \; \overline{mol \; CaCO_3}} = 6.550 \; g \; CaCO_3 = 6.55 \; g \; CaCO_3$

  Check: Units of answer (g $CaCO_3$) are correct. The magnitude of the answer is reasonable because it is larger than grams CaO.

  (c) **Given:** 3.67 g Mg **Find:** g MgO
  Conceptual Plan: g Mg $\rightarrow$ **mol Mg** $\rightarrow$ **mol MgO** $\rightarrow$ **g MgO**

  $\dfrac{mol \; Mg}{24.30 \; g \; Mg} \qquad \dfrac{mol \; MgO}{mol \; Mg} \qquad \dfrac{40.30 \; g \; MgO}{mol \; MgO}$

  Solution: $3.67 \; \bar{g} \, \overline{Mg} \times \dfrac{1 \; \overline{mol \; Mg}}{24.30 \; \bar{g} \, \overline{Mg}} \times \dfrac{1 \; \overline{mol \; MgO}}{1 \; \overline{mol \; Mg}} \times \dfrac{40.30 \; g \; MgO}{1 \; \overline{mol \; MgO}} = 6.086 \; g \; MgO = 6.09 \; g \; MgO$

  Check: The units of the answer (g MgO) are correct. The magnitude of the answer is reasonable because it is larger than grams Mg.

  (d) **Given:** 3.67 g Al **Find:** g Al_2O_3
  Conceptual Plan: g Al $\rightarrow$ **mol Al** $\rightarrow$ **mol Al_2O_3** $\rightarrow$ **g Al_2O_3**

  $\dfrac{mol \; Al}{26.98 \; g \; Al} \qquad \dfrac{2 \; mol \; Al_2O_3}{4 \; mol \; Al} \qquad \dfrac{101.96 \; g \; Al_2O_3}{mol \; Al_2O_3}$

  Solution: $3.67 \; g \; Al \times \dfrac{1 \; \overline{mol \; Al}}{26.98 \; \bar{g} \, \overline{Al}} \times \dfrac{2 \; \overline{mol \; Al_2O_3}}{4 \; \overline{mol \; Al}} \times \dfrac{101.96 \; g \; Al_2O_3}{1 \; \overline{mol \; Al_2O_3}} = 6.934 \; g \; Al_2O_3 = 6.93 \; g \; Al_2O_3$

  Check: The units of the answer (g Al_2O_3) are correct. The magnitude of the answer is reasonable because it is larger than grams Al.

4.71 (a) **Given:** 4.85 g NaOH **Find:** g HCl
  Conceptual Plan: g NaOH $\rightarrow$ **mol NaOH** $\rightarrow$ **mol HCl** $\rightarrow$ **g HCl**

  $\dfrac{mol \; NaOH}{40.01 \; g \; NaOH} \qquad \dfrac{1 \; mol \; HCl}{1 \; mol \; NaOH} \qquad \dfrac{36.46 \; g \; HCl}{1 \; mol \; HCl}$

  Solution: $4.85 \; \bar{g} \, \overline{NaOH} \times \dfrac{1 \; \overline{mol \; NaOH}}{40.01 \; \bar{g} \, \overline{NaOH}} \times \dfrac{1 \; \overline{mol \; HCl}}{1 \; \overline{mol \; NaOH}} \times \dfrac{36.46 \; g \; HCl}{1 \; \overline{mol \; HCl}} = 4.42 \; g \; HCl$

  Check: The units of the answer (g HCl) are correct. The magnitude of the answer is reasonable since it is less than g NaOH.

  (b) **Given:** 4.85 g $Ca(OH)_2$ **Find:** g HNO_3
  Conceptual Plan: g $Ca(OH)_2$ $\rightarrow$ **mol $Ca(OH)_2$** $\rightarrow$ **mol HNO_3** $\rightarrow$ **g HNO_3**

  $\dfrac{mol \; Ca(OH)_2}{74.10 \; g \; Ca(OH)_2} \qquad \dfrac{2 \; mol \; HNO_3}{1 \; mol \; Ca(OH)_2} \qquad \dfrac{63.02 \; g \; HNO_3}{1 \; mol \; HNO_3}$

Solution: $4.85 \ \bar{g} \ \overline{Ca(OH)_2} \times \dfrac{1 \ \overline{mol \ Ca(OH)_2}}{74.10 \ \overline{g \ Ca(OH)_2}} \times \dfrac{2 \ \overline{mol \ HNO_3}}{1 \ \overline{mol \ Ca(OH)_2}} \times \dfrac{63.02 \ g \ HNO_3}{1 \ \overline{mol \ HNO_3}} = 8.25 \ g \ HNO_3$

Check: The units of the answer (g HNO_3) are correct. The magnitude of the answer is reasonable since it is more than g $Ca(OH)_2$.

(c) **Given:** 4.85 g KOH **Find:** g H_2SO_4

Conceptual Plan: g KOH $\rightarrow$ mol KOH $\rightarrow$ mol H_2SO_4 $\rightarrow$ g H_2SO_4

$\dfrac{mol \ KOH}{56.11 \ g \ KOH} \qquad \dfrac{1 \ mol \ H_2SO_4}{2 \ mol \ KOH} \qquad \dfrac{98.09 \ g \ H_2SO_4}{1 \ mol \ H_2SO_4}$

Solution: $4.85 \ \bar{g} \ \overline{NaOH} \times \dfrac{1 \ \overline{mol \ KOH}}{56.11 \ \overline{g \ KOH}} \times \dfrac{1 \ \overline{mol \ H_2SO_4}}{2 \ \overline{mol \ KOH}} \times \dfrac{98.09 \ g \ H_2SO_4}{1 \ \overline{mol \ H_2SO_4}} = 4.24 \ g \ H_2SO_4$

Check: The units of the answer (g H_2SO_4) are correct. The magnitude of the answer is reasonable since it is less than g KOH.

Limiting Reactant, Theoretical Yield, and Percent Yield

4.73   (a)   **Given:** 2 mol Na; 2 mol Br_2 **Find:** limiting reactant

Conceptual Plan: mol Na $\rightarrow$ mol NaBr

$\dfrac{2 \ mol \ NaBr}{2 \ mol \ Na}$ $\rightarrow$ **smallest mol amount determines limiting reactant**

mol Br_2 $\rightarrow$ mol NaBr

$\dfrac{2 \ mol \ NaBr}{1 \ mol \ Br_2}$

Solution: $2 \ \overline{mol \ Na} \times \dfrac{2 \ mol \ NaBr}{2 \ \overline{mol \ Na}} = 2 \ mol \ NaBr$

$2 \ \overline{mol \ Br_2} \times \dfrac{2 \ mol \ NaBr}{1 \ \overline{mol \ Br_2}} = 4 \ mol \ NaBr$

Na is limiting reactant

Check: The answer is reasonable since Na produced the smallest amount of product.

(b)   **Given:** 1.8 mol Na; 1.4 mol Br_2 **Find:** limiting reactant

Conceptual Plan: mol Na $\rightarrow$ mol NaBr

$\dfrac{2 \ mol \ NaBr}{2 \ mol \ Na}$ $\rightarrow$ **smallest mol amount determines limiting reactant**

mol Br_2 $\rightarrow$ mol NaBr

$\dfrac{2 \ mol \ NaBr}{1 \ mol \ Br_2}$

Solution: $1.8 \ \overline{mol \ Na} \times \dfrac{2 \ mol \ NaBr}{2 \ \overline{mol \ Na}} = 1.8 \ mol \ NaBr$

$1.4 \ \overline{mol \ Br_2} \times \dfrac{2 \ mol \ NaBr}{1 \ \overline{mol \ Br_2}} = 2.8 \ mol \ NaBr$

Na is limiting reactant

Check: The answer is reasonable since Na produced the smallest amount of product.

(c)   **Given:** 2.5 mol Na; 1 mol Br_2 **Find:** limiting reactant

Conceptual Plan: mol Na $\rightarrow$ mol NaBr

$\dfrac{2 \ mol \ NaBr}{2 \ mol \ Na}$ $\rightarrow$ **smallest mol amount determines limiting reactant**

mol Br_2 $\rightarrow$ mol NaBr

$\dfrac{2 \ mol \ NaBr}{1 \ mol \ Br_2}$

Solution: $2.5 \ \overline{mol \ Na} \times \dfrac{2 \ mol \ NaBr}{2 \ \overline{mol \ Na}} = 2.5 \ mol \ NaBr$

$1 \ \overline{mol \ Br_2} \times \dfrac{2 \ mol \ NaBr}{1 \ \overline{mol \ Br_2}} = 2 \ mol \ NaBr$

Br_2 is limiting reactant

Check: The answer is reasonable since Br_2 produced the smallest amount of product.

(d) **Given:** 12.6 mol Na; 6.9 mol Br_2 **Find:** limiting reactant
  Conceptual Plan: mol Na $\rightarrow$ mol NaBr

$$\frac{2\ \text{mol NaBr}}{2\ \text{mol Na}} \qquad\qquad \rightarrow \textbf{smallest mol amount determines limiting reactant}$$

  mol Br_2 $\rightarrow$ mol NaBr

$$\frac{2\ \text{mol NaBr}}{1\ \text{mol Br}_2}$$

  Solution: $12.6\ \cancel{\text{mol Na}} \times \dfrac{2\ \text{mol NaBr}}{2\ \cancel{\text{mol Na}}} = 12.6\ \text{mol NaBr}$

  $6.9\ \cancel{\text{mol Br}_2} \times \dfrac{2\ \text{mol NaBr}}{1\ \cancel{\text{mol Br}_2}} = 13.8\ \text{mol NaBr}$

  Na is limiting reactant
  Check: The answer is reasonable since Na produced the smallest amount of product.

4.75 The greatest number of Cl_2 molecules will be formed from reaction mixture (b) and would be 3 molecules Cl_2.

(a) **Given:** 7 molecules HCl, 1 molecule O_2 **Find:** theoretical yield Cl_2
  Conceptual Plan: molecules HCl $\rightarrow$ molecules Cl_2

$$\frac{2\ \text{molecules Cl}_2}{4\ \text{molecules HCl}} \qquad \rightarrow \textbf{smallest molecule amount determines limiting reactant}$$

  molecules O_2 $\rightarrow$ molecules Cl_2

$$\frac{2\ \text{molecules Cl}_2}{1\ \text{molecules O}_2}$$

  Solution: $7\ \cancel{\text{molecules HCl}} \times \dfrac{2\ \text{molecules Cl}_2}{4\ \cancel{\text{molecules HCl}}} = 3\ \text{molecules Cl}_2$

  $1\ \cancel{\text{molecules O}_2} \times \dfrac{2\ \text{molecules Cl}_2}{1\ \cancel{\text{molecules O}_2}} = 2\ \text{molecules Cl}_2$

  Theoretical Yield = 2 molecules Cl_2

(b) **Given:** 6 molecules HCl, 3 molecules O_2 **Find:** theoretical yield Cl_2
  Conceptual Plan: molecules HCl $\rightarrow$ molecules Cl_2

$$\frac{2\ \text{molecules Cl}_2}{4\ \text{molecules HCl}} \qquad \rightarrow \textbf{smallest molecule amount determines limiting reactant}$$

  molecules O_2 $\rightarrow$ molecules Cl_2

$$\frac{2\ \text{molecules Cl}_2}{1\ \text{molecules O}_2}$$

  Solution: $6\ \cancel{\text{molecules HCl}} \times \dfrac{2\ \text{molecules Cl}_2}{4\ \cancel{\text{molecules HCl}}} = 3\ \text{molecules Cl}_2$

  $3\ \cancel{\text{molecules O}_2} \times \dfrac{2\ \text{molecules Cl}_2}{1\ \cancel{\text{molecules O}_2}} = 6\ \text{molecules Cl}_2$

  Theoretical Yield = 3 molecules Cl_2

(c) **Given:** 4 molecules HCl, 5 molecules O_2 **Find:** theoretical yield Cl_2
  Conceptual Plan: molecules HCl $\rightarrow$ molecules Cl_2

$$\frac{2\ \text{molecules Cl}_2}{4\ \text{molecules HCl}} \qquad \rightarrow \textbf{smallest molecule amount determines limiting reactant}$$

  molecules O_2 $\rightarrow$ molecules Cl_2

$$\frac{2\ \text{molecules Cl}_2}{1\ \text{molecules O}_2}$$

  Solution: $4\ \cancel{\text{molecules HCl}} \times \dfrac{2\ \text{molecules Cl}_2}{4\ \cancel{\text{molecules HCl}}} = 2\ \text{molecules Cl}_2$

  $5\ \cancel{\text{molecules O}_2} \times \dfrac{2\ \text{molecules Cl}_2}{1\ \cancel{\text{molecules O}_2}} = 10\ \text{molecules Cl}_2$

  Theoretical Yield = 2 molecules Cl_2

  Answer (b) gives the highest yield of 3
  Check: The units of the answer (molecules Cl_2) are correct. The answer is reasonable based on the limiting reactant in each mixture.

4.77   (a)   **Given:** 4 mol Ti, 4 mol Cl_2 **Find:** theoretical yield $TiCl_4$
          Conceptual Plan: mol Ti $\rightarrow$ mol $TiCl_4$

$$\frac{1 \text{ mol } TiCl_4}{1 \text{ mol Ti}} \qquad \rightarrow \textbf{ smallest mol amount determines limiting reactant}$$

          mol Cl_2 $\rightarrow$ mol $TiCl_4$

$$\frac{1 \text{ mol } TiCl_4}{2 \text{ mol } Cl_2}$$

          Solution: $4 \text{ mol Ti} \times \dfrac{1 \text{ mol } TiCl_4}{1 \text{ mol Ti}} = 4 \text{ mol } TiCl_4$

$$4 \text{ mol } Cl_2 \times \frac{1 \text{ mol } TiCl_4}{2 \text{ mol } Cl_2} = 2 \text{ mol } TiCl_4$$

          Theoretical Yield = 2 mol $TiCl_4$

          Check: The units of the answer (mol $TiCl_4$) are correct. The answer is reasonable since Cl_2 produced the smallest amount of product and is the limiting reactant.

       (b)   **Given:** 7 mol Ti, 17 mol Cl_2 **Find:** theoretical yield $TiCl_4$
          Conceptual Plan: mol Ti $\rightarrow$ mol $TiCl_4$

$$\frac{1 \text{ mol } TiCl_4}{1 \text{ mol Ti}} \qquad \rightarrow \textbf{ smallest mol amount determines limiting reactant}$$

          mol Cl_2 $\rightarrow$ mol $TiCl_4$

$$\frac{1 \text{ mol } TiCl_4}{2 \text{ mol } Cl_2}$$

          Solution: $7 \text{ mol Ti} \times \dfrac{1 \text{ mol } TiCl_4}{1 \text{ mol Ti}} = 7 \text{ mol } TiCl_4$

$$17 \text{ mol } Cl_2 \times \frac{1 \text{ mol } TiCl_4}{2 \text{ mol } Cl_2} = 8.5 \text{ mol } TiCl_4$$

          Theoretical Yield = 7 mol $TiCl_4$

          Check: The units of the answer (mol $TiCl_4$) are correct. The answer is reasonable since Ti produced the smallest amount of product and is the limiting reactant.

       (c)   **Given:** 12.4 mol Ti, 18.8 mol Cl_2 **Find:** theoretical yield $TiCl_4$
          Conceptual Plan: mol Ti $\rightarrow$ mol $TiCl_4$

$$\frac{1 \text{ mol } TiCl_4}{1 \text{ mol Ti}} \qquad \rightarrow \textbf{ smallest mol amount determines limiting reactant}$$

          mol Cl_2 $\rightarrow$ mol $TiCl_4$

$$\frac{1 \text{ mol } TiCl_4}{2 \text{ mol } Cl_2}$$

          Solution: $12.4 \text{ mol Ti} \times \dfrac{1 \text{ mol } TiCl_4}{1 \text{ mol Ti}} = 12.4 \text{ mol } TiCl_4$

$$18.8 \text{ mol } Cl_2 \times \frac{1 \text{ mol } TiCl_4}{2 \text{ mol } Cl_2} = 9.40 \text{ mol } TiCl_4$$

          Theoretical Yield = 9.40 mol $TiCl_4$

          Check: The units of the answer (mol $TiCl_4$) are correct. The answer is reasonable since Cl_2 produced the smallest amount of product and is the limiting reactant.

4.79   **Given:** 4.2 mol ZnS, 6.8 mol O_2 **Find:** mole amount of excess reactant left
     Conceptual Plan: mol ZnS $\rightarrow$ mol ZnO

$$\frac{2 \text{ mol ZnO}}{2 \text{ mol ZnS}} \qquad \rightarrow \textbf{ smallest mol amount determines limiting reactant}$$

     mol O_2 $\rightarrow$ mol ZnO

$$\frac{2 \text{ mol ZnO}}{3 \text{ mol } O_2}$$

     then: mol limiting reactant $\rightarrow$ mol excess reactant required $\rightarrow$ mol excess reactant left

$$\frac{2 \text{ mol ZnS}}{3 \text{ mol } O_2}$$

     Solution: $4.2 \text{ mol ZnS} \times \dfrac{2 \text{ mol ZnO}}{2 \text{ mol ZnS}} = 4.2 \text{ mol ZnO}$

$$6.8 \ \overline{mol \ O_2} \times \frac{2 \ mol \ ZnO}{3 \ \overline{mol \ O_2}} = 4.5 \ mol \ ZnO$$

ZnS is the limiting reactant, therefore O_2 is the excess reactant.

$$4.2 \ \overline{mol \ ZnS} \times \frac{3 \ mol \ O_2}{2 \ \overline{mol \ ZnS}} = 6.3 \ mol \ O_2 \ required$$

$$6.8 \ mol \ O_2 - 6.3 \ mol \ O_2 = 0.5 \ mol \ O_2 \ left$$

Check: The units of the answer (mol O_2) are correct and the magnitude is reasonable since it is less than the original amount of O_2.

4.81   (a)   **Given:** 2.0 g Al, 2.0 g Cl_2 **Find:** theoretical yield in g $AlCl_3$

Conceptual Plan: g Al $\rightarrow$ mol Al $\rightarrow$ mol AlCl$_3$

$$\frac{1 \ mol \ Al}{26.98 \ g \ Al} \qquad \frac{2 \ mol \ AlCl_3}{2 \ mol \ Al} \qquad \rightarrow \textbf{ smallest mol amount determines limiting reactant}$$

g Cl$_2$ $\rightarrow$ mol Cl$_2$ $\rightarrow$ mol AlCl$_3$

$$\frac{1 \ mol \ Cl_2}{70.90 \ g \ Cl_2} \qquad \frac{2 \ mol \ AlCl_3}{3 \ mol \ Cl_2}$$

then: mol AlCl$_3$ $\rightarrow$ g AlCl$_3$

$$\frac{133.3 \ g \ AlCl_3}{mol \ AlCl_3}$$

Solution: $2.0 \ \overline{g \ Al} \times \dfrac{1 \ \overline{mol \ Al}}{26.98 \ \overline{g \ Al}} \times \dfrac{2 \ mol \ AlCl_3}{2 \ \overline{mol \ Al}} = 0.074 \ mol \ AlCl_3$

$$2.0 \ \overline{g \ Cl_2} \times \frac{1 \ \overline{mol \ Cl_2}}{70.90 \ \overline{g \ Cl_2}} \times \frac{2 \ mol \ AlCl_3}{3 \ \overline{mol \ Cl_2}} = 0.0188 \ mol \ AlCl_3$$

$$0.0188 \ mol \ AlCl_3 \times \frac{133.3 \ g \ AlCl_3}{mol \ AlCl_3} = 2.5 \ g \ AlCl_3$$

Check: The units of the answer (g $AlCl_3$) are correct. The answer is reasonable since Cl_2 produced the smallest amount of product and is the limiting reactant.

    (b)   **Given:** 7.5 g Al, 24.8 g Cl_2 **Find:** theoretical yield in g $AlCl_3$

Conceptual Plan: g Al $\rightarrow$ mol Al $\rightarrow$ mol AlCl$_3$

$$\frac{1 \ mol \ Al}{26.98 \ g \ Al} \qquad \frac{2 \ mol \ AlCl_3}{2 \ mol \ Al} \qquad \rightarrow \textbf{ smallest mol amount determines limiting reactant}$$

g Cl$_2$ $\rightarrow$ mol Cl$_2$ $\rightarrow$ mol AlCl$_3$

$$\frac{1 \ mol \ Cl_2}{70.90 \ g \ Cl_2} \qquad \frac{2 \ mol \ AlCl_3}{3 \ mol \ Cl_2}$$

then: mol AlCl$_3$ $\rightarrow$ g AlCl$_3$

$$\frac{133.3 \ g \ AlCl_3}{mol \ AlCl_3}$$

Solution: $7.5 \ \overline{g \ Al} \times \dfrac{1 \ \overline{mol \ Al}}{26.98 \ \overline{g \ Al}} \times \dfrac{2 \ mol \ AlCl_3}{2 \ \overline{mol \ Al}} = 0.2780 \ mol \ AlCl_3$

$$24.8 \ \overline{g \ Cl_2} \times \frac{1 \ \overline{mol \ Cl_2}}{70.90 \ \overline{g \ Cl_2}} \times \frac{2 \ mol \ AlCl_3}{3 \ \overline{mol \ Cl_2}} = 0.2332 \ mol \ AlCl_3$$

$$0.2332 \ mol \ AlCl_3 \times \frac{133.3 \ g \ AlCl_3}{mol \ AlCl_3} = 31.1 \ g \ AlCl_3$$

Check: The units of the answer (g $AlCl_3$) are correct. The answer is reasonable since Cl_2 produced the smallest amount of product and is the limiting reactant.

    (c)   **Given:** 0.235 g Al, 1.15 g Cl_2 **Find:** theoretical yield in g $AlCl_3$

Conceptual Plan: g Al $\rightarrow$ mol Al $\rightarrow$ mol AlCl$_3$

$$\frac{1 \ mol \ Al}{26.98 \ g \ Al} \qquad \frac{2 \ mol \ AlCl_3}{2 \ mol \ Al} \qquad \rightarrow \textbf{ smallest mol amount determines limiting reactant}$$

g Cl$_2$ $\rightarrow$ mol Cl$_2$ $\rightarrow$ mol AlCl$_3$

$$\frac{1 \ mol \ Cl_2}{70.90 \ g \ Cl_2} \qquad \frac{2 \ mol \ AlCl_3}{3 \ mol \ Cl_2}$$

then: mol AlCl$_3$ $\rightarrow$ g AlCl$_3$

$$\frac{133.34 \ g \ AlCl_3}{mol \ AlCl_3}$$

Solution: $0.235 \; \cancel{g \; Al} \times \dfrac{1 \; \cancel{mol \; Al}}{26.98 \; \cancel{g \; Al}} \times \dfrac{2 \; mol \; AlCl_3}{2 \; \cancel{mol \; Al}} = 0.00871\underline{0} \; mol \; AlCl_3$

$1.15 \; \cancel{g \; Cl_2} \times \dfrac{1 \; \cancel{mol \; Cl_2}}{70.90 \; \cancel{g \; Cl_2}} \times \dfrac{2 \; mol \; AlCl_3}{3 \; \cancel{mol \; Cl_2}} = 0.01081 \; mol \; AlCl_3$

$0.00871\underline{0} \; mol \; AlCl_3 \times \dfrac{133.34 \; g \; AlCl_3}{mol \; AlCl_3} = 1.16 \; g \; AlCl_3$

Check: The units of the answer (g AlCl$_3$) are correct. The answer is reasonable since Al produced the smallest amount of product and is the limiting reactant.

4.83 **Given:** 22.55 Fe$_2$O$_3$, 14.78 g CO **Find:** mole amount of excess reactant left
Conceptual Plan: g Fe$_2$O$_3$ $\rightarrow$ mol Fe$_2$O$_3$ $\rightarrow$ mol Fe

$\dfrac{1 \; mol \; Fe_2O_3}{159.7 \; g \; Fe_2O_3} \qquad \dfrac{2 \; mol \; Fe}{1 \; mol \; Fe_2O_3} \rightarrow$ **smallest mol amount determines limiting reactant**

g CO $\rightarrow$ mol CO $\rightarrow$ mol Fe

$\dfrac{1 \; mol \; CO}{28.01 \; g \; CO} \qquad \dfrac{2 \; mol \; Fe}{3 \; mol \; CO}$

then: mol limiting reactant $\rightarrow$ mol excess reactant required $\rightarrow$ mol excess reactant left $\rightarrow$ g excess reactant left

$\dfrac{1 \; mol \; Fe_2O_3}{3 \; mol \; CO} \qquad \dfrac{159.7 \; g \; Fe_2O_3}{1 \; mol \; Fe_2O_3} \qquad$ or $\dfrac{28.01 g \; CO}{1 \; mol \; CO}$

Solution: $22.55 \; g \; \cancel{Fe_2O_3} \times \dfrac{1 \; \cancel{mol \; Fe_2O_3}}{159.7 \; \cancel{g \; Fe_2O_3}} \times \dfrac{2 \; mol \; Fe}{1 \; \cancel{mol \; Fe_2O_3}} = 0.2824 \; mol \; Fe$

$14.78 \; \cancel{g \; CO} \times \dfrac{1 \; \cancel{mol \; CO}}{28.01 \; \cancel{g \; CO}} \times \dfrac{2 \; mol \; Fe}{3 \; \cancel{mol \; CO}} = 0.3518 \; mol \; Fe$

Fe$_2$O$_3$ is the limiting reactant, therefore CO is the excess reactant.

$22.55 \; g \; \cancel{Fe_2O_3} \times \dfrac{1 \; \cancel{mol \; Fe_2O_3}}{159.7 g \; \cancel{Fe_2O_3}} \times \dfrac{3 \; \cancel{mol \; CO}}{1 \; \cancel{mol \; Fe_2O_3}} \times \dfrac{28.01 \; g \; CO}{1 \cancel{mol \; CO}} = 11.86\underline{5} \; g \; CO \; required$

$14.78 \; g \; CO \; - \; 11.87 \; g \; CO \; = \; 2.91 \; g \; CO \; left$

Check: The units of the answer (g CO) are correct and the magnitude is reasonable since it is less than the original amount of CO.

4.85 **Given:** 28.5 g KCl; 25.7 g Pb^{2+}; 29.4 g PbCl$_2$ **Find:** limiting reactant, theoretical yield PbCl$_2$, % yield
Conceptual Plan: g KCl $\rightarrow$ mol KCl $\rightarrow$ mol PbCl$_2$

$\dfrac{1 \; mol \; KCl}{74.55 \; g \; KCl} \qquad \dfrac{1 \; mol \; PbCl_2}{2 \; mol \; KCl} \rightarrow$ **smallest mol amount determines limiting reactant**

g Pb^{2+} $\rightarrow$ mol Pb^{2+} $\rightarrow$ mol PbCl$_2$

$\dfrac{1 \; mol \; Pb^{2+}}{207.2 \; g \; Pb^{2+}} \qquad \dfrac{1 \; mol \; PbCl_2}{1 \; mol \; Pb^{2+}}$

then: mol PbCl$_2$ $\rightarrow$ g PbCl$_2$ then: determine % yield

$\dfrac{278.1 \; g \; PbCl_2}{mol \; PbCl_2} \qquad \dfrac{\text{actual yield g } PbCl_2}{\text{theoretical yield g } PbCl_2} \times 100$

Solution: $28.5 \; \cancel{g \; KCl} \times \dfrac{1 \; \cancel{mol \; KCl}}{74.55 \; \cancel{g \; KCl}} \times \dfrac{1 \; mol \; PbCl_2}{2 \; \cancel{mol \; KCl}} = 0.191\underline{1} \; mol \; PbCl_2$

$25.7 \; \cancel{g \; Pb^{2+}} \times \dfrac{1 \; \cancel{mol \; Pb^{2+}}}{207.2 \; \cancel{g \; Pb^{2+}}} \times \dfrac{1 \; mol \; PbCl_2}{1 \; \cancel{mol \; Pb^{2+}}} = 0.1240 \; mol \; PbCl_2$ Pb^{2+} is the limiting reactant.

$0.12\underline{4}0 \; \cancel{mol \; PbCl_2} \times \dfrac{278.1 \; g \; PbCl_2}{1 \; \cancel{mol \; PbCl_2}} = 34.\underline{5} \; g \; PbCl_2$

$\dfrac{29.4 \; \cancel{g \; PbCl_2}}{34.\underline{5} \; \cancel{g \; PbCl_2}} \times 100 = 85.2\%$

Check: The theoretical yield has the correct units (g PbCl$_2$) and has a reasonable magnitude compared to the mass of Pb^{2+}, the limiting reactant. The % yield is reasonable, under 100%.

4.87   **Given:** 136.4 kg NH_3; 211.4 kg CO_2; 168.4 kg CH_4N_2O
         Find: limiting reactant, theoretical yield CH_4N_2O, % yield
         Conceptual Plan: kg NH_3 → g NH_3 → mol NH_3 → mol CH_4N_2O

$$\frac{1000 \text{ g}}{1 \text{ kg}} \qquad \frac{1 \text{ mol } NH_3}{17.03 \text{ g } NH_3} \qquad \frac{1 \text{ mol } CH_4N_2O}{2 \text{ mol } NH_3}$$

   → smallest amount determines limiting reactant

   kg CO_2 → g CO_2 → mol CO_2 → mol CH_4N_2O

$$\frac{1000 \text{ g}}{1 \text{ kg}} \qquad \frac{1 \text{ mol } CO_2}{44.01 \text{ g } CO_2} \qquad \frac{1 \text{ mol } CH_4N_2O}{1 \text{ mol } CO_2}$$

   then: mol CH_4N_2O → g CH_4N_2O → kg CH_4N_2O   **then: determine % yield**

$$\frac{60.06 \text{ g } CH_4N_2O}{1 \text{ mol } CH_4N_2O} \qquad \frac{1 \text{ kg}}{1000 \text{ g}} \qquad \frac{\text{actual yield kg } CH_4N_2O}{\text{theoretical yield kg } CH_4N_2O} \times 100$$

   Solution: $136.4 \text{ kg } NH_3 \times \dfrac{1000 \text{ g}}{\text{kg}} \times \dfrac{1 \text{ mol } NH_3}{17.03 \text{ g } NH_3} \times \dfrac{1 \text{ mol } CH_4N_2O}{2 \text{ mol } NH_3} = 4004.7 \text{ mol } CH_4N_2O$

   $211.4 \text{ kg } CO_2 \times \dfrac{1000 \text{ g}}{\text{kg}} \times \dfrac{1 \text{ mol } CO_2}{44.01 \text{ g } CO_2} \times \dfrac{1 \text{ mol } CH_4N_2O}{1 \text{ mol } CO_2} = 4803.4 \text{ mol } CH_4N_2O$

   NH_3 is the limiting reactant

   $4004.7 \text{ mol } CH_4N_2O \times \dfrac{60.06 \text{ g } CH_4N_2O}{1 \text{ mol } CH_4N_2O} \times \dfrac{\text{kg}}{1000 \text{ g}} = 240.52 \text{ kg } CH_4N_2O$

   $\dfrac{168.4 \text{ kg } CH_4N_2O}{240.52 \text{ kg } CH_4N_2O} \times 100 = 70.01\%$

   Check: The theoretical yield has the correct units (kg CH_4N_2O) and has a reasonable magnitude compared to the mass of NH_3, the limiting reactant. The % yield is reasonable, under 100%.

Solution Concentration and Solution Stoichiometry

4.89   (a)   **Given:** 3.25 mol LiCl; 2.78 L solution **Find:** molarity LiCl
               Conceptual Plan: mol LiCl, L solution → molarity

$$\text{molarity (M)} = \frac{\text{amount of solute (in moles)}}{\text{volume of solution (in L)}}$$

         Solution: $\dfrac{3.25 \text{ mol LiCl}}{2.78 \text{ L solution}} = 1.169 \text{ mol L}^{-1} = 1.17 \text{ mol L}^{-1}$
         Check: The units of the answer (mol L^{-1}) are correct. The magnitude of the answer is reasonable. Concentrations are usually between 0 mol L^{-1} and 18 mol L^{-1}.

         (b)   **Given:** 28.33 g $C_6H_{12}O_6$; 1.28 L solution **Find:** molarity $C_6H_{12}O_6$
               Conceptual Plan: g $C_6H_{12}O_6$ → mol $C_6H_{12}O_6$, L solution → molarity

$$\frac{\text{mol } C_6H_{12}O_6}{180.16 \text{ g } C_6H_{12}O_6} \qquad \text{molarity (M)} = \frac{\text{amount of solute (in moles)}}{\text{volume of solution (in L)}}$$

         Solution: $28.33 \text{ g } C_6H_{12}O_6 \times \dfrac{1 \text{ mol } C_6H_{12}O_6}{180.16 \text{ g } C_6H_{12}O_6} = 0.15724 \text{ mol } C_6H_{12}O_6$

         $\dfrac{0.15724 \text{ mol } C_6H_{12}O_6}{1.28 \text{ L solution}} = 0.1228 \text{ mol L}^{-1} = 0.123 \text{ mol L}^{-1}$
         Check: The units of the answer (mol L^{-1}) are correct. The magnitude of the answer is reasonable. Concentrations are usually between 0 mol L^{-1} and 18 mol L^{-1}.

         (c)   **Given:** 32.4 mg NaCl; 122.4 mL solution **Find:** molarity NaCl
               Conceptual Plan: mg NaCl → g NaCl → mol NaCl, and mL solution → L solution then molarity

$$\frac{\text{g NaCl}}{1000 \text{ mg NaCl}} \quad \frac{\text{mol NaCl}}{58.45 \text{ g NaCl}} \qquad \frac{\text{L solution}}{1000 \text{ mL solution}} \quad \text{molarity (M)} = \frac{\text{amount of solute (in moles)}}{\text{volume of solution (in L)}}$$

         Solution: $32.4 \text{ mg NaCl} \times \dfrac{1 \text{ g}}{1000 \text{ mg}} \times \dfrac{1 \text{ mol NaCl}}{58.45 \text{ g NaCl}} = 5.543 \times 10^{-4} \text{ mol NaCl}$

$$122.4 \ \overline{\text{mL solution}} \times \frac{1 \text{ L}}{1000 \ \overline{\text{mL}}} = 0.1224 \text{ L}$$

$$\frac{5.543 \times 10^{-4} \text{ mol NaCl}}{0.1224 \text{ L}} = 0.0045\underline{2}87 \text{ mol L}^{-1} \text{ NaCl} = 0.00453 \text{ mol L}^{-1} \text{ NaCl}$$

Check: The units of the answer (mol L^{-1}) are correct. The magnitude of the answer is reasonable. Concentrations are usually between 0 mol L^{-1} and 18 mol L^{-1}.

4.91   (a)   **Given:** 0.556 L; 2.3 mol L^{-1} KCl **Find:** mol KCl
            Conceptual Plan: volume solution x mol L^{-1} = mol

$$\text{Solution: } 0.556 \ \overline{\text{L solution}} \times \frac{2.3 \text{ mol KCl}}{\overline{\text{L solution}}} = 1.3 \text{ mol KCl}$$

            Check: The units of the answer (mol KCl) are correct. The magnitude is reasonable since it is less than 1 L solution.

      (b)   **Given:** 1.8 L; 0.85 mol L^{-1} KCl **Find:** mol KCl
            Conceptual Plan: volume solution x mol L^{-1} = mol

$$\text{Solution: } 1.8 \ \overline{\text{L solution}} \times \frac{0.85 \text{ mol KCl}}{\overline{\text{L solution}}} = 1.5 \text{ mol KCl}$$

            Check: The units of the answer (mol KCl) are correct. The magnitude is reasonable since it is less than 2 L solution.

      (c)   **Given:** 114 mL; 1.85 mol L^{-1} KCl **Find:** mol KCl
            Conceptual Plan: mL solution $\rightarrow$ L solution, then volume solution x mol L^{-1} = mol

$$\frac{1 \text{ L}}{1000 \text{ mL}}$$

$$\text{Solution: } 114 \ \overline{\text{mL solution}} \times \frac{1 \text{ L}}{1000 \ \overline{\text{mL}}} \times \frac{1.85 \text{ mol KCl}}{\overline{\text{L solution}}} = 0.211 \text{ mol KCl}$$

            Check: The units of the answer (mol KCl) are correct. The magnitude is reasonable since it is less than 1 L solution.

4.93   **Given:** 400.0 mL; 1.1 mol L^{-1} NaNO$_3$ **Find:** g NaNO$_3$
      Conceptual Plan: mL solution $\rightarrow$ L solution, then volume solution x mol L^{-1} = mol NaNO$_3$

$$\frac{\text{L solution}}{1000 \text{ mL solution}}$$

            then mol NaNO$_3$ $\rightarrow$ g NaNO$_3$

$$\frac{85.01 \text{ g NaNO}_3}{\text{mol NaNO}_3}$$

$$\text{Solution: } 400.0 \ \overline{\text{mL solution}} \times \frac{1 \text{ L}}{1000 \ \overline{\text{mL}}} \times \frac{1.1 \ \overline{\text{mol NaNO}_3}}{\overline{\text{L solution}}} \times \frac{85.01 \text{ g}}{\overline{\text{mol NaNO}_3}} = 37 \text{ g NaNO}_3$$

      Check: The units of the answer (g NaNO$_3$) are correct. The magnitude is reasonable for the concentration and volume of solution.

4.95   **Given:** V_1 = 123 mL; M_1 = 1.1 mol L^{-1}; V_2 = 500.0 mL **Find:** M_2
      Conceptual Plan: mL $\rightarrow$ L then V_1, M_1, V_2 $\rightarrow$ M_2

$$\frac{1 \text{ L}}{1000 \text{ mL}} \qquad\qquad V_1 M_1 = V_2 M_2$$

$$\text{Solution: } 123 \ \overline{\text{mL}} \times \frac{1 \text{ L}}{1000 \ \overline{\text{mL}}} = 0.123 \text{ L} \qquad 500.0 \ \overline{\text{mL}} \times \frac{1 \text{ L}}{1000 \ \overline{\text{mL}}} = 0.5000 \text{ L}$$

$$M_2 = \frac{V_1 M_1}{V_2} = \frac{(0.123 \ \overline{\text{L}})(1.1 \text{ mol L}^{-1})}{(0.5000 \ \overline{\text{L}})} = 0.27 \text{ mol L}^{-1}$$

      Check: The units of the answer (mol L^{-1}) are correct. The magnitude of the answer is reasonable since it is less than the original concentration.

4.97   **Given:** V_1 = 50 mL; M_1 = 12 mol L^{-1}; M_2 = 0.100 mol L^{-1} **Find:** V_2
      Conceptual Plan: mL $\rightarrow$ L then V_1, M_1, M_2 $\rightarrow$ V_2

$$\frac{1 \text{ L}}{1000 \text{ mL}} \qquad\qquad V_1 M_1 = V_2 M_2$$

Solution: $50 \text{ mL} \times \dfrac{1 \text{ L}}{1000 \text{ mL}} = 0.050 \text{ L}$

$$V_2 = \dfrac{V_1 M_1}{M_2} = \dfrac{(0.050 \text{ L})(12 \text{ mol L}^{-1})}{(0.100 \text{ mol L}^{-1})} = 6.0 \text{ L}$$

Check: The units of the answer (L) are correct. The magnitude of the answer is reasonable since the new concentration is much less than the original; the volume must be larger.

4.99   **Given:** 95.4 mL, 0.102 mol L^{-1} CuCl$_2$; 0.175 mol L^{-1} Na$_3$PO$_4$ **Find:** volume Na$_3$PO$_4$
Conceptual Plan: mL CuCl$_2$ → L CuCl$_2$ → mol CuCl$_2$ → mol Na$_3$PO$_4$ → L Na$_3$PO$_4$ → mL Na$_3$PO$_4$

$$\dfrac{1 \text{ L}}{1000 \text{ mL}} \quad \dfrac{0.102 \text{ mol CuCl}_2}{\text{L}} \quad \dfrac{2 \text{ mol Na}_3\text{PO}_4}{3 \text{ mol CuCl}_2} \quad \dfrac{1 \text{ L}}{0.175 \text{ mol Na}_3\text{PO}_4} \quad \dfrac{1000 \text{ mL}}{\text{L}}$$

Solution: $95.4 \text{ mL CuCl}_2 \times \dfrac{1 \text{ L}}{1000 \text{ mL}} \times \dfrac{0.102 \text{ mol CuCl}_2}{1 \text{ L}} \times \dfrac{2 \text{ mol Na}_3\text{PO}_4}{3 \text{ mol CuCl}_2} \times \dfrac{1 \text{ L}}{0.175 \text{ mol Na}_3\text{PO}_4} \times \dfrac{1000 \text{ mL}}{1 \text{ L}}$

$= 37.1 \text{ mL Na}_3\text{PO}_4$

Check: The units of the answer (mL Na$_3$PO$_4$) are correct. The magnitude of the answer is reasonable since the concentration of Na$_3$PO$_4$ is greater.

4.101   **Given:** 25.0 g H$_2$; 6.0 mol L^{-1} H$_2$SO$_4$ **Find:** volume H$_2$SO$_4$
Conceptual Plan: g H$_2$ → mol H$_2$ → mol H$_2$SO$_4$ → L H$_2$SO$_4$

$$\dfrac{2.016 \text{ g H}_2}{1 \text{ mol H}_2} \quad \dfrac{3 \text{ mol H}_2\text{SO}_4}{3 \text{ mol H}_2} \quad \dfrac{1 \text{ L}}{6.0 \text{ mol H}_2\text{SO}_4}$$

Solution: $25.0 \text{ g H}_2 \times \dfrac{1 \text{ mol H}_2}{2.016 \text{ g H}_2} \times \dfrac{3 \text{ mol H}_2\text{SO}_4}{3 \text{ mol H}_2} \times \dfrac{1 \text{ L}}{6.0 \text{ mol H}_2\text{SO}_4} = 2.1 \text{ L H}_2\text{SO}_4$

Check: The units of the answer (L H$_2$SO$_4$) are correct. The magnitude is reasonable since there are approximately 12 mol H$_2$ and the mole ratio is 1:1.

Cumulative Problems

4.103   **Given:** in 100 g solution, 20.0 g C$_2$H$_6$O$_2$; density of solution = 1.03 g mL^{-1} **Find:** M of solution
Conceptual Plan: g C$_2$H$_6$O$_2$ → mol C$_2$H$_6$O$_2$ and g solution → mL solution → L solution

$$\dfrac{1 \text{ mol C}_2\text{H}_6\text{O}_2}{62.06 \text{ g C}_2\text{H}_6\text{O}_2} \qquad\qquad \dfrac{1.00 \text{ mL}}{1.03 \text{ g}} \qquad \dfrac{1 \text{ L}}{1000 \text{ mL}}$$

then M C$_2$H$_6$O$_2$

$$M = \dfrac{\text{mol C}_2\text{H}_6\text{O}_2}{\text{L solution}}$$

Solution:

$$20.0 \text{ g C}_2\text{H}_6\text{O}_2 \times \dfrac{1 \text{ mol C}_2\text{H}_6\text{O}_2}{62.06 \text{ g C}_2\text{H}_6\text{O}_2} = 0.3222 \text{ mol C}_2\text{H}_6\text{O}_2$$

$$100.0 \text{ g solution} \times \dfrac{1.00 \text{ mL solution}}{1.03 \text{ g solution}} \times \dfrac{1 \text{ L}}{1000 \text{ mL}} = 0.09708 \text{ L}$$

$$M = \dfrac{0.3222 \text{ mol C}_2\text{H}_6\text{O}_2}{0.09708 \text{ L}} = 3.32 \text{ mol L}^{-1} \text{ C}_2\text{H}_6\text{O}_2$$

Check: The units of the answer (mol L^{-1} C$_2$H$_6$O$_2$) are correct. The magnitude of the answer is reasonable since the concentration of solutions is usually between 0 and 18 mol L^{-1}.

4.105   **Given:** 2.5 g NaHCO$_3$ **Find:** g HCl
Conceptual Plan: g NaHCO$_3$ → mol NaHCO$_3$ → mol HCl → g HCl

$$\dfrac{1 \text{ mol NaHCO}_3}{84.02 \text{ g NaHCO}_3} \quad \dfrac{1 \text{ mol HCl}}{1 \text{ mol NaHCO}_3} \quad \dfrac{36.46 \text{ g HCl}}{1 \text{ mol HCl}}$$

Solution: $\text{HCl}(aq) + \text{NaHCO}_3(aq) \rightarrow \text{H}_2\text{O}(l) + \text{CO}_2(g) + \text{NaCl}(aq)$

$$2.5 \text{ g NaHCO}_3 \times \dfrac{1 \text{ mol NaHCO}_3}{84.02 \text{ g NaHCO}_3} \times \dfrac{1 \text{ mol HCl}}{1 \text{ mol NaHCO}_3} \times \dfrac{36.46 \text{ g HCl}}{1 \text{ mol HCl}} = 1.1 \text{ g HCl}$$

Check: The units of the answer (g HCl) are correct. The magnitude of the answer is reasonable since the molar mass of HCl is less than the molar mass of NaHCO$_3$.

4.107   **Given:** 1.0 kg C_8H_{18} **Find:** kg CO_2
Conceptual Plan: kg C_8H_{18} → g C_8H_{18} → mol C_8H_{18} → mol CO_2 → g CO_2 → kg CO_2

$$\frac{1000\ g}{kg} \qquad \frac{1\ mol\ C_8H_{18}}{114.22\ g\ C_8H_{18}} \qquad \frac{16\ mol\ CO_2}{2\ mol\ C_8H_{18}} \qquad \frac{44.01\ g\ CO_2}{1\ mol\ CO_2} \qquad \frac{kg}{1000\ g}$$

Solution: $2\ C_8H_{18}(g) + 25\ O_2(g) \rightarrow 16\ CO_2(g) + 18\ H_2O(g)$

$$1.0\ \cancel{kg\ C_8H_{18}} \times \frac{1000\ \cancel{g}}{\cancel{kg}} \times \frac{1\ \cancel{mol\ C_8H_{18}}}{114.22\ \cancel{g\ C_8H_{18}}} \times \frac{16\ \cancel{mol\ CO_2}}{2\ \cancel{mol\ C_8H_{18}}} \times \frac{44.01\ \cancel{g\ CO_2}}{1\ \cancel{mol\ CO_2}} \times \frac{kg}{1000\ \cancel{g}} = 3.1\ kg\ CO_2$$

Check: The units of the answer (kg CO_2) are correct. The magnitude of the answer is reasonable since the ratio of CO_2 to C_8H_{18} is 8:1.

4.109   **Given:** 3.00 mL $C_4H_6O_3$, $d = 1.08$ g mL^{-1}; 1.25 g $C_7H_6O_3$; 1.22 g $C_9H_8O_4$ **Find:** limiting reactant, theoretical yield $C_9H_8O_4$, and % yield $C_9H_8O_4$
Conceptual Plan: mL $C_4H_6O_3$ → g $C_4H_6O_3$ → mol $C_4H_6O_3$ → mol $C_9H_8O_4$

$$\frac{1.08\ g\ C_4H_6O_3}{1.00\ mL\ C_4H_6O_3} \qquad \frac{1\ mol\ C_4H_6O_3}{102.09\ g\ C_4H_6O_3} \qquad \frac{1\ mol\ C_9H_8O_4}{1\ mol\ C_4H_6O_3}$$

→ **smallest amount determines limiting reactant**

g $C_7H_6O_3$ → mol $C_7H_6O_3$ → mol $C_9H_8O_4$

$$\frac{1\ mol\ C_7H_6O_3}{138.12\ g\ C_7H_6O_3} \qquad \frac{1\ mol\ C_9H_8O_4}{1\ mol\ C_7H_6O_3}$$

then: mol $C_9H_8O_4$ → g $C_9H_8O_4$ **then: determine % yield**

$$\frac{180.1\ g\ C_9H_8O_4}{mol\ C_9H_8O_4} \qquad\qquad \frac{actual\ yield\ g\ C_9H_8O_4}{theoretical\ yield\ g\ C_9H_8O_4} \times 100$$

Solution:

$$3.00\ \cancel{mL\ C_4H_6O_3} \times \frac{1.08\ \cancel{g\ C_4H_6O_3}}{\cancel{mL\ C_4H_6O_3}} \times \frac{1\ \cancel{mol\ C_4H_6O_3}}{102.09\ \cancel{g\ C_4H_6O_3}} \times \frac{1\ mol\ C_9H_8O_4}{1\ \cancel{mol\ C_4H_6O_3}} = 0.03174\ mol\ C_9H_8O_4$$

$$1.25\ \cancel{g\ C_7H_6O_3} \times \frac{1\ \cancel{mol\ C_7H_6O_3}}{138.12\ \cancel{g\ C_7H_6O_3}} \times \frac{1\ mol\ C_9H_8O_4}{1\ \cancel{mol\ C_7H_6O_3}} = 0.009050\ mol\ C_9H_8O_4$$

Salicylic acid is the limiting reactant.

$$0.009050\ \cancel{mol\ C_9H_8O_4} \times \frac{180.1\ g\ C_9H_8O_4}{1\ \cancel{mol\ C_9H_8O_4}} = 1.630\ g\ C_9H_8O_4$$

$$\frac{1.22\ \cancel{g\ C_9H_8O_4}}{1.630\ \cancel{g\ C_9H_8O_4}} \times 100 = 74.8\%$$

Check: The theoretical yield has the correct units (g $C_9H_8O_4$) and has a reasonable magnitude compared to the mass of $C_7H_6O_3$, the limiting reactant. The % yield is reasonable, under 100%.

4.111   **Given:** (a) 11 molecules H_2, 2 molecules O_2; (b) 8 molecules H_2, 4 molecules O_2; (c) 4 molecules H_2, 5 molecules O_2; (d) 3 molecules H_2, 6 molecules O_2 **Find:** loudest explosion based on equation
Conceptual Plan: loudest explosion will occur in the balloon with the mol ratio closest to the balanced equation and that contains the most H_2
Solution: $2H_2(g) + O_2(g) \rightarrow H_2O(l)$
Balloon (a) has enough O_2 to react with 4 molecules H_2; balloon (b) has enough O_2 to react with 8 molecules H_2; balloon (c) has enough O_2 to react with 10 molecules H_2; and balloon (d) has enough O_2 for 3 molecules of H_2 to react. Therefore, balloon (b) will have the loudest explosion because it has the most H_2 that will react.
Check: Answer seems correct since it has the most H_2 with enough O_2 in the balloon to completely react.

4.113   (a)   Skeletal reaction: $HCl(aq) + Hg_2(NO_3)_2(aq) \rightarrow Hg_2Cl_2(s) + HNO_3(aq)$
           Balance Cl: $2HCl(aq) + Hg_2(NO_3)_2(aq) \rightarrow Hg_2Cl_2(s) + 2HNO_3(aq)$
     (b)   Skeletal reaction: $KHSO_3(aq) + HNO_3(aq) \rightarrow H_2O(l) + SO_2(g) + KNO_3(aq)$
           Balanced reaction: $KHSO_3(aq) + HNO_3(aq) \rightarrow H_2O(l) + SO_2(g) + KNO_3(aq)$

(c) Skeletal reaction: $\qquad$ $NH_4Cl(aq) + Pb(NO_3)_2(aq) \rightarrow PbCl_2(s) + NH_4NO_3(aq)$

$\qquad$ Balance Cl: $\qquad$ $2NH_4Cl(aq) + Pb(NO_3)_2(aq) \rightarrow PbCl_2(s) + NH_4NO_3(aq)$

$\qquad$ Balance N: $\qquad$ $2NH_4Cl(aq) + Pb(NO_3)_2(aq) \rightarrow PbCl_2(s) + 2NH_4NO_3(aq)$

(d) Skeletal reaction: $\qquad$ $NH_4Cl(aq) + Ca(OH)_2(aq) \rightarrow NH_3(g) + H_2O(l) + CaCl_2(aq)$

$\qquad$ Balance Cl: $\qquad$ $2NH_4Cl(aq) + Ca(OH)_2(aq) \rightarrow NH_3(g) + H_2O(l) + CaCl_2(aq)$

$\qquad$ Balance N: $\qquad$ $2NH_4Cl(aq) + Ca(OH)_2(aq) \rightarrow 2NH_3(g) + H_2O(l) + CaCl_2(aq)$

$\qquad$ Balance H: $\qquad$ $2NH_4Cl(aq) + Ca(OH)_2(aq) \rightarrow 2NH_3(g) + 2H_2O(l) + CaCl_2(aq)$

4.115 **Given:** 1.5 L solution, 0.050 mol L^{-1} $CaCl_2$, 0.085 mol L^{-1} $Mg(NO_3)_2$ **Find:** g Na_3PO_4

Conceptual Plan: V,M $CaCl_2$ $\rightarrow$ mol $CaCl_2$ and V,M $Mg(NO_3)_2$ $\rightarrow$ mol $Mg(NO_3)_2$

$\qquad\qquad\qquad$ V x M = mol $\qquad\qquad\qquad\qquad\qquad$ V x M = mol

then (mol $CaCl_2$ + mol $Mg(NO_3)_2$) $\rightarrow$ Na_3PO_4 $\rightarrow$ g Na_3PO_4

$\qquad\qquad\qquad\qquad \dfrac{2 \text{ mol } Na_3PO_4}{3 \text{ mol } (CaCl_2 + Mg(NO_3)_2)} \quad \dfrac{163.97 \text{ g } Na_3PO_4}{1 \text{ mol } Na_3PO_4}$

Solution: $\qquad$ $3CaCl_2(aq) + 2Na_3PO_4(aq) \rightarrow Ca_3(PO_4)_2(s) + 6 NaCl(aq)$

$\qquad\qquad\qquad$ $3 Mg(NO_3)_2(aq) + 2Na_3PO_4(aq) \rightarrow Mg_3(PO_4)_2(s) + 6 NaCl(aq)$

$\qquad\qquad\qquad$ $1.5 \text{ L} \times 0.050 \text{ mol L}^{-1} CaCl_2 = 0.07\underline{5} \text{ mol } CaCl_2$

$\qquad\qquad\qquad$ $1.5 \text{ L} \times 0.085 \text{ mol L}^{-1} Mg(NO_3)_2 = 0.1\underline{2}75 \text{ mol } Mg(NO_3)_2$

$0.20\underline{2}5 \; \overline{\text{mol } CaCl_2 \text{ and } Mg(NO_3)_2} \times \dfrac{2 \; \overline{\text{mol } Na_3PO_4}}{3 \; \overline{\text{mol } CaCl_2 \text{ and } Mg(NO_3)_2}} \times \dfrac{163.97 \text{ g mol } Na_3PO_4}{\overline{\text{mol } Na_3PO_4}} = 22 \text{ g mol } Na_3PO_4$

Check: The units of the answer (g Na_3PO_4) are correct. The magnitude of the answer is reasonable since it is needed to remove both the Ca and Mg ions.

4.117 **Given:** 1.0 L, 0.10 mol L^{-1} OH^- **Find:** g Ba

Conceptual Plan: VM $\rightarrow$ mol OH^- $\rightarrow$ mol $Ba(OH)_2$ $\rightarrow$ mol BaO $\rightarrow$ mol Ba $\rightarrow$ g Ba

$\qquad\qquad$ V x M = mol $\quad \dfrac{1 \text{ mol } Ba(OH)_2}{2 \text{ mol } OH} \quad \dfrac{1 \text{ mol } BaO}{1 \text{ mol } Ba(OH)_2} \quad \dfrac{1 \text{ mol } Ba}{1 \text{ mol } BaO} \quad \dfrac{137.3 \text{ g } Ba}{1 \text{ mol } Ba}$

Solution: $BaO(s) + H_2O(l) \rightarrow Ba(OH)_2(aq)$

$1.0 \; \overline{\text{L}} \times \dfrac{0.10 \; \overline{\text{mol } OH^-}}{\overline{\text{L}}} \times \dfrac{1 \; \overline{\text{mol } Ba(OH)_2}}{2 \; \overline{\text{mol } OH^-}} \times \dfrac{1 \; \overline{\text{mol } BaO}}{1 \; \overline{\text{mol } Ba(OH)_2}} \times \dfrac{1 \; \overline{\text{mol } Ba}}{1 \; \overline{\text{mol } BaO}} \times \dfrac{137.3 \text{ g } Ba}{1 \text{ mol } Ba} = 6.9 \text{ g } Ba$

Check: The unit of the answer (g Ba) is correct. The magnitude is reasonable since the molar mass of Ba is large and there are 2 moles hydroxide per mole Ba.

4.119 **Given:** 30.0% $NaNO_3$, \$18.00/100 kg; 20.0% $(NH_4)_2SO_4$, \$16.20/100 kg **Find:** cost per kg of N for the two compounds

Conceptual Plan: mass fertilizer $\rightarrow$ mass $NaNO_3$ $\rightarrow$ mass N $\rightarrow$ cost N per kg, and mass fertilizer $\rightarrow$ mass $(NH_4)_2SO_4$ $\rightarrow$ mass N $\rightarrow$ cost N per kg

Other: % N in $NaNO_3$ = 14.01 g N/84.995 g $NaNO_3$ = 16.48 g N/100 g $NaNO_3$

$\qquad\qquad$ % N in $(NH_4)_2SO_4$ = 42.03 g N/132.14 g $(NH_4)_2SO_4$ = 21.2 g N/100 g $(NH_4)_2SO_4$

Solution:

$\qquad$ $100 \; \overline{\text{kg fertilizer}} \times \dfrac{30.0 \; \overline{\text{kg } NaNO_3}}{100 \; \overline{\text{kg fertilizer}}} \times \dfrac{16.48 \text{ kg N}}{100 \; \overline{\text{kg } NaNO_3}} = 4.944 \text{ kg N}$

$\qquad$ $\dfrac{\$18.00}{100 \; \overline{\text{kg fertilizer}}} \times \dfrac{100 \; \overline{\text{kg fertilizer}}}{4.944 \text{ kg N}} = \dfrac{\$3.64}{\text{kg N}}$

$\qquad$ $100 \; \overline{\text{kg fertilizer}} \times \dfrac{20.0 \; \overline{\text{kg } (NH_4)_2SO_4}}{100 \; \overline{\text{kg fertilizer}}} \times \dfrac{21.2 \text{ kg N}}{100 \; \overline{\text{kg } (NH_4)_2SO_4}} = 4.240 \text{ kg N}$

$\qquad$ $\dfrac{\$16.20}{100 \; \overline{\text{kg fertilizer}}} \times \dfrac{100 \; \overline{\text{kg fertilizer}}}{4.240 \text{ kg N}} = \dfrac{\$3.82}{\text{kg N}}$

$\qquad$ The most economical fertilizer is $NaNO_3$ because of the lower cost per kg of nitrogen.

Check: The units of the cost (\$/kg N) are correct. The answer is reasonable because you compare the cost/kg N directly.

4.121   **Given:** 24.5 g Au, 24.5 g BrF_3, 24.5 g KF **Find:** g $KAuF_4$
Conceptual Plan: g Au → mol Au → mol $KAuF_4$

$$\frac{1 \text{ mol Au}}{196.97 \text{ g Au}} \qquad \frac{2 \text{ mol } KAuF_4}{2 \text{ mol Au}}$$

g BrF_3 → mol BrF_3 → mol $KAuF_4$ → **smallest mol amount determines limiting reactant**

$$\frac{1 \text{ mol } BrF_3}{136.9 \text{ g } BrF_3} \qquad \frac{2 \text{ mol } KAuF_4}{2 \text{ mol } BrF_3}$$

g KF → mol KF → mol $KAuF_4$

$$\frac{1 \text{ mol KF}}{58.10 \text{ g KF}} \qquad \frac{2 \text{ mol } KAuF_4}{2 \text{ mol KF}}$$

then: mol $KAuF_4$ → g $KAuF_4$

$$\frac{312.07 \text{ g } KAuF_4}{\text{mol } KAuF_4}$$

$$2 \text{ Au}(s) + 2BrF_3(l) + 2KF(s) \rightarrow Br_2(l) + 2KAuF_4(s)$$
Oxidation states: 0   + 3– 1   +1 –1   0   +1 +3 – 1

This is a redox reaction since Au increases in oxidation number (oxidation) and Br decreases in number (reduction). BrF_3 is the oxidizing agent, and Au is the reducing agent.
Solution:

$$24.5 \text{ g Au} \times \frac{1 \text{ mol Au}}{196.97 \text{ g Au}} \times \frac{2 \text{ mol } KAuF_4}{2 \text{ mol Au}} = 0.1244 \text{ mol } KAuF_4$$

$$24.5 \text{ g } BrF_3 \times \frac{1 \text{ mol } BrF_3}{136.90 \text{ g } BrF_3} \times \frac{2 \text{ mol } KAuF_4}{2 \text{ mol } BrF_3} = 0.1790 \text{ mol } KAuF$$

$$24.5 \text{ g KF} \times \frac{1 \text{ mol KF}}{58.10 \text{ g KF}} \times \frac{2 \text{ mol } KAuF_4}{2 \text{ mol KF}} = 0.4217 \text{ mol } KAuF_4$$

$$0.1244 \text{ mol } KAuF_4 \times \frac{312.07 \text{ g } KAuF_4}{1 \text{ mol } KAuF_4} = 38.8 \text{ g } KAuF_4$$

Check: Units of the answer (g $KAuF_4$) are correct. The magnitude of the answer is reasonable compared to the mass of the limiting reactant Au.

4.123   **Given:** solution may contain Ag^+, Ca^{2+}, and Cu^{2+} **Find:** determine which ions are present
Conceptual Plan: test the solution sequentially with NaCl, Na_2SO_4, and Na_2CO_3 and see if precipitates form
Solution: Original solution + NaCl yields no reaction: Ag^+ is not present since chlorides are normally soluble, but Ag^+ is an exception.
Original solution with Na_2SO_4 yields a precipitate and solution 2. The precipitate is $CaSO_4$, so Ca^{2+} is present. Sulfates are normally soluble but Ca^{2+} is an exception.
Solution 2 with Na_2CO_3 yields a precipitate. The precipitate is $CuCO_3$, so Cu^{2+} is present. All carbonates, with the exceptions of Group I carbonates and ammonium carbonate, are insoluble.
NET IONIC EQUATIONS:
$$Ca^{2+}(aq) + SO_4{}^{2-}(aq) \rightarrow CaSO_4(s)$$
$$Cu^{2+}(aq) + CO_3{}^{2-}(aq) \rightarrow CuCO_3(s)$$
Check: The answer is reasonable since two different precipitates formed and all the Ca^{2+} was removed before the carbonate was added.

4.125   **Given:** 1.00 g NH_3 **Find:** g PH_3
Conceptual Plan: determine reaction sequence, then g NH_3 → mol NH_3 → mol PH_3 → g PH_3

$$\frac{1 \text{ mol } NH_3}{17.04 \text{ g } NH_3} \qquad \frac{34.00 \text{ g } PH_3}{1 \text{ mol } PH_3}$$

Solution: Balance the reaction sequence:
$$6NH_3 + 71/2 \, O_2 \rightarrow 6NO + 9H_2O$$
$$6NO + P_4 \rightarrow P_4O_6 + 3 N_2$$
$$P_4O_6 + 6H_2O \rightarrow 4H_3PO_3$$
$$4H_3PO_3 \rightarrow PH_3 + 3H_3PO_4$$
Therefore, 6 mol NH_3 produces 1 mol PH_3

$$1.00 \text{ g } NH_3 \times \frac{1 \text{ mol } NH_3}{17.04 \text{ g } NH_3} \times \frac{1 \text{ mol } PH_3}{6 \text{ mol } NH_3} \times \frac{34.00 \text{ g } PH_3}{1 \text{ mol } PH_3} = 0.333 \text{ g } PH_3$$

Check: The unit of the answer is g PH_3, which is correct. The magnitude is reasonable. Even though the molar mass of PH_3 is greater than NH_3, 6 mol of NH_3 are required to produce 1 mol PH_3.

4.127   **Given:** 10.0 kg mixture, 30.35% hexane, 15.85% heptane, 53.80% octane **Find:** total mass CO_2
Conceptual Plan: kg hexane → kmol hexane → kmol CO_2 → kg CO_2

$$\frac{1\text{ kmol }C_6H_{14}}{86.20\text{ kg }C_6H_{14}} \qquad \frac{12\text{ kmol }CO_2}{2\text{ kmol }C_6H_{14}} \qquad \frac{44.01\text{ kg }CO_2}{1\text{ kmol }CO_2}$$

kg heptane → **kmol heptane** → **kmol CO_2** → **kg CO_2**

$$\frac{1\text{ kmol }C_7H_{16}}{100.23\text{ kg }C_7H_{16}} \qquad \frac{7\text{ kmol }CO_2}{1\text{ kmol }C_7H_{16}} \qquad \frac{44.01\text{ kg }CO_2}{1\text{ kmol }CO_2}$$

kg octane → **kmol octane** → **kmol CO_2** → **kg CO_2**

$$\frac{1\text{ kmol }C_8H_{18}}{114.26\text{ kg }C_8H_{18}} \qquad \frac{16\text{ kmol }CO_2}{2\text{ kmol }C_8H_{18}} \qquad \frac{44.01\text{ kg }CO_2}{1\text{ kmol }CO_2}$$

Solution: Balanced Reactions:

$$2C_6H_{14}(l) + 19O_2(g) \rightarrow 12CO_2(g) + 14H_2O(l)$$
$$C_7H_{16}(l) + 11O_2(g) \rightarrow 7CO_2(g) + 8H_2O(l)$$
$$2C_8H_{18}(l) + 25O_2(g) \rightarrow 16CO_2(g) + 18H_2O(l)$$

$$10.0\text{ kg mix} \times \frac{30.35\text{ kg }C_6H_{14}}{100.0\text{ kg mix}} \times \frac{1\text{ kmol }C_6H_{14}}{86.20\text{ kg }C_6H_{14}} \times \frac{12\text{ kmol }CO_2}{2\text{ kmol }C_6H_{14}} \times \frac{44.01\text{kg }CO_2}{1\text{kmol }CO_2} = 9.297\text{ kg }CO_2$$

$$10.0\text{ kg mix} \times \frac{15.85\text{ kg }C_7H_{16}}{100.0\text{ kg mix}} \times \frac{1\text{ kmol }C_7H_{16}}{100.23\text{ kg }C_7H_{16}} \times \frac{7\text{ kmol }CO_2}{1\text{ kmol }C_7H_{16}} \times \frac{44.01\text{kg }CO_2}{1\text{kmol }CO_2} = 4.871\text{ kg }CO_2$$

$$10.0\text{ kg mix} \times \frac{53.80\text{ kg }C_8H_{18}}{100.0\text{ kg mix}} \times \frac{1\text{ kmol }C_8H_{18}}{114.26\text{ kg }C_8H_{18}} \times \frac{16\text{ kmol }CO_2}{2\text{ kmol }C_8H_{18}} \times \frac{44.01\text{kg }CO_2}{1\text{kmol }CO_2} = 16.578\text{ kg }CO_2$$

Total CO_2 = 9.30 kg + 4.87 kg + 16.6 kg = 30.8 kg CO_2
Check: The units of the answer (kg CO_2) are correct. The magnitude of the answer is reasonable since a large amount of CO_2 is produced per mole of hydrocarbon.

Challenge Problems

4.129   **Given:** g C_3H_8 + C_2H_2 = 2.0 g; mol CO_2 = 1.5 mol H_2O **Find:** original g C_2H_2
Conceptual Plan: mol C_3H_8 → **mol CO_2 and mol H_2O and mol C_2H_2** → **mol CO_2 and mol H_2O**
Solution: Let a = mol C_3H_8 and b = mol C_2H_2

$$\begin{array}{ll}
C_3H_8 + 5O_2 \rightarrow 3CO_2 + 4H_2O & \qquad C_2H_2 + 3/2O_2 \rightarrow 2CO_2 + H_2O \\
\quad\text{a} \qquad\qquad 3\text{a} \quad 4\text{a} & \qquad \text{b} \qquad\qquad 2\text{b} \quad\ \text{b}
\end{array}$$

Total mol CO_2 = 3a + 2b   and total mol H_2O = 4a + b
mol CO_2 = 1.5(mol H_2O)
So: 3a + 2b = 1.5(4a + b)

And $\left(a\ \overline{\text{mol }C_3H_8} \times \dfrac{44.11\ C_3H_8}{1\ \overline{\text{mol }C_3H_8}} \right) + \left(b\ \overline{\text{mol }C_2H_2} \times \dfrac{26.01\ C_2H_2}{\overline{\text{mol }C_2H_2}} \right) = 2.0\text{ g}$

Solve simultaneous equations: a = 9.98×10^{-3} mol C_3H_8 and b = 0.0599 mol C_2H_2
Substitute for b and solve for grams C_2H_2.

$$0.060\ \overline{\text{mol }C_2H_2} \times \frac{26.01\ C_2H_2}{\overline{\text{mol }C_2H_2}} = 1.56\text{ g }C_2H_2 = 1.6\text{ g }C_2H_2$$

Check: The units of the answer (g C_2H_2) are correct. The magnitude is reasonable since it is less than the total mass.

4.131   **Given:** 0.100L, 1.22 mol L^{-1} NaI; total mass = 28.1 g **Find:** g AgI
Conceptual Plan: vol, mol L^{-1} → **mol NaI** → **mol I^- ; total mol I^-** → **mol AgI and HgI_2**

Solution: $0.100\ \text{L soln} \times \dfrac{1.22\ \overline{\text{mol NaI}}}{\text{L soln}} \times \dfrac{1\text{ mol }I^-}{\overline{\text{mol NaI}}} = 0.122\text{ mol }I^-$

Let x = mol AgI and y = mol HgI_2

$$x + 2y = 0.122\text{ mol }I^- \text{ so } y = 0.061 - 0.5x$$

$$\left(x \; \overline{\text{mol AgI}} \times \frac{234.77 \text{ g AgI}}{1 \; \overline{\text{mol AgI}}}\right) + \left(y \text{ mol HgI}_2 \times \frac{454.39 \text{ g HgI}_2}{\overline{\text{mol HgI}_2}}\right) = 28.1 \text{ g}$$

Solve the simultaneous equations and $x = 0.0504$ mol AgI

$$0.0504 \; \overline{\text{mol AgI}} \times \frac{234.77 \text{ g AgI}}{1 \; \overline{\text{mol AgI}}} = 11.8 \text{ g AgI}$$

Check: The units of the answer (g AgI) are correct. The magnitude is reasonable since it is less than the total mass.

4.133   **Given:** 3.5×10^{-3} mol L^{-1} Ca $^{2+}$, 1.1×10^{-3} mol L^{-1} Mg^{2+}, 75 L H$_2$O; 0.65 kg detergent/load   **Find:** % by mass
Na$_2$CO$_3$
Conceptual Plan: L H$_2$O $\rightarrow$ mol Ca^{2+} $\rightarrow$ mol Mg^{2+}
Then total moles ions $\rightarrow$ mol CO$_3^{2-}$ $\rightarrow$ mol Na$_2$CO$_3$ $\rightarrow$ g Na$_2$CO$_3$ $\rightarrow$ kg Na$_2$CO$_3$ $\rightarrow$ % Na$_2$CO$_3$

$$\frac{1 \text{ mol CO}_3^{2-}}{1 \text{ mol ion}} \qquad \frac{1 \text{ mol Na}_2\text{CO}_3}{1 \text{ mol CO}_3^{2-}} \qquad \frac{106.01 \text{ g Na}_2\text{CO}_3}{1 \text{ mol Na}_2\text{CO}_3} \qquad \frac{\text{kg}}{1000 \text{ g}} \qquad \frac{\text{kg Na}_2\text{CO}_3}{\text{kg detergent} \times 100}$$

Solution: $75 \text{ L} \times \dfrac{3.5 \times 10^{-3} \text{ mol Ca}^{2+}}{\text{L}} = 0.2625 \text{ mol Ca}^{2+}$

$$75 \text{ L} \times \frac{1.1 \times 10^{-3} \text{ mol Mg}^{2+}}{\text{L}} = 0.0825 \text{ mol Mg}^{2+}$$

$$0.345 \; \overline{\text{mol ions}} \times \frac{1 \; \overline{\text{mol CO}_3^{2-}}}{\overline{\text{mol ions}}} \times \frac{1 \; \overline{\text{mol Na}_2\text{CO}_3}}{\overline{\text{mol CO}_3^{2-}}} \times \frac{106.01 \; \overline{\text{g Na}_2\text{CO}_3}}{1 \; \overline{\text{mol Na}_2\text{CO}_3}} \times \frac{\text{kg Na}_2\text{CO}_3}{1000 \; \overline{\text{g Na}_2\text{CO}_3}} = 0.03657 \text{ kg Na}_2\text{CO}_3$$

$$\frac{0.03657 \; \overline{\text{kg Na}_2\text{CO}_3}}{0.65 \; \overline{\text{kg detergent}}} \times 100 = 5.6\% \text{ Na}_2\text{CO}_3$$

Check: The units of the answer (% Na$_2$CO$_3$) are correct. The magnitude of the answer is reasonable. The percent is less than 100%.

4.135   In designing the unit you would need to consider the theoretical yield and % yield of the reaction, how changing the limiting reactant would affect the reaction, and the stoichiometry between KO$_2$ and O$_2$ in order to determine the mass of KO$_2$ required to produce enough O$_2$ for 10 minutes. You might also consider the speed of the reaction and whether or not the reaction produced heat. Additionally, because your body does not use 100% of the oxygen taken in with each breath, the apparatus would only need to replenish the oxygen used. The percentage of oxygen in air is about 20% and the percentage in exhaled air is about 16%, so we will assume that 4% of the air would need to be replenished with oxygen. (NOTE: The problem can also be solved by finding the amount of KO$_2$ that would be required to react with all of the exhaled CO$_2$.)
Given: air = 4% O$_2$, volume = 5 – 8 L/min, 1 mol gas = 22.4 L gas **Find:** O$_2$ for 10 min breathing time
Conceptual Plan: 10 min $\rightarrow$ vol air $\rightarrow$ vol O$_2$ $\rightarrow$ mol O$_2$ $\rightarrow$ mol KO$_2$ $\rightarrow$ g KO$_2$

$$\frac{8 \text{ L air}}{1 \text{ min}} \qquad \frac{4 \text{ L O}_2}{100 \text{ L air}} \qquad \frac{1 \text{ mol O}_2}{22.4 \text{ L O}_2} \qquad \frac{4 \text{ mol KO}_2}{3 \text{ mol O}_2} \qquad \frac{71.10 \text{ g KO}_2}{1 \text{ mol KO}_2}$$

Solution: $10 \; \overline{\text{min}} \times \dfrac{8 \; \overline{\text{L air}}}{\overline{\text{min}}} \times \dfrac{4 \; \overline{\text{L O}_2}}{100 \; \overline{\text{L air}}} \times \dfrac{1 \; \overline{\text{mol O}_2}}{22.4 \; \overline{\text{L O}_2}} \times \dfrac{4 \; \overline{\text{mol KO}_2}}{3 \; \overline{\text{mol O}_2}} \times \dfrac{71.10 \text{ g KO}_2}{1 \; \overline{\text{mol KO}_2}} = 14 \text{ g KO}_2$

Check: The units of the answer (g KO$_2$) are correct. The magnitude of the answer is reasonable since it is an amount that could be carried in a portable device.

4.137   **Given:** 151 g Na$_2$B$_4$O$_7$ **Find:** g B$_5$H$_9$
Conceptual Plan: g Na$_2$B$_4$O$_7$ $\rightarrow$ mol Na$_2$B$_4$O$_7$ $\rightarrow$ mol B$_5$H$_9$ $\rightarrow$ g B$_5$H$_9$

$$\frac{\text{mol Na}_2\text{B}_4\text{O}_7}{201.22 \text{ g Na}_2\text{B}_4\text{O}_7} \qquad \frac{4 \text{ mol B}_5\text{H}_9}{5 \text{ mol Na}_2\text{B}_4\text{O}_7} \qquad \frac{63.13 \text{ g B}_5\text{H}_9}{\text{mol B}_5\text{H}_9}$$

Solution: All the B in B$_5$H$_9$ goes to the Na$_2$B$_4$O$_7$, so the mole ratio between the two can be used.

$$151 \; \overline{\text{g Na}_2\text{B}_4\text{O}_7} \times \frac{1 \; \overline{\text{mol Na}_2\text{B}_4\text{O}_7}}{201.22 \; \overline{\text{g Na}_2\text{B}_4\text{O}_7}} \times \frac{4 \; \overline{\text{mol B}_5\text{H}_9}}{5 \; \overline{\text{mol Na}_2\text{B}_4\text{O}_7}} \times \frac{63.13 \text{ g B}_5\text{H}_9}{1 \; \overline{\text{mol B}_5\text{H}_9}} = 37.9 \text{ g B}_5\text{H}_9$$

Check: The units of the answer (g B$_5$H$_9$) are correct. The magnitude of the answer is reasonable since the molar mass of B$_5$H$_9$ is less than the molar mass of Na$_2$B$_4$O$_7$.

Conceptual Problems

4.139   The correct answer is d. The molar mass of K and O_2 are comparable. Since the stoichiometry has a ratio of 4 mol K to 1 mol O_2, K will be the limiting reactant when mass of K is less than four times the mass of O_2.

4.141   **Given:** 1 mol L^{-1} solution contains 8 particles   **Find:** amount of solute or solvent needed to obtain new concentration

Conceptual Plan: determine amount of solute particles in each new solution, then determine if solute (if the number is greater) or solvent (if the number is less) needs to be added to obtain the new concentration

Solution: Solution (a) contains 12 particles solute. Concentration is greater than the original, so solute needs

to be added: $12 \; \overline{\text{particles}} \times \dfrac{1 \text{ mol}}{8 \; \overline{\text{particles}}} = 1.5 \text{ mol}$ (1.5 mol – 1.0 mol) = 0.5 mol solute added.

$0.5 \; \overline{\text{mol solute}} \times \dfrac{8 \text{ particles}}{1 \; \overline{\text{mol solute}}} = 4$ solute particles added

Solution (a) is obtained by adding 4 particles solute to 1 L of original solution.

Solution (b) contains 4 particles. Concentration is less than the original so solvent needs to be added.

$4 \; \overline{\text{particles}} \times \dfrac{1 \text{ mol}}{8 \; \overline{\text{particles}}} = 0.5 \text{ mol solute}$ So, 1 L solution contains 0.5 mol = 0.5 mol L^{-1}

$(1 \text{ mol } L^{-1})(1 \text{ L}) = (0.5 \text{ mol } L^{-1})(x)$ $x = 2 \text{ L}$

Solution (b) is obtained by diluting 1 L of the original solution with an additional 1.0 L of solution.

Solution (c) contains 6 particles. Concentration is less than the original, so solvent needs to be added.

$6 \; \overline{\text{particles}} \times \dfrac{1 \text{ mol}}{8 \; \overline{\text{particles}}} = 0.75 \text{ mol solute}$ So, 1 L solution contains 0.75 mol = 0.75 mol L^{-1}

$(1 \text{ mol } L^{-1})(1 \text{ L}) = (0.75 \text{ mol } L^{-1})(x)$ $x = 1.33 \text{ L}$

Solution (c) is obtained by diluting 1 L of the original solution with an additional 0.33 L of solution.

5 Gases

Review Questions

5.1   Pressure is the force exerted per unit area by gas molecules as they strike the surfaces around them. Pressure is caused by collisions of gas molecules with surfaces or other gas molecules.

5.3   When you exhale, you reverse the process of inhalation. The chest cavity muscles relax, which decreases the lung volume, increasing the pressure within the lungs and forcing the air out of the lungs.

5.5   A manometer is a U-shaped tube containing a dense liquid, usually mercury. In an open-ended manometer, one end of the tube is open to atmospheric pressure and the other is attached to a flask containing the gas sample. If the pressure of the gas sample is exactly equal to atmospheric pressure, then the mercury levels on both sides of the tube are the same. If the pressure of the sample is greater than atmospheric pressure, the mercury level on the sample side of the tube is lower than on the side open to the atmosphere. If the pressure of the sample is less than atmospheric pressure, the mercury level on the sample side is higher than on the side open to the atmosphere. This type of manometer always measures the pressure of the gas sample relative to atmospheric pressure. The difference in height between the two levels is equal to the pressure difference from atmospheric pressure.

5.7   For every 10 m of depth that a diver descends in water, they experience an additional 1 atm of pressure due to the weight of the water above them. The pressure regulator used in scuba diving delivers air at a pressure that matches the external pressure; otherwise the diver could not inhale the air. For example, when a diver is at a depth of 20 m below the surface, the regulator delivers air at a pressure of 3 atm to match the 3 atm of pressure around the diver (1 atm due to normal atmospheric pressure and 2 additional atmospheres due to the weight of the water at 20 m). Suppose that a diver inhaled a lungful of air at a pressure of 3 atm and swam quickly to the surface (where the pressure drops to 1 atm) while holding this breath. What would happen to the volume of air in the diver's lungs? Since the pressure decreases by a factor of 3, the volume of the air in the diver's lungs would increase by a factor of 3, severely damaging the diver's lungs and possibly killing the diver.

5.9   Charles's law explains why a hot-air balloon can take flight. The gas that fills a hot-air balloon is warmed with a burner increasing its volume and lowering its density, and causing it to float in the colder, denser surrounding air. Charles's law also explains why the second floor of a house is usually a bit warmer than the ground floor because when air is heated its volume increases, resulting in a lower density. The warm, less dense air tends to rise in a room filled with colder, denser air.

5.11   We know that $V \propto 1/P$ (Boyle's law) $V \propto T$ (Charles's law) $V \propto n$ (Avogadro's law).

       Combining these three expressions we get $V \propto nT/P$. Replace the proportional sign with an equal sign by incorporating R (the ideal gas constant) $V = RnT/P$. Rearranging, we get $PV = nRT$.

5.13   Since $d = \dfrac{P\mathcal{M}}{RT}$ this means that the density will decrease as temperature increases. It will increase as pressure increases or as the molar mass of the gas increases.

5.15   Too much oxygen can also cause physiological problems. Scuba divers breathe pressurized air. At 30 m, a scuba diver breathes air at a total pressure of 4.0 atm, making P_{O_2} about 0.84 atm. This elevated partial pressure of oxygen raises the density of oxygen molecules in the lungs, resulting in a higher concentration of oxygen in body tissues. When P_{O_2} increases beyond 1.4 atm, the increased oxygen concentration in body tissues causes a condition called oxygen toxicity, which results in muscle twitching, tunnel vision, and convulsions.

5.17   In Chapter 4, we learned how the coefficients in chemical equations can be used as conversion factors between number of moles of reactants and number of moles of products in a chemical reaction, and that the molar mass can be used to convert the number of moles to the mass. At STP, each mole of gas occupies 22.7 L. The mass of the product will be as follows:

$$\text{Volume of limiting reagent (L)} \times \frac{1\,\text{mol limiting reagent}}{22.7\,\text{L}} \times \frac{c\,\text{mol product}}{a\,\text{mol limiting reagent}} \times \frac{g\,\text{product}}{1\,\text{mol product}}$$

for the reaction:

a A + b B → c C + d D, where A is the limiting reagent and C is the product of interest.

5.19   Boyle's law states that, for a constant number of particles at constant temperature, the volume of a gas is inversely proportional to its pressure. If you decrease the volume of a gas, you force the gas particles to occupy a smaller space. It follows from kinetic molecular theory that, as long the temperature remains the same, the result is a greater number of collisions with the surrounding surfaces and therefore a greater pressure.

Charles's law states that, for a constant number of particles at constant pressure, the volume of a gas is proportional to its temperature. According to kinetic molecular theory, when you increase the temperature of a gas, the average speed, and thus the average kinetic energy, of the particles increases. Since this greater kinetic energy results in more frequent collisions and more force per collision, the pressure of the gas would increase if its volume were held constant (Gay-Lussac's law). The only way for the pressure to remain constant is for the volume to increase. The greater volume spreads the collisions out over a greater area so that the pressure (defined as force per unit area) is unchanged.

Avogadro's law states that, at constant temperature and pressure, the volume of a gas is proportional to the number of particles. According to kinetic molecular theory, when you increase the number of particles in a gas sample, the number of collisions with the surrounding surfaces increases. Since the greater number of collisions would result in a greater overall force on surrounding surfaces, the only way for the pressure to remain constant is for the volume to increase so that the number of particles per unit volume (and thus the number of collisions) remains constant.

Dalton's law states that the total pressure of a gas mixture is the sum of the partial pressures of its components. In other words, according to Dalton's law, the components in a gas mixture act identically to, and independently of, one another. According to kinetic molecular theory, the particles have negligible size and they do not interact. Consequently, the only property that would distinguish one type of particle from another is its mass. However, even particles of different masses have the same average kinetic energy at a given temperature, so they exert the same force upon a collision with a surface. Consequently, adding components to a gas mixture—even different *kinds* of gases—has the same effect as simply adding more particles. The partial pressures of all the components sum to the overall pressure.

5.21   Gaseous particles travel at tremendous speeds along very haphazard paths. To a perfume molecule, the path from the perfume bottle in the bathroom to your nose 2 m away is much like the path through a busy shopping mall during a clearance sale. The molecule travels only a short distance before it collides with another molecule, changes direction, only to collide again, and so on. The average distance that a molecule travels between collisions is called its mean free path.

5.23   Gases behave ideally when both of the following are true: (a) The volume of the gas particles is small compared to the space between them, and b) the forces between the gas particles are not significant. At high pressures the number of molecules increases, so the volume of the gas particles becomes larger; and since the spacing between the particles is smaller, the interactions become more significant. At low temperatures, the molecules are not moving as fast as at higher temperatures, so when they collide they have a greater opportunity to interact.

Problems by Topic

Converting Between Pressure Units

5.25   (a)   **Given**: 875 mbar **Find**: atm
        Conceptual Plan: mbar → bar → atm

$$\text{Solution: } 875 \ \cancel{\text{mbar}} \times \frac{1 \ \cancel{\text{bar}}}{1000 \ \cancel{\text{mbar}}} \times \frac{0.98692 \ \text{atm}}{1 \ \cancel{\text{bar}}} = 0.864 \ \text{atm}$$

        Check: The units (atm) are correct. The answer makes sense because 1 atm and 1 bar are very close in magnitude.

        (b)   **Given**: 875 mbar **Find**: psi
        Conceptual Plan: mbar → bar → **psi**

$$\text{Solution: } 875 \ \cancel{\text{mbar}} \times \frac{1 \ \cancel{\text{bar}}}{1000 \ \cancel{\text{mbar}}} \times \frac{14.504 \ \text{psi}}{1 \ \cancel{\text{bar}}} = 12.7 \ \text{psi}$$

        Check: The units (psi) are correct. The answer makes sense because 875 mbar (0.875 bar) is less than STP, and there the answer in psi should be less than 14.5 psi.

        (c)   **Given**: 875 mbar **Find**: Pa
        Conceptual Plan: mbar → bar → **Pa**

$$\text{Solution: } 875 \ \cancel{\text{mbar}} \times \frac{1 \ \cancel{\text{bar}}}{1000 \ \cancel{\text{mbar}}} \times \frac{100000 \ \text{Pa}}{1 \ \cancel{\text{bar}}} = 87500 \ \text{Pa}$$

        Check: The units (Pa) are correct. The answer makes sense because the magnitude of the answer is 100 000 larger than 0.875 bar.

        (d)   **Given**: 875 mbar **Find**: torr
        Conceptual Plan: mbar → bar → **torr**

$$\text{Solution: } 875 \ \cancel{\text{mbar}} \times \frac{1 \ \cancel{\text{bar}}}{1000 \ \cancel{\text{mbar}}} \times \frac{750.01 \ \text{torr}}{1 \ \cancel{\text{bar}}} = 656 \ \text{torr}$$

        Check: The units (torr) are correct. The answer makes sense because it is less than 750 torr.

        (e)   **Given**: 875 mbar **Find**: bar
        Conceptual Plan: mbar → **bar**

$$\text{Solution: } 875 \ \cancel{\text{mbar}} \times \frac{1 \ \text{bar}}{1000 \ \cancel{\text{mbar}}} = 0.875 \ \text{bar}$$

        Check: The units (bar) are correct. The answer makes sense because mbar is 1000 times less than bar.

5.27   (a)   **Given**: 1078 hPa **Find**: atm
        Conceptual Plan: hPa → Pa → bar → atm

$$\text{Solution: } 1078 \ \cancel{\text{hPa}} \times \frac{100 \ \cancel{\text{Pa}}}{1 \ \cancel{\text{hPa}}} \times \frac{1 \ \cancel{\text{bar}}}{100000 \ \cancel{\text{Pa}}} \times \frac{0.98692 \ \text{atm}}{1 \ \cancel{\text{bar}}} = 1.064 \ \text{atm}$$

        Check: The units (atm) are correct. The answer makes sense because 1 atm is a larger measurement unit than hPa.

        (b)   **Given**: 1078 hPa **Find**: torr
        Conceptual Plan: hPa → Pa → bar → torr

$$\text{Solution: } 1078 \ \cancel{\text{hPa}} \times \frac{100 \ \cancel{\text{Pa}}}{1 \ \cancel{\text{hPa}}} \times \frac{1 \ \cancel{\text{bar}}}{100000 \ \cancel{\text{Pa}}} \times \frac{750.01 \ \text{torr}}{1 \ \cancel{\text{bar}}} = 808.5 \ \text{torr}$$

        Check: The units (torr) are correct. The answer makes sense because torr is a larger measurement unit than Pa.

(c)   **Given:** 1078 hPa **Find:** kPa
Conceptual Plan: hPa → Pa → kPa

Solution: $1078 \; \cancel{hPa} \times \dfrac{100 \; \cancel{Pa}}{1 \; \cancel{hPa}} \times \dfrac{1 \; kPa}{1000 \; \cancel{Pa}} = 107.8 \; kPa$

Check: The units (kPa) are correct. The answer makes sense because kPa is 10 times larger than hPa.

(d)   **Given:** 1078 hPa **Find:** mbar
Conceptual Plan: hPa → Pa → bar → mbar

Solution: $1078 \; \cancel{hPa} \times \dfrac{100 \; \cancel{Pa}}{1 \; \cancel{hPa}} \times \dfrac{1 \; \cancel{bar}}{100000 \; \cancel{Pa}} \times \dfrac{1000 \; mbar}{1 \; \cancel{bar}} = 1078 \; mbar$

Check: The units (mbar) are correct. The answer makes sense because mbar and hPa are essentially the same thing.

(e)   **Given:** 1078 hPa **Find:** bar
Conceptual Plan: hPa → Pa → bar

Solution: $1078 \; \cancel{hPa} \times \dfrac{100 \; \cancel{Pa}}{1 \; \cancel{hPa}} \times \dfrac{1 \; bar}{100000 \; \cancel{Pa}} = 1.078 \; bar$

Check: The units (bar) are correct. The answer makes sense because bar is 1000 times larger than hPa.

5.29   (a)   **Given:** $P_{bar} = 762.4$ mm Hg and figure   **Find:** P_{gas}
Conceptual plan: Measure height difference then convert cm Hg → mm Hg → mm Hg
$$\dfrac{10 \, mm \, Hg}{1 \, cm \, Hg} \qquad P_{gas} = h + P_{bar}$$

Solution:
$$h = 7.0 \; \cancel{cm \, Hg} \times \dfrac{10 \, mm \, Hg}{1 \, \cancel{cm \, Hg}} = 70 \; mm \; Hg \quad P_{gas} = 70 \; mm \; Hg + 762.4 \; mm \; Hg = 832 \; mm \; Hg$$
Check: The units (mm Hg) are correct. The magnitude of the answer (832 mm Hg) makes physical sense because the mercury column is higher on the right, indicating that the pressure is above barometric pressure. No significant figures to the right of the decimal point can be reported since the mercury height is known only to the 1's place.

(b)   **Given:** $P_{bar} = 762.4$ mm Hg and figure   **Find:** P_{gas}
Conceptual plan: Measure height difference then convert cm Hg → mm Hg → mm Hg
$$\dfrac{10 \, mm \, Hg}{1 \, cm \, Hg} \qquad P_{gas} = h + P_{bar}$$

Solution:
$$h = -4.4 \; \cancel{cm \, Hg} \times \dfrac{10 \, mm \, Hg}{1 \, \cancel{cm \, Hg}} = -44 \; mm \; Hg \quad P_{gas} = -44 \; mm \; Hg + 762.4 \; mm \; Hg = 718 \; mm \; Hg$$
Check: The units (mm Hg) are correct. The magnitude of the answer (718 mm Hg) makes physical sense because the mercury column is higher on the left, indicating that the pressure is below barometric pressure. No significant figures to the right of the decimal point can be reported since the mercury height is known only to the 1's place.

Simple Gas Laws

5.31   **Given:** $V_1 = 5.6$ L, $P_1 = 735$ Torr, and $V_2 = 9.4$ L   **Find:** P_2
Conceptual Plan: $V_1, P_1, V_2 \rightarrow P_2$
$$P_1 V_1 = P_2 V_2$$
Solution:
$P_1 V_1 = P_2 V_2$ Rearrange to solve for P_2.
$$P_2 = P_1 \dfrac{V_1}{V_2} = 735 \; Torr \times \dfrac{5.6 \; \cancel{L}}{9.4 \; \cancel{L}} = 437.872 \; Torr = 4.4 \times 10^2 \; Torr$$
Check: The units (Torr) are correct. The magnitude of the answer (440 Torr) makes physical sense because Boyle's law indicates that as the volume increases, the pressure decreases.

5.33   **Given:** $V_1 = 48.3$ mL, $T_1 = 22\,°C$, and $T_2 = 87\,°C$ **Find:** V_2
Conceptual Plan: °C → K then $V_1, T_1, T_2 \rightarrow V_2$
$$K = °C + 273.15 \qquad \dfrac{V_1}{T_1} = \dfrac{V_2}{T_2}$$

Solution: $T_1 = 22\ °C + 273.15 = 295\ K$ and $T_2 = 87\ °C + 273.15 = 360\ K$

$\dfrac{V_1}{T_1} = \dfrac{V_2}{T_2}$ Rearrange to solve for V_2. $V_2 = V_1 \dfrac{T_2}{T_1} = 48.3\ mL \times \dfrac{360\ K}{295\ K} = 58.9\ mL$

Check: The units (mL) are correct. The magnitude of the answer (59 mL) makes physical sense because Charles's law indicates that as the volume increases, the temperature increases.

5.35   **Given:** $V_1 = 2.46\ L$, $n_1 = 0.158\ mol$, and $\Delta n = 0.113\ mol$ **Find:** V_2

Conceptual Plan: $n_1 \rightarrow n_2$ then $V_1, n_1, n_2 \rightarrow V_2$

$$n_1 + \Delta n = n_2 \qquad \dfrac{V_1}{n_1} = \dfrac{V_2}{n_2}$$

Solution: $n_2 = 0.158\ mol + 0.113\ mol = 0.271\ mol$

$\dfrac{V_1}{n_1} = \dfrac{V_2}{n_2}$ Rearrange to solve for V_2. $V_2 = V_1 \dfrac{n_2}{n_1} = 2.46\ L \times \dfrac{0.271\ \text{mol}}{0.158\ \text{mol}} = 4.21937\ L = 4.22\ L$

Check: The units (L) are correct. The magnitude of the answer (4 L) makes physical sense because Avogadro's law indicates that as the number of moles increases, the volume increases.

Ideal Gas Law

5.37   **Given:** $n = 0.118\ mol$, $P = 0.97\ bar$, and $T = 305\ K$ **Find:** V

Conceptual Plan: $n, P, T \rightarrow V$

$$P V = nRT$$

Solution: $P V = nRT$ Rearrange to solve for V. $V = \dfrac{nRT}{P} = \dfrac{0.118\ \text{mol} \times 0.08314\ \dfrac{L \cdot \text{bar}}{\text{mol} \cdot K} \times 305\ K}{0.97\ \text{bar}} = 3.1\ L$

The volume would be the same for argon gas because the volume of a gas is proportional to the number of moles of a gas, as shown in the ideal gas law. The law does not have a term for mass.

Check: The units (L) are correct. The magnitude of the answer (3 L) makes sense because, as you will see in the next section, one mole of an ideal gas under standard conditions (273 K and 1 bar) occupies 22.7 L. Although these are not standard conditions, they are close enough for a ballpark check of the answer. Since this gas sample contains 0.118 moles, a volume of 3 L is reasonable.

5.39   **Given:** $V = 10.0\ L$, $n = 0.448\ mol$, and $T = 315\ K$ **Find:** P

Conceptual Plan: $n, V, T \rightarrow P$

$$P V = nRT$$

Solution:

$P V = nRT$ Rearrange to solve for P. $P = \dfrac{nRT}{V} = \dfrac{0.448\ \text{mol} \times 0.08314\ \dfrac{L \cdot \text{bar}}{\text{mol} \cdot K} \times 315\ K}{10.0\ L} = 1.17\ \text{bar}$

Check: The units (bar) are correct. The magnitude of the answer (~1 bar) makes sense because, as you will see in the next section, one mole of an ideal gas under standard conditions (273 K and 1 bar) occupies 22.7 L. Although these are not standard conditions, they are close enough for a ballpark check of the answer. Since this gas sample contains 0.448 moles in a volume of 10 L, a pressure of 1 bar is reasonable.

5.41   **Given:** $V = 28.5\ L$, $P = 1.8\ bar$, and $T = 298\ K$ **Find:** n

Conceptual Plan: $V, P, T \rightarrow n$

$$P V = nRT$$

Solution: $P V = nRT$ Rearrange to solve for n. $n = \dfrac{PV}{RT} = \dfrac{1.8\ \text{bar} \times 28.5\ L}{0.08314\ \dfrac{L \cdot \text{bar}}{\text{mol} \cdot K} \times 298\ K} = 2.1\ mol$

Check: The units (mol) are correct. The magnitude of the answer (2 mol) makes sense because, as you will see in the next section, one mole of an ideal gas under standard conditions (273 K and 1 bar) occupies 22.7 L. Although these are not standard conditions, they are close enough for a ballpark check of the answer. Since this gas sample has a volume of 28.5 L, and a pressure of 1.8 bar, ~ 2 mol is reasonable.

5.43   **Given:** $P_1 = 36.0\ psi\ (gauge\ P)$, $V_1 = 11.8\ L$, $T_1 = 12.0\ °C$, $V_2 = 12.2\ L$, and $T_2 = 65.0\ °C$
Find: P_2 and compare to $P_{max} = 38.0\ psi\ (gauge\ P)$

Conceptual Plan: °C → K and gauge P → psi → atm then $P_1, V_1, T_1, V_2, T_2 → P_2$

$$K = °C + 273.15 \qquad psi = gauge\ P + 14.7 \quad \frac{1\ atm}{14.7\ psi} \qquad\qquad \frac{P_1V_1}{T_1} = \frac{P_2V_2}{T_2}$$

Solution: $T_1 = 12.0\ °C + 273.15 = 285.2\ K$ and $T_2 = 65.0\ °C + 273.15 = 338.2\ K$

$$P_1 = 36.0\ psi\ (gauge\ P)\ +\ 14.7\ =\ 50.7\ \cancel{psi} \times \frac{1\ atm}{14.7\ \cancel{psi}} = 3.4\underline{4}898\ atm$$

$$P_{max} = 38.0\ psi\ (gauge\ P)\ +\ 14.7\ =\ 52.7\ \cancel{psi} \times \frac{1\ atm}{14.7\ \cancel{psi}} = 3.59\ atm$$

$\dfrac{P_1V_1}{T_1} = \dfrac{P_2V_2}{T_2}$ Rearrange to solve for P_2. $P_2 = P_1\ \dfrac{V_1}{V_2}\dfrac{T_2}{T_1} = 3.4\underline{4}898\ atm \times \dfrac{11.8\ \cancel{L}}{12.2\ \cancel{L}} \times \dfrac{338.2\ \cancel{K}}{285.2\ \cancel{K}} = 3.96\ atm = 43.5\ psi$

This exceeds the maximum tire rating of 3.59 atm or 38.0 psi (gauge P).

Check: The units (atm) are correct. The magnitude of the answer (3.95 atm) makes physical sense because the relative increase in T is greater than the relative increase in V, so P should increase.

5.45　　**Given:** m (CO_2) = 28.8 g, P = 989 mbar, and T = 22 °C　**Find:** V

Conceptual Plan: °C → K and mbar → bar and g → mol then $n, P, T → V$

$$K = °C + 273.15 \qquad \frac{1\ bar}{1000\ mbar} \qquad \frac{1\ mol}{44.01\ g} \qquad PV = nRT$$

Solution: $T_1 = 22\ °C + 273.15 = 295\ K$, $P = 989\ \cancel{mbar} \times \dfrac{1\ bar}{1000\ \cancel{mbar}} = 0.989\ bar,$

$n = 28.8\ \cancel{g} \times \dfrac{1\ mol}{44.01\ \cancel{g}} = 0.65\underline{4}397\ mol$　$PV = nRT$ Rearrange to solve for V.

$$V = \frac{nRT}{P} = \frac{0.65\underline{4}397\ \cancel{mol} \times 0.08314\ \dfrac{L \cdot \cancel{bar}}{\cancel{mol} \cdot \cancel{K}} \times 295\ \cancel{K}}{0.989\ \cancel{bar}} = 16.2\ L$$

Check: The units (L) are correct. The magnitude of the answer (16 L) makes sense because one mole of an ideal gas under standard conditions (273 K and 1 bar) occupies 22.7 L. Although these are not standard conditions, they are close enough for a ballpark check of the answer. Since this gas sample contains 0.65 moles, a volume of 16 L is reasonable.

5.47　　**Given:** 26.0 g argon, V = 55.0 mL, and T = 295 K　**Find:** P

Conceptual Plan: g → n and mL → L then $n, V, T → P$

$$\frac{1\ mol}{39.95\ g} \qquad \frac{1\ L}{1000\ mL} \qquad PV = nRT$$

Solution: $26.0\ \cancel{g\ Ar} \times \dfrac{1\ mol\ Ar}{39.95\ \cancel{g\ Ar}} = 0.65\underline{0}8135\ mol\ Ar$　$55.0\ \cancel{mL} \times \dfrac{1\ L}{1000\ \cancel{mL}} = 0.0550\ L$

$PV = nRT$ Rearrange to solve for P.

$$P = \frac{nRT}{V} = \frac{0.65\underline{0}8135\ \cancel{mol} \times 0.08314\ \dfrac{L \cdot bar}{\cancel{mol} \cdot \cancel{K}} \times 295\ \cancel{K}}{0.0550\ \cancel{L}} = 290.2\underline{1}904\ bar = 29\underline{0}\ torr = 2.90 \times 10^2\ torr$$

Check: The units (bar) are correct. The magnitude of the answer (300 bar) makes sense because, as you will see in the next section, one mole of an ideal gas under standard conditions (273 K and 1 bar) occupies 22.7 L. Although these are not standard conditions, they can be used for a ballpark check of the answer. Since the volume is ~ $1/400^{th}$ the molar volume and we have ~2/3 of a mole, the resulting pressure should be $(400)(2/3) = 270$ bar.

Given: V_1 = 55.0 mL, P_1 = 29$\underline{0}$ bar, and P_2 = 1.20 bar　**Find:** V_2 (number of 750 mL bottles)

Conceptual Plan: $V_1, P_1, P_2 → V_2$

$$P_1V_1 = P_2V_2$$

Solution: $P_1V_1 = P_2V_2$ Rearrange to solve for V_2.

$$V_2 = V_1\ \frac{P_1}{P_2} = 55.0\ mL \times \frac{290.2\underline{1}904\ \cancel{bar}}{1.20\ \cancel{bar}} = 1.3302 \times 10^4\ \cancel{mL} \times \frac{1\ bottle}{750.0\ \cancel{mL}} = 17.7\ bottles$$

Check: The units (bottles) are correct. The magnitude of the answer (18 bottles) makes physical sense because Boyle's law indicates that as the volume decreases, the pressure increases. The pressure is decreasing by a factor of ~ 250 and so the volume should increase by this factor.

5.49   **Given:** sample a = 5 gas particles, sample b = 10 gas particles, and sample c = 8 gas particles, with all temperatures and volumes the same   **Find:** sample with largest P
Conceptual Plan: $n, V, T \rightarrow P$

$$PV = nRT$$

Solution: $PV = nRT$ Since V and T are constant, this means that $P \propto n$. The sample with the largest number of gas particles will have the highest P. $P_b > P_c > P_a$.

5.51   **Given:** P_1 = 755 Torr, T_1 = 25 °C, and T_2 = 1155 °C   **Find:** P_2
Conceptual Plan: °C $\rightarrow$ K then $P_1, T_1, T_2 \rightarrow P_2$

$$K = °C + 273.15 \qquad \frac{P_1}{T_1} = \frac{P_2}{T_2}$$

Solution: T_1 = 25 °C + 273.15 = 298 K and T_2 = 1155 °C + 273.15 = 1428 K
$\frac{P_1}{T_1} = \frac{P_2}{T_2}$ Rearrange to solve for P_2.

$$P_2 = P_1 \frac{T_2}{T_1} = 755 \text{ Torr} \times \frac{1428 \text{ K}}{298 \text{ K}} = 3.62 \times 10^3 \text{ Torr}$$

Check: The units (Torr) are correct. The magnitude of the answer makes physical sense because there is a significant increase in T, which will increase P significantly.

Molar Volume, Density, and Molar Mass of a Gas

5.53   **Given:** STP and m (Ne) = 33.6 g   **Find:** V
Conceptual Plan: g $\rightarrow$ mol $\rightarrow$ V

$$\frac{1 \text{ mol}}{20.18 \text{ g}} \qquad \frac{22.7 \text{ L}}{1 \text{ mol}}$$

Solution: $33.6 \text{ g} \times \frac{1 \text{ mol}}{20.18 \text{ g}} \times \frac{22.7 \text{ L}}{1 \text{ mol}} = 37.8 \text{ L}$

Check: The units (L) are correct. The magnitude of the answer (38 L) makes sense because one mole of an ideal gas under standard conditions (273 K and 1 bar) occupies 22.7 L and we have about 1.7 mol.

5.55   **Given:** H_2, P = 1655 psi, and T = 20.0 °C   **Find:** d
Conceptual Plan: °C $\rightarrow$ K and psi $\rightarrow$ bar then $P, T, \mathcal{M} \rightarrow d$

$$K = °C + 273.15 \qquad \frac{1 \text{ bar}}{14.50 \text{ psi}} \qquad d = \frac{P\mathcal{M}}{RT}$$

Solution: T = 20.0 °C + 273.15 = 293.2 K $P = 1655 \text{ psi} \times \frac{1 \text{ bar}}{14.50 \text{ psi}} = 114.\underline{1}38 \text{ bar}$

$$d = \frac{P\mathcal{M}}{RT} = \frac{114.138 \text{ bar} \times 2.016 \dfrac{\text{g}}{\text{mol}}}{0.08314 \dfrac{\text{L bar}}{\text{K mol}} \times 293.2 \text{ K}} = 9.44 \text{ g L}^{-1}$$

Check: The units (g L^{-1}) are correct. The magnitude of the answer (9 g L^{-1}) makes physical sense because this is a high pressure, so the gas density will be on the high side.

5.57   **Given:** V = 248 mL, m = 0.433 g, P = 745 mmHg, and T = 28 °C   **Find:** $\mathcal{M}$
Conceptual Plan: °C $\rightarrow$ K mmHg $\rightarrow$ bar mL $\rightarrow$ L then $V, m \rightarrow d$ then $d, P, T \rightarrow \mathcal{M}$

$$K = °C + 273.15 \quad \frac{1 \text{ bar}}{750.01 \text{ mmHg}} \quad \frac{1 \text{ L}}{1000 \text{ mL}} \quad d = \frac{m}{V} \quad d = \frac{P\mathcal{M}}{RT}$$

Solution: T = 28 °C + 273.15 = 301 K $P = 745 \text{ mmHg} \times \frac{1 \text{ bar}}{750.01 \text{ mmHg}} = 0.993\underline{3}2 \text{ bar}$

$$V = 248 \text{ mL} \times \frac{1 \text{ L}}{1000 \text{ mL}} = 0.248 \text{ L} \quad d = \frac{m}{V} = \frac{0.433 \text{ g}}{0.248 \text{ L}} = 1.74\underline{5}97 \text{ g L}^{-1} \quad d = \frac{P\mathcal{M}}{RT} \text{ Rearrange to solve for } \mathcal{M}.$$

$$\mathcal{M} = \frac{dRT}{P} = \frac{1.74\underline{5}97 \dfrac{\text{g}}{\text{L}} \times 0.08314 \dfrac{\text{L} \cdot \text{bar}}{\text{K} \cdot \text{mol}} \times 301 \text{ K}}{0.993\underline{3}2 \text{ bar}} = 44.0 \text{ g mol}^{-1}$$

Check: The units (g mol^{-1}) are correct. The magnitude of the answer (44 g mol^{-1}) makes physical sense because this is a reasonable number for a molecular weight of a gas. The gas is likely CO_2.

5.59   Given: $m = 38.8$ mg, $V = 224$ mL, $T = 55$ °C, and $P = 886$ mbar   Find: $\mathcal{M}$

Conceptual Plan: **mg → g mL → L °C → K mbar → bar then $V, m → d$ then $d, P, T → \mathcal{M}$**

$$\frac{1\,g}{1000\,mg} \quad \frac{1\,L}{1000\,mL} \quad K = °C + 273.15 \quad \frac{1\,bar}{1000\,mbar} \qquad d = \frac{m}{V} \qquad d = \frac{P\mathcal{M}}{RT}$$

Solution: $m = 38.8 \text{ mg} \times \dfrac{1\,g}{1000\,mg} = 0.0388$ g $V = 224 \text{ mL} \times \dfrac{1\,L}{1000\,mL} = 0.224$ L $T = 55$ °C $+ 273.15 = 328$ K

$P = 886 \text{ mbar} \times \dfrac{1\,bar}{1000\,mbar} = 0.886$ bar $d = \dfrac{m}{V} = \dfrac{0.0388\,g}{0.224\,L} = 0.173214$ g L^{-1} $d = \dfrac{P\mathcal{M}}{RT}$

Rearrange to solve for $\mathcal{M}$. $\mathcal{M} = \dfrac{dRT}{P} = \dfrac{0.173214 \dfrac{g}{L} \times 0.08314 \dfrac{L \cdot bar}{K\,mol} \times 328\,K}{0.886\,bar} = 5.33$ g mol^{-1}

Check: The units (g mol^{-1}) are correct. The magnitude of the answer (5.33 g mol^{-1}) makes physical sense because this is a reasonable number for a molecular weight of a gas, especially since the density is on the low side.

Partial Pressure

5.61   Given: $P_{N_2} = 215$ torr, $P_{O_2} = 102$ torr, $P_{He} = 117$ torr, $V = 1.35$ L, and $T = 25.0$ °C

Find: $P_{Total}, m_{N_2}, m_{O_2}, m_{He}$

Conceptual Plan: **°C → K and torr → bar and $P, V, T → n$ then mol → g**

$$K = °C + 273.15 \qquad \frac{1\,bar}{750.01\,torr} \qquad PV = nRT \qquad \mathcal{M}$$

and **$P_{N_2}, P_{O_2}, P_{He} → P_{Total}$**

$$P_{Total} = P_{N_2} + P_{O_2} + P_{He}$$

Solution: $T_1 = 25.0$ °C $+ 273.15 = 298.2$ K, $PV = nRT$ Rearrange to solve for n.

$n = \dfrac{PV}{RT}$ $P_{N_2} = 215 \text{ torr} \times \dfrac{1\,bar}{750.01\,torr} = 0.286667$ bar $n_{N_2} = \dfrac{0.286667\,bar \times 1.35\,L}{0.08314 \dfrac{L \cdot bar}{mol \cdot K} \times 298.2\,K} = 0.01560700$ mol

$0.01560700 \text{ mol} \times \dfrac{28.02\,g}{1\,mol} = 0.437$ g N_2

$P_{O_2} = 102 \text{ torr} \times \dfrac{1\,bar}{750.01\,torr} = 0.135998$ bar $n_{O_2} = \dfrac{0.135998\,bar \times 1.35\,L}{0.08314 \dfrac{L \cdot bar}{mol \cdot K} \times 298.2\,K} = 0.007404252$ mol

$0.007404252 \text{ mol} \times \dfrac{32.00\,g}{1\,mol} = 0.237$ g O_2

$P_{He} = 117 \text{ torr} \times \dfrac{1\,bar}{750.01\,torr} = 0.155998$ bar $n_{He} = \dfrac{0.155998\,bar \times 1.35\,L}{0.08314 \dfrac{L \cdot bar}{mol \cdot K} \times 298.2\,K} = 0.008493113$ mol

$0.008493113 \text{ mol} \times \dfrac{4.003\,g}{1\,mol} = 0.0340$ g He and

$P_{Total} = P_{N_2} + P_{O_2} + P_{He} = 215$ torr $+ 102$ torr $+ 117$ torr $= 434$ torr

Check: The units (g and torr) are correct. The magnitude of the answer (1 g) makes sense because gases are not very dense and these pressures are < 1 bar. Since all of the pressures are small, the total is < 1 bar.

5.63   Given: m (CO_2) $= 1.20$ g, $V = 755$ mL, $P_{N_2} = 725$ mmHg, and $T = 25.0$ °C   Find: P_{Total}

Conceptual Plan: **mL → L and °C → K and g → mol and $n, P, T → V$ then → mmHg**

$$\frac{1\,L}{1000\,mL} \qquad K = °C + 273.15 \qquad \frac{1\,mol}{44.01\,g} \qquad PV = nRT \qquad \frac{750.01\,mmHg}{1\,bar}$$

finally **$P_{CO_2}, P_{N_2} → P_{Total}$**

$$P_{Total} = P_{CO_2} + P_{N_2}$$

Solution: $V = 755 \text{ mL} \times \dfrac{1\,L}{1000\,mL} = 0.755$ L $T = 25.0$ °C $+ 273.15 = 298.2$ K,

$n = 1.20 \text{ g} \times \dfrac{1\,mol}{44.01\,g} = 0.0272665$ mol, $PV = nRT$ Rearrange to solve for P.

$P = \dfrac{nRT}{V} = \dfrac{0.0272665 \text{ mol} \times 0.08314 \dfrac{L \cdot bar}{mol \cdot K} \times 298.2\,K}{0.755\,L} = 0.895365$ bar

$$P_{CO_2} = 0.895365 \ \cancel{bar} \times \frac{750.01 \text{ mmHg}}{1 \ \cancel{bar}} = 672 \text{ mmHg}$$

$$P_{Total} = P_{CO_2} + P_{N_2} = 672 \text{ mmHg} + 725 \text{ mmHg} = 1397 \text{ mmHg or } 1397 \ \cancel{torr} \times \frac{1 \text{ bar}}{750.01 \ \cancel{torr}} = 1.86 \text{ bar}$$

Check: The units (mmHg) are correct. The magnitude of the answer (1400 mmHg) makes sense because it must be greater than 725 mmHg.

5.65 **Given:** $m\,(N_2) = 1.25$ g, $m\,(O_2) = 0.85$ g, $V = 1.55$ L, and $T = 18\ ^\circ C$ **Find:** $\chi_{N_2}, \chi_{O_2}, P_{N_2}, P_{O_2}$
Conceptual Plan: $g \rightarrow$ mol then $n_{N_2}, n_{O_2} \rightarrow \chi_{N_2}$ and $n_{N_2}, n_{O_2} \rightarrow \chi_{O_2}\ ^\circ C \rightarrow K$

$$\mathcal{M} \qquad\qquad \chi_{N_2} = \frac{n_{N_2}}{n_{N_2} + n_{O_2}} \qquad \chi_{O_2} = \frac{n_{O_2}}{n_{N_2} + n_{O_2}} \qquad K = {}^\circ C + 273.15$$

then $n, V, T \rightarrow P$

$$PV = nRT$$

Solution: $n_{N_2} = 1.25 \ \cancel{g} \times \dfrac{1 \text{ mol}}{28.02 \ \cancel{g}} = 0.0446110 \text{ mol}, \quad n_{O_2} = 0.85 \ \cancel{g} \times \dfrac{1 \text{ mol}}{32.00 \ \cancel{g}} = 0.026563 \text{ mol},$

$$T = 18\ ^\circ C + 273.15 = 291 \text{ K}, \quad \chi_{N_2} = \frac{n_{N_2}}{n_{N_2} + n_{O_2}} = \frac{0.0446110 \text{ mol}}{0.0446110 \text{ mol} + 0.026563 \text{ mol}} = 0.626792 = 0.627,$$

$$\chi_{O_2} = \frac{n_{O_2}}{n_{N_2} + n_{O_2}} = \frac{0.026563 \text{ mol}}{0.0446110 \text{ mol} + 0.026563 \text{ mol}} = 0.373212 \text{ We can also calculate this as}$$

$\chi_{O_2} = 1 - \chi_{N_2} = 1 - 0.626792 = 0.373208 = 0.373$ $P\,V = nRT$ Rearrange to solve for P. $P = \dfrac{nRT}{V}$

$$P_{N_2} = \frac{0.044611 \ \cancel{mol} \times 0.08314 \dfrac{\cancel{L} \cdot \text{bar}}{\cancel{mol} \cdot \cancel{K}} \times 291 \ \cancel{K}}{1.55 \ \cancel{L}} = 0.696 \text{ bar}$$

$$P_{O_2} = \frac{0.026563 \ \cancel{mol} \times 0.08314 \dfrac{\cancel{L} \cdot \text{bar}}{\cancel{mol} \cdot \cancel{K}} \times 291 \ \cancel{K}}{1.55 \ \cancel{L}} = 0.415 \text{ bar}$$

Check: The units (none and bar) are correct. The magnitude of the answers makes sense because the mole fractions should total one and since the weight of N_2 is greater than O_2, its mole fraction is larger. The number of moles is <<1, so we expect the pressures to be <1 bar, given the V (1.55 L).

5.67 **Given:** $T = 30.0\ ^\circ C$, $P_{Total} = 732$ mmHg, and $V = 722$ mL **Find:** P_{H_2} and m_{H_2}
Conceptual Plan: $T \rightarrow P_{H_2O}$ then $P_{Total}, P_{H_2O} \rightarrow P_{H_2}$ then mmHg $\rightarrow$ bar and mL $\rightarrow$ L

$$\text{Table 5.4} \qquad\qquad P_{Total} = P_{H_2O} + P_{H_2} \qquad \frac{1 \text{ bar}}{75.01 \text{ mmHg}} \qquad \frac{1 \text{ L}}{1000 \text{ mL}}$$

and $^\circ C \rightarrow K$ $P, V, T \rightarrow n$ then mol $\rightarrow$ g

$$K = {}^\circ C + 273.15 \qquad PV = nRT \qquad \frac{2.016 \text{ g}}{1 \text{ mol}}$$

Solution: Table 5.4 states that at 30° C, $P_{H_2O} = 31.86$ mmHg $\quad P_{Total} = P_{H_2O} + P_{H_2}$
Rearrange to solve for P_{H_2}. $P_{H_2} = P_{Total} - P_{H_2O} = 732$ mmHg $- 31.86$ mmHg $= 700$ mmHg

$$P_{H_2} = 700 \ \cancel{mmHg} \times \frac{1 \text{ bar}}{750.01 \ \cancel{mmHg}} = 0.933321 \text{ bar} \quad V = 722 \ \cancel{mL} \times \frac{1 \text{ L}}{1000 \ \cancel{mL}} = 0.722 \text{ L},$$

$$T = 30.0\ ^\circ C + 273.15 = 303.2 \text{ K}, \quad P\,V = nRT \quad \text{Rearrange to solve for } n. \quad n = \frac{PV}{RT}$$

$$n_{H_2} = \frac{0.933321 \ \cancel{bar} \times 0.722 \ \cancel{L}}{0.08314 \dfrac{\cancel{L} \cdot \cancel{bar}}{\text{mol} \cdot \cancel{K}} \times 303.2 \ \cancel{K}} = 0.0267277 \text{ mol then } 0.0267277 \ \cancel{mol} \times \frac{2.016 \text{ g}}{1 \ \cancel{mol}} = 0.0539 \text{ g } H_2$$

Check: The units (g) are correct. The magnitude of the answer (<< 1 g) makes sense because gases are not very dense, hydrogen is light, the volume is small, and the pressure is ~1 bar.

5.69 **Given:** $T = 25\ ^\circ C$, $P = 0.990$ bar, $V = 0.951$ L. **Find:** P_{H_2} and m_{H_2}
Conceptual Plan: $T \rightarrow P_{H_2O}$, then $P_{Total}, P_{H_2O} \rightarrow P_{H_2}$, then mmHg $\rightarrow$ atm, mL $\rightarrow$ L, and $^\circ C \rightarrow K$,

$$\text{Table 5.4} \qquad\qquad P_{Total} = P_{H_2} + P_{H_2O} \qquad \frac{1 \text{ bar}}{750.01 \text{ mmHg}}$$

then, $P, V, T \rightarrow n \rightarrow g$

Solution: Table 5.4 states that the vapour pressure of H_2O, P_{H_2O}, at 25 °C is 23.78 mmHg. Converting to bar:

$$23.78 \text{ mmHg } x \frac{1 \text{ bar}}{750.01 \text{ mmHg}} = 0.03171 \text{ bar}$$

$$T \text{ (K)} = 25 \text{ °C} + 273.15 = 298.15 \text{ K}$$

$$P_{H_2} = P_{Total} - P_{H_2O} = 0.990 \text{ bar} - 0.03171 \text{ bar} = 0.95\underline{8}29 \text{ bar}$$

$$n = \frac{PV}{RT} = \frac{0.95829 \text{ bar} \times 0.951 \text{ L}}{0.08314 \dfrac{\text{L} \cdot \text{bar}}{\text{mol} \cdot \text{K}} \times 298.15 \text{ K}} = 0.036\underline{7}648 \text{ mol}$$

$$0.036\underline{7}648 \text{ mol } x \frac{2.016 \text{ g } H_2}{1 \text{ mol } H_2} = 0.0741 \text{ g } H_2$$

Check: The units (g) are correct. The magnitude of the answer (<< 1 g) makes sense because gases are not very dense, hydrogen is light, the volume is small, and the pressure is < 1 atm

Reaction Stoichiometry Involving Gases

5.71   **Given:** m (C) = 15.7 g, P = 1.0 bar, and T = 355 K **Find:** V
Conceptual Plan: g C $\rightarrow$ mol C $\rightarrow$ mol H_2 then n (mol H_2), P, T $\rightarrow$ V

$$\frac{1 \text{ mol}}{12.01 \text{ g C}} \qquad \frac{1 \text{ mol } H_2}{1 \text{ mol C}} \qquad\qquad PV = nRT$$

Solution: $15.7 \text{ g C} \times \dfrac{1 \text{ mol C}}{12.01 \text{ g C}} \times \dfrac{1 \text{ mol } H_2}{1 \text{ mol C}} = 1.3\underline{0}724 \text{ mol } H_2$, $PV = nRT$ Rearrange to solve for V.

$$V = \frac{nRT}{P} = \frac{1.30724 \text{ mol} \times 0.08314 \dfrac{\text{L} \cdot \text{bar}}{\text{mol} \cdot \text{K}} \times 355 \text{ K}}{1.0 \text{ bar}} = 39 \text{ L}$$

Check: The units (L) are correct. The magnitude of the answer (39 L) makes sense because we have more than one mole of gas, and so we expect more than 22 L.

5.73   **Given:** P = 748 mmHg, T = 86 °C, and m (CH_3OH) = 25.8 g   **Find:** V_{H_2} and V_{CO}
Conceptual Plan: g CH_3OH $\rightarrow$ mol CH_3OH $\rightarrow$ mol H_2 and mmHg $\rightarrow$ bar and °C $\rightarrow$ K

$$\frac{1 \text{ mol } CH_3OH}{32.04 \text{ g } CH_3OH} \qquad \frac{2 \text{ mol } H_2}{1 \text{ mol } CH_3OH} \qquad \frac{1 \text{ bar}}{750.01 \text{ mmHg}} \qquad K = \text{°C} + 273.15$$

then n (mol H_2), P, T $\rightarrow$ V and mol H_2 $\rightarrow$ mol CO then n (mol CO), P, T $\rightarrow$ V

$$PV = nRT \qquad\qquad \frac{1 \text{ mol CO}}{2 \text{ mol } H_2} \qquad\qquad PV = nRT$$

Solution: $25.8 \text{ g } CH_3OH \times \dfrac{1 \text{ mol } CH_3OH}{32.04 \text{ g } CH_3OH} \times \dfrac{2 \text{ mol } H_2}{1 \text{ mol } CH_3OH} = 1.6\underline{1}049 \text{ mol } H_2$,

$$P_{H_2} = 748 \text{ mmHg} \times \frac{1 \text{ bar}}{750.01 \text{ mmHg}} = 0.99\underline{7}320 \text{ bar}, \quad T = 86 \text{ °C} + 273.15 = 359 \text{ K}, \quad PV = nRT$$

Rearrange to solve for V. $V = \dfrac{nRT}{P}$ $V_{H_2} = \dfrac{1.61049 \text{ mol} \times 0.08314 \dfrac{\text{L} \cdot \text{bar}}{\text{mol} \cdot \text{K}} \times 359 \text{ K}}{0.997320 \text{ bar}} = 48.2 \text{ L } H_2$

$$1.6\underline{1}049 \text{ mol } H_2 \times \frac{1 \text{ mol CO}}{2 \text{ mol } H_2} = 0.8\underline{0}525 \text{ mol CO}, \quad V_{CO} = \frac{0.80525 \text{ mol} \times 0.08314 \dfrac{\text{L} \cdot \text{bar}}{\text{mol} \cdot \text{K}} \times 359 \text{ K}}{0.997320 \text{ bar}} = 24.1 \text{ L CO}$$

Check: The units (L) are correct. The magnitude of the answer (48 L and 24 L) makes sense because we have more than one mole of hydrogen gas and half that of CO and so we expect significantly more than 22 L for hydrogen and half that for CO.

5.75   **Given:** V = 11.8 L and STP   **Find:** m (NaN_3)
Conceptual Plan: V_{N_2} $\rightarrow$ mol N_2 $\rightarrow$ mol NaN_3 $\rightarrow$ g NaN_3

$$\frac{1 \text{ mol } N_2}{22.414 \text{ L } N_2} \qquad \frac{2 \text{ mol } NaN_3}{3 \text{ mol } N_2} \qquad \frac{65.03 \text{ g } NaN_3}{1 \text{ mol } NaN_3}$$

Solution: $11.8 \text{ L } N_2 \times \dfrac{1 \text{ mol } N_2}{22.7 \text{ L } N_2} \times \dfrac{2 \text{ mol } NaN_3}{3 \text{ mol } N_2} \times \dfrac{65.03 \text{ g } NaN_3}{1 \text{ mol } NaN_3} = 22.5 \text{ g } NaN_3$

Check: The units (g) are correct. The magnitude of the answer (23 g) makes sense because we have about a half a mole of nitrogen gas, which translates to even fewer moles of NaN_3 and so we expect significantly less than 65 g.

5.77   **Given**: V_{CH_4} = 25.5 L, P_{CH_4} = 732 torr, and T = 25 °C; mixed with V_{H_2O} = 22.8 L, P_{H_2O} = 702 torr, and T = 125 °C; forms P_{H_2} = 26.2 L at STP **Find**: % Yield

Conceptual Plan: CH$_4$: torr $\rightarrow$ bar and °C $\rightarrow$ K and $P, V, T \rightarrow n_{CH_4} \rightarrow n_{H_2}$

$$\frac{1\,bar}{750.01\,torr} \qquad K = °C + 273.15 \qquad PV = nRT \qquad \frac{3\,mol\,H_2}{1\,mol\,CH_4}$$

H$_2$O: torr $\rightarrow$ K and °C $\rightarrow$ K and $P, V, T \rightarrow n_{H_2O} \rightarrow n_{H_2}$

$$\frac{1\,bar}{750.01\,torr} \qquad K = °C + 273.15 \qquad PV = nRT \qquad \frac{3\,mol\,H_2}{1\,mol\,CH_4}$$

Select smaller n_{H_2} as theoretical yield,
then $L_{H_2} \rightarrow$ mol H$_2$ (actual yield) finally actual yield, theoretical yield $\rightarrow$ % Yield

$$\frac{1\,mol\,H_2}{22.7\,L\,H_2} \qquad\qquad\qquad \% \text{ Yield} = \frac{actual\,yield}{theoretical\,yield} \times 100\%$$

Solution: CH$_4$: P_{CH_4} = 732 torr $\times \dfrac{1\,bar}{750.01\,torr}$ = 0.975987 bar, T = 25 °C + 273.15 = 298 K, $PV = nRT$

Rearrange to solve for n. $n = \dfrac{PV}{RT}$ $n_{CH_4} = \dfrac{0.975987\,bar \times 25.5\,L}{0.08314\,\dfrac{L \cdot bar}{mol \cdot K} \times 298\,K}$ = 1.00452 mol CH$_4$

$$1.00436\;mol\,CH_4 \times \frac{3\,mol\,H_2}{1\,mol\,CH_4} = 3.01308\;mol\,H_2$$

H$_2$O: P_{H_2O} = 702 torr $\times \dfrac{1\,bar}{750.01\,torr}$ = 0.935987 bar, T = 125 °C + 273.15 = 398 K, $n = \dfrac{PV}{RT}$

$n_{H_2O} = \dfrac{0.935987\,bar \times 22.8\,L}{0.08314\,\dfrac{L \cdot bar}{mol \cdot K} \times 398\,K}$ = 0.644929 mol H$_2$O 0.644929 mol H$_2$O $\times \dfrac{3\,mol\,H_2}{1\,mol\,H_2O}$ = 1.93786 mol H$_2$

Water is the limiting reagent since the moles of hydrogen generated is lower.

Theoretical yield = 1.934786 mol H$_2$.

$$26.2\;L\,H_2 \times \frac{1\,mol\,H_2}{22.7\;L\,H_2} = 1.154185\,mol\,H_2 = \text{actual yield}$$

$$\% \text{ Yield} = \frac{actual\,yield}{theoretical\,yield} \times 100\% = \frac{1.154185\;mol\,H_2}{1.934786\;mol\,H_2} \times 100\% = 59.7\%$$

Check: The units (%) are correct. The magnitude of the answer (60%) makes sense because it is between 0 and 100%.

Kinetic Molecular Theory

5.79   (a)   Yes, since the average kinetic energy of a particle is proportional to the temperature in kelvins and the two gases are at the same temperature, they have the same average kinetic energy.

(b)   No, since the helium atoms are lighter, they must move faster to have the same kinetic energy as argon atoms.

(c)   No, since the Ar atoms are moving slower to compensate for their larger mass, they will exert the same pressure on the walls of the container.

(d)   Since He is lighter, it will have the faster rate of effusion.

5.81   **Given**: F_2, Cl_2, Br_2, and T = 298 K **Find**: u_{rms} KE$_{avg}$ for each gas and relative rates of effusion

Conceptual Plan: $\mathcal{M}, T \rightarrow u_{rms} \rightarrow$ KE$_{avg}$

$$u_{rms} = \sqrt{\frac{3RT}{\mathcal{M}}} \qquad KE_{avg} = \tfrac{1}{2} N_A m u_{rms}^2 = \tfrac{3}{2} RT$$

Solution:

$$F_2: \mathcal{M} = \frac{38.00\,g}{1\,mol} \times \frac{1\,kg}{1000\,g} = 0.03800\;kg\,mol^{-1}, u_{rms} = \sqrt{\frac{3RT}{\mathcal{M}}} = \sqrt{\frac{3 \times 8.314\,\dfrac{J}{K \cdot mol} \times 298\,K}{0.03800\,\dfrac{kg}{mol}}} = 442\;m\,s^{-1}$$

Cl_2: $\mathcal{M} = \dfrac{70.90 \ \cancel{g}}{1 \ mol} \times \dfrac{1 \ kg}{1000 \ \cancel{g}} = 0.07090 \ kg \ mol^{-1}$, $u_{rms} = \sqrt{\dfrac{3RT}{\mathcal{M}}} = \sqrt{\dfrac{3 \times 8.314 \dfrac{J}{\cancel{K} \cdot \cancel{mol}} \times 298 \ \cancel{K}}{0.07090 \dfrac{kg}{\cancel{mol}}}} = 324 \ m \ s^{-1}$

Br_2: $\mathcal{M} = \dfrac{159.80 \ \cancel{g}}{1 \ mol} \times \dfrac{1 \ kg}{1000 \ \cancel{g}} = 0.15980 \ kg \ mol^{-1}$, $u_{rms} = \sqrt{\dfrac{3RT}{\mathcal{M}}} = \sqrt{\dfrac{3 \times 8.314 \dfrac{J}{\cancel{K} \cdot \cancel{mol}} \times 298 \ \cancel{K}}{0.15980 \dfrac{kg}{\cancel{mol}}}} = 216 \ m \ s^{-1}$

All molecules have the same kinetic energy:

$$KE_{avg} = \frac{3}{2}RT = \frac{3}{2} \times 8.314 \ \frac{J}{K \cdot mol} \times 298 \ K = 3.72 \times 10^3 \ J \ mol^{-1}$$

Since rate of effusion is proportional to $\sqrt{\dfrac{1}{\mathcal{M}}}$, F_2 will have the fastest rate and Br_2 will have the slowest rate.

Check: The units ($m \ s^{-1}$) are correct. The magnitude of the answer ($200 - 450 \ m \ s^{-1}$) makes sense because it is consistent with what was seen in the text, and the heavier the molecule, the slower the molecule.

5.83   **Given:** $^{238}UF_6$ and $^{235}UF_6$ U-235 = 235.054 amu, U-238 = 238.051 amu
Find: ratio of effusion rates $^{238}UF_6$ / $^{235}UF_6$
Conceptual Plan: $\mathcal{M}(^{238}UF_6)$, $\mathcal{M}(^{235}UF_6)$ $\rightarrow$ **Rate ($^{238}UF_6$)/Rate ($^{235}UF_6$)**

$$\frac{Rate(^{238}UF_6)}{Rate(^{235}UF_6)} = \sqrt{\frac{\mathcal{M}(^{235}UF_6)}{\mathcal{M}(^{238}UF_6)}}$$

Solution: $^{238}UF_6$: $\mathcal{M} = \dfrac{352.05 \ \cancel{g}}{1 \ mol} \times \dfrac{1 \ kg}{1000 \ \cancel{g}} = 0.35205 \ kg \ mol^{-1}$,

$^{235}UF_6$: $\mathcal{M} = \dfrac{349.05 \ \cancel{g}}{1 \ mol} \times \dfrac{1 \ kg}{1000 \ \cancel{g}} = 0.34905 \ kg \ mol^{-1}$,

$\dfrac{Rate(^{238}UF_6)}{Rate(^{235}UF_6)} = \sqrt{\dfrac{\mathcal{M}(^{235}UF_6)}{\mathcal{M}(^{238}UF_6)}} = \sqrt{\dfrac{0.34905 \ \cancel{kg/mol}}{0.35205 \ \cancel{kg/mol}}} = 0.99574$

Check: The units (none) are correct. The magnitude of the answer (<1) makes sense because the heavier molecule has the lower effusion rate since it moves slower.

5.85   **Given:** Ne and unknown gas; and Ne effusion in 76 s and unknown in 155 s
Find: identify unknown gas
Conceptual Plan: $\mathcal{M}(Ne)$, **Rate (Ne), Rate (Unk)** $\rightarrow$ $\mathcal{M}(Kr)$

$$\frac{Rate(Ne)}{Rate(Unk)} = \sqrt{\frac{\mathcal{M}(Unk)}{\mathcal{M}(Ne)}}$$

Solution: Ne: $\mathcal{M} = \dfrac{20.18 \ \cancel{g}}{1 \ mol} \times \dfrac{1 \ kg}{1000 \ \cancel{g}} = 0.02018 \ kg \ mol^{-1}$, $\dfrac{Rate(Ne)}{Rate(Unk)} = \sqrt{\dfrac{\mathcal{M}(Unk)}{\mathcal{M}(Ne)}}$ Rearrange to solve for

$\mathcal{M}(Unk)$. $\mathcal{M}(Unk) = \mathcal{M}(Ne)\left(\dfrac{Rate(Ne)}{Rate(Unk)}\right)^2$ Since Rate α 1/(effusion time),

$\mathcal{M}(Unk) = \mathcal{M}(Ne)\left(\dfrac{Time(Unk)}{Time(Ne)}\right)^2 = 0.02018 \dfrac{kg}{mol} \times \left(\dfrac{155 \ \cancel{s}}{76 \ \cancel{s}}\right)^2 = 0.084 \dfrac{\cancel{kg}}{mol} \times \dfrac{1000 \ g}{1 \ \cancel{kg}} = 84 \ g \ mol^{-1}$ or Kr.

Check: The units ($g \ mol^{-1}$) are correct. The magnitude of the answer (>Ne) makes sense because Ne effused faster and so must be lighter.

5.87   Gas A has the higher molar mass, since it has the slower average velocity. Gas B will have the higher effusion rate, since it has the higher velocity.

5.89   **Given:** O_2 and Cl_2, effusion rate of Cl_2 = 0.315 mol hr^{-1} **Find:** effusion rate of O_2
Conceptual Plan: $\mathcal{M}(O_2)$, $\mathcal{M}(Cl_2)$, **Rate (Cl_2)** $\rightarrow$ **Rate (O_2)**

Solution: $\dfrac{Rate_{O_2}}{Rate_{Cl_2}} = \sqrt{\dfrac{\mathcal{M}_{Cl_2}}{\mathcal{M}_{O_2}}}$

$Rate_{O_2} = Rate_{Cl_2}\sqrt{\dfrac{\mathcal{M}_{Cl_2}}{\mathcal{M}_{O_2}}} = (0.315 \ mol \ hr^{-1})\left(\dfrac{70.90}{32.00}\right)^{1/2} = 0.469 \ mol \ hr^{-1}$

Check: The units (mol hr^{-1}) are correct. The magnitude also makes sense, because effusion increases as molecular mass decreases, and O_2 has a smaller molecular mass.

Real Gases

5.91 The postulate that the volume of the gas particles is small compared to the space between them breaks down at high pressure. At high pressures the number of molecules per unit volume increases, so the volume of the gas particles becomes more significant. Since the spacing between the particles is reduced, the molecules themselves occupy a significant portion of the volume.

5.93 **Given:** Ne, $n = 1.000$ mol, $P = 500.0$ bar, and $T = 355.0$ K **Find:** V(ideal) and V(van der Waals)
Conceptual Plan: $n, P, T \rightarrow V$ and $n, P, T \rightarrow V$

$$PV = nRT \qquad \left(P + \frac{an^2}{V^2} \right)(V - nb) = nRT$$

Solution: $PV = nRT$ Rearrange to solve for V.

$$V = \frac{nRT}{P} = \frac{1.000 \text{ mol} \times 0.08314 \dfrac{\text{L} \cdot \text{bar}}{\text{mol} \cdot \text{K}} \times 355.0 \text{ K}}{500.0 \text{ bar}} = 0.0590294 \text{ L}$$

$$\left(P + \frac{an^2}{V^2} \right)(V - nb) = nRT \text{ Rearrange to solve to } V = \frac{nRT}{\left(P + \dfrac{an^2}{V^2} \right)} + nb$$

Using a = 0.2135 L^2 bar mol^{-2} and b = 0.0171 L mol^{-1} from Table 5.5, and the V from the ideal gas law calculation above, solve for V by successive approximations.

$$V = \frac{1.000 \text{ mol} \times 0.08314 \dfrac{\text{L} \cdot \text{bar}}{\text{mol} \cdot \text{K}} \times 355.0 \text{ K}}{500.0 \text{ bar} + \dfrac{0.2135 \dfrac{\text{L}^2 \cdot \text{bar}}{\text{mol}^2} \times (1.000 \text{ mol})^2}{(0.05826 \text{ L})^2}} + \left(1.000 \text{ mol} \times 0.0171 \dfrac{\text{L}}{\text{mol}} \right) = 0.0695332 \text{ L}$$

Plug in this new value.

$$V = \frac{1.000 \text{ mol} \times 0.08314 \dfrac{\text{L} \cdot \text{bar}}{\text{mol} \cdot \text{K}} \times 355.0 \text{ K}}{500.0 \text{ bar} + \dfrac{0.2135 \dfrac{\text{L}^2 \cdot \text{bar}}{\text{mol}^2} \times (1.000 \text{ mol})^2}{(0.0695332 \text{ L})^2}} + \left(1.000 \text{ mol} \times 0.0171 \dfrac{\text{L}}{\text{mol}} \right) = 0.0713392 \text{ L}$$

Plug in this new value.

$$V = \frac{1.000 \text{ mol} \times 0.08314 \dfrac{\text{L} \cdot \text{bar}}{\text{mol} \cdot \text{K}} \times 355.0 \text{ K}}{500.0 \text{ bar} + \dfrac{0.2135 \dfrac{\text{L}^2 \cdot \text{bar}}{\text{mol}^2} \times (1.000 \text{ mol})^2}{(0.0713392 \text{ L})^2}} + \left(1.000 \text{ mol} \times 0.0171 \dfrac{\text{L}}{\text{mol}} \right) = 0.0715601 \text{ L}$$

Plug in this new value.

$$V = \frac{1.000 \text{ mol} \times 0.08314 \dfrac{\text{L} \cdot \text{bar}}{\text{mol} \cdot \text{K}} \times 355.0 \text{ K}}{500.0 \text{ bar} + \dfrac{0.2135 \dfrac{\text{L}^2 \cdot \text{bar}}{\text{mol}^2} \times (1.000 \text{ mol})^2}{(0.0715601 \text{ L})^2}} + \left(1.000 \text{ mol} \times 0.0171 \dfrac{\text{L}}{\text{mol}} \right) = 0.0715861 \text{ L} = 0.0716 \text{ L}$$

The two values are different because we are at very high pressures. The pressure is corrected from 500.0 bar to 542.1 bar and the final volume correction is 0.0171 L.
Check: The units (L) are correct. The magnitude of the answer (~0.06 L) makes sense because we are at such a high pressure and have one mole of gas.

Cumulative Problems

5.95   **Given:** m (penny) = 2.482 g, T = 25 °C, V = 0.899 L, and P_{Total} = 791 mmHg **Find:** % Zn in penny
Conceptual Plan: $T \rightarrow P_{H_2O}$ then $P_{Total}, P_{H_2O} \rightarrow P_{H_2}$ then mmHg $\rightarrow$ bar and °C $\rightarrow$ K

$$\text{Table 5.4} \qquad\qquad P_{Total} = P_{H_2O} + P_{H_2} \qquad \frac{1\,\text{bar}}{750.01\,\text{mmHg}} \qquad K = °C + 273.15$$

and $P, V, T \rightarrow n_{H_2} \rightarrow n_{Zn} \rightarrow$ **g** $_{Zn} \rightarrow$ **% Zn**

$$PV = nRT \qquad \frac{1\,\text{mol Zn}}{1\,\text{mol H}_2} \quad \frac{65.39\,\text{g Zn}}{1\,\text{mol Zn}} \quad \%Zn = \frac{g_{Zn}}{g_{penny}} \times 100\%$$

Solution: Table 5.4 states that P_{H_2O} = 23.78 mmHg at 25 °C $P_{Total} = P_{H_2O} + P_{H_2}$ Rearrange to solve for P_{H_2}.

$P_{H_2} = P_{Total} - P_{H_2O} = 791$ mmHg $- 23.78$ mmHg $= 767$ mmHg $P_{H_2} = 767\ \overline{\text{mmHg}} \times \dfrac{1\,\text{bar}}{750.01\,\overline{\text{mmHg}}} = 1.022653$ bar

then T = 25 °C + 273.15 = 298 K, $PV = nRT$

Rearrange to solve for n. $n_{H_2} = \dfrac{PV}{RT} = \dfrac{1.022653\ \overline{\text{bar}} \times\ 0.899\ \overline{\text{L}}}{0.08314\ \dfrac{\overline{\text{L}} \cdot \overline{\text{bar}}}{\text{mol} \cdot \overline{\text{K}}} \times 298\ \overline{\text{K}}} = 0.0371075$ mol

$0.0371075\ \overline{\text{mol H}_2} \times \dfrac{1\ \overline{\text{mol Zn}}}{1\ \overline{\text{mol H}_2}} \times \dfrac{65.39\,\text{g Zn}}{1\ \overline{\text{mol Zn}}} = 2.426459$ g Zn

$\%Zn = \dfrac{g_{Zn}}{g_{penny}} \times 100\% = \dfrac{2.426459\ \underline{\text{g}}}{2.482\ \underline{\text{g}}} \times 100\% = 97.8\%$ Zn

Check: The units (% Zn) are correct. The magnitude of the answer (98%) makes sense because it should be between 0 and 100%. We expect about 1/22 a mole of gas, since our conditions are close to STP and we have ~ 1 L of gas.

5.97   **Given:** V = 255 mL, m (flask) = 143.187 g, m (flask + gas) = 143.289 g, P = 356 mbar, and T = 25 °C   **Find:** $\mathcal{M}$
Conceptual Plan: °C $\rightarrow$ K mbar $\rightarrow$ bar mL $\rightarrow$ L m (flask), m (flask + gas) $\rightarrow$ m (gas)

$$K = °C + 273.15 \quad \frac{1\,\text{bar}}{1000\,\text{mbar}} \qquad \frac{1\,\text{L}}{1000\,\text{mL}} \qquad m\ (gas) = m\ (flask + gas) - m\ (flask)$$

then $V, m \rightarrow d$ **then** $d, P, T, \rightarrow \mathcal{M}$

$$d = \frac{m}{V} \qquad\qquad d = \frac{P\mathcal{M}}{RT}$$

Solution: T = 25 °C + 273.15 = 298 K, P = 356 $\overline{\text{mbar}} \times \dfrac{1\,\text{bar}}{1000\ \overline{\text{mbar}}} = 0.356$ bar,

$V = 255\ \overline{\text{mL}} \times \dfrac{1\,\text{L}}{1000\ \overline{\text{mL}}} = 0.255$ L,

$m\ (gas) = m\ (flask + gas) - m\ (flask) = 143.289$ g $- 143.187$g $= 0.102$ g,

$d = \dfrac{m}{V} = \dfrac{0.102\,\text{g}}{0.255\,\text{L}} = 0.400$ g L^{-1}, $d = \dfrac{P\mathcal{M}}{RT}$ Rearrange to solve for $\mathcal{M}$.

$\mathcal{M} = \dfrac{dRT}{P} = \dfrac{0.400\ \dfrac{\text{g}}{\overline{\text{L}}} \times 0.08314 \dfrac{\overline{\text{L}} \cdot \overline{\text{bar}}}{\overline{\text{K}} \cdot \text{mol}} \times 298\ \overline{\text{K}}}{0.356\ \overline{\text{bar}}} = 27.8$ g mol^{-1}

Check: The units (g mol^{-1}) are correct. The magnitude of the answer (28 g mol^{-1}) makes physical sense because this is a reasonable number for a molecular weight of a gas. The gas is likely molecular nitrogen.

5.99   **Given:** V = 158 mL, m (gas) = 0.275 g, P = 556 mmHg, T = 25 °C, gas = 82.66% C and 17.34% H
Find: molecular formula
Conceptual Plan: °C $\rightarrow$ K mmHg $\rightarrow$ bar mL $\rightarrow$ L then $V, m \rightarrow d$

$$K = °C + 273.15 \quad \frac{1\,\text{bar}}{750.01\,\text{mmHg}} \quad \frac{1\,\text{L}}{1000\,\text{mL}} \qquad d = \frac{m}{V}$$

then $d, P, T, \rightarrow \mathcal{M}$ **then** % C, % H, $\mathcal{M} \rightarrow$ **formula**

$$d = \frac{P\mathcal{M}}{RT} \qquad \#C = \frac{\mathcal{M}\,0.8266\,g\,C}{12.01\frac{g\,C}{mol\,C}} \qquad \#H = \frac{\mathcal{M}\,0.1734\,g\,H}{1.008\frac{g\,H}{mol\,H}}$$

Solution: T = 25 °C + 273.15 = 298 K, P = 556 $\overline{\text{mmHg}} \times \dfrac{1\,\text{bar}}{750.01\ \overline{\text{mmHg}}} = 0.741323$ bar,

$V = 158\ \overline{\text{mL}} \times \dfrac{1\,\text{L}}{1000\ \overline{\text{mL}}} = 0.158$ L, $d = \dfrac{m}{V} = \dfrac{0.275\,\text{g}}{0.158\,\text{L}} = 1.74051$ g L^{-1}, $d = \dfrac{P\mathcal{M}}{RT}$ Rearrange to solve for $\mathcal{M}$.

$$\mathcal{M} = \frac{dRT}{P} = \frac{1.74051\,\frac{g}{\cancel{L}} \times 0.08314\,\frac{\cancel{L}\cdot\text{bar}}{\text{K}\cdot\text{mol}} \times 298\text{ K}}{0.741323\,\cancel{\text{bar}}} = 58.2\text{ g mol}^{-1},$$

$$\#C = \frac{\mathcal{M} \times 0.8266\text{ g C}}{12.01\,\frac{\text{g C}}{\text{mol C}}} = \frac{58.2\,\frac{\cancel{\text{g HC}}}{\text{mol HC}} \times \frac{0.8266\,\cancel{\text{g C}}}{1\,\cancel{\text{g HC}}}}{12.01\,\frac{\cancel{\text{g C}}}{\text{mol C}}} = 4.00\,\frac{\text{mol C}}{\text{mol HC}}$$

$$\#H = \frac{\mathcal{M} \times 0.1734\text{ g H}}{1.008\,\frac{\text{g H}}{\text{mol H}}} = \frac{58.2\,\frac{\cancel{\text{g HC}}}{\text{mol HC}} \times \frac{0.1734\,\cancel{\text{g H}}}{1\,\cancel{\text{g HC}}}}{1.008\,\frac{\cancel{\text{g H}}}{\text{mol H}}} = 10.0\,\frac{\text{mol H}}{\text{mol HC}}\ \text{Formula is }C_4H_{10}\text{ or butane.}$$

Check: The answer came up with integer number of C and H atoms in the formula and a molecular weight (58 g mol^{-1}) that is reasonable for a gas.

5.101 **Given**: m (NiO) = 24.78 g, T = 40.0 °C, and P_{Total} = 745 mmHg **Find**: V_{O_2}
Conceptual Plan: $T \rightarrow P_{H_2O}$ then $P_{Total}, P_{H_2O} \rightarrow P_{O_2}$ then mmHg $\rightarrow$ bar and °C $\rightarrow$ K

$$\qquad\qquad Table\ 5.4 \qquad\qquad P_{Total} = P_{H_2O} + P_{O_2} \qquad \frac{1\,\text{bar}}{750.01\,\text{mmHg}} \qquad K = °C + 273.15$$

and $g_{NiO} \rightarrow n_{NiO} \rightarrow n_{O_2}$ then $P, V, T \rightarrow n_{O_2}$

$$\qquad \frac{1\,\text{mol NiO}}{74.69\,\text{g NiO}} \quad \frac{1\,\text{mol O}_2}{2\,\text{mol NiO}} \qquad PV = nRT$$

Solution: Table 5.4 states that P_{H_2O} = 55.40 mmHg at 40°C $P_{Total} = P_{H_2O} + P_{O_2}$ Rearrange to solve for P_{O_2}.
$P_{O_2} = P_{Total} - P_{H_2O} = 745\text{ mmHg} - 55.40\text{ mmHg} = 689.\underline{6}\text{ mmHg}$

$$P_{O_2} = 689.\underline{6}\,\cancel{\text{mmHg}} \times \frac{1\,\text{bar}}{750.01\,\cancel{\text{mmHg}}} = 0.919454\text{ bar} \quad T = 40.0\text{ °C} + 273.15 = 313.2\text{ K,}$$

$$24.78\,\cancel{\text{g NiO}} \times \frac{1\,\cancel{\text{mol NiO}}}{74.69\,\cancel{\text{mol NiO}}} \times \frac{1\,\text{mol O}_2}{2\,\cancel{\text{mol NiO}}} = 0.1658857\text{ mol O}_2 \quad PV = nRT$$

Rearrange to solve for V. $V_{O_2} = \dfrac{nRT}{P} = \dfrac{0.1658857\,\cancel{\text{mol}} \times 0.08314\,\frac{\text{L}\cdot\text{bar}}{\cancel{\text{mol}}\cdot\cancel{\text{K}}} \times 313.2\,\cancel{\text{K}}}{0.919454\,\cancel{\text{bar}}} = 4.70\text{ L}$

Check: The units (L) are correct. The magnitude of the answer (5 L) makes sense because we have much less than 0.5 mole of NiO, so we get less than a mole of oxygen. Thus we expect a volume much less than 22 L.

5.103 **Given**: HCl, K_2S to H_2S, V_{H_2S} = 42.9 mL, P_{H_2S} = 752 mmHg, and T = 25.8 °C **Find**: $m(K_2S)$
Conceptual Plan: read description of reaction and convert words to equation then °C $\rightarrow$ K

$$\qquad\qquad\qquad\qquad\qquad\qquad\qquad\qquad\qquad\qquad\qquad\qquad K = °C + 273.15$$

and mmHg $\rightarrow$ bar and mL $\rightarrow$ L then $P, V, T \rightarrow n_{H_2S} \rightarrow n_{K_2S} \rightarrow g_{K_2S}$

$$\qquad \frac{1\,\text{bar}}{750.01\,\text{mmHg}} \qquad \frac{1\,\text{L}}{1000\,\text{mL}} \qquad PV = nRT \quad \frac{1\,\text{mol K}_2\text{S}}{1\,\text{mol H}_2\text{S}} \quad \frac{1\,\text{mol K}_2\text{S}}{110.27\,\text{g K}_2\text{S}}$$

Solution: 2 HCl (aq) + K_2S (s) $\rightarrow$ H_2S (g) + 2 KCl (aq)

$$T = 25.8\text{ °C} + 273.15 = 299.0\text{ K,}\ P_{H_2S} = 752\,\cancel{\text{mmHg}} \times \frac{1\,\text{bar}}{750.01\,\cancel{\text{mmHg}}} = 1.002653\text{ bar,}$$

$$V_{H_2S} = 42.9\,\cancel{\text{mL}} \times \frac{1\,\text{L}}{1000\,\cancel{\text{mL}}} = 0.0429\text{ L} \qquad PV = nRT\ \text{ Rearrange to solve for }n_{H_2S}.$$

$$n_{H_2S} = \frac{PV}{RT} = \frac{1.002653\,\cancel{\text{bar}} \times 0.0429\,\cancel{\text{L}}}{0.08314\,\frac{\cancel{\text{L}}\cdot\cancel{\text{bar}}}{\text{mol}\cdot\cancel{\text{K}}} \times 299.0\,\cancel{\text{K}}} = 0.001730321\text{ mol}$$

$$0.001730321\,\cancel{\text{mol H}_2\text{S}} \times \frac{1\,\cancel{\text{mol K}_2\text{S}}}{1\,\cancel{\text{mol H}_2\text{S}}} \times \frac{110.27\,\text{g K}_2\text{S}}{1\,\cancel{\text{mol K}_2\text{S}}} = 0.191\text{ g K}_2\text{S}$$

Check: The units (g) are correct. The magnitude of the answer (0.1 g) makes sense because we have such a small volume of gas generated.

5.105 **Given**: T = 22 °C, P = 1.02 bar, and m = 11.83 g **Find**: V_{Total}
Conceptual Plan: °C $\rightarrow$ K and $g_{(NH_4)_2CO_3} \rightarrow n_{(NH_4)_2CO_3} \rightarrow n_{Gas}$ then $P, n, T \rightarrow V$

$$\qquad K = °C + 273.15 \qquad \frac{1\,\text{mol (NH}_4)_2\text{CO}_3}{96.09\,\text{g (NH}_4)_2\text{CO}_3} \quad \frac{(2+1+1=4)\,\text{mol gas}}{1\,\text{mol NH}_4\text{CO}_3} \qquad PV = nRT$$

Solution: $T = 22\,°C + 273.15 = 295$ K,

$$11.83\ \overline{g\ NH_4CO_3} \times \frac{1\ \overline{mol\ (NH_4)_2CO_3}}{96.09\ \overline{g\ (NH_4)_2CO_3}} \times \frac{4\ mol\ gas}{1\ \overline{mol\ (NH_4)_2CO_3}} = 0.492455\ mol\ gas$$

$PV = nRT$ Rearrange to solve for V_{Gas}.

$$V_{Gas} = \frac{nRT}{P} = \frac{0.492455\ \overline{mol\ gas} \times 0.08314\ \frac{L \cdot bar}{\overline{mol} \cdot K} \times 295\ K}{1.02\ \overline{bar}} = 11.8\ L$$

Check: The units (L) are correct. The magnitude of the answer (12 L) makes sense because we have about a half a mole of gas generated.

5.107   **Given:** He and air; $V = 855$ mL, $P = 125$ psi, $T = 25\,°C$, $\rightarrow$ (air) $= 28.8$ g mol^{-1} **Find:** $\Delta = m(air) - m(He)$
Conceptual Plan: mL $\rightarrow$ **L and psi** $\rightarrow$ **bar and** $°C$ $\rightarrow$ **K then** $P, T, \mathcal{M} \rightarrow d$
$$\frac{1\ L}{1000\ mL} \qquad \frac{1\ bar}{14.5\ psi} \qquad K = °C + 273.15 \qquad d = \frac{P\mathcal{M}}{RT}$$

then $d, V \rightarrow m$ **then** $m(air), m(He) \rightarrow \Delta$
$$d = \frac{m}{V} \qquad\qquad \Delta = m(air) - m(He)$$

Solution: $V = 855\ \overline{mL} \times \dfrac{1\ L}{1000\ \overline{mL}} = 0.855\ L$, $P = 125\ \overline{psi} \times \dfrac{1\ bar}{14.5\ \overline{psi}} = 8.62069\ bar$,

$$T = 25\,°C + 273.15 = 298 K,\ d_{air} = \frac{P\mathcal{M}}{RT} = \frac{8.62069\ \overline{bar} \times 28.8\ \frac{g\ air}{\overline{mol\ air}}}{0.08314\ \frac{L \cdot bar}{K \cdot \overline{mol}} \times 298\ K} = 10.0209\ \frac{g\ air}{L},\ d = \frac{m}{V}$$

Rearrange to solve for m. $m = dV$

$$m_{air} = 10.0209\ \frac{g\ air}{L} \times 0.8554\ \overline{L} = 8.571878\ g\ air,\ d_{He} = \frac{P\mathcal{M}}{RT} = \frac{8.62069\ \overline{bar} \times 4.03\ \frac{g\ He}{\overline{mol\ He}}}{0.08314\ \frac{L \cdot bar}{K \cdot \overline{mol}} \times 298\ K} = 1.402234\ \frac{g\ He}{L},$$

$$m_{He} = 1.402234\ \frac{g\ He}{L} \times 0.855\ \overline{L} = 1.19947\ g\ He,$$

$\Delta = m(air) - m(He) = 8.571878\ g\ air - 1.19947\ g\ He = 7.37\ g$
Check: The units (g) are correct. We expect the difference to be less than the difference in the molecular weights since we have less than a mole of gas.

5.109   **Given:** flow $= 335$ L/s, $P_{NO} = 22.4$ torr, $T_{NO} = 955$ K, $P_{NH_3} = 755$ torr, and $T_{NO} = 298$ K, and NH_3 purity $= 65.2\%$ **Find:** flow$_{NH_3}$
Conceptual Plan: torr $\rightarrow$ **bar then** $P_{NO}, V_{NO}/s, T_{NO} \rightarrow n_{NO}/s \rightarrow n_{NH_3}/s$ **(pure)**
$$\frac{1\ bar}{750.01\ torr} \qquad\qquad PV = nRT \qquad \frac{4\ mol\ NH_3}{4\ mol\ NO}$$

then n_{NH_3}/s **(pure)** $\rightarrow$ n_{NH_3}/s **(impure) then** n_{NH_3}/s **(impure),** $P_{NH_3}, T_{NH_3} \rightarrow V_{NH_3}/s$
$$\frac{100\ mol\ NH_3\ impure}{65.2\ mol\ NH_3\ pure} \qquad\qquad PV = nRT$$

Solution: $P_{NO} = 22.4\ \overline{torr} \times \dfrac{1\ bar}{750.01\ \overline{torr}} = 0.029866\ bar$,

$PV = nRT$ Rearrange to solve for n_{NO}. Note that we can substitute V/s for V and get n/s as a result.

$$\frac{n_{NO}}{s} = \frac{PV}{RT} = \frac{0.029866\ \overline{bar} \times 335\ \overline{L}/s}{0.08314\ \frac{\overline{L} \cdot \overline{bar}}{mol \cdot K} \times 955\ K} = 0.126012\ \frac{mol\ NO}{s}$$

$$0.126012\ \frac{\overline{mol\ NO}}{s} \times \frac{4\ \overline{mol\ NH_3}}{4\ \overline{mol\ NO}} \times \frac{100\ mol\ NH_3\ impure}{65.2\ \overline{mol\ NH_3\ pure}} = 0.19327\ \frac{mol\ NH_3\ impure}{s} \qquad PV = nRT$$

Rearrange to solve for V_{NH_3}. Note that we can substitute n/s for n and get V/s as a result.

$$\frac{V_{NH_3}}{s} = \frac{nRT}{P} = \frac{0.19327\ \frac{\overline{mol\ NH_3\ impure}}{s} \times 0.08314\ \frac{L \cdot bar}{\overline{mol} \cdot K} \times 298\ K}{1.007\ \overline{bar}} = 4.76\ L\ s^{-1}\ impure\ NH_3$$

Check: The units (L) are correct. The magnitude of the answer (5 L s^{-1}) makes sense because we expect it to be less than for the NO. The NO is at a very low concentration and a high temperature; when this converts to a much higher pressure and lower temperature this will go down significantly, even though the ammonia is impure. From a practical standpoint, you would like a low flow rate to make it economical.

5.111   **Given:** l = 30.0 cm, w = 20.0 cm, h = 15.0 cm, P = 1.01 bar. **Find:** force (Newtons)
Conceptual Plan: $l, w, h \rightarrow$ **surface area (cm^2), SA (cm^2) $\rightarrow$ SA (m^2), P(bar) $\rightarrow$ P(Pa),**
SA **(cm^2), $P \rightarrow F$**

Solution: SA (cm^2) $= 2(l \cdot w) + 2(l \cdot h) + 2(w \cdot h)$
$$= 2(30.0 \text{ cm x } 20.0 \text{ cm}) + 2(30.0 \text{ cm x } 15.0 \text{ cm}) + 2(20.0 \text{ x } 15.0) = 2700 \text{ cm}^2$$

$$SA(\text{m}^2) = 2700 \text{ cm}^2 \text{ x } \frac{1 \text{ m}^2}{(100 \text{ cm})^2} = 0.2700 \text{ m}^2$$

$$P(Pa) = 1.01 \text{ bar x } \frac{100000 \text{ Pa}}{1 \text{ bar}} = 101000 \text{ Pa} = 101000 \text{ N m}^{-2}$$

$$P = \frac{F}{A} \Rightarrow F = P \cdot A = (101000 \text{ N m}^{-2})(0.27 \text{ m}^2) = 27270 \text{ N} = 2.73 \text{ x } 10^4 \text{ N}$$

The can cannot withstand this force.
Check: The units of the answer (N) is correct. The force is not unreasonable since the area of the can is large.

5.113   **Given:** V_1 = 160.0 L, P_1 = 1855 psi, 3.5 L/balloon, P_2 = 1.01 bar = 14.7 psi, and T = 298 K **Find:** # balloons
Conceptual Plan: $V_1, P_1, P_2 \rightarrow V_2$ **then L $\rightarrow$ # balloons**

$$P_1V_1 = P_2V_2 \qquad \frac{1 \text{ balloon}}{3.5 \text{ L}}$$

Solution: $P_1V_1 = P_2V_2$ Rearrange to solve for V_2. $V_2 = \frac{P_1}{P_2}V_1 = \frac{1855 \text{ psi}}{14.7 \text{ psi}} \text{ x } 160.0 \text{ L} = 20190.5 \text{ L},$

$$20190.5 \text{ L x } \frac{1 \text{ balloon}}{3.5 \text{ L}} = 5800 \text{ balloons}$$

Check: The units (balloons) are correct. The magnitude of the answer (5800) is reasonable since a store does not want to buy a new helium tank very often.

5.115   **Given:** r_1 = 2.5 cm, P_1 = 4.00 atm, T = 298 K, and P_2 = 1.00 atm **Find:** r_2
Conceptual Plan: $r_1 \rightarrow V_1 \; V_1, P_1, P_2 \rightarrow V_2$ **then** $V_2 \rightarrow r_2$

$$V = \frac{4}{3}\pi r^3 \qquad P_1V_1 = P_2V_2 \qquad V = \frac{4}{3}\pi r^3$$

Solution: $V = \frac{4}{3}\pi r^3 = \frac{4}{3} \text{ x } \pi \text{ x } (2.5 \text{ cm})^3 = 65.450 \text{ cm}^3$ $P_1V_1 = P_2V_2$ Rearrange to solve for V_2.

$$V_2 = \frac{P_1}{P_2}V_1 = \frac{4.00 \text{ atm}}{1.00 \text{ atm}} \text{ x } 65.450 \text{ cm}^3 = 261.80 \text{ cm}^3, V = \frac{4}{3}\pi r^3$$

Rearrange to solve for r. $r = \sqrt[3]{\frac{3V}{4\pi}} = \sqrt[3]{\frac{3 \text{ x } 261.80 \text{ cm}^3}{4 \text{ x } \pi}} = 4.0 \text{ cm}$

Check: The units (cm) are correct. The magnitude of the answer (4 cm) is reasonable since the bubble will expand as the pressure is decreased.

5.117   **Given:** 2.0 mol CO : 1.0 mol O$_2$, V = 2.45 L, P_1 = 993 mbar, P_2 = 552 torr, and T = 552 °C
Find: % reacted
Conceptual Plan: from $PV = nRT$ we know that $P \propto n$, looking at the chemical reaction we see that 2 + 1 = 3 moles of gas gets converted to 2 moles of gas. If all the gas reacts, $P_2 = 2/3 \, P_1$.
Calculate $-\Delta P$ for 100% reacted and for actual case. Then calculate % reacted.

$$-\Delta P \, 100\% \, reacted = P_1 - \frac{2}{3}P_1 \quad -\Delta P \, actual = P_1 - P_2 \quad \% \, reacted = \frac{\Delta P \, actual}{\Delta P \, 100\% \, reacted} \text{ x } 100\%$$

Solution:

$$552 \text{ torr x } \frac{1\,000 \text{ mbar}}{750.01 \text{ torr}} = 0.73599 - \Delta P \, 100\% \, reacted = P_1 - \frac{2}{3}P_1 = 993 \text{ mbar} - \frac{2}{3} \, 993 \text{ mbar} = 331 \text{ mbar},$$

$$-\Delta P \, actual = P_1 - P_2 = 993 \text{ mbar} - 735.99 \text{ mbar} = 257 \text{ mbar},$$

$$\% \, reacted = \frac{\Delta P \, actual}{\Delta P \, 100\% \, reacted} \text{ x } 100\% = \frac{257 \text{ mbar}}{331 \text{ mbar}} \text{ x } 100\% = 77.7\%$$

Check: The units (%) are correct. The magnitude of the answer (78%) makes sense because the pressure dropped most of the way to the pressure if all of the reactants had reacted. **Note: There are many ways to solve this problem, including calculating the moles of reactants and products using** $PV = nRT$**.**

5.119   **Given**: $P(\text{Total})_1 = 2.2$ bar $= CO + O_2$, $P(\text{Total})_2 = 1.9$ bar $= CO + O_2 + CO_2$, $V = 1.0$ L, $T = 1.0 \times 10^3$ K
Find: mass CO_2 made
Conceptual Plan: $P(\text{Total})_1 = 2.2$ bar $= P(CO)_1 + P(O_2)_1$, $P(\text{Total})_2 = 1.9$ bar $= P(CO)_2 + P(O_2)_2 + P(CO_2)_2$.
Let $x =$ amount of $P(O_2)$ reacted. From stoichiometry: $P(CO)_2 = P(CO)_1 - 2x$, $P(O_2)_2 = P(O_2)_1 - x$, $P(CO_2)_2 = 2x$. Thus $P(\text{Total})_2 = 1.9$ bar $= P(CO)_1 - 2x + P(O_2)_1 - x + 2x = P(\text{Total})_1 - x$. Using the initial conditions: 1.9 bar $= 2.2$ bar $- x$. So $x = 0.3$ bar and since $2x = P(CO_2)_2 = 0.6$ bar, then $P, V, T \rightarrow n \rightarrow$ g.

$$PV = nRT \, \frac{44.01\,g}{1\,mol}$$

Solution: $PV = nRT$ Rearrange to solve for n.

$$n = \frac{PV}{RT} = \frac{0.6\,\cancel{bar} \times 1.0\,\cancel{L}}{0.08314\,\dfrac{\cancel{L} \cdot \cancel{bar}}{mol \cdot \cancel{K}} \times 1000\,\cancel{K}} = 0.0072167\,mol$$

$$0.00\underline{7}2167\,\cancel{mol} \times \frac{44.01\,g}{1\,\cancel{mol}} = 0.\underline{3}1761\,g\,CO_2 = 0.3\,g\,CO_2$$

Check: The units (g) are correct. The magnitude of the answer (0.3 g) makes sense because we have such a small volume at a very high temperature and such a small pressure. This leads us to expect a very small number of moles.

5.121   **Given**: $h_1 = 22.6$ m, $T_1 = 22\,°C$, and $h_2 = 23.8$ m **Find**: T_2
Conceptual Plan: $°C \rightarrow$ K since $V_{cylinder} \propto h$ **we do not need to know** r **to use** $V_1, T_1, T_2 \rightarrow V_2$

$$K = °C + 273.15 \qquad V = \pi r^2 h \qquad \qquad \frac{V_1}{T_1} = \frac{V_2}{T_2}$$

Solution: $T_1 = 22\,°C + 273.15 = 295K$, $\dfrac{V_1}{T_1} = \dfrac{V_2}{T_2}$ Rearrange to solve for T_2.

$$T_2 = T_1 \times \frac{V_2}{V_1} = T_1 \times \frac{\cancel{\pi r^2} l_2}{\cancel{\pi r^2} l_1} = 295\,K \times \frac{23.8\,\cancel{m}}{22.6\,\cancel{m}} = 311\,K$$

Check: The units (K) are correct. We expect the temperature to increase since the volume increased.

5.123   **Given**: He, $V = 0.35$ L, $P_{max} = 88$ bar, and $T = 299$ K   **Find**: m_{He}
Conceptual Plan: $P, V, T \rightarrow n$ **then** $mol \rightarrow$ **g**

$$PV = nRT \qquad \qquad \mathcal{M}$$

Solution: $PV = nRT$ Rearrange to solve for n.

$$n_{He} = \frac{PV}{RT} = \frac{88\,\cancel{bar} \times 0.35\,\cancel{L}}{0.08314\,\dfrac{\cancel{L} \cdot \cancel{bar}}{mol \cdot \cancel{K}} \times 299\,\cancel{K}} = 1.2553\,mol, \quad 1.\underline{2}553\,\cancel{mol} \times \frac{4.003\,g}{1\,\cancel{mol}} = 5.0\,g\,He$$

Check: The units (g) are correct. The magnitude of the answer (5 g) makes sense because the high pressure and the low volume cancel out (remember 22 L / mol at STP) and so we expect ~ 1 mol and so ~ 4 g.

5.125   **Given**: 15.0 mL HBr in 1.0 min; and 20.3 mL unknown hydrocarbon gas in 1.0 min
Find: formula of unknown gas
Conceptual Plan: **Since these are gases under the same conditions** $V \propto n$, V, time $\rightarrow$ **Rate then**

$$Rate = \frac{V}{time}$$

$\mathcal{M}(\text{HBr})$, Rate (HBr), Rate (Unk) $\rightarrow \mathcal{M}(\text{Unk})$

$$\frac{Rate(HBr)}{Rate(U)} = \sqrt{\frac{\mathcal{M}(U)}{\mathcal{M}(HBr)}}$$

Solution: $Rate(HBr) = \dfrac{V}{time} = \dfrac{15.0\,mL}{1.0\,min} = 15.0\,\dfrac{mL}{min}$, $Rate(Unk) = \dfrac{V}{time} = \dfrac{20.3\,mL}{1.0\,min} = 20.3\,\dfrac{mL}{min}$,

$\dfrac{Rate(HBr)}{Rate(Unk)} = \sqrt{\dfrac{\mathcal{M}(Unk)}{\mathcal{M}(HBr)}}$ Rearrange to solve for $\mathcal{M}(Unk)$.

$$\mathcal{M}(Unk) = \mathcal{M}(HBr)\left(\frac{Rate(HBr)}{Rate(Unk)}\right)^2 = 80.91\,\frac{g}{mol} \times \left(\frac{15.0\,\dfrac{mL}{min}}{20.3\,\dfrac{mL}{min}}\right)^2 = 44.2\,g\,mol^{-1}\,\text{The formula is } C_3H_8, \text{ propane.}$$

Check: The units (g mol^{-1}) are correct. The magnitude of the answer (< HBr) makes sense because the unknown diffused faster and so must be lighter.

5.127 **Given:** 0.583 g neon, $V = 8.00 \times 10^2$ cm^3, $P_{Total} = 1.17$ bar, and $T = 295$ K **Find:** g argon
Conceptual Plan: g $\rightarrow$ *n* and mL $\rightarrow$ L then *n, V, T* $\rightarrow$ P_{Ne} then P_{Ne}, P_{Total} $\rightarrow$ P_{Ar} then

$$\frac{1\,mol}{20.18\,g} \qquad \frac{1\,L}{1000\,mL} \qquad PV = nRT \qquad P_{Total} = P_{Ne} + P_{Ar}$$

$P_{Ar}, V, T \rightarrow n \rightarrow g$
$$PV = nRT \quad \frac{39.95\,g}{1\,mol}$$

Solution: $0.583\,\overline{g\,Ne} \times \dfrac{1\,mol\,Ne}{20.18\,\overline{g\,Ne}} = 0.02888999$ mol Ne $8.00 \times 10^2\,\overline{mL} \times \dfrac{1\,L}{1000\,\overline{mL}} = 0.800$ L

$PV = nRT$ Rearrange to solve for P.

$$P = \frac{nRT}{V} = \frac{0.02888999\,\overline{mol} \times 0.08314\,\frac{L \cdot bar}{mol \cdot K} \times 295\,K}{0.800\,L} = 0.885706\,bar\,Ne$$

$P_{Total} = P_{Ne} + P_{Ar}$ Rearrange to solve for P_{Ar}. $P_{Ar} = P_{Total} - P_{Ne} = 1.17\,bar - 0.885706\,bar = 0.284294$ bar

$PV = nRT$ Rearrange to solve for *n*. $n_{Ar} = \dfrac{PV}{RT} = \dfrac{0.284294\,\overline{bar} \times 0.800\,L}{0.08314\,\frac{L \cdot bar}{mol \cdot K} \times 295\,K} = 0.009273115$ mol Ar

$0.009273115\,\overline{mol\,Ar} \times \dfrac{39.95\,g\,Ar}{1\,\overline{mol\,Ar}} = 0.370461\,g\,Ar = 0.37\,g\,Ar$

Check: The units (g) are correct. The magnitude of the answer (0.4 g) makes sense because the pressure and volume are small.

5.129 **Given:** 75.2% by mass nitrogen + 24.8% by mass krypton, $P_{Total} = 993$ mbar **Find:** P_{Kr}
Solution: Assume 100 g total, so we have 75.2 g N$_2$ and 24.8 g Kr. Converting these masses to moles,
$75.2\,\overline{g\,N_2} \times \dfrac{1\,mol\,N_2}{28.02\,\overline{g\,N_2}} = 2.683797$ mol N$_2$ and $24.8\,\overline{g\,Kr} \times \dfrac{1\,mol\,Kr}{83.80\,\overline{g\,Kr}} = 0.2959427$ mol Kr.

$P_{Kr} = \chi_{Kr}P_{Total} = \dfrac{0.2959427\,mol\,Kr}{2.683797\,mol\,N_2 + 0.2959427\,mol\,Kr}\,993\,mbar\,Kr = 98.6\,mbar\,Kr$

Check: The units (mbar) are correct. The magnitude of the answer (98.6 mbar) makes sense because the mixture is mostly nitrogen by mass, and this dominance is magnified since the molar mass of krypton is larger than the molar mass of nitrogen.

5.131 (a) **Given:** $m_{HC} = 1.75$ g, $V_{CO_2} = 3.17$ L, $P_{CO_2} = 1.0$ bar, $T = 298$ K, $m_{H_2O} = 1.92$ g **Find:** empirical formula for the hydrocarbon
Conceptual Plan: $V_{CO_2}, P_{CO_2}, T \rightarrow n_{CO_2} \rightarrow n_C$; $m_{H_2O}, M_{H_2O} \rightarrow n_{H_2O} \rightarrow n_H$; $n_C, n_H \rightarrow$ Empirical formula

Solution: $n_{CO_2} = \dfrac{PV}{RT} = \dfrac{(1.0\,bar)(3.17\,L)}{(0.08314\,L\,bar\,mol^{-1}\,K^{-1})(298\,K)} = 0.127948$ mol CO$_2$

$n_C = 0.127948\,mol\,CO_2 \times \dfrac{1\,mol\,C}{1\,mol\,CO_2} = 0.127948$ mol C = 0.128 mol C

$n_H = 1.92\,g\,H_2O \times \dfrac{1\,mol\,H_2O}{18.015\,g\,H_2O} \times \dfrac{2\,mol\,H}{1\,mol\,H_2O} = 0.21316$ mol H = 0.213 mol H

$\#\,C\,atoms = \dfrac{0.128}{0.128} = 1$

$\#\,H\,atoms = \dfrac{0.213}{0.128} = 1.66$

Multiplying both numbers by 3 to get a whole number yields the empirical formula C$_3$H$_5$.
Check: Based on the relative mole ratios of C and H, the empirical formula is correct

(b) **Given:** $V_{flask} = 247$ mL, $m_{flask} = 71.814$ g, $m_{flask+HC} = 72.523$, T = 100 °C = 373 K, $P = 813$ torr **Find:** M$_{HC}$
Conceptual Plan: P (torr) $\rightarrow$ P (bar); $V_{flask}, T, P \rightarrow n_{HC}$; $m_{flask}, m_{flask+HC}, n_{HC} \rightarrow$ M$_{HC}$

Solution: $P = 813 \text{ torr} \times \dfrac{1 \text{ bar}}{750.01 \text{ torr}} = 1.08398555 \text{ bar}$

$n_{HC} = \dfrac{PV}{RT} = \dfrac{(1.08398555 \text{ bar})(0.247 \text{ L})}{(0.08314 \text{ L bar mol}^{-1} \text{ K}^{-1})(373 \text{ K})} = 0.0086338 \text{ mol}$

$\mathcal{M} = \dfrac{\Delta m}{n_{HC}} = \dfrac{72.523 \text{ g} - 71.814 \text{ g}}{0.0086338 \text{ mol}} = 82.1 \text{ g mol}^{-1}$

Check: The answer for M is in the correct units. It is also congruous with the molecular formula, because it is a whole number multiple of the empirical formula C_3H_5, which has a mass of 41 g mol^{-1}.

Challenge Problems

5.133   **Given:** $2 \text{ NH}_3 (g) \rightarrow \text{N}_2 (g) + 3 \text{ H}_2 (g)$; $\text{N}_2\text{H}_4 (g) \rightarrow \text{N}_2 (g) + 2 \text{ H}_2 (g)$; initially $P = 0.50$ bar, $T = 300$ K, finally $P = 4.5$ bar, $T = 1200$ K   **Find:** N_2H_4 percent initially

Conceptual Plan: $P_{initial}, T_{initial}, T_{final} \rightarrow P_{final}$ **then determine change in moles of gas**

$$\dfrac{P_{initial}}{T_{initial}} = \dfrac{P_{final}}{T_{final}} \qquad\qquad \dfrac{3 \text{ bar added gas}}{1 \text{ bar NH}_3 \text{ reacted}} \text{ and } \dfrac{2 \text{ bar added gas}}{1 \text{ bar N}_2\text{H}_4 \text{ reacted}}$$

$P_1, P_2 \rightarrow \Delta P$ **write expression for** ΔP **then solve for** $P_{1\text{N}_2\text{H}_4}$ **and** $P_{1\text{NH}_3}$ **finally** $P_{1\text{N}_2\text{H}_4}, P_{1\text{NH}_3} \rightarrow \%$ N_2H_4

$$\Delta P = P_2 - P_1 \quad \Delta P = P_{1\text{NH}_3}\dfrac{3 \text{ bar added gas}}{2 \text{ bar reacted}} + P_{1\text{N}_2\text{H}_4}\dfrac{2 \text{ bar added gas}}{1 \text{ bar reacted}} \text{ where } P_{1,1200K} = P_{1\text{NH}_3} + P_{1\text{N}_2\text{H}_4} \quad \% \text{N}_2\text{H}_4 = \dfrac{P_{\text{N}_2\text{H}_4}}{P_{\text{N}_2\text{H}_4} + P_{\text{NH}_3}} \times 100\%$$

Solution: $\dfrac{P_{initial}}{T_{initial}} = \dfrac{P_{final}}{T_{final}}$ Rearrange to solve for P_{final}. $P_2 = P_1 \times \dfrac{T_2}{T_1} = 0.50 \text{ bar} \times \dfrac{1200 \text{ K}}{300 \text{ K}} = 2.0 \text{ bar}$ if no reaction occurred.

$\Delta P = P_{final} - P_{initial} = 4.5 \text{ bar} - 2.0 \text{ bar} = 2.5 \text{ bar}$, and $P_{1,1200K} = 2.0 \text{ bar} = P_{1\text{NH}_3} + P_{1\text{N}_2\text{H}_4}$ or

$P_{1\text{NH}_3} = 2.0 \text{ bar} - P_{1\text{N}_2\text{H}_4}$.

Substitute this into $\Delta P = P_{1\text{NH}_3}\dfrac{3 \text{ bar added gas}}{2 \text{ bar reacted}} + P_{1\text{N}_2\text{H}_4}\dfrac{2 \text{ bar added gas}}{1 \text{ bar reacted}}$ and solve for $P_{1\text{N}_2\text{H}_4}$.

$\Delta P = 2.5 \text{ bar} = (2.0 \text{ bar} - P_{1\text{N}_2\text{H}_4})\dfrac{3 \text{ bar added gas}}{2 \text{ bar reacted}} + P_{1\text{N}_2\text{H}_4}\dfrac{2 \text{ bar added gas}}{1 \text{ bar reacted}} \rightarrow$

$P_{1\text{N}_2\text{H}_4} = 3.0 \text{ bar} - 2.5 \text{ bar} = 0.5 \text{ bar}$ and $P_{\text{NH}_3} = 2.0 \text{ bar} - 0.5 \text{ bar} = 1.5 \text{ bar}$ finally

$\% \text{N}_2\text{H}_4 = \dfrac{P_{\text{N}_2\text{H}_4}}{P_{\text{N}_2\text{H}_4} + P_{\text{NH}_3}} \times 100\% = \dfrac{0.5 \text{ bar}}{0.5 \text{ bar} + 1.5 \text{ bar}} \times 100\% = \underline{25\%} \text{ N}_2\text{H}_4 = 30\% \text{ N}_2\text{H}_4$

Check: The units (%) are correct. The magnitude of the answer (30%) makes sense because if it were all N_2H_4 the final pressure would have been approximately 6 bar. Since we are closer to the initial pressure than this maximum pressure, less than half of the gas is N_2H_4.

5.135   **Given:** $2 \text{ CO}_2 (g) \rightarrow 2 \text{ CO} (g) + \text{O}_2 (g)$; initially $P = 10.0$ bar, $T = 701$ K, finally $P = 22.5$ bar, $T = 1401$ K

Find: mole percent decomposed

Conceptual Plan: $P_{initial}, T_{initial}, T_{final} \rightarrow P_{final}$ **then determine change in moles of gas**

$$\dfrac{P_{initial}}{T_{initial}} = \dfrac{P_{final}}{T_{final}} \qquad\qquad \dfrac{1 \text{ bar added gas}}{2 \text{ bar CO}_2 \text{ reacted}}$$

$P_1, P_2 \rightarrow \Delta P$ **write expression for** ΔP **then solve for** $P_{\text{CO}_2 \text{ reacted}}$ **finally**

$$\Delta P = P_2 - P_1 \qquad\qquad \Delta P = P_{\text{CO}_2 \text{ reacted}}\dfrac{1 \text{ bar added gas}}{2 \text{ bar CO}_2 \text{ reacted}}$$

$P_{final}, P_{\text{CO}_2 \text{ reacted}} \rightarrow \%$ **CO₂ decomposed**

$$\% \text{CO}_2 \text{ decomposed} = \dfrac{P_{\text{CO}_2 \text{ reacted}}}{P_{final}} \times 100\%$$

Solution: $\dfrac{P_{initial}}{T_{initial}} = \dfrac{P_{final}}{T_{final}}$ Rearrange to solve for P_{final}. $P_2 = P_1 \times \dfrac{T_2}{T_1} = 10.0 \text{ bar} \times \dfrac{1401 \text{ K}}{701 \text{ K}} = 19.985735 \text{ bar}$

$\Delta P = P_{final} - P_{initial} = 22.5 \text{ bar} - 19.985735 \text{ bar} = 2.514265 \text{ bar}$,

$\Delta P = P_{\text{CO}_2 \text{ reacted}}\dfrac{1 \text{ bar added gas}}{2 \text{ bar CO}_2 \text{ reacted}}$ or the pressure increases 1 bar for each 2 bar of gas decomposed, so 5.02853 bar decomposes and then

$$\% CO_2 \text{ decomposed} = \frac{P_{CO_2 \text{ reacted}}}{P_{\text{final}}} \times 100\% = \frac{5.02853 \text{ bar}}{19.875735 \text{ bar}} \times 100\% = 25.1606\% CO_2 \text{ decomposed} =$$

$25\% CO_2$ decomposed

Check: The units (%) are correct. The magnitude of the answer (25%) makes sense because if all of the gas decomposed the final pressure would have been 40 bar. Since we are much closer to the initial pressure than this maximum pressure, much less than half of the gas decomposed.

5.137　**Given:** CH_4: $V = 155$ mL at STP; O_2: $V = 885$ mL at STP; NO: $V = 55.5$ mL at STP; mixed in a flask: $V = 2.0$ L, $T = 275$ K, and 90.0% of limiting reagent used　**Find:** Ps of all components and P_{Total}

Conceptual Plan: CH_4: mL $\rightarrow$ L $\rightarrow$ mol_{CO_4} $\rightarrow$ mol_{CO_2} and

$$\frac{1 \text{ L}}{1000 \text{ mL}} \quad \frac{1 \text{ mol}}{22.7 \text{ L}} \quad \frac{1 \text{ mol CO}_2}{5 \text{ mol NO}}$$

O_2: mL $\rightarrow$ L $\rightarrow$ mol_{O_2} $\rightarrow$ mol_{CO_2} and NO: mL $\rightarrow$ L $\rightarrow$ mol_{NO} $\rightarrow$ mol_{CO_2}

$$\frac{1 \text{ L}}{1000 \text{ mL}} \frac{1 \text{ mol}}{22.7 \text{ L}} \quad \frac{1 \text{ mol CO}_2}{5 \text{ mol O}_2} \qquad\qquad \frac{1 \text{ L}}{1000 \text{ mL}} \frac{1 \text{ mol}}{22.7 \text{ L}} \quad \frac{1 \text{ mol CO}_2}{5 \text{ mol NO}}$$

the smallest yield determines the limiting reagent then initial mol_{NO} $\rightarrow$ reacted mol_{NO} $\rightarrow$ final mol_{NO}

NO is the limiting reagent　　　　90.0%　　　　0.100 x initial mol_{no}

reacted mol_{NO} $\rightarrow$ reacted mol_{CH_4} then initial mol_{CH_4}, reacted mol_{CH_4} $\rightarrow$ final mol_{CH_4} then

$$\frac{1 \text{ mol CH}_4}{5 \text{ mol NO}}$$

initial mol_{CH_4} – reacted mol_{CH_4} = final mol_{CH_4}

final mol_{CH_4}, V, T $\rightarrow$ final P_{CH_4} and reacted mol_{NO} $\rightarrow$ reacted mol_{O_2} then

$$PV = nRT \qquad\qquad \frac{5 \text{ mol O}_2}{5 \text{ mol NO}}$$

initial mol_{O_2}, reacted mol_{O_2} $\rightarrow$ final mol_{O_2} then final mol_{O_2}, V, T $\rightarrow$ final P_{O_2} and

initial mol_{O_2} – reacted mol_{O_2} = final mol_{O_2}　　　$PV = nRT$

final mol_{NO}, V, T $\rightarrow$ final P_{NO} and theoretical mol_{CO_2} from NO $\rightarrow$ final mol_{CO_2}

$$PV = nRT \qquad\qquad\qquad\qquad 90.0\%$$

final mol_{CO_2}, V, T $\rightarrow$ P_{CO_2} then final mol_{CO_2} $\rightarrow$ mol_{H_2O} then mol_{H_2O}, V, T $\rightarrow$ P_{H_2O} and

$$PV = nRT \qquad\qquad \frac{1 \text{ mol H}_2\text{O}}{1 \text{ mol CO}_2} \qquad\qquad PV = nRT$$

final mol_{CO_2} $\rightarrow$ mol_{NO_2} then mol_{NO_2}, V, T $\rightarrow$ P_{NO_2} and final mol_{CO_2} $\rightarrow$ mol_{OH} then

$$\frac{1 \text{ mol NO}_2}{1 \text{ mol CO}_2} \qquad\qquad PV = nRT \qquad\qquad \frac{2 \text{ mol OH}}{1 \text{ mol CO}_2}$$

mol_{OH}, V, T $\rightarrow$ P_{OH} finally P_{CH_4}, P_{O_2}, P_{NO}, P_{CO_2}, P_{H_2O}, P_{NO_2}, P_{OH} $\rightarrow$ P_{Ttotal}

$$PV = nRT \qquad\qquad\qquad P_{\text{Total}} = \sum P$$

Solution: CH_4: $155 \text{ mL} \times \dfrac{1 \text{ L}}{1000 \text{ mL}} \times \dfrac{1 \text{ mol CH}_4}{22.7 \text{ L}} \times \dfrac{1 \text{ mol CO}_2}{1 \text{ mol CH}_4} = 0.00682819$ mol CO_2,

O_2: $885 \text{ mL} \times \dfrac{1 \text{ L}}{1000 \text{ mL}} \times \dfrac{1 \text{ mol O}_2}{22.7 \text{ L}} = 0.0389868$ mol O_2 $\times \dfrac{1 \text{ mol CO}_2}{5 \text{ mol O}_2} = 0.00779735$ mol CO_2

NO: $55.5 \text{ mL} \times \dfrac{1 \text{ L}}{1000 \text{ mL}} \times \dfrac{1 \text{ mol NO}}{22.7 \text{ L}} \times \dfrac{1 \text{ mol CO}_2}{5 \text{ mol NO}} = 0.000488987$ mol CO_2

0.000488987 mol CO_2 is the smallest yield, so NO is the limiting reagent.

$55.5 \text{ mL} \times \dfrac{1 \text{ L}}{1000 \text{ mL}} \times \dfrac{1 \text{ mol NO}}{22.7 \text{ L}} = 0.0024449$ mol NO

reacted mol NO $= 0.900 \times$ mol NO $= 0.900 \times 0.0024449$ mol NO $= 0.00220041$ mol NO,

unreacted mol NO $= 0.100 \times$ mol NO $= 0.100 \times 0.0024449$ mol NO $= 0.00024449$ mol NO,

0.00220041 mol NO $\times \dfrac{1 \text{ mol CH}_4}{5 \text{ mol NO}} = 0.000440082$ mol CH_4 reacted,

0.00682819 mol CH_4 $- 0.000440082$ mol CH_4 reacted $= 0.006388108$ mol CH_4 then $PV = nRT$

Rearrange to solve for P. $P = \dfrac{nRT}{V} = \dfrac{0.006388108 \text{ mol} \times 0.08314 \frac{\text{L} \cdot \text{bar}}{\text{mol} \cdot \text{K}} \times 275 \text{ K}}{2.0 \text{ L}} = 0.0730$ bar CH_4 remaining

0.00220041 mol NO $\times \dfrac{5 \text{ mol O}_2}{5 \text{ mol NO}} = 0.00220041$ mol O_2 reacted,

0.0389868 mol O_2 $- 0.00220041$ mol O_2 reacted $= 0.0367864$ mol O_2

$$P = \frac{nRT}{V} = \frac{0.0367864 \text{ mol} \times 0.08314 \frac{\text{L} \cdot \text{bar}}{\text{mol} \cdot \text{K}} \times 275 \text{ K}}{2.0 \text{ L}} = 0.420 \text{ bar } O_2 \text{ remaining}$$

$$P = \frac{nRT}{V} = \frac{0.00024449 \text{ mol} \times 0.08314 \frac{\text{L} \cdot \text{bar}}{\text{mol} \cdot \text{K}} \times 275 \text{ K}}{2.0 \text{ L}} = 0.00279 \text{ bar } NO \text{ remaining}$$

$$0.00220041 \text{ mol NO} \times \frac{1 \text{ mol } CO_2}{5 \text{ mol NO}} = 0.000440082 \text{ mol } CO_2$$

$$P = \frac{nRT}{V} = \frac{0.000440082 \text{ mol} \times 0.08314 \frac{\text{L} \cdot \text{bar}}{\text{mol} \cdot \text{K}} \times 275 \text{ K}}{2.0 \text{ L}} = 0.00503 \text{ bar } CO_2 \text{ produced}$$

$$0.00220041 \text{ mol NO} \times \frac{1 \text{ mol } H_2O}{5 \text{ mol NO}} = 0.000440082 \text{ mol } H_2O$$

$$P = \frac{nRT}{V} = \frac{0.000440082 \text{ mol} \times 0.08314 \frac{\text{L} \cdot \text{bar}}{\text{mol} \cdot \text{K}} \times 275 \text{ K}}{2.0 \text{ L}} = 0.00503 \text{ bar } H_2O \text{ produced}$$

$$0.00220041 \text{ mol NO} \times \frac{5 \text{ mol } NO_2}{5 \text{ mol NO}} = 0.00220041 \text{ mol } NO_2$$

$$P = \frac{nRT}{V} = \frac{0.00220041 \text{ mol} \times 0.08314 \frac{\text{L} \cdot \text{bar}}{\text{mol} \cdot \text{K}} \times 275 \text{ K}}{2.0 \text{ L}} = 0.0251 \text{ bar } NO_2 \text{ produced}$$

$$0.00220041 \text{ mol NO} \times \frac{2 \text{ mol } OH}{5 \text{ mol NO}} = 0.000880164 \text{ mol } OH$$

$$P = \frac{nRT}{V} = \frac{0.000880164 \text{ mol} \times 0.08314 \frac{\text{L} \cdot \text{bar}}{\text{mol} \cdot \text{K}} \times 275 \text{ K}}{2.0 \text{ L}} = 0.0101 \text{ bar } OH \text{ produced}$$

$$P_{Total} = \sum P$$
$$= 0.0730 \text{ bar} + 0.420 \text{ bar} + 0.00279 \text{ bar} + 0.00503 \text{ bar} + 0.00503 \text{ bar} + 0.0251 \text{ bar} + 0.0101 \text{ bar}$$
$$= 0.541 \text{ bar}$$

Check: The units (bar) are correct. The magnitude of the answers is reasonable. The limiting reagent has the lowest pressure. The product pressures are in line with the ratios of the stoichiometric coefficients.

5.139   **Given:** $P_{CH_4} + P_{C_2H_6} = 0.53$ bar, $P_{CO_2} + P_{H_2O} = 2.2$ bar   **Find:** χ_{CH_4}
Conceptual Plan: Write balanced reactions to determine change in moles of gas for CH_4 and C_2H_6.

$2 CH_4 (g) + 4 O_2 (g) \longrightarrow 4 H_2O (g) + 2 CO_2 (g)$ and $2 C_2H_6 (g) + 7 O_2 (g) \longrightarrow 6 H_2O (g) + 4 CO_2 (g)$ thus $\frac{6 \text{ mol gases}}{2 \text{ mol } CH_4}$ $\frac{10 \text{ mol gases}}{2 \text{ mol } C_2H_6}$

write expression for final pressure, substituting in data given $\longrightarrow \chi_{CH_4}$

$$\chi_{CH_4} = \frac{n_{CH_4}}{n_{CH_4} + n_{C_2H_6}} \text{ and } \chi_{C_2H_6} = 1 - \chi_{CH_4}$$

$P_{CH_4} = \chi_{CH_4} P_{Total}$ $P_{C_2H_6} = \chi_{C_2H_6} P_{Total}$ $P_{Final} = \left(\chi_{CH_4} P_{Total} \times \frac{6 \text{ mol gases}}{2 \text{ mol } CH_4}\right) + \left((1 - \chi_{CH_4}) P_{Total} \times \frac{10 \text{ mol gases}}{2 \text{ mol } C_2H_6}\right)$

Solution:

$$P_{Final} = \left(\chi_{CH_4} \times 0.53 \text{ bar} \times \frac{6 \text{ mol gases}}{2 \text{ mol } CH_4}\right) + \left((1 - \chi_{CH_4}) \times 0.53 \text{ bar} \times \frac{10 \text{ mol gases}}{2 \text{ mol } C_2H_6}\right) = 2.2 \text{ bar}$$

Substitute as above for $\chi_{C_2H_6}$, then to solve for $\chi_{CH_4} = 0.42$.

Check: The units (none) are correct. The magnitude of the answer (0.42) makes sense because if it were all methane the final pressure would have been 1.59 bar, and if it were all ethane the final pressure would have been 2.65 bar. Since we are closer to the latter pressure, we expect the mole fraction of methane to be less than 0.5.

Conceptual Problems

5.141   Since the passengers have more mass than the balloon, they have more momentum than the balloon. The passengers will continue to travel in their original direction longer. The car is slowing so the relative position of the passengers is to move forward and the balloon to move backwards. The opposite happens upon acceleration.

5.143   B is the limiting reactant (2.0 L of B requires 1.0 L A to completely react). The final container will have 0.5 L A and 2.0 L C, so the final volume will be 2.5 L. The change will be ((2.5 L/3.5 L) x 100%) – 100% = – 29%.

5.145   (a)   False – All gases have the same average kinetic energy at the same temperature.

(b)   False – The gases will have the same partial pressures since we have the same number of moles of each.

(c)   False – The average velocity of the B molecules will be less than that of the A molecules since the Bs are heavier.

(d)   True – Since B molecules are heavier they will contribute more to the density ($d = m/V$).

6 Thermochemistry

Review Questions

6.1   Thermochemistry is the study of the relationship between chemistry and energy. It is important because energy and its uses are critical to our society. It is important to understand how much energy is required or released in a process.

6.3   Kinetic energy is energy associated with the motion of an object. Potential energy is energy associated with the position or composition of an object. Examples of kinetic energy are water at the top of Niagara Falls, gas molecules, and a raging river. Examples of potential energy are a curling stone sliding down the ice, a compressed spring, and molecules.

6.5   The SI unit of energy is $kg\frac{m^2}{s^2}$, defined as the joule (J), named after the English scientist James Joule. Other units of energy are the kilojoule (kJ), the calorie (cal), the Calorie (Cal), and the kilowatt-hour (kWh).

6.7   According to the first law, a device that would continually produce energy with no energy input, sometimes known as a perpetual motion machine, cannot exist because the best we can do with energy is break even.

6.9   The internal energy (U) of a system is the sum of the kinetic and potential energies of all of the particles that compose the system. Internal energy is a state function.

6.11   If the reactants have a lower internal energy than the products, ΔU_{sys} is positive and energy flows into the system from the surroundings.

6.13   The internal energy (U) of a system is the sum of the kinetic and potential energies of all of the particles that compose the system. The change in the internal energy of the system (ΔU) must be the sum of the heat transferred (q) and the work done (w): $\Delta U = q + w$.

6.15   The heat capacity of a system is usually defined as the quantity of heat required to change its temperature by 1 °C. Heat capacity (C) is a measure of the system's ability to hold thermal energy without undergoing a large change in temperature. The difference between heat capacity (C) and specific heat capacity (C_s) is that the specific heat capacity is the amount of heat required to raise the temperature of *1 gram* of the substance by 1 °C.

6.17   When two objects of different temperatures come in direct contact heat flows from the higher temperature object to the lower temperature object. The amount of heat lost by the warmer object is equal to the amount of heat gained by the cooler object. The warmer object's temperature will drop and the cooler object's temperature will rise until they reach the same temperature. The magnitude of these temperature changes depends on the mass and heat capacities of the two objects.

6.19   In calorimetry, the thermal energy exchanged between the reaction (defined as the system) and the surroundings is measured by observing the change in temperature of the surroundings. A bomb calorimeter is used to measure the $\Delta_r U$ for combustion reactions. The calorimeter includes a tight fitting, sealed container that forces the reaction to occur at constant volume. A coffee-cup calorimeter is used to measure $\Delta_r H$ for many aqueous reactions. The calorimeter consists of two Styrofoam® coffee cups, one inserted into the other, to provide insulation from the laboratory environment. Since the reaction happens under conditions of constant pressure (open to the atmosphere), $q_r = q_p = \Delta_r H$.

6.21 An endothermic reaction has a positive ΔH and absorbs heat from the surroundings. An endothermic reaction feels cold to the touch. An exothermic reaction has a negative ΔH and gives off heat to the surroundings. An exothermic reaction feels warm to the touch.

6.23 The internal energy of a chemical system is the sum of its kinetic energy and its potential energy. It is this potential energy that absorbs the energy in an endothermic chemical reaction. In an endothermic reaction, as some bonds break and others form, the protons and electrons go from an arrangement of lower potential energy to one of higher potential energy, absorbing thermal energy in the process. This absorption of thermal energy reduces the kinetic energy of the system. This is detected as a drop in temperature.

6.25 (a) If a reaction is multiplied by a factor, the ΔH is multiplied by the same factor.

(b) If a reaction is reversed, the sign of ΔH is reversed.

The relationships hold because H is a state function. Twice as much energy is contained in twice the quantity of reactants or products. If the reaction is reversed, the final and initial states have been switched and the direction of heat flow is reversed.

6.27 The standard state is defined as follows: for a gas, the pure gas at a pressure of exactly 1 bar; for a liquid or solid, the pure substance in its most stable form at a pressure of 1 bar and the temperature of interest (often taken to be 25 °C); and for a substance in solution, a concentration of exactly 1 mol L^{-1}. The standard enthalpy change (ΔH°) is the change in enthalpy for a process when all reactants and products are in their standard states. The superscript degree sign indicates standard states.

6.29 To calculate $\Delta_r H^\circ$, subtract the heats of formations of the reactants multiplied by their stoichiometric coefficients from the heats of formation of the products multiplied by their stoichiometric coefficients. In the form of an equation:

$$\Delta_r H^\circ = \sum n_p \Delta_f H^\circ (\text{products}) - \sum n_r \Delta_f H^\circ (\text{reactants})$$

6.31 One of the main problems associated with the burning of fossil fuels is that, even though they are abundant in the Earth's crust, they are a finite and nonrenewable energy source. The other major problems associated with fossil fuel use are related to the products of combustion. Three major environmental problems associated with the emissions of fossil fuel combustion are air pollution, acid rain, and global warming. One of the main products of fossil fuel combustion is carbon dioxide (CO_2), which is a greenhouse gas.

Problems by Topic

Energy Units

6.33 (a) **Given:** 534 kWh **Find:** J
Conceptual Plan: kWh → J

$$\frac{3.60 \times 10^6 \text{ J}}{1 \text{ kWh}}$$

Solution: $534 \text{ kWh} \times \dfrac{3.60 \times 10^6 \text{ J}}{1 \text{ kWh}} = 1.92 \times 10^9 \text{ J}$

Check: The units (J) are correct. The magnitude of the answer (10^9) makes physical sense because a kWh is much larger than a Joule, so the answer increases.

(b) **Given:** 215 kJ **Find:** Cal
Conceptual Plan: kJ → J → Cal

$$\frac{1000 \text{ J}}{1 \text{ kJ}} \quad \frac{1 \text{ Cal}}{4184 \text{ J}}$$

Solution: $215 \text{ kJ} \times \dfrac{1000 \text{ J}}{1 \text{ kJ}} \times \dfrac{1 \text{ Cal}}{4184 \text{ J}} = 51.4 \text{ Cal}$

Check: The units (Cal) are correct. The magnitude of the answer (51) makes physical sense because a Calorie is about $\frac{1}{4}$ of a kJ, so the answer decreases by a factor of about four.

(c) **Given:** 567 Cal **Find:** J
Conceptual Plan: Cal → J
$$\frac{4184\,J}{1\,Cal}$$
Solution: 567 C̶a̶l̶ x $\frac{4184\,J}{1\,C̶a̶l̶}$ = 2.37 x 10^6 J
Check: The units (J) are correct. The magnitude of the answer (10^6) makes physical sense because a Calorie is much larger than a Joule, so the answer increases.

(d) **Given:** 2.85 x 10^3 J **Find:** cal
Conceptual Plan: J → cal
$$\frac{1\,cal}{4.184\,J}$$
Solution: 2.85 x 10^3 J̶ x $\frac{1\,cal}{4.184\,J̶}$ = 681 cal
Check: The units (cal) are correct. The magnitude of the answer (680) makes physical sense because a J is about $\frac{1}{4}$ the size of a calorie, so the answer decreases by a factor of about four.

6.35 (a) **Given:** 2387 Cal **Find:** J
Conceptual Plan: Cal → J
$$\frac{4184\,J}{1\,Cal}$$
Solution: 2387 C̶a̶l̶ x $\frac{4184\,J}{1\,C̶a̶l̶}$ = 9.987 x 10^6 J
Check: The units (J) are correct. The magnitude of the answer (10^7) makes physical sense because a Calorie is much larger than a Joule, so the answer increases.

(b) **Given:** 2387 Cal **Find:** kJ
Conceptual Plan: Cal → J → kJ
$$\frac{4184\,J}{1\,Cal} \quad \frac{1\,kJ}{1000\,J}$$
Solution: 2387 C̶a̶l̶ x $\frac{4184\,J̶}{1\,C̶a̶l̶}$ x $\frac{1\,kJ}{1000\,J̶}$ = 9.987 x 10^3 kJ
Check: The units (kJ) are correct. The magnitude of the answer (10^3) makes physical sense because a Calorie is larger than a kJ, so the answer increases.

(c) **Given:** 2387 Cal **Find:** kWh
Conceptual Plan: Cal → J → kWh
$$\frac{4184\,J}{1\,Cal} \quad \frac{1\,kWh}{3.60 \times 10^6\,J}$$
Solution: 2387 C̶a̶l̶ x $\frac{4184\,J̶}{1\,C̶a̶l̶}$ x $\frac{1\,kWh}{3.60 \times 10^6\,J̶}$ = 2.774 kWh
Check: The units (kWh) are correct. The magnitude of the answer (3) makes physical sense because a Calorie is much smaller than a kWh, so the answer decreases.

Internal Energy, Heat, and Work

6.37 (d) $\Delta U_{sys} = -\Delta U_{surr}$ If energy change of the system is negative, energy is being transferred from the system to the surroundings, decreasing the energy of the system and increasing the energy of the surroundings. The amount of energy lost by the system must go somewhere, so the amount gained by the surroundings is equal and opposite to that lost by the system.

6.39 (a) The energy exchange is primarily heat since the skin (part of the surroundings) is cooled. There is a small expansion (work) since water is being converted from a liquid to a gas. The sign of ΔU_{sys} is positive since the surroundings cool.

(b)   The energy exchange is primarily work. The sign of ΔU_{sys} is negative since the system is expanding (doing work on the surroundings).

(c)   The energy exchange is primarily heat. The sign of ΔU_{sys} is positive since the system is being heated by the flame.

6.41   **Given:** 622 kJ heat released; 105 kJ work done on surroundings   **Find:** ΔU_{sys}
         Conceptual Plan: interpret language to determine the sign of the two terms then $q, w \rightarrow \Delta U_{sys}$
$$\Delta U = q + w$$

         Solution: Since heat is released from the system to the surroundings, $q = -622$ kJ; since the system is doing work on the surroundings, $w = -105$ kJ. $\Delta U = q + w = -622$ kJ $- 105$ kJ $= -727$ kJ $= -7.27 \times 10^2$ kJ.
         Check: The units (kJ) are correct. The magnitude of the answer (-730) makes physical sense because both terms are negative.

6.43   **Given:** 655 J heat absorbed; 344 J work done on surroundings   **Find:** ΔU_{sys}
         Conceptual Plan: interpret language to determine the sign of the two terms then $q, w \rightarrow \Delta U_{sys}$
$$\Delta U = q + w$$

         Solution: Since heat is absorbed by the system, $q = +655$ J; since the system is doing work on the surroundings, $w = -344$ J. $\Delta U = q + w = 655$ J $- 344$ J $= 311$ J.
         Check: The units (J) are correct. The magnitude of the answer ($+300$) makes physical sense because heat term dominates over the work term.

Heat, Heat Capacity, and Work

6.45   Cooler A had more ice after three hours because most of the ice in cooler B was melted in order to cool the soft drinks that started at room temperature. In cooler A the drinks were already cold and so the ice only needed to maintain this cool temperature.

6.47   **Given:** 1.50 L water, $T_i = 25.0$ °C, $T_f = 100.0$ °C, d $= 1.0$ g mL^{-1} **Find:** q
         Conceptual Plan: L $\rightarrow$ mL $\rightarrow$ g and pull C_s from Table 6.4 and $T_i, T_f \rightarrow \Delta T$ then $m, C_s, \Delta T \rightarrow q$
$$\frac{1000\ mL}{1\ L} \qquad \frac{1.0\ g}{1.0\ mL} \qquad 4.184\ \frac{J}{g \cdot °C} \qquad\qquad \Delta T = T_f - T_i \qquad\qquad q = mC_s\Delta T$$

         Solution: $1.50\ \cancel{L} \times \dfrac{1000\ \cancel{mL}}{1\ \cancel{L}} \times \dfrac{1.0\ g}{1.0\ \cancel{mL}} = 1500$ g and $\Delta T = T_f - T_i = 100.0$ °C $- 25.0$ °C $= 75.0$ °C

         then $q = mC_s\Delta T = 1500\ \cancel{g} \times 4.184 \dfrac{J}{\cancel{g} \cdot \cancel{°C}} \times 75.0\ \cancel{°C} = 4.7 \times 10^5$ J

         Check: The units (J) are correct. The magnitude of the answer (10^6) makes physical sense because there is such a large mass, a significant temperature change, and a high specific heat capacity material.

6.49   (a)   **Given:** 25 g gold, $T_i = 27.0$ °C, $q = 2.35$ kJ   **Find:** T_f
            Conceptual Plan: kJ $\rightarrow$ J and pull C_s from Table 6.4 then $m, C_s, q \rightarrow \Delta T$ then $T_i, \Delta T \rightarrow T_f$
$$\frac{1000\ J}{1\ kJ} \qquad\qquad 0.128\ \frac{J}{g \cdot °C} \qquad\qquad q = mC_s\Delta T \qquad\qquad \Delta T = T_f - T_i$$

            Solution: $2.35\ \cancel{kJ} \times \dfrac{1000\ J}{1\ \cancel{kJ}} = 2350$ J then $q = mC_s\Delta T$. Rearrange to solve for ΔT.

            $\Delta T = \dfrac{q}{mC_s} = \dfrac{2350\ \cancel{J}}{25\ \cancel{g} \times 0.128 \dfrac{\cancel{J}}{\cancel{g} \cdot °C}} = 734.375$ °C finally $\Delta T = T_f - T_i$. Rearrange to solve for T_f.

            $T_f = \Delta T + T_i = 734.375$ °C $+ 27.0$ °C $= 760$ °C

            Check: The units (°C) are correct. The magnitude of the answer (760) makes physical sense because there is such a large amount of heat absorbed, such a small mass, and specific heat capacity. The temperature change should be very large.

    (b)   **Given:** 25 g silver, $T_i = 27.0$ °C, $q = 2.35$ kJ   **Find:** T_f
            Conceptual Plan: kJ $\rightarrow$ J and pull C_s from Table 6.4 then $m, C_s, q \rightarrow \Delta T$ then $T_i, \Delta T \rightarrow T_f$
$$\frac{1000\ J}{1\ kJ} \qquad\qquad 0.235\ \frac{J}{g \cdot °C} \qquad\qquad q = mC_s\Delta T \qquad\qquad \Delta T = T_f - T_i$$

Solution: $2.35 \text{ kJ} \times \dfrac{1000 \text{ J}}{1 \text{ kJ}} = 2350 \text{ J}$ then $q = mC_s\Delta T$. Rearrange to solve for ΔT.

$$\Delta T = \frac{q}{mC_s} = \frac{2350 \text{ J}}{25 \text{ g} \times 0.235 \dfrac{\text{J}}{\text{g} \cdot {}^\circ\text{C}}} = 400 \text{ }^\circ\text{C} \text{ finally } \Delta T = T_f - T_i. \text{ Rearrange to solve for } T_f.$$

$T_f = \Delta T + T_i = 400 \text{ }^\circ\text{C} + 27.0 \text{ }^\circ\text{C} = 430 \text{ }^\circ\text{C}$

Check: The units ($^\circ$C) are correct. The magnitude of the answer (430) makes physical sense because there is such a large amount of heat absorbed, such a small mass, and specific heat capacity. The temperature change should be very large. The temperature change should be less than that of the gold because the specific heat capacity is greater.

(c)   **Given:** 25 g aluminum, $T_i = 27.0 \text{ }^\circ\text{C}$, $q = 2.35$ kJ   **Find:** T_f
Conceptual Plan: kJ $\rightarrow$ J and pull C_s from Table 6.4 then $m, C_s, q \rightarrow \Delta T$ then $T_i, \Delta T \rightarrow T_f$

$$\frac{1000 \text{ J}}{1 \text{ kJ}} \qquad\qquad 0.903 \frac{\text{J}}{\text{g} \cdot {}^\circ\text{C}} \qquad\qquad q = mC_s\Delta T \qquad\qquad \Delta T = T_f - T_i$$

Solution: $2.35 \text{ kJ} \times \dfrac{1000 \text{ J}}{1 \text{ kJ}} = 2350 \text{ J}$ then $q = mC_s\Delta T$. Rearrange to solve for ΔT.

$$\Delta T = \frac{q}{mC_s} = \frac{2350 \text{ J}}{25 \text{ g} \times 0.903 \dfrac{\text{J}}{\text{g} \cdot {}^\circ\text{C}}} = 104.10 {}^\circ\text{C} \text{ finally } \Delta T = T_f - T_i. \text{ Rearrange to solve for } T_f.$$

$T_f = \Delta T + T_i = 104.10 \text{ }^\circ\text{C} + 27.0 \text{ }^\circ\text{C} = 130 \text{ }^\circ\text{C}$

Check: The units ($^\circ$C) are correct. The magnitude of the answer (130) makes physical sense because there is such a large amount of heat absorbed and such a small mass. The temperature change should be less than that of the silver because the specific heat capacity is greater.

(d)   **Given:** 25 g water, $T_i = 27.0 \text{ }^\circ\text{C}$, $q = 2.35$ kJ   **Find:** T_f
Conceptual Plan: kJ $\rightarrow$ J and pull C_s from Table 6.4 then $m, C_s, q \rightarrow \Delta T$ then $T_i, \Delta T \rightarrow T_f$

$$\frac{1000 \text{ J}}{1 \text{ kJ}} \qquad\qquad 4.184 \frac{\text{J}}{\text{g} \cdot {}^\circ\text{C}} \qquad\qquad q = mC_s\Delta T \qquad\qquad \Delta T = T_f - T_i$$

Solution: $2.35 \text{ kJ} \times \dfrac{1000 \text{ J}}{1 \text{ kJ}} = 2350 \text{ J}$ then $q = mC_s\Delta T$. Rearrange to solve for ΔT.

$$\Delta T = \frac{q}{mC_s} = \frac{2350 \text{ J}}{25 \text{ g} \times 4.184 \dfrac{\text{J}}{\text{g} \cdot {}^\circ\text{C}}} = 22.488 {}^\circ\text{C} \text{ finally } \Delta T = T_f - T_i. \text{ Rearrange to solve for } T_f.$$

$T_f = \Delta T + T_i = 22.488 \text{ }^\circ\text{C} + 27.0 \text{ }^\circ\text{C} = 49 \text{ }^\circ\text{C}$

Check: The units ($^\circ$C) are correct. The magnitude of the answer (49) makes physical sense because there is such a large amount of heat absorbed and such a small mass. The temperature change should be less than that of the aluminum because the specific heat capacity is greater.

6.51   **Given:** $V_i = 0.0$ L, $V_f = 2.5$ L, $P = 1.1$ bar   **Find:** w (J)
Conceptual Plan: $V_i, V_f \rightarrow \Delta V$ then $P, \Delta V \rightarrow w$ (L bar) $\rightarrow w$ (J)

$$\Delta V = V_f - V_i \qquad\qquad w = -P\Delta V \qquad\qquad \frac{100.0 \text{ J}}{1 \text{ L} \cdot \text{bar}}$$

Solution: $\Delta V = V_f - V_i = 2.5\text{L} - 0.0\text{L} = 2.5\text{L}$ then

$$w = -P\Delta V = -1.1 \text{ bar} \times 2.5 \text{ L} \times \frac{100.0 \text{ J}}{1 \text{ L} \cdot \text{bar}} = -2.8 \times 10^2 \text{ J}$$

Check: The units (J) are correct. The magnitude of the answer (–2.8) makes physical sense because this is an expansion (negative work) and we have $\sim$ atmospheric pressure and a small volume of expansion.

6.53   **Given:** $q = 565$ J absorbed, $V_i = 0.10$ L, $V_f = 0.85$ L, $P = 1.0$ bar   **Find:** ΔU_{sys}
Conceptual Plan: $V_i, V_f \rightarrow \Delta V$ and interpret language to determine the sign of the heat

$$\Delta V = V_f - V_i \qquad\qquad\qquad\qquad q = +565 \text{ J}$$

then $P, \Delta V \rightarrow w$ (L bar) $\rightarrow w$ (J) finally $q, w \rightarrow \Delta U_{sys}$

$$w = -P\Delta V \qquad \frac{100.0 \text{ J}}{1 \text{ L} \cdot \text{bar}} \qquad\qquad \Delta U = q + w$$

Solution: $\Delta V = V_f - V_i = 0.85 \text{ L} - 0.10 \text{ L} = 0.75 \text{ L}$ then

$$w = -P\Delta V = -1.0 \text{ bar} \times 0.75 \text{ L} \times \frac{100.0 \text{ J}}{1 \text{ L} \cdot \text{bar}} = -75 \text{ J} \quad \Delta U = q + w = +565 \text{ J} - 75 \text{ J} = 490 \text{ J}$$

Check: The units (J) are correct. The magnitude of the answer (500) makes physical sense because the heat absorbed dominated the small expansion work (negative work).

Enthalpy and Thermochemical Stoichiometry

6.55   **Given:** 1 mol fuel, 3452 kJ heat produced; 11 kJ work done on surroundings   **Find:** ΔU_{sys}, ΔH
Conceptual Plan: interpret language to determine the sign of the two terms
then $q \rightarrow \Delta H$ **and** $q, w \rightarrow \Delta U_{sys}$
$$\Delta H = q_p \qquad \Delta U = q + w$$
Solution: Since heat is produced by the system to the surroundings, $q = -3452$ kJ; since the system is doing work on the surroundings, $w = -11$ kJ. $\Delta H = q_p = -3452$ kJ and
$\Delta U = q + w = -3452$ kJ $- 11$ kJ $= -3463$ kJ
Check: The units (kJ) are correct. The magnitude of the answer (–3500) makes physical sense because both terms are negative. We expect significant amounts of energy from fuels.

6.57   (a)   Combustion is an exothermic process; ΔH is negative.

(b)   Evaporation requires an input of energy, so it is endothermic; ΔH is positive.

(c)   Condensation is the reverse of evaporation, so it is exothermic; ΔH is negative.

6.59   **Given:** 177 mL acetone (C_3H_6O), $\Delta_r H° = -1790$ kJ; d = 0.788 g mL^{-1} **Find:** q
Conceptual Plan: mL acetone $\rightarrow$ g acetone $\rightarrow$ mol acetone $\rightarrow$ q
$$\frac{0.788 \text{ g}}{1 \text{ mL}} \qquad \frac{1 \text{ mol}}{58.08 \text{ g}} \qquad \frac{-1790 \text{ kJ}}{1 \text{ mol}}$$
Solution: $177 \text{ mL} \times \dfrac{0.788 \text{ g}}{1 \text{ mL}} \times \dfrac{1 \text{ mol}}{58.08 \text{ g}} \times \dfrac{-1790 \text{ kJ}}{1 \text{ mol}} = -4.30 \times 10^3$ kJ or 4.30×10^3 kJ released

Check: The units (kJ) are correct. The magnitude of the answer (-10^3) makes physical sense because the enthalpy change is negative and we have more than a mole of acetone. We expect more than 1790 kJ to be released.

6.61   **Given:** pork roast, $\Delta_r H° = -2217$ kJ; q needed $= 1.6 \times 10^3$ kJ, 10 % efficiency   **Find:** $m(CO_2)$
Conceptual Plan: q used $\rightarrow$ q generated $\rightarrow$ mol CO_2 $\rightarrow$ g CO_2
$$\frac{100 \text{ kJ generated}}{10 \text{ kJ used}} \qquad \frac{3 \text{ mol}}{2217 \text{ kJ}} \qquad \frac{44.01 \text{ g}}{1 \text{ mol}}$$
Solution: $1.6 \times 10^3 \text{ kJ} \times \dfrac{100 \text{ kJ generated}}{10 \text{ kJ used}} \times \dfrac{3 \text{ mol CO}_2}{2217 \text{ kJ}} \times \dfrac{44.01 \text{ g CO}_2}{1 \text{ mol CO}_2} = 950$ g CO_2
Check: The units (g) are correct. The magnitude of the answer (~1000) makes physical sense because the process is not very efficient and a lot of energy is needed.

Thermal Energy Transfer

6.63   **Given:** silver block, $T_{Agi} = 58.5$ °C, 100.0 g water, $T_{H_2Oi} = 24.8$ °C, $T_f = 26.2$ °C   **Find:** mass of silver block
Conceptual Plan: pull C_s values from Table 6.4 then H_2O: $m, C_s, T_i, T_f \rightarrow q$ Ag: $C_s, T_i, T_f \rightarrow m$
$$\text{Ag: } 0.235 \frac{\text{J}}{\text{g} \cdot °\text{C}} \quad H_2O: 4.184 \frac{\text{J}}{\text{g} \cdot °\text{C}} \qquad q = mC_s(T_f - T_i) \text{ then set } q_{Ag} = -q_{H_2O}$$
Solution: $q = mC_s(T_f - T_i)$ substitute in values and set $q_{Ag} = -q_{H_2O}$.

$$q_{Ag} = m_{Ag}C_{Ag}(T_f - T_{Agi}) = m_{Ag} \times 0.235 \frac{\text{J}}{\text{g} \cdot °\text{C}} \times (26.2 °\text{C} - 58.5 °\text{C}) =$$

$$-q_{H_2O} = -m_{H_2O}C_{H_2O}(T_f - T_{H_2Oi}) = -100.0 \text{ g} \times 4.184 \frac{\text{J}}{\text{g} \cdot °\text{C}} \times (26.2 °\text{C} - 24.8 °\text{C})$$

Rearrange to solve for m_{Ag}.

$$m_{Ag} \times \left(-7.5905 \frac{\text{J}}{\text{g}}\right) = -585.7 \text{ J} \rightarrow m_{Ag} = \frac{-585.7 \text{ J}}{-7.5905 \frac{\text{J}}{\text{g}}} = 77.1622 \text{ g Ag} = 77.2 \text{ g Ag}$$

Check: The units (g) are correct. The magnitude of the answer (77 g) makes physical sense because the heat capacity of water is much greater than the heat capacity of silver.

6.65   **Given:** 31.1 g gold, $T_{Aui} = 69.3\ °C$, 64.2 g water, $T_{H_2Oi} = 27.8\ °C$ **Find:** T_f
Conceptual Plan: pull C_s values from Table 6.4 then $m, C_s, T_i \rightarrow T_f$

$$Au: 0.128\ \frac{J}{g \cdot °C}\quad H_2O: 4.184\ \frac{J}{g \cdot °C}\qquad\qquad q = mC_s(T_f - T_i)\ \text{then set}\ q_{Au} = -q_{H_2O}$$

Solution: $q = mC_s(T_f - T_i)$ substitute in values and set $q_{Au} = -q_{H_2O}$.

$$q_{Au} = m_{Au}C_{Au}(T_f - T_{Aui}) = 31.1\ \text{g} \times 0.128\ \frac{J}{g \cdot °C} \times (T_f - 69.3\ °C) =$$

$$-q_{H_2O} = -m_{H_2O}C_{H_2O}(T_f - T_{H_2Oi}) = -64.2\ \text{g} \times 4.184\ \frac{J}{g \cdot °C} \times (T_f - 27.8\ °C)$$

Rearrange to solve for T_f.

$$3.9808\ \frac{J}{°C} \times (T_f - 69.3\ °C) = -268.613\ \frac{J}{°C} \times (T_f - 27.8\ °C) \rightarrow$$

$$3.9808\ \frac{J}{°C}\ T_f - 275.8694\ J = -268.613\ \frac{J}{°C}\ T_f + 7467.4358\ J \rightarrow$$

$$268.613\ \frac{J}{°C}\ T_f + 3.9808\ \frac{J}{°C}\ T_f = 275.8694\ J + 7467.4358\ J \rightarrow 272.5938\ \frac{J}{°C}\ T_f = 7743.3052\ J \rightarrow$$

$$T_f = \frac{7743.3052\ J}{272.5938\ \frac{J}{°C}} = 28.4\ °C$$

Check: The units (°C) are correct. The magnitude of the answer (28) makes physical sense because the heat transfer is dominated by the water (larger mass and larger specific heat capacity). The final temperature should be closer to the initial temperature of water than of gold.

6.67   **Given:** 6.15 g substance A, $T_{Ai} = 20.5\ °C$, 25.2 g substance B, $T_{Bi} = 52.7\ °C$, $C_s = 1.17\ J\ g^{-1}\ °C^{-1}$, $T_f = 46.7\ °C$
Find: specific heat capacity of substance A
Conceptual Plan: A: $m, T_i, T_f \rightarrow q$ B: $m, C_s, T_i, T_f \rightarrow q$ and solve for C

$$q = mC_s(T_f - T_i)\quad\text{then set}\ q_A = -q_B$$

Solution: $q = mC_s(T_f - T_i)$ substitute in values and set $q_A = -q_B$.

$$q_A = m_A C_A (T_f - T_{Ai}) = 6.15\ g \times C_A \times (46.7\ °C - 20.5\ °C) =$$

$$-q_B = -m_B C_B (T_f - T_{Bi}) = -25.2\ \text{g} \times 1.17\ \frac{J}{g \cdot °C} \times (46.7\ °C - 52.7\ °C)$$

Rearrange to solve for C_A.

$$C_A \times (161.13 g \cdot °C) = 176.904\ J \rightarrow C_A = \frac{176.904\ J}{161.13 g \cdot °C} = 1.097896\ \frac{J}{g \cdot °C} = 1.10\ \frac{J}{g \cdot °C}$$

Check: The units ($J\ g^{-1}\ °C^{-1}$) are correct. The magnitude of the answer ($1\ J\ g^{-1}\ °C^{-1}$) makes physical sense because the mass of substance B is greater than the mass of substance A by a factor of ~4.1, and the temperature change for substance A is greater than the temperature change of substance B by a factor of ~4.4, so the heat capacity of substance A will be a little smaller.

Calorimetry

6.69 $\Delta_r H = q_p$ and $\Delta_r U = q_V = \Delta H - P\Delta V$. Since combustions always involve expansions, expansions do work and therefore have a negative value. Combustions are always exothermic and therefore have a negative value. This means that $\Delta_r U$ is more negative than $\Delta_r H$ and so A (− 25.9 kJ) is the constant volume process and B (− 23.3 kJ) is the constant pressure process.

6.71   **Given:** 0.514 g biphenyl ($C_{12}H_{10}$), bomb calorimeter, $T_i = 25.8\ °C$, $T_f = 29.4\ °C$, $C_{cal} = 5.86\ kJ\ °C^{-1}$ **Find:** $\Delta_r U$
Conceptual Plan: $T_i, T_f \rightarrow \Delta T$ then $\Delta T, C_{cal} \rightarrow q_{cal} \rightarrow q_r$ then g $C_{12}H_{10} \rightarrow$ mol $C_{12}H_{10}$

$$\Delta T = T_f - T_i\qquad q_{cal} = C_{cal}\Delta T\quad q_{cal} = -q_r\qquad \frac{1\ mol}{154.20\ g}$$

then q_r, mol $C_{12}H_{10} \rightarrow \Delta_r U$

$$\Delta_r U = \frac{q_V}{mol\ C_{12}H_{10}}$$

Solution: $\Delta T = T_f - T_i = 29.4\ °C - 25.8\ °C = 3.6\ °C$ then $q_{cal} = C_{cal}\Delta T = 5.86\ \frac{kJ}{°C} \times 3.6\ °C = 21.096\ kJ$

then $q_{cal} = -q_r = -21.096\ kJ$ and $0.514\ \text{g}\ C_{12}H_{10} \times \frac{1\ mol\ C_{12}H_{10}}{154.20\ \text{g}\ C_{12}H_{10}} = 0.00333333\ mol\ C_{12}H_{10}$ then

$$\Delta_r U = \frac{q_V}{\text{mol } C_{12}H_{10}} = \frac{-21.096 \text{ kJ}}{0.00333333 \text{ mol } C_{12}H_{10}} = -6.3 \times 10^3 \text{ kJ mol}^{-1}$$

Check: The units (kJ mol^{-1}) are correct. The magnitude of the answer (-6000) makes physical sense because there is such a large heat generated from a very small amount of biphenyl.

6.73   **Given:** 0.103 g zinc, coffee-cup calorimeter, $T_i = 22.5\,°C$, $T_f = 23.7\,°C$, 50.0 mL solution, d (solution) = 1.0 g mL^{-1}, $C_{soln} = 4.184$ kJ g^{-1} °C^{-1} **Find:** $\Delta_r H$

     Conceptual Plan: $T_i, T_f \rightarrow \Delta T$ and mL soln $\rightarrow$ g soln then $\Delta T, C_{cal} \rightarrow q_{cal} \rightarrow q_r$ then

$$\Delta T = T_f - T_i \qquad \frac{1.0 \text{ g}}{1.0 \text{ mL}} \qquad q_{cal} = m\, C_{soln}\, \Delta T \quad q_{soln} = -q_r$$

     g Zn $\rightarrow$ **mol Zn then** q_r, **mol Zn** $\rightarrow \Delta_r H$

$$\frac{1 \text{ mol}}{65.37 \text{ g}} \qquad\qquad \Delta_r H = \frac{q_p}{\text{mol Zn}}$$

     Solution: $\Delta T = T_f - T_i = 23.7\,°C - 22.5°C = 1.2°C$ and $50.0 \text{ mL} \times \dfrac{1.0 \text{ g}}{1.0 \text{ mL}} = 50.0$ g then

$$q_{soln} = m\, C_{soln}\, \Delta T = 50.0 \text{ g} \times 4.184 \frac{J}{\text{g} \cdot °C} \times 1.2\,°C = 251.0 \text{ J then } q_{soln} = -q_r = -251.0 \text{ J and}$$

$$0.103 \text{ g Zn} \times \frac{1 \text{ mol Zn}}{65.37 \text{ g Zn}} = 0.00157565 \text{ mol Zn then}$$

$$\Delta_r H = \frac{q_p}{mol\ Zn} = \frac{-251.0 \text{ J}}{0.00157565 \text{ mol Zn}} = -1.6 \times 10^5 \text{ J mol}^{-1} = -1.6 \times 10^2 \text{ kJ mol}^{-1}$$

     Check: The units (kJ mol^{-1}) are correct. The magnitude of the answer (-160) makes physical sense because there is such a large heat generated from a very small amount of zinc.

Quantitative Relationships Involving $\Delta_r H$ and Hess's Law

6.75   (a)   Since A + B $\rightarrow$ 2 C has ΔH_1 then 2 C $\rightarrow$ A + B will have a $\Delta H_2 = -\Delta H_1$. When the reaction direction is reversed, it changes from exothermic to endothermic (or vice versa), so the sign of ΔH changes.

       (b)   Since A + $\frac{1}{2}$ B $\rightarrow$ C has ΔH_1 then 2 A + B $\rightarrow$ 2 C will have a $\Delta H_2 = 2\,\Delta H_1$. When the reaction amount doubles, the amount of heat (or ΔH) doubles.

       (c)   Since A $\rightarrow$ B + 2 C has ΔH_1 then $\frac{1}{2}$ A $\rightarrow$ $\frac{1}{2}$ B + C will have a $\Delta H_{1'} = \frac{1}{2}\,\Delta H_1$. When the reaction amount is cut in half, the amount of heat (or ΔH) is cut in half. Then $\frac{1}{2}$ B + C $\rightarrow$ $\frac{1}{2}$ A will have a $\Delta H_2 = -\Delta H_{1'} = -\frac{1}{2}\,\Delta H_1$. When the reaction direction is reversed, it changes from exothermic to endothermic (or vice versa), so the sign of ΔH changes.

6.77   Since the first reaction has Fe_2O_3 as a product and the reaction of interest has it as a reactant, we need to reverse the first reaction. When the reaction direction is reversed, ΔH changes.

     $Fe_2O_3\,(s) \rightarrow 2\ Fe\,(s) + 3/2\ O_2\,(g)$ $\Delta H = +824.2 \text{ kJ mol}^{-1}$

     Since the second reaction has 1 mole CO as a reactant and the reaction of interest has 3 moles of CO as a reactant, we need to multiply the second reaction and the ΔH by 3.

     $3[CO\,(g) + 1/2\ O_2\,(g) \rightarrow CO_2\,(g)]$ $\Delta H = 3(-282.7 \text{ kJ mol}^{-1}) = -848.1 \text{ kJ mol}^{-1}$

     Hess's Law states the ΔH of the net reaction is the sum of the ΔH of the steps. The rewritten reactions are as follows:

     $Fe_2O_3\,(s) \rightarrow 2\ Fe\,(s) + \cancel{3/2\ O_2\,(g)}$ $\Delta H = +824.2 \text{ kJ mol}^{-1}$

     $\underline{3\ CO\,(g) + \cancel{3/2\ O_2\,(g)} \rightarrow 3\ CO_2\,(g)} \qquad\qquad \underline{\Delta H = -848.1 \text{ kJ mol}^{-1}}$

     $Fe_2O_3\,(s) + 3\ CO\,(g) \rightarrow 2\ Fe\,(s) + 3\ CO_2\,(g) \qquad \Delta_r H = -23.9 \text{ kJ mol}^{-1}$

6.79   Since the first reaction has C_5H_{12} as a reactant and the reaction of interest has it as a product, we need to reverse the first reaction. When the reaction direction is reversed, ΔH changes.

     $5\ CO_2\,(g) + 6\ H_2O\,(g) \rightarrow C_5H_{12}\,(l) + 8\ O_2\,(g)$ $\Delta H = +3505.8 \text{ kJ mol}^{-1}$

     Since the second reaction has 1 mole C as a reactant and the reaction of interest has 5 moles of C as a reactant, we need to multiply the second reaction and the ΔH by 5.

     $5[C\,(s) + O_2\,(g) \rightarrow CO_2\,(g)]$ $\Delta H = 5(-393.5 \text{ kJ mol}^{-1}) = -1967.5 \text{ kJ mol}^{-1}$

     Since the third reaction has 2 moles H_2 as a reactant and the reaction of interest has 6 moles of H_2 as a reactant, we need to multiply the third reaction and the ΔH by 3.

     $3[2\ H_2\,(g) + O_2\,(g) \rightarrow 2\ H_2O\,(g)]$ $\Delta H = 3(-483.5 \text{ kJ mol}^{-1}) = -1450.5 \text{ kJ mol}^{-1}$

Hess's Law states the ΔH of the net reaction is the sum of the ΔH of the steps.
The rewritten reactions are as follows:

$5\cancel{CO_2(g)} + \cancel{6 H_2O(g)} \rightarrow C_5H_{12}(l) + \cancel{8 O_2(g)}$	$\Delta H = +3505.8 \text{ kJ mol}^{-1}$
$5 C(s) + \cancel{5 O_2(g)} \rightarrow \cancel{5 CO_2(g)}$	$\Delta H = -1967.5 \text{ kJ mol}^{-1}$
$6 H_2(g) + \cancel{3 O_2(g)} \rightarrow \cancel{6 H_2O(g)}$	$\Delta H = -1450.5 \text{ kJ mol}^{-1}$
$5 C(s) + 6 H_2(g) \rightarrow C_5H_{12}(l)$	$\Delta_r H = +87.8 \text{ kJ mol}^{-1}$

6.81   (a) $\frac{1}{2} N_2(g) + \frac{3}{2} H_2(g) \rightarrow NH_3(g)$ $\Delta_f H^\circ = -45.9 \text{ kJ mol}^{-1}$

       (b) $C(s, graphite) + O_2(g) \rightarrow CO_2(g)$ $\Delta_f H^\circ = -393.5 \text{ kJ mol}^{-1}$

       (c) $2 Fe(s) + \frac{3}{2} O_2(g) \rightarrow Fe_2O_3(s)$ $\Delta_f H^\circ = -824.2 \text{ kJ mol}^{-1}$

       (d) $C(s, graphite) + 2 H_2(g) \rightarrow CH_4(g)$ $\Delta_f H^\circ = -74.6 \text{ kJ mol}^{-1}$

6.83   **Given:** $N_2H_4(l) + N_2O_4(g) \rightarrow 2 N_2O(g) + 2 H_2O(g)$ **Find:** $\Delta_r H^\circ$
      Conceptual Plan: $\Delta_r H^\circ = \sum n_p \Delta_f H^\circ(products) - \sum n_r \Delta_f H^\circ(reactants)$
      Solution:

Reactant/Product	$\Delta_f H^\circ$ (kJ mol^{-1} from Appendix IIB)
$N_2H_4(l)$	50.6
$N_2O_4(g)$	11.1
$N_2O(g)$	81.6
$H_2O(g)$	-241.8

      Be sure to pull data for the correct formula and phase.

$$\Delta_r H^\circ = \sum n_p \Delta_f H^\circ(products) - \sum n_r \Delta_f H^\circ(reactants)$$
$$= [2(\Delta_f H^\circ(N_2O(g))) + 2(\Delta_f H^\circ(H_2O(g)))] - [1(\Delta_f H^\circ(N_2H_4(l))) + 1(\Delta_f H^\circ(N_2O_4(g)))]$$
$$= [2(81.6 \text{ kJ mol}^{-1}) + 2(-241.8 \text{ kJ mol}^{-1})] - [1(50.6 \text{ kJ mol}^{-1}) + 1(11.1 \text{ kJ mol}^{-1})]$$
$$= [-320.4 \text{ kJ mol}^{-1}] - [61.7 \text{ kJ mol}^{-1}]$$
$$= -382.1 \text{ kJ mol}^{-1}$$

      Check: The units (kJ mol^{-1}) are correct. The answer is negative, which means that the reaction is exothermic. The answer is dominated by the negative heat of formation of water.

6.85   (a)   **Given:** $C_2H_4(g) + H_2(g) \rightarrow C_2H_6(g)$ **Find:** $\Delta_r H^\circ$
            Conceptual Plan: $\Delta_r H^\circ = \sum n_p \Delta_f H^\circ(products) - \sum n_r \Delta_f H^\circ(reactants)$
            Solution:

Reactant/Product	$\Delta_f H^\circ$ (kJ mol^{-1} from Appendix IIB)
$C_2H_4(g)$	52.4
$H_2(g)$	0.0
$C_2H_6(g)$	-84.68

            Be sure to pull data for the correct formula and phase.

$$\Delta_r H^\circ = \sum n_p \Delta_f H^\circ(products) - \sum n_r \Delta_f H^\circ(reactants)$$
$$= [1(\Delta_f H^\circ(C_2H_6(g)))] - [1(\Delta_f H^\circ(C_2H_4(g))) + 1(\Delta_f H^\circ(H_2(g)))]$$
$$= [1(-84.68 \text{ kJ mol}^{-1})] - [1(52.4 \text{ kJ mol}^{-1}) + 1(0.0 \text{ kJ mol}^{-1})]$$
$$= [-84.68 \text{ kJ mol}^{-1}] - [52.4 \text{ kJ mol}^{-1}]$$
$$= -137.1 \text{ kJ mol}^{-1}$$

            Check: The units (kJ mol^{-1}) are correct. The answer is negative, which means that the reaction is exothermic. Both hydrocarbon terms are negative, so the final answer is negative.

       (b)   **Given:** $CO(g) + H_2O(g) \rightarrow H_2(g) + CO_2(g)$ **Find:** $\Delta_r H^\circ$
            Conceptual Plan: $\Delta_r H^\circ = \sum n_p \Delta_f H^\circ(products) - \sum n_r \Delta_f H^\circ(reactants)$

Solution:

Reactant/Product	$\Delta_f H°$ (kJ mol^{-1} from Appendix IIB)
CO (g)	− 110.5
H$_2$O (g)	− 241.8
H$_2$ (g)	0.0
CO$_2$ (g)	− 393.5

Be sure to pull data for the correct formula and phase.

$$\Delta_r H° = \sum n_p \Delta_f H°(products) - \sum n_r \Delta_f H°(reactants)$$
$$= [1(\Delta_f H°(H_2 (g))) + 1(\Delta_f H°(CO_2 (g)))] - [1(\Delta_f H°(CO (g))) + 1(\Delta_f H°(H_2O (g)))]$$
$$= [1(0.0 \text{ kJ mol}^{-1}) + 1(− 393.5 \text{ kJ mol}^{-1})] - [1(− 110.5 \text{ kJ mol}^{-1}) + 1(− 241.8 \text{ kJ mol}^{-1})]$$
$$= [− 393.5 \text{ kJ mol}^{-1}] - [− 352.3 \text{ kJ mol}^{-1}]$$
$$= − 41.2 \text{ kJ mol}^{-1}$$

Check: The units (kJ mol^{-1}) are correct. The answer is negative, which means that the reaction is exothermic.

(c) **Given:** 3 NO$_2$ (g) + H$_2$O (l) → 2 HNO$_3$ (aq) + NO (g) **Find:** $\Delta_r H°$

Conceptual Plan: $\Delta_r H° = \sum n_p \Delta_f H°(products) - \sum n_r \Delta_f H°(reactants)$

Solution:

Reactant/Product	$\Delta_f H°$ (kJ mol^{-1} from Appendix IIB)
NO$_2$ (g)	33.2
H$_2$O (l)	− 285.8
HNO$_3$ (aq)	− 207
NO (g)	91.3

Be sure to pull data for the correct formula and phase.

$$\Delta_r H° = \sum n_p \Delta_f H°(products) - \sum n_r \Delta_f H°(reactants)$$
$$= [2(\Delta_f H°(HNO_3 (aq))) + 1(\Delta_f H°(NO (g)))] - [3(\Delta_f H°(NO_2 (g))) + 1(\Delta_f H°(H_2O (l)))]$$
$$= [2(− 207 \text{ kJ mol}^{-1}) + 1(91.3 \text{ kJ mol}^{-1})] - [3(33.2 \text{ kJ mol}^{-1}) + 1(− 285.8 \text{ kJ mol}^{-1})]$$
$$= [− 322.7 \text{ kJ mol}^{-1}] - [− 186.2 \text{ kJ mol}^{-1}]$$
$$= − 137 \text{ kJ mol}^{-1}$$

Check: The units (kJ mol^{-1}) are correct. The answer is negative, which means that the reaction is exothermic.

(d) **Given:** Cr$_2$O$_3$ (s) + 3 CO (g) → 2 Cr (s) + 3 CO$_2$ (g) **Find:** $\Delta_r H°$

Conceptual Plan: $\Delta_r H° = \sum n_p \Delta_f H°(products) - \sum n_r \Delta_f H°(reactants)$

Solution:

Reactant/Product	$\Delta_f H°$ (kJ mol^{-1} from Appendix IIB)
Cr$_2$O$_3$ (s)	− 1139.7
CO (g)	− 110.5
Cr (s)	0.0
CO$_2$ (g)	− 393.5

Be sure to pull data for the correct formula and phase.

$$\Delta_r H° = \sum n_p \Delta_f H°(products) - \sum n_r \Delta_f H°(reactants)$$
$$= [2(\Delta_f H°(Cr (s))) + 3(\Delta_f H°(CO_2 (g)))] - [1(\Delta_f H°(Cr_2O_3 (s))) + 3(\Delta_f H°(CO (g)))]$$
$$= [2(0.0 \text{ kJ mol}^{-1}) + 3(− 393.5 \text{ kJ mol}^{-1})] - [1(− 1139.7 \text{ kJ mol}^{-1}) + 3(− 110.5 \text{ kJ mol}^{-1})]$$
$$= [− 1180.5 \text{ kJ mol}^{-1}] - [− 1471.2 \text{ kJ mol}^{-1}]$$
$$= 290.7 \text{ kJ mol}^{-1}$$

Check: The units (kJ mol^{-1}) are correct. The answer is positive, which means that the reaction is endothermic.

6.87 **Given:** form glucose (C$_6$H$_{12}$O$_6$) and oxygen from sunlight, carbon dioxide, and water **Find:** $\Delta_r H°$

Conceptual Plan: write balanced reaction then $\Delta_r H° = \sum n_p \Delta_f H°(products) - \sum n_r \Delta_f H°(reactants)$

Solution: 6 CO$_2$ (g) + 6 H$_2$O (l) → C$_6$H$_{12}$O$_6$ (s) + 6 O$_2$ (g)

Reactant/Product	$\Delta_f H°$ (kJ mol^{-1} from Appendix IIB)
CO$_2$ (g)	− 393.5
H$_2$O (l)	− 285.8
C$_6$H$_{12}$O (s)	− 1273.3
O$_2$ (g)	0.0

Be sure to pull data for the correct formula and phase.

$\Delta_r H° = \sum n_p \Delta_f H°(products) - \sum n_r \Delta_f H°(reactants)$

$= [1(\Delta_f H°(C_6H_{12}O\ (s))) + 6(\Delta_f H°(O_2\ (g)))] - [6(\Delta_f H°(CO_2\ (g))) + 6(\Delta_f H°(H_2O\ (l)))]$

$= [1(-1273.3\ \text{kJ mol}^{-1}) + 6(0.0\ \text{kJ mol}^{-1})] - [6(-393.5\ \text{kJ mol}^{-1}) + 6(-285.8\ \text{kJ mol}^{-1})]$

$= [-1273.3\ \text{kJ mol}^{-1}] - [-4075.6\ \text{kJ mol}^{-1}]$

$= +2802.5\ \text{kJ mol}^{-1}$

Check: The units (kJ mol^{-1}) are correct. The answer is positive, which means that the reaction is endothermic. The reaction requires the input of light energy, so we expect that this will be an endothermic reaction.

6.89   **Given:** $2\ CH_3NO_2\ (l) + 3/2\ O_2\ (g) \rightarrow 2\ CO_2\ (g) + 3\ H_2O\ (l) + N_2\ (g)$ and $\Delta_r H° = -709.2\ \text{kJ mol}^{-1}$

Find: $\Delta_f H°\ (CH_3NO_2\ (l))$

Conceptual Plan: fill known values into $\Delta_r H° = \sum n_p \Delta_f H°(products) - \sum n_r \Delta_f H°(reactants)$ **and rearrange to solve for** $\Delta_f H°\ (CH_3NO_2\ (l))$

Solution:

Reactant/Product	$\Delta_f H°$(kJ mol^{-1} from Appendix IIB)
$O_2\ (g)$	0.0
$CO_2\ (g)$	-393.5
$H_2O\ (l)$	-285.8
$N_2\ (g)$	0.0

Be sure to pull data for the correct formula and phase.

$\Delta_r H° = \sum n_p \Delta_f H°(products) - \sum n_r \Delta_f H°(reactants)$

$= [2(\Delta_f H°(CO_2\ (g))) + 3(\Delta_f H°(H_2O\ (l))) + 1(\Delta_f H°(N_2\ (g)))] - [2(\Delta_f H°(CH_3NO_2\ (l))) + 3/2(\Delta_f H°(O_2\ (g)))]$

$2(-709.2\ \text{kJ mol}^{-1}) = [2(-393.5\ \text{kJ mol}^{-1}) + 3(-285.8\ \text{kJ mol}^{-1}) + 1(0.0\ \text{kJ mol}^{-1})]$

$- [2(\Delta_f H°(CH_3NO_2(l)) + 3/2(0.0\ \text{kJ mol}^{-1})]$

$-1418.4\ \text{kJ mol}^{-1} = [-1644.4\ \text{kJ mol}^{-1}] - [2(\Delta_f H°(CH_3NO_2(l))]$

$\Delta_f H°(CH_3NO_2(l)) = -113\ \text{kJ mol}^{-1}$

Check: The units (kJ mol^{-1}) are correct. The answer is negative (but not as negative as water and carbon dioxide), which is consistent with an exothermic combustion reaction.

Energy Use and the Environment

6.91   (a)   **Given:** methane, $\Delta_r H° = -802.3\ \text{kJ}$; $q = 1.00 \times 10^2\ \text{kJ}$ **Find:** $m(CO_2)$

        Conceptual Plan: $q \rightarrow \text{mol } CO_2 \rightarrow \text{g } CO_2$

$$\frac{1\ \text{mol}}{-802.3\ \text{kJ}} \qquad \frac{44.01\ \text{g}}{1\ \text{mol}}$$

        Solution: $-1.00 \times 10^2\ \text{kJ} \times \dfrac{1\ \text{mol } CO_2}{-802.3\ \text{kJ}} \times \dfrac{44.01\ \text{g } CO_2}{1\ \text{mol } CO_2} = 5.49\ \text{g } CO_2$

        Check: The units (g) are correct. The magnitude of the answer (~5) makes physical sense because less than a mole of fuel is used.

    (b)   **Given:** propane, $\Delta_r H° = -2217\ \text{kJ}$; $q = 1.00 \times 10^2\ \text{kJ}$ **Find:** $m(CO_2)$

        Conceptual Plan: $q \rightarrow \text{mol } CO_2 \rightarrow \text{g } CO_2$

$$\frac{3\ \text{mol}}{-2217\ \text{kJ}} \qquad \frac{44.01\ \text{g}}{1\ \text{mol}}$$

        Solution: $-1.00 \times 10^2\ \text{kJ} \times \dfrac{3\ \text{mol } CO_2}{-2217\ \text{kJ}} \times \dfrac{44.01\ \text{g } CO_2}{1\ \text{mol } CO_2} = 5.96\ \text{g } CO_2$

        Check: The units (g) are correct. The magnitude of the answer (~6) makes physical sense because less than a mole of fuel is used.

    (c)   **Given:** octane, $\Delta_r H° = -5074.1\ \text{kJ}$; $q = 1.00 \times 10^2\ \text{kJ}$ **Find:** $m(CO_2)$

        Conceptual Plan: $q \rightarrow \text{mol } CO_2 \rightarrow \text{g } CO_2$

$$\frac{8\ \text{mol}}{-5074.1\ \text{kJ}} \qquad \frac{44.01\ \text{g}}{1\ \text{mol}}$$

        Solution: $-1.00 \times 10^2\ \text{kJ} \times \dfrac{8\ \text{mol } CO_2}{-5074.1\ \text{kJ}} \times \dfrac{44.01\ \text{g } CO_2}{1\ \text{mol } CO_2} = 6.94\ \text{g } CO_2$

Check: The units (g) are correct. The magnitude of the answer (~7) makes physical sense because less than a mole of fuel is used.

The methane generated the least carbon dioxide for the given amount of heat, while the octane generated the most carbon dioxide for the given amount of heat.

6.93 **Given:** 7×10^{12} kg/yr octane (C_8H_{18}), $\Delta_r H^\circ = -5074.1$ kJ (using Problem 91), 2×10^{17} kg CO_2 in the atmosphere
Find: $m(CO_2)$ in kg and time to double atmospheric CO_2
Conceptual Plan: use reaction from Problem 91 C_8H_{18} (l) + 25/2 O_2 (g) $\rightarrow$ 8 CO_2 (g) + 9 H_2O (g)
kg (C_8H_{18}) $\rightarrow$ g (C_8H_{18}) $\rightarrow$ mol (C_8H_{18}) $\rightarrow$ mol CO_2 $\rightarrow$ g CO_2 $\rightarrow$ kg CO_2 produced

$$\frac{1000 \text{ g}}{1 \text{ kg}} \quad \frac{1 \text{ mol } C_8H_{18}}{114.22 \text{ g}} \quad \frac{8 \text{ mol } CO_2}{1 \text{ mol } C_8H_{18}} \quad \frac{44.01 \text{ g}}{1 \text{ mol}} \quad \frac{1 \text{ kg}}{1000 \text{ g}}$$

then kg CO_2 $\rightarrow$ yr

$$\frac{2 \times 10^{17} \text{ kg } CO_2}{\left(\dfrac{\text{kg } CO_2 \text{ produced}}{\text{yr}}\right)}$$

Solution:

$$7 \times 10^{12} \text{ kg} \times \frac{1000 \text{ g}}{1 \text{ kg}} \times \frac{1 \text{ mol } C_8H_{18}}{114.22 \text{ g}} \times \frac{8 \text{ mol } CO_2}{1 \text{ mol } C_8H_{18}} \times \frac{44.01 \text{ g } CO_2}{1 \text{ mol } CO_2} \times \frac{1 \text{ kg}}{1000 \text{ g}} = 2.158 \times 10^{13} \text{ kg } CO_2$$

$$= 2 \times 10^{13} \text{ kg } CO_2 \text{ per year}$$

$$\frac{2 \times 10^{17} \text{ kg } CO_2}{\left(\dfrac{2.158 \times 10^{13} \text{ kg } CO_2 \text{ produced}}{\text{yr}}\right)} = 9268 \text{ yr} = 9000 \text{ yr}$$

Check: The units (kg and yr) are correct. The magnitude of the answer (10^{13} kg) makes physical sense because the mass of CO_2 is larger than the hydrocarbon mass in a combustion (since O is much heavier than H).

Cumulative Problems

6.95 **Given:** billiard ball$_A$ = system: m_A = 0.17 kg, v_{A1} = 4.5 m s^{-1} slows to v_{A2} = 3.8 m s^{-1} and v_{A3} = 0; ball$_B$: m_B = 0.17 kg, v_{B1} = 0 and v_{B2} = 3.8 m s^{-1}, and $KE = \frac{1}{2}mv^2$ **Find:** w, q, ΔU_{sys}
Conceptual Plan: $m, v \rightarrow KE$ then $KE_{A3}, KE_{A1} \rightarrow \Delta U_{sys}$ and $KE_{A2}, KE_{A1} \rightarrow q$ and $KE_{B2}, KE_{B1} \rightarrow w_B$

$$KE = \frac{1}{2}mv^2 \qquad \Delta U_{sys} = KE_{A3} - KE_{A1} \qquad q = KE_{A2} - KE_{A1} \qquad w_B = KE_{B2} - KE_{B1}$$

$\Delta U_{sys}, q \rightarrow w_A$ verify that $w_A = -w_B$ so that no heat is transferred to ball$_B$

$$\Delta U = q + w$$

Solution: $KE = \frac{1}{2}mv^2$ since m is in kg and v is in m s^{-1}, KE will be in kg·m^2/s^2, which is joule.

$$KE_{A1} = \frac{1}{2}(0.17 \text{ kg})\left(4.5 \frac{\text{m}}{\text{s}}\right)^2 = 1.7213 \frac{\text{kg} \cdot \text{m}^2}{\text{s}^2} = 1.7213 \text{ J},$$

$$KE_{A2} = \frac{1}{2}(0.17 \text{ kg})\left(3.8 \frac{\text{m}}{\text{s}}\right)^2 = 1.2274 \frac{\text{kg} \cdot \text{m}^2}{\text{s}^2} = 1.2274 \text{ J},$$

$$KE_{A3} = \frac{1}{2}(0.17 \text{ kg})\left(0 \frac{\text{m}}{\text{s}}\right)^2 = 0 \frac{\text{kg} \cdot \text{m}^2}{\text{s}^2} = 0 \text{ J}, \quad KE_{B1} = \frac{1}{2}(0.17 \text{ kg})\left(0 \frac{\text{m}}{\text{s}}\right)^2 = 0 \frac{\text{kg} \cdot \text{m}^2}{\text{s}^2} = 0 \text{ J and}$$

$$KE_{B2} = \frac{1}{2}(0.17 \text{ kg})\left(3.8 \frac{\text{m}}{\text{s}}\right)^2 = 1.2274 \frac{\text{kg} \cdot \text{m}^2}{\text{s}^2} = 1.2274 \text{ J}.$$

$\Delta U_{sys} = KE_{A3} - KE_{A1} = 0 \text{ J} - 1.7213 \text{ J} = -1.7213 \text{ J} = -1.7 \text{ J},$
$q = KE_{A2} - KE_{A1} = 1.2274 \text{ J} - 1.7213 \text{ J} = -0.4939 \text{ J} = -0.5 \text{ J},$
$w_B = KE_{B2} - KE_{B1} = 1.2274 \text{ J} - 0 \text{ J} = 1.2274 \text{ J and}$
$w = \Delta U - q = -1.7213 \text{ J} - -0.4939 \text{ J} = -1.2274 \text{ J} = -1.2 \text{ J}.$
Since $w_A = -w_B$ no heat is transferred to ball$_B$.
Check: The units (J) are correct. Since the ball is initially moving and is stopped at the end, it has lost energy (negative ΔU_{sys}). As the ball slows due to friction, it is releasing heat (negative q). The kinetic energy is transferred to a second ball, so it does work (w negative).

6.97   **Given:** $H_2O\ (l) \rightarrow H_2O\ (g)\ \Delta_rH° = +\ 44.01\ kJ/mol;\ \Delta T_{body} = -\ 0.50\ °C,\ m_{body} = 95\ kg,\ C_{body} = 4.0\ J\ g^{-1}\ °C^{-1}$
Find: m_{H_2O}
Conceptual Plan: kg $\rightarrow$ **g then** $m_{body},\ \Delta T,\ C_{body} \rightarrow q_{body} \rightarrow q_r\ (J) \rightarrow q_r\ (kJ) \rightarrow$ **mol** $H_2O \rightarrow$ **g** H_2O

$$\frac{1000\ g}{1\ kg} \qquad q_{body} = m_{body}C_{body}\Delta T_{body} \qquad q_r = -\ q_{body} \qquad \frac{1\ kJ}{1000\ J} \qquad \frac{1\ mol}{44.01\ kJ} \qquad \frac{18.01\ g}{1\ mol}$$

Solution: $95\ \cancel{kg} \times \dfrac{1000\ g}{1\ \cancel{kg}} = 95000\ g$ then

$$q_{body} = m_{body}C_{body}\Delta T_{body} = 95000\ \cancel{g} \times 4.0\ \frac{J}{\cancel{g}\cdot\cancel{°C}} \times (-\ 0.50\ \cancel{°C}) = -\ 190000\ J\ \text{then}$$

$$q_r = -\ q_{body} = 190000\ \cancel{J} \times \frac{1\ \cancel{kJ}}{1000\ \cancel{J}} \times \frac{1\ \cancel{mol}}{44.01\ \cancel{kJ}} \times \frac{18.01\ g}{1\ \cancel{mol}} = 78\ g\ H_2O$$

Check: The units (g) are correct. The magnitude of the answer (78) makes physical sense because a person can sweat this much on a hot day.

6.99   **Given:** $H_2O\ (s) \rightarrow H_2O\ (l)\ \Delta_fH°\ (H_2O\ (s)) = -\ 291.8\ kJ/mol;\ 355\ mL$ beverage $T_{Bevi} = 25.0\ °C,\ T_{Bevf} = 0.0\ °C,$
$C_{Bev} = 4.184\ J\ g^{-1}\ °C^{-1},\ d_{Bev} = 1.0\ g\ mL^{-1}$ **Find:** $\Delta_rH°$ (ice melting) and m_{ice}
Conceptual Plan: $\Delta_rH° = \sum n_p\Delta_fH°(products) - \sum n_r\Delta_fH°(reactants)$ **mL** $\rightarrow$ **g and** $T_i,\ T_f \rightarrow \Delta T$ **then**

$$\frac{1.0\ g}{1.0\ mL} \qquad \Delta T = T_f - T_i$$

$$m_{H_2O},\ \Delta T_{H_2O},\ C_{H_2O} \rightarrow q_{H_2O} \rightarrow q_r\ (J) \rightarrow q_r\ (kJ) \rightarrow \textbf{mol ice} \rightarrow \textbf{g ice}$$

$$q_{Bev} = m_{Bev}C_{Bev}\Delta T_{Bev} \qquad q_r = -\ q_{Bev} \qquad \frac{1\ kJ}{1000\ J} \qquad \frac{1\ mol}{\Delta_rH°} \qquad \frac{18.01\ g}{1\ mol}$$

Solution:

Reactant/Product	$\Delta_fH°(kJ\ mol^{-1}$ from Appendix IIB)
$H_2O\ (s)$	$-\ 291.8$
$H_2O\ (l)$	$-\ 285.8$

Be sure to pull data for the correct formula and phase.

$$\Delta_rH° = \sum n_p\Delta_fH°(products) - \sum n_r\Delta_fH°(reactants)$$
$$= [1(\Delta_fH°(H_2O\ (l)))] - [1(\Delta_fH°(H_2O\ (s)))]$$
$$= [1(-\ 285.8\ kJ\ mol^{-1})] - [1(-\ 291.8\ kJ\ mol^{-1})]$$
$$= +\ 6.0\ kJ\ mol^{-1}$$

$355\ \cancel{mL} \times \dfrac{1.0\ g}{1.0\ \cancel{mL}} = 355\ g$ and $\Delta T = T_f - T_i = 0.0\ °C - 25.0\ °C = -\ 25.0\ °C$ then

$$q_{Bev} = m_{Bev}C_{Bev}\Delta T_{Bev} = 355\ \cancel{g} \times 4.184\ \frac{J}{\cancel{g}\cdot\cancel{°C}} \times (-\ 25.0\ \cancel{°C}) = -\ 37133\ J\ \text{then}$$

$$q_r = -\ q_{Bev} = -\ 37133\ \cancel{J} \times \frac{1\ \cancel{kJ}}{1000\ \cancel{J}} \times \frac{1\ \cancel{mol}}{-6.0\ \cancel{kJ}} \times \frac{18.01\ g}{1\ \cancel{mol}} = 110\ g\ \text{ice}$$

Check: The units (kJ and g) are correct. The answer is positive, which means that the reaction is endothermic. We expect an endothermic reaction because we know that heat must be added to melt ice. The magnitude of the answer (110 g) makes physical sense because it is much smaller than the weight of the beverage and it would fit in a glass with the beverage.

6.101   **Given:** 25.5 g aluminum, $T_{Ali} = 65.4\ °C$, 55.2 g water, $T_{H_2Oi} = 22.2\ °C$ **Find:** T_f
Conceptual Plan: pull C_s **values from Table 6.4 then** $m,\ C_s,\ T_i \rightarrow T_f$

$$Al:\ 0.903\ \frac{J}{g\cdot°C} \quad H_2O:\ 4.184\ \frac{J}{g\cdot°C} \qquad q = mC_s(T_f - T_i)\ \text{then set}\ q_{Al} = -\ q_{H_2O}$$

Solution: $q = mC_s(T_f - T_i)$ substitute in values and set $q_{Al} = -\ q_{H_2O}$.

$$q_{Al} = m_{Al}C_{Al}(T_f - T_{Ali}) = 25.5\ \cancel{g} \times 0.903\ \frac{J}{\cancel{g}\cdot°C} \times (T_f - 65.4\ °C) =$$

$$-\ q_{H_2O} = -\ m_{H_2O}C_{H_2O}(T_f - T_{H_2Oi}) = -\ 55.2\ \cancel{g} \times 4.184\ \frac{J}{\cancel{g}\cdot°C} \times (T_f - 22.2\ °C)$$

Rearrange to solve for T_f.

$$23.0265\ \frac{J}{°C} \times (T_f - 65.4\ °C) = -\ 230.957\ \frac{J}{°C} \times (T_f - 22.2\ °C) \rightarrow$$

$$23.\underline{0}265 \frac{J}{°C} T_f - 1505.93 \, J = -230.957 \frac{J}{°C} T_f + 5127.25 \, J \rightarrow$$

$$-5127.25 \, J - 1505.93 \, J = -230.957 \frac{J}{°C} T_f - 23.\underline{0}265 \frac{J}{°C} T_f \rightarrow 6633.18 \, J = 253.9835 \frac{J}{°C} T_f \rightarrow$$

$$T_f = \frac{6633.18 \, J}{253.9835 \frac{J}{°C}} = 26.1°C$$

Check: The units (°C) are correct. The magnitude of the answer (26) makes physical sense because the heat transfer is dominated by the water (larger mass and larger specific heat capacity). The final temperature should be closer to the initial temperature of water than of aluminum.

6.103 **Given:** palmitic acid ($C_{16}H_{32}O_2$) combustion $\Delta_fH°$ ($C_{16}H_{32}O_2$ (s)) = -208 kJ mol^{-1}; sucrose ($C_{12}H_{22}O_{11}$) combustion $\Delta_fH°$ ($C_{12}H_{22}O_{11}$ (s)) = -2226.1 kJ mol^{-1} **Find:** $\Delta_rH°$ in kJ mol^{-1} and Cal g^{-1}
Conceptual Plan: write balanced reaction then $\Delta_rH° = \sum n_p \Delta_fH°(products) - \sum n_r \Delta_fH°(reactants)$ **then kJ mol^{-1} $\rightarrow$ J mol^{-1} $\rightarrow$ Cal mol^{-1} $\rightarrow$ Cal g^{-1}**

$$\frac{1000 \, J}{1 \, kJ} \qquad \frac{1 \, Cal}{4184 \, J} \qquad PA: \frac{1 \, mol}{256.42 \, g} \quad S: \frac{1 \, mol}{342.30 \, g}$$

Solution: Combustion is the combination with oxygen to form carbon dioxide and water (l):
$$C_{16}H_{32}O_2 \, (s) + 23 \, O_2 \, (g) \rightarrow 16 \, CO_2 \, (g) + 16 \, H_2O \, (l)$$

Reactant/Product	$\Delta_fH°$(kJ mol^{-1} from Appendix IIB)
$C_{16}H_{32}O_2$ (s)	-208
O_2 (g)	0.0
CO_2 (g)	-393.5
H_2O (l)	-285.8

Be sure to pull data for the correct formula and phase.

$$\Delta_rH° = \sum n_p \Delta_fH°(products) - \sum n_r \Delta_fH°(reactants)$$
$$= [16(\Delta_fH°(CO_2 \, (g))) + 16(\Delta_fH°(H_2O \, (l)))] - [1(\Delta_fH°(C_{16}H_{32}O_2 \, (s))) + 23(\Delta_fH°(O_2 \, (g)))]$$
$$= [16(-393.5 \text{ kJ mol}^{-1}) + 16(-285.8 \text{ kJ mol}^{-1})] - [1(-208 \text{ kJ mol}^{-1}) + 23(0.0 \text{ kJ mol}^{-1})]$$
$$= [-10868.8 \text{ kJ mol}^{-1}] - [-208 \text{ kJ mol}^{-1}]$$
$$= -10,660.8 \text{ kJ mol}^{-1} = -10,661 \text{ kJ mol}^{-1}$$

$$-10,660.8 \frac{kJ}{mol} \times \frac{1000 \, J}{1 \, kJ} \times \frac{1 \, Cal}{4184 \, J} \times \frac{1 \, mol}{256.42 \, g} = -9.9378 \text{ Cal g}^{-1}$$

$$C_{12}H_{22}O_{11} \, (s) + 12 \, O_2 \, (g) \rightarrow 12 \, CO_2 \, (g) + 11 \, H_2O \, (l)$$

Reactant/Product	$\Delta_fH°$(kJ mol^{-1} from Appendix IIB)
$C_{12}H_{22}O_{11}$ (s)	-2226.1
O_2 (g)	0.0
CO_2 (g)	-393.5
H_2O (l)	-285.8

Be sure to pull data for the correct formula and phase.

$$\Delta_rH° = \sum n_p \Delta_fH°(products) - \sum n_r \Delta_fH°(reactants)$$
$$= [12(\Delta_fH°(CO_2 \, (g))) + 11(\Delta_fH°(H_2O \, (l)))] - [1(\Delta_fH°(C_{12}H_{22}O_{11} \, (s))) + 12(\Delta_fH°(O_2 \, (g)))]$$
$$= [12(-393.5 \text{ kJ mol}^{-1}) + 11(-285.8 \text{ kJ mol}^{-1})] - [1(-2226.1 \text{ kJ mol}^{-1}) + 12(0.0 \text{ kJ mol}^{-1})]$$
$$= [-7865.8 \text{ kJ mol}^{-1}] - [-2226.1 \text{ kJ mol}^{-1}]$$
$$= -5639.7 \text{ kJ mol}^{-1}$$

$$-5639.7 \frac{kJ}{mol} \times \frac{1000 \, J}{1 \, kJ} \times \frac{1 \, Cal}{4184 \, J} \times \frac{1 \, mol}{342.30 \, g} = -3.938 \text{ Cal g}^{-1}$$

Check: The units (kJ mol^{-1} and Cal g^{-1}) are correct. The magnitudes of the answers are consistent with the food labels we see every day. Palmitic acid gives more Cal g^{-1} than sucrose.

6.105 At constant P $\Delta_rH = q_P$ and at constant V $\Delta_rU = q_V = \Delta_rH - P\Delta V$. $PV = nRT$ at constant P, and a constant number of moles of gas, as we change the T the only variable that can change is V, so $P\Delta V = nR\Delta T$. Substituting into the equation for Δ_rU we get $\Delta_rU = \Delta_rH - nR\Delta T$ or $\Delta_rH = \Delta_rU + nR\Delta T$.

6.107   **Given:** 16 g peanut butter, bomb calorimeter, $T_i = 22.2$ °C, $T_f = 25.4$ °C, $C_{cal} = 120.0$ kJ °C^{-1}
Find: calories in peanut butter
Conceptual Plan: $T_i, T_f \rightarrow \Delta T$ then $\Delta T, C_{cal} \rightarrow q_{cal} \rightarrow q_r$ (kJ) $\rightarrow q_r$ (kJ) $\rightarrow q_r$ (Cal)

$$\Delta T = T_f - T_i \qquad q_{cal} = -C_{cal}\Delta T \qquad q_r = -q_{cal} \qquad \frac{1000\ J}{1\ kJ} \qquad \frac{1\ Cal}{4184\ J}$$

then q_r **(Cal)** $\rightarrow$ **Cal g^{-1}**

$$\div\ 16\ \text{g peanut butter}$$

Solution: $\Delta T = T_f - T_i = 25.4$ °C $- 22.2$ °C $= 3.2$ °C then $q_{cal} = C_{cal}\Delta T = 120.0\ \dfrac{kJ}{°C} \times 3.2\ °C = \underline{3}84$ kJ

then $q_r = -q_{cal} = -\underline{3}84\ \cancel{kJ} \times \dfrac{1000\ \cancel{J}}{1\ \cancel{kJ}} \times \dfrac{1\ Cal}{4184\ \cancel{J}} = 9\underline{1}.778$ Cal then $\dfrac{9\underline{1}.778\ Cal}{16\ g} = 5.7$ Cal g^{-1}

Check: The units (Cal g^{-1}) are correct. The magnitude of the answer (6) makes physical sense because there is a significant percentage of fat and sugar in peanut butter. The answer is in line with the answers in Problem 103.

6.109   **Given:** $V_1 = 20.0$ L at $P_1 = 3.0$ bar; $P_2 = 1.5$ bar let expand at constant T **Find:** $w, q, \Delta U_{sys}$
Conceptual Plan: $V_1, P_1, P_2 \rightarrow V_2$ then $V_1, V_2 \rightarrow \Delta V$ then $P, \Delta V \rightarrow w$ (L bar) $\rightarrow w$ (J)

$$P_1V_1 = P_2V_2 \qquad \Delta V = V_2 - V_1 \qquad w = -P\Delta V \qquad \frac{100.0\ J}{1\ L\cdot bar}$$

for an ideal gas $\Delta U_{sys} \propto T$, **so since this is a constant temperature process** $\Delta U_{sys} = 0$ **finally** $\Delta U_{sys}, w \rightarrow q$

$$\Delta U = q + w$$

Solution: $P_1V_1 = P_2V_2$. Rearrange to solve for V_2. $V_2 = V_1\dfrac{P_1}{P_2} = (20.0\ \text{L}) \times \dfrac{3.0\ \cancel{bar}}{1.5\ \cancel{bar}} = 40.\text{L}$ and

$\Delta V = V_2 - V_1 = 40.\ \text{L} - 20.0\ \text{L} = 20.\ \text{L}$ then

$w = -P\Delta V = -1.5\ \cancel{bar} \times 20.\ \cancel{L} \times \dfrac{100.0\ J}{1\ \cancel{L}\cdot \cancel{bar}} = -3000\ J = -3.0 \times 10^3\ J \qquad \Delta U = q + w$

Rearrange to solve for q. $q = \Delta U_{sys} - w = +0\ J - (-\underline{3}000\ J) = 3.0 \times 10^3\ J$

Check: The units (J) are correct. Since there is no temperature change, we expect no energy change ($\Delta U_{sys} = 0$). The piston expands and so does work (negative work) and so heat is absorbed (positive q).

6.111   The oxidation of S (g) to SO_3 can be written as follows:
S (g) $+ 3/2\ O_2$ (g) $\rightarrow SO_3$ (g) $\Delta H = -204$ kJ mol^{-1}
The oxidation of SO_2 (g) to SO_3 can be written as follows:
SO_2 (g) $+ 1/2\ O_2$ (g) $\rightarrow SO_3$ (g) $\Delta H = +89.5$ kJ mol^{-1}
The enthalpy of formation reaction for SO_2 (g) under these conditions can be written as follows:
S (g) $+ O_2$ (g) $\rightarrow SO_2$ (g) $\Delta H = ??$
Since the second reaction has 1 mole SO_2 as a reactant and the reaction of interest has 1 mole of SO_2 as a product, we need to reverse the second reaction. When the reaction direction is reversed, ΔH changes sign.
SO_3 (g) $\rightarrow SO_2$ (g) $+ 1/2\ O_2$ (g) $\Delta H = -89.5$ kJ mol^{-1}
Hess's Law states the ΔH of the net reaction is the sum of the ΔH of the steps.
The rewritten reactions are as follows:

S (g) $+ \cancel{3/2\ O_2}$ (g) $\rightarrow \cancel{SO_3(g)}$ $\Delta H = -204$ kJ mol^{-1}
$\cancel{SO_3(g)} \rightarrow SO_2$ (g) $+ \cancel{1/2\ O_2(g)}$ $\Delta H = -89.5$ kJ mol^{-1}

S (g) $+ O_2$ (g) $\rightarrow SO_2$ (g) $\Delta H = -294$ kJmol$^{-1} = \Delta_f H$

Note that this is not under standard conditions, since S is not a solid.

6.113   **Given:** 25.3% methane (CH_4), 38.2% ethane (C_2H_6), and the rest propane (C_3H_8) by volume; $V = 1.55$ L tank, $P = 755$ torr, and $T = 298$ K   **Find:** heat for combustion
Conceptual Plan: percent composition $\rightarrow$ **torr** $\rightarrow$ **bar then** $P, V, T \rightarrow n$ **then**

$$\text{Dalton's Law of Partial Pressures} \qquad \frac{1\ bar}{750.064\ torr} \qquad PV = nRT$$

use data in Problem 91 for methane, and calculate heat of combustion for ethane and propane

$\Delta_r H°$ (CH_4) $= -802.3$ kJ; $\Delta_r H°$ (C_3H_8) $= -2217$ kJ write balanced reaction then $\Delta_r H° = \sum n_p \Delta_f H°$ (*products*) $- \sum n_r \Delta_f H°$ (*reactants*)
then $n, \Delta H \rightarrow q$

Solution: $P_{CH_4} = \dfrac{25.3\ \cancel{\text{torr }CH_4}}{100\ \cancel{\text{torr gas}}} \times 755\ \cancel{\text{torr gas}} \times \dfrac{1\ bar\ CH_4}{750.064\ \cancel{\text{torr}}} = 0.2\underline{5}46649$ bar CH_4,

$$P_{C_2H_6} = \frac{38.2 \text{ torr } C_2H_6}{100 \text{ torr gas}} \times 755 \text{ torr gas} \times \frac{1 \text{ bar } C_2H_6}{750.064 \text{ torr}} = 0.3845139 \text{ bar } C_2H_6,$$

$$P_{C_3H_8} = \frac{100 - (25.3 + 38.2) \text{ torr } C_3H_8}{100 \text{ torr gas}} \times 755 \text{ torr gas} \times \frac{1 \text{ bar } C_3H_8}{750.064 \text{ torr}} = 0.3674020 \text{ bar } C_3H_8$$

$PV = nRT$ Rearrange to solve for n.

$$n_{CH_4} = \frac{PV}{RT} = \frac{0.2546649 \text{ bar } CH_4 \times 1.55 \text{ L}}{0.08314 \dfrac{\text{L} \cdot \text{bar}}{\text{mol} \cdot \text{K}} \times 298 \text{ K}} = 0.01593215 \text{ mol } CH_4,$$

$$n_{C_2H_6} = \frac{PV}{RT} = \frac{0.3845139 \text{ bar } C_2H_6 \times 1.55 \text{ L}}{0.08314 \dfrac{\text{L} \cdot \text{bar}}{\text{mol} \cdot \text{K}} \times 298 \text{ K}} = 0.02405567 \text{ mol } C_2H_6$$

$$n_{C_2H_6} = \frac{PV}{RT} = \frac{0.3674020 \text{ bar } C_3H_8 \times 1.55 \text{ L}}{0.08314 \dfrac{\text{L} \cdot \text{bar}}{\text{mol} \cdot \text{K}} \times 298 \text{ K}} = 0.02298513 \text{ mol } C_3H_8$$

$C_2H_6 (g) + 7/2 O_2 (g) \rightarrow 2 CO_2 (g) + 3 H_2O (g)$

Reactant/Product	$\Delta_f H°$ (kJ mol^{-1} from Appendix IIB)
$C_2H_6 (g)$	− 84.68
$O_2 (g)$	0.0
$CO_2 (g)$	− 393.5
$H_2O (g)$	− 241.8

Be sure to pull data for the correct formula and phase.

$$\begin{aligned}
\Delta_r H° &= \sum n_p \Delta_f H° (products) - \sum n_r \Delta_f H° (reactants) \\
&= [2(\Delta_f H°(CO_2 (g))) + 3(\Delta_f H°(H_2O (g)))] - [1(\Delta_f H°(C_2H_6 (g))) + 7/2(\Delta_f H°(O_2 (g)))] \\
&= [2(- 393.5 \text{ kJ mol}^{-1}) + 3(- 241.8 \text{ kJ mol}^{-1})] - [1(- 84.68 \text{ kJ mol}^{-1}) + 7/2(0.0 \text{ kJ mol}^{-1})] \\
&= [- 1512.4 \text{ kJ mol}^{-1}] - [- 84.68 \text{ kJ mol}^{-1}] \\
&= - 1427.7 \text{ kJ mol}^{-1}
\end{aligned}$$

$C_3H_8 (g) + 5 O_2 (g) \rightarrow 3 CO_2 (g) + 4 H_2O (g)$

Reactant/Product	$\Delta_f H°$ (kJ mol^{-1} from Appendix IIB)
$C_3H_8 (g)$	− 103.85
$O_2 (g)$	0.0
$CO_2 (g)$	− 393.5
$H_2O (g)$	− 241.8

Be sure to pull data for the correct formula and phase.

$$\begin{aligned}
\Delta_r H° &= \sum n_p \Delta_f H° (products) - \sum n_r \Delta_f H° (reactants) \\
&= [3(\Delta_f H°(CO_2 (g))) + 4(\Delta_f H°(H_2O (g)))] - [1(\Delta_f H°(C_3H_8 (g))) + 5(\Delta_f H°(O_2 (g)))] \\
&= [3(- 393.5 \text{ kJ mol}^{-1}) + 4(- 241.8 \text{ kJ mol}^{-1})] - [1(- 103.85 \text{ kJ mol}^{-1}) + 5(0.0 \text{ kJ mol}^{-1})] \\
&= [- 2147.7 \text{ kJ mol}^{-1}] - [- 103.85 \text{ kJ mol}^{-1}] \\
&= - 2043.9 \text{ kJ mol}^{-1}
\end{aligned}$$

$$0.01593215 \text{ mol } CH_4 \times \frac{-802.3 \text{ kJ}}{1 \text{ mol } CH_4} = - 12.782364 \text{ kJ},$$

$$0.02405567 \text{ mol } C_2H_6 \times \frac{-1427.7 \text{ kJ}}{1 \text{ mol } C_2H_6} = - 34.344280 \text{ kJ, and}$$

$$0.02298513 \text{ mol } C_3H_8 \times \frac{-2043.9 \text{ kJ}}{1 \text{ mol } C_3H_8} = - 46.979307 \text{ kJ}$$

The total heat is −12.782364 − 34.344280 − 46.979307 = −94.105951 = −94.1

Check: The units (kJ) are correct. The magnitude of the answer (–100 kJ) makes sense because heats of combustion are typically large and negative.

6.115   **Given:** 1.55 cm copper cube and 1.62 cm aluminum cube, $T_{\text{Metalsi}} = 55.0 °C$, 100.0 mL water, $T_{\text{H}_2\text{Oi}} = 22.2 °C$
Other: density (water) = 0.998 g mL^{-1} **Find:** T_f

Conceptual Plan: pull d values from Table 1.4 then edge length $\rightarrow V \rightarrow m$ then

Cu: 8.96 g mL^{-1} Al: 2.70 g mL^{-1} $\qquad\qquad$ $V = l^3$ $d = m/V$

pull C_s values from Table 6.4   then $m, C_s, T_i \rightarrow T_f$

Cu: 0.385 $\dfrac{J}{g \cdot °C}$ Al: 0.903 $\dfrac{J}{g \cdot °C}$ H$_2$O: 4.184 $\dfrac{J}{g \cdot °C}$ $\quad q = mC_s(T_f - T_i)$ then set $q_{Cu} + q_{Al} = -q_{H_2O}$

Solution: $V_{Cu} = l^3 = (1.55 \text{ cm})^3 = 3.723875 \text{ cm}^3 = 3.723875 \text{ mL}$ and

$V_{Al} = l^3 = (1.62 \text{ cm})^3 = 4.251528 \text{ cm}^3 = 4.251528 \text{ mL}$ then $d = m/V$. Rearrange to solve for m. $m = d\,V$

$m_{Cu} = 8.96 \dfrac{g}{\text{mL}} \times 3.723875 \text{ mL} = 33.36592 \text{ g Cu},$

$m_{Al} = 2.70 \dfrac{g}{\text{mL}} \times 4.251528 \text{ mL} = 11.4791256 \text{ g Al}$ and $m_{H_2O} = 0.998 \dfrac{g}{\text{mL}} \times 100.0 \text{ mL} = 99.8 \text{ g H}_2\text{O}$

$q = mC_s(T_f - T_i)$ substitute in values and set $q_{Cu} + q_{Al} = -q_{H_2O}$.

$q_{Cu} + q_{Al} = m_{Cu}C_{Cu}(T_f - T_{Cui}) + m_{Al}C_{Al}(T_f - T_{Ali}) =$

$\qquad 33.36592 \text{ g} \times 0.385 \dfrac{J}{g \cdot °C} \times (T_f - 55.0 °C) + 11.4791256 \text{ g} \times 0.903 \dfrac{J}{g \cdot °C} \times (T_f - 55.0 °C) =$

$\qquad - q_{H_2O} = - m_{H_2O}C_{H_2O}(T_f - T_{H_2Oi}) = - 99.8 \text{ g} \times 4.184 \dfrac{J}{g \cdot °C} \times (T_f - 22.2 °C)$

Rearrange to solve for T_f.

$12.84588 \dfrac{J}{°C} \times (T_f - 55.0 °C) + 10.36565 \dfrac{J}{°C} \times (T_f - 55.0 °C) = - 417.563 \dfrac{J}{°C} \times (T_f - 22.2 °C) \rightarrow$

$12.84588 \dfrac{J}{°C}T_f - 706.5234 \text{ J} + 10.36565 \dfrac{J}{°C}T_f - 570.1108 \text{ J} = - 417.563 \dfrac{J}{°C}T_f + 9269.899 \text{ J} \rightarrow$

$12.84588 \dfrac{J}{°C}T_f + 10.36565 \dfrac{J}{°C}T_f + 417.563 \dfrac{J}{°C}T_f = + 706.5234 \text{ J} + 570.1108 \text{ J} + 9269.899 \text{ J} \rightarrow$

$440.7745 \dfrac{J}{°C}T_f = 10546.533 \text{ J} \rightarrow T_f = \dfrac{10546.533 \text{ J}}{440.7745 \dfrac{J}{°C}} = 23.92726 °C = 23.9 °C$

Check: The units (°C) are correct. The magnitude of the answer (24) makes physical sense because the heat transfer is dominated by the water (larger mass and larger specific heat capacity). The final temperature should be closer to the initial temperature of water than of copper and aluminum.

6.117 **Given:** $m_{ice} = 2.0 \text{ kg}$, $T_i = -15 °C$, $T_f = 15 °C$, ΔH_{fus} for ice = 6.01 kJ mol^{-1}, $C_{ice} = 2.108$ J g^{-1} °C^{-1}, ΔH_{comb} for methane = $- 891$ kJ mol^{-1} **Find:** volume of methane at STP required to convert ice to water at required temperature.

Conceptual Plan: determine total heat required by summing the heat required to raise temperature of ice from –15 °C to 0 °C, the heat required to melt the ice, and the heat required to raise the temperature of water from 0 °C to 15 °C.

$\qquad 4.184 \text{ J g}^{-1} °C^{-1} \quad q = mC_s \Delta T \quad\quad q = n\Delta H_{fus} \dfrac{1 \text{ mol}}{18.02 \text{ g}} \quad\quad q_{total} = q_1 + q_2 + q_3 \ldots$

Relate the heat required to melt the ice and warm the water to the number moles of methane required to generate that much heat.

$\qquad\qquad q_{ice/water} = -q_{methane} = -n\Delta H_{comb}$

then use the ideal gas law to find the volume.

$\qquad\qquad PV = nRT \quad 0.08314 \dfrac{\text{bar L}}{\text{mol K}}$

Solution: $q_{ice} = mC_s \Delta T = (2.0 \times 10^{-3} \text{ g})(2.108 \text{ J g}^{-1} °C^{-1})(0-(-15)) = 6.324 \times 10^4 \text{ J}$

$q_{melt} = 6.01 \text{ kJ mol}^{-1} \times \dfrac{2.0 \times 10^3 \text{ g}}{18.02 \text{ g mol}^{-1}} = 6.67037 \times 10^2 \text{ kJ} = 6.67037 \times 10^5 \text{ J}$

$q_{water} = mC_s \Delta T = (2.0 \times 10^3 \text{ g})(4.184 \text{ J g}^{-1} °C^{-1})(15-0) = 1.2552 \times 10^5 \text{ J}$

$q_{total} = 6.324 \times 10^4 \text{ J} + 6.67037 \times 10^5 \text{ J} + 1.2552 \times 10^5 \text{ J} = 8.55797 \times 10^5 \text{ J} = 8.55797 \times 10^2 \text{ kJ}$

$$n_{\text{methane}} = \frac{1 \text{ mol}}{891 \text{ kJ}} \times 8.\underline{5}5797 \times 10^2 \text{ kJ} = 0.9\underline{6}049 \text{ mol CH}^4$$

$$V = \frac{nRT}{P} = \frac{(0.96049 \text{ mol})\left(0.08314 \dfrac{\text{bar L}}{\text{mol K}}\right)(273.15 \text{ K})}{1 \text{ bar}} = 21.812 \text{ L} = 22 \text{ L}$$

Check: The volume of one mole of an ideal gas at STP is 22.7 L. Since a little less than one mole of methane is required, the answer of 22 L is reasonable.

6.119 **Given:** for dissolution of NH_4NO_3 $\Delta_r H = 28.1$ kJ mol^{-1}, $C_{\text{beer}} = 1.5$ kJ °C^{-1}, 250 g H_2O, $T_i = 20$ °C, $T_f = 9$ °C, 35% cooling efficiency **Find:** mass of NH_4NO_3 required for cooling.
Conceptual Plan: determine the amount of heat lost to cool the beer and water and then factor in the cooling efficiency to determine the total amount of heat absorbed by the NH_4NO_3.

$$q_{\text{beer}} = C_{\text{beer}} \, \Delta T \quad \frac{1.5 \text{ kJ}}{1 \text{ °C}} \quad q_{\text{water}} = mC_s \, \Delta T \quad \frac{4.184 \text{ J}}{1 \text{ g °C}} \quad \frac{100 \text{ J}}{35 \text{ J}}$$

Use the heat absorbed by the NH_4NO_3 and the enthalpy of dissolution to determine the moles of NH_4NO_3. Convert moles to mass of NH_4NO_3.

$$q = \Delta_r H \times n \quad n = \frac{g}{g \text{ mol}^{-1}} \quad \frac{80.052 \text{ g}}{1 \text{ mol}}$$

Solution:
$q_{\text{beer}} = C_{\text{beer}} \, \Delta T = (1.5 \text{ kJ °C}^{-1})(9\text{--}20) = -1\underline{6}.5 \text{ kJ} = -1.\underline{6}5 \times 10^4 \text{ J}$
$q_{\text{water}} = mC_s \, \Delta T = (250 \text{ g})(4.184 \text{ J g}^{-1} \text{ °C}^{-1})(9\text{--}20) = -1.\underline{1}506 \times 10^4 \text{ J}$

$$q_{\text{total}} = (q_{\text{beer}} + q_{\text{water}})\left(\frac{100 \text{ J}}{35 \text{ J}}\right) = (-1.\underline{6}5 \times 10^4 \text{ J} + -1.\underline{1}506 \times 10^4 \text{ J})\left(\frac{100 \text{ J}}{35 \text{ J}}\right) = -8.\underline{0}017 \times 10^{4} \text{ J} = -8.\underline{0}017 \times 10^1 \text{ kJ}$$

$$q_{\text{NH}_4\text{NO}_3} = -q_{\text{total}} = 8.\underline{0}017 \times 10^1 \text{ kJ} \quad n_{\text{NH}_4\text{NO}_3} = (8.\underline{0}017 \times 10^1 \text{ kJ})\left(\frac{1 \text{ mol}}{28.1 \text{ kJ}}\right) = 2.\underline{8}4759 \text{ mol}$$

$$m_{\text{NH}_4\text{NO}_3} = (2.\underline{8}4759 \text{ mol})\left(\frac{80.052 \text{ g}}{1 \text{ mol}}\right) = 2\underline{2}7.955 \text{ g} = 230 \text{ g}$$

Check: Given the mass of water and beer to cool, plus considering the 35% "cooling power" efficiency of the cold pack, a mass of 230 g of ammonium nitrate is reasonable.

Challenge Problems

6.121 **Given:** 2.5×10^3 kg SUV, $v_1 = 0.0$ mph, $v_2 = 65.0$ mph, octane combustion, 30 % efficiency **Find:** m (CO$_2$)
Conceptual Plan: mi hr^{-1} → m hr^{-1} → m min^{-1} → m s^{-1} then m, v → KE then

$$\frac{1000 \text{ m}}{0.6214 \text{ mi}} \quad \frac{1 \text{ hr}}{60 \text{ min}} \quad \frac{1 \text{ min}}{60 \text{ sec}} \qquad KE = \frac{1}{2}mv^2$$

KE_1, KE_2 → ΔU **used** → ΔU **generated**

$$\Delta U_{\text{sys}} = KE_2 - KE_1 \frac{100 \text{ J generated}}{30 \text{ J used}}$$

use reaction from Problem 91 C$_8$H$_{18}$ (l) + 25/2 O$_2$ (g) → 8 CO$_2$ (g) + 9 H$_2$O (g)

with $\Delta_r H° = -5074.1$ kJ

ΔU **generated (J)** → kJ → mol (C$_8$H$_{18}$) → mol CO$_2$ → g CO$_2$

$$\frac{1 \text{ kJ}}{1000 \text{ J}} \quad \frac{1 \text{ mol C}_8\text{H}_{18}}{5074.1 \text{ kJ}} \quad \frac{8 \text{ mol CO}_2}{1 \text{ mol C}_8\text{H}_{18}} \quad \frac{44.01 \text{ g}}{1 \text{ mol}}$$

Solution: $v_1 = 0.0$ m s^{-1}, 65.0 m̶i̶ h̶r̶$^{-1}$ $\times \dfrac{1000 \text{ m}}{0.6214 \text{ m̶i̶}} \times \dfrac{1 \text{ h̶r̶}}{60 \text{ m̶i̶n̶}} \times \dfrac{1 \text{ m̶i̶n̶}}{60 \text{ sec}} = 29.\underline{0}563$ m s^{-1} then $KE = \dfrac{1}{2}mv^2$

$$KE_1 = \frac{1}{2}(2.5 \times 10^3 \text{ kg})(0)^2 = 0$$

$$KE_2 = \frac{1}{2}(2.5 \times 10^3 \text{ kg})\left(29.\underline{0}563\frac{\text{m}}{\text{s}}\right)^2 = 1.\underline{0}5533 \times 10^6 \frac{\text{kg m}^2}{\text{s}^2} = 1.\underline{0}5533 \times 10^6 \text{ J}$$

$$\Delta U_{\text{sys}} = KE_2 - KE_1 = 1.\underline{0}5533 \times 10^6 \text{ J} - 0 \text{ J} = 1.\underline{0}5533 \times 10^6 \text{ J̶ ̶u̶s̶e̶d̶} \times \frac{100 \text{ J generated}}{30 \text{ J̶ ̶u̶s̶e̶d̶}} =$$

$$= 3.\underline{5}1777 \times 10^6 \text{ J generated}$$

$$3.51777 \times 10^6 \text{ J generated} \times \frac{1 \text{ kJ}}{1000 \text{ J}} \times \frac{1 \text{ mol } C_8H_{18}}{5074.1 \text{ kJ}} \times \frac{8 \text{ mol } CO_2}{1 \text{ mol } C_8H_{18}} \times \frac{44.01 \text{ g } CO_2}{1 \text{ mol } CO_2} = 240 \text{ g } CO_2$$

Check: The units (g) are correct. The magnitude (240) is reasonable, considering the vehicle is so heavy and we generate 8 moles of CO_2 for each mole of octane.

6.123 **Given:** water: $V = 35$ L, $T_i = 25.0\ °C$, $T_f = 100.0\ °C$; fuel = C_7H_{16} , 15% efficiency, $d = 0.78$ g mL^{-1}
Find: V (fuel)
Conceptual Plan: write balanced reaction then $\Delta_r H° = \sum n_p \Delta_f H°(products) - \sum n_r \Delta_f H°(reactants)$ **then**
$\text{L} \to \text{mL} \to \text{g then } T_i, T_f \to \Delta T \text{ then } m, C_s, \Delta T \to q_{H_2O} \text{ (J)} \to q_{H_2O} \text{ (kJ)} \to q_r \text{ (kJ)}$

$\dfrac{1000 \text{ mL}}{1 \text{ L}} \quad \dfrac{1.0 \text{ g}}{1.0 \text{ mL}} \qquad\qquad \Delta T = T_f - T_i \qquad q_{H_2O} = m_{H_2O}C_{H_2O}\Delta T_{H_2O} \dfrac{1 \text{ kJ}}{1000 \text{ J}} \qquad q_r = -q_{H_2O}$

then q_r **generated (J)** $\to$ q_r **used (kJ)** $\to$ **mol** C_7H_{16} $\to$ **g** C_7H_{16} $\to$ **mL** C_7H_{16}

$\dfrac{100 \text{ J generated}}{15 \text{ J needed}} \qquad \dfrac{1 \text{ mol } C_7H_{16}}{\Delta_r H°} \qquad \dfrac{100.21 \text{ g}}{1 \text{ mol}} \qquad \dfrac{1.0 \text{ mL}}{0.78 \text{ g}}$

Solution: Combustion is the combination with oxygen to form carbon dioxide and water:
$C_7H_{16}\ (l) + 11\ O_2\ (g) \to 7\ CO_2\ (g) + 8\ H_2O\ (g)$

Reactant/Product	$\Delta_f H°$ (kJ mol^{-1} from Appendix IIB)
$C_7H_{16}\ (l)$	-224.4
$O_2\ (g)$	0.0
$CO_2\ (g)$	-393.5
$H_2O\ (g)$	-241.8

Be sure to pull data for the correct formula and phase.
$\Delta_r H° = \sum n_p \Delta_f H°(products) - \sum n_r \Delta_f H°(reactants)$
$\quad = [7(\Delta_f H°(CO_2\ (g))) + 8(\Delta_f H°(H_2O\ (g)))] - [1(\Delta_f H°(C_7H_{16}\ (l))) + 11(\Delta_f H°(O_2\ (g)))]$
$\quad = [7(-393.5 \text{ kJ mol}^{-1}) + 8(-241.8 \text{ kJ mol}^{-1})] - [1(-224.4 \text{ kJ mol}^{-1}) + 11(0.0 \text{ kJ mol}^{-1})]$
$\quad = [-4688.9 \text{ kJ mol}^{-1}] - [-224.4 \text{ kJ mol}^{-1}]$
$\quad = -4464.5 \text{ kJ mol}^{-1}$

$35 \text{ L} \times \dfrac{1000 \text{ mL}}{1 \text{ L}} \times \dfrac{1.0 \text{ g}}{1.0 \text{ mL}} = 35000 \text{ g then } \Delta T = T_f - T_i = 100.0\ °C - 25.0\ °C = 75.0\ °C \text{ then}$

$q_{H_2O} = m_{H_2O}C_{H_2O}\Delta T_{H_2O} = 35000 \text{ g} \times 4.184 \dfrac{\text{J}}{\text{g} \cdot °C} \times 75.0\ °C = 1.09725 \times 10^7 \text{ J} \times \dfrac{1 \text{ kJ}}{1000 \text{ J}} = 1.09725 \times 10^4 \text{ kJ}$

$q_r = -q_{H_2O} = -1.09725 \times 10^4 \text{ kJ} \times \dfrac{100 \text{ kJ generated}}{15 \text{ kJ used}} \times \dfrac{1 \text{ mol } C_7H_{16}}{-4467.3 \text{ kJ}} \times \dfrac{100.21 \text{ g } C_7H_{16}}{1 \text{ mol } C_7H_{16}} \times \dfrac{1.0 \text{ mL } C_7H_{16}}{0.78 \text{ g } C_7H_{16}} =$

$= 2100 \text{ mL } C_7H_{16} = 2.1 \text{ L } C_7H_{16}$
Check: The units (mL) are correct. The magnitude (2 L) is a reasonable volume to have to take on a backpacking trip.

6.125 **Given:** $C_{shiraz} = 3.40$ kJ $°C^{-1}$, for shiraz: $T_i = 23.1\ °C$, $T_f = 15.0\ °C$, for ice: $C_{ice} = 2.108$ J g^{-1} $°C^{-1}$, $\Delta H_{fus} = 6.02$ kJ mol^{-1}, for ice/water: $T_i = -5.0\ °C$, $T_f = 15.0\ °C$ **Find:** mass of ice required to cool shiraz.

Conceptual Plan: determine the required heat loss for the shiraz to cool down and equate that to the total heat required to warm the ice, melt the ice, and warm the water to the final temperature.

$q_{shiraz} = C_{shiraz}\Delta T \quad \dfrac{3.40 \text{ kJ}}{1\ °C} \qquad q_{ice} = mC_{ice}\Delta T \quad \dfrac{2.108 \text{ J}}{1 \text{ g } °C} \qquad q_{melt} = n\Delta H_{fus} \quad \dfrac{1 \text{ mol}}{18.02 \text{ g}} \qquad q_{water} = mC_{water}\Delta T \quad \dfrac{4.184 \text{ J}}{1 \text{ g } °C}$

Substitute into the equation and solve for mass.

$q_{shiraz} = -(q_{ice} + q_{melt} + q_{water})$

Solution: $q_{shiraz} = C_{shiraz}\Delta T = (3.40 \text{ kJ } °C^{-1})(15.0\ °C - 23.1\ °C) = -27.54 \text{ kJ} = -2.754 \times 10^4 \text{ J}$

$q_{shiraz} = -(q_{ice} + q_{melt} + q_{water})$

$-2.754 \times 10^4 = -\left(m\left(\dfrac{2.108 \text{ J}}{1 \text{ g } °C}\right) \right)(0.0\ °C - (-5.0\ °C)) + m\dfrac{6.02 \times 10^3 \text{ J}}{1 \text{ mol}} \dfrac{1 \text{ mol}}{18.02 \text{ g}} + m\left(\dfrac{4.184 \text{ J}}{1 \text{ g } °C}\right)(15.0\ °C - 0.0\ °C))$

$2.754 \times 10^4 = 10.54m + 334.073m + 62.76m \qquad 2.754 \times 10^4 = 407.373m \qquad m = 67.604 \text{ g} = 67.6 \text{ g}$

Check: Because water has a higher heat capacity than the wine it should take a mass of ice less than a typical bottle of wine to cool the wine to the desired temperature. Taking other factors into consideration (heat required to warm the ice and heat required to melt the ice), a mass of 67.6 g is reasonable.

6.127   **Given:** the relationship between temperature and kinetic energy for an ideal gas   **Find:** molar heat capacity at constant volume (C_v) and molar heat capacity and constant pressure (C_p)

Conceptual Plan: use the kinetic energy formula and substitute the velocity with the root mean square velocity of a gas, then find ΔU under the different conditions of constant volume and pressure.

$$KE = \frac{1}{2}mv^2 \quad \mu_{rms} = \sqrt{\frac{3RT}{M}} \quad \Delta U = q + w$$

Solution:

$KE = \frac{1}{2}mv^2$, for an ideal gas $v = u_{rms} = \sqrt{\frac{3RT}{M}}$ and so $KE_{avg} = \frac{1}{2}N_A mu_{rms}^2 = \frac{3}{2}RT$ then

$\Delta U_{sys} = KE_2 - KE_1 = \frac{3}{2}RT_2 - \frac{3}{2}RT_1 = \frac{3}{2}R\Delta T$. At constant V $\Delta U_{sys} = C_V\Delta T$ so $C_V = \frac{3}{2}R$.

At constant P, $\Delta U_{sys} = q + w = q_P - P\Delta V = \Delta H - P\Delta V$, but since $PV = nRT$, for one mole of an ideal gas at constant P $P\Delta V = R\Delta T$, so $\Delta U_{sys} = q + w = q_P - P\Delta V = \Delta H - P\Delta V = \Delta H - R\Delta T$ then

$\frac{3}{2}R\Delta T = \Delta H - R\Delta T$ or $\Delta H = \frac{5}{2}R\Delta T = C_P\Delta T$ so $C_P = \frac{5}{2}R$.

6.129   **Given:** $\Delta H_{vap} = 40.7$ kJ mol^{-1} at $T = 373$ K, 454 g H_2O **Find:** $q, w, \Delta U, \Delta H$ for evaporation of water

Conceptual Plan: convert mass of water to moles and use the enthalpy of vaporization to find q,

$$mol = \frac{g}{g\ mol^{-1}} \quad \frac{1\ mol}{18.02\ g} \quad q = n\Delta H_{vap}$$

Then find the difference in volume between the liquid and gaseous water using density and the ideal gas law (assume $P = 1$ bar), then

$$d = \frac{m}{V} \quad d_{H_2O} = \frac{0.9998\ g}{mL} \quad PV = nRT \quad 0.08314\ \frac{bar\ L}{mol\ K} \quad \Delta V = V_G - V_L$$

determine the work and ΔU

$$w = -P\Delta V\frac{100\ J}{1L\ bar} \quad \Delta U = q + w$$

Solution:

$q = \Delta H = 454\ g \times \frac{1\ mol}{18.02\ g} \times \frac{40.7\ kJ}{1\ mol} = 1025.405\ kJ = 1030\ kJ$ and $w = -P\Delta V$. Assume that $P = 1$ bar

(exactly) and $\Delta V = V_G - V_L$, where $V_L = 454\ g \times \frac{1\ mL}{0.9998\ g} \times \frac{1\ L}{1000\ mL} = 0.4540908\ L$ and $PV = nRT$.

Rearrange to solve for V_G. $V_G = \frac{nRT}{P} = \dfrac{454\ g \times \frac{1\ mol}{18.02\ g} \times 0.08314\ \frac{L\cdot bar}{mol\cdot K} \times 373\ K}{1\ bar} = 781.3038\ L$

$\Delta V = V_G - V_L = 781.3038\ L - 0.4540908\ L = 780.8497\ L$ and so

$w = -P\Delta V = -1.0\ bar \times 780.8497\ L \times \frac{100.0\ J}{1\ L\cdot bar} = -78084.97\ J = -7.81 \times 10^4\ J = -78.1\ kJ.$

Finally $\Delta U = q + w = 1025.405\ kJ - 78.08497\ kJ = 947.320\ kJ = 950\ kJ.$

6.131   **Given:** equation for combustion of octane (see problem 91.c), $\Delta_r H = -1303$ kJ mol^{-1} at 298 K   **Find:** $\Delta_r U$

Conceptual Plan: assume the volume of the liquid is negligible compared to the volume of the gases and determine the volume change for the reaction

$$\Delta V = V_G - V_L = \Delta V_G \quad PV = nRT \quad 0.08314\ \frac{bar\ L}{mol\ K}$$

then (assuming P = 1 bar) find work and use the work and the given heat for 1 mole of octane to determine ΔU

$$\Delta w = -P\Delta V \frac{100\,\text{J}}{1\text{L bar}} \qquad \Delta U = q + w$$

Solution:

C_8H_{18} (l) + 25/2 O_2 (g) $\rightarrow$ 8 CO_2 (g) + 9 H_2O (l); $q = \Delta H = -1303$ kJ mol^{-1}, and $w = -P\Delta V$. Assume that $P = 1$ bar (exactly) and $\Delta V = \Delta V_G$ since the gas volumes are so much larger than the liquid volumes. The change in the number of moles of gas $\Delta n_G = 8\ \text{mol} - \frac{25}{2}\text{mol} = -4.5$ mol and $P\Delta V = \Delta nRT$. Rearrange to solve for ΔV_G. $\Delta V_G = \frac{\Delta nRT}{P} = \frac{-4.5\ \cancel{\text{mol}} \times 0.08314 \frac{\text{L}\cdot\cancel{\text{bar}}}{\cancel{\text{mol}}\cdot\text{K}} \times 298\ \text{K}}{1\ \cancel{\text{bar}}} = -111.4907$ L and so

$w = -P\Delta V = -1.0\ \cancel{\text{bar}} \times (-111.4907\ \cancel{\text{L}}) \times \frac{100.0\ \text{J}}{1\ \cancel{\text{L}}\cdot\cancel{\text{bar}}} = +11149.07\ \text{J} = +11000\ \text{J} = +11\ \text{kJ}.$

Finally $\Delta U = q + w = -1303\ \text{kJ} + 11.14907\ \text{kJ} = -1291.8509\ \text{kJ} = -1292\ \text{kJ}.$

Conceptual Problems

6.133   (d)   Only one answer is possible. $\Delta U_{sys} = -\Delta U_{surr}$.

6.135   (a)   At constant P, $\Delta U_{sys} = q + w = q_P + w = \Delta H + w$ so $\Delta U_{sys} - w = \Delta H = q$.

6.137   The aluminum cylinder will be cooler after 1 hour because it has a lower heat capacity than water (less heat needs to be pulled out for every °C temperature change).

6.139   **Given:** 2418 J heat produced; 5 J work done on surroundings at constant P **Find:** ΔU, ΔH, q, and w
       Conceptual Plan: interpret language to determine the sign of the two terms then $q, w \rightarrow \Delta U_{sys}$
       $$\Delta U = q + w$$
       Solution: Since heat is released from the system to the surroundings, $q = -2418$ J.
       Since the system is doing work on the surroundings, $w = -5$ kJ. At constant P, $\Delta H = q = -2.418$ kJ;
       $\Delta U = q + w = -2418\ \text{J} - 5\ \text{J} = -2423\ \text{J} = -2\ \text{kJ}.$
       Check: The units (kJ) are correct. The magnitude of the answer (–2) makes physical sense because both terms are negative and the amount of work done is negligibly small.

6.141   (b)   If ΔV is positive and the reaction is endothermic, then $w = -P\Delta V < 0$. Since $\Delta U_{sys} = q + w = q_P + w = \Delta H + w$ if w is negative then $\Delta H > \Delta U_{sys}$. If ΔV is positive and the reaction is exothermic, then $\Delta H < \Delta U$.

7 The Quantum-Mechanical Model of the Atom

Review Questions

7.1   When a particle is absolutely small it means that you cannot observe it without disturbing it. When you observe the particle, it behaves differently than when you do not observe it. Electrons fit this description.

7.3   The quantum-mechanical model of the atom is important because it explains how electrons exist in atoms and how those electrons determine the chemical and physical properties of elements.

7.5   The wavelength (λ) of the wave is the distance in space between adjacent crests and is measured in units of distance. The amplitude of the wave is the vertical height of a crest. The more closely spaced the waves, that is, the shorter the wavelength, the more energy there is. The amplitude of the electric and magnetic field waves in light determine the intensity or brightness of the light. The higher the amplitude, the more energy the wave has.

7.7   For visible light, wavelength determines the colour. Red light has a wavelength of 750 nm, the longest wavelength of visible light, and blue has a wavelength of 500 nm.

7.9   (a)   Gamma rays(γ) – the wavelength range is 10^{-11} to 10^{-15} m. Gamma rays are produced by the sun, other stars, and certain unstable atomic nuclei on Earth. Human exposure to gamma rays is dangerous because the high energy of gamma rays can damage biological molecules.

        (b)   X-rays – the wavelength range is 10^{-8} to 10^{-11} m. X-rays are used in medicine. X-rays pass through many substances that block visible light and are therefore used to image bones and internal organs. X-rays are sufficiently energetic to damage biological molecules so, while several yearly exposures to X-rays are harmless, excessive exposure increases cancer risk.

        (c)   Ultraviolet radiation (UV) – the wavelength range is 0.4×10^{-6} to 10^{-8} m. Ultraviolet radiation is most familiar as the component of sunlight that produces a sunburn or suntan. While not as energetic as gamma rays or X-rays, ultraviolet light still carries enough energy to damage biological molecules. Excessive exposure to ultraviolet light increases the risk of skin cancer and cataracts and causes premature wrinkling of the skin.

        (d)   Visible light – the wavelength range is 0.75×10^{-6} to 0.4×10^{-6} m (750 nm to 400 nm). Visible light, as long as the intensity is not too high, does not carry enough energy to damage biological molecules. It does, however, cause certain molecules in our eyes to change their shape, sending a signal to the brain that results in vision.

        (e)   Infrared radiation (IR) – the wavelength range is 0.75×10^{-6} to 10^{-3} m. The heat you feel when you place your hand near a hot object is infrared radiation. All warm objects, including human bodies, emit infrared light. Although infrared light is invisible to our eyes, infrared sensors can detect it and are often used in night vision technology to "see" in the dark.

(f)   Microwave radiation – the wavelength range is 10^{-3} to 10^{-1} m. Microwave radiation is used in radar and in microwave ovens. Microwave radiation is efficiently absorbed by water and can therefore heat substances that contain water.

(g)   Radio waves – the wavelength range is 10^{-1} to 10^5 m. Radio waves are used to transmit the signals responsible for AM and FM radio, cellular telephones, television, and other forms of communication.

7.11   Diffraction occurs when a wave encounters an obstacle or a slit that is comparable in size to its wavelength. The wave bends around the slit. The diffraction of light through two slits separated by a distance comparable to the wavelength of the light results in an interference pattern. Each slit acts as a new wave source, and the two new waves interfere with each other. This results in a pattern of bright and dark lines.

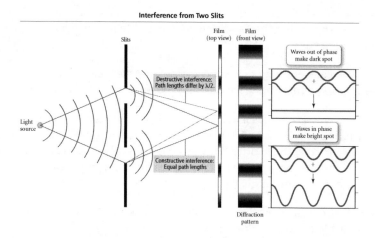

7.13   Because of the results of the experiments with the photoelectric effect, Einstein proposed that light energy must come in packets. The amount of energy in a light packet depends on its frequency (wavelength). The emission of electrons depends on whether or not a single photon has sufficient energy to dislodge a single electron.

7.15   An emission spectrum occurs when an atom absorbs energy and re-emits that energy as light. The light emitted contains distinct wavelengths for each element. The emission spectrum of a particular element is always the same and can be used to identify the element. A white light spectrum is continuous, meaning that there are no sudden interruptions in the intensity of the light as a function of wavelengths. It consists of all wavelengths. Emission spectra are not continuous. They consist of bright lines at specific wavelengths, with complete darkness in between.

7.17   Electron diffraction occurs when an electron beam is aimed at two closely spaced slits, and a series of detectors is arranged to detect the electrons after they pass through the slits. An interference pattern similar to that observed for light is recorded behind the slits. Electron diffraction is evidence of the wave nature of electrons.

7.19   Complementary properties are those that exclude one another. The more you know about one, the less you know about the other. Which of two complementary properties you observe depends on the experiment you perform. In electron diffraction, when you try to observe which hole the electron goes through (particle nature) you lose the interference pattern (wave nature). When you try to observe the interference pattern, you cannot determine which hole the electron goes through.

7.21   A trajectory is a path that is determined by the particle's velocity (the speed and direction of travel), its position, and the forces acting on it. Both position and velocity are required to predict a trajectory.

7.23   Deterministic means that the present determines the future. That means that under the identical condition, identical results will occur.

7.25   A probability distribution map is a statistical map that shows where an electron is likely to be found under a given set of conditions.

7.27   An orbital is a probability distribution map showing where the electron is likely to be found.

7.29   The principal quantum number (n) is an integer and has possible values of 1,2,3, etc. The principal quantum number determines the overall size and energy of an orbital.

7.31   The magnetic quantum number (m_l) is an integer ranging from $-l$ to $+l$. For example, if $l = 1$, $m_l = -1, 0, +1$. The magnetic quantum number specifies the orientation of the orbital.

7.33   The probability density is the probability per unit volume of finding the electron at a point in space. The radial distribution function represents the total probability of finding the electron within a thin spherical shell at a distance r from the nucleus. In contrast to probability density, which has a maximum at the nucleus for an s orbital, the radial distribution function has a value of zero at the nucleus. It increases to a maximum and then decreases again with increasing r.

7.35   The sublevels are s ($l = 0$), which can hold a maximum of two electrons; p ($l = 1$), which can hold a maximum of six electrons; d ($l = 2$), which can hold a maximum of 10 electrons; and f ($l = 3$), which can hold a maximum of 14 electrons.

7.37   Electron spin is a fundamental property of electrons. It is more correctly expressed as saying the electron has inherent angular momentum. The value m_s is the spin quantum number. An electron with $m_s = +1/2$ has a spin opposite of an electron with $m_s = -1/2$.

7.39   An electron configuration shows the particular orbitals that are occupied by electrons in an atom. Some examples are H = $1s^1$, He = $1s^2$, and Li = $1s^2 2s^1$.

7.41   Shielding or screening occurs when one electron is blocked from the full effects of the nuclear charge so that the electron experiences only a part of the nuclear charge. It is the inner (core) electrons that shield the outer electrons from the full nuclear charge.

7.43   The sublevels within a principle level split in multielectron atoms because of penetration of the outer electrons into the region of the core electrons. The sublevels in hydrogen are not split because they are empty in the ground state.

7.45   The Pauli exclusion principle states the following: No two electrons in an atom can have the same four quantum numbers.

Since two electrons occupying the same orbital have three identical quantum numbers (n, l, m_l), they must have different spin quantum numbers. The Pauli exclusion principle implies that each orbital can have a maximum of only two electrons, with opposing spins.

7.47   The radial probability diagram for a 2s orbital would consist of two peaks (at ~50 and 300 pm) with a node between the peaks. The peaks would be of different heights, with the smaller peak being closer to the nucleus. The radial probability diagram for a 3p orbital has similar features but the peaks occur at distances further from the nucleus and are generally wider than the peaks in the 2s orbital.

Problems by Topic

Electromagnetic Radiation

7.49   **Given:** distance to sun = 1.496 x 10^8 km **Find:** time for light to travel from sun to Earth
Conceptual Plan: distance km $\rightarrow$ distance m $\rightarrow$ time

$$\frac{1000 \text{ m}}{\text{km}} \qquad \text{time} = \frac{\text{distance}}{3.00 \text{ x } 10^8 \text{ m s}^{-1}}$$

Solution: $1.496 \text{ x } 10^8 \text{ km} \text{ x} \frac{1000 \text{ m}}{\text{km}} \text{ x } \frac{\text{s}}{3.00 \text{ x } 10^8 \text{ m}} = 499 \text{ s}$

Check: The units of the answer, seconds, are correct. The magnitude of the answer is reasonable, since it corresponds to about 8 min.

7.51   (i)   By increasing wavelength the order is d) ultraviolet < c) infrared < b) microwaves < a) radio waves.

        (ii)   By increasing energy the order is a) radio waves < b) microwaves < c) infrared < d) ultraviolet.

7.53   (a)   **Given:** λ = 632.8 nm **Find:** frequency (ν)
               Conceptual Plan: nm $\rightarrow$ m $\rightarrow$ ν
               $$\frac{m}{10^9\,nm} \qquad \nu = \frac{c}{\lambda}$$
               Solution: $632.8\,nm \times \dfrac{m}{10^9\,nm} = 6.328 \times 10^{-7}\,m \qquad \nu = \dfrac{3.00 \times 10^8\,m}{s} \times \dfrac{1}{6.328 \times 10^{-7}\,m} = 4.74 \times 10^{14}\,s^{-1}$
               Check: The units of the answer, s^{-1}, are correct. The magnitude of the answer seems reasonable since wavelength and frequency are inversely proportional.

        (b)   **Given:** λ = 503 nm **Find:** frequency (ν)
               Conceptual Plan: nm $\rightarrow$ m $\rightarrow$ ν
               $$\frac{m}{10^9\,nm} \qquad \nu = \frac{c}{\lambda}$$
               Solution: $503\,nm \times \dfrac{m}{10^9\,nm} = 5.03 \times 10^{-7}\,m \qquad \nu = \dfrac{3.00 \times 10^8\,m}{s} \times \dfrac{1}{5.03 \times 10^{-7}\,m} = 5.96 \times 10^{14}\,s^{-1}$
               Check: The units of the answer, s^{-1}, are correct. The magnitude of the answer seems reasonable since wavelength and frequency are inversely proportional.

        (c)   **Given:** λ = 0.052 nm **Find:** frequency (ν)
               Conceptual Plan: nm $\rightarrow$ m $\rightarrow$ ν
               $$\frac{m}{10^9\,nm} \qquad \nu = \frac{c}{\lambda}$$
               Solution: $0.052\,nm \times \dfrac{m}{10^9\,nm} = 5.2 \times 10^{-11}\,m \qquad \nu = \dfrac{3.00 \times 10^8\,m}{s} \times \dfrac{1}{5.2 \times 10^{-11}\,m} = 5.8 \times 10^{18}\,s^{-1}$
               Check: The units of the answer, s^{-1}, are correct. The magnitude of the answer seems reasonable since wavelength and frequency are inversely proportional.

7.55   (a)   **Given:** frequency (ν) from 5 a. = $4.74 \times 10^{14}\,s^{-1}$ **Find:** energy
               Conceptual Plan: ν $\rightarrow$ E
               $$E = h\nu \quad h = 6.626 \times 10^{-34}\,J\,s$$
               Solution: $6.626 \times 10^{-34}\,J\,s \times \dfrac{4.74 \times 10^{14}}{s} = 3.14 \times 10^{-19}\,J$
               Check: The units of the answer, J, are correct. The magnitude of the answer is reasonable since we are talking about the energy of one photon.

        (b)   **Given:** frequency (ν) from 5 b. = $5.96 \times 10^{14}\,s^{-1}$ **Find:** energy
               Conceptual Plan: ν $\rightarrow$ E
               $$E = h\nu \quad h = 6.626 \times 10^{-34}\,J\,s$$
               Solution: $6.626 \times 10^{-34}\,J\,s \times \dfrac{5.96 \times 10^{14}}{s} = 3.95 \times 10^{-19}\,J$
               Check: The units of the answer, J, are correct. The magnitude of the answer is reasonable since we are talking about the energy of one photon.

        (c)   **Given:** frequency (ν) from 5 c. = $5.8 \times 10^{18}\,s^{-1}$ **Find:** energy
               Conceptual Plan: ν $\rightarrow$ E
               $$E = h\nu \quad h = 6.626 \times 10^{-34}\,J\,s$$
               Solution: $6.626 \times 10^{-34}\,J\,s \times \dfrac{5.8 \times 10^{18}}{s} = 3.8 \times 10^{-15}\,J$
               Check: The units of the answer, J, are correct. The magnitude of the answer is reasonable since we are talking about the energy of one photon.

7.57   **Given:** λ = 532 nm and E_{pulse} = 3.85 mJ **Find:** number of photons
        Conceptual Plan: nm $\rightarrow$ m $\rightarrow$ E_{photon} $\rightarrow$ number of photons
        $$\frac{m}{10^9\,nm} \qquad E = \frac{hc}{\lambda}; \; h = 6.626 \times 10^{-34}\,J\,s \qquad \frac{E_{pulse}}{E_{photon}}$$

Solution: $532 \, \text{nm} \times \dfrac{\text{m}}{10^9 \, \text{nm}} = 5.32 \times 10^{-7} \, \text{m}$ $E = \dfrac{6.626 \times 10^{-34} \, \text{J s} \times \dfrac{3.00 \times 10^8 \, \text{m}}{\text{s}}}{5.32 \times 10^{-7} \, \text{m}} = 3.7\underline{3}64 \times 10^{-19} \, \text{J photon}^{-1}$

$3.85 \, \text{mJ} \times \dfrac{\text{J}}{1000 \, \text{mJ}} \times \dfrac{1 \, \text{photon}}{3.7364 \times 10^{-19} \, \text{J}} = 1.03 \times 10^{16} \, \text{photons}$

Check: The units of the answer, number of photons, are correct. The magnitude of the answer is reasonable for the amount of energy involved.

7.59   (a)   **Given:** $\lambda = 1500 \, \text{nm}$ **Find:** E for 1 mol photons

Conceptual Plan: $\text{nm} \rightarrow \text{m} \rightarrow E_{\text{photon}} \rightarrow E(\text{J})_{\text{mol}} \rightarrow E(\text{kJ})_{\text{mol}}$

$\dfrac{\text{m}}{10^9 \, \text{nm}}$ $E = \dfrac{hc}{\lambda}; \; h = 6.626 \times 10^{-34} \, \text{J s}$ $\dfrac{\text{mol}}{6.022 \times 10^{23} \, \text{photons}}$ $\dfrac{\text{kJ}}{1000 \, \text{J}}$

Solution:

$1500 \, \text{nm} \times \dfrac{\text{m}}{10^9 \, \text{nm}} = 1.500 \times 10^{-6} \, \text{m}$ $E = \dfrac{6.626 \times 10^{-34} \, \text{J s} \times \dfrac{3.00 \times 10^8 \, \text{m}}{\text{s}}}{1.500 \times 10^{-6} \, \text{m}} = 1.3\underline{2}52 \times 10^{-19} \, \text{J photon}^{-1}$

$\dfrac{1.3\underline{2}52 \times 10^{-19} \, \text{J}}{\text{photon}} \times \dfrac{6.022 \times 10^{23} \, \text{photons}}{\text{mol}} \times \dfrac{\text{kJ}}{1000 \, \text{J}} = 79.8 \, \text{kJ mol}^{-1}$

Check: The units of the answer, kJ mol^{-1}, are correct. The magnitude of the answer is reasonable for a wavelength in the infrared region.

(b)   **Given:** $\lambda = 500 \, \text{nm}$ **Find:** E for 1 mol photons

Conceptual Plan: $\text{nm} \rightarrow \text{m} \rightarrow E_{\text{photon}} \rightarrow E_{\text{mol}} \rightarrow E(\text{kJ})_{\text{mol}}$

$\dfrac{\text{m}}{10^9 \, \text{nm}}$ $E = \dfrac{hc}{\lambda}; \; h = 6.626 \times 10^{-34} \, \text{J s}$ $\dfrac{\text{mol}}{6.022 \times 10^{23} \, \text{photons}}$ $\dfrac{\text{kJ}}{1000 \, \text{J}}$

Solution:

$500 \, \text{nm} \times \dfrac{\text{m}}{10^9 \, \text{nm}} = 5.00 \times 10^{-7} \, \text{m}$ $E = \dfrac{6.626 \times 10^{-34} \, \text{J s} \times \dfrac{3.00 \times 10^8 \, \text{m}}{\text{s}}}{5.00 \times 10^{-7} \, \text{m}} = 3.9\underline{7}56 \times 10^{-19} \, \text{J photon}^{-1}$

$\dfrac{3.9\underline{7}56 \times 10^{-19} \, \text{J}}{\text{photon}} \times \dfrac{6.022 \times 10^{23} \, \text{photons}}{\text{mol}} \times \dfrac{\text{kJ}}{1000 \, \text{J}} = 239 \, \text{kJ mol}^{-1}$

Check: The units of the answer, kJ mol^{-1}, are correct. The magnitude of the answer is reasonable for a wavelength in the visible region.

(c)   **Given:** $\lambda = 150 \, \text{nm}$ **Find:** E for 1 mol photons

Conceptual Plan: $\text{nm} \rightarrow \text{m} \rightarrow E_{\text{photon}} \rightarrow E_{\text{mol}} \rightarrow E(\text{kJ})_{\text{mol}}$

$\dfrac{\text{m}}{10^9 \, \text{nm}}$ $E = \dfrac{hc}{\lambda}; \; h = 6.626 \times 10^{-34} \, \text{J s}$ $\dfrac{\text{mol}}{6.022 \times 10^{23} \, \text{photons}}$ $\dfrac{\text{kJ}}{1000 \, \text{J}}$

Solution:

$1.50 \, \text{nm} \times \dfrac{\text{m}}{10^9 \, \text{nm}} = 1.50 \times 10^{-7} \, \text{m}$ $E = \dfrac{6.626 \times 10^{-34} \, \text{J s} \times \dfrac{3.00 \times 10^8 \, \text{m}}{\text{s}}}{1.50 \times 10^{-7} \, \text{m}} = 1.3\underline{2}52 \times 10^{-18} \, \text{J photon}^{-1}$

$\dfrac{1.3\underline{2}52 \times 10^{-18} \, \text{J}}{\text{photon}} \times \dfrac{6.022 \times 10^{23} \, \text{photons}}{\text{mol}} \times \dfrac{\text{kJ}}{1000 \, \text{J}} = 798 \, \text{kJ mol}^{-1}$

Check: The units of the answer, kJ mol^{-1}, are correct. The magnitude of the answer is reasonable for a wavelength in the ultraviolet region. Note: The energy increases from the IR to the VIS to the UV as expected.

The Wave Nature of Matter and the Uncertainty Principle

7.61   The interference pattern would be a series of light and dark lines.

7.63   **Given:** $m = 9.109 \times 10^{-31}$ kg, $\lambda = 0.20$ nm **Find:** v
Conceptual Plan: $m, \lambda \rightarrow v$

$$v = \frac{h}{m\lambda}$$

Solution: $\dfrac{6.626 \times 10^{-34} \dfrac{kg \cdot m^2}{s^2} \cdot s}{(9.109 \times 10^{-31} \, kg)(0.20 \, nm)\left(\dfrac{1m}{1 \times 10^9 \, nm}\right)} = 3.6 \times 10^6 \text{ m s}^{-1}$

Check: The units of the answer, m s^{-1}, are correct. The magnitude of the answer is large, as would be expected for the speed of the electron.

7.65   **Given:** $m = 9.109 \times 10^{-31}$ kg; $v = 1.35 \times 10^5$ m s^{-1} **Find:** λ
Conceptual Plan: $m,v \rightarrow \lambda$

$$\lambda = \frac{h}{mv}$$

Solution: $\dfrac{6.626 \times 10^{-34} \dfrac{kg \cdot m^2}{s^2} \cdot s}{(9.109 \times 10^{-31} \, kg)\left(\dfrac{1.35 \times 10^5 \, m}{s}\right)} = 5.39 \times 10^{-9} \text{ m} = 5.39 \text{ nm}$

Check: The units of the answer, m, are correct. The magnitude is reasonable since we are looking at an electron.

7.67   **Given:** $m = 143$ g; $v = 95$ mph **Find:** λ
Conceptual Plan: $m,v \rightarrow \lambda$

$$\lambda = \frac{h}{mv}$$

Solution: $\dfrac{6.626 \times 10^{-34} \dfrac{kg \cdot m^2}{s^2} \cdot s}{(143 \, g)\left(\dfrac{kg}{1000 \, g}\right)\left(\dfrac{95 \, mi}{hr}\right)\left(\dfrac{1.609 \, km}{mi}\right)\left(\dfrac{1000 \, m}{km}\right)\left(\dfrac{hr}{3600 \, s}\right)} = 1.1 \times 10^{-34} \text{ m}$

The value of the wavelength, 1.1×10^{-34} m, is so small it will not have an effect on the trajectory of the baseball.
Check: The units of the answer, m, are correct. The magnitude of the answer is very small, as would be expected for the de Broglie wavelength of a baseball.

7.69   **Given:** $\Delta x = 552$ pm, $m = 9.109 \times 10^{-31}$ kg **Find:** Δv
Conceptual Plan: $\Delta x, m \rightarrow \Delta v$

$$\Delta x \times m\Delta v \geq \frac{h}{4\pi}$$

Solution: $\dfrac{6.626 \times 10^{-34} \dfrac{kg \cdot m^2}{s^2} \cdot s}{4(3.141)(9.109 \times 10^{-31} \, kg)(552 \, pm)\left(\dfrac{m}{1 \times 10^{12} \, pm}\right)} = 1.05 \times 10^5 \text{ m s}^{-1}$

Check: The units of the answer, m s^{-1}, are correct. The magnitude is reasonable for the uncertainty in the speed of an electron.

Photoelectric Effect

7.71   **Given:** for aluminum $\phi = 412$ kJ mol^{-1}, $E_{light} = 471$ kJ mol^{-1}, $m_e = 9.11 \times 10^{-31}$ kg **Find:** velocity of electrons emitted
Conceptual Plan: Determine the energy of each photon and then calculate the difference between the photon energy and the work function to find the kinetic energy of the electron.

$$\frac{6.022 \times 10^{23} \text{ photons}}{1 \text{ mol}} \qquad \frac{1000 \text{ J}}{1 \text{ kJ}} \qquad KE_{electron} = E_{photon} - \phi$$

Use the kinetic energy of the electron and the mass of the electron to find the velocity.

$$KE = \frac{1}{2} mv^2$$

Solution: $E_{photon} = \dfrac{1 \text{ mol}}{6.022 \times 10^{23} \text{ photons}} \times \dfrac{471 \text{ kJ}}{1 \text{ mol}} \times \dfrac{1000 \text{ J}}{1 \text{ kJ}} = 7.8\underline{2}13 \times 10^{-19} \text{ J}$

$\phi = \dfrac{1 \text{ mol}}{6.022 \times 10^{23} \text{ electrons}} \times \dfrac{412 \text{ kJ}}{1 \text{ mol}} \times \dfrac{1000 \text{ J}}{1 \text{ kJ}} = 6.8\underline{4}16 \times 10^{-19} \text{ J}$

$KE_{electron} = E_{photon} - \phi = 7.8\underline{2}13 \times 10^{-19} \text{ J} - 6.8\underline{4}16 \times 10^{-19} \text{ J} = 9.7\underline{9}7 \times 10^{-20} \text{ J}$

$KE = \dfrac{1}{2} mv^2 \quad v = \sqrt{\dfrac{KE}{(0.5)(m)}} = \sqrt{\dfrac{9.797 \times 10^{-20} \text{ J}}{(0.5)(9.11 \times 10^{-31} \text{ kg})}} = 4.6\underline{3}7697 \times 10^5 \text{ m s}^{-1} = 4.64 \times 10^5 \text{ m s}^{-1}$

Check: The units (m s^{-1}) are correct and the magnitude of the velocity (10^5) is reasonable for an electron.

Orbitals and Quantum Numbers

7.73   Since the size of the orbital is determined by the n quantum, with the size increasing with increasing n, an electron in a 2s orbital is closer, on average, to the nucleus than an electron in a 3s orbital.

7.75   The value of l is an integer that lies between 0 and $n - 1$.

(a)   When $n = 1$, l can only be $l = 0$.

(b)   When $n = 2$, l can be $l = 0$ or $l = 1$.

(c)   When $n = 3$, l can be $l = 0$, $l = 1$, or $l = 2$.

(d)   When $n = 4$, l can be $l = 0$, $l = 1$, $l = 2$, or $l = 3$.

7.77   Set c cannot occur together as a set of quantum numbers to specify an orbital. l must lie between 0 and $n - 1$, so for $n = 3$, l can only be as high as 2.

7.79   The 2s orbital would be the same shape as the 1s orbital but would be larger in size and the 3p orbitals would have the same shape as the 2p orbitals but would be larger in size. Also, the 2s and 3p orbitals would have more nodes.

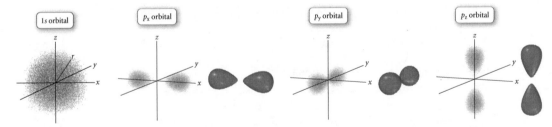

Atomic Spectroscopy

7.81   When the atom emits the photon of energy that was needed to raise the electron to the $n = 2$ level, the photon has the same energy as the energy absorbed to move the electron to the excited state. Therefore, the electron has to be in $n = 1$ (the ground state) following the emission of the photon.

7.83   According to the quantum-mechanical model, the higher the n level the higher the energy. So, the transition from $3p \rightarrow 1s$ would be a greater energy difference than a transition from $2p \rightarrow 1s$. The lower energy transition would have the longer wavelength. Therefore, the $2p \rightarrow 1s$ transition would produce a longer wavelength.

7.85   (a)   **Given:** $n = 2 \rightarrow n = 1$ **Find:** λ

Conceptual Plan: $n = 1, n = 2 \rightarrow \Delta E_{atom} \rightarrow \Delta E_{photon} \rightarrow \lambda$

$$\Delta E_{atom} = E_1 - E_2 \qquad \Delta E_{atom} \rightarrow -\Delta E_{photon} \qquad E = \frac{hc}{\lambda}$$

Solution:

$\Delta E = E_1 - E_2$

$= -2.18 \times 10^{-18} \text{J}\left(\dfrac{1}{1^2}\right) - \left[-2.18 \times 10^{-18}\left(\dfrac{1}{2^2}\right)\right] = -2.18 \times 10^{-18} \text{ J}\left[\left(\dfrac{1}{1^2}\right) - \left(\dfrac{1}{2^2}\right)\right] = -1.635 \times 10^{-18} \text{J}$

$\Delta E_{photon} = -\Delta E_{atom} = 1.635 \times 10^{-18} \text{J} \quad \lambda = \dfrac{hc}{E} = \dfrac{(6.626 \times 10^{-34} \text{J} \cdot \text{s})(3.00 \times 10^8 \text{m s}^{-1})}{1.635 \times 10^{-18} \text{J}} = 1.22 \times 10^{-7} \text{ m}$

This transition would produce a wavelength in the UV region.

Check: The units of the answer, m, are correct. The magnitude of the answer is reasonable since it is in the region of UV radiation.

(b)   **Given:** $n = 3 \to n = 1$ **Find:** λ

       Conceptual Plan: $n = 1, n = 3 \to \Delta E_{atom} \to \Delta E_{photon} \to \lambda$

           $\Delta E_{atom} = E_1 - E_3 \qquad \Delta E_{atom} \to -\Delta E_{photon} \qquad E = \dfrac{hc}{\lambda}$

       Solution:

$\Delta E = E_1 - E_3$

$= -2.18 \times 10^{-18} \text{J}\left(\dfrac{1}{1^2}\right) - \left[-2.18 \times 10^{-18}\left(\dfrac{1}{3^2}\right)\right] = -2.18 \times 10^{-18} \text{ J}\left[\left(\dfrac{1}{1^2}\right) - \left(\dfrac{1}{3^2}\right)\right] = -1.938 \times 10^{-18} \text{ J}$

$\Delta E_{photon} = -\Delta E_{atom} = 1.938 \times 10^{-18} \text{J} \quad \lambda = \dfrac{hc}{E} = \dfrac{(6.626 \times 10^{-34} \text{ J} \cdot \text{s})(3.00 \times 10^8 \text{ m s}^{-1})}{1.938 \times 10^{-18} \text{ J}} = 1.03 \times 10^{-7} \text{ m}$

This transition would produce a wavelength in the UV region.

Check: The units of the answer, m, are correct. The magnitude of the answer is reasonable since it is in the region of UV radiation.

(c)   **Given:** $n = 4 \to n = 2$ **Find:** λ

       Conceptual Plan: $n = 2, n = 4 \to \Delta E_{atom} \to \Delta E_{photon} \to \lambda$

           $\Delta E_{atom} = E_2 - E_4 \qquad \Delta E_{atom} \to -\Delta E_{photon} \qquad E = \dfrac{hc}{\lambda}$

       Solution:

$\Delta E = E_2 - E_4$

$= -2.18 \times 10^{-18} \text{J}\left(\dfrac{1}{2^2}\right) - \left[-2.18 \times 10^{-18}\left(\dfrac{1}{4^2}\right)\right] = -2.18 \times 10^{-18} \text{ J}\left[\left(\dfrac{1}{2^2}\right) - \left(\dfrac{1}{4^2}\right)\right] = -4.087 \times 10^{-19} \text{ J}$

$\Delta E_{photon} = -\Delta E_{atom} = 4.087 \times 10^{-19} \text{J} \quad \lambda = \dfrac{hc}{E} = \dfrac{(6.626 \times 10^{-34} \text{ J} \cdot \text{s})(3.00 \times 10^8 \text{ m s}^{-1})}{4.087 \times 10^{-19} \text{ J}} = 4.86 \times 10^{-7} \text{ m}$

This transition would produce a wavelength in the visible region.

Check: The units of the answer, m, are correct. The magnitude of the answer is reasonable since it is in the region of visible light.

(d)   **Given:** $n = 5 \to n = 2$ **Find:** λ

       Conceptual Plan: $n = 2, n = 5 \to \Delta E_{atom} \to \Delta E_{photon} \to \lambda$

           $\Delta E_{atom} = E_2 - E_5 \qquad \Delta E_{atom} \to -\Delta E_{photon} \qquad E = \dfrac{hc}{\lambda}$

       Solution:

$\Delta E = E_2 - E_5$

$= -2.18 \times 10^{-18} \text{J}\left(\dfrac{1}{2^2}\right) - \left[-2.18 \times 10^{-18}\left(\dfrac{1}{5^2}\right)\right] = -2.18 \times 10^{-18} \text{ J}\left[\left(\dfrac{1}{2^2}\right) - \left(\dfrac{1}{5^2}\right)\right] = -4.578 \times 10^{-19} \text{ J}$

$\Delta E_{photon} = -\Delta E_{atom} = 4.578 \times 10^{-19} \text{J} \quad \lambda = \dfrac{hc}{E} = \dfrac{(6.626 \times 10^{-34} \text{ J} \cdot \text{s})(3.00 \times 10^8 \text{ m s}^{-1})}{4.578 \times 10^{-19} \text{ J}} = 4.34 \times 10^{-7} \text{ m}$

This transition would produce a wavelength in the visible region.

Check: The units of the answer, m, are correct. The magnitude of the answer is reasonable since it is in the region of visible light.

7.87   **Given:** $n(\text{initial}) = 7$ $\lambda = 397$ nm **Find:** $n(\text{final})$

       Conceptual Plan: $\lambda \to \Delta E_{photon} \to \Delta E_{atom} \to n = x, n = 7$

           $E = \dfrac{hc}{\lambda} \qquad \Delta E_{photon} \to -\Delta E_{atom} \qquad \Delta E_{atom} = E_x - E_7$

Solution: $E = \dfrac{hc}{\lambda} = \dfrac{(6.626 \times 10^{-34}\,\text{J} \cdot \cancel{s})(3.00 \times 10^{8}\,\cancel{m}\,\cancel{s}^{-1})}{(397\,\cancel{nm})\left(\dfrac{\cancel{m}}{10^{9}\,\cancel{nm}}\right)} = 5.0\underline{0}7 \times 10^{-19}\,\text{J}$

$\Delta E_{atom} = -\Delta E_{photon} = -5.0\underline{0}7 \times 10^{-19}\,\text{J}$

$\Delta E = E_x - E_7 = -5.0\underline{0}7 \times 10^{-19} = -2.18 \times 10^{-18}\,\text{J}\left(\dfrac{1}{x^2}\right) - \left[-2.18 \times 10^{-18}\left(\dfrac{1}{7^2}\right)\right] = -2.18 \times 10^{-18}\,\text{J}\left[\left(\dfrac{1}{x^2}\right) - \left(\dfrac{1}{7^2}\right)\right]$

$0.2297 = \left(\dfrac{1}{x^2}\right) - \left(\dfrac{1}{7^2}\right) \qquad 0.25229 = \left(\dfrac{1}{x^2}\right) \qquad x^2 = 3.998 \quad x = 2$

Check: The answer is reasonable since it is an integer less than the initial value of 7.

Electron Configurations of Atoms and Ions and Magnetic Properties

7.89   (a)   Si   Silicon has 14 electrons. Distribute two of these into the 1s orbital, two into the 2s orbital, six into the 2p orbital, two into the 3s orbital, and two into the 3p orbital. $1s^2 2s^2 2p^6 3s^2 3p^2$

        (b)   O   Oxygen has 8 electrons. Distribute two of these into the 1s orbital, two into the 2s orbital, and four into the 2p orbital. $1s^2 2s^2 2p^4$

        (c)   K   Potassium has 19 electrons. Distribute two of these into the 1s orbital, two into the 2s orbital, six into the 2p orbital, two into the 3s orbital, six into the 3p orbital, and one into the 4s orbital. $1s^2 2s^2 2p^6 3s^2 3p^6 4s^1$

        (d)   Ne   Neon has 10 electrons. Distribute two of these into the 1s orbital, two into the 2s orbital, and six into the 2p orbital. $1s^2 2s^2 2p^6$

7.91   (a)   N   Nitrogen has 7 electrons and has the electron configuration $1s^2 2s^2 2p^3$. Draw a box for each orbital, putting the lowest energy orbital (1s) on the far left and proceeding to orbitals of higher energy to the right. Distribute the 7 electrons into the boxes representing the orbitals, allowing a maximum of two electrons per orbital and remembering Hund's rule. You can see from the diagram that nitrogen has 3 unpaired electrons.

$$\boxed{\downarrow\uparrow}\quad \boxed{\downarrow\uparrow}\quad \boxed{\uparrow}\,\boxed{\uparrow}\,\boxed{\uparrow}$$
$$1s\qquad\quad 2s\qquad\qquad 2p$$

        (b)   F   Fluorine has 9 electrons and has the electron configuration $1s^2 2s^2 2p^5$. Draw a box for each orbital, putting the lowest energy orbital (1s) on the far left and proceeding to orbitals of higher energy to the right. Distribute the 9 electrons into the boxes representing the orbitals, allowing a maximum of two electrons per orbital and remembering Hund's rule. You can see from the diagram that fluorine has 1 unpaired electron.

$$\boxed{\downarrow\uparrow}\quad \boxed{\downarrow\uparrow}\quad \boxed{\downarrow\uparrow}\,\boxed{\downarrow\uparrow}\,\boxed{\uparrow}$$
$$1s\qquad\quad 2s\qquad\qquad 2p$$

        (c)   Mg   Magnesium has 12 electrons and has the electron configuration $1s^2 2s^2 2p^6 3s^2$. Draw a box for each orbital, putting the lowest energy orbital (1s) on the far left and proceeding to orbitals of higher energy to the right. Distribute the 12 electrons into the boxes representing the orbitals, allowing a maximum of two electrons per orbital and remembering Hund's rule. You can see from the diagram that magnesium has no unpaired electrons.

$$\boxed{\downarrow\uparrow}\quad \boxed{\downarrow\uparrow}\quad \boxed{\downarrow\uparrow}\,\boxed{\downarrow\uparrow}\,\boxed{\downarrow\uparrow}\quad \boxed{\downarrow\uparrow}$$
$$1s\qquad\quad 2s\qquad\qquad 2p\qquad\qquad 3s$$

        (d)   Al   Aluminum has 13 electrons and has the electron configuration $1s^2 2s^2 2p^6 3s^2 3p^1$. Draw a box for each orbital, putting the lowest energy orbital (1s) on the far left and proceeding to orbitals of higher energy to the right. Distribute the 13 electrons into the boxes representing the orbitals, allowing a maximum of two electrons per orbital and remembering Hund's rule. You can see from the diagram that aluminum has 1 unpaired electron.

$$\boxed{\downarrow\uparrow}\quad \boxed{\downarrow\uparrow}\quad \boxed{\downarrow\uparrow}\,\boxed{\downarrow\uparrow}\,\boxed{\downarrow\uparrow}\quad \boxed{\downarrow\uparrow}\quad \boxed{\uparrow}\,\boxed{}\,\boxed{}$$
$$1s\qquad\quad 2s\qquad\qquad 2p\qquad\qquad 3s\qquad\qquad 3p$$

7.93   (a) O^{2-} Begin by writing the electron configuration of the neutral atom.

O $1s^2 2s^2 2p^4$

Since this ion has a 2 – charge, add two electrons to write the electron configuration of the ion.

O^{2-} $1s^2 2s^2 2p^6$ This is isoelectronic with Ne.

(b) Br^- Begin by writing the electron configuration of the neutral atom.

Br $[Ar]4s^2 3d^{10} 4p^5$

Since this ion has a 1 – charge, add one electron to write the electron configuration of the ion.

Br^- $[Ar]4s^2 3d^{10} 4p^6$ This is isoelectronic with Kr.

(c) Sr^{2+} Begin by writing the electron configuration of the neutral atom.

Sr $[Kr]5s^2$

Since this ion has a 2+ charge, remove two electrons to write the electron configuration of the ion.

Sr^{2+} [Kr]

(d) Co^{3+} Begin by writing the electron configuration of the neutral atom.

Co $[Ar]4s^2 3d^7$

Since this ion has a 3+ charge, remove three electrons to write the electron configuration of the ion. Since it is a transition metal, remove the electrons from the 4s orbital before removing electrons from the 3d orbitals.

Co^{3+} $[Ar]4s^0 3d^6$

(e) Cu^{2+} Begin by writing the electron configuration of the neutral atom. Remember, Cu is one of our exceptions.

Cu $[Ar]4s^1 3d^{10}$

Since this ion has a 2+ charge, remove two electrons to write the electron configuration of the ion. Since it is a transition metal, remove the electrons from the 4s orbital before removing electrons from the 3d orbitals.

Cu^{2+} $[Ar]4s^0 3d^9$

7.95   Identify the noble gas that precedes the element and put it in square brackets.

Determine the outer principal quantum level for the s orbital. Subtract one to obtain the quantum level for the d orbital. If the element is in the third or fourth transition series, include $(n-2)f$ electrons in the configuration. Count across the row to see how many electrons are in the neutral atom.

For an ion, remove the required number of electrons, first from the s and then from the d orbitals.

(a)   Ni; Ni^{2+}

The noble gas that precedes Ni is Ar. Ni is in the fourth period so the orbitals we use are 4s and 3d and Ni has 10 more electrons than Ar.

Ni $[Ar]4s^2 3d^8$

Ni will lose electrons from the 4s and then from the 3d.

Ni^{2+} $[Ar]4s^0 3d^8$

(b)   Mn; Mn^{4+}

The noble gas that precedes Mn is Ar. Mn is in the fourth period so the orbitals we use are 4s and 3d and Mn has seven more electrons than Ar.

Mn $[Ar]4s^2 3d^5$

Mn will lose electrons from the 4s and then from the 3d.

Mn^{4+} $[Ar]4s^0 3d^3$

(c)   Y; Y^+

The noble gas that precedes Y is Kr. Y is in the fifth period so the orbitals we use are 5s and 4d and Y has three more electrons than Kr.

Y $[Kr]5s^2 4d^1$

Y will lose electrons from the 5s and then from the 4d.

Y^+ $[Kr]5s^1 4d^1$

(d)   Ta; Ta^{2+}

The noble gas that precedes Ta is Xe. Ta is in the sixth period so the orbitals we use are 6s, 5d, and 4f and Ta has 19 more electrons than Xe.

Ta $[Xe]6s^24f^{14}5d^3$
Ta will lose electrons from the 6s and then from the 5d.
Ta^{2+} $[Xe]6s^04f^{14}5d^3$

7.97   (a) V^{5+} Begin by writing the electron configuration of the neutral atom.
V $[Ar]4s^23d^3$
Since this ion has a 5+ charge, remove five electrons to write the electron configuration of the ion. Since it is a transition metal, remove the electrons from the 4s orbital before removing electrons from the 3d orbitals.
V^{5+} $[Ar]4s^03d^0 = [Ne]3s^23p^6$

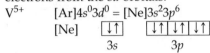
3s   3p

V^{5+} is diamagnetic.

(b) Cr^{3+} Begin by writing the electron configuration of the neutral atom. Remember, Cr is one of our exceptions.
Cr $[Ar]4s^13d^5$
Since this ion has a 3+ charge, remove three electrons to write the electron configuration of the ion. Since it is a transition metal, remove the electrons from the 4s orbital before removing electrons from the 3d orbitals.
Cr^{3+} $[Ar]4s^03d^3$

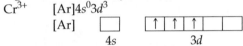
4s   3d

Cr^{3+} is paramagnetic.

(c) Ni^{2+} Begin by writing the electron configuration of the neutral atom.
Ni $[Ar]4s^23d^8$
Since this ion has a 2+ charge, remove two electrons to write the electron configuration of the ion. Since it is a transition metal, remove the electrons from the 4s orbital before removing electrons from the 3d orbitals.
Ni^{2+} $[Ar]4s^03d^8$

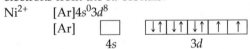
4s   3d

Ni^{2+} is paramagnetic.

(d) Fe^{3+} Begin by writing the electron configuration of the neutral atom.
Fe $[Ar]4s^23d^6$
Since this ion has a 3+ charge, remove three electrons to write the electron configuration of the ion. Since it is a transition metal, remove the electrons from the 4s orbital before removing electrons from the 3d orbitals.
Fe^{3+} $[Ar]4s^03d^5$

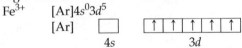
4s   3d

Fe^{3+} is paramagnetic.

Cumulative Problems

7.99   **Given:** 348 kJ mol^{-1} **Find:** λ
Conceptual Plan: kJ mol^{-1} $\rightarrow$ kJ molec^{-1} $\rightarrow$ J molec^{-1} $\rightarrow$ λ

$$\frac{6.022 \times 10^{23} \text{ C} - \text{C bonds}}{\text{mol C} - \text{C bonds}} \quad \frac{1000 \text{ J}}{\text{kJ}} \qquad E = \frac{hc}{\lambda}$$

Solution: $\dfrac{348 \text{ kJ}}{\text{mol C} - \text{C bonds}} \times \dfrac{\text{mol C} - \text{C bonds}}{6.022 \times 10^{23} \text{ C} - \text{C bonds}} \times \dfrac{1000 \text{ J}}{\text{kJ}} = 5.77\underline{9} \times 10^{-19} \text{ J}$

$$\lambda = \frac{(6.626 \times 10^{-34} \text{ J} \cdot \text{s})(3.00 \times 10^8 \text{ m s}^{-1})}{5.77\underline{9} \times 10^{-19} \text{ J}} = 3.44 \times 10^{-7} \text{m} = 344 \text{ nm}$$

Check: The units of the answer, m or nm, are correct. The magnitude of the answer is reasonable since this wavelength is in the UV region.

7.101   **Given:** E_{pulse} = 5.0 watts; d = 5.5 mm; hole = 1.2 mm; λ = 532 nm **Find:** photon s^{-1}
Conceptual Plan: fraction of beam through hole $\rightarrow$ fraction of power and then E_{photon} $\rightarrow$ number photons s^{-1}

$$\frac{\text{area hole}}{\text{area beam}} \qquad \text{fraction x power} \qquad E = \frac{hc}{\lambda} \qquad \frac{\text{power } s^{-1}}{E \text{ photon}^{-1}}$$

Solution: $A = \pi r^2 \dfrac{\pi(0.60 \text{ mm})^2}{\pi(2.75 \text{ mm})^2} = 0.0476 \qquad 0.0476 \times 5.0 \text{ watts} \times \dfrac{J s^{-1}}{\text{watt}} = 0.238 \text{ J s}^{-1}$

$$E_{photon} = \frac{(6.626 \times 10^{-34} \text{ J} \cdot \text{s})(3.00 \times 10^8 \text{ m s}^{-1})}{(532 \text{ nm})\left(\dfrac{\text{m}}{10^9 \text{ nm}}\right)} = 3.736 \times 10^{-19} \text{ J photon}^{-1}$$

$$\frac{0.238 \text{ J s}^{-1}}{3.736 \times 10^{-19} \text{ J photon}^{-1}} = 6.4 \times 10^{17} \text{ photons s}^{-1}$$

Check: The units of the answer, number of photons s^{-1}, are correct. The magnitude of the answer is reasonable.

7.103   **Given:** KE = 506 eV **Find:** λ
Conceptual Plan: $KE_{ev} \rightarrow KE_J \rightarrow v \rightarrow \lambda$

$$\frac{1.602 \times 10^{-19} J}{eV} \qquad KE = 1/2 \, mv^2 \qquad \lambda = \frac{h}{mv}$$

Solution:

$$506 \text{ eV}\left(\frac{1.602 \times 10^{-19} J}{eV}\right)\left(\frac{\dfrac{kg \cdot m^2}{s^2}}{J}\right) = \frac{1}{2}(9.11 \times 10^{-31} \text{ kg}) \, v^2$$

$$v^2 = \frac{506 \text{ eV}\left(\dfrac{1.602 \times 10^{-19} J}{eV}\right)\left(\dfrac{\dfrac{kg \cdot m^2}{s^2}}{J}\right)}{\dfrac{1}{2}(9.11 \times 10^{-31} \text{ kg})} = 1.7796 \times 10^{14} \frac{m^2}{s^2}$$

$$v = 1.334 \times 10^7 \text{ m s}^{-1} \qquad \lambda = \frac{h}{mv} = \frac{6.626 \times 10^{-34} \dfrac{kg \cdot m^2}{s^2} \cdot s}{(9.11 \times 10^{-31} \text{ kg})(1.334 \times 10^7 \text{ m s}^{-1})} = 5.45 \times 10^{-11} \text{ m} = 0.0545 \text{ nm}$$

Check: The units of the answer, m or nm, are correct. The magnitude of the answer is reasonable because a de Broglie wavelength is usually a very small number.

7.105   **Given:** $n = 1 \rightarrow n = \infty$ **Find:** E; λ
Conceptual Plan: $n = \infty$, $n = 1 \rightarrow \Delta E_{atom} \rightarrow \Delta E_{photon} \rightarrow \lambda$

$$\Delta E_{atom} = E_\infty - E_1 \qquad \Delta E_{atom} \rightarrow \Delta E_{photon} \qquad E = \frac{hc}{\lambda}$$

Solution: $\Delta E = E_\infty - E_1 = 0 - \left[-2.18 \times 10^{-18}\left(\dfrac{1}{1^2}\right)\right] = +2.18 \times 10^{-18} \text{ J}$

$$\Delta E_{photon} = -\Delta E_{atom} = +2.18 \times 10^{-18} \text{ J}$$

$$\lambda = \frac{hc}{E} = \frac{(6.626 \times 10^{-34} \text{ J} \cdot \text{s})(3.00 \times 10^8 \text{ m s}^{-1})}{2.18 \times 10^{-18} \text{ J}} = 9.12 \times 10^{-8} \text{ m} = 91.2 \text{ nm}$$

Check: The units of the answers, J for E and m or nm for part 1, are correct. The magnitude of the answer is reasonable because it would require more energy to completely remove the electron than just moving it to a higher n level. This results in a shorter wavelength.

7.107   (a)   **Given:** $n = 1$ **Find:** number of orbitals if $l = 0 \rightarrow n$
Conceptual Plan: value $n \rightarrow$ values $l \rightarrow$ values $m_l \rightarrow$ number of orbitals

$$l = 0 \rightarrow n \qquad\qquad m_l = -1 \rightarrow +1 \text{ total } m_l$$

Solution:

$n =$	1	
$l =$	0	1
$m_l =$	0	-1, 0, +1

total 4 orbitals

Check: The total orbitals will be equal to the number of l sublevels^2.

(b)   **Given:** $n = 2$ **Find:** number of orbitals if $l = 0 \to n$
Conceptual Plan: value $n \to$ **values** $l \to$ **values** $m_l \to$ **number of orbitals**

$$l = 0 \to n \qquad\qquad m_l = -1 \to +1 \text{ total } m_l$$

Solution:

$n =$	2		
$l =$	0	1	2
$m_l =$	0	$-1, 0, +1$	$-2,-1,0,1,2$

total 9 orbitals

Check: The total orbitals will be equal to the number of l sublevels^2.

(c)   **Given:** $n = 3$ **Find:** number of orbitals if $l = 0 \to n$
Conceptual Plan: value $n \to$ **values** $l \to$ **values** $m_l \to$ **number of orbitals**

$$l = 0 \to n \qquad\qquad m_l = -1 \to +1 \text{ total } m_l$$

Solution:

$n =$	3			
$l =$	0	1	2	3
$m_l =$	0	$-1, 0, +1$	$-2,-1,0,1,2$	$-3,-2,-1,0,1,2,3$

total 16 orbitals

Check: The total orbitals will be equal to the number of l sublevels^2.

7.109   **Given:** $\lambda = 1875$ nm; 1282 nm; 1093 nm **Find:** equivalent transitions
Conceptual Plan: $\lambda \to E_{photon} \to E_{atom} \to n$

$$E = \frac{hc}{\lambda} \qquad E_{photon} = -E_{atom} \qquad E = -2.18 \times 10^{-18} \text{J} \left(\frac{1}{n_f^2} - \frac{1}{n_i^2} \right)$$

Solution: Since the wavelength of the transitions are longer wavelengths than those obtained in the visual region, the electron must relax to a higher n level. Therefore, we can assume that the electron returns to the $n = 3$ level.

For $\lambda = 1875$ nm: $E = \dfrac{(6.626 \times 10^{-34} \text{ J} \cdot \text{s})(3.00 \times 10^8 \text{ m s}^{-1})}{1875 \text{ nm}\left(\dfrac{\text{m}}{10^9 \text{ nm}}\right)} = 1.060 \times 10^{-19} \text{ J}$ $1.060 \times 10^{-19} \text{ J} = -1.060 \times 10^{-19} \text{ J}$

$$-1.060 \times 10^{-19} \text{ J} = -2.18 \times 10^{-18} \left(\frac{1}{3^2} - \frac{1}{n^2} \right); n = 4$$

For $\lambda = 1282$ nm: $E = \dfrac{(6.626 \times 10^{-34} \text{ J} \cdot \text{s})(3.00 \times 10^8 \text{ m s}^{-1})}{1282 \text{ nm}\left(\dfrac{\text{m}}{10^9 \text{ nm}}\right)} = 1.551 \times 10^{-19} \text{ J}$ $1.551 \times 10^{-19} \text{ J} = -1.551 \times 10^{-19} \text{ J}$

$$-1.551 \times 10^{-19} = -2.18 \times 10^{-18} \left(\frac{1}{3^2} - \frac{1}{n^2} \right); n = 5$$

For $\lambda = 1093$ nm: $E = \dfrac{(6.626 \times 10^{-34} \text{ J} \cdot \text{s})(3.00 \times 10^8 \text{ m s}^{-1})}{1093 \text{ nm}\left(\dfrac{\text{m}}{10^9 \text{ nm}}\right)} = 1.819 \times 10^{-19} \text{ J}$ $1.819 \times 10^{-19} \text{ J} = -1.819 \times 10^{-19} \text{ J}$

$$-1.819 \times 10^{-19} \text{ J} = -2.18 \times 10^{-18} \left(\frac{1}{3^2} - \frac{1}{n^2} \right); n = 6$$

Check: The values obtained are all integers, which is correct. The values of n: 4,5,6, are reasonable. The values of n increase as the wavelength decreases because the two n levels involved are further apart and more energy is released as the electron relaxes to the $n = 3$ level.

7.111   **Given:** $\phi = 193$ kJ mol^{-1} **Find:** threshold frequency(ν)
Conceptual Plan: ϕ kJ mol$^{-1} \to \phi$ kJ atom$^{-1} \to \phi$ J atom$^{-1} \to \nu$

$$\frac{6.022 \times 10^{23} \text{ atoms}}{\text{mol}} \qquad \frac{1000 \text{ J}}{\text{kJ}} \qquad \phi = h\nu$$

Solution: $\nu = \dfrac{\phi}{h} = \dfrac{\left(\dfrac{193 \text{ kJ}}{\text{mol}}\right)\left(\dfrac{\text{mol}}{6.022 \times 10^{23} \text{ atoms}}\right)\left(\dfrac{1000 \text{ J}}{\text{kJ}}\right)}{6.626 \times 10^{-34} \text{ J} \cdot \text{s}} = 4.84 \times 10^{14} \text{ s}^{-1}$

Check: The units of the answer, s^{-1}, are correct. The magnitude of the answer puts the frequency in the infrared range and is a reasonable answer.

7.113   **Given:** $\nu_{low} = 30 \text{ s}^{-1}$ $\nu_{hi} = 1.5 \times 10^4 \text{ s}^{-1}$; speed $= 344 \text{ m s}^{-1}$ **Find:** $\lambda_{low} - \lambda_{hi}$

       Conceptual Plan: $\nu_{low} \rightarrow \lambda_{low}$ and $\nu_{hi} = \lambda_{hi}$ then $\lambda_{low} - \lambda_{hi}$

$$\lambda\nu = \text{speed}$$

       Solution: $\lambda = \dfrac{\text{speed}}{\nu}$ $\lambda_{low} = \dfrac{344 \text{ m s}^{-1}}{30 \text{ s}^{-1}} = 11 \text{ m}$ $\lambda_{hi} = \dfrac{344 \text{ m s}^{-1}}{1.5 \times 10^4 \text{ s}^{-1}} = 0.023 \text{ m}$ $11 \text{ m} - 0.023 \text{ m} = 11 \text{ m}$

       Check: The units of the answer, m, are correct. The magnitude is reasonable since the value is only determined by the low frequency value because of significant figures.

7.115   **Given:** $\lambda = 792 \text{ nm}$, V = 100.0 mL, P = 55.7 mtorr, T = 25°C **Find:** E to dissociate 15.0%

       Conceptual Plan: $\lambda \rightarrow E \text{ molecule}^{-1}$ and then P.V.T $\rightarrow$ n $\rightarrow$ molecules

$$E = \frac{hc}{\lambda} \qquad\qquad n = \frac{PV}{RT} \qquad\qquad \frac{6.022 \times 10^{23} \text{ molecules}}{\text{mole}}$$

       Solution: $E = \dfrac{(6.626 \times 10^{-34} \text{ J} \cdot \text{s})(3.00 \times 10^8 \text{ m s}^{-1})}{792 \text{ nm}\left(\dfrac{\text{m}}{10^9 \text{ nm}}\right)} = 2.51 \times 10^{-19} \text{ J molecule}^{-1}$

$$\frac{(55.7 \text{ mtorr})\left(\dfrac{1 \text{ torr}}{1000 \text{ mtorr}}\right)\left(\dfrac{1 \text{ bar}}{760 \text{ torr}}\right)(100.0 \text{ mL})\left(\dfrac{\text{L}}{1000 \text{ mL}}\right)\left(\dfrac{6.022 \times 10^{23} \text{ molecules}}{\text{mol}}\right)}{\left(\dfrac{0.0821 \text{ Lbar}}{\text{mol K}}\right)(298 \text{ K})} = 1.80 \times 10^{17} \text{ molecules}$$

       $(1.80 \times 10^{17} \text{ molecules})(0.15\%) = 2.70 \times 10^{16} \text{ molecules dissociated}$

       $(2.51 \times 10^{-19} \text{ J molecule}^{-1})(2.70 \times 10^{16} \text{ molecules}) = 6.777 \times 10^{-3} \text{ J} = 6.78 \times 10^{-3} \text{ J}$

       Check: The units of the answer, J, are correct. The magnitude is reasonable since it is for a part of a mole of molecules.

7.117   **Given:** 20.0 mW, 1.00 hr., 2.29×10^{20} photons **Find:** λ

       Conceptual Plan: mW $\rightarrow$ W $\rightarrow$ J $\rightarrow$ J photon^{-1} $\rightarrow$ λ

$$\frac{W}{1000 \text{ mW}} \quad E = W \times s \qquad \frac{E}{\text{number of photons}} \qquad \lambda = \frac{hc}{E}$$

       Solution: $(20.0 \text{ mW})\left(\dfrac{1 \text{ W}}{1000 \text{ mW}}\right)\left(\dfrac{\dfrac{J}{s}}{W}\right)\left(\dfrac{3600 \text{ s}}{2.29 \times 10^{20} \text{ photons}}\right) = 3.14 \times 10^{-19} \text{ J photon}^{-1}$

$$\frac{(6.626 \times 10^{-34} \text{ J} \cdot \text{s})(3.00 \times 10^8 \text{ m s}^{-1})\left(\dfrac{10^9 \text{ nm}}{\text{m}}\right)}{3.14 \times 10^{-19} \text{ J}} = 632 \text{ nm}$$

       Check: The units of the answer, nm, are correct. The magnitude is reasonable because it is in the red range.

7.119   Write the electron configuration of vanadium.

       V: $[\text{Ar}] 4s^2 3d^3$

       Since this ion has a 3+ charge, remove three electrons to write the electron configuration of the ion. Since it is a transition metal, remove the electrons from the $4s$ orbital before removing electrons from the $3d$ orbitals.

       V^{3+}: $[\text{Ar}] 4s^0 3d^2$

       Both vanadium and the V^{3+} ion have unpaired electrons and are paramagnetic.

7.121   (a)   Cr $[\text{Ar}]4s^1 3d^5$ (b)   Cu $[\text{Ar}]4s^1 3d^{10}$

               Cr^+ $[\text{Ar}]4s^0 3d^5$ Cu^+ $[\text{Ar}]4s^0 3d^{10}$

               Cr^{2+} $[\text{Ar}]4s^0 3d^4$ Cu^{2+} $[\text{Ar}]4s^0 3d^9$

               Cr^{3+} $[\text{Ar}]4s^0 3d^3$

Challenge Problems

7.123   (a)   **Given:** $n = 1$, $n = 2$, $n = 3$, L = 155 pm **Find:** E_1, E_2, E_3

           Conceptual Plan: $n \rightarrow E$

$$E_n = \frac{n^2 h^2}{8 \text{ m L}^2}$$

Solution:

$$E_1 = \frac{1^2(6.626 \times 10^{-34}\text{ J}\cdot\text{s})^2}{8(9.11 \times 10^{-31}\text{ kg})(155\text{ pm})^2\left(\dfrac{\text{m}}{10^{12}\text{ pm}}\right)^2} = \frac{1(6.626 \times 10^{-34})^2\text{ J}^2\text{ s}^2}{8(9.11 \times 10^{-31}\text{ kg})(155 \times 10^{-12})^2\text{ m}^2}$$

$$= \frac{1(6.626 \times 10^{-34})^2\left(\dfrac{\text{kg}\cdot\text{m}^2}{\text{s}^2}\right)\text{J s}^2}{8(9.11 \times 10^{-31}\text{ kg})(155 \times 10^{-12})^2\text{ m}^2} = 2.51 \times 10^{-18}\text{ J}$$

$$E_2 = \frac{2^2(6.626 \times 10^{-34}\text{ J}\cdot\text{s})^2}{8(9.11 \times 10^{-31}\text{ kg})(155\text{ pm})^2\left(\dfrac{\text{m}}{10^{12}\text{ pm}}\right)^2} = \frac{4(6.626 \times 10^{-34})^2\text{ J}^2\text{ s}^2}{8(9.11 \times 10^{-31}\text{ kg})(155 \times 10^{-12})^2\text{m}^2}$$

$$= \frac{4(6.626 \times 10^{-34})^2\left(\dfrac{\text{kg}\cdot\text{m}^2}{\text{s}^2}\right)\text{J s}^2}{8(9.11 \times 10^{-31}\text{kg})(155 \times 10^{-12})^2\text{ m}^2} = 1.00 \times 10^{-17}\text{ J}$$

$$E_3 = \frac{3^2(6.626 \times 10^{-34}\text{ J}\cdot\text{s})^2}{8(9.11 \times 10^{-31}\text{ kg})(155\text{ pm})^2\left(\dfrac{\text{m}}{10^{12}\text{ pm}}\right)^2} = \frac{9(6.626 \times 10^{-34})^2\text{ J}^2\text{ s}^2}{8(9.11 \times 10^{-31}\text{ kg})(155 \times 10^{-12})^2\text{ m}^2}$$

$$= \frac{9(6.626 \times 10^{-34})^2\left(\dfrac{\text{kg}\cdot\text{m}^2}{\text{s}^2}\right)\text{J s}^2}{8(9.11 \times 10^{-31}\text{ kg})(155 \times 10^{-12})^2\text{ m}^2} = 2.26 \times 10^{-17}\text{ J}$$

Check: The units of the answers, J, are correct. The answers seem reasonable since the energy is increasing with increasing n level.

(b) **Given:** $n = 1 \rightarrow n = 2$ and $n = 2 \rightarrow n = 3$ **Find:** λ
Conceptual Plan: $n = 1, n = 2 \rightarrow \Delta E_{\text{atom}} \rightarrow \Delta E_{\text{photon}} \rightarrow \lambda$

$$\Delta E_{\text{atom}} = E_2 - E_1 \qquad \Delta E_{\text{atom}} \rightarrow \quad -\Delta E_{\text{photon}}\quad E = \frac{hc}{\lambda}$$

Solution: Using the energies calculated in part a
$$E_2 - E_1 = (1.00 \times 10^{-17}\text{ J} - 2.51 \times 10^{-18}\text{ J}) = 7.49 \times 10^{-18}\text{ J}$$
$$\lambda = \frac{(6.626 \times 10^{-34}\text{ J}\cdot\text{s})(3.00 \times 10^{8.}\text{ m s}^{-1})}{7.49 \times 10^{-18}\text{ J}} = 2.65 \times 10^{-8}\text{ m} = 26.5\text{ nm}$$
$$E_3 - E_2 = (2.26 \times 10^{-17}\text{ J} - 1.00 \times 10^{-17}\text{ J}) = 1.26 \times 10^{-17}\text{ J}$$
$$\lambda = \frac{(6.626 \times 10^{-34}\text{ J}\cdot\text{s})(3.00 \times 10^{8.}\text{ m s}^{-1})}{1.26 \times 10^{-17}\text{ J}} = 1.58 \times 10^{-8}\text{ m} = 15.8\text{ nm}$$
These wavelengths would lie in the UV region.
Check: The units of the answers, m, are correct. The magnitude of the answers is reasonable based on the energies obtained for the levels.

7.125 For the 1s orbital in the Excel spreadsheet, call column A: r; and column B: $\psi(1s)$. Make the values for r column A: 0–200. In column B, put the equation for the wave function written as follows: =(POWER(1/3.1415,1/2))*(1/POWER(53,3/2))*(EXP(-A2/53)). Go to make chart, choose xy scatter.

e.g., sample values
r ψ (1s)
0 7.000146224
1 7.000143491
2 7.000140809
3 7.000138177
4 7.000135594
5 7.00013306
6 7.000130573

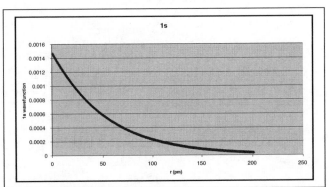

For the 2s orbital in the same Excel spreadsheet, call column A: r; and column C: $\psi(2s)$. Use the same values for r in column A: 0–200. In column C, put the equation for the wave function written as follows: =(POWER(1/((32)*(3.1415)),1/2))*(1/POWER(53,3/2))*(2-(A2/53))*(EXP(-A2/53)). Go to make chart, choose xy scatter.

e.g., sample values

r ψ (2s)

0 7.0000516979
1 7.000050253
2 7.0000488441
3 7.0000474702
4 7.0000461307
5 7.0000448247
6 7.0000435513

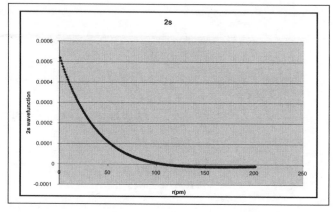

Note: The plot for the 2s orbital extends below the x axis. The x-intercept represents the radial node of the orbital.

7.127 **Given:** threshold frequency = $2.25 \times 10^{14}\ s^{-1}$; $\lambda = 5.00 \times 10^{-7}$ m **Find:** v of electron
Conceptual Plan: v $\rightarrow$ ϕ and then λ $\rightarrow$ E and then $\rightarrow$ KE $\rightarrow$ v

$$\phi = h\nu \qquad E = \frac{hc}{\lambda} \qquad KE = E - \phi \qquad KE = 1/2\ mv^2$$

Solution:

$$\phi = (6.626 \times 10^{-34}\ J \cdot s)(2.25 \times 10^{14}\ s^{-1}) = 1.491 \times 10^{-19}\ J \quad E = \frac{(6.626 \times 10^{-34}\ J \cdot s)(3.00 \times 10^8\ m\ s^{-1})}{5.00 \times 10^{-7}\ m} = 3.976 \times 10^{-19}\ J$$

$$KE = 3.976 \times 10^{-19}\ J - 1.491 \times 10^{-19}\ J = 2.485 \times 10^{-19}\ J \quad v^2 = \frac{2.485 \times 10^{-19}\ \frac{kg \cdot m^2}{s^2}}{\frac{1}{2}(9.11 \times 10^{-31}\ kg)} = 5.455 \times 10^{11}\ \frac{m^2}{s^2}$$

$v = 7.39 \times 10^5\ m\ s^{-1}$

Check: The units of the answer, m s^{-1}, are correct. The magnitude of the answer is reasonable for the speed of an electron.

7.129 **Given:** t = 5.0 fs, λ_{low} = 722 nm **Find:** ΔE, and λ_{high}
Conceptual Plan: t $\rightarrow$ ΔE and then λ_{low} $\rightarrow$ E_{high} $\rightarrow$ E_{low} $\rightarrow$ λ_{high}

$$\Delta t \times \Delta E \geq \frac{h}{4\pi} \qquad E = \frac{hc}{\lambda} \qquad E - \Delta E \qquad \lambda = \frac{hc}{E}$$

Solution: $\dfrac{6.626 \times 10^{-34}\ J \cdot s}{4(3.141)(5.0\ fs)\left(\dfrac{s}{1 \times 10^{15}\ fs}\right)} = 1.055 \times 10^{-20}\ J$

$$E = \frac{(6.626 \times 10^{-34}\ J \cdot s)(3.00 \times 10^8\ m\ s^{-1})}{722\ nm\left(\dfrac{m}{10^9\ nm}\right)} = 2.75 \times 10^{-19}\ J$$

$2.75 \times 10^{-19}\ J - 1.06 \times 10^{-20}\ J = 2.64 \times 10^{-19}\ J$

$$\frac{(6.626 \times 10^{-34}\ J \cdot s)(3.00 \times 10^8\ m\ s^{-1})\left(\dfrac{10^9\ nm}{m}\right)}{(2.64 \times 10^{-19}\ J)} = 752.9\ nm = 7.5 \times 10^2\ nm$$

Check: The units of the answer, nm, are correct. The magnitude of the answer is reasonable since it is a longer wavelength but it is close to the original wavelength.

7.131   **Given:** $r = 1.8$ m **Find:** λ
Conceptual Plan: $r \rightarrow C$
$$C = 2\pi r$$
Solution: $(2)(3.141)(1.8m) = 11.3$ m = the circumference of the orbit. So the largest wavelength that would fit the orbit would be 11 m.
Check: The units of the answer, m, are correct. The magnitude of the wave is about the circumference of the orbit.

7.133   **Given:** $r = 100.00$ pm, $q_{proton} = 1.60218 \times 10^{-19}$ C, $q_{electron} = -1.60218 \times 10^{-19}$ C
Find: IE in kJ mol^{-1} and λ of ionization
Conceptual Plan: $r, q_{proton}, q_{electron}, \rightarrow E_{atom} \rightarrow E_{mol}$ and then $E_{atom} \rightarrow \lambda$

$$E = \frac{1}{4\pi\epsilon_0}\frac{q_p q_e}{r} \qquad \frac{1000 J}{kJ} \qquad \frac{6.022 \times 0^{23}\, atom}{mol} \qquad\qquad \lambda = \frac{hc}{E}$$

Solution: $E = \dfrac{1}{(4)(3.141)\left(8.85 \times 10^{-12}\,\frac{C^2}{J\,m}\right)} \times \dfrac{(1.602 \times 10^{-19} C)(-1.602 \times 10^{-19} C)}{(100.00\, pm)\left(\frac{1\, m}{1 \times 10^{12}\, pm}\right)} = -2.308 \times 10^{-18}$ J atom^{-1}

-2.308×10^{-18} J/ atom $\times \dfrac{6.022 \times 10\, atom}{mol} \times \dfrac{kJ}{(1000 J)} = -1.39 \times 10^3$ kJ mol^{-1}

$IE = 0 - (-1.39 \times 10^3$ kJ mol$^{-1}) = 1.39 \times 10^3$ kJ mol^{-1}

$$\lambda = \frac{(6.626 \times 10^{-34}\, J s)(3.00 \times 10^8\, m\, s^{-1})\left(\frac{1 \times 10^9\, nm}{m}\right)}{(2.308 \times 10^{-18}\, J)} = 86.1\ nm$$

Check: The units of the answer (kJ mol^{-1}) are correct. The magnitude of the answer is reasonable since the value is positive and energy must be added to the atom to remove the electron. The units of the wavelength (nm) are correct and the magnitude is reasonable based on the ionization energy.

Conceptual Problems

7.135   (a)   Since the interference pattern is caused by single electrons interfering with themselves, the pattern remains the same even when the rate of the electrons passing through the slits is one electron per minute. It will simply take longer for the full pattern to develop.

(b)   When a light is placed behind the slits, it flashes to indicate which hole the electron passed through, but the interference pattern is now absent. With the laser on, the electrons hit positions directly behind each slit, as if they were ordinary particles.

(c)   Diffraction occurs when a wave encounters an obstacle of a slit that is comparable in size to its wavelength. The wave bends around the slit. The diffraction of light through two slits separated by a distance comparable to the wavelength of the light results in an interference pattern. Each slit acts as a new wave source, and the two new waves interfere with each other, which results in a pattern of bright and dark lines.

(d)   Since the mass of the bullets and their particle size are not absolutely small, the bullets will not produce an interference pattern when they pass through the slits. The de Broglie wavelength produced by the bullets will not be sufficiently large enough to interfere with the bullet trajectory and no interference pattern will be observed.

8 Periodic Properties of the Elements

Review Questions

8.1   A periodic property is one that is predictable based on the element's position within the periodic table.

8.3   The first attempt to organize the elements according to similarities in their properties was made by the German chemist Johann Dobereiner. He grouped elements into triads; three elements with similar properties. A more complex approach was attempted by the English chemist John Newlands. He organized elements into octaves, analogous to musical notes. When arranged this way, the properties of every eighth element were similar.

8.5   The periodic law was based on the observations that the properties of elements recur and certain elements have similar properties. The theory that explains the existence of the periodic law is quantum-mechanical theory.

8.7   Valence electrons are those that are important in chemical bonding. For main-group elements, the valence electrons are those in the outermost principal energy level. For transition elements, we also count the outermost d electrons among the valence even though they are not in the outermost principal energy level. The chemical properties of an element depend on its valence electrons, which are important in bonding because they are held most loosely. This is why the elements in a column of the periodic table have similar chemical properties: they have the same number of valence electrons.

8.9   The number of columns in a block corresponds to the maximum number of electrons that can occupy the particular sublevel of that block. The s block has two columns corresponding to one s orbital holding a maximum of two electrons. The p block has six columns corresponding to the three p orbitals with two electrons each.

8.11   For groups 1 and 2, the number of valence electrons is equal to the group number. For example, calcium is in group 2 has two valence electrons. For groups 13 to 18, the number of valence electrons is equal to the group number minus 10. For example, oxygen is in group 16 so it has $16 - 10$ = 6 valence electrons. We subtract 10 to account for the electrons in the completely filled d block, which are not considered to be valence electrons.

8.13   To use the periodic table to write the electron configuration, find the noble gas that precedes the element. The element has the inner electron configuration of that noble gas. Place the symbol for the noble gas in [ ]. Obtain the outer electron configuration by tracing the element across the period and assigning electrons in the appropriate orbitals.

8.15   (a)   The alkali metals (group 1) have one valence electron and are among the most reactive metals because their outer electron configuration (ns^1) is one electron beyond a noble gas configuration. They react to lose the ns^1 electron, obtaining a noble gas configuration. This is why the group 1 metals tend to form 1+ cations.

(b)   The alkaline earth metals (group 2) have two valence electrons, have an outer electron configuration of ns^2, and also tend to be reactive metals. They lose their ns^2 electrons to form 2+ cations.

(c)   The halogens (group 17) have seven valence electrons and have an outer electron configuration of ns^2np^5. They are among the most reactive nonmetals. They are only one electron short of a noble gas configuration and tend to react to gain that one electron, forming 1– anions.

(d)   The oxygen family (group 16) has six valence electrons and has an outer electron configuration of ns^2np^4. They are two electrons short of a noble gas configuration and tend to react to gain those two electrons, forming 2– anions.

8.17   The effective nuclear charge (Z_{eff}) is the average or net charge from the nucleus experienced by the electrons in the outermost levels. Shielding is the blocking of nuclear charge from the outermost electrons. The shielding is primarily due to the inner (core) electrons, although there is some interaction and shielding from the electron repulsions of the outer electrons with each other.

8.19   Slater's rules are a set of empirical rules for estimating the shielding constant, S, which, in turn, allows an estimation of the effective nuclear charge for a given electron in an atom. Slater's rules assign different shielding contributions to all of the other electrons based on their shell and orbital type in relation to the electron in question. For example, electrons in the same shell (same n) as the electron in question will have different shielding contributions than electrons in the $n - 1$ shell.

8.21   The lanthanoid contraction refers to a levelling off of atomic radius as one goes down a group in the d block. For example, we would normally expect Pt to be larger than Pd because it has more electrons and protons and the valence electrons are in a period with a higher n value. However, the atomic radii of Pt and Pd are about the same. The origin of the lanthanide contraction is related to electrons occupying the large f orbitals, which are not effective at shielding the outermost d or s electrons from the nuclear charge. As a result, the valence electrons are held more tightly by the nucleus, offsetting the usual increase in size we see when moving down a group in the periodic table.

8.23   The ionization energy (IE) of an atom or ion is the energy required to remove an electron from the atom or ion in the gaseous state. The ionization energy is always positive because removing an electron always takes energy. The energy required to remove the first electron is called the first ionization energy (IE_1). The energy required to remove the second electron is called the second ionization energy (IE_2). The second IE is always greater than the first IE.

8.25   Exceptions occur with elements Be, Mg, and Ca in group 2 having a higher first ionization energy than elements B, Al, and Ga in group 13. This exception is caused by the change in going from the s block to the p block. The result is that the electrons in the s orbital shield the electron in the p orbital from the nuclear charge, making it easier to remove.

Another exception occurs with N, P, and As in group 15 having a higher first ionization energy than O, S, and Se in group 16. This exception is caused by the repulsion between electrons when they must occupy the same orbital. Group 15 has 3 p electrons while group 16 has 4 p electrons. In the group 15 elements the p orbitals are half-filled, which makes the configuration particularly stable. The fourth group 16 electron must pair with another electron, making it easier to remove.

8.27   The electron affinity (EA) of an atom or ion is the energy change associated with the gaining of an electron by the atom in the gaseous state. The electron affinity is usually—though not always—negative because an atom or ion usually releases energy when it gains an electron. The trends in electron affinity are not as regular as trends in other properties. For main-group elements, electron affinity generally becomes more negative as you move to the right across a row in the periodic table. There is not a corresponding trend in electron affinity going down a column.

8.29   (a)   The reactions of the alkali metals with halogens result in the formation of metal halides.
$$2\,M(s) + X_2 \rightarrow 2\,MX(s)$$

(b)   Alkali metals react with water to form the dissolved alkali metal ion, the hydroxide ion, and hydrogen gas.
$$2\,M(s) + 2\,H_2O(l) \rightarrow 2\,M^+(aq) + 2\,OH^-(aq) + H_2(g)$$

Problems by Topic

Electron Configurations and the Periodic Table

8.31 (a) P The atomic number of P is 15. The noble gas that precedes P in the periodic table is neon, so the inner electron configuration is [Ne]. Obtain the outer electron configuration by tracing the elements between Ne and P and assigning electrons to the appropriate orbitals. Begin with [Ne]. Because P is in row 3, add two $3s$ electrons. Next, add three $3p$ electrons as you trace across the p block to P, which is in the third column of the p block.

P [Ne]$3s^2 3p^3$

(b) Ge The atomic number of Ge is 32. The noble gas that precedes Ge in the periodic table is argon, so the inner electron configuration is [Ar]. Obtain the outer electron configuration by tracing the elements between Ar and Ge and assigning electrons to the appropriate orbitals. Begin with [Ar]. Because Ge is in row 4, add two $4s$ electrons. Next, add ten $3d$ electrons as you trace across the d block. Finally add two $4p$ electrons as you trace across the p block to Ge, which is in the second column of the p block.

Ge [Ar]$4s^2 3d^{10} 4p^2$

(c) Zr The atomic number of Zr is 40. The noble gas that precedes Zr in the periodic table is krypton, so the inner electron configuration is [Kr]. Obtain the outer electron configuration by tracing the elements between Kr and Zr and assigning electrons to the appropriate orbitals. Begin with [Kr]. Because Zr is in row 5, add two $5s$ electrons. Next, add two $4d$ electrons as you trace across the d block to Zr, which is in the second column.

Zr [Kr]$5s^2 4d^2$

(d) I The atomic number of I is 53. The noble gas that precedes I in the periodic table is krypton, so the inner electron configuration is [Kr]. Obtain the outer electron configuration by tracing the elements between Kr and I and assigning electrons to the appropriate orbitals. Begin with [Kr]. Because I is in row 5, add two $5s$ electrons. Next, add ten $4d$ electrons as you trace across the d block. Finally, add five $5p$ electrons as you trace across the p block to I, which is in the fifth column of the p block.

I [Kr]$5s^2 4d^{10} 5p^5$

8.33 (a) Li is in period 2 and the first column in the s block, so Li has one $2s$ electron.

(b) Cu is in period 4 and the ninth column in the d block ($n - 1$), so Cu should have nine $3d$ electrons, however, it is one of our exceptions, so it has ten $3d$ electrons.

(c) Br is in period 4 and the fifth column of the p block, so Br has five $4p$ electrons.

(d) Zr is in period 5 and the second column of the d block ($n - 1$), so Zr has two $4d$ electrons.

8.35 (a) In period 4, an element with five valence electrons could be V or As.

(b) In period 4, an element with four $4p$ electrons would be in the fourth column of the p block and is Se.

(c) In period 4, an element with three $3d$ electrons would be in the third column of the d block ($n - 1$) and is V.

(d) In period 4, an element with a complete outer shell would be in the sixth column of the p block and is Kr.

8.37 (a) Ba is in column 2, so it has two valence electrons.

(b) Cs is in column 1, so it has one valence electron.

(c) Ni is in column 10, so it has 10 valence electrons (eight from the d block and two from the s block).

(d) S is in column 16, so it has six valence electrons (two from the s block and four from the p block).

8.39   (a)   The outer electron configuration ns^2 would belong to a reactive metal in the alkaline earth family.

        (b)   The outer electron configuration ns^2np^6 would belong to an unreactive nonmetal in the noble gas family.

        (c)   The outer electron configuration ns^2np^5 would belong to a reactive nonmetal in the halogen family.

        (d)   The outer electron configuration ns^2np^2 would belong to an element in the carbon family. If $n = 2$, the element is a nonmetal; if $n = 3$ or 4, the element is a metalloid; and if $n = 5$ or 6, the element is a metal.

Effective Nuclear Charge and Atomic Radius

8.41   The valence electrons in nitrogen would experience a greater effective nuclear charge. Be has four protons and N has seven protons. Both atoms have two core electrons that predominately contribute to the shielding, while the valence electrons will contribute a slight shielding effect. So, Be has an effective nuclear charge of slightly more than 2+ and N has an effective nuclear charge of slightly more than 5+.

8.43   (a)   K(19) [Ar]$4s^1$ $Z_{eff} = Z -$ core electrons $= 19 - 18 = 1+$

        (b)   Ca(20) [Ar]$4s^2$ $Z_{eff} = Z -$ core electrons $= 20 - 18 = 2+$

        (c)   O(8) [He]$2s^22p^4$ $Z_{eff} = Z -$ core electrons $= 8 - 2 = 6+$

        (d)   C(6) [He]$2s^22p^2$ $Z_{eff} = Z -$ core electrons $= 6 - 2 = 4+$

8.45   **Given:** fourth period elements **Find:** Z_{eff} for each element using Slater's rules and then use the values to explain the trend in atomic radii
        Conceptual Plan: Write the electron configuration for each element, grouping subshells by n value. Use Slater's rules to calculate the shielding constant, S, and then subtract S from the atomic number to determine Z_{eff}. Use Z_{eff} to explain the trend in atomic radii.
        Solution:

Element	Z	Electron configuration	S	$Z_{eff} (= Z - S)$
K	19	$1s^22s^22p^63s^23p^64s^1$	Other e⁻ in same valence shell: 0 Core e⁻ in $n - 1$: 8 Core e⁻ in $< n - 1$: 10 $S = 8(0.85) + 10(1.00) = 16.8$	$19 - 6.80 = 2.20$
Ca	20	$1s^22s^22p^63s^23p^64s^2$	Other e⁻ in same valence shell: 1 Core e⁻ in $n - 1$: 8 Core e⁻ in $< n - 1$: 10 $S = 1(0.35) + 8(0.85) + 10(1.00) = 17.15$	$20 - 17.15 = 2.85$
Sc	21	$1s^22s^22p^63s^23p^63d^14s^2$	Other e⁻ in same valence shell: 1 Core e⁻ in $n - 1$: 9 Core e⁻ in $< n - 1$: 10 $S = 1(0.35) + 9(0.85) + 10(1.00) = 18.00$	$21 - 18.00 = 3.00$
Ti	22	$1s^22s^22p^63s^23p^63d^24s^2$	Other e⁻ in same valence shell: 1 Core e⁻ in $n - 1$: 10 Core e⁻ in $< n - 1$: 10 $S = 1(0.35) + 10(0.85) + 10(1.00) = 18.85$	$22 - 18.85 = 3.15$
V	23	$1s^22s^22p^63s^23p^63d^34s^2$	Other e⁻ in same valence shell: 1 Core e⁻ in $n - 1$: 11 Core e⁻ in $< n - 1$: 10 $S = 1(0.35) + 11(0.85) + 10(1.00) = 19.70$	$23 - 19.70 = 3.30$
Cr	24	$1s^22s^22p^63s^23p^63d^54s^1$	Other e⁻ in same valence shell: 0 Core e⁻ in $n - 1$: 13 Core e⁻ in $< n - 1$: 10 $S = 13(0.85) + 10(1.00) = 21.05$	$24 - 21.05 = 2.95$
Mn	25	$1s^22s^22p^63s^23p^63d^54s^2$	Other e⁻ in same valence shell: 1 Core e⁻ in $n - 1$: 13 Core e⁻ in $< n - 1$: 10 $S = 1(0.35) + 13(0.85) + 10(1.00) = 21.40$	$25 - 21.40 = 3.60$

Fe	26	$1s^2 2s^2 2p^6 3s^2 3p^6 3d^6 4s^2$	Other e$^-$ in same valence shell: 1 Core e$^-$ in $n-1$: 14 Core e$^-$ in $< n-1$: 10 $S = 1(0.35) + 14(0.85) + 10(1.00) = 22.25$	$26 - 22.25 = 3.75$
Co	27	$1s^2 2s^2 2p^6 3s^2 3p^6 3d^7 4s^2$	Other e$^-$ in same valence shell: 1 Core e$^-$ in $n-1$: 15 Core e$^-$ in $< n-1$: 10 $S = 1(0.35) + 15(0.85) + 10(1.00) = 23.10$	$27 - 23.10 = 3.90$
Ni	28	$1s^2 2s^2 2p^6 3s^2 3p^6 3d^8 4s^2$	Other e$^-$ in same valence shell: 1 Core e$^-$ in $n-1$: 16 Core e$^-$ in $< n-1$: 10 $S = 1(0.35) + 16(0.85) + 10(1.00) = 23.95$	$28 - 23.95 = 4.05$
Cu	29	$1s^2 2s^2 2p^6 3s^2 3p^6 3d^{10} 4s^1$	Other e$^-$ in same valence shell: 0 Core e$^-$ in $n-1$: 18 Core e$^-$ in $< n-1$: 10 $S = 18(0.85) + 10(1.00) = 25.3$	$29 - 25.3 = 3.70$
Zn	30	$1s^2 2s^2 2p^6 3s^2 3p^6 3d^{10} 4s^2$	Other e$^-$ in same valence shell: 1 Core e$^-$ in $n-1$: 18 Core e$^-$ in $< n-1$: 10 $S = 1(0.35) + 18(0.85) + 10(1.00) = 25.65$	$30 - 25.65 = 4.35$
Ga	31	$1s^2 2s^2 2p^6 3s^2 3p^6 3d^{10} 4s^2 4p^1$	Other e$^-$ in same valence shell: 2 Core e$^-$ in $n-1$: 18 Core e$^-$ in $< n-1$: 10 $S = 2(0.35) + 18(0.85) + 10(1.00) = 26.00$	$31 - 26.00 = 5.00$
Ge	32	$1s^2 2s^2 2p^6 3s^2 3p^6 3d^{10} 4s^2 4p^2$	Other e$^-$ in same valence shell: 3 Core e$^-$ in $n-1$: 18 Core e$^-$ in $< n-1$: 10 $S = 3(0.35) + 18(0.85) + 10(1.00) = 26.35$	$32 - 26.35 = 5.65$
As	33	$1s^2 2s^2 2p^6 3s^2 3p^6 3d^{10} 4s^2 4p^3$	Other e$^-$ in same valence shell: 4 Core e$^-$ in $n-1$: 18 Core e$^-$ in $< n-1$: 10 $S = 4(0.35) + 18(0.85) + 10(1.00) = 26.70$	$33 - 26.70 = 6.30$
Se	34	$1s^2 2s^2 2p^6 3s^2 3p^6 3d^{10} 4s^2 4p^4$	Other e$^-$ in same valence shell: 5 Core e$^-$ in $n-1$: 18 Core e$^-$ in $< n-1$: 10 $S = 5(0.35) + 18(0.85) + 10(1.00) = 27.05$	$34 - 27.05 = 6.95$
Br	35	$1s^2 2s^2 2p^6 3s^2 3p^6 3d^{10} 4s^2 4p^5$	Other e$^-$ in same valence shell: 6 Core e$^-$ in $n-1$: 18 Core e$^-$ in $< n-1$: 10 $S = 6(0.35) + 18(0.85) + 10(1.00) = 27.40$	$35 - 27.40 = 7.60$
Kr	36	$1s^2 2s^2 2p^6 3s^2 3p^6 3d^{10} 4s^2 4p^6$	Other e$^-$ in same valence shell: 7 Core e$^-$ in $n-1$: 18 Core e$^-$ in $< n-1$: 10 $S = 7(0.35) + 18(0.85) + 10(1.00) = 27.75$	$36 - 27.75 = 8.25$

The effective nuclear charge increases as you move from left to right across the period and the outermost valence electrons are drawn closer to the nucleus. As a result, the radius of the atom becomes smaller.

8.47   (a)   Al or In   In atoms are larger than Al atoms because as you trace the path between Al and In on the periodic table you move down a column. Atomic size increases as you move down a column because the outermost electrons occupy orbitals with a higher principal quantum number that are therefore larger, resulting in a larger atom.

       (b)   Si or N   Si atoms are larger than N atoms because as you trace the path between N and Si on the periodic table you move down a column (atomic size increases) and then to the left across a period (atomic size increases). These effects add together for an overall increase.

(c)   P or Pb   Pb atoms are larger than P atoms because as you trace the path between P and Pb on the periodic table you move down a column (atomic size increases) and then to the left across a period (atomic size increases). These effects add together for an overall increase.

(d)   C or F   C atoms are larger than F atoms because as you trace the path between C and F on the periodic table you move to the right within the same period. As you move to the right across a period, the effective nuclear charge experienced by the outermost electrons increases, which results in a smaller size.

8.49   Ca, Rb, S, Si, Ge, F   F is above and to the right of the other elements, so we start with F as the smallest atom. As you trace a path from F to S you move to the left (size increases) and down (size increases), next you move left from S to Si (size increases), then down to Ge (size increases), next move to the left to Ca (size increases), and then to the left and down to Rb (size increases). So, in order of increasing atomic radii F < S < Si < Ge < Ca < Rb.

Ionic Electron Configurations, Ionic Radii, Magnetic Properties, and Ionization Energy

8.51   (a)   Li or Li$^+$ An Li atom is larger than Li$^+$ because cations are smaller than the atoms from which they are formed.

(b)   I$^-$ or Cs$^+$ An I$^-$ ion is larger than a Cs$^+$ ion because, although they are isoelectronic, I$^-$ has two fewer protons than Cs$^+$, resulting in a lesser pull on the electrons and therefore a larger radius.

(c)   Cr or Cr^{3+} A Cr atom is larger than Cr^{3+} because cations are smaller than the atoms from which they are formed.

(d)   O or O^{2-} An O^{2-} ion is larger than an O atom because anions are larger than the atoms from which they are formed.

8.53   Since all the species are isoelectronic, the radius will depend on the number of protons in each species. The fewer the protons, the larger the radius.
F: $Z = 9$; Ne: $Z = 10$; O: $Z = 8$; Mg: $Z = 12$; Na: $Z = 11$
So: $O^{2-} > F^- > Ne > Na^+ > Mg^{2+}$

Ionic Radii

8.55   **Given:** radius of O = 73 pm, radius of O^{2-} = 140 pm **Find:** Z_{eff} for each species using Slater's rules and then use the values to explain the different radii
Conceptual Plan: Write the electron configuration for each atom/ion, grouping subshells by n value. Use Slater's rules to calculate the shielding constant, S, and then subtract S from the atomic number to determine Z_{eff}. Use Z_{eff} to explain the radii of the ion versus the neutral atom.

Species	Z	e$^-$ configuration	S	$Z_{eff} (= Z - S)$	Radius (pm)
O	8	$1s^2 2s^2 2p^4$	Other e$^-$ in same valence shell: 5 Core e$^-$ in $n - 1$: 2 Core e$^-$ in $< n - 1$: 0 $S = 5(0.35) + 2(0.85) = 3.45$	$8 - 3.45 = 4.55$	73
O^{2-}	8	$1s^2 2s^2 2p^6$	Other e$^-$ in same valence shell: 7 Core e$^-$ in $n - 1$: 2 Core e$^-$ in $< n - 1$: 0 $S = 7(0.35) + 2(0.85) = 4.15$	$8 - 4.15 = 3.85$	140

The effective nuclear charge experienced by the valence electrons in O is greater than that experienced by valence electrons in O^{2-}. As a result, the O atom has a smaller atomic radius.

8.57   **Given:** radius of Ga = 135 pm, radius of Ga^{3+} = 62 pm **Find:** Z_{eff} for each species using Slater's rules and then use the values to explain the different radii

Conceptual Plan: Write the electron configuration for each atom/ion, grouping subshells by n value. Use Slater's rules to calculate the shielding constant, S, and then subtract S from the atomic number to determine Z_{eff}. Use Z_{eff} to explain the radii of the ion versus the neutral atom.

Species	Z	e⁻ configuration	S	$Z_{eff} (= Z - S)$
Ga	31	$1s^2 2s^2 2p^6 3s^2 3p^6 3d^{10} 4s^2 4p^1$	Other e⁻ in same valence shell: 2 Core e⁻ in $n-1$: 18 Core e⁻ in $< n-1$: 10 $S = 2(0.35) + 18(0.85) + 10(1.00) = 26.00$	$31 - 26.00 = 5.00$
Ga^{3+}	31	$1s^2 2s^2 2p^6 3s^2 3p^6 3d^{10}$	Other e⁻ in same valence shell: 17 Core e⁻ in $n-1$: 8 Core e⁻ in $< n-1$: 2 $S = 17(0.35) + 8(1.00) + 2(1.00) = 15.95$	$31 - 15.95 = 15.05$

The effective nuclear charge experienced by the valence electrons in Ga^{3+} is much greater than that experienced by valence electrons in Ga. As a result, the Ga^{3+} ion has a much smaller ionic radius.

Ionization Energy

8.59　(a)　Br or Bi　　Br has a higher ionization energy than Bi because as you trace the path between Br and Bi on the periodic table you move down a column (ionization energy decreases) and then to the left across a period (ionization energy decreases). These effects sum together for an overall decrease.

　　　(b)　Na or Rb　　Na has a higher ionization energy than Rb because as you trace a path between Na and Rb on the periodic table you move down a column. Ionization energy decreases as you go down a column because of the increasing size of orbitals with increasing n.

　　　(c)　As or At　　Based on periodic trends alone, it is impossible to tell which has a higher ionization energy because as you trace the path between As and At you go to the right across a period (ionization energy increases) and then down a column (ionization energy decreases). These effects tend to oppose each other, and it is not obvious which will dominate.

　　　(d)　P or Sn　　P has a higher ionization energy than Sn because as you trace the path between P and Sn on the periodic table you move down a column (ionization energy decreases) and then to the left across a period (ionization energy decreases). These effects sum together for an overall decrease.

8.61　Since ionization energy increases as you move to the right across a period and increases as you move up a column, the element with the smallest first ionization energy would be the element farthest to the left and lowest down on the periodic table. So, In has the smallest ionization energy; as you trace a path to the right and up on the periodic table, the next element reached is Si; continuing up and to the right you reach N; and then continuing to the right you reach F. So, in the order of increasing first ionization energy the elements are In < Si < N < F.

8.63　The jump in ionization energy occurs when you change from removing a valence electron to removing a core electron. To determine where this jump occurs you need to look at the electron configuration of the atom.

　　　(a)　Be　$1s^2 2s^2$　　The first and second ionization energies involve removing 2s electrons, while the third ionization energy removes a core electron, so the jump will occur between the second and third ionization energies.

　　　(b)　N　$1s^2 2s^2 2p^3$　　The first five ionization energies involve removing the 2p and 2s electrons, while the sixth ionization energy removes a core electron, so the jump will occur between the fifth and sixth ionization energies.

　　　(c)　O　$1s^2 2s^2 2p^4$　　The first six ionization energies involve removing the 2p and 2s electrons, while the seventh ionization energy removes a core electron, so the jump will occur between the sixth and seventh ionization energies.

(d)   Li $1s^2 2s^1$ The first ionization energy involves removing a $2s$ electron, while the second ionization energy removes a core electron, so the jump will occur between the first and second ionization energies.

8.65   **Given:** Mg **Find:** Z_{eff} for Mg, Mg^+, and Mg^{2+} and compare the values to the ionization energies
Conceptual Plan: Write the electron configuration for each atom or ion, grouping subshells by n value. Use Slater's rules to calculate the shielding constant, S, and then subtract S from the atomic number to determine Z_{eff}. Use Z_{eff} to explain the trend in the first three ionization energies.

Species	Z	e$^-$ configuration	S	Z_{eff} (= Z − S)
Mg	12	$1s^2 2s^2 2p^6 3s^2$	Other e$^-$ in same valence shell: 1 Core e$^-$ in $n-1$: 8 Core e$^-$ in $< n-1$: 2 $S = 1(0.35) + 8(0.85) + 2(1.00) = 9.15$	$12 - 9.15 = 2.85$
Mg^+	12	$1s^2 2s^2 2p^6 3s^1$	Other e$^-$ in same valence shell: 0 Core e$^-$ in $n-1$: 8 Core e$^-$ in $< n-1$: 2 $S = 8(0.85) + 2(1.00) = 8.80$	$12 - 8.80 = 3.20$
Mg^{2+}	12	$1s^2 2s^2 2p^6$	Other e$^-$ in same valence shell: 7 Core e$^-$ in $n-1$: 2 Core e$^-$ in $< n-1$: 0 $S = 7(0.35) + 2(0.85) = 4.15$	$12 - 4.15 = 7.85$

The ionization energies of Mg, Mg^+, and Mg^{2+} are 731, 1450, and 7730 kJ mol^{-1}, respectively. The large increase in ionization energy on going from Mg^+ to Mg^{2+} corresponds to the removal of a core electron from the $n = 2$ shell in Mg^{2+}. A similar increase in effective nuclear charge is seen on going from Mg^+ to Mg^{2+}, illustrating that the electrons in the $n = 2$ shell of Mg^{2+} are more strongly attracted to the nucleus.

Electron Affinities and Metallic Character

8.67   (a)   Na or Rb   Na has a more positive electron affinity than Rb. In column 1 electron affinity becomes less positive as you go down the column.

(b)   B or S   S has a more positive electron affinity than B. As you trace from B to S in the periodic table you move to the right, which shows the value of the electron affinity becoming more positive. Also, as you move from period 2 to period 3 the value of the electron affinity becomes more positive. Both of these trends sum together for the value of the electron affinity to become more positive.

(c)   C or N   C has the more positive electron affinity. As you trace from C to N across the periodic table you would normally expect N to have the more positive electron affinity. However, N has a half-filled p sublevel, which lends it extra stability, therefore it is harder to add an electron.

(d)   Li or F   F has the more positive electron affinity. As you trace from Li to F on the periodic table you move to the right in the period. As you go to the right across a period the value of the electron affinity generally becomes more positive.

8.69   (a)   Sr or Sb   Sr is more metallic than Sb because as we trace the path between Sr and Sb on the periodic table we move to the right within the same period. Metallic character decreases as you go to the right.

(b)   As or Bi   Bi is more metallic because as we trace a path between As and Bi on the periodic table we move down a column in the same family (metallic character increases).

(c)   Cl or O   Based on periodic trends alone, we cannot tell which is more metallic because as we trace the path between O and Cl we go to the right across a period (metallic character decreases) and then down a column (metallic character increases). These effects tend to oppose each other, and it is not easy to tell which will predominate.

    (d)   S or As   As is more metallic than S because as we trace the path between S and As on the periodic table we move down a column (metallic character increases) and then to the left across a period (metallic character increases). These effects add together for an overall increase.

8.71   The order of increasing metallic character is S < Se < Sb < In < Ba < Fr.

Metallic character decreases as you move left to right across a period and decreases as you move up a column; therefore, the element with the least metallic character will be to the top right of the periodic table. So, of these elements, S has the least metallic character. As you move down the column the next element is Se; as you continue down and then to the right you reach Sb; continuing to the right goes to In; going down the column and then to the right comes to Ba; and then down the column and to the right is Fr.

Chemical Behaviour of the Alkali Metals and the Halogens

8.73   Alkaline earth metals react with halogens to form metal halides. Write the formulas for the reactants and the metal halide product.

$$Sr(s) + I_2(g) \rightarrow SrI_2(s)$$

8.75   Alkali metals react with water to form the dissolved metal ion, the hydroxide ion, and hydrogen gas. Write the skeletal equation including each of these and then balance it.

$$Li(s) + H_2O(l) \rightarrow Li^+(aq) + OH^-(aq) + H_2(g)$$
$$2\,Li(s) + 2\,H_2O(l) \rightarrow 2\,Li^+(aq) + 2\,OH^-(aq) + H_2(g)$$

8.77   The halogens react with hydrogen to form hydrogen halides. Write the skeletal reaction with each of the halogen and hydrogen as the reactants and the hydrogen halide compound as the product and balance the equation.

$$H_2(g) + Br_2(g) \rightarrow HBr(g)$$
$$H_2(g) + Br_2(g) \rightarrow 2\,HBr(g)$$

Cumulative Problems

8.79   Br: $1s^2 2s^2 2p^6 3s^2 3p^6 4s^2 3d^{10} 4p^5$
Kr: $1s^2 2s^2 2p^6 3s^2 3p^6 4s^2 3d^{10} 4p^6$

Krypton has a completely filled p sublevel, giving it chemical stability. Bromine needs one electron to achieve a completely filled p sublevel and therefore has a highly positive electron affinity. It therefore easily takes on an electron and is reduced to the bromide ion, giving it the added stability of the filled p sublevel.

8.81   Since K^+ has a 1+ charge you would need a cation with a similar size and a 1+ charge. Looking at the ions in the same family, Na^+ would be too small and Rb^+ would be too large. If we then consider Ar^+ and Ca^+ we would have ions of similar size and charge. Between these two Ca^+ would be the easier to achieve because the first ionization energy of Ca is similar to that of K, while the first ionization energy of Ar is much larger. However, the second ionization energy of Ca is relatively low, making it easy to lose the second electron.

8.83   C has an outer shell electron configuration of $ns^2 np^2$; based on this you would expect Si and Ge, which are in the same family, to be most like carbon. Ionization energies for both Si and Ge are similar and tend to be slightly lower than C, but all are intermediate in the range of first ionization energies. The electron affinities of Si and Ge are close to that of C.

8.85   (a)   N: $[He]2s^2 2p^3$ Mg: $[Ne]3s^2$ O: $[He]2s^2 2p^4$
                F: $[He]2s^2 2p^5$ Al: $[Ne]3s^2 3p^1$

        (b)   Mg > Al > N > O > F

        (c)   Al < Mg < O < N < F   (from the table)

        (d)   Mg and Al would have the largest radius because they are in period $n = 3$; Al is smaller than Mg because radius decreases as you move to the right across the period. F is smaller than O, and O is smaller than N because as you move to the right across the period radius decreases.

The first ionization energy of Al is smaller than the first ionization energy of Mg because Al loses the electron from the 3p orbital, which is shielded by the electrons in the 3s orbital; while Mg loses the electron from the filled 3s orbital, which has added stability because it is a filled orbital. The first ionization energy of O is lower than the first ionization energy of N because N has a half-filled 2p orbital, which adds extra stability, thus making it harder to remove the electron. The fourth electron in the O 2p orbitals experiences added electron–electron repulsion because it must pair with another electron in the same 2p orbital, thus making it easier to remove.

8.87   As you move to the right across a row in the periodic table for the main-group elements the effective nuclear charge (Z_{eff}) experienced by the electrons in the outermost principal energy level increases, resulting in a stronger attraction between the outermost electrons and the nucleus, and therefore a smaller atomic radii.

Across the row of transition elements the number of electrons in the outermost principal energy level (highest n value) is nearly constant. As another proton is added to the nucleus with each successive element, another electron is added, but that electron goes into an $n_{highest} - 1$ orbital (a core level). The number of outermost electrons stays constant and they experience a roughly constant effective nuclear charge, keeping the radius approximately constant after the first couple of elements in the series.

8.89   The noble gases all have a filled outer quantum level, very high first ionization energies, and positive values for the electron affinity and are thus particularly unreactive. The lighter noble gases will not form any compounds because the ionization energies of He and Ne are both over 2000 kJ mol^{-1}. Since ionization energy decreases as you move down a column we find that the heavier noble gases, Ar, Kr, and Xe, do form some compounds. They have ionization energies that are close to the ionization energy of H and can thus be forced to lose an electron.

8.91   Group 16: ns^2np^4 Group 17: ns^2np^5
The electron affinity of the group 17 elements are more positive than the group 16 elements in the same period because group 17 requires only one electron to achieve the noble gas configuration ns^2np^6, while the group 16 elements require two electrons. Adding one electron to the group 16 element will not give them any added stability and leads to extra electron–electron repulsions, so the value of the electron affinity is less positive than that for group 17.

8.93 $35 = Br = [Ar]4s^23d^{10}4p^5$ $53 = I = [Kr]5s^24d^{10}5p^5$
Br and I are both halogens with an outermost electron configuration of ns^2np^5; the next element with the same outermost electron configuration is 85, At.

8.95   (i) $10 - 2 = 8 \rightarrow$ O; $12 - 2 = 10 \rightarrow$ Ne; $58 - 5 = 53 \rightarrow$ I; $11 - 2 = 9 \rightarrow$ F; $7 - 2 = 5 \rightarrow$ B; $44 - 5 = 39 \rightarrow$ Y; $63 - 6 = 57 \rightarrow$ La; $66 - 6 = 60 \rightarrow$ Nd   One If by Land

        (ii) $9 - 2 = 7 \rightarrow$ N; $99 - 7 = 92 \rightarrow$ U; $30 - 4 = 26 \rightarrow$ Fe; $95 - 7 = 88 \rightarrow$ Ra; $19 - 3 = 16 \rightarrow$ S $47 - 5 = 42 \rightarrow$ Mo; $79 - 6 = 73 \rightarrow$ Ta   (backwards) Atoms Are Fun

Challenge Problems

8.97   (a)   Using Excel, make a table of radius, atomic number, and density. Using xy scatter, make a chart of radius vs. density. With an exponential trendline, estimate the density of argon and xenon. Also, make a chart of atomic number vs. density. With a linear trendline, estimate the density of argon and xenon.

element	radius(pm)	atomic number	density
He	32	2	0.16
Ne	70	10	0.81
Ar	98	18	
Kr	112	36	3.38
Xe	130	54	
Rn		86	8.96
		118	

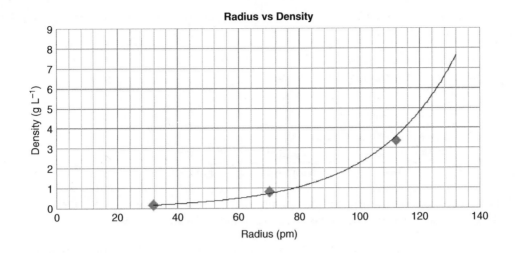

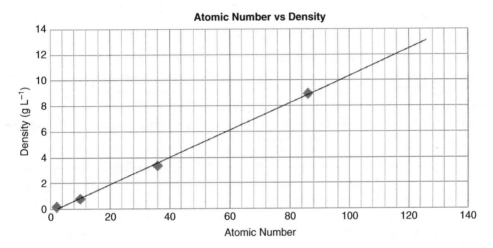

From the radius vs. density chart, Ar has a density of ~ 2 g L^{-1} and Xe has a density of ~ 7 g L^{-1}. From the atomic number vs. density chart, Ar has a density of ~1.8 g L^{-1} and Xe has a density of ~6 g L^{-1}.

(b)   Using the chart of atomic number vs. density, element 118 would be predicted to have a density of ~ 13 g L^{-1}.

(c)   **Given:** Ne: M = 20.18 g mol^{-1}; r = 70 pm   **Find:** mass of neon; d neon
Conceptual Plan: M $\rightarrow$ m_{atom} **and then** r $\rightarrow$ vol_{atom} **and then** $\rightarrow$ d

$$\frac{6.022 \times 10^{23} \text{atoms}}{\text{mol}} \qquad V = \frac{4}{3}\pi r^3 \qquad d = \frac{\text{mass}}{\text{vol}}$$

Solution: $\dfrac{20.18 \text{ g}}{\text{mol}} \times \dfrac{\text{mol}}{6.022 \times 10^{23} \text{ atoms}} = 3.35 \times 10^{-23} \text{ g atom}^{-1}$

$V = \dfrac{4}{3} \times 3.14 \times (70 \text{ pm})^3 \times \left(\dfrac{\text{m}}{10^{12} \text{ pm}}\right)^3 \times \dfrac{\text{L}}{0.0010 \text{ m}^3} = 1.\underline{4}4 \times 10^{-27} \text{ L}$

$d = \dfrac{3.35 \times 10^{-23} \text{ g}}{1.\underline{4}4 \times 10^{-27} \text{ L}} = 2.\underline{3}3 \times 10^4 = 2.3 \times 10^4 \text{ g L}^{-1}$

Check: The units of the answer (g L^{-1}) are correct. This density is significantly larger than the actual density of neon gas. This suggests that a L of neon is composed of primarily empty space.

(d)   **Given:** Ne: M = 20.18 g mol^{-1}, d = 0.90 g L^{-1}; Kr: M = 83.30 g mol^{-1}, d = 3.75 g L^{-1}; Ar: M = 39.95 g mol^{-1}
Find: d of argon in g L^{-1}

Conceptual Plan: $d \rightarrow$ mol L$^{-1} \rightarrow$ atoms L^{-1} for Kr and Ne and then atoms L$^{-1} \rightarrow$ mol L$^{-1} \rightarrow d$ for Ar

$$\text{mol} = \frac{\text{mass}}{\text{molar mass}} \quad \frac{6.022 \times 10^{23}\,\text{atoms}}{\text{mol}} \qquad \frac{\text{mol}}{6.022 \times 10^{23}\,\text{atoms}} \qquad \frac{39.95\,\text{g}}{\text{mol}}$$

Solution: for Ne:
$$\frac{0.90\,\text{g}}{\text{L}} \times \frac{\text{mol}}{20.18\,\text{g}} \times \frac{6.022 \times 10^{23}\,\text{atoms}}{\text{mol}} = 2.69 \times 10^{22}\,\text{atoms L}^{-1}$$

for Kr:
$$\frac{3.75\,\text{g}}{\text{L}} \times \frac{\text{mol}}{83.80\,\text{g}} \times \frac{6.022 \times 10^{23}\,\text{atoms}}{\text{mol}} = 2.69 \times 10^{22}\,\text{atoms L}^{-1}$$

for Ar:
$$\frac{2.69 \times 10^{22}\,\text{atoms}}{\text{L}} \times \frac{\text{mol}}{6.022 \times 10^{23}\,\text{atoms}} \times \frac{39.95\,\text{g}}{\text{mol}} = 1.78\,\text{g L}^{-1}$$

This value is similar to the value calculated in part a. The value of the density calculated from the radius was 2 g L^{-1} and the value of the density calculated from the atomic number was 1.8 g L^{-1}.
Check: The units of the answer (g L^{-1}) are correct. The value of the answer agrees with the published value.

8.99   The density increases as you move to the right across the first transition series. For the first transition series, the mass increases as you move to the right across the periodic table. However, the radius of the transition series elements stays nearly constant as you move to the right across the periodic table, thus the volume will remain nearly constant. Since density is mass/volume the density of the elements increases.

8.101   The element that would fill the 8s and 8p orbitals would have atomic number 168. The element is in the noble gas family and would have the properties of noble gases. It would have the electron configuration of $[118]8s^2 5g^{18} 6f^{14} 7d^{10} 8p^6$. The outer shell electron (highest n level) configuration would be $8s^2 8p^6$. The element would be relatively inert, have a first ionization energy less than 1037 kJ mol^{-1} (the first ionization energy of Rn), and have a positive electron affinity. It would be difficult to form compounds with most elements but would be able to form compounds with fluorine and oxygen.

8.103   When you move down the column from Al to Ga, the size of the atom actually decreases because not much shielding is contributed by the 3d electrons in the Ga atom, while there is a large increase in the nuclear charge; therefore, the effective nuclear charge is greater for Ga than for Al, so the ionization energy does not decrease. As you go from In to Tl, the ionization energy actually increases because the 4f electrons do not contribute to the shielding of the outermost electrons and there is a large increase in the effective nuclear charge.

8.105   The second electron is added to an ion with a 1 − charge, so there is a large repulsive force that has to be overcome to add the second electron. Thus, it will require energy to add the second electron, and the second electron affinity will have a negative value.

8.107   **Given:** Ra, Z = 88   **Find:** Z for next two alkaline earth metals
         Solution: The next element would lie in period 8, column 2. The largest currently known element is 116 in period 7, column 16. To reach period 8 column 2 you need to add 4 protons and would have Z = 120.

         The alkaline earth metal following 120 would lie in period 9 column 2. To reach this column, you need to add 18 g-block element protons, 10 d-block element protons, 14 f-block element protons, 6 p-block element protons, and then 2 s-block element protons. This would give Z = 170.

8.109   Francium would have an electron configuration of $[\text{Rn}]7s^1$; the atomic radius would be > 265 pm (atomic radius of Cs); the first ionization energy would be less than 376 kJ mol^{-1}; the density would be greater than 1.879 g cm^{-3}; and the normal melting would be less than 29°C.

         (a) $2\text{Fr}(s) + 2\text{H}_2\text{O}(l) \rightarrow 2\text{Fr}^+(aq) + 2\text{OH}^-(aq) + \text{H}_2(g)$

         (b) $2\text{Fr}(s) + 1/2\text{O}_2(g) \rightarrow \text{Fr}_2\text{O}(s)$

         (c) $2\text{Fr}(s) + \text{Cl}_2(g) \rightarrow 2\text{FrCl}(s)$

8.111   **Given:** Li, Na, K, Rb **Find:** Z_{eff} for each species using Slater's rules and then determine if Z_{eff} explains the variation in ionic radius

Conceptual Plan: Write the electron configuration for each ion, grouping subshells by n value. Use Slater's rules to calculate the shielding constant, S, and then subtract S from the atomic number to determine Z_{eff}. Use Z_{eff} to explain the variation in ionic radius.

Species	Z	e⁻ configuration	S	$Z_{eff} (= Z - S)$	Radius (pm)
Li	3	$1s^2 2s^1$	Other e⁻ in same valence shell: 0	$3 - 1.70 = 1.30$	152
			Core e⁻ in $n - 1$: 2		
			Core e⁻ in $< n - 1$: 0		
			$S = 2(0.85) = 1.7$		
Na	11	$1s^2 2s^2 2p^6 3s^1$	Other e⁻ in same valence shell: 0	$11 - 8.80 = 2.20$	186
			Core e⁻ in $n - 1$: 8		
			Core e⁻ in $< n - 1$: 2		
			$S = 8(0.85) + 2(1.00) = 8.80$		
K	19	$1s^2 2s^2 2p^6 3s^2 3p^6 4s^1$	Other e⁻ in same valence shell: 0	$19 - 16.80 = 2.20$	227
			Core e⁻ in $n - 1$: 8		
			Core e⁻ in $< n - 1$: 10		
			$S = 8(0.85) + 10(1.00) = 16.80$		
Rb	37	$1s^2 2s^2 2p^6 3s^2 3p^6 3d^{10} 4s^2 4p^6 5s^1$	Other e⁻ in same valence shell: 0	$37 - 34.80 = 2.20$	248
			Core e⁻ in $n - 1$: 8		
			Core e⁻ in $< n - 1$: 28		
			$S = 8(0.85) + 28(1.00) = 34.80$		

Na, K, and Rb all have the same Z_{eff} but different atomic radii. The variation in atomic radii as we go down a group can be explained by taking the valence level n into consideration. As n increases the valence orbitals become larger and the atomic radii increase. For example, an element with $n = 2$ valence electrons (Li) will have a smaller radius than an element with $n = 5$ valence electrons (Rb).

Conceptual Problems

8.113   If six electrons rather than eight electrons led to a stable configuration, the electron configuration of the stable configuration would be $ns^2 np^4$.

    (a)   A noble gas would have the electron configuration $ns^2 np^4$. This could correspond to the O atom.

    (b)   A reactive nonmetal would have one less electron than the stable configuration. This would have the electron configuration $ns^2 np^3$. This could correspond to the N atom.

    (c)   A reactive metal would have one more electron than the stable configuration. This would have the electron configuration of ns^1. This could correspond to the Li atom.

8.115   The $4s$ electrons in calcium have relatively low ionization energies ($IE_1 = 590$ kJ mol⁻¹; $IE_2 = 1145$ kJ mol⁻¹) because they are valence electrons. The energetic cost for calcium to lose a third electron is extraordinarily high because the next electron to be lost is a core electron. Similarly, the electron affinity of fluorine to gain one electron (328 kJ mol⁻¹) is highly exothermic because the added electron completes fluoride's valence shell. The gain of a second electron by the negatively charged fluoride anion would not be favourable. Therefore, we would expect calcium and fluoride to combine in a 1:2 ratio.

9 Chemical Bonding I: Lewis Theory

Review Questions

9.1 Bonding theories are central to chemistry because they explain how atoms bond together to form molecules. Bonding theories explain why some combinations of atoms are stable and others are not.

9.3 The three types of bonds are ionic bonds, which occur between metals and nonmetals and are characterized by the transfer of electrons; covalent bonds, which occur between nonmetals and are characterized by the sharing of electrons; and metallic bonds, which occur between metals and are characterized by electrons being pooled.

9.5 Bonds are formed when atoms attain a stable electron configuration. Since the stable configuration usually has eight electrons in the outermost shell, this is known as the octet rule.

9.7 In Lewis theory, we represent ionic bonding by moving electron dots from the metal to the nonmetal and then allowing the resultant ions to form a crystalline lattice composed of alternating cations and anions. The cation loses its valence electron(s) and is left with an octet in the previous principal energy level; the anion gains electron(s) to form an octet. The Lewis structure of the anion is usually written within brackets with the charge in the upper right-hand corner, outside the brackets. The positive and negative charges attract one another, resulting in the compound.

9.9 Lattice energy is the energy associated with forming a crystalline lattice of alternating cations and anions from the gaseous ions. Since the cations are positively charged and the anions are negatively charged there is a lowering of potential—as described by Coulomb's law—when the ions come together to form a lattice. That energy is emitted as heat when the lattice forms.

9.11 The Born–Haber cycle is a hypothetical series of steps that represents the formation of an ionic compound from its constituent elements. The steps are chosen so that the change in enthalpy of each step is known except for the last one, which is the lattice energy. In terms of the formation of NaCl, the steps are as follows:
Step 1: The formation of gaseous sodium from solid sodium (sublimation energy of sodium)
Step 2: The formation of a chlorine atom from a chlorine molecule (bond energy of chlorine)
Step 3: The ionization of gaseous sodium (ionization energy of sodium)
Step 4: The addition of an electron to gaseous chlorine (the negative electron affinity of chlorine)
Step 5: The formation of the crystalline solid from the gaseous ions (the lattice energy)

The overall reaction is the formation of NaCl(s), so we can use Hess's law to determine the lattice energy.
$$\Delta_f H^\circ = \Delta_r H_{\text{step 1}} + \Delta_r H_{\text{step 2}} + \Delta_r H_{\text{step 3}} + \Delta_r H_{\text{step 4}} + \Delta_r H_{\text{step 5}}$$
$\Delta_f H^\circ$ = sublimation energy + ½ bond energy + ionization energy + negative electron affinity + lattice energy
Since all the terms are known except the lattice energy, we can calculate the lattice energy.

9.13 We modelled ionic solids as a lattice of individual ions held together by coulombic forces, which are equal in all directions. To melt the solid, these forces must be overcome, which requires a significant amount of heat. Therefore, the model accounts for the high melting points of ionic solids.

9.15   A pair of electrons that is shared between two atoms is called a bonding pair, while a pair of electrons that is associated with only one atom—and therefore, not involved in bonding—is called a lone pair.

9.17   Generally, combinations of atoms that can satisfy the octet rule on each atom are stable, while those combinations that do not satisfy the octet rule are not stable.

9.19   Electronegativity is the ability of an atom to attract electrons to itself in a chemical bond. This results in a polar bond. Electronegativity generally increases across a period in the periodic table. And electronegativity generally decreases down a column (group) in the periodic table. The most electronegative element is fluorine.

9.21   Percent ionic character is defined as the ratio of a bond's actual dipole moment to the dipole moment it would have if the electron were completely transferred from one atom to the other, multiplied by 100.

A bond in which an electron is completely transferred from one atom to another would have 100% ionic character. However, no bond is 100% ionic. Percent ionic character generally increases as the electronegativity difference increases. In general, bonds with greater than 50% ionic character are referred to as ionic bonds.

9.23   To calculate the dipole moment we use $\mu = qr$:

For 100 pm: $\mu = 1.6 \times 10^{-19} \, \cancel{C} \times 100 \, \cancel{pm} \times \dfrac{\cancel{m}}{10^{12} \, \cancel{pm}} \times \dfrac{D}{3.34 \times 10^{-30} \, \cancel{C} \cdot \cancel{m}} = 4.8 \, D$

For 200 pm: $\mu = 1.6 \times 10^{-19} \, \cancel{C} \times 200 \, \cancel{pm} \times \dfrac{\cancel{m}}{10^{12} \, \cancel{pm}} \times \dfrac{D}{3.34 \times 10^{-30} \, \cancel{C} \cdot \cancel{m}} = 9.6 \, D$

9.25   The total number of electrons for a Lewis structure of a molecule is the sum of the valence electrons of each atom in the molecule.

The total number of electrons for the Lewis structure of an ion is found by summing the number of valence electrons for each atom and then subtracting one electron for each positive charge or adding one electron for each negative charge.

9.27   In some cases we can write resonance structures that are not equivalent. One possible resonance structure may be somewhat better than another. In such cases the true structure may still be represented as an average of the resonance structures, but with the better resonance structure contributing more to the true structure. Multiple nonequivalent resonance structures may be weighted differently in their contributions to the true overall structure of a molecule.

9.29   The octet rule has some exceptions because not all atoms always have eight electrons surrounding them. The two major categories are 1) odd octets—electron species, molecules, or ions with an odd number of electrons, for example, NO, and 2) incomplete octets—molecules or ions with fewer than eight electrons around an atom, for example, BF_3.

9.31   The bond energy of a chemical bond is the energy required to break 1 mol of the bond in the gas phase. Since breaking bonds is endothermic and forming bonds is exothermic we can calculate the overall enthalpy change as a sum of the enthalpy changes associated with breaking the required bonds in the reactants and forming the required bonds in the products.

9.33   When metal atoms bond together to form a solid, each metal atom donates one or more electrons to an electron sea.

Problems by Topic

Valence Electrons and Dot Structures

9.35   N : $1s^2 2s^2 2p^3$ $\cdot \overset{\displaystyle \cdot \cdot}{\underset{\displaystyle \cdot}{N}} :$ The electrons included in the Lewis structure are $2s^2 2p^3$.

9.37   (a)   Al: $1s^2 2s^2 2p^6 3s^2 3p^1$

$\cdot \overset{\displaystyle \cdot}{Al} \cdot$

(b) Na$^+$: $1s^22s^22p^6$

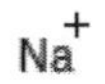

Na$^+$

(c) Cl: $1s^22s^22p^63s^23p^5$

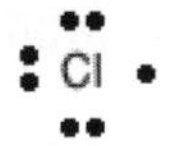

:Cl·

(d) Cl$^-$: $1s^22s^22p^63s^23p^6$

:Cl:$^-$

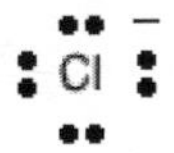

Ionic Lewis Structures and Lattice Energy

9.39 (a) NaF: Draw the Lewis structures for Na and F based on their valence electrons. Na: $3s^1$ F: $2s^22p^5$

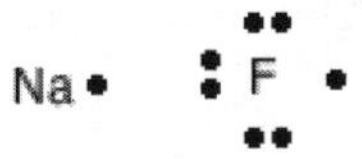

Na· :F·

Sodium must lose one electron and be left with the octet from the previous shell, while fluorine needs to gain one electron to get an octet.

Na$^+$ [:F:]$^-$

(b) CaO: Draw the Lewis structures for Ca and O based on their valence electrons. Ca: $4s^2$ O: $2s^22p^4$

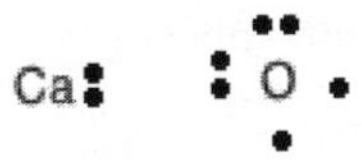

Ca: :O·

Calcium must lose two electrons and be left with the octet from the previous shell, while oxygen needs to gain two electrons to get an octet.

Ca^{2+} [:O:]$^{2-}$

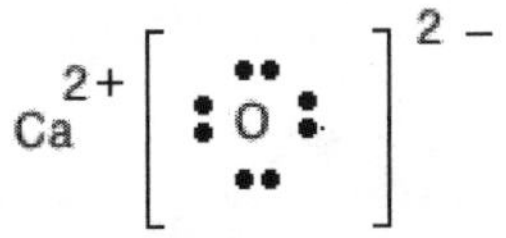

(c) SrBr$_2$: Draw the Lewis structures for Sr and Br based on their valence electrons. Sr: $5s^2$ Br: $4s^24p^5$

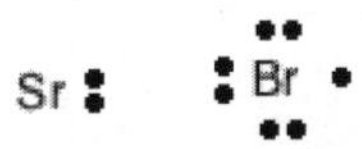

Sr: :Br·

Strontium must lose two electrons and be left with the octet from the previous shell, while bromine needs to gain one electron to get an octet.

Sr^{2+} 2[:Br:]$^-$

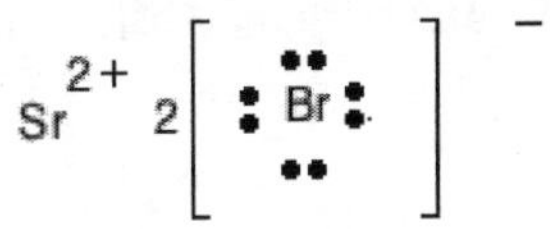

(d) K$_2$O: Draw the Lewis structures for K and O based on their valence electrons. K: $4s^1$ O: $2s^22p^4$

K· :O·

Potassium must lose one electron and be left with the octet from the previous shell, while oxygen needs to gain two electrons to get an octet.

2K$^+$ [:O:]$^{2-}$

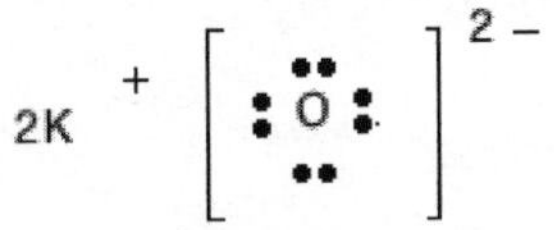

9.41   (a)   Sr and Se: Draw the Lewis structures for Sr and Se based on their valence electrons.

Sr: $5s^2$ Se: $4s^24p^4$

Sr $\vdots$ $\vdots$Se $\cdot$

Strontium must lose two electrons and be left with the octet from the previous shell, while selenium needs to gain two electrons to get an octet.

$$Sr^{2+} \quad \left[\; \vdots Se \vdots \; \right]^{2-}$$

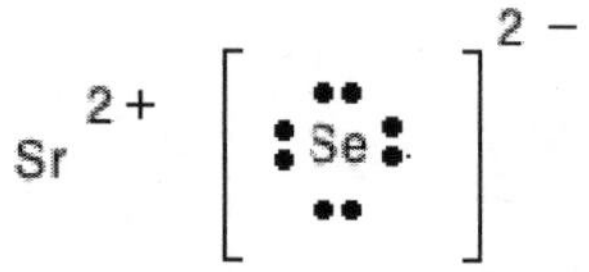

Thus, we need one Sr^{2+} and one Se^{2-}. Write the formula with subscripts (if necessary) to indicate the number of atoms.

SrSe

(b)   Ba and Cl: Draw the Lewis structures for Ba and Cl based on their valence electrons.

Ba: $6s^2$ Cl: $3s^23p^5$

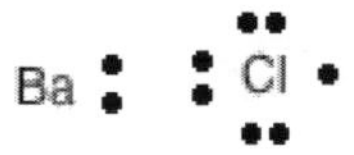

Ba $\vdots$ $\vdots$ Cl $\cdot$

Barium must lose two electrons and be left with the octet from the previous shell, while chlorine needs to gain one electron to get an octet.

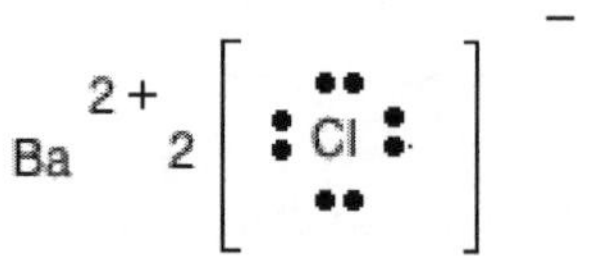

$$Ba^{2+} \quad 2 \left[\; \vdots Cl \vdots \; \right]^{-}$$

Thus, we need one Ba^{2+} and two Cl^-. Write the formula with subscripts (if necessary) to indicate the number of atoms.

$BaCl_2$

(c)   Na and S: Draw the Lewis structures for Na and S based on their valence electrons.

Na: $3s^1$ S: $3s^23p^4$

Na $\cdot$ $\vdots$ S $\cdot$

Sodium must lose one electron and be left with the octet from the previous shell, while sulfur needs to gain two electrons to get an octet.

$$2\,Na^{+} \quad \left[\; \vdots S \vdots \; \right]^{2-}$$

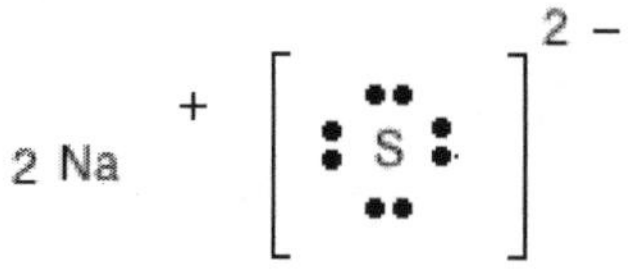

Thus, we need two Na^+ and one S^{2-}. Write the formula with subscripts (if necessary) to indicate the number of atoms.

Na_2S

(d)   Al and O: Draw the Lewis structures for Al and O based on their valence electrons.

Al: $3s^23p^1$ O: $2s^22p^4$

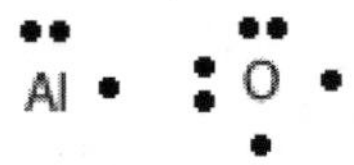

Al $\cdot$ $\vdots$ O $\cdot$

Aluminum must lose three electrons and be left with the octet from the previous shell, while oxygen needs to gain two electrons to get an octet.

$$2\,Al^{3+} \quad 3 \left[\; \vdots O \vdots \; \right]^{2-}$$

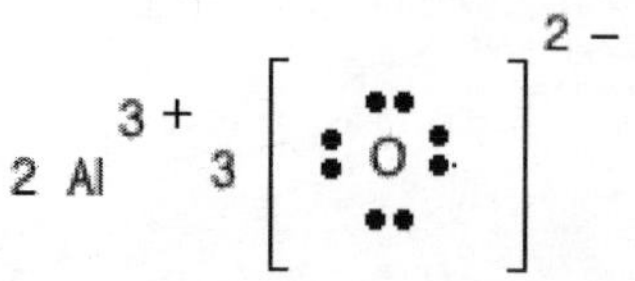

Thus, we need two Al^{3+} and three O^{2-} in order to lose and gain the same number of electrons. Write the formula with subscripts (if necessary) to indicate the number of atoms.

$$Al_2O_3$$

9.43 As the size of the alkaline metal ions increases down the column, so does the distance between the metal cation and the oxide anion. Therefore, the magnitude of the lattice energy of the oxides decreases, making the formation of the oxides less exothermic and the compounds less stable. Since the ions cannot get as close to each other, they therefore do not release as much energy.

9.45 Cesium is slightly larger than barium, but oxygen is slightly larger than fluorine, so we cannot use size to explain the difference in the lattice energy. However, the charge on cesium ion is 1+ and the charge on fluoride ion is 1−, while the charge on barium ion is 2+ and the charge on oxide ion is 2−. The coulombic equation states that the magnitude of the potential also depends on the product of the charges. Since the product of the charges for CsF = 1−, and the product of the charges for BaO = 4−, the stabilization for BaO relative to CsF should be about four times greater, which is what we see in its much more exothermic lattice energy.

9.47 **Given:** $\Delta_f H° KCl = -436.5$ kJ mol^{-1}; $IE_1(K) = 419$ kJ mol^{-1}; $\Delta_{sub}H(K) = 89.0$ kJ mol^{-1}; $Cl_2(g)$ bond energy = 243 kJ mol^{-1}; $EA(Cl) = -349$ kJ mol^{-1} **Find:** lattice energy
Conceptual Plan:

$$K(s)+1/2Cl_2(g) \xrightarrow{\Delta_{sub}H} K(g)+ 1/2Cl_2(g) \xrightarrow{IE_1} K^+(g)+ 1/2Cl_2(g) \xrightarrow{\text{bond energy}} K^+(g)+Cl(g) \xrightarrow{EA} K^+(g)+Cl^-(g) \xrightarrow{\text{lattice energy}} KCl(s)$$

$$\Delta_f H°$$

Solution: $\Delta_f H° = \Delta_{sub}H + IE_1 + 1/2$ bond energy $+ EA +$ lattice energy

$$-436.5\,\frac{kJ}{mol} = +89.0\,\frac{kJ}{mol} + 419\,\frac{kJ}{mol} + \frac{1}{2}(243)\,\frac{kJ}{mol} + (-349)\,\frac{kJ}{mol} + \text{lattice energy}$$

$$\text{lattice energy} = -717\text{ kJ mol}^{-1}$$

Simple Covalent Lewis Structures, Electronegativity, and Bond Polarity

9.49 (a) Hydrogen: Write the Lewis structure of each atom based on the number of valence electrons.

H•   •H

When the two hydrogen atoms share their electrons, they each get two electrons, which is a stable configuration for hydrogen.

H —— H

(b) The halogens: Write the Lewis structure of each atom based on the number of valence electrons.

:Ẍ•   •Ẍ:

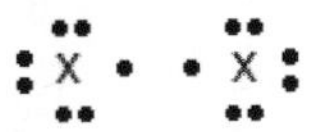

If the two halogens pair together they can each achieve an octet, which is a stable configuration. So, the halogens are predicted to exist as diatomic molecules.

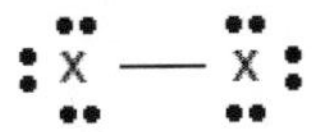

:Ẍ —— Ẍ:

(c) Oxygen: Write the Lewis structure of each atom based on the number of valence electrons.

:Ö•   •Ö:

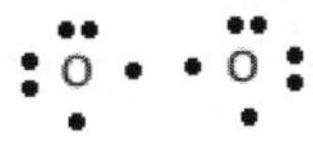

In order to achieve a stable octet on each oxygen, the oxygen atoms will need to share two electron pairs. So, oxygen is predicted to exist as a diatomic molecule with a double bond.

:Ö == Ö:

(d) Nitrogen: Write the Lewis structure of each atom based on the number of valence electrons.

In order to achieve a stable octet on each nitrogen, the nitrogen atoms will need to share three electron pairs. So, nitrogen is predicted to exist as a diatomic molecule with a triple bond.

$$N \equiv N$$

9.51 (a) PH_3: Write the Lewis structure for each atom based on the number of valence electrons.

Phosphorus will share an electron pair with each hydrogen in order to achieve a stable octet.

(b) SCl_2: Write the Lewis structure for each atom based on the number of valence electrons.

The sulfur will share an electron pair with each chlorine in order to achieve a stable octet.

(c) HI: Write the Lewis structure for each atom based on the number of valence electrons.

The iodine will share an electron pair with hydrogen in order to achieve a stable octet.

(d) CH_4: Write the Lewis structure for each atom based on the number of valence electrons.

The carbon will share an electron pair with each hydrogen in order to achieve a stable octet.

9.53 (a) SF_2: Write the Lewis structure for each atom based on the number of valence electrons.

The sulfur will share an electron pair with each fluorine in order to achieve a stable octet.

$$
\overset{\displaystyle ..}{\underset{\displaystyle |}{\overset{..}{:}S}} \!-\! \overset{..}{\underset{..}{F}:}
$$

$$
\overset{..}{:}F\overset{}{:}
$$

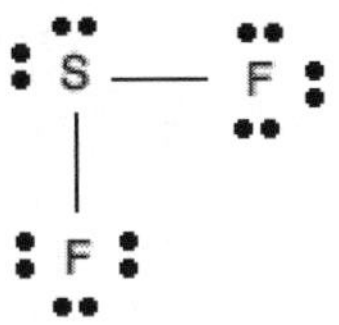

(b) SiH$_4$: Write the Lewis structure for each atom based on the number of valence electrons.

H •   • Ṡi •

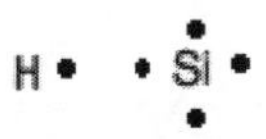

The silicon will share an electron pair with each hydrogen in order to achieve a stable octet.

```
        H
        |
  H —— Si —— H
        |
        H
```

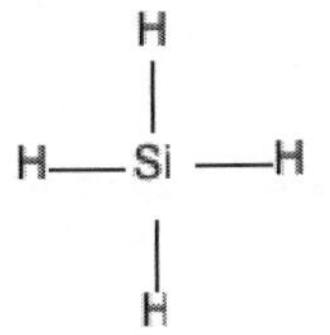

(c) HCOOH Write the Lewis structure for each atom based on the number of valence electrons.

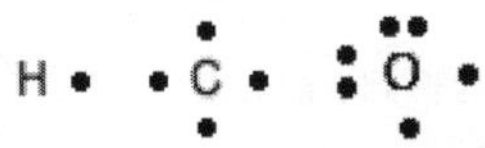

H •   • Ċ •   : Ö •

The carbon will share an electron pair with hydrogen, an electron pair with the interior oxygen, and two electron pairs with the terminal oxygen in order to achieve a stable octet. The terminal oxygen will share two electron pairs with carbon in order to achieve a stable octet. The interior oxygen with share an electron pair with carbon and an electron pair with hydrogen in order to achieve a stable octet.

```
      :O:
       ‖
  H —— C —— O —— H
            ••
```

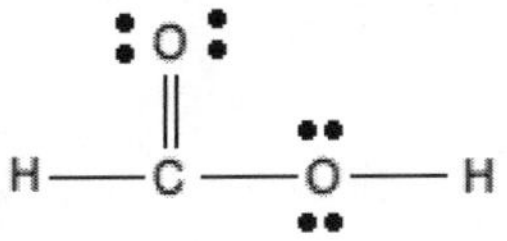

(d) CH$_3$SH Write the Lewis structure for each atom based on the number of valence electrons.

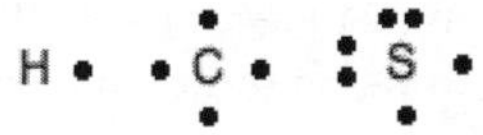

H •   • Ċ •   : S̈ •

The carbon will share an electron pair with each hydrogen and an electron pair with sulfur in order to achieve a stable octet. The sulfur will share an electron pair with carbon and an electron pair with hydrogen in order to achieve a stable octet.

```
        H
        |
        ••
  H —— C —— S —— H
        |   ••
        H
```

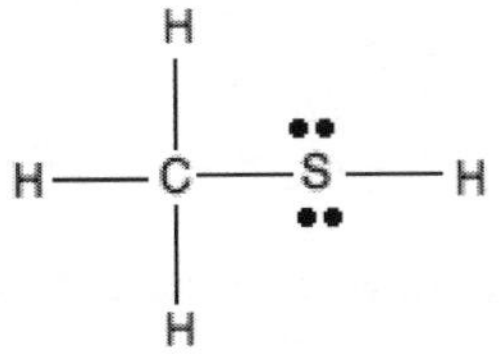

9.55 (a) Br and Br: pure covalent From Figure 9.12 we find the electronegativity of Br is 2.5. Since both atoms are the same, the electronegativity difference (ΔEN) = 0, and using Table 9.3 we classify this bond as pure covalent.

(b) C and Cl: polar covalent From Figure 9.12 we find the electronegativity of C is 2.5 and Cl is 3.0. The electronegativity difference (ΔEN) is ΔEN = 3.0 – 2.5 = 0.5. Using Table 9.3 we classify this bond as polar covalent.

(c) C and S: pure covalent From Figure 9.12 we find the electronegativity of C is 2.5 and S is 2.5. The electronegativity difference (ΔEN) is ΔEN = 2.5 – 2.5 = 0. Using Table 9.3 we classify this bond as pure covalent.

(d)   Sr and O: ionic   From Figure 9.12 we find the electronegativity of Sr is 1.0 and O is 3.5. The electronegativity difference (ΔEN) is ΔEN = 3.5 – 1.0 = 2.5. Using Table 9.3 we classify this bond as ionic.

9.57   CO: Write the Lewis structure for each atom based on the number of valence electrons.

The carbon will share three electron pairs with oxygen in order to achieve a stable octet.

The oxygen atom is more electronegative than the carbon atom, so the oxygen will have a partial negative charge and the carbon will have a partial positive charge.

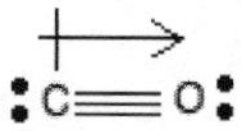

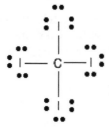

To estimate the percent ionic character, determine the difference in electronegativity between carbon and oxygen.

From Figure 9.12 we find the electronegativity of C is 2.5 and O is 3.5. The electronegativity difference (ΔEN) is ΔEN = 3.5 – 2.5 = 1.0.

From Figure 9.14, we can estimate a percent ionic character of 25%.

Covalent Lewis Structures, Resonance, and Formal Charge

9.59   (a)   CI$_4$:   Calculate the total number of electrons for the Lewis structure by summing the number of valence electrons of each atom in the molecule.

(number of valence e$^-$ for C) + 4(number of valence e$^-$ for I) = 4 + 4(7) = 32

Write the correct skeletal structure for the molecule, including bonds between C and each of the I atoms.

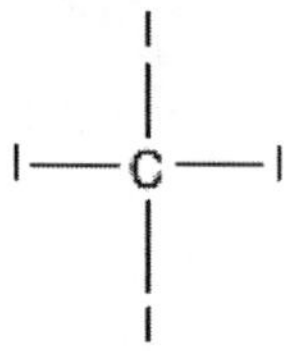

$$
\begin{array}{ccc}
 & \text{I} & \\
 & | & \\
\text{I} & \!\!-\text{C}-\!\! & \text{I} \\
 & | & \\
 & \text{I} & \\
\end{array}
$$

Each bond accounts for two electrons, leaving 24 electrons to place in the Lewis structure. Put nonbonding (also called lone-pair) electrons on terminal atoms.

$$
\begin{array}{ccc}
 & \ddot{\text{I}} & \\
 & | & \\
\ddot{\text{I}} & \!\!-\text{C}-\!\! & \ddot{\text{I}} \\
 & | & \\
 & \ddot{\text{I}} & \\
\end{array}
$$

All 32 valence electrons are used. All atoms have octets; the structure is complete.

(b)   N$_2$O: Calculate the total number of electrons for the Lewis structure by summing the number of valence electrons of each atom in the molecule.

2(number of valence e$^-$ for N) + (number of valence e$^-$ for O) = 2(5) + 6 = 16

Write the correct skeletal structure for the molecule, including bonds between one N atom and each of the other atoms. N is the less electronegative, so it is central.

N —— N —— O

Each bond accounts for two electrons, leaving 12 electrons to place in the Lewis structure. Put nonbonding (also called lone-pair) electrons on terminal atoms.

$$:\!\ddot{\text{N}}\!-\!\text{N}\!-\!\ddot{\text{O}}\!:$$

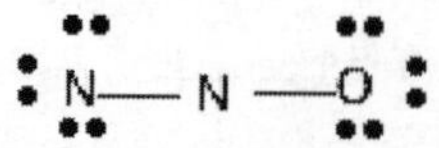

All 16 valence electrons are used. If any atom lacks an octet, form double or triple bonds as necessary.

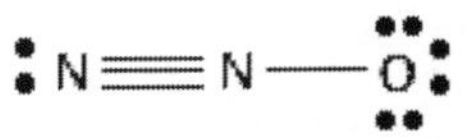

$$:N \equiv N - \overset{\displaystyle ..}{\underset{\displaystyle ..}{O}}:$$

All atoms have octets; the structure is complete.

(c) SiH$_4$: Calculate the total number of electrons for the Lewis structure by summing the number of valence electrons of each atom in the molecule.

(number of valence e$^-$ for Si) + 4(number of valence e$^-$ for H) = 4 + 4(1) = 8

Write the correct skeletal structure for the molecule, including bonds between Si and each of the H atoms. H is always terminal, so Si is the central atom.

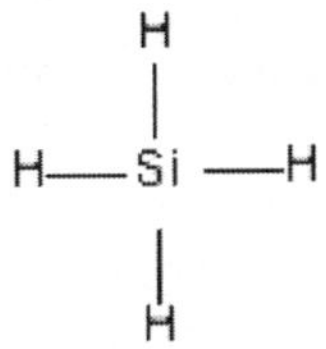

$$\begin{array}{c} H \\ | \\ H - Si - H \\ | \\ H \end{array}$$

Each bond accounts for two electrons; all eight valence electrons are used. All atoms (except H) have octets; the structure is complete.

(d) Cl$_2$CO: Calculate the total number of electrons for the Lewis structure by summing the number of valence electrons of each atom in the molecule.

(number of valence e$^-$ for C) + 2(number of valence e$^-$ for Cl) + (number of valence e$^-$ for O) = 4 + 2(7) + 6 = 24

Write the correct skeletal structure for the molecule, including bonds between C and each of the other atoms. C is the less electronegative, so it is central.

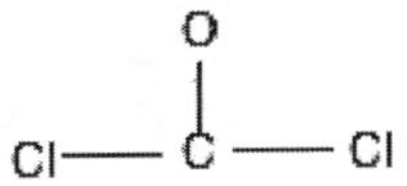

$$\begin{array}{c} O \\ | \\ Cl - C - Cl \end{array}$$

Each bond accounts for two electrons, leaving 18 electrons to place in the Lewis structure. Put nonbonding (also called lone-pair) electrons on terminal atoms.

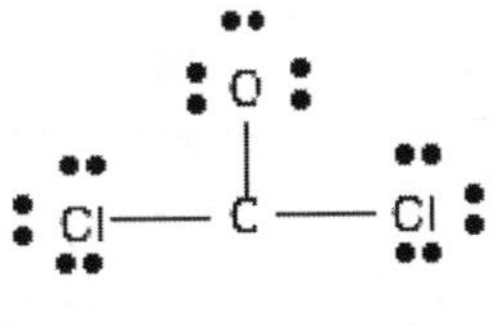

$$\begin{array}{c} :\overset{\displaystyle ..}{O}: \\ | \\ :\overset{..}{Cl} - C - \overset{..}{Cl}: \end{array}$$

All 24 valence electrons are used. If any atom lacks an octet, form double or triple bonds as necessary.

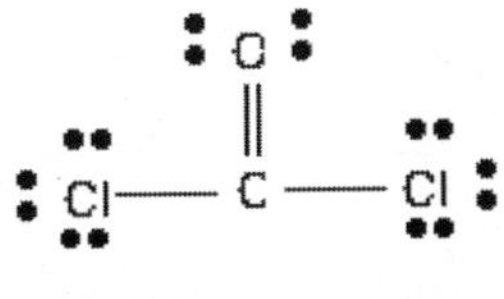

$$\begin{array}{c} :\overset{\displaystyle ..}{O}: \\ \parallel \\ :\overset{..}{Cl} - C - \overset{..}{Cl}: \end{array}$$

All atoms have octets; the structure is complete.

9.61 (a) N$_2$H$_2$: Calculate the total number of electrons for the Lewis structure by summing the number of valence electrons of each atom in the molecule.

2(number of valence e$^-$ for N) + 2(number of valence e$^-$ for H) = 2(5) + 2(1) = 12

Write the correct skeletal structure for the molecule, including bonds between each of the atoms, with H always terminal.

$$H - N - N - H$$

Each bond accounts for two electrons, leaving six electrons to place in the Lewis structure. Since the terminal atoms are H, put lone pairs on the central atoms that do not already have a complete octet.

$$H \!-\! \overset{\displaystyle ..}{N} \!-\! \overset{\displaystyle ..}{\underset{\displaystyle ..}{N}} \!-\! H$$

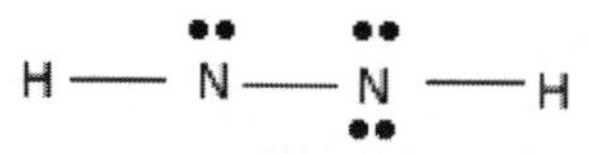

All 12 valence electrons are used. If any atom lacks an octet, form double or triple bonds as necessary.

$$H \!-\! \overset{\displaystyle ..}{N} \!=\! \overset{\displaystyle ..}{N} \!-\! H$$

All atoms have octets (except H); the structure is complete.

(b) N_2H_4:   Calculate the total number of electrons for the Lewis structure by summing the number of valence electrons of each atom in the molecule.

2(number of valence e⁻ for N) + 4(number of valence e⁻ for H) = 2(5) + 4(1) = 14

Write the correct skeletal structure for the molecule, including bonds between each of the atoms, with H always terminal.

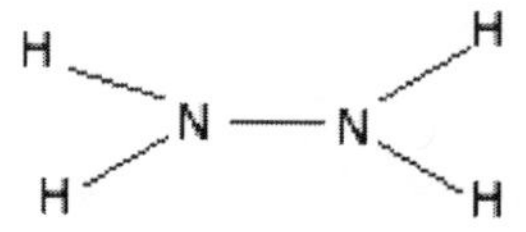

Each bond accounts for two electrons, leaving four electrons to place in the Lewis structure. Since the terminal atoms are H, put lone pairs on the central atoms that do not already have a complete octet.

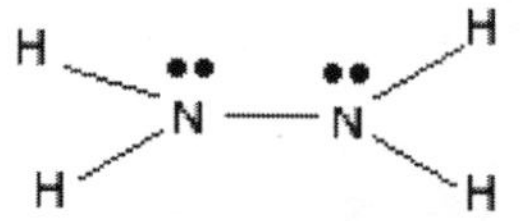

All 14 valence electrons are used. All atoms have octets (except H); the structure is complete.

(c) C_2H_2:   Calculate the total number of electrons for the Lewis structure by summing the number of valence electrons of each atom in the molecule.

2(number of valence e⁻ for C) + 2(number of valence e⁻ for H) = 2(4) + 2(1) = 10

Write the correct skeletal structure for the molecule, including bonds between each of the atoms, with H always terminal.

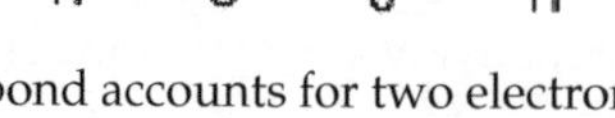

$$H \!-\! C \!-\! C \!-\! H$$

Each bond accounts for two electrons, leaving four electrons to place in the Lewis structure. Since the terminal atoms are H, put lone pairs on the central atoms that do not already have a complete octet.

$$H \!-\! C \!-\! \overset{\displaystyle ..}{\underset{\displaystyle ..}{C}} \!-\! H$$

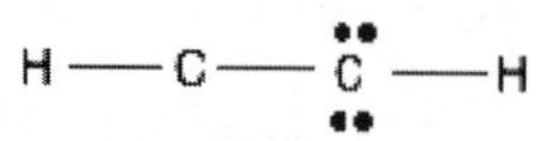

All 10 valence electrons are used. If any atom lacks an octet, form double or triple bonds as necessary.

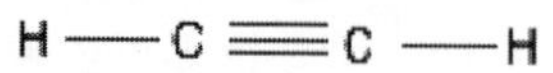

$$H \!-\! C \!\equiv\! C \!-\! H$$

All atoms have octets (except H); the structure is complete.

(d) C_2H_4:   Calculate the total number of electrons for the Lewis structure by summing the number of valence electrons of each atom in the molecule.

2(number of valence e⁻ for C) + 4(number of valence e⁻ for H) = 2(4) + 4(1) = 12

Write the correct skeletal structure for the molecule, including bonds between each of the atoms, with H always terminal.

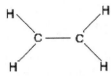

Each bond accounts for two electrons, leaving two electrons to place in the Lewis structure. Since the terminal atoms are H, put lone pairs on the central atoms that do not already have a complete octet.

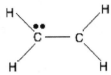

All 12 valence electrons are used. If any atom lacks an octet, form double or triple bonds as necessary.

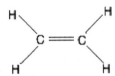

All atoms have octets (except H); the structure is complete.

9.63   (a) SeO_2:   Calculate the total number of electrons for the Lewis structure by summing the number of valence electrons of each atom in the molecule.

    (number of valence e⁻ for Se) + 2(number of valence e⁻ for O) = 6 + 2(6) = 18

Write the correct skeletal structure for the molecule, including bonds between each of the atoms. Se is the less electronegative, so it is central.

$$O \text{——} Se \text{——} O$$

Each bond accounts for two electrons, leaving 14 electrons to place in the Lewis structure. Put lone pairs on terminal atoms and then on the central atom.

$$\ddot{\underset{..}{O}} \text{——} Se \text{——} \ddot{\underset{..}{O}}$$

All 18 valence electrons are used.
If any atom lacks an octet, form double or triple bonds as necessary.

$$\ddot{\underset{..}{O}} \text{——} Se \text{==} \ddot{\underset{..}{O}}$$

All atoms have octets; the structure is complete. However, the double bond can form from either oxygen atom, so there are two resonance forms.

$$\ddot{\underset{..}{O}} \text{——} Se \text{==} \ddot{\underset{..}{O}} \longleftrightarrow \ddot{\underset{..}{O}} \text{==} Se \text{——} \ddot{\underset{..}{O}}$$

Calculate the formal charge on each atom by finding the number of valence electrons and subtracting the number of lone-pair electrons and one-half the number of bonding electrons.

$$\ddot{\underset{..}{O}} \text{——} Se \text{==} \ddot{\underset{..}{O}} \longleftrightarrow \ddot{\underset{..}{O}} \text{==} Se \text{——} \ddot{\underset{..}{O}}$$

	O	Se	O	O	Se	O
number of valence electrons	6	6	6	6	6	6
- number of lone-pair electrons	6	2	4	4	2	6
- 1/2(number of bonding electrons)	1	3	2	2	3	1
Formal charge	−1	+1	0	0	+1	−1

(b) $CO_3{}^{2-}$:   Calculate the total number of electrons for the Lewis structure by summing the number of valence electrons of each atom in the ion and adding 2 for the 2 – charge.

3(number of valence e^- for O) + (number of valence e^- for C) + 2 = 3(6) + 4 + 2 = 24

Write the correct skeletal structure for the ion, including bonds between each of the atoms. C is the less electronegative atom, so it is central.

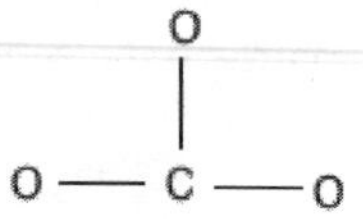

Each bond accounts for two electrons, leaving 18 electrons to place in the Lewis structure. Put lone pairs on terminal atoms.

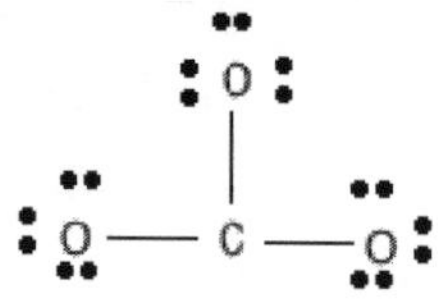

All 24 valence electrons are used.

If any atoms lack an octet, form double or triple bonds as necessary.

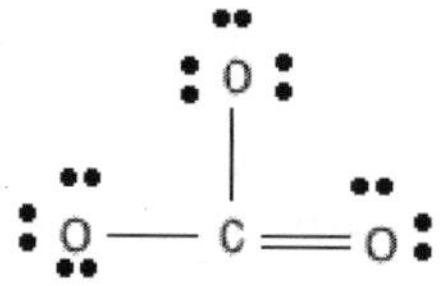

Lastly, write the Lewis structure in brackets with the charge of the ion in the upper right-hand corner.

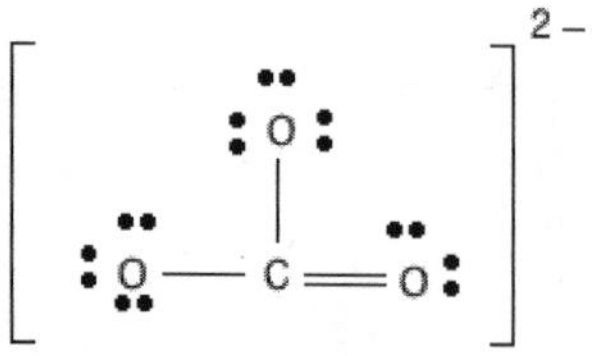

All atoms have octets; the structure is complete. However, the double bond can form from any oxygen atom, so there are three resonance forms.

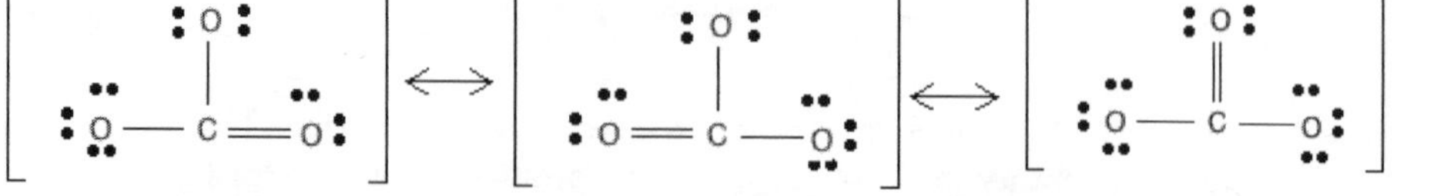

Calculate the formal charge on each atom by finding the number of valence electrons and subtracting the number of lone-pair electrons and one-half the number of bonding electrons.

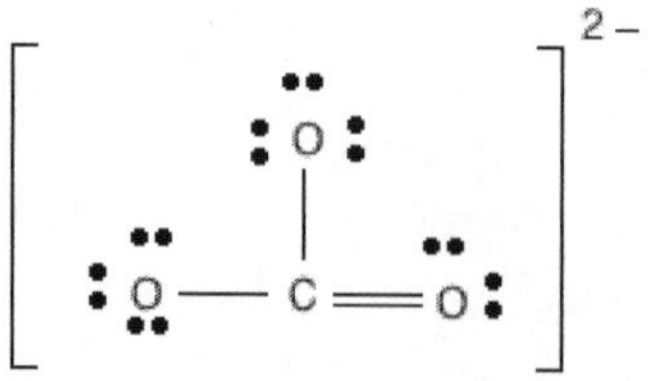

	O_{left}	O_{top}	O_{right}	C
number of valence electrons	6	6	6	4
- number of lone-pair electrons	6	6	4	0
- 1/2(number of bonding electrons)	1	1	2	4
Formal charge	−1	−1	0	0

The sum of the formal charges is – 2, which is the overall charge of the ion. The other resonance forms would have the same values for the single and double bonded oxygen atoms and for the carbon atom.

(c)   ClO⁻:   Calculate the total number of electrons for the Lewis structure by summing the number of valence electrons of each atom in the ion and adding 1 for the 1 – charge.

(number of valence e⁻ for O) + (number of valence e⁻ for Cl) + 1 = 6 + 7 + 1 = 14

Write the correct skeletal structure for the ion, including bonds between each of the atoms.

Cl —— O

Each bond accounts for two electrons, leaving 12 electrons to place in the Lewis structure. Put lone pairs on terminal atoms.

:Cl —— O:

All 14 valence electrons are used.

Lastly, write the Lewis structure in brackets with the charge of the ion in the upper right-hand corner.

[:Cl —— O:]⁻

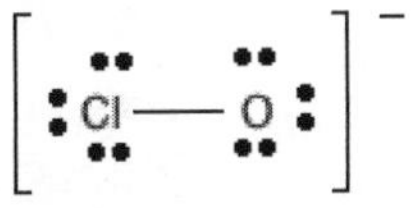

All atoms have octets; the structure is complete.

Calculate the formal charge on each atom by finding the number of valence electrons and subtracting the number of lone-pair electrons and one-half the number of bonding electrons.

	Cl	O
number of valence electrons	7	6
- number of lone-pair electrons	6	6
- 1/2(number of bonding electrons)	1	1
Formal charge	0	–1

The sum of the formal charges is – 1, which is the overall charge of the ion.

(d)   NO₂⁻:   Calculate the total number of electrons for the Lewis structure by summing the number of valence electrons of each atom in the ion and adding 1 for the 1 – charge.

2(number of valence e⁻ for O) + (number of valence e⁻ for N) + 1 = 2(6) + 5 + 1 = 18

Write the correct skeletal structure for the ion, including bonds between each of the atoms. N is the less electronegative atom, so it is central

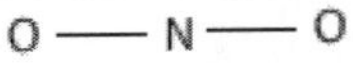

O —— N —— O

Each bond accounts for two electrons, leaving 14 electrons to place in the Lewis structure. Put lone pairs on terminal atoms and then on the central atom.

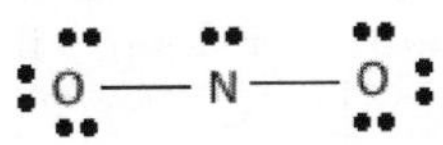

:O —— N —— O:

All 14 valence electrons are used.

If any atom lacks an octet, form double or triple bonds as necessary.

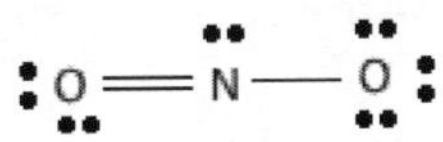

:O ══ N —— O:

Lastly, write the Lewis structure in brackets with the charge of the ion in the upper right-hand corner.

[:O ══ N —— O:]⁻

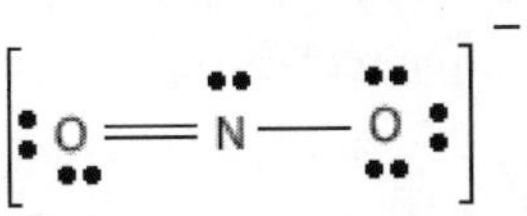

All atoms have octets; the structure is complete. However, the double bond can form from either oxygen atom, so there are two resonance forms.

Calculate the formal charge on each atom by finding the number of valence electrons and subtracting the number of lone-pair electrons and one-half the number of bonding electrons. Using the left side structure:

	O	N	O
number of valence electrons	6	5	6
- number of lone-pair electrons	4	2	6
- 1/2(number of bonding electrons)	2	3	1
Formal charge	0	0	−1

The sum of the formal charges is − 1, which is the overall charge of the ion.

9.65

Calculate the formal charge on each atom in structure I by finding the number of valence electrons and subtracting the number of lone-pair electrons and one-half the number of bonding electrons.

	H_{left}	H_{top}	C	S
number of valence electrons	1	1	4	6
- number of lone-pair electrons	0	0	0	4
- 1/2(number of bonding electrons)	1	1	4	2
Formal charge	0	0	0	0

The sum of the formal charges is 0, which is the overall charge of the molecule.
Calculate the formal charge on each atom in structure II by finding the number of valence electrons and subtracting the number of lone-pair electrons and one-half the number of bonding electrons.

	H_{left}	H_{top}	S	C
number of valence electrons	1	1	6	4
- number of lone-pair electrons	0	0	0	4
- 1/2(number of bonding electrons)	1	1	4	2
Formal charge	0	0	+2	−2

The sum of the formal charges is 0, which is the overall charge of the molecule.
Structure I is the better Lewis structure because it has the least amount of formal charge on each atom.

9.67 does not provide a significant contribution to the resonance hybrid as it has a +1 formal charge on a very electronegative oxygen.

	O_{left}	O_{right}	C
number of valence electrons	6	6	4
- number of lone-pair electrons	2	6	0
- 1/2(number of bonding electrons)	3	1	4
Formal charge	+1	−1	0

Odd-Electron Species, Incomplete Octets, and Hypercoordinate Species

9.69 (a) BCl_3: Calculate the total number of electrons for the Lewis structure by summing the number of valence electrons of each atom in the molecule.

(number of valence e⁻ for B) + 3(number of valence e⁻ for Cl) = 3 +3(7) = 24
Write the correct skeletal structure for the molecule, including bonds between each of the atoms. B is the less electronegative, so it is central.

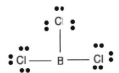

Each bond accounts for two electrons, leaving 18 electrons to place in the Lewis structure. Put lone pairs on terminal atoms.

All 24 valence electrons are used.
B has an incomplete octet. If we complete the octet, there is a formal charge of − 1 on the B, which is less electronegative than Cl.

(b)   NO₂: Calculate the total number of electrons for the Lewis structure by summing the number of valence electrons of each atom in the molecule.
(number of valence e⁻ for N) + 2(number of valence e⁻ for O) = 5 +2(6) = 17
Write the correct skeletal structure for the molecule, including bonds between each of the atoms. N is the less electronegative, so it is central.

O —— N —— O

Each bond accounts for two electrons, leaving 13 electrons to place in the Lewis structure. Put lone pairs on terminal atoms and any remaining electrons on the central atom.

All 17 valence electrons are used. If any atom lacks an octet form double or triple bonds as necessary to complete the octet.

N has seven electrons and it is left as an incomplete octet.

(c)   BH₃: Calculate the total number of electrons for the Lewis structure by summing the number of valence electrons of each atom in the molecule.
(number of valence e⁻ for B) + 3(number of valence e⁻ for H) = 3 +3(1) = 6
Write the correct skeletal structure for the molecule, including bonds between each of the atoms. B is the less electronegative, so it is central.

Each bond accounts for two electrons, leaving no further electrons to place in the Lewis structure.
All six valence electrons are used.

B has an incomplete octet. H cannot double bond, so it is not possible to complete the octet on B with a double bond.

9.71 (a) PO_4^{3-}: Calculate the total number of electrons for the Lewis structure by summing the number of valence electrons of each atom in the ion and adding 3 for the 3 − charge.

4(number of valence e^- for O) + (number of valence e^- for P) + 3 = 4(6) + 5 + 3 = 32

Write the correct skeletal structure for the ion, including bonds between each of the atoms. P is less electronegative, so it is central.

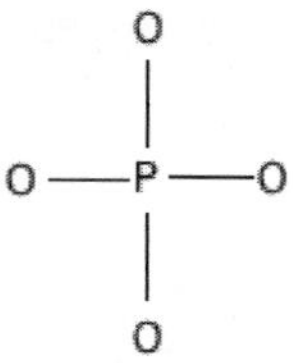

Each bond accounts for two electrons, leaving 24 electrons to place in the Lewis structure. Put lone pairs on terminal atoms.

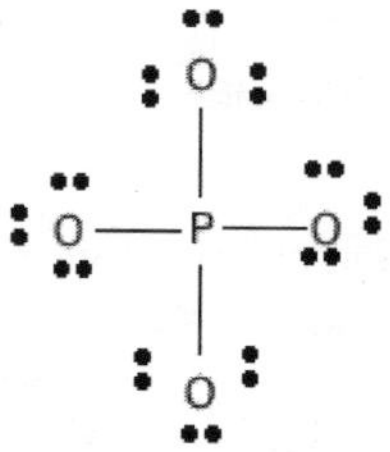

All 32 valence electrons are used.

Lastly, write the Lewis structure in brackets with the charge of the ion in the upper right-hand corner.

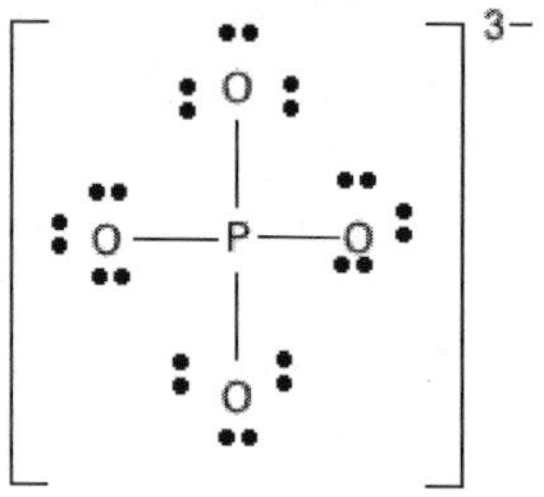

All atoms have octets; the structure is complete.

Calculate the formal charge on each atom by finding the number of valence electrons and subtracting the number of lone-pair electrons and one-half the number of bonding electrons.

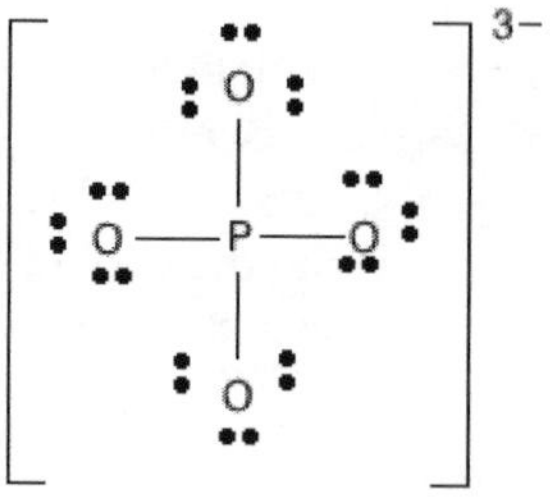

	O_{left}	O_{top}	O_{right}	O_{bottom}	P
number of valence electrons	6	6	6	6	5
- number of lone-pair electrons	6	6	6	6	0
- 1/2(number of bonding electrons)	1	1	1	1	4
Formal charge	−1	−1	−1	−1	+1

The sum of the formal charges is −3, which is the overall charge of the ion. However, we can write a resonance structure with a double bond to an oxygen, which leads to lower formal charges on P and O.

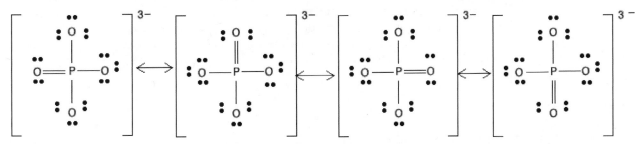

Using the leftmost structure, calculate the formal charge on each atom by finding the number of valence electrons and subtracting the number of lone-pair electrons and one-half the number of bonding electrons.

	O_{left}	O_{top}	O_{right}	O_{bottom}	P
number of valence electrons	6	6	6	6	5
- number of lone-pair electrons	4	6	6	6	0
- 1/2(number of bonding electrons)	2	1	1	1	5
Formal charge	0	–1	–1	–1	0

The sum of the formal charges is –3, which is the overall charge of the ion. These resonance forms would all have the lower formal charges associated with the double bonded O and P.

(b) CN^-:   Calculate the total number of electrons for the Lewis structure by summing the number of valence electrons of each atom in the ion and adding 1 for the 1 – charge.

(number of valence e⁻ for C) + (number of valence e⁻ for N) + 1 = 4 + 5 + 1 = 10

Write the correct skeletal structure for the ion, including bonds between each of the atoms.

C —— N

Put lone pairs on terminal atoms, starting with the most electronegative atom.

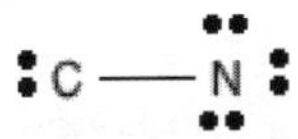

:C —— N:

All 10 valence electrons are used.
If any atom lacks an octet, form double or triple bonds as necessary.

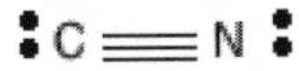

:C ⩬ N:

Lastly, write the Lewis structure in brackets with the charge of the ion in the upper right-hand corner.

[:C ⩬ N:]⁻

All atoms have octets; the structure is complete.
Calculate the formal charge on each atom by finding the number of valence electrons and subtracting the number of lone-pair electrons and one-half the number of bonding electrons.

[:C ⩬ N:]⁻

	C	N
number of valence electrons	4	5
- number of lone-pair electrons	2	2
- 1/2(number of bonding electrons)	3	3
Formal charge	–1	0

The sum of the formal charges is – 1, which is the overall charge of the ion.

(c) $SO_3{}^{2-}$:   Calculate the total number of electrons for the Lewis structure by summing the valence electrons of each atom in the ion and adding 2 for the 2 – charge.

3(number of valence e⁻ for O) + (number of valence e⁻ for S) + 2 = 3(6) + 6 + 2 = 26

Write the correct skeletal structure for the ion, including bonds between each of the atoms. S is less electronegative, so it is central.

Each bond accounts for two electrons, leaving 20 electrons to place in the Lewis structure. Put lone pairs on terminal atoms and then on the central atom.

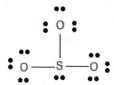

All 26 valence electrons are used.

Lastly, write the Lewis structure in brackets with the charge of the ion in the upper right-hand corner.

Calculate the formal charge on each atom by finding the number of valence electrons and subtracting the number of lone-pair electrons and one-half the number of bonding electrons.

	O_{left}	O_{top}	O_{right}	S
number of valence electrons	6	6	6	6
- number of lone-pair electrons	6	6	6	2
- 1/2(number of bonding electrons)	1	1	1	3
Formal charge	–1	–1	–1	+1

The sum of the formal charges is –2, which is the overall charge of the ion. However, we can write a resonance structure with a double bond to an oxygen, which leads to a lower formal charge.

Using the leftmost resonance form, calculate the formal charge on each atom by finding the number of valence electrons and subtracting the number of lone-pair electrons and one-half the number of bonding electrons.

	O_{left}	O_{top}	O_{right}	S
number of valence electrons	6	6	6	6
- number of lone-pair electrons	4	6	6	2
- 1/2(number of bonding electrons)	2	1	1	4
Formal charge	0	−1	−1	0

The sum of the formal charges is −2, which is the overall charge of the ion. These resonance forms would all have the lower formal charge on the double bonded O and S.

(d) ClO_2^- : Calculate the total number of electrons for the Lewis structure by summing the number of valence electrons of each atom in the ion and adding 1 for the 1 − charge.

2(number of valence e^- for O) + (number of valence e^- for Cl) + 1 = 2(6) + 7 + 1 = 20

Write the correct skeletal structure for the ion, including bonds between each of the atoms. Cl is less electronegative, so it is central.

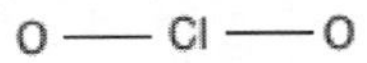

$$O \!-\! Cl \!-\! O$$

Each bond accounts for two electrons, leaving 16 electrons to place in the Lewis structure. Put lone pairs on terminal atoms and then on the central atom.

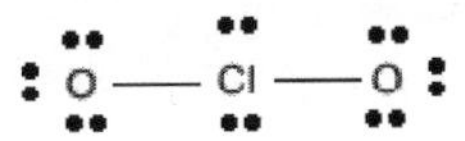

All 20 valence electrons are used.

Lastly, write the Lewis structure in brackets with the charge of the ion in the upper right-hand corner.

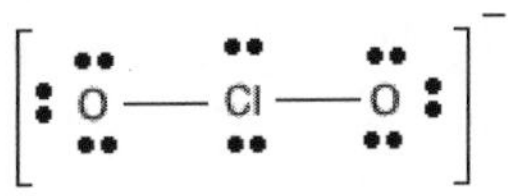

All atoms have octets; the structure is complete.

Calculate the formal charge on each atom by finding the number of valence electrons and subtracting the number of lone-pair electrons and one-half the number of bonding electrons.

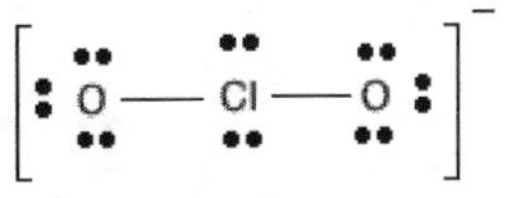

	O_{left}	O_{right}	Cl
number of valence electrons	6	6	7
- number of lone-pair electrons	6	6	4
- 1/2(number of bonding electrons)	1	1	2
Formal charge	−1	−1	+1

The sum of the formal charges is −1, which is the overall charge of the ion. However, we can write a resonance structure with a double bond to an oxygen, which leads to a lower formal charge.

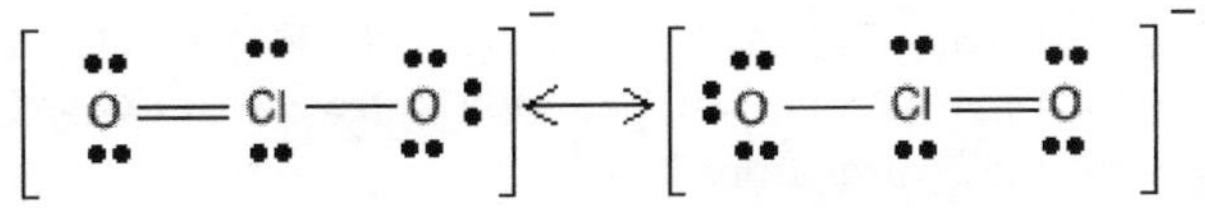

Using the leftmost resonance form, calculate the formal charge on each atom by finding the number of valence electrons and subtracting the number of lone-pair electrons and one-half the number of bonding electrons.

	O_{left}	O_{right}	Cl
number of valence electrons	6	6	7
- number of lone-pair electrons	4	6	4
- 1/2(number of bonding electrons)	2	1	3
Formal charge	0	−1	0

The sum of the formal charges is −1, which is the overall charge of the ion. These resonance forms would all have the lower formal charge on the double bonded O and Cl.

9.73 (a) PF_5: Calculate the total number of electrons for the Lewis structure by summing the number of valence electrons of each atom in the molecule.

(number of valence e^- for P) + 5(number of valence e^- for F) = 5 +5(7) = 40

Write the correct skeletal structure for the molecule, including bonds between each of the atoms. P is less electronegative, so it is central.

Each bond accounts for two electrons, leaving 30 electrons to place in the Lewis structure. Put lone pairs on terminal atoms.

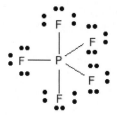

An alternative Lewis structure in which the octet rule is obeyed by the central atom would be:

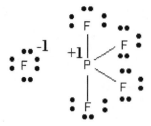

(b) I_3^-: Calculate the total number of electrons for the Lewis structure by summing the number of valence electrons of each atom in the ion and adding 1 for the 1 – charge.

3(number of valence e^- for I) + 1 = 3(7) + 1 = 22

Write the correct skeletal structure for the ion, including bonds between each of the atoms.

I —— I —— I

Each bond accounts for two electrons, leaving 18 electrons to place in the Lewis structure. Put lone pairs on terminal atoms to give a complete octet. Place any remaining electrons around the central atom.

Lastly, write the Lewis structure in brackets with the charge of the ion in the upper right-hand corner.

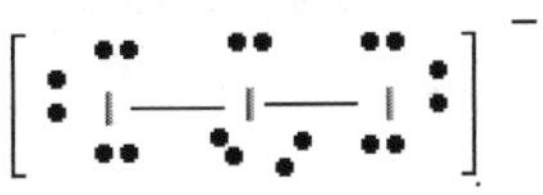

An alternative Lewis structure in which the octet rule is obeyed by the central atom would be:

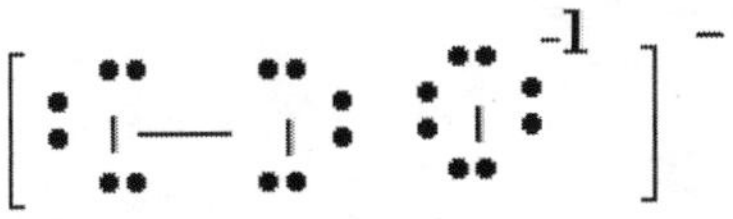

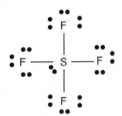

(c)   SF₄: Calculate the total number of electrons for the Lewis structure by summing the number of valence electrons of each atom in the molecule.

(number of valence e⁻ for S) + 4(number of valence e⁻ for F) = 6 + 4(7) = 34

Write the correct skeletal structure for the molecule, including bonds between each of the atoms. S is less electronegative, so it is central

$$
\begin{array}{c}
\text{F} \\
| \\
\text{F} - \text{S} - \text{F} \\
| \\
\text{F}
\end{array}
$$

Each bond accounts for two electrons, leaving 26 electrons to place in the Lewis structure. Put lone pairs on terminal atoms to give a complete octet. Place any remaining electrons around the central atom.

An alternative Lewis structure in which the octet rule is obeyed by the central atom would be:

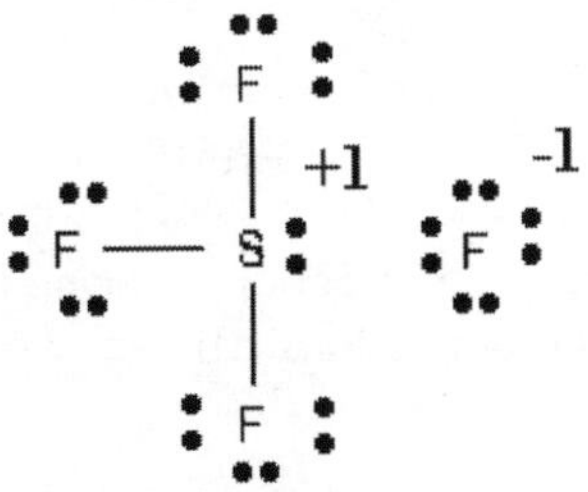

(d)   GeF₄: Calculate the total number of electrons for the Lewis structure by summing the number of valence electrons of each atom in the molecule.

(number of valence e⁻ for Ge) + 4(number of valence e⁻ for F) = 4 + 4(7) = 32

Write the correct skeletal structure for the molecule, including bonds between each of the atoms. Ge is less electronegative, so it is central.

$$
\begin{array}{c}
\text{F} \\
| \\
\text{F} - \text{Ge} - \text{F} \\
| \\
\text{F}
\end{array}
$$

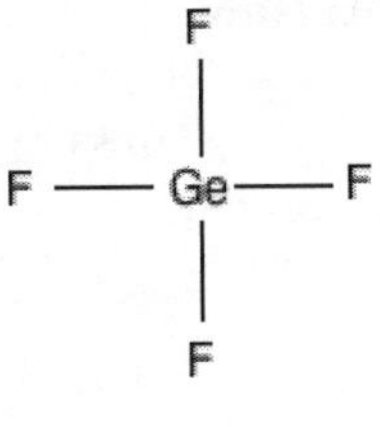

Each bond accounts for two electrons, leaving 24 electrons to place in the Lewis structure. Put lone pairs on terminal atoms.

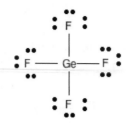

All atoms have octets; the structure is complete.

Bond Energies and Bond Lengths

9.75   Bond strength: $H_3CCH_3 < H_2CCH_2 < HCCH$
Bond length: $H_3CCH_3 > H_2CCH_2 > HCCH$
Write the Lewis structures for the two compounds. Compare the C–C bonds. Triple bonds are stronger than double bonds, which are stronger than single bonds. Also, single bonds are longer than double bonds, which are longer than triple bonds.
HCCH $(10\ e^-)$ $H_2CCH_2\ (12\ e^-)$ $H_3CCH_3 (14\ e^-)$

9.77   Rewrite the reaction using the Lewis structures of the molecules involved.

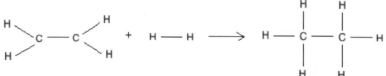

Bonds Broken		**Bonds Formed**	
C = C	$+611$ kJ mol^{-1}	2 C – H	$-2(414)$ kJ mol^{-1}
H – H	$+436$ kJ mol^{-1}	C – C	-347 kJ mol^{-1}

$\Sigma\ \Delta_r H$ bonds broken: $+1047$ kJ mol^{-1} $\Sigma\ \Delta_r H$ bonds formed: -1175 kJ mol^{-1}
$\Delta_r H = \Sigma\ (\Delta_r H$ bonds broken$) + \Sigma\ (\Delta_r H$ bonds formed$)$
       $= +1047$ kJ mol^{-1} $- 1175$ kJ mol^{-1}
       $= -128$ kJ mol^{-1}

9.79   Rewrite the reaction using the Lewis structures of the molecules involved.

$$C\ +\ 2\ H—\overset{\bullet\bullet}{\underset{\bullet\bullet}{O}}—H\ \longrightarrow\ 2\ H—H\ +\ \overset{\bullet\bullet}{\underset{\bullet\bullet}{O}}=C=\overset{\bullet\bullet}{\underset{\bullet\bullet}{O}}$$

Bonds Broken		**Bonds Formed**	
4 O – H	$+4(464)$ kJ mol^{-1}	2C = O	$-2(799)$ kJ mol^{-1}
		2H – H	$-2(436)$ kJ mol^{-1}

$\Sigma\ \Delta_r H$ bonds broken: $+1856$ kJ mol^{-1} $\Sigma\ \Delta_r H$ bonds formed: -2470 kJ mol^{-1}
$\Delta_r H = \Sigma\ (\Delta_r H$ bonds broken$) + \Sigma\ (\Delta_r H$ bonds formed$)$
       $= +1856$ kJ mol^{-1} $- 2470$ kJ mol^{-1}
       $= -614$ kJ mol^{-1}

9.81   CH$_3$—NH$_2$ contains a C—N bond, which according to Table 9.1 has a bond energy of 305 kJ mol^{-1}. CH$_2$=NH contains a C=N bond, which according to Table 9.1 has a bond energy of 615 kJ mol^{-1}. Since a higher frequency absorption corresponds to a stronger bond, then the absorption at 1050 cm^{-1} belongs to the C—N stretch and the absorption at 1640 cm^{-1} belongs to the C=N stretch.

Cumulative Problems

9.83   (a)   BI$_3$: This is a covalent compound between two nonmetals.
Calculate the total number of electrons for the Lewis structure by summing the number of valence electrons of each atom in the molecule.

(number of valence e$^-$ for B) + (number of valence e$^-$ for I) = 3 +3(7) = 24

Write the correct skeletal structure for the molecule.

Each bond accounts for two electrons, leaving 18 electrons to place in the Lewis structure. Put lone pairs on terminal atoms.

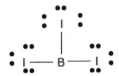

(b)   K$_2$S: This is an ionic compound between a metal and nonmetal.
Draw the Lewis structures for K and S based on their valence electrons.   K: $4s^1$ S: $3s^23p^4$

K•   •S:

Potassium must lose one electron and be left with the octet from the previous shell, while sulfur needs to gain two electrons to get an octet.

2 K$^+$ [:S:]$^{2-}$

(c)   HCFO: This is a covalent compound between nonmetals.
Calculate the total number of electrons for the Lewis structure by summing the number of valence electrons of each atom in the molecule.

(number of valence e$^-$ for H) + (number of valence e$^-$ for C) + (number of valence e$^-$ for F) + (number of valence e$^-$ for O) = 1 + 4 + 7 + 6 = 18

Write the correct skeletal structure for the molecule. C is less electronegative, so it is central; H is terminal.

O
|
H——C——F

Each bond accounts for two electrons, leaving 12 electrons to place in the Lewis structure. Put lone pairs on terminal atoms.

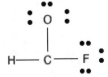

If any atom lacks an octet, form double or triple bonds as necessary to give them octets.

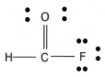

(d) PBr_3: This is a covalent compound between two nonmetals.
Calculate the total number of electrons for the Lewis structure by summing the number of valence electrons of each atom in the molecule.

(number of valence e⁻ for P) + 3(number of valence e⁻ for Br) = 5 + 3(7) = 26.

Write the correct skeletal structure for the molecule.

Each bond accounts for two electrons, leaving 20 electrons to place in the Lewis structure. Put lone pairs on terminal atoms and then on the central atom.

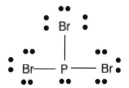

9.85 (a) $BaCO_3$: Ba^{2+}

Answer:

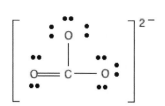

Method for arriving at answer:

1) Determine the cation and anion.
    Ba^{2+} CO_3^{2-}

2) Write the Lewis structure for the barium cation based on the valence electrons.
    Ba $5s^2$ Ba^{2+} $5s^0$

Ba • Ba^{2+}

Ba must lose two electrons and be left with the octet from the previous shell.

3) Write the Lewis structure for the covalent anion.

Calculate the total number of electrons for the Lewis structure by summing the number of valence electrons of each atom in the ion and adding two for the 2 − charge.

(number of valence e⁻ for C) + 3(number of valence e⁻ for O) = 4 + 3(6) + 2 = 24

Write the correct skeletal structure for the ion.

Each bond accounts for two electrons, leaving 18 electrons to place in the Lewis structure. Put lone pairs on terminal atoms.

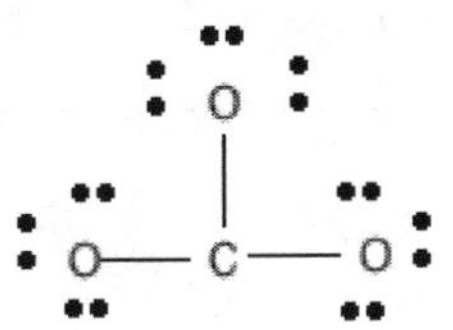

If any atom lacks an octet, form double or triple bonds as necessary.

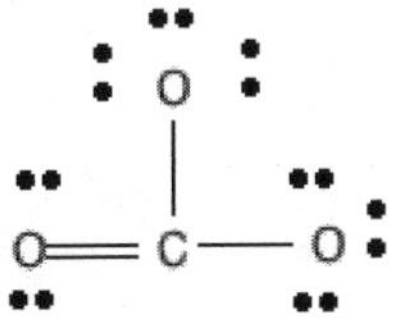

Lastly, write the Lewis structure in brackets with the charge of the ion in the upper right-hand corner.

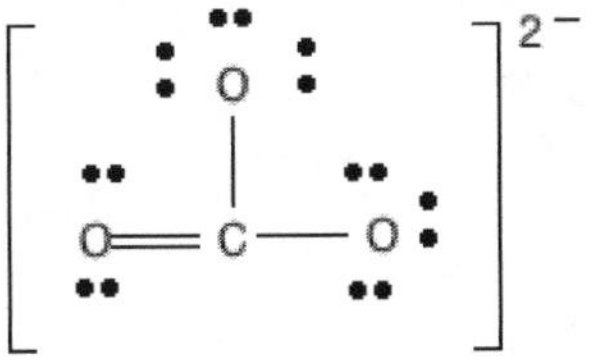

The double bond can be between the C and any of the oxygen atoms, so there are resonance structures.

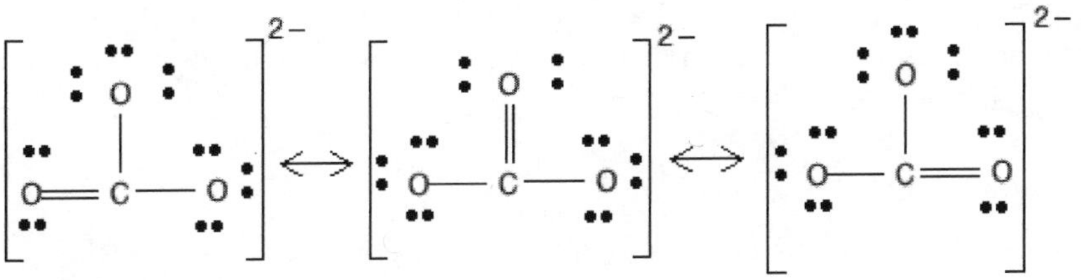

(b) $Ca(OH)_2$: Ca^{2+}

Answer:

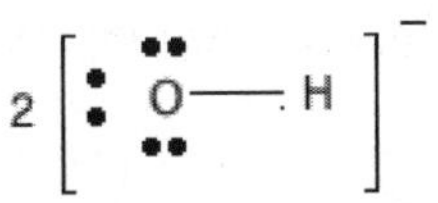

Method for arriving at answer:

1) Determine the cation and anion.

Ca^{2+} OH^-

2) Write the Lewis structure for the calcium cation based on the valence electrons.

Ca $4s^2$ Ca^{2+} $4s^0$

Ca must lose two electrons and be left with the octet from the previous shell.

3) Write the Lewis structure for the covalent anion.

Calculate the total number of electrons for the Lewis structure by summing the valence electrons of each atom in the ion and adding one for the 1 – charge.

(number of valence e⁻ for H) + (number of valence e⁻ for O) +1 = 1 + 6 +1 = 8

Write the correct skeletal structure for the ion.

O———H

Each bond accounts for two electrons, leaving six electrons to place in the Lewis structure. Put lone pairs on terminal atoms except H.

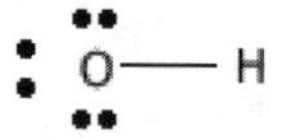

$$: \ddot{O} - H$$

Lastly, write the Lewis structure in brackets with the charge of the ion in the upper right-hand corner.

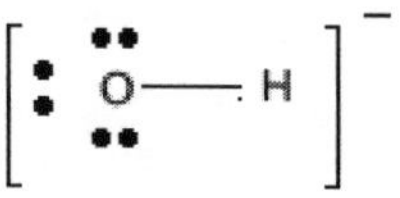

$$\left[: \ddot{O} - \cdot H \right]^-$$

(c) KNO_3: K^+

Answer:

$$\left[\begin{array}{c} : \ddot{O} : \\ | \\ \ddot{O} = N - \ddot{O} : \end{array} \right]^-$$

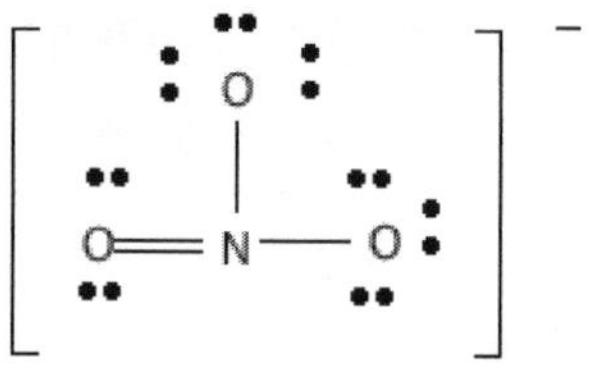

Method for arriving at answer:

1) Determine the cation and anion.

$$K^+ \qquad NO_3^-$$

2) Write the Lewis structure for the potassium cation based on the valence electrons.

$$K\ 4s^1 \qquad K^+\ 4s^0$$

$$K\cdot \qquad K^+$$

K must lose one electron and be left with the octet from the previous shell.

3) Write the Lewis structure for the covalent anion.

Calculate the total number of electrons for the Lewis structure by summing the valence electrons of each atom in the ion and adding one for the 1 – charge.

(number of valence e⁻ for N) + (number of valence e⁻ for O) = 5 + 3(6) +1 = 24

Write the correct skeletal structure for the ion.

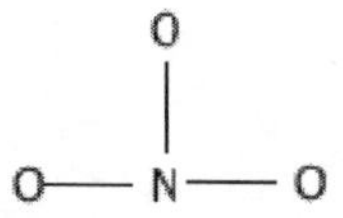

$$\begin{array}{c} O \\ | \\ O - N - O \end{array}$$

Each bond accounts for two electrons, leaving 18 electrons to place in the Lewis structure. Put lone pairs on terminal atoms.

$$\begin{array}{c} : \ddot{O} : \\ | \\ : \ddot{O} - N - \ddot{O} : \end{array}$$

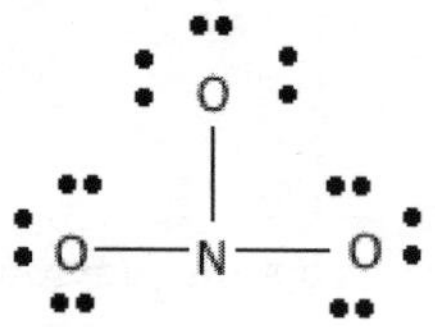

If any atom lacks an octet, form double or triple bonds as necessary.

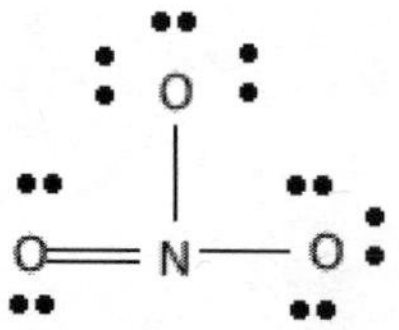

$$\begin{array}{c} : \ddot{O} : \\ | \\ \ddot{O} = N - \ddot{O} : \end{array}$$

Lastly, write the Lewis structure in brackets with the charge of the ion in the upper right-hand corner.

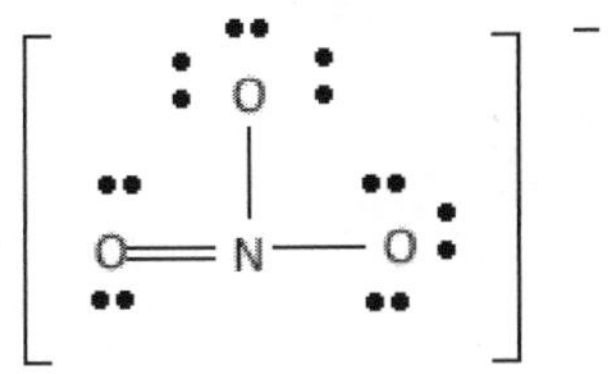

The double bond can be between the N and any of the oxygen atoms, so there are resonance structures.

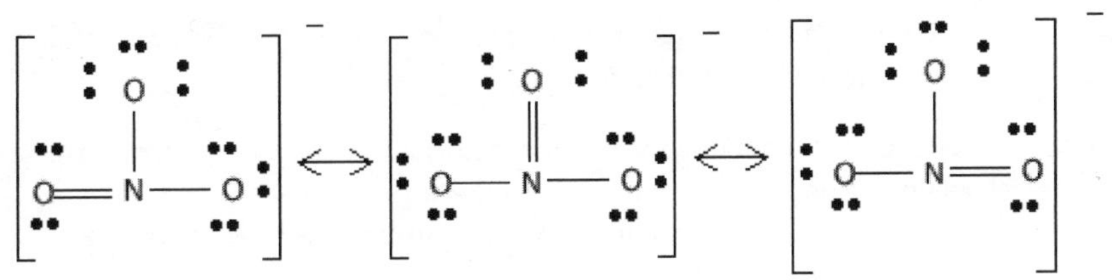

(d) LiIO: Li^+

Answer:

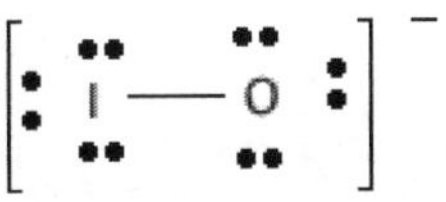

Method for arriving at answer:

1) Determine the cation and anion.

Li^+ IO^-

2) Write the Lewis structure for the lithium cation based on the valence electrons.

$Li\ 2s^1$ $Li^+\ 2s^0$

Li• Li^+

Li must lose one electron and be left with the octet from the previous shell.

3) Write the Lewis structure for the covalent anion.

Calculate the total number of electron for the Lewis structure by summing the number of valence electrons of each atom in the ion and adding one for the 1 – charge.

(number of valence e⁻ for I) + (number of valence e⁻ for O) = 7 + 6 + 1 = 14

Write the correct skeletal structure for the ion.

I — O

Each bond accounts for two electrons, leaving 12 electrons to place in the Lewis structure. Put lone pairs on terminal atoms.

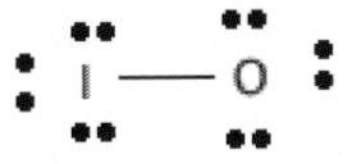

Lastly, write the Lewis structure in brackets with the charge of the ion in the upper right-hand corner.

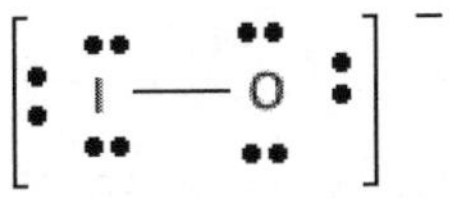

9.87   (a) C_4H_8: Calculate the total number of electrons for the Lewis structure by summing the number of valence electrons of each atom in the molecule.

4(number of valence e⁻ for C) + 8(number of valence e⁻ for H) = 4(4) + 8(1) = 24

Write the correct skeletal structure for the molecule.

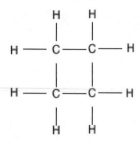

Each bond accounts for two electrons, leaving 0 electrons to place in the Lewis structure. All atoms have octets except H.

(b) C_4H_4: Calculate the total number of electrons for the Lewis structure by summing the number of valence electrons of each atom in the molecule.

4(number of valence e⁻ for C) + 4(number of valence e⁻ for H) = 4(4) + 4(1) = 20

Write the correct skeletal structure for the molecule.

$$H \text{—} C \text{—} C \text{—} H$$
$$H \text{—} C \text{—} C \text{—} H$$

Each bond accounts for two electrons, leaving four electrons to place in the Lewis structure. Put lone pairs on any non-hydrogen atoms.

$$H \text{—} \overset{..}{C} \text{—} \overset{..}{C} \text{—} H$$
$$H \text{—} C \text{—} C \text{—} H$$

Complete octets by forming double bonds on alternating carbons; draw resonance structures.

$$
\begin{array}{ccc}
H \text{—} C \text{—} C \text{—} H & & H \text{—} C \text{=} C \text{—} H \\
\| \quad \| & \longleftrightarrow & | \quad | \\
H \text{—} C \text{—} C \text{—} H & & H \text{—} C \text{=} C \text{—} H
\end{array}
$$

(c) C_6H_{12}:   Calculate the total number of electrons for the Lewis structure by summing the valence electrons of each atom in the molecule.

6(number of valence e⁻ for C) + 12(number of valence e⁻ for H) = 6(4) + 12(1) = 36

Write the correct skeletal structure for the molecule.

Each bond accounts for two electrons, leaving 0 electrons to place in the Lewis structure. All 36 electrons are used and all atoms have octets except H.

(d) C_6H_6:   Calculate the total number of electrons for the Lewis structure by summing the number of valence electrons of each atom in the molecule.

6(number of valence e⁻ for C) + 6(number of valence e⁻ for H) = 6(4) + 6(1) = 30

Write the correct skeletal structure for the molecule.

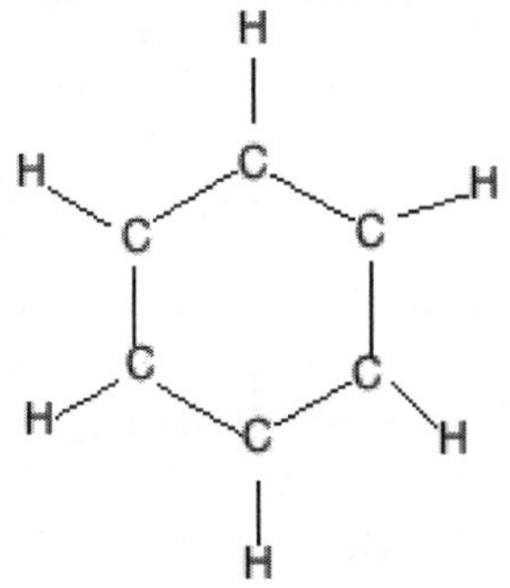

Each bond accounts for two electrons, leaving six electrons to place in the Lewis structure. Put lone pairs on non-hydrogen atoms.

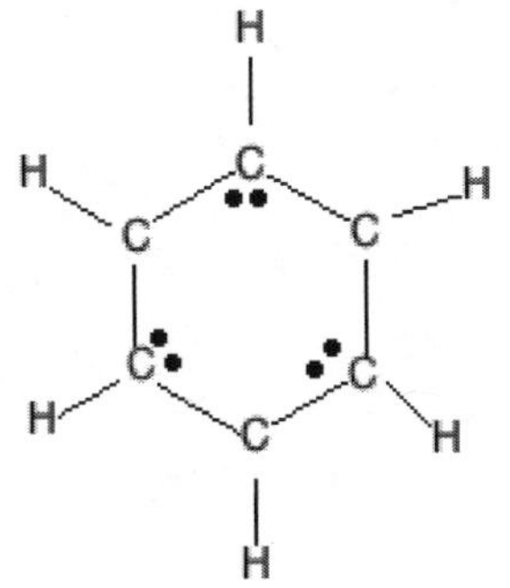

Complete octets by forming double bonds on alternating carbons; draw resonance structures.

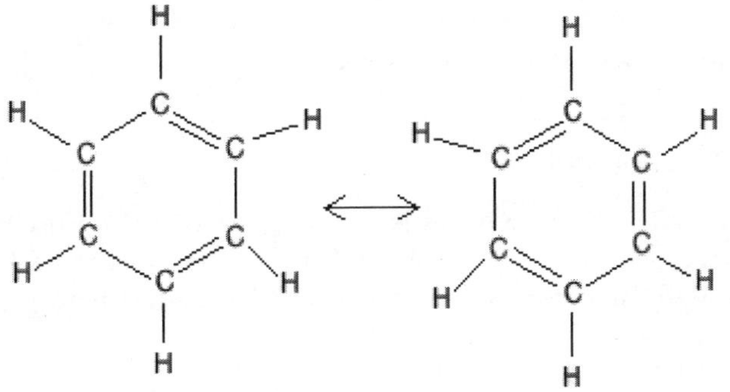

9.89   **Given:** 26.01% C; 4.38% H; 69.52% O; molar mass = 46.02 g mol^{-1}
        Find: molecular formula and Lewis structure
        Conceptual Plan: convert mass to mol of each element $\rightarrow$ **pseudoformula** $\rightarrow$ **empirical formula**

$$\frac{1 \text{ mol C}}{12.01 \text{ g C}} \qquad \frac{1 \text{ mol H}}{1.008 \text{ g H}} \qquad \frac{1 \text{ mol O}}{16.00 \text{ g O}} \qquad \text{divide by smallest number}$$

$\rightarrow$ **molecular formula** $\rightarrow$ **Lewis structure**

empirical formula x n

Solution: $26.01 \text{ g C} \times \dfrac{1 \text{ mol C}}{12.01 \text{ g C}} = 2.166 \text{ mol C}$

$4.38 \text{ g H} \times \dfrac{1 \text{ mol H}}{1.008 \text{ g H}} = 4.3\underline{4}5 \text{ mol H}$

$69.52 \text{ g O} \times \dfrac{1 \text{ mol O}}{16.00 \text{ g O}} = 4.3\underline{4}5 \text{ mol O}$

$C_{2.166}H_{4.345}O_{4.345}$

$C_{\frac{2.166}{2.166}}H_{\frac{4.345}{2.166}}O_{\frac{4.345}{2.166}} \rightarrow CH_2O_2$

The correct empirical formula is CH_2O_2.

empirical formula mass = $(12.01 \text{ g mol}^{-1}) + 2(1.008 \text{ g mol}^{-1}) + 2(16.00 \text{ g mol}^{-1}) = 46.03 \text{ g mol}^{-1}$

$$n = \frac{\text{molar mass}}{\text{formula molar mass}} = \frac{46.02 \text{ g mol}^{-1}}{46.03 \text{ g mol}^{-1}} = 1$$

molecular formula   = CH_2O_2 x 1
                                      = CH_2O_2

Calculate the total number of electrons for the Lewis structure by summing the number of valence electrons of each atom in the molecule.

       (number of valence e⁻ for C) + 2(number of valence e⁻ for O) + 2(number of valence e⁻ for H)
       = 4 + 2(6) + 2(1) = 18

Write the correct skeletal structure for the molecule.

Each bond accounts for two electrons, leaving 10 electrons to place in the Lewis structure. Put lone pairs on terminal, nonhydrogen atoms and then on the central atoms.

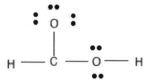

Complete the octet on C by forming a double bond.

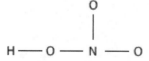

9.91   To determine the values of the lattice energy, it is necessary to look them up online. The lattice energy of Al_2O_3 is –15,916 kJ mol⁻¹, the value for Fe_2O_3 is –14,774 kJ mol⁻¹. The thermite reaction is exothermic due to the energy released when the Al_2O_3 lattice forms. The lattice energy of Al_2O_3 is more negative than the lattice energy of Fe_2O_3.

9.93 HNO_3 Calculate the total number of electrons for the Lewis structure by summing the number of valence electrons of each atom in the molecule.

       3(number of valence e⁻ for O) + (number of valence e⁻ for N) + (number of valence e⁻ for H) = 3(6) + 5 +1 = 24

Write the correct skeletal structure for the molecule.

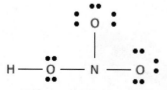

Each bond accounts for two electrons, leaving 16 electrons to place in the Lewis structure. Put lone pairs on terminal atoms.

All 24 valence electrons are used.

If any atoms lack an octet, form double or triple bonds as necessary. The double bond can be formed to any of the three oxygen atoms, so there are three resonance forms.

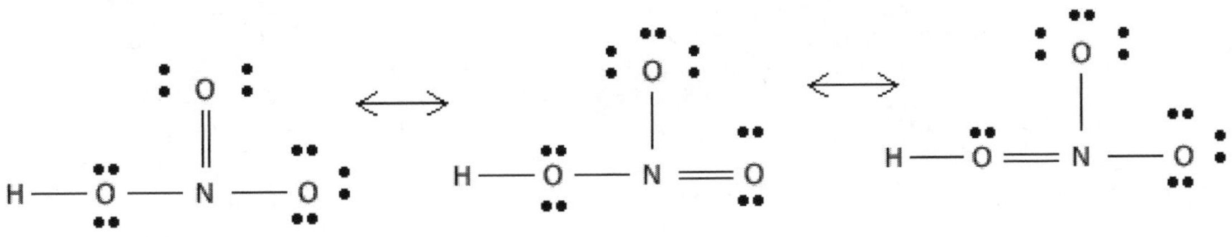

All atoms have octets (except H); the structure is complete.

To determine which resonance hybrid(s) is most important, calculate the formal charge on each atom in each structure by finding the number of valence electrons and subtracting the number of lone-pair electrons and one-half the number of bonding electrons.

	Structure I					Structure II				
	O_{left}	O_{top}	O_{right}	N	H	O_{left}	O_{top}	O_{right}	N	H
number of valence electrons	6	6	6	5	1	6	6	6	5	1
- number of lone-pair electrons	4	4	6	0	0	4	6	4	0	0
- 1/2(number of bonding electrons)	2	2	1	4	1	2	1	2	4	1
Formal charge	0	0	–1	+1	0	0	–1	0	+1	0

	Structure III				
	O_{left}	O_{top}	O_{right}	N	H
number of valence electrons	6	6	6	5	1
- number of lone-pair electrons	2	6	6	0	0
- 1/2(number of bonding electrons)	3	1	1	4	1
Formal charge	+1	–1	–1	+1	0

The sum of the formal charges is 0 for each structure, which is the overall charge of the molecule. However, in structures I and II the individual formal charges are lower. These two forms would contribute equally to the structure of HNO_3. Structure III would be less important since the individual formal charges are higher.

9.95 CNO^- Determine the number of valence electrons.

(valence e⁻ from C) + (valence e⁻ from N) + (valence e⁻ from O) + 1(from the negative charge)

4 + 5 + 6 + 1 = 16

Write the skeletal structure:

C — N — O

Each bond accounts for two electrons, leaving 12 electrons to place in the Lewis structure. Put lone pairs on terminal atoms to give a complete octet.

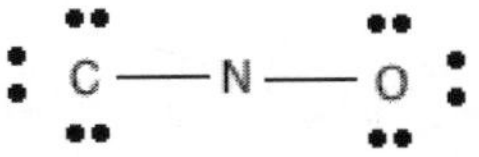

If any atoms lack an octet, form double or triple bonds as necessary.

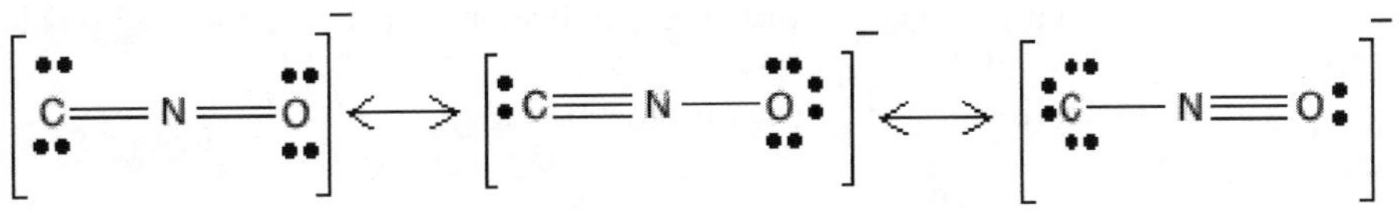

Determine the formal charge on each atom for each structure.

	Structure I			Structure II		
	C	N	O	C	N	O
number of valence electrons	4	5	6	4	5	6
- number of lone-pair electrons	4	0	4	2	0	6
- 1/2(number of bonding electrons)	2	4	2	3	4	1
Formal charge	–2	+1	0	–1	+1	–1

	Structure III		
	C	N	O
number of valence electrons	4	5	6
- number of lone-pair electrons	6	0	2
- 1/2(number of bonding electrons)	1	4	3
Formal charge	–3	+1	+1

Structures I, II, and III all follow the octet rule but have varying degrees of negative formal charge on carbon, which is the least electronegative atom. Also, the amount of formal charge is very high in all three resonance forms. Although structure II is the best of the resonance forms, none of these resonance forms contribute strongly to the stability of the fulminate ion and the ion is not very stable.

9.97 $HCSNH_2$: Calculate the total number of electrons for the Lewis structure by summing the number of valence electrons of each atom in the molecule.

(number of valence e^- for N) + (number of valence e^- for S) + (number of valence e^- for C) + 3(number of valence e^- for H) = 5 + 6 + 4 + 3(1) = 18

Write the correct skeletal structure for the molecule.

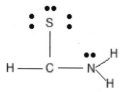

Put lone pairs on terminal atoms and on the central atoms beginning with the most electronegative and proceeding until there are no more electrons.

Complete the octet on C by forming a double bond.

9.99   (a) O_2^-:   Calculate the total number of electrons for the Lewis structure by summing the number of valence electrons of each atom in the radical and adding 1 for the 1 – charge.

2(number of valence e^- for O) + 1 = 2(6) + 1 = 13

Write the correct skeletal structure for the radical.

O ——— O

Each bond accounts for two electrons, leaving 11 electrons to place in the Lewis structure. Put lone pairs on terminal atoms.

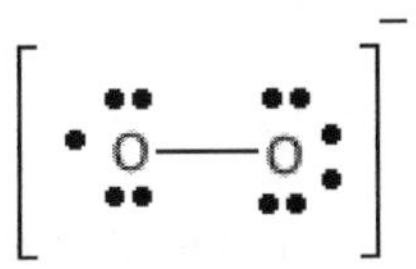

$$\left[\cdot \ddot{O} \!-\! \ddot{O} \colon \right]^{-}$$

All 13 valence electrons are used.

O has an incomplete octet. It has seven electrons because we have an odd number of valence electrons.

(b) O^-:   Write the Lewis structure based on the valence electrons $2s^2 2p^5$.

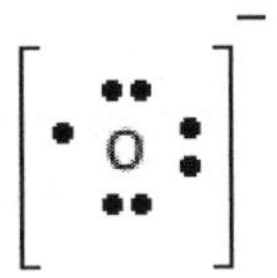

$$\left[\cdot \ddot{O} \colon \right]^{-}$$

O has an incomplete octet. It has seven electrons because we have an odd number of valence electrons.

(c)   OH: Calculate the total number of electrons for the Lewis structure by summing the number of valence electrons of each atom in the molecule.

(number of valence e^- for O) + (number of valence e^- for H) = 6 + 1 = 7

Write the correct skeletal structure for the molecule.

$$H \!-\! O$$

Each bond accounts for two electrons, leaving five electrons to place in the Lewis structure. Put lone pairs on terminal, nonhydrogen atoms.

$$H \!-\! \dot{\ddot{O}}$$

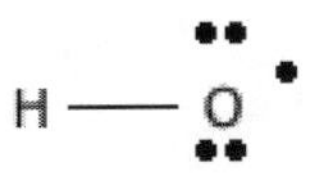

All seven valence electrons are used.

O has an incomplete octet. It has seven electrons because we have an odd number of valence electrons.

(d) CH_3OO: Calculate the total number of electrons for the Lewis structure by summing the number of valence electrons of each atom in the molecule.

3(number of valence e^- for H) + (number of valence e^- for C) + 2(number of valence e^- for O) = 3(1) + 4 + 2(6) = 19

Write the correct skeletal structure for the radical. C is the least electronegative atom, so it is central.

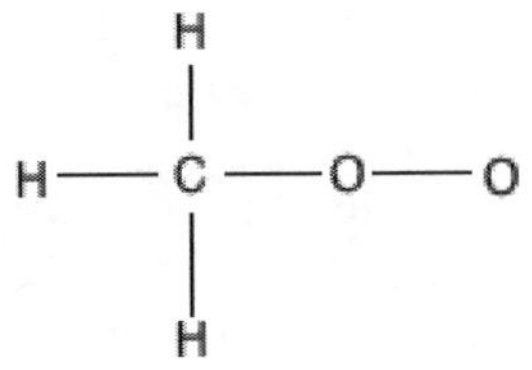

$$
\begin{array}{c}
H \\
| \\
H \!-\! C \!-\! O \!-\! O \\
| \\
H
\end{array}
$$

Each bond accounts for two electrons, leaving nine electrons to place in the Lewis structure. Put lone pairs on terminal, nonhydrogen atoms and then on the central atoms.

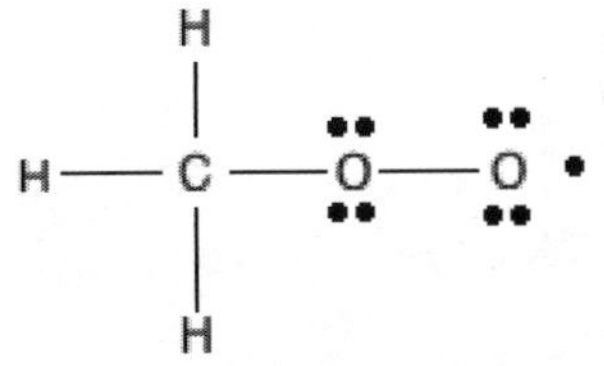

$$
\begin{array}{c}
H \\
| \\
H \!-\! C \!-\! \ddot{O} \!-\! \dot{\ddot{O}} \\
| \\
H
\end{array}
$$

All 19 valence electrons are used.

O has an incomplete octet. It has seven electrons because we have an odd number of valence electrons.

9.101   Rewrite the reaction for the combustion of hydrogen using the Lewis structures of the molecules involved.

$$H-H\ (g)\ +1/2\ \overset{\cdot\cdot}{\underset{\cdot\cdot}{O}}=\overset{\cdot\cdot}{\underset{\cdot\cdot}{O}}\ (g)\ \rightarrow\ H-\overset{\cdot\cdot}{\underset{\cdot\cdot}{O}}-H$$

Bonds Broken	**Bonds Formed**
H – H + 436 kJ mol^{-1}	2 O – H –2 (464) kJ mol^{-1}
½ O = O +½ (498) kJ mol^{-1}	

$\Sigma\ \Delta_r H$ bonds broken: +685 kJ mol^{-1} $\Sigma\ \Delta_r H$ bonds formed: –928 kJ mol^{-1}

$\Delta_r H = \Sigma\ (\Delta_r H$ bonds broken$) + \Sigma\ (\Delta_r H$ bonds formed$)$
$\quad\quad = +685$ kJ mol^{-1} – 928 kJ mol^{-1}
$\quad\quad = -243$ kJ mol^{-1}

$CH_4(g) + 2O_2(g)\ \rightarrow\ CO_2(g) + 2H_2O(g)$

Rewrite the reaction for the combustion of methane using the Lewis structures of the molecules involved.

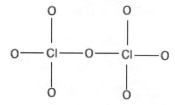

Bonds Broken	**Bonds Formed**
4 C – H + 4(414) kJ mol^{-1}	2 C = O –2(799) kJ mol^{-1}
2 O = O + 2(498) kJ mol^{-1}	4 O – H –4(464) kJ mol^{-1}

$\Sigma\ \Delta_r H$ bonds broken: +2652 kJ mol^{-1} $\Sigma\ \Delta_r H$ bonds formed: – 3454 kJ mol^{-1}

$\Delta_r H = \Sigma\ (\Delta_r H$ bonds broken$) + \Sigma\ (\Delta_r H$ bonds formed$)$
$\quad\quad = +2652$ kJ mol^{-1} – 3454 kJ mol^{-1}
$\quad\quad = -802$ kJ mol^{-1}

Compare the following:

	kJ mol^{-1}	kJ g^{-1}
H$_2$	–243	–121
CH$_4$	–802	–50.0

The numbers shown in the table were calculated as shown below.
The molar mass of H$_2$ is 2.016 g mol^{-1} so

$$\frac{-243\ kJ}{1\ mol}\times\frac{1\ mol}{2.016\ g}=-121\ kJ\ g^{-1}$$

The molar mass of CH$_4$ is 16.04 g mol^{-1} so

$$\frac{-802\ kJ}{1\ mol}\times\frac{1\ mol}{16.04\ g}=-50.0\ kJ\ g^{-1}$$

So, methane yields more energy per mole but hydrogen yields more energy per gram.

9.103   (a)   Cl$_2$O$_7$:   Calculate the total number of electrons for the Lewis structure by summing the valence electrons of each atom in the molecule.

2(number of valence e$^-$ for Cl) + 7(number of valence e$^-$ for O) = 2(7)5 + 7(6) = 56

Write the correct skeletal structure for the molecule.

$$\begin{array}{ccc} O & & O \\ | & & | \\ O-Cl-O-Cl-O \\ | & & | \\ O & & O \end{array}$$

Each bond accounts for two electrons, leaving 40 electrons to place in the Lewis structure. Put lone pairs on terminal atoms and then on any central atom that does not already have a complete octet.

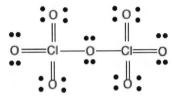

This structure is correct. However, another structure can be drawn where double bonds are formed to minimize formal charge.

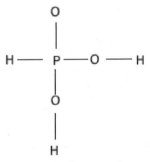

(b) H_3PO_3: Calculate the total number of electrons for the Lewis structure by summing the valence electrons of each atom in the molecule.

(number of valence e^- for P) + 3(number of valence e^- for O) + 3(number of valence e^- for H) = 5 + 3(6) + 3(1) = 26

Write the correct skeletal structure for the molecule.

$$\begin{array}{c} O \\ | \\ H — P — O — H \\ | \\ O \\ | \\ H \end{array}$$

Each bond accounts for two electrons, leaving 14 electrons to place in the Lewis structure. Put lone pairs on terminal (nonhydrogen) atoms and then on central atoms.

$$\begin{array}{c} :\!\overset{..}{O}\!: \\ | \\ H — P — \overset{..}{O} — H \\ | \\ :\!O\!: \\ | \\ H \end{array}$$

This structure is correct. However, another structure can be drawn where double bonds are formed to minimize formal charge.

$$\begin{array}{c} :\!\overset{..}{O}\!: \\ \| \\ H — P — \overset{..}{O} — H \\ | \\ :\!\overset{..}{O}\!: \\ | \\ H \end{array}$$

(c) H_3AsO_4: Calculate the total number of electrons for the Lewis structure by summing the valence electrons of each atom in the molecule.

(number of valence e⁻ for As) + 4(number of valence e⁻ for O) + 3(number of valence e⁻ for H) = 5 + 4(6) + 3(1) = 32

Write the correct skeletal structure for the molecule.

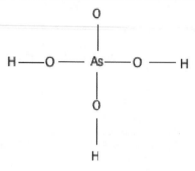

Each bond accounts for two electrons, leaving 18 electrons to place in the Lewis structure. Put lone pairs on terminal (nonhydrogen) atoms to give a complete octet.

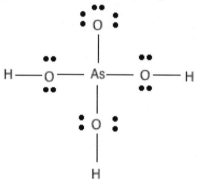

This structure is correct. However, another structure can be drawn where double bonds are formed to minimize formal charge.

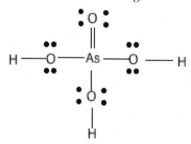

9.105 $Na^+F^- < Na^+O^{2-} < Mg^{2+}F^- < Mg^{2+}O^{2-} < Al^{3+}O^{2-}$

The lattice energy is proportional to the magnitude of the charge and inversely proportional to the distance between the atoms. Na^+F^- would have the smallest lattice energy because the magnitude of the charges on Na and F are the smallest. $Mg^{2+}F^-$ and Na^+O^{2-} both have the same magnitude formal charge, the O^{2-} is larger than F^- in size, and Na^+ is larger than Mg^{2+}, so Na^+O^{2-} should be less than $Mg^{2+}F^-$. The magnitude of the charge makes $Mg^{2+}O^{2-} < Al^{3+}O^{2-}$.

9.107   **Given:** heat atomization CH_4 = 1660 kJ mol⁻¹, CH_2Cl_2 = 1495 kJ mol⁻¹ **Find:** bond energy C – Cl
Write the reaction using the Lewis structure.

H—C—H(g) ⟶ C(g) + 4 H(g)

Determine the number and kinds of bonds broken and then ΔH atomization = Σ bonds broken.

ΔH atomization = Σ 4 (C – H) bonds broken

$$\frac{1660 \text{ kJ}}{1 \text{ mol CH}_4} \times \frac{1 \text{ mol CH}_4}{4 \text{ C} - \text{H bonds}} = 415 \text{ kJ/C} - \text{H bond}$$

Write the reaction using the Lewis structure.

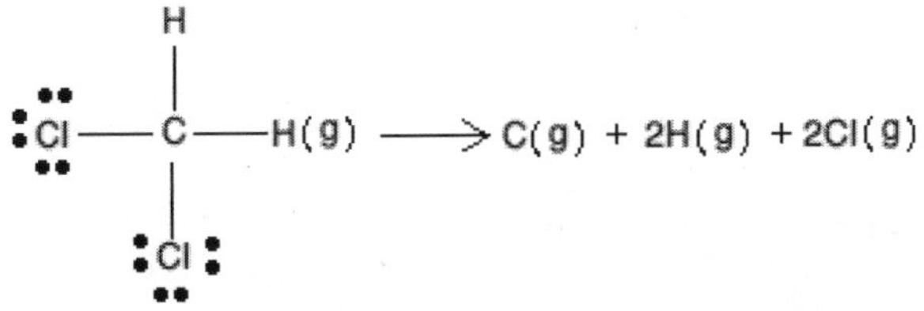

Determine the number and kinds of bonds broken and ΔH atomization = Σ bonds broken.

ΔH atomization = Σ 2 (C – H) bonds broken + 2(C – Cl) bonds broken

1495 kJ mol^{-1} = 2(415 kJ mol^{-1}) + 2 (x)   x = 333 kJ mol^{-1} for the C – Cl bond energy

Check: The bond energy found (333 kJ mol^{-1}) is very close to the table value of 339 kJ mol^{-1}.

9.109   **Given:** 7.743% H **Find:** Lewis structure

Conceptual Plan: %H → %C → mass C,H → mol C,H → pseudoformula → empirical formula

$$100\% - \%H \qquad \text{Assume 100 g sample} \qquad \frac{1 \text{ mol C}}{12.01 \text{ g}} \quad \frac{1 \text{ mol N}}{1.008 \text{ g}} \qquad \text{divide by smallest number}$$

Solution: %C = 100% - 7.743% = 92.568% C

In a 100.00 g sample; 7.743 g H, 92.568 g C

$$7.743 \text{ g H} \times \frac{1 \text{ mol H}}{1.008 \text{ g H}} = 7.682 \text{ mol H}$$

$$92.568 \text{ g C} \times \frac{1 \text{ mol C}}{12.011 \text{ g C}} = 7.7069 \text{ mol C}$$

$$C_{7.7068}H_{7.682}$$
$$C_{\frac{7.7068}{7.682}}H_{\frac{7.682}{7.682}} \rightarrow CH$$

The empirical formula is CH. The smallest molecular formula would be C_2H_2.

Calculate the total number of electrons for the Lewis structure by summing the valence electrons of each atom in the molecule.

2(number of valence e$^-$ for C) + 2(number of valence e$^-$ for H) = 2(4) + 2(1) = 10 e$^-$

Write the correct skeletal structure for the molecule.

H —— C —— C —— H

Each bond accounts for two electrons, leaving four electrons to place in the Lewis structure. Put lone pairs on the central atoms, since the hydrogens are complete with two.

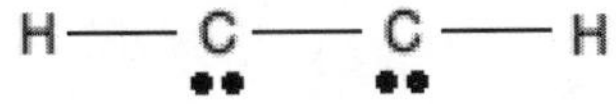

Complete the octet on C by forming a triple bond.

H —— C ≡≡≡ C —— H

Challenge Problems

9.111

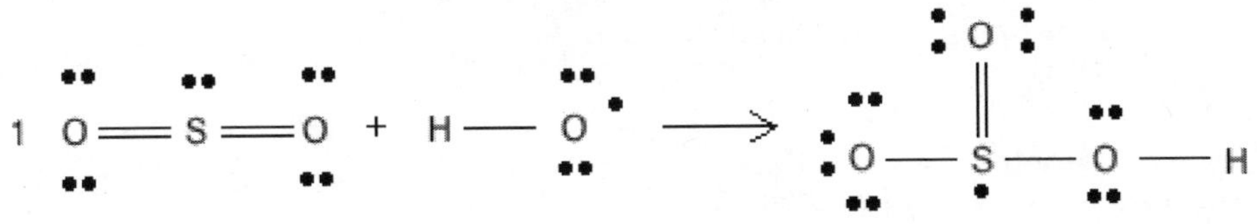

Step 1:

Bonds Broken	**Bonds Formed**
$S = O$ +523 kJ mol^{-1}	$2S - O$ $-2(265)$ kJ mol^{-1}

$\Sigma \, \Delta_r H$ bonds broken: +523 kJ mol^{-1} $\Sigma \, \Delta_r H$ bonds formed: −530 kJ mol^{-1}

$\Delta_r H_{\text{step 1}} = \Sigma \, (\Delta_r H$ bonds broken) $+ \Sigma \, (\Delta_r H$ bonds formed)

$\quad\quad\quad = +523$ kJ mol^{-1} − 530 kJ mol^{-1}

$\quad\quad\quad = -7$ kJ mol^{-1}

Step 2:

Bonds Broken	**Bonds Formed**
$O - H$ +464 kJ mol^{-1}	$H - O$ − 464 kJ mol^{-1}
$O = O$ +498 kJ mol^{-1}	$O - O$ −142 kJ mol^{-1}

$\Sigma \, \Delta_r H$ bonds broken: +962 kJ mol^{-1} $\Sigma \, \Delta_r H$ bonds formed: −606 kJ mol^{-1}

$\Delta_r H_{\text{step2}} = \Sigma \, (\Delta_r H$ bonds broken) $+ \Sigma \, (\Delta_r H$ bonds formed)

$\quad\quad\quad = +962$ kJ mol^{-1} − 606 kJ mol^{-1}

$\quad\quad\quad = +356$ kJ mol^{-1}

NOTE: Since the O – H bond is both broken and formed in the reaction it cancels out and the calculation could be simplified as follows:

Bonds Broken	**Bonds Formed**
$O = O$ +498 kJ mol^{-1}	$O - O$ −142 kJ mol^{-1}

$\Sigma \, \Delta_r H$ bonds broken: +498 kJ mol^{-1} $\Sigma \, \Delta_r H$ bonds formed: −142 kJ mol^{-1}

$\Delta_r H_{\text{step 2}} = \Sigma \, (\Delta_r H$ bonds broken) $+ \Sigma \, (\Delta_r H$ bonds formed)

$\quad\quad\quad = +498$ kJ mol^{-1} − 142 kJ mol^{-1}

$\quad\quad\quad = + 356$ kJ mol^{-1}

Step 3:

Bonds Broken	**Bonds Formed**
$O - H$ +464 kJ mol^{-1}	$H - O$ − 464 kJ mol^{-1}
$S - O$ +265 kJ mol^{-1}	$S - O$ − 265 kJ mol^{-1}
	$S = O$ − 523 kJ mol^{-1}

NOTE: O – H and S – O occur on both sides, so cancel them out leaving:

Bonds Broken	**Bonds Formed**
	$S = O$ −523 kJ mol^{-1}

$\Sigma \, \Delta_r H$ bonds broken: none $\Sigma \, \Delta_r H$ bonds formed: −523 kJ mol^{-1}

$\Delta_r H_{\text{step 3}} = \Sigma \, (\Delta_r H$ bonds broken) $+ \Sigma \, (\Delta_r H$ bonds formed)

$\quad\quad\quad = 0 - 523$ kJ mol^{-1}

$\quad\quad\quad = - 523$ kJ mol^{-1}

Hess's law states that ΔH for the reaction is the sum of ΔH of the steps:

$\Delta_r H = (- 7$ kJ mol$^{-1}) + (+356$ kJ mol$^{-1}) + (- 523$ kJ mol$^{-1}) = - 174$ kJ mol^{-1}

9.113   **Given:** $\mu = 1.08$ D HCl, 20% ionic and $\mu = 1.82$ D HF, 45% ionic **Find:** r
Conceptual Plan: $\mu \rightarrow \mu_{calc} \rightarrow r$

% ionic character $= \dfrac{\mu}{\mu_{calc}} \times 100$

Solution: For HCl $\mu_{calc} = \dfrac{1.08}{0.20} = 5.4$ D

$$\dfrac{5.4 \text{ D} \times \dfrac{3.34 \times 10^{-30} \text{ C} \cdot \text{m}}{\text{D}} \times \dfrac{10^{12} \text{ pm}}{\text{m}}}{1.6 \times 10^{-19} \text{ C}} = 113 \text{ pm}$$

For HF $\mu_{calc} = \dfrac{1.82}{0.45} = 4.04$ D

$$\dfrac{4.04 \text{ D} \times \dfrac{3.34 \times 10^{-30} \text{ C} \cdot \text{m}}{\text{D}} \times \dfrac{10^{12} \text{ pm}}{\text{m}}}{1.6 \times 10^{-19} \text{ C}} = 84 \text{ pm}$$

From Table 9.2, the bond length of HCl = 127 pm, and HF = 92 pm. Both of these values are slightly higher than the calculated values.

9.115   In order for the four P atoms to be equivalent, they must all be in the same electronic environment. That is, they must all see the same number of bonds and lone-pair electrons. The only way to achieve this is with a tetrahedral configuration where the P atoms are at the four points of the tetrahedron.

9.117   **Given:** $\Delta_f H° \text{PI}_3(s) = -24.7$ kJ mol^{-1}; P – I = 184 kJ mol^{-1}; I – I = 151 kJ mol^{-1}; $\Delta_f H° \text{P}(g) = 334$ kJ mol^{-1}; $\Delta_f H° \text{I}_2(g) = 62$ kJ mol^{-1} **Find:** $\Delta_{sub} H \text{PI}_3(s)$
Conceptual Plan: $\text{PI}_3(s) \rightarrow \text{PI}_3(g)$; use Hess's law
Solution:

Reaction	ΔH(kJ mol^{-1})	
$\text{PI}_3(s) \rightarrow \text{P}(s) + 3/2\ \text{I}_2(s)$	+ 24.7	(this is the reverse of the formation reaction)
$\text{P}(s) \rightarrow \text{P}(g)$	+334	(formation of P(g))
$3/2\ \text{I}_2(s) \rightarrow 3/2\ \text{I}_2(g)$	3/2(62)	(formation of I$_2$(g))
$3/2\ \text{I}_2(g) \rightarrow 3\ \text{I}(g)$	3/2(151)	(breaking I – I bond)
$\text{P}(g) + 3\text{I}(g) \rightarrow \text{PI}_3(g)$	– 3(184)	(forming P – I bond)
$\text{PI}_3(s) \rightarrow \text{PI}_3(g)$	+126	(sublimation of PI$_3$(s))

9.119   **Given:** H_2S_4 linear **Find:** oxidation number of each S
Calculate the total number of electrons for the Lewis structure by summing the number of valence electrons of each atom in the molecule.
4(number of valence e$^-$ for S) + 2(number of valence e$^-$ for H) = 4(6) + 2(1) = 26
Write the correct skeletal structure for the molecule.

H —— S —— S —— S —— S —— H

Distribute the electrons among the atoms, giving octets (except H) to as many atoms as possible.

H —— S —— S —— S —— S —— H

Determine the oxidation number on each atom. EN(H) < EN(S), so the electrons in the H – S bond belong to the S atom, while the electrons in the S – S bonds split between the two S atoms.

O. N. = valence electrons – electrons that belong to the atom

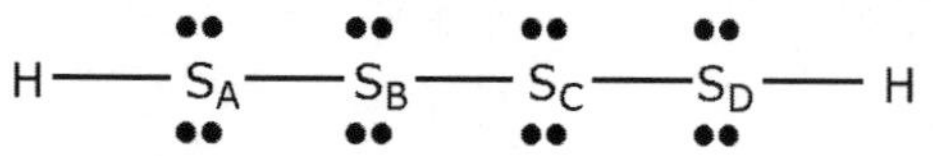

$H = 1 - 0 = +1$ for each H
$S_A = 6 - 7 = -1$
$S_B = 6 - 6 = 0$
$S_C = 6 - 6 = 0$
$S_D = 6 - 7 = -1$

9.121 **Given:** $\Delta_f H$ $SO_2 = -296.8$ kJ mol^{-1}, $S(g) = 277.2$ kJ mol^{-1}, break $O = O$ bond 498 kJ mol^{-1}
Find: S = O bond energy
Conceptual Plan: Use $\Delta_f H$ for SO_2 and $S(g)$ and the bond energy of O_2 to determine heat of atomization of SO_2.

Reaction		ΔH	(kJ mol^{-1})
$SO_2(g)$	$\rightarrow$ ~~S(s, rhombic) + O₂(g)~~		+296.8
~~S(s, rhombic)~~	$\rightarrow$ S(g)		+277.2
~~O=O(g)~~	$\rightarrow$ 2 O(g)		+498
$SO_2(g)$	$\rightarrow$ S(g) + 2 O(g)		+1072

Write the reaction using the Lewis structure.

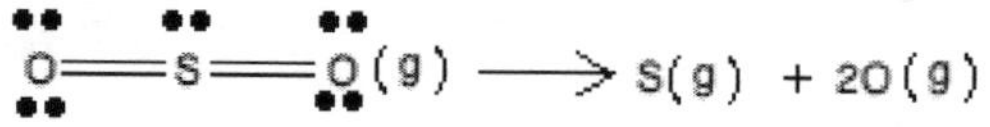

Determine the number and kinds of bonds broken and then ΔH atomization = bonds broken.
ΔH atomization = 2 Σ (S=O) bonds broken.
1072 kJ mol^{-1} = 2 (S=O) bonds broken.
S=O bond energy = 536 kJ mol^{-1}.
Check: The S=O bond energy is close to the table value of 523 kJ mol^{-1}.

Conceptual Problems

9.123 When we say that a compound is "energy rich" we mean that it gives off a great amount of energy when it reacts. It means that there is a lot of energy stored in the compound. This energy is released when the weak bonds in the compound break and much stronger bonds are formed in the product, thereby releasing energy.

9.125 Lewis theory is successful because it allows us to understand and predict many chemical observations. We can use it to determine the formulae of ionic compounds and to account for the low melting points and boiling points of molecular compounds compared to ionic compounds. Lewis theory allows us to predict what molecules or ions will be stable, which will be more reactive, and which will not exist. Lewis theory, however, does not really tell us anything about how the bonds in the molecules and ions form. It does not give us a way to account for the paramagnetism of oxygen. And, by itself, Lewis theory does not really tell us anything about the shape of the molecule or ion.

10 Chemical Bonding II: Molecular Shapes, Valence Bond Theory, and Molecular Orbital Theory

Review Questions

10.1   The properties of molecules are directly related to their shape. The sensation of taste, immune response, the sense of smell, and many types of drug action all depend on shape-specific interactions between molecules and proteins.

10.3   The five basic electron geometries are
(1)   Linear, which has two electron groups.
(2)   Trigonal planar, which has three electron groups.
(3)   Tetrahedral, which has four electron groups.
(4)   Trigonal bipyramid, which has five electron groups.
(5)   Octahedral, which has six electron groups.
An electron group is defined as a lone pair of electrons, a single bond, a multiple bond, or even a single electron.

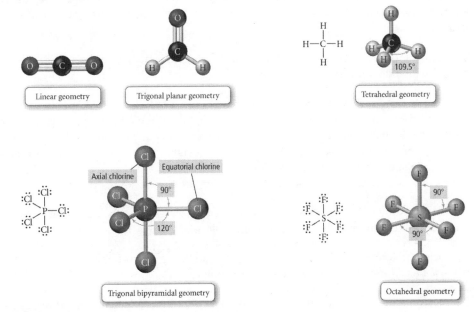

10.5   (a)   Four electron groups give tetrahedral electron geometry, while three bonding groups and one lone pair give a trigonal pyramidal molecular geometry.

        (b)   Four electron groups give a tetrahedral electron geometry, while two bonding groups and two lone pairs give a bent molecular geometry.

(c)   Five electron groups give a trigonal bipyramidal electron geometry, while four bonding groups and one lone pair give a seesaw molecular geometry.

(d)   Five electron groups give a trigonal bipyramidal electron geometry, while three bonding groups and two lone pairs give a T-shaped molecular geometry.

(e)   Five electron groups give a trigonal bipyramidal electron geometry, while two bonding groups and three lone pairs give a linear geometry.

(f)   Six electron groups give an octahedral electron geometry, while five bonding groups and one lone pair give a square pyramidal molecular geometry.

(g)   Six electron groups give an octahedral electron geometry, while four bonding groups and two lone pairs give a square planar molecular geometry.

10.7   To determine if a molecule is polar, do the following:

1.   Draw the Lewis structure for the molecule and determine the molecular geometry.

2.   Determine whether the molecule contains polar bonds.

3.   Determine whether the polar bonds add together to form a net dipole moment.

Polarity is important because polar and nonpolar molecules have different properties. Polar molecules interact strongly with other polar molecules, but do not interact with nonpolar molecules, and vice versa.

10.9   According to valence bond theory, the shape of the molecule is determined by the geometry of the overlapping orbitals.

10.11   Hybridization is a mathematical procedure in which the standard atomic orbitals are combined to form new atomic orbitals called hybrid orbitals. Hybrid orbitals are still localized on individual atoms, but they have different shapes and energies from those of standard atomic orbitals. They are necessary in valence bond theory because they correspond more closely to the actual distribution of electrons in chemically bonded atoms.

10.13   The number of standard atomic orbitals added together always equals the number of hybrid orbitals formed. The total number of orbitals is conserved.

10.15   The double bond in Lewis theory is simply two pairs of electrons that are shared between the same two atoms. However, in valence bond theory we see that the double bond is made up of two different kinds of bonds. The double bond in valence bond theory consists of one σ bond and one π bond. Valence bond theory shows us that rotation about a double bond is severely restricted. Because of the side-by-side overlap of the p orbitals, the π bond must essentially break for rotation to occur. The single bond consists of overlap that results in a σ bond. Since the overlap is linear, rotation is not restricted.

10.17   In molecular orbital theory, atoms will bond when the electrons in the atoms can lower their energy by occupying the molecular orbitals of the resultant molecule.

10.19   A bonding molecular orbital is lower in energy than the atomic orbitals from which it is formed. There is an increased electron density in the internuclear region.

10.21   The electrons in orbitals behave like waves. The bonding molecular orbital arises from the constructive interference between the atomic orbitals and is lower in energy than the atomic orbitals. The antibonding molecular orbital arises from the destructive interference between the atomic orbitals and is higher in energy than the atomic orbitals.

10.23   Molecular orbitals can be approximated by a linear combination of atomic orbitals (AOs). The total number of MOs formed from a particular set of AOs will always equal the number of AOs used.

10.25

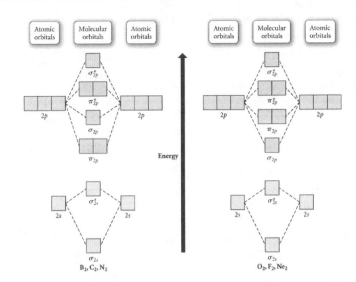

10.27   A paramagnetic species has unpaired electrons in molecular orbitals of equal energy. A paramagnetic species is attracted to a magnetic field. The magnetic property is a direct result of the unpaired electrons. The spin and angular momentum of the electrons generate tiny magnetic fields. A diamagnetic species has all of the electrons paired. The magnetic fields caused by the electron spin and orbital angular momentum tend to cancel each other. A diamagnetic species is not attracted to a magnetic field and is, in fact, slightly repelled.

10.29   Nonbonding orbitals are atomic orbitals not involved in a bond and will remain localized on the atom.

Problems by Topic

VSEPR Theory and Molecular Geometry

10.31   Four electron groups: A trigonal pyramidal molecular geometry has three bonding groups and one lone pair of electrons, so there are four electron pairs on atom A.

10.33   (a)   4 total electron groups, 4 bonding groups, 0 lone pairs
                A tetrahedral molecular geometry has four bonding groups and no lone pairs. So, there are four total electron groups, four bonding groups, and no lone pairs.

        (b)   5 total electron groups, 3 bonding groups, 2 lone pairs
                A T-shaped molecular geometry has three bonding groups and two lone pairs. So, there are five total electron groups, three bonding groups, and two lone pairs.

        (c)   6 total electron groups, 5 bonding groups, 1 lone pairs
                A square pyramidal molecular geometry has five bonding groups and one lone pair. So, there are six total electron groups, five bonding groups, and one lone pair.

10.35   (a) PF_3:   Electron geometry–tetrahedral; molecular geometry–trigonal pyramidal; bond angle = 109.5°
                         Because of the lone pair, the bond angle will be less than 109.5°.
                         Draw a Lewis structure for the molecule:
                         PF_3 has 26 valence electrons.

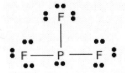

Determine the total number of electron groups around the central atom:
There are four electron groups on P.
Determine the number of bonding groups and the number of lone pairs around the central atom:
There are three bonding groups and one lone pair.
Use Table 10.1 to determine the electron geometry, molecular geometry, and bond angles:
Four electron groups give a tetrahedral electron geometry; three bonding groups and one lone pair give a trigonal pyramidal molecular geometry; the idealized bond angles for tetrahedral geometry are 109.5°. The lone pair will make the bond angle less than idealized.

(b) SBr_2:   Electron geometry–tetrahedral; molecular geometry–bent; bond angle = 109.5°
Because of the lone pairs, the bond angle will be less than 109.5°.
Draw a Lewis structure for the molecule:
SBr_2 has 20 valence electrons.

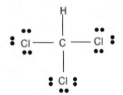

Determine the total number of electron groups around the central atom:
There are four electron groups on S.
Determine the number of bonding groups and the number of lone pairs around the central atom:
There are two bonding groups and two lone pairs.
Use Table 10.1 to determine the electron geometry, molecular geometry, and bond angles:
Four electron groups give a tetrahedral electron geometry; two bonding groups and two lone pairs give a bent molecular geometry; the idealized bond angles for tetrahedral geometry are 109.5°. The lone pairs will make the bond angle less than idealized.

(c) $CHCl_3$: Electron geometry–tetrahedral; molecular geometry–tetrahedral; bond angle = 109.5°
Because there are no lone pairs, the bond angle will be 109.5°.
Draw a Lewis structure for the molecule:
$CHCl_3$ has 26 valence electrons.

$$\overset{\displaystyle H}{\underset{\displaystyle :\ddot{C}l:}{:\ddot{C}l - \underset{|}{\overset{|}{C}} - \ddot{C}l:}}$$

Determine the total number of electron groups around the central atom:
There are four electron groups on C.
Determine the number of bonding groups and the number of lone pairs around the central atom:
There are four bonding groups and no lone pairs.
Use Table 10.1 to determine the electron geometry, molecular geometry, and bond angles:
Four electron groups give a tetrahedral electron geometry; four bonding groups and no lone pairs give a tetrahedral molecular geometry; the idealized bond angles for tetrahedral geometry are 109.5°; however, because the attached atoms have different electronegativities the bond angles are less than idealized.

(d) CS_2:   Electron geometry–linear; molecular geometry–linear; bond angle = 180°
Because there are no lone pairs, the bond angle will be 180°.
Draw a Lewis structure for the molecule:
CS_2 has 16 valence electrons.

$$\ddot{S} = C = \ddot{S}$$

Determine the total number of electron groups around the central atom:
There are two electron groups on C.

Determine the number of bonding groups and the number of lone pairs around the central atom:
There are two bonding groups and no lone pairs.
Use Table 10.1 to determine the electron geometry, molecular geometry, and bond angles:
Two electron groups give a linear geometry; two bonding groups and no lone pairs give a linear
molecular geometry; the idealized bond angle is $180°$. The molecule will not deviate from this.

10.37 H_2O will have the smaller bond angle because lone pair–lone pair repulsions are greater than lone
pair–bonding pair repulsions.

Draw the Lewis structures for both structures:
H_3O^+ has eight valence electrons. H_2O has eight valence electrons.

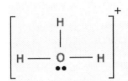

There are three bonding groups and   There are two bonding groups and
one lone pair.   two lone pairs.

Both have four electron groups, but the two lone pairs in H_2O will cause the bond angle to be smaller
because of the lone pair–lone pair repulsions.

10.39   (a) SF_4 Draw a Lewis structure for the molecule:
SF_4 has 34 valence electrons.

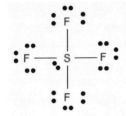

Determine the total number of electron groups around the central atom:
There are five electron groups on S.
Determine the number of bonding groups and the number of lone pairs around the central atom:
There are four bonding groups and one lone pair.
Use Table 10.1 to determine the electron geometry and molecular geometry:
The electron geometry is trigonal bipyramidal so the molecular geometry is seesaw.
Sketch the molecule:

(b) ClF_3 Draw a Lewis structure for the molecule:
ClF_3 has 28 valence electrons.

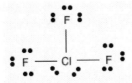

Determine the total number of electron groups around the central atom:
There are five electron groups on Cl.

Determine the number of bonding groups and the number of lone pairs around the central atom:
There are three bonding groups and two lone pairs.
Use Table 10.1 to determine the electron geometry and molecular geometry:
The electron geometry is trigonal bipyramidal so the molecular geometry is T-shaped.
Sketch the molecule:

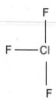

(c)   IF$_2$$^-$ Draw a Lewis structure for the ion:
IF$_2$$^-$ has 22 valence electrons.

$$\left[\ddot{\overset{..}{F}} - \overset{..}{\underset{..}{I}} - \overset{..}{\underset{..}{F}} \right]^-$$

Determine the total number of electron groups around the central atom:
There are five electron groups on I.
Determine the number of bonding groups and the number of lone pairs around the central atom:
There are two bonding groups and three lone pairs.
Use Table 10.1 to determine the electron geometry and molecular geometry:
The electron geometry is trigonal bipyramidal so the molecular geometry is linear.
Sketch the ion:

$$[F — I — F]^-$$

(d)   IBr$_4$$^-$ Draw a Lewis structure for the ion:
IBr$_4$$^-$ has 36 valence electrons.

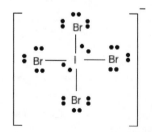

Determine the total number of electron groups around the central atom:
There are six electron groups on I.
Determine the number of bonding groups and the number of lone pairs around the central atom:
There are four bonding groups and two lone pairs.
Use Table 10.1 to determine the electron geometry and molecular geometry:
The electron geometry is octahedral so the molecular geometry is square planar.
Sketch the ion:

$$\left[\begin{matrix} Br & & Br \\ & I & \\ Br & & Br \end{matrix} \right]^-$$

10.41   (a) C_2H_2 Draw the Lewis structure:

$$H \longrightarrow C \equiv C \longrightarrow H$$

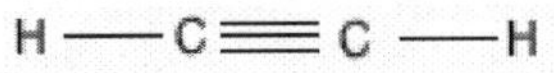

Atom	Number of Electron Groups	Number of Lone Pairs	Molecular Geometry
Left C	2	0	Linear
Right C	2	0	Linear

Sketch the molecule:

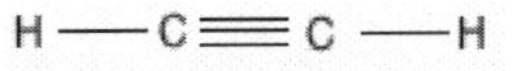

$$H \longrightarrow C \equiv C \longrightarrow H$$

(b) C_2H_4 Draw the Lewis structure:

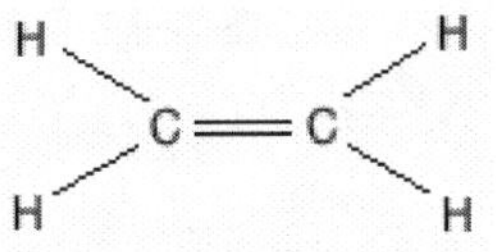

Atom	Number of Electron Groups	Number of Lone Pairs	Molecular Geometry
Left C	3	0	Trigonal planar
Right C	3	0	Trigonal planar

Sketch the molecule:

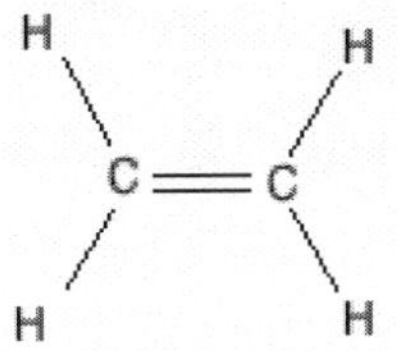

(c) C_2H_6 Draw the Lewis structure:

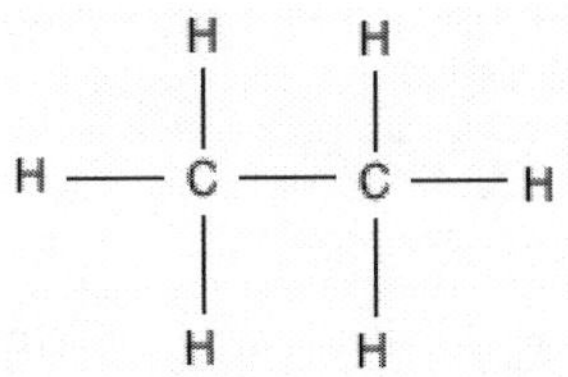

Atom	Number of Electron Groups	Number of Lone Pairs	Molecular Geometry
Left C	4	0	Tetrahedral
Right C	4	0	Tetrahedral

Sketch the molecule:

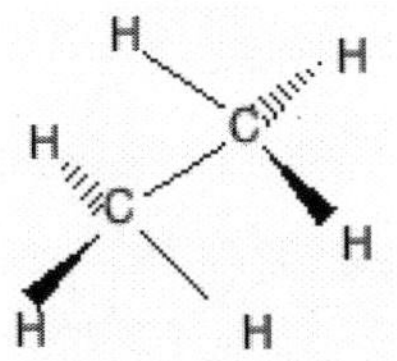

10.43   (a)   Four pairs of electrons give a tetrahedral electron geometry. The lone pair would cause lone pair–bonded pair repulsions and would have a trigonal pyramidal molecular geometry.

        (b)   Five pairs of electrons give a trigonal bipyramidal electron geometry. The lone pair occupies an equatorial position in order to minimize lone pair–bonded pair repulsions and the molecule would have a seesaw molecular geometry.

        (c)   Six pairs of electrons give an octahedral electron geometry. The two lone pairs would occupy opposite positions in order to minimize lone pair–lone pair repulsions. The molecular geometry would be square planar.

10.45   (a) CH_3OH Draw the Lewis structure and determine the geometry about each interior atom:

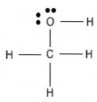

Sketch the molecule:

Atom	Number of Electron Groups	Number of Lone Pairs	Molecular Geometry
C	4	0	Tetrahedral
O	4	2	Bent

Sketch the molecule:

      (b) CH_3OCH_3 Draw the Lewis structure and determine the geometry about each interior atom:

Atom	Number of Electron Groups	Number of Lone Pairs	Molecular Geometry
C	4	0	Tetrahedral
O	4	2	Bent
C	4	0	Tetrahedral

Sketch the molecule:

(c) H_2O_2 Draw the Lewis structure and determine the geometry about each interior atom:

$$H — \overset{..}{\underset{..}{O}} — \overset{..}{\underset{..}{O}} — H$$

Atom	Number of Electron Groups	Number of Lone Pairs	Molecular Geometry
O	4	2	Bent
O	4	2	Bent

Sketch the molecule:

$$\underset{H}{\diagdown}\overset{\diagup}{O} — O\overset{\diagdown}{\underset{H}{}}$$

Molecular Shape and Polarity

10.47   Draw the Lewis structure for CO_2 and CCl_4 and determine the molecular geometry and then the polarity.

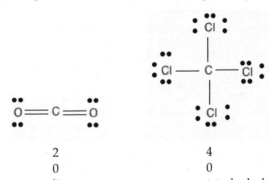

Number of electron groups on C	2	4
Number of lone pairs	0	0
Molecular geometry	linear	tetrahedral

Even though each molecule contains polar bonds, the sum of the bond dipoles gives a net dipole of zero for each molecule.
The linear molecular geometry of CO_2 will have bond vectors that are equal and opposite. $\longleftarrow \quad \longrightarrow$
The tetrahedral molecular geometry of CCl_4 will have bond vectors that are equal and have a net dipole of zero.

10.49   (a) PF_3 – polar

Draw the Lewis structure and determine the molecular geometry:
The molecular geometry from Exercise 35 is trigonal pyramidal.

Determine if the molecule contains polar bonds:
The electronegativities of P = 2.1 and F = 4. Therefore the bonds are polar.

Determine whether the polar bonds add together to form a net dipole:
Because the molecule is trigonal pyramidal, the three dipole moments sum to a nonzero net dipole moment. The molecule is polar. See Table 10.2 on page 381 in the text to see how dipole moments add to determine polarity.

(b) SBr_2 – nonpolar

Draw the Lewis structure and determine the molecular geometry:
The molecular geometry from Exercise 35 is bent.

Determine if the molecule contains polar bonds:
The electronegativities of S = 2.5 and Br = 2.8. Therefore the bonds are nonpolar.

Even though the molecule is bent, since the bonds are nonpolar, the molecule is nonpolar.

(c) $CHCl_3$ – polar

Draw the Lewis structure and determine the molecular geometry:
The molecular geometry from Exercise 35 is tetrahedral.

Determine if the molecule contains polar bonds:
The electronegativities of C = 2.5, H = 2.1, and Cl = 3.0. Therefore the bonds are polar.

Determine whether the polar bonds add together to form a net dipole:
Because the bonds have different dipole moments due to the different atoms involved, the four dipole moments sum to a nonzero net dipole moment. The molecule is polar. See Table 10.2 on page 381 in the text to see how dipole moments add to determine polarity.

(d) CS_2 – nonpolar

Draw the Lewis structure and determine the molecular geometry:
The molecular geometry from Exercise 35 is linear.

Determine if the molecule contains polar bonds:
The electronegativities of C = 2.5 and S = 2.5. Therefore the bonds are nonpolar. Also, the molecule is linear, which would result in a zero net dipole even if the bonds were polar.
The molecule is nonpolar. See Table 10.2 on page 381 in the text to see how dipole moments add to determine polarity.

10.51   (a) ClO_3^- – polar

Draw the Lewis structure and determine the molecular geometry:

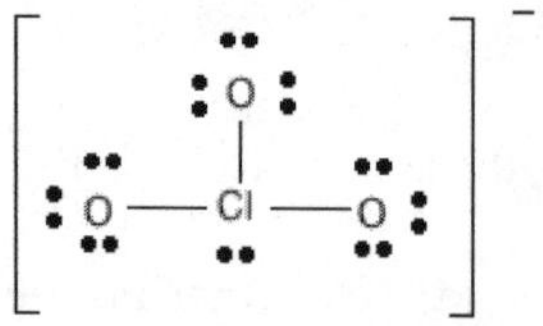

Four electron pairs with one lone pair give a trigonal pyramidal molecular geometry.

Determine if the molecule contains polar bonds:
The electronegativities of Cl = 3.0 and O = 3.5. Therefore the bonds are polar.

Determine whether the polar bonds add together to form a net dipole:
Because the molecular geometry is trigonal pyramidal, the three dipole moments sum to a nonzero net dipole moment. The molecule is polar. See Table 10.2 on page 381 in the text to see how dipole moments add to determine polarity.

(b) SCl_2 – polar

Draw the Lewis structure and determine the molecular geometry:

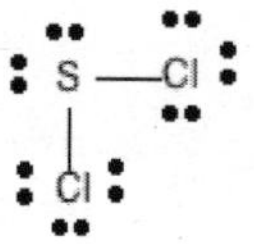

Four electron pairs with two lone pairs give a bent molecular geometry.

Determine if the molecule contains polar bonds:
The electronegativities of S = 2.5 and Cl = 3.0. Therefore the bonds are polar.

Determine whether the polar bonds add together to form a net dipole:
Because the molecular geometry is bent, the two dipole moments sum to a nonzero net dipole moment. The molecule is polar. See Table 10.2 on page 381 in the text to see how dipole moments add to determine polarity.

(c) SCl_4 – polar
Draw the Lewis structure and determine the molecular geometry:

Five electron pairs with one lone pair give a seesaw molecular geometry.

Determine if the molecule contains polar bonds:
The electronegativities of S = 2.5 and Cl = 3.0. Therefore the bonds are polar.

Determine whether the polar bonds add together to form a net dipole:
Because the molecular geometry is seesaw, the four equal dipole moments sum to a nonzero net dipole moment. The molecule is polar.
The seesaw molecular geometry will not have offsetting bond vectors.

(d) $BrCl_5$ – nonpolar
Draw the Lewis structure and determine the molecular geometry.

Six electron pairs with one lone pair give square pyramidal molecular geometry.

Determine if the molecule contains polar bonds:
The electronegativity of Br = 2.8 and Cl = 3.0. The difference is only 0.2, therefore the bonds are nonpolar. Even though the molecular geometry is square pyramidal, the five bonds are nonpolar so there is no net dipole. The molecule is nonpolar.

Valence Bond Theory

10.53   (a)   Be $2s^2$ No bonds can form. Beryllium contains no unpaired electrons, so no bonds can form without hybridization.

(b)   P $3s^2 3p^3$ Three bonds can form. Phosphorus contains three unpaired electrons, so three bonds can form without hybridization.

(c)   F $2s^2 2p^5$ One bond can form. Fluorine contains one unpaired electron, so one bond can form without hybridization.

10.55 PH$_3$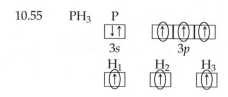

The unhybridized bond angles should be 90°. So, without hybridization, there is good agreement between valence bond theory and the actual bond angle of 93.3°.

10.57 C $2s^2 2p^2$

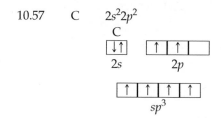

10.59 Both sp^2 and sp hybridization allow the formation of at least one π bond.

10.61 (a) CCl$_4$ Write the Lewis structure for the molecule:

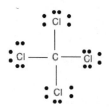

Use VSEPR to predict the electron geometry:
Four electron groups around the central atom give a tetrahedral electron geometry.

Select the correct hybridization for the central atom based on the electron geometry:
Tetrahedral electron geometry has sp^3 hybridization.

Sketch the molecule and label the bonds:

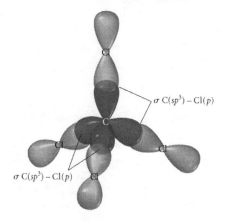

(b) NH_3 Write the Lewis structure for the molecule:

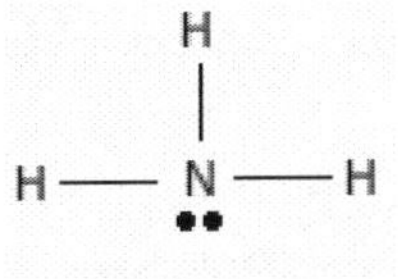

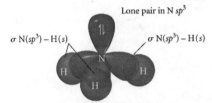

Use VSEPR to predict the electron geometry:
Four electron groups around the central atom give a tetrahedral electron geometry.

Select the correct hybridization for the central atom based on the electron geometry:
Tetrahedral electron geometry has sp^3 hybridization.

Sketch the molecule and label the bonds:

Lone pair in N sp^3

$\sigma\ N(sp^3) - H(s)$ $\sigma\ N(sp^3) - H(s)$

(c) OF_2 Write the Lewis structure for the molecule:

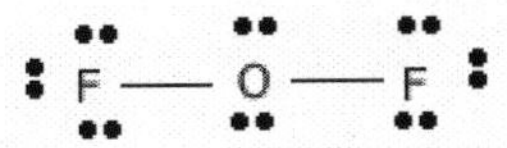

Use VSEPR to predict the electron geometry:
Four electron groups around the central atom give a tetrahedral electron geometry.

Select the correct hybridization for the central atom based on the electron geometry:
Tetrahedral electron geometry has sp^3 hybridization.

Sketch the molecule and label the bonds:

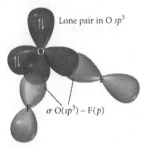

Lone pair in O sp^3

$\sigma\ O(sp^3) - F(p)$

(d) CO_2 Write the Lewis structure for the molecule:

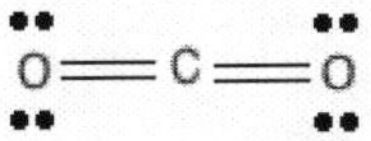

Use VSEPR to predict the electron geometry:
Two electron groups around the central atom give a linear electron geometry.

Select the correct hybridization for the central atom based on the electron geometry:
Linear electron geometry has sp hybridization.

Sketch the molecule and label the bonds:

$\pi\ C(p_y) - O(p_y)$ $\pi\ C(p_z) - O(p_z)$

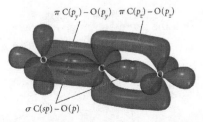

$\sigma\ C(sp) - O(p)$

10.63   (a) $COCl_2$ Write the Lewis structure for the molecule:

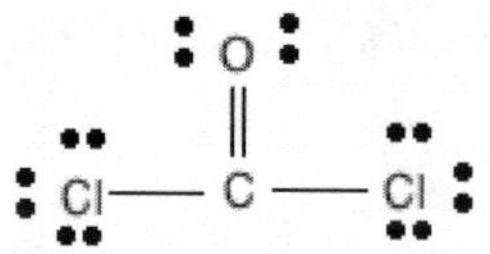

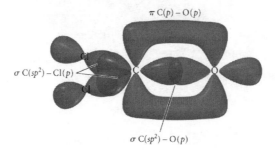

Use VSEPR to predict the electron geometry:
Three electron groups around the central atom give a trigonal planar electron geometry.

Select the correct hybridization for the central atom based on the electron geometry:
Trigonal planar electron geometry has sp^2 hybridization.

Sketch the molecule and label the bonds:

$\pi \; C(p) - O(p)$

$\sigma \; C(sp^2) - Cl(p)$

$\sigma \; C(sp^2) - O(p)$

(b) NH_2^- Write the Lewis structure for the molecule:

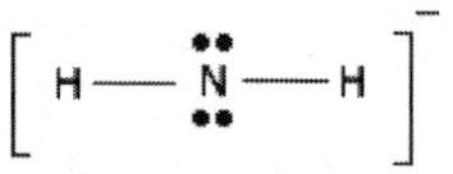

$$\left[H - \overset{\displaystyle ..}{\underset{\displaystyle ..}{N}} - H \right]^-$$

Use VSEPR to predict the electron geometry:
Four electron groups around the central atom give a tetrahedral electron geometry.

Select the correct hybridization for the central atom based on the electron geometry:
Tetrahedral electron geometry has sp^3 hybridization.

Sketch the molecule and label the bonds:

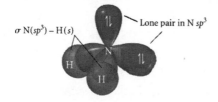

$\sigma \; N(sp^3) - H(s)$

Lone pair in N sp^3

(c) CO_3^{2-} Write the Lewis structure for the molecule:

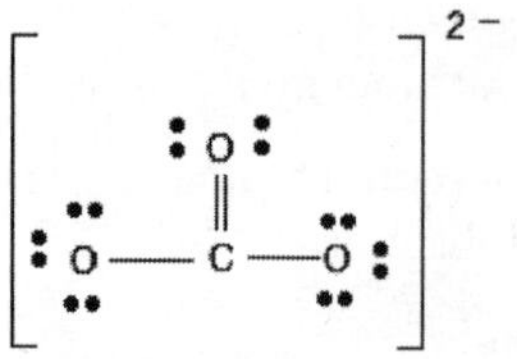

$$\left[\begin{array}{c} :\overset{..}{O}: \\ \| \\ :\overset{..}{O} - C - \overset{..}{O}: \end{array} \right]^{2-}$$

Use VSEPR to predict the electron geometry:
Three electron groups around the central atom give a trigonal planar electron geometry.

Select the correct hybridization for the central atom based on the electron geometry:
Trigonal planar electron geometry has sp^2 hybridization.

Sketch the molecule and label the bonds:

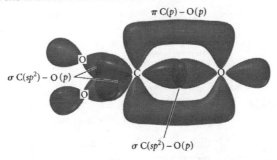

10.65   (a) N_2H_2 Write the Lewis structure for the molecule:

$$H \!-\! \overset{\bullet\bullet}{N} \!=\! \overset{\bullet\bullet}{N} \!-\! H$$

Use VSEPR to predict the electron geometry:
Three electron groups around each interior atom give a trigonal planar electron geometry.

Select the correct hybridization for the central atoms based on the electron geometry:
Trigonal planar electron geometry has sp^2 hybridization.

Sketch the molecule and label the bonds:

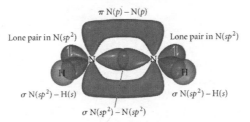

(b) N_2H_4 Write the Lewis structure for the molecule:

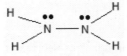

Use VSEPR to predict the electron geometry:
Four electron groups around each interior atom gives tetrahedral electron geometry.

Select the correct hybridization for the central atoms based on the electron geometry:
Tetrahedral electron geometry has sp^3 hybridization.

Sketch the molecule and label the bonds:

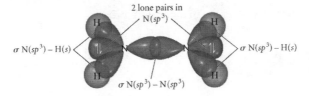

(c) CH_3NH_2 Write the Lewis structure for the molecule:

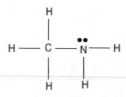

Use VSEPR to predict the electron geometry:
Four electron groups around the C give a tetrahedral electron geometry around the C atom, and four electron groups around the N give a tetrahedral geometry around the N atom.

Select the correct hybridization for the central atoms based on the electron geometry:
Tetrahedral electron geometry has sp^3 hybridization of both C and N.

Sketch the molecule and label the bonds:

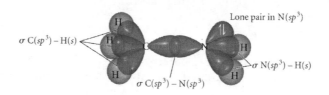

10.67

C – 1 and C – 2 each have four electron pairs around the atom, which is tetrahedral electron pair geometry. Tetrahedral electron pair geometry is sp^3 hybridization.
C – 3 has three electron groups around the atom, which is trigonal planar electron pair geometry. Trigonal planar electron pair geometry is sp^2 hybridization.
O has four electron pairs around the atom, which is tetrahedral electron pair geometry. Tetrahedral electron pair geometry is sp^3 hybridization.
N has four electron pairs around the atom, which is tetrahedral electron pair geometry. Tetrahedral electron pair geometry is sp^3 hybridization.

Molecular Orbital Theory

10.69 $1s + 1s$ constructive interference results in a bonding orbital:

10.71 Be_2^+ has seven electrons. Be_2^- has nine electrons.

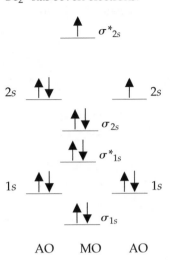

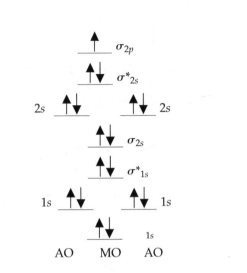

AO = Atomic Orbital; MO = Molecular Orbital

Bond order $= \dfrac{4-3}{2} = \dfrac{1}{2}$ stable   Bond order $= \dfrac{5-4}{2} = \dfrac{1}{2}$ stable

10.73   The bonding and antibonding molecular orbitals from the combination of p_z and p_z atomic orbitals lie along the internuclear axis.

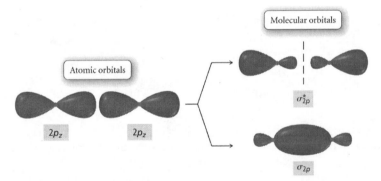

10.75   (a) 4 valence electrons   (b) 6 valence electrons   (c) 8 valence electrons   (d) 9 valence electrons

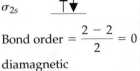   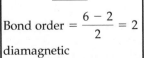   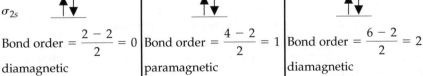   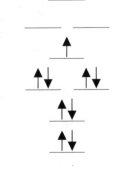

Bond order $= \dfrac{2-2}{2} = 0$ Bond order $= \dfrac{4-2}{2} = 1$ Bond order $= \dfrac{6-2}{2} = 2$

diamagnetic   paramagnetic   diamagnetic   paramagnetic

10.77   (a)   Write an energy level diagram for the molecular orbitals in H_2^{2-}. The ion has four valence electrons. Assign the electrons to the molecular orbitals beginning with the lowest energy orbitals and following Hund's rule.

σ^*_{1s} ↑↓

σ_{1s} ↑↓   Bond order $= \dfrac{2-2}{2} = 0.$ With a bond order of 0, the ion will not exist.

(b)   Write an energy level diagram for the molecular orbitals in Ne_2. The molecule has 16 valence electrons. Assign the electrons to the molecular orbitals beginning with the lowest energy orbitals and following Hund's rule.

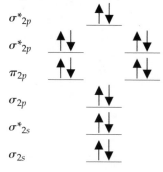

σ^*_{2p} ↑↓

σ^*_{2p} ↑↓   ↑↓

π_{2p} ↑↓   ↑↓

σ_{2p} ↑↓

σ^*_{2s} ↑↓

σ_{2s} ↑↓

Bond order $= \dfrac{8-8}{2} = 0.$ With a bond order of 0, the molecule will not exist.

(c)   Write an energy level diagram for the molecular orbitals in He_2^{2+}. The ion has two valence electrons. Assign the electrons to the molecular orbitals beginning with the lowest energy orbitals and following Hund's rule.

σ^*_{1s} _____

σ_{1s} ↑↓

Bond order $= \dfrac{2-0}{2} = 1.$ With a bond order of 1, the ion will exist.

(d)   Write an energy level diagram for the molecular orbitals in F_2^{2-}. The molecule has 16 valence electrons. Assign the electrons to the molecular orbitals beginning with the lowest energy orbitals and following Hund's rule.

σ^*_{2p} ↑↓

σ^*_{2p} ↑↓   ↑↓

π_{2p} ↑↓   ↑↓

σ_{2p} ↑↓

σ^*_{2s} ↑↓

σ_{2s} ↑↓

Bond order $= \dfrac{8-8}{2} = 0.$ With a bond order of 0, the ion will not exist.

10.79 C_2^- has the highest bond order, the highest bond energy, and the shortest bond.

Write an energy level diagram for the molecular orbitals in each of the C_2 species.

Assign the electrons to the molecular orbitals beginning with the lowest energy orbitals and following Hund's rule for each of the species.

C_2 (8 valence electrons); C_2^+ (7 valence electrons): C_2^- (9 valence electrons)

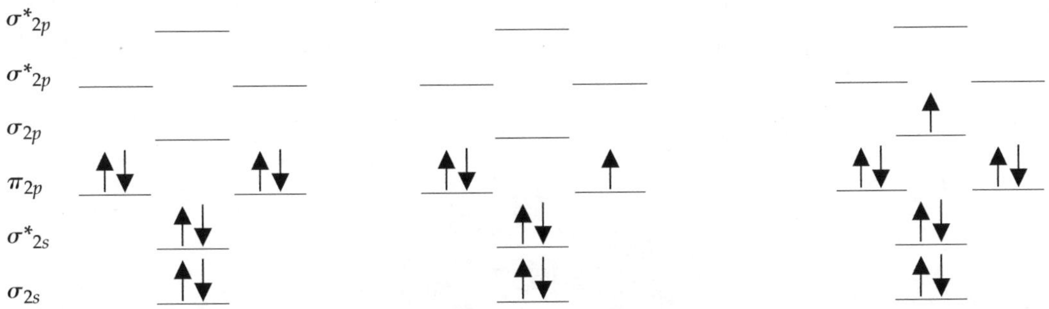

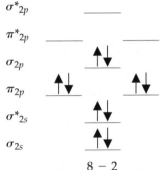

$$\text{Bond order} = \frac{6-2}{2} = 2 \qquad \text{Bond order} = \frac{5-2}{2} = 1.5 \qquad \text{Bond order} = \frac{7-2}{2} = 2.5$$

C_2^- has the highest bond order at 2.5. Bond order is directly related to bond energy, so C_2^- has the largest bond energy and bond order is inversely related to bond length, so C_2^- has the shortest bond length.

10.81   Write an energy level diagram for the molecular orbitals in CO using N_2 energy ordering.
Assign the electrons to the molecular orbitals beginning with the lowest energy orbitals and following Hund's rule.
CO has 10 valence electrons.

$$\text{Bond order} = \frac{8-2}{2} = 3$$

The electron density is toward the O atom since it is more electronegative.

Cumulative Problems

10.83   (a) COF_2 Write the Lewis structure for the molecule:

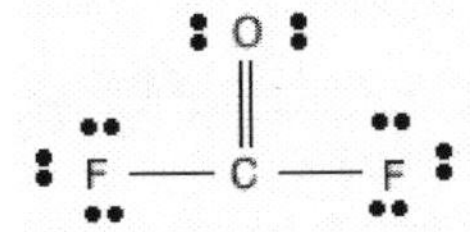

Use VSEPR to predict the electron geometry:
Three electron groups around the central atom give a trigonal planar electron geometry. Three bonding pairs of electrons give a trigonal planar molecular geometry.

Determine if the molecule contains polar bonds:
The electronegativities of C = 2.5, O = 3.5, and F = 4.0 Therefore the bonds are polar.

Determine whether the polar bonds add together to form a net dipole:
Even though a trigonal planar molecular geometry normally is nonpolar, because the bonds have different dipole moments, the sum of the dipole moments is not zero. The molecule is polar. See Table 10.2 on page 381 in the text to see how dipole moments add to determine polarity.

Select the correct hybridization for the central atom based on the electron geometry:
Trigonal planar geometry has sp^2 hybridization.

Sketch the molecule and label the bonds:

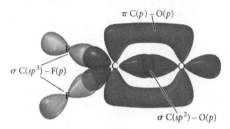

(b) S_2Cl_2 Write the Lewis structure for the molecule:

$$:\!\ddot{Cl} - \ddot{S} - \ddot{S} - \ddot{Cl}:$$

Use VSEPR to predict the electron geometry:
Four electron groups around the central atom give a tetrahedral electron geometry. Two bonding pairs and two lone pairs of electrons give a bent molecular geometry.

Determine if the molecule contains polar bonds:
The electronegativities of S = 2.5 and Cl = 3.0. Therefore the bonds are polar.

Determine whether the polar bonds add together to form a net dipole:
In a bent molecular geometry the sum of the dipole moments is not zero. The molecule is polar. See Table 10.2 on page 381 in the text to see how dipole moments add to determine polarity.

Select the correct hybridization for the central atom based on the electron geometry:
Tetrahedral geometry has sp^3 hybridization.

Sketch the molecule and label the bonds:

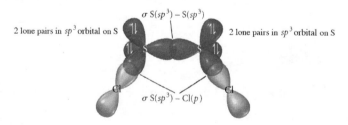

10.85   (a)   serine

C – 1 and C – 3 each have four electron groups around the atom. Four electron pairs give a tetrahedral electron geometry; tetrahedral electron geometry has sp^3 hybridization. Four bonding pairs and zero lone pairs give a tetrahedral molecular geometry.

C – 2 has three electron groups around the atom. Three electron pairs give a trigonal planar geometry; trigonal planar geometry has sp^2 hybridization. Three bonding pairs and zero lone pairs give a trigonal planar molecular geometry.

N has four electron groups around the atom. Four electron pairs give a tetrahedral electron geometry; tetrahedral electron geometry has sp^3 hybridization. Three bonding pairs and one lone pair give a trigonal pyramidal molecular geometry.

O – 1 and O – 2 each have four electron groups around the atom. Four electron pairs give a tetrahedral electron geometry; tetrahedral electron geometry has sp^3 hybridization. Two bonding pairs and two lone pairs give a bent molecular geometry.

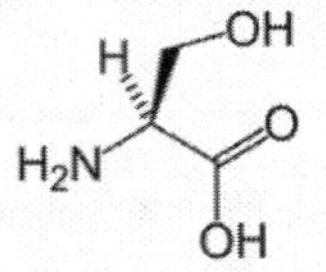

(b)   asparagine

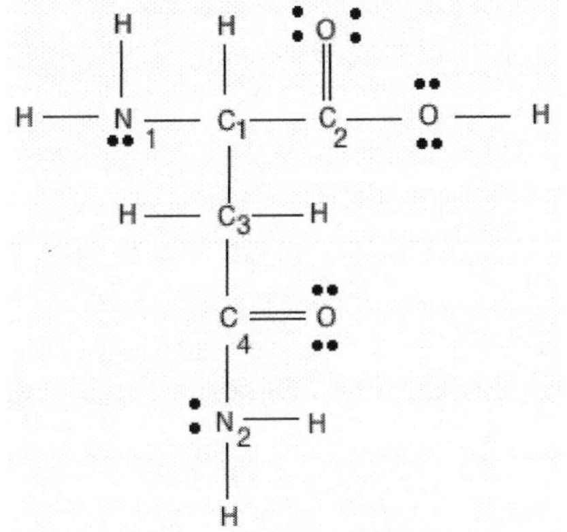

C – 1 and C – 3 each have four electron groups around the atom. Four electron groups give a tetrahedral electron geometry; tetrahedral electron geometry has sp^3 hybridization. Four bonding groups and zero lone pairs give a tetrahedral molecular geometry.

C – 2 and C – 4 each have three electron groups around the atom. Three electron groups give a trigonal planar geometry; trigonal planar geometry has sp^2 hybridization. Three bonding pairs and zero lone groups give a trigonal planar molecular geometry.

N – 1 and N – 2 each have four electron groups around the atom. Four electron groups give a tetrahedral electron geometry; tetrahedral electron geometry has sp^3 hybridization. Three bonding groups and one lone pair give a trigonal pyramidal molecular geometry.

O has four electron groups around the atom. Four electron groups give a tetrahedral electron geometry; tetrahedral electron geometry has sp^3 hybridization. Two bonding groups and two lone pairs give a bent molecular geometry.

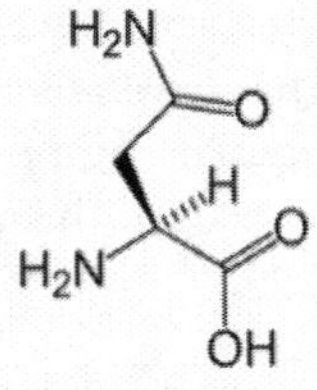

(c)   cysteine

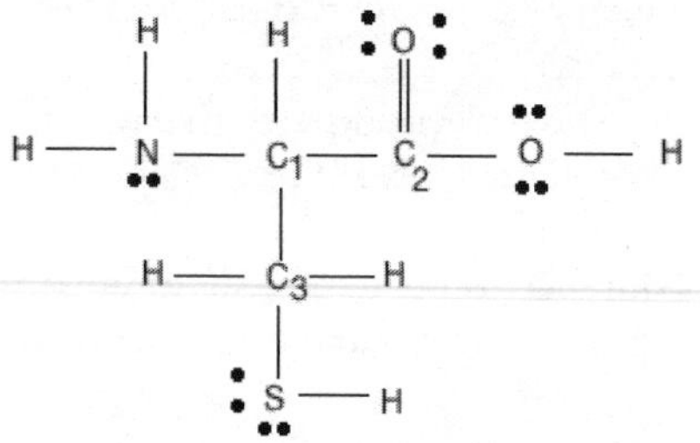

C – 1 and C – 3 each have four electron groups around the atom. Four electron pairs give a tetrahedral electron geometry; tetrahedral electron geometry has sp^3 hybridization. Four bonding pairs and zero lone pairs give a tetrahedral molecular geometry.

C – 2 has three electron groups around the atom. Three electron groups give a trigonal planar geometry; trigonal planar geometry has sp^2 hybridization. Three bonding groups and zero lone pairs give a trigonal planar molecular geometry.

N has four electron groups around the atom. Four electron groups give a tetrahedral electron geometry; tetrahedral electron geometry has sp^3 hybridization. Three bonding groups and one lone pair give a trigonal pyramidal molecular geometry.

O and S have four electron groups around the atom. Four electron groups give a tetrahedral electron geometry; tetrahedral electron geometry has sp^3 hybridization. Two bonding groups and two lone pairs give a bent molecular geometry.

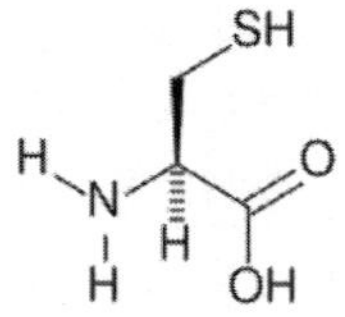

10.87   4 π bonds; 25 σ bonds; the lone pair on the Os and N – 2 occupy sp^2 orbitals; the lone pairs on N – 1, N – 3, and N – 4 occupy sp^3 orbitals.

caffeine

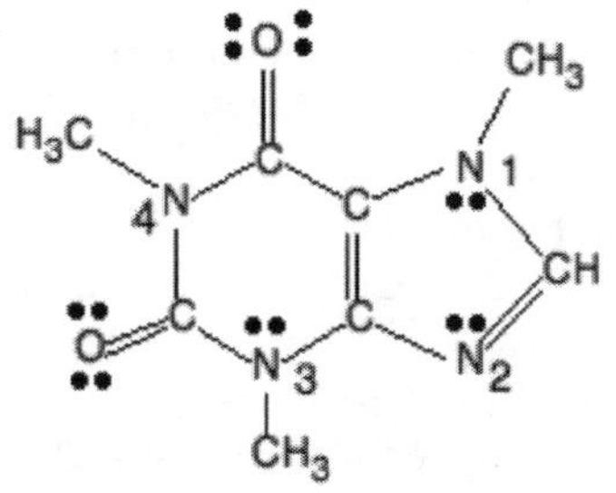

10.89   (a)   Water soluble: The 4 C – OH bonds, the C = O bond, and the C – O bonds in the ring make the molecule polar. Because of the large electronegativity difference between the C and O, each of the bonds will have a dipole moment. The sum of the dipole moments does NOT give a net zero dipole moment, so the molecule is polar. Since it is polar, it will be water soluble.

            (b)   Fat soluble: There is only one C – O bond in the molecule. The dipole moment from this bond is not enough to make the molecule polar because of all of the nonpolar components of the molecule. The C – H bonds in the structure lead to a net dipole of zero for most of the sites in the molecule. Since the molecule is nonpolar, it is fat soluble.

            (c)   Water soluble: The carboxylic acid function (COOH group) along with the N atom in the ring make the molecule polar. Because of the electronegativity difference between the C and O and the C and N atoms, the bonds will have a dipole moment and the net dipole moment of the molecule is NOT zero, so the molecule is polar. Since the molecule is polar, it is water soluble.

(d)   Fat soluble: The two O atoms in the structure contribute a very small amount to the net dipole moment of this molecule. The majority of the molecule is nonpolar because there is no net dipole moment at the interior C atoms. Because the molecule is nonpolar it is fat soluble.

10.91   ClF has 14 valence electrons. Assign the electrons to the lowest energy MOs first and then follow Hund's rule. The MOs are formed from the $2s$ and $2p$ orbitals on F and the $3s$ and $3p$ orbitals on Cl.

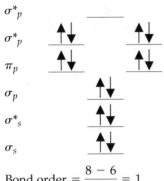

Bond order $= \dfrac{8 - 6}{2} = 1$

10.93   BrF (14 valence electrons)

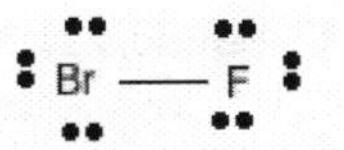

:Br —— F:

no central atom, no hybridization, no electron structure

BrF$_2^-$ (22 valence electrons)

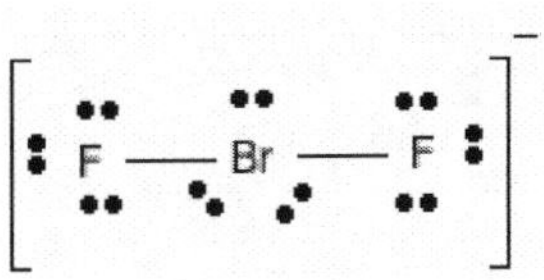

[:F —— Br —— F:]$^-$

There are five electron pairs on the central atom so the electron geometry is trigonal bipyramidal. The two bonding pairs and three lone pairs give a linear molecular geometry. An electron geometry of trigonal bipyramidal has sp^3d hybridization.

BrF$_3$ (28 valence electrons)

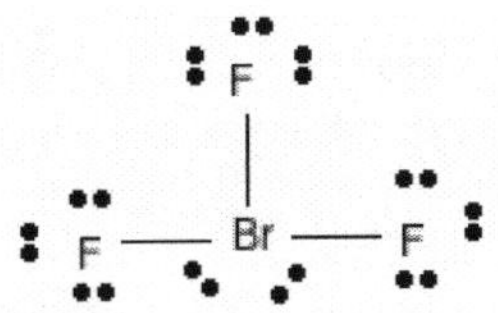

:F:
|
:F —— Br —— F:

There are five electron pairs on the central atom so the electron geometry is trigonal bipyramidal. The three bonding pairs and two lone pairs give a T-shaped molecular geometry. An electron geometry of trigonal bipyramidal has sp^3d hybridization.

BrF$_4^-$ (36 valence electrons)

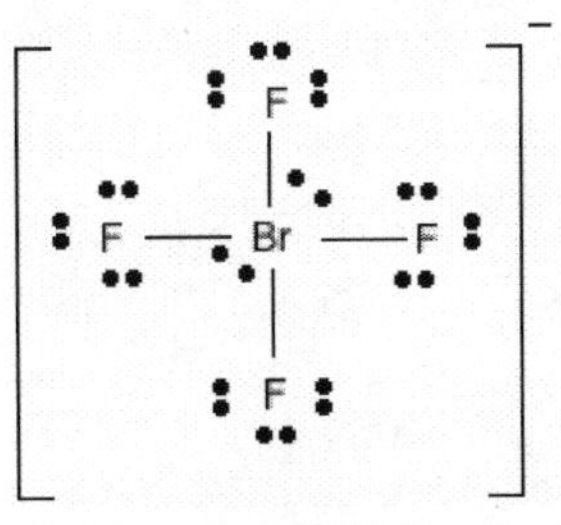

[:F:
|
:F —— Br —— F:
|
:F:]$^-$

There are six electron pairs on the central atom so the electron geometry is octahedral. The four bonding pairs and two lone pairs give a square planar molecular geometry. An electron geometry of octahedral has sp^3d^2 hybridization.

BrF$_5$ (42 valence electrons)

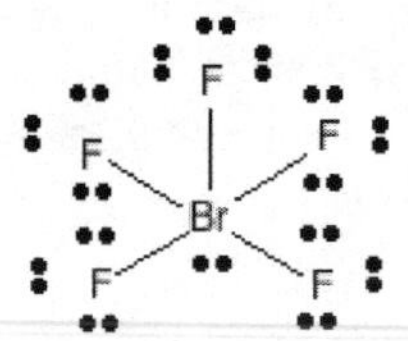

> There are six electron pairs on the central atom so the electron geometry is octahedral. The five bonding pairs and one lone pair give a square pyramidal molecular geometry. An electron geometry of octahedral has sp^3d^2 hybridization.

10.95   Draw the Lewis structure: C$_4$H$_6$Cl$_2$ (36 valence electrons)

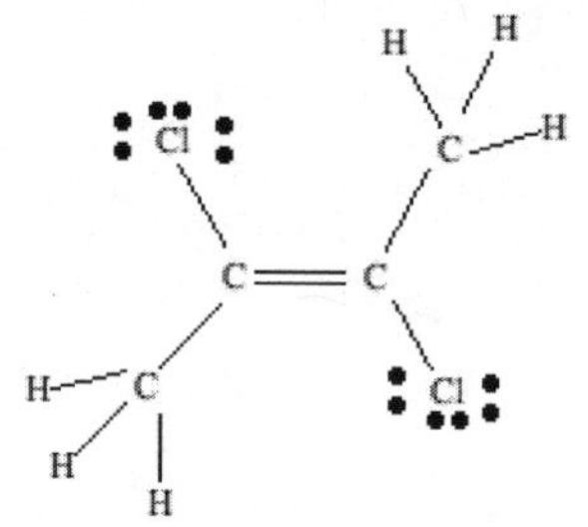

Even though the C – Cl bonds are polar, the net dipole will since the C – Cl bonds and the C – CH$_3$ bonds are on opposite sides of the double bond. This will result in bond vectors that cancel each other.

10.97   (a)   N$_2$O$_5$ Draw the Lewis structure: (40 valence electrons)

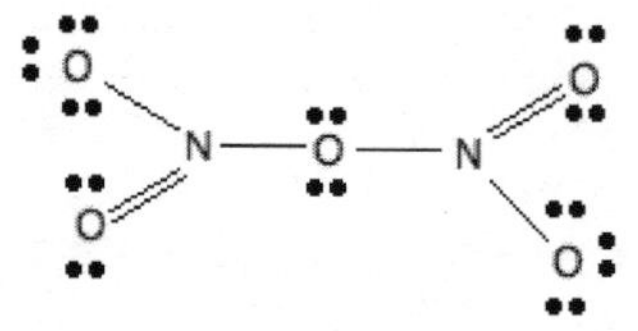

> Each N has a trigonal planar electron geometry so there are three sp^2 hybrid orbitals on each N. The central O has tetrahedral electron geometry, so there are four sp^3 hybrid orbitals. There are a total of 10 hybrid orbitals.

(b)   C$_2$H$_5$NO Draw the Lewis structure: (24 valence electrons)

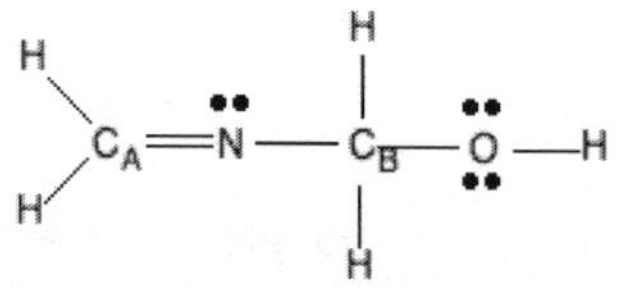

> C$_A$ has a trigonal planar electron geometry, so there are three sp^2 hybrid orbitals.
> N has a trigonal planar electron geometry, so there are three sp^2 hybrid orbitals.
> C$_B$ has a tetrahedral electron geometry, so there are four sp^3 hybrid orbitals.
> O has a tetrahedral electron geometry, so there are four sp^3 hybrid orbitals.
> There are a total of 14 hybrid orbitals.

(c)   BrCN   Draw the Lewis structure: (16 valence electrons)

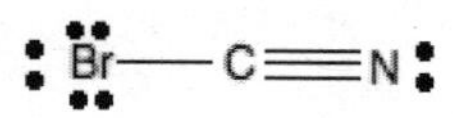

> The C has linear electron geometry, so there are two sp hybrid orbitals.

Challenge Problems

10.99   According to valence bond theory, CH_4, NH_3, and H_2O are all sp^3 hybridized. This hybridization results in a tetrahedral electron group configuration with a 109.5° bond angle. NH_3 and H_2O deviate from this idealized bond angle because their lone electron pairs exist in their own sp^3 orbitals. The presence of lone pairs lowers the tendency for the central atom's orbitals to hybridize. As a result, as lone pairs are added, the bond angle moves from the 109.5° hybrid angle toward the 90° unhybridized angle.

10.101   Using the MO diagram for NH_3 assign the eight valence electrons to the molecular orbitals. Start with the lowest energy orbital first and follow Hund's rule.

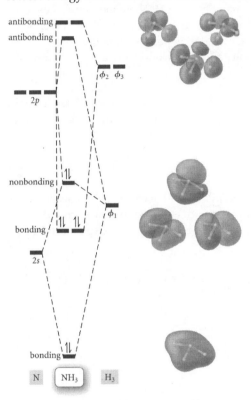

Bond order $= \dfrac{6 - 0}{2} = 3$.

With a bond order of 3, the molecule is stable.

10.103   For each, write the Lewis structure.
Determine electron pair geometry around each central atom.
Determine the molecular geometry, determine idealized bond angles, and predict actual bond angles.

NO_2

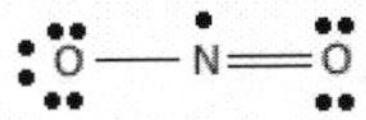

Two bonding groups and a lone electron give a trigonal planar electron geometry; the molecular geometry will be bent. Trigonal planar electron geometry has idealized bond angles of 120°. The bond angle is expected to be slightly less than 120° because of the lone electron occupying the third sp^2 orbital.

$NO_2{}^+$

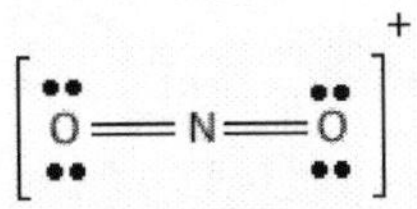

Two bonding groups of electrons and no lone pairs give a linear electron geometry and molecular geometry. Linear electron geometry has a bond angle of 180°.

NO_2^-

Two bonding groups of electrons and one lone pair give a trigonal planar electron geometry; the molecular geometry will be bent.

Trigonal planar electron geometry has idealized bond angles of 120°. The bond angle is expected to be less than 120° because of the lone-pair electrons occupying the third sp^2 orbital. Further, the bond angle should be less than the bond angle in NO_2 because the presence of lone pairs lowers the tendency for the central atom's orbitals to hybridize. As a result, as lone pairs are added, the bond angle moves further from the 120° hybrid angle to the 90° unhybridized angle and the two electrons will increase this tendency.

10.105   Both VSEPR theory and hybridization would predict a bond angle of 180°. However, gaseous BaF_2 has a bond angle of 108°. This may be because the $5d$ orbitals are very close in energy to the $6s$ orbitals on the Ba. Thus, these may contribute to the bonding scheme rather than the $6p$ orbitals.

Conceptual Problems

10.107   A molecule with four bond groups and one lone pair would need five equivalent positions around the central atom. In two dimensions, this could be accommodated with a pentagon shape around the central atom. The idealized bond angles would be 72°; however, because of the lone pair occupying one of the positions, the bond angles would be less than 72°.

11 Liquids, Solids, and Intermolecular Forces

Review Questions

11.1   The key to the gecko's sticky feet lies in the millions of microhairs, called setae, that line its toes. Each seta is between 30 and 130 μm long and branches out to end in several hundred flattened tips called spatulae. This unique structure allows the gecko's toes to have unusually close contact with the surfaces it climbs. The close contact allows intermolecular forces—which are significant only at short distances—to hold the gecko to the wall.

11.3   The main properties of liquids are that liquids have much higher densities in comparison to gases and generally have lower densities in comparison to solids; liquids have an indefinite shape and assume the shape of their container; liquids have a definite volume; and liquids are not easily compressed.

11.5   Solids may be crystalline, in which case the atoms or molecules that compose them are arranged in a well-ordered three-dimensional array, or they may be amorphous, in which case the atoms or molecules that compose them have no long-range order.

11.7   Since there is the most molecular motion in the gas phase and the least molecular motion in the solid phase (atoms are pushed closer together), a substance will be converted from a solid then to a liquid and finally to a gas as the temperature increases. The strength of the intermolecular interactions is least in the gas phase, since there are large distances between particles and they are moving very fast. Intermolecular forces are stronger in liquids and solids, where molecules are "touching" one another. The strength of the interactions in the condensed phases will determine at what temperature the substance will melt and boil.

11.9   Intermolecular forces, even the strongest ones, are generally much weaker than bonding forces. The reason for the relative weakness of intermolecular forces compared to bonding forces is related to Coulomb's law $\left(E = \dfrac{1}{4\pi\epsilon_o} \dfrac{q_1 q_2}{r} \right)$. Bonding forces are the result of large charges (the charges on protons and electrons, q_1 and q_2) interacting at very close distances (r). Intermolecular forces are the result of smaller charges interacting at greater distances.

11.11   The dipole–dipole force exists in all molecules that are polar. Polar molecules have permanent dipoles that interact with the permanent dipoles of neighbouring molecules. The positive end of one permanent dipole is attracted to the negative end of another; this attraction is the dipole–dipole force.

11.13   The hydrogen bond is a sort of super dipole–dipole force. Polar molecules containing hydrogen atoms bonded directly to fluorine, oxygen, or nitrogen exhibit an intermolecular force called hydrogen bonding. The large electronegativity difference between hydrogen and these electronegative elements means that the H atoms will have fairly large partial positive charges (δ+), while the F, O, or N atoms will have fairly large partial negative charges (δ-). In addition, since these atoms are all quite small, they can approach one another very closely. The result is a strong attraction between the hydrogen in each of these molecules and the F, O, or N on its neighbours, an attraction called a hydrogen bond.

11.15   Surface tension is the tendency of liquids to minimize their surface area. Molecules at the surface have relatively fewer neighbours with which to interact, because there are no molecules above the surface. Consequently, molecules at the surface are inherently less stable—they have higher potential energy—than those in the interior. In order to increase the surface area of the liquid, some molecules from the interior have to be moved to the surface, a process requiring energy. The surface tension of a liquid is the energy required to increase the surface area by a unit amount. Surface tension decreases with decreasing intermolecular forces.

11.17   Capillary action is the ability of a liquid to flow against gravity up a narrow tube. Capillary action results from a combination of two forces: the attraction between molecules in a liquid, called cohesive forces, and the attraction between these molecules and the surface of the tube, called adhesive forces. The adhesive forces cause the liquid to spread out over the surface of the tube, while the cohesive forces cause the liquid to stay together. If the adhesive forces are greater than the cohesive forces (as is the case for water in a glass tube), the attraction to the surface draws the liquid up the tube while the cohesive forces pull along those molecules not in direct contact with the tube walls. The liquid rises up the tube until the force of gravity balances the capillary action—the thinner the tube, the higher the rise. If the adhesive forces are smaller than the cohesive forces (as is the case for liquid mercury), the liquid does not rise up the tube at all (and in fact will drop to a level below the level of the surrounding liquid).

11.19   The molecules that leave the liquid are the ones at the high end of the energy curve—the most energetic. If no additional heat enters the liquid, the average energy of the entire collection of molecules goes down—much as the class average on an exam goes down if you eliminate the highest-scoring students. So vaporization is an endothermic process; it takes energy to vaporize the molecules in a liquid. Also, vaporization requires overcoming the intermolecular forces that hold liquids together. Since energy must be absorbed to pull the molecules apart, the process is endothermic. Condensation is the opposite process, so it must be exothermic. Also, gas particles have more energy than those in the liquid. It is the least energetic of these that condense, adding energy to the liquid.

11.21   The heat of vaporization ($\Delta_{vap}H$) is the amount of heat required to vaporize one mole of a liquid to a gas. The heat of vaporization of a liquid can be used to calculate the amount of heat energy required to vaporize a given mass of the liquid (or the amount of heat given off by the condensation of a given mass of liquid), and can be used to compare the volatility of two substances.

11.23   When a system in dynamic equilibrium is disturbed, the system responds so as to minimize the disturbance and return to a state of equilibrium.

11.25   The boiling point of a liquid is the temperature at which its vapour pressure equals the external pressure. The normal boiling point of a liquid is the temperature at which its vapour pressure equals 1.01325 bar (= 1 atm = 760 Torr). The standard boiling point of a liquid is the temperature at which its vapour pressure equals 1 bar.

11.27   As the temperature rises, more liquid vaporizes and the pressure within the container increases. As more and more gas is forced into the same amount of space, the density of the gas becomes higher and higher. At the same time, the increasing temperature causes the density of the liquid to become lower and lower. At the critical temperature, the meniscus between the liquid and gas disappears and the gas and liquid phases commingle to form a supercritical fluid.

11.29   Fusion, or melting, is the phase transition from solid to liquid. The term fusion is used for melting because, if you heat several crystals of a solid, they will fuse into a continuous liquid upon melting. Fusion is endothermic because solids have less kinetic energy than liquids, so energy must be added to a solid to get it to melt.

11.31   There are two horizontal lines (i.e., heat is added, but the temperature stays constant) in the heating curve because there are two endothermic phase changes. The heat that is added is used to change the phase from solid to liquid or liquid to gas.

11.33   A phase diagram is simply a map of the phase of a substance as a function of pressure (on the y-axis) and temperature (on the x-axis).

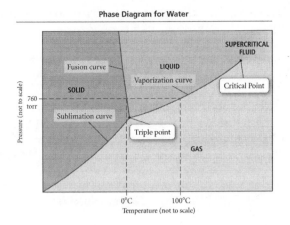

Phase Diagram for Water

11.35   Water has only a few electrons, so it is not very polarizable, yet it is a liquid at room temperature. Water's high boiling point can be understood by examining the structure of the water molecule. The bent geometry of the water molecule and the highly polar nature of the O–H bonds result in a molecule with a significant dipole moment. Water's two O–H bonds (hydrogen directly bonded to oxygen) allow a water molecule to form strong hydrogen bonds with four other water molecules, resulting in a relatively high boiling point. Water's high polarity also allows it to dissolve many other polar and ionic compounds, and even a number of nonpolar gases such as oxygen and carbon dioxide (by inducing a dipole moment in their molecules). Water has an exceptionally high specific heat capacity. One significant difference between the phase diagram of water and that of other substances is that the fusion curve for water has a negative slope. The fusion curve within the phase diagrams for most substances has a positive slope because increasing pressure favours the denser phase, which for most substances is the solid phase. This negative slope means that ice is less dense than liquid water, and so ice floats. The solid phase sinks in the liquid of most other substances.

11.37   A crystalline lattice is the regular arrangements of atoms within a crystalline solid. The crystalline lattice can be represented by a small collection of atoms, ions, or molecules—a fundamental building block called the unit cell. When the unit cell is repeated over and over—like tiles in a floor or the pattern in a wallpaper design, but in three dimensions—the entire lattice can be reproduced.

11.39   Atoms in a simple cubic cell structure have a coordination number of 6, an edge length of $2r$, and 1 atom in the unit cell. Atoms in a body-centred cubic cell structure have a coordination number of 8, an edge length of $4r/\sqrt{3}$, and 2 atoms in the unit cell. Atoms in a face-centred cubic cell structure have a coordination number of 12, an edge length of $2\sqrt{2}r$, and 4 atoms in the unit cell.

11.41   The three types of solids are molecular solids, ionic solids, and atomic solids. Molecular solids are those solids whose composite units are molecules. The lattice sites in a crystalline molecular solid are therefore occupied by molecules. Ice (solid H_2O) and dry ice (solid CO_2) are examples of molecular solids. Molecular solids are held together by the kinds of intermolecular forces—dispersion forces, dipole–dipole forces, and hydrogen bonding. Ionic solids are those solids whose composite units are ions. Table salt (NaCl) and calcium fluoride (CaF_2) are good examples of ionic solids. Ionic solids are held together by the coulombic interactions that occur between the cations and anions occupying the lattice sites in the crystal, which is an ionic bond. Atomic solids are those solids whose composite units are individual atoms. Atomic solids can themselves be divided into three categories—nonbonding atomic solids, metallic atomic solids, and network covalent atomic solids—each held together by a different kind of force. Nonbonding atomic solids, which include only the noble gases in their solid form, are held together by relatively weak dispersion forces. Metallic atomic solids, such as iron or gold, are held together by metallic bonds, which in the simplest model are represented by the interaction of metal cations with a sea of electrons that surround them. Network covalent atomic solids, such as diamond, graphite, and silicon dioxide, are held together by covalent bonds.

11.43   Cesium chloride (CsCl) is a good example of an ionic compound containing cations and anions of similar size (Cs^+ radius = 167 pm; Cl^- radius = 181 pm). In the cesium chloride structure, the chloride ions occupy the lattice sites of a simple cubic cell and one cesium ion lies in the very centre of the cell, as shown in Figure 11.54. Notice that the cesium chloride unit cell contains one chloride anion ($8 \times 1/8 = 1$) and one cesium cation (the cesium ion in the middle belongs entirely to the unit cell) for a ratio of Cs to Cl of 1:1, just as in the formula for the compound.

The crystal structure of sodium chloride must accommodate the more disproportionate sizes of Na^+ (radius = 97 pm) and Cl^- (radius = 181 pm). The larger chloride anion could theoretically fit many of the smaller sodium cations around it, but charge neutrality requires that each sodium cation be surrounded by an equal number of chloride anions. The structure that minimizes the energy is shown in Figure 11.55 and has a coordination number of 6 (each chloride anion is surrounded by six sodium cations and vice versa). You can visualize this structure, called the rock salt structure, as chloride anions occupying the lattice sites of a face-centred cubic structure with the smaller sodium cations occupying the holes between the anions. (Alternatively, you can visualize this structure as the sodium cations occupying the lattice sites of a face-centred cubic structure with the larger chloride anions occupying the spaces between the cations.) Each unit cell contains four chloride anions ($[8 \times 1/8] + [6 \times \frac{1}{2}] = 4$) and four sodium cations ($12 \times \frac{1}{4}$) resulting in a ratio of 1:1, just as in the formula of the compound.

You can visualize this structure (shown in Figure 11.56), called the zinc blende structure, as sulfide anions occupying the lattice sites of a face-centred cubic structure with the smaller zinc cations occupying four of the eight tetrahedral holes located directly beneath each corner atom. A tetrahedral hole is the empty space that lies in the centre of a tetrahedral arrangement of four atoms. Each unit cell contains four sulfide anions ($[8 \times 1/8] + [6 \times \frac{1}{2}] = 4$) and four zinc cations (each of the four zinc cations is completely contained within the unit cell), resulting in a ratio of 1:1, just as in the formula of the compound.

11.45   Atomic solids can themselves be divided into three categories—nonbonding atomic solids, metallic atomic solids, and network covalent atomic solids. Nonbonding atomic solids, which include only the noble gases in their solid form, are held together by relatively weak dispersion forces. Metallic atomic solids, such as iron or gold, are held together by metallic bonds, which in the simplest model are represented by the interaction of metal cations with a sea of electrons that surround them. Network covalent atomic solids, such as diamond, graphite, and silicon dioxide, are held together by covalent bonds.

11.47   The band gap is an energy gap that exists between the valence band and conduction band. In metals, the valence band and conduction band are always energetically continuous—the energy difference between the top of the valence band and the bottom of the conduction band is infinitesimally small. In semiconductors, the band gap is small, allowing some electrons to be promoted at ordinary temperatures resulting in limited conductivity. In insulators, the band gap is large, and electrons are not promoted into the conduction band at ordinary temperatures, resulting in no electrical conductivity.

Problems by Topic
Intermolecular Forces

11.49   (a)   dispersion forces

(b)   dispersion forces, dipole–dipole forces, and hydrogen bonding

(c)   dispersion forces and dipole–dipole forces

(d)   dispersion forces

11.51   (a)   dispersion forces and dipole–dipole forces

(b)   dispersion forces, dipole–dipole forces, and hydrogen bonding

(c)   dispersion forces

(d)   dispersion forces

11.53   (a) CH_4 < (b) CH_3CH_3 < (c) CH_3CH_2Cl < (d) CH_3CH_2OH. The first two molecules only exhibit dispersion forces, so the boiling point increases with increasing number of electrons. The third molecule also exhibits dipole–dipole forces, which are stronger than dispersion forces. The last molecule exhibits hydrogen bonding. Since these are by far the strongest intermolecular forces in this group, the last molecule has the highest boiling point.

11.55   (a) CH_3OH has the higher boiling point since it exhibits hydrogen bonding.

(b) CH_3CH_2OH has the higher boiling point since it exhibits hydrogen bonding.

(c) CH_3CH_3 has the higher boiling point since it has the larger number of electrons.

11.57   (a) Br_2 has the higher vapour pressure since it has the smaller number of electrons.

(b) H_2S has the higher vapour pressure since it does not exhibit hydrogen bonding.

(c) PH_3 has the higher vapour pressure since it does not exhibit hydrogen bonding.

11.59   (a)   This will not form a homogeneous solution, since one is polar and one is nonpolar.

(b)   This will form a homogeneous solution. There will be ion–dipole interactions between the K^+ and Cl^- ions and the water molecules. There will also be dispersion forces, dipole–dipole forces, and hydrogen bonding between the water molecules.

(c)   This will form a homogeneous solution. There will be dispersion forces present among all of the molecules.

(d)   This will form a homogeneous solution. There will be dispersion forces, dipole–dipole forces, and hydrogen bonding among all of the molecules.

Surface Tension, Viscosity, and Capillary Action

11.61   Water will have the higher surface tension since it exhibits hydrogen bonding, a strong intermolecular force. Acetone cannot form hydrogen bonds.

11.63   Compound A will have the higher viscosity since it can interact with other molecules along the entire molecule. The more branched isomer has a smaller surface area allowing for fewer interactions. Also the molecule is very flexible and the molecules can get tangled with each other.

11.65   In a clean glass tube the water can generate strong adhesive interactions with the glass (due to the dipoles at the surface of the glass). Water experiences adhesive forces with glass that are stronger than its cohesive forces, causing it to climb the surface of a glass tube. When grease or oil coats the glass this interferes with the formation of these adhesive interactions with the glass, since oils are nonpolar and cannot interact strongly with the dipoles in the water. Without experiencing these strong intermolecular forces with oil, the water's cohesive forces will be greater and it will be drawn away from the surface of the tube.

Vaporization and Vapour Pressure

11.67   The water in the 12 cm diameter beaker will evaporate more quickly because there is more surface area for the molecules to evaporate from. The vapour pressure will be the same in the two containers because the vapour pressure is the pressure of the gas when it is in dynamic equilibrium with the liquid (evaporation rate = condensation rate). The vapour pressure is dependent only on the substance and the temperature. The 12 cm diameter container will reach this dynamic equilibrium faster.

11.69   The boiling point and higher heat of vaporization of oil are much higher than that of water, so it will not vaporize as quickly as the water. The evaporation of water cools your skin because evaporation is an endothermic process.

11.71   **Given:** 915 kJ from candy bar, water $d = 1.00$ g mL^{-1} **Find:** L(H_2O) vaporized at 100.0 °C
Other: $\Delta_{vap}H° = 40.7$ kJ mol^{-1}

Conceptual Plan: $q \rightarrow$ mol $H_2O \rightarrow$ g $H_2O \rightarrow$ mL $H_2O \rightarrow$ L H_2O

$$\frac{1 \text{ mol}}{40.7 \text{ kJ}} \qquad \frac{18.01 \text{ g}}{1 \text{ mol}} \qquad \frac{1.00 \text{ mL}}{1.00 \text{ g}} \qquad \frac{1 \text{ L}}{1000 \text{ mL}}$$

Solution: $915 \text{ kJ} \times \dfrac{1 \text{ mol}}{40.7 \text{ kJ}} \times \dfrac{18.02 \text{ g}}{1 \text{ mol}} \times \dfrac{1.00 \text{ mL}}{1 \text{ g}} \times \dfrac{1 \text{ L}}{1000 \text{ mL}} = 0.405 \text{ L } H_2O$

Check: The units (L) are correct. The magnitude of the answer (< 1 L) makes physical sense because we are vaporizing about 22 moles of water.

11.73   **Given:** 0.95 g water condenses on iron block 75.0 g at $T_i = 22\ °C$ **Find:** T_f (iron block)
Other: $\Delta_{vap}H° = 44.0 \text{ kJ mol}^{-1}$; $C_{Fe} = 0.449 \text{ J g}^{-1}\ °C^{-1}$ from text
Conceptual Plan: g $H_2O \rightarrow$ mol $H_2O \rightarrow q_{H_2O}$ (kJ) $\rightarrow q_{H_2O}$ (J) $\rightarrow q_{Fe}$ then $q_{Fe}, m_{Fe}, T_i \rightarrow T_f$

$$\frac{1 \text{ mol}}{18.01 \text{ g}} \qquad \frac{-44.0 \text{ kJ}}{1 \text{ mol}} \qquad \frac{1000 \text{ J}}{1 \text{ kJ}} \qquad -q_{H_2O} = q_{Fe} \qquad q = mC_s(T_f - T_i)$$

Solution: $0.95 \text{ g} \times \dfrac{1 \text{ mol}}{18.02 \text{ g}} \times \dfrac{-44.0 \text{ kJ}}{1 \text{ mol}} \times \dfrac{1000 \text{ J}}{1 \text{ kJ}} = -2319.64 \text{ J}$ then $-q_{H_2O} = q_{Fe} = 2319.64 \text{ J}$ then

$q = m\ C_s(T_f - T_i)$. Rearrange to solve for T_f.

$$T_f = \frac{m\ C_s\ T_i + q}{m\ C_s} = \frac{\left(75.0 \text{ g} \times 0.449\ \dfrac{\text{J}}{\text{g}\cdot°C} \times 22\ °C\right) + 2319.64 \text{ J}}{75.0 \text{ g} \times 0.449\ \dfrac{\text{J}}{\text{g}\cdot°C}} = 91\ °C.$$

Check: The units (°C) are correct. The temperature rose, which is consistent with heat being added to the block. The magnitude of the answer (91 °C) makes physical sense because even though we have $\sim \frac{1}{20}$ of a mole, the energy involved in condensation is very large.

11.75   **Given:**

Temperature (K)	Pressure (mbar)
200	87.1
210	179.1
220	340.9
230	608.0
235	795.9

Find: $\Delta_{vap}H°$ (NH_3) and normal boiling point

Conceptual Plan: To find the heat of vaporization, use Excel or similar software to make a plot of the natural log of vapour pressure (ln P) as a function of the inverse of the temperature in K (1/T). Then fit the points to a line and determine the slope of the line. Since the slope = $-\Delta_{vap}H/R$, we find the heat of vaporization as follows:

slope = $-\Delta_{vap}H/R \rightarrow \Delta_{vap}H = -$ slope x R then J $\rightarrow$ kJ.

$$\frac{1 \text{ kJ}}{1000 \text{ J}}$$

For the normal boiling point, use the equation of the best fit line, substitute 1013.25 mbar for the pressure and calculate the temperature.

Solution: Data was plotted in Excel.
The slope of the best fitting line is -2969.3 K, the ln β, is 19.321.

$$\Delta_{vap}H = -\text{slope} \times R = -(-2969.3 \text{ K}) \times \left(\frac{8.314 \text{ J}}{\text{K mol}}\right) = \frac{2.46868 \times 10^4 \text{ J}}{\text{mol}} \times \frac{1 \text{ kJ}}{1000 \text{ J}} = 24.7 \text{ kJ mol}^{-1}$$

To find the temperature:

$$\ln P = -2969.3 \text{ K}\left(\frac{1}{T}\right) + 19.321 \rightarrow$$

$$\ln 1013.25 = -2969.3 \text{ K}\left(\frac{1}{T}\right) + 19.321 \rightarrow$$

$$2969.3 \text{ K}\left(\frac{1}{T}\right) = 19.321 - 6.92092 \rightarrow$$

$$T = \frac{2969.3 \text{ K}}{12.40008} = 239 \text{ K}$$

Check: The units (kJ mol^{-1} and K) are correct. The magnitude of the answers (25 kJ mol^{-1} and 239 K) are consistent with other values in the text.

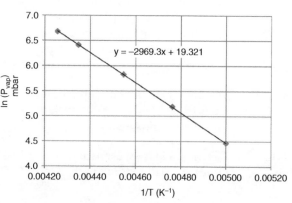

11.77   **Given:** ethanol, $\Delta_{vap}H° = 38.56$ kJ mol^{-1}; normal boiling point = 78.4 °C   **Find:** $P_{Ethanol}$ at 15 °C
Conceptual Plan: °C $\rightarrow$ K and kJ $\rightarrow$ J then $\Delta_{vap}H°, T_1, P_1, T_2 \rightarrow P_2$

$$K = °C + 273.15 \qquad \frac{1000\ J}{1\ kJ} \qquad \ln\frac{P_2}{P_1} = \frac{-\Delta_{vap}H}{R}\left(\frac{1}{T_2} - \frac{1}{T_1}\right)$$

Solution: $T_1 = 78.4$ °C + 273.15 = 351.6 K; $T_2 = 15$ °C + 273.15 = 288 K;

$\dfrac{38.56\ \cancel{kJ}}{mol} \times \dfrac{1000\ J}{1\ \cancel{kJ}} = 3.856 \times 10^4\ \dfrac{J}{mol}$ $P_1 = 1.01$ bar $\ln\dfrac{P_2}{P_1} = \dfrac{-\Delta_{vap}H}{R}\left(\dfrac{1}{T_2} - \dfrac{1}{T_1}\right)$. Substitute values in

equation. $\ln\dfrac{P_2}{1.01\ bar} = \dfrac{-3.856 \times 10^4\ \dfrac{\cancel{J}}{\cancel{mol}}}{8.314\ \dfrac{\cancel{J}}{K\cdot\cancel{mol}}}\left(\dfrac{1}{288\ K} - \dfrac{1}{351.6\ K}\right) = -2.9\underline{1}302 \rightarrow$

$\dfrac{P_2}{1.01\ bar} = e^{-2.91302} = 0.05\underline{4}311 \rightarrow P_2 = 0.054311 \times 1.01$ bar = 0.05\underline{4}8 bar = 55 mbar

Check: The units (bar) are correct. Since 15 °C is significantly below the boiling point, we expect the answer to be much less than 1.01 bar.

Sublimation and Fusion

11.79   **Given:** 65.8 g water freezes   **Find:** energy released   **Other:** $\Delta_{fus}H° = 6.02$ kJ mol^{-1} from text
Conceptual Plan: g $H_2O \rightarrow$ mol $H_2O \rightarrow q_{H_2O}$ (kJ) $\rightarrow q_{H_2O}$ (J)

$$\frac{1\ mol}{18.01\ g} \qquad \frac{-6.02\ kJ}{1\ mol} \qquad \frac{1000\ J}{1\ kJ}$$

Solution: $65.8\ \cancel{g} \times \dfrac{1\ \cancel{mol}}{18.02\ \cancel{g}} \times \dfrac{-6.02\ \cancel{kJ}}{1\ \cancel{mol}} \times \dfrac{1000\ J}{1\ \cancel{kJ}} = -219\underline{8}2$ J $= 2.20 \times 10^4$ J released or 22.0 kJ released

Check: The units (J) are correct. The magnitude (22000 J) makes sense since we are freezing about 3 moles of water. Freezing is exothermic, so heat is released.

11.81   **Given:** 8.5 g ice; 255 g water   **Find:** ΔT of water
Other: $\Delta_{fus}H° = 6.0$ kJ mol^{-1}; $C_{H_2O} = 4.18$ J g^{-1} °C^{-1} from text
Conceptual Plan: The first step is to calculate how much heat is removed from the water to melt the ice.
$q_{ice} = -q_{water}$ so g (ice) $\rightarrow$ mol (ice) $\rightarrow q_{fus}$(kJ) $\rightarrow q_{fus}$ (J) $\rightarrow q_{water}$ (J) then $q, m, C_s \rightarrow \Delta T_1$

$$\frac{1\ mol}{18.01\ g} \qquad \frac{6.0\ kJ}{1\ mol} \qquad \frac{1000\ J}{1\ kJ} \qquad q_{water} = -q_{ice} \qquad q = mC_s\Delta T_1$$

Now we have slightly cooled water (at a temperature of T_1) in contact with 0.0 °C water, and we can calculate a second temperature drop of the water due to mixing of the water that was ice with the initially room temperature water, so $q_{ice} = -q_{water}$ with $m, C_s \rightarrow \Delta T_2$ with $\Delta T_1\ \Delta T_2 \rightarrow \Delta T_{Total}$.

$$q = m\ C_s\Delta T_2 \text{ then set } q_{ice} = -q_{water} \quad \Delta T_{Total} = \Delta T_1 + \Delta T_2$$

Solution: $8.5\ \cancel{g} \times \dfrac{1\ \cancel{mol}}{18.01\ \cancel{g}} \times \dfrac{6.0\ \cancel{kJ}}{1\ \cancel{mol}} \times \dfrac{1000\ J}{1\ \cancel{kJ}} = 2.8\underline{3}176 \times 10^3$ J, $q_{water} = -q_{ice} = -2.8\underline{3}176 \times 10^3$ J

$q = mC_s\Delta T$. Rearrange to solve for ΔT. $\Delta T_1 = \dfrac{q}{mC_s} = \dfrac{-2.83176 \times 10^3\ \cancel{J}}{255\ \cancel{g} \times 4.18\ \dfrac{\cancel{J}}{\cancel{g}\cdot °C}} = -2.\underline{6}567$ °C.

$q = mC_s\Delta T$ substitute in values and set $q_{ice} = -q_{H_2O}$.

$q_{ice} = m_{ice}C_{ice}\left(T_f - T_{icei}\right) = 8.5\ \cancel{g} \times 4.18\ \dfrac{J}{\cancel{g}\cdot °C} \times \left(T_f - 0.0\ °C\right) =$

$-q_{water} = -m_{water}C_{water}\Delta T_{water2} = -255\ \cancel{g} \times 4.18\ \dfrac{J}{\cancel{g}\cdot °C} \times \Delta T_{water2} \rightarrow$

$8.5\ T_f = -255\Delta T_{water2} = -255(T_f - T_{f1})$. Rearrange to solve for T_f. $8.5\ T_f + 255\ T_f = 255\ T_{f1} \rightarrow$

$263.5\ T_f = 255\ T_{f1} \rightarrow T_f = 0.96774\ T_{f1}$ but $\Delta T_1 = (T_{f1} - T_{i1}) = -2.\underline{6}567$ °C which says that

$T_{f1} = T_{i1} - 2.\underline{6}567$ °C and $\Delta T_{Total} = (T_f - T_{i1})$ so

$\Delta T_{Total} = 0.96774\ T_{f1} - T_{i1} = 0.96774(T_{i1} - 2.\underline{6}567\ °C) - T_{i1} = -2.\underline{6}567$ °C $- 0.03226\ T_{i1}$.

This implies that the larger the initial temperature of the water, the larger the temperature drop. If the initial temperature was 90 °C, the temperature drop would be 5.6 °C. If the initial temperature was 25 °C, the temperature drop would be 3.5 °C. If the initial temperature was 5 °C, the temperature drop would be

2.8 °C. This makes physical sense because the lower the initial temperature of the water, the less kinetic energy it initially has and the smaller the heat transfer from the water to the melted ice will be.

Check: The units (°C) are correct. The temperature drop from the melting of the ice is only 2.7 °C because the mass of the water is so much larger than the ice.

11.83 **Given:** 10.0 g ice $T_i = -10.0$ °C to steam at $T_f = 110.0$ °C **Find:** heat required (kJ)
Other: $\Delta_{fus}H° = 6.02$ kJ mol^{-1}; $\Delta_{vap}H° = 40.7$ kJ mol^{-1}; $C_{ice} = 2.09$ J g^{-1} °C^{-1}; $C_{water} = 4.18$ J g^{-1} °C^{-1}; $C_{steam} = 2.01$ J g^{-1} °C^{-1}

Conceptual Plan: Follow the heating curve in Figure 11.39. $q_{Total} = q_1 + q_2 + q_3 + q_4 + q_5$ where q_1, q_3, and q_5 are heating of a single phase then J $\rightarrow$ kJ and q_2 and q_4 are phase transitions.

$$q = mC_S(T_f - T_i) \qquad \frac{1\ kJ}{1000\ J} \qquad q = m \times \frac{1\ mol}{18.01\ g} \times \frac{\Delta H}{1\ mol}$$

Solution:

$$q_1 = m_{ice}C_{ice}(T_{icef} - T_{icei}) = 10.0\ g \times 2.09\ \frac{J}{g \cdot °C} \times (0.0\ °C - (-10.0\ °C)) = 209\ J \times \frac{1\ kJ}{1000\ J} = 0.209\ kJ,$$

$$q_2 = m \times \frac{1\ mol}{18.01\ g} \times \frac{\Delta_{fus}H}{1\ mol} = 10.0\ g \times \frac{1\ mol}{18.01\ g} \times \frac{6.02\ kJ}{1\ mol} = 3.\underline{3}43\ kJ,$$

$$q_3 = m_{water}C_{water}(T_{waterf} - T_{wateri}) = 10.0\ g \times 4.18\ \frac{J}{g \cdot °C} \times (100.0\ °C - 0.0\ °C) = 4180\ J \times \frac{1\ kJ}{1000\ J} = 4.18\ kJ,$$

$$q_4 = m \times \frac{1\ mol}{18.01\ g} \times \frac{\Delta_{vap}H}{1\ mol} = 10.0\ g \times \frac{1\ mol}{18.01\ g} \times \frac{40.7\ kJ}{1\ mol} = 22.5\underline{9}9\ kJ,$$

$$q_5 = m_{steam}C_{steam}(T_{steamf} - T_{steami}) = 10.0\ g \times 2.01\ \frac{J}{g \cdot °C} \times (110.0\ °C - 100.0\ °C)$$

$$= 201\ J \times \frac{1\ kJ}{1000\ J} = 0.201\ kJ.$$

$q_{Total} = q_1 + q_2 + q_3 + q_4 + q_5 = 0.209$ kJ $+ 3.\underline{3}43$ kJ $+ 4.18$ kJ $+ 22.5\underline{9}9$ kJ $+ 0.201$ kJ $= 30.5$ kJ

Check: The units (kJ) are correct. The total amount of heat is dominated by the vaporization step. Since we have less than 1 mole we expect less than 41 kJ.

Phase Diagrams

11.85 (a) solid

  (b) liquid

  (c) gas

  (d) supercritical fluid

  (e) solid/liquid equilibrium

  (f) liquid/gas equilibrium

  (g) solid/liquid/gas equilibrium

11.87 **Given:** nitrogen, normal boiling point = 77.3 K, normal melting point = 63.1 K, critical temperature = 126.2 K, critical pressure = 2.55×10^4 Torr, triple point at 63.1 K and 94.0 Torr
Find: sketch phase diagram. Does nitrogen have a stable liquid phase at 1 atm?

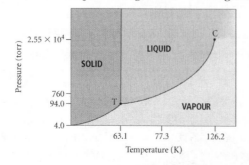

Nitrogen has a stable liquid phase at 1 atm.

Note that the axes are not to scale.

11.89   (a)   0.036 mbar, the higher of the two triple points

   (b)   The rhombic phase is more dense because if we start in the monoclinic phase at 100 °C and increase the pressure, we will cross into the rhombic phase.

The Uniqueness of Water

11.91   Water has a low molar mass (18.01 g mol^{-1}), yet it is a liquid at room temperature. Water's high boiling point for its molar mass can be understood by examining the structure of the water molecule. The bent geometry of the water molecule and the highly polar nature of the O–H bonds result in a molecule with a significant dipole moment. Water's two O–H bonds (hydrogen directly bonded to oxygen) allow a water molecule to form very strong hydrogen bonds with four other water molecules, resulting in a relatively high boiling point.

11.93   Water has an exceptionally high specific heat capacity, which has a moderating effect on the climate of coastal cities. Also, its high $\Delta_{vap}H$ causes water evaporation and condensation to have a strong effect on temperature. A tremendous amount of heat can be stored in large bodies of water. Heat will be absorbed or released from large bodies of water preferentially over land around it. In some cities, such as Vancouver, for example, the daily fluctuation in temperature can be less than 10 °C. This same moderating effect occurs over the entire planet, two-thirds of which is covered by water. In other words, without water, the daily temperature fluctuations on our planet might be more like those on Mars, where temperature fluctuations of 63 °C have been measured between early morning and midday.

Types of Solids and Their Structures

11.95   **Given:** X-ray with λ = 154 pm, maximum reflection angle of θ = 28.3°; assume n = 1
   Find: distance between layers
   Conceptual Plan: λ , θ, $n \rightarrow d$
   $$n\lambda = 2\,d\,\sin\theta$$

   Solution: $n\lambda = 2\,d\,\sin\theta$. Rearrange to solve for d. $d = \dfrac{n\,\lambda}{2\,\sin\theta} = \dfrac{1 \times 154 \text{ pm}}{2\,\sin 28.3°} = 162$ pm.

   Check: The units (pm) are correct. The magnitude (164 pm) makes sense since n = 1 and the $\sin$ is always < 1. The number is consistent with interatomic distances.

11.97   (a)   8 corner atoms x (1/8 atom / unit cell) = 1 atom / unit cell

   (b)   8 corner atoms x (1/8 atom / unit cell) + 1 atom in centre = (1 + 1) atoms / unit cell = 2 atoms / unit cell

   (c)   8 corner atoms x (1/8 atom / unit cell) + 6 face-centred atoms x (1/2 atom / unit cell) = (1 + 3) atoms / unit cell = 4 atoms / unit cell

11.99   **Given:** platinum, face-centred cubic structure, r = 139 pm **Find:** edge length of unit cell and density (g cm^{-3})
   Conceptual Plan: $r \rightarrow l$ and $l \rightarrow V(pm^3) \rightarrow V(cm^3)$ and $\mathcal{M}$, FCC structure $\rightarrow m$ then $m, V \rightarrow d$
   $$l = 2\sqrt{2}\,r \qquad V = l^3 \qquad \frac{(1 \text{ cm})^3}{(10^{10} \text{ pm})^3} \qquad m = \frac{4 \text{ atoms}}{\text{unit cell}} \times \frac{\mathcal{M}}{N_A} \qquad d = m/V$$

   Solution: $l = 2\sqrt{2}\,r = 2\sqrt{2} \times 139$ pm $= 393.151$ pm $= 393$ pm and

   $$V = l^3 = (393.151 \text{ pm})^3 \times \frac{(1 \text{ cm})^3}{(10^{10} \text{ pm})^3} = 6.07682 \times 10^{-23} \text{ cm}^3 \text{ and}$$

   $$m = \frac{4 \text{ atoms}}{\text{unit cell}} \times \frac{\mathcal{M}}{N_A} = \frac{4 \text{ atoms}}{\text{unit cell}} \times \frac{195.09 \text{ g}}{1 \text{ mol}} \times \frac{1 \text{ mol}}{6.022 \times 10^{23} \text{ atoms}} = 1.295848 \times 10^{-21} \frac{\text{g}}{\text{unit cell}} \text{ then}$$

   $$d = \frac{m}{V} = \frac{1.295848 \times 10^{-21} \dfrac{\text{g}}{\text{unit cell}}}{6.07682 \times 10^{-23} \dfrac{\text{cm}^3}{\text{unit cell}}} = 21.3 \text{ g cm}^{-3}$$

   Check: The units (pm and g cm^{-3}) are correct. The magnitude (393 pm) makes sense because it must be larger than the radius of an atom. The magnitude (21 g cm^{-3}) is consistent for Pt from Chapter 1.

11.101 **Given:** rhodium, face-centred cubic structure, $d = 12.41$ g cm^{-3} **Find:** r (Rh)

Conceptual Plan: $\mathcal{M}$, FCC structure $\rightarrow$ m then $m, V \rightarrow d$ then $V(cm^3) \rightarrow l$ (cm) $\rightarrow l$ (pm) then $l \rightarrow r$

$$m = \frac{4 \text{ atoms}}{\text{unit cell}} \times \frac{\mathcal{M}}{N_A} \qquad d = m/V \qquad V = l^3 \qquad \frac{10^{10} \text{ pm}}{1 \text{ cm}} \qquad l = 2\sqrt{2}\,r$$

Solution: $m = \dfrac{4 \text{ atoms}}{\text{unit cell}} \times \dfrac{\mathcal{M}}{N_A} = \dfrac{4 \text{ atoms}}{\text{unit cell}} \times \dfrac{102.905 \text{ g}}{1 \text{ mol}} \times \dfrac{1 \text{ mol}}{6.022 \times 10^{23} \text{ atoms}} = 6.835271 \times 10^{-22}\,\dfrac{\text{g}}{\text{unit cell}}$

then $d = \dfrac{m}{V}$. Rearrange to solve for V. $V = \dfrac{m}{d} = \dfrac{6.835271 \times 10^{-22}\,\dfrac{\text{g}}{\text{unit cell}}}{12.41 \text{ g cm}^{-3}} = 5.507873 \times 10^{-23}\,\dfrac{\text{cm}^3}{\text{unit cell}}$

then $V = l^3$. Rearrange to solve for l.

$l = \sqrt[3]{V} = \sqrt[3]{5.507873 \times 10^{-23} \text{ cm}^3} = 3.804831 \times 10^{-8} \text{ cm} \times \dfrac{10^{10} \text{ pm}}{1 \text{ cm}} = 380.4831 \text{ pm}$ then $l = 2\sqrt{2}r$.

Rearrange to solve for r. $r = \dfrac{l}{2\sqrt{2}} = \dfrac{380.4831 \text{ pm}}{2\sqrt{2}} = 134.5$ pm.

Check: The units (pm) are correct. The magnitude (135 pm) is consistent with an atomic diameter.

11.103 **Given:** polonium, simple cubic structure, $d = 9.3$ g cm^{-3}; $r = 167$ pm; $\mathcal{M} = 209$ g mol^{-1} **Find:** estimate N_A

Conceptual Plan: $r \rightarrow l$ and $l \rightarrow V(pm^3) \rightarrow V(cm^3)$ then $d, V \rightarrow m$ then $\mathcal{M}$, SC structure $\rightarrow m$

$$l = 2r \qquad V = l^3 \qquad \frac{(1 \text{ cm})^3}{(10^{10} \text{ pm})^3} \qquad d = m/V \qquad m = \frac{1 \text{ atom}}{\text{unit cell}} \times \frac{\mathcal{M}}{N_A}$$

Solution: $l = 2r = 2 \times 167 \text{ pm} = 334 \text{ pm}$ and $V = l^3 = (334 \text{ pm})^3 \times \dfrac{(1 \text{ cm})^3}{(10^{10} \text{ pm})^3} = 3.72597 \times 10^{-23} \text{ cm}^3$ then

$d = \dfrac{m}{V}$. Rearrange to solve for m. $m = d\,V = 9.3\,\dfrac{\text{g}}{\text{cm}^3} \times \dfrac{3.72597 \times 10^{-23} \text{ cm}^3}{\text{unit cell}} = 3.46515 \times 10^{-22}\,\dfrac{\text{g}}{\text{unit cell}}$

then $m = \dfrac{1 \text{ atom}}{\text{unit cell}} \times \dfrac{\mathcal{M}}{N_A}$. Rearrange to solve for N_A.

$N_A = \dfrac{1 \text{ atom}}{\text{unit cell}} \times \dfrac{\mathcal{M}}{m} = \dfrac{1 \text{ atom}}{\text{unit cell}} \times \dfrac{209 \text{ g}}{1 \text{ mol}} \times \dfrac{1 \text{ unit cell}}{3.46515 \times 10^{-22} \text{ g}} = 6.0 \times 10^{23}$ atoms mol^{-1}.

Check: The units (atoms mol^{-1}) are correct. The magnitude (6×10^{23}) is consistent with Avogadro's number.

11.105 (a) atomic, since Ar is an atom

(b) molecular, since water is a molecule

(c) ionic, since K_2O is an ionic solid

(d) atomic, since iron is a metal

11.107 LiCl has the highest melting point since it is the only ionic solid in the group. The other three solids are held together by intermolecular forces, while LiCl is held together by stronger coulombic interactions between the cations and anions of the crystal lattice.

11.109 (a) TiO_2 because it is a covalent solid

(b) $SiCl_4$ because it has a higher molar mass and therefore has stronger dispersion forces

(c) Xe because it has a higher molar mass and therefore has stronger dispersion forces

(d) CaO because the ions have greater charge and therefore stronger coulombic interactions

11.111 The Ti atoms occupy the corner positions and the centre of the unit cell: 8 corner atoms x (1/8 atom / unit cell) + 1 atom in centre = (1 + 1) Ti atoms / unit cell = 2 Ti atoms / unit cell. The O atoms occupy four positions on the top and bottom faces and two positions inside the unit cell: 4 face-centred atoms x (1/2 atom / unit cell) + 2 atoms in the interior = (2 + 2) O atoms / unit cell = 4 O atoms / unit cell. Therefore there are 2 Ti atoms / unit cell and 4 O atoms / unit cell, so the ratio Ti:O is 2:4 or 1:2. The formula for the compound is TiO_2.

11.113   In CsCl: The Cs atoms occupy the centre of the unit cell: 1 atom in centre = 1 Cs atom / unit cell. The Cl atoms occupy corner positions of the unit cell: 8 corner atoms x (1/8 atom / unit cell) = 1 Cl atom / unit cell. Therefore there is 1 Cl atom / unit cell and 1 Cl atom / unit cell, so the ratio Cs:Cl is 1:1. The formula for the compound is CsCl, as expected.

In $BaCl_2$: The Ba atoms occupy the corner positions and the face-centred positions of the unit cell: 8 corner atoms x (1/8 atom / unit cell) + 6 face-centred atoms x (1/2 atom / unit cell) = (1 + 3) Ba atoms / unit cell = 4 Ba atoms / unit cell. The Cl atoms occupy eight positions inside the unit cell: 8 Cl atoms / unit cell. Therefore there are 4 Ba atoms / unit cell and 8 Cl atoms / unit cell, so the ratio Ba:Cl is 4:8 or 1:2. The formula for the compound is $BaCl_2$, as expected.

Band Theory

11.115   (a)   Zn should have little or no band gap because it is the only metal in the group.

11.117   (a)   p-type semiconductor: Ge is Group 14 and Ga is Group 13, so the Ga will generate electron "holes."

          (b)   n-type semiconductor: Si is Group 14 and As is Group 15, so the As will add electrons to the conduction band.

Cumulative Problems

11.119   The general trend is that melting point increases with increasing number of electrons. This is due to the fact that the electrons of the larger molecules are held more loosely and a stronger dipole moment can be induced more easily. HF is the exception to the rule. It has a relatively high melting point due to strong intermolecular forces due to hydrogen bonding.

11.121   (a)   i < iii < ii

          Cr – Cl will have the highest boiling point because it has a dipole moment and the other molecules do not. Boiling point will increase with increased dipole moment. Oxygen has a greater number of electrons than nitrogen and therefore a bigger electron cloud causing greater dispersion forces and thus a higher boiling point than nitrogen.

          (b)   iv < i < iii < ii

          Compounds iv and i have only dispersion forces therefore the molecule with the larger number of electrons has the higher boiling point. Compound iii has dipole–dipole interactions in addition to dispersion forces, which increased the boiling point and Compound ii has H-bonding, dipole–dipole interactions, and dispersion forces and thus has the highest boiling point of the four compounds.

11.123   (a)   All molecules shown in the plot partake in hydrogen bonding, but water is able to form a network of hydrogen bonds. The boiling point for water, therefore, does not follow an "expected" trend based on the figure.

          (b)   The boiling points of the alcohols increase as the alkyl chain gets larger because they have more electrons and are more polarizable. The dispersion forces are thus increased.

11.125   **Given:** P_{H_2O} = 23.76 Torr at 25 °C; 1.25 g water in 1.5 L container   **Find:** m (H_2O) as liquid
          Conceptual Plan: °C $\rightarrow$ K and Torr $\rightarrow$ atm then $P, V, T \rightarrow$ mol (g) $\rightarrow$ g (g) then g (g), g (l)$_i$ $\rightarrow$ g (l)$_f$

$$K = °C + 273.15 \qquad \frac{1\ atm}{760\ Torr} \qquad PV = nRT \qquad \frac{18.01\ g}{1\ mol} \qquad g\ (l)_f = g\ (l)_i - g\ (g)$$

Solution: T = 25 °C + 273.15 = 298 K, $23.76\ \cancel{Torr} \times \dfrac{1\ atm}{760\ \cancel{Torr}}$ = 0.0312632 atm then $PV = nRT$.

Rearrange to solve for n. $n = \dfrac{PV}{RT} = \dfrac{0.0312632\ \cancel{atm} \times 1.5\ \cancel{L}}{0.08206\ \dfrac{\cancel{L} \cdot \cancel{atm}}{K \cdot mol} \times 298\ K}$ = 0.00191768 mol in the gas phase then

$0.00191768 \text{ mol} \times \dfrac{18.01 \text{ g}}{1 \text{ mol}} = 0.0345375 \text{ g}$ in gas phase then

$g\,(l)_f = g\,(l)_i - g\,(g) = 1.25 \text{ g} - 0.0345375 \text{ g} = 1.22 \text{ g}$ remaining as liquid. Yes, there is 1.22 g of liquid.

Check: The units (g) are correct. The magnitude (1.2 g) is expected since very little material is expected to be in the gas phase.

11.127 Since we are starting at a temperature that is higher and a pressure that is lower than the triple point, the phase transitions will be gas → liquid → solid, or condensation followed by freezing.

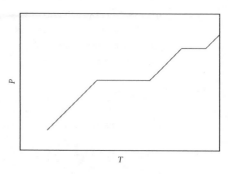

11.129 The ideal gas law assumes that there are no forces between the molecules. At these high pressures, ammonia molecules are closer to one another, so the hydrogen bonds between ammonia molecules are able to take effect and will pull on one another strongly, decreasing the volume. This is different than for something like argon, where even at these high pressures, the weak dispersion forces have little effect on the volume. Argon will better obey the ideal gas law, even at these pressures.

11.131 **Given:** Ice: $T_1 = 0\ ^\circ\text{C}$ exactly, $m = 53.5$ g; Water: $T_1 = 75\ ^\circ\text{C}$, $m = 115$ g **Find:** T_f

Other: $\Delta_{fus}H^\circ = 6.0$ kJ mol^{-1}; $C_{water} = 4.18$ J g^{-1} $^\circ$C^{-1}

Conceptual Plan: $q_{ice} = -q_{water}$ so g (ice) $\rightarrow$ mol (ice) $\rightarrow$ q_{fus}(kJ) $\rightarrow$ q_{fus} (J) $\rightarrow$ q_{water} (J) then

$\dfrac{1 \text{ mol}}{18.01 \text{ g}}$ $\dfrac{6.02 \text{ kJ}}{1 \text{ mol}}$ $\dfrac{1000 \text{ J}}{1 \text{ kJ}}$ $q_{water} = -q_{ice}$

$q, m, C_s \rightarrow \Delta T$ then $T_i, \Delta T \rightarrow T_2$ now we have slightly cooled water in contact with 0.0 $^\circ$C water

$q = mC_s\Delta T$ $\Delta T = T_2 - T_i$

so $q_{ice} = -q_{water}$ with $m, C_s, T_i \rightarrow T_f$

$q = mC_s(T_f - T_i)$ then set $q_{ice} = -q_{water}$

Solution: $53.5 \text{ g} \times \dfrac{1 \text{ mol}}{18.01 \text{ g}} \times \dfrac{6.02 \text{ kJ}}{1 \text{ mol}} \times \dfrac{1000 \text{ J}}{1 \text{ kJ}} = 1.78828 \times 10^4$ J, $q_{water} = -q_{ice} = -1.78828 \times 10^4$ J

$q = mC_s\Delta T$. Rearrange to solve for ΔT. $\Delta T = \dfrac{q}{mC_s} = \dfrac{-1.78828 \times 10^4 \text{ J}}{115 \text{ g} \times 4.18 \dfrac{\text{J}}{\text{g} \cdot {}^\circ\text{C}}} = -37.2017\ ^\circ$C then

$\Delta T = T_2 - T_i$. Rearrange to solve for T_2. $T_2 = \Delta T + T_i = -37.2017\ ^\circ$C $+ 75\ ^\circ$C $= 37.798\ ^\circ$C

$q = mC_s(T_f - T_i)$ substitute in values and set $q_{ice} = -q_{water}$.

$q_{ice} = m_{ice}C_{ice}(T_f - T_{icei}) = 53.5 \text{ g} \times 4.18 \dfrac{\text{J}}{\text{g} \cdot {}^\circ\text{C}} \times (T_f - 0.0\ ^\circ\text{C}) =$

$-q_{water} = -m_{water}C_{water}(T_f - T_{water2}) = -115 \text{ g} \times 4.18 \dfrac{\text{J}}{\text{g} \cdot {}^\circ\text{C}} \times (T_f - 37.798\ ^\circ\text{C})$.

Rearrange to solve for T_f.

$53.5T_f = -115(T_f - 37.798\ ^\circ\text{C}) \rightarrow 53.5\,T_f = -115\,T_f + 4346.8\ ^\circ\text{C} \rightarrow -4346.8\ ^\circ\text{C} = -168.5\,T_f$

$\rightarrow T_f = \dfrac{-4346.8\ ^\circ\text{C}}{-168.5} = 25.8\ ^\circ\text{C} = 26\ ^\circ\text{C}.$

Check: The units ($^\circ$C) are correct. The temperature is between the two initial temperatures. Since the ice mass is about half the water mass, we are not surprised that the temperature is closer to the original ice temperature.

11.133 **Given:** Home: 6.0 m x 10.0 m x 2.2 m; $T = 30\ ^\circ$C, $P_{H_2O} = 85\%$ of $P^\circ_{H_2O}$ **Find:** m (H$_2$O) removed

Other: $P^\circ_{H_2O} = 31.8$ Torr from text

Conceptual Plan: $l, w, h \rightarrow V\,(m^3) \rightarrow V\,(cm^3) \rightarrow V\,(L)$ and $P^\circ_{H_2O} \rightarrow P_{H_2O}$ (Torr) $\rightarrow P_{H_2O}$ (atm) and

$$V = lwh \qquad \frac{(100\ cm)^3}{(1\ m)^3} \qquad \frac{1\ L}{1000\ cm^3} \qquad P_{H2O} = 0.85\,P^\circ_{H_2O} \qquad \frac{1\ atm}{760\ Torr}$$

$°C \rightarrow K$ then $P, V, T \rightarrow mol\,(H_2O) \rightarrow g\,(H_2O)$

$$K = °C + 273.15 \qquad PV = nRT \qquad \frac{18.01\ g}{1\ mol}$$

Solution: $V = l\,w\,h = 6.0\ m \times 10.0\ m \times 2.2\ m = 132\ m^3 \times \dfrac{(100\ cm)^3}{(1\ m)^3} \times \dfrac{1\ L}{1000\ cm^3} = 1.32 \times 10^5\ L,$

$P_{H_2O} = 0.85\,P^\circ_{H_2O} = 0.85 \times 31.8\ Torr \times \dfrac{1\ atm}{760\ Torr} = 0.035566\ atm,\ T = 30\ °C + 273.15 = 303\ K,$

then $PV = nRT$. Rearrange to solve for n.

$$n = \frac{PV}{RT} = \frac{0.035566\ atm \times 1.32 \times 10^5\ L}{0.08206\ \dfrac{L\cdot atm}{K\cdot mol} \times 303\ K} = 188.81\ mol\ \text{then}\ 188.81\ mol \times \frac{18.01\ g}{1\ mol} = 3400\ g\ \text{to remove.}$$

Check: The units (g) are correct. The magnitude of the answer (3400 g) makes sense since the volume of the house is so large. We are removing almost 200 moles of water.

11.135 CsCl has a higher melting point than AgI because of its higher coordination number. In CsCl, one anion bonds to eight cations (and vice versa), while in AgI, one anion bonds only to four cations.

11.137 (a) Atoms are connected across the face diagonal (c), so $c = 4r$.

(b) From the Pythagorean Theorem $c^2 = a^2 + b^2$, from part (a) $c = 4r$, and for a cubic structure $a = l, b = l$ so
$(4r)^2 = l^2 + l^2 \rightarrow 16r^2 = 2l^2 \rightarrow 8r^2 = l^2 \rightarrow l = \sqrt{8r^2} \rightarrow l = 2\sqrt{2}r.$

11.139 **Given:** diamond, V (unit cell) $= 0.0454\ nm^3$; $d = 3.52\ g\ cm^{-3}$ **Find:** number of carbon atoms in a unit cell
Conceptual Plan: $V(nm^3) \rightarrow V(cm^3)$ then $d, V \rightarrow m \rightarrow mol \rightarrow atoms$

$$\frac{(1\ cm)^3}{(10^7\ nm)^3} \qquad d = m/V \qquad \frac{1\ mol}{12.01\ g} \qquad \frac{6.022 \times 10^{23}\ atoms}{1\ mol}$$

Solution: $0.0454\ nm^3 \times \dfrac{(1\ cm)^3}{(10^7\ nm)^3} = 4.54 \times 10^{-23}\ cm^3$ then $d = \dfrac{m}{V}$. Rearrange to solve for m.

$m = d\,V = 3.52\ \dfrac{g}{cm^3} \times 4.54 \times 10^{-23}\ cm^3 = 1.59808 \times 10^{-22}\ g$ then

$$\frac{1.59808 \times 10^{-22}\ g}{\text{unit cell}} \times \frac{1\ mol}{12.01\ g} \times \frac{6.022 \times 10^{23}\ atoms}{1\ mol} = 8.01\ \frac{C\ atoms}{\text{unit cell}} = 8\ \frac{C\ atoms}{\text{unit cell}}$$

Check: The units (atoms) are correct. The magnitude (8) makes sense because it is a fairly small number and our answer is within calculation error of an integer.

11.141 (a) $CO_2\,(s) \rightarrow CO_2\,(g)$ at 194.7 K

(b) $CO_2\,(s) \rightarrow$ triple point at 216.5 K $\rightarrow CO_2\,(g)$ just above 216.5 K

(c) $CO_2\,(s) \rightarrow CO_2\,(l)$ at somewhat above 216 K $\rightarrow CO_2\,(g)$ at around 250 K

(d) $CO_2\,(s) \rightarrow CO_2$ above the critical point where there is no distinction between liquid and gas. This change occurs at about 300 K.

11.143 **Given:** metal, $d = 7.8748\ g\ cm^{-3}$; $l = 0.28664\ nm$, body-centred cubic lattice **Find:** $\mathcal{M}$
Conceptual Plan: $l \rightarrow V(nm^3) \rightarrow V(cm^3)$ then $d, V \rightarrow m$ then m, FCC structure $\rightarrow \mathcal{M}$

$$V = l^3 \qquad \frac{(1\ cm)^3}{(10^7\ nm)^3} \qquad d = m/V \qquad m = \frac{2\ atoms}{\text{unit cell}} \times \frac{\mathcal{M}}{N_A}$$

Solution: $V = l^3 = (0.28664\ nm)^3 = 0.02355105602\ nm^3 \times \dfrac{(1\ cm)^3}{(10^7\ nm)^3} = 2.355105602 \times 10^{-23}\ cm^3$ then $d = \dfrac{m}{V}$.

Rearrange to solve for m. $m = d\,V = 7.8748\ \dfrac{g}{cm^3} \times 2.355105602 \times 10^{-23}\ cm^3 = 1.854598559 \times 10^{-22}\ g$

then $m = \dfrac{2 \text{ atoms}}{\text{unit cell}} \times \dfrac{M}{N_A}$. Rearrange to solve for M.

$$M = \dfrac{\text{unit cell}}{2 \text{ atoms}} \times N_A \times m = \dfrac{\text{unit cell}}{2 \text{ atoms}} \times \dfrac{6.022 \times 10^{23} \text{ atoms}}{1 \text{ mol}} \times \dfrac{1.854598559 \times 10^{-22} \text{ g}}{\text{unit cell}} = 55.842 \text{ g mol}^{-1}$$

$= 55.84 \text{ g mol}^{-1}$ iron.

Check: The units (g mol^{-1}) are correct. The magnitude (55.8) makes sense because it is a reasonable atomic mass for a metal and it is close to iron.

Challenge Problems

11.145   **Given:** KCl, rock salt structure **Find:** density (g cm^{-3}) **Other:** r (K$^+$) = 133 pm; r (Cl$^-$) = 181 pm from Chapter 8
Conceptual Plan: Rock salt structure is a face-centred cubic structure with anions at the lattice points and cations in the holes between lattice sites $\rightarrow$ **assume** $r = r(\text{Cl}^-)$**, but** $M = M(\text{KCl})$
$r(\text{K}^+), r(\text{Cl}^-) \rightarrow l$ **and** $l \rightarrow V(\text{pm}^3) \rightarrow V(\text{cm}^3)$ **and, FCC structure** $\rightarrow m$ **then** $m, V \rightarrow d$.

from Figure 11.55 $l = 2r(\text{Cl}^-) + 2r(\text{K}^+)$ $V = l^3 \dfrac{(1\text{cm})^3}{(10^{10}\text{pm})^3}$ $m = \dfrac{4 \text{ formula units}}{\text{unit cell}} \times \dfrac{M}{N_A}$ $d = m/V$

Solution: $l = 2r(\text{Cl}^-) + 2r(\text{K}^+) = 2(181 \text{ pm}) + 2(133 \text{ pm}) = 628 \text{ pm}$ and

$$V = l^3 = (628 \text{ pm})^3 \times \dfrac{(1 \text{ cm})^3}{(10^{10} \text{ pm})^3} = 2.47673 \times 10^{-22} \text{ cm}^3 \text{ and}$$

$$m = \dfrac{4 \text{ formula units}}{\text{unit cell}} \times \dfrac{M}{N_A} = \dfrac{4 \text{ formula units}}{\text{unit cell}} \times \dfrac{74.55 \text{ g}}{1 \text{ mol}} \times \dfrac{1 \text{ mol}}{6.022 \times 10^{23} \text{ formula units}}$$

$$= 4.951976 \times 10^{-22} \dfrac{\text{g}}{\text{unit cell}}$$

then $d = \dfrac{m}{V} = \dfrac{4.951976 \times 10^{-22} \dfrac{\text{g}}{\text{unit cell}}}{2.47673 \times 10^{-22} \dfrac{\text{cm}^3}{\text{unit cell}}} = 1.99940 \text{ g cm}^{-3} = 2.00 \text{ g cm}^{-3}$

Check: The units (g cm^{-3}) are correct. The magnitude (2 g cm^{-3}) is reasonable for a salt density. The published value is 1.98 g cm^{-3}. This method of estimating the density gives a value that is close to the experimentally measured density.

11.147   Decreasing the pressure will decrease the temperature of liquid nitrogen. Because the nitrogen is boiling, its temperature must be constant at a given pressure. As the pressure decreases, the boiling point decreases, and therefore so does the temperature. Remember that vaporization is an endothermic process, so as the nitrogen vaporizes it will remove heat from the liquid, dropping its temperature. If the pressure drops below the pressure of the triple point, the phase change will shift from vaporization to sublimation and the liquid nitrogen will become solid.

11.149   **Given:** cubic closest-packing structure = cube with touching spheres of radius = r on alternating corners of a cube   **Find:** body diagonal of cube and radius of tetrahedral hole
Solution: The cell edge length = l and $l^2 + l^2 = (2r)^2 \rightarrow 2l^2 = 4r^2 \rightarrow l^2 = 2r^2$. Since body diagonal = BD is the hypotenuse of the right triangle formed by the face diagonal and the cell edge we have $(BD)^2 = l^2 + (2r)^2 = 2r^2 + 4r^2 = 6r^2 \rightarrow BD = \sqrt{6}r$. The radius of the tetrahedral hole = r_T is half the body diagonal minus the radius of the sphere or

$$r_T = \dfrac{BD}{2} - r = \dfrac{\sqrt{6}r}{2} - r = \left(\dfrac{\sqrt{6}}{2} - 1\right)r = \left(\dfrac{\sqrt{6} - 2}{2}\right)r = \left(\dfrac{\sqrt{3}\sqrt{2} - \sqrt{2}\sqrt{2}}{\sqrt{2}\sqrt{2}}\right)r$$

$$= \left(\dfrac{\sqrt{3} - \sqrt{2}}{\sqrt{2}}\right)r \approx 0.22474r.$$

11.151   **Given:** 1.00 L water, T_i = 298 K, T_f = 373 K - vapour; P_{CH_4} = 1.00 atm **Find:** V (CH$_4$)
Other: $\Delta_{comb}H^\circ$ (CH$_4$) = 890.4 kJ mol^{-1}; C_{water} = 75.2 J mol^{-1} K^{-1}; $\Delta_{vap}H^\circ$ (H$_2$O) = 40.7 kJ mol^{-1}, d = 1.00 g mL^{-1}
Conceptual Plan: L $\rightarrow$ mL $\rightarrow$ g $\rightarrow$ mol then heat liquid water: $n, C_s, T_i, T_f \rightarrow q_{1water}$ **(J)**

$\dfrac{1000 \text{ mL}}{1 \text{ L}}$ $\dfrac{1.00 \text{ g}}{1.00 \text{ mL}}$ $\dfrac{1 \text{ mol}}{18.01 \text{ g}}$ $\qquad q = mC_S(T_f - T_i)$

vaporize water: n_{water}, $\Delta_{vap}H°$ $\rightarrow$ q_{2water} (J) then calculate total heat q_{1water}, q_{2water} $\rightarrow$ q_{water} (J) then

$$q = n\Delta H \qquad\qquad q_{1water} + q_{2water} = q_{water}$$

q_{water}(J) $\rightarrow$ $-q_{CH_4comb}$ (J) $\rightarrow$ n_{CH_4} finally n_{CH_4}, P, T $\rightarrow$ V

$$q_{water} = -q_{CH_4comb} \qquad q = n\Delta H \qquad\qquad PV = nRT$$

Solution: $1.00 \text{ L} \times \dfrac{1000 \text{ mL}}{1 \text{ L}} \times \dfrac{1.00 \text{ g}}{1.00 \text{ mL}} \times \dfrac{1 \text{ mol}}{18.01 \text{ g}} = 55.5247 \text{ mol } H_2O$

$q_{1water} = n_{water}C_{water}(T_f - T_i) = 55.5247 \text{ mol} \times 75.2 \dfrac{J}{\text{mol} \cdot K} \times (373 \text{ K} - 298 \text{ K}) = 3.1315936 \times 10^5 \text{ J}$

$= 313.15936 \text{ kJ}$,

$q_{2water} = n\Delta_{vap}H = 55.5247 \text{ mol} \times 40.7 \dfrac{kJ}{\text{mol}} = 2.259855 \times 10^3 \text{ kJ}$

$q_{1water} + q_{2water} = q_{water} = 313.15936 \text{ kJ} + 2.259855 \times 10^3 \text{ kJ} = 2.57301465 \times 10^3 \text{ kJ}$

$q_{water} = -q_{CH_4comb} = 2.57301465 \times 10^3 \text{ kJ}$ then $q_{CH_4comb} = n\Delta_{CH_4comb}H$. Rearrange to solve for n.

$n_{CH_4} = \dfrac{q_{CH_4}}{\Delta_{CH_4comb}H} = \dfrac{-2.57301465 \times 10^3 \text{ kJ}}{-890.4 \dfrac{kJ}{\text{mol}}} = 2.8897289 \text{ mol}$ then $PV = nRT$.

Rearrange to solve for V. $V = \dfrac{nRT}{P} = \dfrac{2.8897289 \text{ mol} \times 0.08206 \dfrac{L \cdot atm}{\text{mol} \cdot K} \times 298 \text{ K}}{1.00 \text{ atm}} = 70.665085 \text{ L} = 70.7 \text{ L}.$

Check: The units (L) are correct. The volume (71 L) is reasonable since we are using about 3 moles of methane.

11.153 $\quad P_{Total} = P_{N_2} + P_{H_2O} + P_{ethanol}$
P_{N_2}: Use Boyle's law to calculate $P_1V_1 = P_2V_2$. Rearrange to solve for P_2.

$P_2 = P_1\dfrac{V_1}{V_2} = 1.01 \text{ bar} \times \dfrac{1.0 \text{ L}}{3.0 \text{ L}} = 0.3367 \text{ bar}$

For water and ethanol, we need to calculate the pressure if all of the liquid were to vaporize in the 3.0 L apparatus. $PV = nRT$. Rearrange to solve for P.

$P_{water} = \dfrac{nRT}{V} = 2.0 \text{ g} \times \dfrac{1 \text{ mol}}{18.01 \text{ g}} \times 8.314462 \times 10^{-2} \dfrac{L \cdot bar}{K \cdot mol} \times 308 \text{ K} \times \dfrac{1}{3.00 \text{ L}} = 0.9479 \text{ bar } H_2O$

Since this pressure is greater than the vapour pressure of water at this temperature (0.05576 bar), then $P_{H_2O} = 0.05576 \text{ bar}$.

$P_{ethanol} = \dfrac{nRT}{V} = 0.50 \text{ g} \times \dfrac{1 \text{ mol}}{46.07 \text{ g}} \times 8.314462 \times 10^{-2} \dfrac{L \cdot bar}{K \cdot mol} \times 308 \text{ K} \times \dfrac{1}{3.00 \text{ L}} = 0.09264 \text{ bar ethanol}$

Since this pressure is less than the vapour pressure of ethanol at this temperature (0.1356 bar), all of the liquid will vaporize and $P_{ethanol} = 0.09264 \text{ bar}$.
Finally, the total pressure is
$P_{Total} = P_{N_2} + P_{water} + P_{ethanol} = 0.3367 \text{ bar} + 0.05576 \text{ bar} + 0.09264 \text{ bar}$
$= 0.4851 \text{ bar} = 0.46 \text{ bar or } 0.48 \text{ atm}$ (Remember 1 atm = 1.01 bar)

Conceptual Problems

11.155　A container with a larger surface area will evaporate more quickly because there is more surface area for the molecules to evaporate from. Vapour pressure is the pressure of the gas when it is in dynamic equilibrium with the liquid (evaporation rate = condensation rate). The vapour pressure is dependent only on the substance and the temperature. The larger the surface area, the more quickly it will reach this equilibrium state.

11.157　The triple point will be at a lower temperature since the fusion equilibrium line has a positive slope. This means that we will be increasing both temperature and pressure as we travel from the triple point to the normal melting point.

11.159   The liquid segment will have the least steep slope because it takes the most kJ mol^{-1} to raise the temperature of the phase.

11.161   The heat of fusion of a substance is always smaller than the heat of vaporization because the number of interactions between particles that are broken is less in fusion than in vaporization. When we melt a solid, the particles have increased mobility, but are still strongly interacting with other liquid particles. In vaporization, all of the interactions between particles must be broken (gas particles have essentially no intermolecular interactions) and the particles must absorb enough energy to move much more rapidly.

12 Solutions

Review Questions

12.1   As seawater moves through the intestine, it flows past cells that line the digestive tract, which consist of largely fluid interiors surrounded by membranes. Although cellular fluids themselves contain dissolved ions, including sodium and chloride, the fluids are more dilute than seawater. Nature's tendency toward mixing (which tends to produce solutions of uniform concentration), together with the selective permeability of the cell membranes (which allow water to flow in and out, but restrict the flow of dissolved solids), cause a flow of solvent out of the body's cells and into the seawater.

12.3   A substance is soluble in another substance if they can form a homogeneous mixture. The solubility of a substance is the amount of the substance that will dissolve in a given amount of solvent. Many different units can be used to express solubility, including grams of solute per 100 grams of solvent, grams of solute per litre of solvent, moles of solute per litre of solution, and moles of solute per kilogram of solvent.

12.5   Entropy is a measure of energy randomization or energy dispersion in a system. When two substances mix to form a solution there is an increase in randomness due to the fact that the components are no longer segregated to separate regions. This makes the formation of a solution energetically favourable, even when it is endothermic.

12.7   A solution always forms if the solvent–solute interactions are comparable to, or stronger than, the solvent–solvent interactions and the solute–solute interactions.

12.9   Step 1: Separate the solute into its constituent particles. This step is always endothermic (positive ΔH) because energy is required to overcome the forces that hold the solute together.

   Step 2: Separate the solvent particles from each other to make room for the solute particles. This step is also endothermic because energy is required to overcome the intermolecular forces among the solvent particles.

   Step 3: Mix the solute particles with the solvent particles. This step is exothermic because energy is released as the solute particles interact with the solvent particles through the various types of intermolecular forces.

12.11   In any solution formation, the initial rate of dissolution far exceeds the rate of deposition. But as the concentration of dissolved solute increases, the rate of deposition also increases. Eventually the rate of dissolution and deposition become equal—dynamic equilibrium has been reached.

   A saturated solution is a solution in which the dissolved solute is in dynamic equilibrium with the solid (or undissolved) solute. If you add additional solute to a saturated solution, it will not dissolve.

   An unsaturated solution is a solution containing less than the equilibrium amount of solute. If you add additional solute to an unsaturated solution, it will dissolve.

A supersaturated solution is a solution containing more than the equilibrium amount of solute. Such solutions are unstable and the excess solute normally precipitates out of the solution. However, in some cases, if left undisturbed, a supersaturated solution can exist for an extended period of time.

12.13   The solubility of gases in liquids decreases with increasing temperature. The decreasing solubility of gases with increasing temperature results in a lower oxygen concentration available for fish and other aquatic life in warm waters.

12.15   Henry's law quantifies the solubility of gases with increasing pressure as follows: $S_{gas} = k_H P_{gas}$, where S_{gas} is the solubility of the gas; k_H is a constant of proportionality (called the Henry's law constant) that depends on the specific solute, solvent, and temperature; and P_{gas} is the partial pressure of the gas. The equation simply shows that the solubility of a gas in a liquid is directly proportional to the pressure of the gas above the liquid. If the solubility of a gas is known at a certain temperature, the solubility at another pressure at this temperature can be calculated.

12.17   Parts by mass and parts by volume are ratios of masses and volume, respectively. A parts by mass concentration is the ratio of the mass of the solute to the mass of the solution, all multiplied by a multiplication factor, where percent by mass (%) is the desired unit, the factor = 100; where parts per million by mass (ppm) is the desired unit, the factor = 10^6; and for parts per billion by mass (ppb), the factor = 10^9. The size of the multiplication factor depends on the concentration of the solution. For example, in percent by mass, the

multiplication factor is 100%, so percent by mass $= \dfrac{\text{mass solute}}{\text{mass solution}} \times 100\%$. A solution with a concentration of 28% by mass contains 28 g of solute per 100 g of solution.

12.19   Raoult's law quantifies the relationship between the vapour pressure of a solution and its concentration as $P_{solution} = \chi_{solvent} P^{\circ}_{solvent}$, where $P_{solution}$ is the vapour pressure of the solution, $\chi_{solvent}$ is the mole fraction of the solvent, and $P^{\circ}_{solvent}$ is the vapour pressure of the pure solvent. This equation allows you to calculate the vapour pressure of a solution or to calculate the concentration of a solution, given the vapour pressure of the solution.

12.21   If the solute–solvent interactions are particularly strong (stronger than solvent–solvent interactions), then the solute tends to prevent the solvent from vaporizing as easily as it would otherwise and the vapour pressure of the solution will be less than that predicted by Raoult's law. If the solute–solvent interactions are particularly weak (weaker than solvent–solvent interactions), then the solute tends to allow more vaporization than would occur with just the solvent and the vapour pressure of the solution will be greater than predicted by Raoult's law.

12.23   Colligative properties are properties that depend on the amount of solute and not the type of solute. Examples of colligative properties are vapour pressure lowering, freezing point depression, boiling point elevation, and osmotic pressure.

12.25   The van't Hoff factor (i) is the ratio of moles of particles in solution to moles of formula units dissolved: $i = \dfrac{\text{moles of particles}}{\text{moles of formula units dissolved}}$. The van't Hoff factor often does not match its theoretical value due to the fact that the ionic solute is not completely dissolved into the expected number of ions, leaving ion pairs in solution. The result is that the number of particles in the solution is not as high as theoretically expected.

12.27   The Tyndall effect is the scattering of light by a colloidal dispersion. The Tyndall effect is often used as a test to determine whether a mixture is a solution or a colloid, since solutions contain completely dissolved solute molecules that are too small to scatter light.

Problems by Topic

Solubility

12.29   (a)   hexane, toluene, or CCl_4; dispersion forces

        (b)   water, methanol, acetone; dispersion, dipole–dipole, hydrogen bonding

(c)   hexane, toluene, or CCl_4; dispersion forces

(d)   water, acetone, methanol, ethanol; dispersion, ion–dipole

12.31 $HOCH_2CH_2CH_2OH$ would be more soluble in water because it has –OH groups on both ends of the molecule, so it can hydrogen bond on both ends.

12.33   (a)   water; dispersion, dipole–dipole, hydrogen bonding

          (b)   hexane; dispersion forces

          (c)   water; dispersion, dipole–dipole

          (d)   water; dispersion, dipole–dipole, hydrogen bonding

Energetics of Solution Formation

12.35   (a)   Endothermic

          (b)   The lattice energy is greater in magnitude than the heat of hydration.

          (c)

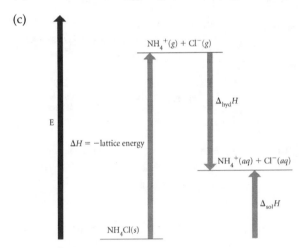

          (d) The solution forms because chemical systems tend toward greater entropy.

12.37   **Given:** $AgNO_3$: lattice energy $= -820$; kJ mol^{-1}, $\Delta_{soln}H = +22.6$ kJ mol^{-1} **Find:** $\Delta_{hyd}H$
          Conceptual Plan: Lattice Energy, $\Delta_{soln}H \rightarrow \Delta_{hyd}H$
          $$\Delta_{soln}H = \Delta_{solute}H + \Delta_{hyd}H \ where \ \Delta_{solute}H = -\Delta_{lattice}H$$
          Solution: $\Delta_{soln}H = \Delta_{solute}H + \Delta_{hyd}H$ where $\Delta_{solute}H = -\Delta_{lattice}H$ so $\Delta_{hyd}H = \Delta_{soln}H + \Delta_{lattice}H$
          $\Delta_{hyd}H = 22.6$ kJ mol^{-1} $- 820$ kJ mol^{-1} $= -797$ kJ mol^{-1}
          Check: The units (kJ mol^{-1}) are correct. The magnitude of the answer (-800) makes physical sense because the lattice energy is so negative, and thus it dominates the calculation.

12.39   **Given:** LiI: Lattice Energy $= -7.3 \times 10^2$ kJ mol^{-1}, $\Delta_{hyd}H = -793$ kJ mol^{-1}; 15.0 g LiI
          Find: $\Delta_{soln}H$ and heat evolved
          Conceptual Plan: Lattice Energy, $\Delta_{hyd}H \rightarrow \Delta_{soln}H$ and g $\rightarrow$ mol then mol, $\Delta_{soln}H \rightarrow q$
          $$\Delta_{soln}H = \Delta_{solute}H + \Delta_{hyd}H \ where \ \Delta_{solute}H = -\Delta_{lattice}H \qquad \frac{1\ mol}{133.843\ g} \qquad q = n\,\Delta_{soln}H$$
          Solution: $\Delta_{soln}H = \Delta_{solute}H + \Delta_{hyd}H$ where $\Delta_{solute}H = -\Delta_{lattice}H$ so $\Delta_{soln}H = \Delta_{hyd}H - \Delta_{lattice}H$
          $\Delta_{soln}H = -793$ kJ mol^{-1} $- (-730$ kJ mol^{-1}) $= -63$ kJ mol^{-1} $= -6.3 \times 10^1$ kJ mol^{-1} and

          $15.0 \ \text{g} \times \dfrac{1\ mol}{133.843\ \text{g}} = 0.112072$ mol then

          $q = n\Delta_{soln}H = 0.112072 \ \text{mol} \times -6.3 \times 10^1 \ \dfrac{kJ}{\text{mol}} = -7.0$ kJ or 7 kJ released

          Check: The units (kJ mol^{-1} and kJ) are correct. The magnitude of the answer (-60) makes physical sense because the lattice energy and the heat of hydration are about the same. The magnitude of the heat (7)

makes physical sense since 15 g is much less than a mole, and thus the amount of heat released is going to be small.

Solution Equilibrium and Factors Affecting Solubility

12.41   The solution is unsaturated since we are dissolving 25 g of NaCl per 100 g of water and the solubility from the figure is ~ 35 g NaCl per 100 g of water at 25° C.

12.43   At 40 °C the solution has 45 g of KNO_3 per 100 g of water and it can contain up to 63 g of KNO_3 per 100 g of water. At 0 °C the solubility from the figure is ~ 14 g KNO_3 per 100 g of water, so ~ 31 g KNO_3 per 100 g of water will precipitate out of solution.

12.45   Since the solubility of gases decreases as the temperature increases, boiling will cause dissolved oxygen to be removed from the solution.

12.47   Henry's law says that as pressure increases, nitrogen will more easily dissolve in blood. To reverse this process, divers should ascend to lower pressures.

12.49   **Given:** room temperature, 80.0 L aquarium, $P_{Total} = 1.0$ bar; $\chi_{N_2} = 0.78$ **Find:** m (N_2)
Other: $k_H(N_2) = 6.1 \times 10^{-4}$ mol L^{-1} bar^{-1} at 25 °C
Conceptual Plan: $P_{Total}, \chi_{N_2} \rightarrow P_{N_2}$ then $P_{N_2}, k_H(N_2) \rightarrow S_{N_2}$ then $L \rightarrow$ mol $\rightarrow$ g

$$P_{N_2} = \chi_{N_2} P_{Total} \qquad S_{N_2} = k_H(N_2)P_{N_2} \quad M = \frac{\text{amount solute (moles)}}{\text{volume solution (L)}} \frac{28.01 \text{ g } N_2}{1 \text{ mol } N_2}$$

Solution: $P_{N_2} = \chi_{N_2} P_{Total} = 0.78 \times 1.0$ bar $= 0.78$ bar then

$S_{N_2} = k_H(N_2)P_{N_2} = 6.1 \times 10^{-4} \dfrac{\text{mol}}{\text{L} \cdot \text{bar}} \times 0.78 \text{ bar} = 4.758 \times 10^{-4}$ mol L^{-1} then

$80.0 \text{ L} \times 4.758 \times 10^{-4} \dfrac{\text{mol}}{\text{L}} \times \dfrac{28.01 \text{ g}}{1 \text{ mol}} = 1.1$ g
Check: The units (g) are correct. The magnitude of the answer (1) seems reasonable since we have 80 L of water and expect much less than a mole of nitrogen.

Concentrations of Solutions

12.51   **Given:** NaCl and water; 112 g NaCl in 1.00 L solution **Find:** M, m, and mass percent
Other: $d = 1.08$ g mL^{-1}
Conceptual Plan: $g_{NaCl} \rightarrow$ mol and $L \rightarrow$ mL $\rightarrow g_{soln}$ and $g_{soln}\ g_{NaCl} \rightarrow g_{H_2O} \rightarrow kg_{H_2O}$ then

$$\frac{1 \text{ mol NaCl}}{58.44 \text{ g NaCl}} \qquad \frac{1000 \text{ mL}}{1 \text{ L}} \quad \frac{1.08 \text{ g}}{1 \text{ mL}} \qquad g_{H_2O} = g_{soln} - g_{NaCl} \quad \frac{1 \text{ kg}}{1000 \text{ g}}$$

mol, $V \rightarrow$ M and mol, $kg_{H_2O} \rightarrow m$ and $g_{soln}\ g_{NaCl} \rightarrow$ mass percent

$$M = \frac{\text{amount solute (moles)}}{\text{volume solution (L)}} \quad m = \frac{\text{amount solute (moles)}}{\text{mass solvent (kg)}} \quad \text{mass percent} = \frac{\text{mass solute}}{\text{mass solution}} \times 100\%$$

Solution: $112 \text{ g NaCl} \times \dfrac{1 \text{ mol NaCl}}{58.44 \text{ g NaCl}} = 1.9164956$ mol NaCl and

$1.00 \text{ L} \times \dfrac{1000 \text{ mL}}{1 \text{ L}} \times \dfrac{1.08 \text{ g}}{1 \text{ mL}} = 1080$ g soln and

$g_{H_2O} = g_{soln} - g_{NaCl} = 1080 \text{ g} - 112 \text{ g} = 968 \text{ g } H_2O \times \dfrac{1 \text{ kg}}{1000 \text{ g}} = 0.968$ kg H_2O then

$M = \dfrac{\text{amount solute (moles)}}{\text{volume solution (L)}} = \dfrac{1.9164956 \text{ mol NaCl}}{1.00 \text{ L soln}} = 1.92$ mol L^{-1} and

$m = \dfrac{\text{amount solute (moles)}}{\text{mass solvent (kg)}} = \dfrac{1.9164956 \text{ mol NaCl}}{0.968 \text{ kg } H_2O} = 2.0$ mol kg^{-1} and

$\text{mass percent} = \dfrac{\text{mass solute}}{\text{mass solution}} \times 100\% = \dfrac{112 \text{ g NaCl}}{1080 \text{ g soln}} \times 100\% = 10.4\%$ by mass.

Check: The units (mol L^{-1}, mol kg^{-1}, and percent by mass) are correct. The magnitude of the answer (2 mol L^{-1}) seems reasonable since we have 112 g NaCl, which is a couple of moles, and we have 1 L. The magnitude of the answer (2 m) seems reasonable since it is a little higher than the molarity, which we expect since we only use the solvent weight in the denominator. The magnitude of the answer (10%) seems reasonable since we have 112 g NaCl and just over 1000 g of solution.

12.53   **Given:** initial solution: 50.0 mL of 5.00 mol L^{-1} KI; final solution contains: 3.05 g KI in 25.0 mL
Find: final volume to dilute initial solution to
Conceptual Plan: final solution: $g_{KI} \rightarrow$ **mol and mL** $\rightarrow$ **L then mol, $V \rightarrow M_2$ then $M_1, V_1, M_2 \rightarrow V_2$**

$$\frac{1 \text{ mol KI}}{166.006 \text{ g KI}} \qquad \frac{1 \text{ L}}{1000 \text{ mL}} \qquad M = \frac{\text{amount solute (moles)}}{\text{volume solution (L)}} \qquad M_1V_1 = M_2V_2$$

Solution: $3.05 \text{ g KI} \times \dfrac{1 \text{ mol KI}}{166.006 \text{ g KI}} = 0.01837283 \text{ mol KI}$ and $25.0 \text{ mL} \times \dfrac{1 \text{ L}}{1000 \text{ mL}} = 0.0250 \text{ mL}$

then $M = \dfrac{\text{amount solute (moles)}}{\text{volume solution (L)}} = \dfrac{0.01837283 \text{ mol KI}}{0.0250 \text{L soln}} = 0.7349132 \text{ mol L}^{-1}$ then $M_1V_1 = M_2V_2$.

Rearrange to solve for V_2. $V_2 = \dfrac{M_1}{M_2} \times V_1 = \dfrac{5.00 \text{ mol L}^{-1}}{0.7349132 \text{ mol L}^{-1}} \times 50.0 \text{ mL} \times \dfrac{1 \text{ L}}{1000 \text{ mL}}$

$= 0.340 \text{ L diluted volume.}$

Check: The units (L) are correct. The magnitude of the answer (0.340 L) seems reasonable since we are starting with a concentration of 5 mol L^{-1} and ending with a concentration of less than 1 mol L^{-1}.

12.55   **Given:** AgNO$_3$ and water; 3.4% Ag by mass, 4.8 L solution   **Find:** m (Ag)   **Other:** $d = 1.01$ g mL^{-1}
Conceptual Plan: L $\rightarrow$ mL $\rightarrow$ g$_{soln}$ $\rightarrow$ g$_{Ag}$

$$\frac{1000 \text{ mL}}{1 \text{ L}} \qquad \frac{1.01 \text{ g}}{1 \text{ mL}} \qquad \frac{3.4 \text{ g Ag}}{100 \text{ g soln}}$$

Solution: $4.8 \text{ L} \times \dfrac{1000 \text{ mL}}{1 \text{ L}} \times \dfrac{1.01 \text{ g}}{1 \text{ mL}} = 4848 \text{ g soln}$ then

$4848 \text{ g soln} \times \dfrac{3.4 \text{ g Ag}}{100 \text{ g soln}} = 160 \text{ g Ag} = 1.6 \times 10^2 \text{ g Ag.}$

Check: The units (g) are correct. The magnitude of the answer (160 g) seems reasonable since we have almost 5000 g solution.

12.57   **Given:** Ca^{2+} and water; 0.0085% Ca^{2+} by mass, 1.2 g Ca   **Find:** m (water)
Conceptual Plan: g$_{Ca}$ $\rightarrow$ g$_{soln}$ $\rightarrow$ g$_{H_2O}$

$$\frac{100 \text{ g soln}}{0.0085 \text{ g Ca}} \qquad g_{H_2O} = g_{soln} - g_{Ca}$$

Solution: $1.2 \text{ g Ca} \times \dfrac{100 \text{ g soln}}{0.0085 \text{ g Ca}} = 14118 \text{ g soln}$ then

$g_{H_2O} = g_{soln} - g_{Ca} = 14118 \text{ g} - 1.2 \text{ g} = 1.4 \times 10^4 \text{ g water.}$

Check: The units (g) are correct. The magnitude of the answer (10^4 g) seems reasonable since we have such a low concentration of Ca.

12.59   **Given:** concentrated HNO$_3$: 70.3% HNO$_3$ by mass, $d = 1.41$ g mL^{-1}; final solution: 1.15 L of 0.100 mol L^{-1} HNO$_3$
Find: describe final solution preparation
Conceptual Plan: $M_2, V_2 \rightarrow$ mol$_{HNO_3}$ $\rightarrow$ g$_{HNO_3}$ $\rightarrow$ g$_{conc\ acid}$ $\rightarrow$ mL$_{conc\ acid}$ **then describe method**

$$\text{mol} = MV \qquad \frac{63.02 \text{ g HNO}_3}{1 \text{ mol HNO}_3} \qquad \frac{100 \text{ g conc acid}}{70.3 \text{ g HNO}_3} \qquad \frac{1 \text{ mL}}{1.41 \text{ g}}$$

Solution: mol $= M V = 0.100 \dfrac{\text{mol HNO}_3}{1 \text{ L soln}} \times 1.15 \text{ L soln} = 0.115 \text{ mol HNO}_3$ then

$0.115 \text{ mol HNO}_3 \times \dfrac{63.02 \text{ g HNO}_3}{1 \text{ mol HNO}_3} \times \dfrac{100 \text{ g conc acid}}{70.3 \text{ g HNO}_3} \times \dfrac{1 \text{ mL conc acid}}{1.41 \text{ g conc acid}} = 7.31 \text{ mL conc acid.}$

Prepare the solution by putting about 1.00 L of distilled water in a container. Carefully pour in the 7.31 mL of the concentrated acid, mix the solution, and allow it to cool. Finally add enough water to generate the total volume of solution (1.15 L). It is important to add acid to water, and not the reverse, since there is such a large amount of heat released upon mixing.

Check: The units (mL) are correct. The magnitude of the answer (7 g) seems reasonable since we are starting with such a very concentrated solution and diluting it to a low concentration.

12.61   (a)   **Given:** 1.00×10^2 mL of 0.500 mol L^{-1} KCl   **Find:** describe final solution preparation
Conceptual Plan: mL $\rightarrow$ L then $M, V \rightarrow$ mol$_{KCl} \rightarrow$ g$_{KCl}$ then describe method

$$\frac{1 \text{ L}}{1000 \text{ mL}} \qquad \text{mol} = M\,V \qquad \frac{74.56 \text{ g KCl}}{1 \text{ mol KCl}}$$

Solution: $1.00 \times 10^2 \text{ mL} \times \dfrac{1 \text{ L}}{1000 \text{ mL}} = 0.100$ L

$\text{mol} = M\,V = 0.500 \dfrac{\text{mol KCl}}{1 \text{ L soln}} \times 0.100 \text{ L soln} = 0.0500$ mol KCl

then $0.0500 \text{ mol KCl} \times \dfrac{74.56 \text{ g KCl}}{1 \text{ mol KCl}} = 3.73$ g KCl.

Prepare the solution by carefully adding 3.73 g KCl to a 100 mL volumetric flask. Add ~ 75 mL of distilled water and agitate the solution until the salt dissolves completely. Finally, add enough water to generate a total volume of solution (add water to the mark on the flask).
Check: The units (g) are correct. The magnitude of the answer (4 g) seems reasonable since we are making a small volume of solution and the formula weight of KCl is ~ 75 g mol^{-1}.

(b)   **Given:** 1.00×10^2 g of 0.500 m KCl   **Find:** describe final solution preparation
Conceptual Plan:

$m \rightarrow$ mol$_{KCl}$(1 kg solvent)$^{-1} \rightarrow$ g$_{KCl}$(1 kg solvent)$^{-1}$ then g$_{KCl}$(1 kg solvent)$^{-1}$, g$_{soln} \rightarrow$ g$_{KCl}$, g$_{H_2O}$

$$m = \frac{\text{amount solute (moles)}}{\text{mass solvent (kg)}} \qquad \frac{74.56 \text{ g KCl}}{1 \text{ mol KCl}} \qquad\qquad g_{soln} = g_{KCl} + g_{H_2O}$$

then describe method

Solution: $m = \dfrac{\text{amount solute (moles)}}{\text{mass solvent (kg)}}$ so $0.500\ m = \dfrac{0.500 \text{ mol KCl}}{1 \text{ kg } H_2O}$ so

$\dfrac{0.500 \text{ mol KCl}}{1 \text{ kg } H_2O} \times \dfrac{74.56 \text{ g KCl}}{1 \text{ mol KCl}} = \dfrac{37.28 \text{ g KCl}}{1000 \text{ g } H_2O}$ $g_{soln} = g_{KCl} + g_{H_2O}$ so $g_{soln} - g_{KCl} = g_{H_2O}$

substitute into ratio $\dfrac{37.28 \text{ g KCl}}{1037.28 \text{ g solution}} = \dfrac{x \text{ g KCl}}{500 \text{ g solution}}$.   Cross multiply, and solve for grams KCl.

$0.03728(100 \text{ g soln} - x \text{ g KCl}) = x \text{ g KCl} \rightarrow 3.\underline{7}28 - 0.03728\,(x \text{ g KCl}) = x \text{ g KCl} \rightarrow$

$3.\underline{7}28 = 1.03728\,(x \text{ g KCl}) \rightarrow \dfrac{3.\underline{7}28}{1.03728} = x \text{ g KCl} = 3.59$ g KCl then

$g_{H_2O} = g_{soln} - g_{KCl} = 100 \text{ g} - 3.59 \text{ g} = 96.41$ g H_2O.

Prepare the solution by carefully adding 3.59 g KCl to a container with 96.41 g of distilled water and agitate the solution until the salt dissolves completely.
Check: The units (g) are correct. The magnitude of the answer (3.6 g) seems reasonable since we are making a small volume of solution and the formula weight of KCl is ~ 75 g mol^{-1}.

(c)   **Given:** 1.00×10^2 g of 5.0% KCl by mass   **Find:** describe final solution preparation
Conceptual Plan: g$_{soln} \rightarrow$ g$_{KCl}$ then g$_{KCl}$, g$_{soln} \rightarrow$ g$_{H_2O}$

$$\frac{5.0 \text{ g KCl}}{100 \text{ g soln}} \qquad\qquad g_{soln} = g_{KCl} + g_{H_2O}$$

then describe method

Solution: $1.00 \times 10^2 \text{ g soln} \times \dfrac{5.0 \text{ g KCl}}{100 \text{ g soln}} = 5.0$ g KCl then $g_{soln} = g_{KCl} + g_{H_2O}$.

So $g_{H_2O} = g_{soln} - g_{KCl} = 100 \text{ g} - 5.0 \text{ g} = 95$ g H_2O.
Prepare the solution by carefully adding 5.0 g KCl to a container with 95 g of distilled water and agitate the solution until the salt dissolves completely.
Check: The units (g) are correct. The magnitude of the answer (5 g) seems reasonable since we are making a small volume of solution and the solution is 5% by mass KCl.

12.63   (a)   **Given:** 28.4 g of glucose ($C_6H_{12}O_6$) in 355 g water; final volume = 378 mL   **Find:** molarity
Conceptual Plan: mL $\rightarrow$ L and g $_{C_6H_{12}O_6} \rightarrow$ mol $_{C_6H_{12}O_6}$ then mol $_{C_6H_{12}O_6}$, $V \rightarrow$ **M**

$$\frac{1 \text{ L}}{1000 \text{ mL}} \qquad \frac{1 \text{ mol } C_6H_{12}O_6}{180.16 \text{ g } C_6H_{12}O_6} \qquad M = \frac{\text{amount solute (moles)}}{\text{volume solution (L)}}$$

Solution: $378 \; \cancel{mL} \times \dfrac{1 \; L}{1000 \; \cancel{mL}} = 0.378 \; L$ and

$28.4 \; \cancel{g \; C_6H_{12}O_6} \times \dfrac{1 \; mol \; C_6H_{12}O_6}{180.16 \; \cancel{g \; C_6H_{12}O_6}} = 0.15\underline{7}638 \; mol \; C_6H_{12}O_6$

$M = \dfrac{\text{amount solute (moles)}}{\text{volume solution (L)}} = \dfrac{0.15\underline{7}638 \; mol \; C_6H_{12}O_6}{0.378 \; L} = 0.417 \; mol \; L^{-1}$

Check: The units ($mol \; L^{-1}$) are correct. The magnitude of the answer ($0.4 \; mol \; L^{-1}$) seems reasonable since we have 1/8 mole in about 1/3 L.

(b)   **Given:** 28.4 g of glucose ($C_6H_{12}O_6$) in 355 g water; final volume = 378 mL **Find:** molality
  Conceptual Plan: $g_{H_2O} \rightarrow kg_{H_2O}$ and $g_{C_6H_{12}O_6} \rightarrow mol_{C_6H_{12}O_6}$ then $mol_{C_6H_{12}O_6}, \; kg_{H_2O} \rightarrow m$

$$\dfrac{1 \; kg}{1000 \; g} \qquad \qquad \dfrac{1 \; mol \; C_6H_{12}O_6}{180.16 \; g \; C_6H_{12}O_6} \qquad m = \dfrac{\text{amount solute (moles)}}{\text{mass solvent (kg)}}$$

Solution: $355 \; \cancel{g} \times \dfrac{1 \; kg}{1000 \; \cancel{g}} = 0.355 \; kg$ and

$28.4 \; \cancel{g \; C_6H_{12}O_6} \times \dfrac{1 \; mol \; C_6H_{12}O_6}{180.16 \; \cancel{g \; C_6H_{12}O_6}} = 0.15\underline{7}638 \; mol \; C_6H_{12}O_6$

$m = \dfrac{\text{amount solute (moles)}}{\text{mass solvent (kg)}} = \dfrac{0.15\underline{7}638 \; mol \; C_6H_{12}O_6}{0.355 \; kg} = 0.444 \; mol \; kg^{-1}$

Check: The units ($mol \; kg^{-1}$) are correct. The magnitude of the answer ($0.4 \; mol \; kg^{-1}$) seems reasonable since we have 1/8 mole in about 1/3 kg.

(c)   **Given:** 28.4 g of glucose ($C_6H_{12}O_6$) in 355 g water; final volume = 378 mL **Find:** percent by mass
  Conceptual Plan: $g_{C_6H_{12}O_6}, \; g_{H_2O} \rightarrow g_{soln}$ then $g_{C_6H_{12}O_6}, \; g_{soln} \rightarrow$ **percent by mass**

$$g_{soln} = g_{C_6H_{12}O_6} + g_{H_2O} \qquad \text{mass percent} = \dfrac{\text{mass solute}}{\text{mass solution}} \times 100\%$$

Solution: $g_{soln} = g_{C_6H_{12}O_6} + g_{H_2O} = 28.4 \; g + 355 \; g = 38\underline{3}.4 \; g \; soln$ then

$\text{mass percent} = \dfrac{\text{mass solute}}{\text{mass solution}} \times 100\% = \dfrac{28.4 \; g \; C_6H_{12}O_6}{38\underline{3}.4 \; g \; soln} \times 100\% = 7.41 \; \text{percent by mass.}$

Check: The units (percent by mass) are correct. The magnitude of the answer (7%) seems reasonable since we are dissolving 28 g in 355 g.

(d)   **Given:** 28.4 g of glucose ($C_6H_{12}O_6$) in 355 g water; final volume = 378 mL **Find:** mole fraction
  Conceptual Plan:

$g_{C_6H_{12}O_6} \rightarrow mol_{C_6H_{12}O_6}$ and $g_{H_2O} \rightarrow mol_{H_2O}$ then $mol_{C_6H_{12}O_6}, \; mol_{H_2O} \rightarrow \chi_{C_6H_{12}O_6}$

$$\dfrac{1 \; mol \; C_6H_{12}O_6}{180.16 \; g \; C_6H_{12}O_6} \qquad \dfrac{1 \; mol \; H_2O}{18.02 \; g \; H_2O} \qquad \chi = \dfrac{\text{amount solute (in moles)}}{\text{total amount of solute and solvent (in moles)}}$$

Solution: $28.4 \; \cancel{g \; C_6H_{12}O_6} \times \dfrac{1 \; mol \; C_6H_{12}O_6}{180.16 \; \cancel{g \; C_6H_{12}O_6}} = 0.15\underline{7}638 \; mol \; C_6H_{12}O_6$ and

$355 \; \cancel{g \; H_2O} \times \dfrac{1 \; mol \; H_2O}{18.02 \; \cancel{g \; H_2O}} = 19.\underline{7}003 \; mol \; H_2O$ then

$\chi = \dfrac{\text{amount solute (in moles)}}{\text{total amount of solute and solvent (in moles)}} = \dfrac{0.15\underline{7}638 \; \cancel{mol}}{0.15\underline{7}638 \; \cancel{mol} + 19.\underline{7}003 \; \cancel{mol}} = 0.00794$

Check: The units (none) are correct. The magnitude of the answer (0.008) seems reasonable since we have many more grams of water and water has a much lower molecular weight.

(e)   **Given:** 28.4 g of glucose ($C_6H_{12}O_6$) in 355 g water; final volume = 378 mL **Find:** mole percent
  Conceptual Plan: use answer from part (d) then $\chi_{C_6H_{12}O_6} \rightarrow$ **mole percent**
$$\chi \times 100\%$$

Solution: mole percent $= \chi \times 100\% = 0.00794 \times 100\% = 0.794 \; \text{mole percent}$

Check: The units (%) are correct. The magnitude of the answer (0.8) seems reasonable since we have many more grams of water, water has a much lower molecular weight than glucose, and we are increasing the answer from part (d) by a factor of 100.

12.65   **Given:** 3.0% H_2O_2 by mass, $d = 1.01$ g mL^{-1} **Find:** molarity
         Conceptual Plan:
         Assume exactly 100 g of solution; $g_{solution} \rightarrow g_{H_2O_2} \rightarrow mol_{H_2O_2}$ and $g_{solution} \rightarrow mL_{solution} \rightarrow L_{solution}$

$$\frac{3.0 \text{ g } H_2O_2}{100 \text{ g solution}} \quad \frac{1 \text{ mol } H_2O_2}{34.02 \text{ g } H_2O_2} \qquad\qquad \frac{1 \text{ mL}}{1.01 \text{ g}} \quad \frac{1 \text{ L}}{1000 \text{ mL}}$$

then $mol_{H_2O_2}, L_{solution} \rightarrow M$

$$M = \frac{\text{amount solute (moles)}}{\text{volume solution (L)}}$$

Solution: $100 \, \overline{\text{g solution}} \times \dfrac{3.0 \, \overline{\text{g } H_2O_2}}{100 \, \overline{\text{g solution}}} \times \dfrac{1 \text{ mol } H_2O_2}{34.02 \, \overline{\text{g } H_2O_2}} = 0.0881834$ mol H_2O_2 and

$100 \, \overline{\text{g solution}} \times \dfrac{1 \, \overline{\text{mL solution}}}{1.01 \, \overline{\text{g solution}}} \times \dfrac{1 \text{ L solution}}{1000 \, \overline{\text{mL solution}}} = 0.0990099$ L solution then

$M = \dfrac{\text{amount solute (moles)}}{\text{volume solution (L)}} = \dfrac{0.0881834 \text{ mol } H_2O_2}{0.0990099 \text{ L solution}} = 0.89$ mol L^{-1} H_2O_2.

Check: The units (mol L^{-1}) are correct. The magnitude of the answer (1) seems reasonable since we are starting with a low concentration solution and pure water is ~ 55.5 mol L^{-1}.

12.67   **Given:** 36% HCl by mass   **Find:** molality and mole fraction
         Conceptual Plan: Assume exactly 100 g of solution; $g_{solution} \rightarrow g_{HCl} \rightarrow mol_{HCl}$ and $g_{HCl}, g_{solution} \rightarrow$

$$\frac{36 \text{ g HCl}}{100 \text{ g solution}} \quad \frac{1 \text{ mol HCl}}{36.46 \text{ g HCl}} \qquad\qquad g_{soln} = g_{HCl} + g_{H_2O}$$

$g_{solvent} \rightarrow kg_{solvent}$ then $mol_{HCl}, kg_{solvent} \rightarrow m$ and $g_{solvent} \rightarrow mol_{solvent}$ then $mol_{HCl}, mol_{solvent} \rightarrow \chi_{HCl}$

$$\frac{1 \text{ kg}}{1000 \text{ g}} \qquad m = \frac{\text{amount solute (moles)}}{\text{mass solvent (kg)}} \quad \frac{1 \text{ mol } H_2O}{18.02 \text{ g } H_2O} \quad \chi = \frac{\text{amount solute (in moles)}}{\text{total amount of solute and solvent (in moles)}}$$

Solution: $100 \, \overline{\text{g solution}} \times \dfrac{36 \text{ g HCl}}{100 \, \overline{\text{g solution}}} = 36 \, \overline{\text{g HCl}} \times \dfrac{1 \text{ mol HCl}}{36.46 \, \overline{\text{g HCl}}} = 0.987383$ mol HCl and

$g_{soln} = g_{HCl} + g_{H_2O}$. Rearrange to solve for $g_{solvent}$. $g_{H_2O} = g_{soln} - g_{HCl} = 100 \text{ g} - 36 \text{ g} = 64 \text{ g } H_2O$

$64 \, \overline{\text{g } H_2O} \times \dfrac{1 \text{ kg } H_2O}{1000 \, \overline{\text{g } H_2O}} = 0.064$ kg H_2O then

$m = \dfrac{\text{amount solute (moles)}}{\text{mass solvent (kg)}} = \dfrac{0.987383 \text{ mol HCl}}{0.064 \text{ kg}} = 15$ mol kg^{-1} HCl and

$64 \, \overline{\text{g } H_2O} \times \dfrac{1 \text{ mol } H_2O}{18.02 \, \overline{\text{g } H_2O}} = 3.55161$ mol H_2O then

$\chi = \dfrac{\text{amount solvent (in moles)}}{\text{total amount of solute and solvent (in moles)}} = \dfrac{0.987383 \, \overline{\text{mol}}}{0.987383 \, \overline{\text{mol}} + 3.55161 \, \overline{\text{mol}}} = 0.22$.

Check: The units (mol kg^{-1} and unitless) are correct. The magnitudes of the answers (15 and 0.2) seem reasonable since we are starting with a high concentration solution and the molar mass of water is much less than that of HCl.

Vapour Pressure of Solutions

12.69   The level has decreased more in the beaker filled with pure water. The dissolved salt in the seawater decreases the vapour pressure and subsequently lowers the rate of vaporization.

12.71   **Given:** 24.5 g of glycerin ($C_3H_8O_3$) in 135 mL water at 30 °C; $P^{\circ}_{H_2O} = 31.8$ Torr   **Find:** P_{H_2O}
         Other: $d\,(H_2O) = 1.00$ g mL^{-1}; glycerin is not an ionic solid
         Conceptual Plan: g $_{C_3H_8O_3} \rightarrow$ mol $_{C_3H_8O_3}$ and mL$_{H_2O} \rightarrow g_{H_2O} \rightarrow mol_{H_2O}$ then mol $_{C_3H_8O_3},$ mol$_{H_2O} \rightarrow \chi_{H_2O}$

$$\frac{1 \text{ mol } C_3H_8O_3}{92.09 \text{ g } C_3H_8O_3} \qquad\qquad \frac{1.00 \text{ g}}{1 \text{ mL}} \quad \frac{1 \text{ mol } H_2O}{18.01 \text{ g } H_2O} \quad \chi = \frac{\text{amount solute (in moles)}}{\text{total amount of solute and solvent (in moles)}}$$

then $\chi_{H_2O}, P^{\circ}_{H_2O} \rightarrow P_{H_2O}$

$$P_{solution} = \chi_{solvent} P^{\circ}_{solvent}$$

Solution: $24.5 \ \cancel{\text{g C}_3\text{H}_8\text{O}_3} \times \dfrac{1 \text{ mol C}_3\text{H}_8\text{O}_3}{92.09 \ \cancel{\text{g C}_3\text{H}_8\text{O}_3}} = 0.2660441 \text{ mol C}_3\text{H}_8\text{O}_3$ and

$135 \ \cancel{\text{mL}} \times \dfrac{1.00 \ \cancel{\text{g}}}{1 \ \cancel{\text{mL}}} \times \dfrac{1 \text{ mol H}_2\text{O}}{18.01 \ \cancel{\text{g H}_2\text{O}}} = 7.495836 \text{ mol H}_2\text{O}$ then

$\chi = \dfrac{\text{amount solvent (in moles)}}{\text{total amount of solute and solvent (in moles)}} = \dfrac{7.495836 \ \cancel{\text{mol}}}{0.2660441 \ \cancel{\text{mol}} + 7.495836 \ \cancel{\text{mol}}} = 0.9657243$ then

$P_{\text{solution}} = \chi_{\text{solvent}} P^{\circ}_{\text{solvent}} = 0.9657243 \times 31.8 \text{ Torr} = 30.7 \text{ Torr}$

Check: The units (Torr) are correct. The magnitude of the answer (31 Torr) seems reasonable since it is a drop from the pure vapour pressure. Very few moles of glycerin are added, so the pressure will not drop much.

12.73   **Given:** 50.0 g of heptane (C_7H_{16}) and 50.0 g of octane (C_8H_{18}) at 25 °C; $P^{\circ}_{C_7H_{16}} = 45.8$ Torr; $P^{\circ}_{C_8H_{18}} = 10.9$ Torr

(a)   **Find:** $P_{C_7H_{16}}, \ P_{C_8H_{18}}$

Conceptual Plan: $\text{g } C_7H_{16} \to \text{mol } C_7H_{16}$ and $\text{g } C_8H_{18} \to \text{mol } C_8H_{18}$ then $\text{mol } C_7H_{16},$

$\dfrac{1 \text{ mol C}_7\text{H}_{16}}{100.20 \text{ g C}_7\text{H}_{16}} \qquad \dfrac{1 \text{ mol C}_8\text{H}_{18}}{114.22 \text{ g C}_8\text{H}_{18}} \qquad \chi_{C_7H_{16}} = \dfrac{\text{amount C}_7\text{H}_{16} \text{ (in moles)}}{\text{total amount (in moles)}}$

$\text{mol } C_8H_{18} \to \chi_{C_7H_{16}}, \chi_{C_8H_{18}}$ then $\chi_{C_7H_{16}}, \ P^{\circ}_{C_7H_{16}} \to P_{C_7H_{16}}$ and $\chi_{C_8H_{18}}, \ P^{\circ}_{C_8H_{18}} \to P_{C_8H_{18}}$

$\chi_{C_8H_{18}} = 1 - \chi_{C_7H_{16}} \qquad\qquad\qquad P_{C_7H_{16}} = \chi_{C_7H_{16}} P^{\circ}_{C_7H_{16}} \qquad\qquad\qquad P_{C_8H_{18}} = \chi_{C_8H_{18}} P^{\circ}_{C_8H_{18}}$

Solution: $50.0 \ \cancel{\text{g C}_7\text{H}_{16}} \times \dfrac{1 \text{ mol C}_7\text{H}_{16}}{100.20 \ \cancel{\text{g C}_7\text{H}_{16}}} = 0.499002 \text{ mol C}_7\text{H}_{16}$ and

$50.0 \ \cancel{\text{g C}_8\text{H}_{18}} \times \dfrac{1 \text{ mol C}_8\text{H}_{18}}{114.22 \ \cancel{\text{g C}_8\text{H}_{18}}} = 0.437752 \text{ mol C}_8\text{H}_{18}$ then

$\chi_{C_7H_{16}} = \dfrac{\text{amount C}_7\text{H}_{16} \text{ (in moles)}}{\text{total amount (in moles)}} = \dfrac{0.499002 \ \cancel{\text{mol}}}{0.499002 \ \cancel{\text{mol}} + 0.437752 \ \cancel{\text{mol}}} = 0.532693$ and

$\chi_{C_8H_{18}} = 1 - \chi_{C_7H_{16}} = 1 - 0.532693 = 0.467307$ then

$P_{C_7H_{16}} = \chi_{C_7H_{16}} P^{\circ}_{C_7H_{16}} = 0.532693 \times 45.8 \text{ Torr} = 24.4 \text{ Torr}$ and

$P_{C_8H_{18}} = \chi_{C_8H_{18}} P^{\circ}_{C_8H_{18}} = 0.467307 \times 10.9 \text{ Torr} = 5.09 \text{ Torr}$

Check: The units (Torr) are correct. The magnitudes of the answers (24 and 5 Torr) seem reasonable because we expect a drop in half from the pure vapour pressures since we have roughly a 50:50 mole ratio of the two components.

(b)   **Find:** P_{Total}

Conceptual Plan: $P_{C_7H_{16}}, \ P_{C_8H_{18}} \to P_{\text{Total}}$

$P_{\text{Total}} = P_{C_7H_{16}} + P_{C_8H_{18}}$

Solution: $P_{\text{Total}} = P_{C_7H_{16}} + P_{C_8H_{18}} = 24.4 \text{ Torr} + 5.09 \text{ Torr} = 29.5 \text{ Torr}$

Check: The units (Torr) are correct. The magnitude of the answer (30 Torr) seems reasonable considering the two pressures.

(c)   **Find:** mass percent composition of the gas phase

Conceptual Plan: since $n \ \alpha \ P$ and we are calculating a mass percent, which is a ratio of masses, we can simply convert 1 Torr to 1 mole so

$P_{C_7H_{16}}, \ P_{C_8H_{18}} \to n_{C_7H_{16}}, \ n_{C_8H_{18}}$ then $\text{mol}_{C_7H_{16}} \to \text{g}_{C_7H_{16}}$ and $\text{mol } C_8H_{18} \to \text{g } C_8H_{18}$

$\dfrac{100.20 \text{ g C}_7\text{H}_{16}}{1 \text{ mol C}_7\text{H}_{16}} \qquad\qquad \dfrac{114.22 \text{ g C}_8\text{H}_{18}}{1 \text{ mol C}_8\text{H}_{18}}$

then $\text{g}_{C_7H_{16}}, \text{g } C_8H_{18} \to$ **mass percents**

$\text{mass percent} = \dfrac{\text{mass solute}}{\text{mass solution}} \times 100\%$

Solution: so $n_{C_7H_{16}} = 24.4 \text{ mol}$ and $n_{C_8H_{18}} = 5.09 \text{ mol}$ then

$24.4 \ \cancel{\text{mol C}_7\text{H}_{16}} \times \dfrac{100.20 \text{ g C}_7\text{H}_{16}}{1 \ \cancel{\text{mol C}_7\text{H}_{16}}} = 2444.88 \text{ g C}_7\text{H}_{16}$ and

$5.09 \ \cancel{\text{mol C}_8\text{H}_{18}} \times \dfrac{114.22 \text{ g C}_8\text{H}_{18}}{1 \ \cancel{\text{mol C}_8\text{H}_{18}}} = 581.380 \text{ g C}_8\text{H}_{18}$ then

$\text{mass percent} = \dfrac{\text{mass solute}}{\text{mass solution}} \times 100\% = \dfrac{2444.88 \ \cancel{\text{g C}_7\text{H}_{16}}}{2444.88 \ \cancel{\text{g C}_7\text{H}_{16}} + 581.380 \ \cancel{\text{g C}_8\text{H}_{18}}} \times 100\% =$

$= 80.8 \text{ percent by mass } C_7H_{16}$

then 100% − 80.8% = 19.2 percent by mass C_8H_{18}

Check: The units (%) are correct. The magnitudes of the answers (81% and 19%) seem reasonable considering the two pressures.

(d) The two mass percents are different because the vapour is richer in the more volatile component (the lighter molecule).

12.75 **Given:** 4.08 g of chloroform ($CHCl_3$) and 9.29 g of acetone (CH_3COCH_3); at 35 °C $P^{\circ}_{CHCl_3}$ = 295 Torr; $P^{\circ}_{CH_3COCH_3}$ = 332 Torr; assume ideal behaviour; $P_{Total\ measured}$ = 312 Torr
Find: P_{CHCl_3}, $P_{CH_3COCH_3}$, P_{Total}, and if the soln is ideal.
Conceptual Plan: $g_{CHCl_3} \rightarrow mol_{CHCl_3}$ and $g_{CH_3COCH_3} \rightarrow mol_{CH_3COCH_3}$ then

$$\frac{1\ mol\ CHCl_3}{119.38\ g\ CHCl_3} \qquad \frac{1\ mol\ CH_3COCH_3}{58.08\ g\ CH_3COCH_3}$$

mol_{CHCl_3}, $mol_{CH_3COCH_3} \rightarrow \chi_{CHCl_3}$, $\chi_{CH_3COCH_3}$ then χ_{CHCl_3}, $P^{\circ}_{CHCl_3} \rightarrow P_{CHCl_3}$ and

$$\chi_{CHCl_3} = \frac{amount\ CHCl_3\ (in\ moles)}{total\ amount\ (in\ moles)} \qquad \chi_{CH_3COCH_3} = 1 - \chi_{CHCl_3} \qquad P_{CHCl_3} = \chi_{CHCl_3}P^{\circ}_{CHCl_3}$$

$\chi_{CH_3COCH_3}$, $P^{\circ}_{CH_3COCH_3} \rightarrow P_{CH_3COCH_3}$ then P_{CHCl_3}, $P_{CH_3COCH_3} \rightarrow P_{Total}$ then **compare values**

$$P_{CH_3COCH_3} = \chi_{CH_3COCH_3}P^{\circ}_{CH_3COCH_3} \qquad\qquad P_{Total} = P_{CHCl_3} + P_{CH_3COCH_{33}}$$

Solution:

$$4.08\ \overline{g\ CHCl_3} \times \frac{1\ mol\ CHCl_3}{119.38\ \overline{g\ CHCl_3}} = 0.0341766\ mol\ CHCl_3\ and$$

$$9.29\ \overline{g\ CH_3COCH_3} \times \frac{1\ mol\ CH_3COCH_3}{58.08\ \overline{g\ CH_3COCH_3}} = 0.159952\ mol\ CH_3COCH_3\ then$$

$$\chi_{CHCl_3} = \frac{amount\ CHCl_3\ (in\ moles)}{total\ amount\ (in\ moles)} = \frac{0.0341766\ \overline{mol}}{0.0341766\ \overline{mol} + 0.159952\ \overline{mol}} = 0.176052\ and$$

$$\chi_{CH_3COCH_3} = 1 - \chi_{CHCl_3} = 1 - 0.176052 = 0.823948\ then$$

$$P_{CHCl_3} = \chi_{CHCl_3}P^{\circ}_{CHCl_3} = 0.176052 \times 295\ Torr = 51.9\ Torr\ and$$

$$P_{CH_3COCH_3} = \chi_{CH_3COCH_3}P^{\circ}_{CH_3COCH_3} = 0.823948 \times 332\ Torr = 274\ Torr\ then$$

$$P_{Total} = P_{CHCl_3} + P_{CH_3COCH_3} = 51.9\ Torr + 274\ Torr = 326\ Torr.$$

Since 326 Torr ≠ 312 Torr, the solution is not behaving ideally. The chloroform–acetone interactions are stronger than the chloroform–chloroform and acetone–acetone interactions.

Check: The units (Torr) are correct. The magnitude of the answer seems reasonable since each is a fraction of the pure vapour pressure. We are not surprised that the solution is not ideal, since the types of bonds in the two molecules are very different.

Freezing Point Depression, Boiling Point Elevation, and Osmosis

12.77 **Given:** 55.8 g of glucose ($C_6H_{12}O_6$) in 455 g water **Find:** T_f and T_b **Other:** K_f = 1.86 °C m^{-1}; K_b = 0.512 °C m^{-1};
Conceptual Plan: $g_{H_2O} \rightarrow kg_{H_2O}$ and $g_{C_6H_{12}O_6} \rightarrow mol_{C_6H_{12}O_6}$ then $mol_{C_6H_{12}O_6}$, $kg_{H_2O} \rightarrow m$

$$\frac{1\ kg}{1000\ g} \qquad\qquad \frac{1\ mol\ C_6H_{12}O_6}{180.16\ g\ C_6H_{12}O_6} \qquad\qquad m = \frac{amount\ solute\ (moles)}{mass\ solvent\ (kg)}$$

$m, K_f \rightarrow \Delta T_f \rightarrow T_f$ and $m, K_b \rightarrow \Delta T_b \rightarrow T_b$

$$\Delta T_f = K_f m \qquad T_f = T^{\circ}_f - \Delta T_f \qquad \Delta T_b = K_b m \qquad \Delta T_b = T_b - T^{\circ}_b$$

Solution: $455\ \overline{g} \times \dfrac{1\ kg}{1000\ \overline{g}} = 0.455\ kg$ and $55.8\ \overline{g\ C_6H_{12}O_6} \times \dfrac{1\ mol\ C_6H_{12}O_6}{180.16\ \overline{g\ C_6H_{12}O_6}} = 0.309725\ mol\ C_6H_{12}O_6$ then

$$m = \frac{amount\ solute\ (moles)}{mass\ solvent\ (kg)} = \frac{0.309725\ mol\ C_6H_{12}O_6}{0.455\ kg} = 0.680714\ m\ or\ 0.680714\ mol\ kg^{-1}\ then$$

$$\Delta T_f = K_f m = 1.86\ \frac{°C}{\overline{m}} \times 0.680714\ \overline{m} = 1.27\ °C\ then\ T_f = T^{\circ}_f - \Delta T_f = 0.00\ °C - 1.27\ °C = -1.27\ °C\ and$$

$$\Delta T_b = K_b m = 0.512\ \frac{°C}{\overline{m}} \times 0.680714\ \overline{m} = 0.349\ °C\ and\ \Delta T_b = T_b - T^{\circ}_b\ so$$

$$T_b = T^{\circ}_b + \Delta T_b = 100.000\ °C + 0.349\ °C = 100.349\ °C$$

Check: The units (°C) are correct. The magnitudes of the answers seem reasonable since the molality is ~ 2/3. The shift in boiling point is less than the shift in freezing point because the constant for boiling is smaller than the constant for freezing.

12.79   **Given:** 17.5 g of unknown nonelectrolyte in 100.0 g water, $T_f = -1.8 \,°C$ **Find:** molar mass
Other: $K_f = 1.86 \,°C\, m^{-1}$
Conceptual Plan: $g_{H_2O} \rightarrow kg_{H_2O}$ and $T_f \rightarrow \Delta T_f$ then $\Delta T_f, K_f \rightarrow m$ then $m, kg_{H_2O} \rightarrow mol_{Unk}$

$$\frac{1 \text{ kg}}{1000 \text{ g}} \qquad T_f = T_f^° - \Delta T_f \qquad \Delta T_f = K_f m \qquad m = \frac{\text{amount solute (moles)}}{\text{mass solvent (kg)}}$$

then $g_{Unk}, mol_{Unk} \rightarrow$ molar mass

$$\text{molar mass} = \frac{g_{Unk}}{mol_{Unk}}$$

Solution: $100.0 \text{ g} \times \dfrac{1 \text{ kg}}{1000 \text{ g}} = 0.1000 \text{ kg}$ and $T_f = T_f^° - \Delta T_f$ so

$\Delta T_f = T_f^° - T_f = 0.00 \,°C - (-1.8\,°C) = +1.8\,°C$ $\Delta T_f = K_f m$. Rearrange to solve for m.

$$m = \frac{\Delta T_f}{K_f} = \frac{1.8\,°C}{1.86\,\dfrac{°C}{m}} = 0.96774 \, m \text{ then } m = \frac{\text{amount solute (moles)}}{\text{mass solvent (kg)}} \text{ so}$$

$$mol_{Unk} = m_{Unk} \times kg_{H_2O} = 0.96774 \,\frac{\text{mol Unk}}{kg} \times 0.1000 \text{ kg} = 0.096774 \text{ mol Unk then}$$

$$\text{molar mass} = \frac{g_{Unk}}{mol_{Unk}} = \frac{17.5 \text{ g}}{0.096774 \text{ mol}} = 180 \text{ g mol}^{-1} = 1.8 \times 10^2 \text{ g mol}^{-1}.$$

Check: The units (g mol^{-1}) are correct. The magnitude of the answer (180 g mol^{-1}) seems reasonable since the molality is ~ 0.1 and we have ~18 g. It is a reasonable molecular weight for a solid or liquid.

12.81   **Given:** 24.6 g of glycerin ($C_3H_8O_3$) in 250.0 mL of solution at 298 K **Find:** Π
Conceptual Plan: $mL_{soln} \rightarrow L_{soln}$ and $g_{C_3H_8O_3} \rightarrow mol_{C_3H_8O_3}$ then $mol_{C_3H_8O_3}, L_{soln} \rightarrow M$ then

$$\frac{1 \text{ L}}{1000 \text{ mL}} \qquad\qquad \frac{1 \text{ mol } C_3H_8O_3}{92.09 \text{ g } C_3H_8O_3} \qquad\qquad M = \frac{\text{amount solute (moles)}}{\text{volume solution (L)}}$$

$M, T \rightarrow \Pi$

$$\Pi = M\,RT$$

Solution:
$$250.0 \text{ mL} \times \frac{1 \text{ L}}{1000 \text{ mL}} = 0.2500 \text{ L and } 24.6 \text{ g } C_3H_8O_3 \times \frac{1 \text{ mol } C_3H_8O_3}{92.09 \text{ g } C_3H_8O_3} = 0.267130 \text{ mol } C_3H_8O_3 \text{ then}$$

$$M = \frac{\text{amount solute (moles)}}{\text{volume solution (L)}} = \frac{0.267130 \text{ mol } C_3H_8O_3}{0.2500 \text{ L}} = 1.06852 \text{ mol L}^{-1} \text{ then}$$

$$\Pi = M\,RT = 1.06852 \,\frac{\text{mol}}{L} \times 0.08314 \,\frac{\text{bar} \cdot L}{\text{mol} \cdot K} \times 298 \text{ K} = 26.5 \text{ bar}$$

Check: The units (bar) are correct. The magnitude of the answer (26 bar) seems reasonable since the molarity is ~ 1.

12.83   **Given:** 27.55 mg unknown protein in 25.0 mL solution; $\Pi = 3.22$ Torr at 25 °C **Find:** molar mass$_{\text{unknown protein}}$
Conceptual Plan: $°C \rightarrow K$ and Torr $\rightarrow$ bar then $\Pi, T \rightarrow M$ then $mL_{soln} \rightarrow L_{soln}$ then

$$K = °C + 273.15 \qquad \frac{1 \text{ bar}}{750.01 \text{ Torr}} \qquad \Pi = M\,RT \qquad \frac{1 \text{ L}}{1000 \text{ mL}}$$

$L_{soln}, M \rightarrow mol_{\text{unknown protein}}$ and mg $\rightarrow$ g then $g_{\text{unknown protein}}, mol_{\text{unknown protein}} \rightarrow$ molar mass$_{\text{unknown protein}}$

$$M = \frac{\text{amount solute (moles)}}{\text{volume solution (L)}} \qquad\qquad \frac{1 \text{ g}}{1000 \text{ mg}} \qquad\qquad \text{molar mass} = \frac{g_{\text{unknown protein}}}{mol_{\text{unknown protein}}}$$

Solution: $25 \,°C + 273.15 = 298 \text{ K}$ and $3.22 \text{ Torr} \times \dfrac{1 \text{ bar}}{750.01 \text{ Torr}} = 0.00429328 \text{ bar } \Pi = M\,RT$ for M.

$$M = \frac{\Pi}{RT} = \frac{0.00429328 \text{ bar}}{0.08314 \,\dfrac{\text{bar} \cdot L}{\text{mol} \cdot K} \times 298 \text{ K}} = 1.73286 \times 10^{-4} \text{ mol L}^{-1} \text{ then } 25.0 \text{ mL} \times \frac{1 \text{ L}}{1000 \text{ mL}} = 0.0250 \text{ L then}$$

$$M = \frac{\text{amount solute (moles)}}{\text{volume solution (L)}}. \text{ Rearrange to solve for } mol_{\text{unknown protein}}.$$

$$mol_{\text{unknown protein}} = M \times L = 1.73286 \times 10^{-4} \,\frac{\text{mol}}{L} \times 0.0250 \text{ L} = 4.33214 \times 10^{-6} \text{ mol and}$$

$$27.55 \ \overline{\text{mg}} \times \frac{1 \ \text{g}}{1000 \ \overline{\text{mg}}} = 0.02755 \ \text{g} \ \text{then molar mass} = \frac{\text{g}_{\text{unknown protein}}}{\text{mol}_{\text{unknown protein}}} = \frac{0.02755 \ \text{g}}{4.33214 \times 10^{-6} \ \text{mol}} = 6.36 \times 10^3 \ \text{g mol}^{-1}.$$

Check: The units (g mol^{-1}) are correct. The magnitude of the answer (6400 g mol^{-1}) seems reasonable for a large biological molecule. A small amount of material is put into 0.025 L, so the concentration is very small and the molecular weight is large.

12.85   (a)   **Given:** 0.100 m of K$_2$S, completely dissociated   **Find:** T_f, T_b

           Other: $K_f = 1.86 \ °C \ m^{-1}$; $K_b = 0.512 \ °C \ m^{-1}$;

           Conceptual Plan: $m, i, K_f \rightarrow \Delta T_f$ then $\Delta T_f \rightarrow T_f$ and $m, i, K_b \rightarrow \Delta T_b$ then $\Delta T_b \rightarrow T_b$

$$\Delta T_f = K_f \, i m_{i=3} \qquad T_f = T_f° - \Delta T_f \qquad \Delta T_b = K_b \, i m_{i=3} \qquad T_b = T_b° + \Delta T_b$$

           Solution: $\Delta T_f = K_f \, i m = 1.86 \dfrac{°C}{m} \times 3 \times 0.100 \ m = 0.558 \ °C$ then

$$T_f = T_f° - \Delta T_f = 0.000 \ °C - 0.558 \ °C = -0.558 \ °C \text{ and}$$

$$\Delta T_b = K_b \, im = 0.512 \dfrac{°C}{m} \times 3 \times 0.100 \ m = 0.154 \ °C \text{ then}$$

$$T_b = T_b° - \Delta T_b = 100.000 \ °C + 0.154 \ °C = 100.154 \ °C.$$

           Check: The units (°C) are correct. The magnitudes of the answers (– 0.6 °C and 100.2 °C) seem reasonable since the molality of the particles is 0.3. The shift in boiling point is less than the shift in freezing point because the constant for boiling is larger than the constant for freezing.

    (b)   **Given:** 21.5 g CuCl$_2$ in 4.50 x 10^2 g water, completely dissociated   **Find:** T_f, T_b

           Other: $K_f = 1.86 \ °C \ m^{-1}$; $K_b = 0.512 \ °C \ m^{-1}$;

           Conceptual Plan: g$_{\text{H}_2\text{O}} \rightarrow$ kg$_{\text{H}_2\text{O}}$ and g$_{\text{CuCl}_2} \rightarrow$ mol$_{\text{CuCl}_2}$ then mol$_{\text{CuCl}_2}$, kg$_{\text{H}_2\text{O}} \rightarrow m$

$$\frac{1 \ \text{kg}}{1000 \ \text{g}} \qquad\qquad \frac{1 \ \text{mol CuCl}_2}{134.46 \ \text{g CuCl}_2} \qquad\qquad m = \frac{\text{amount solute (moles)}}{\text{mass solvent (kg)}}$$

           $m, i, K_f \rightarrow \Delta T_f \rightarrow T_f$ and $m, i, K_b \rightarrow \Delta T_b \rightarrow T_b$

$$\Delta T_f = K_f \, im_{i=3} \quad T_f = T_f° - \Delta T_f \qquad \Delta T_b = K_b \, im_{i=3} \quad T_b = T_b° + \Delta T_b$$

           Solution:

$$4.5 \times 10^2 \ \text{g} \times \frac{1 \ \text{kg}}{1000 \ \text{g}} = 0.450 \ \text{kg} \text{ and } 21.5 \ \overline{\text{g CuCl}_2} \times \frac{1 \ \text{mol CuCl}_2}{134.46 \ \overline{\text{g CuCl}_2}} = 0.159904 \ \text{mol CuCl}_2 \text{ then}$$

$$m = \frac{\text{amount solute (moles)}}{\text{mass solvent (kg)}} = \frac{0.159904 \ \text{mol CuCl}_2}{0.450 \ \text{kg}} = 0.355341 \ m \text{ then}$$

$$\Delta T_f = K_f \, im = 1.86 \dfrac{°C}{m} \times 3 \times 0.355341 \ m = 1.98 \ °C \text{ then}$$

$$T_f = T_f° - \Delta T_f = 0.000 \ °C - 1.98 \ °C = -1.98 \ °C \text{ and}$$

$$\Delta T_b = K_b \, im = 0.512 \dfrac{°C}{m} \times 3 \times 0.355341 \ m = 0.546 \ °C \text{ then}$$

$$T_b = T_b° - \Delta T_b = 100.000 \ °C + 0.546 \ °C = 100.546 \ °C.$$

           Check: The units (°C) are correct. The magnitudes of the answers (– 2 °C and 100.5 °C) seem reasonable since the molality of the particles is ~ 1. The shift in boiling point is less than the shift in freezing point because the constant for boiling is larger than the constant for freezing.

    (c)   **Given:** 5.5% by mass NaNO$_3$, completely dissociated   **Find:** T_f, T_b

           Other: $K_f = 1.86 \ °C \ m^{-1}$; $K_b = 0.512 \ °C \ m^{-1}$;

           Conceptual Plan: percent by mass $\rightarrow$ g$_{\text{NaNO}_3}$, g$_{\text{H}_2\text{O}}$ then g$_{\text{H}_2\text{O}} \rightarrow$ kg$_{\text{H}_2\text{O}}$ and g$_{\text{NaNO}_3} \rightarrow$ mol$_{\text{NaNO}_3}$

$$\text{mass percent} = \frac{\text{mass solute}}{\text{mass solution}} \times 100\% \qquad \frac{1 \ \text{kg}}{1000 \ \text{g}} \qquad \frac{1 \ \text{mol NaNO}_3}{84.99 \ \text{g NaNO}_3}$$

           then mol$_{\text{NaNO}_3}$, kg$_{\text{H}_2\text{O}} \rightarrow m$ **then** $m, i, K_f \rightarrow \Delta T_f \rightarrow T_f$ and $m, i, K_b \rightarrow \Delta T_b \rightarrow T_b$

$$m = \frac{\text{amount solute (moles)}}{\text{mass solvent (kg)}} \qquad \Delta T_f = K_f \, im_{i=2} \quad T_f = T_f° - \Delta T_f \qquad \Delta T_b = K_b \, im_{i=2} \quad T_b = T_b° + \Delta T_b$$

           Solution: mass percent $= \dfrac{\text{mass solute}}{\text{mass solution}} \times 100\%$ so 5.5% by mass NaNO$_3$ means 5.5 g NaNO$_3$ and

$$100.0 \ \text{g} - 5.5 \ \text{g} = 94.5 \ \text{g water. Then } 94.5 \ \text{g} \times \frac{1 \ \text{kg}}{1000 \ \text{g}} = 0.0945 \ \text{kg and}$$

$$5.5 \ \overline{\text{g NaNO}_3} \times \frac{1 \ \text{mol NaNO}_3}{84.99 \ \overline{\text{g NaNO}_3}} = 0.064713 \ \text{mol NaNO}_3 \text{ then}$$

$$m = \frac{\text{amount solute (moles)}}{\text{mass solvent (kg)}} = \frac{0.064713 \text{ mol NaNO}_3}{0.0945 \text{ kg}} = 0.68480 \; m \text{ then}$$

$$\Delta T_f = K_f \, im = 1.86 \frac{°C}{m} \times 2 \times 0.68480 \; m = 2.5 °C \text{ then}$$

$$T_f = T_f° - \Delta T_f = 0.000 °C - 2.3 °C = -2.5 °C \text{ and}$$

$$\Delta T_b = K_b \, im = 0.512 \frac{°C}{m} \times 2 \times 0.68480 \; m = 0.70 °C \text{ then}$$

$$T_b = T_b° - \Delta T_b = 100.000 °C + 0.64 °C = 100.70 °C.$$

Check: The units (°C) are correct. The magnitudes of the answers (− 2.5 °C and 100.7 °C) seem reasonable since the molality of the particles is ∼ 1. The shift in boiling point is less than the shift in freezing point because the constant for boiling is larger than the constant for freezing.

12.87   (a)   **Given:** 0.100 m of $FeCl_3$ **Find:** T_f **Other:** $K_f = 1.86 °C \, m^{-1}$; $i_{measured} = 3.4$
Conceptual Plan: $m, i, K_f \rightarrow \Delta T_f$ then $\Delta T_f \rightarrow T_f$

$$\Delta T_f = K_f \, im \qquad\qquad T_f = T_f° - \Delta T_f$$

Solution: $\Delta T_f = K_f \, im = 1.86 \dfrac{°C}{m} \times 3.4 \times 0.100 \; m = 0.632 °C$ then

$$T_f = T_f° - \Delta T_f = 0.000 °C - 0.632 °C = -0.632 °C.$$

Check: The units (°C) are correct. The magnitude of the answer (− 0.6 °C) seems reasonable since the theoretical molality of the particles is 0.4.

(b)   **Given:** 0.085 mol L^{-1} of K_2SO_4 at 298 K   **Find:** Π **Other:** $i_{measured} = 2.6$
Conceptual Plan: $M, i, T \rightarrow \Pi$

$$\Pi = iM \, RT$$

Solution: $\Pi = iM \, RT = 2.6 \times 0.085 \dfrac{\text{mol}}{L} \times 0.08314 \dfrac{\text{bar} \cdot L}{\text{mol} \cdot K} \times 298 \; K = 5.5 \text{ bar}$

Check: The units (bar) are correct. The magnitude of the answer (5 bar) seems reasonable since the molarity of particles is ∼ 0.2 m.

(c)   **Given:** 1.22% by mass $MgCl_2$ **Find:** T_b **Other:** $K_b = 0.512 °C \, m^{-1}$; $i_{measured} = 2.7$
Conceptual Plan: percent by mass $\rightarrow g_{MgCl_2}, g_{H_2O}$ then $g_{H_2O} \rightarrow kg_{H_2O}$ and $g_{MgCl_2} \rightarrow$ **mol** $_{MgCl_2}$ **then**

$$\text{mass percent} = \frac{\text{mass solute}}{\text{mass solution}} \times 100\% \qquad \frac{1 \text{ kg}}{1000 \text{ g}} \qquad \frac{1 \text{ mol MgCl}_2}{95.22 \text{ g MgCl}_2}$$

mol $_{MgCl_2}, kg_{H_2O} \rightarrow m$ **then** $m, i, K_b \rightarrow \Delta T_b \rightarrow T_b$

$$m = \frac{\text{amount solute (moles)}}{\text{mass solvent (kg)}} \qquad \Delta T_b = K_b \, im \quad T_b = T_b° + \Delta T_b$$

Solution: mass percent $= \dfrac{\text{mass solute}}{\text{mass solution}} \times 100\%$ so 1.22% by mass $MgCl_2$ means 1.22 g $MgCl_2$ and

$$100.00 \text{ g} - 1.22 \text{ g} = 98.78 \text{ g water. Then } 98.78 \text{ g} \times \frac{1 \text{ kg}}{1000 \text{ g}} = 0.09878 \text{ kg and}$$

$$1.22 \text{ g MgCl}_2 \times \frac{1 \text{ mol MgCl}_2}{95.23 \text{ g MgCl}_2} = 0.0128110 \text{ mol MgCl}_2 \text{ then}$$

$$m = \frac{\text{amount solute (moles)}}{\text{mass solvent (kg)}} = \frac{0.0128110 \text{ mol MgCl}_2}{0.09878 \text{ kg}} = 0.129693 \; m \text{ then}$$

$$\Delta T_b = K_b \, im = 0.512 \frac{°C}{m} \times 2.7 \times 0.129706 \; m = 0.18 °C \text{ then}$$

$$T_b = T_b° - \Delta T_b = 100.000 °C + 0.18 °C = 100.18 °C.$$

Check: The units (°C) are correct. The magnitude of the answer (100.2 °C) seems reasonable since the molality of the particles is ∼ 1/3.

12.89   **Given:** 0.100 mol L^{-1} of ionic solution, $\Pi = 8.3$ bar at 25 °C   **Find:** $i_{measured}$
Conceptual Plan: °C $\rightarrow$ K then $\Pi, M, T \rightarrow i$

$$K = °C + 273.15 \qquad\qquad \Pi = iM \, RT$$

Solution: 25 °C + 273.15 = 298 K then $\Pi = iM \, RT$. Rearrange to solve for i.

$$i = \frac{\Pi}{MRT} = \frac{8.3 \text{ bar}}{0.100 \frac{\text{mol}}{L} \times 0.08314 \frac{\text{bar} \cdot L}{\text{mol} \cdot K} \times 298 \text{ K}} = 3.4.$$

Check: The units (none) are correct. The magnitude of the answer (3) seems reasonable for an ionic solution with a high osmotic pressure.

12.91   **Given:** 5.50% NaCl by mass in water at 25 °C **Find:** P_{H_2O} **Other:** $P^{\circ}_{H_2O} = 23.78$ Torr

Conceptual Plan: % NaCl by mass $\rightarrow$ g_{NaCl}, g_{H_2O} then $g_{NaCl} \rightarrow$ mol $_{NaCl}$ and

$$\frac{5.50 \text{ g NaCl}}{100 \text{ g (NaCl + H}_2\text{O)}} \qquad \frac{1 \text{ mol NaCl}}{58.44 \text{ g NaCl}}$$

$g_{H_2O} \rightarrow$ mol $_{H_2O}$ then mol $_{NaCl}$, mol $_{H_2O} \rightarrow \chi_{H_2O}$ then χ_{H_2O}, $P^{\circ}_{H_2O} \rightarrow P_{H_2O}$

$$\frac{1 \text{ mol H}_2\text{O}}{18.01 \text{ g H}_2\text{O}} \qquad \chi = \frac{\text{amount solute (in moles)}}{\text{total amount of solute and solvent (in moles)}} \qquad P_{\text{solution}} = \chi_{\text{solvent}} P^{\circ}_{\text{solvent}}$$

Solution: $\dfrac{5.50 \text{ g NaCl}}{100 \text{ g (NaCl + H}_2\text{O)}}$ means 5.50 g NaCl and $(100 \text{ g} - 5.50 \text{ g}) = 94.5$ g H_2O then

$5.50 \text{ g NaCl} \times \dfrac{1 \text{ mol NaCl}}{58.44 \text{ g NaCl}} = 0.0941136$ mol NaCl and $94.5 \text{ g H}_2\text{O} \times \dfrac{1 \text{ mol H}_2\text{O}}{18.01 \text{ g H}_2\text{O}} = 5.24708$ mol H_2O the

number of moles of solute $= i_{NaCl} \times n_{NaCl}$ so $\chi_{\text{solv}} = \dfrac{\text{amount solvent (in moles)}}{\text{total amount solute and solvent particles (in moles)}} =$

$\dfrac{5.24708 \text{ mol}}{5.24708 \text{ mol} + 2(0.0941136 \text{ mol})} = 0.96536$ then $P_{\text{soln}} = \chi_{\text{solv}} P^{\circ}_{\text{solv}} = 0.96536 \times 23.78 \text{ Torr} = 23.0 \text{ Torr}$

Check: The units (Torr) are correct. The magnitude of the answer (23 Torr) seems reasonable since it is a drop from the pure vapour pressure. Only a fraction of a mole of NaCl is added, so the pressure will not drop much.

Cumulative Problems

12.93   Chloroform is polar and has stronger solute–solvent interactions than nonpolar carbon tetrachloride.

12.95   The main intermolecular interactions keeping both methanol and water in the liquid phase at room temperatures are hydrogen bonds. Therefore, disrupting the methanol–methanol and water–water hydrogen bonds to form similar methanol–water hydrogen bonds is roughly thermoneutral.

To dissolve pentanol, however, the dispersion forces between the alkyl chains in pentanol are disrupted, as are the hydrogen bonds in water. The interactions between water and the alkyl chain that would be formed upon dissolving pentanol would not give back the same amount of energy as those disrupted, so the dissolution would be energetically unfeasible. Note that there would be hydrogen bonds between the O–H group of pentanol and water, but that is not enough to dissolve the pentanol in water. Instead, a film on the surface of the water would be formed.

12.97   **Given:** $KClO_4$: lattice energy $= -599$ kJ mol^{-1}, $\Delta_{\text{hyd}}H = -548$ kJ mol^{-1}; 10.0 g $KClO_4$ in 100.00 mL solution **Find:** $\Delta_{\text{soln}}H$ and ΔT **Other:** $C_s = 4.05$ J g^{-1} °C^{-1}; $d = 1.05$ g mL^{-1}

Conceptual Plan: lattice energy, $\Delta_{\text{hyd}}H \rightarrow \Delta_{\text{soln}}H$ and g $\rightarrow$ mol then mol, $\Delta_{\text{soln}}H \rightarrow q(\text{kJ}) \rightarrow q(\text{J})$

$$\Delta_{\text{soln}}H = \Delta_{\text{solute}}H + \Delta_{\text{hyd}}H \text{ where } \Delta_{\text{solute}}H = -\Delta_{\text{lattice}}H \quad \frac{1 \text{ mol}}{138.56 \text{ g}} \qquad q = n \Delta H_{\text{soln}} \quad \frac{1000 \text{ J}}{1 \text{ kJ}}$$

then mL$_{\text{soln}} \rightarrow$ g$_{\text{soln}}$ then q, g$_{\text{soln}}$, $C_s \rightarrow \Delta T$

$$\frac{1.05 \text{ g}}{1 \text{ mL}} \qquad q = m C_s \Delta T$$

Solution: $\Delta_{\text{soln}}H = \Delta_{\text{solute}}H + \Delta_{\text{hyd}}H$ where $\Delta_{\text{solute}}H = -\Delta_{\text{lattice}}H$ so $\Delta_{\text{soln}}H = \Delta_{\text{hyd}}H - \Delta_{\text{lattice}}H$

$\Delta_{\text{soln}}H = -548 \text{ kJ mol}^{-1} - (-599 \text{ kJ mol}^{-1}) = +51 \text{ kJ mol}^{-1}$ and $10.0 \text{ g} \times \dfrac{1 \text{ mol}}{138.56 \text{ g}} = 0.0721709$ mol then

$q = n \Delta_{\text{soln}}H = 0.0721709 \text{ mol} \times 51 \dfrac{\text{kJ}}{\text{mol}} = +3.6807 \text{ kJ} \times \dfrac{1000 \text{ J}}{1 \text{ kJ}} = +3680.7$ J absorbed then

$100.0 \text{ mL} \times \dfrac{1.05 \text{ g}}{1 \text{ mL}} = 105$ g. Since heat is absorbed when $KClO_4$ dissolves, the temperature will

drop or $q = -3680.7$ J and $q = m C_s \Delta T$. Rearrange to solve for ΔT.

$$\Delta T = \frac{q}{m\,C_s} = \frac{-3680.7 \text{ J}}{105 \text{ g} \times 4.05 \frac{\text{J}}{\text{g} \cdot {}^\circ\text{C}}} = -8.7\,{}^\circ\text{C}.$$

Check: The units (kJ mol^{-1} and °C) are correct. The magnitude of the answer (51 kJ mol^{-1}) makes physical sense because the lattice energy is larger than the heat of hydration. The magnitude of the temperature change (-9 °C) makes physical sense since heat is absorbed and the heat of solution is fairly small.

12.99　　**Given:** argon, 0.0537 L; 25 °C, $P_{Ar} = 1.0$ bar to make 1.0 L saturated solution　**Find:** $k_H(Ar)$
　　　　Conceptual Plan: °C $\rightarrow$ K and $P_{Ar}, V, T \rightarrow$ mol$_{Ar}$ then mol$_{Ar}, V_{soln}, P_{Ar} \rightarrow k_H(Ar)$

$$\text{K} = {}^\circ\text{C} + 273.15 \qquad\qquad PV = nRT \qquad\qquad S_{Ar} = k_H(Ar)P_{Ar} \text{ with } S_{Ar} = \frac{\text{mol}_{Ar}}{L_{soln}}$$

　　　　Solution: 25 °C + 273.15 = 298 K and $PV = nRT$. Rearrange to solve for n.

$$n = \frac{PV}{RT} = \frac{1.0 \text{ bar} \times 0.0537 \text{ L}}{0.08314 \dfrac{\text{bar} \cdot \text{L}}{\text{mol} \cdot \text{K}} \times 298 \text{ K}} = 0.00219597 \text{ mol then } S_{Ar} = k_H(Ar)P_{Ar} \text{ with } S_{Ar} = \frac{\text{mol}_{Ar}}{L_{soln}}.$$

　　　　Substitute in values and rearrange to solve for k_H.

$$k_H(Ar) = \frac{\text{mol}_{Ar}}{L_{soln}P_{Ar}} = \frac{0.00219597 \text{ mol}}{1.0 \text{ L}_{soln} \times 1.0 \text{ bar}} = 2.2 \times 10^{-3} \text{ mol L}^{-1}\text{bar}^{-1}.$$

　　　　Check: The units (mol L^{-1} bar^{-1}) are correct. The magnitude of the answer (10^{-3}) seems reasonable since it is consistent with other values in the text.

12.101　**Given:** 0.001 ppm by mass Hg = legal limit; 0.0040 ppm by mass Hg = contaminated water; 50.0 mg Hg ingested　**Find:** volume of contaminated water
　　　　Conceptual Plan: mg$_{Hg}$ $\rightarrow$ g$_{Hg}$ $\rightarrow$ g$_{H_2O}$ $\rightarrow$ mL$_{H_2O}$ $\rightarrow$ L$_{H_2O}$

$$\frac{1 \text{ g}}{1000 \text{ mg}} \qquad \frac{10^6 \text{ g water}}{0.0040 \text{ g Hg}} \qquad \frac{1 \text{ mL}}{1.00 \text{ g}} \qquad \frac{1 \text{ L}}{1000 \text{ mL}}$$

　　　　Solution: $50.0 \text{ mg Hg} \times \dfrac{1 \text{ g Hg}}{1000 \text{ mg Hg}} \times \dfrac{10^6 \text{ g water}}{0.0040 \text{ g Hg}} \times \dfrac{1 \text{ mL water}}{1.00 \text{ g water}} \times \dfrac{1 \text{ L water}}{1000 \text{ mL water}} = 1.3 \times 10^4 \text{ L water.}$

　　　　Check: The units (L) are correct. The magnitude of the answer (10^4 L) seems reasonable since the concentration is so low.

12.103　**Given:** 12.5% NaCl by mass in water at 55 °C; 2.5 L vapour　**Find:** g $_{H_2O}$ in vapour
　　　　Other: $P^\circ_{H_2O} = 118$ Torr, $i_{NaCl} = 2.0$ (complete dissociation)
　　　　Conceptual Plan: % NaCl by mass $\rightarrow$ g$_{NaCl}$, g $_{H_2O}$ then g $_{NaCl}$ $\rightarrow$ mol $_{NaCl}$ and g $_{H_2O}$ $\rightarrow$ mol $_{H_2O}$

$$\frac{12.5 \text{ g NaCl}}{100 \text{ g (NaCl + H}_2\text{O)}} \qquad\qquad \frac{1 \text{ mol NaCl}}{58.44 \text{ g NaCl}} \qquad\qquad \frac{1 \text{ mol H}_2\text{O}}{18.01 \text{ g H}_2\text{O}}$$

　　　　then mol $_{NaCl}$, mol $_{H_2O}$ $\rightarrow$ χ $_{NaCl}$ $\rightarrow$ χ $_{H_2O}$ then χ $_{H_2O}$, $P^\circ_{H_2O}$ $\rightarrow$ P_{H_2O}

$$\chi = \frac{\text{amount solute (in moles)}}{\text{total amount of solute and solvent (in moles)}} \quad \chi_{H_2O} = 1 - i_{NaCl}\,\chi_{NaCl} \quad P_{solution} = \chi_{solvent}P^\circ_{solvent}$$

　　　　then Torr $\rightarrow$ atm and °C $\rightarrow$ K　$P, V, T \rightarrow$ mol$_{H_2O}$ $\rightarrow$ g$_{H_2O}$

$$\frac{1 \text{ atm}}{760 \text{ Torr}} \qquad \text{K} = {}^\circ\text{C} + 273.15 \quad PV = nRT \qquad \frac{18.01 \text{ g H}_2\text{O}}{1 \text{ mol H}_2\text{O}}$$

　　　　Solution: $\dfrac{12.5 \text{ g NaCl}}{100 \text{ g (NaCl + H}_2\text{O)}}$ means 12.5 g NaCl and (100 g − 12.5 g) = 87.5 g H$_2$O then

$$12.5 \text{ g NaCl} \times \frac{1 \text{ mol NaCl}}{58.44 \text{ g NaCl}} = 0.213895 \text{ mol NaCl and } 87.5 \text{ g H}_2\text{O} \times \frac{1 \text{ mol H}_2\text{O}}{18.01 \text{ g H}_2\text{O}} = 4.85572 \text{ mol H}_2\text{O}$$

　　　　then $\chi = \dfrac{\text{amount solute (in moles)}}{\text{total amount of solute and solvent (in moles)}} = \dfrac{0.213895 \text{ mol}}{0.213895 \text{ mol} + 4.85572 \text{ mol}} = 0.0421916$

　　　　then $\chi_{H_2O} = 1 - i_{NaCl}\chi_{NaCl} = 1 - (2.0 \times 0.0421916) = 0.915617$ then

　　　　$P_{solution} = \chi_{solvent}P^\circ_{solvent} = 0.915617 \times 118 \text{ Torr} = 108.043 \text{ Torr H}_2\text{O}$ then

$$108.043 \text{ Torr H}_2\text{O} \times \frac{1 \text{ atm}}{760 \text{ Torr}} = 0.142162 \text{ atm}$$

　　　　and 55 °C + 273.15 = 328 K then $PV = nRT$. Rearrange to solve for n.

$$n = \frac{PV}{RT} = \frac{0.142162 \text{ atm} \times 2.5 \text{ L}}{0.08206 \dfrac{\text{L} \cdot \text{atm}}{\text{K} \cdot \text{mol}} \times 328 \text{ K}} = 0.013204 \text{ mol then}$$

$$0.013204 \overline{\text{mol H}_2\text{O}} \times \frac{18.02 \text{ g H}_2\text{O}}{1 \overline{\text{mol H}_2\text{O}}} = 0.24 \text{ g H}_2\text{O}.$$

Check: The units (g) are correct. The magnitude of the answer (0.2 g) seems reasonable since there is very little mass in a vapour.

12.105   **Given:** $T_b = 106.5$ °C aqueous solution   **Find:** T_f **Other:** $K_f = 1.86$ °C m^{-1}; $K_b = 0.512$ °C m^{-1}
Conceptual Plan: $T_b \rightarrow \Delta T_b$ then $\Delta T_b, K_b \rightarrow m$ then $m, K_f \rightarrow \Delta T_f \rightarrow T_f$
$$T_b = T_b^\circ + \Delta T_b \qquad \Delta T_b = K_b m \qquad \Delta T_f = K_f m \quad T_f = T_f^\circ - \Delta T_f$$
Solution: $T_b = T_b^\circ + \Delta T_b$ so $\Delta T_b = T_b - T_b^\circ = 106.5$ °C $- 100.0$ °C $= 6.5$ °C then $\Delta T_b = K_b m$.

Rearrange to solve for m. $m = \dfrac{\Delta T_b}{K_b} = \dfrac{6.5 \text{ °C}}{0.512 \dfrac{\text{°C}}{m}} = 12.695 \; m$ then

$\Delta T_f = K_f m = 1.86 \dfrac{\text{°C}}{m} \times 12.695 \; m = 23.6$ °C then $T_f = T_f^\circ - \Delta T_f = 0.000$ °C $- 23.6$ °C °C $= -24$ °C.

Check: The units (°C) are correct. The magnitude of the answer (– 24 °C) seems reasonable since the shift in boiling point is less than the shift in freezing point because the constant for boiling is smaller than the constant for freezing.

12.107   (a)   **Given:** 0.90% NaCl by mass per volume; isotonic aqueous solution at 25 °C; KCl; $i = 1.9$
Find: % KCl by mass per volume
Conceptual Plan: Isotonic solutions will have the same number of particles. Since i is the same,
$$\frac{1 \text{ mol KCl}}{1 \text{ mol NaCl}}$$
the new % mass per volume will be the mass ratio of the two salts.
$$\text{percent by mass per volume} = \frac{\text{mass solute}}{V} \times 100\% \quad \frac{1 \text{ mol NaCl}}{58.44 \text{ g NaCl}} \text{ and } \frac{74.56 \text{ g KCl}}{1 \text{ mol KCl}}$$

Solution: percent by mass per volume $= \dfrac{\text{mass solute}}{V} \times 100\% =$

$$= \frac{0.0090 \overline{\text{ g NaCl}}}{V} \times \frac{1 \overline{\text{mol NaCl}}}{58.44 \overline{\text{ g NaCl}}} \times \frac{1 \overline{\text{mol KCl}}}{1 \overline{\text{mol NaCl}}} \times \frac{74.56 \text{ g KCl}}{1 \overline{\text{mol KCl}}} \times 100\%$$

$= 1.1\%$ KCl by mass per volume
Check: The units (% KCl by mass per volume) are correct. The magnitude of the answer (1.1) seems reasonable since the molar mass of KCl is larger than the molar mass of NaCl.

(b)   **Given:** 0.90% NaCl by mass per volume; isotonic aqueous solution at 25 °C; NaBr; $i = 1.9$
Find: % NaBr by mass per volume
Conceptual Plan: Isotonic solutions will have the same number of particles. Since i is the same,
$$\frac{1 \text{ mol NaBr}}{1 \text{ mol NaCl}}$$
the new % mass per volume will be the mass ratio of the two salts.
$$\text{percent by mass per volume} = \frac{\text{mass solute}}{V} \times 100\% \quad \frac{1 \text{ mol NaCl}}{58.44 \text{ g NaCl}} \text{ and } \frac{102.90 \text{ g NaBr}}{1 \text{ mol NaBr}}$$

Solution: percent by mass per volume $= \dfrac{\text{mass solute}}{V} \times 100\% =$

$$= \frac{0.0090 \overline{\text{ g NaCl}}}{V} \times \frac{1 \overline{\text{mol NaCl}}}{58.44 \overline{\text{ g NaCl}}} \times \frac{1 \overline{\text{mol NaBr}}}{1 \overline{\text{mol NaCl}}} \times \frac{102.90 \text{ g NaBr}}{1 \overline{\text{mol NaBr}}} \times 100\%$$

$= 1.6\%$ NaBr by mass per volume
Check: The units (% NaBr by mass per volume) are correct. The magnitude of the answer (1.6) seems reasonable since the molar mass of NaBr is larger than the molar mass of NaCl.

(c)   **Given:** 0.90% NaCl by mass per volume; isotonic aqueous solution at 25 °C; glucose ($C_6H_{12}O_6$); $i = 1.9$ **Find:** % glucose by mass per volume
Conceptual Plan: Isotonic solutions will have the same number of particles. Since glucose is a nonelectrolyte the i is not the same, then use the mass ratio of the two compounds.
$$\frac{1.9 \text{ mol C}_6\text{H}_{12}\text{O}_6}{1 \text{ mol NaCl}} \quad \text{percent by mass per volume} = \frac{\text{mass solute}}{V} \times 100\% \quad \frac{1 \text{ mol NaCl}}{58.44 \text{ g NaCl}} \text{ and } \frac{180.16 \text{ g C}_6\text{H}_{12}\text{O}_6}{1 \text{ mol C}_6\text{H}_{12}\text{O}_6}$$

Solution: percent by mass per volume $= \dfrac{\text{mass solute}}{V} \times 100\% =$

$= \dfrac{0.0090 \; \overline{\text{g NaCl}}}{V} \times \dfrac{1 \; \overline{\text{mol NaCl}}}{58.44 \; \overline{\text{g NaCl}}} \times \dfrac{1.9 \; \overline{\text{mol C}_6\text{H}_{12}\text{O}_6}}{1 \; \overline{\text{mol NaCl}}} \times \dfrac{180.16 \; \text{g C}_6\text{H}_{12}\text{O}_6}{1 \; \overline{\text{mol C}_6\text{H}_{12}\text{O}_6}} \times 100\%$

$= 5.3\% \; \text{C}_6\text{H}_{12}\text{O}_6$ by mass per volume

Check: The units (% $\text{C}_6\text{H}_{12}\text{O}_6$ by mass per volume) are correct. The magnitude of the answer (5.3) seems reasonable since the molar mass of $\text{C}_6\text{H}_{12}\text{O}_6$ is larger than the molar mass of NaCl and we need more moles of $\text{C}_6\text{H}_{12}\text{O}_6$ since it is a nonelectrolyte.

12.109   **Given:** 4.5701 g of MgCl_2 and 43.238 g water, $P_{\text{soln}} = 0.3672$ bar, $P_{\text{soln}}^\circ = 0.3854$ bar at 348.0 K **Find:** i_{measured}

Conceptual Plan: $g_{\text{MgCl}_2} \rightarrow \text{mol}_{\text{MgCl}_2}$ and $g_{\text{H}_2\text{O}} \rightarrow \text{mol}_{\text{H}_2\text{O}}$ then $P_{\text{soln}}, P_{\text{soln}}^\circ, \rightarrow \chi_{\text{MgCl}_2}$

$$\dfrac{1 \text{ mol MgCl}_2}{95.218 \text{ g MgCl}_2} \qquad\qquad \dfrac{1 \text{ mol H}_2\text{O}}{18.015 \text{ g H}_2\text{O}} \qquad\qquad P_{\text{Soln}} = (1 - \chi_{\text{MgCl}_2})P_{\text{H}_2\text{O}}^\circ$$

then mol $_{\text{MgCl}_2}$, mol$_{\text{H}_2\text{O}}$, $\chi_{\text{MgCl}_2} \rightarrow i$

$$\chi_{\text{MgCl}_2} = \dfrac{i \,(\text{moles MgCl}_2)}{\text{moles H}_2\text{O} + i \,(\text{moles MgCl}_2)}$$

Solution: $4.5701 \; \overline{\text{g MgCl}_2} \times \dfrac{1 \text{ mol MgCl}_2}{95.218 \; \overline{\text{g MgCl}_2}} = 0.047996177 \text{ mol MgCl}_2$ and

$43.238 \; \overline{\text{g H}_2\text{O}} \times \dfrac{1 \text{ mol H}_2\text{O}}{18.015 \; \overline{\text{g H}_2\text{O}}} = 2.4001110 \text{ mol H}_2\text{O}$ then $P_{\text{soln}} = (1 - \chi_{\text{MgCl}_2})P_{\text{H}_2\text{O}}^\circ$ so

$$\chi_{\text{MgCl}_2} = 1 - \dfrac{P_{\text{soln}}}{P_{\text{H}_2\text{O}}^\circ} = 1 - \dfrac{0.3672 \text{ bar}}{0.3854 \text{ bar}} = 0.04722366$$

Solve for i.

$i(0.047996177) = 0.04722366(2.4001110 + i\,(0.047996177)) \rightarrow$

$i(0.047996177 - 0.002266555) = 0.1133420 \rightarrow i = \dfrac{0.1133420}{0.04572962} = 2.479$

Check: The units (none) are correct. The magnitude of the answer (2.5) seems reasonable for MgCl_2 since we expect i to be 3 if it completely dissociates. Since Mg is small and doubly charged, we expect a significant drop from 3.

12.111   **Given:** $T_b = 375.3$ K aqueous solution   **Find:** $P_{\text{H}_2\text{O}}$ at 338 K   **Other:** $P_{\text{H}_2\text{O}}^\circ = 0.2467$ bar; $K_b = 0.512 \; ^\circ\text{C } m^{-1}$, $T_b^\circ = 100 \; ^\circ\text{C}$ or 373.15 K

Conceptual Plan: $T_b \rightarrow \Delta T_b$ then $\Delta T_b, K_b \rightarrow m$ assume 1 kg water kg $_{\text{H}_2\text{O}} \rightarrow \text{mol}_{\text{H}_2\text{O}}$ then

$$T_b = T_b^\circ + \Delta T_b \qquad\qquad \Delta T_b = K_b m \qquad\qquad \dfrac{1 \text{ mol H}_2\text{O}}{18.01 \text{ g H}_2\text{O}}$$

$m \rightarrow \text{mol}_{\text{Solute}}$ then mol$_{\text{H}_2\text{O}}$, mol $_{\text{Solute}} \rightarrow \chi_{\text{H}_2\text{O}}$ then $\chi_{\text{H}_2\text{O}}, P_{\text{H}_2\text{O}}^\circ \rightarrow P_{\text{H}_2\text{O}}$

$$m = \dfrac{\text{amount solute (moles)}}{\text{mass solvent (kg)}} \qquad \chi_{\text{H}_2\text{O}} = \dfrac{\text{moles H}_2\text{O}}{\text{moles H}_2\text{O} + \text{moles solute}} \qquad P_{\text{H}_2\text{O}} = \chi_{\text{H}_2\text{O}} P_{\text{H}_2\text{O}}^\circ$$

Solution: $T_b = T_b^\circ + \Delta T_b$ so $\Delta T_b = T_b - T_b^\circ = 375.3 \text{ K} - 373.15 \text{ K} = 2.15 \text{ K} = 2.15 \; ^\circ\text{C}$ then

$\Delta T_b = K_b m$. Rearrange to solve for m. $m = \dfrac{\Delta T_b}{K_b} = \dfrac{2.2 \; ^\circ\text{C}}{0.512 \; \frac{^\circ\text{C}}{m}} = 4.296875 \; m$ then

$1000 \; \overline{\text{g H}_2\text{O}} \times \dfrac{1 \text{ mol H}_2\text{O}}{18.01 \; \overline{\text{g H}_2\text{O}}} = 55.50930 \text{ mol H}_2\text{O}$ then

$m = \dfrac{\text{amount solute (moles)}}{\text{mass solvent (kg)}} = \dfrac{x \text{ mol}}{1 \text{ kg}} = 4.199219 \; m$ so $x = 4.199219 \text{ mol}$ then

$\chi_{\text{H}_2\text{O}} = \dfrac{\text{moles H}_2\text{O}}{\text{moles H}_2\text{O} + \text{moles solute}} = \dfrac{55.50930 \; \overline{\text{mol}}}{55.50930 \; \overline{\text{mol}} + 4.199219 \; \overline{\text{mol}}} = 0.929671$. Since neither m nor χ is

temperature dependant the $\chi_{\text{H}_2\text{O}}$ at 375.3 K is the same as $\chi_{\text{H}_2\text{O}}$ at 338 K.

So at 338 K $P_{\text{H}_2\text{O}} = \chi_{\text{H}_2\text{O}} P_{\text{H}_2\text{O}}^\circ = 0.929671 \times 0.2467 \text{ bar} = 0.229 \text{ bar}$.

Check: The units (bar) are correct. The magnitude of the answer (0.229 bar) seems reasonable since the mole fraction is lowered by ~ 7%.

12.113   **Given:** equal masses of carbon tetrachloride (CCl_4) and chloroform ($CHCl_3$) at 316 K; $P^{\circ}_{CCl_4}$ = 0.354 bar; $P^{\circ}_{CHCl_3}$ = 0.526 bar **Find:** χ_{CCl_4}, χ_{CHCl_3} in vapour; and P_{CHCl_3} in flask of condensed vapour

Conceptual Plan: assume 100 grams of each $g_{CCl_4} \rightarrow mol_{CCl_4}$ and $g_{CHCl_3} \rightarrow mol_{CHCl_3}$ then

$$\frac{1 \text{ mol } CCl_4}{153.82 \text{ g } CCl_4} \qquad\qquad \frac{1 \text{ mol } CHCl_3}{119.38 \text{ g } CHCl_3}$$

mol_{CCl_4}, $mol_{CHCl_3} \rightarrow \chi_{CCl_4}$, χ_{CHCl_3} then χ_{CCl_4}, $P^{\circ}_{CCl_4} \rightarrow P_{CCl_4}$ and χ_{CHCl_3}, $P^{\circ}_{CHCl_3} \rightarrow P_{CHCl_3}$ then

$$\chi_{CCl_4} = \frac{\text{amount } CCl_4 \text{ (in moles)}}{\text{total amount (in moles)}} \quad \chi_{CHCl_3} = 1 - \chi_{CCl_4} \qquad P_{CCl_4} = \chi_{CCl_4} P^{\circ}_{CCl_4} \qquad P_{CHCl_3} = \chi_{CHCl_3} P^{\circ}_{CHCl_3}$$

P_{CCl_4}, $P_{CHCl_3} \rightarrow P_{Total}$ then since $n \, \alpha \, P$ and we are calculating a mass percent, which is a ratio of masses,

$$P_{Total} = P_{CCl_4} + P_{CHCl_3}$$

we can simply convert 1 bar to 1 mole so P_{CCl_4}, $P_{CHCl_3} \rightarrow n_{CCl_4}$, n_{CHCl_3} then

$$\chi_{CCl_4} = \frac{\text{amount } CCl_4 \text{ (in moles)}}{\text{total amount (in moles)}}$$

mol_{CCl_4}, $mol_{CHCl_3} \rightarrow \chi_{CCl_4}$, χ_{CHCl_3} **then for the second vapour** χ_{CHCl_3}, $P^{\circ}_{CHCl_3} \rightarrow P_{CHCl_3}$

$$\chi_{CHCl_3} = 1 - \chi_{CCl_4} \qquad\qquad\qquad\qquad P_{CHCl_3} = \chi_{CHCl_3} P^{\circ}_{CHCl_3}$$

Solution: $100.00 \; \cancel{g \; CCl_4} \times \dfrac{1 \text{ mol } CCl_4}{153.82 \; \cancel{g \; CCl_4}} = 0.65011051 \text{ mol } CCl_4$ and

$100.00 \; \cancel{g \; CHCl_3} \times \dfrac{1 \text{ mol } CHCl_3}{119.38 \; \cancel{g \; CHCl_3}} = 0.83766125 \text{ mol } CHCl_3$ then

$\chi_{CCl_4} = \dfrac{\text{amount } CCl_4 \text{ (in moles)}}{\text{total amount (in moles)}} = \dfrac{0.65011051 \; \cancel{mol}}{0.65011051 \; \cancel{mol} + 0.83766125 \; \cancel{mol}} = 0.43696925$ and

$\chi_{CHCl_3} = 1 - \chi_{CCl_4} = 1 - 0.43696925 = 0.56303075$ then

$P_{CCl_4} = \chi_{CCl_4} P^{\circ}_{CCl_4} = 0.43696925 \times 0.354 \text{ bar} = 0.154687 \text{ bar}$ and

$P_{CHCl_3} = \chi_{CHCl_3} P^{\circ}_{CHCl_3} = 0.56303075 \times 0.526 \text{ bar} = 0.296154 \text{ bar}$ then

$P_{Total} = P_{CCl_4} + P_{CHCl_3} = 0.154687 \text{ bar} + 0.296154 \text{ bar} = 0.450841 \text{ bar}$ then

$mol_{CCl_4} = 0.154687 \text{ mol}$ and $mol_{CHCl_3} = 0.296154 \text{ mol}$ then

$\chi_{CCl_4} = \dfrac{\text{amount } CCl_4 \text{ (in moles)}}{\text{total amount (in moles)}} = \dfrac{0.154687 \; \cancel{mol}}{0.154687 \; \cancel{mol} + 0.296154 \; \cancel{mol}} = 0.343108 = 0.343$ in the first vapour

and $\chi_{CHCl_3} = 1 - \chi_{CCl_4} = 1 - 0.343108 = 0.656892 = 0.657$ in the first vapour; then in the second vapour

$P_{CHCl_3} = \chi_{CHCl_3} P^{\circ}_{CHCl_3} = 0.656892 \times 0.526 \text{ bar} = 0.345525 \text{ bar} = 0.346 \text{ bar}$.

Check: The units (none and bar) are correct. The magnitudes of the answers seem reasonable since we expect the lighter component to be found preferentially in the vapour phase. This effect is magnified in the second vapour.

12.115   **Given:** 49.0% H_2SO_4 by mass, d = 1.39 g cm^{-3}, 25.0 cm^3 diluted to 99.8 cm^3 **Find:** molarity

Conceptual Plan: initial $V_{solution} \rightarrow g_{solution} \rightarrow g_{H_2SO_4} \rightarrow mol_{H_2SO_4}$ and final $V_{solution} \rightarrow L_{solution}$

$$\frac{1.39 \text{ g}}{1 \text{ cm}^3} \qquad \frac{49.0 \text{ g } H_2SO_4}{100 \text{ g solution}} \quad \frac{1 \text{ mol } H_2SO_4}{98.09 \text{ g } H_2SO_4} \qquad\qquad \frac{1 \text{ mL}}{1 \text{ cm}^3} \quad \frac{1 \text{ L}}{1000 \text{ mL}}$$

then $mol_{H_2SO_4}$, $L_{solution} \rightarrow M$

$$M = \frac{\text{amount solute (moles)}}{\text{volume solution (L)}}$$

Solution:

$25.0 \; \cancel{cm^3 \text{ solution}} \dfrac{1 \; \cancel{mL}}{1 \; \cancel{cm^{-3}}} \times \dfrac{1.39 \; \cancel{g \text{ solution}}}{1 \; \cancel{mL \text{ solution}}} \times \dfrac{49.0 \; \cancel{g \; H_2SO_4}}{100 \; \cancel{g \text{ solution}}} \times \dfrac{1 \text{ mol } H_2SO_4}{98.09 \; \cancel{g \; H_2SO_4}} = 0.1735906 \text{ mol } H_2SO_4$ and

$99.8 \; \cancel{cm^3 \text{ solution}} \dfrac{1 \; \cancel{mL}}{1 \; \cancel{cm^{-3}}} \times \dfrac{1 \text{ L solution}}{1000 \; \cancel{mL \text{ solution}}} = 0.0998 \text{ L solution}$ then

$M = \dfrac{\text{amount solute (moles)}}{\text{volume solution (L)}} = \dfrac{0.1735906 \text{ mol } H_2SO_4}{0.0998 \text{ L solution}} = 1.74 \text{ mol L}^{-1} \; H_2SO_4$.

Check: The units (mol L^{-1}) are correct. The magnitude of the answer (1.74 mol L^{-1}) seems reasonable since the solutions is ~ 1/6 surfuric acid.

12.117   **Given:** 10.05 g of unknown compound in 50.0 mL water, $T_f = -3.16$ °C, mass percent composition of the compound is 60.97% C, 11.94% H, and the rest is O **Find:** molecular formula

Other: $K_f = 1.86$ °C m^{-1}; $d = 1.00$ g mL^{-1}

Conceptual Plan: $g_{H_2O} \rightarrow kg_{H_2O}$ and $T_f \rightarrow \Delta T_f$ then $\Delta T_f, K_f \rightarrow m$ then $m, kg_{H_2O} \rightarrow mol_{Unk}$

$$\frac{1 \text{ kg}}{1000 \text{ g}} \qquad T_f = T_f^\circ - \Delta T_f \qquad \Delta T_f = K_f m \qquad m = \frac{\text{amount solute (moles)}}{\text{mass solvent (kg)}}$$

then $g_{Unk}, mol_{Unk} \rightarrow$ **molar mass** $\rightarrow g_C, g_H, g_O \rightarrow mol_C, mol_H, mol_O \rightarrow$ **molecular formula**

$$\text{molar mass} = \frac{g_{Unk}}{mol_{Unk}} \quad \text{mass percents} \quad \frac{1 \text{ mol C}}{12.01 \text{ g C}} \frac{1 \text{ mol H}}{1.008 \text{ g H}} \frac{1 \text{ mol O}}{16.00 \text{ g O}}$$

Solution: $50.0 \text{ mL} \times \dfrac{1 \text{ g}}{1 \text{ mL}} \times \dfrac{1 \text{ kg}}{1000 \text{ g}} = 0.0500$ kg and $T_f = T_f^\circ - \Delta T_f$ so

$\Delta T_f = T_f^\circ - T_f = 0.00$ °C $-$ -3.16 °C $= +3.16$ °C $\Delta T_f = K_f m$. Rearrange to solve for m.

$$m = \frac{\Delta T_f}{K_f} = \frac{3.16 \text{ °C}}{1.86 \dfrac{\text{°C}}{m}} = 1.69892 \ m \text{ then } m = \frac{\text{amount solute (moles)}}{\text{mass solvent (kg)}} \text{ so}$$

$$mol_{Unk} = m_{Unk} \times kg_{H_2O} = 1.69892 \frac{\text{mol Unk}}{\text{kg}} \times 0.0500 \text{ kg} = 0.08494624 \text{ mol Unk then}$$

$$\text{molar mass} = \frac{g_{Unk}}{mol_{Unk}} = \frac{10.05 \text{ g}}{0.08494624 \text{ mol}} = 118.3101 \text{ g mol}^{-1} \text{ then}$$

$$\frac{118.3101 \ \overline{g \text{ Unk}}}{1 \text{ mol Unk}} \times \frac{60.97 \ \overline{g \text{ C}}}{100 \ \overline{g \text{ Unk}}} \times \frac{1 \text{ mol C}}{12.01 \ \overline{g \text{ C}}} = \frac{6.01 \text{ mol C}}{1 \text{ mol Unk}}$$

$$\frac{118.3101 \ \overline{g \text{ Unk}}}{1 \text{ mol Unk}} \times \frac{11.94 \ \overline{g \text{ H}}}{100 \ \overline{g \text{ Unk}}} \times \frac{1 \text{ mol H}}{1.008 \ \overline{g \text{ H}}} = \frac{14.0 \text{ mol H}}{1 \text{ mol Unk}} \text{ and}$$

$$\frac{118.3101 \ \overline{g \text{ Unk}}}{1 \text{ mol Unk}} \times \frac{(100 - (60.97 + 11.94)) \overline{g \text{ O}}}{100 \ \overline{g \text{ Unk}}} \times \frac{1 \text{ mol O}}{16.00 \ \overline{g \text{ O}}} = \frac{2.00 \text{ mol O}}{1 \text{ mol Unk}}.$$

So the molecular formula is $C_6H_{14}O_2$.

Check: The units (formula) are correct. The magnitude of the answer (formula with ~ 118 vapour) seems reasonable since the molality is ~ 1.7 and we have ~10 g. It is a reasonable molecular weight for a solid or liquid. The formula does have the correct molar mass.

12.119   **Given:** 100.0 mL solution 13.5% by mass NaCl, $d = 1.12$ g mL^{-1}; $T_b = 104.4$ °C **Find:** g NaCl or water to add

Other: $K_b = 0.512$ °C m^{-1}; $i_{measured} = 1.8$

Conceptual Plan: $T_b \rightarrow \Delta T_b$ then $\Delta T_b, i, K_b \rightarrow m$ then $mL_{solution} \rightarrow g_{solution} \rightarrow g_{NaCl} \rightarrow mol_{NaCl}$ then

$$\Delta T_b = T_b - T_b^\circ \qquad \Delta T_b = K_b im \qquad \frac{1.12 \text{ g solution}}{1 \text{ mL solution}} \quad \frac{13.5 \text{ g NaCl}}{100 \text{ g solution}} \quad \frac{1 \text{ mol NaCl}}{58.44 \text{ g NaCl}}$$

$m, mol_{NaCl} \rightarrow kg_{H_2O} \rightarrow g_{H_2O}$ and $g_{solution}, g_{NaCl} \rightarrow g_{H_2O}$ then **compare the initial and final g_{H_2O} then**

$$m = \frac{\text{amount solute (moles)}}{\text{mass solvent (kg)}} \frac{1000 \text{ g}}{1 \text{ kg}} \qquad g_{solution} = g_{NaCl} + g_{H_2O}$$

calculate the total NaCl in final solution by scaling-up the amount from the initial solution. Then calculate the difference between the needed and starting amounts of NaCl.

Solution: $\Delta T_b = T_b - T_b^\circ = 104.4$ °C $- 100.0$ °C $= 4.4$ °C then $\Delta T_b = K_b im$.

Rearrange to solve for m. $m = \dfrac{\Delta T_b}{K_b i} = \dfrac{4.4 \text{ °C}}{0.512 \dfrac{\text{°C}}{m} \times 1.8} = 4.774306 \ m$ NaCl then

$$100.0 \ \overline{\text{mL solution}} \times \frac{1.12 \text{ g solution}}{1 \ \overline{\text{mL solution}}} = 112 \ \overline{\text{g solution}} \times \frac{13.5 \text{ g NaCl}}{100 \ \overline{\text{g solution}}} = 15.13 \ \overline{\text{g NaCl}} \times \frac{1 \text{ mol NaCl}}{58.44 \ \overline{\text{g NaCl}}}$$

$= 0.2587269$ mol NaCl

then $m = \dfrac{\text{amount solute (moles)}}{\text{mass solvent (kg)}}$. Rearrange to solve for kg_{H_2O}.

$$kg_{H_2O} = \frac{mol_{NaCl}}{m} = \frac{0.2587269 \ \overline{\text{mol NaCl}}}{4.774306 \ \dfrac{\overline{\text{mol NaCl}}}{1 \text{ kg}_{H_2O}}} = 0.0541915 \ kg_{H_2O} \times \frac{1000 \ g_{H_2O}}{1 \ \overline{kg_{H_2O}}} = 54.1915 \ g_{H_2O} \text{ in final solution}$$

then $g_{solution} = g_{NaCl} + g_{H_2O} = 112$ g solution $- 15.12$ g NaCl $= 96.88$ g H_2O in initial solution. Comparing the initial and final solutions, there is a lot more water in the initial solution so NaCl needs to be added.

In the solution with a boiling point of 104.4 °C, $\dfrac{15.12 \text{ g NaCl}}{54.1915 \text{ g H}_2\text{O}} = \dfrac{x \text{ g NaCl}}{96.88 \text{ g H}_2\text{O}}$. Solve for x g NaCl.

x g NaCl $= \dfrac{15.12 \text{ g NaCl}}{54.1915 \text{ g H}_2\text{O}} \times 96.88 \text{ g H}_2\text{O} = 27.031$ g NaCl so the amount to be added is

27.031 g NaCl $- 15.12$ g NaCl $= 11.911$ g NaCl $= 12$ g NaCl.

Check: The units (g) are correct. The magnitude of the answer (12 g) seems reasonable since there is approximately twice as much water as is desired in the initial solution, so the NaCl amount needs to be approximately doubled.

12.121   **Given:** 100 mL solvent (CS_2), $T_{b,solvent} = 46.2$ °C, $T_{b,solution} = 47.7$ °C, $d = 1.26$ g cm^{-3}; add 10 g white phosphorous
Find: molar mass and molecular formula of white phosphorous
Other: $K_b = 2.37$ °C kg mol^{-1}
Conceptual Plan: mL$_{solvent}$ → kg$_{solvent}$ then ΔT_b, K_b → m and m, kg$_{solvent}$ → moles solute

$$\dfrac{1.26 \text{ g}}{1 \text{ cm}^{-3}} \quad \dfrac{1 \text{ kg}}{1000 \text{ g}} \qquad\qquad \Delta T_b = K_b m \qquad m = \dfrac{\text{amount solute (moles)}}{\text{mass solvent (kg)}}$$

→ molar mass solute → molecular formula

$$\text{molar mass} = \dfrac{g_{solute}}{n_{solute}} \qquad \text{ratio of masses}$$

Solution:

$$100 \text{ mL}_{solvent} \times \dfrac{1 \text{ cm}^3}{1 \text{ mL}} \times \dfrac{1.26 \text{ g}}{1 \text{ cm}^3} \times \dfrac{1 \text{ kg}}{1000 \text{ g}} = 0.126 \text{ kg}$$

$$\Delta T_b = K_b m \quad m = \dfrac{\Delta T_b}{K_b} = \dfrac{(47.7 - 46.2)°C}{2.37 \text{ °C kg mol}^{-1}} = \dfrac{1.5 \text{ mol}}{2.37 \text{ kg}} = 0.632911 \text{ mol kg}^{-1}$$

$$m = \dfrac{\text{amount solute (mole)}}{\text{mass solvent (kg)}} \to \text{moles solute} = m \times \text{mass solvent (kg)} \to \text{moles solute}$$

$$= 0.632911 \dfrac{\text{mol}}{\text{kg}} \times 0.126 \text{ kg} = 0.797468 \text{ mol solute}$$

$$\text{molar mass} = \dfrac{\text{mass solute}}{\text{moles solute}} = \dfrac{10 \text{ g white phosphorous}}{0.797468 \text{ mol}} = 125.39 \text{ g mol}^{-1} \text{ This is the molar mass of white}$$

phosphorous. Molecular formula = empirical formula x ratio of masses →

$$\text{Ratio of masses} = \dfrac{\text{molar mass of white phosphorous}}{\text{molar mass of phosphorous}}$$

$$= \dfrac{125.39 \text{ g mol}^{-1}}{30.97 \text{ g mol}^{-1}} = 4.0. \text{ Therefore the molecular formula for white phosphorous is } P_4.$$

Challenge Problems

12.123   **Given:** N_2: $k_H(N_2) = 6.1 \times 10^{-4}$ mol L^{-1} bar^{-1} at 25 °C; 14.6 mg L^{-1} at 50 °C and 100 kPa; $P_{N_2} = 78$ kPa; O_2: $k_H(O_2) = 1.3 \times 10^{-3}$ mol L^{-1} bar^{-1} at 25 °C; 27.8 mg L^{-1} at 50 °C and 100 kPa; $P_{O_2} = 21$ kPa; and 1.5 L water
Find: V (N_2) and V (O_2)
Conceptual Plan: at 25 °C: P_{N_2}, $k_H(N_2)$ → S_{N_2} **then L → mol**

$$S_{N_2} = k_H(N_2)P_{N_2} \qquad\qquad S_{N_2}$$

at 50 °C: L → mL → mg → g → mol then mol$_{25 °C}$, mol$_{25 °C}$ **→** mol$_{removed}$ **then °C → K**

$$\dfrac{1000 \text{ mL}}{1 \text{ L}} \quad \dfrac{14.6 \text{ mg}}{1 \text{ L}} \quad \dfrac{1 \text{ g}}{1000 \text{ mg}} \quad \dfrac{1 \text{ mol}}{28.01 \text{ g}} \qquad\qquad \text{mol}_{removed} = \text{mol}_{25 °C} - \text{mol}_{50 °C} \qquad K = °C + 273.15$$

then P, n, T → V

$$PV = nRT$$

at 25 °C: P_{O_2}, $k_H(O_2)$ $\rightarrow$ S_{O_2} then L $\rightarrow$ mol

$$S_{O_2} = k_H(O_2)P_{O_2} \qquad S_{O_2}$$

at 50 °C: L $\rightarrow$ mL $\rightarrow$ mg $\rightarrow$ g $\rightarrow$ mol then mol$_{25\,°C}$, mol$_{25\,°C}$ $\rightarrow$ mol$_{removed}$ then °C $\rightarrow$ K

$$\frac{1000\ mL}{1\ L} \quad \frac{27.8\ mg}{1\ L} \quad \frac{1\ g}{1000\ mg} \quad \frac{1\ mol}{32.00\ g} \qquad\qquad mol_{removed} = mol_{25\,°C} - mol_{50\,°C} \qquad K = °C + 273.15$$

then P, n, T $\rightarrow$ V

$$PV = nRT$$

Solution: at 25 °C:

$$S_{N_2} = k_H(N_2)P_{N_2} = 6.1 \times 10^{-4}\ \frac{mol}{L \cdot bar} \times 78\ kPa \times \frac{1\ bar}{100\ kPa} = 4.\underline{7}58 \times 10^{-4}\ mol\ L^{-1}\ then$$

$$1.5\ \cancel{L} \times 4.\underline{7}58 \times 10^{-4}\ \frac{mol}{\cancel{L}} = 0.00071\underline{3}71\ mol$$

at 50 °C: $1.5\ \cancel{L} \times \dfrac{14.6\ \cancel{mg}}{1\ \cancel{L} \cdot 100\ \cancel{kPa}} \times 78\ \cancel{kPa} \times \dfrac{1\ \cancel{g}}{1000\ \cancel{mg}} \times \dfrac{1\ mol}{28.01\ \cancel{g}} = 0.000609\underline{8}5\ mol\ then$

$mol_{removed} = mol_{25\,°C} - mol_{50\,°C} = 0.00071371\ mol - 0.00060985\ mol = 1.\underline{0}39 \times 10^{-4}\ mol\ N_2$

then 50 °C + 273.15 = 323 K then $PV = nRT$. Rearrange to solve for V.

$$V = \frac{nRT}{P} = \frac{1.\underline{0}39 \times 10^{-4}\ mol \times 0.08314\ \dfrac{L \cdot bar}{mol \cdot K} \times 323K}{100\ kPa \times \dfrac{1\ bar}{100\ kPa}} = 0.002\underline{7}903\ L\ N_2$$

at 25 °C:

$$S_{O_2} = k_H(O_2)\ P_{O_2} = 1.3 \times 10^{-3}\ \frac{mol}{L \cdot bar} \times 21\ kPa \times \frac{1\ bar}{100\ kPa} = 2.73 \times 10^{-4}\ mol\ L^{-1}\ then$$

$$1.5\ \cancel{L} \times 2.\underline{7}3 \times 10^{-4}\ \frac{mol}{\cancel{L}} = 0.00040\underline{9}5\ mol$$

at 50 °C: $1.5\ \cancel{L} \times \dfrac{27.8\ \cancel{mg}}{1\ \cancel{L} \cdot 100\ \cancel{kPa}} \times 21\ \cancel{kPa} \times \dfrac{1\ \cancel{g}}{1000\ \cancel{mg}} \times \dfrac{1\ mol}{32.00\ \cancel{g}} = 0.000273\underline{6}6\ mol\ then$

$mol_{removed} = mol_{25\,°C} - mol_{50\,°C} = 0.0004095\ mol - 0.00027366\ mol = 1.\underline{3}58 \times 10^{-4}\ mol\ O_2$

then 50 °C + 273.15 = 323 K then $PV = nRT$. Rearrange to solve for V.

$$V = \frac{nRT}{P} = \frac{1.\underline{3}58 \times 10^{-4}\ mol \times 0.08314\ \dfrac{L \cdot bar}{mol \cdot K} \times 323\ K}{100\ kPa \times \dfrac{1\ bar}{100\ kPa}} = 0.003\underline{6}470\ L\ O_2\ finally$$

$V_{Total} = V_{N_2} + V_{O_2} = 0.0027903\ L + 0.0036470\ L = 0.0064\ L$.

Check: The units (L) are correct. The magnitude of the answer (0.006 L) seems reasonable since we have so little dissolved gas at room temperature and most is still soluble at 50 °C.

12.125 **Given:** 1.10 g glucose ($C_6H_{12}O_6$) and sucrose ($C_{12}H_{22}O_{11}$) mixture in 25.0 mL solution and Π = 3.78 bar at 298 K **Find:** percent composition of mixture

Conceptual Plan: Π, T $\rightarrow$ M then mL$_{soln}$ $\rightarrow$ L$_{soln}$ then L$_{soln}$, M $\rightarrow$ mol$_{mixture}$ then

$$\Pi = M\,RT \qquad\qquad \frac{1\ L}{1000\ mL} \qquad\qquad M = \frac{amount\ solute\ (moles)}{volume\ solution\ (L)}$$

mol$_{mixture}$, g$_{mixture}$ $\rightarrow$ mol$_{C_6H_{12}O_6}$, mol$_{C_{12}H_{22}O_{11}}$ then

$$g_{mixture} = mol\ C_6H_{12}O_6 \times \frac{180.16\ g\ C_6H_{12}O_6}{1\ mol\ C_6H_{12}O_6} + mol\ C_{12}H_{22}O_{11} \times \frac{342.30\ g\ C_{12}H_{22}O_{11}}{1\ mol\ C_{12}H_{22}O_{11}}\ \textit{with}\ mol_{mixture} = mol_{C_6H_{12}O_6} + mol_{C_{12}H_{22}O_{11}}$$

mol$_{C_6H_{12}O_6}$ $\rightarrow$ g$_{C_6H_{12}O_6}$ and mol$_{C_{12}H_{22}O_{11}}$ $\rightarrow$ g$_{C_{12}H_{22}O_{11}}$ and g$_{C_6H_{12}O_6}$, g$_{C_{12}H_{22}O_{11}}$ $\rightarrow$ **mass percents**

$$\frac{180.16\ g\ C_6H_{12}O_6}{1\ mol\ C_6H_{12}O_6} \qquad \frac{342.30\ g\ C_{12}H_{22}O_{11}}{1\ mol\ C_{12}H_{22}O_{11}} \qquad mass\ percent = \frac{mass\ solute}{mass\ solution} \times 100\%$$

Solution: $\Pi = MRT$. Rearrange to solve for M.

$$M = \frac{\Pi}{RT} = \frac{3.78\ bar}{0.08314\ \dfrac{L \cdot bar}{mol \cdot K} \times 298\ K} = 0.1525\underline{6}9\ \frac{mol\ mixture}{L}\ then\ 25.0\ \cancel{mL} \times \frac{1\ L}{1000\ \cancel{mL}} = 0.0250\ L$$

then $M = \dfrac{\text{amount solute (moles)}}{\text{volume solution (L)}}$ so

$\text{mol}_{\text{mixture}} = M \times L_{\text{soln}} = 0.152569 \dfrac{\text{mol mixture}}{\text{L}} \times 0.00381422 \text{ L} = 0.00381422 \text{ mol mixture}$ then

$g_{\text{mixture}} = \overline{\text{mol } C_6H_{12}O_6} \times \dfrac{180.16 \text{ g } C_6H_{12}O_6}{1 \overline{\text{mol } C_6H_{12}O_6}} + \overline{\text{mol } C_{12}H_{22}O_{11}} \times \dfrac{342.30 \text{ g } C_{12}H_{22}O_{11}}{1 \overline{\text{mol } C_{12}H_{22}O_{11}}}$ with

$\text{mol}_{\text{mixture}} = \text{mol } C_6H_{12}O_6 + \text{mol } C_{12}H_{22}O_{11}$ so

$1.10 \text{ g} = \text{mol } C_6H_{12}O_6 \times \dfrac{180.16 \text{ g } C_6H_{12}O_6}{1 \text{ mol } C_6H_{12}O_6} + (0.00381422 \text{ mol} - \text{mol } C_6H_{12}O_6) \times \dfrac{342.30 \text{ g } C_{12}H_{22}O_{11}}{1 \text{ mol } C_{12}H_{22}O_{11}} \rightarrow$

$1.10 = 180.16 \times \text{mol } C_6H_{12}O_6 + 1.305607 - 342.30 \times \text{mol } C_6H_{12}O_6 \rightarrow 162.14 \, x \text{ mol } C_6H_{12}O_6$
$= 0.205607 \rightarrow$

$x \text{ mol } C_6H_{12}O_6 = \dfrac{0.205607}{162.14} = 0.00126808 \text{ mol } C_6H_{12}O_6$ then

$\text{mol}_{C_{12}H_{22}O_{11}} = \text{mol}_{\text{mixture}} - \text{mol}_{C_6H_{12}O_6} = 0.00381422 \text{ mol} - 0.00126808 \text{ mol}$
$= 0.0025461 \text{ mol } C_{12}H_{22}O_{11}$ then

$0.00126808 \overline{\text{mol } C_6H_{12}O_6} \times \dfrac{180.16 \text{ g } C_6H_{12}O_6}{1 \overline{\text{mol } C_6H_{12}O_6}} = 0.22845 \text{ g } C_6H_{12}O_6$ and

$0.0025461 \overline{\text{mol } C_{12}H_{22}O_{11}} \times \dfrac{342.30 \text{ g } C_{12}H_{22}O_{11}}{1 \overline{\text{mol } C_{12}H_{22}O_{11}}} = 0.871543 \text{ g } C_{12}H_{22}O_{11}$ and finally

$\text{mass percent} = \dfrac{\text{mass solute}}{\text{mass solution}} \times 100\% = \dfrac{0.22845 \overline{\text{g } C_6H_{12}O_6}}{0.22845 \overline{\text{g } C_6H_{12}O_6} + 0.87154 \overline{\text{g } C_{12}H_{22}O_{11}}} \times 100\%$

$= 20.8\% \, C_6H_{12}O_6$ by mass and $100.00\% - 20.8\% = 78.2\% \, C_{12}H_{22}O_{11}$ by mass.

Check: The units (% by mass) are correct. We expect the percent by $C_6H_{12}O_6$ to be larger than that for $C_{12}H_{22}O_{11}$ since the $g_{\text{mixture}}/\text{mol}_{\text{mixture}} = 285$ g mol^{-1}, which is closer to $C_{12}H_{22}O_{11}$ than $C_6H_{12}O_6$ and the molar mass of $C_{12}H_{22}O_{11}$ is larger than the molar mass of $C_6H_{12}O_6$. In addition, and most definitively, the masses obtained for sucrose and glucose sum to 1.1 g, the initial amount of solid dissolved.

12.127 **Given:** isopropyl alcohol ($(CH_3)_2CHOH$) and propyl alcohol ($CH_3CH_2CH_2OH$) at 313 K; solution 2/3 by mass isopropyl alcohol $P_{2/3} = 0.110$ bar; solution 1/3 by mass isopropyl alcohol $P_{1/3} = 0.089$ bar;
Find: P°_{iso} and P°_{pro} and explain why they are different
Conceptual Plan: since these are isomers, they have the same molar mass and so the fraction by mass is the same as the mole fraction, so mole fractions, P_{soln}s → P°s

$$\chi_{\text{iso}} = \dfrac{\text{amount iso (in moles)}}{\text{total amount (in moles)}} \quad \chi_{\text{pro}} = 1 - \chi_{\text{iso}} \quad P_{\text{iso}} = \chi_{\text{iso}} P^\circ_{\text{iso}} \quad P_{\text{pro}} = \chi_{\text{pro}} P^\circ_{\text{pro}} \text{ and } P_{\text{soln}} = P_{\text{iso}} + P_{\text{pro}}$$

Solution:
Solution 1: $\chi_{\text{iso}} = 2/3$ and $\chi_{\text{iso}} = 1/3$ $P_{\text{soln}} = P_{\text{iso}} + P_{\text{pro}}$ so 0.110 bar $= 2/3 P^\circ_{\text{iso}} + 1/3 P^\circ_{\text{pro}}$.

Solution 2: $\chi_{\text{iso}} = 1/3$ and $\chi_{\text{iso}} = 2/3$ $P_{\text{soln}} = P_{\text{iso}} + P_{\text{pro}}$ so 0.089 bar $= 1/3 P^\circ_{\text{iso}} + 2/3 P^\circ_{\text{pro}}$. We now have two equations and two unknowns and a number of ways to solve this. One way is to rearrange the first equation for P°_{iso} and then substitute into the other equation. Thus, $P^\circ_{\text{iso}} = 3/2(0.110 \text{ bar} - 1/3 P^\circ_{\text{pro}})$ and

$0.089 \text{ bar} = \dfrac{1}{3}\dfrac{3}{2}(0.110 \text{ bar} - 1/3 \, P^\circ_{\text{pro}}) + \dfrac{2}{3} P^\circ_{\text{pro}} \rightarrow 0.089 \text{ bar} = 0.0550 \text{ bar} - \dfrac{1}{6} P^\circ_{\text{pro}} + \dfrac{2}{3} P^\circ_{\text{pro}} \rightarrow$

$\dfrac{1}{2} P^\circ_{\text{pro}} = 0.0340 \text{ bar} \rightarrow P^\circ_{\text{pro}} = 0.0680 \text{ bar} = 0.068 \text{ bar}$ and then

$P^\circ_{\text{iso}} = 3/2(0.110 \text{ bar} - 1/3 P^\circ_{\text{pro}}) = 3/2(0.110 \text{ bar} - 1/3(0.0680 \text{ bar})) = 0.131 \text{ bar}$.
The major intermolecular attractions are between the OH groups. The OH group at the end of the chain in propyl alcohol is more accessible than the one in the middle of the chain in isopropyl alcohol. In addition, the molecular shape of propyl alcohol is a straight chain of carbon atoms, while that of isopropyl alcohol has a branched chain and is more like a ball. The contact area between two ball-like objects is smaller than that of two chain-like objects. The smaller contact area in isopropyl alcohol means the molecules do not attract each other as strongly as do those of propyl alcohol. As a result of both of these factors, the vapour pressure of isopropyl alcohol is higher.
Check: The units (bar) are correct. The magnitude of the answer seems reasonable since the solution partial pressures are both ~0.1 bar.

12.129   **Given:** 0.1000 m H_2SO_4 solution; complete dissociation to H^+ and HSO_4^-; limited dissociation to SO_4^{2-};
$T_f = 272.76$ K **Find:** m (SO_4^{2-}) **Other:** $K_f = 1.86$ K m^{-1}
Conceptual Plan: $T_f \rightarrow \Delta T_f$ then $m, \Delta T_f, K_f \rightarrow i \rightarrow m$ (SO_4^{2-})

$$T_f = T_f^\circ - \Delta T_f \qquad\qquad \Delta T_f = K_f im \quad m\,(SO_4^{2-}) = m\ H_2SO_4\ (i-2.0)/2$$

Solution: $T_f = T_f^\circ - \Delta T_f$. Rearrange to solve for ΔT_f. So

$\Delta T_f = T_f^\circ - T_f = 273.15$ K $- 272.76$ K $= -0.39$ K then $\Delta T_f = K_f im$. Rearrange to solve for i.

$$i = \frac{\Delta T_f}{K_f m} = \frac{0.39\ \text{K}}{1.86\ \dfrac{\text{K}}{m} \times 0.1000\ m} = 2.0\underline{9}68.$$

Remember that when H_2SO_4 completely dissociates, two particles are formed (H^+ and HSO_4^-), so $i = 2$.
When HSO_4^- dissociates two particles are generated (SO_4^{2-} and H^+).

$m(SO_4^{2-})$ $=$ m H_2SO_4 $i-2 = (0.1000\ m)$ $2.0\underline{9}68 - 2 = 0.0097\ m = 0.0097\ m$ SO_4^{2-}.

Check: The units (m) are correct. The magnitude of the answer (0.01 m) seems reasonable since not much of the HSO_4^- dissociates.

12.131   **Given:** $Na_2CO_3 + NaHCO_3 = 11.60$ g in 1.00 L; treat 300.0 cm³ of solution with HNO_3 and collect 0.940 L CO_2
at 298 K and 0.972 bar **Find:** M(Na_2CO_3) and M($NaHCO_3$)
Conceptual Plan: $P, V, T \rightarrow n$ in 300.0 cm³ then n in 300.0 cm³ $\rightarrow n$ in 1.00 L then

$$PV = nRT \qquad\qquad\qquad \text{take ratio of volumes}$$

set up equations for the total mass and the total moles and solve. Then calculate concentrations.

$g_{Na_2CO_3} + g_{NaHCO_3} = 11.60$ g $\quad\dfrac{105.99\ \text{g}\ Na_2CO_3}{1\ \text{mol}\ Na_2CO_3}\ \dfrac{84.01\ \text{g}\ NaHCO_3}{1\ \text{mol}\ NaHCO_3}\quad n_{Na_2CO_3} + n_{NaHCO_3} = n.$

Solution: $PV = nRT$. Rearrange to solve for n. $n = \dfrac{PV}{RT}$

$$n_{CO_2} = \frac{0.972\ \text{bar} \times 0.940\ \text{L}}{0.08314\ \dfrac{\text{L} \cdot \text{bar}}{\text{mol} \cdot \text{K}} \times 298\ \text{K}} = 0.03687804\ \text{mol}\ CO_2 \text{ in } 300.0 \text{ cm}^3.$$ Then take ratio of moles to volume to

get the moles in 1.00 L

$$\frac{0.03687804\ \text{mol}\ CO_2}{300.0\ \text{cm}^3} \times 1000\ \text{cm}^3 = 0.1229268\ \text{mol}\ CO_2 \text{ in } 1.00 \text{ L since one mole of } CO_2 \text{ is generated for each}$$

mole of carbonate. So n $=$ $n_{Na_2CO_3} + n_{NaHCO_3} = 0.1229268$ mol and $g_{Na_2CO_3} + g_{NaHCO_3} = 11.60$ g or

$g_{Na_2CO_3} = 11.60$ g $- g_{NaHCO_3}$ using molar masses and substituting

$$n_{Na_2CO_3} + n_{NaHCO_3} = 0.1229268\ \text{mol} = g_{Na_2CO_3} \times \frac{1\ \text{mol}\ Na_2CO_3}{105.99\ \text{g}\ Na_2CO_3} + g_{NaHCO_3} \times \frac{1\ \text{mol}\ NaHCO_3}{84.01\ \text{g}\ NaHCO_3} =$$

$$(11.60\ \text{g} - g_{NaHCO_3}) \times \frac{1\ \text{mol}\ Na_2CO_3}{105.99\ \text{g}\ Na_2CO_3} + g_{NaHCO_3} \times \frac{1\ \text{mol}\ NaHCO_3}{84.01\ \text{g}\ NaHCO_3}$$

$$\rightarrow 0.1229268\ \text{mol} = 0.10\underline{9}44429\ \text{mol} - g_{NaHCO_3} \times 0.009434852\ \frac{\text{mol}}{\text{g}} + g_{NaHCO_3}\ 0.011\underline{9}03345\ \frac{\text{mol}}{\text{g}}$$

$$\rightarrow 0.0134825\ \text{mol} = g_{NaHCO_3} \times 0.002\underline{4}68493\ \frac{\text{mol}}{\text{g}} \rightarrow$$

$$g_{NaHCO_3} = \frac{0.0134825\ \text{mol}}{0.002\underline{4}68493\ \dfrac{\text{mol}}{\text{g}}} = 5.4\underline{6}1838\ \text{g}\ NaHCO_3 = 5.5\ \text{g}\ NaHCO_3 \text{ and then } g_{Na_2CO_3} =$$

11.60 g $- g_{NaHCO_3} = 11.60$ g $- 5.4\underline{6}1838$ g $NaHCO_3 = 6.1\underline{3}8162$ g $Na_2CO_3 = 6.1$ g Na_2CO_3 then M = mol L^{-1}

$$\frac{5.4\underline{6}1838\ \overline{\text{g}\ NaHCO_3} \times \dfrac{1\ \text{mol}\ NaHCO_3}{84.01\ \overline{\text{g}\ NaHCO_3}}}{1.00\ \text{L}} = 0.065\ \text{mol}\ L^{-1}\ NaHCO_3 \text{ and}$$

$$\frac{6.1\underline{3}8162\ \overline{\text{g}\ Na_2CO_3} \times \dfrac{1\ \text{mol}\ Na_2CO_3}{105.99\ \overline{\text{g}\ Na_2CO_3}}}{1.00\ \text{L}} = 0.058\ \text{mol}\ L^{-1}\ Na_2CO_3.$$

Check: The units (mol L^{-1}) are correct. The magnitude of the answers (0.052 mol L^{-1} and 0.073 mol L^{-1}) makes sense because the number of moles of CO_2 is small (0.12 mol L^{-1}). The balance of the two components make sense because if it were all Na_2CO_3 the number of moles would have been 0.109 moles (11.6/105.99) and if it were all $NaHCO_3$ the number of moles would have been 0.138 moles (11.6/84.01)—the actual number of moles is roughly in the middle of these two values.

Conceptual Problems

12.133   The water should not be immediately cycled back into the river. As the water was warmed, dissolved oxygen would have been released, since the amount of a gas able to be dissolved into a liquid decreases as the temperature of the liquid increases. As such, the water returned to the river would lack dissolved oxygen if it was still hot. To preserve the dissolved oxygen necessary for the survival of fish and other aquatic life, the water must first be cooled.

12.135   (b) NaCl. If all of the substances have the same cost per kilogram, we need to determine which substance will generate the largest number of particles per kilogram (or gram). $HOCH_2CH_2OH$ generates 1 mol particle / 62.07 g; NaCl generates 2 mol particles / 58.44 g; KCl generates 2 mol particles / 74.56 g; $MgCl_2$ generates 3 mol particles / 95.22 g; and $SrCl_2$ generates 3 mol particles / 158.53 g. So NaCl will generate 1 mole of particles for each 29 g.

12.137   NaCl molality = 0.02 m, the boiling point will be 100.02 °C. Adding salt to boiling water is for gastronomic reasons (taste), not to decrease the cooking time by increasing the boiling point.

13 Chemical Kinetics

Review Questions

13.1 Unlike mammals, which actively regulate their body temperature through metabolic activity, lizards are ectotherms—their body temperature depends on their surroundings. When splashed with cold water, a lizard's body simply gets colder. The drop in body temperature immobilizes the lizard because its movement depends on chemical reactions that occur within its muscles, and the rates of those reactions—how fast they occur—are highly sensitive to temperature. In other words, when the temperature drops, the reactions that produce movement occur more slowly; therefore the movement itself slows down. Cold reptiles are lethargic, unable to move very quickly. For this reason, reptiles try to maintain their body temperature in a narrow range by moving between sun and shade.

13.3 The rate of a chemical reaction is measured as a change in the amounts of reactants or products (usually in terms of concentration) divided by the change in time. Typical units are molarity per second ($mol \ L^{-1} \ s^{-1}$), molarity per minute ($mol \ L^{-1} \ min^{-1}$), and molarity per year ($mol \ L^{-1} \ yr^{-1}$), depending on how fast the reaction proceeds.

13.5 The average rate of the reaction can be calculated for any time interval as $\text{Rate} = -\dfrac{1}{a}\dfrac{[A]_{t_2} - [A]_{t_1}}{t_2 - t_1} = -\dfrac{1}{b}\dfrac{[B]_{t_2} - [B]_{t_1}}{t_2 - t_1} = \dfrac{1}{c}\dfrac{[C]_{t_2} - [C]_{t_1}}{t_2 - t_1} = \dfrac{1}{d}\dfrac{[D]_{t_2} - [D]_{t_1}}{t_2 - t_1}$ for the chemical reaction $a A + b B \rightarrow c C + d D$. The instantaneous rate of the reaction is the rate at any one point in time, represented by the instantaneous slope of the plot of concentration versus time at that point. We can obtain the instantaneous rate from the slope of the tangent to this curve at the point of interest.

13.7 The reaction order cannot be determined by the stoichiometry of the reaction. It can only be determined by running controlled experiments where the concentrations of the reactants are varied and the reaction rates are measured and analyzed.

13.9 The rate law shows the relationship between the rate of a reaction and the concentrations of the reactants. The integrated rate law for a chemical reaction is a relationship between the concentration of a reactant and time.

13.11 The half-life, lifetime, and decay time are the amount of time it takes for the initial concentration to reduce to $1/2$, $1/e$, and $1/n$ of their original concentrations, respectively.

	zero order	first order	second order
decay time	$t = \dfrac{\left(\frac{n-1}{n}\right)[A]_0}{k}$	$t = \dfrac{\ln(n)}{k}$	$t = \dfrac{n-1}{k[A]_0}$
half-life	$t = \dfrac{[A]_0}{2k}$	$t_{1/2} = \dfrac{0.693}{k}$	$t = \dfrac{1}{k[A]_0}$
decay to $1/5$ original concentration	$t = \dfrac{5[A]_0}{4k}$	$t = \dfrac{\ln(5)}{k}$	$t = \dfrac{4}{k[A]_0}$

13.13   The modern form of the Arrhenius equation, which relates the rate constant (k) and the temperature in kelvin (T), is as follows: $k = A\,e^{-E_a/RT}$, where R is the gas constant (8.314 J mol^{-1} K^{-1}), A is a constant called the frequency factor (or the pre-exponential factor), and E_a is called the activation energy (or activation barrier). The frequency factor is the number of times that the reactants approach the activation barrier per unit time. The exponential factor ($-E_a/RT$) is the fraction of approaches that are successful in surmounting the activation barrier and forming products. The exponential factor increases with increasing temperature, but decreases with an increasing value for the activation energy. As the temperature increases, the number of collisions increases and the number of molecules having enough thermal energy to surmount the activation barrier increases. At any given temperature, a sample of molecules will have a distribution of energies, as shown in Figure 13.14. Under common circumstances, only a small fraction of the molecules have enough energy to make it over the activation barrier. Because of the shape of the energy distribution curve, however, a small change in temperature results in a large difference in the number of molecules having enough energy to surmount the activation barrier.

13.15   In the collision model, a chemical reaction occurs after a sufficiently energetic collision between the two reactant molecules. In collision theory, therefore, each approach to the activation barrier is a collision between the reactant molecules. The value of the frequency factor should simply be the number of collisions that occur per second. In the collision model $k = pz\,e^{-E_a/RT}$, where the frequency factor (A) has been separated into two separate parts—p is called the orientation factor and z is the collision frequency. The collision frequency is simply the number of collisions that occur per unit time. The orientation factor says that if two molecules are to react with each other, they must collide in such a way that allows the necessary bonds to break and form. The small orientation factor indicates that the orientational requirements for this reaction are fairly stringent—the molecules must be aligned in a very specific way for the reaction to occur. When two molecules with sufficient energy and the correct orientation collide, something unique happens: the electrons on one of the atoms or molecules are attracted to the nuclei of the other; some bonds begin to weaken while other bonds begin to form and, if all goes well, the reactants go through the transition state and are transformed into the products and a chemical reaction occurs.

13.17   An elementary step is a single step in a reaction mechanism. Elementary steps cannot be broken down into simpler steps—they occur as they are written. Elementary steps are characterized by their molecularity, the number of reactant particles involved in the step. The molecularity of the three most common types of elementary steps are as follows: unimolecular - A $\rightarrow$ products and Rate = k[A]; bimolecular - A + A $\rightarrow$ products and Rate = k[A]^2; and bimolecular - A + B $\rightarrow$ products and Rate = k[A][B]. Elementary steps in which three reactant particles collide, called termolecular steps, are very rare because the probability of three particles simultaneously colliding is small.

13.19   Reaction intermediates are species that are formed in one step of a mechanism and consumed in another step. An intermediate is not found in the balanced equation for the overall reaction, but plays a key role in the mechanism.

13.21   In homogeneous catalysis, the catalyst exists in the same phase as the reactants. In heterogeneous catalysis, the catalyst exists in a phase different from the reactants. The most common type of heterogenous catalyst is a solid catalyst.

13.23   Enzymes are biological catalysts that increase the rates of biochemical reactions. Enzymes are large protein molecules with complex three-dimensional structures. Within that structure is a specific area called the active site. The properties and shape of the active site are just right to bind the reactant molecule, usually called the substrate. The substrate fits into the active site in a manner that is analogous to a key fitting into a lock.

Problems by Topic

Reaction Rates

13.25   (a) $\text{Rate} = -\dfrac{1}{2}\dfrac{\Delta[\text{HBr}]}{\Delta t} = \dfrac{\Delta[\text{H}_2]}{\Delta t} = \dfrac{\Delta[\text{Br}_2]}{\Delta t}$

         (b)   **Given:** first 25.0 s; 0.600 mol L^{-1} to 0.512 mol L^{-1} **Find:** average rate

Conceptual Plan: t_1, t_2, $[HBr]_1$, $[HBr]_2$ $\rightarrow$ average rate

$$\text{Rate} = -\frac{1}{2}\frac{\Delta[HBr]}{\Delta t}$$

Solution:

$$\text{Rate} = -\frac{1}{2}\frac{[HBr]_{t_2} - [HBr]_{t_1}}{t_2 - t_1} = -\frac{1}{2}\frac{0.512 \text{ mol L}^{-1} - 0.600 \text{ mol L}^{-1}}{25.0 \text{ s} - 0.0 \text{ s}}$$

$$= 1.76 \times 10^{-3} \text{ mol L}^{-1}\text{s}^{-1} = 1.8 \times 10^{-3} \text{ mol L}^{-1}\text{s}^{-1}$$

Check: The units (mol L^{-1} s^{-1}) are correct. The magnitude of the answer (10^{-3} mol L^{-1} s^{-1}) makes physical sense because rates are always positive and we are not changing the concentration much in 25 s.

(c)   **Given:** 1.50 L vessel, first 15.0 s of reaction, and part (b) data **Find:** mol$_{Br_2}$ formed
Conceptual Plan: Average rate, t_1, t_2, $\rightarrow$ Δ [Br$_2$] then Δ [Br$_2$], L $\rightarrow$ mol$_{Br_2}$ formed

$$\text{Rate} = \frac{\Delta[Br_2]}{\Delta t} \qquad\qquad [\ ] = \frac{mol_{Br_2}}{L}$$

Solution: Rate $= 1.76 \times 10^{-3}$ mol L^{-1} s$^{-1} = \dfrac{\Delta[Br_2]}{\Delta t} = \dfrac{\Delta[Br_2]}{15.0 \text{ s} - 0.0 \text{ s}}$. Rearrange to solve for $\Delta[Br_2]$.

$\Delta[Br_2] = 1.76 \times 10^{-3}\dfrac{\text{mol L}^{-1}}{\text{s}} \times 15.0 \text{ s} = 0.0264$ mol L^{-1} then $[\ ] = \dfrac{mol_{Br_2}}{L}$. Rearrange to solve for

mol$_{Br_2}$.

$0.264 \dfrac{\text{mol Br}_2}{L} \times 1.50 \text{ L} = 0.040$ mol Br$_2$.

Check: The units (mol) are correct. The magnitude of the answer (0.04 mol) makes physical sense because the time is shorter than in part (b) and we need to divide by 2 and multiply by 1.5 because of the stoichiometric coefficient difference and the volume of the vessel, respectively.

13.27   (a)   Rate $= -\dfrac{1}{2}\dfrac{\Delta[A]}{\Delta t} = -\dfrac{\Delta[B]}{\Delta t} = \dfrac{1}{3}\dfrac{\Delta[C]}{\Delta t}$

(b)   **Given:** $\dfrac{\Delta[A]}{\Delta t} = -0.100$ mol L^{-1} s^{-1} **Find:** $\dfrac{\Delta[B]}{\Delta t}$, and $\dfrac{\Delta[C]}{\Delta t}$

Conceptual Plan: $\dfrac{\Delta[A]}{\Delta t} \rightarrow \dfrac{\Delta[B]}{\Delta t}$, and $\dfrac{\Delta[C]}{\Delta t}$

$$\text{Rate} = -\frac{1}{2}\frac{\Delta[A]}{\Delta t} = -\frac{\Delta[B]}{\Delta t} = \frac{1}{3}\frac{\Delta[C]}{\Delta t}$$

Solution: Rate $= -\dfrac{1}{2}\dfrac{\Delta[A]}{\Delta t} = -\dfrac{\Delta[B]}{\Delta t} = \dfrac{1}{3}\dfrac{\Delta[C]}{\Delta t}$. Substitute in value and solve for the two desired

values. $-\dfrac{1}{2}\dfrac{-0.100 \text{ mol L}^{-1}}{\text{s}} = -\dfrac{\Delta[B]}{\Delta t}$ so $\dfrac{\Delta[B]}{\Delta t} = -0.0500$ mol L^{-1} s^{-1} and

$-\dfrac{1}{2}\dfrac{-0.100 \text{ mol L}^{-1}}{\text{s}} = \dfrac{1}{3}\dfrac{\Delta[C]}{\Delta t}$

so $\dfrac{\Delta[C]}{\Delta t} = 0.150$ mol L^{-1} s^{-1}.

Check: The units (mol L^{-1} s^{-1}) are correct. The magnitude of the answer (-0.05 mol L^{-1} s^{-1}) makes physical sense because fewer moles of B are reacting for every mole of A and the change in concentration with time is negative since this is a reactant. The magnitude of the answer (0.15 mol L^{-1} s^{-1}) makes physical sense because more moles of C are being formed for every mole of A reacting and the change in concentration with time is positive since this is a product.

13.29   **Given:** $Cl_2(g) + 3 F_2(g) \rightarrow 2 ClF_3(g)$; $\Delta[Cl_2]/\Delta t = -0.012$ mol L^{-1} s^{-1} **Find:** $\Delta[F_2]/\Delta t$; $\Delta[ClF_3]/\Delta t$; and Rate
Conceptual Plan: Write the expression for the rate with respect to each species then

$$\text{Rate} = -\frac{\Delta[Cl_2]}{\Delta t} = -\frac{1}{3}\frac{\Delta[F_2]}{\Delta t} = \frac{1}{2}\frac{\Delta[ClF_3]}{\Delta t}$$

rate expression, $\dfrac{\Delta[Cl_2]}{\Delta t} \rightarrow \dfrac{\Delta[F_2]}{\Delta t}$; $\dfrac{\Delta[ClF_3]}{\Delta t}$; **Rate**

$$\text{Rate} = -\frac{\Delta[Cl_2]}{\Delta t} = -\frac{1}{3}\frac{\Delta[F_2]}{\Delta t} = \frac{1}{2}\frac{\Delta[ClF_3]}{\Delta t}$$

Solution: Rate $= -\dfrac{\Delta[Cl_2]}{\Delta t} = -\dfrac{1}{3}\dfrac{\Delta[F_2]}{\Delta t} = \dfrac{1}{2}\dfrac{\Delta[ClF_3]}{\Delta t}$ so

$-\dfrac{\Delta[Cl_2]}{\Delta t} = -\dfrac{1}{3}\dfrac{\Delta[F_2]}{\Delta t}$. Rearrange to solve for $\dfrac{\Delta[F_2]}{\Delta t}$.

$\dfrac{\Delta[F_2]}{\Delta t} = 3\dfrac{\Delta[Cl_2]}{\Delta t} = 3(-0.012 \text{ mol L}^{-1}\text{s}^{-1}) = -0.036 \text{ mol L}^{-1}\text{s}^{-1}$

and $-\dfrac{\Delta[Cl_2]}{\Delta t} = \dfrac{1}{2}\dfrac{\Delta[ClF_3]}{\Delta t}$. Rearrange to solve for $\dfrac{\Delta[ClF_3]}{\Delta t}$.

$\dfrac{\Delta[ClF_3]}{\Delta t} = -2\dfrac{\Delta[Cl_2]}{\Delta t} = -2(-0.012 \text{ mol L}^{-1}\text{s}^{-1}) = 0.024 \text{ mol L}^{-1}\text{s}^{-1}$

Rate $= -\dfrac{\Delta[Cl_2]}{\Delta t} = -(-0.012 \text{ mol L}^{-1}\text{s}^{-1}) = 0.012 \text{ mol L}^{-1}\text{s}^{-1}$

Check: The units (mol L^{-1} s^{-1}) are correct. The magnitude of the answers (-0.036 mol L^{-1} s^{-1} and 0.024 mol L^{-1} s^{-1}) makes physical sense because F_2 is being used at three times the rate of Cl_2, ClF_3 is being formed at two times the rate of Cl_2 disappearance, and Cl_2 has a stoichiometric coefficient of 1.

13.31   (a)   **Given:** $[C_4H_8]$ versus time data **Find:** average rate between 0 and 10 s, and between 40 and 50 s

           Conceptual Plan: $t_1, t_2, [C_4H_8]_1, [C_4H_8]_2 \rightarrow$ **average rate**

$$\text{Rate} = -\dfrac{\Delta[C_4H_8]}{\Delta t}$$

           Solution: For 0 to 10 s Rate $= -\dfrac{[C_4H_8]_{t_2} - [C_4H_8]_{t_1}}{t_2 - t_1} = -\dfrac{0.913 \text{ mol L}^{-1} - 1.000 \text{ mol L}^{-1}}{10.\,\text{s} - 0.\,\text{s}}$

$$= 8.7 \times 10^{-3} \text{ mol L}^{-1}\text{s}^{-1} \text{ and for 40 to 50 s:}$$

Rate $= -\dfrac{[C_4H_8]_{t_2} - [C_4H_8]_{t_1}}{t_2 - t_1} = -\dfrac{0.637 \text{ mol L}^{-1} - 0.697 \text{ mol L}^{-1}}{50.\,\text{s} - 40.\,\text{s}}$

$$= 6.0 \times 10^{-3} \text{ mol L}^{-1}\text{s}^{-1}.$$

           Check: The units (mol L^{-1} s^{-1}) are correct. The magnitude of the answer (10^{-3} mol L^{-1} s^{-1}) makes physical sense because rates are always positive and we are not changing the concentration much in 10 s. Also reactions slow as they proceed because the concentration of the reactants is decreasing.

    (b)   **Given:** $[C_4H_8]$ versus time data **Find:** $\dfrac{\Delta[C_2H_4]}{\Delta t}$ between 20 and 30 s

           Conceptual Plan: $t_1, t_2, [C_4H_8]_1, [C_4H_8]_2 \rightarrow \dfrac{\Delta[C_2H_4]}{\Delta t}$

$$\text{Rate} = -\dfrac{\Delta[C_4H_8]}{\Delta t} = \dfrac{1}{2}\dfrac{\Delta[C_2H_4]}{\Delta t}$$

           Solution: Rate $= -\dfrac{[C_4H_8]_{t_2} - [C_4H_8]_{t_1}}{t_2 - t_1} = -\dfrac{0.763 \text{ mol L}^{-1} - 0.835 \text{ mol L}^{-1}}{30.\,\text{s} - 20.\,\text{s}}$

$$= 7.2 \times 10^{-3} \text{ mol L}^{-1}\text{s}^{-1} = \dfrac{1}{2}\dfrac{\Delta[C_2H_4]}{\Delta t}.$$

Rearrange to solve for $\dfrac{\Delta[C_2H_4]}{\Delta t}$. So $\dfrac{\Delta[C_2H_4]}{\Delta t} = 2(7.2 \times 10^{-3} \text{ mol L}^{-1}\text{s}^{-1}) = 1.4 \times 10^{-2} \text{ mol L}^{-1}\text{s}^{-1}$.

           Check: The units (mol L^{-1} s^{-1}) are correct. The magnitude of the answer (10^{-2} mol L^{-1} s^{-1}) makes physical sense because rate of product formation is always positive and we are not changing the concentration much in 10 s. The rate of change of the product is faster than the decline of the reactant because of the stoichiometric coefficients.

13.33   (a)   **Given:** $[Br_2]$ versus time plot

           Find: (i) average rate between 0 and 25 s; (ii) instantaneous rate at 25 s; and (iii) instantaneous rate of HBr formation at 50 s

           Conceptual Plan: (i) $t_1, t_2, [Br_2]_1, [Br_2]_2 \rightarrow$ **average rate then**

$$\text{Rate} = -\dfrac{\Delta[Br_2]}{\Delta t}$$

(ii) draw tangent at 25 s and determine slope $\rightarrow$ instantaneous rate then

$$Rate = -\frac{\Delta[Br_2]}{\Delta t}$$

(iii) draw tangent at 50 s and determine slope $\rightarrow$ instantaneous rate $\rightarrow$ $\dfrac{\Delta[HBr]}{\Delta t}$

$$Rate = -\frac{\Delta[Br_2]}{\Delta t} \qquad\qquad Rate = \frac{1}{2}\frac{\Delta[HBr]}{\Delta t}$$

Solution:

(i) $Rate = -\dfrac{[Br_2]_{t_2} - [Br_2]_{t_1}}{t_2 - t_1} = -\dfrac{0.75 \text{ mol L}^{-1} - 1.00 \text{ mol L}^{-1}}{25 \text{ s} - 0.\text{ s}}$

$= 1.0 \times 10^{-2} \text{ mol L}^{-1}\text{s}^{-1}$

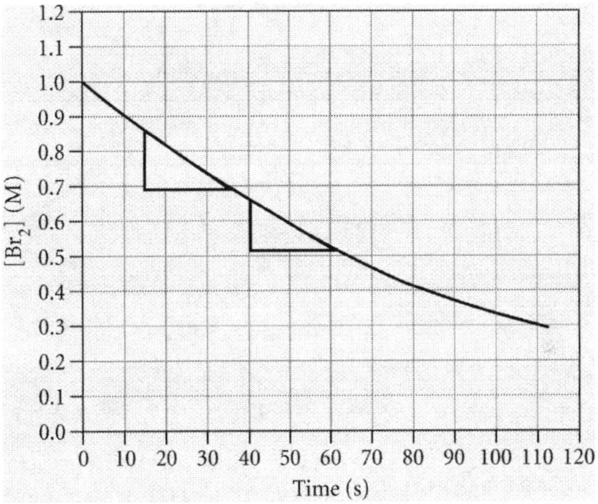

and (ii) at 25 s:

$Slope = \dfrac{\Delta y}{\Delta x} = \dfrac{0.68 \text{ mol L}^{-1} - 0.85 \text{ mol L}^{-1}}{35 \text{ s} - 15 \text{ s}}$

$= -8.5 \times 10^{-3} \text{ mol L}^{-1}\text{s}^{-1}$

since the slope $= \dfrac{\Delta[Br_2]}{\Delta t}$ and $Rate = -\dfrac{\Delta[Br_2]}{\Delta t}$,

then $Rate = -(-8.5 \times 10^{-3} \text{ mol L}^{-1}\text{ s}^{-1})$

$= 8.5 \times 10^{-3} \text{ mol L}^{-1}\text{ s}^{-1}$

(iii) at 50 s:

$Slope = \dfrac{\Delta y}{\Delta x} = \dfrac{0.53 \text{ mol L}^{-1} - 0.66 \text{ mol L}^{-1}}{60.\text{ s} - 40.\text{ s}}$

$= -6.5 \times 10^{-3} \text{ mol L}^{-1}\text{s}^{-1}$

since the slope $= \dfrac{\Delta[Br_2]}{\Delta t}$ and

$Rate = -\dfrac{\Delta[Br_2]}{\Delta t} = \dfrac{1}{2}\dfrac{\Delta[HBr]}{\Delta t}$ then

$\dfrac{\Delta[HBr]}{\Delta t} = -2\dfrac{\Delta[Br_2]}{\Delta t} = -2(-6.5 \times 10^{-3} \text{ mol L}^{-1}\text{s}^{-1}) = 1.3 \times 10^{-2} \text{ mol L}^{-1}\text{s}^{-1}$

Check: The units (mol L^{-1} s^{-1}) are correct. The magnitude of the first answer is larger than the second answer because the rate is slowing down and the first answer includes the initial portion of the data. The magnitudes of the answers (10^{-3} mol L^{-1} s^{-1}) make physical sense because rates are always positive and we are not changing the concentration much.

(b) **Given:** [Br$_2$] versus time data; and [HBr]$_0$ = 0 mol L^{-1} **Find:** plot [HBr] with time

Conceptual Plan: Since $Rate = -\dfrac{\Delta[Br_2]}{\Delta t} = \dfrac{1}{2}\dfrac{\Delta[HBr]}{\Delta t}$. **The rate of change of [HBr] will be twice that of [Br$_2$]. The plot will start at the origin.**

Solution:

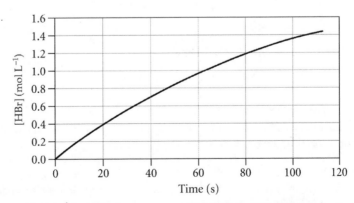

Check: The units (mol L^{-1} versus s) are correct. The plot makes sense because the plot has the same general shape of the original plot, only we are increasing instead of decreasing and our concentration axis by a factor of two (to account for the difference in stoichiometric coefficients).

The Rate Law and Reaction Orders

13.35 (a) **Given:** Rate versus [A] plot **Find:** reaction order
Conceptual Plan: Look at shape of plot and match to possibilities.
Solution: The plot is a linear plot, so Rate α [A] or the reaction is first order.
Check: The order of the reaction is a common reaction order.

(b) **Given:** part (a) **Find:** sketch plot of [A] versus time
**Conceptual Plan: Using the result from part (a), shape plot of [A] versus time should be curved
with [A] decreasing. Use 1.0 mol L^{-1} as initial concentration.**
Solution:

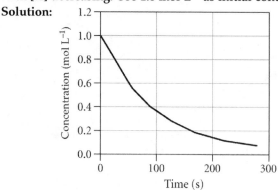

Check: The plot has a shape that matches the one in the text for first-order plots.

(c) **Given:** part (a) **Find:** write a rate law and estimate k
Conceptual Plan: Using the result from part (a), the slope of the plot is the rate constant.
Solution: Slope $= \dfrac{\Delta y}{\Delta x} = \dfrac{0.010\ \frac{\overline{\text{mol L}}^{-1}}{\text{s}} - 0.00\ \frac{\overline{\text{mol L}}^{-1}}{\text{s}}}{1.0\ \overline{\text{mol L}}^{-1} - 0.0\ \overline{\text{mol L}}^{-1}} = 0.010\ \text{s}^{-1}$ so Rate $= k\,[A]^1$ or Rate $= k\,[A]$ or
Rate $= 0.010\ \text{s}^{-1}\,[A]$

Check: The units (s^{-1}) are correct. The magnitude of the answer ($10^{-2}\ \text{s}^{-1}$) makes physical sense because
of the rate and concentration data. Remember that concentration is in units of mol L^{-1}, so plugging
the rate constant into the equation has the units of the rate as mol $L^{-1}\,\text{s}^{-1}$, which is correct.

13.37 **Given:** reaction order: (a) first-order; (b) second-order; and (c) zero-order   **Find:** units of k
Conceptual Plan: Using rate law, rearrange to solve for k.
Rate $= k\,[A]^n$, where n = reaction order
Solution: For all cases rate has units of mol $L^{-1}\,\text{s}^{-1}$ and [A] has units of mol L^{-1}

(a) Rate $= k\,[A]^1 = k\,[A]$ so $k = \dfrac{\text{Rate}}{[A]} = \dfrac{\frac{\overline{\text{mol L}}^{-1}}{\text{s}}}{\overline{\text{mol L}}^{-1}} = \text{s}^{-1}$;

(b) Rate $= k\,[A]^2$ so $k = \dfrac{\text{Rate}}{[A]^2} = \dfrac{\frac{\overline{\text{mol L}}^{-1}}{\text{s}}}{\overline{\text{mol L}}^{-1}\cdot \text{mol L}^{-1}} = \text{L mol}^{-1}\,\text{s}^{-1}$;

(c) Rate $= k\,[A]^0 = k = \text{mol L}^{-1}\,\text{s}^{-1}$.
Check: The units (s^{-1}, L mol^{-1} s^{-1}, and mol L^{-1} s^{-1}) are correct. The units for k change with the reaction order
so that the units on the rate remain as mol L^{-1} s^{-1}.

13.39 **Given:** A, B, and C react to form products. Reaction is first order in A, second order in B, and zero order in C
Find: (a) rate law; (b) overall order of reaction; (c) factor change in rate if [A] doubled; (d) factor change in rate
if [B] doubled; (e) factor change in rate if [C] doubled; and (f) factor change in rate if [A], [B], and [C] doubled.

Conceptual Plan:

(a) **Using general rate law form, substitute in values for orders.**

$$\text{Rate} = k\,[A]^m\,[B]^n\,[C]^p, \text{ where } m, n, \text{ and } p = \text{reaction orders}$$

(b) **Using rate law in part (a) add up all reaction orders.**

$$\textit{overall reaction order} = m + n + p$$

(c) **through (f) Using rate law from part (a) substitute in concentration changes.**

$$\frac{\text{Rate 2}}{\text{Rate 1}} = \frac{k\,[A]_2^1\,[B]_2^2}{k\,[A]_1^1\,[B]_1^2}$$

Solution:

(a) $m = 1$, $n = 2$, and $p = 0$ so Rate $= k\,[A]^1[B]^2[C]^0$ or Rate $= k\,[A][B]^2$.

(b) $\textit{overall reaction order} = m + n + p = 1 + 2 + 0 = 3$ so it is a third-order reaction overall.

(c) $\dfrac{\text{Rate 2}}{\text{Rate 1}} = \dfrac{k\,[A]_2^1\,[B]_2^2}{k\,[A]_1^1\,[B]_1^2}$ and $[A]_2 = 2\,[A]_1$, $[B]_2 = [B]_1$, $[C]_2 = [C]_1$, so $\dfrac{\text{Rate 2}}{\text{Rate 1}} = \dfrac{\cancel{k}\,(2[A]_1)^1\,\cancel{[B]_1^2}}{\cancel{k}\,[A]_1^1\,\cancel{[B]_1^2}} = 2$ so the reaction rate doubles (factor of 2).

(d) $\dfrac{\text{Rate 2}}{\text{Rate 1}} = \dfrac{k\,[A]_2^1\,[B]_2^2}{k\,[A]_1^1\,[B]_1^2}$ and $[A]_2 = [A]_1$, $[B]_2 = 2\,[B]_1$, $[C]_2 = [C]_1$, so $\dfrac{\text{Rate 2}}{\text{Rate 1}} = \dfrac{\cancel{k}\,\cancel{[A]_1}\,(2\,[B]_1)^2}{\cancel{k}\,\cancel{[A]_1^1}\,[B]_1^2} = 2^2 = 4$ so the reaction rate quadruples (factor of 4).

(e) $\dfrac{\text{Rate 2}}{\text{Rate 1}} = \dfrac{k\,[A]_2^1\,[B]_2^2}{k\,[A]_1^1\,[B]_1^2}$ and $[A]_2 = [A]_1$, $[B]_2 = [B]_1$, $[C]_2 = 2\,[C]_1$, so $\dfrac{\text{Rate 2}}{\text{Rate 1}} = \dfrac{\cancel{k}\,\cancel{[A]_1}\,\cancel{[B]_1^2}}{\cancel{k}\,\cancel{[A]_1^1}\,\cancel{[B]_1^2}} = 1$ so the reaction rate is unchanged (factor of 1).

(f) $\dfrac{\text{Rate 2}}{\text{Rate 1}} = \dfrac{k\,[A]_2^1\,[B]_2^2}{k\,[A]_1^1\,[B]_1^2}$ and $[A]_2 = 2\,[A]_1$, $[B]_2 = 2\,[B]_1$, $[C]_2 = 2\,[C]_1$, so

$$\frac{\text{Rate 2}}{\text{Rate 1}} = \frac{\cancel{k}\,(2\,[A]_1)^1\,(2\,[B]_1)^2}{\cancel{k}\,[A]_1^1\,[B]_1^2} = 2 \times 2^2 = 8$$

so the reaction rate goes up by a factor of 8.

Check: The units (none) are correct. The rate law is consistent with the orders given and the overall order is larger than any of the individual orders. The factors are consistent with the reaction orders. The larger the order, the larger the factor. When all concentrations are changed the rate changes the most. If a reactant is not in the rate law, then changing its concentration has no effect on the reaction rate.

13.41 **Given:** table of $[A]$ versus initial rate **Find:** rate law and k

Conceptual Plan: Using general rate law form, compare rate ratios to determine reaction order.

$$\frac{\text{Rate 2}}{\text{Rate 1}} = \frac{k\,[A]_2^n}{k\,[A]_1^n}$$

Then use one of the concentration/initial rate pairs to determine k.

$$\text{Rate} = k[A]^n$$

Solution: $\dfrac{\text{Rate 2}}{\text{Rate 1}} = \dfrac{k\,[A]_2^n}{k\,[A]_1^n}$ Comparing the first two sets of data $\dfrac{0.210\ \cancel{\text{mol L}^{-1}\text{s}^{-1}}}{0.053\ \cancel{\text{mol L}^{-1}\text{s}^{-1}}} = \dfrac{\cancel{k}\,(0.200\ \cancel{\text{mol L}^{-1}})^n}{\cancel{k}\,(0.100\ \cancel{\text{mol L}^{-1}})^n}$ and

$3.9623 = 2^n$ so $n = 2$. If we compare the first and the last data sets $\dfrac{0.473\ \cancel{\text{mol L}^{-1}\text{s}^{-1}}}{0.053\ \cancel{\text{mol L}^{-1}\text{s}^{-1}}} = \dfrac{\cancel{k}\,(0.300\ \cancel{\text{mol L}^{-1}})^n}{\cancel{k}\,(0.100\ \cancel{\text{mol L}^{-1}})^n}$

and $8.9245 = 3^n$ so $n = 2$.

This second comparison is not necessary, but it increases our confidence in the reaction order. So Rate $= k\,[A]^2$. Selecting the second data set and rearranging the rate equation

$$k = \frac{\text{Rate}}{[A]^2} = \frac{0.210\ \dfrac{\text{mol L}^{-1}}{\text{s}}}{(0.200\ \text{mol L}^{-1})^2} = 5.25\ \text{L mol}^{-1}\text{s}^{-1} \text{ so Rate} = 5.25\ \text{L mol}^{-1}\text{s}^{-1}[A]^2.$$

Check: The units (none and $L \, mol^{-1} \, s^{-1}$) are correct. The rate law is a common form. The rate is changing more rapidly than the concentration, so second order is consistent. The rate constant is consistent with the units necessary to get rate as $mol \, L^{-1} \, s^{-1}$ and the magnitude is reasonable since we have a second-order reaction.

13.43   **Given**: table of $[NO_2]$ and $[F_2]$ versus initial rate   **Find**: rate law, k, and overall order
Conceptual Plan: Using general rate law form, compare rate ratios to determine reaction order of each reactant.

$$\frac{\text{Rate 2}}{\text{Rate 1}} = \frac{k \, [NO_2]_2^m \, [F_2]_2^n}{k \, [NO_2]_1^m \, [F_2]_1^n}$$

Then use one of the concentration/initial rate pairs to determine k.

$$\text{Rate} = k[NO_2]^m \, [F_2]^n$$

Solution: $\dfrac{\text{Rate 2}}{\text{Rate 1}} = \dfrac{k \, [NO_2]_2^m \, [F_2]_2^n}{k \, [NO_2]_1^m \, [F_2]_1^n}$ Comparing the first two sets of data:

$$\frac{0.051 \, \cancel{mol \, L^{-1} s^{-1}}}{0.026 \, \cancel{mol \, L^{-1} s^{-1}}} = \frac{\cancel{k} \, (0.200 \, \cancel{mol \, L^{-1}})^m \, (\cancel{0.100 \, mol \, L^{-1}})^n}{\cancel{k} \, (0.100 \, \cancel{mol \, L^{-1}})^m \, (\cancel{0.100 \, mol \, L^{-1}})^n}$$ and $1.9615 = 2^m$ so $m = 1$. If we compare the

second and the third data sets: $\dfrac{0.411 \, mol \, L^{-1} s^{-1}}{0.051 \, mol \, L^{-1} s^{-1}} = \dfrac{k \, (0.400 \, mol \, L^{-1})^1 \, (0.400 \, mol \, L^{-1})^n}{k \, (0.200 \, mol \, L^{-1})^1 \, (0.100 \, mol \, L^{-1})^n}$

$8.\underline{0}588 = (2.00)(4.00)^n$ which simplifies to $4.\underline{0}294 = (4.00)^n$ and so $n = 1$. So Rate $= k \, [NO_2][F_2]$. Selecting

the last data set and rearranging the rate equation $k = \dfrac{\text{Rate}}{[NO_2][F_2]} = \dfrac{0.411 \, \dfrac{\cancel{mol \, L^{-1}}}{s}}{(0.400 \, \cancel{mol \, L^{-1}})(0.400 \, mol \, L^{-1})}$

$= 2.57 \, L \, mol^{-1} \, s^{-1}$ so Rate $= 2.57 \, L \, mol^{-1} \, s^{-1} [NO_2][F_2]$ and the reaction is second order overall.

Check: The units (none and $L \, mol^{-1} \, s^{-1}$) are correct. The rate law is a common form. The rate is changing as rapidly as each concentration is changing, which is consistent with first order in each reactant. The rate constant is consistent with the units necessary to get rate as $mol \, L^{-1} \, s^{-1}$ and the magnitude is reasonable since we have a second-order reaction.

The Integrated Rate Law and Half-Life

13.45   (a)   The reaction is zero order. Since the slope of the plot is independent of the concentration, there is no dependence of the concentration of the reactant in the rate law.

(b)   The reaction is first order. The expression for the half-life of a first-order reaction is $t_{1/2} = \dfrac{0.693}{k}$, which is independent of the reactant concentration.

(c)   The reaction is second order. The integrated rate expression for a second-order reaction is $\dfrac{1}{[A]_t} = k \, t + \dfrac{1}{[A]_0}$, which is linear when the inverse of the concentration is plotted versus time.

13.47   **Given**: table of $[AB]$ versus time   **Find**: reaction order, k, and $[AB]$ at 25 s
Conceptual Plan: Look at the data and see if any common reaction orders can be eliminated. If the data do not show an equal concentration drop with time, then zero order can be eliminated. Look for changes in the half-life (compare time for concentration to drop to one-half of any value). If the half-life is not constant, then the first order can be eliminated. If the half-life is getting longer as the concentration drops, this might suggest second order. Plot the data as indicated by the appropriate rate law. Determine k from the slope of the plot. Finally calculate the $[AB]$ at 25 s by using the appropriate integrated rate expression.
Solution: By the preceding logic, we can eliminate both the zero-order and the first-order reactions. (Alternatively, you could make all three plots and only one should be linear.) This suggests that we should have a second-order reaction. Plot $1/[AB]$ versus time.

Since $\dfrac{1}{[AB]_t} = k\,t + \dfrac{1}{[AB]_0}$, the slope will be the rate

constant. The slope can be determined by measuring $\Delta y/\Delta x$ on the plot or by using functions, such as "add trendline" in Excel. Thus the rate constant is $0.0225\ \text{L mol}^{-1}\,\text{s}^{-1}$ and the rate law is Rate $= 0.0225\ \text{L mol}^{-1}\,\text{s}^{-1}[AB]^2$.

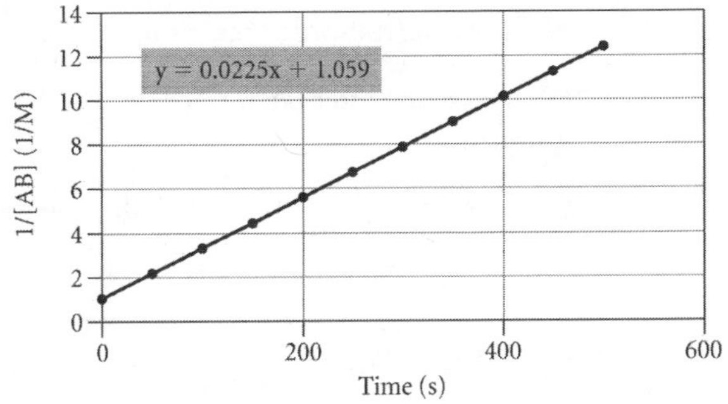

Finally, use $\dfrac{1}{[AB]_t} = k\,t + \dfrac{1}{[AB]_0}$; substitute in the

values of $[AB]_0$, 25 s, and k; and rearrange to solve

for $[AB]$ at 25 s. $[AB]_t = \dfrac{1}{k\,t + \dfrac{1}{[AB]_0}} = \dfrac{1}{(0.0225\ \text{L mol}^{-1}\,\text{s}^{-1})\,(25\ \text{s}) + \left(\dfrac{1}{0.950\ \text{mol L}^{-1}}\right)} = 0.619\ \text{mol L}^{-1}.$

Check: The units (none, $\text{L mol}^{-1}\,\text{s}^{-1}$, and mol L^{-1}) are correct. The rate law is a common form. The plot was extremely linear, confirming second-order kinetics. The rate constant is consistent with the units necessary to get rate as $\text{mol L}^{-1}\,\text{s}^{-1}$ and the magnitude is reasonable since we have a second-order reaction. The $[AB]$ at 25 s is in between the values at 0 s and 50 s.

13.49   **Given:** table of $[C_4H_8]$ versus time **Find:** reaction order, k, and reaction rate when $[C_4H_8] = 0.25\ \text{mol L}^{-1}$
Conceptual Plan: Look at the data and see if any common reaction orders can be eliminated. If the data do not show an equal concentration drop with time, then zero order can be eliminated. Look for changes in half-life (compare time for concentration to drop to one-half of any value). If the half-life is not constant, then first order can be eliminated. If the half-life is getting longer as the concentration drops, this might suggest second order. Plot the data as indicated by the appropriate rate law. Determine k from the slope of the plot. Finally calculate the reaction rate when $[C_4H_8] = 0.25\ \text{mol L}^{-1}$ by using the rate law.

Solution: By the preceding logic, we can see that the reaction is most likely first order. It takes about 60 s for the concentration to be cut in half for any concentration. Plot $\ln\,[C_4H_8]$ versus time. Since $\ln[A]_t = -k\,t + \ln[A]_0$, the negative of the slope will be the rate constant. The slope can be determined by measuring $\Delta y/\Delta x$ on the plot or by using functions, such as "add trendline" in Excel. Thus the rate constant is $0.0112\ \text{s}^{-1}$ and the rate law is Rate $= 0.0112\ \text{s}^{-1}[C_4H_8]$. Finally, use Rate $= 0.0112\ \text{s}^{-1}[C_4H_8]$, substitute in the values of $[C_4H_8]$. Rate $= 0.0112\ \text{s}^{-1}[0.25\ \text{mol L}^{-1}] = 2.8 \times 10^{-3}\ \text{mol L}^{-1}\,\text{s}^{-1}.$

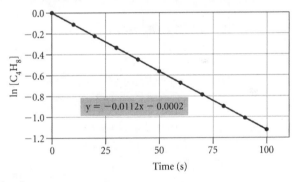

Check: The units (none, s^{-1}, and $\text{mol L}^{-1}\,\text{s}^{-1}$) are correct. The rate law is a common form. The plot was extremely linear, confirming first-order kinetics. The rate constant is consistent with the units necessary to get rate as $\text{mol L}^{-1}\,\text{s}^{-1}$ and the magnitude is reasonable since we have a first-order reaction. The rate when $[C_4H_8] = 0.\,25\ \text{mol L}^{-1}$ is consistent with the average rate using 90 s and 100 s.

13.51   **Given:** plot of $\ln\,[A]$ versus time has slope $= -\,0.0045\ \text{s}^{-1}$; $[A]_0 = 0.250\ \text{mol L}^{-1}$
Find: (a) k, (b) rate law, (c) $t_{1/2}$, (d) τ, and (e) $[A]$ after 225 s
Conceptual Plan:

(a)   **A plot of $\ln\,[A]$ versus time is linear for a first-order reaction. Using $\ln[A]_t = -k\,t + \ln[A]_0$, the rate constant is the negative of the slope.**

(b)   **Rate law is first order. Add rate constant from part (a).**

(c)   **For a first-order reaction, $t_{1/2} = \dfrac{0.693}{k}$. Substitute in k from part (a).**

(d)   For a first-order reaction, $\tau = \dfrac{1}{k}$. Substitute in for k from part (a).

(e)   Use the integrated rate law, $\ln[A]_t = -kt + \ln[A]_0$, and substitute in k and the initial concentration.

Solution:

(a)   Since the rate constant is the negative of the slope, $k = 4.5 \times 10^{-3}\ s^{-1}$.

(b)   Since the reaction is first order, Rate $= 4.5 \times 10^{-3}\ s^{-1}\ [A]$.

(c) $t_{1/2} = \dfrac{0.693}{k} = \dfrac{0.693}{0.0045\ s^{-1}} = 1.5 \times 10^2\ s$

(d) $\tau = \dfrac{1}{k} = \dfrac{1}{4.5 \times 10^{-3}\ s^{-1}} = 2.2 \times 10^{-2}\ s$

(e) $\ln[A]_t = -kt + \ln[A]_0$, and substitute in k and the initial concentration. So
$\ln[A]_t = -(0.0045\ s^{-1})(225\ s) + \ln 0.250\ mol\ L^{-1} = -2.39879$ and $[A]_{250\ s} = e^{-2.39879} = 0.0908\ mol\ L^{-1}$.
Check: The units (s^{-1}, none, s, and mol L^{-1}) are correct. The rate law is a common form. The rate constant is consistent with value of the slope. The half-life and lifetime are consistent with a small value of k. The concentration at 225 s is consistent with being between one and two half-lives.

13.53   **Given:** decomposition of SO_2Cl_2, first order; $k = 1.42 \times 10^{-4}\ s^{-1}$
Find: (a) $t_{1/2}$; (b) t to decrease to 30% of $[SO_2Cl_2]_0$; (c) t to 0.78 mol L^{-1} when $[SO_2Cl_2]_0 = 1.00$ mol L^{-1}; and
(d) $[SO_2Cl_2]$ after 2.00×10^2 s and 5.00×10^2 s when $[SO_2Cl_2]_0 = 0.150$ mol L^{-1}
Conceptual Plan:

(a) $k \rightarrow t_{1/2}$
$t_{1/2} = \dfrac{0.693}{k}$

(b) $[SO_2Cl_2]_0,\ 30\%\ of\ [SO_2Cl_2]_0,\ k \rightarrow t$
$\ln[A]_t = -kt + \ln[A]_0$

(c) $[SO_2Cl_2]_0,\ [SO_2Cl_2]_t,\ k \rightarrow t$
$\ln[A]_t = -kt + \ln[A]_0$

(d) $[SO_2Cl_2]_0,\ t,\ k \rightarrow [SO_2Cl_2]_t$
$\ln[A]_t = -kt + \ln[A]_0$

Solution:

(a) $t_{1/2} = \dfrac{0.693}{k} = \dfrac{0.693}{1.42 \times 10^{-4}\ s^{-1}} = 4.88 \times 10^3\ s$

(b) $[SO_2Cl_2]_t = 0.30\ [SO_2Cl_2]_0$. Since $\ln[SO_2Cl_2]_t = -kt + \ln[SO_2Cl_2]_0$ rearrange to solve for t.
$t = -\dfrac{1}{k} \ln \dfrac{[SO_2Cl_2]_t}{[SO_2Cl_2]_0} = -\dfrac{1}{1.42 \times 10^{-4}\ s^{-1}} \ln \dfrac{0.30\ \cancel{[SO_2Cl_2]_0}}{\cancel{[SO_2Cl_2]_0}} = 8.5 \times 10^3\ s$

(c) $[SO_2Cl_2]_t = 0.78$ mol L^{-1}; $[SO_2Cl_2]_0 = 1.00$ mol L^{-1}. Since $\ln[SO_2Cl_2]_t = -kt + \ln[SO_2Cl_2]_0$ rearrange to
solve for t. $t = -\dfrac{1}{k} \ln \dfrac{[SO_2Cl_2]_t}{[SO_2Cl_2]_0} = -\dfrac{1}{1.42 \times 10^{-4}\ s^{-1}} \ln \dfrac{0.78\ \cancel{mol\ L^{-1}}}{1.00\ \cancel{mol\ L^{-1}}} = 1.7 \times 10^3\ s$.

(d) $[SO_2Cl_2]_0 = 0.150$ mol L^{-1} and 2.00×10^2 s in
$\ln[SO_2Cl_2]_t = -\left(1.42 \times 10^{-4}\ s^{-1}\right)\left(2.00 \times 10^2\ s\right) + \ln 0.150\ mol\ L^{-1} = -1.92552 \rightarrow$
$[SO_2Cl_2]_t = e^{-1.92552} = 0.146$ mol L^{-1}
$[SO_2Cl_2]_0 = 0.150$ M and 5.00×10^2 s in

$$\ln[SO_2Cl_2]_t = -\left(1.42 \times 10^{-4}\,s^{-1}\right)\left(5.00 \times 10^2\,s\right) + \ln 0.150\,mol\,L^{-1} = -1.96812 \rightarrow$$

$$[SO_2Cl_2]_t = e^{-1.96812} = 0.140\,mol\,L^{-1}$$

Check: The units (s, s, s, and mol L^{-1}) are correct. The rate law is a common form. The half-life is consistent with a small value of k. The time to 30% is consistent with two half-lives. The time to 0.78 mol L^{-1} is consistent with being less than one half-life. The final concentrations are consistent with the time being less than one half-life.

13.55   **Given:** $t_{1/2}$ for radioactive decay of U-238 = 4.5 billion years and independent of $[U\text{-}238]_0$
    Find: t to decrease by 10%; number U-238 atoms today when 1.5×10^{18} atoms formed 13.8 billion years ago
    Conceptual Plan: $t_{1/2}$ **independent of concentration implies first order kinetics,** $t_{1/2} \rightarrow k$ **then**

$$t_{1/2} = \frac{0.693}{k}$$

90% of $[U\text{-}238]_0$, $k \rightarrow t$ and $[U\text{-}238]_0$, t, $k \rightarrow [U\text{-}238]_t$

$$\ln[A]_t = -kt + \ln[A]_0 \qquad \ln[A]_t = -kt + \ln[A]_0$$

Solution: $t_{1/2} = \dfrac{0.693}{k}$ rearrange to solve for k. $k = \dfrac{0.693}{t_{1/2}} = \dfrac{0.693}{4.5 \times 10^9\,yr} = 1.54 \times 10^{-10}\,yr^{-1}$ then

$[U\text{-}238]_t = 0.10\,[U\text{-}238]_0$. Since $\ln[U\text{-}238]_t = -kt + \ln[U\text{-}238]_0$ rearrange to solve for t.

$$t = -\frac{1}{k}\ln\frac{[U\text{-}238]_t}{[U\text{-}238]_0} = -\frac{1}{1.54 \times 10^{-10}\,yr^{-1}}\ln\frac{0.90\,[U\text{-}238]_0}{[U\text{-}238]_0} = 6.8 \times 10^8\,yr$$

and $[U\text{-}238]_0 = 1.5 \times 10^{18}$ atoms; $t = 13.8 \times 10^9\,yr$

$\ln[U\text{-}238]_t = -kt + \ln[U\text{-}238]_0 = -(1.54 \times 10^{-10}\,yr^{-1})(13.8 \times 10^9\,yr)$

$+\ln(1.5 \times 10^{18}\,\text{atoms}) = 39.726797 \rightarrow$

$[U\text{-}238]_t = e^{39.726797} = 1.8 \times 10^{17}$ atoms.

Check: The units (yr and atoms) are correct. The time to 10% decay is consistent with less than one half-life. The final concentration is consistent with the time being about three half-lives.

The Effect of Temperature and the Collision Model

13.57

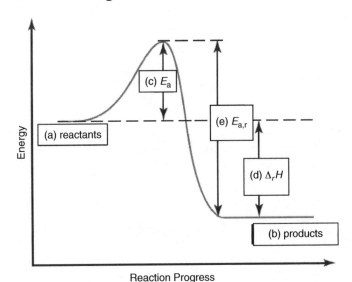

13.59   **Given:** activation energy = 56.8 kJ mol^{-1}, frequency factor = $1.5 \times 10^{11}\,s^{-1}$, 25 °C **Find:** rate constant
    Conceptual Plan: °C $\rightarrow$ **K and kJ mol^{-1} $\rightarrow$ J mol^{-1} then** E_a, T, $A \rightarrow k$

$$K = °C + 273.15 \qquad \frac{1000\,J}{1\,kJ} \qquad k = A\,e^{-E_a/RT}$$

Solution: $T = 25°C + 273.15 = 298\,K$ and $\dfrac{56.8\,kJ}{mol} \times \dfrac{1000\,J}{1\,kJ} = 5.68 \times 10^4\,J\,mol^{-1}$ then

$$k = A\,e^{-E_a/RT} = (1.5 \times 10^{11}\,\text{s}^{-1})\,e^{\dfrac{-5.68 \times 10^4 \frac{J}{mol}}{\left(8.314 \frac{J}{K \cdot mol}\right) 298\,K}} = 17\,\text{s}^{-1}$$

Check: The units (s^{-1}) are correct. The rate constant is consistent with a large activation energy and a large frequency factor.

13.61   **Given:** plot of $\ln k$ versus $1/T$ (in K) is linear with a slope of -7445 K **Find:** E_a

Conceptual Plan: Since $\ln k = \dfrac{-E_a}{R}\left(\dfrac{1}{T}\right) + \ln A$ a plot of $\ln k$ versus $1/T$ will have a slope = $-E_a/R$.

Solution: Since the slope = -7445 K $= -E_a/R$ then

$$E_a = -(slope)R = -(-7445\,\text{K})\left(8.314\,\frac{J}{K \cdot mol}\right)\left(\frac{1\,kJ}{1000\,J}\right) = 61.90\,\text{kJ mol}^{-1}.$$

Check: The units (kJ mol^{-1}) are correct. The activation energy is typical for many reactions.

13.63   **Given:** table of rate constant versus T **Find:** E_a and A

Conceptual Plan: Since $\ln k = \dfrac{-E_a}{R}\left(\dfrac{1}{T}\right) + \ln A$ a plot of $\ln k$ versus $1/T$ will have a slope = $-E_a/R$ and a y-intercept = $\ln A$.

Solution: The slope can be determined by measuring $\Delta y/\Delta x$ on the plot or by using functions, such as "add trendline" in Excel. Since the slope = -30189 K $= -E_a/R$ then $E_a = -(slope)R =$

$$-(-30189\,\text{K})\left(8.314\,\frac{J}{K \cdot mol}\right)\left(\frac{1\,kJ}{1000\,J}\right) =$$

$= 251$ kJ mol^{-1} and intercept = $27.399 = \ln A$ then $A = e^{intercept} = e^{27.399} = 7.93 \times 10^{11}\,\text{s}^{-1}$.

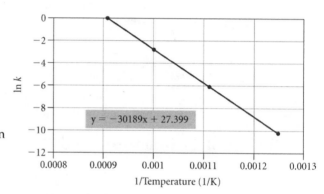

Check: The units (kJ mol^{-1} and s^{-1}) are correct. The plot was extremely linear, confirming Arrhenius behaviour. The activation and frequency factor are typical for many reactions.

13.65   **Given:** table of rate constant versus T **Find:** E_a and A

Conceptual Plan: Since $\ln k = \dfrac{-E_a}{R}\left(\dfrac{1}{T}\right) + \ln A$ a plot of $\ln k$ versus $1/T$ will have a slope = $-E_a/R$ and an intercept = $\ln A$.

Solution: The slope can be determined by measuring $\Delta y/\Delta x$ on the plot or by using functions, such as "add trendline" in Excel. Since the slope = -2767.2 K $= -E_a/R$ then $E_a = -(slope)R =$

$$= -(-2767.2\,\text{K})\left(8.314\,\frac{J}{K \cdot mol}\right)\left(\frac{1\,kJ}{1000\,J}\right) =$$

$= 23.0$ kJ mol^{-1} and intercept = $25.112 = \ln A$ then $A = e^{intercept} = e^{25.112} = 8.05 \times 10^{10}\,\text{s}^{-1}$.

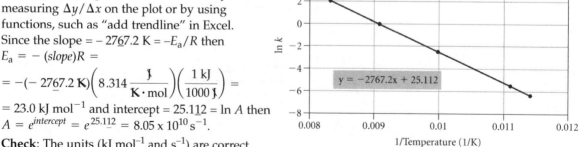

Check: The units (kJ mol^{-1} and s^{-1}) are correct. The plot was extremely linear, confirming Arrhenius behaviour. The activation and frequency factor are typical for many reactions.

13.67   **Given:** rate constant = $0.0117\,\text{s}^{-1}$ at 400.0 K, and $0.689\,\text{s}^{-1}$ at 450.0 K **Find:** (a) E_a and (b) rate constant at 425 K

Conceptual Plan:

(a) $k_1, T_1, k_2, T_2 \rightarrow E_a$ then J mol$^{-1} \rightarrow$ kJ mol^{-1}

$$\ln\left(\frac{k_2}{k_1}\right) = \frac{E_a}{R}\left(\frac{1}{T_1} - \frac{1}{T_2}\right) \qquad \frac{1\,kJ}{1000\,J}$$

(b) $E_a, k_1, T_1, T_2 \rightarrow k_2$

$$\ln\left(\frac{k_2}{k_1}\right) = \frac{E_a}{R}\left(\frac{1}{T_1} - \frac{1}{T_2}\right)$$

Solution:

(a) $\ln\left(\frac{k_2}{k_1}\right) = \frac{E_a}{R}\left(\frac{1}{T_1} - \frac{1}{T_2}\right)$. Rearrange to solve for E_a.

$$E_a = \frac{R\ln\left(\frac{k_2}{k_1}\right)}{\left(\frac{1}{T_1} - \frac{1}{T_2}\right)} = \frac{8.314\,\dfrac{J}{K \cdot mol}\ln\left(\dfrac{0.689\,s^{-1}}{0.0117\,s^{-1}}\right)}{\left(\dfrac{1}{400.\,K} - \dfrac{1}{450.\,K}\right)} = 1.22 \times 10^5\,\frac{J}{mol} \times \frac{1\,kJ}{1000\,J} = 122\,kJ\,mol^{-1}.$$

(b) $\ln\left(\frac{k_2}{k_1}\right) = \frac{E_a}{R}\left(\frac{1}{T_1} - \frac{1}{T_2}\right)$ with $k_1, = 0.0117\,s^{-1}$, $T_1 = 400.0$ K, $T_2 = 425$ K. Rearrange to solve for k_2.

$$\ln k_2 = \frac{E_a}{R}\left(\frac{1}{T_1} - \frac{1}{T_2}\right) + \ln k_1 = \frac{1.22 \times 10^5\,\dfrac{J}{mol}}{8.314\,\dfrac{J}{K \cdot mol}}\left(\frac{1}{400.\,K} - \frac{1}{425\,K}\right) + \ln 0.0117\,s^{-1} = -2.2902 \rightarrow$$

$k_2 = e^{-2.2902} = 0.101\,s^{-1}.$

Check: The units (kJ mol^{-1} and s^{-1}) are correct. The activation energy is typical for a reaction. The rate constant at 425 K is in between the values given at 400 K and 450 K.

13.69   **Given:** rate constant doubles from 10.0 °C to 20.0 °C   **Find:** E_a

Conceptual Plan: °C $\rightarrow$ K then $k_1, T_1, k_2, T_2 \rightarrow E_a$ then J mol^{-1} $\rightarrow$ kJ mol^{-1};

$$K = °C + 273.15 \qquad \ln\left(\frac{k_2}{k_1}\right) = \frac{E_a}{R}\left(\frac{1}{T_1} - \frac{1}{T_2}\right) \qquad \frac{1\,kJ}{1000\,J}$$

Solution: $T_1 = 10.0$ °C + 273.15 = 283.2 K and $T_2 = 20.0$ °C + 273.15 = 293.2 K and $k_2 = 2\,k_1$ then

$\ln\left(\frac{k_2}{k_1}\right) = \frac{E_a}{R}\left(\frac{1}{T_1} - \frac{1}{T_2}\right)$. Rearrange to solve for E_a.

$$E_a = \frac{R\ln\left(\frac{k_2}{k_1}\right)}{\left(\frac{1}{T_1} - \frac{1}{T_2}\right)} = \frac{8.314\,\dfrac{J}{K \cdot mol}\ln\left(\dfrac{2\,k_1}{k_1}\right)}{\left(\dfrac{1}{283.2\,K} - \dfrac{1}{293.2\,K}\right)} = 4.7851 \times 10^4\,\frac{J}{mol} \times \frac{1\,kJ}{1000\,J} = 47.85\,kJ\,mol^{-1}.$$

Check: The units (kJ mol^{-1}) are correct. The activation energy is typical for a reaction.

13.71   Reaction (a) would have the faster rate because the orientation factor, p, would be larger for this reaction since the reactants are symmetrical.

Reaction Mechanisms

13.73   Since the first reaction is the slow step, it is the rate-determining step. Using this first step to determine the rate law, Rate = k_1 [AB]^2. Since this is the observed rate law, this mechanism is consistent with the experimental data.

13.75   (a)   The overall reaction is the sum of the steps in the mechanism:

$$NO_2Cl\,(g) \rightleftharpoons NO_2\,(g) + \cancel{Cl\,(g)}$$
$$NO_2Cl\,(g) + \cancel{Cl\,(g)} \rightarrow NO_2\,(g) + Cl_2\,(g)$$
$$\overline{2\,NO_2Cl\,(g) \rightleftharpoons 2\,NO_2\,(g) + Cl_2\,(g)}$$

(b)   The rate law for the production of NO$_2$ is Rate = k_2[NO$_2$Cl][Cl]. However Cl is an intermediate and its concentration cannot appear in the rate law. Using the steady-state approximation, the rate of production of Cl is equal to its rate of consumption. That is,

$k_1[NO_2Cl] = k_{-1}[NO_2][Cl] + k_2[NO_2Cl][Cl]$, which simplifies to

$k_1[NO_2Cl] = (k_{-1}[NO_2] + k_2[NO_2Cl])[Cl]$ and then rearranges to $[Cl] = \dfrac{k_1[NO_2Cl]}{k_{-1}[NO_2] + k_2[NO_2Cl]}$.

Substituting this back into the first rate equation (Rate = $k_2[NO_2Cl][Cl]$) gives

$$\text{Rate} = \frac{k_1k_2[NO_2Cl]^2}{k_{-1}[NO_2] + k_2[NO_2Cl]}$$

Catalysis

13.77   Heterogeneous catalysts require a large surface area because catalysis can only happen at the active sites on the surface. A greater surface area means greater opportunity for the substrate to react, which results in a speedier reaction.

13.79   Assume rate ratio $\propto$ k ratio (since concentration terms will cancel each other) and $k = A\,e^{-E_a/RT}$. $T = 25\,°C + 273.15 = 298$ K, $E_{a_1} = 1.25 \times 10^5$ J mol^{-1}, and $E_{a_2} = 5.5 \times 10^4$ J mol^{-1}. Ratio of rates will be

$$\frac{k_2}{k_1} = \frac{\cancel{A}\,e^{-E_{a_2}/RT}}{\cancel{A}\,e^{-E_{a_1}/RT}} = \frac{e^{\frac{-5.5 \times 10^4\,\frac{J}{mol}}{\left(8.314\,\frac{J}{K\cdot mol}\right)298\,K}}}{e^{\frac{-1.25 \times 10^5\,\frac{J}{mol}}{\left(8.314\,\frac{J}{K\cdot mol}\right)298\,K}}} = \frac{e^{-22.199}}{e^{-50.453}} = 2 \times 10^{12}.$$

Cumulative Problems

13.81   **Given:** table of [CH$_3$CN] versus time   **Find:** (a) reaction order, k; (b) $t_{1/2}$; and (c) t for 90% conversion
Conceptual Plan: (a) and (b) Look at the data and see if any common reaction orders can be eliminated. If the data does not show an equal concentration drop with time, then zero order can be eliminated. Look for changes in the half-life (compare time for concentration to drop to one-half of any value). If the half-life is not constant, then the first order can be eliminated. If the half-life is getting longer as the concentration drops, this might suggest second order. Plot the data as indicated by the appropriate rate law or if it is first order and there is an obvious half-life in the data, a plot is not necessary. Determine k from the slope of the plot (or using the half-life equation for first order). (c) Finally calculate the time to 90% conversion using the appropriate integrated rate equation.
Solution: (a) and (b) By the preceding logic, we can see that the reaction is first order. It takes 15.0 h for the concentration to be cut in half for any concentration (1.000 mol L^{-1} to 0.501 mol L^{-1}; 0.794 mol L^{-1} to 0.398

mol L^{-1}; and 0.631 mol L^{-1} to 0.316 mol L^{-1}), so $t_{1/2} = 15.0$ h. Then use $t_{1/2} = \dfrac{0.693}{k}$ and rearrange to solve for k.
$k = \dfrac{0.693}{t_{1/2}} = \dfrac{0.693}{15.0\,h} = 0.0462\,h^{-1}$.

(c)   [CH$_3$CN]$_t$ = 0.10 [CH$_3$CN]$_0$. Since $\ln[CH_3CN]_t = -kt + \ln[CH_3CN]_0$ rearrange to solve for t
$$t = -\frac{1}{k}\ln\frac{[CH_3CN]_t}{[CH_3CN]_0} = -\frac{1}{0.0462\,h^{-1}}\ln\frac{0.10\,\cancel{[CH_3CN]_0}}{\cancel{[CH_3CN]_0}} = 49.8\,h.$$
Check: The units (none, h^{-1}, h, and h) are correct. The rate law is a common form. The data showed a constant half-life very clearly. The rate constant is consistent with the units necessary to get rate as mol L^{-1} s^{-1} and the magnitude is reasonable since we have a first-order reaction. The time to 90% conversion is consistent with a time between three and four half-lives.

13.83   **Given:** Rate $= k\dfrac{[A][C]^2}{[B]^{1/2}} = 0.0115$ mol L^{-1} s^{-1} at certain initial concentrations of A, B, and C; double A and C concentration and triple B concentration   **Find:** reaction rate

Conceptual Plan: $[A]_1, [B]_1, [C]_1,$ **Rate 1,** $[A]_2, [B]_2, [C]_2 \rightarrow$ **Rate 2**

$$\frac{\text{Rate 2}}{\text{Rate 1}} = \frac{k \dfrac{[A]_2[C]_2^2}{[B]_2^{1/2}}}{k \dfrac{[A]_1[C]_1^2}{[B]_1^{1/2}}}$$

Solution: $\dfrac{\text{Rate 2}}{\text{Rate 1}} = \dfrac{k \dfrac{[A]_2[C]_2^2}{[B]_2^{1/2}}}{k \dfrac{[A]_1[C]_1^2}{[B]_1^{1/2}}}$. Rearrange to solve for Rate 2. $\text{Rate 2} = \dfrac{k \dfrac{[A]_2[C]_2^2}{[B]_2^{1/2}}}{k \dfrac{[A]_1[C]_1^2}{[B]_1^{1/2}}}$

Rate 1 $[A]_2 = 2[A]_1, [B]_2 = 3[B]_1, [C]_2 = 2[C]_1,$ and Rate 1 = 0.0115 mol L^{-1} s^{-1} so

$$\text{Rate 2} = \frac{\cancel{k}\dfrac{2\,\cancel{[A]_1}(2\cancel{[C]_1})^2}{(3\,\cancel{[B]_1})^{1/2}}}{\cancel{k}\dfrac{\cancel{[A]_1}\cancel{[C]_1^2}}{\cancel{[B]_1^{1/2}}}}\,0.0115 \text{ mol L}^{-1}\text{s}^{-1} = \frac{2^3}{3^{1/2}}\,0.0115 \text{ mol L}^{-1}\text{s}^{-1} = 0.0531 \text{ mol L}^{-1}\text{s}^{-1}.$$

Check: The units (mol L^{-1} s^{-1}) are correct. They should increase because we have a factor of eight (2^3) divided by the square root of three (1.73).

13.85   **Given:** table of P_{Total} versus time **Find:** rate law, k, and P_{Total} at 2.00×10^4 s

Conceptual Plan: Since two moles of gas are generated for each mole of CH$_3$CHO decomposed, $P_{\text{CH}_3\text{CHO}}$ = $P_{\text{Total}}^\circ - (P_{\text{Total}} - P_{\text{Total}}^\circ)$. Look at the data and see if any common reaction orders can be eliminated. If the data does not show an equal P_{Total} rise (or $P_{\text{CH}_3\text{CHO}}$ drop) with time, then zero order can be eliminated. There is not enough data to look for changes in the half-life (compare time for $P_{\text{CH}_3\text{CHO}}$ to drop to one-half of any value). It does appear that the half-life is getting longer, so the first order can be eliminated. Plot the data as indicated by the appropriate rate law. Determine k from the slope of the plot. Finally calculate the $P_{\text{CH}_3\text{CHO}}$ at 2.00×10^4 s using the appropriate integrated rate expression and then convert this to P_{Total} using the reaction stoichiometry.

Solution: Calculate $P_{\text{CH}_3\text{CHO}} = P_{\text{Total}}^\circ - (P_{\text{Total}} - P_{\text{Total}}^\circ)$.

Time (s)	P_{Total} (bar)	$P_{\text{CH}_3\text{CHO}}$ (bar)
0	0.22	0.22
1000	0.24	0.20
3000	0.27	0.17
7000	0.31	0.13

By the preceding logic, we can eliminate both the zero-order and the first-order reactions. (Alternatively, you could make all three plots and only one should be linear.) This suggests that we should have a second-order reaction. Plot $1/P_{\text{CH}_3\text{CHO}}$ versus time. Since $\dfrac{1}{P_{\text{CH}_3\text{CHO}}} = kt + \dfrac{1}{P_{\text{CH}_3\text{CHO}}^\circ}$, the slope will be the rate constant. The slope can be determined by measuring $\Delta y / \Delta x$ on the plot or by using functions, such as "add trendline" in Excel. Thus the rate constant is 4.5×10^{-4} bar^{-1} s^{-1} and the rate law is Rate = 4.5×10^{-4} bar^{-1} s^{-1} $P_{\text{CH}_3\text{CHO}}^2$.

Finally, use $\dfrac{1}{P_{\text{CH}_3\text{CHO}}} = kt + \dfrac{1}{P_{\text{CH}_3\text{CHO}}^\circ}$;

substitute in the values of $P_{\text{CH}_3\text{CHO}}^\circ$, 2.00×10^4 s, and k; and rearrange to solve for $P_{\text{CH}_3\text{CHO}}^\circ$ at 2.00×10^4 s.

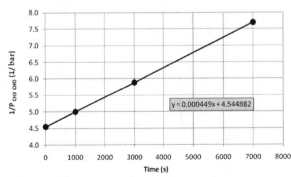

$$P_{\text{CH}_3\text{CHO}} = \frac{1}{kt + \dfrac{1}{P_{\text{CH}_3\text{CHO}}^\circ}} =$$

$$\frac{1}{(4.5 \times 10^{-4}\,\text{bar}^{-1}\,\text{s}^{-1})(2.00 \times 10^4\,\text{s}) + \left(\dfrac{1}{0.22\,\text{bar}}\right)} =$$

0.0738255 bar = 0.074 bar

Finally, from the first equation in the solution $P_{Total} = 2P_{Total}^{\circ} - P_{CH_3CHO} = 2(0.22\ bar) - 0.0738255\ bar = 0.366175\ bar = 0.37\ bar$.

Check: The units (none, $bar^{-1}\ s^{-1}$, and bar) are correct. The rate law is a common form. The plot was extremely linear, confirming second-order kinetics. The rate constant is consistent with the units necessary to get rate as $bar^{-1}\ s^{-1}$ and the magnitude is reasonable since we have a second-order reaction. The P_{Total} at 2.00×10^4 s is consistent with the changes that we see in the data table through 7000 s.

13.87 **Given:** N_2O_5 decomposes to NO_2 and O_2, first order in $[N_2O_5]$; $t_{1/2} = 2.81$ h at 25 °C; $V = 1.5$ L, $P_{N_2O_5}^{\circ} = 745$ torr **Find:** P_{O_2} after 215 minutes

Conceptual Plan: Write a balanced reaction. Then $t_{1/2} \rightarrow k$ **then** °C $\rightarrow$ K **and torr** $\rightarrow$ **bar then**

$$N_2O_5 \rightarrow 2\,NO_2 + \tfrac{1}{2}\,O_2 \qquad t_{1/2} = \frac{0.693}{k} \qquad K = °C + 273.15 \qquad \frac{1\ bar}{750.064\ torr}$$

$P_{N_2O_5}^{\circ}, V, T \rightarrow n/V$ **then min** $\rightarrow$ **h then** $[N_2O_5]_0, t, k \rightarrow [N_2O_5]_t$ **then** $[N_2O_5]_0, [N_2O_5]_t \rightarrow [O_2]_t$

$$PV = nRT \qquad \frac{1\ h}{60\ min} \qquad \ln[A]_t = -kt + \ln[A]_0 \qquad [O_2]_t = ([N_2O_5]_0 - [N_2O_5]_t) \times \frac{1/2\ mol\ O_2}{1\ mol\ N_2O_5}$$

then $[O_2]_t, V, T \rightarrow P_{O_2}^{\circ}$ **and finally bar** $\rightarrow$ **torr**

$$PV = nRT \qquad \frac{750.064\ torr}{1\ bar}$$

Solution: $t_{1/2} = \dfrac{0.693}{k}$ and rearrange to solve for k. $k = \dfrac{0.693}{t_{1/2}} = \dfrac{0.693}{2.81\ h} = 0.246619\ h^{-1}$. Then

$T = 25\ °C + 273.15 = 298$ K. $745\ \cancel{torr} \times \dfrac{1\ bar}{750.064\ \cancel{torr}} = 0.993249$ bar then $PV = nRT$. Rearrange to solve for n/V.

$\dfrac{n}{V} = \dfrac{P}{RT} = \dfrac{0.993249\ \cancel{bar}}{0.08314\ \dfrac{L \cdot \cancel{bar}}{K \cdot mol} \times 298\ K} = 0.0400896\ mol\ L^{-1}$ then $215\ \cancel{min} \times \dfrac{1\ h}{60\ \cancel{min}} = 3.58333$ h.

Since $\ln[N_2O_5]_t = -kt + \ln[N_2O_5]_0 = -(0.246619\ h^{-1})(3.58333h) + \ln(0.0400896\ mol\ L^{-1}) = -4.10036 \rightarrow$

$[N_2O_5]_t = e^{-4.10036} = 0.0165667\ mol\ L^{-1}$ then

$[O_2]_t = ([N_2O_5]_0 - [N_2O_5]_t) \times \dfrac{1/2\ mol\ O_2}{1\ mol\ N_2O_5} = (0.0400896\ \dfrac{\cancel{mol\ N_2O_5}}{L} - 0.0165667\ \dfrac{\cancel{mol\ N_2O_5}}{L}) \times \dfrac{1/2\ mol\ O_2}{1\ \cancel{mol\ N_2O_5}}$

$= 0.0117614\ mol\ L^{-1}\ O_2$

then finally $PV = nRT$ and rearrange to solve for P.

$P = \dfrac{n}{V}RT = 0.0117614\ \dfrac{mol}{\cancel{L}} \times 0.08314\ \dfrac{\cancel{L} \cdot bar}{\cancel{K} \cdot \cancel{mol}} \times 298\ \cancel{K} = 0.2913971\ \cancel{bar} \times \dfrac{750.064\ torr}{1\ \cancel{bar}} = 219$ torr.

Check: The units (torr) are correct. The pressure is reasonable because it must be less than one-half of the original pressure.

13.89 **Given:** I_2 formation from I atoms, second order in I; $k = 1.5 \times 10^{10}\ L\ mol^{-1}\ s^{-1}$, $[I]_0 = 0.0100\ mol\ L^{-1}$ **Find:** t to decrease by 95%

Conceptual Plan: $[I]_0, [I]_t, k \rightarrow t$

$$\frac{1}{[A]_t} = kt + \frac{1}{[A]_0}$$

Solution: $[I]_t = 0.05\,[I]_0 = 0.05 \times 0.0100\ mol\ L^{-1} = 0.0005\ mol\ L^{-1}$. Since $\dfrac{1}{[I]_t} = kt + \dfrac{1}{[I]_0}$ rearrange to solve for t.

$t = \dfrac{1}{k}\left(\dfrac{1}{[I]_t} - \dfrac{1}{[I]_0}\right) = \dfrac{1}{(1.5 \times 10^{10}\ \cancel{L\ mol^{-1}}\ s^{-1})}\left(\dfrac{1}{0.0005\ \cancel{mol\ L^{-1}}} - \dfrac{1}{0.0100\ \cancel{mol\ L^{-1}}}\right)$

$= 1.267 \times 10^{-7}\ s = 1 \times 10^{-7}\ s$.

Check: The units (s) are correct. We expect the time to be extremely small because the rate constant is so large.

13.91 **Given:** $AB(aq) \rightarrow A(g) + B(g)$; $k = 0.0118\ L\ mol^{-1}\ s^{-1}$; 250.0 mL of 0.100 mol L^{-1} AB; collect gas over water $T = 25.0\ °C$, $P_{Total} = 755.1$ kPa, and $V = 200.0$ mL; $P_{H_2O}^{\circ} = 23.8$ kPa **Find:** t

Conceptual Plan: $P_{Total}, P_{H_2O} \rightarrow P_A + P_B$ **then kPa** $\rightarrow$ **bar and mL** $\rightarrow$ **L**

$$P_{Total} = P_{H_2O} + P_A + P_B \qquad \frac{1\ bar}{750.064\ kPa} \qquad \frac{1\ L}{1000\ mL}$$

and °C $\rightarrow$ K $\quad$ $P, V, T \rightarrow n_{A+B} \rightarrow \Delta n_{AB}$ **then** $[AB]_0, V_{AB}, \Delta n_{AB} \rightarrow [AB]$ **then** $k, [AB] \rightarrow t$

$$K = °C + 273.15 \qquad PV = nRT \qquad \Delta n_{AB} = \tfrac{1}{2}\,n_{A+B} \qquad [AB] = [AB]_0 - \frac{\Delta n_{AB}}{V_{AB} \times \dfrac{1\ L}{1000\ mL}} \qquad \frac{1}{[AB]_t} = kt + \frac{1}{[AB]_0}$$

Solution: $P_{Total} = P_{H_2O} + P_A + P_B$. Rearrange to solve for $P_A + P_B$. $P_A + P_B = P_{Total} - P_{H_2O} = 755.1$ kPa – 23.8 kPa = 731.3 kPa

$$P_A + P_B = 731.3 \text{ kPa} \times \frac{1 \text{ bar}}{750.064 \text{ kPa}} = 0.97498347 \text{ bar} \quad V = 200.0 \text{ mL} \times \frac{1 \text{ L}}{1000 \text{ mL}} = 0.2000 \text{ L,}$$

$T = 25.0 \,°C + 273.15 = 298.2$ K, $PV = nRT$. Rearrange to solve for n. $n = \dfrac{PV}{RT}$

$$n_{H_2} = \frac{0.97498347 \text{ bar} \times 0.2000 \text{ L}}{0.08314 \dfrac{\text{L} \cdot \text{bar}}{\text{mol} \cdot \text{K}} \times 298.2 \text{ K}} = 0.007865196 \text{ mol A} + \text{B. Since one mole each of A and B are generated}$$

for each mole of AB reacting $\Delta n_{AB} = \frac{1}{2} n_{A+B} = \frac{1}{2}$ (0.007865196 mol A + B) = 0.003932598 mol AB then

$$[AB] = [AB]_0 - \frac{\Delta n_{AB}}{V_{AB} \times \dfrac{1 \text{ L}}{1000 \text{ mL}}} = 0.100 \text{ mol L}^{-1} - \frac{0.003932598 \text{ mol AB}}{250.0 \text{ mL} \times \dfrac{1 \text{ L}}{1000 \text{ mL}}}$$

$$= 0.100 \text{ mol L}^{-1} - 0.015730393 \text{ mol L}^{-1}$$

$$= 0.0842696 \text{ mol L}^{-1}.$$

Since $\dfrac{1}{[AB]_t} = kt + \dfrac{1}{[AB]_0}$ rearrange to solve for t.

$$t = \frac{1}{k}\left(\frac{1}{[XY]_t} - \frac{1}{[XY]_0}\right) = \frac{1}{(0.0118 \text{ L mol}^{-1}\text{s}^{-1})}\left(\frac{1}{0.0842696 \text{ mol L}^{-1}} - \frac{1}{0.100 \text{ mol L}^{-1}}\right)$$

$$= 158.1928 \text{ s} = 160 \text{ s.}$$

Check: The units (s) are correct. The magnitude of the answer (160 s) makes sense because the rate constant is 0.0118 L mol^{-1} s^{-1} and a small volume of gas is generated.

13.93 (a) There are two elementary steps in the reaction mechanism because there are two peaks in the reaction progress diagram.

(b)

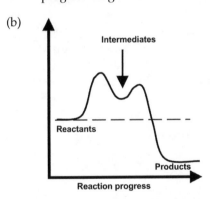

(c) The first step is the rate-limiting step because it has the higher activation energy.

(d) The overall reaction is exothermic because the products are at a lower energy than the reactants.

13.95 **Given:** *n*-butane desorption from single crystal aluminum oxide, first order; $k = 0.128$ s^{-1} at 150 K; initially completely covered
Find: (a) $t_{1/2}$; (b) t for 25% and for 50% to desorb; (c) fraction remaining after 10 s and 20 s
Conceptual Plan: (a) $k \rightarrow t_{1/2}$ (b) $[C_4H_{10}]_0, [C_4H_{10}]_t, k \rightarrow t$ (c) $[C_4H_{10}]_0, t, k \rightarrow [C_4H_{10}]_t$

$$t_{1/2} = \frac{0.693}{k} \qquad\qquad \ln[A]_t = -kt + \ln[A]_0 \qquad\qquad \ln[A]_t = -kt + \ln[A]_0$$

Solution:

(a) $t_{1/2} = \dfrac{0.693}{k} = \dfrac{0.693}{0.128 \text{ s}^{-1}} = 5.41 \text{ s}$

(b) $\ln[C_4H_{10}]_t = -kt + \ln[C_4H_{10}]_0$. Rearrange to solve for t. For 25% desorbed $[C_4H_{10}]_t = 0.75 \, [C_4H_{10}]_0$

and $t = -\dfrac{1}{k} \ln \dfrac{[C_4H_{10}]_t}{[C_4H_{10}]_0} = -\dfrac{1}{0.128 \text{ s}^{-1}} \ln \dfrac{0.75 \,[\cancel{C_4H_{10}]_0}}{[\cancel{C_4H_{10}]_0}} = 2.2 \text{ s. For 50\% desorbed}$

$[C_4H_{10}]_t = 0.50 \,[C_4H_{10}]_0$ and $t = -\dfrac{1}{k} \ln \dfrac{[C_4H_{10}]_t}{[C_4H_{10}]_0} = -\dfrac{1}{0.128 \text{ s}^{-1}} \ln \dfrac{0.50 \,[\cancel{C_4H_{10}]_0}}{[\cancel{C_4H_{10}]_0}} = 5.4 \text{ s.}$

(c)   For 10 s $\ln[C_4H_{10}]_t = -kt + \ln[C_4H_{10}]_0 = -(0.128\,\text{s}^{-1})(10\,\cancel{\text{s}}) + \cancel{\ln(1.00)} = -1.2\underline{8} \rightarrow$

$[C_4H_{10}]_t = e^{-1.28} = 0.28 = \text{fraction covered}$

for 20 s $\ln [C_4H_{10}]_t = -kt + \ln[C_4H_{10}]_0 = -(0.128 \text{ s}^{-1})(20\,\cancel{\text{s}}) + \cancel{\ln(1.00)} = -2.5\underline{6} \rightarrow$

$[C_4H_{10}]_t = e^{-2.56} = 0.077 = \text{fraction covered.}$

Check: The units (s, s, s, none, and none) are correct. The half-life is reasonable considering the size of the rate constant. The time to 25% desorbed is less than one half-life. The time to 50% desorbed is the half-life. The fraction at 10 s is consistent with about two half-lives. The fraction covered at 20 s is consistent with about four half-lives.

13.97   (a)   **Given:** table of rate constant versus T **Find:** E_a and A

Conceptual Plan: First convert temperature data into kelvin (°C + 273.15 = K). Since

$\ln k = \dfrac{-E_a}{R} \left(\dfrac{1}{T}\right) + \ln A$ a plot of $\ln k$ versus $1/T$ will have a slope $= -E_a/R$ and an intercept $= \ln A$.

Solution: The slope can be determined by measuring $\Delta y/\Delta x$ on the plot or by using functions, such as "add trendline" in Excel. Since the slope $= -10\underline{7}59 \text{ K} = -E_a/R$ then

$E_a = -(slope)R =$

$= -(-10\underline{7}70 \text{ K})\left(8.314 \dfrac{\text{J}}{\text{K} \cdot \text{mol}}\right)\left(\dfrac{1 \text{ kJ}}{1000 \text{ J}}\right)$

$= 89.5 \text{ kJ mol}^{-1}$

and intercept $= 26.7\underline{8}5 = \ln A$ then

$A = e^{intercept} = e^{26.785} = 4.29 \times 10^{11} \text{ L mol}^{-1}\text{s}^{-1}.$

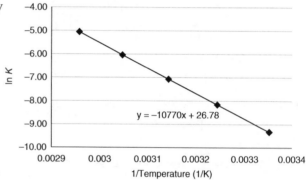

Check: The units (kJ mol^{-1} and L mol^{-1} s^{-1}) are correct. The plot was extremely linear, confirming Arrhenius behaviour. The activation and frequency factor are typical for many reactions.

(b)   **Given:** part (a) results **Find:** k at 15 °C

Conceptual Plan: °C $\rightarrow$ K then $T, E_a, A \rightarrow k$

$\qquad\qquad$°C + 273.15 = K$\qquad\qquad \ln k = \dfrac{-E_a}{R}\left(\dfrac{1}{T}\right) + \ln A$

Solution: 15 °C + 273.15 = 288 K then

$\ln k = \dfrac{-E_a}{R}\left(\dfrac{1}{T}\right) + \ln A = \dfrac{-89.5 \dfrac{\cancel{\text{kJ}}}{\cancel{\text{mol}}} \times \dfrac{1000 \cancel{\text{J}}}{1 \cancel{\text{kJ}}}}{8.314 \dfrac{\cancel{\text{J}}}{\text{K} \cdot \cancel{\text{mol}}}}\left(\dfrac{1}{288 \text{ K}}\right) + \ln(4.29 \times 10^{11} \text{ L mol}^{-1}\text{s}^{-1}) = -10.594 \rightarrow$

$k = e^{-10.594} = 2.5 \times 10^{-5} \text{ L mol}^{-1} \text{s}^{-1}.$

Check: The units (L mol^{-1} s^{-1}) are correct. The value of the rate constant is less than the value at 25 °C.

(c)   **Given:** part (a) results, 0.155 mol L^{-1} C_2H_5Br and 0.250 mol L^{-1} OH$^-$ at 75 °C **Find:** initial reaction rate

Conceptual Plan: °C $\rightarrow$ K then $T, E_a, A \rightarrow k$ then k, [C_2H_5Br], [OH$^-$] $\rightarrow$ initial reaction rate

$\qquad\qquad$°C + 273.15 = K$\qquad\quad \ln k = \dfrac{-E_a}{R}\left(\dfrac{1}{T}\right) + \ln A \qquad\qquad$ Rate $= k\,[C_2H_5Br][OH^-]$

Solution: 75 °C + 273.15 = 348 K then

$\ln k = \dfrac{-E_a}{R}\left(\dfrac{1}{T}\right) + \ln A = \dfrac{-89.5 \dfrac{\cancel{\text{kJ}}}{\cancel{\text{mol}}} \times \dfrac{1000 \cancel{\text{J}}}{1 \cancel{\text{kJ}}}}{8.314 \dfrac{\cancel{\text{J}}}{\text{K} \cdot \cancel{\text{mol}}}}\left(\dfrac{1}{348 \text{ K}}\right) + \ln(4.29 \times 10^{11} \text{ L mol}^{-1}\text{s}^{-1}) = -4.\underline{1}149 \rightarrow$

$k = e^{-4.\underline{1}656} = 1.\underline{5}149 \times 10^{-2} \text{ L mol}^{-1}\text{s}^{-1}.$

Rate $= k\,[C_2H_5Br][OH^-] = (1.5780 \times 10^{-2}\,\cancel{L\,mol^{-1}}\,s^{-1})(0.155\,\cancel{mol\,L^{-1}})(0.250\,mol\,L^{-1})$

$= 6.1 \times 10^{-4}\,mol\,L^{-1}\,s^{-1}$.

Check: The units ($mol\,L^{-1}\,s^{-1}$) are correct. The value of the rate is reasonable considering the value of the rate constant (larger than in the table) and the fact that the concentrations are less than 1 mol L^{-1}.

13.99 (a) No, because the activation energy is zero. This means that the rate constant ($k = A\,e^{-E_a/RT}$) will be independent of temperature.

(b) No bond is broken and the two radicals (CH_3) attract each other.

(c) Formation of diatomic gases from atomic gases.

13.101 **Given:** $t_{1/2}$ for radioactive decay of C-14 = 5730 years; bone has 19.5% C-14 in living bone
Find: age of bone
Conceptual Plan: Radioactive decay implies first-order kinetics, $t_{1/2} \rightarrow k$ **then 19.5% of** $[C-14]_0,\ k \rightarrow t$

$$t_{1/2} = \frac{0.693}{k} \qquad\qquad \ln[A]_t = -kt + \ln[A]_0$$

Solution: $t_{1/2} = \dfrac{0.693}{k}$ rearrange to solve for k. $k = \dfrac{0.693}{t_{1/2}} = \dfrac{0.693}{5730\,yr} = 1.20942 \times 10^{-4}\,yr^{-1}$ then

$[C-14]_t = 0.195\,[C-14]_0$. Since $\ln[C-14]_t = -kt + \ln[C-14]_0$ rearrange to solve for t.

$t = -\dfrac{1}{k}\ln\dfrac{[C-14]_t}{[C-14]_0} = -\dfrac{1}{1.20942 \times 10^{-4}\,yr^{-1}}\ln\dfrac{0.195\,\cancel{[C-14]_0}}{\cancel{[C-14]_0}} = 1.35 \times 10^4\,yr$.

Check: The units (yr) are correct. The time to 19.5% decay is consistent with the time being between two and three half-lives.

13.103 (a) The rate law for mechanism I is Rate $= k_1[H_2][I_2]$. The rate law is first order in both H_2 and I_2, which agrees with the experimental data, so the mechanism is valid.

(b) The rate law for the production of HI is Rate $= k_2[H_2][I]^2$. However, I is an intermediate and its concentration cannot appear in the rate law. Using the steady-state approximation, the rate of production of I is equal to its rate of consumption. That is,

$k_1[I_2] = k_{-1}[I]^2 + k_2[H_2][I]^2$ which simplifies to $k_1[I_2]= (k_{-1} + k_2[H_2])\,[I]^2$ and then rearranges to

$$[I]^2 = \frac{k_1\,[I_2]}{k_{-1} + k_2\,[H_2]}$$

Substituting this back into the first rate equation (Rate $= k_2[H_2][I]^2$) gives Rate $= \dfrac{k_1\,k_2\,[I_2][H_2]}{k_{-1} + k_2\,[H_2]}$. Under low H_2 pressures the $k_2[H_2]$ term in the denominator becomes insignificant and the rate law simplifies to Rate $= \dfrac{k_1\,k_2}{k_{-1}}\,[I_2][H_2]$. This predicts a reaction which is first order in both H_2 and I_2, which agrees with the experimental data and makes mechanism II valid.

(c) Under high pressures of H_2, k_{-1} becomes small compared to $k_2[H_2]$ and the rate law simplifies to Rate $= k_1[I_2]$ which is first order overall and zero order in H_2.

13.105 (a) The rate law for the production of NOBr is Rate $= k_2[NO][NOBr_2]$. However, $NOBr_2$ is an intermediate and its concentration cannot appear in the rate law. Using the steady-state approximation, the rate of production of $NOBr_2$ is equal to its rate of consumption. That is,

$k_1[NO][Br_2] = k_{-1}[NOBr_2] + k_2\,[NO][NOBr_2]$ which simplifies to

$k_1[NO][Br_2] = (k_{-1} + k_2\,[NO])\,[NOBr_2]$ and then

$$[NOBr_2] = \frac{k_1\,[NO][Br_2]}{k_{-1} + k_2\,[NO]}$$

Substituting this back into the first rate equation (Rate = k_2[NO][NOBr$_2$]) gives Rate = $\dfrac{k_2 k_1 [NO]^2 [Br_2]}{k_{-1} + k_2 [NO]}$.

(b)   At very high NO concentrations k_2[NO] becomes large in comparison to k_{-1} and the rate law simplifies to Rate = $\dfrac{k_2 k_1 [NO]\cancel{[NO]}[Br_2]}{\cancel{k_2 [NO]}}$ = k_1[NO][Br$_2$] which is second order overall.

(c)   At very low NO concentrations k_2[NO] becomes small in comparison to k_{-1} and the rate law simplifies to Rate = $\dfrac{k_2 k_1}{k_{-1}}$ [NO]^2 [Br$_2$] which is third order overall.

13.107 (a)   For a zero-order reaction, the rate is independent of the concentration. If the first half goes in the first 100 minutes, the second half will go in the second 100 minutes. This means that there will be none or 0% left at 200 minutes.

(b)   For a first-order reaction, the half-life is independent of concentration. This means that if half of the reactant decomposes in the first 100 minutes, then half of this (or another 25% of the original amount) will decompose in the second 100 minutes. This means that at 200 minutes 50% + 25% = 75% has decomposed or 25% remains.

(c)   For a second-order reaction, $t_{1/2} = \dfrac{1}{k[A]_0}$ = 100 min and the integrated rate expression is

$\dfrac{1}{[A]_t} = kt + \dfrac{1}{[A]_0}$. We can rearrange the first expression to solve for k as $k = \dfrac{1}{100\ \text{min}\ [A]_0}$. Substituting

this and 200 minutes into the integrated rate expression, we get $\dfrac{1}{[A]_t} = \dfrac{200\ \cancel{\text{min}}}{100\ \cancel{\text{min}}\ [A]_0} + \dfrac{1}{[A]_0} \rightarrow$

$\dfrac{1}{[A]_t} = \dfrac{3}{[A]_0} \rightarrow \dfrac{[A]_t}{[A]_0} = \dfrac{1}{3}$ or 33% remains.

13.109 Using the energy diagram shown and using Hess's Law, we can see that the activation energy for the decomposition is equal to the activation energy for the formation reaction plus the heat of formation of 2 moles of HI or

$E_{\text{a formation}} = E_{\text{a decomposition}} + 2\Delta H_f^\circ(HI)$. So
$E_{\text{a formation}} = 185\ \text{kJ} + 2\ \text{mol}\ (-\ 5.65\ \text{kJ mol}^{-1}) = 174\ \text{kJ}$.
Check: Since the reaction is endothermic, we expect the activation energy in the reverse direction to be less in the forward direction.

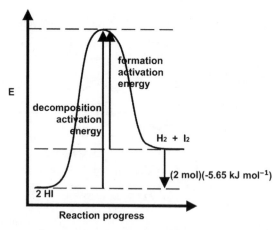

Note: energy axis is not to scale.

13.111 **Given:** $k = 2.71 \times 10^{-4}\ \text{s}^{-1}$ at 573 K, $P_{SO_2Cl_2} = 2.000\ \text{bar}$ **Find:** a) pressure of SO$_2$Cl$_2$ after 1.00 hour, b) total pressure after 1 hour.

Conceptual Plan: a) t (hr) $\rightarrow$ t (s) then $k, t, P_0 \rightarrow P_t$

$$\dfrac{3600\ s}{1\ hr} \qquad \ln[A]_t = -kt + \ln[A]_0$$

b) $\Delta P_{SO_2Cl_2} \rightarrow P_{SO_2},\ P_{Cl_2} \rightarrow P_{total}$

$\Delta P = P_{\text{initial}} - P_t\ SO_2Cl_2 \rightarrow\ SO_2 + Cl_2 \qquad P_{\text{total}} = P_1 + P_2 + P_3\ \ldots$

Solution: a) $t = 1.00\ \text{hr} \times \dfrac{3600\ s}{1\ hr} = 3.60 \times 10^3\ \text{s}$. Since $P \propto \dfrac{n}{V}$ the pressures can be used in the first-order integrated rate law:

$\ln[A]_t = -kt + \ln[A]_0 = -(2.71 \times 10^{-4}\,\text{s}^{-1})(3.60 \times 10^3\,\text{s}) + \ln(2.000) = -0.97\underline{56} + 0.693\underline{17} = -0.28\underline{243}$

$\ln[A]_t = -0.28\underline{243} \rightarrow [A]_t = 0.754\,\text{bar} = P_{(SO_2Cl_2)_t}$

b) $\Delta P_{SO_2Cl_2} = P_{(SO_2Cl_2)_{initial}} - P_{(SO_2Cl_2)_t} = 2.000\,\text{bar} - 0.754\,\text{bar} = 1.246\,\text{bar}$. In the balanced equation, the moles of SO_2 and Cl_2 produced are equal to the moles of SO_2Cl_2 consumed. Therefore, $\Delta P_{SO_2Cl_2} = P_{SO_2} = P_{Cl_2} = 1.246\,\text{bar}$.

$P_{total} = P_{(SO_2Cl_2)_t} + P_{SO_2} + P_{Cl_2} = 0.754\,\text{bar} + 1.246\,\text{bar} + 1.246\,\text{bar} = 3.246\,\text{bar}$.

Check: The units (bar) are correct. The total pressure is higher than the initial pressure because for every mole of gas consumed two moles of gas are being produced.

13.113   **Given:** a) $A = 6.1 \times 10^{13}\,\text{s}^{-1}$, $E_a = 260\,\text{kJ mol}^{-1}$, $T = 723\,\text{K}$ **Find:** a) rate constant at 723 K and b) t for 15.0% isomerization

Conceptual Plan: a) $A, E_a, T \rightarrow k$ and then b) $k, [A]_0, [A]_t \rightarrow t$

$$k = Ae^{-\frac{Ea}{RT}} \qquad\qquad \ln[A]_t = -kt + \ln[A]_0$$

Solution: a) $k = Ae^{-\frac{E_a}{RT}} = (6.1 \times 10^{13}\,\text{s}^{-1})e^{-\frac{260 \times 10^3\,\text{J mol}^{-1}}{(8.314\,\text{J K}^{-1}\text{mol}^{-1})\,(723\,\text{K})}}$

$k = (6.1 \times 10^{13}\,\text{s}^{-1})\,e^{-43.2539} = 1.00 \times 10^{-5}\,\text{s}^{-1}$

b) After 15% isomerization there is 85% of the *cis*-but-2-ene remaining. If $[A]_0 = 1\,\text{mol L}^{-1}$ then $[A]_t = 0.85\,\text{mol L}^{-1}$.

$\ln[A]_t = -kt + \ln[A]_0 \rightarrow \ln(0.85) = -(1.00 \times 10^{-5}\,\text{s}^{-1})t + \ln(1.00)$, which rearranges to

$t = \dfrac{\ln(0.85)}{-1.00 \times 10^5\,\text{s}^{-1}} = 1.63 \times 10^4\,\text{s} = 4.51\,\text{hours}$.

Check: The units (s^{-1}, s) are correct. The magnitude of the time (16300 s) is appropriate in comparison to the half-life ($t_{1/2} = 0.693/k = 69300\,\text{s}$) which represents the time for 50% isomerization.

Challenge Problems

13.115   (a)   Since the rate-determining step involves the collision of two molecules, the expected reaction order would be second order.

(b)   The proposed mechanism is

$CH_3NC + CH_3NC \underset{k_2}{\overset{k_1}{\rightleftharpoons}} CH_3NC^* + CH_3NC$ (fast)

$CH_3NC^* \overset{k_3}{\rightarrow} CH_3CN$ (slow). So the sum matches the overall reaction.

$\overline{CH_3NC \rightarrow CH_3CN}$

CH_3NC^* is the activated molecule. Since the second step is the rate-determining step, Rate $= k_3[CH_3NC^*]$. Since CH_3NC^* is an intermediate, its concentration cannot appear in the rate law. Using the fast equilibrium in the first step, we see that $k_1[CH_3NC]^2 = k_2[CH_3NC^*][CH_3NC]$ or $[CH_3NC^*] = \dfrac{k_1}{k_2}[CH_3NC]$. Substituting this into the first rate expression we get that Rate $= k_3\dfrac{k_1}{k_2}[CH_3NC]$, which simplifies to Rate $= k[CH_3NC]$. This matches the experimental observation of first order and the mechanism is valid.

13.117   Rate $= k[A]^2$ and Rate $= -\dfrac{d[A]}{dt}$ so $\dfrac{d[A]}{dt} = -k[A]^2$. Moving the A terms to the left and the t and constants to the right we have $\dfrac{d[A]}{[A]^2} = -k\,dt$. Integrating we get $\displaystyle\int_{[A]_0}^{[A]} \dfrac{d[A]}{[A]^2} = -\int_0^t k\,dt$. When we evaluate this integral $-[A]_{[A]_0}^{-1|[A]} = -k\,t_0^t \rightarrow -[A]_t^{-1} - (-[A]_0^{-1}) = -k\,t \rightarrow [A]_t^{-1} = k\,t + [A]_0^{-1}$ or

$\dfrac{1}{[A]_t} = k\,t + \dfrac{1}{[A]_0}$ which is the desired integrated rate law.

13.119   For this mechanism, the overall reaction is the sum of the steps in the mechanism:

$$Cl_2(g) \underset{k_2}{\overset{k_1}{\rightleftharpoons}} 2Cl(g)$$

$$\cancel{Cl(g)} + CO(g) \underset{k_4}{\overset{k_3}{\rightleftharpoons}} \cancel{ClCO(g)}$$

$$\cancel{ClCO(g)} + Cl_2(g) \xrightarrow{k_5} Cl_2CO(g) + \cancel{Cl(g)}$$

$$\overline{CO(g) + 2\,Cl_2(g) \rightarrow Cl_2CO(g) + 2\,Cl(g)}$$

There is no overall reaction given. Since the third step is the rate-determining step, Rate = k_5 [ClCO] [Cl$_2$]. Since ClCO is an intermediate, its concentration cannot appear in the rate law. Using the fast equilibrium in the second step, we see that k_3[Cl] [CO] = k_4 [ClCO] or [ClCO] = $\dfrac{k_3}{k_4}$[Cl] [CO]. Substituting this expression into the first rate expression we get Rate = $k_5 \dfrac{k_3}{k_4}$ [Cl] [CO] [Cl$_2$]. Since Cl is an intermediate, its concentration cannot appear in the rate law. Using the fast equilibrium in the first step, we see that k_1[Cl$_2$] = k_2 [Cl]^2 or

[Cl] = $\sqrt{\dfrac{k_1}{k_2}}$[Cl$_2$]. Substituting this expression into last first rate expression we get that

Rate = $k_5 \dfrac{k_3}{k_4}\sqrt{\dfrac{k_1}{k_2}}$[Cl$_2$] [CO] [Cl$_2$] = $k_5 \dfrac{k_3}{k_4}\sqrt{\dfrac{k_1}{k_2}}$[CO] [Cl$_2$]$^{3/2}$. Simplifying this expression we see

Rate = k [CO] [Cl$_2$]$^{3/2}$.

13.121   For the elementary reaction $2\,NOCl(g) \underset{k_{-1}}{\overset{k_1}{\rightleftharpoons}} 2NO(g) + Cl_2(g)$ we see that k_1 [NOCl]^2 = k_{-1} [NO]^2 [Cl$_2$]. For each mole of NOCl that reacts, one mole of NO and one-half mole of Cl$_2$ are generated. Since before any reaction only NOCl is present, [NO] = 2 [Cl$_2$]. Substituting this into the first expression, we get that k_1 [NOCl]^2 = k_{-1} (2[Cl$_2$])^2 [Cl$_2$] $\rightarrow$ k_1 [NOCl]^2 = 4 k_{-1} [Cl$_2$]^3. Rearranging and substituting the specific values into this expression we get

$$[Cl_2] = \sqrt[3]{\dfrac{k_1}{4k_{-1}}}[NOCl]^{2/3} = \sqrt[3]{\dfrac{7.8 \times 10^{-2}\,\dfrac{L^2}{mol^2 \cdot s}}{4\left(4.7 \times 10^2\,\dfrac{L^2}{mol^2 \cdot s}\right)}}\left(0.12\,mol\,L^{-1}\right)^{2/3} = 0.00842237\,mol\,L^{-1}Cl_2$$

= 0.0084 mol L–1 Cl$_2$ and [Cl$_2$] = 2 [NO] = 2$\left(0.00842237\,mol\,L^{-1}\right)$ = 0.0168447 mol L^{-1} NO
= 0.017 mol L^{-1} NO.

13.123   (a)   **Given:** V$_{max}$ = k_2[E]$_0$, equation 13.33 from text **Find:** K$_M$ when rate = $\dfrac{1}{2}$ V$_{max}$

Conceptual Plan: Start with equation 13.33 and then substitute rate with $\dfrac{1}{2}$ V$_{max}$ and k_2[E]$_0$ with V$_{max}$. Rearrange to isolate for K$_M$.

Solution:

$$Rate = \dfrac{k_2\,[E]_0\,[S]}{[S] + K_M}$$

$$\dfrac{1}{2}\,V_{max} = \dfrac{V_{max}\,[S]}{[S] + K_M}$$

$$\left(\dfrac{1}{2}\,V_{max}\right)([S] + K_M) = V_{max}[S]$$

$$[S] + K_M = \frac{2\,V_{max}\,[S]}{V_{max}} = 2[S]$$

$$K_M = 2[S] - [S]$$

$$K_M = [S]$$

The Michaelis constant is the concentration of substrate that yields a rate of $\frac{1}{2}\,V_{max}$.

(b)   **Given:** $V_{max} = 1.98$ mmol $L^{-1}\,s^{-1}$, $K_M = 18$ mmol L^{-1} **Find:** rate at different S concentrations

Conceptual Plan: Start with equation 13.33, substitute $k_2[E]_0$ with given V_{max} and insert the different concentrations of S. Solve for rate.

Solution: For $[S] = 0.1$ mmol L^{-1}:

$$\text{Rate} = \frac{k_2\,[E]_0\,[S]}{[S] + K_M} = \frac{V_{max}\,[S]}{[S] + K_M} = \frac{(1.98 \text{ mmol } L^{-1}\,s^{-1})\,(0.1 \text{ mmol } L^{-1})}{0.1 \text{ mmol } L^{-1} + 18 \text{ mmol } L^{-1}} = 0.0109 \text{ mmol } L^{-1}$$

For $[S] = 1$ mmol L^{-1}:

$$\text{Rate} = \frac{k_2\,[E]_0\,[S]}{[S] + K_M} = \frac{V_{max}\,[S]}{[S] + K_M} = \frac{(1.98 \text{ mmol } L^{-1}\,s^{-1})\,(1 \text{ mmol } L^{-1})}{1 \text{ mmol } L^{-1} + 18 \text{ mmol } L^{-1}} = 0.104 \text{ mmol } L^{-1}$$

For $[S] = 10$ mmol L^{-1}:

$$\text{Rate} = \frac{k_2\,[E]_0\,[S]}{[S] + K_M} = \frac{V_{max}\,[S]}{[S] + K_M} = \frac{(1.98 \text{ mmol } L^{-1}\,s^{-1})\,(10 \text{ mmol } L^{-1})}{10 \text{ mmol } L^{-1} + 18 \text{ mmol } L^{-1}} = 0.707 \text{ mmol } L^{-1}$$

For $[S] = 100$ mmol L^{-1}:

$$\text{Rate} = \frac{k_2\,[E]_0\,[S]}{[S] + K_M} = \frac{V_{max}\,[S]}{[S] + K_M} = \frac{(1.98 \text{ mmol } L^{-1}s^{-1})\,(100 \text{ mmol } L^{-1})}{100 \text{ mmol } L^{-1} + 18 \text{ mmol } L^{-1}} = 1.68 \text{ mmol } L^{-1}$$

For $[S] = 1000$ mmol L^{-1}:

$$\text{Rate} = \frac{k_2\,[E]_0\,[S]}{[S] + K_M} = \frac{V_{max}\,[S]}{[S] + K_M} = \frac{(1.98 \text{ mmol } L^{-1}\,s^{-1})\,(1000 \text{ mmol } L^{-1})}{1000 \text{ mmol } L^{-1} + 18 \text{ mmol } L^{-1}} = 1.94 \text{ mmol } L^{-1}$$

Check: The units (mmol L^{-1}) are correct. Ten-fold increases in substrate concentration do not result in similar increases in the rate because [S] appears in the numerator and denominator. The V_{max} term, which is based on k_2 and $[E]_0$, plays a larger role in determining the overall rate.

13.125   The rate law for the production of E is Rate = $k_3[EZ]$. However EZ is an intermediate and its concentration cannot appear in the rate law. Using the second step and assuming the rate of the forward reaction is equal to the rate of the reverse reaction we can say:

$k_2[EA][B] = k_{-2}[EZ][C]$ which rearranges to $[EZ] = \dfrac{k_2\,[EA][B]}{k_{-2}\,[C]}$.

However, EA is also an intermediate and must be represented in other terms. Using the first reaction and assuming that the rate of the forward reaction equals the rate of the reverse reaction we can say:

$k_1[E][A] = k_{-1}[EA]$ which rearranges to $[EA] = \dfrac{k_1\,[E][A]}{k_{-1}}$. This is substituted back into the expression for EZ:

$$[EZ] = \frac{k_2\,[EA][B]}{k_{-2}\,[C]} = \frac{k_2\,[B]}{k_{-2}\,[C]}\,\frac{k_1\,[E][A]}{k_{-1}}$$ and this in turn gets substituted back into the original rate equation:

$$\text{Rate} = k_3[EZ] = k_3\,\frac{k_2\,[B]}{k_{-2}\,[C]}\,\frac{k_1[E][A]}{k_{-1}} = \frac{k_1\,k_2\,k_3[E][A][B]}{k_{-1}\,k_{-2}\,[C]}.$$

Conceptual Problems

13.127   Reaction A is second order. A plot of 1/[A] versus time will be linear $\left(\dfrac{1}{[A]_t} = kt + \dfrac{1}{[A]_0} \right)$. Reaction B is first

order. A plot of ln [A] versus time will be linear $(\ln[A]_t = -kt + \ln[A]_0)$.

13.129   At high pressures of H_2 there is a significant amount of H_2 adsorbed on the surface and the rate becomes solely dependent on the rate at which the ethane becomes adsorbed.

14 Chemical Equilibrium

Review Questions

14.1 Like adult hemoglobin, fetal hemoglobin is in equilibrium with oxygen. However, the equilibrium constant for fetal hemoglobin is larger than the equilibrium constant for adult hemoglobin, meaning that the reaction tends to go farther in the direction of the product. Consequently, fetal hemoglobin loads oxygen at a lower oxygen concentration than adult hemoglobin. In the placenta, fetal blood flows in close proximity to maternal blood, without the two ever mixing. Because of the different equilibrium constants, the maternal hemoglobin unloads oxygen, which the fetal hemoglobin then binds and carries into its own circulatory system. Nature has thus evolved a chemical system through which the mother's hemoglobin can in effect hand off oxygen to the hemoglobin of the fetus.

14.3 (a) For solution-phase reactions the equilibrium constant is expressed as $K_c = \dfrac{[C]^c[D]^d}{[A]^a[B]^b}$.

(b) For gas-phase reactions the equilibrium constant is expressed as $K_P = \dfrac{P_C^c P_D^d}{P_A^a P_B^b}$.

14.5 If you reverse the equation, invert the equilibrium constant. $K_{reverse} = \dfrac{1}{K_{forward}}$.

If you multiply the coefficients in the equation by a factor, raise the equilibrium constant to the same factor. That is, if you multiply the reaction by n, raise the equilibrium constant K to the n. $K' = K^n$.

14.7 K is the thermodynamic equilibrium constant and is defined in terms of activities. K_c is the equilibrium constant with respect to concentrations expressed as molarities, while K_P is the equilibrium constant with respect to partial pressures expressed in bar. K_c and K_P can be related through $K_P = K_c(RT)^{\Delta n}$.

14.9 The thermodynamic equilibrium constant is expressed in terms of activities. The activities or pure solids and pure liquids are equal to one, so they are omitted from the equilibrium constant expression.

14.11 When we know the initial amounts of the reactants and products and the equilibrium amount of one reactant or product, the other equilibrium amounts can be deduced from the stoichiometry of the reaction. From the initial and equilibrium amount of the one reactant, we can find the change in amount for that reactant. Using the stoichiometry of the reaction, we can determine the equilibrium amounts of the other reactants and products. We generally use an ICE table (I = Initial C = Change E = Equilibrium) to keep track of the changes.

14.13 Standard states are defined as 1 mol L^{-1} concentration, or 1 bar pressure. So the value of Q when the reactants and products are in their standard states is 1.

14.15 To solve a problem given initial amounts and the equilibrium constant you would prepare an ICE table, calculate Q, compare Q and K, predict the direction of the reaction, represent the change with x, sum the table, determine the equilibrium values, put the equilibrium values in the equilibrium expression, and solve for x. Determine the reactant and product amounts.

14.17   According to Le Châtelier's principle, when a chemical system at equilibrium is disturbed, the system shifts in a direction that minimizes the disturbance.

14.19   If a chemical system is at equilibrium,
decreasing the volume causes the reaction to shift in the direction that has the fewer moles of gas particles.
increasing the volume causes the reaction to shift in the direction that has the greater number of moles of gas particles.
if a reaction has an equal number of moles of gas on both sides of the chemical equation, then a change in volume produces no effect on the equilibrium.
adding an inert gas to the mixture at a fixed volume has no effect on the equilibrium.

Problems by Topic

Equilibrium and the Equilibrium-Constant Expression

14.21   (a) $K_P = \dfrac{(P_{H_2})^2 P_{S_2}}{(P_{H_2S})^2}$. The partial pressure of H_2 and H_2S in the equilibrium constant expression both need to be squared.

(b) $K_c = \dfrac{[Cu^{2+}]}{[Ag^+]^2}$. The concentrations of both silver and copper are not in the equilibrium constant expression since they are solids.

(c) $K = (P_{H_2})^2[OH^-]^2[Li^+]$. Both the partial pressure of hydrogen and the concentration of hydroxide need to be squared, and since all the species represented in the expression are products they belong in the numerator.

14.23   With an equilibrium constant of 1.4×10^{-5}, the value of the equilibrium constant is small, therefore, the concentration of reactants will be greater than the concentration of products. This is independent of the initial concentration of the reactants and products.

14.25   (i) has 10 H_2 and 10 I_2
(ii) has 7 H_2 and 7 I_2 and 6 HI
(iii) has 5 H_2 and 5 I_2 and 10 HI
(iv) has 4 H_2 and 4 I_2 and 12 HI
(v) has 3 H_2 and 3 I_2 and 14 HI
(vi) has 3 H_2 and 3 I_2 and 14 HI

(a)   Concentration of (v) and (vi) are the same, so the system reached equilibrium at (v).

(b)   If a catalyst was added to the system, the system would reach the conditions at (v) sooner since a catalyst speeds up the reaction but does not change the equilibrium conditions.

(c)   The final figure (vi) would have the same amount of reactants and products since a catalyst speeds up the reaction, but does not change the equilibrium concentrations.

14.27   (a)   If you reverse the reaction, invert the equilibrium constant. So $K' = \dfrac{1}{K} = \dfrac{1}{9.1 \times 10^6} = 1.1 \times 10^{-7}$.

The reactants will be favoured.

(b)   If you multiply the coefficients in the equation by a factor, raise the equilibrium constant to the same factor.
So $K' = (K)^{1/2} = (9.1 \times 10^6)^{1/2} = 3.0 \times 10^3$. The products will be favoured.

(c)   Begin with the reverse of the reaction and invert the equilibrium constant.

$$K_{reverse} = \frac{1}{K} = \frac{1}{9.1 \times 10^6} = 1.1 \times 10^{-7}$$

Then multiply the reaction by 2 and raise the value of $K_{reverse}$ to the 2nd power.

$K' = (K_{reverse})^2 = (1.1 \times 10^{-7})^2 = 1.2 \times 10^{-14}$. The reactants will be favoured.

14.29   To find the equilibrium constant for reaction 3, you need to combine reactions 1 and 2 to get reaction 3. Begin by reversing reaction 2, then multiply reaction 1 by 2 and add the two new reactions. When you add reactions you multiply the values of K.

$N_2(g) + O_2(g) \rightleftharpoons 2\cancel{NO}(g)$	$K_1 = \dfrac{1}{K} = \dfrac{1}{2.1 \times 10^{30}} = 4.76 \times 10^{-31}$
$2\cancel{NO}(g) + Br_2(g) \rightleftharpoons 2\,NOBr(g)$	$K_2 = (K)^2 = (5.3)^2 = 28.09$
$N_2(g) + O_2(g) + Br_2(g) \rightleftharpoons 2\,NOBr(g)$	$K_3 = K_1 K_2 = (4.76 \times 10^{-31})(28.09) = 1.3 \times 10^{-29}$

K_p, K_c, and Heterogeneous Equilibria

14.31   (a)   **Given:** $K_p = 6.26 \times 10^{-22}$ T = 298K   **Find:** K_c
Conceptual Plan: $K_p \rightarrow K_c$
$$K_p = K_c(RT)^{\Delta n}$$
Solution: Δn = mol product gas – mol reactant gas = 2 – 1 = 1

$$K_c = \frac{K_p}{(RT)^{\Delta n}} = \frac{6.26 \times 10^{-22}}{(0.08314 \frac{\text{bar L}}{\text{mol K}} \times 298 \text{ K})^1} = 2.53 \times 10^{-23}$$

Check: Substitute into the equation and confirm that you get the original value of K_p.

$$K_p = K_c(RT)^{\Delta n} = (2.53 \times 10^{-23})(0.08314 \frac{\text{bar L}}{\text{mol K}} \times 298 \text{ K})^1 = 6.26 \times 10^{-22}$$

(b)   **Given:** $K_p = 7.7 \times 10^{24}$ T = 298K   **Find:** K_c
Conceptual Plan: $K_p \rightarrow K_c$
$$K_p = K_c(RT)^{\Delta n}$$
Solution: Δn = mol product gas – mol reactant gas = 4 – 2 = 2

$$K_c = \frac{K_p}{(RT)^{\Delta n}} = \frac{7.7 \times 10^{24}}{(0.08314 \frac{\text{bar L}}{\text{mol K}} \times 298 \text{ K})^2} = 1.3 \times 10^{22}$$

Check: Substitute into the equation and confirm that you get the original value of K_p.

$$K_p = K_c(RT)^{\Delta n} = (1.3 \times 10^{22})(0.08314 \frac{\text{bar L}}{\text{mol K}} \times 298 \text{ K})^2 = 7.7 \times 10^{24}$$

(c)   **Given:** $K_p = 81.9$ T = 298K   **Find:** K_c
Conceptual Plan: $K_p \rightarrow K_c$
$$K_p = K_c(RT)^{\Delta n}$$
Solution: Δn = mol product gas – mol reactant gas = 2 – 2 = 0

$$K_c = \frac{K_p}{(RT)^{\Delta n}} = \frac{81.9}{(0.08314 \frac{\text{bar L}}{\text{mol K}} \times 298 \text{ K})^0} = 81.9$$

Check: Substitute into the equation and confirm that you get the original value of K_p.

$$K_p = K_c(RT)^{\Delta n} = (81.9)(0.08314 \frac{\text{bar L}}{\text{mol K}} \times 298 \text{ K})^0 = 81.9$$

14.33   (a)   Since H_2O is a liquid, it is omitted from the equilibrium expression. $K_c = \dfrac{[HCO_3^-][OH^-]}{[CO_3^{2-}]}$

(b)   Since $KClO_3$ and KCl are both solids, they are omitted from the equilibrium expression. $K_c = [O_2]^3$

(c)   Since H_2O is a liquid, it is omitted from the equilibrium expression. $K_c = \dfrac{[H_3O^+][F^-]}{[HF]}$

(d)   Since H_2O is a liquid, it is omitted from the equilibrium expression. $K_c = \dfrac{[NH_4^+][OH^-]}{[NH_3]}$

Relating the Equilibrium Constant to Equilibrium Concentrations and Equilibrium Partial Pressures

14.35   **Given:** At equilibrium: $P_{CO} = 0.105$ bar, $P_{H_2} = 0.114$ bar, $P_{CH_3OH} = 0.185$ bar   **Find:** K
        Conceptual Plan: Balanced reaction → **equilibrium expression** → K

        Solution: $K = \dfrac{P_{CH_3OH}}{P_{CO}(P_{H_2})^2} = \dfrac{(0.185)}{(0.105)(0.114)^2} = 136$

        Check: The answer is reasonable since the pressure of products is greater than the pressure of reactants and the equilibrium constant should be greater than 1.

14.37   At 350 K: **Given:** At equilibrium: $P_{N_2} = 0.121$ bar, $P_{H_2} = 0.105$ bar, $P_{NH_3} = 0.565$ bar **Find:** K
        Conceptual Plan: Balanced reaction → **equilibrium expression** → K

        Solution: $K = \dfrac{(P_{NH_3})^2}{P_{N_2}(P_{H_2})^3} = \dfrac{(0.565)^2}{(0.121)(0.105)^3} = 2.28 \times 10^3$

        Check: The value is reasonable since the pressure of the products is greater than the pressures of the reactants.

        At 415 K: **Given:** At equilibrium: $P_{N_2} = 0.110$ bar, $P_{NH_3} = 0.128$ bar, $K = 13.2$ **Find:** P_{H_2}
        Conceptual Plan: Balanced reaction → **equilibrium expression** → P_{H_2}

        Solution: $K = \dfrac{(P_{NH_3})^2}{P_{N_2}(P_{H_2})^3}$ $13.2 = \dfrac{(0.128)^2}{(0.110)(x)^3}$ $x = 0.224$

        Check: Plug the value for x back into the equilibrium expression and check to see if the same equilibrium constant is obtained.

$$\dfrac{(0.128)^2}{(0.110)(0.224)^3} = 13.2$$

        At 515 K: **Given:** At equilibrium: $P_{N_2} = 0.120$ bar, $P_{H_2} = 0.140$ bar, $K = 0.0512$ **Find:** P_{NH_3}
        Conceptual Plan: Balanced reaction → **equilibrium expression** → P_{NH_3}

        Solution: $K = \dfrac{(P_{NH_3})^2}{P_{N_2}(P_{H_2})^3}$ $0.0512 = \dfrac{(x)^2}{(0.120)(.140)^3}$ $x = 0.00411$

        Check: Plug the value for x back into the equilibrium expression and check to see if the same equilibrium constant is obtained.

$$\dfrac{(0.00411)^2}{(0.120)(0.140)^3} = 0.0512$$

14.39   **Given:** $P_{NO} = 108$ mbar, $P_{Br_2} = 126$ mbar, $K = 32.9$ **Find:** P_{BrNO}
        Conceptual Plan: Balanced reaction → **equilibrium expression** → P_{BrNO}

        Solution: $P_{NO} = 108$ mbar $\times \dfrac{1\ bar}{1000\ mbar} = 0.108$ bar

                $P_{Br_2} = 126$ mbar $\times \dfrac{1\ bar}{1000\ mbar} = 0.126$ bar

        $K = \dfrac{(P_{BrNO})^2}{P_{Br_2}(P_{NO})^2}$ $32.9 = \dfrac{(x)^2}{(0.126)(0.108)^2}$ $x = P_{BrNO} = 0.220$ bar

Check: Plug the value for x back into the equilibrium expression and check to see if the same equilibrium constant is obtained.

$$\frac{(0.220)^2}{(0.126)(0.108)^2} = 32.9$$

14.41 **Given:** $[Fe^{3+}]_{initial} = 2.4 \times 10^{-4}$ mol L^{-1}; $[SCN^-]_{initial} = 8.0 \times 10^{-4}$ mol L^{-1}; $[FeSCN^{2+}]_{eq} = 1.7 \times 10^{-4}$ mol L^{-1} **Find:** K
Conceptual Plan: 1. **Prepare ICE table**
2. **Calculate concentration change for known value**
3. **Calculate concentration changes for other reactants/products**
4. **Determine equilibrium concentration**
5. **Write the equilibrium expression and determine K**

Solution: Fe^{3+}(aq) + SCN$^-$(aq) ⇌ FeSCN^{3+}(aq)

	[Fe^{3+}]	[SCN$^-$]	[FeSCN^{3+}]
I	2.4×10^{-4}	8.0×10^{-4}	0
C	-1.7×10^{-4}	-1.7×10^{-4}	$+1.7 \times 10^{-4}$
E	7.0×10^{-5}	6.3×10^{-4}	1.7×10^{-4}

$$K = \frac{[FeSCN^{2+}]}{[Fe^{3+}][SCN^-]} = \frac{(1.7 \times 10^{-4})}{(7.0 \times 10^{-5})(6.3 \times 10^{-4})} = 3.9 \times 10^3$$

14.43 **Given:** 3.67 L flask, 0.371 g H$_2$ initial, 17.93 g I$_2$ initial, 17.72 g HI equilibrium **Find:** K
Conceptual Plan: g → mol → mol L^{-1} and then
$$n = \frac{g}{\text{molar mass}} \quad [\,] = \frac{n}{V}$$
1. **Prepare ICE table**
2. **Calculate concentration change for known value**
3. **Calculate concentration changes for other reactants/products**
4. **Determine equilibrium concentration**
5. **Write the equilibrium expression and determine K**

Solution: 0.371 g H$_2 \times \dfrac{1 \text{ mol H}_2}{2.016 \text{ g H}_2} = 0.184$ mol H$_2 \dfrac{0.184 \text{ mol H}_2}{3.67 \text{ L}} = 0.05014$ mol L^{-1}. This is an initial concentration.

17.93 g I$_2 \times \dfrac{1 \text{ mol I}_2}{253.80 \text{ g I}_2} = 0.070646$ mol I$_2 \dfrac{0.070646 \text{ mol I}_2}{3.67 \text{ L}} = 0.019249$ mol L^{-1}. This is an initial concentration.

17.72 g HI $\times \dfrac{1 \text{ mol HI}}{127.91 \text{ g HI}} = 0.13853$ mol HI $\dfrac{0.13853 \text{ mol HI}}{3.67 \text{ L}} = 0.037747$ mol L^{-1}. This is an equilibrium concentration.

H$_2$(g) + I$_2$(g) ⇌ 2 HI(g)

	[H$_2$]	[I$_2$]	[HI]
I	0.05014	0.019249	0
C	-0.0188733	-0.0188733	0.037747
E	0.0312667	0.0003757	0.037747

Since HI gained 0.037747 mol L^{-1}, then H$_2$ and I$_2$ had to lose $0.037747/2 = 0.0188733$ mol L^{-1} based on the stoichiometry of the balanced equation.

$$K = \frac{[HI]^2}{[H_2][I_2]} = \frac{(0.037747)^2}{(0.0312667)(0.0003757)} = 121.29 = 120$$

The Reaction Quotient and Reaction Direction

14.45 **Given:** $K = 8.5 \times 10^{-3}$; $P_{NH_3} = 0.226$ bar, $P_{H_2S} = 0.266$ bar **Find:** Will solid form or decompose?
Conceptual Plan: Calculate $Q \to$ compare Q and K

Solution: $Q = P_{NH_3}P_{H_2S} = (0.266)(0.266) = 0.0708$

$Q = 0.0708$ and $K = 8.5 \times 10^{-3}$ so $Q > K$ and the reaction will shift to the left, so more solid will form.

14.47 **Given:** 6.55 g Ag_2SO_4, 1.5 L solution, $K = 1.1 \times 10^{-5}$ **Find:** Will more solid dissolve?

Conceptual Plan: g $Ag_2SO_4 \rightarrow$ mol $Ag_2SO_4 \rightarrow [Ag_2SO_4] \rightarrow [Ag^+],[SO_4^{-2}] \rightarrow$ calculate Q and compare to K.

$$\frac{1 \text{ mol } Ag_2SO_4}{311.81 \text{ g}} \qquad [\,] = \frac{\text{mol } Ag_2SO_4}{\text{vol solution}} \qquad Q = [Ag^+]^2[SO_4^{2-}]$$

Solution: $6.55 \, \overline{\text{g } Ag_2SO_4} \left(\dfrac{1 \text{ mol } Ag_2SO_4}{311.81 \, \overline{\text{g}Ag_2SO_4}} \right) = 0.0210 \text{ mol } Ag_2SO_4$

$$\frac{0.0210 \text{ mol } Ag_2SO_4}{1.5 \text{ L solution}} = 0.01\underline{4}0 \text{ mol L}^{-1} \, Ag_2SO_4$$

$[Ag^+] = 2[Ag_2SO_4] = 2(0.01\underline{4}0 \text{ mol L}^{-1}) = 0.0280 \text{ mol L}^{-1}$ $[SO_4^{2-}] = [Ag_2SO_4] = 0.01\underline{4}0 \text{ mol L}^{-1}$

$Q = [Ag^+]^2[SO_4^{2-}] = (0.0280)^2(0.01\underline{4}0) = 1.1 \times 10^{-5}$

$Q = K$ so the system is at equilibrium and is a saturated solution. Therefore, if more solid is added it will not dissolve.

Finding Equilibrium Concentrations from Initial Concentrations and the Equilibrium Constant

14.49 (a) **Given:** $[A] = 1.0 \text{ mol L}^{-1}$, $[B] = 0.0$, $K = 4.0$; $a = 1, b = 1$ **Find:** $[A]$, $[B]$ at equilibrium

Conceptual Plan: Prepare an ICE table, calculate Q, compare Q and K, predict the direction of the reaction, represent the change with x, sum the table, determine the equilibrium values, put the equilibrium values in the equilibrium expression, and solve for x. Determine $[A]$ and $[B]$.

Solution: $A(g) \leftrightarrows B(g)$

	[A]	[B]
I	1.0	0
C	$-x$	$+x$
E	$1.0 - x$	x

$Q = \dfrac{[B]}{[A]} = \dfrac{0}{1} = 0$ $Q < K$ therefore, the reaction will proceed to the right by x.

$K = \dfrac{[B]}{[A]} = \dfrac{(x)}{(1.0 - x)} = 4.0$ $x = 0.80$

$[A] = 1.0 - 0.80 = 0.20 \text{ mol L}^{-1}$ $[B] = 0.80 \text{ mol L}^{-1}$

Check: Plug the values into the equilibrium expression: $K = \dfrac{0.80}{0.20} = 4.0$.

(b) **Given:** $[A] = 1.0 \text{ mol L}^{-1}$, $[B] = 0.0$, $K = 4.0$; $a = 2, b = 2$ **Find:** $[A]$, $[B]$ at equilibrium

Conceptual Plan: Prepare an ICE table, calculate Q, compare Q and K, predict the direction of the reaction, represent the change with x, sum the table, determine the equilibrium values, put the equilibrium values in the equilibrium expression, and solve for x. Determine $[A]$ and $[B]$.

Solution: $2 A(g) \leftrightarrows 2 B(g)$

	[A]	[B]
I	1.0	0
C	$-2x$	$+2x$
E	$1.0 - 2x$	$2x$

$Q = \dfrac{[B]^2}{[A]^2} = \dfrac{0}{1} = 0$ $Q < K$ therefore, the reaction will proceed to the right by x.

$K = \dfrac{[B]^2}{[A]^2} = \dfrac{(2x)^2}{(1.0 - 2x)^2} = 4.0$ $x = 0.3\underline{3}$

$[A] = 1.0 - 2(0.3\underline{3}) = 0.3\underline{3} = 0.33 \text{ mol L}^{-1}$ $[B] = 2(0.3\underline{3}) = 0.66 = 0.66 \text{ mol L}^{-1}$

Check: Plug the values into the equilibrium expression: $K = \dfrac{(0.66)^2}{(0.33)^2} = 4.0$.

(c) **Given:** [A] = 1.0 mol L^{-1}, [B] = 0.0, K = 4.0; a = 1, b = 2 **Find:** [A], [B] at equilibrium
Conceptual Plan: Prepare an ICE table, calculate Q, compare Q and K, predict the direction of the reaction, represent the change with x, sum the table, determine the equilibrium values, put the equilibrium values, in the equilibrium expression, and solve for x. Determine [A] and [B].
Solution: A(g) $\leftrightharpoons$ 2 B(g)

	[A]	[B]
I	1.0	0
C	-x	+2x
E	1.0 - x	2x

$$Q = \frac{[B]^2}{[A]} = \frac{0}{1} = 0 \quad Q < K \text{ therefore, the reaction will proceed to the right by } x.$$

$$K = \frac{[B]^2}{[A]} = \frac{(2x)^2}{(1.0 - x)} = 4.0 \quad 4x^2 + 4x - 4 = 0 \text{ Solve using the quadratic equation, Appendix I.}$$

$x = -1.62$ or $x = 0.62$, therefore, $x = 0.62$.
[A] = 1.0 - 0.62 = 0.38 mol L^{-1} [B] = 2x = 2(0.62) = 1.2̲4 mol L^{-1} = 1.2 mol L^{-1}

Check: Plug the values into the equilibrium expression: $K = \dfrac{(1.24)^2}{0.38} = 4.0.$

14.51 **Given:** [N$_2$O$_4$] = 0.0500 mol L^{-1}, [NO$_2$] = 0, K = 0.538 **Find:** [N$_2$O$_4$], [NO$_2$] at equilibrium
Conceptual Plan: Prepare an ICE table, calculate Q, compare Q and K, predict the direction of the reaction, represent the change with x, sum the table, determine the equilibrium values, put the equilibrium values in the equilibrium expression, and solve for x. Determine [N$_2$O$_4$] and [NO$_2$].
Solution: Since the reaction of interest is in the gas phase $K = K_P$. In order to calculate the equilibrium concentrations in mol L^{-1} we need to first convert to K_c.

$$K_c = \frac{K_P}{(RT)^{\Delta n}} = \frac{0.538 \text{ bar}}{\left(0.08314 \dfrac{\text{bar L}}{\text{mol K}}\right)(313\text{K})} = 0.020\underline{6}7 \text{ mol L}^{-1}$$

N$_2$O$_4$ (g) $\leftrightharpoons$ 2 NO$_2$(g)

	[N$_2$O$_4$]	[NO$_2$]
I	0.0500	0
C	-x	+2x
E	0.0500 - x	2x

$$Q = \frac{[NO_2]^2}{[N_2O_4]} = \frac{0}{0.0500} = 0 \quad Q < K \text{ therefore, the reaction will proceed to the right by } x.$$

$$K_c = \frac{[NO_2]^2}{[N_2O_4]} \quad 0.020\underline{6}7 = \frac{(2x)^2}{(0.0500 - x)} \quad (2x)^2 - (0.020\underline{6}7)(0.0500 - x) = 0$$

$4x^2 + 0.020\underline{6}7x - 0.0010\underline{3}3 = 0$

$$\frac{-b \pm \sqrt{b^2 - 4ac}}{2a} = \frac{-0.02067 \pm \sqrt{(0.02067)^2 - 4(4)(-0.001033)}}{2(4)} = \frac{-0.02067 \pm \sqrt{0.01696}}{8}$$

$x = 0.013\underline{6}9$ or $x = -0.018\underline{8}6$, therefore $x = 0.013\underline{6}9$.
[N$_2$O$_4$] = 0.0500 - 0.013\underline{6}9 = 0.0363 mol L^{-1}, [NO$_2$] = 2x = 2(0.013\underline{6}9) = 0.0274 mol L^{-1}

Check: Plug the values into the equilibrium expression. $K_c = \dfrac{(0.0274)^2}{0.0363} = 0.020\underline{6}8.$ This is the K_c value.

14.53 **Given:** P_{CO} = 2.28 bar, K = 80.3 **Find:** P_{CO_2} and P_{CO} at equilibrium
Conceptual Plan: Prepare an ICE table, calculate Q, compare Q and K, predict the direction of the reaction, represent the change with x, sum the table, determine the equilibrium values, put the equilibrium values in the equilibrium expression, and solve for x. Determine [CO], [Cl$_2$], and [COCl$_2$].

Solution:

$$NiO(s) + CO(g) \rightleftharpoons Ni(s) + CO_2(g)$$

	P_{CO}	P_{CO_2}
I	2.28	0
C	$-x$	$+x$
E	$2.28 - x$	x

$$Q = \frac{P_{CO_2}}{P_{CO}} = \frac{0}{(2.28)} = 0 \quad Q < K \text{ therefore, the reaction will proceed to the right by } x.$$

$$K = \frac{P_{CO_2}}{P_{CO}} = \frac{x}{(2.28 - x)} = 80.3 \quad 80.3(2.28 - x) = x$$

$x = 2.25$ bar

$P_{CO_2} = 2.25$ bar, $P_{CO} = 2.28 - 2.25 = 0.03$ bar

Check: Since the equilibrium constant is so large, the reaction goes essentially to completion; therefore, it is reasonable that the concentration of product is 2.25 bar.

14.55   **Given:** $[HC_2H_3O_2] = 0.210$ mol L^{-1}, $[H_3O^+] = 0.0$, $[C_2H_3O_2^-] = 0.0$, $K = 1.8 \times 10^{-5}$
Find: $[HC_2H_3O2]$, $[H_2O^+]$, $[C_2H_3O_2^-]$ at equilibrium
Conceptual Plan: Prepare an ICE table, calculate Q, compare Q and K, predict the direction of the reaction, represent the change with x, sum the table, determine the equilibrium values, put the equilibrium values in the equilibrium expression, and solve for x. Determine [CO], [Cl$_2$], and [COCl$_2$].
Solution:

$$HC_2H_3O_2(aq) + H_2O(l) \rightleftharpoons H_3O^+(aq) + C_2H_3O_2^-(aq)$$

	$[HC_2H_3O_2]$	$[H_2O]$	$[H_3O^+]$	$[C_2H_3O_2^-]$
I	0.210		0	0
C	$-x$		$+x$	$+x$
E	$0.210 - x$		x	x

$$Q = \frac{[H_3O^+][C_2H_3O_2^-]}{[HC_2H_3O_2]} = \frac{0}{(0.210)} = 0 \quad Q < K \text{ therefore, the reaction will proceed to the right by } x.$$

$$K = \frac{[H_3O^+][C_2H_3O_2^-]}{[HC_2H_3O_2]} = \frac{(x)(x)}{(0.210 - x)} = 1.8 \times 10^{-5}$$

Assume x is small compared to 0.210.

$x^2 = 0.210(1.8 \times 10^{-5})$

$x = 0.00194$ Check assumption: $\dfrac{0.00194}{0.210} \times 100 = 0.92\%$; assumption valid.

$[H_3O^+] = [C_2H_3O_2^-] = 0.00194$ mol L^{-1}

$[HC_2H_3O_2] = 0.210 - 0.00194 = 0.20\underline{8}1 = 0.208$ mol L^{-1}

Check: Plug the values into the equilibrium expression: $K = \dfrac{(0.00194)(0.00194)}{(0.208)} = 1.81 \times 10^{-5}$; the answer is the same to two significant figures with the true value, so answers are valid.

14.57   **Given:** $P_{ClF} = 0.500$ bar, $K = 1.75 \times 10^{-6}$ **Find:** Pressures of all reactants and products at equilibrium.
Conceptual Plan: Prepare an ICE table, calculate Q, compare Q and K, predict the direction of the reaction, represent the change with x, sum the table, determine the equilibrium values, put the equilibrium values in the equilibrium expression, and solve for x. Determine P_{ClF}, P_{Cl_2}, P_{F_2} at equilibrium.
Solution:

$$2\,ClF(g) \rightleftharpoons Cl_2(g) + F_2(g)$$

	P_{ClF}	P_{Cl_2}	P_{F_2}	
I	0.500	0	0	Since there are no initial products, $Q < K$
C	$-2x$	$+x$	$+x$	and the reaction will proceed to the right.
E	$0.500 - 2x$	x	x	

$$K = \frac{P_{F_2} P_{Cl_2}}{(P_{ClF})^2} = 1.75 \times 10^{-6} = \frac{(x)^2}{(0.500 - 2x)^2}. \quad \text{Simplify by taking the square root of both sides.}$$

$$\sqrt{1.75 \times 10^{-6}} = 1.3\underline{2}2 \times 10^{-3} = \frac{x}{0.500 - 2x}. \quad \text{Assume } x \text{ is small compared to } 0.500.$$

$1.3\underline{2}2 \times 10^{-3} = \dfrac{x}{0.500}$ $x = 6.6\underline{1}4 \times 10^{-4}$ Check assumption: $\dfrac{6.614 \times 10^{-4}}{0.500} \times 100 = 0.132\%$

Assumption valid. $x = 6.6\underline{1}4 \times 10^{-4} = P_{Cl_2} = P_{F_2} = 6.61 \times 10^{-4}$ bar

$P_{ClF} = 0.500 - 2x = 0.500 - 2(6.\,6\underline{1}4 \times 10^{-4}) = 0.499$ bar

Check: Plug the values into the equilibrium expression:

$K = \dfrac{P_{F_2}P_{Cl_2}}{(P_{ClF})^2} = \dfrac{(6.61 \times 10^{-4})^2}{(0.499)^2} = 1.75 \times 10^{-6}$. This is the equilibrium constant.

14.59   (a)   **Given:** [A] = 1.0 mol L^{-1}, [B] = [C] = 0.0, K = 1.0 **Find:** [A], [B], [C] at equilibrium

Conceptual Plan: Prepare an ICE table, calculate Q, compare Q and K, predict the direction of the reaction, represent the change with x, sum the table, determine the equilibrium values, put the equilibrium values in the equilibrium expression, and solve for x. Determine [A], [B], and [C].

Solution:

	A (g) $\leftrightarrows$	B (g) +	C (g)
	[A]	[B]	[C]
I	1.0	0	0
C	-x	+x	+x
E	1.0 - x	x	x

$Q = \dfrac{[B][C]}{[A]} = \dfrac{0}{(1.0)} = 0$ $Q < K$ therefore, the reaction will proceed to the right by x.

$K = \dfrac{[B][C]}{[A]} = \dfrac{(x)(x)}{(1.0 - x)} = 1.0$

$x^2 = 1.0(1.0 - x)$

$x^2 + x - 1 = 0$

$\dfrac{-b \pm \sqrt{b^2 - 4ac}}{2a}$ $\dfrac{-1 \pm \sqrt{1^2 - 4(1)(-1)}}{2(1)}$

$x = 0.6\underline{1}8$ or $x = -1.618$, therefore, $x = 0.6\underline{1}8$.

[B] = [C] = $x = 0.6\underline{1}8 = 0.62$ mol L^{-1}

[A] = $1.0 - 0.6\underline{1}8 = 0.382 = 0.38$ mol L^{-1}

Check: Plug the values into the equilibrium expression:

$K = \dfrac{(0.62)(0.62)}{(0.38)} = 1.01 = 1.0$. This is the equilibrium constant, so the values are correct.

  (b)   **Given:** [A] = 1.0 mol L^{-1}, [B] = [C] = 0.0, K = 0.010 **Find:** [A], [B], [C] at equilibrium

Conceptual Plan: Prepare an ICE table, calculate Q, compare Q and K, predict the direction of the reaction, represent the change with x, sum the table, determine the equilibrium values, put the equilibrium values in the equilibrium expression, and solve for x. Determine [A], [B], and [C].

Solution:

	A (g) $\leftrightarrows$	B (g) +	C (g)
	[A]	[B]	[C]
I	1.0	0	0
C	-x	+x	+x
E	1.0 - x	x	x

$Q = \dfrac{[B][C]}{[A]} = \dfrac{0}{(1.0)} = 0$ $Q < K$ therefore, the reaction will proceed to the right by x.

$K = \dfrac{[B][C]}{[A]} = \dfrac{(x)(x)}{(1.0 - x)} = 0.010$

$x^2 = 0.010(1.0 - x)$

$x^2 + 0.010x - 0.010 = 0$

$\dfrac{-b \pm \sqrt{b^2 - 4ac}}{2a}$ $\dfrac{-(0.010) \pm \sqrt{(0.010)^2 - 4(1)(-0.010)}}{2(1)}$

$x = 0.09512$ or $x = -0.1015$, therefore, $x = 0.09512$.

$[B] = [C] = x = 0.09512 = 0.095$ mol L^{-1}

$[A] = 1.0 - 0.09512 = 0.90488 = 0.90$ mol L^{-1}

Check: Plug the values into the equilibrium expression:

$K = \dfrac{(0.095)(0.095)}{(0.90)} = 0.01002 = 0.010$. This is the equilibrium constant, so the values are correct.

(c)   **Given:** $[A] = 1.0$ mol L^{-1}, $[B] = [C] = 0.0$, $K = 1.0 \times 10^{-5}$ **Find:** $[A]$, $[B]$, $[C]$ at equilibrium

Conceptual Plan: Prepare an ICE table, calculate Q, compare Q and K, predict the direction of the reaction, represent the change with x, sum the table, determine the equilibrium values, put the equilibrium values in the equilibrium expression, and solve for x. Determine $[A]$, $[B]$, and $[C]$.

Solution:

$$A\ (g) \leftrightharpoons B\ (g) + C\ (g)$$

	$[A]$	$[B]$	$[C]$
I	1.0	0	0
C	$-x$	$+x$	$+x$
E	$1.0 - x$	x	x

$Q = \dfrac{[B][C]}{[A]} = \dfrac{0}{(1.0)} = 0$ $Q < K$ therefore, the reaction will proceed to the right by x.

$K = \dfrac{[B][C]}{[A]} = \dfrac{(x)(x)}{(1.0 - x)} = 1.0 \times 10^{-5}$

Assume x is small compared to 1.0.

$x^2 = 1.0(1.0 \times 10^{-5})$

$x = 0.00316$ Check assumption: $\dfrac{0.00316}{1.0} \times 100 = 0.32\%$; assumption valid.

$[B] = [C] = x = 0.00316 = 0.0032$ mol L^{-1}

$[A] = 1.0 - 0.00316 = 0.9968 = 1.0$ mol L^{-1}

Check: Plug the values into the equilibrium expression:

$K = \dfrac{(0.0032)(0.0032)}{(1.0)} = 1.024 \times 10^{-5} = 1.0 \times 10^{-5}$.

This is the equilibrium constant, so the values are correct

Le Châtelier's Principle

14.61   **Given:** $CO(g) + Cl_2(g) \leftrightharpoons COCl_2(g)$ at equilibrium   **Find:** What is the effect of each of the following?

(a) $COCl_2$ is added to the reaction mixture: Adding $COCl_2$ increases the concentration of $COCl_2$ and causes the reaction to shift to the left.

(b) Cl_2 is added to the reaction mixture: Adding Cl_2 increases the concentration of Cl_2 and causes the reaction to shift to the right.

(c) $COCl_2$ is removed from the reaction mixture: Removing the $COCl_2$ decreases the concentration of $COCl_2$ and causes the reaction to shift to the right.

14.63   **Given:** $2KClO_3(s) \leftrightharpoons 2KCl(s) + 3O_2(g)$ at equilibrium **Find:** What is the effect of each of the following?

(a) O_2 is removed from the reaction mixture: Removing the O_2 decreases the concentration of O_2 and causes the reaction to shift to the right.

(b)   KCl is added to the reaction mixture: Adding KCl does not cause any change in the reaction. KCl is a solid and the concentration remains constant, so the addition of more solid does not change the equilibrium concentration.

(c) $KClO_3$ is added to the reaction mixture: Adding $KClO_3$ does not cause any change in the reaction. $KClO_3$ is a solid and the concentration remains constant, so the addition of more solid does not change the equilibrium concentration.

(d) O_2 is added to the reaction mixture: Adding O_2 increases the concentration of O_2 and causes the reaction to shift to the left.

14.65   (a)   **Given:** $I_2(g) \rightleftharpoons 2I(g)$ at equilibrium   **Find:** the effect of increasing the volume
        The chemical equation has 2 moles of gas on the right and 1 mole of gas on the left. Increasing the volume of the reaction mixture decreases the pressure and causes the reaction to shift to the right (toward the side with more moles of gas particles).

        (b)   **Given:** $2H_2S(g) \rightleftharpoons 2H_2(g) + S_2(g)$ **Find:** the effect of decreasing the volume
        The chemical equation has 3 moles of gas on the right and 2 moles of gas on the left. Decreasing the volume of the reaction mixture increases the pressure and causes the reaction to shift to the left (toward the side with fewer moles of gas particles).

        (c)   **Given:** $I_2(g) + Cl_2(g) \rightleftharpoons 2ICl(g)$ **Find:** the effect of decreasing the volume
        The chemical equation has 2 moles of gas on the right and 2 moles of gas on the left. Decreasing the volume of the reaction mixture increases the pressure but causes no shift in the reaction because the moles are equal on both sides.

14.67   **Given:** $C(s) + CO_2(g) \rightleftharpoons 2CO(g)$ is endothermic   **Find:** the effect of increasing the temperature
        Since the reaction is endothermic we can think of the heat as a reactant: Increasing the temperature is equivalent to adding a reactant, causing the reaction to shift to the right. This will cause an increase in the concentration of products and a decrease in the concentration of reactant; therefore, the value of K will increase.
        Find: the effect of decreasing the temperature
        Since the reaction is endothermic we can think of the heat as a reactant: Decreasing the temperature is equivalent to removing a reactant, causing the reaction to shift to the left. This will cause a decrease in the concentration of products and an increase in the concentration of reactants; therefore, the value of K will decrease.

14.69   **Given:** $C(s) + 2H_2(g) \rightleftharpoons CH_4(g)$ is exothermic   **Find:** determine which will favour CH_4

        (a)   Adding more C to the reaction mixture does NOT favour CH_4. Adding C does not cause any change in the reaction. C is a solid and the concentration remains constant, so the addition of more solid does not change the equilibrium concentration.

        (b)   Adding more H_2 to the reaction mixture favours CH_4. Adding H_2 increases the concentration of H_2, causing the reaction to shift to the right.

        (c)   Raising the temperature of the reaction mixture does NOT favour CH_4. Since the reaction is exothermic we can think of heat as a product: Raising the temperature is equivalent to adding a product, causing the reaction to shift to the left.

        (d)   Lowering the volume of the reaction mixture favours CH_4. The chemical equation has 1 mole of gas on the right and 2 moles of gas on the left. Decreasing the volume of the reaction mixture increases the pressure and causes the reaction to shift to the right (toward the side with fewer moles of gas particles).

        (e)   Adding a catalyst to the reaction mixture does NOT favour CH_4. A catalyst added to the reaction mixture only speeds up the reaction, it does not change the equilibrium concentration.

        (f)   Adding neon gas to the reaction mixture does NOT favour CH_4. Adding an inert gas to a reaction mixture at a fixed volume has no effect on the equilibrium.

Cumulative Problems

14.71   (a)   To find the value of K for the new equation, combine the two given equations to yield the new equation. Reverse equation 1, and use $1/K_1$ and then add to equation 2. To find K for equation 3 use $(1/K_1)(K_2)$.

$HbO_2(aq)$	$\rightleftharpoons$	$Hb(aq) + O_2(aq)$	$K_1 = 1/1.8$
$Hb(aq) + CO(aq)$	$\rightleftharpoons$	$HbCO(aq)$	$K_2 = 306$
$HbO_2(aq) + CO(aq)$	$\rightleftharpoons$	$HbCO(aq) + O_2(aq)$	$K_3 = K_1K_2 = (1/1.8)(306) = 170$

(b)   **Given:** $O_2 = 20\%$, $CO = 0.10\%$ **Find:** the ratio $\dfrac{[HbCO]}{[HbO_2]}$

Conceptual Plan: Determine the equilibrium expression and then determine $\dfrac{[HbCO]}{[HbO_2]}$

Solution: $K = \dfrac{[HbCO][O_2]}{[HbO_2][CO]}$ $170 = \dfrac{[HbCO](20.0)}{[HbO_2](0.10)}$ $\dfrac{[HbCO]}{[HbO_2]} = 170\left(\dfrac{0.10}{20.0}\right) = \dfrac{0.85}{1.0}$

Since the ratio is almost 1:1, 0.10% CO will replace about 50% of the O_2 in the blood. The CO blocks the uptake of O_2 by the blood and is therefore highly toxic.

14.73   (a)   **Given:** 4.45 g CO_2, 10.0 L, 1200 K, 2.00 g C, $K = 48.3$ **Find:** Total pressure

Conceptual Plan: g CO_2 → mol CO_2 and g C → mol C and then determine Limiting Reactant

$$\frac{1 \text{ mol } CO_2}{44.01 \text{ g } CO_2} \qquad \frac{1 \text{ mol } C}{12.01 \text{ g } C}$$

and then mol CO_2 → $P\ CO_2$. Prepare an ICE table, represent the change with

$$PV = nRT$$

x, **sum the table, determine the equilibrium values, put the equilibrium values in the equilibrium expression, and solve for** *x*.

Solution: $CO_2(g) + C(s) \rightleftharpoons 2\ CO(g)$

$$4.45 \text{ g } CO_2 \times \frac{1 \text{ mol}}{44.01 \text{ g } CO_2} = 0.1011 \text{ mol } CO_2 \quad 2.00 \text{ g } C \times \frac{1 \text{ mol}}{12.01 \text{ g } C} = 0.1665 \text{ mol } C$$

Since the stoichiometry is 1:1, the CO_2 is the limiting reactant.

$$P_{CO_2} = \frac{(0.1011 \text{ mol})\left(0.08314 \dfrac{\text{bar L}}{\text{mol K}}\right)(1200 \text{ K})}{10.0 \text{ L}} = 1.009 \text{ bar}$$

	$CO_2(g) + C(s)$	$\rightleftharpoons$	$2\ CO(g)$
	P_{CO_2}		P_{CO}
I	1.01		0
C	-*x*		+2*x*
E	1.01 - *x*		2*x*

The reaction will proceed to the right by *x*.

$K = \dfrac{P_{CO}^2}{P_{CO_2}} = \dfrac{(2x)^2}{(1.01 - x)} = 48.3$. Solve using the quadratic equation, found in Appendix I.

$x = 0.937$ bar

$P_{CO_2} = 1.01 \text{ bar} - 0.937 \text{ bar} = 0.073 \text{ bar}$ $P_{CO} = 2(0.937 \text{ bar}) = 1.87 \text{ bar}$

P total = 1.95 bar

Check: Plug the values for the partial pressure into the equilibrium expression: $\dfrac{(1.87)^2}{0.073} = 48$, which is the value of the equilibrium constant.

(b)   **Given:** 4.45 g CO_2, 10.0 L, 1200 K, 0.50 g C, $K = 5.78$ **Find:** Total pressure

Conceptual Plan: g CO_2 → mol CO_2 and g C → mol C and then determine Limiting Reactant

$$\frac{1 \text{ mol } CO_2}{44.01 \text{ g } CO_2} \qquad \frac{1 \text{ mol } C}{12.01 \text{ g } C}$$

and then mol CO_2 → P_{CO_2}, and mol C → mol CO → P_{CO}

$$PV = nRT \qquad\qquad PV = nRT$$

Solution: $CO_2(g) + C(s) \rightleftharpoons 2\ CO(g)$

$$4.45 \text{ g } CO_2 \times \frac{1 \text{ mol}}{44.01 \text{ g } CO_2} = 0.1011 \text{ mol } CO_2 \quad 0.50 \text{ g } C \times \frac{1 \text{ mol}}{12.01 \text{ g } C} = 0.0416 \text{ mol } C$$

Since the stoichiometry is 1:1, the C is the limiting reactant; therefore, the moles of CO formed will be determined from the reaction, not the equilibrium.

$$0.0416 \text{ mol } C \times \frac{2 \text{ mol } CO}{1 \text{ mol } C} = 0.0832 \text{ mol } CO$$

	$CO_2(g) + C(s)$		$\rightleftharpoons$	$2\ CO(g)$
I	0.1011	0.0416		0
C	-0.0416	-0.0416		+2(0.0416)
E	0.0595	0		0.0832

$$P_{CO_2} = \frac{(0.0595 \text{ mol})\left(0.08314 \frac{\text{bar L}}{\text{mol K}}\right)(1200 \text{ K})}{10.0 \text{ L}} = 0.593 \text{ bar}$$

$$P_{CO} = \frac{(0.0832 \text{ mol})\left(0.08314 \frac{\text{bar L}}{\text{mol K}}\right)(1200 \text{ K})}{10.0 \text{ L}} = 0.830 \text{ bar}$$

$P_{total} = 0.593 + 0.830 = 1.42 \text{ bar}$

Check: The pressure is less than the equilibrium pressure, which is reasonable since the C was the limiting reactant.

14.75   **Given:** $V = 10.0$ L, $T = 650$K, 1.0 g MgO, $P_{CO_2} = 0.0260$ bar, $K = 0.042$
Find: mass $MgCO_3$ when volume is 0.100 L
Conceptual Plan: P (10.0L) $\rightarrow$ P(0.100L). **Prepare an ICE table, represent the change with x, sum the table, determine the equilibrium value, put the equilibrium values in the equilibrium expression, and solve for x. Then determine moles CO_2, the limiting reactant, and the mass of $MgCO_3$ formed.**

$$P_1V_1=P_2V_2 \quad PV=nRT$$

$P_1V_1 = P_2V_2 \quad (0.0260 \text{ bar})(10.0 \text{ L}) = (x)(0.100 \text{ L}) \quad x = 2.60 \text{ bar}$

$$MgCO_3(s) \leftrightarrows MgO(s) + CO_2(g)$$

I			2.60
C			-x
E			2.60 - x

$K = P_{CO_2} = 0.042 = 2.60 - x \quad x = 2.558 \text{ bar}$

$$n_{CO_2} = \frac{(2.558 \text{ bar})0.100 \text{ L}}{\left(0.08314 \frac{\text{bar L}}{\text{mol K}}\right)(650 \text{ K})} = 0.004733 \text{ mol } CO_2 \quad 1.0 \text{ g MgO} \times \frac{1 \text{ mol}}{40.30 \text{ g MgO}} = 0.0248 \text{ mol MgO}$$

Therefore, CO_2 is the limiting reactant and produces 0.004733 mol $MgCO_3$.

$$0.004733 \text{ mol MgCO}_3 \times \frac{84.31 \text{ g MgCO}_3}{1 \text{ mol MgCO}_3} = 0.40 \text{ g MgCO}_3$$

14.77   **Given:** $C_2H_4(g) + Cl_2(g) \leftrightarrows C_2H_4Cl_2(g)$ is exothermic **Find:** Which of the following will maximize $C_2H_4Cl_2$?

(a)   Increasing the reaction volume will not maximize $C_2H_4Cl_2$. The chemical equation has 1 mole of gas on the right and 2 moles of gas on the left. Increasing the volume of the reaction mixture decreases the pressure and causes the reaction to shift to the left (toward the side with more moles of gas particles).

(b)   Removing $C_2H_4Cl_2$ as it forms will maximize $C_2H_4Cl_2$. Removing the $C_2H_4Cl_2$ will decrease the concentration of $C_2H_4Cl_2$ and will cause the reaction to shift to the right, producing more $C_2H_4Cl_2$.

(c)   Lowering the reaction temperature will maximize $C_2H_4Cl_2$. The reaction is exothermic so we can think of heat as a product. Lowering the temperature will cause the reaction to shift to the right, producing more $C_2H_4Cl_2$.

(d)   Adding Cl_2 will maximize $C_2H_4Cl_2$. Adding Cl_2 increases the concentration of Cl_2 so the reaction shifts to the right, which will produce more $C_2H_4Cl_2$.

14.79   **Given:** Reaction 1 at equilibrium: $P_{H_2} = 0.170$ bar, $P_{I_2} = 0.120$ bar, $P_{HI} = 1.26$ bar. Reaction 2: $P_{H_2} = P_{I_2} = 0.135$ bar, $P_{HI} = 1.10$ bar **Find:** Is reaction 2 at equilibrium? If not, what is the P_{HI} at equilibrium? **Conceptual Plan: Use equilibrium partial pressures to determine K. Use K to determine if reaction 2 is at equilibrium. Prepare an ICE table, calculate Q, compare Q and K, predict the direction of the reaction, represent the change with x, sum the table, determine the equilibrium values, put the equilibrium values in the equilibrium expression, and solve for x. Determine P_{HI}.**

Solution: $H_2(g) + I_2(g) \leftrightarrows 2 HI(g)$

	P_{H_2}	P_{I_2}	P_{HI}
Reaction 1:	0.170	0.120	1.26

$$K = \frac{P_{HI}^2}{P_{H_2}P_{I_2}} = \frac{(1.26)^2}{(0.170)(0.120)} = 77.\underline{8}2$$

$$Q = \frac{P_{HI}^2}{P_{H_2}P_{I_2}} = \frac{1.10^2}{(0.135)(0.135)} = 66.\underline{3}9. \quad Q < K \text{ so the reaction shifts to the right.}$$

$$H_2(g) \quad + \quad I_2(g) \quad \leftrightarrows \quad 2\,HI(g)$$

Reaction 2:	P_{H_2}	P_{I_2}	P_{HI}
I	0.135	0.135	1.10
C	$-x$	$-x$	$+2x$
E	0.135 - x	0.135 - x	1.10 + 2x

$$K = \frac{P_{HI}^2}{P_{H_2}P_{I_2}} = \frac{(1.10 + 2x)^2}{(0.135 - x)(0.135 - x)} = 77.\underline{8}2$$

$$\sqrt{\frac{(1.10 + 2x)^2}{(0.135 - x)(0.135 - x)}} = \sqrt{77.\underline{8}2}$$

$$\frac{(1.10 + 2x)}{(0.135 - x)} = 8.\underline{8}21$$

$$x = 0.00839$$

$$P_{H_2} = P_{I_2} = 0.135 - x = 0.135 - 0.00839 = 0.12\underline{6}6 \text{ bar;}$$

$$P_{HI} = 1.10 + 2x = 1.10 + 2(0.0433) = 1.117 \text{ bar}$$

Check: Plug the values into the equilibrium expression:

$$K = \frac{(1.117)^2}{(0.1266)^2} = 77.\underline{8}5. \text{ This value is close to the original equilbirium constant.}$$

14.81   **Given:** 200.0-L container; 1.27 kg N_2; 0.310 kg H_2; 725 K; $K = 5.3 \times 10^{-5}$ **Find:** mass in g of NH_3 and % yield
Conceptual Plan: $K_p \rightarrow K_c$ and then $\text{kg} \rightarrow \text{g} \rightarrow \text{mol} \rightarrow \text{mol L}^{-1}$ and then prepare an ICE table. Represent the

$$K_p = K_c(RT)^{\Delta n} \qquad \frac{1000\,\text{g}}{\text{kg}} \qquad \frac{\text{g}}{\text{molar mass}} \qquad \frac{\text{mol}}{\text{vol}}$$

change with x, sum the table, determine the equilibrium values, put the equilibrium values in the equilibrium expression, and solve for x. Determine $[NH_3]$. Then $\text{mol L}^{-1} \rightarrow \text{mol} \rightarrow \text{g}$ and then determine

$$\text{mol L}^{-1} \times \text{vol} \quad \text{mol} \times \text{molar mass}$$

theoretical yield $NH_3 \rightarrow$ % yield.

determine limiting reactant $\dfrac{\text{actual yield}}{\text{theoretical yield}}$

Solution: $K_p = K_c(RT)^{\Delta n}$ $K_c = \dfrac{K_p}{(RT)^{\Delta n}} = \dfrac{5.3 \times 10^{-5}}{\left(\left(0.08314\,\dfrac{\text{bar L}}{\text{mol K}}\right)(725\text{K})\right)^{-2}} = 0.19\underline{2}6$

$$n_{N_2} = 1.27\,\text{kg N}_2 \times \frac{1000\,\text{g}}{\text{kg}} \times \frac{1\,\text{mol N}_2}{28.00\,\text{g N}_2} = 45.\underline{3}57\,\text{mol N}_2 \quad [N_2] = \frac{45.357\,\text{mol}}{200.0\,\text{L}} = 0.226\underline{7}8$$

$$n_{H_2} = 0.310\,\text{kg H}_2 \times \frac{1000\,\text{g}}{\text{kg}} \times \frac{1\,\text{mol H}_2}{2.016\,\text{g H}_2} = 153.77\,\text{mol H}_2 \quad [H_2] = \frac{153.77\,\text{mol}}{200.0\,\text{L}} = 0.768\underline{8}5$$

$$N_2(g) \quad + \quad 3\,H_2(g) \quad \leftrightarrows \quad 2\,NH_3(g)$$

Reaction 1:	$[N_2]$	$[H_2]$	$[NH_3]$
I	0.22$\underline{6}$8	0.76$\underline{8}$9	0
C	$-x$	$-3x$	$+2x$
E	0.2268 - x	0.7689 - 3x	2x

Reaction shifts to the right.

$$K = \frac{[NH_3]^2}{[N_2][H_2]^3} = \frac{(2x)^2}{(0.2268 - x)(0.7689 - 3x)^3} = 0.19\underline{2}6$$

Assume x is small compared to 0.2268 and 3x is small compared to 0.7689.

$$\frac{(2x)^2}{(0.2268)(0.7689)^3} = 0.19\underline{2}6 \; x = 0.07045 \qquad x = 0.07045 \text{ is the solution to the problem.}$$

Check assumptions: $\dfrac{0.07045}{0.2268} \times 100\% = 31.0$ not valid and $\dfrac{3(0.07045)}{0.7689} \times 100\% = 27.5\%$

Use method of successive substitution to solve for x. This yields $x = 0.0465$.

$[NH_3] = 2x = 2(0.0465) = 0.0930$ mol L^{-1}

Check: Plug the values into the equilibrium expression:

$$K = \frac{(0.0930)^2}{(0.2268 - 0.0465)(0.7689 - 3(0.0465))^3} = 0.1924.$$

This value is close to the original equilibrium constant.

Determine grams NH$_3$: $0.0930 \; \dfrac{\overline{\text{mol NH}_3}}{\text{L}} \times \dfrac{200.0 \, \text{L}}{} \times \dfrac{17.02 \text{ g NH}_3}{\overline{\text{mol NH}_3}} = 316.6 \text{ g} = 3.2 \times 10^2 \text{ g}$

Determine the theoretical yield: Determine the limiting reactant:

$1.27 \, \overline{\text{kg N}_2} \times \dfrac{1000 \, \text{g}}{\text{kg}} \times \dfrac{1 \, \overline{\text{mol N}_2}}{28.0 \, \overline{\text{g N}_2}} \times \dfrac{2 \, \overline{\text{mol NH}_3}}{1 \, \overline{\text{mol N}_2}} \times \dfrac{17.02 \text{ g NH}_3}{\overline{\text{mol NH}_3}} = 1544 \text{ g NH}_3$

$0.310 \, \overline{\text{kg H}_2} \times \dfrac{1000 \, \text{g}}{\text{kg}} \times \dfrac{1 \, \overline{\text{mol H}_2}}{2.016 \, \overline{\text{g H}_2}} \times \dfrac{2 \, \overline{\text{mol NH}_3}}{3 \, \overline{\text{mol H}_2}} \times \dfrac{17.02 \text{ g NH}_3}{\overline{\text{mol NH}_3}} = 1745 \text{ g NH}_3$

N_2 produces the least amount of NH$_3$, therefore, it is the limiting reactant and the theoretical yield is 1.54×10^3 g NH$_3$.

$\% \text{ yield} = \dfrac{3.2 \times 10^2 \, \text{g}}{1.54 \times 10^3 \, \text{g}} \times 100 = 21\%$

14.83 **Given:** At equilibrium: $P_{CO} = 0.30$ bar; $P_{Cl_2} = 0.10$ bar; $P_{COCl_2} = 0.60$ bar, add 0.40 bar Cl$_2$
Find: P_{CO} when system returns to equilibrium
Conceptual Plan: Use equilibrium partial pressures to determine K. For the new conditions prepare an ICE table, represent the change with x, sum the table, determine the equilibrium values, put the equilibrium values in the equilibrium expression, and solve for x. Determine P_{CO}.
Solution: $CO(g) + Cl_2(g) \leftrightharpoons COCl_2(g)$
Condition 1: $\begin{array}{ccc} P_{CO} & P_{Cl_2} & P_{COCl_2} \\ 0.30 & 0.10 & 0.60 \end{array}$

$$K = \frac{P_{COCl_2}}{P_{CO} P_{Cl_2}} = \frac{(0.60)}{(0.30)(0.10)} = 20.$$

 $CO(g) + Cl_2(g) \leftrightharpoons COCl_2(g)$

Condition 2:

	P_{CO}	P_{Cl_2}	P_{COCl_2}
I	0.30	0.10+0.40	0.60
C	-x	-x	+x
E	0.30 - x	0.50 - x	0.60 + x

Reaction shifts to the right because the concentration of Cl$_2$ was increased.

$$K = \frac{P_{COCl_2}}{P_{CO} P_{Cl_2}} = \frac{(0.60 + x)}{(0.30 - x)(0.50 - x)} = 20$$

$20x^2 - 17x + 2.4 = 0$

$\dfrac{-b \pm \sqrt{b^2 - 4ac}}{2a} = \dfrac{-(-17) \pm \sqrt{(-17)^2 - 4(20)(2.4)}}{2(20)}$

$x = 0.67$ or 0.18, so $x = 0.18$.

$P_{CO} = 0.30 - 0.18 = 0.12$ bar; $P_{Cl_2} = 0.50 - 0.18 = 0.32$; $P_{COCl_2} = 0.60 + 0.18 = 0.78$ bar

Check: Plug the values into the equilibrium expression:

$$K = \frac{(0.78)}{(0.12)(0.32)} = 20.3 = 20. \text{ This is the same as the original equilibrium constant.}$$

14.85 **Given:** $K = 0.76$; P_{total} at equilibrium $= 1.00$ **Find:** $P_{initial}$ CCl$_4$
Conceptual Plan: Prepare an ICE table, represent the P_{CCl_4} with A and the change with x, sum the table, determine the equilibrium values, use the total pressure, and solve for A in terms of x. Determine partial pressure of each at equilibrium, use the equilibrium expression to determine x, and then determine A.
Solution: $CCl_4(g) \leftrightharpoons C(s) + 2 Cl_2(g)$

	P_{CCl_4}	P_C	P_{Cl_2}
I	A	constant	0
C	-x		+2x
E	$A - x$		2x

$$P_{Total} = P_{CCl_4} + P_{Cl_2} \quad 1.0 = A - x + 2x \quad A = 1.00 - x$$

$$P_{CCl_4} = (A - x) = (1.00 - x) - x = 1.00 - 2x; \; P_{Cl_2} = (2x)$$

$$K = \frac{P_{Cl_2}^2}{P_{CCl_4}} = \frac{(2x)^2}{(1.00 - 2x)} = 0.76$$

$$4x^2 + 1.52x - 0.76 = 0 \quad x = 0.285 \text{ or } -0.665, \text{ so } x = 0.2\underline{8}5$$

$$A = 1.00 - x = 1.00 - 0.285 = 0.715 = 0.72 \text{ bar}$$

Check: Plug values into equilibrium expression:

$$K = \frac{P_{Cl_2}^2}{P_{CCl_4}} = \frac{(2x)^2}{(A - x)} = \frac{(2(0.285))^2}{(0.715 - 0.285)} = 0.755 = 0.76. \text{ This is the original equilibrium constant.}$$

14.87   **Given:** $V = 0.654$ L, $T = 1000$ K, $K = 3.9 \times 10^{-2}$ **Find:** mass CaO as equilibrium

Conceptual Plan: $K \rightarrow P_{CO_2} \rightarrow n_{(CO_2)} \rightarrow n_{(CaO)} \rightarrow g$

$$\quad\quad\quad\quad\quad\quad\quad\quad PV = nRT \quad\; \text{stoichiometry} \quad\; g = n(\text{molar mass})$$

Solution: Since $CaCO_3$ and CaO are solids, they are not included in the equilibrium expression.

$$K = P_{CO_2} = 3.9 \times 10^{-2} \quad n = \frac{PV}{RT} = \frac{(3.9 \times 10^{-2} \, \cancel{\text{bar}})(0.654 \, \cancel{L})}{\left(0.08314 \, \dfrac{\cancel{\text{bar}} \cdot \cancel{L}}{\text{mol} \cdot \cancel{K}}\right)(1000 \, \cancel{K})} = 3.0\underline{6}7 \times 10^{-4} \text{ mol } CO_2$$

$$3.0\underline{6}7 \times 10^{-4} \; \cancel{\text{mol } CO_2} \times \frac{1 \; \cancel{\text{mol CaO}}}{1 \; \cancel{\text{mol } CO_2}} \times \frac{56.1 \text{ g CaO}}{1 \; \cancel{\text{mol CaO}}} = 0.0172 \text{ g} = 0.017 \text{ g CaO}$$

Check: The small value of K would give a small amount of products, so we would not expect to have a large mass of CaO formed.

14.89   **Given:** $K = 3.10$, Initial $P_{CO} = 215$ mbar, $P_{Cl_2} = 245$ mbar **Find:** mole fraction $COCl_2$

Conceptual Plan: P in mbar $\rightarrow$ P in bar. **Prepare an ICE table, represent the change with x, sum the table,**

$$\quad\quad\quad\quad\quad\quad\quad\quad\quad\quad \frac{1 \text{ bar}}{1000 \text{ mbar}}$$

determine the equilibrium values, use the total pressure, and solve for mole fraction.

$$\quad\quad\quad\quad\quad\quad\quad\quad\quad\quad\quad\quad\quad\quad\quad\quad\quad\quad \frac{P_{COCl_2}}{P_{Total}}$$

Solution: $P_{CO} = (215 \; \cancel{\text{mbar}}) \left(\dfrac{1 \text{ bar}}{1000 \; \cancel{\text{mbar}}}\right) = 0.215 \text{ bar} \quad P_{Cl_2} = (245 \; \cancel{\text{mbar}}) \left(\dfrac{1 \text{ bar}}{1000 \; \cancel{\text{mbar}}}\right) = 0.245 \text{ bar}$

	$CO(g)$	$+ \; Cl_2(g)$	$\rightleftharpoons$	$COCl_2(g)$	
I	0.215	0.245		0	$Q < K$ so reaction shifts to the right.
C	-x	-x		+x	
E	0.215 - x	0.245 - x		x	

$$K = \frac{P_{COCl_2}}{P_{CO}P_{Cl_2}} = \frac{x}{(0.215 - x)(0.245 - x)} = 3.10$$

$$x = 0.7082 \text{ or } 0.074\underline{3}8, \text{ so } x = 0.074\underline{3}8$$

$$P_{Cl_2} = 0.245 - 0.07438 = 0.1706 \text{ bar}, P_{COCl_2} = 0.07438 \text{ bar}, P_{CO} = 0.215 - 0.07438 = 0.1406 \text{ bar}$$

$$\text{mole fraction } COCl_2 = \frac{P_{COCl_2}}{P_{CO} + P_{Cl_2} + P_{COCl_2}} = \frac{0.07438}{0.07438 + 0.1406 + 0.1706} = 0.192$$

Check: Plug the equilibrium pressures into the equilibrium expression:

$$K = \frac{0.0743}{(0.141)(0.171)} = 3.081 \sim 3.10. \text{ This is the equilibrium constant, so the answer is reasonable.}$$

Challenge Problems

14.91   (a)   **Given:** $P_{NO} = 522$ mbar, $P_{O_2} = 421$ mbar; at equilibrium, $P_{total} = 748$ mbar **Find:** K

Conceptual Plan: **Prepare an ICE table, represent the change with x, sum the table, determine the equilibrium values, use the total pressure, and solve for x.** mbar $\rightarrow$ bar $\rightarrow$ K

Solution:

	$2 \, NO(g) \;+$	$O_2(g)$	$\rightleftharpoons$	$2 \, NO_2(g)$
	P_{NO}	P_{O_2}		P_{NO_2}
I	522 mbar	421 mbar		0
C	-2x	-x		+2x
E	522 - 2x	421 - x		2x

$P_{Total} = P_{NO} + P_{O_2} + P_{NO_2}$ $748 = 522 - 2x + (421 - x) + 2x$

$x = 195$ mbar $P_{NO} = (522 - 2(195) = 132$ mbar;

$P_{O_2} = (421 - 195) = 226$ mbar; $P_{NO_2} = 2(195) = 390$ mbar

$P_{NO} = 132 \text{ mbar} \times \dfrac{1 \text{ bar}}{1000 \text{ mbar}} = 0.132$ bar; $P_{O_2} = 226 \text{ mbar} \times \dfrac{1 \text{ bar}}{1000 \text{ mbar}} = 0.226$ bar;

$P_{NO_2} = 390 \text{ mbar} \times \dfrac{1 \text{ bar}}{1000 \text{ mbar}} = 0.390$ bar

$K = \dfrac{P_{NO_2}^2}{P_{NO}^2 P_{O_2}} = \dfrac{(0.390)^2}{(0.132)^2(0.226)} = 38.\underline{6}25 = 38.6$

(b)   **Given:** $= P_{NO} = 255$ mbar, $P_{O_2} = 185$ mbar, $K = 38.6$ **Find:** equilibrium P_{NO_2}
Conceptual Plan:
mbar $\rightarrow$ bar and then prepare an ICE table. Represent the change with x, sum the table,
$$\dfrac{1 \text{ bar}}{1000 \text{ mbar}}$$
determine the equilibrium values, put the equilibrium values in the equilibrium expression, and
solve for x. Determine P_{NO_2}.

Solution: $P_{NO} = 255 \text{ mbar} \times \dfrac{1 \text{ bar}}{1000 \text{ mbar}} = 0.255$ bar $P_{O_2} = 185 \text{ mbar} \times \dfrac{1 \text{ bar}}{1000 \text{ mbar}} = 0.185$ bar

	$2 \text{ NO}(g)$ +	$\text{O}_2(g)$ $\leftrightharpoons$	$2 \text{ NO}_2(g)$
	P_{NO}	P_{O_2}	P_{NO_2}
I	0.255	0.185	0
C	-2x	-x	+2x
E	0.255 - 2x	0.185 - x	2x

$K = \dfrac{P_{NO_2}^2}{P_{NO}^2 P_{O_2}} = \dfrac{(2x)^2}{(0.255 - 2x)^2(0.185 - x)} = 38.6$

Solve using successive approximations or a cubic equation calculator found on the internet.

$x = 0.084\underline{5}6$ $P_{NO_2} = 2x = 2(0.084\underline{5}6) = 0.169\underline{1}$ bar

Check: Plug the values into the equilibrium expression:

$K = \dfrac{(0.1691)^2}{(0.08588)^2(0.1004)} = 38.\underline{6}16 = 38.6$. This is the original equilibrium constant.

14.93   **Given:** P_{NOCl} at equilibrium $= 115$ mbar; $K = 0.27$, $T = 700$ K   **Find:** initial pressure NO, Cl_2
Conceptual Plan: mbar $\rightarrow$ bar and then prepare an ICE table. **Represent the change with x, sum the table,**
$$\dfrac{1 \text{ bar}}{1000 \text{ mbar}}$$
**determine the equilibrium values, put the equilibrium values in the equilibrium expression, and determine
initial pressure.**

Solution: $115 \text{ mbar} \times \dfrac{1 \text{ bar}}{1000 \text{ mbar}} = 0.115$ bar

	$2 \text{ NO}(g) +$	$Cl_2(g) \leftrightharpoons$	$2 \text{ NOCl}(g)$
	P_{NO}	P_{Cl_2}	P_{NOCl}
I	A	A	0
C	-2x	-x	+2x
E	A - 2x	A - x	0.115
	A - 0.115	A - 0.0756	

Let A = initial pressure of NO and Cl_2.

$2x = 0.115$, so $x = 0.0575$

$K = \dfrac{P_{NOCL}^2}{P_{NO}^2 P_{Cl_2}} = \dfrac{(0.115)^2}{(A - 0.115)^2(A - 0.0575)} = 0.27$

Solve using successive approximations or a cubic equation calculator found on the internet.

$A = 0.463$

$P_{NO} = P_{Cl_2} = A = 0.463$ bar

Check: Plug the values into the equilibrium expression:

$$K = \frac{P_{NOCL}^2}{P_{NO}^2 P_{Cl_2}} = \frac{(0.115)^2}{(0.463 - 0.115)^2(0.463 - 0.0575)} = 0.269.$$

This is the same as the original equilibrium constant

14.95   **Given:** $P = 0.750$ atm, density $= 0.520$ g/L, $T = 337°C$ **Find:** K_c

Conceptual Plan: Prepare an ICE table, represent the P_{CCl_4} with A and the change with x, sum the table, determine the equilibrium values, use the total pressure, and solve for A in terms of x. Determine partial pressure of each at equilibrium in terms of x, use the density to determine the apparent molar mass, and

$$d = \frac{PM}{RT}$$

then use the mole fraction (in terms of P) and the molar mass of each gas to determine x.

$$\chi_A = \frac{P_A}{P_{Total}}$$

Solution: $2\,NO_2(g) \rightleftharpoons 2\,NO(g) + O_2(g)$

	P_{NO_2}	P_{NO}	P_{O_2}
I	A	0	0
C	$-2x$	$+2x$	$+x$
E	$A - 2x$	$2x$	x

$P_{Total} = P_{NO_2} + P_{NO} + P_{O_2}$ $0.750 = A - 2x + 2x + x$ $A = 0.750 - x$

$P_{NO_2} = (A - 2x) = (0.750 - x) - 2x = (0.750 - 3x)$; $P_{NO} = (2x)$; $P_{O_2} = x$

$$d = \frac{PM}{RT} \quad M = \frac{dRT}{P} = \frac{\left(0.520\,\frac{g}{L}\right)\left(0.0821\,\frac{L \cdot atm}{mol \cdot K}\right)(610\,K)}{0.750\,atm} = 34.72\,g/mol$$

$$M = \chi_{NO_2}M_{NO_2} + \chi_{NO}M_{NO} + \chi_{O_2}M_{O_2} = \frac{P_{NO_2}}{P_{total}}M_{NO_2} + \frac{P_{NO}}{P_{total}}M_{NO} + \frac{P_{O_2}}{P_{total}}M_{O_2}$$

$P_{Total}M = P_{NO_2}M_{NO_2} + P_{NO}M_{NO} + P_{O_2}M_{O_2}$

$(0.750)(34.7) = (0.750 - 3x)(46.0) + 2x(30.0) + x(32.0)$

$x = 0.184$

$$K_p = \frac{P_{NO}^2 P_{O_2}}{P_{NO_2}^2} = \frac{(2x)^2(x)}{(0.750 - 3x)} = \frac{(2(0.184))^2(0.184)}{(0.750 - 3(0.184))^2} = 0.6356$$

$$K_p = K_c(RT)^{\Delta n} \quad 0.6356 = K_c((0.0821\,\frac{L \cdot atm}{mol \cdot K})(610K))^1$$

$$K_c = 1.27 \times 10^{-2}$$

14.97   (a)   **Given:** $K = 1.8 \times 10^{-10}$ **Find:** concentrations of Ag^+ and Cl^- at equilibrium

Conceptual Plan: Prepare an ICE table, represent the change with x, sum the table, determine the equilibrium values, and solve for x.

Solution: $AgCl(s) \rightleftharpoons Ag^+(aq) + Cl^-(aq)$

	[AgCl]	[Ag$^+$]	[Cl$^-$]
I	constant	0	0
C		$+x$	$+x$
E		x	x

$K = [Ag^+][Cl^-] = (x)(x) = 1.8 \times 10^{-10}$ $x = 1.34 \times 10^{-5} = [Ag^+] = [Cl^-] = 1.3 \times 10^{-5}$ mol L^{-1}

(b)   **Given:** $K = 1.6 \times 10^7$, AgCl(s) in 0.100 mol L^{-1} NH$_3$ **Find:** [Cl$^-$] at equilibrium

Conceptual Plan: Combine the reaction from part (a) with the given reaction to get an overall reaction that contains $NH_3(aq)$ and $AgCl(s)$. Prepare an ICE table. Represent the change with x, sum the table, determine the equilibrium values, put the equilibrium values in the equilibrium expression, and solve for x. Determine the equilibrium concentration of Cl$^-$.

Solution: $AgCl(s) \rightleftharpoons \cancel{Ag^+(aq)} + Cl^-(aq)$ $K_1 = 1.8 \times 10^{-10}$

$\underline{\cancel{Ag^+(aq)} + 2NH_3(aq) \rightleftharpoons Ag(NH_3)_2^+(aq)}$ $K_2 = 1.6 \times 10^7$

$AgCl(s) + 2NH_3(aq) \rightleftharpoons Ag(NH_3)_2^+(aq) + Cl^-(aq)$ $K = K_1K_2 = 2.88 \times 10^{-3}$

$$AgCl(s) + 2NH_3(aq) \rightleftharpoons Ag(NH_3)_2^+(aq) + Cl^-(aq)$$

	[AgCl]	[NH$_3$]	[Ag(NH$_3$)$_2^+$]	[Cl$^-$]
I	constant	0.100	0	0
C		$-2x$	$+x$	$+x$
E		0.100 - 2x	$+x$	$+x$

$$K = \frac{[Cl^-][Ag(NH_3)_2^+]}{[NH_3]^2} = 2.\underline{8}8 \times 10^{-3} = \frac{(x)(x)}{(0.100 - 2x)^2}.$$ Simplify by taking the square root of both sides.

$$\sqrt{2.88 \times 10^{-3}} = 0.05\underline{3}6656 = \frac{(x)}{(0.100 - 2x)}.$$ Solve for x. $(0.05\underline{3}6656)(0.100 - 2x) = x$

$x = 4.\underline{8}46 \times 10^{-3} = [Cl^-] = 4.8 \times 10^{-3}$ mol L^{-1}

Check: The concentration of Cl$^-$ in the solution with ammonia is higher than the concentration of Cl$^-$ in aqueous solution (1.34×10^{-5} mol L^{-1}), supporting the statement that the addition of ammonia increases the solubility of AgCl(s).

Conceptual Problems

14.99   For reaction mixture d, the x *is small* approximation is most likely to apply. Since the equilibrium constant is very small, at equilibrium the concentration of products will be small. In mixtures b and c, you would have to lose a large amount of product and the x *is small* approximation will not apply. In mixture a, the initial concentration is smaller than in mixture d, so while it is a good approximation it is a better approximation for mixture d.

14.101 $K_p = 0.50$ means that P(products) < P(reactants). If the reactants and products are in their standard states, then P of each reactant and product = 1.0. So $Q > K$ and to reach equilibrium the reaction will have to shift to the left.

15 Acids and Bases

15.1 The pain of heartburn is caused by hydrochloric acid, which is excreted in the stomach to kill microorganisms and activate enzymes that break down food. The hydrochloric acid can sometimes back up out of the stomach and into the esophagus, a phenomenon known as acid reflux. When hydrochloric acid comes in contact with the lining of the esophagus, the H^+ ions irritate the esophageal tissues, resulting in a burning sensation. The simplest way to relieve mild heartburn is to swallow repeatedly. Saliva contains bicarbonate ion (HCO_3^-) that acts as a base and, when swallowed, neutralizes some of the acid in the esophagus. Heartburn can also be treated with antacids such as Tums, milk of magnesia, or Mylanta. These over-the-counter medications contain more base than does saliva and therefore do a better job of neutralizing the esophageal acid.

15.3 A carboxylic acid is an organic acid that contains the following group of atoms: $H-O-\overset{\overset{\textstyle O}{\|}}{C}-$. Carboxylic acids are often found in substances derived from living organisms. Examples include citric acid, malic acid, and acetic acid.

15.5 The hydronium ion is H_3O^+. In water, H^+ ions always associate with H_2O molecules to form hydronium ions and other associated species with the general formula $H(H_2O)_n^+$.

15.7 According to Huheey, "The differences between the various acid–base concepts are not concerned with which is right, but which is most convenient to use in a particular situation." There is no single correct definition; we use the definition that is best for a particular situation.

15.9 A conjugate acid–base pair are two substances related to each other by the transfer of a proton. In the reaction:

$NH_3(aq) + H_2O(l) \rightleftharpoons NH_4^+(aq) + OH^-(aq)$, the conjugate pairs are NH_3/NH_4^+ and H_2O/OH^-.

15.11 A diprotic acid is one that contains two ionizable protons. An example is H_2SO_4.

A triprotic acid is one that contains three ionizable protons. An example is H_3PO_4.

15.13 The autoionization of water is $H_2O(l) + H_2O(l) \rightleftharpoons H_3O^+(aq) + OH^-(aq)$
and has the ion product constant for water $K_w = [H_3O^+][OH^-]$.

It can also be written $H_2O(l) \rightleftharpoons H^+(aq) + OH^-(aq)$ and the ion product constant for water is $K_w = [H^+][OH^-]$.
At 25 $^\circ$C, $K_w = 1.0 \times 10^{-14}$.

15.15 We define pH as pH $= -\log[H_3O^+]$. At 25 $^\circ$C, an acidic solution has a pH < 7, a basic solution has a pH > 7, and a neutral solution has a pH $= 7$.

15.17 We can neglect the contribution of the autoionization of water to the H_3O^+ concentration in a solution of a strong or weak acid because it is negligible compared to the concentration from the acid itself. Even the weakest of the weak acids has an ionization constant that is four orders of magnitude larger than that of water.

15.19   The percent ionization is defined as percent ionization $= \dfrac{\text{concentration of ionized acid}}{\text{initial concentration of acid}} \times 100\%$. The percent
ionization of a weak acid decreases with the increasing concentration of the acid.

15.21 $B(aq) + H_2O(l) \rightleftharpoons BH^+(aq) + OH^-(aq)$

15.23   At 25 °C, the product of K_a for an acid and K_b for its conjugate base is $K_w = 1.0 \times 10^{-14}$.

15.25   For most polyprotic acids, K_{a_1} is much larger than K_{a_2}. Therefore, the amount of H_3O^+ contributed by the
first ionization step is much larger than that contributed by the second or third ionization step. In addition,
the production of H_3O^+ by the first step inhibits additional production of H_3O^+ by the second step because
of Le Châtelier's principle.

15.27   For an H—Y binary acid, the factors affecting the ease with which this hydrogen will be donated are the
polarity of the bond and the strength of the bond.

15.29   A Lewis acid is an electron pair acceptor. A Lewis base is an electron pair donor.

15.31   The combustion of fossil fuels produces oxides of sulfur and nitrogen, which react with oxygen and water
to form sulfuric and nitric acids. These acids then combine with rain to form acid rain. Acid rain is a significant problem in the more eastern parts of North America.

Problems by Topic
The Nature and Definitions of Acids and Bases

15.33   (a)   acid $HNO_3(aq) \rightarrow H^+(aq) + NO_3^-(aq)$

         (b)   acid $NH_4^+(aq) \rightleftharpoons H^+(aq) + NH_3(aq)$

         (c)   base $KOH(aq) \rightarrow K^+(aq) + OH^-(aq)$

         (d)   acid $HC_2H_3O_2(aq) \rightleftharpoons H^+(aq) + C_2H_3O_2^-(aq)$

15.35   (a)   Since H_2CO_3 donates a proton to H_2O, it is the acid. After H_2CO_3 donates the proton, it becomes
                HCO_3^-, the conjugate base. Since H_2O accepts a proton, it is the base. After H_2O accepts the proton,
                it becomes H_3O^+, the conjugate acid.

         (b)   Since H_2O donates a proton to NH_3, it is the acid. After H_2O donates the proton, it becomes OH^-, the
                conjugate base. Since NH_3 accepts a proton, it is the base. After NH_3 accepts the proton, it becomes
                NH_4^+, the conjugate acid.

         (c)   Since HNO_3 donates a proton to H_2O, it is the acid. After HNO_3 donates the proton, it becomes NO_3^-,
                the conjugate base. Since H_2O accepts a proton, it is the base. After H_2O accepts the proton, it becomes
                H_3O^+, the conjugate acid.

         (d)   Since H_2O donates a proton to C_5H_5N, it is the acid. After H_2O donates the proton, it becomes OH^-,
                the conjugate base. Since C_5H_5N accepts a proton, it is the base. After C_5H_5N accepts the proton, it
                becomes $C_5H_5NH^+$, the conjugate acid.

15.37   (a) Cl^- $HCl(aq) + H_2O(l) \rightarrow H_3O^+(aq) + Cl^-(aq)$

         (b) HSO_3^- $H_2SO_3(aq) + H_2O(l) \rightleftharpoons H_3O^+(aq) + HSO_3^-(aq)$

         (c) CHO_2^- $HCHO_2(aq) + H_2O(l) \rightleftharpoons H_3O^+(aq) + CHO_2^-(aq)$

         (d) F^- $HF(aq) + H_2O(l) \rightleftharpoons H_3O^+(aq) + F^-(aq)$

15.39 $H_2PO_4^- (aq) + H_2O(l) \rightleftharpoons H_3O^+ (aq) + HPO_4^{2-} (aq)$

          $H_2PO_4^- (aq) + H_2O(l) \rightleftharpoons H_3PO_4(aq) + OH^- (aq)$

Acid Strength and K_a

15.41   (a) HNO_3 is a strong acid.

          (b)   HCl is a strong acid.

          (c)   HBr is a strong acid.

          (d) H_2SO_3 is a weak acid. $H_2SO_3(aq) + H_2O(l) \rightleftharpoons H_3O^+(aq) + HSO_3^-(aq)$

                  $K_a = \dfrac{[H_3O^+][HSO_3^-]}{[H_2SO_3]}$

15.43   (a) contains no HA, 10 H^+, and 10 A^-

          (b) contains 3 HA, 3 H^+, and 7 A^-

          (c) contains 9 HA, 1 H^+, and 1 A^-

          So, solution a > solution b > solution c.

15.45   (a) F^- is a stronger base than Cl^-.
                  F^- is the conjugate base of HF (a weak acid), Cl^- is the conjugate base of HCl (a strong acid); the weaker the acid, the stronger the conjugate base.

          (b) NO_2^- is a stronger base than NO_3^-.
                  NO_2^- is the conjugate base of HNO_2 (a weak acid), NO_3^- is the conjugate base of HNO_3 (a strong acid); the weaker the acid, the stronger the conjugate base.

          (c) ClO^- is a stronger base than F^-.
                  F^- is the conjugate base of HF ($K_a = 3.5 \times 10^{-4}$), ClO^- is the conjugate base of HClO ($K_a = 2.9 \times 10^{-8}$), and HClO is the weaker acid; the weaker the acid, the stronger the conjugate base.

Autoionization of Water and pH

15.47   (a)   **Given:** $K_w = 1.0 \times 10^{-14}$, $[H_3O^+] = 1.2 \times 10^{-8}$ mol L^{-1} **Find:** $[OH^-]$
                  Conceptual Plan: $[H_3O^+] \rightarrow [OH^-]$
                           $K_w = 1.0 \times 10^{-14} = [H_3O^+][OH^-]$
                  Solution:
                  $K_w = 1.0 \times 10^{-14} = (1.2 \times 10^{-8})[OH^-]$
                  $[OH^-] = 8.3 \times 10^{-7}$ mol L^{-1}
                  $[OH^-] > [H_3O^+]$ so the solution is basic.

          (b)   **Given:** $K_w = 1.0 \times 10^{-14}$, $[H_3O^+] = 8.5 \times 10^{-5}$ mol L^{-1} **Find:** $[OH^-]$
                  Conceptual Plan: $[H_3O^+] \rightarrow [OH^-]$
                           $K_w = 1.0 \times 10^{-14} = [H_3O^+][OH^-]$
                  Solution:
                  $K_w = 1.0 \times 10^{-14} = (8.5 \times 10^{-5})[OH^-]$
                  $[OH^-] = 1.2 \times 10^{-10}$ mol L^{-1}
                  $[H_3O^+] > [OH^-]$ so the solution is acidic.

          (c)   **Given:** $K_w = 1.0 \times 10^{-14}$, $[H_3O^+] = 3.5 \times 10^{-2}$ mol L^{-1} **Find:** $[OH^-]$
                  Conceptual Plan: $[H_3O^+] \rightarrow [OH^-]$
                           $K_w = 1.0 \times 10^{-14} = [H_3O^+][OH^-]$

Solution:
$K_w = 1.0 \times 10^{-14} = (3.5 \times 10^{-2})[\text{OH}^-]$
$[\text{OH}^-] = 2.9 \times 10^{-13} \text{ mol L}^{-1}$
$[\text{H}_3\text{O}^+] > [\text{OH}^-]$ so the solution is acidic.

15.49　(a)　**Given:** $[\text{H}_3\text{O}^+] = 1.7 \times 10^{-8} \text{ mol L}^{-1}$ **Find:** pH and pOH
　　　Conceptual Plan: $[\text{H}_3\text{O}^+] \rightarrow \text{pH} \rightarrow \text{pOH}$
　　　　　　　　　pH = -log[H₃O⁺]　pH + pOH = 14
　　　Solution: $\text{pH} = -\log(1.7 \times 10^{-8}) = 7.77$　　$\text{pOH} = 14.00 - 7.77 = 6.23$
　　　pH > 7 so the solution is basic.

　　(b)　**Given:** $[\text{H}_3\text{O}^+] = 1.0 \times 10^{-7} \text{ mol L}^{-1}$ **Find:** pH and pOH
　　　Conceptual Plan: $[\text{H}_3\text{O}^+] \rightarrow \text{pH} \rightarrow \text{pOH}$
　　　　　　　　　pH = -log[H₃O⁺]　pH + pOH = 14
　　　Solution: $\text{pH} = -\log(1.0 \times 10^{-7}) = 7.00$　　$\text{pOH} = 14.00 - 7.00 = 7.00$
　　　pH = 7 so the solution is neutral.

　　(c)　**Given:** $[\text{H}_3\text{O}^+] = 2.2 \times 10^{-6} \text{ mol L}^{-1}$ **Find:** pH and pOH
　　　Conceptual Plan: $[\text{H}_3\text{O}^+] \rightarrow \text{pH} \rightarrow \text{pOH}$
　　　　　　　　　pH = -log[H₃O⁺]　pH + pOH = 14
　　　Solution: $\text{pH} = -\log(2.2 \times 10^{-6}) = 5.66$　　$\text{pOH} = 14.00 - 5.66 = 8.34$
　　　pH < 7 so the solution is acidic.

15.51　$\text{pH} = -\log[\text{H}_3\text{O}^+]$ $K_w = 1.0 \times 10^{-14} = [\text{H}_3\text{O}^+][\text{OH}^-]$

$[\text{H}_3\text{O}^+]$	$[\text{OH}^-]$	pH	Acidic or Basic
7.1×10^{-4}	1.4×10^{-11}	**3.15**	acidic
3.7×10^{-9}	2.7×10^{-6}	8.43	basic
8×10^{-12}	1×10^{-3}	**11.1**	basic
6.3×10^{-4}	**1.6×10^{-11}**	3.20	acidic

$[\text{H}_3\text{O}^+] = 10^{-3.15} = 7.1 \times 10^{-4}$　　$[\text{OH}^-] = \dfrac{1.0 \times 10^{-14}}{7.1 \times 10^{-4}} = 1.4 \times 10^{-11}$

$[\text{OH}^-] = \dfrac{1.0 \times 10^{-14}}{3.7 \times 10^{-9}} = 2.7 \times 10^{-6}$　$\text{pH} = -\log(3.7 \times 10^{-9}) = 8.43$

$[\text{H}_3\text{O}^+] = 10^{-11.1} = 8 \times 10^{-12}$　　　$[\text{OH}^-] = \dfrac{1.0 \times 10^{-14}}{8 \times 10^{-12}} = 1 \times 10^{-3}$

$[\text{H}_3\text{O}^+] = \dfrac{1.0 \times 10^{-14}}{1.6 \times 10^{-11}} = 6.3 \times 10^{-4}$　$\text{pH} = -\log(6.3 \times 10^{-4}) = 3.20$

15.53　**Given:** $K_w = 2.4 \times 10^{-14}$ at 37 °C **Find:** $[\text{H}_3\text{O}^+]$, pH
　　　Conceptual Plan: $K_w \rightarrow [\text{H}_3\text{O}^+] \rightarrow \text{pH}$
　　　　　　　　　$K_w = [\text{H}_3\text{O}^+][\text{OH}^-]$　pH = -log[H₃O⁺]
　　　Solution: $\text{H}_2\text{O}(l) + \text{H}_2\text{O}(l) \rightleftharpoons \text{H}_3\text{O}^+(aq) + \text{OH}^-(aq)$
　　　　　　$K_w = [\text{H}_3\text{O}^+][\text{OH}^-]$
　　　　　　$[\text{H}_3\text{O}^+] = [\text{OH}^-] = \sqrt{K_w} = \sqrt{2.4 \times 10^{-14}} = 1.5 \times 10^{-7}$
　　　　　　$\text{pH} = -\log[\text{H}_3\text{O}^+] = -\log(1.5 \times 10^{-7}) = 6.81$
　　　Check: The value of K_w increased, indicating more products formed, so the $[\text{H}_3\text{O}^+]$ increases and the pH decreases from the values at 25 °C.

Acid Solutions

15.55   (a)   **Given:** 0.25 mol L^{-1} HCl (strong acid) **Find:** $[H_3O^+]$, $[OH^-]$, pH
Conceptual Plan: $[HCl] \rightarrow [H_3O^+] \rightarrow pH$ and then $[H_3O^+] \rightarrow [OH^-]$

$$[HCl] \rightarrow [H_3O^+] \quad pH = -\log[H_3O^+] \qquad [H_3O^+][OH^-] = 1.0 \times 10^{-14}$$

Solution: 0.25 mol L^{-1} HCl $= 0.25$ mol L^{-1} H_3O^+ pH $= -\log(0.25) = 0.60$
$[OH^-] = 1.0 \times 10^{-14}/0.25$ mol $L^{-1} = 4.0 \times 10^{-14}$ mol L^{-1}
Check: HCl is a strong acid with a relatively high concentration, so we expect the pH to be low and the $[OH^-]$ to be small.

(b)   **Given:** 0.015 mol L^{-1} HNO_3 (strong acid) **Find:** $[H_3O^+]$, $[OH^-]$, pH
Conceptual Plan: $[HNO_3] \rightarrow [H_3O^+] \rightarrow pH$ and then $[H_3O^+] \rightarrow [OH^-]$

$$[HNO_3] \rightarrow [H_3O^+] \quad pH = -\log[H_3O^+] \qquad [H_3O^+][OH^-] = 1.0 \times 10^{-14}$$

Solution: 0.015 mol L^{-1} $HNO_3 = 0.015$ mol L^{-1} H_3O^+ pH $= -\log(0.015) = 1.82$
$[OH^-] = 1.0 \times 10^{-14}/0.015$ mol $L^{-1} = 6.7 \times 10^{-13}$ mol L^{-1}
Check: HNO_3 is a strong acid, so we expect the pH to be low and the $[OH^-]$ to be small.

(c)   **Given:** 0.052 mol L^{-1} HBr and 0.020 mol L^{-1} HNO_3 (strong acids) **Find:** $[H_3O^+]$, $[OH^-]$, pH
Conceptual Plan: $[HBr] + [HNO_3] \rightarrow [H_3O^+] \rightarrow pH$ and then $[H_3O^+] \rightarrow [OH^-]$

$$[HBr] + [HNO_3] \rightarrow [H_3O^+] \quad pH = -\log[H_3O^+] \qquad [H_3O^+][OH^-] = 1.0 \times 10^{-14}$$

Solution: 0.052 mol L^{-1} HBr $= 0.052$ mol L^{-1} H_3O^+ and 0.020 mol L^{-1} $HNO_3 = 0.020$ mol L^{-1} H_3O^+
Total $H_3O^+ = 0.052$ mol $L^{-1} + 0.020$ mol $L^{-1} = 0.072$ mol L^{-1} pH $= -\log(0.072) = 1.14$
$[OH^-] = 1.0 \times 10^{-14}/0.072$ mol $L^{-1} = 1.4 \times 10^{-13}$ mol L^{-1}
Check: HBr and HNO_3 are both strong acids and completely dissociate. This gives a relatively high concentration, so we expect the pH to be low and the $[OH^-]$ to be small.

(d)   **Given:** $HNO_3 = 0.655\%$ by mass, $d_{solution} = 1.01$ g mL^{-1} **Find:** $[H_3O^+]$, $[OH^-]$, pH
Conceptual Plan:
% mass $HNO_3 \rightarrow$ g $HNO_3 \rightarrow$ mol HNO_3 and then g soln $\rightarrow$ mL soln $\rightarrow$ L soln $\rightarrow$ mol L^{-1} HNO_3

$$\frac{\%}{100} \qquad \frac{1 \text{ mol } HNO_3}{63.018 \text{ g } HNO_3} \qquad\qquad \frac{1.01 \text{ g soln}}{1 \text{ mL soln}} \quad \frac{1000 \text{ mL soln}}{1 \text{ L soln}} \quad \frac{\text{mol } HNO_3}{\text{L soln}}$$

$\rightarrow$ **M** $H_3O^+ \rightarrow pH$ and then $[H_3O^+] \rightarrow [OH^-]$

$$[HNO_3] \rightarrow [H_3O^+] \qquad pH = -\log[H_3O^+] \; [H_3O^+][OH^-] = 1.0 \times 10^{-14}$$

Solution: $\dfrac{0.655 \text{ g } HNO_3}{100 \text{ g soln}} \times \dfrac{1 \text{ mol } HNO_3}{63.018 \text{ g } HNO_3} \times \dfrac{1.01 \text{ g soln}}{1 \text{ mL soln}} \times \dfrac{1000 \text{ mL soln}}{1 \text{ L soln}} = 0.105$ mol L^{-1} HNO_3

0.105 mol L^{-1} $HNO_3 = 0.105$ mol L^{-1} H_3O^+ pH $= -\log(0.105) = 0.979$
$[OH^-] = 1.00 \times 10^{-14}/0.105$ mol $L^{-1} = 9.52 \times 10^{-14}$ mol L^{-1}
Check: HNO_3 is a strong acid and completely dissociates. This gives a relatively high concentration, so we expect the pH to be low and the $[OH^-]$ to be small.

15.57   (a)   **Given:** pH $= 1.25$, 0.250 L **Find:** g HI
Conceptual Plan: pH $\rightarrow [H_3O^+] \rightarrow [HI] \rightarrow$ mol HI $\rightarrow$ g HI

$$pH = -\log[H_3O^+] \qquad [H_3O^+] \rightarrow [HI] \text{ mol} = MV \quad \frac{127.9 \text{ g HI}}{1 \text{ mol HI}}$$

Solution: $[H_3O^+] = 10^{-1.25} = 0.056$ mol $L^{-1} = [HI]$ $\dfrac{0.056 \text{ mol HI}}{L} \times 0.250 \text{ L} \times \dfrac{127.9 \text{ g HI}}{\text{mol HI}} = 1.8$ g HI

(b)   **Given:** pH $= 1.75$, 0.250 L **Find:** g HI
Conceptual Plan: pH $\rightarrow [H_3O^+] \rightarrow [HI] \rightarrow$ mol HI $\rightarrow$ g HI

$$pH = -\log[H_3O^+] \qquad [H_3O^+] \rightarrow [HI] \qquad \text{mol} = MV \quad \frac{127.9 \text{ g HI}}{1 \text{ mol HI}}$$

Solution: $[H_3O^+] = 10^{-1.75} = 0.0178$ mol $L^{-1} = [HI]$ $\dfrac{0.0178 \text{ mol HI}}{1 \text{ L}} \times 0.250 \text{ L} \times \dfrac{127.9 \text{ g HI}}{1 \text{ mol HI}}$

$= 0.57$ g HI

(c) **Given:** pH = 2.85, 0.250 L **Find:** g HI

Conceptual Plan: pH → $[H_3O^+]$ → [HI] → mol HI → g HI

$$pH = -log[H_3O^+] \qquad [H_3O^+] \rightarrow [HI] \qquad mol = MV \qquad \frac{127.9 \text{ g HI}}{1 \text{ mol HI}}$$

Solution: $[H_3O^+] = 10^{-2.85} = 0.0014$ mol L^{-1} = [HI] $\frac{0.0014 \text{ mol HI}}{1 \text{ L}}$ x 0.250 L x $\frac{127.9 \text{ g HI}}{1 \text{ mol HI}}$ = 0.045 g HI

15.59 **Given:** 224 mL HCl, 27.2 °C, 1.02 atm, 1.5 L solution **Find:** pH

Conceptual Plan: vol HCl → mol HCl → [HCl] → $[H_3O^+]$ → pH

$$PV = nRT \qquad M = \frac{mol \text{ HCl}}{vol \text{ soln}} \qquad [HCl] = [H_3O^+] \quad pH = -log[H_3O^+]$$

Solution: $n = \dfrac{(1.02 \text{ atm})(224 \text{ mL})\left(\dfrac{1 \text{ L}}{1000 \text{ mL}}\right)}{\left(\dfrac{0.0821 \text{ L atm}}{mol \text{ K}}\right)((27.2 + 273.15) \text{ K})} = 0.00927$ mol

$[HCl] = \dfrac{0.00927 \text{ mol}}{1.5 \text{ L}} = 0.00618$ mol $L^{-1} = [H_3O^+]$ pH = -log(0.00618) = 2.21

15.61 **Given:** 0.100 mol L^{-1} benzoic acid. $K_a = 6.5$ x 10^{-5} **Find:** $[H_3O^+]$, pH

Conceptual Plan: Write a balanced reaction. Prepare an ICE table, represent the change with x, sum the table, determine the equilibrium values, put the equilibrium values in the equilibrium expression, and solve for x. Determine $[H_3O^+]$ and pH.

Solution: $HC_7H_5O_2(aq) + H_2O(l) \rightleftharpoons H_3O^+(aq) + C_7H_5O_2^-(aq)$

I	0.100	0	0
C	- x	+x	+x
E	0.100 – x	x	x

$$K_a = \frac{[H_3O^+][C_7H_5O_2^-]}{[HC_7H_5O_2]} = \frac{(x)(x)}{(0.100 - x)} = 6.5 \text{ x } 10^{-5}$$

Assume x is small compared to 0.100.

$x^2 = (6.5$ x $10^{-5})(0.100)$ $x = 2.5$ x 10^{-3} mol $L^{-1} = [H_3O^+]$

Check assumption: $\dfrac{2.5 \text{ x } 10^{-3}}{0.100}$ x 100% = 2.5%; assumption valid.

pH = $-log(2.5$ x $10^{-3}) = 2.60$

15.63 (a) **Given:** 0.500 mol L^{-1} HNO_2; $K_a = 4.6$ x 10^{-4} **Find:** pH

Conceptual Plan: Write a balanced reaction. Prepare an ICE table, represent the change with x, sum the table, determine the equilibrium values, put the equilibrium values in the equilibrium expression, and solve for x. Determine $[H_3O^+]$ and pH.

Solution: $HNO_2(aq) + H_2O(l) \rightleftharpoons H_3O^+(aq) + NO_2^-(aq)$

I	0.500	0	0
C	- x	+x	+x
E	0.500 – x	x	x

$$K_a = \frac{[H_3O^+][NO_2^-]}{[HNO_2]} = \frac{(x)(x)}{(0.500 - x)} = 4.6 \text{ x } 10^{-4}$$

Assume x is small compared to 0.500.

$x^2 = (4.6$ x $10^{-4})(0.500)$ $x = 0.015$ mol $L^{-1} = [H_3O^+]$

Check assumption: $\dfrac{0.015}{0.500}$ x 100% = 3.0% assumption valid.

pH = -log(0.015) = 1.82

(b) **Given:** 0.100 mol L^{-1} HNO_2; $K_a = 4.6$ x 10^{-4} **Find:** pH

Conceptual Plan: Write a balanced reaction. Prepare an ICE table, represent the change with x, sum the table, determine the equilibrium values, put the equilibrium values in the equilibrium expression, and solve for x. Determine $[H_3O^+]$ and pH.

Solution: $HNO_2(aq) + H_2O(l) \rightleftharpoons H_3O^+(aq) + NO_2^-(aq)$

I	0.100	0	0
C	$-x$	$+x$	$+x$
E	$0.100 - x$	x	x

$$K_a = \frac{[H_3O^+][NO_2^-]}{[HNO_2]} = \frac{(x)(x)}{(0.100 - x)} = 4.6 \times 10^{-4}$$

Assume x is small compared to 0.100.

$x^2 = (4.6 \times 10^{-4})(0.100) \qquad x = 0.0068 \text{ mol L}^{-1} = [H_3O^+]$

Check assumption: $\dfrac{0.0068}{0.100} \times 100\% = 6.8\%$; assumption not valid, solve using quadratic equation.

$x^2 = (4.6 \times 10^{-4})(0.100 - x) \quad x^2 + 4.6 \times 10^{-4}x - 4.6 \times 10^{-5} = 0$

$x = 0.00656$

$pH = -\log(0.00656) = 2.18$

(c) **Given:** $0.1000 \text{ mol L}^{-1} HNO_2$; $K_a = 4.6 \times 10^{-4}$ **Find:** pH

Conceptual Plan: Write a balanced reaction. Prepare an ICE table, represent the change with x, sum the table, determine the equilibrium values, put the equilibrium values in the equilibrium expression, and solve for x. Determine $[H_3O^+]$ and pH.

Solution: $HNO_2(aq) + H_2O(l) \rightleftharpoons H_3O^+(aq) + NO_2^-(aq)$

I	0.0100	0	0
C	$-x$	$+x$	$+x$
E	$0.0100 - x$	x	x

$$K_a = \frac{[H_3O^+][NO_2^-]}{[HNO_2]} = \frac{(x)(x)}{(0.0100 - x)} = 4.6 \times 10^{-4}$$

Assume x is small compared to 0.100.

$x^2 = (4.6 \times 10^{-4})(0.0100) \qquad x = 0.0021 \text{ mol L}^{-1} = [H_3O^+]$

Check assumption: $\dfrac{0.0021}{0.0100} \times 100\% = 21\%$; assumption not valid, solve with quadratic equation.

$x^2 = (4.6 \times 10^{-4})(0.0100 - x) \quad x^2 + 4.6 \times 10^{-4}x - 4.6 \times 10^{-6} = 0$

$x = 0.0019$

$pH = -\log(0.0019) = 2.72$

15.65 **Given:** 15.0 mL glacial acetic, $d = 1.05 \text{ g mL}^{-1}$, dilute to 1.50 L, $K_a = 1.8 \times 10^{-5}$ **Find:** pH

Conceptual Plan: mL acetic acid $\rightarrow$ g acetic acid $\rightarrow$ mol acetic acid $\rightarrow$ mol L^{-1} and then write a balanced reaction.

$$\frac{1.05 \text{ g}}{1 \text{ mL}} \qquad \frac{1 \text{ mol acetic acid}}{60.05 \text{ g acetic acid}} \qquad M = \frac{\text{mol}}{\text{L}}$$

Prepare an ICE table, represent the change with x, sum the table, determine the equilibrium values, put the equilibrium values in the equilibrium expression, and solve for x. Determine $[H_3O^+]$ and pH.

Solution: $15.0 \text{ mL} \times \dfrac{1.05 \text{ g}}{1 \text{ mL}} \times \dfrac{1 \text{ mol}}{60.05 \text{ g}} \times \dfrac{1}{1.50 \text{ L}} = 0.1748 \text{ mol L}^{-1}$

$HC_2H_3O_2(aq) + H_2O(l) \rightleftharpoons H_3O^+(aq) + C_2H_3O_2^-(aq)$

I	0.1748	0	0
C	$-x$	$+x$	$+x$
E	$0.1748 - x$	x	x

$$K_a = \frac{[H_3O^+][C_2H_3O_2^-]}{[HC_2H_3O_2]} = \frac{(x)(x)}{(0.1748 - x)} = 1.8 \times 10^{-5}$$

Assume x is small compared to 0.1748.

$x^2 = (1.8 \times 10^{-5})(0.1748) \qquad x = 0.00177 \text{ mol L}^{-1} = [H_3O^+]$

Check assumption: $\dfrac{0.00177}{0.1748} \times 100\% = 1.0\%$ assumption valid.

$pH = -\log(0.00177) = 2.75$

15.67 **Given:** 0.185 mol L^{-1} HA, pH = 2.95 **Find:** K_a

Conceptual Plan: pH → $[H_3O^+]$ and then write a balanced reaction. Prepare an ICE table, calculate equilibrium concentrations, and then plug into the equilibrium expression to solve for K_a.

Solution: $[H_3O^+] = 10^{-2.95} = 0.00112$ mol $L^{-1} = [A^-]$

	HA(aq) + H$_2$O(l) $\rightleftharpoons$	H$_3$O$^+$$(aq)$ +	A$^-$ (aq)
I	0.185	0	0
C	$-x$	$+x$	$+x$
E	0.185 − 0.00112	0.00112	0.00112

$$K_a = \frac{[H_3O^+][A^-]}{[HA]} = \frac{(0.00112)(0.00112)}{(0.185 - 0.00112)} = 6.8 \times 10^{-6}$$

15.69 **Given:** 0.125 mol L^{-1} HCN, $K_a = 4.9 \times 10^{-10}$ **Find:** % ionization

Conceptual Plan: Write a balanced reaction. Prepare an ICE table, represent the change with x, sum the table, determine the equilibrium values, put the equilibrium values in the equilibrium expression, solve for x, and then x → % ionization.

$$\% \text{ ionization} = \frac{x}{[\text{HCN}]_{\text{original}}} \times 100\%$$

Solution: HCN(aq) + H$_2$O(l) $\rightleftharpoons$ H$_3$O$^+$$(aq)$ + CN$^-$ (aq)

	HCN	H$_3$O$^+$	CN$^-$
I	0.125	0	0
C	$-x$	$+x$	$+x$
E	0.125 − x	x	x

$$K_a = \frac{[H_3O^+][CN^-]}{[HCN]} = \frac{(x)(x)}{(0.125 - x)} = 4.9 \times 10^{-10}$$

Assume x is small compared to 0.125.

$x^2 = (4.9 \times 10^{-10})(0.125)$ $\quad x = 7.83 \times 10^{-6}$

$$\% \text{ ionization} = \frac{7.83 \times 10^{-6}}{0.125} \times 100\% = 0.0063\% \text{ ionized}$$

15.71 (a) **Given:** 1.00 mol L^{-1} HC$_2$H$_3$O$_2$, $K_a = 1.8 \times 10^{-5}$ **Find:** % ionization

Conceptual Plan: Write a balanced reaction. Prepare an ICE table, represent the change with x, sum the table, determine the equilibrium values, put the equilibrium values in the equilibrium expression, solve for x, and then x → % ionization.

$$\% \text{ ionization} = \frac{x}{[\text{HC}_2\text{H}_3\text{O}_2]_{\text{original}}} \times 100\%$$

Solution: HC$_2$H$_3$O$_2$ (aq) + H$_2$O(l) $\rightleftharpoons$ H$_3$O$^+$$(aq)$ + C$_2$H$_3$O$_2^-$ (aq)

	HC$_2$H$_3$O$_2$	H$_3$O$^+$	C$_2$H$_3$O$_2^-$
I	1.00	0	0
C	$-x$	$+x$	$+x$
E	1.00 − x	x	x

$$K_a = \frac{[H_3O^+][C_2H_3O_2^-]}{[HC_2H_3O_2]} = \frac{(x)(x)}{(1.00 - x)} = 1.8 \times 10^{-5}$$

Assume x is small compared to 1.00.

$x^2 = (1.8 \times 10^{-5})(1.00)$ $\quad x = 0.00424$

$$\% \text{ ionization} = \frac{0.00424}{1.00} \times 100\% = 0.42\% \text{ ionized}$$

(b) **Given:** 0.500 mol L^{-1} HC$_2$H$_3$O$_2$, $K_a = 1.8 \times 10^{-5}$ **Find:** % ionization

Conceptual Plan: Write a balanced reaction. Prepare an ICE table, represent the change with x, sum the table, determine the equilibrium values, put the equilibrium values in the equilibrium expression, solve for x, and then x → % ionization.

$$\% \text{ ionization} = \frac{x}{[\text{HC}_2\text{H}_3\text{O}_2]_{\text{original}}} \times 100\%$$

Solution: HC$_2$H$_3$O$_2$$(aq)$ + H$_2$O(l) $\rightleftharpoons$ H$_3$O$^+$$(aq)$ + C$_2$H$_3$O$_2^-$ (aq)

	HC$_2$H$_3$O$_2$	H$_3$O$^+$	C$_2$H$_3$O$_2^-$
I	0.500	0	0
C	$-x$	$+x$	$+x$
E	0.500 − x	x	x

$$K_a = \frac{[H_3O^+][C_2H_3O_2^-]}{[HC_2H_3O_2]} = \frac{(x)(x)}{(0.500 - x)} = 1.8 \times 10^{-5}$$

Assume x is small compared to 0.500.

$x^2 = (1.8 \times 10^{-5})(0.500)$ $x = 0.00300$

% ionization $= \dfrac{0.00300}{0.500} \times 100\% = 0.60\%$ ionized

(c)   **Given:** 0.100 mol L^{-1} HC$_2$H$_3$O$_2$, $K_a = 1.8 \times 10^{-5}$ **Find:** % ionization
Conceptual Plan: Write a balanced reaction. Prepare an ICE table, represent the change with x, sum the table, determine the equilibrium values, put the equilibrium values in the equilibrium expression, solve for x, and then $x \rightarrow$ % ionization.

$$\% \text{ ionization} = \frac{x}{[HC_2H_3O_2]_{original}} \times 100\%$$

Solution: HC$_2$H$_3$O$_2$(aq) + H$_2$O(l) $\rightleftharpoons$ H$_3$O$^+$(aq) + C$_2$H$_3$O$_2^-$ (aq)

I	0.100	0	0
C	- x	+x	+x
E	0.100 – x	x	x

$$K_a = \frac{[H_3O^+][C_2H_3O_2^-]}{[HC_2H_3O_2]} = \frac{(x)(x)}{(0.100 - x)} = 1.8 \times 10^{-5}$$

Assume x is small compared to 1.00.

$x^2 = (1.8 \times 10^{-5})(0.100)$ $x = 0.00134$

% ionization $= \dfrac{0.00134}{0.100} \times 100\% = 1.3\%$ ionized

(d)   **Given:** 0.0500 mol L^{-1} HC$_2$H$_3$O$_2$, $K_a = 1.8 \times 10^{-5}$ **Find:** % ionization
Conceptual Plan: Write a balanced reaction. Prepare an ICE table, represent the change with x, sum the table, determine the equilibrium values, put the equilibrium values in the equilibrium expression, solve for x, and then $x \rightarrow$ % ionization.

$$\% \text{ ionization} = \frac{x}{[HC_2H_3O_2]_{original}} \times 100\%$$

Solution: HC$_2$H$_3$O$_2$(aq) + H$_2$O(l) $\rightleftharpoons$ H$_3$O$^+$(aq) + C$_2$H$_3$O$_2^-$ (aq)

I	0.0500	0	0
C	- x	+x	+x
E	0.0500 – x	x	x

$$K_a = \frac{[H_3O^+][C_2H_3O_2^-]}{[HC_2H_3O_2]} = \frac{(x)(x)}{(0.0500 - x)} = 1.8 \times 10^{-5}$$

Assume x is small compared to 0.0500.

$x^2 = (1.8 \times 10^{-5})(0.0500)$ $x = 9.49 \times 10^{-4}$

% ionization $= \dfrac{9.49 \times 10^{-4}}{0.0500} \times 100\% = 1.9\%$ ionized

15.73   **Given:** 0.148 mol L^{-1} HA, 1.55% dissociation **Find:** K_a
Conceptual Plan: mol L^{-1} $\rightarrow$ [H$_3$O$^+$] $\rightarrow$ K_a and then write a balanced reaction, determine equilibrium concentration, and plug into the equilibrium expression.
Solution: (0.148 mol L^{-1} HA)(0.0155) = 0.002294 mol L^{-1} = [H$_3$O$^+$] = [A$^-$]

HA(aq) + H$_2$O(l) $\rightleftharpoons$ H$_3$O$^+$(aq) + A$^-$(aq)

I	0.148	0	0
C	- x	+x	+x
E	0.148 – 0.002294	0.002294	0.002294

$$K_a = \frac{[H_3O^+][A^-]}{[HA]} = \frac{(0.002294)(0.002294)}{(0.148 - 0.002294)} = 3.61 \times 10^{-5}$$

15.75   (a)   **Given:** 0.250 mol L^{-1} HF, $K_a = 3.5 \times 10^{-4}$ **Find:** pH, % dissociation
Conceptual Plan: Write a balanced reaction. Prepare an ICE table, represent the change with x,

sum the table, determine the equilibrium values, put the equilibrium values in the equilibrium expression, solve for x, and then $x \rightarrow$ % ionization.

$$\% \text{ ionization} = \frac{x}{[\text{HF}]_{\text{original}}} \times 100\%$$

Solution: $HF(aq) + H_2O(l) \rightleftharpoons H_3O^+(aq) + F^-(aq)$

I	0.250	0	0
C	$-x$	$+x$	$+x$
E	$0.250 - x$	x	x

$$K_a = \frac{[H_3O^+][F^-]}{[HF]} = \frac{(x)(x)}{(0.250 - x)} = 3.5 \times 10^{-4}$$

Assume x is small compared to 0.250.

$$x^2 = (3.5 \times 10^{-4})(0.250) \qquad x = 0.00935 \text{ mol L}^{-1} = [H_3O^+]$$

$$\frac{0.00935}{0.250} \times 100\% = 3.7\%$$

$$pH = -\log(0.00935) = 2.03$$

(b) **Given:** 0.100 mol L^{-1} HF, $K_a = 3.5 \times 10^{-4}$ **Find:** pH, % dissociation

Conceptual Plan: Write a balanced reaction. Prepare an ICE table, represent the change with x, sum the table, determine the equilibrium values, put the equilibrium values in the equilibrium expression, solve for x, and then $x \rightarrow$ % ionization.

$$\% \text{ ionization} = \frac{x}{[\text{HF}]_{\text{original}}} \times 100\%$$

Solution: $HF(aq) + H_2O(l) \rightleftharpoons H_3O^+(aq) + F^-(aq)$

I	0.100	0	0
C	$-x$	$+x$	$+x$
E	$0.100 - x$	x	x

$$K_a = \frac{[H_3O^+][F^-]}{[HF]} = \frac{(x)(x)}{(0.100 - x)} = 3.5 \times 10^{-4}$$

Assume x is small compared to 0.100.

$$x^2 = (3.5 \times 10^{-4})(0.100) \qquad x = 0.00592 \text{ mol L}^{-1} = [H_3O^+]$$

Check assumption: $\dfrac{0.00592}{0.100} \times 100\% = 5.9\%$; assumption not valid, solve using quadratic equation

$$x^2 + 3.5 \times 10^{-4} x - 3.5 \times 10^{-5} = 0$$

$$x = 0.00574 \text{ or } -0.00609$$

$$pH = -\log(0.00574) = 2.24$$

$$\% \text{ dissociation} = \frac{0.00574}{0.100} \times 100\% = 5.7\%$$

(c) **Given:** 0.050 mol L^{-1} HF, $K_a = 3.5 \times 10^{-4}$ **Find:** pH, % dissociation

Conceptual Plan: Write a balanced reaction. Prepare an ICE table, represent the change with x, sum the table, determine the equilibrium values, put the equilibrium values in the equilibrium expression, solve for x, and then $x \rightarrow$ % ionization.

$$\% \text{ ionization} = \frac{x}{[\text{HF}]_{\text{original}}} \times 100\%$$

Solution: $HF(aq) + H_2O(l) \rightleftharpoons H_3O^+(aq) + F^-(aq)$

I	0.050	0	0
C	$-x$	$+x$	$+x$
E	$0.050 - x$	x	x

$$K_a = \frac{[H_3O^+][F^-]}{[HF]} = \frac{(x)(x)}{(0.050 - x)} = 3.5 \times 10^{-4}$$

Assume x is small compared to 0.050.

$$x^2 = (3.5 \times 10^{-4})(0.050) \qquad x = 0.00418 \text{ mol L}^{-1} = [H_3O^+]$$

Check assumption: $\dfrac{0.00418}{0.050} \times 100\% = 8.4\%$; assumption not valid, solve using quadratic equation

$x^2 + 3.5 \times 10^{-4} x - 1.75 \times 10^{-5} = 0$
$x = 0.00401 \text{ or } -0.00436$
$pH = -\log(0.00401) = 2.40$
% dissociation $= \dfrac{0.00401}{0.050} \times 100\% = 8.0\%$

15.77 (a) **Given:** 0.115 mol L^{-1} HBr (strong acid), 0.125 mol L^{-1} CH$_3$COO$^-$ (weak acid) **Find:** pH
Conceptual Plan: Since the mixture is a strong acid and a weak acid, the strong acid will dominate. Use the concentration of the strong acid to determine [H$_3$O$^+$] and then pH.
Solution: 0.115 mol L^{-1} HBr = 0.115 mol L^{-1} H$_3$O$^+$ pH = $-\log(0.115)$ = 0.939

(b) **Given:** 0.150 mol L^{-1} HNO$_2$ (weak acid), 0.085 mol L^{-1} HNO$_3$ (strong acid) **Find:** pH
Conceptual Plan: Since the mixture is a strong acid and a weak acid, the strong acid will dominate. Use the concentration of the strong acid to determine [H$_3$O$^+$] and then pH.
Solution: 0.085 mol L^{-1} HNO$_3$ = 0.085 mol L^{-1} H$_3$O$^+$ pH = $-\log(0.085)$ = 1.07

(c) **Given:** 0.185 mol L^{-1} HCHO$_2$, $K_a = 1.8 \times 10^{-4}$; 0.225 mol L^{-1} CH$_3$COOH, $K_a = 1.8 \times 10^{-5}$ **Find:** pH
Conceptual Plan: Since the mixture is a weak acid and a weak acid, and the K values are only 10^1 apart, you need to find [H$_3$O$^+$] from each reaction. Write a balanced reaction. Prepare an ICE table, represent the change with x, sum the table, determine the equilibrium values, put the equilibrium values in the equilibrium expression, and solve for x.
Solution: HCHO$_2$ (aq) + H$_2$O(l) $\rightleftharpoons$ H$_3$O$^+$(aq) + CHO$_2^-$ (aq)

I	0.185	0	0
C	$-x$	$+x$	$+x$
E	$0.185 - x$	x	x

$K_a = \dfrac{[H_3O^+][CHO_2^-]}{[HCHO_2]} = \dfrac{(x)(x)}{(0.185 - x)} = 1.8 \times 10^{-4}$
Assume x is small compared to 0.100.
$x^2 = (1.8 \times 10^{-4})(0.185)$ $x = 0.00577$ mol L^{-1}

CH3COOH (aq) + H$_2$O(l) $\rightleftharpoons$ H$_3$O$^+$(aq) + CH$_3$COO$^-$ (aq)

I	0.225	0.00577	0
C	$-x$	$+x$	$+x$
E	$0.225 - x$	$0.00577 + x$	x

$K_a = \dfrac{[H_3O^+][CH_3COO^-]}{[CH3COOH]} = \dfrac{(0.00577 + x)(x)}{(0.225 - x)} = 1.8 \times 10^{-5}$
Assume x is small compared to 0.225.
$x^2 + 0.00602x - 4.05 \times 10^{-6} = 0$ $x = 0.00061$ mol L^{-1}
$[H_3O^+] = 0.00577$ mol L^{-1} + x = 0.00577 mol L^{-1} + 0.00061 mol L^{-1} = 0.006389 mol L^{-1}
pH = $-\log(0.006389)$ = 2.19

(d) **Given:** 0.050 mol L^{-1} CH$_3$COOH, $K_a = 1.8 \times 10^{-5}$; 0.050 mol L^{-1} HCN, $K_a = 4.9 \times 10^{-10}$ **Find:** pH
Conceptual Plan: Since the values of K are more than 10^1 apart, the acid with the larger K will dominate the reaction. Write a balanced reaction. Prepare an ICE table, represent the change with x, sum the table, determine the equilibrium values, put the equilibrium values in the equilibrium expression, and solve for x.
Solution: CH$_3$COOH(aq) + H$_2$O(l) $\rightleftharpoons$ H$_3$O$^+$(aq) + CH$_3$COO$^-$ (aq)

I	0.0500	0	0
C	$-x$	$+x$	$+x$
E	$0.0500 - x$	x	x

$K_a = \dfrac{[H_3O^+][CH_3COO^-]}{[CH_3COOH]} = \dfrac{(x)(x)}{(0.0500 - x)} = 1.8 \times 10^{-5}$
Assume x is small compared to 0.0500.
$x^2 = (1.8 \times 10^{-5})(0.0500)$ $x = 9.49 \times 10^{-4}$ mol L^{-1}
pH = $-\log(9.49 \times 10^{-4})$ = 3.02

Base Solutions

15.79   (a)   **Given:** 0.15 mol L^{-1} NaOH   **Find:** [OH$^-$], [H$_3$O$^+$], pH, pOH

Conceptual Plan: [NaOH] $\rightarrow$ [OH$^-$] $\rightarrow$ [H$_3$O$^+$] $\rightarrow$ pH $\rightarrow$ pOH

$$K_w = [H_3O^+][OH^-] \qquad pH = -\log[H_3O^+] \qquad pH + pOH = 14$$

Solution: [OH$^-$] = [NaOH] = 0.15 mol L^{-1}

$$[H_3O^+] = \frac{K_w}{[OH^-]} = \frac{1.0 \times 10^{-14}}{0.15 \text{ mol L}^{-1}} = 6.7 \times 10^{-14} \text{ mol L}^{-1}$$

pH = $-\log(6.7 \times 10^{-14})$ = 13.17

pOH = 14.00 − 13.18 = 0.83

(b)   **Given:** 1.5 x 10^{-3} mol L^{-1} Ca(OH)$_2$ **Find:** [OH$^-$], [H$_3$O$^+$], pH, pOH

Conceptual Plan: [Ca(OH)$_2$] $\rightarrow$ [OH$^-$] $\rightarrow$ [H$_3$O$^+$] $\rightarrow$ pH $\rightarrow$ pOH

$$K_w = [H_3O^+][OH^-] \qquad pH = -\log[H_3O^+] \qquad pH + pOH = 14$$

Solution: [OH$^-$] = 2[Ca(OH)$_2$] = 2(1.5 x 10^{-3}) = 0.0030 mol L^{-1}

$$[H_3O^+] = \frac{K_w}{[OH^-]} = \frac{1.0 \times 10^{-14}}{0.0030 \text{ mol L}^{-1}} = 3.33 \times 10^{-12} \text{ mol L}^{-1}$$

pH = $-\log(3.33 \times 10^{-12})$ = 11.48

pOH = 14.00 − 11.48 = 2.52

(c)   **Given:** 4.8 x 10^{-4} mol L^{-1} Sr(OH)$_2$ **Find:** [OH$^-$], [H$_3$O$^+$], pH, pOH

Conceptual Plan: [Sr(OH)$_2$] $\rightarrow$ [OH$^-$] $\rightarrow$ [H$_3$O$^+$] $\rightarrow$ pH $\rightarrow$ pOH

$$K_w = [H_3O^+][OH^-] \qquad pH = -\log[H_3O^+] \qquad pH + pOH = 14$$

Solution: [OH$^-$] = [Sr(OH)$_2$] = 2(4.8 x 10^{-4}) = 9.6 x 10^{-4} mol L^{-1}

$$[H_3O^+] = \frac{K_w}{[OH^-]} = \frac{1.0 \times 10^{-14}}{9.6 \times 10^{-4} \text{ mol L}^{-1}} = 1.04 \times 10^{-11} \text{ mol L}^{-1}$$

pH = $-\log(1.04 \times 10^{-11})$ = 10.98

pOH = 14.00 − 10.98 = 3.02

(d)   **Given:** 8.7 x 10^{-5} mol L^{-1} KOH   **Find:** [OH$^-$], [H$_3$O$^+$], pH, pOH

Conceptual Plan: [KOH] $\rightarrow$ [OH$^-$] $\rightarrow$ [H$_3$O$^+$] $\rightarrow$ pH $\rightarrow$ pOH

$$K_w = [H_3O^+][OH^-] \qquad pH = -\log[H_3O^+] \qquad pH + pOH = 14$$

Solution: [OH$^-$] = [KOH] = 8.7 x 10^{-5} mol L^{-1}

$$[H_3O^+] = \frac{K_w}{[OH^-]} = \frac{1.0 \times 10^{-14}}{8.7 \times 10^{-5} \text{ mol L}^{-1}} = 1.1 \times 10^{-10} \text{ mol L}^{-1}$$

pH = $-\log(1.1 \times 10^{-10})$ = 9.94

pOH = 14.00 − 9.94 = 4.06

15.81   **Given:** 3.85% KOH by mass, d = 1.01 g mL^{-1} **Find:** pH

Conceptual Plan:

% mass $\rightarrow$ g KOH $\rightarrow$ mol KOH and mass soln $\rightarrow$ mL soln $\rightarrow$ L soln $\rightarrow$ mol L^{-1} KOH $\rightarrow$ [OH$^-$]

$$\frac{1 \text{ mol KOH}}{56.01 \text{ g KOH}} \qquad \frac{1.01 \text{ g soln}}{1 \text{ mL soln}} \quad \frac{1000 \text{ mL soln}}{1 \text{ L soln}} \quad \frac{\text{mol KOH}}{\text{L soln}}$$

$\rightarrow$ pOH $\rightarrow$ pH

$$pOH = -\log[OH^-] \quad pH + pOH = 14$$

Solution: $\dfrac{3.85 \text{ g KOH}}{100.0 \text{ g soln}} \times \dfrac{1 \text{ mol KOH}}{56.01 \text{ g KOH}} \times \dfrac{1.01 \text{ g soln}}{1 \text{ mL soln}} \times \dfrac{1000 \text{ mL soln}}{1 \text{ L soln}} = 0.6942 \text{ mol L}^{-1}$ KOH

[OH$^-$] = [KOH] = 0.6942 mol L^{-1} pOH = -log(0.6942) = 0.159   pH = 14.000 - 0.159 = 13.841

15.83   **Given:** 3.55 L, pH = 12.4; 0.855 mol L^{-1} KOH   **Find:** vol

Conceptual Plan: pH $\rightarrow$ [H$_3$O$^+$] $\rightarrow$ [OH$^-$] and then $V_1M_1 = V_2M_2$

$$[H_3O^+] = 10^{-pH} \quad 1.0 \times 10^{-14} = [H_3O^+][OH^-] \quad V_1M_1 = V_2M_2$$

Solution: [H$_3$O$^+$] = 10$^{-12.4}$ = 3.98 x 10^{-13} mol L^{-1} 1.0 x 10^{-14} = (3.98 x 10^{-13} mol L^{-1})[OH$^-$]

[OH$^-$] = 0.02512 mol L^{-1}

$V_1M_1 = V_2M_2$ V_1(0.855 mol L^{-1}) = (3.55 L)(0.0251 mol L^{-1}) V_1 = 0.104 L

15.85 (a) $NH_3(aq) + H_2O(l) \rightleftharpoons NH_4^+(aq) + OH^-(aq)$ $\qquad K_b = \dfrac{[NH_4^+][OH^-]}{[NH_3]}$

(b) $HCO_3^-(aq) + H_2O(l) \rightleftharpoons H_2CO_3(aq) + OH^-(aq)$ $\qquad K_b = \dfrac{[H_2CO_3][OH^-]}{[HCO_3^-]}$

(c) $CH_3NH_2(aq) + H_2O(l) \rightleftharpoons CH_3NH_3^+(aq) + OH^-(aq)$ $\qquad K_b = \dfrac{[CH_3NH_3^+][OH^-]}{[CH_3NH_2]}$

15.87 **Given:** 0.15 mol L^{-1} NH_3, $K_b = 1.76 \times 10^{-5}$ **Find:** [OH⁻], pH, pOH
Conceptual Plan: Write a balanced reaction. Prepare an ICE table, represent the change with x, sum the table, determine the equilibrium values, put the equilibrium values in the equilibrium expression, and solve for x.
$x = [OH^-] \rightarrow pOH \rightarrow pH$
$\qquad$ pOH = -log[OH⁻] pH + pOH = 14
Solution: $NH_3(aq) + H_2O(l) \rightleftharpoons NH_4^+(aq) + OH^-(aq)$

I	0.15	0	0
C	-x	+x	+x
E	0.15 - x	x	x

$K_b = \dfrac{[NH_4^+][OH^-]}{[NH_3]} = \dfrac{(x)(x)}{(0.15 - x)} = 1.76 \times 10^{-5}$
Assume x is small.
$x^2 = (1.76 \times 10^{-5})(0.15)$ $\quad x = [OH^-] = 0.00162$ mol L^{-1}
$pOH = -\log(0.00162) = 2.79$
$pH = 14.00 - 2.79 = 11.21$

15.89 **Given:** $pK_b = 10.4$, 455 mg L^{-1} caffeine **Find:** pH
Conceptual Plan: $pK_b \rightarrow K_b$ and then mg $L^{-1} \rightarrow$ g $L^{-1} \rightarrow$ mol L^{-1} and then write a balanced reaction. Prepare an ICE table, represent the change with x, sum the table, determine the equilibrium values, put the equilibrium values in the equilibrium expression, and solve for x.
$x = [OH^-] \rightarrow pOH \rightarrow pH$
$\qquad$ pOH = -log[OH⁻] pH + pOH = 14
Solution: $K_b = 10^{-10.4} = 3.98 \times 10^{-11}$

$$\dfrac{455 \text{ mg caffeine}}{\text{L soln}} \times \dfrac{1 \text{ g caffeine}}{1000 \text{ mg caffeine}} \times \dfrac{1 \text{ mol caffeine}}{194.19 \text{ g caffeine}} = 0.002343 \text{ mol } L^{-1} \text{ caffeine}$$

$C_8H_{10}N_4O_2(aq) + H_2O(l) \rightleftharpoons HC_8H_{10}N_4O_2^+(aq) + OH^-(aq)$

I	0.002343	0	0
C	-x	+x	+x
E	0.002343 - x	x	x

$K_b = \dfrac{[HC_8H_{10}N_4O_2^+][OH^-]}{[C_8H_{10}N_4O_2]} = \dfrac{(x)(x)}{(0.002343 - x)} = 3.98 \times 10^{-11}$
Assume x is small.
$x^2 = (3.98 \times 10^{-11})(0.002343)$ $\quad x = [OH^-] = 3.05 \times 10^{-7}$ mol L^{-1}
Check assumption: $\dfrac{3.05 \times 10^{-7} \text{ mol } L^{-1}}{0.002343} \times 100\% = 0.013\%$; assumption is valid
$pOH = -\log(3.05 \times 10^{-7}) = 6.5$
$pH = 14.00 - 6.5 = 7.5$

15.91 **Given:** 0.150 mol L^{-1} morphine, pH = 10.5 **Find:** K_b
Conceptual Plan:
pH $\rightarrow$ pOH $\rightarrow$ [OH⁻] and then write a balanced equation, prepare an ICE table, and determine
$\qquad$ pH = pOH = 14 pOH = -log[OH⁻]
equilibrium concentrations $\longrightarrow K_b$.

Solution: $pOH = 14.0 - 10.5 = 3.5$ $[OH^-] = 10^{-3.5} = 3.16 \times 10^{-4}$ mol L^{-1} = $[Hmorphine^+]$

$$morphine(aq) + H_2O(l) \rightleftharpoons Hmorphine^+(aq) + OH^-(aq)$$

I	0.150	0	0
C	-x	+x	+x
E	0.150 - x	3.16×10^{-4}	3.16×10^{-4}

$$K_b = \frac{[Hmorphine^+][OH^-]}{[morphine]} = \frac{(3.16 \times 10^{-4})(3.16 \times 10^{-4})}{(0.150 - 3.16 \times 10^{-4})} = 6.68 \times 10^{-7} = 7 \times 10^{-7}$$

Acid–Base Properties of Ions and Salts

15.93   (a)   pH-neutral: Br^- is the conjugate base of a strong acid; therefore, it is pH-neutral.

   (b)   weak base: ClO^- is the conjugate base of a weak acid; therefore, it is a weak base.
   $$ClO^-(aq) + H_2O(l) \rightleftharpoons HClO(aq) + OH^-(aq)$$

   (c)   weak base: CN^- is the conjugate base of a weak acid; therefore, it is a weak base.
   $$CN^-(aq) + H_2O(l) \rightleftharpoons HCN(aq) + OH^-(aq)$$

   (d)   pH-neutral: Cl^- is the conjugate base of a strong acid; therefore, it is pH-neutral.

15.95   **Given:** $[F^-] = 0.140$ mol L^{-1}, $K_a(HF) = 3.5 \times 10^{-4}$ **Find:** $[OH^-]$, pOH
   Conceptual Plan: Determine K_b. Write a balanced reaction. Prepare an ICE table, represent the change

$$K_b = \frac{K_w}{K_a}$$

   with x, sum the table, determine the equilibrium values, put the equilibrium values in the equilibrium expression, and solve for x. Determine $[OH^-]$ $\rightarrow$ pOH $\rightarrow$ pH.

$$pOH = -\log[OH^-] \quad pH + pOH = 14$$

   Solution: $F^-(aq) + H_2O(l) \rightleftharpoons HF(aq) + OH^-(aq)$

I	0.140	0	0
C	-x	+x	+x
E	0.140 - x	x	x

$$K_b = \frac{K_w}{K_a} = \frac{1.0 \times 10^{-14}}{3.5 \times 10^{-4}} = \frac{(x)(x)}{(0.140 - x)}$$

   Assume x is small.
   $x = 2.0 \times 10^{-6}$ mol $L^{-1} = [OH^-]$ $pOH = -\log(2.0 \times 10^{-6}) = 5.70$
   $pH = 14.00 - 5.70 = 8.30$

15.97   (a)   weak acid: NH_4^+ is the conjugate acid of a weak base; therefore, it is a weak acid.
   $$NH_4^+(aq) + H_2O(l) \rightleftharpoons H_3O^+(aq) + NH_3(aq)$$

   (b)   pH-neutral: Na^+ is the counterion of a strong base; therefore, it is pHneutral.

   (c)   weak acid: The Co^{3+} cation is a small, highly charged metal cation; therefore, it is a weak acid.

   $$Co(H_2O)_6^{3+}(aq) + H_2O(l) \rightleftharpoons Co(H_2O)_5(OH)^{2+}(aq) + H_3O^+(aq)$$

   (d)   weak acid: $CH_2NH_3^+$ is the conjugate acid of a weak base; therefore, it is a weak acid.
   $$CH_2NH_3^+(aq) + H_2O(l) \rightleftharpoons H_3O^+(aq) + CH_2NH_2(aq)$$

15.99   (a)   acidic: $FeCl_3$ Fe^{3+} is a small, highly charged metal cation and is therefore acidic. Cl^- is the conjugate base of a strong acid; therefore, it is pH-neutral.

   (b)   basic: NaF Na^+ is the counterion of a strong base; therefore, it is pH-neutral. F^- is the conjugate base of a weak acid; therefore, it is basic.

   (c)   acidic: NH_4Br NH_4^+ is the conjugate acid of a weak base; therefore, it is acidic. Br^- is the conjugate base of a strong acid; therefore, it is pH-neutral.

(d)   acidic: $C_6H_5NH_3NO_2$ $C_6H_5NH_3^+$ is the conjugate acid of a weak base; therefore, it is a weak acid. NO_2^-
       is the conjugate base of a weak acid; therefore, it is a weak base. To determine pH, compare K values.

$$K_a\,(C_6H_5NH_3^+) = \frac{1.0 \times 10^{-14}}{3.9 \times 10^{-10}} = 2.6 \times 10^{-5} \quad K_b(NO_2^-) = \frac{1.0 \times 10^{-14}}{4.6 \times 10^{-4}} = 2.2 \times 10^{-11}$$

$K_a > K_b$; therefore, the solution is acidic.

15.101   Identify each species and determine the acid, base, or neutral properties.

NaCl pH-neutral: Na^+ is the counterion of a strong base; therefore, it is pH-neutral. Cl^- is the conjugate base
of a strong acid; therefore, it is pH-neutral.

NH_4Cl acidic: NH_4^+ is the conjugate acid of a weak base; therefore, it is acidic. Cl^- is the conjugate base of
a strong acid; therefore, it is pH-neutral.

$NaHCO_3$ basic: Na^+ is the counterion of a strong base; therefore, it is pH-neutral. HCO_3^- is the conjugate
base of a weak acid; therefore, it is basic.

NH_4ClO_2 acidic: NH_4^+ is the conjugate acid of a weak base; therefore, it is acidic. ClO_2^- is the conjugate base
of a weak acid; therefore, it is basic. $K_a(NH_4^+) = 5.6 \times 10^{-10}$; $K_b(ClO_2^-) = 9.1 \times 10^{-13}$

NaOH strong base

Increasing acidity: $NaOH < NaHCO_3 < NaCl < NH_4ClO_2 < NH_4Cl$

15.103   (a)   **Given:** 0.10 mol L^{-1} NH_4Cl **Find:** pH
             **Conceptual Plan: Identify each species and determine which will contribute to pH. Write a
             balanced reaction. Prepare an ICE table, represent the change with x, sum the table, determine
             the equilibrium values, put the equilibrium values in the equilibrium expression, and solve for
             x. Determine $[H_3O^+] \rightarrow$ pH.**
             Solution: NH_4^+ is the conjugate acid of a weak base; therefore, it is acidic. Cl^- is the conjugate base of
             a strong acid; therefore, it is pH-neutral.

$$NH_4^+(aq) + H_2O(l) \rightleftharpoons NH_3\,(aq) + H_3O^+(aq)$$

I	0.10	0	0
C	$-x$	$+x$	$+x$
E	$0.10 - x$	x	x

$$K_a = \frac{K_w}{K_b} = \frac{1.0 \times 10^{-14}}{1.8 \times 10^{-5}} = 5.56 \times 10^{-10} = \frac{(x)(x)}{(0.10 - x)}$$

Assume x is small.

$x = 7.\underline{4}5 \times 10^{-6}$ mol $L^{-1} = [H_3O^+]$ pH $= -\log(7.\underline{4}5 \times 10^{-6}) = 5.13$

(b)   **Given:** 0.10 mol L^{-1} CH_3COOH **Find:** pH
       **Conceptual Plan: Identify each species and determine which will contribute to pH. Write a
       balanced reaction. Prepare an ICE table, represent the change with x, sum the table, determine
       the equilibrium values, put the equilibrium values in the equilibrium expression, and solve for
       x. Determine $[OH^-] \rightarrow$ pOH $\rightarrow$ pH.**
       pOH $= -\log[OH^-]$ pH $+$ pOH $= 14$
       Solution: Na^+ is the counterion of a strong base; therefore, it is pH-neutral. CH_3COO^- is the conju-
       gate base of a weak acid; therefore, it is basic.

$$CH_3COO^-(aq) + H_2O(l) \rightleftharpoons HCH_3COOH(aq) + OH^-(aq)$$

I	0.10 mol L^{-1}	0	0
C	$-x$	$+x$	$+x$
E	$0.10 - x$	x	x

$$K_b = \frac{K_w}{K_a} = \frac{1.0 \times 10^{-14}}{1.8 \times 10^{-5}} = 5.56 \times 10^{-10} = \frac{(x)(x)}{(0.10 - x)}$$

Assume x is small.

$x = 7.\underline{4}5 \times 10^{-6}$ mol $L^{-1} = [OH^-]$ pOH $= -\log(7.\underline{4}5 \times 10^{-6}) = 5.13$
pH $= 14.00 - 5.13 = 8.87$

(c)   **Given:** 0.10 mol L^{-1} NaCl **Find:** pH
Conceptual Plan: Identify each species and determine which will contribute to pH.
Solution: Na$^+$ is the counterion of a strong base; therefore, it is pH-neutral. Cl$^-$ is the conjugate base of a strong acid; therefore, it is pH-neutral.
pH = 7.0

15.105   **Given:** 0.15 mol L^{-1} KF **Find:** concentration of all species
Conceptual Plan: Identify each species and determine which will contribute to pH. Write a balanced reaction. Prepare an ICE table, represent the change with x, sum the table, determine the equilibrium values, put the equilibrium values in the equilibrium expression, and solve for x. Then, determine [OH$^-$] $\rightarrow$ [H$_3$O$^+$].
$$K_w = [H_3O^+][OH^-]$$
Solution: K$^+$ is the counterion of a strong base; therefore, it is pH-neutral. F$^-$ is the conjugate base of a weak acid; therefore, it is basic.

	F$^-$(aq) + H$_2$O(l) $\rightleftharpoons$	HF (aq) +	OH$^-$(aq)
I	0.15	0	0
C	-x	+x	+x
E	0.15 $-$ x	x	x

$$K_b = \frac{K_w}{K_a} = \frac{1.0 \times 10^{-14}}{3.5 \times 10^{-4}} = \frac{(x)(x)}{(0.15 - x)}$$

Assume x is small.

$$x = 2.1 \times 10^{-6} \text{ mol L}^{-1} = [OH^-] = [HF] \qquad [H_3O^+] = \frac{K_w}{[OH^-]} = \frac{1.0 \times 10^{-14}}{2.1 \times 10^{-6} \text{ mol L}^{-1}} = 4.8 \times 10^{-9}$$

[K$^+$] = 0.15 mol L^{-1}
[F$^-$] = (0.15 $-$ 2.1 $\times$ 10^{-6}) = 0.15 mol L^{-1}
[HF] = 2.1 $\times$ 10^{-6} mol L^{-1}
[OH$^-$] = 2.1 $\times$ 10^{-6} mol L^{-1}
[H$_3$O$^+$] = 4.8 $\times$ 10^{-9} mol L^{-1}

Polyprotic Acids

15.107 $H_3PO_4(aq) + H_2O(l) \rightleftharpoons H_3O^+(aq) + H_2PO_4^-(aq) \qquad K_{a_1} = \dfrac{[H_3O^+][H_2PO_4^-]}{[H_3PO_4]}$

$H_2PO_4^-(aq) + H_2O(l) \rightleftharpoons H_3O^+(aq) + HPO_4^{2-}(aq) \qquad K_{a_2} = \dfrac{[H_3O^+][HPO_4^{2-}]}{[H_2PO_4^-]}$

$HPO_4^{2-}(aq) + H_2O(l) \rightleftharpoons H_3O^+(aq) + PO_4^{3-}(aq) \qquad K_{a_3} = \dfrac{[H_3O^+][PO_4^{3-}]}{[HPO_4^{2-}]}$

15.109   (a)   **Given:** 0.350 mol L^{-1} H$_3$PO$_4$, K_{a_1} = 7.5 $\times$ 10^{-3}, K_{a_2} = 6.2 $\times$ 10^{-8} **Find:** [H$_3$O$^+$], pH
Conceptual Plan: K_{a_1} **is much larger than** K_{a_2}**, so use** K_{a_1} **to calculate [H$_3$O$^+$]. Write a balanced reaction. Prepare an ICE table, represent the change with x, sum the table, determine the equilibrium values, put the equilibrium values in the equilibrium expression, and solve for x.**
Solution: H$_3$PO$_4$(aq) + H$_2$O(l) $\rightleftharpoons$ H$_3$O$^+$(aq) + H$_2$PO$_4^-$(aq)

	H$_3$PO$_4$(aq) + H$_2$O(l) $\rightleftharpoons$	H$_3$O$^+$(aq) +	H$_2$PO$_4^-$(aq)
I	0.350	0	0
C	- x	+x	+x
E	0.350 $-$ x	x	x

$$K_a = \frac{[H_3O^+][H_2PO_4^-]}{[H_3PO_4]} = \frac{(x)(x)}{(0.350 - x)} = 7.5 \times 10^{-3}$$

Assume x is small compared to 0.350.
$$x^2 = (7.5 \times 10^{-3})(0.350) \qquad x = 0.0512 \text{ mol L}^{-1} = [H_3O^+]$$

Check assumption: $\dfrac{0.0512}{0.350}$ x 100% = 14.4% assumption not valid, solve with quadratic equation.

$$x^2 + 7.5 \times 10^{-3} x - 0.002625 = 0 \qquad x = 0.04762 \text{ mol L}^{-1} = [H_3O^+]$$
pH = $-$log(0.04762) = 1.32

(b)   **Given:** 0.350 mol L^{-1} H$_2$C$_2$O$_4$, K_{a_1} = 6.0 x 10^{-2}, K_{a_2} = 6.0 x 10^{-5} **Find:** [H$_3$O$^+$], pH

Conceptual Plan: K_{a_1} is much larger than K_{a_2}, so use K_{a_1} to calculate [H$_3$O$^+$]. Write a balanced reaction. Prepare an ICE table, represent the change with x, sum the table, determine the equilibrium values, put the equilibrium values in the equilibrium expression, and solve for x.

Solution: H$_2$C$_2$O$_4$(aq) + H$_2$O(l) $\rightleftharpoons$ H$_3$O$^+$(aq) + HC$_2$O$_4$$^-$(aq)

I	0.350	0	0
C	- x	+x	+x
E	0.350 – x	x	x

$$K_a = \frac{[H_3O^+][HC_2O_4^-]}{[H_2C_2O_4]} = \frac{(x)(x)}{(0.350 - x)} = 6.0 \times 10^{-2}$$

$x^2 + 6.0 \times 10^{-2} x - 0.021 = 0$ $x = 0.1179 = 0.12$ mol L^{-1} = [H$_3$O$^+$]

pH = $-\log(0.12) = 0.92$

15.111   **Given:** 0.500 mol L^{-1} H$_2$SO$_3$, K_{a_1} = 1.6 x 10^{-2}, K_{a_2} = 6.4 x 10^{-8} **Find:** concentration of all species

Conceptual Plan: K_{a_1} is much larger than K_{a_2} so, use K_{a_1} to calculate [H$_3$O$^+$]. Write a balanced reaction. Prepare an ICE table, represent the change with x, sum the table, determine the equilibrium values, put the equilibrium values in the equilibrium expression, and solve for x.

Solution: H$_2$SO$_3$(aq) + H$_2$O(l) $\rightleftharpoons$ H$_3$O$^+$(aq) + HSO$_3$$^-$(aq)

I	0.500	0	0
C	- x	+x	+x
E	0.500 – x	x	x

$$K_{a_1} = \frac{[H_3O^+][HSO_3^-]}{[H_2SO_3]} = \frac{(x)(x)}{(0.500 - x)} = 1.6 \times 10^{-2}$$

$x^2 + 1.6 \times 10^{-2} x - 0.0080 = 0$ $x = 0.0818 = 0.082$ mol L^{-1} = [H$_3$O$^+$] = [HSO$_3$$^-$]

Use the values from reaction 1 in reaction 2.

HSO$_3$$^-$(aq) + H$_2$O(l) $\rightleftharpoons$ H$_3$O$^+$(aq) + SO$_3$$^{2-}$(aq)

I	0.0818	0.0818	0
C	- y	+y	+y
E	0.0818 – y	0.0818 + y	y

$$K_{a_2} = \frac{[H_3O^+][SO_3^{2-}]}{[HSO_3^-]} = \frac{(0.0818 + y)(y)}{(0.0818 - y)} = 6.4 \times 10^{-8}$$

Assume y is small. Then, $y = 6.4 \times 10^{-8}$.

[H$_2$SO$_3$] = 0.500 – 0.0818 = 0.418 mol L^{-1}

[HSO$_3$$^-$] = x = 0.0818 = 0.082 mol L^{-1}

[SO$_3$$^{2-}$] = y = 6.4 x 10^{-8} mol L^{-1}

[H$_3$O$^+$] = x + y = 0.0818 = 0.082 mol L^{-1}

$$[OH^-] = \frac{K_w}{[H_3O^+]} = \frac{1.0 \times 10^{-14}}{0.0818 \text{ mol L}^{-1}} = 1.2 \times 10^{-13} \text{ mol L}^{-1}$$

15.113   (a)   **Given:** [H$_2$SO$_4$] = 0.50 mol L^{-1} K_{a_2} = 0.012 **Find:** [H$_3$O$^+$], pH

Conceptual Plan: The first ionization step is strong. Use K_{a_2} and reaction 2. Write a balanced reaction. Prepare an ICE table, represent the change with x, sum the table, determine the equilibrium values, put the equilibrium values in the equilibrium expression, and solve for x.

Solution: H$_2$SO$_4$(aq) + H$_2$O(l) $\rightarrow$ H$_3$O$^+$(aq) + HSO$_4$$^-$(aq) strong

[H$_3$O$^+$] = [HSO$_4$$^-$] = 0.50 mol L^{-1}

HSO$_4$$^-$(aq) + H$_2$O(l) $\rightleftharpoons$ H$_3$O$^+$(aq) + SO$_4$$^{2-}$(aq)

I	0.50	0.50	0
C	- x	+x	+x
E	0.50 – x	0.50 + x	x

$$K_a = \frac{[H_3O^+][SO_4^{2-}]}{[HSO_4^-]} = \frac{(0.50 + x)(x)}{(0.50 - x)} = 0.012$$

$x^2 + 0.512 x - 0.006 = 0$ $x = 0.0115$ mol L^{-1} = [H$_3$O$^+$] from second ionization step

[H$_3$O$^+$] = 0.50 + 0.012 = 0.51 mol L^{-1}

pH = - $\log(0.51) = 0.29$

(b)   **Given:** $[H_2SO_4] = 0.10$ mol L^{-1}, $K_{a_2} = 0.012$ **Find:** $[H_3O^+]$, pH

Conceptual Plan: The first ionization step is strong. Use K_{a_2} and reaction 2. Write a balanced reaction. Prepare an ICE table, represent the change with x, sum the table, determine the equilibrium values, put the equilibrium values in the equilibrium expression, and solve for x.

Solution: $H_2SO_4(aq) + H_2O(l) \longrightarrow H_3O^+(aq) + HSO_4^-(aq)$ strong

$[H_3O^+] = [HSO_4^-] = 0.10$ mol L^{-1}

$HSO_4^-(aq) + H_2O(l) \rightleftharpoons H_3O^+(aq) + SO_4^{2-}(aq)$

I	0.10	0.10	0
C	$-x$	$+x$	$+x$
E	$0.10 - x$	$0.10 + x$	x

$K_{a_2} = \dfrac{[H_3O^+][SO_4^{2-}]}{[HSO_4^-]} = \dfrac{(0.10 + x)(x)}{(0.10 - x)} = 0.012$

$x^2 + 0.112x - 0.0012 = 0$ $x = 0.009848$

$\dfrac{0.009848}{0.10}$ x 100% = 9.8% contribution of second ionizations step not negligible

$[H_3O^+] = 0.10 + 0.0085 = 0.1085 = 0.11$ mol L^{-1}

pH = $-\log(0.11) = 0.96$

(c)   **Given:** $[H_2SO_4] = 0.050$ mol L^{-1}, $K_{a_2} = 0.012$ **Find:** $[H_3O^+]$, pH

Conceptual Plan: The first ionization step is strong. Use K_{a_2} and reaction 2. Write a balanced reaction. Prepare an ICE table, represent the change with x, sum the table, determine the equilibrium values, put the equilibrium values in the equilibrium expression, and solve for x.

Solution: $H_2SO_4(aq) + H_2O(l) \longrightarrow H_3O^+(aq) + HSO_4^-(aq)$ strong

$[H_3O^+] = [HSO_4^-] = 0.050$ mol L^{-1}

$HSO_4^-(aq) + H_2O(l) \rightleftharpoons H_3O^+(aq) + SO_4^{2-}(aq)$

I	0.050	0.050	0
C	$-x$	$+x$	$+x$
E	$0.050 - x$	$0.050 + x$	x

$K_{a_2} = \dfrac{[H_3O^+][SO_4^{2-}]}{[HSO_4^-]} = \dfrac{(0.050 + x)(x)}{(0.050 - x)} = 0.012$

$x^2 + 0.062\,x - 0.006 = 0$ $x = 0.008509$

$\dfrac{0.008509}{0.050}$ x 100% = 17% contribution of second ionization step not negligible

$[H_3O^+] = 0.050 + 0.0085 = 0.0585 = 0.059$ mol L^{-1} pH = $-\log(0.059) = 1.23$

Molecular Structure and Acid Strength

15.115   (a)   HCl is the stronger acid. HCl is the weaker bond; therefore, it is more acidic.

(b)   HF is the stronger acid. The electron affinity of F is greater than O, making F^- the more stable conjugate base and HF the stronger acid.

(c) H_2Se is the stronger acid. The H—Se bond is weaker; therefore, it is more acidic.

15.117   (a) H_2SO_4 is the stronger acid because it has more oxygen atoms.

(b) $HClO_2$ is the stronger acid because it has more oxygen atoms.

(c)   HClO is the stronger acid because Cl is more electronegative than Br.

(d) CCl_3COOH is the stronger acid because Cl is more electronegative than H.

15.119 S^{2-} is the stronger base. Base strength is determined from the corresponding acid. The weaker the acid, the stronger the base. H_2S is the weaker acid because it has a stronger bond.

15.121   A base is an electron pair donor under the Lewis definition. So any factor that leads to more electron density being put on the basic site will make it a better electron pair donor and a stronger base. Site ii is more basic because the methyl (CH_3) group acts as electron density donor (it is less electronegative than nitrogen). The methyl group will add electron density to the nitrogen at site ii making it more effective at donating an electron pair and a stronger base than the nitrogen at site i.

Lewis Acids and Bases

15.123   (a)   Lewis acid: Fe^{3+} has an empty d orbital and can accept lone-pair electrons.

(b)   Lewis acid: BH_3 has an empty p orbital to accept a lone pair of electrons.

(c)   Lewis base: NH_3 has a lone pair of electrons to donate.

(d)   Lewis base: F^- has lone-pair electrons to donate.

15.125   (a) Fe^{3+} accepts an electron pair from H_2O, so Fe^{3+} is the Lewis acid and H_2O is the Lewis base.

(b) Zn^{2+} accepts an electron pair from NH_3, so Zn^{2+} is the Lewis acid and NH_3 is the Lewis base.

(c)   The empty p orbital on B accepts an electron pair from $(CH_3)_3N$, so BF_3 is the Lewis acid and $(CH_3)_3N$ is the Lewis base.

Cumulative Problems

15.127   (a)   Weak acid. The beaker contains 10 HF molecules, 2 H_3O^+ ions, and 2 F^- ions. Since both the molecule and the ions exist in solution, the acid is a weak acid.

(b)   Strong acid. The beaker contains 12 H_3O^+ ions and 12 I^- ions. Since the molecule is completely ionized in solution, the acid is a strong acid.

(c)   Weak acid. The beaker contains 10 $HCHO_2$ molecules, 2 H_3O^+ ions, and 2 CHO_2^- ions. Since both the molecule and the ions exist in solution, the acid is a weak acid.

(d)   Strong acid. The beaker contains 12 H_3O^+ ions and 12 NO_3^- ions. Since the molecule is completely ionized in solution, the acid is a strong acid.

15.129 $HbH^+(aq) + O_2(aq) \rightleftharpoons HbO_2(aq) + H^+(aq)$

Using Le Châtelier's principle, if the $[H^+]$ increases, the reaction will shift left, if the $[H^+]$ decreases, the reaction will shift right. So, if the pH of blood is too acidic (low pH; $[H^+]$ increased), the reaction will shift to the left. This will lead to less HbO_2 in the blood and decrease the oxygen-carrying capacity of the hemoglobin in the blood.

15.131   **Given:** 4.00×10^2 mg $Mg(OH)_2$, 2.00×10^2 mL HCl solution, pH = 1.3
Find: volume neutralized, % neutralized.
Conceptual Plan:
mg $Mg(OH)_2$ → g $Mg(OH)_2$ → mol $Mg(OH)_2$ and then pH → $[H_3O^+]$ and then mol $Mg(OH)_2$ →

$$\frac{1 \text{ g } Mg(OH)_2}{1000 \text{ } Mg(OH)_2} \qquad \frac{1 \text{ mol } Mg(OH)_2}{58.33 \text{g } Mg(OH)_2} \qquad\qquad \text{pH} = -\log [H_3O^+] \qquad\qquad \frac{2 \text{ mol 2 OH}^-}{1 \text{ mol } Mg(OH)_2}$$

mol OH^- → mol H_3O^+ → vol H_3O^+ → % neutralized.

$$\frac{1 \text{ mol } H_3O^+}{1 \text{ mol } OH^-} \qquad \frac{\text{mol } H_3O^+}{M(H_3O^+)} \quad \frac{\text{vol HCl neutralized}}{\text{total vol HCl}} \times 100\%$$

Solution: $[H_3O^+] = 10^{-1.3} = 0.05011$ mol L^{-1} = 0.05 mol L^{-1}

$$4.00 \times 10^2 \text{ mg } Mg(OH)_2 \times \frac{1 \text{ g } Mg(OH)_2}{1000 \text{ mg } Mg(OH)_2} \times \frac{1 \text{ mol } Mg(OH)_2}{58.33 \text{ g } Mg(OH)_2} \times \frac{2 \text{ mol } OH^-}{1 \text{ mol } Mg(OH)_2}$$

$$\times \frac{1 \text{ mol } H_3O^+}{1 \text{ mol } OH^-} \times \frac{1 \text{ L}}{0.0501 \text{ mol } H_3O^+} \times \frac{1000 \text{ mL}}{1 \text{ L}} = 273.8 \text{ mL} = 274 \text{ mL neutralized}$$

Stomach contains 2.00×10^2 mL HCl at pH = 1.3 and 4.00×10^2 mg will neutralize 274 mL of pH 1.3 HCl, so all of the stomach acid will be neutralized.

15.133   **Given:** pH of Great Lakes acid rain = 4.5, West Coast = 5.4
Find: $[H_3O^+]$ and ratio of Great Lakes/West Coast
Conceptual Plan: pH $\rightarrow$ $[H_3O^+]$, and then ratio of $[H_3O^+]$ Great Lakes to West Coast.

$$pH = -\log[H_3O^+]$$

Solution: Great Lakes: $[H_3O^+] = 10^{-4.5} = 3.16 \times 10^{-5}$ mol L^{-1}

West Coast: $[H_3O^+] = 10^{-5.4} = 3.98 \times 10^{-6}$ mol L^{-1}

$$\frac{\text{Great Lakes}}{\text{West Coast}} = \frac{3.16 \times 10^{-5}\,\cancel{\text{mol L}^{-1}}}{3.98 \times 10^{-6}\,\cancel{\text{mol L}^{-1}}} = 7.94 = 8 \text{ times more acidic}$$

15.135   **Given:** 6.5×10^2 mg aspirin, $pK_a = 3.5$ **Find:** pH of solution
Conceptual Plan:

mg aspirin $\rightarrow$ g aspirin $\rightarrow$ mol aspirin and then [aspirin] and pK_a

$$\frac{1 \text{ g aspirin}}{1000 \text{ mg aspirin}} \quad \frac{1 \text{ mol aspirin}}{180.16 \text{ g aspirin}} \qquad \frac{\text{mol aspirin}}{\text{L soln}} \quad pK_a = -\log K_a$$

$\rightarrow K_a$. **Write a balanced reaction. Prepare an ICE table, represent the change with x, sum the table, determine the equilibrium values, put the equilibrium values in the equilibrium expression, and solve for x. Determine $[H_3O^+] \rightarrow$ pH.**

$$pH = -\log[H_3O^+]$$

Solution: $\dfrac{6.5 \times 10^2 \,\cancel{\text{mg aspirin}}}{1} \times \dfrac{1 \,\cancel{\text{g aspirin}}}{1000 \,\cancel{\text{mg aspirin}}} \times \dfrac{1 \text{ mol aspirin}}{180.16 \,\cancel{\text{g aspirin}}} \times \dfrac{1}{0.24 \text{ L}} = 0.01\underline{5}0$ mol L^{-1} aspirin

$K_a = 10^{-3.5} = 3.1\underline{6} \times 10^{-4}$

$\text{aspirin}(aq) + H_2O(l) \rightleftharpoons H_3O^+(aq) + \text{aspirin}^-(aq)$

I	0.01$\underline{5}$0	0	0
C	$-x$	$+x$	$+x$
E	0.01$\underline{5}$0 $- x$	x	x

$$K_a = \frac{[H_3O^+][\text{aspirin}^-]}{[\text{aspirin}]} = \frac{(x)(x)}{(0.0150 - x)} = 3.1\underline{6} \times 10^{-4}$$

$x^2 + 3.16 \times 10^{-4}x - 4.74 \times 10^{-6} = 0$ $x = 2.0\underline{2} \times 10^{-3}$ mol L$^{-1} = [H_3O^+]$

$pH = -\log(2.0\underline{2} \times 10^{-3}) = 2.7$

15.137   (a)   **Given:** 0.0100 mol L^{-1} HClO$_4$ **Find:** pH
Conceptual Plan: $[HClO_4] \rightarrow [H_3O^+] \rightarrow$ pH

$$[HClO_4] \rightarrow [H_3O^+] \quad pH = -\log[H_3O^+]$$

Solution: 0.0100 mol L^{-1} HClO$_4$ = 0.0100 mol L^{-1} H$_3$O$^+$ pH = $-\log(0.0100) = 2.000$

(b)   **Given:** 0.115 mol L^{-1} HClO$_2$, $K_a = 1.1 \times 10^{-2}$ **Find:** pH
Conceptual Plan: Write a balanced reaction. Prepare an ICE table, represent the change with x, sum the table, determine the equilibrium values, put the equilibrium values in the equilibrium expression, and solve for x. Determine $[H_3O^+]$ and pH.
Solution: $HClO_2(aq) + H_2O(l) \rightleftharpoons H_3O^+(aq) + ClO_2^-(aq)$

I	0.115	0	0
C	$-x$	$+x$	$+x$
E	0.115 $- x$	x	x

$$K_a = \frac{[H_3O^+][ClO_2^-]}{[HClO_2]} = \frac{(x)(x)}{(0.115 - x)} = 1.1 \times 10^{-2}$$

Assume x is small compared to 0.115.

$x^2 = (1.1 \times 10^{-2})(0.115)$ $x = 0.035\underline{6}$ mol L$^{-1} = [H_3O^+]$

Check assumption: $\dfrac{0.0356}{0.115}$ x 100% = 30.9% Assumption not valid, solve with quadratic equation.

$x^2 + 1.1 \times 10^{-2}x - 0.001265 = 0$

$x = 0.030\underline{4}9$ mol L^{-1} or -0.0415 mol L^{-1}

pH $= -\log(0.030\underline{4}9) = 1.52$

(c) **Given:** 0.045 mol L^{-1} Sr(OH)$_2$ **Find:** pH
Conceptual Plan: [Sr(OH)$_2$] → **[OH$^-$]** → **[H$_3$O$^+$]** → **pH**

$$K_w = [H_3O^+][OH^-] \quad pH = -\log[H_3O^+] \quad pH + pOH = 14$$

Solution: [OH$^-$] = [Sr(OH)$_2$] = 2(0.045) = 0.090 mol L^{-1}

$$[H_3O^+] = \dfrac{K_w}{[OH^-]} = \dfrac{1.0 \times 10^{-14}}{0.090 \text{ mol L}^{-1}} = 1.\underline{1}1 \times 10^{-13} \text{ mol L}^{-1}$$

pH $= -\log(1.\underline{1}1 \times 10^{-13}) = 12.95$

(d) **Given:** 0.0852 mol L^{-1} KCN, $K_a = 4.9 \times 10^{-10}$ **Find:** pH
Conceptual Plan: Identify each species and determine which will contribute to pH. Write a balanced reaction. Prepare an ICE table, represent the change with x, sum the table, determine the equilibrium values, put the equilibrium values in the equilibrium expression, and solve for x. Determine [OH$^-$] → **pOH** → **pH.**

$$pOH = -\log[OH^-] \quad pH + pOH = 14$$

Solution: K$^+$ is the counterion of a strong base; therefore, it is pH-neutral. CN$^-$ is the conjugate base of a weak acid; therefore, it is basic.

	CN$^-$(aq) + H$_2$O(l) $\rightleftharpoons$ HCN (aq)+	OH$^-$(aq)	
I	0.0852	0	0
C	-x	+x	+x
E	0.0852 − x	x	x

$$K_b = \dfrac{K_w}{K_a} = \dfrac{1.0 \times 10^{-14}}{4.9 \times 10^{-10}} = 2.0\underline{4} \times 10^{-5} = \dfrac{(x)(x)}{(0.0852 - x)}$$

Assume x is small.

$x = 1.\underline{3}2 \times 10^{-3}$ mol L^{-1} = [OH$^-$]   pOH $= -\log(1.\underline{3}2 \times 10^{-3}) = 2.88$

pH $= 14.00 - 2.88 = 11.12$

(e) **Given:** 0.155 mol L^{-1} NH$_4$Cl, K_b (NH$_3$) $= 1.8 \times 10^{-5}$ **Find:** pH
Conceptual Plan: Identify each species and determine which will contribute to pH. Write a balanced reaction. Prepare an ICE table, represent the change with x, sum the table, determine the equilibrium values, put the equilibrium values in the equilibrium expression, and solve for x. Determine [H$_3$O$^+$] → **pH.**
Solution: NH$_4^+$ is the conjugate acid of a weak base; therefore, it is acidic. Cl$^-$ is the conjugate base of a strong acid; therefore, it is pH-neutral.

	NH$_4^+$(aq) + H$_2$O(l) $\rightleftharpoons$ NH$_3$(aq) +	H$_3$O$^+$(aq)	
I	0.155	0	0
C	-x	+x	+x
E	0.155 − x	x	x

$$K_a = \dfrac{K_w}{K_b} = \dfrac{1 \times 10^{-14}}{1.8 \times 10^{-5}} = 5.\underline{5}6 \times 10^{-10} = \dfrac{(x)(x)}{(0.155 - x)}$$

Assume x is small.

$x = 9.\underline{2}8 \times 10^{-6}$ mol L^{-1} = [H$_3$O$^+$]   pH $= -\log(9.\underline{2}8 \times 10^{-6}) = 5.03$

15.139 (a) **Given:** 0.0550 mol L^{-1} HI (strong acid), 0.00850 mol L^{-1} HF (weak acid) **Find:** pH
Conceptual Plan: Since the mixture is a strong acid and a weak acid, the strong acid will dominate. Use the concentration of the strong acid to determine [H$_3$O$^+$] and then pH.
Solution: 0.0550 mol L^{-1} HI = 0.0550 mol L^{-1} H$_3$O$^+$ pH = -log(0.0550) = 1.260

(b) **Given:** 0.112 mol L^{-1} NaCl (salt), 0.0953 mol L^{-1} KF (salt) **Find:** pH
Conceptual Plan: Identify each species and determine which will contribute to pH. Write a balanced

reaction. **Prepare an ICE table, represent the change with x, sum the table, determine the equilibrium values, put the equilibrium values in the equilibrium expression, and solve for x. Determine $[H_3O^+] \rightarrow$ pH.**

Solution: Na^+ is the counterion of a strong base; therefore, it is pH-neutral. Cl^- is the conjugate base of a strong acid; therefore, it is pH-neutral. K^+ is the counterion of a strong base; therefore, it is pH-neutral. F^- is the conjugate base of a weak acid. Therefore, it will produce a basic solution.

$$F^-(aq) + H_2O(l) \rightleftharpoons HF(aq) + OH^-(aq)$$

I	0.0953	0	0
C	$-x$	$+x$	$+x$
E	$0.0953 - x$	x	x

$$K_b = \frac{K_w}{K_a} = \frac{1.0 \times 10^{-14}}{3.5 \times 10^{-4}} = \frac{(x)(x)}{(0.0953 - x)}$$

Assume x is small.

$x = 1.650 \times 10^{-6}$ mol $L^{-1} = [OH^-]$ pOH $= -\log(1.650 \times 10^{-6}) = 5.78$

pH $= 14.00 - 5.78 = 8.22$

(c)   **Given:** 0.132 mol L^{-1} NH_4Cl (salt), 0.150 mol L^{-1} HNO_3 (strong acid) **Find:** pH
Conceptual Plan: Since the mixture is a strong acid and a salt, the strong acid will dominate. Use the concentration of the strong acid to determine $[H_3O^+]$ and then pH.
Solution: 0.150 mol L^{-1} HNO_3 = 0.150 mol L^{-1} H_3O^+ pH $= -\log(0.150) = 0.824$

(d)   **Given:** 0.0887 mol L^{-1} $NaC_7H_5O_2$ (salt) 0.225 mol L^{-1} KBr (salt)
Conceptual Plan: Identify each species and determine which will contribute to pH. Write a balanced reaction. Prepare an ICE table, represent the change with x, sum the table, determine the equilibrium values, put the equilibrium values in the equilibrium expression, and solve for x. Determine $[H_3O^+] \rightarrow$ pH.
Solution: Na^+ is the counterion of a strong base; therefore, it is pH-neutral. $C_7H_5O_2^-$ is the conjugate base of a weak acid. Therefore, it will produce a basic solution. K^+ is the counterion of a strong base; therefore, it is pH-neutral. Cl^- is the conjugate base of a strong acid; therefore, it is pH-neutral.

$$C_7H_5O_2^-(aq) + H_2O(l) \rightleftharpoons HC_7H_5O_2(aq) + OH^-(aq)$$

I	0.0887	0	0
C	$-x$	$+x$	$+x$
E	$0.0887 - x$	x	x

$$K_b = \frac{K_w}{K_a} = \frac{1.0 \times 10^{-14}}{6.5 \times 10^{-5}} = \frac{(x)(x)}{(0.0887 - x)}$$

Assume x is small.

$x = 3.694 \times 10^{-6}$ mol $L^{-1} = [OH^-]$ pOH $= -\log(3.694 \times 10^{-6}) = 5.43$

pH $= 14.00 - 5.43 = 8.57$

(e)   **Given:** 0.0450 mol L^{-1} HCl (strong acid), 0.0225 mol L^{-1} HNO_3 (strong acid) **Find:** pH
Conceptual Plan: Since the mixture is a strong acid and a strong acid, $[H_3O^+]$ is the sum of the concentration of both acids. Then determine pH.
Solution: 0.0450 mol L^{-1} HCl = 0.0450 mol L^{-1} H_3O^+, 0.0225 mol L^{-1} HNO_3 = 0.0225 mol L^{-1} H_3O^+
$[H_3O^+] = 0.0450 + 0.0225 = 0.0675$ mol L^{-1} pH $= -\log(0.0675) = 1.171$

15.141   (a)   sodium cyanide = NaCN   nitric acid = HNO_3
$$H^+(aq) + CN^-(aq) \rightleftharpoons HCN(aq)$$

(b)   ammonium chloride = NH_4Cl sodium hydroxide = NaOH
$$NH_4^+(aq) + OH^-(aq) \rightleftharpoons NH_3(aq) + H_2O(l)$$

(c)   sodium cyanide = NaCN   ammonium bromide = NH_4Br
$$NH_4^+(aq) + CN^-(aq) \rightleftharpoons NH_3(aq) + HCN(aq)$$

(d)   potassium hydrogen sulfate = $KHSO_4$ lithium acetate = $LiC_2H_3O_2$
$$HSO_4^-(aq) + C_2H_3O_2^-(aq) \rightleftharpoons SO_4^{2-}(aq) + HC_2H_3O_2(aq)$$

(e)   sodium hypochlorite = $NaClO$ ammonia = NH_3
No reaction, both are bases.

15.143   **Given:** 1.0 mol L^{-1} urea, pH = 7.050 **Find:** K_a Hurea$^+$
Conceptual Plan: pH $\rightarrow$ pOH $\rightarrow$ [OH$^-$] $\rightarrow$ K_b(urea) $\rightarrow$ K_a(Hurea$^+$). Write a balanced reaction.
$$pH + pOH = 14 \quad pOH = -\log[OH^-]$$
Prepare an ICE table, represent the change with x, sum the table, determine the equilibrium values, put the equilibrium values in the equilibrium expression, and determine K_b.
Solution: pOH = 14.000 − 7.050 = 6.950 mol L^{-1} OH$^-$ = $10^{-6.950}$ = 1.1$\underline{2}$2 x 10^{-7} mol L^{-1}

	urea(aq) + H$_2$O(l) $\rightleftharpoons$	Hurea$^+$(aq) +	OH$^-$(aq)
I	1.0	0	0
C	−x	+x	+x
E	1.0 − 1.1$\underline{2}$2 x 10^{-7}	1.1$\underline{2}$2 x 10^{-7}	1.1$\underline{2}$2 x 10^{-7}

$$K_b = \frac{[\text{Hurea}^+][\text{OH}^-]}{[\text{urea}]} = \frac{(1.1\underline{2}2 \times 10^{-7})(1.1\underline{2}2 \times 10^{-7})}{(1.0 - 1.1\underline{2}2 \times 10^{-7})} = 1.2\underline{5}89 \times 10^{-14}$$

$$K_a = \frac{K_w}{K_b} = \frac{1.00 \times 10^{-14}}{1.2\underline{5}89 \times 10^{-14}} = 0.794\underline{3} = 0.794$$

15.145   **Given:** Ca(Lact)$_2$, [Ca^{2+}] = 0.26 mol L^{-1}, pH = 8.40 **Find:** K_a lactic acid
Conceptual Plan: [Ca^{2+}] $\rightarrow$ [Lact$^-$] ; determine K_b lactate ion. Prepare an ICE table, represent the
$$\frac{2 \text{ mol lactate ion}}{1 \text{ mol Ca}^{2+}}$$
change with x, sum the table, and determine the equilibrium constant. $K_b \rightarrow K_a$
$$K_a = \frac{K_w}{K_b}$$

Solution: 0.26 mol L^{-1} Ca^{2+} $\left(\dfrac{2 \text{ mol lact}^-}{1 \text{ mol Ca}^{2+}}\right)$ = 0.52 mol L^{-1} lact$^-$

	Lact$^-$(aq) + H$_2$O(l) $\rightleftharpoons$	Hlact(aq) +	OH$^-$(aq)
I	0.52	0	0
C	−x	+x	+x
E	0.52 − x	x	x

pH = 8.40 [H$_3$O$^+$] = $10^{-8.40}$ = 4.0 x 10^{-9} [OH$^-$] = $\dfrac{1.0 \times 10^{-14}}{4.0 \times 10^{-9}}$ = 2.5 x 10^{-6} mol L^{-1} = x

$$K_b = \frac{[\text{Hlact}][\text{OH}^-]}{[\text{lact}^-]} = \frac{(2.5 \times 10^{-6})(2.5 \times 10^{-6})}{(0.52 - 2.5 \times 10^{-6})} = 1.2 \times 10^{-11}$$

$$K_a = \frac{K_w}{K_b} = \frac{1.0 \times 10^{-14}}{1.2 \times 10^{-11}} = 8.3 \times 10^{-4}$$

15.147   **Given:** 2,4–D = $C_8H_6Cl_2O_3$, pK_a = 2.73, 190 g L^{-1} **Find:** pH
Conceptual Plan: g L^{-1} $\rightarrow$ mol L^{-1} then pK_a $\rightarrow$ K_a
$$\frac{1 \text{ mol } 2,4-D}{221.03 \text{ g } 2,4-D} \qquad pK_a = -\log K_a$$
Write a balanced reaction. Prepare an ICE table, represent the change with x, sum the table, determine the equilibrium values, put the equilibrium values in the equilibrium expression, and solve for x. Determine [H$_3$O$^+$] and pH.
Solution: $\dfrac{190 \text{ g}}{1 \text{ L}} \times \dfrac{1 \text{ mol}}{221.03 \text{ g}}$ = 0.8$\underline{5}$956 mol L^{-1} 2,4–D $K_a = 10^{-2.73} = 1.\underline{8}6 \times 10^{-3}$

	C$_8$H$_6$Cl$_2$O$_3$(aq) + H$_2$O(l) $\rightleftharpoons$	H$_3$O$^+$(aq) +	C$_8$H$_5$Cl$_2$O$_3^-$(aq)
I	0.8$\underline{5}$956 mol L^{-1}	0	0
C	−x	+x	+x
E	0.8$\underline{5}$958 − x	x	x

$$K_a = \frac{[\text{H}_3\text{O}^+][\text{C}_8\text{H}_5\text{Cl}_2\text{O}_3^-]}{[\text{C}_8\text{H}_6\text{Cl}_2\text{O}_3]} = \frac{(x)(x)}{0.85956 - x} = 1.86 \times 10^{-3}. \text{ Solve using quadratic equation.}$$

$x^2 + 1.\underline{8}6 \times 10^{-3}x - 1.\underline{5}99 \times 10^{-3}$. $x = 0.03\underline{9}068$ mol $L^{-1} = [H_3O^+]$

pH $= -\log[H_3O^+] = -\log(0.03\underline{9}068) = 1.41$

Challenge Problems

15.149   The calculation is incorrect because it neglects the contribution from the autoionization of water.
HI is a strong acid, so $[H_3O^+]$ from HI $= 1.0 \times 10^{-7}$ mol L^{-1}.

$$H_2O(l) + H_2O(l) \rightleftharpoons H_3O^+(aq) + OH^-(aq)$$

		H_3O^+	OH^-
I		1×10^{-7}	0
C	$-x$	$+x$	$+x$
E		$1 \times 10^{-7} + x$	x

$K_w = [H_3O^+][OH^-] = 1.0 \times 10^{-14}$

$(1 \times 10^{-7} + x)(x) = 1.0 \times 10^{-14}$ $x^2 + 1 \times 10^{-7}x - 1.0 \times 10^{-14} = 0$

$x = 6.18 \times 10^{-8}$ mol L^{-1}

$[H_3O^+] = (1 \times 10^{-7} + x) = (1 \times 10^{-7} + 6.18 \times 10^{-8}) = 1.618 \times 10^{-7}$ mol L^{-1}

pH $= -\log(1.618 \times 10^{-7}) = 6.79$

15.151   **Given:** 0.00115 mol L^{-1} HCl, 0.01000 mol L^{-1} $HClO_2$, $K_a = 1.1 \times 10^{-2}$ **Find:** pH
Conceptual Plan: Use HCl to determine $[H_3O^+]$. Use $[H_3O^+]$ and $HClO_2$ to determine dissociation of $HClO_2$. Write a balanced reaction, prepare an ICE table, calculate equilibrium concentrations, and plug into the equilibrium expression.
Solution: 0.00115 mol L^{-1} HCl $= 0.00115$ mol L^{-1} H_3O^+

$$HClO_2(aq) + H_2O(l) \rightleftharpoons H_3O^+(aq) + ClO_2^-(aq)$$

		H_3O^+	ClO_2^-
I	0.0100	0.00115	0
C	$-x$	$+x$	$+x$
E	$0.01000 - x$	$0.00115 + x$	x

$K_a = \dfrac{[H_3O^+][ClO_2^-]}{[HClO_2]} = \dfrac{(0.00115 + x)(x)}{(0.0100 - x)} = 1.1 \times 10^{-2}$

$x^2 + 0.01215x - 1.1 \times 10^{-4} = 0$ $x = 0.006045$ mol L^{-1}

$[H_3O^+] = 0.00115 + 0.006045 = 0.007\underline{1}95$ mol L^{-1}

pH $= -\log(0.007\underline{1}95) = 2.14$

15.153   **Given:** 1.0 mol L^{-1} HA, $K_a = 1.0 \times 10^{-8}$; $K = 4.0$ for reaction 2 **Find:** $[H^+]$, $[A^-]$, $[HA_2^-]$
Conceptual Plan: Combine reaction 1 and reaction 2 then determine the equilibrium expression and the value of K. Prepare an ICE table, calculate equilibrium concentrations, and then plug into the equilibrium expression.
Solution:

			$K = 1.0 \times 10^{-8}$
$HA(aq)$	$\rightleftharpoons$	$H^+(aq) + A^-(aq)$	$K = 1.0 \times 10^{-8}$
$HA(aq) + A^-(aq)$	$\rightleftharpoons$	$HA_2^-(aq)$	$K = 4.0$
$2HA(aq)$	$\rightleftharpoons$	$H^+(aq) + HA_2^-(aq)$	$K = 4.0 \times 10^{-8}$

		H^+	HA_2^-
I	1.0	0	0
C	$-2x$	$+x$	$+x$
E	$1.0 - 2x$	x	x

$K = \dfrac{[H^+][HA_2^-]}{[HA]^2} = 4.0 \times 10^{-8} = \dfrac{(x)(x)}{(1.0 - 2x)^2}$

Take the square root of both sides of the equation. $x = 1.9992 \times 10^{-4}$ mol L^{-1}

		H^+		A^-	$K = 1.0 \times 10^{-8}$
	$HA(aq) \rightleftharpoons$	$H^+(aq)$	$+$	$A^-(aq)$	$K = 1.0 \times 10^{-8}$
I	1.0	1.9992×10^{-4}		0.0	
C	$-2y$	$+y$		$+y$	
E	$1.0 - 2y$	$1.9992 \times 10^{-4} + y$		y	

$K = \dfrac{[H^+][A^-]}{[HA]} = 1.0 \times 10^{-8} = \dfrac{(1.9992 \times 10^{-4} + y)(y)}{(1.0 - 2y)}$

$y^2 + 1.9992 \times 10^{-4}y - 1.0 \times 10^{-8} = 0$ $y = 4.\underline{1}4 \times 10^{-5}$ mol L^{-1}

$[H^+] = x + y = 1.9992 \times 10^{-4} + 4.14 \times 10^{-5} = 2.4 \times 10^{-4}$ mol L^{-1}

$[A^-] = y = 4.14 \times 10^{-5}$ mol L^{-1}

$[HA_2^-] = x = 2.0 \times 10^{-4}$ mol L^{-1}

15.155 **Given:** 0.200 mol NH_4CN, 1.00 L, K_b (NH_3) = 1.76 × 10^{-5}, K_a (HCN) = 4.9 × 10^{-10} **Find:** pH

Conceptual Plan: K_b NH_3 → K_a NH_4^+; K_a HCN → K_b CN^- **Prepare an ICE table, represent the**

$$K_a K_b = K_w$$

change with x, sum the table, and determine the equilibrium conditions.

Solution: $K_a(NH_4^+) = \dfrac{1.0 \times 10^{-14}}{1.76 \times 10^{-5}} = 5.68 \times 10^{-10}$ $\quad K_b(CN^-) = \dfrac{1.0 \times 10^{-14}}{4.9 \times 10^{-10}} = 2.0 \times 10^{-5}$

0.200 mol L^{-1} NH_4CN = 0.200 mol L^{-1} NH_4^+ and 0.200 mol L^{-1} CN^-

Since the value for K for CN^- is greater than the K for NH_4^+, the CN^- reaction will be larger and the solution will be basic.

	$CN^-(aq)$	+ $H_2O(l)$	$\rightleftharpoons$	$HCN(aq)$	+ $OH^-(aq)$
I	0.200			0	0
C	-x			+x	+x
E	0.200 - x			x	x

$K_b = \dfrac{[HCN][OH^-]}{[CN^-]} = 2.0 \times 10^{-5} = \dfrac{(x)(x)}{(0.200 - x)}$ $\quad$ Solve using the quadratic equation.

$x = 0.0020$ mol L^{-1} = $[OH^-]$

$[H_3O^+] = \dfrac{1.0 \times 10^{-14}}{0.0020} = 5.0 \times 10^{-12}$ $\quad$ pH = $-\log (5.0 \times 10^{-12})$ = 11.30

15.157 **Given:** mixture Na_2CO_3 and $NaHCO_3$ = 82.2 g, 1.0 L, pH = 9.95, K_a H_2CO_3 = K_{a_1} = 4.3 × 10^{-7}, K_{a_2} = 5.6 × 10^{-11}

Find: mass $NaHCO_3$

Conceptual Plan: Let x = g $NaHCO_3$, y = g Na_2CO_3 → mol $NaHCO_3$, Na_2CO_3 → [$NaHCO_3$], [Na_2CO_3]

$$\frac{1 \text{ mol } NaHCO_3}{84.01 \text{ g } NaHCO_3} \quad \frac{1 \text{ mol } Na_2CO_3}{105.99 \text{ g } NaHCO_3} \qquad M = \frac{\text{mol}}{L}$$

→ [HCO_3^-], [CO_3^{2-}], K_a(HCO_3^-) → K_b(CO_3^{2-}). Prepare an ICE table, represent the change with z,

$$\frac{1 \text{ mol } HCO_3^-}{1 \text{ mol } NaHCO_3} \quad \frac{1 \text{ mol } CO_3^{2-}}{1 \text{ mol } Na_2CO_3} \quad K_b = \frac{K_w}{K_a}$$

sum the table, and determine the equilibrium conditions.

Solution: Let x = g $NaHCO_3$ and y = g Na_2CO_3 $x + y$ = 82.2, so y = 82.2 - x

$\text{mol } NaHCO_3 = x \text{ g } NaHCO_3\left(\dfrac{1 \text{ mol } NaHCO_3}{84.01 \text{ g } NaHCO_3}\right) = \dfrac{x}{84.01}$

$[HCO_3^-] = \dfrac{\left(\dfrac{x}{84.01} \text{ mol } NaHCO_3\right)}{1 \text{ L}}\dfrac{1 \text{ mol } HCO_3^-}{1 \text{ mol } NaHCO_3} = \dfrac{x}{84.01}$ mol L^{-1} HCO_3^-

$\text{mol } Na_2CO_3 = 82.2 - x \text{ g } Na_2CO_3\left(\dfrac{1 \text{ mol}}{105.99 \text{ g } Na_2CO_3}\right) = \dfrac{82.2 - x}{105.99}$ mol Na_2CO_3

$[CO_3^{2-}] = \dfrac{\left(\dfrac{82.2 - x}{105.99} \text{ mol } Na_2CO_3\right)}{1 \text{ L}}\dfrac{1 \text{ mol } CO_3^{2-}}{1 \text{ mol } Na_2CO_3} = \dfrac{82.2 - x}{105.99}$ mol L^{-1} CO_3^{2-}

Since the pH of the solution is basic, it is the hydrolysis of CO_3^{2-} that dominates in the solution.

$K_b(CO_3^{2-}) = \dfrac{1.0 \times 10^{-14}}{5.6 \times 10^{-11}} = 1.78 \times 10^{-4}$ and: $[H_3O^+] = 10^{-9.95} = 1.12 \times 10^{-10}$ mol L^{-1}

$[OH^-] = \dfrac{1.0 \times 10^{-14}}{1.12 \times 10^{-10}} = 8.91 \times 10^{-5}$ mol L^{-1}

$$CO_3{}^{2-}(aq) + H_2O(l) \rightleftharpoons HCO_3{}^-(aq) + OH^-(aq)$$

I	$\dfrac{82.2 - x}{105.99}$	$\dfrac{x}{84.01}$
C	$-z$	$+z$
E	$\left(\dfrac{82.2 - x}{105.99}\right) - z$	$\left(\dfrac{x}{84.01}\right) + z \quad 8.91 \times 10^{-5}$

$$K_b(CO_3{}^{2-}) = 1.78 \times 10^{-4} = \frac{[HCO_3{}^-][OH^-]}{[CO_3{}^{2-}]} = \frac{\left(\left(\dfrac{x}{84.01}\right) - z\right)(8.91 \times 10^{-5})}{\left(\dfrac{82.2 - x}{105.99}\right) - z} \quad \text{Assume } z \text{ is small.}$$

$$\frac{1.78 \times 10^{-4}}{8.91 \times 10^{-5}} = \frac{\left(\dfrac{x}{84.01}\right)}{\left(\dfrac{82.2 - x}{105.99}\right)} \qquad x = 50.38 = 50.4 \text{ g NaHCO}_3$$

Conceptual Problems

15.159   Solution b would be most acidic.

(a)   0.0100 mol L^{-1} HCl (strong acid) and 0.0100 mol L^{-1} KOH (strong base), since the concentrations are equal, the acid and base will completely neutralize each other and the resulting solution will be pH-neutral.

(b)   0.0100 mol L^{-1} HF (weak acid) and 0.0100 mol L^{-1} KBr (salt). K_a (HF) = 3.5 x 10^{-4}. The weak acid will produce an acidic solution. K$^+$ is the counterion of a strong base and is pH-neutral. Br$^-$ is the conjugate base of a strong acid and is pH-neutral.

(c)   0.0100 mol L^{-1} NH$_4$Cl (salt) and 0.100 mol L^{-1} CH$_3$NH$_3$Br. K_b(NH$_3$) = 1.8 x 10^{-5}, K_b(CH$_3$NH$_2$) = 4.4 x 10^{-4}. NH$_4{}^+$ is the conjugate acid of a weak base and CH$_3$NH$_3{}^+$ is the conjugate acid of a weak base. Cl$^-$ and Br$^-$ are the conjugate bases of strong acids and will be pH-neutral. The solution will be acidic. However, because the K_a for the conjugate acids in this solution is smaller K_a for HF, the solution will be acidic, but not as acidic as HF.

(d)   0.100 mol L^{-1} NaCN (salt) and 0.100 mol L^{-1} CaCl$_2$. Na$^+$ and Ca^{2+} ion are the counterion of a strong base; therefore, they are pH-neutral. Cl$^-$ is the conjugate base of a strong acid and is pH-neutral. CN$^-$ is the conjugate base of a weak acid and will produce a basic solution.

15.161   CH$_3$COOH < CH$_2$ClCOOH < CHCl$_2$COOH < CCl$_3$COOH

Since Cl is more electronegative than H, as you add Cl you increase the number of electronegative atoms, which pulls the electron density away from the O—H group, polarizing the O—H bond, making it more acidic.

16 Aqueous Ionic Equilibrium

Review Questions

16.1   The pH range of human blood is between 7.36 and 7.42. This nearly constant blood pH is maintained by buffers that are chemical systems that resist pH changes, neutralizing an added acid or base. An important buffer system in blood is a mixture of carbonic acid (H_2CO_3) and bicarbonate ion (HCO_3^-).

16.3   The buffer capacity refers to how much added acid or base a buffer can effectively neutralize without causing a large change in the pH of the solution. The factors that affect buffer capacity are the absolute concentrations of the acid and its conjugate base as well as the relative concentrations of the buffer components. The buffer capacity increases as the relative concentrations of the buffer components become more similar to each other.

16.5   The Henderson–Hasselbalch equation $\left(pH = pK_a + \log \dfrac{[\text{base}]}{[\text{acid}]} \right)$ allows easy calculation of the pH of a buffer solution from the initial concentrations of the buffer components as long as the *x is small* approximation is valid.

16.7   When the concentration of the conjugate acid and base components of a buffer system are equal, the pH is equal to the pK_a of the weak acid of the buffer system. When a small amount of a strong acid is added, it will react with the conjugate base of the buffer system, converting it to the weak acid of the buffer system. Thus the weak acid concentration increases, the conjugate base concentration decreases, and the pH drops slightly at most. When a small amount of a strong base is added, it will react with the weak acid of the buffer system, converting it to the conjugate base of the buffer system. Thus the weak acid concentration decreases, the conjugate base concentration increases, and the pH rises slightly at most.

16.9   The factors that influence the effectiveness of a buffer are the relative amounts of the acid and conjugate base (the closer they are to each other the more effective the buffer) and the absolute concentrations of the acid and conjugate base (the higher the absolute concentrations the more effective the buffer).

16.11 In an acid–base titration, a basic (or acidic) solution of unknown concentration is reacted with an acidic (or basic) solution of known concentration. The known solution is slowly added to the unknown one while the pH is monitored with either a pH meter or an indicator (a substance whose colour depends on the pH). As the acid and base combine, they neutralize each other. At the equivalence point—the point in the titration when the number of moles of base is stoichiometrically equal to the number of moles of acid—the titration is complete. When this point is reached, neither reactant is in excess and the number of moles of the reactants are related by the reaction stoichiometry.

16.13 The volume required to get to the equivalence point is only dependent on the concentration and volume of acid or base to be titrated and the base or acid used to do the titration, because the equivalence point is dependent on the stoichiometry of the balanced reaction of the acid and base. The stoichiometry only considers the number of moles involved, not the strength of the reactants involved.

16.15   (a)   The initial pH is that of the weak acid solution to be titrated. Calculate the pH by working an equilibrium problem (similar to Examples 15.5 and 15.6) using the concentration of the weak acid as the initial concentration.

       (b)   Between the initial pH and the equivalence point, the solution becomes a buffer. Use the reaction stoichiometry to compute the amounts of each buffer component and then use the Henderson–Hasselbalch equation to compute the pH (as in Example 16.3).

       (c)   Halfway to the equivalence point, the buffer components are exactly equal and pH = pK_a.

       (d)   At the equivalence point, the acid has all been converted into its conjugate base. Calculate the pH by working an equilibrium problem for the ionization of water by the ion acting as a weak base (similar to Example 15.14). (Compute the concentration of the ion acting as a weak base by dividing the number of moles of the ion by the total volume at the equivalence point.)

       (e)   Beyond the equivalence point, OH^- is in excess. You can ignore the weak base and calculate the $[OH^-]$ by subtracting the initial number of moles of acid from the number of moles of added OH^- and dividing by the total volume, then convert to pOH using $-\log[OH^-]$ and then to pH using pH + pOH = 14.00.

16.17   The volume required to get to the first equivalence point is identical to the volume between the first and second equivalence points, because the equivalence point is dependent on the stoichiometry of the balanced reaction of the acid and base. The stoichiometry only considers the number of moles involved, not the strength of the reactants involved. There are the same number of moles of the first acidic proton and the second acidic proton.

16.19   An indicator (HIn) is itself a weak organic acid that has a different colour than its conjugate base (In^-). The colour of a solution containing an indicator depends on the relative concentrations of HIn and In^-. As the $[H_3O^+]$ changes during the titration, the above relative concentrations of HIn and In^- change accordingly. At low pH, the $[H_3O^+]$ is high, the equilibrium favours the acid species, and the colour is that of the acid species. As the titration proceeds, the $[H_3O^+]$ decreases, shifting toward higher concentrations of the conjugate base, and the colour changes. Because the colour of an indicator is intense, only a small amount is required—an amount that will not affect the pH of the solution or the equivalence point of the neutralization reaction.

16.21   The molar solubility, S, is simply the solubility in units of moles per litre (mol L^{-1}). The molar solubility of a compound, A_mX_n, can be computed directly from K_{sp} by solving for S in the expression: $K_{sp} = (mS)^m (nS)^n = m^m n^n S^{m+n}$.

16.23   At relatively low concentrations, uncommon ions will not affect the solubility equilibrium. However, at higher concentrations, the presence of uncommon ions may lead to ion pair formation because the solvent cannot keep the ions separate. Ion pair formation can lead to an increase in the solubility of an insoluble salt.

16.25 Q is the reaction quotient, the product of the concentrations of the ionic components raised to their stoichiometric coefficients, and K is the product of the concentrations of the ionic components raised to their stoichiometric coefficients at equilibrium. For a solution containing an ionic compound: If $Q < K_{sp}$, the solution is unsaturated. More of the solid ionic compound can dissolve in the solution: If $Q = K_{sp}$, the solution is saturated, the solution is holding the equilibrium amount of the dissolved ions, and additional solid will not dissolve in the solution. If $Q > K_{sp}$, the solution is supersaturated and under most circumstances, the excess solid will precipitate out.

16.27   Qualitative analysis is a systematic way to determine the metal ions present in an unknown solution by the selective precipitation of the ions. The word qualitative means involving quality or kind. So qualitative analysis involves finding the kind of ions present in the solution. Quantitative analysis is concerned with quantity, or the amounts of substances in a solution or mixture.

Problems by Topic
The Common Ion Effect and Buffers

16.29   The only solution that HNO_2 will ionize less in is (d) 0.10 mol L^{-1} $NaNO_2$. It is the only solution that generates a common ion NO_2^- with nitrous acid.

16.31   (a)   **Given:** 0.20 mol L^{-1} HCOOH and 0.15 mol L^{-1} HCOONa   **Find:** pH   **Other:** K_a (HCOOH) = 1.8 x 10^{-4}
Conceptual Plan: mol L^{-1} HCOONa $\rightarrow$ mol L^{-1} HCOONa then mol L^{-1} HCOOH, mol L^{-1}

$$HCOONa \ (aq) \rightarrow Na^+ \ (aq) + HCOO^- \ (aq)$$

$HCOO^- \rightarrow [H_3O^+] \rightarrow$ pH

$$\text{ICE Table} \quad pH = -\log [H_3O^+]$$

Solution: Since 1 $HCOO^-$ ion is generated for each HCOONa, $[HCOO^-]$ = 0.15 mol L^{-1} $HCOO^-$.

$$HCOOH \ (aq) + H_2O \ (l) \rightleftharpoons H_3O^+ \ (aq) + HCOO^-(aq)$$

	[HCOOH]	[H₃O⁺]	[HCOO⁻]
I	0.20	≈0	0.15
C	−x	+x	+x
E	0.20 − x	+x	0.15 + x

$$K_a = \frac{[H_3O^+][HCOO^-]}{[HCOOH]} = 1.8 \times 10^{-4} = \frac{x(0.15 + x)}{0.20 - x}$$ Assume x is small ($x \ll 0.15 < 0.20$) so

$$\frac{x(0.15 + x)}{0.20 - x} = 1.8 \times 10^{-4} = \frac{x(0.15)}{0.20}$$ and $x = 2.4 \times 10^{-4}$ mol L^{-1} = $[H_3O^+]$. Confirm that the more stringent assumption is valid.

$$\frac{2.4 \times 10^{-4}}{0.15} \times 100\% = 0.16\%$$ so assumption is valid. Finally,

$$pH = -\log [H_3O^+] = -\log (2.4 \times 10^{-4}) = 3.62$$

Check: The units (none) are correct. The magnitude of the answer makes physical sense because pH should be greater than $-\log (0.20)$ = 0.70 because this is a weak acid and there is a common ion effect.

(b)   **Given:** 0.16 mol L^{-1} NH_3 and 0.22 mol L^{-1} NH_4Cl **Find:** pH   **Other:** K_b (NH_3) = 1.79 x 10^{-5}
Conceptual Plan: mol L^{-1} NH_4Cl $\rightarrow$ mol L^{-1} NH_4^+ then mol L^{-1} NH_3, mol L^{-1} NH_4^+ $\rightarrow$

$$NH_4Cl \ (aq) \rightarrow NH_4^+ \ (aq) + Cl^- \ (aq)$$
ICE Table

$[OH^-] \rightarrow [H_3O^+] \rightarrow$ pH

$$K_w = [H_3O^+][OH^-] \quad pH = -\log [H_3O^+]$$

Solution: Since 1 NH_4^+ ion is generated for each NH_4Cl, $[NH_4^+]$ = 0.22 mol L^{-1} NH_4^+.

$$NH_3 \ (aq) + H_2O \ (l) \rightleftharpoons NH_4^+ \ (aq) + OH^-(aq)$$

	[NH₃]	[NH₄⁺]	[OH⁻]
I	0.16	0.22	≈0
C	−x	+x	+x
E	0.16 − x	0.22 + x	+x

$$K_b = \frac{[NH_4^+][OH^-]}{[NH_3]} = 1.79 \times 10^{-5} = \frac{(0.22 + x)x}{0.16 - x}$$

Assume x is small ($x \ll 0.16 < 0.22$) so $\frac{(0.22 + x)x}{0.16 - x} = 1.79 \times 10^{-5} = \frac{(0.22)x}{0.16}$ and

$x = 1.30182 \times 10^{-5}$ mol L^{-1} = $[OH^-]$. Confirm that the more stringent assumption is valid.

$$\frac{1.30182 \times 10^{-5}}{0.16} \times 100\% = 8.1 \times 10^{-3}\%$$ so assumption is valid.

$$K_w = [H_3O^+][OH^-] \text{ so } [H_3O^+] = \frac{K_w}{[OH^-]} = \frac{1.0 \times 10^{-14}}{1.30182 \times 10^{-5}} = 7.6816 \times 10^{-10} \text{ mol } L^{-1}.$$

Finally, pH = $-\log [H_3O^+]$ = $-\log (7.6816 \times 10^{-10})$ = 9.11

Check: The units (none) are correct. The magnitude of the answer makes physical sense because pH should be less than 14 + log (0.16) = 13.2 because this is a weak base and there is a common ion effect.

16.33   **Given:** 0.15 mol L^{-1} HC$_7$H$_5$O$_2$ in pure water and in 0.10 mol L^{-1} NaC$_7$H$_5$O$_2$
Find: % ionization in both solutions   **Other:** K_a (HC$_7$H$_5$O$_2$) = 6.5 x 10^{-5}
Conceptual Plan: pure water: mol L^{-1} HC$_7$H$_5$O$_2$ → [H$_3$O$^+$] → % ionization then in NaC$_7$H$_5$O$_2$ solution:

$$\text{ICE Table} \qquad \text{% ionization} = \frac{[\text{H}_3\text{O}^+]_{equil}}{[\text{HC}_7\text{H}_5\text{O}_2]_0} \times 100\%$$

mol L^{-1} NaC$_7$H$_5$O$_2$ → mol L^{-1} C$_7$H$_5$O$_2^-$ then mol L^{-1} HC$_7$H$_5$O$_2$, mol L^{-1} C$_7$H$_5$O$_2^-$ →

$$\text{NaC}_7\text{H}_5\text{O}_{2(aq)} \rightarrow \text{Na}^+ (aq) + \text{C}_7\text{H}_5\text{O}_2^- (aq) \qquad\qquad\qquad \text{ICE Table}$$

[H$_3$O$^+$] →   % ionization

$$\text{% ionization} = \frac{[\text{H}_3\text{O}^+]_{equil}}{[\text{HC}_7\text{H}_5\text{O}_2]_0} \times 100\%$$

Solution: in pure water:

	HC$_7$H$_5$O$_2$ (aq) + H$_2$O (l) $\rightleftharpoons$ H$_3$O$^+$ (aq) + C$_7$H$_5$O$_2^-$(aq)		
	[HC$_7$H$_5$O$_2$]	[H$_3$O$^+$]	[C$_7$H$_5$O$_2^-$]
I	0.15	≈0	0
C	−x	+x	+x
E	0.15 − x	+x	+x

$$K_a = \frac{[\text{H}_3\text{O}^+][\text{C}_7\text{H}_5\text{O}_2^-]}{[\text{HC}_7\text{H}_5\text{O}_2]} = 6.5 \times 10^{-5} = \frac{x^2}{0.15 - x}$$

Assume x is small (x << 0.10) so $\dfrac{x^2}{0.15 - x} = 6.5 \times 10^{-5} = \dfrac{x^2}{0.15}$ and x = 3.1225 x 10^{-3} mol L^{-1} = [H$_3$O$^+$]. Then

$$\text{% ionization} = \frac{[\text{H}_3\text{O}^+]_{equil}}{[\text{HC}_7\text{H}_5\text{O}_2]_0} \times 100\% = \frac{3.1225 \times 10^{-3}}{0.15} \times 100\% = 2.1\%, \text{ which also confirms that the}$$

assumption is valid (since it is less than 5%). In NaC$_7$H$_5$O$_2$ solution: Since 1 C$_7$H$_5$O$_2^-$ ion is generated for each NaC$_7$H$_5$O$_2$, [C$_7$H$_5$O$_2^-$] = 0.10 mol L^{-1} C$_7$H$_5$O$_2^-$.

	HC$_7$H$_5$O$_2$ (aq) + H$_2$O (l) $\rightleftharpoons$ H$_3$O$^+$ (aq) + C$_7$H$_5$O$_2^-$(aq)		
	[HC$_7$H$_5$O$_2$]	[H$_3$O$^+$]	[C$_7$H$_5$O$_2^-$]
I	0.15	≈0	0.10
C	−x	+x	+x
E	0.15 − x	+x	0.10 + x

$$K_a = \frac{[\text{H}_3\text{O}^+][\text{C}_7\text{H}_5\text{O}_2^-]}{[\text{HC}_7\text{H}_5\text{O}_2]} = 6.5 \times 10^{-5} = \frac{x(0.10 + x)}{0.15 - x} \quad \text{Assume x is small (x << 0.10 < 0.15) so}$$

$$\frac{x(0.10 + x)}{0.15 - x} = 6.5 \times 10^{-5} = \frac{x(0.10)}{0.15} \text{ and } x = 9.75 \times 10^{-5} \text{ mol L}^{-1} = [\text{H}_3\text{O}^+], \text{ then}$$

$$\text{% ionization} = \frac{[\text{H}_3\text{O}^+]_{equil}}{[\text{HC}_7\text{H}_5\text{O}_2]_0} \times 100\% = \frac{9.75 \times 10^{-5}}{0.15} \times 100\% = 0.065\%, \text{ which also confirms that the}$$

assumption is valid (since it is less than 5%). The percent ionization in the sodium benzoate solution is less than in pure water because of the common ion effect. An increase in one of the products (benzoate ion) shifts the equilibrium to the left, so less acid dissociates.
Check: The units (%) are correct. The magnitude of the answer makes physical sense because the acid is weak and so the percent ionization is low. With a common ion present, the percent ionization decreases.

16.35   (a)   **Given:** 0.15 mol L^{-1} HF   **Find:** pH   **Other:** K_a (HF) = 3.5 x 10^{-4}
Conceptual Plan: mol L^{-1} HF → [H$_3$O$^+$] → pH

$$\text{ICE Table} \qquad \text{pH} = -\log [\text{H}_3\text{O}^+]$$

Solution:

	HF (aq) + H$_2$O (l) $\rightleftharpoons$ H$_3$O$^+$ (aq) + F$^-$(aq)		
	[HF]	[H$_3$O$^+$]	[F$^-$]
I	0.15	≈0	0
C	−x	+x	+x
E	0.15 − x	+x	+x

$$K_a = \frac{[\text{H}_3\text{O}^+][\text{F}^-]}{[\text{HF}]} = 3.5 \times 10^{-4} = \frac{x^2}{0.15 - x} \quad \text{Assume x is small (x << 0.15) so}$$

$$\frac{x^2}{0.15 - x} = 3.5 \times 10^{-4} = \frac{x^2}{0.15} \text{ and } x = 7.\underline{2}457 \times 10^{-3} \text{ mol L}^{-1} = [H_3O^+]. \text{ Confirm that}$$

assumption is valid $\dfrac{7.\underline{2}457 \times 10^{-3}}{0.15} \times 100\% = 4.8\% < 5\%$ so assumption is valid.

Finally, pH $= -\log [H_3O^+] = -\log (7.\underline{2}457 \times 10^{-3}) = 2.14$.

Check: The units (none) are correct. The magnitude of the answer makes physical sense because pH should be greater than $-\log (0.15) = 0.82$ because this is a weak acid.

(b) **Given:** 0.15 mol L^{-1} NaF   **Find:** pH **Other:** K_a (HF) = 3.5 x 10^{-4}

Conceptual Plan: mol L^{-1} NaF $\rightarrow$ mol L^{-1} F$^-$ and K_a $\rightarrow$ K_b then mol L^{-1} F$^-$ $\rightarrow$ [OH$^-$] $\rightarrow$ [H$_3$O$^+$]

$$\text{NaF } (aq) \rightarrow \text{Na}^+ (aq) + \text{F}^- (aq) \qquad K_w = K_a K_b \qquad\qquad \text{ICE Table } \quad K_w = [H_3O^+][OH^-]$$

$\rightarrow$ pH

pH $= -\log [H_3O^+]$

Solution: Since 1 F$^-$ ion is generated for each NaF, [F$^-$] = 0.15 mol L^{-1} F$^-$. Since $K_w = K_a K_b$, rearrange to

solve for K_b. $K_b = \dfrac{K_w}{K_a} = \dfrac{1.0 \times 10^{-14}}{3.5 \times 10^{-4}} = 2.\underline{8}571 \times 10^{-11}$

$$\text{F}^- (aq) + \text{H}_2\text{O} (l) \rightleftharpoons \text{HF} (aq) + \text{OH}^- (aq)$$

	[F$^-$]	[HF]	[OH$^-$]
I	0.15	0	≈ 0
C	$-x$	$+x$	$+x$
E	$0.15 - x$	$+x$	$+x$

$K_b = \dfrac{[HF][OH^-]}{[F^-]} = 2.\underline{8}571 \times 10^{-11} = \dfrac{x^2}{0.15 - x}$

Assume x is small ($x << 0.15$) so $\dfrac{x^2}{0.15 - x} = 2.\underline{8}571 \times 10^{-11} = \dfrac{x^2}{0.15}$ and $x = 2.\underline{0}702 \times 10^{-6}$ mol L^{-1} = [OH$^-$].

Confirm that assumption is valid $\dfrac{2.\underline{0}702 \times 10^{-6}}{0.15} \times 100\% = 0.0014\% < 5\%$ so assumption is valid.

$K_w = [H_3O^+][OH^-]$ so $[H_3O^+] = \dfrac{K_w}{[OH^-]} = \dfrac{1.0 \times 10^{-14}}{2.\underline{0}702 \times 10^{-6}} = 4.\underline{8}305 \times 10^{-9}$ mol L^{-1}.

Finally, pH $= -\log [H_3O^+] = -\log (4.\underline{8}305 \times 10^{-9}) = 8.32$.

Check: The units (none) are correct. The magnitude of the answer makes physical sense because pH should be slightly basic, since the fluoride ion is a very weak base.

(c) **Given:** 0.15 mol L^{-1} HF and 0.15 mol L^{-1} NaF **Find:** pH **Other:** K_a (HF) = 3.5 x 10^{-4}

Conceptual Plan: mol L^{-1} NaF $\rightarrow$ mol L^{-1} F$^-$ then mol L^{-1} HF, mol L^{-1} F$^-$ $\rightarrow$ [H$_3$O$^+$] $\rightarrow$ pH

$$\text{NaF } (aq) \rightarrow \text{Na}^+ (aq) + \text{F}^- (aq) \qquad\qquad \text{ICE Table} \quad \text{pH} = -\log [H_3O^+]$$

Solution: Since 1 F$^-$ ion is generated for each NaF, [F$^-$] = 0.15 mol L^{-1} F$^-$.

$$\text{HF } (aq) + \text{H}_2\text{O} (l) \rightleftharpoons \text{H}_3\text{O}^+ (aq) + \text{F}^- (aq)$$

	[HF]	[H$_3$O$^+$]	[F$^-$]
I	0.15	≈ 0	0.15
C	$-x$	$+x$	$+x$
E	$0.15 - x$	$+x$	$0.15 + x$

$K_a = \dfrac{[H_3O^+][F^-]}{[HF]} = 3.5 \times 10^{-4} = \dfrac{x(0.15 + x)}{0.15 - x}$

Assume x is small ($x << 0.15$) so $\dfrac{x(0.15 + \cancel{x})}{0.15 - \cancel{x}} = 3.5 \times 10^{-4} = \dfrac{x(\cancel{0.15})}{\cancel{0.15}}$ and $x = 3.5 \times 10^{-4}$ mol L^{-1} = [H$_3$O$^+$].

Confirm that assumption is valid $\dfrac{3.5 \times 10^{-4}}{0.15} \times 100\% = 0.23\% < 5\%$ so assumption is valid.

Finally, pH $= -\log [H_3O^+] = -\log (3.5 \times 10^{-4}) = 3.46$.

Check: The units (none) are correct. The magnitude of the answer makes physical sense because pH should be greater than in part (a) (2.14) because of the common ion effect suppressing the dissociation of the weak acid.

16.37   When an acid (such as HCl) is added it will react with the conjugate base of the buffer system as follows: $HCl + CH_3COONa \rightarrow CH_3COOH + NaCl$. When a base (such as NaOH) is added it will react with the weak acid of the buffer system as follows: $NaOH + CH_3COOH \rightarrow H_2O + CH_3COONa$. The reaction generates the other buffer system component.

16.39   (a)   **Given:** 0.20 mol L^{-1} HCOOH and 0.15 mol L^{-1} HCOONa **Find:** pH **Other:** K_a (HCOOH) = 1.8 x 10^{-4}
                Conceptual Plan: Identify acid and base components then mol L^{-1} HCOONa $\rightarrow$ mol L^{-1} HCOO$^-$ then

           acid = HCOOH   base = HCOO$^-$ HCOONa (aq) $\rightarrow$ Na$^+$ (aq) + HCOO$^-$ (aq)

           K_a, **mol L^{-1} HCOOH, mol L^{-1} HCOO$^-$ $\rightarrow$ pH.**

           $$pH = pK_a + \log \frac{[base]}{[acid]}$$

           Solution: Acid = HCOOH, so [acid] = [HCOOH] = 0.20 mol L^{-1}. Base = HCOO$^-$. Since 1 HCOO$^-$ ion is generated for each HCOONa, [HCOO$^-$] = 0.15 mol L^{-1} HCOO$^-$ = [base]. Then

           $$pH = pK_a + \log \frac{[base]}{[acid]} = -\log (1.8 \times 10^{-4}) + \log \frac{0.15 \ \overline{mol \ L}^{-1}}{0.20 \ \overline{mol \ L}^{-1}} = 3.62.$$

           Note that in order to use the Henderson–Hasselbalch equation, the assumption that x is small must be valid. This was confirmed in Problem 31.
           Check: The units (none) are correct. The magnitude of the answer makes physical sense because pH should be less than the pK_a of the acid because there is more acid than base. The answer agrees with Problem 31.

          (b)   **Given:** 0.16 mol L^{-1} NH$_3$ and 0.22 mol L^{-1} NH$_4$Cl   **Find:** pH **Other:** K_b (NH$_3$) = 1.79 x 10^{-5}
                Conceptual Plan: Identify acid and base components then mol L^{-1} NH$_4$Cl $\rightarrow$ mol L^{-1} NH$_4^+$ and K_b $\rightarrow$

           acid = NH$_4^+$ base = NH$_3$ NH$_4$Cl (aq) $\rightarrow$ NH$_4^+$ (aq) + Cl$^-$ (aq) $pK_b = -\log K_b$

           $pK_b \rightarrow pK_a$

           $14 = pK_a + pK_b$

           then pK_a, mol L^{-1} NH$_3$, mol L^{-1} NH$_4^+$ $\rightarrow$ pH.

           $$pH = pK_a + \log \frac{[base]}{[acid]}$$

           Solution: Base = NH$_3$, [base] = [NH$_3$] = 0.16 mol L^{-1}. Acid = NH$_4^+$. Since 1 NH$_4^+$ ion is generated for each NH$_4$Cl, [NH$_4^+$] = 0.18 mol L^{-1} NH$_4^+$ = [acid].
           Since K_b (NH$_3$) = 1.79 x 10^{-5}, $pK_b = -\log K_b = -\log (1.79 \times 10^{-5}) = 4.75$. Since $14 = pK_a + pK_b$,

           $$pK_a = 14 - pK_b = 14 - 4.75 = 9.25 \text{ then } pH = pK_a + \log \frac{[base]}{[acid]} = 9.25 + \log \frac{0.16 \ \overline{mol \ L}^{-1}}{0.22 \ \overline{mol \ L}^{-1}} = 9.11.$$

           Note that in order to use the Henderson–Hasselbalch equation, the assumption that x is small must be valid. This was confirmed in Problem 31.
           Check: The units (none) are correct. The magnitude of the answer makes physical sense because pH should be less than the pK_a of the acid because there is more acid than base. The answer agrees with Problem 31, within the error of the value.

16.41   (a)   **Given:** 0.135 mol L^{-1} HClO and 0.155 mol L^{-1} KClO **Find:** pH **Other:** K_a (HClO) = 2.9 x 10^{-8}
                Conceptual Plan: Identify acid and base components then mol L^{-1} KClO $\rightarrow$ mol L^{-1} ClO$^-$ then

           acid = HClO   base = ClO$^-$ KClO (aq) $\rightarrow$ K$^+$ (aq) + ClO$^-$ (aq)

           mol L^{-1} HClO, mol L^{-1} ClO$^-$ $\rightarrow$ pH.

           $$pH = pK_a + \log \frac{[base]}{[acid]}$$

           Solution: Acid = HClO, so [acid] = [HClO] = 0.135 mol L^{-1}. Base = ClO$^-$. Since 1 ClO$^-$ ion is generated for each KClO, [ClO$^-$] = 0.155 mol L^{-1} ClO$^-$ = [base]. Then

           $$pH = pK_a + \log \frac{[base]}{[acid]} = -\log (2.9 \times 10^{-8}) + \log \frac{0.155 \ \overline{mol \ L}^{-1}}{0.135 \ \overline{mol \ L}^{-1}} = 7.60.$$

           Check: The units (none) are correct. The magnitude of the answer makes physical sense because pH should be greater than the pK_a of the acid because there is more base than acid.

(b)   **Given:** 1.05% by mass $C_2H_5NH_2$ and 1.10% by mass $C_2H_5NH_3Br$ **Find:** pH
Other: K_b $(C_2H_5NH_2) = 5.6 \times 10^{-4}$
Conceptual Plan: Assume exactly 100 g of solution. Since both components are in the same solution (i.e., the same final volume of solution), the ratio of the moles of each component is the same as the ratio of the molarity of these components and only the relative number of moles needs to be calculated. $g_{Solution} \rightarrow g_{C_2H_5NH_2} \rightarrow$ **mol** $C_2H_5NH_2$ **and** $g_{solution} \rightarrow g$ $C_2H_5NH_3Br \rightarrow$ **mol** $C_2H_5NH_3Br$

$$\frac{1.05 \text{ g } C_2H_5NH_2}{100 \text{ g solution}} \quad \frac{1 \text{ mol } C_2H_5NH_2}{45.09 \text{ g } C_2H_5NH_2} \qquad\qquad \frac{1.10 \text{ g } C_2H_5NH_3Br}{100 \text{ g solution}} \quad \frac{1 \text{ mol } C_2H_5NH_3Br}{125.99 \text{ g } C_2H_5NH_3Br}$$

identify acid and base components then mol L^{-1} $C_2H_5NH_3Br \rightarrow$ **mol** L^{-1} $C_2H_5NH_3^+$ **and**

$$\text{acid} = C_2H_5NH_3^+ \text{ base} = C_2H_5NH_2 \qquad\qquad C_2H_5NH_3Br \text{ (aq)} \rightarrow C_2H_5NH_3^+ \text{ (aq)} + Br^- \text{ (aq)}$$

$K_b \rightarrow pK_b \rightarrow pK_a$ **then** pK_a**, mol** L^{-1} $C_2H_5NH_2$**, mol** L^{-1} $C_2H_5NH_3^+ \rightarrow$ **pH**

$$pK_b = -\log K_b \quad 14 = pK_a + pK_b \qquad\qquad\qquad\qquad pH = pK_a + \log \frac{[\text{base}]}{[\text{acid}]}$$

Solution:

$$100 \ \cancel{\text{g solution}} \times \frac{1.05 \ \cancel{\text{g } C_2H_5NH_2}}{100 \ \cancel{\text{g solution}}} \times \frac{1 \text{ mol } C_2H_5NH_2}{45.09 \ \cancel{\text{g } C_2H_5NH_2}} = 0.0232\underline{8}676 \text{ mol } C_2H_5NH_2 \text{ and}$$

$$100 \ \cancel{\text{g solution}} \times \frac{1.10 \ \cancel{\text{g } C_2H_5NH_3Br}}{100 \ \cancel{\text{g solution}}} \times \frac{1 \text{ mol } C_2H_5NH_3Br}{125.99 \ \cancel{\text{g } C_2H_5NH_3Br}} = 0.00873\underline{0}852 \text{ mol } C_2H_5NH_3Br$$

Then base = $C_2H_5NH_2$, moles of base = mol $C_2H_5NH_2 = 0.0232\underline{8}676$ mol; acid = $C_2H_5NH_3^+$.
Since 1 $C_2H_5NH_3^+$ ion is generated for each $C_2H_5NH_3Br$, mol $C_2H_5NH_3^+ = 0.00873\underline{0}852$ mol.
Since K_b $(C_2H_5NH_2) = 5.6 \times 10^{-4}$, $pK_b = -\log K_b = -\log (5.6 \times 10^{-4}) = 3.25$.
Since $14 = pK_a + pK_b$, $pK_a = 14 - pK_b = 14 - 3.25 = 10.75$ then

$$pH = pK_a + \log \frac{\text{mol base}}{\text{mol acid}} = 10.75 + \log \frac{0.0232\underline{8}676 \ \cancel{\text{mol}}}{0.00873\underline{0}852 \ \cancel{\text{mol}}} = 11.18.$$

Check: The units (none) are correct. The magnitude of the answer makes physical sense because pH should be greater than the pK_a of the acid because there is more base than acid.

(c)   **Given:** 10.0 g CH_3COOH and 10.0 g CH_3COONa in 150.0 mL solution **Find:** pH
Other: K_a $(CH_3COOH) = 1.8 \times 10^{-5}$
Conceptual Plan: Identify acid and base components then mL $\rightarrow$ **L and g** CH_3COOH $\rightarrow$ **mol**

$$\text{acid} = CH_3COOH \text{ base} = CH_3COO^- \qquad\qquad \frac{1 \text{ L}}{1000 \text{ mL}} \quad \frac{1 \text{ mol } CH_3COOH}{60.05 \text{ g } CH_3COOH}$$

CH_3COOH **then mol** CH_3COOH**, L** $\rightarrow$ **mol** L^{-1} CH_3COOH **and g** CH_3COONa $\rightarrow$ **mol** CH_3COONa

$$M = \frac{\text{mol}}{\text{L}} \qquad\qquad\qquad \frac{1 \text{ mol } CH_3COONa}{82.04 \text{ g } CH_3COONa}$$

then mol CH_3COONa**, L** $\rightarrow$ **mol** L^{-1} CH_3COONa $\rightarrow$ **mol** L^{-1} CH_3COO^- **then mol** L^{-1} CH_3COOH**,**

$$M = \frac{\text{mol}}{\text{L}} \qquad\qquad CH_3COONa \text{ (aq)} \rightarrow Na^+ \text{(aq)} + CH_3COO^- \text{(aq)}$$

mol L^{-1} CH_3COO^- $\rightarrow$ **pH.**

$$pH = pK_a + \log \frac{[\text{base}]}{[\text{acid}]}$$

Solution: $150.0 \ \cancel{\text{mL}} \times \dfrac{1 \text{ L}}{1000 \ \cancel{\text{mL}}} = 0.1500$ L and

$$10.0 \ \cancel{\text{g } CH_3COOH} \times \frac{1 \text{ mol } CH_3COOH}{60.05 \ \cancel{\text{g } CH_3COOH}} = 0.16\underline{6}528 \text{ mol } CH_3COOH$$

then $M = \dfrac{\text{mol}}{\text{L}} = \dfrac{0.16\underline{6}528 \text{ mol } CH_3COOH}{0.1500 \text{ L}} = 1.1\underline{1}019 \text{ mol } L^{-1} \ CH_3COOH$ and

$$10.0 \ \cancel{\text{g } CH_3COONa} \times \frac{1 \text{ mol } CH_3COONa}{82.04 \ \cancel{\text{g } CH_3COONa}} = 0.12\underline{1}892 \text{ mol } CH_3COONa \text{ then}$$

$M = \dfrac{\text{mol}}{\text{L}} = \dfrac{0.12\underline{1}892 \text{ mol } CH_3COONa}{0.1500 \text{ L}} = 0.81\underline{2}612 \text{ mol } L^{-1} \ CH_3COONa.$ Acid = CH_3COOH, so

$[\text{acid}] = [CH_3COOH] = 1.1\underline{1}019 \text{ mol } L^{-1}$ and base = CH_3COO^-. Since 1 CH_3COO^- ion is generated

for each CH_3COONa, $[CH_3COO^-] = 0.81\underline{2}612 \text{ mol } L^{-1}$ $CH_3COO^- = [\text{base}]$. Then

$$pH = pK_a + \log \frac{[\text{base}]}{[\text{acid}]} = -\log (1.8 \times 10^{-5}) + \log \frac{0.81\underline{2}612 \ \cancel{\text{mol } L^{-1}}}{1.1\underline{1}019 \ \cancel{\text{mol } L^{-1}}} = 4.61.$$

Check: The units (none) are correct. The magnitude of the answer makes physical sense because pH should be less than the pK_a of the acid because there is more acid than base.

16.43 (a) **Given:** 50.0 mL of 0.15 mol L^{-1} HCOOH and 75.0 mL of 0.13 mol L^{-1} HCOONa **Find:** pH
Other: K_a (HCOOH) = 1.8 x 10^{-4}
Conceptual Plan: Identify acid and base components then mL HCOOH, mL HCOONa → total mL then

$$\text{acid = HCOOH} \quad \text{base = HCOO}^- \qquad\qquad \text{total mL = mL HCOOH + mL HCOONa}$$

mL HCOOH, mol L^{-1} HCOOH, total mL → buffer mol L^{-1} HCOOH and

$$M_1 V_1 = M_2 V_2$$

mL HCOONa, mol L^{-1} HCOONa, total mL → buffer mol L^{-1} HCOONa → buffer mol L^{-1} HCOO$^-$ then

$$M_1 V_1 = M_2 V_2 \qquad \text{HCOONa } (aq) \rightarrow \text{Na}^+ (aq) + \text{HCOO}^- (aq)$$

K_a, mol L^{-1} HCOOH, mol L^{-1} HCOO$^-$ → pH.

$$pH = pK_a + \log \frac{[\text{base}]}{[\text{acid}]}$$

Solution: Total mL = mL HCOOH + mL HCOONa = 50.0 mL + 75.0 mL = 125.0 mL. Then since $M_1 V_1 = M_2 V_2$ rearrange to solve for M_2.

$$M_2 = \frac{M_1 V_1}{V_2} = \frac{(0.15 \text{ mol L}^{-1})(50.0 \text{ mL})}{125.0 \text{ mL}} = 0.060 \text{ mol L}^{-1} \text{ HCOOH and}$$

$$M_2 = \frac{M_1 V_1}{V_2} = \frac{(0.13 \text{ mol L}^{-1})(75.0 \text{ mL})}{125.0 \text{ mL}} = 0.078 \text{ mol L}^{-1} \text{ HCOONa. Acid = HCOOH, so [acid]}$$

= [HCOOH] = 0.060 mol L^{-1}.

Base = HCOO$^-$. Since 1 HCOO$^-$ ion is generated for each HCOONa, [HCOO$^-$] = 0.078 mol L^{-1} HCOO$^-$

= [base]. Then $pH = pK_a + \log \frac{[\text{base}]}{[\text{acid}]} = -\log (1.8 \times 10^{-4}) + \log \frac{0.078 \text{ mol L}^{-1}}{0.060 \text{ mol L}^{-1}} = 3.86.$

Check: The units (none) are correct. The magnitude of the answer makes physical sense because pH should be greater than the pK_a of the acid because there is more base than acid.

(b) **Given:** 125.0 mL of 0.10 mol L^{-1} NH$_3$ and 250.0 mL of 0.10 mol L^{-1} NH$_4$Cl **Find:** pH
Other: K_b (NH$_3$) = 1.79 x 10^{-5}
Conceptual Plan: Identify acid and base components then mL NH$_3$, mL NH$_4$Cl → total mL then

$$\text{acid = NH}_4^+ \quad \text{base = NH}_3 \qquad\qquad \text{total mL = mL NH}_3 + \text{mL NH}_4\text{Cl}$$

mL NH$_3$, mol L^{-1} NH$_3$, total mL → buffer mol L^{-1} NH$_3$ and

$$M_1 V_1 = M_2 V_2$$

mL NH$_4$Cl, mol L^{-1} NH$_4$Cl, total mL → buffer mol L^{-1} NH$_4$Cl → buffer mol L^{-1} NH$_4^+$ and K_b →

$$M_1 V_1 = M_2 V_2 \qquad \text{NH}_4\text{Cl } (aq) \rightarrow \text{NH}_4^+ (aq) + \text{Cl}^- (aq) \qquad pK_b = -\log K_b$$

pK_b → pK_a

$$14 = pK_a + pK_b$$

then pK_a, mol L^{-1} NH$_3$, mol L^{-1} NH$_4^+$ → pH.

$$pH = pK_a + \log \frac{[\text{base}]}{[\text{acid}]}$$

Solution: Total mL = mL NH$_3$ + mL NH$_4$Cl = 125.0 mL + 250.0 mL = 375.0 mL. Then since $M_1 V_1 = M_2 V_2$ rearrange to solve for M_2.

$$M_2 = \frac{M_1 V_1}{V_2} = \frac{(0.10 \text{ mol L}^{-1})(125.0 \text{ mL})}{375.0 \text{ mL}} = 0.033333 \text{ mol L}^{-1} \text{ NH}_3 \text{ and}$$

$$M_2 = \frac{M_1 V_1}{V_2} = \frac{(0.10 \text{ mol L}^{-1})(250.0 \text{ mL})}{375.0 \text{ mL}} = 0.066667 \text{ mol L}^{-1} \text{ NH}_4\text{Cl. Base = NH}_3, \text{[base] = [NH}_3] =$$

0.033333 mol L^{-1} acid = NH$_4^+$. Since 1 NH$_4^+$ ion is generated for each NH$_4$Cl, [NH$_4^+$] =

0.0666667 mol L^{-1} NH$_4^+$ = [acid]. Since K_b (NH$_3$) = 1.79 x 10^{-5},

$pK_b = -\log K_b = -\log (1.79 \times 10^{-5}) = 4.75.$ Since $14 = pK_a + pK_b$,

$$pK_a = 14 - pK_b = 14 - 4.75 = 9.25 \text{ then } pH = pK_a + \log \frac{[\text{base}]}{[\text{acid}]} = 9.25 + \log \frac{0.033333 \text{ mol L}^{-1}}{0.066667 \text{ mol L}^{-1}} = 8.95.$$

Check: The units (none) are correct. The magnitude of the answer makes physical sense because pH should be less than the pK_a of the acid because there is more acid than base.

16.45   **Given:** NaF / HF buffer at pH = 4.00 **Find:** [NaF] / [HF] **Other:** K_a (HF) = 3.5 x 10^{-4}
             Conceptual Plan: Identify acid and base components then pH, K_a → [NaF] / [HF].

$$\text{acid} = \text{HF} \quad \text{base} = \text{F}^- \qquad\qquad \text{pH} = pK_a + \log \frac{[\text{base}]}{[\text{acid}]}$$

Solution: $\text{pH} = pK_a + \log \dfrac{[\text{base}]}{[\text{acid}]} = -\log(3.5 \times 10^{-4}) + \log \dfrac{[\text{NaF}]}{[\text{HF}]} = 4.00$. Solve for [NaF]/[HF].

$\log \dfrac{[\text{NaF}]}{[\text{HF}]} = 4.00 - 3.46 = 0.54 \rightarrow \dfrac{[\text{NaF}]}{[\text{HF}]} = 10^{0.54} = 3.5.$

Check: The units (none) are correct. The magnitude of the answer makes physical sense because the pH is greater than the pK_a of the acid, so there needs to be more base than acid.

16.47   **Given:** 150.0 mL buffer of 0.15 mol L^{-1} benzoic acid at pH = 4.25 **Find:** mass sodium benzoate
             Other: K_a ($HC_7H_5O_2$) = 6.5 x 10^{-5}
             Conceptual Plan: Identify acid and base components then pH, K_a, [$HC_7H_5O_2$] → [$NaC_7H_5O_2$]

$$\text{acid} = HC_7H_5O_2 \quad \text{base} = C_7H_5O_2^- \qquad\qquad \text{pH} = pK_a + \log \frac{[\text{base}]}{[\text{acid}]}$$

mL → L then [$NaC_7H_5O_2$], L → mol $NaC_7H_5O_2$ → g $NaC_7H_5O_2$.

$$\frac{1\ \text{L}}{1000\ \text{mL}} \qquad M = \frac{\text{mol}}{\text{L}} \qquad \frac{144.11\ \text{g } NaC_7H_5O_2}{1\ \text{mol } NaC_7H_5O_2}$$

Solution: $\text{pH} = pK_a + \log \dfrac{[\text{base}]}{[\text{acid}]} = -\log(6.5 \times 10^{-5}) + \log \dfrac{[NaC_7H_5O_2]}{0.15\ \text{mol } L^{-1}} = 4.25$. Solve for [$NaC_7H_5O_2$].

$\log \dfrac{[NaC_7H_5O_2]}{0.15\ \text{mol } L^{-1}} = 4.25 - 4.19 = 0.0\underline{6}291 \rightarrow \dfrac{[NaC_7H_5O_2]}{0.15\ \text{mol } L^{-1}} = 10^{0.06291} = 1.1\underline{5}59 \rightarrow$

$[NaC_7H_5O_2] = 0.1\underline{7}338\ \text{mol } L^{-1}.$

Convert to moles using $M = \dfrac{\text{mol}}{\text{L}}$.

$\dfrac{0.1\underline{7}338\ \text{mol } NaC_7H_5O_2}{1\ \cancel{L}} \times 0.150\ \cancel{L} = 0.026007\ \cancel{\text{mol } NaC_7H_5O_2} \times \dfrac{144.11\ \text{g } NaC_7H_5O_2}{1\ \cancel{\text{mol } NaC_7H_5O_2}} = 3.7\ \text{g } NaC_7H_5O_2$.

Check: The units (g) are correct. The magnitude of the answer makes physical sense because the volume of solution is small and the concentration is low, so much less than a mole is needed.

16.49   **(a)**   **Given:** 250.0 mL buffer 0.250 mol L^{-1} CH_3COOH and 0.250 mol L^{-1} CH_3COONa **Find:** initial pH
             Other: K_a (CH_3COOH) = 1.8 x 10^{-5}
             Conceptual Plan: Identify acid and base components then mol L^{-1} CH_3COONa → mol L^{-1}

$$\text{acid} = CH_3COOH \quad \text{base} = CH_3COO^- \qquad CH_3COONa\ (aq) \rightarrow Na^+\ (aq) + CH_3COO^-\ (aq)$$

CH_3COO^- then mol L^{-1} CH_3COOH, mol L^{-1} CH_3COO^- → pH.

$$\text{pH} = pK_a + \log \frac{[\text{base}]}{[\text{acid}]}$$

Solution: Acid = CH_3COOH, so [acid] = [CH_3COOH] = 0.250 mol L^{-1}. Base = CH_3COO^-. Since 1 CH_3COO^- ion is generated for each CH_3COONa, [CH_3COO^-] = 0.250 mol L^{-1} CH_3COO^- = [base]. Then

$\text{pH} = pK_a + \log \dfrac{[\text{base}]}{[\text{acid}]} = -\log(1.8 \times 10^{-5}) + \log \dfrac{0.250\ \cancel{\text{mol } L^{-1}}}{0.250\ \cancel{\text{mol } L^{-1}}} = 4.74.$

Check: The units (none) are correct. The magnitude of the answer makes physical sense because pH is equal to the pK_a of the acid because there are equal amounts of acid and base.

(b)   **Given:** 250.0 mL buffer 0.250 mol L^{-1} CH_3COOH and 0.250 mol L^{-1} CH_3COONa, add 0.0050 mol HCl
             Find: pH **Other:** K_a (CH_3COOH) = 1.8 x 10^{-5}
             Conceptual Plan: Part I: Stoichiometry:
             mL → L then [CH_3COONa], L → mol CH_3COONa and [CH_3COOH], L → mol CH_3COOH

$$\frac{1\ \text{L}}{1000\ \text{mL}} \qquad\qquad M = \frac{\text{mol}}{\text{L}} \qquad\qquad M = \frac{\text{mol}}{\text{L}}$$

write balanced equation then

$$HCl + CH_3COONa \rightarrow CH_3COOH + NaCl$$

mol CH_3COONa, mol CH_3COOH, mol HCl → mol CH_3COONa, mol CH_3COOH then

set up stoichiometry table

Part II: Equilibrium:
mol CH$_3$COONa, mol CH$_3$COOH, L, K_a → pH

$$pH = pK_a + \log \frac{[\text{base}]}{[\text{acid}]}$$

Solution: $250.0 \text{ mL} \times \dfrac{1 \text{ L}}{1000 \text{ mL}} = 0.2500 \text{ L}$ then

$\dfrac{0.250 \text{ mol CH}_3\text{COOH}}{1 \text{ L}} \times 0.2500 \text{ L} = 0.0625 \text{ mol CH}_3\text{COOH}$ and

$\dfrac{0.250 \text{ mol CH}_3\text{COONa}}{1 \text{ L}} \times 0.2500 \text{ L} = 0.0625 \text{ mol CH}_3\text{COONa}$. Set up a table to track changes:

$$\text{HCl } (aq) + \text{CH}_3\text{COONa } (aq) \rightarrow \text{CH}_3\text{COOH } (aq) + \text{NaCl } (aq)$$

	HCl	CH$_3$COONa	CH$_3$COOH	NaCl
Before addition	≈ 0 mol	0.0625 mol	0.0625 mol	0 mol
Addition	0.0050 mol	—	—	—
After addition	≈ 0 mol	0.0575 mol	0.0675 mol	0.0050 mol

Since the amount of HCl is small, there are still significant amounts of both buffer components, so the Henderson–Hasselbalch equation can be used to calculate the new pH.

$$pH = pK_a + \log \frac{[\text{base}]}{[\text{acid}]} = -\log(1.8 \times 10^{-5}) + \log \frac{\dfrac{0.0575 \text{ mol}}{0.2500 \text{ L}}}{\dfrac{0.0675 \text{ mol}}{0.2500 \text{ L}}} = 4.68.$$

Check: The units (none) are correct. The magnitude of the answer makes physical sense because the pH dropped slightly when acid was added.

(c) **Given:** 250.0 mL buffer 0.250 mol L^{-1} CH$_3$COOH and 0.250 mol L^{-1} CH$_3$COONa, add 0.0050 mol NaOH
Find: pH   **Other:** K_a (CH$_3$COOH) = 1.8 x 10^{-5}
Conceptual Plan: Part I: Stoichiometry:
mL → L then [CH$_3$COONa], L → mol CH$_3$COONa and [CH$_3$COOH], L → mol CH$_3$COOH

$\dfrac{1 \text{ L}}{1000 \text{ mL}}$ $M = \dfrac{\text{mol}}{\text{L}}$ $M = \dfrac{\text{mol}}{\text{L}}$

write balanced equation then

$\text{NaOH} + \text{CH}_3\text{COOH} \rightarrow \text{H}_2\text{O} + \text{CH}_3\text{COONa}$

mol CH$_3$COONa, mol CH$_3$COOH, mol NaOH → mol CH$_3$COONa, mol CH$_3$COOH then

set up stoichiometry table

Part II: Equilibrium:
mol CH$_3$COONa, mol CH$_3$COOH, L, K_a → pH

$$pH = pK_a + \log \frac{[\text{base}]}{[\text{acid}]}$$

Solution: $250.0 \text{ mL} \times \dfrac{1 \text{ L}}{1000 \text{ mL}} = 0.2500 \text{ L}$ then

$\dfrac{0.250 \text{ mol CH}_3\text{COOH}}{1 \text{ L}} \times 0.2500 \text{ L} = 0.0625 \text{ mol CH}_3\text{COOH}$ and

$\dfrac{0.250 \text{ mol CH}_3\text{COONa}}{1 \text{ L}} \times 0.2500 \text{ L} = 0.0625 \text{ mol CH}_3\text{COONa}$ set up a table to track changes:

$$\text{NaOH } (aq) + \text{CH}_3\text{COOH } (aq) \rightarrow \text{CH}_3\text{COONa } (aq) + \text{H}_2\text{O } (l)$$

	NaOH	CH$_3$COOH	CH$_3$COONa	H$_2$O
Before addition	≈ 0 mol	0.0625 mol	0.0625 mol	—
Addition	0.0050 mol	—	—	—
After addition	≈ 0 mol	0.0575 mol	0.0675 mol	—

Since the amount of NaOH is small, there are still significant amounts of both buffer components, so the Henderson–Hasselbalch equation can be used to calculate the new pH.

$$pH = pK_a + \log \frac{[\text{base}]}{[\text{acid}]} = -\log(1.8 \times 10^{-5}) + \log \frac{\dfrac{0.0675 \text{ mol}}{0.2500 \text{ L}}}{\dfrac{0.0575 \text{ mol}}{0.2500 \text{ L}}} = 4.81.$$

Check: The units (none) are correct. The magnitude of the answer makes physical sense because the pH rose slightly when base was added.

16.51   (a)   **Given:** 500.0 mL pure water   **Find:** initial pH and after adding 0.010 mol HCl
Conceptual Plan: pure water has a pH of 7.00 then mL → L then mol HCl, L → [H$_3$O$^+$] → pH

$$\frac{1\,L}{1000\,mL} \qquad M = \frac{mol}{L} \qquad pH = -\log[H_3O^+]$$

Solution: Pure water has a pH of 7.00 so initial pH = 7.00, $500.0\,\overline{mL} \times \dfrac{1\,L}{1000\,\overline{mL}} = 0.5000\,L$,

then $M = \dfrac{mol}{L} = \dfrac{0.010\,mol\,HCl}{0.5000\,L} = 0.020\,mol\,L^{-1}$ HCl. Since HCl is a strong acid, it dissociates completely, so pH $= -\log[H_3O^+] = -\log(0.020) = 1.70$.

Check: The units (none) are correct. The magnitudes of the answers make physical sense because the pH starts neutral and then drops significantly when acid is added and there is no buffer present.

(b)   **Given:** 500.0 mL buffer 0.125 mol L^{-1} CH$_3$COOH and 0.115 mol L^{-1} CH$_3$COONa
Find: initial pH and after adding 0.010 mol HCl **Other:** K_a (CH$_3$COOH) = 1.8 x 10^{-5}
Conceptual Plan: initial pH:
Identify acid and base components then mol L^{-1} CH$_3$COONa → mol L^{-1} CH$_3$COO$^-$ then

$$\text{acid} = CH_3COOH \quad \text{base} = CH_3COO^- \qquad\qquad CH_3COONa\,(aq) \longrightarrow Na^+\,(aq) + CH_3COO^-\,(aq)$$

mol L^{-1} CH$_3$COOH, mol L^{-1} CH$_3$COO$^-$ → pH

$$pH = pK_a + \log\frac{[\text{base}]}{[\text{acid}]}$$

pH after HCl addition: Part I: Stoichiometry:
mL → L then [CH$_3$COONa], L → mol CH$_3$COONa and [CH$_3$COOH], L → mol CH$_3$COOH

$$\frac{1\,L}{1000\,mL} \qquad\qquad M = \frac{mol}{L} \qquad\qquad\qquad M = \frac{mol}{L}$$

write balanced equation then

HCl + CH$_3$COONa → CH$_3$COOH + NaCl

mol CH$_3$COONa, mol CH$_3$COOH, mol HCl → mol CH$_3$COONa, mol CH$_3$COOH then

set up stoichiometry table

Part II: Equilibrium:
mol CH$_3$COONa, mol CH$_3$COOH, L, K_a → pH

$$pH = pK_a + \log\frac{[\text{base}]}{[\text{acid}]}$$

Solution: Initial pH: Acid = CH$_3$COOH, so [acid] = [CH$_3$COOH] = 0.125 mol L^{-1}. Base = CH$_3$COO$^-$. Since 1 CH$_3$COO$^-$ ion is generated for each CH$_3$COONa, [CH$_3$COO$^-$] = 0.115 mol L^{-1} CH$_3$COO$^-$ = [base]. Then

$$pH = pK_a + \log\frac{[\text{base}]}{[\text{acid}]} = -\log(1.8 \times 10^{-5}) + \log\frac{0.115\,\overline{mol\,L^{-1}}}{0.125\,\overline{mol\,L^{-1}}} = 4.71.$$

pH after HCl addition:

$500.0\,\overline{mL} \times \dfrac{1\,L}{1000\,\overline{mL}} = 0.5000\,L$ then $\dfrac{0.125\,mol\,CH_3COOH}{1\,\overline{L}} \times 0.5000\,\overline{L} = 0.0625\,mol\,CH_3COOH$ and

$\dfrac{0.115\,mol\,CH_3COONa}{1\,\overline{L}} \times 0.5000\,\overline{L} = 0.0575\,mol\,CH_3COONa$. Set up a table to track changes:

	HCl (aq)	+ CH$_3$COONa (aq)	→ CH$_3$COOH (aq)	+ NaCl (aq)
Before addition	≈ 0 mol	0.0575 mol	0.0625 mol	0 mol
Addition	0.010 mol	—	—	—
After addition	≈ 0 mol	0.0475 mol	0.0725 mol	0.10 mol

Since the amount of HCl is small, there are still significant amounts of both buffer components, so the Henderson–Hasselbalch equation can be used to calculate the new pH.

$$pH = pK_a + \log\frac{[\text{base}]}{[\text{acid}]} = -\log(1.8 \times 10^{-5}) + \log\frac{\dfrac{0.0475\,\overline{mol}}{\overline{0.5000\,L}}}{\dfrac{0.0725\,\overline{mol}}{\overline{0.5000\,L}}} = 4.56.$$

Check: The units (none) are correct. The magnitudes of the answers make physical sense because the pH started below the pK_a of the acid and it dropped slightly when acid was added.

(c) **Given:** 500.0 mL buffer 0.155 mol L^{-1} CH$_3$CH$_2$NH$_2$ and 0.145 mol L^{-1} CH$_3$CH$_2$NH$_3$Cl
Find: initial pH and after adding 0.010 mol HCl   **Other:** K_b (CH$_3$CH$_2$NH$_2$) = 5.6 x 10^{-4}
Conceptual Plan: initial pH:
Identify acid and base components then mol L^{-1} CH$_3$CH$_2$NH$_3$Cl → mol L^{-1} CH$_3$CH$_2$NH$_3^+$

$\quad$ acid = C$_2$H$_5$NH$_3^+$ base = C$_2$H$_5$NH$_2$ $\qquad\qquad$ C$_2$H$_5$NH$_3$Cl (aq) → C$_2$H$_5$NH$_3^+$ (aq) + Cl$^-$ (aq)

and K_b → pK_b → pK_a then pK_a, mol L^{-1} CH$_3$CH$_2$NH$_2$, mol L^{-1} CH$_3$CH$_2$NH$_3^+$ → pH

$\quad pK_b = -\log K_b \quad 14 = pK_a + pK_b \qquad\qquad\qquad\qquad\qquad\qquad\qquad pH = pK_a + \log \dfrac{[\text{base}]}{[\text{acid}]}$

pH after HCl addition: Part I: Stoichiometry:
mL → L then [CH$_3$CH$_2$NH$_2$], L → mol CH$_3$CH$_2$NH$_2$ and

$\qquad \dfrac{1\text{ L}}{1000\text{ mL}} \qquad\qquad\qquad M = \dfrac{\text{mol}}{\text{L}}$

[CH$_3$CH$_2$NH$_3$Cl], L → mol CH$_3$CH$_2$NH$_3$Cl write balanced equation then

$\qquad\qquad M = \dfrac{\text{mol}}{\text{L}} \qquad\qquad\qquad$ HCl + CH$_3$CH$_2$NH$_2$ → CH$_3$CH$_2$NH$_3$Cl

mol CH$_3$CH$_2$NH$_2$, mol CH$_3$CH$_2$NH$_3$Cl, mol HCl → mol CH$_3$CH$_2$NH$_2$, mol CH$_3$CH$_2$NH$_3$Cl then

$\qquad\qquad\qquad\qquad\qquad\qquad$ set up stoichiometry table

Part II: Equilibrium:
mol CH$_3$CH$_2$NH$_2$, mol CH$_3$CH$_2$NH$_3$Cl, L, K_a → pH

$\qquad\qquad\qquad pH = pK_a + \log \dfrac{[\text{base}]}{[\text{acid}]}$

Solution: Base = CH$_3$CH$_2$NH$_2$, [base] = [CH$_3$CH$_2$NH$_2$] = 0.155 mol L^{-1}, acid = CH$_3$CH$_2$NH$_3^+$. Since 1 CH$_3$CH$_2$NH$_3^+$ ion is generated for each CH$_3$CH$_2$NH$_3$Cl, [CH$_3$CH$_2$NH$_3^+$] = 0.145 mol L^{-1} CH$_3$CH$_2$NH$_3^+$ = [acid].

Since K_b (CH$_3$CH$_2$NH$_2$) = 5.6 x 10^{-4}, $pK_b = -\log K_b = -\log (5.6$ x $10^{-4}) = 3.25$. Since $14 = pK_a + pK_b$, $pK_a = 14 - pK_b = 14 - 3.25 = 10.75$ then

$$pH = pK_a + \log \dfrac{[\text{base}]}{[\text{acid}]} = 10.75 + \log \dfrac{0.155 \text{ mol L}^{-1}}{0.145 \text{ mol L}^{-1}} = 10.78.$$

pH after HCl addition: $500.0 \text{ mL} \times \dfrac{1 \text{ L}}{1000 \text{ mL}} = 0.5000$ L then

$\dfrac{0.155 \text{ mol CH}_3\text{CH}_2\text{NH}_2}{1 \text{ L}}$ x 0.5000 L = 0.0775 mol CH$_3$CH$_2$NH$_2$ and

$\dfrac{0.145 \text{ mol CH}_3\text{CH}_2\text{NH}_3\text{Cl}}{1 \text{ L}}$ x 0.5000 L = 0.0725 mol CH$_3$CH$_2$NH$_3$Cl. Set up a table to track changes:

	HCl (aq) +	CH$_3$CH$_2$NH$_2$ (aq) →	CH$_3$CH$_2$NH$_3$Cl (aq)
Before addition	≈ 0 mol	0.0775 mol	0.0725 mol
Addition	0.010 mol	—	—
After addition	≈ 0 mol	0.06$\underline{7}$5 mol	0.08$\underline{2}$5 mol

Since the amount of HCl is small, there are still significant amounts of both buffer components, so the Henderson–Hasselbalch equation can be used to calculate the new pH.

$$pH = pK_a + \log \dfrac{[\text{base}]}{[\text{acid}]} = 10.75 + \log \dfrac{\dfrac{0.0675 \text{ mol}}{0.5000 \text{ L}}}{\dfrac{0.0825 \text{ mol}}{0.5000 \text{ L}}} = 10.66.$$

Check: The units (none) are correct. The magnitudes of the answers make physical sense because the initial pH should be greater than the pK_a of the acid because there is more base than acid and the pH drops slightly when acid is added.

16.53 **Given:** 350.00 mL 0.150 mol L^{-1} HF and 0.150 mol L^{-1} NaF buffer
Find: mass NaOH to raise pH to 4.00 and mass NaOH to raise pH to 4.00 with buffer concentrations raised to 0.350 mol L^{-1}
Other: K_a (HF) = 3.5 x 10^{-4}

Conceptual Plan: Identify acid and base components. Since [NaF] = [HF] then initial pH = pK_a.

$$acid = HF \quad base = F^- \qquad\qquad pH = pK_a$$

final pH, pK_a → [NaF]/[HF] and mL → L then [HF], L → mol HF and [NaF], L → mol NaF

$$pH = pK_a + \log \frac{[base]}{[acid]} \qquad \frac{1\ L}{1000\ mL} \qquad M = \frac{mol}{L} \qquad M = \frac{mol}{L}$$

then write balanced equation then

$$NaOH + HF \rightarrow NaF + H_2O$$

mol HF, mol NaF, [NaF]/[HF] → mol NaOH → g NaOH.

$$set\ up\ stoichiometry\ table \quad \frac{40.00\ g\ NaOH}{1\ mol\ NaOH}$$

Finally, when the buffer concentrations are raised to 0.350 mol L^{-1}, simply multiply the g NaOH by ratio of concentrations (0.350 mol L^{-1} / 0.150 mol L^{-1}).

Solution: Initial pH = pK_a = $-\log(3.5 \times 10^{-4})$ = 3.46 then

$$pH = pK_a + \log\frac{[base]}{[acid]} = -\log(3.5 \times 10^{-4}) + \log\frac{[NaF]}{[HF]} = 4.00.\ \text{Solve for [NaF]/[HF].}$$

$$\log\frac{[NaF]}{[HF]} = 4.00 - 3.46 = 0.54 \rightarrow \frac{[NaF]}{[HF]} = 10^{0.54} = 3.5.\quad 350.0\ mL \times \frac{1\ L}{1000\ mL} = 0.3500\ L\ then$$

$$\frac{0.150\ mol\ HF}{1\ L} \times 0.3500\ L = 0.0525\ mol\ HF\ and\ \frac{0.150\ mol\ NaF}{1\ L} \times 0.3500\ L = 0.0525\ mol\ NaF$$

Set up a table to track changes:

	NaOH (aq)	+ HF (aq)	→ NaF (aq)	+ H$_2$O (l)
Before addition	≈ 0 mol	0.0525 mol	0.0125 mol	—
Addition	x	—	—	—
After addition	≈ 0 mol	(0.0525 − x) mol	(0.0525 + x) mol	—

Since $\frac{[NaF]}{[HF]} = 3.5 = \frac{(0.0525 + x)\ mol}{(0.0525 - x)\ mol}$, solve for x. Note that the ratio of moles is the same as the ratio of concentrations, since the volume for both terms is the same. $3.5(0.0525 - x) = (0.0525 + x) \rightarrow$
$0.18375 - 3.5x = 0.0525 + x \rightarrow 0.13125 = 4.5x \rightarrow x = 0.029167\ mol\ NaOH$ then

$$0.029167\ mol\ NaOH \times \frac{40.00\ g\ NaOH}{1\ mol\ NaOH} = 1.1667\ g\ NaOH = 1.2\ g\ NaOH.\ \text{Finally multiply the NaOH mass}$$

by the ratio of concentrations $1.1667\ g\ NaOH \times \frac{0.350\ mol\ L^{-1}}{0.150\ mol\ L^{-1}} = 2.7\ g\ NaOH.$

Check: The units (g) are correct. The magnitudes of the answers make physical sense because there is much less than a mole of each of the buffer components, so there must be much less than a mole of NaOH. The higher the buffer concentrations, the higher the buffer capacity and the mass of NaOH it can neutralize.

16.55 (a) Yes, this will be a buffer because NH$_3$ is a weak base and NH$_4^+$ is its conjugate acid. The ratio of base to acid is 0.10/0.15 = 0.67, so the pH will be within 1 pH unit of the pK_a.

(b) No, this will not be a buffer solution because HCl is a strong acid and NaOH is a strong base.

(c) Yes, this will be a buffer because HF is a weak acid and the NaOH will convert 20.0/50.0 = 40% of the acid to its conjugate base.

(d) No, this will not be a buffer solution because both components are bases.

(e) No, this will not be a buffer solution because both components are bases.

16.57 (a) **Given:** blood buffer 0.024 mol L^{-1} HCO$_3^-$ and 0.0012 mol L^{-1} H$_2$CO$_3$, pK_a = 6.1 **Find:** initial pH
Conceptual Plan: Identify acid and base components then mol L^{-1} HCO$_3^-$, mol L^{-1} H$_2$CO$_3$ → pH

$$acid = H_2CO_3 \quad base = HCO_3^- \qquad\qquad pH = pK_a + \log\frac{[base]}{[acid]}$$

Solution: Acid = H$_2$CO$_3$, so [acid] = [H$_2$CO$_3$] = 0.0012 mol L^{-1}. Base = HCO$_3^-$, so [base] = [HCO$_3^-$] = 0.024 mol L^{-1} HCO$_3^-$. Then $pH = pK_a + \log\frac{[base]}{[acid]} = 6.1 + \log\frac{0.024\ mol\ L^{-1}}{0.0012\ mol\ L^{-1}} = 7.4.$

Check: The units (none) are correct. The magnitude of the answer makes physical sense because pH is greater than the pK_a of the acid because there is more base than acid.

(b) **Given:** 5.0 L of blood buffer **Find:** mass HCl to lower pH to 7.0
Conceptual Plan: final pH, pK_a → [HCO$_3^-$]/[H$_2$CO$_3$] then [HCO$_3^-$], L → mol HCO$_3^-$ and

$$pH = pK_a + \log\frac{[base]}{[acid]} \qquad M = \frac{mol}{L}$$

[H$_2$CO$_3$], L → mol H$_2$CO$_3$ then write balanced equation then

$$M = \frac{mol}{L} \qquad H^+ + HCO_3^- \to H_2CO_3$$

mol HCO$_3^-$, mol H$_2$CO$_3$, [HCO$_3^-$]/[H$_2$CO$_3$] → mol HCl → g HCl

set up stoichiometry table $\dfrac{36.46 \text{ g HCl}}{1 \text{ mol HCl}}$

Solution: $pH = pK_a + \log\frac{[base]}{[acid]} = 6.1 + \log\frac{[HCO_3^-]}{[H_2CO_3]} = 7.0$. Solve for [HCO$_3^-$]/[H$_2CO_3$].

$$\log\frac{[HCO_3^-]}{[H_2CO_3]} = 7.0 - 6.1 = 0.9 \to \frac{[HCO_3^-]}{[H_2CO_3]} = 10^{0.9} = 7.9433. \text{ Then}$$

$$\frac{0.024 \text{ mol HCO}_3^-}{1 \text{ L}} \times 5.0 \text{ L} = 0.12 \text{ mol HCO}_3^- \text{ and } \frac{0.0012 \text{ mol H}_2CO_3}{1 \text{ L}} \times 5.0 \text{ L} = 0.0060 \text{ mol H}_2CO_3$$

Since HCl is a strong acid, [HCl] = [H$^+$], and set up table to track changes:

	H$^+$ (aq)	+ HCO$_3^-$ (aq)	→ H$_2$CO$_3$ (aq)
Before addition	≈ 0 mol	0.12 mol	0.0060 mol
Addition	x	—	—
After addition	≈ 0 mol	(0.12 − x) mol	(0.0060 + x) mol

Since $\dfrac{[HCO_3^-]}{[H_2CO_3]} = 7.9433 = \dfrac{(0.12 - x) \text{ mol}}{(0.0060 + x) \text{ mol}}$, solve for x. Note that the ratio of moles is the same as the ratio of concentrations, since the volume for both terms is the same.

$7.9433 (0.0060 + x) = (0.12 - x) \to 0.0476598 + 7.9433 x = 0.12 - x \to 8.9433 x = 0.07234 \to$

$x = 0.0080888$ mol HCl then $0.0080888 \text{ mol HCl} \times \dfrac{36.46 \text{ g HCl}}{1 \text{ mol HCl}} = 0.29492$ g HCl = 0.3 g HCl.

Check: The units (g) are correct. The amount of acid needed is small because the concentrations of the buffer components are very low and the buffer starts only 0.4 pH units above the final pH.

(c) **Given:** 5.0 L of blood buffer **Find:** mass NaOH to raise pH to 7.8
Conceptual Plan: final pH, pK_a → [HCO$_3^-$]/[H$_2$CO$_3$] then [HCO$_3^-$], L → mol HCO$_3^-$ and

$$pH = pK_a + \log\frac{[base]}{[acid]} \qquad M = \frac{mol}{L}$$

[H$_2$CO$_3$], L → mol H$_2$CO$_3$ then write balanced equation then

$$M = \frac{mol}{L} \qquad OH^- + H_2CO_3 \to HCO_3^- + H_2O$$

mol HCO$_3^-$, mol H$_2$CO$_3$, [HCO$_3^-$]/[H$_2$CO$_3$] → mol NaOH → g NaOH

set up stoichiometry table $\dfrac{40.00 \text{ g NaOH}}{1 \text{ mol NaOH}}$

Solution: $pH = pK_a + \log\frac{[base]}{[acid]} = 6.1 + \log\frac{[HCO_3^-]}{[H_2CO_3]} = 7.8$.

Solve for [HCO$_3^-$]/[H$_2$CO$_3$]. $\log\frac{[HCO_3^-]}{[H_2CO_3]} = 7.8 - 6.1 = 1.7 \to \frac{[HCO_3^-]}{[H_2CO_3]} = 10^{1.7} = 50.11872$. Then

$$\frac{0.024 \text{ mol HCO}_3^-}{1 \text{ L}} \times 5.0 \text{ L} = 0.12 \text{ mol HCO}_3^- \text{ and } \frac{0.0012 \text{ mol H}_2CO_3}{1 \text{ L}} \times 5.0 \text{ L} = 0.0060 \text{ mol H}_2CO_3$$

Since NaOH is a strong base, [NaOH] = [OH$^-$], and set up table to track changes:

	OH$^-$ (aq)	+ H$_2$CO$_3$ (aq)	→ HCO$_3^-$ (aq)	+ H$_2$O (l)
Before addition	≈ 0 mol	0.0060 mol	0.12 mol	—
Addition	x	—	—	
After addition	≈ 0 mol	(0.0060 − x) mol	(0.12 + x) mol	

Since $\dfrac{[HCO_3^-]}{[H_2CO_3]} = 50.11872 = \dfrac{(0.12 + x) \text{ mol}}{(0.0060 - x) \text{ mol}}$, solve for x. Note that the ratio of moles is the same as the ratio of concentrations, since the volume for both terms is the same.

$50.\underline{11872}(0.0060 - x) = (0.12 + x) \rightarrow 0.3\underline{0071} - 50.\underline{11872}x = 0.12 + x \rightarrow 51.\underline{11872}x = 0.1\underline{8071}$

$\rightarrow x = 0.00\underline{35351}$ mol NaOH then

$0.00\underline{35351}$ $\overline{\text{mol NaOH}}$ $\times \dfrac{40.00 \text{ g NaOH}}{1 \overline{\text{mol NaOH}}} = 0.1\underline{4141}$ g NaOH = 0.14 g NaOH.

Check: The units (g) are correct. The amount of base needed is small because the concentrations of the buffer components are very low.

16.59   **Given:** CH_3COOH/CH_3COOK, $HClO_2/KClO_2$, NH_3/NH_4Cl, and $HClO/KClO$ potential buffer systems to create buffer at pH = 7.20 **Find:** best buffer system and ratio of component masses
Other: K_a $(CH_3COOH) = 1.8 \times 10^{-5}$, K_a $(HClO_2) = 1.8 \times 10^{-4}$, K_b $(NH_3) = 1.79 \times 10^{-5}$, K_a $(HClO) = 2.9 \times 10^{-8}$
Conceptual Plan: calculate pK_a of all potential buffer acids for the base $K_b \rightarrow pK_b \rightarrow pK_a$ then

$$pK_a = -\log K_a \qquad\qquad pK_b = -\log K_b \quad 14 = pK_a + pK_b$$

and choose the pK_a that is closest to 7.20. Then pH, $K_a \rightarrow$ [base]/[acid] $\rightarrow$ mass base/mass acid

$$pH = pK_a + \log \frac{[\text{base}]}{[\text{acid}]} \frac{\text{molar mass (base)}}{\text{molar mass (acid)}}$$

Solution: for CH_3COOH/CH_3COOK: $pK_a = -\log K_a = -\log (1.8 \times 10^{-5}) = 4.74$; for $HClO_2/KClO_2$:

$pK_a = -\log K_a = -\log (1.8 \times 10^{-4}) = 3.74$; for NH_3/NH_4Cl:

$pK_b = -\log K_b = -\log (1.79 \times 10^{-5}) = 4.75$.

Since $14 = pK_a + pK_b$, $pK_a = 14 - pK_b = 14 - 4.75 = 9.25$; and for $HClO/KClO$:

$pK_a = -\log K_a = -\log (2.9 \times 10^{-8}) = 7.54$. So the HClO/KClO buffer system has the pK_a that is the

closest to 7.20. So, $pH = pK_a + \log \dfrac{[\text{base}]}{[\text{acid}]} = 7.54 + \log \dfrac{[\text{KClO}]}{[\text{HClO}]} = 7.1$. Solve for [KClO]/[HClO].

$\log \dfrac{[\text{KClO}]}{[\text{HClO}]} = 7.20 - 7.54 = -0.34 \rightarrow \dfrac{[\text{KClO}]}{[\text{HClO}]} = 10^{-0.34} = 0.4\underline{57088}$. Then convert to mass ratio using

$\dfrac{\text{molar mass (base)}}{\text{molar mass (acid)}}, \quad 0.4\underline{57088} \dfrac{\dfrac{\overline{\text{KClO mol}}}{\text{L}}}{\dfrac{\overline{\text{HClO mol}}}{\text{L}}} \times \dfrac{\dfrac{90.55 \text{ g KClO}}{\overline{\text{mol KClO}}}}{52.46 \text{ g HClO} \overline{\text{mol HClO}}} = 0.79 \dfrac{\text{g KClO}}{\text{g HClO}}$

Check: The units (none and g base/g acid) are correct. The buffer system with the K_a closest to 10^{-7} is the best choice. The magnitude of the answer makes physical sense because the buffer needs more acid than base (and this fact is not overcome by the heavier molar mass of the base).

16.61   **Given:** 500.0 mL of 0.100 mol L^{-1} HNO_2 / 0.150 mol L^{-1} KNO_2 buffer and a) 250 mg NaOH, b) 350 mg KOH, c) 1.25 g HBr, and d) 1.35 g HI **Find:** if buffer capacity is exceeded
Conceptual Plan: mL $\rightarrow$ L then [HNO_2], L $\rightarrow$ mol HNO_2 and [KNO_2], L $\rightarrow$ mol KNO_2 then

$$\dfrac{1 \text{ L}}{1000 \text{ mL}} \qquad\qquad M = \dfrac{\text{mol}}{\text{L}} \qquad\qquad M = \dfrac{\text{mol}}{\text{L}}$$

then calculate moles of acid or base to be added to the buffer mg $\rightarrow$ g $\rightarrow$ mol then

$$\dfrac{1 \text{ g}}{1000 \text{ mg}} \text{ molar mass}$$

compare the added amount to the buffer amount of the opposite component. Ratio of base/acid must be between 0.1 and 10 to maintain the buffer integrity.

Solution: 500.00 $\overline{\text{mL}}$ $\times \dfrac{1 \text{ L}}{1000 \overline{\text{mL}}} = 0.5000$ L then $\dfrac{0.100 \text{ mol } HNO_2}{1 \text{ L}} \times 0.5000$ $\overline{\text{L}} = 0.0500$ mol HNO_2 and

$\dfrac{0.150 \text{ mol } KNO_2}{1 \text{ L}} \times 0.5000$ $\overline{\text{L}} = 0.0750$ mol KNO_2

(a)   For NaOH: 250 $\overline{\text{mg NaOH}} \times \dfrac{1 \overline{\text{g NaOH}}}{1000 \overline{\text{mg NaOH}}} \times \dfrac{1 \text{ mol NaOH}}{40.00 \overline{\text{g NaOH}}} = 0.00\underline{625}$ mol NaOH. Since the buffer

contains 0.0500 mol acid, the amount of acid is reduced by $0.00625/0.0500 = 12.5\%$ and the ratio of base/acid is still between 0.1 and 10. The buffer capacity is not exceeded.

(b)   For KOH: $350 \; \overline{mg \; KOH} \times \dfrac{1 \; \overline{g \; KOH}}{1000 \; \overline{mg \; KOH}} \times \dfrac{1 \; mol \; KOH}{56.11 \; \overline{g \; KOH}} = 0.00624 \; mol \; KOH$. Since the buffer contains 0.0500 mol acid, the amount of acid is reduced by 0.00624/0.0500 = 12.5% and the ratio of base/acid is still between 0.1 and 10. The buffer capacity is not exceeded.

(c)   For HBr: $1.25 \; \overline{g \; HBr} \times \dfrac{1 \; mol \; HBr}{80.91 \; \overline{g \; HBr}} = 0.0154496 \; mol \; HBr$. Since the buffer contains 0.0750 mol base, the amount of acid is reduced by 0.0154/0.0750 = 20.6% and the ratio of base/acid is still between 0.1 and 10. The buffer capacity is not exceeded.

(d)   For HI: $1.35 \; \overline{g \; HI} \times \dfrac{1 \; mol \; HI}{127.91 \; \overline{g \; HI}} = 0.0105545 \; mol \; HI$. Since the buffer contains 0.0750 mol base, the amount of acid is reduced by 0.0106/0.0750 = 14.1% and the ratio of base/acid is still between 0.1 and 10. The buffer capacity is not exceeded.

16.63   (a)   **Given:** 12.5 mL of 0.100 mol L^{-1} HCl and 25.0 mL of 0.100 mol L^{-1} Tris **Find:** pH
        Other: pK_a (TrisH$^+$) = 8.10
        Conceptual plan: Write a balanced equation then mL $\rightarrow$ L and L, mol L^{-1} $\rightarrow$ mol

$$\dfrac{1 \; L}{1000 \; mL} \qquad\qquad M = \dfrac{mol}{L}$$

HCl $\rightarrow$ mol H$_3$O$^+$

$H_3O^+ \; (aq) + Tris \; (aq) \;\; \rightarrow TrisH^+ \; (aq)$

Then mL $\rightarrow$ L then L, mol L^{-1} $\rightarrow$ mol Tris. Set up a table to track the changes and then

$$\dfrac{1 \; L}{1000 \; mL} \qquad\qquad M = \dfrac{mol}{L}$$

mol Tris, mol TrisH$^+$, pK_a $\rightarrow$ pH

$$pH = pK_a + \log \dfrac{[base]}{[acid]}$$

Solution: Mole HCl = $12.5 \; \overline{mL} \times \dfrac{1 \; \overline{L}}{1000 \; \overline{mL}} \times \dfrac{0.100 \; mol}{\overline{L}} = 1.25 \times 10^{-3} \; mol = 1.25 \times 10^{-3} \; mol \; H_3O^+$ since

HCl is a strong acid. Mole Tris = $25.0 \; \overline{mL} \times \dfrac{1 \; \overline{L}}{1000 \; \overline{mL}} \times \dfrac{0.100 \; mol}{\overline{L}} = 2.50 \times 10^{-3} \; mol \; Tris$. Set up a table to track changes:

	H$_3$O$^+$ (aq)	+	Tris (aq)	$\rightarrow$	TrisH$^+$ (aq)
Initial	1.25×10^{-3} mol		2.50×10^{-3} mol		0
Change	-1.25×10^{-3} mol		-1.25×10^{-3} mol		$+1.25 \times 10^{-3}$ mol
Final	≈ 0		1.25×10^{-3} mol		1.25×10^{-3} mol

There is a mixture of a weak acid (TrisH$^+$) and its conjugate base (Tris) which form a buffer. There are equal amounts of acid and base and the K_a (= $10^{-8.10}$ = 7.9×10^{-9}) is small so use of the Henderson–Hasselbalch equation is appropriate. Since everything is in the same volume, the moles are proportional to the molarities.

$$pH = pK_a + \log \dfrac{[base]}{[acid]} = 8.10 + \log \dfrac{1.25 \times 10^{-3} \; \overline{mol}}{1.25 \times 10^{-3} \; \overline{mol}} = 8.10$$

Check: The units (none) are appropriate and the pH is equal to the pK_a because there are equal amounts of acid and base.

(b)   **Given:** 1.25×10^{-3} mol Tris (from part a), 1.25×10^{-3} mol TrisH$^+$ (from part a), 0.0002 mol H$_3$O$^+$ produced **Find:** pH after reaction **Other:** pK_a (TrisH$^+$) = 8.10
        Conceptual Plan: Write a balanced equation then set up a table to track the changes and determine change in moles of acid and base.

$H_3O^+ \; (aq) + Tris \; (aq) \; \rightarrow \; TrisH^+ \; (aq)$

Then mol Tris, mol TrisH$^+$, pK_a → pH

$$pH = pK_a + \log \frac{[\text{base}]}{[\text{acid}]}$$

Solution:

	H_3O^+ (aq)	+	Tris (aq)	→	TrisH$^+$ (aq)
Before addition	≈0		1.25×10^{-3} mol		1.25×10^{-3} mol
Addition	0.0002 mol		—		—
After addition	≈0		1.05×10^{-3} mol		1.45×10^{-3} mol

The ratio of Tris/TrisH$^+$ is 0.72, so the buffer is still effective. Since everything is in the same volume, the moles are proportional to the molarities. Use the Henderson–Hasselbalch equation to solve for pH:

$$pH = pK_a + \log \frac{[\text{base}]}{[\text{acid}]} = 8.10 + \log \frac{1.05 \times 10^{-3} \text{ mol}}{1.45 \times 10^{-3} \text{ mol}} = 8.10 - 0.140 = 7.96$$

Check: The units (none) are appropriate and the pH is lower than the pK_a because there is more acid than base.

Titrations, pH Curves, and Indicators

16.65 (i) The equivalence point of a titration is where the pH rises sharply as base is added. The pH at the equivalence point is the midpoint of the sharp rise at ~ 50 mL added base. For (a) the pH = ~ 8 and for (b) the pH = ~ 7.

(ii) Graph (a) represents a weak acid and graph (b) represents a strong acid. A strong acid titration starts at a lower pH, has a flatter initial region and a sharper rise at the equivalence point than a weak acid. The pH at the equivalence point of a strong acid is neutral, while the pH at the equivalence point of a weak acid is basic.

16.67 **Given:** 20.0 mL 0.200 mol L^{-1} KOH and 0.200 mol L^{-1} CH$_3$NH$_2$ titrated with 0.100 mol L^{-1} HI

(a) **Find:** volume of base to reach equivalence point
Conceptual Plan: The answer for both titrations will be the same since the initial concentration and volumes of the bases are the same. Write balanced equation then mL → L then

$$HI + KOH \rightarrow KI + H_2O \text{ and } HI + CH_3NH_2 \rightarrow CH_3NH_3I \qquad \frac{1 \text{ L}}{1000 \text{ mL}}$$

[base], L → mol base then set mol base = mol acid and [HI], mol HI → L HI → mL HI

$$M = \frac{\text{mol}}{\text{L}} \qquad \text{balanced equation has 1:1 stoichiometry} \qquad M = \frac{\text{mol}}{\text{L}} \quad \frac{1000 \text{ mL}}{1 \text{ L}}$$

Solution: $20.0 \text{ mL base} \times \frac{1 \text{ L}}{1000 \text{ mL}} = 0.0200$ L base then

$\frac{0.200 \text{ mol base}}{1 \text{ L}} \times 0.0200 \text{ L} = 0.00400$ mol base. So mol base = 0.00400 mol = mol HI then

$0.00400 \text{ mol HI} \times \frac{1 \text{ L HI}}{0.100 \text{ mol HI}} = 0.0400 \text{ L HI} \times \frac{1000 \text{ mL}}{1 \text{ L}} = 40.0$ mL HI for both titrations.

Check: The units (mL) are correct. The volume of acid is twice the volume of bases because the concentration of the base is twice that of the acid in each case. The answer for both titrations is the same because the stoichiometry is the same for both titration reactions.

(b) The pH at the equivalence point will be neutral for KOH (since it is a strong base) and it will be acidic for CH$_3$NH$_2$ (since it is a weak base).

(c) The initial pH will be lower for CH$_3$NH$_2$ (since it is a weak base) and will only partially dissociate and not raise the pH as high as KOH (since it is a strong base and so it dissociates completely) at the same base concentration.

(d)   The titration curves will look like the following:

KOH:

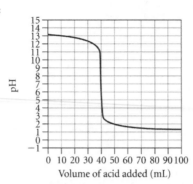

CH$_3$NH$_2$:

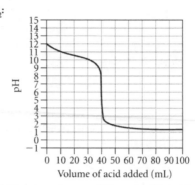

Important features to include are a high initial pH (if strong base, pH is over 13 and lower for a weak base), flat initial region (very flat for strong base, not as flat for weak base where pH halfway to equivalence point is the pK_b of the base), sharp drop at equivalence point, pH at equivalence point (neutral for strong base and lower for weak base), and then flatten out at low pH.

16.69   (a)   The equivalence point of a titration is where the pH rises sharply as base is added. The volume at the equivalence point is ~ 30 mL. The pH at the equivalence point is the midpoint of the sharp rise at ~ 30 mL added base, which is pH = ~ 9.

        (b)   At 0 mL the pH is calculated by doing an equilibrium calculation of a weak acid in water (as done in Chapter 15).

        (c)   The pH one-half way to the equivalence point is equal to the pK_a of the acid, or ~ 15 mL.

        (d)   The pH at the equivalence point, or ~ 30 mL, is calculated by doing an equilibrium problem with the K_b of the conjugate base. At the equivalence point, all of the acid has been converted to its conjugate base.

        (e)   Beyond the equivalence point (> 30 mL) there is excess base. All of the acid has been converted to its conjugate base and so the pH is calculated by focusing on this excess base concentration.

16.71   **Given:** 35.0 mL of 0.175 mol L^{-1} HBr titrated with 0.200 mol L^{-1} KOH

        (a)   **Find:** initial pH
                Conceptual Plan: Since HBr is a strong acid, it will dissociate completely, so initial pH = − log [H$_3$O$^+$] = − log [HBr].
                Solution: pH = − log [HBr] = − log 0.175 = 0.757
                Check: The units (none) are correct. The pH is reasonable since the concentration is greater than 0.1 mol L^{-1} and the acid dissociates completely, the pH is less than 1.

        (b)   **Find:** volume of base to reach equivalence point
                Conceptual Plan: Write balanced equation then mL → L then [HBr], L → mol HBr then

                HBr + KOH → KBr + H$_2$O $\dfrac{1\ \text{L}}{1000\ \text{mL}}$ $M = \dfrac{\text{mol}}{\text{L}}$

                set mol acid (HBr) = mol base (KOH) and [KOH], mol KOH → L KOH → mL KOH.

                balanced equation has 1:1 stoichiometry $M = \dfrac{\text{mol}}{\text{L}}$ $\dfrac{1000\ \text{mL}}{1\ \text{L}}$

                Solution: 35.0 mL HBr × $\dfrac{1\ \text{L}}{1000\ \text{mL}}$ = 0.0350 L HBr then

                $\dfrac{0.175\ \text{mol HBr}}{1\ \text{L}}$ × 0.0350 L = 0.006125 mol HBr.

                So mol acid = mol HBr = 0.006125 mol = mol KOH then

                0.006125 mol KOH × $\dfrac{1\ \text{L}}{0.200\ \text{mol KOH}}$ = 0.030625 L KOH × $\dfrac{1000\ \text{mL}}{1\ \text{L}}$ = 30.6 mL KOH.

                Check: The units (mL) are correct. The volume of base is a little less than the volume of acid because the concentration of the base is a little greater than that of the acid.

(c) **Find:** pH after adding 10.0 mL of base

Conceptual Plan: Use calculations from part (b). Then mL $\rightarrow$ L then [KOH], L $\rightarrow$ mol KOH then

$$\frac{1\ L}{1000\ mL} \qquad M = \frac{mol}{L}$$

mol HBr, mol KOH $\rightarrow$ mol excess HBr and L HBr, L KOH $\rightarrow$ total L then

set up stoichiometry table $\qquad\qquad$ L HBr + L KOH = total L

mol excess HBr, L $\rightarrow$ [HBr] $\rightarrow$ pH.

$$M = \frac{mol}{L} \quad pH = -\log[HBr]$$

Solution: $10.0\ \overline{mL\ KOH} \times \dfrac{1\ L}{1000\ \overline{mL}} = 0.0100\ L\ KOH$ then

$\dfrac{0.200\ mol\ KOH}{1\ \cancel{L}} \times 0.0100\ \cancel{L} = 0.00200\ mol\ KOH.$

Since KOH is a strong base, [KOH] = [OH$^-$], and set up a table to track changes:

$$KOH\ (aq)\ +\ HBr\ (aq)\ \rightarrow\ KBr\ (aq)\ +\ H_2O\ (l)$$

Before addition	≈ 0 mol	0.006125 mol	0 mol	—
Addition	0.00200 mol	—	—	—
After addition	≈ 0 mol	0.004125 mol	0.00200 mol	—

Then 0.0350 L HBr + 0.0100 L KOH = 0.0450 L total volume.

So mol excess acid = mol HBr = 0.004125 mol in 0.0450 L so

$[HBr] = \dfrac{0.004125\ mol\ HBr}{0.0450\ L} = 0.0916667\ mol\ L^{-1}$ and

$pH = -\log[HBr] = -\log 0.0916667 = 1.038.$

Check: The units (none) are correct. The pH is a little higher than the initial pH, which is expected since this is a strong acid.

(d) **Find:** pH at equivalence point

Solution: Since this is a strong acid–strong base titration, the pH at the equivalence point is neutral or 7.

(e) **Find:** pH after adding 5.0 mL of base beyond the equivalence point

Conceptual Plan: Use calculations from parts (b) & (c). Then the pH is only dependent on the amount of excess base and the total solution volumes.

mL excess $\rightarrow$ L excess then [KOH], L excess $\rightarrow$ mol KOH excess

$$\frac{1\ L}{1000\ mL} \qquad\qquad M = \frac{mol}{L}$$

then L HBr, L KOH to equivalence point, L KOH excess $\rightarrow$ total L then

L HBr + L KOH to equivalence point + L KOH excess = total L

mol excess KOH, total L $\rightarrow$ [KOH] = [OH$^-$] $\rightarrow$ [H$_3$O$^+$] $\rightarrow$ pH

$$M = \frac{mol}{L} \qquad K_w = [H_3O^+][OH^-] \quad pH = -\log[H_3O^+]$$

Solution: $5.0\ \overline{mL\ KOH} \times \dfrac{1\ L}{1000\ \overline{mL}} = 0.0050\ L\ KOH$ excess then

$\dfrac{0.200\ mol\ KOH}{1\ \cancel{L}} \times 0.0050\ \cancel{L} = 0.0010\ mol\ KOH$ excess. Then 0.0350 L HBr + 0.0306 L KOH + 0.0050 L

KOH = 0.0706 L total volume. $[KOH\ excess] = \dfrac{0.0010\ mol\ KOH\ excess}{0.0706\ L} = 0.014164\ mol\ L^{-1}$

KOH excess

Since KOH is a strong base, [KOH] excess = [OH$^-$]. $K_w = [H_3O^+][OH^-]$ so

$[H_3O^+] = \dfrac{K_w}{[OH^-]} = \dfrac{1.0 \times 10^{-14}}{0.014164} = 7.06 \times 10^{-13}\ mol\ L^{-1}.$ Finally,

$pH = -\log[H_3O^+] = -\log(7.06 \times 10^{-13}) = 12.15.$

Check: The units (none) are correct. The pH is rising sharply at the equivalence point, so the pH after 5 mL past the equivalence point should be quite basic.

16.73   **Given:** 25.0 mL of 0.115 mol L^{-1} RbOH titrated with 0.100 mol L^{-1} HCl

(a)   **Find:** initial pH
Conceptual Plan: Since RbOH is a strong base, it will dissociate completely, so
[RbOH] = [OH$^-$] $\rightarrow$ [H$_3$O$^+$] $\rightarrow$ pH.
$$K_w = [\text{H}_3\text{O}^+][\text{OH}^-] \quad \text{pH} = -\log[\text{H}_3\text{O}^+]$$
Solution: Since RbOH is a strong base, [RbOH] excess = [OH$^-$]. $K_w = [\text{H}_3\text{O}^+][\text{OH}^-]$ so

$$[\text{H}_3\text{O}^+] = \frac{K_w}{[\text{OH}^-]} = \frac{1.0 \times 10^{-14}}{0.115} = 8.69565 \times 10^{-14} \text{ mol L}^{-1} \text{ and}$$

$$\text{pH} = -\log[\text{H}_3\text{O}^+] = -\log(8.69565 \times 10^{-14}) = 13.06.$$

Check: The units (none) are correct. The pH is reasonable since the concentration is greater than 0.1 mol L^{-1} and the base dissociates completely, the pH is greater than 13.

(b)   **Find:** volume of acid to reach equivalence point
Conceptual Plan: Write balanced equation then mL $\rightarrow$ L then [RbOH], L $\rightarrow$ mol RbOH then
$$\text{HCl} + \text{RbOH} \rightarrow \text{RbCl} + \text{H}_2\text{O} \qquad \frac{1 \text{ L}}{1000 \text{ mL}} \qquad M = \frac{\text{mol}}{\text{L}}$$
set mol base (RbOH) = mol acid (HCl) and [HCl], mol HCl $\rightarrow$ L HCl $\rightarrow$ mL HCl.
$$\text{balanced equation has 1:1 stoichiometry} \qquad M = \frac{\text{mol}}{\text{L}} \quad \frac{1000 \text{ mL}}{1 \text{ L}}$$
Solution: $25.0 \text{ mL RbOH} \times \dfrac{1 \text{ L}}{1000 \text{ mL}} = 0.0250 \text{ L RbOH}$ then

$\dfrac{0.115 \text{ mol RbOH}}{1 \text{ L}} \times 0.0250 \text{ L} = 0.002875 \text{ mol RbOH}$. So mol base = mol RbOH = 0.002875 mol = mol

HCl then $0.002875 \text{ mol HCl} \times \dfrac{1 \text{ L}}{0.100 \text{ mol HCl}} = 0.02875 \text{ L HCl} \times \dfrac{1000 \text{ mL}}{1 \text{ L}} = 28.8 \text{ mL HCl.}$

Check: The units (mL) are correct. The volume of acid is greater than the volume of base because the concentration of the base is a little greater than that of the acid.

(c)   **Find:** pH after adding 5.0 mL of acid
Conceptual Plan: Use calculations from part (b). Then mL $\rightarrow$ L then [HCl], L $\rightarrow$ mol HCl then
$$\frac{1 \text{ L}}{1000 \text{ mL}} \qquad M = \frac{\text{mol}}{\text{L}}$$
mol RbOH, mol HCl $\rightarrow$ mol excess RbOH and L RbOH, L HCl $\rightarrow$ total L then
$$\text{set up stoichiometry table} \qquad \text{L RbOH + L HCl = total L}$$
mol excess RbOH, L $\rightarrow$ [RbOH] = [OH$^-$] $\rightarrow$ [H$_3$O$^+$] $\rightarrow$ pH.
$$M = \frac{\text{mol}}{\text{L}} \qquad K_w = [\text{H}_3\text{O}^+][\text{OH}^-] \quad \text{pH} = -\log[\text{H}_3\text{O}^+]$$
Solution: $5.0 \text{ mL HCl} \times \dfrac{1 \text{ L}}{1000 \text{ mL}} = 0.0050 \text{ L HCl}$ then $\dfrac{0.100 \text{ mol HCl}}{1 \text{ L}} \times 0.0050 \text{ L} = 0.00050 \text{ mol HCl.}$

Since HCl is a strong acid, [HCl] = [H$_3$O$^+$]. Set up a table to track changes:

	HCl (aq)	+	RbOH (aq)	$\rightarrow$	RbCl (aq)	+	H$_2$O (l)
Before addition	0 mol		0.002875 mol		0 mol		—
Addition	0.00050 mol		—		—		—
After addition	$\approx$ 0 mol		0.002375 mol		0.00050 mol		—

Then 0.0250 L RbOH + 0.0050 L HCl = 0.0300 L total volume. So mol excess base = mol RbOH =

0.002375 mol in 0.0300 L so $[\text{RbOH}] = \dfrac{0.002375 \text{ mol RbOH}}{0.0300 \text{ L}} = 0.0791667 \text{ mol L}^{-1}$. Since RbOH is a strong

base, [RbOH] excess = [OH$^-$]. $K_w = [\text{H}_3\text{O}^+][\text{OH}^-]$ so $[\text{H}_3\text{O}^+] = \dfrac{K_w}{[\text{OH}^-]} = \dfrac{1.0 \times 10^{-14}}{0.0791667}$

$= 1.26316 \times 10^{-13} \text{ mol L}^{-1}$ and $\text{pH} = -\log[\text{H}_3\text{O}^+] = -\log(1.26316 \times 10^{-13}) = 12.90.$

Check: The units (none) are correct. The pH is a little lower than the initial pH, which is expected since this is a strong base.

(d)   **Find:** pH at equivalence point
Solution: Since this is a strong acid–strong base titration, the pH at the equivalence point is neutral or 7.

(e) **Find:** pH after adding 5.0 mL of acid beyond the equivalence point
Conceptual Plan: Use calculations from parts (b) and (c). Then the pH is only dependent on the amount of excess acid and the total solution volumes. Then
mL excess $\rightarrow$ L excess then [HCl], L excess $\rightarrow$ mol HCl excess

$$\frac{1\,L}{1000\,mL} \qquad\qquad M = \frac{mol}{L}$$

then L RbOH, L HCl to equivalence point, L HCl excess $\rightarrow$ total L then

L RbOH + L HCl to equivalence point + L HCl excess = total L

mol excess HCl, total L $\rightarrow$ [HCl] = [H$_3$O$^+$] $\rightarrow$ pH.

$$M = \frac{mol}{L} \qquad\qquad pH = -\log[H_3O^+]$$

Solution: $5.0\ \overline{mL\ HCl} \times \dfrac{1\,L}{1000\ \overline{mL}} = 0.0050\ L\ HCl$ excess then

$\dfrac{0.100\ mol\ HCl}{1\ \overline{L}} \times 0.0050\ \overline{L} = 0.00050\ mol\ HCl$ excess. Then $0.0250\ L\ RbOH + 0.0288\ L\ HCl + 0.0050\ L$

$HCl = 0.0588\ L$ total volume. $[HCl\ excess] = \dfrac{0.00050\ mol\ HCl\ excess}{0.0588\ L} = 0.008\underline{5}034\ mol\ L^{-1}\ HCl$ excess

Since HCl is a strong acid, [HCl] excess $= [H_3O^+]$.
Finally, $pH = -\log[H_3O^+] = -\log(0.008\underline{5}034) = 2.07$.
Check: The units (none) are correct. The pH is dropping sharply at the equivalence point, so the pH after 5 mL past the equivalence point should be quite acidic.

16.75 **Given:** 20.0 mL of 0.105 mol L^{-1} CH$_3$COOH titrated with 0.125 mol L^{-1} NaOH   **Other:** K_a (CH$_3$COOH) $= 1.8 \times 10^{-5}$

(a) **Find:** initial pH
Conceptual Plan: Since CH$_3$COOH is a weak acid, set up an equilibrium problem using the initial concentration.
So mol L^{-1} CH$_3$COOH $\rightarrow$ [H$_3$O$^+$] $\rightarrow$ pH

ICE Table $pH = -\log[H_3O^+]$

Solution:

$$CH_3COOH\ (aq) + H_2O\ (l) \rightleftharpoons H_3O^+\ (aq) + CH_3COO^-\ (aq)$$

	[CH$_3$COOH]	[H$_3$O$^+$]	[CH$_3$COO$^-$]
I	0.105	≈ 0	0
C	$-x$	$+x$	$+x$
E	$0.105 - x$	x	x

$K_a = \dfrac{[H_3O^+][CH_3COO^-]}{[CH_3COOH]} = 1.8 \times 10^{-5} = \dfrac{x^2}{0.105 - x}$ Assume x is small ($x \ll 0.105$) so

$\dfrac{x^2}{0.105 - x} = 1.8 \times 10^{-5} = \dfrac{x^2}{0.105}$ and $x = 1.\underline{3}748 \times 10^{-3}\ mol\ L^{-1} = [H_3O^+]$. Confirm that the assumption is valid.

$\dfrac{1.\underline{3}748 \times 10^{-3}}{0.105} \times 100\% = 1.3\% < 5\%$, so the assumption is valid. Finally,

$pH = -\log[H_3O^+] = -\log(1.\underline{3}748 \times 10^{-3}) = 2.86$.
Check: The units (none) are correct. The magnitude of the answer makes physical sense because pH should be greater than $-\log(0.105) = 0.98$ because this is a weak acid.

(b) **Find:** volume of base to reach equivalence point
Conceptual Plan: Write a balanced equation then mL $\rightarrow$ L then [CH$_3$COOH], L $\rightarrow$ mol

CH$_3$COOH + NaOH $\rightarrow$ CH$_3$COONa + H$_2$O $\dfrac{1\,L}{1000\,mL}$ $M = \dfrac{mol}{L}$

CH$_3$COOH then set mol acid(CH$_3$COOH) = mol base(NaOH) and [NaOH], mol NaOH $\rightarrow$ L NaOH $\rightarrow$ mL NaOH.

balanced equation has 1:1 stoichiometry $M = \dfrac{mol}{L}\qquad \dfrac{1000\,mL}{1\,L}$

Solution: $20.0\ \overline{mL\ CH_3COOH} \times \dfrac{1\,L}{1000\ \overline{mL}} = 0.0200\ L\ CH_3COOH$ then

$$\frac{0.105 \text{ mol CH}_3\text{COOH}}{1 \text{ L}} \times 0.0200 \text{ L} = 0.00210 \text{ mol CH}_3\text{COOH}.$$

So mol acid = mol CH_3COOH = 0.00210 mol = mol NaOH then

$$0.00210 \overline{\text{mol NaOH}} \times \frac{1 \text{ L}}{0.125 \overline{\text{mol NaOH}}} = 0.0168 \text{ L NaOH} \times \frac{1000 \text{ mL}}{1 \text{ L}} = 16.8 \text{ mL NaOH}.$$

Check: The units (mL) are correct. The volume of base is a little less than the volume of acid because the concentration of the base is a little greater than that of the acid.

(c) **Find:** pH after adding 5.0 mL of base

Conceptual Plan: Use calculations from part (b). Then mL $\rightarrow$ L **then** [NaOH], L $\rightarrow$ mol NaOH **then**

$$\frac{1 \text{ L}}{1000 \text{ mL}} \qquad M = \frac{\text{mol}}{\text{L}}$$

mol CH_3COOH, mol NaOH $\rightarrow$ **mol excess CH_3COOH, mol CH_3COO^- and**

$$\text{set up stoichiometry table}$$

L CH_3COOH, L NaOH $\rightarrow$ **total L then**

$$\text{L CH}_3\text{COOH} + \text{L NaOH} = \text{total L}$$

mol excess CH_3COOH, L $\rightarrow$ **[CH_3COOH] and mol excess CH_3COO^-, L** $\rightarrow$ **[CH_3COO^-] then**

$$M = \frac{\text{mol}}{\text{L}} \qquad M = \frac{\text{mol}}{\text{L}}$$

mol L^{-1} CH_3COOH, mol L^{-1} CH_3COO^- $\rightarrow$ **[H_3O^+]** $\rightarrow$ **pH.**

$$\text{ICE Table} \quad \text{pH} = -\log[\text{H}_3\text{O}^+]$$

Solution: $5.0 \overline{\text{mL NaOH}} \times \dfrac{1 \text{ L}}{1000 \overline{\text{mL}}} = 0.0050 \text{ L NaOH}$ then

$\dfrac{0.125 \text{ mol NaOH}}{1 \text{ L}} \times 0.0050 \text{ L} = 0.000625 \text{ mol NaOH}$. Set up a table to track changes:

	NaOH (aq) +	CH_3COOH (aq) $\rightarrow$	CH_3COONa (aq) +	H_2O (l)
Before addition	0 mol	0.00210 mol	0 mol	—
Addition	0.000625 mol	—	—	—
After addition	≈ 0 mol	0.001475 mol	0.000625 mol	—

Then 0.0200 L CH_3COOH + 0.0050 L NaOH = 0.0250 L total volume. Then

$$[CH_3COOH] = \frac{0.001475 \text{ mol CH}_3\text{COOH}}{0.0250 \text{ L}} = 0.0590 \text{ mol L}^{-1} \text{ and}$$

$$[CH_3COONa] = \frac{0.000625 \text{ mol CH}_3\text{COO}^-}{0.0250 \text{ L}} = 0.025 \text{ mol L}^{-1}.$$

Since 1 CH_3COO^- ion is generated for each CH_3COONa, $[CH_3COO^-]$ = 0.025 mol L^{-1} CH_3COO^-.

CH_3COOH (aq) + H_2O (l) $\rightleftharpoons$	H_3O^+ (aq) +	CH_3COO^-(aq)	
	[CH_3COOH]	[H_3O^+]	[CH_3COO^-]
I	0.0590	≈ 0	0.025
C	$-x$	$+x$	$+x$
E	$0.0590 - x$	x	$0.025 + x$

$$K_a = \frac{[H_3O^+][CH_3COO^-]}{[CH_3COOH]} = 1.8 \times 10^{-5} = \frac{x(0.025 + x)}{0.0590 - x} \text{ Assume } x \text{ is small } (x \ll 0.025 < 0.0590) \text{ so}$$

$$\frac{x(0.025 + \cancel{x})}{0.0590 - \cancel{x}} = 1.8 \times 10^{-5} = \frac{x(0.025)}{0.0590} \text{ and } x = 4.248 \times 10^{-5} \text{ mol L}^{-1} = [\text{H}_3\text{O}^+]. \text{ Confirm that the assumption is valid.}$$

$$\frac{4.248 \times 10^{-5}}{0.025} \times 100\% = 0.17\% < 5\%, \text{ so the assumption is valid.}$$

Finally, pH $= -\log[\text{H}_3\text{O}^+] = -\log(4.248 \times 10^{-5}) = 4.37$.

Check: The units (none) are correct. The pH is a little higher than the initial pH, which is expected since some of the acid has been neutralized.

(d) **Find:** pH at one-half of the equivalence point

Conceptual Plan: Since this is a weak acid–strong base titration, the pH at one-half the equivalence point is the pK_a of the weak acid.

Solution: pH = pK_a = $-\log K_a$ = $-\log(1.8 \times 10^{-5})$ = 4.74.

Check: The units (none) are correct. Since this is a weak acid–strong base titration, the pH at one-half the equivalence point is the pK_a of the weak acid, so it should be a little below 5.

(e) **Find:** pH at equivalence point

Conceptual Plan: Use calculations from part (b). Then, since all of the weak acid has been converted to its conjugate base, the pH is only dependent on the hydrolysis reaction of the conjugate base. The mol CH_3COO^- = initial mol CH_3COOH and L CH_3COOH, L NaOH to equivalence point → total L then

$$L\ CH_3COOH + L\ NaOH = total\ L$$

mol excess CH_3COO^-, L → [CH_3COO^-] and K_a → K_b then do an equilibrium calculation:

$$M = \frac{mol}{L} \qquad\qquad K_w = K_a K_b$$

[CH_3COO^-], K_b → [OH^-] → [H_3O^+] → pH.

$$set\ up\ ICE\ table \quad K_w = [H_3O^+][OH^-] \qquad pH = -\log[H_3O^+]$$

Solution: mol CH_3COO^- = initial mol CH_3COOH = 0.00210 mol and total volume = L CH_3COOH + L NaOH = 0.020 L + 0.0168 L = 0.0368 L then

$$[CH_3COO^-] = \frac{0.00210\ mol\ CH_3COO^-}{0.0368\ L} = 0.0570652\ mol\ L^{-1}\ and\ K_w = K_a K_b.\ Rearrange\ to\ solve\ for\ K_b.$$

$$K_b = \frac{K_w}{K_a} = \frac{1.0 \times 10^{-14}}{1.8 \times 10^{-5}} = 5.\underline{5}556 \times 10^{-10}.\ Set\ up\ an\ ICE\ table$$

$$CH_3COO^-\ (aq) + H_2O\ (l) \rightleftharpoons CH_3COOH\ (aq) + OH^-\ (aq)$$

	[CH_3COO^-]	[CH_3COOH]	[OH^-]
I	0.057\underline{0}652	≈0	≈0
C	$-x$	$+x$	$+x$
E	0.057\underline{0}652 $-x$	x	x

$$K_b = \frac{[CH_3COOH][OH^-]}{[CH_3COO^-]} = 5.\underline{5}556 \times 10^{-10} = \frac{x^2}{0.0570652 - x}\ Assume\ x\ is\ small\ (x \ll 0.057)\ so$$

$$\frac{x^2}{0.0570652 - \underline{x}} = 5.\underline{5}556 \times 10^{-10} = \frac{x^2}{0.0570652}\ and\ x = 5.\underline{6}305 \times 10^{-6}\ mol\ L^{-1} = [OH^-].$$

Confirm that the assumption is valid. $\dfrac{5.6305 \times 10^{-6}}{0.0570652} \times 100\% = 0.0099\% < 5\%$, so the assumption is valid.

$$K_w = [H_3O^+][OH^-]\ so\ [H_3O^+] = \frac{K_w}{[OH^-]} = \frac{1.0 \times 10^{-14}}{5.6305 \times 10^{-6}} = 1.\underline{7}760 \times 10^{-9}\ mol\ L^{-1}.$$

Finally, pH $= -\log[H_3O^+] = -\log(1.\underline{7}760 \times 10^{-9}) = 8.75$.

Check: The units (none) are correct. Since this is a weak acid–strong base titration, the pH at the equivalence point is basic.

(f) **Find:** pH after adding 5.0 mL of base beyond the equivalence point

Conceptual Plan: Use calculations from parts (b) and (c). Then the pH is only dependent on the amount of excess base and the total solution volumes.

mL excess → L excess then [NaOH], L excess → mol NaOH excess

$$\frac{1\ L}{1000\ mL} \qquad\qquad M = \frac{mol}{L}$$

then L CH_3COOH, L NaOH to equivalence point, L NaOH excess → total L then

$$L\ CH_3COOH + L\ NaOH\ to\ equivalence\ point + L\ NaOH\ excess = total\ L$$

mol excess NaOH, total L → [NaOH] = [OH^-] → [H_3O^+] → pH

$$M = \frac{mol}{L} \qquad K_w = [H_3O^+][OH^-] \qquad pH = -\log[H_3O^+]$$

Solution: 5.0 mL NaOH $\times \dfrac{1\ L}{1000\ mL} = 0.0050\ L\ NaOH\ excess\ then$

$\dfrac{0.125\ mol\ NaOH}{1\ L} \times 0.0050\ L = 0.000625\ mol\ NaOH\ excess.$ Then 0.0200 L CH_3COOH + 0.0168 L NaOH + 0.0050 L NaOH = 0.0418 L total volume.

$$[\text{NaOH excess}] = \frac{0.000625 \text{ mol NaOH excess}}{0.0418 \text{ L}} = 0.01\underline{4}9522 \text{ mol L}^{-1} \text{ NaOH excess. Since NaOH is}$$

a strong base, [NaOH] excess = [OH$^-$]. The strong base overwhelms the weak base and is

insignificant in the calculation. $K_w = [\text{H}_3\text{O}^+][\text{OH}^-]$ so $[\text{H}_3\text{O}^+] = \dfrac{K_w}{[\text{OH}^-]} = \dfrac{1.0 \times 10^{-14}}{0.01\underline{4}9522}$

$= 6.\underline{6}88 \times 10^{-13} \text{ mol L}^{-1}$. Finally, pH $= -\log[\text{H}_3\text{O}^+] = -\log(6.\underline{6}88 \times 10^{-13}) = 12.17$.

Check: The units (none) are correct. The pH is rising sharply at the equivalence point, so the pH after 5 mL past the equivalence point should be quite basic.

16.77   **Given:** 25.0 mL of 0.175 mol L^{-1} CH$_3$NH$_2$ titrated with 0.150 mol L^{-1} HBr   **Other:** K_b (CH$_3$NH$_2$) = 4.4 × 10^{-4}

(a)   **Find:** initial pH

Conceptual Plan: Since CH$_3$NH$_2$ is a weak base, set up an equilibrium problem using the initial concentration, so mol L^{-1} CH$_3$NH$_2$ → [OH$^-$] → [H$_3$O$^+$] → pH.

ICE Table $K_w = [\text{H}_3\text{O}^+][\text{OH}^-]$ pH $= -\log[\text{H}_3\text{O}^+]$

Solution:

CH$_3$NH$_2$ (aq) + H$_2$O (l) ⇌	CH$_3$NH$_3^+$ (aq) +	OH$^-$ (aq)
[CH$_3$NH$_2$]	[CH$_3$NH$_3^+$]	[OH$^-$]
I 0.175	0	≈ 0
C $-x$	$+x$	$+x$
E 0.175 $- x$	x	x

$$K_b = \frac{[\text{CH}_3\text{NH}_3^+][\text{OH}^-]}{[\text{CH}_3\text{NH}_2]} = 4.4 \times 10^{-4} = \frac{x^2}{0.175 - x}$$

Assume x is small ($x \ll 0.175$) so $\dfrac{x^2}{0.175 - \cancel{x}} = 4.4 \times 10^{-4} = \dfrac{x^2}{0.175}$ and $x = 8.\underline{7}750 \times 10^{-3} \text{ mol L}^{-1} = [\text{OH}^-]$.

Confirm that the assumption is valid. $\dfrac{8.\underline{7}750 \times 10^{-3}}{0.175} \times 100\% = 5.0\%$, so the assumption is valid.

$$K_w = [\text{H}_3\text{O}^+][\text{OH}^-] \text{ so } [\text{H}_3\text{O}^+] = \frac{K_w}{[\text{OH}^-]} = \frac{1.0 \times 10^{-14}}{8.\underline{7}750 \times 10^{-3}} = 1.\underline{1}396 \times 10^{-12} \text{ mol L}^{-1}.$$

Finally, pH $= -\log[\text{H}_3\text{O}^+] = -\log(1.\underline{1}396 \times 10^{-12}) = 11.94$.

Check: The units (none) are correct. The magnitude of the answer makes physical sense because pH should be less than 14 + log (0.175) = 13.2 because this is a weak base.

(b)   **Find:** volume of acid to reach equivalence point

Conceptual Plan: Write a balanced equation, then mL → L then [CH$_3$NH$_2$], L → mol CH$_3$NH$_2$

HBr + CH$_3$NH$_2$ → CH$_3$NH$_3$Br + H$_2$O $\dfrac{1 \text{ L}}{1000 \text{ mL}}$ $M = \dfrac{\text{mol}}{\text{L}}$

then set mol base (CH$_3$NH$_2$) = mol acid (HBr) and [HBr], mol HBr → L HBr → mL HBr.

balanced equation has 1:1 stoichiometry $M = \dfrac{\text{mol}}{\text{L}}$ $\dfrac{1000 \text{ mL}}{1 \text{ L}}$

Solution: 25.0 $\cancel{\text{mL CH}_3\text{NH}_2} \times \dfrac{1 \text{ L}}{1000 \cancel{\text{mL}}} = 0.0250 \text{ L CH}_3\text{NH}_2$ then

$\dfrac{0.175 \text{ mol CH}_3\text{NH}_2}{1 \cancel{\text{L}}} \times 0.0250 \cancel{\text{L}} = 0.004\underline{3}75 \text{ mol CH}_3\text{NH}_2$. So mol base = mol CH$_3NH_2$ = 0.004375 mol

= mol HBr then 0.004375 $\cancel{\text{mol HBr}} \times \dfrac{1 \text{ L}}{0.150 \cancel{\text{mol HBr}}} = 0.0291667 \cancel{\text{L HBr}} \times \dfrac{1000 \text{ mL}}{1 \cancel{\text{L}}} = 29.2 \text{ mL HBr}.$

Check: The units (mL) are correct. The volume of acid is greater than the volume of base because the concentration of the base is a little greater than that of the acid.

(c)   **Find:** pH after adding 5.0 mL of acid

Conceptual Plan: Use calculations from part (b). Then mL → L then [HBr], L → mol HBr

$\dfrac{1 \text{ L}}{1000 \text{ mL}}$ $M = \dfrac{\text{mol}}{\text{L}}$

then mol CH$_3$NH$_2$, mol HBr → mol excess CH$_3$NH$_2$ and L CH$_3$NH$_2$, L HBr → total L.

set up stoichiometry table   L CH$_3$NH$_2$ + L HBr = total L

Since there are significant concentrations of both the acid and the conjugate base species, this is a buffer solution and so the Henderson–Hasselbalch equation $\left(\text{pH} = pK_a + \log \frac{[\text{base}]}{[\text{acid}]} \right)$ can be used. Convert K_b to K_a using $K_w = K_a K_b$. Also note that the ratio of concentrations is the same as the ratio of moles, since the volume is the same for both species.

Solution: $5.0 \; \cancel{\text{mL HBr}} \times \dfrac{1 \text{ L}}{1000 \; \cancel{\text{mL}}} = 0.0050 \text{ L HBr}$ then $\dfrac{0.150 \text{ mol HBr}}{1 \cancel{\text{L}}} \times 0.0050 \; \cancel{\text{L}} = 0.00075 \text{ mol HBr}$.

Set up a table to track changes:

$$\text{HBr } (aq) + \text{CH}_3\text{NH}_2 \; (aq) \rightarrow \text{CH}_3\text{NH}_3\text{Br } (aq)$$

Before addition	0 mol	0.004375 mol	0 mol
Addition	0.00075 mol	—	—
After addition	≈ 0 mol	0.003625 mol	0.000750 mol

then $K_w = K_a K_b$ so

$K_a = \dfrac{K_w}{K_b} = \dfrac{1.0 \times 10^{-14}}{4.4 \times 10^{-4}} = 2.2727 \times 10^{-11} \text{ mol L}^{-1}$, then use the Henderson–Hasselbalch equation, since

the solution is a buffer. $\text{pH} = pK_a + \log \dfrac{[\text{base}]}{[\text{acid}]} = -\log (2.2727 \times 10^{-11}) + \log \dfrac{0.003625}{0.000750} = 11.33$

Check: The units (none) are correct. The pH is a little lower than the last pH, which is expected since some of the base has been neutralized.

(d) **Find:** pH at one-half of the equivalence point
Conceptual Plan: Since this is a weak base–strong acid titration, the pH at one-half the equivalence point is the pK_a of the conjugate acid of the weak base.

Solution: $\text{pH} = pK_a = -\log K_a = -\log (2.2727 \times 10^{-11}) = 10.64$.

Check: The units (none) are correct. Since this is a weak acid–strong base titration, the pH at one-half the equivalence point is the pK_a of the conjugate acid of the weak base, so it should be a little below 11.

(e) **Find:** pH at equivalence point
Conceptual Plan: Use calculations from above. Since all of the weak base has been converted to its conjugate acid, the pH is only dependent on the hydrolysis reaction of the conjugate acid. The mol CH_3NH_3^+ = initial mol CH_3NH_2 and
L CH_3NH_2, L HBr to equivalence point $\rightarrow$ total L then mol CH_3NH_3^+, L $\rightarrow$ [CH_3NH_3^+]

$$\text{L CH}_3\text{NH}_2 + \text{L HBr} = \text{total L} \qquad M = \frac{\text{mol}}{\text{L}}$$

then do an equilibrium calculation: [CH_3NH_3^+], K_a $\rightarrow$ [H_3O^+] $\rightarrow$ pH.

$$\text{set up ICE table} \qquad \text{pH} = -\log [\text{H}_3\text{O}^+]$$

Solution: mol base = mol acid = mol $\text{CH}_3\text{NH}_3^+ = 0.004375$ mol. Then total volume = L CH_3NH_2 +

L HBr $= 0.0250 \text{ L} + 0.0292 \text{ L} = 0.0542$ then $[\text{CH}_3\text{NH}_3^+] = \dfrac{0.004375 \text{ mol CH}_3\text{NH}_3^+}{0.0542 \text{ L}} = 0.0807196 \text{ mol L}^{-1}$.

$$\text{CH}_3\text{NH}_3^+ \; (aq) + \text{H}_2\text{O} \; (l) \rightleftharpoons \text{CH}_3\text{NH}_2 \; (aq) + \text{H}_3\text{O}^+(aq)$$

	[CH_3NH_3^+]	[CH_3NH_2]	[H_3O^+]
Set up an ICE table: I	0.0807196	≈ 0	≈ 0
C	$-x$	$+x$	$+x$
E	$0.0807196 - x$	x	x

$K_a = \dfrac{[\text{CH}_3\text{NH}_2] [\text{H}_3\text{O}^+]}{[\text{CH}_3\text{NH}_3^+]} = 2.2727 \times 10^{-11} = \dfrac{x^2}{0.0807196 - x}$ Assume x is small ($x \ll 0.0807$) so

$\dfrac{x^2}{0.0807196 - \cancel{x}} = 2.2727 \times 10^{-11} = \dfrac{x^2}{0.0807196}$ and $x = 1.3544 \times 10^{-6} = [\text{H}_3\text{O}^+]$.

Confirm that the assumption is valid. $\dfrac{1.3544 \times 10^{-6}}{0.0807106} \times 100\% = 0.0017\% < 5\%$, so the assumption is valid.

Finally, $\text{pH} = -\log [\text{H}_3\text{O}^+] = -\log (1.3544 \times 10^{-6}) = 5.87$.

Check: The units (none) are correct. Since this is a weak base–strong acid titration, the pH at the equivalence point is acidic.

(f)   **Find:** pH after adding 5.0 mL of acid beyond the equivalence point
        Conceptual Plan: Use calculations from parts (b) and (c). Then the pH is only dependent on the amount of excess acid and the total solution volumes.
        mL excess $\rightarrow$ L excess then [HBr], L excess $\rightarrow$ mol HBr excess

$$\frac{1\,L}{1000\,mL} \qquad\qquad\qquad M = \frac{mol}{L}$$

then L CH_3NH_2, L HBr to equivalence point, L HBr excess $\rightarrow$ total L then

L CH_3NH_2 + L HBr to equivalence point + L HBr excess = total L

mol excess HBr, total L $\rightarrow$ [HBr] = [H_3O^+] $\rightarrow$ pH

$$M = \frac{mol}{L} \qquad\qquad pH = -\log[H_3O^+]$$

Solution: $5.0 \ \overline{mL \ HBr} \times \dfrac{1\,L}{1000 \ \overline{mL}} = 0.0050$ L HBr excess then

$\dfrac{0.150 \text{ mol HBr}}{1 \ \overline{L}} \times 0.0050 \ \overline{L} = 0.00075$ mol HBr excess. Then 0.0250 L CH_3NH_2 + 0.0292 L HBr + 0.0050 L HBr = 0.0592 L total volume.

$[\text{HBr excess}] = \dfrac{0.00075 \text{ mol HBr excess}}{0.0592 \text{ L}} = 0.012669$ mol L^{-1} HBr excess

Since HBr is a strong acid, [HBr] excess = [H_3O^+]. The strong acid overwhelms the weak acid and is insignificant in the calculation. Finally, pH $= -\log[H_3O^+] = -\log(0.012669) = 1.90$.
Check: The units (none) are correct. The pH is dropping sharply at the equivalence point, so the pH after 5 mL past the equivalence point should be quite acidic.

16.79   (i)   Acid a is more concentrated, since the equivalence point (where sharp pH rise occurs) is at a higher volume of added base.

        (ii)   Acid b has the larger K_a, since the pH at a volume of added base equal to half of the equivalence point volume is lower.

16.81   **Given:** 0.229 g unknown monoprotic acid titrated with 0.112 mol L^{-1} NaOH and curve
        Find: molar mass and pK_a of acid
        Conceptual Plan: The equivalence point is where sharp pH rise occurs. The pK_a is the pH at a volume of added base equal to half of the equivalence point volume. Then mL NaOH $\rightarrow$ L NaOH

$$\frac{1\,L}{1000\,mL}$$

then [NaOH], L NaOH $\rightarrow$ mol NaOH = mol acid then mol NaOH, g acid $\rightarrow$ molar mass.

$$M = \frac{mol}{L} \qquad\qquad\qquad \frac{g\ acid}{mol\ acid}$$

Solution: The equivalence point is at 25 mL NaOH. The pH at 0.5 x 25 mL = 13 mL is ~3 = pK_a. Then

$25 \ \overline{mL \ NaOH} \times \dfrac{1\,L}{1000 \ \overline{mL}} = 0.025$ L NaOH then

$\dfrac{0.112 \text{ mol NaOH}}{1 \ \overline{L}} \times 0.025 \ \overline{L} = 0.0028$ mol NaOH $= 0.0028$ mol acid then

molar mass $= \dfrac{0.229 \text{ g acid}}{0.0028 \text{ mol acid}} = 82$ g mol^{-1}.

Check: The units (none and g mol^{-1}) are correct. The pK_a is consistent with a weak acid. The molar mass is reasonable for an acid (must be > 20 g mol^{-1}– lightest acid is HF).

16.83   **Given:** 20.0 mL of 0.125 mol L^{-1} sulfurous acid (H_2SO_3) titrated with 0.1014 mol L^{-1} KOH **Find:** volume of base added
        Conceptual Plan: Since this is a diprotic acid, each proton is titrated sequentially. Write balanced equations.

$H_2SO_3 + OH^- \rightarrow HSO_3^- + H_2O$ and $HSO_3^- + OH^- \rightarrow SO_3^{2-} + H_2O$

Then mL $\rightarrow$ L then [H_2SO_3], L $\rightarrow$ mol H_2SO_3 then set mol base (H_2SO_3) = mol acid (KOH) and

$$\frac{1\,L}{1000\,mL} \qquad\qquad M = \frac{mol}{L} \qquad\qquad \text{balanced equation has 1:1 stoichiometry}$$

[KOH], mol KOH $\rightarrow$ L KOH $\rightarrow$ mL KOH the volume to the second equivalence point will be

$$M = \frac{mol}{L} \qquad \frac{1000\,mL}{1\,L}$$

double the volume to the first equivalence point.

Solution: $20.0 \ \overline{mL \ H_2SO_3} \times \dfrac{1\,L}{1000 \ \overline{mL}} = 0.0200$ L H_2SO_3 then

$\dfrac{0.115 \text{ mol } H_2SO_3}{1 \cancel{L}} \times 0.0200 \cancel{L} = 0.00230 \text{ mol } H_2SO_3$. So mol base = mol H_2SO_3 = 0.00230 mol = mol KOH

then $0.00230 \overline{\cancel{\text{mol KOH}}} \times \dfrac{1 \text{ L}}{0.1014 \overline{\cancel{\text{mol KOH}}}} = 0.02268245 \cancel{\text{L KOH}} \times \dfrac{1000 \text{ mL}}{1 \cancel{L}} = 22.7 \text{ mL KOH to first}$

equivalence point. The volume to the second equivalence point is simply twice this amount, or 45.4 mL to the second equivalence point.

Check: The units (mL) are correct. The volume of base is greater than the volume of acid because the concentration of the acid is a little greater than that of the base. The volume to the second equivalence point is twice the volume to the first equivalence point.

16.85 The indicator will be in its acid form at an acidic pH, so the colour in the HCl sample will be red. The colour change will occur over the pH range from $pH = pK_a - 1.0$ to $pH = pK_a + 1.0$, so the colour will start to change at $pH = 5.0 - 1.0 = 4.0$ and finish changing by $pH = 5.0 + 1.0 = 6.0$.

16.87 Since the exact conditions of the titration are not given, a rough calculation will suffice. Looking at the pattern of earlier problems, the pH at the equivalence point of a titration of a weak acid and a strong base is the hydrolysis of the conjugate base of the weak acid that has been diluted by a factor of roughly 2 with base. If it is assumed that the initial concentration of the weak acid is $\sim 0.1 \text{ mol L}^{-1}$, then the conjugate base concentration will be $\sim 0.05 \text{ mol L}^{-1}$. From earlier calculations it can be seen that the $K_b = \dfrac{K_w}{K_a} = \dfrac{[OH^-]^2}{0.05}$ thus

$[OH^-] = \sqrt{\dfrac{0.05 K_w}{K_a}} = \sqrt{\dfrac{5 \times 10^{-16}}{K_a}}$ and the $pH = 14 + \log \sqrt{\dfrac{5 \times 10^{-16}}{K_a}}$.

(a) For HF, the $K_a = 3.5 \times 10^{-4}$ and so the above equation approximates the pH at the equivalence point of ~ 8.0. Looking at Table 16.1, phenol red or *m*-nitrophenol will change at the appropriate pH range.

(b) For HCl, the pH at the equivalence point is 7, since HCl is a strong acid. Looking at Table 16.1, alizarin, bromthymol blue, or phenol red will change at the appropriate pH range.

(c) For HCN, the $K_a = 4.9 \times 10^{-10}$ and so the above equation approximates the pH at the equivalence point of ~ 11.0. Looking at Table 16.1, alizarin yellow R will change at the appropriate pH range.

Solubility Equilibria

16.89 For the dissolution reaction, start with the ionic compound as a solid and put it in equilibrium with the appropriate cation and anion, making sure to include the appropriate stoichiometric coefficients. The K_{sp} expression is the product of the concentrations of the cation and anion concentrations raised to their stoichiometric coefficients.

(a) $BaSO_4 (s) \rightleftharpoons Ba^{2+} (aq) + SO_4^{2-} (aq)$ and $K_{sp} = [Ba^{2+}] [SO_4^{2-}]$.

(b) $PbBr_2 (s) \rightleftharpoons Pb^{2+} (aq) + 2 Br^- (aq)$ and $K_{sp} = [Pb^{2+}] [Br^-]^2$.

(c) $Ag_2CrO_4 (s) \rightleftharpoons 2 Ag^+ (aq) + CrO_4^{2-} (aq)$ and $K_{sp} = [Ag^+]^2 [CrO_4^{2-}]$.

16.91 **Given:** ionic compound formula and Table 16.2 of K_{sp} values **Find:** molar solubility (*S*)
Conceptual Plan: The expression of the solubility product constant of A_mX_n is $K_{sp} = [A^{n+}]^m [X^{m-}]^n$. The molar solubility of a compound, A_mX_n, can be computed directly from K_{sp} by solving for *S* in the expression $K_{sp} = (mS)^m (nS)^n = m^m n^n S^{m+n}$.
Solution:

(a) For AgBr, $K_{sp} = 5.35 \times 10^{-13}$, $A = Ag^+$, $m = 1$, $X = Br^-$, and $n = 1$ so $K_{sp} = 5.35 \times 10^{-13} = S^2$. Rearrange to solve for *S*. $S = \sqrt{5.35 \times 10^{-13}} = 7.31 \times 10^{-7} \text{ mol L}^{-1}$.

(b) For $Mg(OH)_2$, $K_{sp} = 2.06 \times 10^{-13}$, $A = Mg^{2+}$, $m = 1$, $X = OH^-$, and $n = 2$ so $K_{sp} = 2.06 \times 10^{-13} = 2^2 S^3$.
Rearrange to solve for *S*. $S = \sqrt[3]{\dfrac{2.06 \times 10^{-13}}{4}} = 3.72 \times 10^{-5} \text{ mol L}^{-1}$.

(c)   For CaF_2, $K_{sp} = 1.46 \times 10^{-10}$, $A = Ca^{2+}$, $m = 1$, $X = F^-$, and $n = 2$ so $K_{sp} = 1.46 \times 10^{-10} = 2^2 S^3$. Rearrange

to solve for S. $S = \sqrt[3]{\dfrac{1.46 \times 10^{-10}}{4}} = 3.32 \times 10^{-4}$ mol L^{-1}.

Check: The units (mol L^{-1}) are correct. The molar solubilities are much less than one and dependent not only on the value of the K_{sp}, but also the stoichiometry of the ionic compound. The more ions that are generated, the greater the molar solubility for the same value of the K_{sp}.

16.93   **Given:** ionic compound formula and molar solubility (S)   **Find:** K_{sp}
Conceptual Plan: The expression of the solubility product constant of $A_m X_n$ is $K_{sp} = [A^{n+}]^m [X^{m-}]^n$.
The molar solubility of a compound, $A_m X_n$, can be computed directly from K_{sp} by solving for S in the expression $K_{sp} = (mS)^m (nS)^n = m^m n^n S^{m+n}$.
Solution:

(a)   For NiS, $S = 3.27 \times 10^{-11}$ mol L^{-1}, $A = Ni^{2+}$, $m = 1$, $X = S^{2-}$, and $n = 1$ so $K_{sp} = S^2 = (3.27 \times 10^{-11})^2 = 1.07 \times 10^{-21}$.

(b)   For PbF_2, $S = 5.63 \times 10^{-3}$ mol L^{-1}, $A = Pb^{2+}$, $m = 1$, $X = F^-$, and $n = 2$ so $K_{sp} = 2^2 S^3 = 2^2 (5.63 \times 10^{-3})^3 = 7.14 \times 10^{-7}$.

(c)   For MgF_2, $S = 2.65 \times 10^{-4}$ mol L^{-1}, $A = Mg^{2+}$, $m = 1$, $X = F^-$, and $n = 2$ so $K_{sp} = 2^2 S^3 = 2^2 (2.65 \times 10^{-4})^3 = 7.44 \times 10^{-11}$.

Check: The units (none) are correct. The K_{sp} values are much less than one and dependent not only on the value of the solubility, but also the stoichiometry of the ionic compound. The more ions that are generated, the smaller the K_{sp} for the same value of the S.

16.95   **Given:** ionic compound formulas AX and AX_2 and $K_{sp} = 1.5 \times 10^{-5}$ **Find:** higher molar solubility (S)
Conceptual Plan: The expression of the solubility product constant of $A_m X_n$ is $K_{sp} = [A^{n+}]^m [X^{m-}]^n$.
The molar solubility of a compound, $A_m X_n$, can be computed directly from K_{sp} by solving for S in the expression $K_{sp} = (mS)^m (nS)^n = m^m n^n S^{m+n}$.
Solution: For AX, $K_{sp} = 1.5 \times 10^{-5}$, $m = 1$, and $n = 1$ so $K_{sp} = 1.5 \times 10^{-5} = S^2$. Rearrange to solve for S.
$S = \sqrt{1.5 \times 10^{-5}} = 3.9 \times 10^{-3}$ mol L^{-1}. For AX_2, $K_{sp} = 1.5 \times 10^{-5}$, $m = 1$, and $n = 2$ so $K_{sp} = 1.5 \times 10^{-5} = 2^2 S^3$.

Rearrange to solve for S. $S = \sqrt[3]{\dfrac{1.5 \times 10^{-5}}{4}} = 1.6 \times 10^{-2}$ mol L^{-1}. Since 10^{-2} mol L$^{-1} > 10^{-3}$ mol L^{-1}, AX_2 has

a higher molar solubility.
Check: The units (mol L^{-1}) are correct. The more ions that are generated, the greater the molar solubility for the same value of the K_{sp}.

16.97   **Given:** $Fe(OH)_2$ in 100.0 mL solution   **Find:** grams of $Fe(OH)_2$ **Other:** $K_{sp} = 4.87 \times 10^{-17}$
Conceptual Plan: The expression of the solubility product constant of $A_m X_n$ is $K_{sp} = [A^{n+}]^m [X^{m-}]^n$.
The molar solubility of a compound, $A_m X_n$, can be computed directly from K_{sp} by solving for S in the expression $K_{sp} = (mS)^m (nS)^n = m^m n^n S^{m+n}$. Then solve for S, then mL $\rightarrow$ L then $\dfrac{1\,L}{1000\,mL}$

S, L $\rightarrow$ **mol Fe(OH)$_2$** $\rightarrow$ **g Fe(OH)$_2$.**
$$M = \frac{mol}{L} \qquad \frac{89.87\ g\ Fe(OH)_2}{1\ mol\ Fe(OH)_2}$$
Solution: For $Fe(OH)_2$, $K_{sp} = 4.87 \times 10^{-17}$, $A = Fe^{2+}$, $m = 1$, $X = OH^-$, and $n = 2$ so $K_{sp} = 4.87 \times 10^{-17} = 2^2 S^3$.

Rearrange to solve for S. $S = \sqrt[3]{\dfrac{4.87 \times 10^{-17}}{4}} = \underline{2.30050} \times 10^{-6}$ mol L^{-1}. Then 100.0 mL $\times \dfrac{1\,L}{1000\,mL} = 0.1000\,L$

then $\dfrac{\underline{2.30050} \times 10^{-6}\ mol\ Fe(OH)_2}{1\,L} \times 0.1000\,L = \underline{2.30050} \times 10^{-7}\ mol\ Fe(OH)_2 \times \dfrac{89.87\ g\ Fe(OH)_2}{1\ mol\ Fe(OH)_2}$

= 2.07×10^{-5} g $Fe(OH)_2$.

Check: The units (g) are correct. The solubility rules from Chapter 4 (most hydroxides are insoluble) suggest that very little $Fe(OH)_2$ will dissolve, so the magnitude of the answer is not surprising.

16.99   The solution that has the least amount of OH$^-$ (aq) would have the lowest pH (most acidic). All the compounds are hydroxides, so the least soluble compound would generate the lowest amount of OH$^-$ (aq) and make a solution with the lowest pH. From previous questions, we have learned that the greater the number of ions generated the greater the molar solubility for compounds with the same K_{sp}. So, initially we are looking for the compound that generates the fewest number of ions. Compounds iv and v both generate 4 (3 OH^- and one M^{3+}) ions in solution. Compounds ii and iii both generate 3 (2 OH^- and one M^{2+}) ions in solution. KOH generates two ions, however, it is a strong base and completely dissociates so it actually generates the most OH^-. The choice is between compounds ii and iii, which both generate the same number of ions. In order to select between the two we need to compare their K_{sp} values. The compound with the smaller K_{sp} will have the lower molar solubility, so compound iii should be the least soluble and generate a solution with the lowest pH.

16.101 (a) **Given:** BaF_2 **Find:** molar solubility (S) in pure water **Other:** K_{sp} (BaF_2) = 2.45 x 10^{-5}
Conceptual Plan: The expression of the solubility product constant of A_mX_n is $K_{sp} = [A^{n+}]^m [X^{m-}]^n$. The molar solubility of a compound, A_mX_n, can be computed directly from K_{sp} by solving for S in the expression $K_{sp} = (mS)^m (nS)^n = m^m n^n S^{m+n}$.
Solution: BaF_2, K_{sp} = 2.45 x 10^{-5}, A = Ba^{2+}, m = 1, X = F^-, and n = 2 so K_{sp} = 2.45 x 10^{-5} = 2^2S^3.

Rearrange to solve for S. $S = \sqrt[3]{\dfrac{2.45 \times 10^{-5}}{4}}$ = 1.83 x 10^{-2} mol L^{-1}.

(b) **Given:** BaF_2 **Find:** molar solubility (S) in 0.10 mol L^{-1} $Ba(NO_3)_2$ **Other:** K_{sp} (BaF_2) = 2.45 x 10^{-5}
Conceptual Plan: mol L^{-1} $Ba(NO_3)_2$ $\rightarrow$ mol L^{-1} Ba^{2+} then mol L^{-1} Ba^{2+}, K_{sp} $\rightarrow$ S

$$Ba(NO_3)_2 \;(s) \rightarrow Ba^{2+} \;(aq) + 2\,NO_3^- \;(aq) \qquad \text{ICE Table}$$

Solution: Since 1 Ba^{2+} ion is generated for each $Ba(NO_3)_2$, $[Ba^{2+}]$ = 0.10 mol L^{-1}.

$BaF_2 \;(s) \rightleftharpoons$	$Ba^{2+} \;(aq)$	+	$2\,F^- \;(aq)$
I	0.10		0
C	+S		+$2S$
E	0.10 + S		$2S$

K_{sp} (BaF_2) = $[Ba^{2+}]\,[F^-]^2$ = 2.45 x 10^{-5} = $(0.10 + S)(2S)^2$.

Assume $S \ll 0.10$, 2.45 x 10^{-5} = $(0.10)(2S)^2$, and S = 7.83 x 10^{-3} mol L^{-1}. Confirm that the assumption is valid.

$\dfrac{7.83 \times 10^{-3}}{0.10}$ x 100% = 7.8% > 5%, so the assumption is not valid. Since expanding the expression will give a third order polynomial, that is not easily solved directly. Solve by successive approximations. Substitute S = 7.83 x 10^{-3} mol L^{-1} for the S term that is part of a sum (i.e., the one in (0.10 + S)). Thus, 2.45 x 10^{-5} = $(0.10 + 7.83 \times 10^{-3})(2S)^2$ and S = 7.53 x 10^{-3} mol L^{-1}. Substitute this new S value again. Thus, 2.45 x 10^{-5} = $(0.10 + 7.53 \times 10^{-3})(2S)^2$ and S = 7.55 x 10^{-3} mol L^{-1}. Substitute this new S value again. Thus, 2.45 x 10^{-5} = $(0.10 + 7.55 \times 10^{-3})(2S)^2$ and S = 7.55 x 10^{-3} mol L^{-1}. So the solution has converged and S = 7.55 x 10^{-3} mol L^{-1}.

(c) **Given:** BaF_2 **Find:** molar solubility (S) in 0.15 mol L^{-1} NaF **Other:** K_{sp} (BaF_2) = 2.45 x 10^{-5}
Conceptual Plan: mol L^{-1} NaF $\rightarrow$ mol L^{-1} F^- then mol L^{-1} F^-, K_{sp} $\rightarrow$ S

$$NaF \;(s) \rightarrow Na^+ \;(aq) + F^- \;(aq) \qquad \text{ICE Table}$$

Solution: Since 1 F^- ion is generated for each NaF, $[F^-]$ = 0.15 mol L^{-1}.

$BaF_2 \;(s) \rightleftharpoons$	$Ba^{2+} \;(aq)$	+	$2\,F^- \;(aq)$
I	0		0.15
C	+S		+$2S$
E	S		0.15 + $2S$

K_{sp} (BaF_2) = $[Ba^{2+}]\,[F^-]^2$ = 2.45 x 10^{-5} = $(S)(0.15 + 2S)^2$.

Since $2S \ll 0.15$, 2.45 x 10^{-5} = $(S)(0.15)^2$, and S = 1.09 x 10^{-3} mol L^{-1}. Confirm that the assumption is valid. $\dfrac{2\,(1.09 \times 10^{-3})}{0.15}$ x 100% = 1.5% < 5%, so the assumption is valid.

Check: The units (mol L^{-1}) are correct. The solubility of the BaF_2 decreases in the presence of a common ion. The effect of the anion is greater because the K_{sp} expression has the anion concentration squared.

16.103 **Given:** $Ca(OH)_2$ **Find:** molar solubility (S) in buffers at a) pH = 4, b) pH = 7, and c) pH = 9
Other: K_{sp} ($Ca(OH)_2$) = 4.68 x 10^{-6}

Conceptual Plan: pH → **[H₃O⁺]** → **[OH⁻] then mol L⁻¹ OH⁻, K_{sp}** → **S**

$$[H_3O^+] = 10^{-pH} \quad K_w = [H_3O^+][OH^-]$$ set up ICE table

Solution:

(a) pH = 4, so $[H_3O^+] = 10^{-pH} = 10^{-4} = 1 \times 10^{-4}$ mol L⁻¹ then $K_w = [H_3O^+][OH^-]$ so

	$Ca(OH)_2\ (s)$	$\rightleftharpoons$	$Ca^{2+}\ (aq)$	$+\ 2\ OH^-\ (aq)$
I			0	1×10^{-10}
C			+S	—
E			S	1×10^{-10}

$$[OH^-] = \frac{K_w}{[H_3O^+]} = \frac{1.0 \times 10^{-14}}{1 \times 10^{-4}} = 1 \times 10^{-10} \text{ mol L}^{-1} \text{ then}$$

$K_{sp}\ (Ca(OH)_2) = [Ca^{2+}][OH^-]^2 = 4.68 \times 10^{-6} = S\ (1 \times 10^{-10})^2$ and $S = 5 \times 10^{14}$ mol L⁻¹.

(b) pH = 7, so $[H_3O^+] = 10^{-pH} = 10^{-7} = 1 \times 10^{-7}$ mol L⁻¹ then $K_w = [H_3O^+][OH^-]$ so

$$[OH^-] = \frac{K_w}{[H_3O^+]} = \frac{1.0 \times 10^{-14}}{1 \times 10^{-7}} = 1 \times 10^{-7} \text{ mol L}^{-1} \text{ then}$$

	$Ca(OH)_2\ (s)$	$\rightleftharpoons$	$Ca^{2+}\ (aq)$	$+\ 2\ OH^-(aq)$
I			0	1×10^{-7}
C			+S	—
E			S	1×10^{-7}

$K_{sp}\ (Ca(OH)_2) = [Ca^{2+}][OH^-]^2 = 4.68 \times 10^{-6} = S\ (1 \times 10^{-7})^2$ and $S = 5 \times 10^8$ mol L⁻¹.

(c) pH = 9, so $[H_3O^+] = 10^{-pH} = 10^{-9} = 1 \times 10^{-9}$ mol L⁻¹ then $K_w = [H_3O^+][OH^-]$ so

	$Ca(OH)_2\ (s)$	$\rightleftharpoons$	$Ca^{2+}\ (aq)$	$+\ 2\ OH^-(aq)$
I			0	1×10^{-5}
C			+S	—
E			S	1×10^{-5}

$$[OH^-] = \frac{K_w}{[H_3O^+]} = \frac{1.0 \times 10^{-14}}{1 \times 10^{-9}} = 1 \times 10^{-5} \text{ mol L}^{-1} \text{ then}$$

$K_{sp}\ (Ca(OH)_2) = [Ca^{2+}][OH^-]^2 = 4.68 \times 10^{-6} = S\ (1 \times 10^{-5})^2$. and $S = 5 \times 10^4$ mol L⁻¹.

Check: The units (mol L⁻¹) are correct. The solubility of the $Ca(OH)_2$ decreases as the pH increases (and the hydroxide ion concentration increases). Realize that these molar solubilities are not achievable because the saturation point of pure $Ca(OH)_2$ is ~ 30 mol L⁻¹. The bottom line is that as long as the hydroxide concentration can be controlled with a buffer, the $Ca(OH)_2$ will be very soluble.

16.105 (a) $BaCO_3$ will be more soluble in acidic solutions because CO_3^{2-} is basic. In acidic solutions it can be converted to HCO_3^- and H_2CO_3. These species are not CO_3^{2-} so they do not appear in the K_{sp} expression.

(b) CuS will be more soluble in acidic solutions because S^{2-} is basic. In acidic solutions it can be converted to HS^- and H_2S. These species are not S^{2-} so they do not appear in the K_{sp} expression.

(c) AgCl will not be more soluble in acidic solutions because Cl^- will not react with acidic solutions, because HCl is a strong acid.

(d) PbI_2 will not be more soluble in acidic solutions because I^- will not react with acidic solutions, because HI is a strong acid.

Precipitation and Qualitative Analysis

16.107 **Given:** 0.015 mol L⁻¹ NaF and 0.010 mol L⁻¹ $Ca(NO_3)_2$ **Find:** Will a precipitate form? If so, identify it.
Other: $K_{sp}\ (CaF_2) = 1.46 \times 10^{-10}$
Conceptual Plan: Look at all possible combinations and consider the solubility rules from Chapter 4. Salts of alkali metals (Na) are very soluble, so NaF and $NaNO_3$ will be very soluble. Nitrate compounds are very soluble, so $NaNO_3$ will be very soluble. The only possibility for a precipitate is CaF_2. Determine if a precipitate will form by determining the concentration of the Ca^{2+} and F^- in solution. Then compute the reaction quotient, Q. If $Q > K_{sp}$ then a precipitate will form.
Solution: Since the only possible precipitate is CaF_2, calculate the concentrations of Ca^{2+} and F^-. NaF (s) → Na⁺ (aq) + F⁻ (aq). Since 1 F⁻ ion is generated for each NaF, $[F^-]$ = 0.015 mol L⁻¹.

$Ca(NO_3)_2$ (s) → Ca^{2+} (aq) + 2 NO_3^- (aq). Since 1 Ca^{2+} ion is generated for each $Ca(NO_3)_2$, $[Ca^{2+}]$ = 0.010 mol L^{-1}. Then calculate Q (CaF_2), A = Ca^{2+}, m = 1, X = F^-, and n = 2. Since Q= $[A^{n+}]^m$ $[X^{m-}]^n$, then Q (CaF_2) = $[Ca^{2+}]$ $[F^-]^2$ = (0.010) $(0.015)^2$ = 2.3 x 10^{-6} > 1.46 x 10^{-10} = K_{sp} (CaF_2) , so a precipitate will form.
Check: The units (none) are correct. The solubility of the CaF_2 is low, and the concentration of ions are extremely large compared to the K_{sp}, so a precipitate will form.

16.109 **Given:** 75.0 mL of NaOH with pOH = 2.58 and 125.0 mL of 0.0018 mol L^{-1} $MgCl_2$ **Find:** Will a precipitate form? If so, identify it. **Other:** K_{sp} ($Mg(OH)_2$) = 2.06 x 10^{-13}
Conceptual Plan: Look at all possible combinations and consider the solubility rules from Chapter 4. Salts of alkali metals (Na) are very soluble, so NaOH and NaCl will be very soluble. Chloride compounds are generally very soluble, so $MgCl_2$ and NaCl will be very soluble. The only possibility for a precipitate is $Mg(OH)_2$. Determine if a precipitate will form by determining the concentration of the Mg^{2+} and OH^- in solution. Since pH, not NaOH concentration, is given pOH → $[OH^-]$ then

$$[OH^-] = 10^{-pOH}$$

mix solutions and calculate diluted concentrations mL NaOH, mL $MgCl_2$ → mL total then

$$mL\ NaOH + mL\ MgCl_2 = total\ mL$$

mL, initial M → final M then compute the reaction quotient, Q.

$$M_1 V_1 = M_2 V_2$$

If Q > K_{sp} then a precipitate will form.
Solution: Since the only possible precipitate is $Mg(OH)_2$, calculate the concentrations of Mg^{2+} and OH^-.
For NaOH at pOH = 2.58, so $[OH^-]$ = 10^{-pOH} = $10^{-2.58}$ = 2.63027 x 10^{-3} mol L^{-1} and
$MgCl_2$ (s) → Mg^{2+} (aq) + 2 Cl^- (aq). Since 1 Mg^{2+} ion is generated for each $MgCl_2$, $[Mg^{2+}]$ = 0.0018 mol L^{-1}.
Then total mL = mL NaOH + mL $MgCl_2$ = 75.0 mL + 125.0 mL = 200.0 mL. Then $M_1 V_1 = M_2 V_2$,

rearrange to solve for M_2. $M_2 = M_1 \dfrac{V_1}{V_2}$ = 2.63027 x 10^{-3} mol L^{-1} OH^- x $\dfrac{75.0\ \text{mL}}{200.0\ \text{mL}}$

= 9.8635 x 10^{-4} mol L^{-1} OH^- and

$M_2 = M_1 \dfrac{V_1}{V_2}$ = 0.0018 mol L^{-1} Mg^+ x $\dfrac{125.0\ \text{mL}}{200.0\ \text{mL}}$ = 1.125 x 10^{-3} mol L^{-1} Mg^{2+}. Calculate Q ($Mg(OH)_2$),

A = Mg^{2+}, m = 1, X = OH^-, and n = 2. Since Q= $[A^{n+}]^m$ $[X^{m-}]^n$, then Q ($Mg(OH)_2$) = $[Mg^{2+}]$ $[OH^-]^2$

= (1.125 x 10^{-3})(9.8635 x 10^{-4})^2 = 1.1 x 10^{-9} > 2.06 x 10^{-13} = K_{sp} ($Mg(OH)_2$), so a precipitate will form.
Check: The units (none) are correct. The solubility of the $Mg(OH)_2$ is low, and the NaOH (a base) is high enough that the product of the concentration of ions are large compared to the K_{sp}, so a precipitate will form.

16.111 **Given:** KOH as precipitation agent in a) 0.015 mol L^{-1} $CaCl_2$, b) 0.0025 mol L^{-1} $Fe(NO_3)_2$, and c) 0.0018 mol L^{-1} $MgBr_2$
Find: concentration of KOH necessary to form a precipitate
Other: K_{sp} ($Ca(OH)_2$) = 4.68 x 10^{-6}, K_{sp} ($Fe(OH)_2$) = 4.87 x 10^{-17}, K_{sp} ($Mg(OH)_2$) = 2.06 x 10^{-13}
Conceptual Plan: The solubility rules from Chapter 4 state that most hydroxides are insoluble, so all precipitates will be hydroxides. Determine the concentration of the cation in solution. Since all metals have

an oxidation state of +2 and $[OH^-]$ = $[KOH]$, all of the K_{sp} = [cation] $[KOH]^2$ and so $[KOH] = \sqrt{\dfrac{K_{sp}}{[\text{cation}]}}$.

Solution:

(a) $CaCl_2$ (s) → Ca^{2+} (aq) + 2 Cl^- (aq). Since 1 Ca^{2+} ion is generated for each $CaCl_2$, $[Ca^{2+}]$ = 0.015 mol L^{-1}.

Then $[KOH] = \sqrt{\dfrac{K_{sp}}{[\text{cation}]}} = \sqrt{\dfrac{4.68 \times 10^{-6}}{0.015}}$ = 0.018 mol L^{-1} KOH.

(b) $Fe(NO_3)_2$ (s) → Fe^{2+} (aq) + 2 NO_3^- (aq). Since 1 Fe^{2+} ion is generated for each $Fe(NO_3)_2$, $[Fe^{2+}]$ = 0.0025 mol L^{-1}.

Then $[KOH] = \sqrt{\dfrac{K_{sp}}{[\text{cation}]}} = \sqrt{\dfrac{4.87 \times 10^{-17}}{0.0025}}$ = 1.4 x 10^{-7} mol L^{-1} KOH.

(c) $MgBr_2 (s) \rightarrow Mg^{2+} (aq) + 2\,Br^- (aq)$. Since 1 Mg^{2+} ion is generated for each $MgBr_2$, $[Mg^{2+}] = 0.0018$ M.

Then $[KOH] = \sqrt{\dfrac{K_{sp}}{[\text{cation}]}} = \sqrt{\dfrac{2.06 \times 10^{-13}}{0.0018}} = 1.1 \times 10^{-5}$ mol L^{-1} KOH.

Check: The units (mol L^{-1}) are correct. Since all cations have an oxidation state of +2, it can be seen that the [KOH] needed to precipitate the hydroxide is lower the smaller the K_{sp}.

16.113   **Given:** solution with 0.010 mol L^{-1} Ba^{2+} and 0.020 mol L^{-1} Ca^{2+} add Na_2SO_4 to form precipitates
Find: (a) which ion precipitates first and minimum $[Na_2SO_4]$ needed; and (b) [first cation] when second cation precipitates **Other:** K_{sp} ($BaSO_4$) = 1.07×10^{-10}, K_{sp} ($CaSO_4$) = 7.10×10^{-5}
Conceptual Plan: (a) The precipitates that will form are $BaSO_4$ and $CaSO_4$.
Use the equation derived in Problem 20 to define K_{sp}. Substitute in concentration of cation and solve for
for ionic compound, A_mX_n, $K_{sp} = [A^{n+}]^m [X^{m-}]^n$
concentration of anion to form precipitate. The cation with the lower anion concentration will precipitate first.

(b)   Substitute the higher anion concentration into the K_{sp} expression for the first cation to precipitate and calculate the amount of this first cation to remain in solution.
Solution:

(a)   Derive expression for K_{sp} ($BaSO_4$), A = Ba^{2+}, m = 1, X = $SO_4{}^{2-}$, and n = 1. Since K_{sp} = $[Ba^{2+}] [SO_4{}^{2-}]$, then K_{sp} ($BaSO_4$) = 1.07×10^{-10} = 0.010 $[SO_4{}^{2-}]$. Solve for $[SO_4{}^{2-}]$. $[SO_4{}^{2-}]$ = 1.07×10^{-8} mol L^{-1} $SO_4{}^{2-}$. Since $Na_2SO_4 (s) \rightarrow 2\,Na^+ (aq) + SO_4{}^{2-} (aq)$, 1 $SO_4{}^{2-}$ ion is generated for each Na_2SO_4, $[Na_2SO_4]$ = 1.1 $\times 10^{-8}$ mol L^{-1} Na_2SO_4 to precipitate $BaSO_4$. Derive expression for K_{sp} ($CaSO_4$), A = Ca^{2+}, m = 1, X = $SO_4{}^{2-}$, and n = 1. Since K_{sp} = $[Ca^{2+}] [SO_4{}^{2-}]$, then K_{sp} ($CaSO_4$) = 7.10×10^{-5} = 0.020 $[SO_4{}^{2-}]$. Solve for $[SO_4{}^{2-}]$. $[SO_4{}^{2-}]$ = 0.0036 mol L^{-1} $SO_4{}^{2-}$ = 0.0036 mol L^{-1} Na_2SO_4 = $[Na_2SO_4]$ to precipitate $CaSO_4$. Since 1.1×10^{-8} mol L^{-1} Na_2SO_4 << 0.0036 mol L^{-1} Na_2SO_4, the Ba^{2+} will precipitate first.

(b)   Since Ca^{2+} will not precipitate until $[Na_2SO_4]$ = 0.0036 mol L^{-1} Na_2SO_4, substitute this value into the K_{sp} expression for $BaSO_4$. So K_{sp} ($BaSO_4$) = $[Ba^{2+}] [SO_4{}^{2-}]$ = 1.07×10^{-10} = $[Ba^{2+}]$ 0.0036. Solve for $[Ba^{2+}]$ = 3.0×10^{-8} mol L^{-1} Ba^{2+}.

Check: The units (none, mol L^{-1}, and mol L^{-1}) are correct. Comparing the two K_{sp} values, it can be seen that the Ba^{2+} will precipitate first since the solubility product is so much lower. Since the K_{sp} value is so low, the concentration of precipitating agent is very low. Since the $CaSO_4$ K_{sp} value is so much higher, the higher $[SO_4{}^{2-}]$ to precipitate Ca will force the concentration of Ba^{2+} to very low levels.

Complex Ion Equilbria

16.115   **Given:** solution with 1.1×10^{-3} mol L^{-1} $Zn(NO_3)_2$ and 0.150 mol L^{-1} NH_3 **Find:** $[Zn^{2+}]$ at equilibrium
Other: K_f ($Zn(NH_3)_4{}^{2+}$) = 2.8×10^9
Conceptual Plan: Write a balanced equation and expression for K_f. Use initial concentrations to set up an ICE table. Since the K_f is so large, assume that the reaction essentially goes to completion. Solve for $[Zn^{2+}]$ at equilibrium.
Solution: $Zn(NO_3)_2 (s) \rightarrow Zn^{2+} (aq) + 2\,NO_3{}^- (aq)$. Since 1 Zn^{2+} ion is generated for each $Zn(NO_3)_2$, $[Zn^{2+}]$ = 1.1×10^{-3} mol L^{-1}. Balanced equation is:

$Zn^{2+} (aq) + 4\,NH_3 (aq) \rightleftharpoons Zn(NH_3)_4{}^{2+} (aq)$ Set up an ICE table with initial concentrations.

	$[Zn^{2+}]$	$[NH_3]$	$[Zn(NH_3)_4{}^{2+}]$
I	1.1×10^{-3}	0.150	0
C	$\approx -1.1 \times 10^{-3}$	$\approx -4(1.1 \times 10^{-3})$	$\approx +1.1 \times 10^{-3}$
E	x	0.14<u>5</u>6	1.1×10^{-3}

Since K_f is so large and since initially $[NH_3] > 4\,[Zn^{2+}]$ the reaction essentially goes to completion. Then write an equilibrium expression and solve for x.

$K_f = \dfrac{[Zn(NH_3)_4{}^{2+}]}{[Zn^{2+}][NH_3]^4} = 2.8 \times 10^9 = \dfrac{1.1 \times 10^{-3}}{x\,(0.14\underline{5}6)^4}$ So $x = 8.7 \times 10^{-10}$ mol L^{-1} Zn^{2+}. Since x is insignificant

compared to the initial concentration, the assumption is valid.

Check: The units (mol L^{-1}) are correct. Since K_f is so large, the reaction essentially goes to completion and $[Zn^{2+}]$ is extremely small.

16.117 **Given:** $FeS(s) + 6 CN^-(aq) \rightleftharpoons Fe(CN)_6^{4-}(aq) + S^{2-}(aq)$ use K_{sp} and K_f values   **Find:** K

Other: $K_f (Fe(CN)_6^{4-}) = 1.5 \times 10^{35}$, $K_{sp} (FeS) = 3.72 \times 10^{-19}$

Conceptual Plan: Identify the appropriate solid and complex ion. Write balanced equations for dissolving the solid and forming the complex ion. Add these two reactions to get the desired overall reaction. Using the rules from Chapter 14, multiply the individual reaction Ks to get the overall K for the sum of these reactions.

Solution: Identify the solid as FeS and the complex ion as $Fe(CN)_6^{4-}$. Write the individual reactions and add them together.

$$FeS(s) \rightleftharpoons \cancel{Fe^{2+}(aq)} + S^{2-}(aq) \qquad\qquad K_{sp} = 1.5 \times 10^{-19}$$
$$\underline{\cancel{Fe^{2+}(aq)} + 6 CN^-(aq) \rightleftharpoons Fe(CN)_6^{4-}(aq) \qquad\qquad K_f = 3.72 \times 10^{35}}$$
$$FeS(s) + 6 CN^-(aq) \rightleftharpoons Fe(CN)_6^{4-}(aq) + S^{2-}(aq)$$

Since the overall reaction is the simple sum of the two reactions, the overall reaction $K = K_f \times K_{sp} = (1.5 \times 10^{35}) \times (3.72 \times 10^{-19}) = 5.6 \times 10^{16}$.

Check: The units (none) are correct. Since K_f is so large, it overwhelms the K_{sp} and the overall reaction is very spontaneous.

16.119 **Given:** $K_{sp} (Ag_2S) = 6.2 \times 10^{-51}$, $K_f (Ag(NH_3)_2^+) = 1.6 \times 10^7$, $[NH_3] = 5.0$ mol L^{-1} **Find:** molar solubility of Ag_2S.

Conceptual Plan: Identify the appropriate solid and complex ion. Write balanced equations for dissolving the solid and forming the complex ion. Add these two reactions to get the desired overall reaction. Using the rules from Chapter 14, multiply the individual reaction Ks to get the overall K for the sum of these reactions. Then refer to the stoichiometry of the reaction and prepare an ICE table showing the equilibrium concentrations of the ions relative to S, the amount of Ag_2S that dissolves.

Solution: $Ag_2S(s) \rightleftharpoons \cancel{2Ag^+(aq)} + S^{2-}(aq) \qquad\qquad K_{sp} = 6.2 \times 10^{-51}$

$$\underline{\cancel{2Ag^+(aq)} + 4 NH_3(aq) \rightleftharpoons 2 Ag(NH_3)_2^+(aq) \qquad\qquad K' = (K_f)^2 = (1.6 \times 10^7)^2}$$

$$Ag_2S(s) + 4 NH_3(aq) \rightleftharpoons 2 Ag(NH_3)_2^+(aq) + S^{2-}(aq) \qquad K = K_{sp}(K_f)^2 = 1.\underline{5}87 \times 10^{-36}$$

$$Ag_2S(s) + 4 NH_3(aq) \rightleftharpoons 2 Ag(NH_3)_2^+(aq) + S^{2-}(aq)$$

	[Ag₂S]	[NH₃]	[Ag(NH₃)₂⁺]	[S²⁻]
I	constant	5.0	0	0
C		−4S	+2S	+S
E		5.0 − 4S	2S	+S

$$K = \frac{[S^{2-}][Ag(NH_3)_2^+]^2}{[NH_3]^4} = 1.\underline{5}87 \times 10^{-36} = \frac{(2S)^2(S)}{(5.0 - 4S)^4}.$$ Assume S is small compared to 5.0, simplify and solve

for S. $1.\underline{5}87 \times 10^{-36} = \frac{4S^3}{(5.0)^4}$ then $S = \sqrt[3]{\frac{(625)(1.587 \times 10^{-36})}{4}} = 6.3 \times 10^{-12}$ mol L^{-1}. S is very small compared

to the concentration of NH_3 so the assumption is valid.

Check: The units (mol L^{-1}) are correct. The molar solubility of Ag_2S in the presence of NH_3 is greater than

the solubility of Ag_2S in water $(S = \sqrt[3]{\frac{6.2 \times 10^{-51}}{4}} = 1.2 \times 10^{-17}$ mol L$^{-1})$.

Cumulative Problems

16.121 **Given:** 150.0 mL solution of 2.05 g sodium benzoate and 2.47 g benzoic acid **Find:** pH

Other: $K_a (HC_7H_5O_2) = 6.5 \times 10^{-5}$

Conceptual Plan: g $NaC_7H_5O_2 \rightarrow$ mol $NaC_7H_5O_2$ and g $HC_7H_5O_2 \rightarrow$ mol $HC_7H_5O_2$

$$\frac{1 \text{ mol } NaC_7H_5O_2}{144.11 \text{ g } NaC_7H_5O_2} \qquad\qquad \frac{1 \text{ mol } HC_7H_5O_2}{122.13 \text{ g } HC_7H_5O_2}$$

Since the two components are in the same solution, the ratio of [base]/[acid] = (mol base)/(mol acid). Then K_a, mol $NaC_7H_5O_2$, mol $HC_7H_5O_2$ → pH.

$$pH = pK_a + \log \frac{[base]}{[acid]}$$

Solution: $2.05 \; \overline{g \; NaC_7H_5O_2} \times \dfrac{1 \; mol \; NaC_7H_5O_2}{144.11 \; \overline{g \; NaC_7H_5O_2}} = 0.014225\underline{2} \; mol \; NaC_7H_5O_2$ and

$2.47 \; \overline{g \; HC_7H_5O_2} \times \dfrac{1 \; mol \; HC_7H_5O_2}{122.13 \; \overline{g \; HC_7H_5O_2}} = 0.020224\underline{4} \; mol \; HC_7H_5O_2$ then

$$pH = pK_a + \log \frac{[base]}{[acid]} = pK_a + \log \frac{mol \; base}{mol \; acid} = -\log(6.5 \times 10^{-5}) + \log \frac{0.014225\underline{2} \; \overline{mol}}{0.020224\underline{4} \; \overline{mol}} = 4.03.$$

Check: The units (none) are correct. The magnitude of the answer makes physical sense because the pH is a little lower than the pK_a of the acid because there is more acid than base in the buffer solution.

16.123   **Given:** 150.0 mL of 0.25 mol L^{-1} HCOOH and 75.0 mL of 0.20 mol L^{-1} NaOH **Find:** pH **Other:** K_a (HCOOH) = 1.8×10^{-4}

Conceptual Plan: In this buffer, the base is generated by converting some of the formic acid to the formate ion. **Part I: Stoichiometry:**

mL → L then L, initial HCOOH mol L^{-1} → mol HCOOH then mL → L then

$$\frac{1 \; L}{1000 \; mL} \qquad\qquad M = \frac{mol}{L} \qquad\qquad \frac{1 \; L}{1000 \; mL}$$

L, initial NaOH mol L^{-1} → mol NaOH then write a balanced equation then

$$M = \frac{mol}{L} \qquad\qquad NaOH + HCOOH \rightarrow H_2O + HCOONa$$

mol HCOOH, mol NaOH → mol HCOONa, mol HCOOH then

set up stoichiometry table

Part II: Equilibrium:

Since the two components are in the same solution, the ratio of [base]/[acid] = (mol base)/(mol acid). Then K_a, mol HCOONa, mol HCOOH → pH.

$$pH = pK_a + \log \frac{[base]}{[acid]}$$

Solution: $150.0 \; \overline{mL} \times \dfrac{1 \; L}{1000 \; \overline{mL}} = 0.1500 \; L$ then

$0.1500 \; \overline{L \; HCHO_2} \times \dfrac{0.25 \; mol \; HCHO_2}{1 \; \overline{L \; HCHO_2}} = 0.037\underline{5} \; mol \; HCOOH.$

Then $75.0 \; \overline{mL} \times \dfrac{1 \; L}{1000 \; \overline{mL}} = 0.0750 \; L$ then $0.0750 \; \overline{L \; NaOH} \times \dfrac{0.20 \; mol \; NaOH}{1 \; \overline{L \; NaOH}} = 0.015 \; mol \; NaOH$ then set up a table to track changes:

	NaOH (aq)	+ HCOOH (aq)	→ HCOONa (aq)	+ H₂O (l)
Before addition	0 mol	0.037$\underline{5}$ mol	0 mol	—
Addition	0.015 mol	—	—	—
After addition	≈0 mol	0.022$\underline{5}$ mol	0.015 mol	—

Since the amount of NaOH is small, there are significant amounts of both buffer components, so the Henderson–Hasselbalch equation can be used to calculate the pH.

$$pH = pK_a + \log \frac{[base]}{[acid]} = pK_a + \log \frac{mol \; base}{mol \; acid} = -\log(1.8 \times 10^{-4}) + \log \frac{0.015 \; \overline{mol}}{0.022\underline{5} \; \overline{mol}} = 3.57.$$

Check: The units (none) are correct. The magnitude of the answer makes physical sense because the pH is a little lower than the pK_a of the acid because there is more acid than base in the buffer solution.

16.125   **Given:** 1.0 L of buffer of 0.25 mol NH_3 and 0.25 mol NH_4Cl; adjust to pH = 8.75

Find: mass NaOH or HCl **Other:** K_b (NH_3) = 1.79×10^{-5}

Conceptual Plan: To decide which reagent needs to be added to adjust pH, calculate the initial pH. Since the mol NH_3 = mol NH_4Cl, the pH = pK_a so K_b → pK_b → pK_a then

acid = NH_4^+ base = NH_3 $\qquad\qquad pK_b = -\log K_b \quad 14 = pK_a + pK_b$

final pH, pK_a → $[NH_3]/[NH_4^+]$ then $[NH_3]$, L → mol NH_3 and $[NH_4^+]$, L → mol NH_4^+

$$pH = pK_a + \log \frac{[base]}{[acid]} \qquad\qquad M = \frac{mol}{L} \qquad\qquad M = \frac{mol}{L}$$

then write a balanced equation then

$$H^+ + NH_3 \rightarrow NH_4^+$$

mol NH$_3$, mol NH$_4^+$, [NH$_3$]/[NH$_4^+$] $\rightarrow$ mol HCl $\rightarrow$ g HCl.

set up stoichiometry table $\dfrac{36.46 \text{ g HCl}}{1 \text{ mol HCl}}$

Solution: Since K_b (NH$_3$) = 1.79 x 10^{-5}, pK_b = $-$ log K_b = $-$ log (1.79 x 10^{-5}) = 4.75. Since 14 = pK_a + pK_b,

pK_a = 14 $-$ pK_b = 14 $-$ 4.75 = 9.25. Since the desired pH is lower (8.75), HCl (a strong acid) needs to be

added. Then pH = pK_a + log $\dfrac{[\text{base}]}{[\text{acid}]}$ = 9.25 + log $\dfrac{[NH_3]}{[NH_4^+]}$ = 8.75. Solve for $\dfrac{[NH_3]}{[NH_4^+]}$.

log $\dfrac{[NH_3]}{[NH_4^+]}$ = 8.75 $-$ 9.25 = $-0.50 \rightarrow \dfrac{[NH_3]}{[NH_4^+]}$ = 10$^{-0.50}$ = 0.31623. Then

$\dfrac{0.25 \text{ mol NH}_3}{1 \text{ Ł}}$ x 1.0 Ł = 0.25 mol NH$_3$ and

$\dfrac{0.25 \text{ mol NH}_4\text{Cl}}{1 \text{ Ł}}$ x 1.0 Ł = 0.25 mol NH$_4$Cl = 0.25 mol NH$_4^+$. Since HCl is a strong acid, [HCl] = [H$^+$], and

set up a table to track changes:

	H$^+$ (aq)	+	NH$_3$ (aq)	$\rightarrow$	NH$_4^+$ (aq)
Before addition	$\approx$0 mol		0.25 mol		0.25 mol
Addition	x		—		—
After addition	$\approx$0 mol		(0.25 $-$ x) mol		(0.25 + x) mol

Since $\dfrac{[NH_3]}{[NH_4^+]}$ = 0.31623 = $\dfrac{(0.25 - x) \text{ mol}}{(0.25 + x) \text{ mol}}$, solve for x. Note that the ratio of moles is the same as the ratio of

concentrations, since the volume for both terms is the same. 0.31623 (0.25 + x) = (0.25 $-$ x) $\rightarrow$

0.0790575 + 0.31623 x = 0.25 $-$ x $\rightarrow$ 1.31623 x = 0.17094 $\rightarrow$ x = 0.12987 mol HCl then

0.12987 mol HCl x $\dfrac{36.46 \text{ g HCl}}{1 \text{ mol HCl}}$ = 4.7 g HCl.

Check: The units (g) are correct. The magnitude of the answer makes physical sense because there is much less than a mole of each of the buffer components, so there must be much less than a mole of HCl.

16.127 (a) **Given:** potassium hydrogen phthalate = KHP = KHC$_8$H$_4$O$_4$ titration with NaOH
Find: balanced equation
Conceptual Plan: The reaction will be a titration of the acid proton, leaving the phthalate ion intact. The K will not be titrated since it is basic.
Solution: NaOH (aq) + KHC$_8$H$_4$O$_4$ (aq) $\rightarrow$ Na$^+$ (aq) + K$^+$ (aq) + C$_8$H$_4$O$_4{}^{2-}$ (aq) + H$_2$O (l)
Check: An acid–base reaction generates a salt (soluble here) and water. There is only one acidic proton in KHP.

(b) **Given:** 0.5527 g KHP titrated with 25.87 mL of NaOH solution   **Find:** [NaOH]
Conceptual Plan:
g KHP $\rightarrow$ mol KHP $\rightarrow$ mol NaOH and mL $\rightarrow$ L then mol NaOH and mL $\rightarrow$ mol L^{-1} NaOH

$\dfrac{1 \text{ mol KHP}}{204.22 \text{ g KHP}}$ 1:1 from balanced equation $\dfrac{1 \text{ L}}{1000 \text{ mL}}$ $M = \dfrac{\text{mol}}{\text{L}}$

Solution: 0.5527 g KHP x $\dfrac{1 \text{ mol KHP}}{204.22 \text{ g KHP}}$ = 0.002706395 mol KHP; mol KHP = mol acid = mol base =

0.002706395 mol NaOH then 25.87 mL x $\dfrac{1 \text{ L}}{1000 \text{ mL}}$ = 0.02587 L then

[NaOH] = $\dfrac{0.002706395 \text{ mol NaOH}}{0.02587 \text{ L}}$ = 0.1046 mol L^{-1} NaOH.

Check: The units (mol L^{-1}) are correct. The magnitude of the answer makes physical sense because there is much less than a mole of acid. The magnitude of the moles of acid and base are smaller than the volume of base in litres.

16.129   **Given:** 0.25 mol weak acid with 10.0 mL of 3.00 mol L^{-1} KOH diluted to 1.5000 L has pH = 3.85   **Find:** pK_a of acid

Conceptual Plan: mL $\rightarrow$ L then mol L^{-1} KOH, L $\rightarrow$ mol KOH then write a balanced reaction

$$\frac{1 \text{ L}}{1000 \text{ mL}} \qquad\qquad M = \frac{\text{mol}}{\text{L}} \qquad\qquad KOH + HA \rightarrow NaA + H_2O$$

added mol KOH, initial mol acid $\rightarrow$ equil. mol KOH, equil. mol acid then

set up stoichiometry table

equil. mol KOH, equil. mol acid, pH $\rightarrow$ pK_a.

$$pH = pK_a + \log \frac{[\text{base}]}{[\text{acid}]}$$

Solution: $10.00 \text{ mL} \times \dfrac{1 \text{ L}}{1000 \text{ mL}} = 0.01000 \text{ L}$ then $0.01000 \text{ L KOH} \times \dfrac{3.00 \text{ mol KOH}}{1 \text{ L KOH}} = 0.0300 \text{ mol KOH}$

Since KOH is a strong base, [KOH] = [OH^-], and set up a table to track changes:

	KOH (aq)	+ HA (aq)	$\rightarrow$ KA (aq)	+ H_2O (l)
Before addition	$\approx$0 mol	0.25 mol	0 mol	—
Addition	0.0300 mol	—	—	—
After addition	$\approx$0 mol	0.22 mol	0.0300 mol	—

Since the ratio of base to acid is between 0.1 and 10, it is a buffer solution. Note that the ratio of moles is the same as the ratio of concentrations, since the volume for both terms is the same.

$$pH = pK_a + \log \frac{[\text{base}]}{[\text{acid}]} = pK_a + \log \frac{0.0300 \text{ mol}}{0.22 \text{ mol}} = 3.85. \text{ Solve for } pK_a.$$

$$pK_a = 3.85 - \log \frac{0.0300 \text{ mol}}{0.22 \text{ mol}} = 4.72.$$

Check: The units (none) are correct. The magnitude of the answer makes physical sense because there is more acid than base at equilibrium, so the pK_a is higher than the pH of the solution.

16.131   **Given:** 0.552 g ascorbic acid dissolved in 20.00 mL and titrated with 28.42 mL of 0.1103 mol L^{-1} KOH solution; pH = 3.72 when 10.0 mL KOH added   **Find:** molar mass and K_a of acid

Conceptual Plan: mL $\rightarrow$ L then mol L^{-1} KOH, L $\rightarrow$ mol KOH $\rightarrow$ mol acid then mol acid, g acid $\rightarrow$ $\mathcal{M}$

$$\frac{1 \text{ L}}{1000 \text{ mL}} \qquad M = \frac{\text{mol}}{\text{L}} \quad \text{1:1 for monoprotic acid} \qquad \text{molar mass} = \frac{\text{g acid}}{\text{mol acid}}$$

For the second part of the problem:

mL $\rightarrow$ L then mol L^{-1} KOH, L $\rightarrow$ mol KOH then write a balanced reaction

$$\frac{1 \text{ L}}{1000 \text{ mL}} \qquad\qquad M = \frac{\text{mol}}{\text{L}} \qquad\qquad KOH + HA \rightarrow NaA + H_2O$$

added mol KOH, initial mol acid $\rightarrow$ equil. mol KOH, equil. mol acid then

set up stoichiometry table

equil. mol KOH, equil. mol acid, pH $\rightarrow$ pK_a $\rightarrow$ K_a.

$$pH = pK_a + \log \frac{[\text{base}]}{[\text{acid}]} \quad pK_a = -\log K_a$$

Solution: $28.42 \text{ mL} \times \dfrac{1 \text{ L}}{1000 \text{ mL}} = 0.02842 \text{ L}$ then

$0.02842 \text{ L KOH} \times \dfrac{0.1103 \text{ mol KOH}}{1 \text{ L KOH}} = 0.003134726 \text{ mol KOH} = \text{mol base} = \text{mol acid} = 0.003134726 \text{ mol}$

ascorbic acid then molar mass $= \dfrac{\text{g acid}}{\text{mol acid}} = \dfrac{0.552 \text{ g acid}}{0.003134726 \text{ mol acid}} = 176 \text{ g mol}^{-1}$. For the second part of

the problem, $10.00 \text{ mL} \times \dfrac{1 \text{ L}}{1000 \text{ mL}} = 0.01000 \text{ L}$ then $0.01000 \text{ L KOH} \times \dfrac{0.1103 \text{ mol KOH}}{1 \text{ L KOH}}$

$= 0.001103 \text{ mol KOH}$. Since KOH is a strong base, [KOH] = [OH^-], and set up a table to track changes:

	KOH (aq)	+ HA (aq)	$\rightarrow$ KA (aq)	+ H_2O (l)
Before addition	$\approx$0 mol	0.003134726 mol	0 mol	—
Addition	0.001103 mol	—	—	—
After addition	$\approx$0 mol	0.002031726 mol	0.001103 mol	—

Since the ratio of base to acid is between 0.1 and 10, it is a buffer solution. Note that the ratio of moles is the same as the ratio of concentrations, since the volume for both terms is the same.

$$pH = pK_a + \log\frac{[\text{base}]}{[\text{acid}]} = pK_a + \log\frac{0.001103 \text{ mol}}{0.002031726 \text{ mol}} = 3.72. \text{ Solve for } pK_a.$$

$$pK_a = 3.72 - \log\frac{0.001103}{0.002031726} = 3.98529 \text{ and so } pK_a = -\log K_a$$

or $K_a = 10^{-pK_a} = 10^{-3.98529} = 1.0 \times 10^{-4}$.

Check: The units (g mol^{-1} and none) are correct. The magnitude of the answer makes physical sense because there is much less than a mole of acid and about a half a gram of acid, so the molar mass will be high. The number is reasonable for an acid (must be > 20 g mol^{-1} – lightest acid is HF). The K_a is reasonable because the pK_a is within 1 unit of the pH when the titration solution is behaving as a buffer.

16.133 **Given:** saturated $CaCO_3$ solution; precipitate 1.00×10^2 mg $CaCO_3$ **Find:** volume of solution evaporated
Other: K_{sp} ($CaCO_3$) = 4.96×10^{-9}
Conceptual Plan: mg $CaCO_3$ $\rightarrow$ g $CaCO_3$ $\rightarrow$ mol $CaCO_3$

$$\frac{1 \text{ g } CaCO_3}{1000 \text{ mg } CaCO_3} \qquad \frac{1 \text{ mol } CaCO_3}{100.09 \text{ g } CaCO_3}$$

The expression of the solubility product constant of A_mX_n is $K_{sp} = [A^{n+}]^m [X^{m-}]^n$. The molar solubility of a compound, A_mX_n, can be computed directly from K_{sp} by solving for S in the expression $K_{sp} = (mS)^m (nS)^n = m^m n^n S^{m+n}$. Then mol $CaCO_3$, S $\rightarrow$ L.

$$M = \frac{mol}{L}$$

Solution: $1.00 \times 10^2 \text{ mg } CaCO_3 \times \dfrac{1 \text{ g } CaCO_3}{1000 \text{ mg } CaCO_3} \times \dfrac{1 \text{ mol } CaCO_3}{100.09 \text{ g } CaCO_3} = 9.99101 \times 10^{-4}$ mol $CaCO_3$ then

$K_{sp} = 4.96 \times 10^{-9}$, $A = Ca^{2+}$, $m = 1$, $X = CO_3^{2-}$, and $n = 1$ so $K_{sp} = 4.96 \times 10^{-9} = S^2$. Rearrange to solve for S.

$S = \sqrt{4.96 \times 10^{-9}} = 7.04273 \times 10^{-5}$ mol L^{-1}. Finally,

$$9.99101 \times 10^{-4} \text{ mol } CaCO_3 \times \frac{1 \text{ L}}{7.04273 \times 10^{-5} \text{ mol } CaCO_3} = 14.2 \text{ L}.$$

Check: The units (L) are correct. The volume should be large since the solubility is low.

16.135 **Given:** $[Ca^{2+}] = 9.2$ mg dL^{-1} and K_{sp} ($Ca_2P_2O_7$) = 8.64×10^{-13} **Find:** $[P_2O_7^{4-}]$ to form precipitate
Conceptual Plan: mg Ca^{2+} dL^{-1} $\rightarrow$ g Ca^{2+} dL^{-1} $\rightarrow$ mol Ca^{2+} dL^{-1} $\rightarrow$ mol Ca^{2+} L^{-1} then

$$\frac{1 \text{ g } Ca^{2+}}{1000 \text{ mg } Ca^{2+}} \qquad \frac{1 \text{ mol } Ca^{2+}}{40.08 \text{ g } Ca^{2+}} \qquad \frac{10 \text{ dL}}{1 \text{ L}}$$

write a balanced equation and expression for K_{sp}. Then $[Ca^{2+}]$, K_{sp} $\rightarrow$ $[P_2O_7^{4-}]$.

Solution: $9.2 \dfrac{\text{mg } Ca^{2+}}{\text{dL}} \times \dfrac{1 \text{ g } Ca^{2+}}{1000 \text{ mg } Ca^{2+}} \times \dfrac{1 \text{ mol } Ca^{2+}}{40.08 \text{ g } Ca^{2+}} \times \dfrac{10 \text{ dL}}{1 \text{ L}} = 2.29541 \times 10^{-3}$ mol L^{-1} Ca^{2+} then write

equation $Ca_2P_2O_7$ (s) $\rightarrow$ 2 Ca^{2+} (aq) + $P_2O_7^{4-}$ (aq). So $K_{sp} = [Ca^{2+}]^2 [P_2O_7^{4-}] = 8.64 \times 10^{-13} = (2.29541 \times 10^{-3})^2 [P_2O_7^{4-}]$. Solve for $[P_2O_7^{4-}]$ then $[P_2O_7^{4-}] = 1.6 \times 10^{-7}$ mol L^{-1}.

Check: The units (mol L^{-1}) are correct. Since K_{sp} is so small and the calcium concentration is relatively high, the diphosphate concentration required is at a very low level.

16.137 **Given:** CuS in 0.150 mol L^{-1} NaCN **Find:** molar solubility (S)
Other: K_f ($Cu(CN)_4^{2-}$) = 1.0×10^{25}, K_{sp} (CuS) = $[Cu^{2+}][S^{2-}]$ = 1.27×10^{-36}
Conceptual Plan: Identify the appropriate solid and complex ion. Write balanced equations for dissolving the solid and forming the complex ion. Add these two reactions to get the desired overall reaction. Using the rules from Chapter 14, multiply the individual reaction Ks to get the overall K for the sum of these reactions. Then mol L^{-1} NaCN, K $\rightarrow$ S.

ICE Table

Solution: Identify the solid as CuS and the complex ion as $Cu(CN)_4^{2-}$. Write the individual reactions and add them together.

CuS (s) $\rightleftharpoons$ Cu^{2+} (aq) + S^{2-} (aq)	$K_{sp} = 1.27 \times 10^{-36}$
Cu^{2+} (aq) + 4 CN^- (aq) $\rightleftharpoons$ $Cu(CN)_4^{2-}$ (aq)	$K_f = 1.0 \times 10^{25}$
CuS (s) + 4 CN^- (aq) $\rightleftharpoons$ $Cu(CN)_4^{2-}$ (aq) + S^{2-} (aq)	

Since the overall reaction is the simple sum of the two reactions, the overall reaction $K = K_f K_{sp} =$ $(1.0 \times 10^{25}) \times (1.27 \times 10^{-36}) = 1.27 \times 10^{-11}$. NaCN (s) $\rightarrow$ Na$^+$ (aq) + CN$^-$ (aq). Since 1 CN$^-$ ion is generated for each NaCN, [CN$^-$] = 0.150 mol L^{-1}. Set up an ICE table:

$$CuS\ (s) + 4\ CN^-\ (aq) \rightleftharpoons Cu(CN)_4^{2-}\ (aq) + S^{2-}\ (aq)$$

	[CN$^-$]	[Cu(CN)$_4^{2-}$]	[X^{2-}]
I	0.150	0	0
C	$-4S$	$+S$	$+S$
E	0.150 $-$ 4S	S	S

$$K = \frac{[Cu(CN)_4^{2-}][S^{2-}]}{[CN^-]^4} = 1.27 \times 10^{-11} = \frac{S^2}{(0.150 - 4S)^4}.$$

Assume S is small (4S << 0.150) so $\dfrac{S^2}{(0.150 - \cancel{4S})^4} = 1.27 \times 10^{-11} = \dfrac{S^2}{(0.150)^4}$ and $S = 8.0183 \times 10^{-8} =$

8.0×10^{-8} mol L^{-1}. Confirm that the assumption is valid. $\dfrac{4(8.0183 \times 10^{-8})}{0.150} \times 100\% = 0.00021\% \ll 5\%$, so the

assumption is valid.

Check: The units (mol L^{-1}) are correct. Since K_f is large, the overall K is larger than the original K_{sp} and the solubility of CuS increases over that of pure water ($\sqrt{1.27 \times 10^{-36}} = 1.13 \times 10^{-18}$ mol L^{-1}).

16.139   **Given:** 100.0 mL of 0.36 mol L^{-1} NH$_2$OH and 50.0 mL of 0.26 mol L^{-1} HCl and K_b (NH$_2$OH) = 1.10 $\times$ 10^{-8}
Find: pH
Conceptual Plan: Identify acid and base components, mL $\rightarrow$ L then [NH$_2$OH], L $\rightarrow$ mol NH$_2$OH

$$acid = NH_3OH^+ \quad base = NH_2OH \qquad \frac{1\ L}{1000\ mL} \qquad M = \frac{mol}{L}$$

then mL $\rightarrow$ L then [HCl], L $\rightarrow$ mol HCl then write balanced equation then

$$\frac{1\ L}{1000\ mL} \qquad M = \frac{mol}{L} \qquad HCl + NH_2OH \rightarrow NH_3OHCl$$

mol NH$_2$OH, mol HCl $\rightarrow$ mol excess NH$_2$OH, mol NH$_3$OH$^+$.

set up stoichiometry table

Since there are significant amounts of both the acid and the conjugate base species, this is a buffer solution and so the Henderson–Hasselbalch equation $\left(\text{pH} = \text{p}K_a + \log \dfrac{[\text{base}]}{[\text{acid}]} \right)$ can be used. Convert K_b to

K_a **using $K_w = K_a K_b$. Also note that the ratio of concentrations is the same as the ratio of moles, since the volume is the same for both species.**

Solution: $100\ \cancel{mL\ NH_2OH} \times \dfrac{1\ L}{1000\ \cancel{mL}} = 0.1\ L\ NH_2OH$ then

$\dfrac{0.36\ mol\ NH_2OH}{1\ \cancel{L}} \times 0.1000\ \cancel{L} = 0.036\ mol\ NH_2OH$. $50.0\ \cancel{mL\ HCl} \times \dfrac{1\ L}{1000\ \cancel{mL}} = 0.0500\ L\ HCl$ then

$\dfrac{0.26\ mol\ HCl}{1\ \cancel{L}} \times 0.0500\ \cancel{L} = 0.013\ mol\ HCl$. Set up a table to track changes:

$$HCl\ (aq) + NH_2OH\ (aq) \rightarrow NH_3OHCl\ (aq)$$

	HCl (aq)	NH$_2$OH (aq)	NH$_3$OHCl (aq)
Before addition	0 mol	0.036 mol	0 mol
Addition	0.013 mol	—	—
After addition	$\approx$0 mol	0.023 mol	0.013 mol

Then $K_w = K_a K_b$ so $K_a = \dfrac{K_w}{K_b} = \dfrac{1.0 \times 10^{-14}}{1.10 \times 10^{-8}} = 9.0909 \times 10^{-7}$ mol L^{-1} then use Henderson–Hasselbalch

equation, since the solution is a buffer. Note that the ratio of moles is the same as the ratio of concentrations, since the volume for both terms is the same.

$$pH = pK_a + \log \frac{[base]}{[acid]} = -\log(9.0909 \times 10^{-7}) + \log \frac{0.023\ \cancel{mol}}{0.013\ \cancel{mol}} = 6.28918 = 6.29.$$

Check: The units (none) are correct. The magnitude of the answer makes physical sense because pH should be more than the pK_a of the acid because there is more base than acid.

16.141 **Given:** 25.0 mL of NaOH titrated with 19.6 mL of 0.189 mol L^{-1} HCl solution; 10.0 mL of H_3PO_4 titrated with 34.9 mL of NaOH **Find:** concentration of H_3PO_4 solution
Conceptual Plan: Write the first balanced reaction then mL $\rightarrow$ L then mol L^{-1} HCl, L $\rightarrow$ mol HCl $\rightarrow$ mol NaOH

$$HCl + NaOH \rightarrow NaCl + H_2O \qquad \frac{1\,L}{1000\,mL} \qquad M = \frac{mol}{L} \qquad 1:1$$

then mL $\rightarrow$ L then mol NaOH, L $\rightarrow$ mol L^{-1} NaOH then write 2nd balanced reaction then mL $\rightarrow$ L
$$\frac{1\,L}{1000\,mL} \qquad H_3PO_4 + 3\,NaOH \rightarrow Na_3PO_4 + 3\,H_2O \qquad \frac{1\,L}{1000\,mL}$$

then mol L^{-1} NaOH, L $\rightarrow$ mol NaOH $\rightarrow$ mol H_3PO_4 then mL $\rightarrow$ L then mol H_3PO_4, L $\rightarrow$ mol L^{-1} H_3PO_4.
$$M = \frac{mol}{L} \qquad 3:1 \qquad \frac{1\,L}{1000\,mL} \qquad M = \frac{mol}{L}$$

Solution: In the first titration, $19.6\ \overline{mL} \times \dfrac{1\,L}{1000\ \overline{mL}} = 0.0196$ L then

$0.0196\ \overline{L\ HCl} \times \dfrac{0.189\ mol\ HCl}{1\ \overline{L\ HCl}} = 0.0037044\ \overline{mol\ HCl} \times \dfrac{1\ mol\ NaOH}{1\ \overline{mol\ HCl}} = 0.0037044\ mol\ NaOH$ then

$25.0\ \overline{mL} \times \dfrac{1\,L}{1000\ \overline{mL}} = 0.0250$ L then $\dfrac{0.0037044\ mol\ NaOH}{0.0250\ L\ NaOH} = 0.148176\ mol\ L^{-1}\ NaOH$. In the second

titration, $34.9\ \overline{mL} \times \dfrac{1\,L}{1000\ \overline{mL}} = 0.0349$ L then $0.0349\ \overline{L\ NaOH} \times \dfrac{0.148176\ mol\ NaOH}{1\ \overline{L\ NaOH}}$

$= 0.00517134\ \overline{mol\ NaOH} \times \dfrac{1\ mol\ H_3PO_4}{3\ \overline{mol\ NaOH}} = 0.00172378\ mol\ H_3PO_4$ then $10.0\ \overline{mL} \times \dfrac{1\,L}{1000\ \overline{mL}} = 0.0100$ L

then $\dfrac{0.00172378\ mol\ H_3PO_4}{0.0100\ L\ H_3PO_4} = 0.172\ mol\ L^{-1}\ H_3PO_4$.

Check: The units (mol L^{-1}) are correct. The magnitude of the answer makes physical sense because the concentration of NaOH is a little lower than the HCl (because the volume of NaOH is greater than HCl) and the concentration of H_3PO_4 is more than the NaOH (because the ratio of the volume of NaOH to volume of H_3PO_4 is just over 3 and H_3PO_4 is a triprotic acid).

16.143 **Given:** $(CH_3)_2NH/(CH_3)_2NH_2Cl$ buffer at pH = 10.43 **Find:** relative masses of $(CH_3)_2NH$ and $(CH_3)_2NH_2Cl$
Other: $K_b\ ((CH_3)_2NH) = 5.4 \times 10^{-4}$
Conceptual Plan: $K_b \rightarrow pK_b \rightarrow pK_a$ then pH, $pK_a \rightarrow$ [$(CH_3)_2NH$] / [$(CH_3)_2NH_2^+$] then

$$pK_b = -\log K_b \quad 14 = pK_a + pK_b \quad acid = (CH_3)_2NH_2^+ \quad base = (CH_3)_2NH \qquad pH = pK_a + \log\frac{[base]}{[acid]}$$

[$(CH_3)_2NH$]/[$(CH_3)_2NH_2^+$] $\rightarrow$ g $(CH_3)_2NH$ / g $(CH_3)_2NH_2^+$
$$\frac{45.09\ g\ (CH_3)_2NH}{1\ mol\ (CH_3)_2NH} \qquad \frac{81.54\ g\ (CH_3)_2NH_2Cl}{1\ mol\ (CH_3)_2NH_2Cl}$$

Solution: Since $K_b\ ((CH_3)_2NH) = 5.4 \times 10^{-4}$, $pK_b = -\log K_b = -\log(5.4 \times 10^{-4}) = 3.27$.

Since $14 = pK_a + pK_b$, $pK_a = 14 - pK_b = 14 - 3.27 = 10.73$. Since [acid] = [$(CH_3)_2NH_2^+$] = [$(CH_3)_2NH_2Cl$]

and [base] = [$(CH_3)_2NH$] then $pH = pK_a + \log\dfrac{[base]}{[acid]} = 10.73 + \log\dfrac{[(CH_3)_2NH]}{[(CH_3)_2NH_2Cl]} = 10.43$. Solve for

$\dfrac{[(CH_3)_2NH]}{[(CH_3)_2NH_2Cl]}$. $\log\dfrac{[(CH_3)_2NH]}{[(CH_3)_2NH_2Cl]} = 10.43 - 10.73 = -0.30 \rightarrow \dfrac{[(CH_3)_2NH]}{[(CH_3)_2NH_2Cl]} = 10^{-0.30} = 0.501187$.

Then $\dfrac{0.501187\ \overline{mol\ (CH_3)_2NH}}{1\ \overline{mol\ (CH_3)_2NH_2Cl}} \times \dfrac{45.09\ g\ (CH_3)_2NH}{1\ \overline{mol\ (CH_3)_2NH}} \times \dfrac{1\ \overline{mol\ (CH_3)_2NH_2Cl}}{81.54\ g\ (CH_3)_2NH_2Cl} = \dfrac{0.277147\ g\ (CH_3)_2NH}{g\ (CH_3)_2NH_2Cl}$

$= \dfrac{0.28\ g\ (CH_3)_2NH}{g\ (CH_3)_2NH_2Cl}$ or $\dfrac{3.6\ g\ (CH_3)_2NH_2Cl}{g\ (CH_3)_2NH}$.

Check: The units (g/g) are correct. The magnitude of the answer makes physical sense since there are more moles of acid than base in the buffer (pH < pK_a) and the molar mass of the acid is greater than the molar mass of the base. Thus, the ratio of the mass of the base to the mass of the acid is expected to be less than 1.

16.145 **Given:** $HC_7H_5O_2$ / $C_7H_5O_2Na$ buffer at pH = 4.55, complete dissociation of $C_7H_5O_2Na$, $d = 1.01$ g mL^{-1}; $T_f = -2.0\ °C$ **Find:** [$HC_7H_5O_2$] and [$C_7H_5O_2Na$] **Other:** $K_a\ (HC_7H_5O_2) = 6.5 \times 10^{-5}$, $K_f = 1.86\ °C\ m^{-1}$
Conceptual Plan: $K_a \rightarrow pK_a$ then pH, $pK_a \rightarrow$ [$C_7H_5O_2Na$] / [$HC_7H_5O_2$] and $T_f \rightarrow \Delta T_f$ then

$$pK_a = -\log K_a \quad acid = HC_7H_5O_2 \quad base = C_7H_5O_2^- \quad pH = pK_a + \log\frac{[base]}{[acid]} \qquad T_f = T_f^\circ - \Delta T_f$$

ΔT_f, i, K_f $\rightarrow$ m then assume 1 kg water (or 1000 g water).

$$\Delta T_f = K_f m \qquad\qquad m = \frac{\text{amount solute (moles)}}{\text{mass solvent (kg)}}$$

Assume that $HC_7H_5O_2$ does not dissociate and $C_7H_5O_2Na$ completely dissociates, then mol particles = mol $HC_7H_5O_2$ +2(mol $C_7H_5O_2Na$). Use $[C_7H_5O_2Na]$ / $[HC_7H_5O_2]$ and total mol particles = mol $[HC_7H_5O_2]$ +2(mol $C_7H_5O_2Na$) to solve for mol $HC_7H_5O_2$ and mol $C_7H_5O_2Na$. Then

mol $HC_7H_5O_2$ $\rightarrow$ g mol $HC_7H_5O_2$ and mol $C_7H_5O_2Na$ $\rightarrow$ g $C_7H_5O_2Na$ then

$$\frac{122.12 \text{ g } HC_7H_5O_2}{1 \text{ mol } HC_7H_5O_2} \qquad\qquad \frac{143.94 \text{ g } C_7H_5O_2Na}{1 \text{ mol } C_7H_5O_2Na}$$

g $HC_7H_5O_2$, g $C_7H_5O_2Na$, g water $\rightarrow$ g solution $\rightarrow$ mL solution $\rightarrow$ L solution then

$$\text{g } HC_7H_5O_2 + \text{g } C_7H_5O_2Na + \text{g water} = \text{g solution} \qquad d = \frac{1 \text{ mL}}{1.01 \text{ g}} \qquad \frac{1 \text{ L}}{1000 \text{ mL}}$$

mol $HC_7H_5O_2$, L $\rightarrow$ mol L^{-1} $HC_7H_5O_2$ and mol $C_7H_5O_2Na$, L $\rightarrow$ mol L^{-1} $C_7H_5O_2Na$.

$$M = \frac{\text{mol}}{\text{L}} \qquad\qquad M = \frac{\text{mol}}{\text{L}}$$

Solution: Since K_a ($HC_7H_5O_2$) = 6.5 x 10^{-5}, pK_a = $-$ log K_a = $-$ log (6.5 x 10^{-5}) = 4.19. Since [acid] = $[HC_7H_5O_2]$ and [base] = $[C_7H_5O_2^-]$ = $[C_7H_5O_2Na]$ then

$$pH = pK_a + \log \frac{[\text{base}]}{[\text{acid}]} = 4.19 + \log \frac{[C_7H_5O_2Na]}{[HC_7H_5O_2]} = 4.55. \text{ Solve for } \frac{[C_7H_5O_2Na]}{[HC_7H_5O_2]}.$$

$$\log \frac{[C_7H_5O_2Na]}{[HC_7H_5O_2]} = 4.55 - 4.19 = 0.36 \rightarrow \frac{[C_7H_5O_2Na]}{[HC_7H_5O_2]} = 10^{0.36} = 2.29087. \text{ Then } T_f = T_f^\circ - \Delta T_f \text{ so}$$

$\Delta T_f = T_f^\circ - T_f = 0.0 \,°C - (-2.0 \,°C) = 2.0 \,°C$ then $\Delta T_f = K_f\, m$. Rearrange to solve for m.

$$m = \frac{\Delta T_f}{K_f} = \frac{2.0 \,°C}{1.86 \frac{°C}{m}} = 1.07527 \frac{\text{mol particles}}{\text{kg solvent}}. \text{ Assume 1 kg water, so we have 1.07527 mol particles.}$$

Assume that $HC_7H_5O_2$ does not dissociate and $C_7H_5O_2Na$ completely dissociates, then 1.07527 mol particles = mol $HC_7H_5O_2$ +2(mol $C_7H_5O_2Na$). Use $[C_7H_5O_2Na]$ / $[HC_7H_5O_2]$ = 2.29087 and 1.07527 mol particles = mol $[HC_7H_5O_2]$ +2(mol $C_7H_5O_2Na$) to solve for mol $HC_7H_5O_2$ and mol $C_7H_5O_2Na$. So, mol $C_7H_5O_2Na$ = 2.29087(mol $HC_7H_5O_2$) $\rightarrow$ 1.07527 mol particles = mol $HC_7H_5O_2$ + 2 (2.29087 mol $HC_7H_5O_2$) $\rightarrow$ 1.07527 mol particles = 5.58174 mol $HC_7H_5O_2$ $\rightarrow$ mol $HC_7H_5O_2$ = 0.192641 mol and mol $C_7H_5O_2Na$ = 2.29087 x mol $HC_7H_5O_2$ = 2.29087 x 0.192641 mol $HC_7H_5O_2$ = 0.441315 mol $C_7H_5O_2Na$

$$0.192641 \text{ mol } HC_7H_5O_2 \text{ x } \frac{122.12 \text{ g } HC_7H_5O_2}{1 \text{ mol } HC_7H_5O_2} = 23.5253 \text{ g } HC_7H_5O_2 \text{ and}$$

$$0.441315 \text{ mol } C_7H_5O_2Na \text{ x } \frac{143.94 \text{ g } C_7H_5O_2Na}{1 \text{ mol } C_7H_5O_2Na} = 63.5229 \text{ g } C_7H_5O_2Na \text{ then}$$

23.5253 g mol $HC_7H_5O_2$ + 63.5229 g $C_7H_5O_2Na$ + 1000 g water = 1087.048 g solution then

$$1087.048 \text{ g solution x } \frac{1 \text{ mL}}{1.01 \text{ g}} \text{ x } \frac{1 \text{ L}}{1000 \text{ mL}} = 1.076285 \text{ L. Finally,}$$

$$\frac{0.192641 \text{ mol } HC_7H_5O_2}{1.076285 \text{ L}} = 0.178987 \text{ mol } L^{-1} HC_7H_5O_2 = 0.18 \text{ mol } L^{-1} HC_7H_5O_2 \text{ and}$$

$$\frac{0.441315 \text{ mol } C_7H_5O_2Na}{1.076285 \text{ L}} = 0.410035 \text{ mol } L^{-1} C_7H_5O_2Na = 0.41 \text{ mol } L^{-1} C_7H_5O_2Na.$$

Check: The units (mol L^{-1} and mol L^{-1}) are correct. The magnitude of the answer makes physical sense since there are more moles of base than acid in the buffer (pH > pK_a).

16.147 **Given:** pH = 9.41, saturated solution of $Fe(OH)_2$ **Find:** K_{sp}
Conceptual Plan: pH $\rightarrow$ $[H_3O^+]$ then K_w, $[H_3O^+]$ $\rightarrow$ $[OH^-]$. Balanced equation, $[OH^-]$ $\rightarrow$ $[Fe^{2+}]$ then

$$pH = -\log [H_3O^+] \qquad\qquad K_w = [H_3O^+][OH^-] \qquad\qquad Fe(OH)_2 \rightarrow Fe^{2+} + 2 OH^-$$

$[Fe^{2+}]$, $[OH^-]$ $\rightarrow$ K_{sp}

$$K_{sp} = [A^{n+}]^m [X^{m-}]^n$$

Solution: pH = -log$[H_3O^+]$ $\rightarrow$ $[H_3O^+]$ = $10^{-9.41}$ = 3.89 x 10^{-10} mol L^{-1}. K_w = $[H_3O^+][OH^-]$ = 1.0 x 10^{-14} then

$$[OH^-] = \frac{K_w}{[H_3O^+]} = \frac{1.0 \text{ x } 10^{-14}}{3.89 \text{ x } 10^{-10}} = 2.5707 \text{ x } 10^{-5} \text{ mol } L^{-1}. \text{ From } Fe(OH)_2 \text{ (s)} \rightarrow Fe^{2+} \text{ (aq)} + 2 OH^- \text{ (aq), the}$$

ratio of $[OH^-]:[Fe^{2+}]$ is 2:1, so $[Fe^{2+}] = \frac{1}{2}[OH^-] = \frac{1}{2}(2.\underline{5}707 \times 10^{-5} \text{ mol L}^{-1}) = 1.\underline{2}854 \times 10^{-5} \text{ mol L}^{-1}$. For $Fe(OH)_2$, $A = Fe^{2+}$, $m = 1$, $X = OH^-$, and $n = 2$ therefore $K_{sp} = [Fe^{2+}][OH^-]^2 = (1.\underline{2}854 \times 10^{-5} \text{ mol L}^{-1})(2.\underline{5}707 \times 10^{-5}$ mol $L^{-1})^2 = 8.5 \times 10^{-15}$.

Check: The units (none) are correct and the magnitude (10^{-15}) is appropriate for a K_{sp} value.

Challenge Problems

16.149   **Given:** 10.0 L of 75 ppm $CaCO_3$ and 55 ppm $MgCO_3$ (by mass)
Find: mass Na_2CO_3 to precipitate 90.0% of ions
Other: $K_{sp}(CaCO_3) = 4.96 \times 10^{-9}$ and $K_{sp}(MgCO_3) = 6.82 \times 10^{-6}$
Conceptual Plan: Assume that the density of water is 1.00 g mL^{-1}. L water → mL water → g water then

$$\frac{1000 \text{ mL}}{1 \text{ L}} \qquad \frac{1.00 \text{ g water}}{1 \text{ mL}}$$

g water → g $CaCO_3$ → mol $CaCO_3$ → mol Ca^{2+} and g water → g $MgCO_3$ → mol $MgCO_3$ then

$$\frac{75 \text{ g } CaCO_3}{10^6 \text{ g water}} \quad \frac{1 \text{ mol } CaCO_3}{100.09 \text{ g } CaCO_3} \quad \frac{1 \text{ mol } Ca^{2+}}{1 \text{ mol } CaCO_3} \qquad \frac{55 \text{ g } MgCO_3}{10^6 \text{ g water}} \quad \frac{1 \text{ mol } MgCO_3}{84.32 \text{ g } MgCO_3}$$

mol $MgCO_3$ → mol Mg^{2+} then comparing the two K_{sp} values, essentially all of the Ca^{2+} will

$$\frac{1 \text{ mol } Mg^{2+}}{1 \text{ mol } MgCO_3}$$

precipitate before the Mg^{2+} will begin to precipitate. Since 90.0% of the ions are to be precipitates, there will be 10.0% of the ions left in the solution (all will be Mg^{2+}).

$$(0.100)(\text{mol } Ca^{2+} + \text{mol } Mg^{2+})$$

Calculate the moles of ions remaining in solution. Then mol Mg^{2+}, L → mol L^{-1} Mg^{2+}.

$$M = \frac{\text{mol}}{L}$$

The solubility product constant (K_{sp}) is the equilibrium expression for a chemical equation representing the dissolution of an ionic compound. The expression of the solubility product constant of A_mX_n is K_{sp} = $[A^{n+}]^m [X^{m-}]^n$. Use this equation to mol L^{-1} Mg^{2+}, K_{sp} → mol L^{-1} CO_3^{2-} then mol L^{-1} CO_3^{2-}, L → mol CO_3^{2-}

$$\text{for ionic compound, } A_mX_n, \, K_{sp} = [A^{n+}]^m [X^{m-}]^n. \qquad M = \frac{\text{mol}}{L}$$

then mol CO_3^{2-} → mol Na_2CO_3 → g Na_2CO_3.

$$\frac{1 \text{ mol } CO_3^{2-}}{1 \text{ mol } Na_2CO_3} \qquad \frac{105.99 \text{ g } Na_2CO_3}{1 \text{ mol } Na_2CO_3}$$

Solution: $10.0 \text{ L} \times \dfrac{1000 \text{ mL}}{1 \text{ L}} \times \dfrac{1.00 \text{ g water}}{1 \text{ mL}} = 1.00 \times 10^4$ g water then

$1.00 \times 10^4 \text{ g water} \times \dfrac{75 \text{ g } CaCO_3}{10^6 \text{ g water}} \times \dfrac{1 \text{ mol } CaCO_3}{100.09 \text{ g } CaCO_3} \times \dfrac{1 \text{ mol } Ca^{2+}}{1 \text{ mol } CaCO_3} = 0.0074933 \text{ mol } Ca^{2+}$ and

$1.00 \times 10^4 \text{ g water} \times \dfrac{55 \text{ g } MgCO_3}{10^6 \text{ g water}} \times \dfrac{1 \text{ mol } MgCO_3}{84.32 \text{ g } MgCO_3} \times \dfrac{1 \text{ mol } Mg^{2+}}{1 \text{ mol } MgCO_3} = 0.0065228 \text{ mol } Mg^{2+}$ so the ions

remaining in solution after 90.0% precipitate out $= (0.100)(\text{mol } Ca^{2+} + \text{mol } Mg^{2+})$

$= (0.100)(0.0074933 \text{ mol } Ca^{2+} + 0.0065228 \text{ mol } Mg^{2+}) = 0.00140161 \text{ mol ions}$

so $\dfrac{0.00140161 \text{ mol } Mg^{2+}}{10.0 \text{ L}} = 0.000140161 \text{ mol L}^{-1} Mg^{2+}$. Then $K_{sp} = 6.82 \times 10^{-6}$, $A = Mg^{2+}$, $m = 1$, $X = CO_3^{2-}$, and

$n = 1$, so $K_{sp} = 6.82 \times 10^{-6} = [Mg^{2+}][CO_3^{2-}] = (0.00140161)[CO_3^{2-}]$. Rearrange to solve for $[CO_3^{2-}]$.

So $[CO_3^{2-}] = 0.0486583 \text{ mol L}^{-1}$. Then

$\dfrac{0.0486583 \text{ mol } CO_3^{2-}}{1 \text{ L}} \times 10.0 \text{ L} \times \dfrac{1 \text{ mol } Na_2CO_3}{1 \text{ mol } CO_3^{2-}} \times \dfrac{105.99 \text{ g } Na_2CO_3}{1 \text{ mol } Na_2CO_3} = 51.6 \text{ g } Na_2CO_3$.

Check: The units (g) are correct. The mass is reasonable to put in a washing machine load.

16.151   **Given:** excess $Mg(OH)_2$ in 1.00 L of 1.0 mol L^{-1} NH_4Cl has pH = 9.00 **Find:** $K_{sp}(Mg(OH)_2)$
Other: $K_b(NH_3) = 1.76 \times 10^{-5}$
Conceptual Plan: mol L^{-1} NH_4Cl → mol L^{-1} NH_4^+ and K_b → K_a then final pH → $[H_3O^+]$ then

$$NH_4Cl \, (aq) \rightarrow NH_4^+ \, (aq) + Cl^- \, (aq) \qquad K_w = K_a K_b \qquad [H_3O^+] = 10^{-pH}$$

mol L^{-1} NH$_4^+$, mol L^{-1} H$_3$O$^+$, K_a → x. Since x is significant compared to initial mol L^{-1} NH$_4^+$ this is a buffer solution.

ICE Table

The NH$_4^+$ is neutralized with Mg(OH)$_2$. Since Mg(OH)$_2$ (s) $\rightleftharpoons$ Mg^{2+} (aq) + 2 OH$^-$(aq) there are 2 moles of OH$^-$ generated for each mole of Mg(OH)$_2$ dissolved. Thus $\frac{1}{2}$ (x mol OH$^-$) = mol Mg(OH)$_2$ was dissolved in 1.00 L of solution. Since there is 1.00 L solution mol Mg(OH)$_2$ = [Mg^{2+}] and [H$_3$O$^+$] → [OH$^-$].

$$K_w = [H_3O^+][OH^-]$$

Finally, write an expression for K_{sp} (Mg(OH)$_2$) and substitute in values for [Mg^{2+}] and [OH$^-$].

Solution: Since 1 NH$_4^+$ ion is generated for each NH$_4$Cl, [NH$_4^+$] = 1.0 mol L^{-1} NH$_4^+$. Since $K_w = K_a K_b$, rearrange to solve for K_a. $K_a = \dfrac{K_w}{K_b} = \dfrac{1.0 \times 10^{-14}}{1.76 \times 10^{-5}} = 5.\underline{6}818 \times 10^{-10}$. Final pH = 9.00, so

[H$_3$O$^+$] = 10^{-pH} = $10^{-9.00}$ = 1.0 × 10^{-9} mol L^{-1}. Set up an ICE Table:

NH$_4^+$ (aq) + H$_2$O (l) $\rightleftharpoons$ H$_3$O$^+$ (aq) + NH$_3$ (aq)

	[NH$_4^+$]	[H$_3$O$^+$]	[NH$_3$]
I	1.0	≈0	0
C	−x	+x	+x
E	1.0 − x	1 × 10^{-9}	x

$$K_a = \frac{[H_3O^+][NH_3]}{[NH_4^+]} = 5.\underline{6}818 \times 10^{-10} = \frac{(1.0 \times 10^{-9})x}{1.0 - x}.$$

Solve for x. $5.\underline{6}818 \times 10^{-10} (1.0 - x) = (1.0 \times 10^{-9})x$ → $5.\underline{6}818 \times 10^{-10} = (1.0 \times 10^{-9} + 5.\underline{6}818 \times 10^{-10})x$ → $x = 0.3\underline{6}2318$, so this is a buffer solution. Since there is 1.00 L of solution, 0.362318 mol of NH$_4^+$ is neutralized with Mg(OH)$_2$. Since Mg(OH)$_2$ (s) $\rightleftharpoons$ Mg^{2+} (aq) + 2 OH$^-$ (aq) there are 2 moles of OH$^-$ generated for each mole of Mg(OH)$_2$ dissolved. Thus $\frac{1}{2}$ (0.3\underline{6}2318 mol OH$^-$) = 0.1\underline{8}1159 mol Mg(OH)$_2$ was dissolved in 1.00 L of solution. Thus the [Mg^{2+}] = 0.1\underline{8}1159 mol L^{-1}. Since K_w = [H$_3$O$^+$][OH$^-$] so

$$[OH^-] = \frac{K_w}{[H_3O^+]} = \frac{1.0 \times 10^{-14}}{1.0 \times 10^{-9}} = 1.0 \times 10^{-5} \text{ mol L}^{-1} \text{ then}$$

K_{sp} (Mg(OH)$_2$) = [Mg^{2+}][OH$^-$]^2 = (0.1\underline{8}1159)(1.0 × 10^{-5})^2 = 1.8 × 10^{-11}.

Check: The units (none) are correct. The magnitude of the answer makes physical sense because the concentration of NH$_4$Cl is high and so it took a significant amount of Mg(OH)$_2$ to raise the pH to 9.00. Note that this number disagrees with the accepted value for the K_{sp} (Mg(OH)$_2$). This is most likely due to errors in the measurements in this experiment.

16.153 (a) **Given:** Au(OH)$_3$ in pure water **Find:** molar solubility (S) **Other:** K_{sp} = 5.5 × 10^{-46}

Conceptual Plan: Use equations derived in Problems 20 and 21 and solve for S. Then

for ionic compound, A$_m$X$_n$, K_{sp} = [A^{n+}]^m [X^{m-}]^n = m^m n^n S^{m+n}.

check answer for validity.

Solution: For Au(OH)$_3$, K_{sp} = 5.5 × 10^{-46}, A = Au^{3+}, m = 1, X = OH$^-$, and n = 3 so K_{sp} = [Au^{3+}][OH$^-$]^3

= 5.5 × 10^{-46} = 3^3S^4. Rearrange to solve for S. $S = \sqrt[4]{\dfrac{5.5 \times 10^{-46}}{27}} = 2.1 \times 10^{-12}$ mol L^{-1}. This answer

suggests that the [OH$^-$] = 3(2.1 × 10^{-12} mol L^{-1}) = 6.3 × 10^{-12} mol L^{-1}. This result is lower than found in pure water (1.0 × 10^{-7} mol L^{-1}), so substitute this value for [OH$^-$] and solve for S = [Au^{3+}]. So K_{sp} = [Au^{3+}][OH$^-$]^3 = 5.5 × 10^{-46} = S (1.0 × 10^{-7} mol L^{-1})^3 and solving for S gives S = 5.5 × 10^{-25} mol L^{-1}.

Check: The units (mol L^{-1}) are correct. Since K_{sp} is so small the autoionization of water must be considered and the solubility is smaller than normally anticipated.

(b) **Given:** Au(OH)$_3$ in 1.0 mol L^{-1} HNO$_3$ **Find:** molar solubility (S) **Other:** K_{sp} = 5.5 × 10^{-46}

Conceptual Plan: Since HNO$_3$ is a strong acid, it will neutralize the gold(III) hydroxide (through the reaction of H$^+$ with OH$^-$ to form water (the reverse of the autoionization of water equilibrium). Write balanced equations for dissolving the solid and for the neutralization reaction. Add these two reactions to get the desired overall reaction. Using the rules from Chapter 14, multiply the individual reaction Ks to get the overall K for the sum of these reactions. then mol L^{-1} HNO$_3$, K → S.

ICE Table

Solution: Identify the solid as $Au(OH)_3$. Write the individual reactions and add them together.

$Au(OH)_3$ (s) $\rightleftharpoons$ Au^{3+} (aq) + $3 \overline{OH^-}$ $\overline{(aq)}$ $K_{sp} = 5.5 \times 10^{-46}$

$\underline{3 H^+ (aq) + 3 \overline{OH^-} \overline{(aq)} \rightleftharpoons 3 H_2O (l)}$ $\left(\dfrac{1}{K_w}\right)^3 = \left(\dfrac{1}{1.0 \times 10^{-14}}\right)^3$

$Au(OH)_3$ (s) + $3 H^+$ (aq) $\rightleftharpoons$ Au^{3+} (aq) + $3 H_2O$ (l)

Since the overall reaction is the sum of the dissolution reaction and three times the reverse of the autoionization of water reaction, the overall reaction

$K = K_{sp}\left(\dfrac{1}{K_w}\right)^3 = (5.5 \times 10^{-46})\left(\dfrac{1}{1.0 \times 10^{-14}}\right)^3 = 5.5 \times 10^{-4} = \dfrac{[Au^{3+}]}{[H^+]^3}$ then since HNO_3 is a strong

acid, it will completely dissociate to H^+ and NO_3^-. Set up an ICE table.

$Au(OH)_3$ (s) + $3 H^+$ (aq) $\rightleftharpoons$ Au^{3+} (aq) + $3 H_2O$ (l)

	$[H^+]$	$[Au^{3+}]$
I	1.0	0
C	$-3S$	$+S$
E	$1.0 - 3S$	S

$K = \dfrac{[Au^{3+}]}{[H^+]^3} = 5.5 \times 10^{-4} = \dfrac{S}{(1.0 - 3S)^3}.$

Assume S is small ($3S << 1.0$) so $\dfrac{S}{(1.0 - 3\cancel{S})^3} = 5.5 \times 10^{-4} \text{ mol L}^{-1} = \dfrac{S}{(1.0)^3} = S.$ Confirm that the

assumption is valid. $\dfrac{3(5.5 \times 10^{-4})}{1.0}$ x 100% = 0.017% $\ll$ 5%, so the assumption is valid.

Check: The units (mol L^{-1}) are correct. K is much larger than the original K_{sp} so the solubility of $Au(OH)_3$ increases over that of pure water.

16.155   **Given:** 1.00 L of 0.100 mol L^{-1} $MgCO_3$ **Find:** volume of 0.100 mol L^{-1} Na_2CO_3 to precipitate 99% of Mg^{2+} ions   **Other:** K_{sp} ($MgCO_3$) = 6.82 x 10^{-6}
Conceptual Plan:
Since 99% of the Mg^{2+} ions are to be precipitated, there will be 1% of the ions left in solution.
$$(0.01)(0.100 \text{ mol L}^{-1} Mg^{2+})$$
Let x = required volume (in L). Calculate the amount of CO_3^{2-} added and the amount of Mg^{2+} that does not precipitate and remains in solution. Use these to calculate the $[Mg^{2+}]$ and $[CO_3^{2-}]$. The solubility product constant (K_{sp}) is the equilibrium expression for a chemical equation representing the dissolution of an ionic compound. The expression of the solubility product constant of A_mX_n is $K_{sp} = [A^{n+}]^m [X^{m-}]^n$. Substitute these expressions in this equation to $[Mg^{2+}], [CO_3^{2-}], K_{sp} \rightarrow x$
$$\text{for ionic compound, } A_mX_n, \ K_{sp} = [A^{n+}]^m [X^{m-}]^n.$$
Solution: Since 99% of the Mg^{2+} ions are to be precipitated, there will be 1% of the ions left in solution or $(0.01)(0.100 \text{ mol L}^{-1} Mg^{2+}) = 0.001 \text{ mol L}^{-1} Mg^{2+}$. Let x = required volume (in L). The volume of the solution after precipitation is $(1.00 + x)$. The amount of CO_3^{2-} added = $(0.100 \text{ mol L}^{-1})(x \text{ L}) = 0.100x$ mol CO_3^{2-}. The amount of Mg^{2+} that does not precipitate and remains in solution is $(0.100 \text{ mol L}^{-1})(1.00 \text{ L})(0.001)$ = 1.00×10^{-3} mol and the amount that precipitates = 0.099 mol, which is also equal to the amount of CO_3^{2-} used. The amount of CO_3^{2-} remaining in solution is $(0.10x - 0.099)$. Thus, $[Mg^{2+}] = 1.00 \times 10^{-3} \text{ mol}/(1.00 + x)$ L and $[CO_3^{2-}] = (0.10x - 0.099) \text{ mol}/(1.00 + x)$ L. Then $K_{sp} = 6.82 \times 10^{-6}$, A = Mg^{2+}, m = 1, X = CO_3^{2-}, and

$n = 1$, so $K_{sp} = 6.82 \times 10^{-6} = [Mg^{2+}] [CO_3^{2-}] = \dfrac{(1.00 \times 10^{-3})(0.10x - 0.099)}{(1.00 + x)^2}$. Rearrange to solve for x.

$1.00 + 2.00x + x^2 = \dfrac{1.0 \times 10^{-4}x - 9.9 \times 10^{-5}}{6.82 \times 10^{-6}} \rightarrow 0 = x^2 - 12.6628x + 15.4526$. Using quadratic equation,

$x = 1.\underline{3}68$ L = 1.4 L

Check: The units (L) are correct. The necessary concentration is very low, so the volume is fairly large.

16.157   **Given:** 1.0 L solution with 0.10 mol L^{-1} Ba(OH)$_2$ and excess Zn(OH)$_2$ **Find:** pH
Other: K_{sp} (Zn(OH)$_2$) = 3 x 10^{-15}, K_f (Zn(OH)$_4{}^{2-}$) = 2 x 10^{15}
Conceptual Plan: Since [Ba(OH)$_2$] = 0.10 mol L^{-1} then [OH$^-$] = 0.20 mol L^{-1}. **Write balanced equations for the solubility of Zn(OH)$_2$ and reaction with excess OH$^-$ and expressions for K_{sp} and K_f. Use initial concentrations to set up an ICE table. Solve for [OH$^-$] at equilibrium. Then [OH$^-$] $\rightarrow$ [H$_3$O$^+$] $\rightarrow$ pH.**

$$K_w = [H_3O^+][OH^-] \quad pH = -\log[H_3O^+]$$

Solution: Write two reactions and combine.

$$Zn(OH)_2(s) \rightleftharpoons Zn^{2+}(aq) + 2\,OH^-(aq) \quad \text{with} \quad K_{sp} = [Zn^{2+}][OH^-]^2 = 3 \times 10^{-15}$$

$$Zn^{2+}(aq) + 42\,OH^-(aq) \rightleftharpoons Zn(OH)_4{}^{2-}(aq) \quad \text{with } K_f = \frac{[Zn(OH)_4{}^{2-}]}{[Zn^{2+}][OH^-]^4} = 2 \times 10^{15}$$

$$Zn(OH)_2(s) + 2\,OH^-(aq) \rightleftharpoons Zn(OH)_4{}^{2-}(aq)$$

$$\text{with } K = K_{sp}\,K_f = [Zn^{2+}][OH^-]^2\frac{[Zn(OH)_4{}^{2-}]}{[Zn^{2+}][OH^-]^2} = (3 \times 10^{-15})(2 \times 10^{15})$$

$$K = \frac{[Zn(OH)_4{}^{2-}]}{[OH^-]^2} = 6. \text{ Set up an ICE table with initial concentration and solve for } x.$$

$$Zn(OH)_2(s) + 2\,OH^-(aq) \rightleftharpoons Zn(OH)_4{}^{2-}(aq)$$

	[OH$^-$]	[Zn(OH)$_4{}^{2-}$]
I	0.20	0
C	$-2x$	$+x$
E	$0.20 - 2x$	x

$$K = \frac{[Zn(OH)_4{}^{2-}]}{[OH^-]^2} = \frac{x}{(0.20 - 2x)^2} = 6$$

$x = 6(0.20 - 2x)^2 \rightarrow x = 6(4x^2 - 0.80x + 0.040) \rightarrow x = 24x^2 - 4.8x + 0.24 \rightarrow$

$0 = 24x^2 - 5.8x + 0.24$ Using quadratic equation, $x = 0.0530049 \rightarrow$

So [OH$^-$] = 0.20 - 2x = 0.20 - 2(0.0530049) = 0.093990 mol L^{-1} OH$^-$. then $K_w = [H_3O^+][OH^-]$ so

$$[H_3O^+] = \frac{K_w}{[OH^-]} = \frac{1.0 \times 10^{-14}}{0.093990} = 1.06394 \times 10^{-13} \text{ mol L}^{-1}. \text{ Finally,}$$

$$pH = -\log[H_3O^+] = -\log(1.06394 \times 10^{-13}) = 12.97.$$

Check: The units (none) are correct. Since the pH of the solution before the addition of the Zn(OH)$_2$ is 13.30, the reaction decreases the [OH$^-$] and the pH drops.

Conceptual Problems

16.159   If the concentration of the acid is greater than the concentration of the base, then the pH will be less than the pK_a. If the concentration of the acid is equal to the concentration of the base, then the pH will be equal to the pK_a. If the concentration of the acid is less than the concentration of the base, then the pH will be greater than the pK_a.

(a)   pH < pK_a

(b)   pH > pK_a

(c)   pH = pK_a, the OH$^-$ will convert half of the acid to base

(d)   pH > pK_a, the OH$^-$ will convert more than half of the acid to base

16.161   Only (b) is correct. The volume to the first equivalence point will be the same since the number of moles of acid is the same. The pH profiles of the three titrations will be different.

16.163   (a)   The solubility will be unchanged since the pH is constant and there are no common ions added.

(b)   The solubility will be less because extra fluoride ions are added, suppressing the solubility of the fluoride ionic compound.

(c)   The solubility will increase because some of the fluoride ion will be converted to HF, and so more of the ionic compound can be dissolved.

17 Gibbs Energy and Thermodynamics

Review Questions

17.1 A perpetual motion machine is a machine that perpetually moves without any energy input. This machine is not possible because if the machine is to be in motion, energy will be used or lost. Over time, if there is no energy input, the machine will run down and stop moving.

17.3 In thermodynamics, the spontaneity of a reaction is the direction in which and extent to which a chemical reaction proceeds. Kinetics is the speed of the reaction—how fast a reaction takes place. A reaction may be thermodynamically spontaneous, but kinetically slow at a given temperature. For example, the conversion of diamond to graphite is thermodynamically spontaneous. But your diamonds will not become worthless anytime soon because the process is extremely slow kinetically. Although the rate of a spontaneous process can be increased by the use of a catalyst, a nonspontaneous process cannot be made spontaneous by the use of a catalyst. Catalysts affect only the rate of a reaction, not the spontaneity.

17.5 The entropy of a gas increases when it expands into a vacuum because the number of possible states increases (such as where the particle is located).

17.7 The entropy of a state is proportional to the number of energetically equivalent ways to arrange the components of the system to achieve a particular state. This implies the state with the highest entropy also has the greatest dispersal of energy.

17.9 The entropy of a sample of matter increases as it changes state from a solid to a liquid and then to a gas, because the amount of molecular motion and the amount of thermal energy is the greatest in the gas phase and is least in the solid phase.

17.11 The change in Gibbs energy for a process is proportional to the negative of ΔS_{univ}. Since ΔS_{univ} is a criterion for spontaneity, $\Delta_r G$ is also a criterion for spontaneity (although opposite in sign).

17.13 The third law of thermodynamics states that the entropy of a perfect crystal at absolute zero (0 K) is zero. For enthalpy we defined a standard state so that we could define a "zero" for the scale. This is not necessary for entropy because there is an absolute zero.

17.15 The larger the molar mass, the greater the entropy at 25 °C. For a given state of matter, entropy generally increases with increasing molecular complexity.

17.17 The three ways of calculating the $\Delta_r G°$ are to
- use tabulated values of standard enthalpies of formation to calculate $\Delta_r H°$ and use tabulated values of standard entropies to calculate $\Delta_r S°$; then use the values of $\Delta_r H°$ and $\Delta_r S°$ calculated in these ways to calculate the standard Gibbs energy change for a reaction by using the equation $\Delta_r G° = \Delta_r H° - T\Delta_r S°$.
- use tabulated values of the standard Gibbs energies of formation to calculate $\Delta_r G°$ using an equation similar to that used for standard enthalpy of a reaction: $\Delta_r G° = \sum n_p \Delta_f G°(\text{products}) - \sum n_r \Delta_f G°(\text{reactants})$.

- use a reaction pathway or stepwise reaction to sum the changes in Gibbs energy for each of the steps in a manner similar to that used in Chapter 6 for enthalpy of stepwise reactions.

The method to calculate the Gibbs energy of a reaction at temperatures other than at 25 °C is the first method. The second method is only applicable at 25 °C. The third method is only applicable at the temperature of the individual reactions, generally 25 °C.

17.19   The standard free energy change for a reaction ($\Delta_rG°$) applies only to standard conditions. For a gas, standard conditions are those in which the pure gas is present at a partial pressure of 1 bar. For nonstandard conditions, we need to calculate Δ_rG (not $\Delta_rG°$) to predict spontaneity.

17.21   The Gibbs energy of reaction under nonstandard conditions (Δ_rG) can be calculated from $\Delta_rG°$ using the relationship $\Delta_rG = \Delta_rG° + RT \ln Q$, where Q is the reaction quotient (defined in Section 14.6), T is the temperature in K, and R is the gas constant in the appropriate units (8.314 J K^{-1} mol^{-1}).

Problems by Topic

Entropy, the Second Law of Thermodynamics, and the Direction of Spontaneous Change

17.23   (a) and (c) are spontaneous processes.

17.25   System B has the greatest entropy. There is only one energetically equivalent arrangement for System A. However, the particles of System B may exchange positions for a second energetically equivalent arrangement.

17.27   (a) $\Delta S_{sys} > 0$ because a gas is being generated.

   (b) $\Delta S_{sys} < 0$ because 2 moles of gas are being converted to 1 mole of gas.

   (c) $\Delta S_{sys} < 0$ because a gas is being converted to a solid.

   (d) $\Delta S_{sys} < 0$ because 4 moles of gas are being converted to 2 moles of gas.

17.29   (a) $\Delta S_{sys} > 0$, because 6 moles of gas are being converted to 7 moles of gas. Since $\Delta_rH° < 0$ and $\Delta S_{surr} > 0$, the reaction is spontaneous at all temperatures.

   (b) $\Delta S_{sys} < 0$ because 2 moles of different gases are being converted to 2 moles of one gas. Since $\Delta_rH° > 0$ and $\Delta S_{surr} < 0$, the reaction is nonspontaneous at all temperatures.

   (c) $\Delta S_{sys} < 0$, because 3 moles of gas are being converted to 2 moles of gas. Since $\Delta_rH° > 0$ and $\Delta S_{surr} < 0$, the reaction is nonspontaneous at all temperatures.

   (d) $\Delta S_{sys} > 0$, because 9 moles of gas are being converted to 10 moles of gas. Since $\Delta_rH° < 0$ and $\Delta S_{surr} > 0$, the reaction is spontaneous at all temperatures.

17.31   (a)   **Given:** $\Delta_rH° = -385$ kJ mol^{-1}, $T = 298$ K **Find:** ΔS_{surr}
   Conceptual Plan: kJ $\rightarrow$ J then $\Delta_rH°$, $T \rightarrow \Delta S_{surr}$

$$\frac{1000 \text{ J}}{1 \text{ kJ}} \qquad \Delta S_{surr} = \frac{-\Delta H_{sys}}{T}$$

   Solution: -385 kJ mol$^{-1} \times \dfrac{1000 \text{ J}}{1 \text{ kJ}} = -385\,000$ J mol^{-1} then

$$\Delta S_{surr} = \frac{-\Delta H_{sys}}{T} = \frac{-(-385\,000 \text{ J mol}^{-1})}{298 \text{ K}} = 1290 \text{ J K}^{-1} \text{ mol}^{-1} = 1.29 \times 10^3 \text{ J K}^{-1} \text{ mol}^{-1}$$

   Check: The units (J K^{-1} mol^{-1}) are correct. The magnitude of the answer (10^3 J K^{-1} mol^{-1}) makes sense because the kJ mol^{-1} and the temperature started with very similar values and then a factor of 10^3 was applied.

   (b)   **Given:** $\Delta_rH° = -385$ kJ mol^{-1}, $T = 77$ K **Find:** ΔS_{surr}
   Conceptual Plan: kJ $\rightarrow$ J then $\Delta_rH°$, $T \rightarrow \Delta S_{surr}$

$$\frac{1000 \text{ J}}{1 \text{ kJ}} \qquad \Delta S_{surr} = \frac{-\Delta H_{sys}}{T}$$

Solution: $-385 \text{ kJ mol}^{-1} \times \dfrac{1000 \text{ J}}{1 \text{ kJ}} = -385\,000 \text{ J mol}^{-1}$ then

$$\Delta S_{surr} = \dfrac{-\Delta H_{sys}}{T} = \dfrac{-(-385\,000 \text{ J mol}^{-1})}{77 \text{ K}} = 5.00 \times 10^3 \text{ J K}^{-1} \text{ mol}^{-1}$$

Check: The units ($\text{J K}^{-1} \text{ mol}^{-1}$) are correct. The magnitude of the answer ($5 \times 10^3 \text{ J K}^{-1} \text{ mol}^{-1}$) makes sense because the temperature is much lower than in part (a), so the answer should increase.

(c) **Given:** $\Delta_r H° = +114 \text{ kJ mol}^{-1}$, $T = 298 \text{ K}$ **Find:** ΔS_{surr}
Conceptual Plan: kJ $\rightarrow$ J then $\Delta_r H°, T \rightarrow \Delta S_{surr}$
$$\dfrac{1000 \text{ J}}{1 \text{ kJ}} \qquad\qquad \Delta S_{surr} = \dfrac{-\Delta H_{sys}}{T}$$

Solution: $+114 \text{ kJ mol}^{-1} \times \dfrac{1000 \text{ J}}{1 \text{ kJ}} = +114\,000 \text{ J mol}^{-1}$ then

$$\Delta S_{surr} = \dfrac{-\Delta H_{sys}}{T} = \dfrac{-114\,000 \text{ J mol}^{-1}}{298 \text{ K}} = -383 \text{ J K}^{-1} \text{ mol}^{-1}$$

Check: The units ($\text{J K}^{-1} \text{ mol}^{-1}$) are correct. The magnitude of the answer ($-400 \text{ J K}^{-1} \text{ mol}^{-1}$) makes sense because the kJ mol^{-1} are less and of the opposite sign than part (a), so the answer should decrease.

(d) **Given:** $\Delta_r H° = +114 \text{ kJ mol}^{-1}$, $T = 77 \text{ K}$ **Find:** ΔS_{surr}
Conceptual Plan: kJ $\rightarrow$ J then $\Delta_r H°, T \rightarrow \Delta S_{surr}$
$$\dfrac{1000 \text{ J}}{1 \text{ kJ}} \qquad\qquad \Delta S_{surr} = \dfrac{-\Delta H_{sys}}{T}$$

Solution: $+114 \text{ kJ mol}^{-1} \times \dfrac{1000 \text{ J}}{1 \text{ kJ}} = +114\,000 \text{ J mol}^{-1}$ then

$$\Delta S_{surr} = \dfrac{-\Delta H_{sys}}{T} = \dfrac{-114\,000 \text{ J mol}^{-1}}{77 \text{ K}} = -1480 \text{ J K}^{-1} \text{ mol}^{-1} = -1.48 \times 10^3 \text{ J K}^{-1} \text{ mol}^{-1}$$

Check: The units ($\text{J K}^{-1} \text{ mol}^{-1}$) are correct. The magnitude of the answer ($-2 \times 10^3 \text{ J K}^{-1} \text{ mol}^{-1}$) makes sense because the temperature is much lower than in part (c), so the answer should increase.

17.33 (a) **Given:** $\Delta_r H° = +115 \text{ kJ mol}^{-1}$, $\Delta_r S° = -263 \text{ J K}^{-1} \text{ mol}^{-1}$, $T = 298 \text{ K}$ **Find:** ΔS_{univ} and spontaneity
Conceptual Plan: kJ $\rightarrow$ J then $\Delta_r H°, T \rightarrow \Delta S_{surr}$ then $\Delta_r S°, \Delta S_{surr} \rightarrow \Delta S_{univ}$
$$\dfrac{1000 \text{ J}}{1 \text{ kJ}} \qquad\qquad \Delta S_{surr} = \dfrac{-\Delta H_{sys}}{T} \qquad\qquad \Delta S_{univ} = \Delta S_{sys} + \Delta S_{surr}$$

Solution: $115 \text{ kJ mol}^{-1} \times \dfrac{1000 \text{ J}}{1 \text{ kJ}} = 115\,000 \text{ J mol}^{-1}$ then

$$\Delta S_{surr} = \dfrac{-\Delta H_{sys}}{T} = \dfrac{-(115\,000 \text{ J mol}^{-1})}{298 \text{ K}} = -385.906 \text{ J K}^{-1} \text{ mol}^{-1} \text{ then } \Delta S_{univ} = \Delta S_{sys} + \Delta S_{surr}$$

$= -263 \text{ J K}^{-1} \text{ mol}^{-1} - 385.906 \text{ J K}^{-1} \text{ mol}^{-1} = -649 \text{ J K}^{-1} \text{ mol}^{-1}$ so the reaction is nonspontaneous.
Check: The units ($\text{J K}^{-1} \text{ mol}^{-1}$) are correct. The magnitude of the answer ($-650 \text{ J K}^{-1} \text{ mol}^{-1}$) makes sense because both terms were negative, so the reaction is nonspontaneous.

(b) **Given:** $\Delta_r H° = -115 \text{ kJ mol}^{-1}$, $\Delta_r S° = +263 \text{ J K}^{-1} \text{ mol}^{-1}$, $T = 298 \text{ K}$ **Find:** ΔS_{univ} and spontaneity
Conceptual Plan: kJ $\rightarrow$ J then $\Delta_r H°, T \rightarrow \Delta S_{surr}$ then $\Delta_r S°, \Delta S_{surr} \rightarrow \Delta S_{univ}$
$$\dfrac{1000 \text{ J}}{1 \text{ kJ}} \qquad\qquad \Delta S_{surr} = \dfrac{-\Delta H_{sys}}{T} \qquad\qquad \Delta S_{univ} = \Delta S_{sys} + \Delta S_{surr}$$

Solution: $-115 \text{ kJ mol}^{-1} \times \dfrac{1000 \text{ J}}{1 \text{ kJ}} = -115\,000 \text{ J mol}^{-1}$ then

$$\Delta S_{surr} = \dfrac{-\Delta H_{sys}}{T} = \dfrac{-(-115\,000 \text{ J mol}^{-1})}{298 \text{ K}} = 385.906 \text{ J K}^{-1} \text{ mol}^{-1} \text{ then } \Delta S_{univ} = \Delta S_{sys} + \Delta S_{surr}$$

$= +263 \text{ J K}^{-1} \text{ mol}^{-1} + 385.906 \text{ J K}^{-1} \text{ mol}^{-1} = +649 \text{ J K}^{-1} \text{ mol}^{-1}$ so the reaction is spontaneous.
Check: The units ($\text{J K}^{-1} \text{ mol}^{-1}$) are correct. The magnitude of the answer ($+650 \text{ J K}^{-1} \text{ mol}^{-1}$) makes sense because both terms were positive, so the reaction is spontaneous.

(c)   **Given:** $\Delta_r H° = -115$ kJ mol^{-1}, $\Delta_r S° = -263$ J K^{-1} mol^{-1}, $T = 298$ K   **Find:** ΔS_{univ} and spontaneity

Conceptual Plan: kJ $\rightarrow$ **J then** $\Delta_r H°$, T $\rightarrow$ ΔS_{surr} **then** $\Delta_r S°$, ΔS_{surr} $\rightarrow$ ΔS_{univ}

$$\frac{1000\ \text{J}}{1\ \text{kJ}} \qquad\qquad \Delta S_{surr} = \frac{-\Delta H_{sys}}{T} \qquad\qquad \Delta S_{univ} = \Delta S_{sys} + \Delta S_{surr}$$

Solution: -115 kJ mol^{-1} $\times \dfrac{1000\ \text{J}}{1\ \text{kJ}} = -115\,000$ J mol^{-1} then

$$\Delta S_{surr} = \frac{-\Delta H_{sys}}{T} = \frac{-(-115\,000\ \text{J mol}^{-1})}{298\ \text{K}} = +385.906\ \text{J K}^{-1}\ \text{mol}^{-1}$$

then $\Delta S_{univ} = \Delta S_{sys} + \Delta S_{surr} = -263$ J K^{-1} mol^{-1} + 385.906 J K^{-1} mol^{-1} = $+123$ J K^{-1} mol^{-1} so the reaction is spontaneous.

Check: The units (J K^{-1} mol^{-1}) are correct. The magnitude of the answer (120 J K^{-1} mol^{-1}) makes sense because the larger term was positive, so the reaction is spontaneous.

(d)   **Given:** $\Delta_r H° = -115$ kJ mol^{-1}, $\Delta_r S° = -263$ J K^{-1} mol^{-1}, $T = 615$ K   **Find:** ΔS_{univ} and spontaneity

Conceptual Plan: kJ $\rightarrow$ **J then** $\Delta_r H°$, T $\rightarrow$ ΔS_{surr} **then** $\Delta_r S°$, ΔS_{surr} $\rightarrow$ ΔS_{univ}

$$\frac{1000\ \text{J}}{1\ \text{kJ}} \qquad\qquad \Delta S_{surr} = \frac{-\Delta H_{sys}}{T} \qquad\qquad \Delta S_{univ} = \Delta S_{sys} + \Delta S_{surr}$$

Solution: -115 kJ mol^{-1} $\times \dfrac{1000\ \text{J}}{1\ \text{kJ}} = -115\,000$ J mol^{-1} then

$$\Delta S_{surr} = \frac{-\Delta H_{sys}}{T} = \frac{-(-115\,000\ \text{J mol}^{-1})}{615\ \text{K}} = +186.992\ \text{J K}^{-1}\ \text{mol}^{-1}\ \text{then}$$

$\Delta S_{univ} = \Delta S_{sys} + \Delta S_{surr} = -263$ J K^{-1} mol^{-1} + 186.992 J K^{-1} mol^{-1} = -76 J K^{-1} mol^{-1} so the reaction is nonspontaneous.

Check: The units (J K^{-1} mol^{-1}) are correct. The magnitude of the answer (-80 J K^{-1} mol^{-1}) makes sense because the larger term was negative, so the reaction is nonspontaneous.

17.35   **Given:** $\Delta_r H = +40.65$ kJ mol^{-1}, $T = 100$ °C   **Find:** $\Delta_r S$ for vaporization of water.

Conceptual Plan: kJ $\rightarrow$ **J and °C** $\rightarrow$ **K, then** $\Delta_r H$, T $\rightarrow$ $\Delta_r S$

$$\frac{1000\ \text{J}}{1\ \text{kJ}} \qquad \text{K} = °\text{C} + 273.15 \qquad \Delta_r S = \frac{\Delta_r H}{T}$$

Solution: 40.65 kJ mol^{-1} $\times \dfrac{1000\ \text{J}}{1\ \text{kJ}} = 4.065 \times 10^4$ J mol^{-1} then $T = 100 + 273.15 = 373.15$ K

$$\Delta_r S = \frac{\Delta_r H}{T} = \frac{4.065 \times 10^4\ \text{J mol}^{-1}}{373.15\ \text{K}} = 108.9\ \text{J K}^{-1}\ \text{mol}^{-1}$$

Check: The units (J K^{-1} mol^{-1}) are correct. The entropy is positive because we are converting a liquid to a gas.

Standard Entropy Changes and Gibbs Energy

17.37   (a)   **Given:** $\Delta_r H° = +115$ kJ mol^{-1}, $\Delta_r S° = -263$ J K^{-1} mol^{-1}, $T = 298$ K   **Find:** $\Delta_r G°$ and spontaneity

Conceptual Plan: J K^{-1} mol^{-1} $\rightarrow$ **kJ K^{-1} mol^{-1} then** $\Delta_r H°$, $\Delta_r S°$, T $\rightarrow$ $\Delta_r G°$

$$\frac{1000\ \text{J}}{1\ \text{kJ}} \qquad\qquad \Delta_r G° = \Delta_r H° - T\Delta_r S°$$

Solution: -263 J K^{-1} mol^{-1} $\times \dfrac{1\ \text{kJ}}{1000\ \text{J}} = -0.263$ kJ K^{-1} mol^{-1} then

$\Delta_r G° = \Delta_r H° - T\Delta_r S° = +115$ kJ mol^{-1} $- (298\ \text{K})(-0.263$ kJ K^{-1} mol$^{-1})$

$= +1.93 \times 10^2$ kJ mol^{-1} = $+1.93 \times 10^5$ J mol^{-1} so the reaction is nonspontaneous.

Check: The units (kJ mol^{-1}) are correct. The magnitude of the answer ($+190$ kJ mol^{-1}) makes sense because both terms were positive, so the reaction is nonspontaneous.

(b)   **Given:** $\Delta_r H° = -115$ kJ mol^{-1}, $\Delta_r S° = +263$ J K^{-1} mol^{-1}, $T = 298$ K   **Find:** $\Delta_r G°$ and spontaneity

Conceptual Plan: J K^{-1} mol^{-1} $\rightarrow$ **kJ K^{-1} mol^{-1} then** $\Delta_r H°$, $\Delta_r S°$, T $\rightarrow$ $\Delta_r G°$

$$\frac{1000\ \text{J}}{1\ \text{kJ}} \qquad\qquad \Delta_r G° = \Delta_r H° - T\Delta_r S°$$

Solution: $+263$ J K^{-1} mol^{-1} x $\dfrac{1\ kJ}{1000\ J}$ $= +0.263$ kJ K^{-1} mol^{-1} then

$\Delta_r G° = \Delta_r H° - T\Delta_r S° = -115$ kJ mol^{-1} $- (298\ K)(0.263$ kJ K^{-1} mol$^{-1})$ $= -193$ kJ mol^{-1}

$= -1.93 \times 10^2$ kJ mol^{-1} $= -1.93 \times 10^5$ J mol^{-1} so the reaction is spontaneous.

Check: The units (kJ mol^{-1}) are correct. The magnitude of the answer (–190 kJ mol^{-1}) makes sense because both terms were negative, so the reaction is spontaneous.

(c) **Given:** $\Delta_r H° = -115$ kJ mol^{-1}, $\Delta_r S° = -263$ J K^{-1} mol^{-1}, $T = 298$ K **Find:** $\Delta_r G°$ and spontaneity

Conceptual Plan: J K^{-1} mol^{-1} $\rightarrow$ kJ K^{-1} mol^{-1} then $\Delta_r H°$, $\Delta_r S°$, $T \rightarrow \Delta_r G°$

$\dfrac{1000\ J}{1\ kJ}$ $\qquad \Delta_r G° = \Delta_r H° - T\Delta_r S°$

Solution: -263 J K^{-1} mol^{-1} x $\dfrac{1\ kJ}{1000\ J}$ $= -0.263$ kJ K^{-1} mol^{-1} then $\Delta_r G° = \Delta_r H° - T\Delta_r S°$

$= -115$ kJ mol^{-1} $- (298\ K)(-0.263$ kJ K^{-1} mol$^{-1})$ $= -36.626$ kJ mol^{-1} $= -3.7 \times 10^1$ kJ mol^{-1}

$= -3.7 \times 10^4$ J mol^{-1} so the reaction is spontaneous.

Check: The units (kJ mol^{-1}) are correct. The magnitude of the answer (–40 kJ mol^{-1}) makes sense because the larger term was negative, so the reaction is spontaneous.

(d) **Given:** $\Delta_r H° = -115$ kJ mol^{-1}, $\Delta_r S° = -263$ J K^{-1} mol^{-1}, $T = 615$ K **Find:** $\Delta_r G°$ and spontaneity

Conceptual Plan: J K^{-1} mol^{-1} $\rightarrow$ kJ K^{-1} mol^{-1} then $\Delta_r H°$, $\Delta_r S°$, $T \rightarrow \Delta_r G°$

$\dfrac{1000\ J}{1\ kJ}$ $\qquad \Delta_r G° = \Delta_r H° - T\Delta_r S°$

Solution: -263 J K^{-1} mol^{-1} x $\dfrac{1\ kJ}{1000\ J}$ $= -0.263$ kJ K^{-1} mol^{-1} then

$\Delta_r G° = \Delta_r H° - T\Delta_r S° = -115$ kJ mol^{-1} $- (615\ K)(-0.263$ kJ K^{-1} mol$^{-1})$ $= +47$ kJ mol^{-1}

$= +4.7 \times 10^4$ J mol^{-1} so the reaction is nonspontaneous.

Check: The units (kJ mol^{-1}) are correct. The magnitude of the answer (+50 kJ mol^{-1}) makes sense because the larger term was positive, so the reaction is nonspontaneous.

17.39 **Given:** $\Delta_r H° = -2217$ kJ mol^{-1}, $\Delta_r S° = +101.1$ J K^{-1} mol^{-1}, $T = 25$ °C **Find:** $\Delta_r G°$ and spontaneity

Conceptual Plan: °C $\rightarrow$ K then J K^{-1} mol^{-1} $\rightarrow$ kJ K^{-1} mol^{-1} then $\Delta_r H°$, $\Delta_r S°$, $T \rightarrow \Delta_r G°$

K = 273.15 + °C $\qquad \dfrac{1\ kJ}{1000\ J}$ $\qquad \Delta_r G° = \Delta_r H° - T\Delta_r S°$

Solution: $T = 273.15 + 25$ °C $= 298$ K then $+101.1$ J K^{-1} mol^{-1} x $\dfrac{1\ kJ}{1000\ J}$ $= +0.1011$ kJ K^{-1} mol^{-1} then

$\Delta_r G° = \Delta_r H° - T\Delta_r S° = -2217$ kJ mol^{-1} $- (298\ K)(0.1011$ kJ K^{-1} mol$^{-1})$ $= -2247$ kJ mol^{-1}

$= -2.247 \times 10^6$ J mol^{-1} so the reaction is spontaneous.

Check: The units (kJ mol^{-1}) are correct. The magnitude of the answer (–2250 kJ mol^{-1}) makes sense because both terms are negative, so the reaction is spontaneous.

17.41

ΔH	ΔS	ΔG	Low Temp.	High Temp.
–	+	–	Spontaneous	Spontaneous
–	–	Temp. dependent	Spontaneous	Nonspontaneous
+	+	Temp. dependent	Nonspontaneous	Spontaneous
+	–	+	Nonspontaneous	Nonspontaneous

17.43 The molar entropy of a substance increases with increasing temperature. The kinetic energy and the molecular motion increases. The substance will have access to an increased number of energy levels.

17.45 (a) CO_2 (g) because it has greater molar mass/complexity.

(b) CH_3OH (g) because it is in the gas phase.

(c) CO_2 (g) because it has greater molar mass/complexity.

(d) SiH_4 (g) because it has greater molar mass.

(e) $CH_3CH_2CH_3$ (g) because it has greater molar mass/complexity.

(f)   NaBr (aq) because a solution has more entropy than a solid crystal.

17.47   (a)   He (g) < Ne (g) < SO_2 (g) < NH_3 (g) < CH_3CH_2OH (g). All are in the gas phase. From He to Ne there is an increase in molar mass; beyond that, the molecules increase in complexity.

(b) H_2O (s) < H_2O (l) < H_2O (g). Entropy increases as we go from a solid to a liquid to a gas.

(c) CH_4 (g) < CF_4 (g) < CCl_4 (g). Entropy increases as the molar mass increases.

17.49   (a)   **Given:** C_2H_4 (g) + H_2 (g) $\rightarrow$ C_2H_6 (g)   **Find:** $\Delta_r S°$
       Conceptual Plan: $\Delta_r S° = \sum n_p S°\text{(products)} - \sum n_r S°\text{(reactants)}$
       Solution:

Reactant/Product	$S°$(J K^{-1} mol^{-1} from Appendix IIB)
C_2H_4 (g)	219.3
H_2 (g)	130.7
C_2H_6 (g)	229.2

Be sure to pull data for the correct formula and phase.

$\Delta_r S° = \sum n_p S°\text{(products)} - \sum n_r S°\text{(reactants)}$
$= [1(S°(C_2H_6 \text{ (g)}))] - [1(S°(C_2H_4 \text{ (g)})) + 1(S°(H_2 \text{ (g)}))]$
$= [1(229.2 \text{ J K}^{-1} \text{ mol}^{-1})] - [1(219.3 \text{ J K}^{-1} \text{ mol}^{-1}) + 1(130.7 \text{ J K}^{-1} \text{ mol}^{-1})]$
$= [229.2 \text{ J K}^{-1} \text{ mol}^{-1}] - [350.0 \text{ J K}^{-1} \text{ mol}^{-1}]$
$= -120.8 \text{ J K}^{-1} \text{ mol}^{-1}$ The moles of gas are decreasing.

Check: The units (J K^{-1} mol^{-1}) are correct. The answer is negative, which is consistent with 2 moles of gas going to 1 mole of gas.

(b)   **Given:** C (s) + H_2O (g) $\rightarrow$ CO (g) + H_2 (g)   **Find:** $\Delta_r S°$
       Conceptual Plan: $\Delta_r S° = \sum n_p S°\text{(products)} - \sum n_r S°\text{(reactants)}$
       Solution:

Reactant/Product	$S°$(J K^{-1} mol^{-1} from Appendix IIB)
C (s)	5.7
H_2O (g)	188.8
CO (g)	197.7
H_2 (g)	130.7

Be sure to pull data for the correct formula and phase.

$\Delta_r S° = \sum n_p S°\text{(products)} - \sum n_r S°\text{(reactants)}$
$= [1(S°(CO \text{ (g)})) + 1(S°(H_2 \text{ (g)}))] - [1(S°(C \text{ (s)})) + 1(S°(H_2O \text{ (g)}))]$
$= [1(197.7 \text{ J K}^{-1} \text{ mol}^{-1}) + 1(130.7 \text{ J K}^{-1} \text{ mol}^{-1})] - [1(5.7 \text{ J K}^{-1} \text{ mol}^{-1}) + 1(188.8 \text{ J K}^{-1} \text{ mol}^{-1})]$
$= [328.4 \text{ J K}^{-1} \text{ mol}^{-1}] - [194.5 \text{ J K}^{-1} \text{ mol}^{-1}]$
$= +133.9 \text{ J K}^{-1} \text{ mol}^{-1}$ The moles of gas are increasing.

Check: The units (J K^{-1} mol^{-1}) are correct. The answer is positive, which is consistent with 1 mole of gas going to 2 moles of gas.

(c)   **Given:** CO (g) + H_2O (g) $\rightarrow$ H_2 (g) + CO_2 (g)   **Find:** $\Delta_r S°$
       Conceptual Plan: $\Delta_r S° = \sum n_p S°\text{(products)} - \sum n_r S°\text{(reactants)}$
       Solution:

Reactant/Product	$S°$(J K^{-1} mol^{-1} from Appendix IIB)
CO (g)	197.7
H_2O (g)	188.8
H_2 (g)	130.7
CO_2 (g)	213.8

Be sure to pull data for the correct formula and phase.

$\Delta_r S° = \sum n_p S°(products) - \sum n_r S°(reactants)$

$= [1(S°(H_2 (g))) + 1(S°(CO_2 (g)))] - [1(S°(CO (g))) + 1(S°(H_2O (g)))]$

$= [1(130.7 \text{ J K}^{-1} \text{ mol}^{-1}) + 1(213.8 \text{ J K}^{-1} \text{ mol}^{-1})] - [1(197.7 \text{ J K}^{-1} \text{ mol}^{-1})$

$+ 1(188.8 \text{ J K}^{-1} \text{ mol}^{-1})]$

$= [344.5 \text{ J K}^{-1} \text{ mol}^{-1}] - [386.5 \text{ J K}^{-1} \text{ mol}^{-1}]$

$= -42.0 \text{ J K}^{-1} \text{ mol}^{-1}$

The change is small because the number of moles of gas is constant.

Check: The units (J K^{-1} mol^{-1}) are correct. The answer is small and negative, which is consistent with a constant number of moles of gas. Water molecules are bent and carbon dioxide molecules are linear, so the water has more complexity. Also, carbon monoxide is more complex than hydrogen gas.

(d)   **Given:** 2 H$_2$S (g) + 3 O$_2$ (g) → 2 H$_2$O (l) + 2 SO$_2$ (g) **Find:** $\Delta_r S°$
      Conceptual Plan: $\Delta_r S° = \sum n_p S°(\textbf{products}) - \sum n_r S°(\textbf{reactants})$
      Solution:

Reactant/Product	$S°$(J K^{-1} mol^{-1} from Appendix IIB)
H$_2$S (g)	205.8
O$_2$ (g)	205.2
H$_2$O (l)	70.0
SO$_2$ (g)	248.2

Be sure to pull data for the correct formula and phase.

$\Delta_r S° = \sum n_p S°(products) - \sum n_r S°(reactants)$

$= [2(S°(H_2O (l))) + 2(S°(SO_2 (g)))] - [2(S°(H_2S (g))) + 3(S°(O_2 (g)))]$

$= [2(70.0 \text{ J K}^{-1} \text{ mol}^{-1}) + 2(248.2 \text{ J K}^{-1} \text{ mol}^{-1})] - [2(205.8 \text{ J K}^{-1} \text{ mol}^{-1})$

$+ 3(205.2 \text{ J K}^{-1} \text{ mol}^{-1})]$

$= [636.4 \text{ J K}^{-1} \text{ mol}^{-1}] - [1027.2 \text{ J K}^{-1} \text{ mol}^{-1}]$

$= -390.8 \text{ J K}^{-1} \text{ mol}^{-1}$

The number of moles of gas is decreasing.

Check: The units (J K^{-1} mol^{-1}) are correct. The answer is negative, which is consistent with a decrease in the number of moles of gas.

17.51   **Given:** CH$_2$Cl$_2$ (g) formed from elements in standard states **Find:** $\Delta_r S°$ and rationalize sign
        Conceptual Plan: Write a balanced reaction, then $\Delta_r S° = \sum n_p S°(\textbf{products}) - \sum n_r S°(\textbf{reactants})$
        Solution: C (s) + H$_2$ (g) + Cl$_2$ (g) → CH$_2$Cl$_2$ (g)

Reactant/Product	$S°$(J K^{-1} mol^{-1} from Appendix IIB)
C (s)	5.7
H$_2$ (g)	130.7
Cl$_2$ (g)	223.1
CH$_2$Cl$_2$ (g)	270.2

Be sure to pull data for the correct formula and phase.

$\Delta_r S° = \sum n_p S°(products) - \sum n_r S°(reactants)$

$= [1(S°(CH_2Cl_2 (g)))] - [1(S°(C (s))) + 1(S°(H_2 (g))) + 1(S°(Cl_2 (g)))]$

$= [1(270.2 \text{ J K}^{-1} \text{ mol}^{-1})] - [1(5.7 \text{ J K}^{-1} \text{ mol}^{-1}) + 1(130.7 \text{ J K}^{-1} \text{ mol}^{-1}) + 1(223.1 \text{ J K}^{-1} \text{ mol}^{-1})]$

$= [270.2 \text{ J K}^{-1} \text{ mol}^{-1}] - [359.5 \text{ J K}^{-1} \text{ mol}^{-1}]$

$= -89.3 \text{ J K}^{-1} \text{ mol}^{-1}$

The moles of gas are decreasing.

Check: The units (J K^{-1} mol^{-1}) are correct. The answer is negative, which is consistent with 2 moles of gas going to 1 mole of gas.

17.53   **Given:** methanol (CH$_3$OH) combustion at 25 °C **Find:** $\Delta_r H°$, $\Delta_r S°$, $\Delta_r G°$, and spontaneity
        Conceptual Plan: Write a balanced reaction then $\Delta_r H° = \sum n_p \Delta_f H°(\textbf{products}) - \sum n_r \Delta_f H°(\textbf{reactants})$

then $\Delta_r S° = \sum n_p S°(\text{products}) - \sum n_r S°(\text{reactants})$ then °C → K then J K^{-1} mol^{-1} → kJ K^{-1} mol^{-1} then

$$K = 273.15 + °C \qquad \frac{1 \text{ kJ}}{1000 \text{ J}}$$

$\Delta_r H°, \Delta_r S°, T \rightarrow \Delta_r G°.$

$\Delta_r G° = \Delta_r H° - T\Delta_r S°$

Solution: Menthanol is combined with oxygen to form carbon dioxide and water.

2 CH$_3$OH (l) + 3 O$_2$ (g) → 2 CO$_2$ (g) + 4 H$_2$O (g)

Reactant/Product	$\Delta_f H°$(kJ mol^{-1} from Appendix IIB)
CH$_3$OH (l)	−238.6
O$_2$ (g)	0.0
CO$_2$ (g)	−393.5
H$_2$O (g)	−241.8

Be sure to pull data for the correct formula and phase.

$\Delta_r H° = \sum n_p \Delta_f H°(\text{products}) - \sum n_r \Delta_f H°(\text{reactants})$

$= [2(\Delta_f H°(\text{CO}_2 (g))) + 4(\Delta_f H°(\text{H}_2\text{O} (g)))] - [2(\Delta_f H°(\text{CH}_3\text{OH} (l))) + 3(\Delta_f H°(\text{O}_2 (g)))]$

$= [2(-393.5 \text{ kJ mol}^{-1}) + 4(-241.8 \text{ kJ mol}^{-1})] - [2(-238.6 \text{ kJ mol}^{-1}) + 3(0.0 \text{ kJ mol}^{-1})]$

$= [-1754.2 \text{ kJ mol}^{-1}] - [-477.2 \text{ kJ mol}^{-1}]$

$= -1277 \text{ kJ mol}^{-1}$ then

Reactant/Product	$S°$(J K^{-1} mol^{-1} from Appendix IIB)
CH$_3$OH (l)	126.8
O$_2$ (g)	205.2
CO$_2$ (g)	213.8
H$_2$O (g)	188.8

Be sure to pull data for the correct formula and phase.

$\Delta_r S° = \sum n_p S°(\text{products}) - \sum n_r S°(\text{reactants})$

$= [2(S°(\text{CO}_2 (g))) + 4(S°(\text{H}_2\text{O} (g)))] - [2(S°(\text{CH}_3\text{OH} (l))) + 3(S°(\text{O}_2 (g)))]$

$= [2(213.8 \text{ J K}^{-1} \text{ mol}^{-1}) + 4(188.8 \text{ J K}^{-1} \text{ mol}^{-1})] - [2(126.8 \text{ J K}^{-1} \text{ mol}^{-1}) + 3(205.2 \text{ J K}^{-1} \text{ mol}^{-1})]$

$= [1182.8 \text{ J K}^{-1} \text{ mol}^{-1}] - [869.2 \text{ J K}^{-1} \text{ mol}^{-1}]$

$= 313.6 \text{ J K}^{-1} \text{ mol}^{-1}$

then $T = 273.15 + 25 °C = 298 K$ then $+313.6 \text{ J K}^{-1} \text{ mol}^{-1} \times \dfrac{1 \text{ kJ}}{1000 \text{ J}} = +0.3136 \text{ kJ K}^{-1} \text{ mol}^{-1}$ then

$\Delta_r G° = \Delta_r H° - T\Delta_r S° = -1277 \text{ kJ mol}^{-1} - (298 \text{ K})(+0.3136 \text{ kJ K}^{-1} \text{ mol}^{-1}) = -1370 \text{ kJ mol}^{-1}$

so the reaction is spontaneous.

Check: The units (kJ mol^{-1}, J K^{-1} mol^{-1}, and kJ mol^{-1}) are correct. Combustion reactions are exothermic and we see a large negative enthalpy. We expect a large positive entropy because we have an increase in the number of moles of gas. The free energy is the sum of two negative terms so we expect a large negative free energy and the reaction is spontaneous.

17.55   (a)   **Given:** N$_2$O$_4$ (g) → 2 NO$_2$ (g) at 25 °C

        Find: $\Delta_r H°, \Delta_r S°, \Delta_r G°$, spontaneity. Can temperature be changed to make it spontaneous?

        Conceptual Plan: $\Delta_r H° = \sum n_p \Delta_f H°(\text{products}) - \sum n_r \Delta_f H°(\text{reactants})$ then

        $\Delta_r S° = \sum n_p S°(\text{products}) - \sum n_r S°(\text{reactants})$ then °C → K then J K^{-1} mol^{-1} → kJ K^{-1} mol^{-1} then

$$K = 273.15 + °C \qquad \frac{1 \text{ kJ}}{1000 \text{ J}}$$

        $\Delta_r H°, \Delta_r S°, T \rightarrow \Delta_r G°$

            $\Delta_r G° = \Delta_r H° - T\Delta_r S°$

        Solution:

Reactant/Product	$\Delta_f H°$(kJ mol^{-1} from Appendix IIB)
N$_2$O$_4$ (g)	9.16
NO$_2$ (g)	33.2

        Be sure to pull data for the correct formula and phase.

$$\Delta_r H° = \sum n_p \Delta_f H°(\text{products}) - \sum n_r \Delta_f H°(\text{reactants})$$
$$= [2(\Delta_f H°(NO_2 \, (g)))] - [1(\Delta_f H°(N_2O_4 \, (g)))]$$
$$= [2(33.2 \text{ kJ mol}^{-1})] - [1(9.16 \text{ kJ mol}^{-1})]$$
$$= [66.4 \text{ kJ mol}^{-1}] - [9.16 \text{ kJ mol}^{-1}]$$
$$= +57.2 \text{ kJ mol}^{-1} \text{ then}$$

Reactant/Product	$S°(\text{J K}^{-1} \text{ mol}^{-1}$ from Appendix IIB)
$N_2O_4 \, (g)$	304.4
$NO_2 \, (g)$	240.1

Be sure to pull data for the correct formula and phase.

$$\Delta_r S° = \sum n_p S°(\text{products}) - \sum n_r S°(\text{reactants})$$
$$= [2(S°(NO_2 \, (g)))] - [1(S°(N_2O_4 \, (g)))]$$
$$= [2(240.1 \text{ J K}^{-1} \text{ mol}^{-1})] - [1(304.4 \text{ J K}^{-1} \text{ mol}^{-1})]$$
$$= [480.2 \text{ J K}^{-1} \text{ mol}^{-1}] - [304.4 \text{ J K}^{-1} \text{ mol}^{-1}]$$
$$= +175.8 \text{ J K}^{-1} \text{ mol}^{-1} \text{ then } T = 273.15 + 25 \text{ °C} = 298 \text{ K then}$$

$$+175.8 \text{ J K}^{-1} \text{ mol}^{-1} \times \frac{1 \text{ kJ}}{1000 \text{ J}} = +0.1758 \text{ kJ K}^{-1} \text{ mol}^{-1} \text{ then}$$

$$\Delta_r G° = \Delta_r H° - T\Delta_r S° = +57.2 \text{ kJ mol}^{-1} - (298 \text{ K})(+0.1758 \text{ kJ K}^{-1} \text{ mol}^{-1}) = +4.8 \text{ kJ mol}^{-1}$$

$= +4.8 \times 10^3 \text{ J mol}^{-1}$ so the reaction is nonspontaneous. It can be made spontaneous by raising the temperature.

Check: The units (kJ mol⁻¹, J K⁻¹ mol⁻¹, and kJ mol⁻¹) are correct. The reaction requires the breaking of a bond, so we expect that this will be an endothermic reaction. We expect a positive entropy change because we are increasing the number of moles of gas. Since the positive enthalpy term dominates at room temperature, the reaction is nonspontaneous. The second term can dominate if we raise the temperature high enough.

(b)   **Given:** $NH_4Cl \, (s) \rightarrow HCl \, (g) + NH_3 \, (g)$ at 25 °C
Find: $\Delta_r H°$, $\Delta_r S°$, $\Delta_r G°$, spontaneity. Can temperature be changed to make it spontaneous?
Conceptual Plan: $\Delta_r H° = \sum n_p \Delta_f H°(\text{products}) - \sum n_r \Delta_f H°(\text{reactants})$ then

$\Delta_r S° = \sum n_p S°(\text{products}) - \sum n_r S°(\text{reactants})$ then °C → K then J K⁻¹ mol⁻¹ → kJ K⁻¹ mol⁻¹ then

$$K = 273.15 + °C \qquad \frac{1 \text{ kJ}}{1000 \text{ J}}$$

$$\Delta_r H°, \Delta_r S°, T \rightarrow \Delta_r G°$$
$$\Delta_r G° = \Delta_r H° - T\Delta_r S°$$

Solution:

Reactant/Product	$\Delta_f H°(\text{kJ mol}^{-1}$ from Appendix IIB)
$NH_4Cl \, (s)$	−314.4
$HCl \, (g)$	−92.3
$NH_3 \, (g)$	−45.9

Be sure to pull data for the correct formula and phase.

$$\Delta_r H° = \sum n_p \Delta_f H°(\text{products}) - \sum n_r \Delta_f H°(\text{reactants})$$
$$= [1(\Delta_f H°(HCl \, (g))) + 1(\Delta_f H°(NH_3 \, (g)))] - [1(\Delta_f H°(NH_4Cl \, (g)))]$$
$$= [1(-92.3 \text{ kJ mol}^{-1}) + 1(-45.9 \text{ kJ mol}^{-1})] - [1(-314.4 \text{ kJ mol}^{-1})]$$
$$= [-138.2 \text{ kJ mol}^{-1}] - [-314.4 \text{ kJ mol}^{-1}]$$
$$= +176.2 \text{ kJ mol}^{-1} \text{ then}$$

Reactant/Product	$S°(\text{J K}^{-1} \text{ mol}^{-1}$ from Appendix IIB)
$NH_4Cl \, (s)$	94.6
$HCl \, (g)$	186.9
$NH_3 \, (g)$	192.8

Be sure to pull data for the correct formula and phase.

$$\Delta_r S° = \sum n_p S°(\text{products}) - \sum n_r S°(\text{reactants})$$
$$= [1(S°(\text{HCl }(g))) + 1(S°(\text{NH}_3 (g)))] - [1(S°(\text{NH}_4\text{Cl }(g)))]$$
$$= [1(186.9 \text{ J K}^{-1} \text{ mol}^{-1}) + 1(192.8 \text{ J K}^{-1} \text{ mol}^{-1})] - [1(94.6 \text{ J K}^{-1} \text{ mol}^{-1})]$$
$$= [379.7 \text{ J K}^{-1} \text{ mol}^{-1}] - [94.6 \text{ J K}^{-1} \text{ mol}^{-1}]$$
$$= +285.1 \text{ J K}^{-1} \text{ mol}^{-1}$$

then $T = 273.15 + 25 °C = 298 \text{ K}$ then $+285.1 \text{ J K}^{-1} \text{ mol}^{-1} \times \dfrac{1 \text{ kJ}}{1000 \text{ J}} = +0.2851 \text{ kJ K}^{-1} \text{ mol}^{-1}$ then

$$\Delta_r G° = \Delta_r H° - T\Delta_r S° = +176.2 \text{ kJ mol}^{-1} - (298 \text{ K})(+0.2851 \text{ kJ K}^{-1} \text{ mol}^{-1}) = +91.2 \text{ kJ mol}^{-1}$$

so the reaction is nonspontaneous. It can be made spontaneous by raising the temperature.
Check: The units (kJ mol⁻¹, J K⁻¹ mol⁻¹, and kJ mol⁻¹) are correct. The reaction requires the breaking of a bond, so we expect that this will be an endothermic reaction. We expect a positive entropy change because we are increasing the number of moles of gas. Since the positive enthalpy term dominates at room temperature, the reaction is nonspontaneous. The second term can dominate if we raise the temperature high enough.

(c)   **Given:** $3 \text{ H}_2 (g) + \text{Fe}_2\text{O}_3 (s) \rightarrow 2 \text{ Fe }(s) + 3 \text{ H}_2\text{O }(l)$ at 25 °C **Find:** $\Delta_r H°, \Delta_r S°, \Delta_r G°$, spontaneity. Can temperature be changed to make it spontaneous?
Conceptual Plan: $\Delta_r H° = \sum n_p \Delta_f H°(\text{products}) - \sum n_r \Delta_f H°(\text{reactants})$ then
$\Delta_r S° = \sum n_p S°(\text{products}) - \sum n_r S°(\text{reactants})$ then °C $\rightarrow$ K then J K⁻¹ mol⁻¹ $\rightarrow$ kJ K⁻¹ mol⁻¹ **then**

$$\text{K} = 273.15 + °C \qquad\qquad \dfrac{1 \text{ kJ}}{1000 \text{ J}}$$

$$\Delta_r H°, \Delta_r S°, T \rightarrow \Delta_r G°$$
$$\Delta_r G° = \Delta_r H° - T\Delta_r S°$$

Solution:

Reactant/Product	$\Delta_f H°$(kJ mol⁻¹ from Appendix IIB)
H₂ (g)	0.0
Fe₂O₃ (s)	−824.2
Fe (s)	0.0
H₂O (l)	−285.8

Be sure to pull data for the correct formula and phase.
$$\Delta_r H° = \sum n_p \Delta_f H°(\text{products}) - \sum n_r \Delta_f H°(\text{reactants})$$
$$= [2(\Delta_f H°(\text{Fe }(s))) + 3(\Delta_f H°(\text{H}_2\text{O }(l)))] - [3(\Delta_f H°(\text{H}_2 (g))) + 1(\Delta_f H°(\text{Fe}_2\text{O}_3 (s)))]$$
$$= [2(0.0 \text{ kJ mol}^{-1}) + 3(-285.8 \text{ kJ mol}^{-1})] - [3(0.0 \text{ kJ mol}^{-1}) + 1(-824.2 \text{ kJ mol}^{-1})]$$
$$= [-857.4 \text{ kJ mol}^{-1}] - [-824.2 \text{ kJ mol}^{-1}]$$
$$= -33.2 \text{ kJ mol}^{-1} \text{ then}$$

Reactant/Product	$S°$(J K⁻¹ mol⁻¹ from Appendix IIB)
H₂ (g)	130.7
Fe₂O₃ (s)	87.4
Fe (s)	27.3
H₂O (l)	70.0

Be sure to pull data for the correct formula and phase.
$$\Delta_r S° = \sum n_p S°(\text{products}) - \sum n_r S°(\text{reactants})$$
$$= [2(S°(\text{Fe }(s))) + 3(S°(\text{H}_2\text{O }(l)))] - [3(S°(\text{H}_2 (g))) + 1(S°(\text{Fe}_2\text{O}_3 (s)))]$$
$$= [2(27.3 \text{ J K}^{-1} \text{ mol}^{-1}) + 3(70.0 \text{ J K}^{-1} \text{ mol}^{-1})] - [3(130.7 \text{ J K}^{-1} \text{ mol}^{-1}) + 1(87.4 \text{ J K}^{-1} \text{ mol}^{-1})]$$
$$= [264.6 \text{ J K}^{-1} \text{ mol}^{-1}] - [479.5 \text{ J K}^{-1} \text{ mol}^{-1}]$$
$$= -214.9 \text{ J K}^{-1} \text{ mol}^{-1}$$

then $T = 273.15 + 25 °C = 298 \text{ K}$ then $-214.9 \text{ J K}^{-1} \text{ mol}^{-1} \times \dfrac{1 \text{ kJ}}{1000 \text{ J}} = -0.2149 \text{ kJ K}^{-1} \text{ mol}^{-1}$ then

$$\Delta_r G° = \Delta_r H° - T\Delta_r S° = -33.2 \text{ kJ mol}^{-1} - (298 \text{ K})(-0.2149 \text{ kJ K}^{-1} \text{ mol}^{-1}) = 30.8 \text{ kJ mol}^{-1}$$

so the reaction is nonspontaneous. It can be made spontaneous by lowering the temperature.

Check: The units (kJ mol^{-1}, J K^{-1} mol^{-1}, and kJ mol^{-1}) are correct. The reaction requires breaking and forming of bonds with the net result being exothermic. We expect a negative entropy because we are going from a mixture of gas and solid to gas and liquid. This process is the opposite of rusting, so we are not surprised that it is nonspontaneous.

(d) **Given:** N_2 (g) + 3 H_2 (g) $\rightarrow$ 2 NH_3 (g) at 25 °C
Find: $\Delta_r H°$, $\Delta_r S°$, $\Delta_r G°$, spontaneity. Can temperature be changed to make it spontaneous?
Conceptual Plan: $\Delta_r H° = \sum n_p \Delta_f H°$(products) $- \sum n_r \Delta_f H°$(reactants) then

$\Delta_r S° = \sum n_p S°$(products) $- \sum n_r S°$(reactants) then °C $\rightarrow$ K then J K^{-1} mol^{-1} $\rightarrow$ kJ K^{-1} mol^{-1} then

$$K = 273.15 + °C \qquad \frac{1\text{ kJ}}{1000\text{ J}}$$

$\Delta_r H°$, $\Delta_r S°$, $T \rightarrow \Delta_r G°$

$$\Delta_r G° = \Delta_r H° - T\Delta_r S°$$

Solution:

Reactant/Product	$\Delta_f H°$(kJ mol^{-1} from Appendix IIB)
N_2 (g)	0.0
H_2 (g)	0.0
NH_3 (g)	−45.9

Be sure to pull data for the correct formula and phase.

$\Delta_r H° = \sum n_p \Delta_f H°$(products) $- \sum n_r \Delta_f H°$(reactants)

$= [2(\Delta_f H°(NH_3\ (g)))] - [1(\Delta_f H°(N_2\ (g))) + 3(\Delta_f H°(H_2\ (g)))]$

$= [2(-45.9\text{ kJ mol}^{-1})] - [1(0.0\text{ kJ mol}^{-1}) + 3(0.0\text{ kJ mol}^{-1})]$

$= [-91.8\text{ kJ mol}^{-1}] - [0.0\text{ kJ mol}^{-1}]$

$= -91.8$ kJ mol^{-1} then

Reactant/Product	$S°$(J K^{-1} mol^{-1} from Appendix IIB)
N_2 (g)	191.6
H_2 (g)	130.7
NH_3 (g)	192.8

Be sure to pull data for the correct formula and phase.

$\Delta_r S° = \sum n_p S°$(products) $- \sum n_r S°$(reactants)

$= [2(S°(NH_3\ (g)))] - [1(S°(N_2\ (g))) + 3(S°(H_2\ (g)))]$

$= [2(192.8\text{ J K}^{-1}\text{ mol}^{-1})] - [1(191.6\text{ J K}^{-1}\text{ mol}^{-1}) + 3(130.7\text{ J K}^{-1}\text{ mol}^{-1})]$

$= [385.6\text{ J K}^{-1}\text{ mol}^{-1}] - [583.7\text{ J K}^{-1}\text{ mol}^{-1}]$

$= -198.1$ J K^{-1} mol^{-1}

then $T = 273.15 + 25$ °C $= 298$ K then -198.1 J K^{-1} mol^{-1} $\times \dfrac{1\text{ kJ}}{1000\text{ J}} = -0.1981$ kJ K^{-1} mol^{-1} then

$\Delta_r G° = \Delta_r H° - T\Delta_r S° = -91.8$ kJ mol^{-1} $- (298\text{ K})(-0.1981\text{ kJ K}^{-1}\text{ mol}^{-1}) = -32.8$ kJ mol^{-1}

so the reaction is spontaneous.

Check: The units (kJ mol^{-1}, J K^{-1} mol^{-1}, and kJ mol^{-1}) are correct. The reaction requires the breaking of a bond, so we expect that this will be an endothermic reaction. We expect a positive entropy change because we are increasing the number of moles of gas. Since the negative enthalpy term dominates at room temperature, the reaction is spontaneous. The second term can dominate if we raise the temperature high enough.

17.57 (a) **Given:** N_2O_4 (g) $\rightarrow$ 2 NO_2 (g) at 25 °C **Find:** $\Delta_r G°$, spontaneity, and compare to Problem 55.
Determine which method would show how free energy changes with temperature.
Conceptual Plan: $\Delta_r G° = \sum n_p \Delta_f G°$(products) $- \sum n_r \Delta_f G°$(reactants) **then compare to Problem 55**
Solution:

Reactant/Product	$\Delta_f G°$(kJ mol^{-1} from Appendix IIB)
N_2O_4 (g)	99.8
NO_2 (g)	51.3

Be sure to pull data for the correct formula and phase.

$$\Delta_r G^\circ = \sum n_p \Delta_f G^\circ (\text{products}) - \sum n_r \Delta_f G^\circ (\text{reactants})$$
$$= [2(\Delta_f G^\circ (\text{NO}_2\ (g)))] - [1(\Delta_f G^\circ (\text{N}_2\text{O}_4\ (g)))]$$
$$= [2(51.3\ \text{kJ mol}^{-1})] - [1(99.8\ \text{kJ mol}^{-1})]$$
$$= [102.6\ \text{kJ mol}^{-1}] - [99.8\ \text{kJ mol}^{-1}]$$
$$= +2.8\ \text{kJ mol}^{-1}$$

so the reaction is nonspontaneous. The value is similar to Problem 55.

Check: The units (kJ mol^{-1}) are correct. The free energy of the products is greater than the reactants, so the answer is positive and the reaction is nonspontaneous. The answer is the same as in Problem 55 within the error of the calculation.

(b)   **Given:** $\text{NH}_4\text{Cl}\ (s) \rightarrow \text{HCl}\ (g) + \text{NH}_3\ (g)$ at 25 °C
Find: $\Delta_r G^\circ$, spontaneity, and compare to Problem 55
Conceptual Plan: $\Delta_r G^\circ = \sum n_p \Delta_f G^\circ (\textbf{products}) - \sum n_r \Delta_f G^\circ (\textbf{reactants})$ **then compare to Problem 55**
Solution:

Reactant/Product	$\Delta_f G^\circ (\text{kJ mol}^{-1}$ from Appendix IIB)
$\text{NH}_4\text{Cl}\ (s)$	−202.9
$\text{HCl}\ (g)$	−95.3
$\text{NH}_3\ (g)$	−16.4

Be sure to pull data for the correct formula and phase.
$$\Delta_r G^\circ = \sum n_p \Delta_f G^\circ (\text{products}) - \sum n_r \Delta_f G^\circ (\text{reactants})$$
$$= [1(\Delta_f G^\circ (\text{HCl}\ (g))) + 1(\Delta_f G^\circ (\text{NH}_3\ (g)))] - [1(\Delta_f G^\circ (\text{NH}_4\text{Cl}\ (g)))]$$
$$= [1(-95.3\ \text{kJ mol}^{-1}) + 1(-16.4\ \text{kJ mol}^{-1})] - [1(-202.9\ \text{kJ mol}^{-1})]$$
$$= [-111.7\ \text{kJ mol}^{-1}] - [-202.9\ \text{kJ mol}^{-1}]$$
$$= +91.2\ \text{kJ mol}^{-1}$$

so the reaction is nonspontaneous. The result is the same as in Problem 55.

Check: The units (kJ mol^{-1}) are correct. The answer matches Problem 55.

(c)   **Given:** $3\ \text{H}_2\ (g) + \text{Fe}_2\text{O}_3\ (s) \rightarrow 2\ \text{Fe}\ (s) + 3\ \text{H}_2\text{O}\ (l)$ at 25 °C
Find: $\Delta_r G^\circ$, spontaneity, and compare to Problem 55
Conceptual Plan: $\Delta_r G^\circ = \sum n_p \Delta_f G^\circ (\textbf{products}) - \sum n_r \Delta_f G^\circ (\textbf{reactants})$ **then compare to Problem 55**
Solution:

Reactant/Product	$\Delta_f G^\circ (\text{kJ mol}^{-1}$ from Appendix IIB)
$\text{H}_2\ (g)$	0.0
$\text{Fe}_2\text{O}_3\ (s)$	−742.2
$\text{Fe}\ (s)$	0.0
$\text{H}_2\text{O}\ (l)$	−237.1

Be sure to pull data for the correct formula and phase.
$$\Delta_r G^\circ = \sum n_p \Delta_f G^\circ (\text{products}) - \sum n_r \Delta_f G^\circ (\text{reactants})$$
$$= [2(\Delta_f G^\circ (\text{Fe}\ (s))) + 3(\Delta_f G^\circ (\text{H}_2\text{O}\ (l)))] - [3(\Delta_f G^\circ (\text{H}_2\ (g))) + 1(\Delta_f G^\circ (\text{Fe}_2\text{O}_3\ (s)))]$$
$$= [2(0.0\ \text{kJ mol}^{-1}) + 3(-237.1\ \text{kJ mol}^{-1})] - [3(0.0\ \text{kJ mol}^{-1}) + 1(-742.2\ \text{kJ mol}^{-1})]$$
$$= [-711.3\ \text{kJ mol}^{-1}] - [-742.2\ \text{kJ mol}^{-1}]$$
$$= +30.9\ \text{kJ mol}^{-1}$$

so the reaction is nonspontaneous. The value is similar to that in Problem 55.

Check: The units (kJ mol^{-1}) are correct. The answer is the same as in Problem 55 within the error of the calculation.

(d)   **Given:** $\text{N}_2\ (g) + 3\ \text{H}_2\ (g) \rightarrow 2\ \text{NH}_3\ (g)$ at 25 °C
Find: $\Delta_r G^\circ$, spontaneity, and compare to Problem 55
Conceptual Plan: $\Delta_r G^\circ = \sum n_p \Delta_f G^\circ (\textbf{products}) - \sum n_r \Delta_f G^\circ (\textbf{reactants})$ **then compare to Problem 55**
Solution:

Reactant/Product	$\Delta_f G^\circ (\text{kJ mol}^{-1}$ from Appendix IIB)
$\text{N}_2\ (g)$	0.0
$\text{H}_2\ (g)$	0.0
$\text{NH}_3\ (g)$	−16.4

Be sure to pull data for the correct formula and phase.

$$\Delta_r G^\circ = \sum n_p \Delta_f G^\circ(\text{products}) - \sum n_r \Delta_f G^\circ(\text{reactants})$$
$$= [2(\Delta_f G^\circ(NH_3\ (g)))] - [1(\Delta_f G^\circ(N_2\ (g))) + 3(\Delta_f G^\circ(H_2\ (g)))]$$
$$= [2(-16.4\ \text{kJ mol}^{-1})] - [1(0.0\ \text{kJ mol}^{-1}) + 3(0.0\ \text{kJ mol}^{-1})]$$
$$= [-32.8\ \text{kJ mol}^{-1}] - [0.0\ \text{kJ mol}^{-1}]$$
$$= -32.8\ \text{kJ mol}^{-1}$$

so the reaction is spontaneous. The result is the same as in Problem 55.

Check: The units (kJ mol^{-1}) are correct. The answer matches Problem 55.

Values calculated by the two methods are comparable. The method using $\Delta_r H^\circ$ and $\Delta_r S^\circ$ is longer, but it can be used to determine how $\Delta_r G^\circ$ changes with temperature.

17.59   **Given:** 2 NO (g) + O$_2$ (g) → 2 NO$_2$ (g) **Find:** $\Delta_r G^\circ$ and spontaneity at (a) 298 K, (b) 715 K, and (c) 855 K
Conceptual Plan: $\Delta_r H^\circ = \sum n_p \Delta_f H^\circ(\text{products}) - \sum n_r \Delta_f H^\circ(\text{reactants})$ then

$\Delta_r S^\circ = \sum n_p S^\circ(\text{products}) - \sum n_r S^\circ(\text{reactants})$ then J K^{-1} mol^{-1} → kJ K^{-1} mol^{-1} then $\Delta_r H^\circ, \Delta_r S^\circ, T \rightarrow \Delta_r G^\circ$

$$\frac{1\ \text{kJ}}{1000\ \text{J}}$$
$$\Delta_r G^\circ = \Delta_r H^\circ - T\Delta_r S^\circ$$

Solution:

Reactant/Product	$\Delta_f H^\circ$(kJ mol^{-1} from Appendix IIB)
NO (g)	91.3
O$_2$ (g)	0.0
NO$_2$ (g)	33.2

Be sure to pull data for the correct formula and phase.

$$\Delta_r H^\circ = \sum n_p \Delta_f H^\circ(\text{products}) - \sum n_r \Delta_f H^\circ(\text{reactants})$$
$$= [2(\Delta_f H^\circ(NO_2\ (g)))] - [2(\Delta_f H^\circ(NO\ (g))) + 1(\Delta_f H^\circ(O_2\ (g)))]$$
$$= [2(33.2\ \text{kJ mol}^{-1})] - [2(91.3\ \text{kJ mol}^{-1}) + 1(0.0\ \text{kJ mol}^{-1})]$$
$$= [66.4\ \text{kJ mol}^{-1}] - [182.6\ \text{kJ mol}^{-1}]$$
$$= -116.2\ \text{kJ mol}^{-1}\ \text{then}$$

Reactant/Product	S°(J K^{-1} mol^{-1} from Appendix IIB)
NO (g)	210.8
O$_2$ (g)	205.2
NO$_2$ (g)	240.1

Be sure to pull data for the correct formula and phase.

$$\Delta_r S^\circ = \sum n_p S^\circ(\text{products}) - \sum n_r S^\circ(\text{reactants})$$
$$= [2(S^\circ(NO_2\ (g)))] - [2(S^\circ(NO\ (g))) + 1(S^\circ(O_2\ (g)))]$$
$$= [2(240.1\ \text{J K}^{-1}\ \text{mol}^{-1})] - [2(210.8\ \text{J K}^{-1}\ \text{mol}^{-1}) + 1(205.2\ \text{J K}^{-1}\ \text{mol}^{-1})]$$
$$= [480.2\ \text{J K}^{-1}\ \text{mol}^{-1}] - [626.8\ \text{J K}^{-1}\ \text{mol}^{-1}]$$
$$= -146.6\ \text{J K}^{-1}\ \text{mol}^{-1}$$

$$-146.6\ \text{J K}^{-1}\ \text{mol}^{-1} \times \frac{1\ \text{kJ}}{1000\ \text{J}} = -0.1466\ \text{kJ K}^{-1}\ \text{mol}^{-1}\ \text{then}$$

(a) $\Delta_r G^\circ = \Delta_r H^\circ - T\Delta_r S^\circ = -116.2\ \text{kJ mol}^{-1} - (298\ \text{K})(-0.1466\ \text{kJ K}^{-1}\ \text{mol}^{-1}) = -72.5\ \text{kJ mol}^{-1}$
       so the reaction is spontaneous.

(b) $\Delta_r G^\circ = \Delta_r H^\circ - T\Delta_r S^\circ = -116.2\ \text{kJ mol}^{-1} - (715\ \text{K})(-0.1466\ \text{kJ K}^{-1}\ \text{mol}^{-1}) = -11.4\ \text{kJ mol}^{-1}$
       so the reaction is spontaneous.

(c) $\Delta_r G^\circ = \Delta_r H^\circ - T\Delta_r S^\circ = -116.2\ \text{kJ mol}^{-1} - (855\ \text{K})(-0.1466\ \text{kJ K}^{-1}\ \text{mol}^{-1}) = +9.1\ \text{kJ mol}^{-1}$
       so the reaction is nonspontaneous.

Check: The units (kJ mol^{-1}) are correct. The enthalpy term dominates at low temperatures, making the reaction spontaneous. As the temperature increases, the decrease in entropy starts to dominate and in the last case the reaction is nonspontaneous.

17.61   Since the first reaction has Fe_2O_3 as a product and the reaction of interest has it as a reactant, we need to reverse the first reaction. When the reaction direction is reversed, $\Delta_r G°$ changes.

Fe_2O_3 (s) → 2 Fe (s) + 3/2 O_2 (g) $\Delta_r G° = +742.2$ kJ mol^{-1}

Since the second reaction has 1 mole of CO as a reactant and the reaction of interest has 3 moles of CO as a reactant, we need to multiply the second reaction and the $\Delta_r G°$ by 3.

3 [CO (g) +1/2 O_2 (g) → CO_2 (g)] $\Delta_r G° = 3(-257.2$ kJ mol$^{-1}) = -771.6$ kJ mol^{-1}

Hess's law states the $\Delta_r G°$ of the net reaction is the sum of the $\Delta_r G°$ of the steps.

The rewritten reactions are:

Fe_2O_3 (s) → 2 Fe (s) + ~~3/2 O₂ (g)~~	$\Delta_r G° = +742.2$ kJ mol^{-1}
3 CO (g) + ~~3/2 O₂ (g)~~ → 3 CO_2 (g)	$\Delta_r G° = -771.6$ kJ mol^{-1}
Fe_2O_3 (s) + 3 CO (g) → 2 Fe (s) + 3 CO_2 (g)	$\Delta_r G° = -29.4$ kJ mol^{-1}

Gibbs Energy Changes, Nonstandard Conditions, and the Equilibrium Constant

17.63   (a)   **Given:** I_2 (s) → I_2 (g) at 25.0 °C **Find:** $\Delta_r G°$

Conceptual Plan: $\Delta_r G° = \sum n_p \Delta_f G°(\text{products}) - \sum n_r \Delta_f G°(\text{reactants})$

Solution:

Reactant/Product	$\Delta_f G°$(kJ mol^{-1} from Appendix IIB)
I_2 (s)	0.0
I_2 (g)	19.3

Be sure to pull data for the correct formula and phase.

$\Delta_r G° = \sum n_p \Delta_f G°(\text{products}) - \sum n_r \Delta_f G°(\text{reactants})$

$= [1(\Delta_f G°(I_2 (g)))] - [1(\Delta_f G°(I_2 (s)))]$

$= [1(19.3$ kJ mol$^{-1})] - [1(0.0$ kJ mol$^{-1})]$

$= +19.3$ kJ mol^{-1} so the reaction is nonspontaneous.

Check: The units (kJ mol^{-1}) are correct. The answer is positive because gases have higher free energy than solids and the free energy change of the reaction is the same as free energy of formation of gaseous iodine.

(b)   **Given:** I_2 (s) → I_2 (g) at 25.0 °C (i) $P_{I_2} = 1.00$ mbar; (ii) $P_{I_2} = 0.100$ mbar **Find:** $\Delta_r G$

Conceptual Plan: °C → K and mbar → bar then $\Delta_r G°, P_{I_2}, T$ → $\Delta_r G$

$$K = 273.15 + °C \qquad \frac{1 \text{ bar}}{1000 \text{ mbar}} \qquad \Delta_r G = \Delta_r G° + RT \ln Q \quad \text{where } Q = P_{I_2}$$

Solution: $T = 273.15 + 25.0$ °C $= 298.2$ K and (i) 1.00 ~~mbar~~ $\times \dfrac{1 \text{ bar}}{1000 \text{ mbar}} = 1.00 \times 10^{-3}$ bar

then $\Delta_r G = \Delta_r G° + RT \ln Q = \Delta_r G° + RT \ln P_{I_2}$

$= +19.3$ kJ mol^{-1}

$+ \left(8.314 \dfrac{J}{K \cdot mol}\right)\left(\dfrac{1 \text{ kJ}}{1000 \text{ J}}\right)(298.2 \text{ K}) \ln (1.00 \times 10^{-3})$

$= + 2.2$ kJ mol^{-1} so the reaction is nonspontaneous.

Then (ii) 0.100 ~~mbar~~ $\times \dfrac{1 \text{ bar}}{1000 \text{ mbar}} = 1.00 \times 10^{-4}$ bar then

$\Delta_r G = \Delta_r G° + RT \ln Q = \Delta_r G° + RT \ln P_{I_2} = +19.3$ kJ mol^{-1}

$+ \left(8.314 \dfrac{J}{K \cdot mol}\right)\left(\dfrac{1 \text{ kJ}}{1000 \text{ J}}\right)(298.2 \text{ K}) \ln (1.00 \times 10^{-4}) = -3.5$ kJ mol^{-1} so the reaction is spontaneous.

Check: The units (kJ mol^{-1}) are correct. The answer is positive at higher pressure because the pressure is higher than the vapour pressure of iodine. Once the desired pressure is below the vapour pressure (4.1×10^{-4} bar at 25.0 °C), the reaction becomes spontaneous.

(c)   Iodine sublimes at room temperature because there is an equilibrium between the solid and the gas phases. The vapour pressure is low (4.1×10^{-4} bar at 25.0 °C), so a small amount of iodine can remain in the gas phase, which is consistent with the free energy values.

17.65   **Given:** $CH_3OH\,(g) \rightleftharpoons CO\,(g) + 2\,H_2\,(g)$ at 125 °C, $P_{CH_3OH} = 0.855$ bar, $P_{CO} = 0.125$ bar, $P_{H_2} = 0.183$ bar
Find: $\Delta_r G$
Conceptual Plan:
$\Delta_r G° = \sum n_p \Delta_f G°(\text{products}) - \sum n_r \Delta_f G°(\text{reactants})$ then °C $\rightarrow$ K then $\Delta_r G°, P_{CH_3OH}, P_{CO}, P_{H_2}, T \rightarrow \Delta_r G$

$$K = 273.15 + °C \qquad \Delta_r G = \Delta_r G° + RT \ln Q \quad \text{where } Q = \frac{P_{CO} P_{H_2}^2}{P_{CH_3OH}}$$

Solution:

Reactant/Product	$\Delta_f G°$(kJ mol^{-1} from Appendix IIB)
$CH_3OH\,(g)$	-162.3
$CO\,(g)$	-137.2
$H_2\,(g)$	0.0

Be sure to pull data for the correct formula and phase.
$$\begin{aligned}
\Delta_r G° &= \sum n_p \Delta_f G°(\text{products}) - \sum n_r \Delta_f G°(\text{reactants}) \\
&= [1(\Delta_f G°(CO\,(g))) + 2(\Delta_f G°(H_2\,(g)))] - [1(\Delta_f G°(CH_3OH\,(g)))] \\
&= [1(-137.2\text{ kJ mol}^{-1}) + 2(0.0\text{ kJ mol}^{-1})] - [1(-162.3\text{ kJ mol}^{-1})] \\
&= [-137.2\text{ kJ mol}^{-1}] - [-162.3\text{ kJ mol}^{-1}] \\
&= +25.1\text{ kJ mol}^{-1}
\end{aligned}$$

$T = 273.15 + 125$ °C $= 398$ K then $Q = \dfrac{P_{CO} P_{H_2}^2}{P_{CH_3OH}} = \dfrac{(0.125)(0.183)^2}{0.855} = 0.00489605$ then

$$\Delta_r G = \Delta_r G° + RT \ln Q = +25.1\text{ kJ mol}^{-1} + \left(8.314\,\frac{\text{J}}{\text{K}\cdot\text{mol}}\right)\left(\frac{1\text{ kJ}}{1000\text{ J}}\right)(398\text{ K}) \ln(0.00489605)$$

$= +7.5$ kJ mol^{-1} so the reaction is nonspontaneous.
Check: The units (kJ mol^{-1}) are correct. The standard free energy for the reaction was positive and the fact that Q was less than one made the free energy smaller, but the reaction at these conditions is still not spontaneous.

17.67   (a)   **Given:** $2\,CO\,(g) + O_2\,(g) \rightleftharpoons 2\,CO_2\,(g)$ at 25 °C **Find:** K
Conceptual Plan:
$\Delta_r G° = \sum n_p \Delta_f G°(\text{products}) - \sum n_r \Delta_f G°(\text{reactants})$ then °C $\rightarrow$ K then $\Delta_r G°, T \rightarrow K$

$$K = 273.15 + °C \qquad \Delta_r G° = -RT \ln K$$

Solution:

Reactant/Product	$\Delta_f G°$(kJ mol^{-1} from Appendix IIB)
$CO\,(g)$	-137.2
$O_2\,(g)$	0.0
$CO_2\,(g)$	-394.4

Be sure to pull data for the correct formula and phase.
$$\begin{aligned}
\Delta_r G° &= \sum n_p \Delta_f G°(\text{products}) - \sum n_r \Delta_f G°(\text{reactants}) \\
&= [2(\Delta_f G°(CO_2\,(g)))] - [2(\Delta_f G°(CO\,(g))) + 1(\Delta_f G°(O_2\,(g)))] \\
&= [2(-394.4\text{ kJ mol}^{-1})] - [2(-137.2\text{ kJ mol}^{-1}) + 1(0.0\text{ kJ mol}^{-1})] \\
&= [-788.8\text{ kJ mol}^{-1}] - [-274.4\text{ kJ mol}^{-1}] \\
&= -514.4\text{ kJ mol}^{-1}
\end{aligned}$$

$T = 273.15 + 25$ °C $= 298$ K then

$\Delta_r G° = -RT \ln K$. Rearrange to solve for K.

$$K = e^{\frac{-\Delta_r G°}{RT}} = e^{\dfrac{-(-514.4\text{ kJ mol}^{-1}) \times \frac{1000\text{ J}}{1\text{ kJ}}}{\left(8.314\,\frac{\text{J}}{\text{K}\cdot\text{mol}}\right)(298\text{ K})}} = e^{207.623} = 1.48 \times 10^{90}.$$

Check: The units (none) are correct. The standard free energy for the reaction was very negative and so we expect a very large K. The reaction is spontaneous, so mostly products are present at equilibrium.

(b)   **Given:** $2\,H_2S\,(g) \rightleftharpoons 2\,H_2\,(g) + S_2\,(g)$ at 25 °C **Find:** K
Conceptual Plan:
$\Delta_r G° = \sum n_p \Delta_f G°(\text{products}) - \sum n_r \Delta_f G°(\text{reactants})$ then °C $\rightarrow$ K then $\Delta_r G°, T \rightarrow K$

$$K = 273.15 + °C \qquad \Delta_r G° = -RT \ln K$$

Solution:

Reactant/Product	$\Delta_f G°$(kJ mol^{-1} from Appendix IIB)
H_2S (g)	−33.4
H_2 (g)	0.0
S_2 (g)	79.7

Be sure to pull data for the correct formula and phase.

$$\Delta_r G° = \sum n_p \Delta_f G°(\text{products}) - \sum n_r \Delta_f G°(\text{reactants})$$
$$= [2(\Delta_f G°(H_2 \ (g))) + 1(\Delta_f G°(S_2 \ (g)))] - [2(\Delta_f G°(H_2S \ (g)))]$$
$$= [2(0.0 \text{ kJ mol}^{-1})] + 1(79.7 \text{ kJ mol}^{-1})] - [2(-33.4 \text{ kJ mol}^{-1})]$$
$$= [79.7 \text{ kJ mol}^{-1}] - [-66.8 \text{ kJ mol}^{-1}]$$
$$= +146.5 \text{ kJ mol}^{-1}$$

$T = 273.15 + 25 \ °C = 298 \text{ K}$ then

$\Delta_r G° = -RT \ln K$. Rearrange to solve for K.

$$K = e^{\frac{-\Delta_r G°}{RT}} = e^{\frac{-146.5 \text{ kJ mol}^{-1} \times \frac{1000 \text{ J}}{1 \text{ kJ}}}{\left(8.314 \frac{\text{J}}{\text{K} \cdot \text{mol}}\right)(298 \text{ K})}} = e^{-59.\underline{1}305} = 2.09 \times 10^{-26}.$$

Check: The units (none) are correct. The standard free energy for the reaction was positive and so we expect a small K. The reaction is nonspontaneous and so mostly reactants are present at equilibrium.

17.69   **Given:** $I_2 \ (g) + Cl_2 \ (g) \rightleftharpoons 2 \ ICl \ (g)$ $K = 6.91 \times 10^3$ at 460 K   **Find:** $\Delta_r G°$ at (a) standard conditions, (b) equilibrium, and (c) $P_{ICl} = 2.55$ bar, $P_{I_2} = 0.325$ bar, $P_{Cl_2} = 0.221$ bar

         Conceptual Plan: (a) $K, T \rightarrow \Delta_r G°$ then (b) at equilibrium then

$$\Delta_r G° = -RT \ln K$$

         (c) $\Delta_r G°, P_{ICl}, P_{I_2}, P_{Cl_2}, T \rightarrow \Delta_r G$

$$\Delta_r G = \Delta_r G° + RT \ln Q \text{ where } Q = \frac{P_{ICl}^2}{P_{I_2} P_{Cl_2}}$$

Solution:

(a) $\Delta_r G° = -RT \ln K = -\left(8.314 \frac{\text{J}}{\text{K} \cdot \text{mol}}\right)\left(\frac{1 \text{ kJ}}{1000 \text{ J}}\right)(460 \text{ K}) \ln (6.91 \times 10^3) = -33.8 \text{ kJ mol}^{-1}$

(b)   at equilibrium $\Delta_r G = 0$

(c) $Q = \frac{P_{ICl}^2}{P_{I_2} P_{Cl_2}} = \frac{(2.55)^2}{(0.325)(0.221)} = 90.\underline{5}325$ then

         $\Delta_r G = \Delta_r G° + RT \ln Q = -33.8 \text{ kJ mol}^{-1} + \left(8.314 \frac{\text{J}}{\text{K} \cdot \text{mol}}\right)\left(\frac{1 \text{ kJ}}{1000 \text{ J}}\right)(460 \text{ K}) \ln (90.\underline{5}325)$

         $= -16.6 \text{ kJ mol}^{-1}$

Check: The units (kJ mol^{-1}) are correct. The K was greater than 1 so we expect a negative standard free energy for the reaction. At equilibrium, by definition, the free energy change is zero. Since the conditions give a $Q < K$, the reaction needs to proceed in the forward direction and is spontaneous.

17.71   (a)   **Given:** $2 \ CO \ (g) + O_2 \ (g) \rightleftharpoons 2 \ CO_2 \ (g)$ at 25 °C   **Find:** K at 525 K

         Conceptual Plan: $\Delta_r H° = \sum n_p \Delta_f H°(\text{products}) - \sum n_r \Delta_f H°(\text{reactants})$ then

         $\Delta_r S° = \sum n_p S°(\text{products}) - \sum n_r S°(\text{reactants})$ then J K^{-1} mol^{-1} $\rightarrow$ kJ K^{-1} mol^{-1} then

$$\frac{1 \text{ kJ}}{1000 \text{ J}}$$

         $\Delta_r H°, \Delta_r S°, T \rightarrow \Delta_r G$ then $\Delta_r G°, T \rightarrow K$

$$\Delta_r G° = \Delta_r H° - T_r \Delta S° \qquad\qquad \Delta_r G° = -RT \ln K$$

         Solution:

Reactant/Product	$\Delta_f H°$(kJ mol^{-1} from Appendix IIB)
CO (g)	−110.5
O_2 (g)	0.0
CO_2 (g)	−393.5

Be sure to pull data for the correct formula and phase.

$$\Delta_r H° = \sum n_p \Delta_f H°(\text{products}) - \sum n_r \Delta_f H°(\text{reactants})$$
$$= [2(\Delta_f H°(CO_2 (g)))] - [2(\Delta_f H°(CO (g))) + 1(\Delta_f H°(O_2 (g)))]$$
$$= [2(-393.5 \text{ kJ mol}^{-1})] - [2(-110.5 \text{ kJ mol}^{-1}) + 1(0.0 \text{ kJ mol}^{-1})] \text{ then}$$
$$= [-787.0 \text{ kJ mol}^{-1}] - [-221.0 \text{ kJ mol}^{-1}]$$
$$= -566.0 \text{ kJ mol}^{-1}$$

Reactant/Product	$S°$(J K^{-1} mol^{-1} from Appendix IIB)
CO (g)	197.7
O$_2$ (g)	205.2
CO$_2$ (g)	213.8

Be sure to pull data for the correct formula and phase.
$$\Delta_r S° = \sum n_p S°(\text{products}) - \sum n_r S°(\text{reactants})$$
$$= [2(S°(CO_2 (g)))] - [2(S°(CO (g))) + 1(S°(O_2 (g)))]$$
$$= [2(213.8 \text{ J K}^{-1} \text{ mol}^{-1})] - [2(197.7 \text{ J K}^{-1} \text{ mol}^{-1}) + 1(205.2 \text{ J K}^{-1} \text{ mol}^{-1})] \text{ then}$$
$$= [427.6 \text{ J K}^{-1} \text{ mol}^{-1}] - [600.6 \text{ J K}^{-1} \text{ mol}^{-1}]$$
$$= -173.0 \text{ J K}^{-1} \text{ mol}^{-1}$$

$$-173.0 \text{ J K}^{-1} \text{ mol}^{-1} \times \frac{1 \text{ kJ}}{1000 \text{ J}} = -0.1730 \text{ kJ K}^{-1} \text{ mol}^{-1} \text{ then}$$

$$\Delta_r G° = \Delta_r H° - T\Delta_r S° = -566.0 \text{ kJ mol}^{-1} - (525 \text{ K})(-0.1730 \text{ kJ K}^{-1} \text{ mol}^{-1})$$

$$= -475.2 \text{ kJ mol}^{-1} = -4.752 \times 10^5 \text{ J mol}^{-1} \text{ then}$$

$$\Delta_r G° = -RT \ln K. \text{ Rearrange to solve for } K.$$

$$K = e^{\frac{-\Delta_r G°}{RT}} = e^{\frac{-(-4.752 \times 10^5 \text{ J mol}^{-1})}{\left(8.314 \frac{\text{J}}{\text{K} \cdot \text{mol}}\right)(525 \text{ K})}} = e^{108.864} = 1.90 \times 10^{47}.$$

Check: The units (none) are correct. The free energy change is very negative, indicating a spontaneous reaction. This results in a very large K.

(b)   **Given:** 2 H$_2$S (g) $\rightleftharpoons$ 2 H$_2$ (g) + S$_2$ (g) at 25 °C **Find:** K at 525 K
    Conceptual Plan: $\Delta_r H° = \sum n_p \Delta_f H°(\text{products}) - \sum n_r \Delta_f H°(\text{reactants})$ then

$\Delta_r S° = \sum n_p S°(\text{products}) - \sum n_r S°(\text{reactants})$ then J K^{-1} mol^{-1} $\rightarrow$ kJ K^{-1} mol^{-1} then $\Delta_r H°$, $\Delta_r S°$,

$$\frac{1 \text{ kJ}}{1000 \text{ J}}$$

$$T \rightarrow \Delta_r G \text{ then } \Delta_r G°, T \rightarrow K$$

$$\Delta_r G° = \Delta_r H° - T\Delta_r S° \quad \Delta_r G° = -RT \ln K$$

Solution:

Reactant/Product	$\Delta_f H°$(kJ mol^{-1} from Appendix IIB)
H$_2$S (g)	−20.6
H$_2$ (g)	0.0
S$_2$ (g)	128.6

Be sure to pull data for the correct formula and phase.
$$\Delta_r H° = \sum n_p \Delta_f H°(\text{products}) - \sum n_r \Delta_f H°(\text{reactants})$$
$$= [2(\Delta_f H°(H_2 (g))) + 1(\Delta_f H°(S_2 (g)))] - [2(\Delta_f H°(H_2 S (g)))]$$
$$= [2(0.0 \text{ kJ mol}^{-1}) + 1(128.6 \text{ kJ mol}^{-1})] - [2(-20.6 \text{ kJ mol}^{-1})]$$
$$= [128.6 \text{ kJ mol}^{-1}] - [-41.2 \text{ kJ mol}^{-1}]$$
$$= +169.8 \text{ kJ mol}^{-1} \text{ then}$$

Reactant/Product	$S°$(J K^{-1} mol^{-1} from Appendix IIB)
H$_2$S (g)	205.8
H$_2$ (g)	130.7
S$_2$ (g)	228.2

Be sure to pull data for the correct formula and phase.

$$\Delta_r S° = \sum n_p S°(\text{products}) - \sum n_r S°(\text{reactants})$$
$$= [2(S°(H_2\ (g))) + 1(S°(S_2\ (g)))] - [2(S°(H_2S\ (g)))]$$
$$= [2(130.7\ \text{J K}^{-1}\ \text{mol}^{-1}) + 1(228.2\ \text{J K}^{-1}\ \text{mol}^{-1})] - [2(205.8\ \text{J K}^{-1}\ \text{mol}^{-1})]$$
$$= [489.6\ \text{J K}^{-1}\ \text{mol}^{-1}] - [411.6\ \text{J K}^{-1}\ \text{mol}^{-1}]$$
$$= +78.0\ \text{J K}^{-1}\ \text{mol}^{-1}$$

then $+78.0\ \text{J K}^{-1}\ \text{mol}^{-1} \times \dfrac{1\ \text{kJ}}{1000\ \text{J}} = +0.0780\ \text{kJ K}^{-1}\ \text{mol}^{-1}$ then

$$\Delta_r G° = \Delta_r H° - T\Delta_r S° = +169.8\ \text{kJ mol}^{-1} - (525\ \text{K})(+0.0780\ \text{kJ K}^{-1}\ \text{mol}^{-1}) = +128.\underline{8}5\ \text{kJ mol}^{-1}$$
$$= +1.2\underline{8}85 \times 10^5\ \text{J mol}^{-1}\ \text{then}$$

$\Delta_r G° = -R\,T\,\ln K$. Rearrange to solve for K.

$$K = e^{\frac{-\Delta_r G°}{RT}} = e^{\frac{-1.2885 \times 10^5\ \text{J mol}^{-1}}{\left(8.314\frac{\text{J}}{\text{K} \cdot \text{mol}}\right)(525\ \text{K})}} = e^{-29.\underline{5}199} = 1.51 \times 10^{-13}.$$

Check: The units (none) are correct. The free energy change is positive, indicating a nonspontaneous reaction. This results in a very small K.

17.73   **Given:** table of K versus temperature **Find:** $\Delta_r H°$, $\Delta_r S°$
Conceptual Plan: Plot ln K versus 1/T. The slope will be $-\Delta_r H°/R$ and the intercept will be $\Delta_r S°/R$.

Solution: Plot $\ln K$ versus $1/T$. Since $\ln K = -\dfrac{\Delta_r H°}{R}\dfrac{1}{T} + \dfrac{\Delta_r S°}{R}$, the negative of the slope will be

$-\dfrac{\Delta_r H°}{R}$ and the intercept will be $\dfrac{\Delta_r S°}{R}$. The slope can be determined by measuring $\Delta y / \Delta x$ on the plot or by

using functions, such as "add trendline" in Excel. Since the slope is 1124.9 K,

$$\Delta_r H° = -\text{slope } R = -(1124.9\ \text{K})\left(8.314\frac{\text{J}}{\text{K} \cdot \text{mol}}\right)\left(\frac{1\ \text{kJ}}{1000\ \text{J}}\right) = -9.\underline{3}52\ \text{kJ mol}^{-1} = -9.35\ \text{kJ mol}^{-1}.$$

Since the intercept is 2.6$\underline{6}$22 K^{-1}, $\Delta_r S° = \text{intercept } R = \left(\dfrac{2.6\underline{6}22}{\text{K}}\right)\left(8.314\ \dfrac{\text{J}}{\text{K} \cdot \text{mol}}\right) = 22.\underline{1}33\ \text{J K}^{-1}\ \text{mol}^{-1}$

$= 22.1\ \text{J K}^{-1}\ \text{mol}^{-1}.$

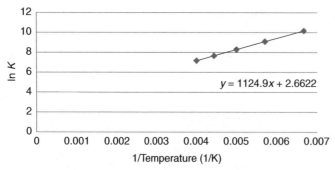

Check: The units are correct (kJ mol^{-1} and J K^{-1} mol^{-1}). The plot is very linear. The numbers are typical for reactions.

17.75   **Given:** $\Delta_r H° = -25.8$ kJ mol^{-1}, $K = 1.4 \times 10^3$ at 298 K **Find:** K at 655 K
Conceptual Plan: $\Delta_r H°, K_1, T_1, T_2 \rightarrow K_2$
$$\ln K = -\frac{\Delta_r H°}{R}\frac{1}{T} + \frac{\Delta_r S°}{R}$$

Solution: Since $\ln K = -\dfrac{\Delta_r H°}{R}\dfrac{1}{T} + \dfrac{\Delta_r S°}{R}$, $\ln K_1 + \dfrac{\Delta_r H°}{R}\dfrac{1}{T_1} = \dfrac{\Delta_r S°}{R} = \ln K_2 + \dfrac{\Delta_r H°}{R}\dfrac{1}{T_2}$.

Rearrange to solve for K_2.

$$\ln K_2 = \ln K_1 + \frac{\Delta_r H°}{R}\left(\frac{1}{T_1} - \frac{1}{T_2}\right) = \ln(1.4 \times 10^3) + \frac{-25.8\ \text{kJ}}{8.314\ \dfrac{\text{J}}{\text{K} \cdot \text{mol}}} \times \dfrac{1000\ \text{J}}{1\ \text{kJ}}\left(\frac{1}{298\ \text{K}} - \frac{1}{655\ \text{K}}\right) = 1.\underline{5}6852\ \text{and so}$$

$$K_2 = e^{1.56852} = 4.\underline{7}9954 = 4.8$$

Check: The units are correct (none). Since the reaction is exothermic, we expect the K to decrease with increasing temperature.

Cumulative Problems

17.77 (a) +, since vapours have higher entropy than liquids.

(b) –, since solids have less entropy than liquids.

(c) –, since there is only one microstate for the final macrostate and there are six microstates for the initial macrostate.

17.79 (a) **Given**: $N_2\ (g) + O_2\ (g) \rightarrow 2\ NO\ (g)$ **Find**: $\Delta_r G°$ and K at 25 °C
Conceptual Plan: $\Delta_r H° = \sum n_p \Delta_f H°\text{(products)} - \sum n_r \Delta_f H°\text{(reactants)}$ then
$\Delta_r S° = \sum n_p S°\text{(products)} - \sum n_r S°\text{(reactants)}$ then °C → K then J K^{-1} mol^{-1} → kJ K^{-1} mol^{-1} then

$$K = 273.15 + °C \qquad \frac{1\ kJ}{1000\ J}$$

$\Delta_r H°, \Delta_r S°, T \rightarrow \Delta_r G$ then $\Delta_r G°, T \rightarrow K$
$$\Delta_r G° = \Delta_r H° - T\Delta_r S° \qquad \Delta_r G° = -RT \ln K$$
Solution:

Reactant/Product	$\Delta_f H°$(kJ mol^{-1} from Appendix IIB)
$N_2\ (g)$	0.0
$O_2\ (g)$	0.0
$NO\ (g)$	91.3

Be sure to pull data for the correct formula and phase.
$$\begin{aligned}\Delta_r H° &= \sum n_p \Delta_f H°\text{(products)} - \sum n_r \Delta_f H°\text{(reactants)}\\ &= [2(\Delta_f H°(NO\ (g)))] - [1(\Delta_f H°(N_2\ (g))) + 1(\Delta_f H°(O_2\ (g)))]\\ &= [2(91.3\ kJ\ mol^{-1})] - [1(0.0\ kJ\ mol^{-1}) + 1(0.0\ kJ\ mol^{-1})]\\ &= [182.6\ kJ\ mol^{-1}] - [0.0\ kJ\ mol^{-1}]\\ &= +182.6\ kJ\ mol^{-1}\ \text{then}\end{aligned}$$

Reactant/Product	$S°$(J K^{-1} mol^{-1} from Appendix IIB)
$N_2\ (g)$	191.6
$O_2\ (g)$	205.2
$NO\ (g)$	210.8

Be sure to pull data for the correct formula and phase.
$$\begin{aligned}\Delta_r S° &= \sum n_p S°\text{(products)} - \sum n_r S°\text{(reactants)}\\ &= [2(S°(NO\ (g)))] - [1(S°(N_2\ (g))) + 1(S°(O_2\ (g)))]\\ &= [2(210.8\ J\ K^{-1}\ mol^{-1})] - [1(191.6\ J\ K^{-1}\ mol^{-1}) + 1(205.2\ J\ K^{-1}\ mol^{-1})]\\ &= [421.6\ J\ K^{-1}\ mol^{-1}] - [396.8\ J\ K^{-1}\ mol^{-1}]\\ &= +24.8\ J\ K^{-1}\ mol^{-1}\end{aligned}$$

then $T = 273.15 + 25\ °C = 298\ K$ then $+24.8\ J\ K^{-1}\ mol^{-1} \times \dfrac{1\ kJ}{1000\ J} = +0.0248\ kJ\ K^{-1}\ mol^{-1}$ then

$\Delta_r G° = \Delta_r H° - T\Delta_r S° = +182.6\ kJ\ mol^{-1} - (298\ K)(0.0248\ kJ\ K^{-1}\ mol^{-1}) = +175.2\ kJ\ mol^{-1}$
$= +1.752 \times 10^5\ J\ mol^{-1}$ then $\Delta_r G° = -RT \ln K$. Rearrange to solve for K.

$$K = e^{\frac{-\Delta_r G°}{RT}} = e^{\frac{-1.752 \times 10^5\ J\,mol^{-1}}{\left(8.314\frac{J}{K\,\cdot\,mol}\right)(298\ K)}} = e^{-70.7144} = 1.95 \times 10^{-31}$$ so the reaction is nonspontaneous and at equilibrium mostly reactants are present.
Check: The units (kJ mol^{-1} and none) are correct. The enthalpy is twice the enthalpy of formation of NO. We expect a very small entropy change because the number of moles of gas is unchanged. Since the positive enthalpy term dominates at room temperature, the free energy change is very positive and the reaction in the forward direction is nonspontaneous. This results in a very small K.

(b)   **Given:** N_2 (g) + O_2 (g) → 2 NO (g) **Find:** $\Delta_rG°$ at 2000 K

Conceptual Plan: Use results from part (a) $\Delta_rH°$, $\Delta_rS°$, T → $\Delta_rG°$ then $\Delta_rG°$, T → K

$$\Delta_rG° = \Delta_rH° - T\Delta_rS° \qquad\qquad \Delta_rG° = -RT \ln K$$

Solution: $\Delta_rG° = \Delta_rH° - T\Delta_rS° = +182.6 \text{ kJ mol}^{-1} - (2000 \text{ K})(0.0248 \text{ kJ K}^{-1}\text{ mol}^{-1})$

$= +133.0 \text{ kJ mol}^{-1} = +1.330 \times 10^5 \text{ J mol}^{-1}$ then $\Delta_rG° = -RT \ln K$. Rearrange to solve for K.

$$K = e^{\frac{-\Delta_rG°}{RT}} = e^{\frac{-1.330 \times 10^5 \text{ J mol}^{-1}}{\left(8.314\frac{\text{J}}{\text{K} \cdot \text{mol}}\right)(2000 \text{ K})}} = e^{-7.998557} = 3.36 \times 10^{-4} \text{ so the forward reaction is}$$

becoming more spontaneous.

Check: The units (kJ mol^{-1} and none) are correct. As the temperature rises, the entropy term becomes more significant. The free energy change is reduced and the K increases. The reaction is still nonspontaneous.

17.81   **Given:** C_2H_4 (g) + X_2 (g) → $C_2H_4X_2$ (g) where X = Cl, Br, and I

Find: $\Delta_rH°$, $\Delta_rS°$, $\Delta_rG°$ and K at 25 °C and spontaneity trends with X and temperature

Conceptual Plan: $\Delta_rH° = \sum n_p\Delta_fH°$(products) $-$ $\sum n_r\Delta_fH°$(reactants) then

$\Delta_rS° = \sum n_pS°$(products) $-$ $\sum n_rS°$(reactants) then °C → K then J K^{-1} mol^{-1} → kJ K^{-1} mol^{-1} then

$$K = 273.15 + °C \qquad\qquad \frac{1 \text{ kJ}}{1000 \text{ J}}$$

$\Delta_rH°$, $\Delta_rS°$, T → $\Delta_rG°$

$$\Delta_rG° = \Delta_rH° - T\Delta_rS°$$

Solution:

Reactant/Product	$\Delta_fH°$(kJ mol^{-1} from Appendix IIB)
C_2H_4 (g)	52.4
Cl_2 (g)	0.0
$C_2H_4Cl_2$ (g)	−129.7

Be sure to pull data for the correct formula and phase.

$\Delta_rH° = \sum n_p\Delta_fH°$(products) $-$ $\sum n_r\Delta_fH°$(reactants)

$= [1(\Delta_fH°(C_2H_4Cl_2 \text{ (g)}))] - [1(\Delta_fH°(C_2H_4 \text{ (g)})) + 1(\Delta_fH°(Cl_2 \text{ (g)}))]$

$= [1(-129.7 \text{ kJ mol}^{-1})] - [1(52.4 \text{ kJ mol}^{-1}) + 1(0.0 \text{ kJ mol}^{-1})]$

$= [-129.7 \text{ kJ mol}^{-1}] - [52.4 \text{ kJ mol}^{-1}]$

$= -182.1 \text{ kJ mol}^{-1}$ then

Reactant/Product	$S°$(J K^{-1} mol^{-1} from Appendix IIB)
C_2H_4 (g)	219.3
Cl_2 (g)	223.1
$C_2H_4Cl_2$ (g)	308.0

Be sure to pull data for the correct formula and phase.

$\Delta_rS° = \sum n_pS°$(products) $-$ $\sum n_rS°$(reactants)

$= [1(S°(C_2H_4Cl_2 \text{ (g)}))] - [1(S°(C_2H_4 \text{ (g)})) + 1(S°(Cl_2 \text{ (g)}))]$

$= [1(308.0 \text{ J K}^{-1}\text{ mol}^{-1})] - [1(219.3 \text{ J K}^{-1}\text{ mol}^{-1}) + 1(223.1 \text{ J K}^{-1}\text{ mol}^{-1})]$

$= [308.0 \text{ J K}^{-1}\text{ mol}^{-1}] - [442.4 \text{ J K}^{-1}\text{ mol}^{-1}]$

$= -134.4 \text{ J K}^{-1}\text{ mol}^{-1}$

then $T = 273.15 + 25$ °C $= 298$ K then $-134.4 \text{ J K}^{-1}\text{ mol}^{-1} \times \frac{1 \text{ kJ}}{1000 \text{ J}} = -0.1344 \text{ kJ K}^{-1}\text{ mol}^{-1}$ then

$\Delta_rG° = \Delta_rH° - T\Delta_rS° = -182.1 \text{ kJ mol}^{-1} - (298 \text{ K})(-0.1344 \text{ kJ K}^{-1}\text{ mol}^{-1}) = -142.0 \text{ kJ mol}^{-1}$

$= -1.420 \times 10^5 \text{ J mol}^{-1}$ then $\Delta_rG° = -RT \ln K$. Rearrange to solve for K.

$$K = e^{\frac{-\Delta_rG°}{RT}} = e^{\frac{-(-1.420 \times 10^5 \text{ J mol}^{-1})}{\left(8.314\frac{\text{J}}{\text{K} \cdot \text{mol}}\right)(298 \text{ K})}} = e^{57.334} = 7.94 \times 10^{24} \text{ so the reaction is spontaneous.}$$

Reactant/Product	$\Delta_f H°$(kJ mol^{-1} from Appendix IIB)
C_2H_4 (g)	52.4
Br_2 (g)	30.9
$C_2H_4Br_2$ (g)	38.3

Be sure to pull data for the correct formula and phase.

$\Delta_r H° = \sum n_p \Delta_f H°(\text{products}) - \sum n_r \Delta_f H°(\text{reactants})$

$= [1(\Delta_f H°(C_2H_4Br_2 \, (g)))] - [1(\Delta_f H°(C_2H_4 \, (g))) + 1(\Delta_f H°(Br_2 \, (g)))]$

$= [1(38.3 \text{ kJ mol}^{-1})] - [1(52.4 \text{ kJ mol}^{-1}) + 1(30.9 \text{ kJ mol}^{-1})]$

$= [38.3 \text{ kJ mol}^{-1}] - [83.3 \text{ kJ mol}^{-1}]$

$= -45.0 \text{ kJ mol}^{-1}$ then

Reactant/Product	$S°$(J K^{-1} mol^{-1} from Appendix IIB)
C_2H_4 (g)	219.3
Br_2 (g)	245.5
$C_2H_4Br_2$ (g)	330.6

Be sure to pull data for the correct formula and phase.

$\Delta_r S° = \sum n_p S°(\text{products}) - \sum n_r S°(\text{reactants})$

$= [1(S°(C_2H_4Br_2 \, (g)))] - [1(S°(C_2H_4 \, (g))) + 1(S°(Br_2 \, (g)))]$

$= [1(330.6 \text{ J K}^{-1} \text{ mol}^{-1})] - [1(219.3 \text{ J K}^{-1} \text{ mol}^{-1}) + 1(245.5 \text{ J K}^{-1} \text{ mol}^{-1})]$

$= [330.6 \text{ J K}^{-1} \text{ mol}^{-1}] - [464.8 \text{ J K}^{-1} \text{ mol}^{-1}]$

$= -134.2 \text{ J K}^{-1} \text{ mol}^{-1}$

then $-134.2 \text{ J K}^{-1} \text{ mol}^{-1} \times \dfrac{1 \text{ kJ}}{1000 \text{ J}} = -0.1342 \text{ kJ K}^{-1} \text{ mol}^{-1}$

then $\Delta_r G° = \Delta_r H° - T\Delta_r S° = -45.0 \text{ kJ mol}^{-1} - (298 \text{ K})(-0.1342 \text{ kJ K}^{-1} \text{ mol}^{-1}) = -5.0 \text{ kJ mol}^{-1}$

$= -5.0 \times 10^3 \text{ J mol}^{-1}$ then $\Delta_r G° = -RT \ln K$

Rearrange to solve for K. $K = e^{\frac{-\Delta_r G°}{RT}} = e^{\frac{-(-5.0008 \times 10^3 \text{ J mol}^{-1})}{\left(8.314\frac{\text{J}}{\text{K} \cdot \text{mol}}\right)(298 \text{ K})}} = e^{2.021495} = 7.5$ so the reaction is spontaneous.

Reactant/Product	$\Delta_f H°$(kJ mol^{-1} from Appendix IIB)
C_2H_4 (g)	52.4
I_2 (g)	62.42
$C_2H_4I_2$ (g)	66.5

Be sure to pull data for the correct formula and phase.

$\Delta_r H° = \sum n_p \Delta_f H°(\text{products}) - \sum n_r \Delta_f H°(\text{reactants})$

$= [1(\Delta_f H°(C_2H_4I_2 \, (g)))] - [1(\Delta_f H°(C_2H_4 \, (g))) + 1(\Delta_f H°(I_2 \, (g)))]$

$= [1(66.5 \text{ kJ mol}^{-1})] - [1(52.4 \text{ kJ mol}^{-1}) + 1(62.42 \text{ kJ mol}^{-1})]$

$= [66.5 \text{ kJ mol}^{-1}] - [114.82 \text{ kJ mol}^{-1}]$

$= -48.32 \text{ kJ mol}^{-1}$ then

Reactant/Product	$S°$(J K^{-1} mol^{-1} from Appendix IIB)
C_2H_4 (g)	219.3
I_2 (g)	260.69
$C_2H_4I_2$ (g)	347.8

Be sure to pull data for the correct formula and phase.

$\Delta_r S° = \sum n_p S°(\text{products}) - \sum n_r S°(\text{reactants})$

$= [1(S°(C_2H_4I_2 \, (g)))] - [1(S°(C_2H_4 \, (g))) + 1(S°(I_2 \, (g)))]$

$= [1(347.8 \text{ J K}^{-1} \text{ mol}^{-1})] - [1(219.3 \text{ J K}^{-1} \text{ mol}^{-1}) + 1(260.69 \text{ J K}^{-1} \text{ mol}^{-1})]$

$= [347.8 \text{ J K}^{-1} \text{ mol}^{-1}] - [479.99 \text{ J K}^{-1} \text{ mol}^{-1}]$

$= -132.2 \text{ J K}^{-1} \text{ mol}^{-1}$

then $-132.2 \text{ J K}^{-1} \text{ mol}^{-1} \times \dfrac{1 \text{ kJ}}{1000 \text{ J}} = -0.1322 \text{ kJ K}^{-1} \text{ mol}^{-1}$

then $\Delta_r G° = \Delta_r H° - T\Delta_r S° = -48.32 \text{ kJ mol}^{-1} - (298 \text{ K})(-0.1322 \text{ kJ K}^{-1} \text{ mol}^{-1}) = -8.9244 \text{ kJ mol}^{-1}$

$= -8.9244 \times 10^3 \text{ J mol}^{-1}$ then $\Delta_r G° = -RT \ln K$. Rearrange to solve for K.

$$K = e^{\frac{-\Delta_r G°}{RT}} = e^{\dfrac{-(-8.9244 \times 10^3 \text{ J mol}^{-1})}{\left(8.314 \frac{\text{J}}{\text{K} \cdot \text{mol}}\right)(298 \text{ K})}} = e^{3.6021} = 37 \text{ and the reaction is spontaneous.}$$

Cl_2 is the most spontaneous in the forward direction; Br_2 is the least. The entropy change in the reactions is very constant. The spontaneity is determined by the standard enthalpy of formation of the dihalogenated ethane. Higher temperatures make the forward reactions less spontaneous.

Check: The units (kJ mol^{-1} and none) are correct. The enthalpy change becomes less negative as we move to larger halogens. The enthalpy term dominates at room temperature, the free energy change is the same sign as the enthalpy change. The more negative the Gibbs energy change, the larger the K.

17.83   (a)   **Given:** $N_2O (g) + NO_2 (g) \rightleftharpoons 3 NO (g)$ at 298 K   **Find:** $\Delta_r G°$

   Conceptual Plan: $\Delta_r G° = \sum n_p \Delta_f G°(\text{products}) - \sum n_r \Delta_f G°(\text{reactants})$

   Solution:

Reactant/Product	$\Delta_f G°$(kJ mol^{-1} from Appendix IIB)
$N_2O (g)$	103.7
$NO_2 (g)$	51.3
$NO (g)$	87.6

   Be sure to pull data for the correct formula and phase.

   $\Delta_r G° = \sum n_p \Delta_f G°(\text{products}) - \sum n_r \Delta_f G°(\text{reactants})$
   $= [3(\Delta_f G°(NO (g)))] - [1(\Delta_f G°(N_2O (g))) + 1(\Delta_f G°(NO_2 (g)))]$
   $= [3(87.6 \text{ kJ mol}^{-1})] - [1(103.7 \text{ kJ mol}^{-1}) + 1(51.3 \text{ kJ mol}^{-1})]$
   $= [262.8 \text{ kJ mol}^{-1}] - [155.0 \text{ kJ mol}^{-1}]$
   $= +107.8 \text{ kJ mol}^{-1}$

   The reaction is nonspontaneous.

   Check: The units (kJ mol^{-1}) are correct. The standard free energy for the reaction was positive, so the reaction is nonspontaneous.

   (b)   **Given:** $P_{N_2O} = P_{NO_2} = 1.0$ bar initially   **Find:** P_{NO} when reaction ceases to be spontaneous

   Conceptual Plan: Reaction will no longer be spontaneous when $Q = K$, so $\Delta_r G°, T \rightarrow K$.

   $$\Delta_r G° = -RT \ln K$$

   Then solve the equilibrium problem to get gas pressures, since $K << 1$ the amount of NO generated will be very, very small compared to 1.0 bar, so, within experimental error, $P_{N_2O} = P_{NO_2} = 1.0$ bar. Simply solve for P_{NO}.

   $$K = \frac{P_{NO}^3}{P_{N_2O} P_{NO_2}}$$

   Solution: $\Delta_r G° = -RT \ln K$. Rearrange to solve for K.

   $$K = e^{\frac{-\Delta_r G°}{RT}} = e^{\dfrac{-(+107.8 \text{ kJ mol}^{-1}) \times \frac{1000 \text{ J}}{1 \text{ kJ}}}{\left(8.314 \frac{\text{J}}{\text{K} \cdot \text{mol}}\right)(298 \text{ K})}} = e^{-43.5103} = 1.27 \times 10^{-19}. \text{ Since } K = \frac{P_{NO}^3}{P_{N_2O} P_{NO_2}}, \text{ rearrange to}$$

   solve for P_{NO}. $P_{NO}^3 = \sqrt[3]{K \, P_{N_2O} P_{NO_2}} = \sqrt[3]{(1.27 \times 10^{-19})(1.0)(1.0)} = 5.0 \times 10^{-7}$ bar.
   Note that the assumption that P_{N_2O} was very, very small was valid.

   Check: The units (bar) are correct. Since the Gibbs energy change was positive, the K was very small. This leads us to expect that very little NO will be formed.

   (c)   **Given:** $N_2O (g) + NO_2 (g) \rightleftharpoons 3 NO (g)$ **Find:** temperature for spontaneity

   Conceptual Plan: $\Delta_r H° = \sum n_p \Delta_f H°(\text{products}) - \sum n_r \Delta_f H°(\text{reactants})$ then

$\Delta_r S° = \sum n_p S°(\text{products}) - \sum n_r S°(\text{reactants})$ then $J\,K^{-1}\,mol^{-1} \rightarrow kJ\,K^{-1}\,mol^{-1}$ then $\Delta_r H°, \Delta_r S° \rightarrow T$

$$\frac{1\ kJ}{1000\ J}$$

$$\Delta_r G° = \Delta_r H° - T\Delta_r S°$$

Solution:

Reactant/Product	$\Delta_f H°(kJ\,mol^{-1}$ from Appendix IIB)
$N_2O\ (g)$	81.6
$NO_2\ (g)$	33.2
$NO\ (g)$	91.3

Be sure to pull data for the correct formula and phase.

$\Delta_r H° = \sum n_p \Delta_f H°(\text{products}) - \sum n_r \Delta_f H°(\text{reactants})$

$= [3(\Delta_f H°(NO\ (g)))] - [1(\Delta_f H°(N_2O\ (g))) + 1(\Delta_f H°(NO_2\ (g)))]$

$= [3(91.3\ kJ\,mol^{-1})] - [1(81.6\ kJ\,mol^{-1}) + 1(33.2\ kJ\,mol^{-1})]$

$= [273.9\ kJ\,mol^{-1}] - [114.8\ kJ\,mol^{-1}]$

$= +159.1\ kJ\,mol^{-1}$ then

Reactant/Product	$S°(J\,K^{-1}\,mol^{-1}$ from Appendix IIB)
$N_2O\ (g)$	220.0
$NO_2\ (g)$	240.1
$NO\ (g)$	210.8

Be sure to pull data for the correct formula and phase.

$\Delta_r S° = \sum n_p S°(\text{products}) - \sum n_r S°(\text{reactants})$

$= [3(S°(NO\ (g)))] - [1(S°(N_2O\ (g))) + 1(S°(NO_2\ (g)))]$

$= [3(210.8\ J\,K^{-1}\,mol^{-1})] - [1(220.0\ J\,K^{-1}\,mol^{-1}) + 1(240.1\ J\,K^{-1}\,mol^{-1})]$

$= [632.4\ J\,K^{-1}\,mol^{-1}] - [460.1\ J\,K^{-1}\,mol^{-1}]$

$= +172.3\ J\,K^{-1}\,mol^{-1}$

then $+172.3\ J\,K^{-1}\,mol^{-1} \times \dfrac{1\ kJ}{1000\ J} = +0.1723\ kJ\,K^{-1}\,mol^{-1}$. Since $\Delta_r G° = \Delta_r H° - T\Delta_r S°$, set $\Delta_r G = 0$

and rearrange to solve for T. $T = \dfrac{\Delta_r H}{\Delta_r S°} = \dfrac{+159.1\ kJ\,mol^{-1}}{0.1723\ kJ\,K^{-1}\,mol^{-1}} = +923.4\ K.$

Check: The units (K) are correct. The reaction can be made more spontaneous by raising the temperature, because the entropy change is positive (increase in the number of moles of gas).

17.85 (a) **Given:** ATP (aq) + $H_2O\ (l) \rightarrow$ ADP (aq) + $P_i\ (aq)$ $\Delta_r G° = -30.5\ kJ\,mol^{-1}$ at 298 K **Find:** K

Conceptual Plan: $\Delta_r G°, T \rightarrow K$

$$\Delta_r G° = -RT\ \ln K$$

Solution: $\Delta_r G° = -RT\ \ln K$. Rearrange to solve for K.

$K = e^{\frac{-\Delta_r G°}{RT}} = e^{\dfrac{-(-30.5\ kJ\,mol^{-1}) \times \frac{1000\ J}{1\ kJ}}{\left(8.314\ \frac{J}{K\cdot mol}\right)(298\ K)}} = e^{12.3104} = 2.22 \times 10^5.$

Check: The units (none) are correct. The free energy change is negative and the reaction is spontaneous. This results in a large K.

(b) **Given:** oxidation of glucose drives reforming of ATP

Find: $\Delta_r G°$ of oxidation of glucose and moles ATP formed per mole of glucose

Conceptual Plan: write a balanced reaction for glucose oxidation then

$\Delta_r G° = \sum n_p \Delta_f G°(\text{products}) - \sum n_r \Delta_f G°(\text{reactants})$ then $\Delta_r G°s \rightarrow$ **mol ATP/mol glucose.**

$$\frac{\Delta_r G°\ \text{glucose oxidation}}{\Delta_r G°\ \text{ATP hydrolysis}}$$

Solution: $C_6H_{12}O_6\ (s) + 6\,O_2\ (g) \rightarrow 6\,CO_2\ (g) + 6\,H_2O\ (l)$

Reactant/Product	$\Delta_f G°(kJ\,mol^{-1}$ from Appendix IIB)
$C_6H_{12}O_6\ (s)$	-910.4
$O_2\ (g)$	0.0
$CO_2\ (g)$	-394.4
$H_2O\ (l)$	-237.1

Be sure to pull data for the correct formula and phase.

$$\Delta_r G° = \sum n_p \Delta_f G°(\text{products}) - \sum n_r \Delta_f G°(\text{reactants})$$

$$= [6(\Delta_f G°(CO_2\ (g))) + 6(\Delta_f G°(H_2O\ (l)))] - [1(\Delta_f G°(C_6H_{12}O_6\ (s))) + 6(\Delta_f G°(O_2\ (g)))]$$

$$= [6(-394.4\ \text{kJ mol}^{-1}) + 6(-237.1\ \text{kJ mol}^{-1})] - [1(-910.4\ \text{kJ mol}^{-1}) + 6(0.0\ \text{kJ mol}^{-1})]$$

$$= [-3789.0\ \text{kJ mol}^{-1}] - [-910.4\ \text{kJ mol}^{-1}]$$

$$= -2878.6\ \text{kJ mol}^{-1}$$

So the reaction is very spontaneous. $\dfrac{2878.6\ \dfrac{\text{kJ generated}}{\text{mol glucose oxidized}}}{30.5\ \dfrac{\text{kJ needed}}{\text{mol ATP reformed}}} = 94.4\ \dfrac{\text{mol ATP reformed}}{\text{mol glucose oxidized}}$

Check: The units (mol) are correct. The Gibbs energy change for the glucose oxidation is large compared to the ATP hydrolysis, so we expect to reform many moles of ATP.

17.87   (a)   **Given:** 2 CO (g) + 2 NO (g) → N$_2$ (g) + 2 CO$_2$ (g) **Find:** $\Delta_r G°$ and effect of increasing T on $\Delta_r G°$
Conceptual Plan: $\Delta_r G° = \sum n_p \Delta_f G°(\text{products}) - \sum n_r \Delta_f G°(\text{reactants})$

Solution:

Reactant/Product	$\Delta_f G°$(kJ mol^{-1} from Appendix IIB)
CO (g)	-137.2
NO (g)	87.6
N$_2$ (g)	0.0
CO$_2$ (g)	-394.4

Be sure to pull data for the correct formula and phase.

$$\Delta_r G° = \sum n_p \Delta_f G°(\text{products}) - \sum n_r \Delta_f G°(\text{reactants})$$

$$= [1(\Delta_f G°(N_2\ (g))) + 2(\Delta_f G°(CO_2\ (g)))] - [2(\Delta_f G°(CO\ (g))) + 2(\Delta_f G°(NO\ (g)))]$$

$$= [1(0.0\ \text{kJ mol}^{-1}) + 2(-394.4\ \text{kJ mol}^{-1})] - [2(-137.2\ \text{kJ mol}^{-1}) + 2(87.6\ \text{kJ mol}^{-1})]$$

$$= [-788.8\ \text{kJ mol}^{-1}] - [-99.2\ \text{kJ mol}^{-1}]$$

$$= -689.6\ \text{kJ mol}^{-1}$$

Since the number of moles of gas is decreasing, the entropy change is negative and so $\Delta_r G°$ will become less negative with increasing temperature.
Check: The units (kJ mol^{-1}) are correct. The Gibbs energy change is negative since the carbon dioxide has such a low Gibbs energy of formation.

(b)   **Given:** 5 H$_2$ (g) + 2 NO (g) → 2 NH$_3$ (g) + 2 H$_2$O (g) **Find:** $\Delta_r G°$ and effect of increasing T on $\Delta_r G°$
Conceptual Plan: $\Delta_r G° = \sum n_p \Delta_f G°(\text{products}) - \sum n_r \Delta_f G°(\text{reactants})$

Solution:

Reactant/Product	$\Delta_f G°$(kJ mol^{-1} from Appendix IIB)
H$_2$ (g)	0.0
NO (g)	87.6
NH$_3$ (g)	-16.4
H$_2$O (g)	-228.6

Be sure to pull data for the correct formula and phase.

$$\Delta_r G° = \sum n_p \Delta_f G°(\text{products}) - \sum n_r \Delta_f G°(\text{reactants})$$

$$= [2(\Delta_f G°(NH_3\ (g))) + 2(\Delta_f G°(H_2O\ (g)))] - [5(\Delta_f G°(H_2\ (g))) + 2(\Delta_f G°(NO\ (g)))]$$

$$= [2(-16.4\ \text{kJ mol}^{-1}) + 2(-228.6\ \text{kJ mol}^{-1})] - [5(0.0\ \text{kJ mol}^{-1}) + 2(87.6\ \text{kJ mol}^{-1})]$$

$$= [-490.0\ \text{kJ mol}^{-1}] - [175.2\ \text{kJ mol}^{-1}]$$

$$= -665.2\ \text{kJ mol}^{-1}$$

Since the number of moles of gas is decreasing, the entropy change is negative and so $\Delta_r G°$ will become less negative with increasing temperature.
Check: The units (kJ mol^{-1}) are correct. The Gibbs energy change is negative since ammonia and water have such a low Gibbs energy of formation.

(c)   **Given:** 2 H$_2$ (g) + 2 NO (g) → N$_2$ (g) + 2 H$_2$O (g) **Find:** $\Delta_r G°$ and effect of increasing T on $\Delta_r G°$
Conceptual Plan: $\Delta_r G° = \sum n_p \Delta_f G°(\text{products}) - \sum n_r \Delta_f G°(\text{reactants})$

Solution:

Reactant/Product	$\Delta_f G°$(kJ mol^{-1} from Appendix IIB)
H_2 (g)	0.0
NO (g)	87.6
N_2 (g)	0.0
H_2O (g)	-228.6

Be sure to pull data for the correct formula and phase.

$$\Delta_r G° = \sum n_p \Delta_f G°(\text{products}) - \sum n_r \Delta_f G°(\text{reactants})$$
$$= [1(\Delta_f G°(N_2 \, (g))) + 2(\Delta_f G°(H_2O \, (g)))] - [2(\Delta_f G°(H_2 \, (g))) + 2(\Delta_f G°(NO \, (g)))]$$
$$= [1(0.0 \text{ kJ mol}^{-1}) + 2(-228.6 \text{ kJ mol}^{-1})] - [2(0.0 \text{ kJ mol}^{-1}) + 2(87.6 \text{ kJ mol}^{-1})]$$
$$= [-457.2 \text{ kJ mol}^{-1}] - [175.2 \text{ kJ mol}^{-1}]$$
$$= -632.4 \text{ kJ mol}^{-1}$$

Since the number of moles of gas is decreasing, the entropy change is negative and so $\Delta_r G°$ will become less negative with increasing temperature.

Check: The units (kJ mol^{-1}) are correct. The Gibbs energy change is negative since water has such a low Gibbs energy of formation.

(d) **Given:** $2 \, NH_3 \, (g) + 2 \, O_2 \, (g) \rightarrow N_2O \, (g) + 3 \, H_2O \, (g)$ **Find:** $\Delta_r G°$ and effect of increasing T on $\Delta_r G°$
Conceptual Plan: $\Delta_r G° = \sum n_p \Delta_f G°(\textbf{products}) - \sum n_r \Delta_f G°(\textbf{reactants})$

Solution:

Reactant/Product	$\Delta_f G°$(kJ mol^{-1} from Appendix IIB)
NH_3 (g)	-16.4
O_2 (g)	0.0
N_2O (g)	103.7
H_2O (g)	-228.6

Be sure to pull data for the correct formula and phase.

$$\Delta_r G° = \sum n_p \Delta_f G°(\text{products}) - \sum n_r \Delta_f G°(\text{reactants})$$
$$= [1(\Delta_f G°(N_2O \, (g))) + 3(\Delta_f G°(H_2O \, (g)))] - [2(\Delta_f G°(NH_3 \, (g))) + 2(\Delta_f G°(O_2 \, (g)))]$$
$$= [1(103.7 \text{ kJ mol}^{-1}) + 3(-228.6 \text{ kJ mol}^{-1})] - [2(-16.4 \text{ kJ mol}^{-1}) + 2(0.0 \text{ kJ mol}^{-1})]$$
$$= [-582.1 \text{ kJ mol}^{-1}] - [-32.8 \text{ kJ mol}^{-1}]$$
$$= -549.3 \text{ kJ mol}^{-1}$$

Since the number of moles of gas is constant the entropy change will be small and slightly negative, so the magnitude of $\Delta_r G°$ will decrease with increasing temperature.

Check: The units (kJ mol^{-1}) are correct. The Gibbs energy change is negative since water has such a low Gibbs energy of formation. The entropy change is negative once the $S°$ values are reviewed ($\Delta_r S° = -9.6$ J K^{-1} mol^{-1}).

17.89 With one exception, the formation of any oxide of nitrogen at 298 K requires more moles of gas as reactants than are formed as products. For example, 1 mole of N_2O requires 0.5 moles of O_2 and 1 mole of N_2; 1 mole of N_2O_3 requires 1 mole of N_2 and 1.5 moles of O_2, and so on. The exception is NO, where 1 mole of NO requires 0.5 moles of O_2 and 0.5 moles of N_2: $\frac{1}{2} N_2(g) + \frac{1}{2} O_2(g) \rightarrow NO(g)$. This reaction has a positive $\Delta_r S°$ because what is essentially mixing of the N and O has taken place in the product.

17.91 **Given:** $X_2 \, (g) \rightarrow 2 \, X \, (g)$; $P_{\text{initial } X_2} = 755$ torr, $P_{\text{final } X} = 103$ torr at 298 K; $P_{\text{initial } X_2} = 748$ torr, $P_{\text{final } X} = 532$ torr at 755 K **Find:** $\Delta_r H°$

Conceptual Plan: at each temperature $P_{\text{initial } X_2}, P_{\text{final } X} \rightarrow K$ **then** $K_1, K_2, T_1, T_2 \rightarrow \Delta_r H°$

$$\text{Use stoichiometry to calculate } [X_2]_{\text{final}} \text{ and } K = \frac{P_X^2}{P_{X_2}} \qquad \ln K = -\frac{\Delta_r H°}{R} \frac{1}{T} + \frac{\Delta_r S°}{R}$$

Solution: Use stoichiometry of $X_2 \, (g) \rightarrow 2 \, X \, (g)$; $P_{\text{final } X_2} = P_{\text{initial } X_2} - \frac{1}{2} P_{\text{final } X}$ so that at $T_1 = 298$ K

$P_{\text{final } X_2} = P_{\text{initial } X_2} - \frac{1}{2} P_{\text{final } X} = 755 \text{ torr} - \frac{1}{2} (103 \text{ torr}) = 70\underline{3}.5$ torr and at $T_{12} = 755$ K $P_{\text{final } X_2}$

$= P_{\text{initial } X_2} - \frac{1}{2}$

$P_{\text{final } X} = 748 \text{ torr} - \frac{1}{2} (532 \text{ torr}) = 482$ torr. Then $K = \frac{P_X^2}{P_{X_2}}$ so that at $T_1 = 298$ K

$$K_1 = \frac{P_X^2}{P_{X_2}} = \frac{(103)^2}{703.5} = 15.08031 \text{ and at } T_2 = 755 \text{ K. } K_2 = \frac{P_X^2}{P_{X_2}} = \frac{(532)^2}{482} = 587.1867.$$

Since $\ln K = -\dfrac{\Delta_r H^\circ}{R}\dfrac{1}{T} + \dfrac{\Delta_r S^\circ}{R}$, $\ln K_1 + \dfrac{\Delta_r H^\circ}{R}\dfrac{1}{T_1} = \dfrac{\Delta_r S^\circ}{R} = \ln K_2 + \dfrac{\Delta_r H^\circ}{R}\dfrac{1}{T_2}$.

Rearrange to solve for $\Delta_r H^\circ$.

$$\Delta_r H^\circ = \frac{\ln\dfrac{K_2}{K_1}}{\left(\dfrac{1}{T_1} - \dfrac{1}{T_2}\right)} R = \frac{\ln\left(\dfrac{587.1867}{15.08031}\right)}{\left(\dfrac{1}{298\text{ K}} - \dfrac{1}{755\text{ K}}\right)} \times 8.314\,\frac{\text{J}}{\text{K}\cdot\text{mol}} \times \frac{1\text{ kJ}}{1000\text{ J}} = 14.9889\text{ kJ mol}^{-1} = 15.0\text{ kJ mol}^{-1}$$

Check: The units are correct (kJ mol^{-1}). Since K increases with increasing temperature the reaction is expected to be endothermic.

17.93 (a) $\Delta S_{univ} > 0$. The process is spontaneous. It is slow unless a spark is applied.

(b) $\Delta S_{univ} > 0$. Although the change in the system is not spontaneous, the overall change, which includes such processes as combustion or water flow to generate electricity, is spontaneous.

(c) $\Delta S_{univ} > 0$, The acorn oak/tree system is becoming more ordered, so the processes associated with growth are not spontaneous. But they are driven by spontaneous processes such as the generation of heat by the sun and the reactions that produce energy in the cell.

17.95 At equilibrium ($P_{H_2O} = 18.3$ mbar), $\Delta_r G = 0$.

$$Q = P_{H_2O}^6 = \left(\frac{18.3\text{ mbar}}{\dfrac{1000\text{ mbar}}{1\text{ bar}}}\right)^6 = (0.0183\text{ bar})^6 = 3.7558 \times 10^{-11} \text{ and}$$

$\Delta_r G = \Delta_r G^\circ + RT \ln Q = 0$. Rearrange to solve for $\Delta_r G^\circ$ (at $P_{H_2O} = 1$ bar = standard conditions)

$$\Delta_r G^\circ = \Delta_r G - RT \ln Q = 0 - \left(8.314\frac{\text{J}}{\text{K}\cdot\text{mol}}\right)\left(\frac{1\text{ kJ}}{1000\text{ J}}\right)(298\text{ K}) \ln(3.7558 \times 10^{-11}) = 59.474\text{ kJ mol}^{-1}$$

$$= 59.5\text{ kJ mol}^{-1}.$$

17.97 **Given:** For vaporization of water $\Delta_r H^\circ = 40.6$ kJ mol^{-1}, normal boiling point ($P = 1$ bar, $T = 100$ °C)
Find: temperature of standard boiling point ($P = 1$ bar).
Conceptual Plan: atm $\to$ bar and °C $\to$ K, then $P_1, P_2 \to K_1, K_2$

$$\frac{1.01325\text{ bar}}{1\text{ atm}} \qquad K = {}^\circ\text{C} + 273.15 \qquad H_2O\,(l) \to H_2O\,(g)\ \ K = P_{H_2O}$$

$\Delta_r H^\circ, K_1, K_2, T_1 \to T_2$

$$\ln K = -\frac{\Delta_r H^\circ}{R}\frac{1}{T} + \frac{\Delta_r S^\circ}{R}$$

Solution: $P_1 = 1\text{ atm} \times \dfrac{1.01325\text{ bar}}{1\text{ atm}} = 1.01325\text{ bar} = K_1$ and $T_1 = 100 + 273.15 = 373.15$ K. $P_2 = 1$ bar $= K_2$.

Since $\ln K = -\dfrac{\Delta_r H^\circ}{R}\dfrac{1}{T} + \dfrac{\Delta_r S^\circ}{R}$, $\ln K_1 + \dfrac{\Delta_r H^\circ}{R}\dfrac{1}{T_1} = \dfrac{\Delta_r S^\circ}{R} = \ln K_2 + \dfrac{\Delta_r H^\circ}{R}\dfrac{1}{T_2}$ which simplifies to

$\ln K_1 + \dfrac{\Delta_r H^\circ}{R}\dfrac{1}{T_1} = \ln K_2 + \dfrac{\Delta_r H^\circ}{R}\dfrac{1}{T_2}$ and then rearranged to $\ln\dfrac{K_1}{K_2} = \dfrac{\Delta_r H^\circ}{R}\left(\dfrac{1}{T_2} - \dfrac{1}{T_1}\right)$. Substitute and solve

for T_2. $\ln\dfrac{1.01325}{1} = \dfrac{40.6 \times 10^3\text{ J mol}^{-1}}{8.314\text{ J K}^{-1}\text{mol}^{-1}}\left(\dfrac{1}{T_2} - \dfrac{1}{373.15}\right) \to 0.01316 = 4.883 \times 10^3\text{ K}\left(\dfrac{1}{T_2} - \dfrac{1}{373.15}\right)$

$2.695 \times 10^{-6}\text{ K}^{-1} = \dfrac{1}{T_2} - 2.6799 \times 10^{-3}\text{ K}^{-1} \to \dfrac{1}{T_2} = 2.6826 \times 10^{-3}\text{ K}^{-1}$ and $T_2 = 372.77$ K or 99.62 °C

Check: The units (K) are correct. The magnitude of the answer (< 100 °C) makes sense since 1 bar is equal to a little less than 1 atm.

Challenge Problems

17.99 (a) **Given:** glutamate (aq) + NH_3 (aq) → glutamine (aq) + H_2O (l) $\Delta_r G° = +14.2$ kJ mol^{-1} at 298 K **Find:** K
Conceptual Plan: $\Delta_r G°, T \rightarrow K$
$$\Delta_r G° = -RT \ln K$$
Solution: $\Delta_r G° = -RT \ln K$. Rearrange to solve for K.

$$K = e^{\frac{-\Delta_r G°}{RT}} = e^{\frac{-(+14.2 \text{ kJ mol}^{-1}) \times \frac{1000 \text{ J}}{1 \text{ kJ}}}{\left(8.314 \frac{\text{J}}{\text{K} \cdot \text{mol}}\right)(298 \text{ K})}} = e^{-5.73142} = 3.24 \times 10^{-3}.$$

Check: The units (none) are correct. The free energy change is positive and the reaction is nonspontaneous. This results in a small K.

(b) **Given:** pair ATP hydrolysis with glutamate/NH_3 reaction **Find:** show coupled reactions, $\Delta_r G°$ and K
Conceptual Plan: **Use the reaction mechanism shown, where A = NH_3 and B = glutamate ($C_5H_8O_4N^-$),**
then calculate $\Delta_r G°$ by adding free energies of reactions then $\Delta_r G°, T \rightarrow K$.
$$\Delta_r G° = -RT \ln K$$

Solution:

NH_3 (aq)+ATP (aq)+$\cancel{H_2O}$ $\cancel{(l)}$ → $\cancel{NH_3 - P_i(aq)}$+ADP (aq)	$\Delta_r G° = -30.5$ kJ mol^{-1}
$\cancel{NH_3 - P_i(aq)}$+ $C_5H_8O_4N^-$ (aq) → $C_5H_{10}O_3N_2$ (aq)+$\cancel{H_2O}$ $\cancel{(l)}$+$P_i(aq)$	$\Delta_r G° = +14.2$ kJ mol^{-1}
NH_3 (aq)+$C_5H_8O_4N^-$ (aq)+ATP (aq) → $C_5H_{10}O_3N_2$ (aq)+ADP (aq)+$P_i(aq)$	$\Delta_r G° = -16.3$ kJ mol^{-1}

then $\Delta_r G° = -RT \ln K$. Rearrange to solve for K.

$$K = e^{\frac{-\Delta_r G°}{RT}} = e^{\frac{-(-16.3 \text{ kJ mol}^{-1}) \times \frac{1000 \text{ J}}{1 \text{ kJ}}}{\left(8.314 \frac{\text{J}}{\text{K} \cdot \text{mol}}\right)(298 \text{ K})}} = e^{6.57902} = 7.20 \times 10^2.$$

Check: The units (none) are correct. The free energy change is negative and the reaction is spontaneous. This results in a large K.

17.101 (a) **Given:** $\frac{1}{2}$ H_2 (g) + $\frac{1}{2}$ Cl_2 (g) → HCl (g), define standard state as 2 bar **Find:** $\Delta_f G°$
Conceptual Plan: $\Delta_f G°, P_{H_2}, P_{Cl_2}, P_{HCl}, T \rightarrow$ new $\Delta_f G°$
$$\Delta_r G = \Delta_r G° + RT \ln Q \text{ where } Q = \frac{P_{HCl}}{P_{H_2}^{1/2} P_{Cl_2}^{1/2}}$$
Solution: $\Delta_f G° = -95.3$ kJ mol^{-1} and $Q = \dfrac{P_{HCl}}{P_{H_2}^{1/2} P_{Cl_2}^{1/2}} = \dfrac{2}{2^{1/2} \, 2^{1/2}} = 1$ then

$$\Delta_r G = \Delta_r G° + RT \ln Q = -95.3 \frac{\text{kJ}}{\text{mol}} + \left(8.314 \frac{\text{J}}{\text{K} \cdot \text{mol}}\right)\left(\frac{1 \text{ kJ}}{1000 \text{ J}}\right)(298 \text{ K}) \ln (1) =$$

-95.3 kJ mol^{-1}
Since the number of moles of reactants and products are the same, the decrease in volume affects the entropy of both equally, so there is no change in $\Delta_f G°$.
Check: The units (kJ mol^{-1}) are correct. The Q is 1, so $\Delta_f G°$ is unchanged under the new standard conditions.

(b) **Given:** N_2 (g) + $\frac{1}{2}$ O_2 (g) → N_2O (g), define standard state as 2 bar **Find:** $\Delta_f G°$
Conceptual Plan: $\Delta_f G°, P_{N_2}, P_{O_2}, P_{N_2O}, T \rightarrow$ new $\Delta_f G°$
$$\Delta_r G = \Delta_r G° + RT \ln Q \text{ where } Q = \frac{P_{N_2O}}{P_{N_2} P_{O_2}^{1/2}}$$
Solution: $\Delta_f G° = +103.7$ kJ mol^{-1} and $Q = \dfrac{P_{N_2O}}{P_{N_2} P_{O_2}^{1/2}} = \dfrac{2}{2 \, 2^{1/2}} = \dfrac{1}{\sqrt{2}}$ then

$$\Delta_r G = \Delta_r G° + RT \ln Q = +103.7 \frac{\text{kJ}}{\text{mol}} + \left(8.314 \frac{\text{J}}{\text{K} \cdot \text{mol}}\right)\left(\frac{1 \text{ kJ}}{1000 \text{ J}}\right)(298 \text{ K}) \ln \left(\frac{1}{\sqrt{2}}\right) =$$

$+102.8$ kJ mol^{-1}

The entropy of the reactants (1.5 mol) is decreased more than the entropy of the product (1 mol). Since the product is relatively more favoured at lower volume, $\Delta_f G°$ is less positive.

Check: The units (kJ mol^{-1}) are correct. The Q is less than one, so $\Delta_f G°$ is reduced under the new standard conditions.

(c)   **Given:** ½ H$_2$ (g) → H (g), define standard state as 2 bar   **Find:** $\Delta_f G°$
Conceptual Plan: $\Delta_f G°, P_{H_2}, P_H, T$ new $\Delta_f G°$

$$\Delta_r G = \Delta_r G° + RT \ln Q \text{ where } Q = \frac{P_H}{P_{H_2}^{1/2}}$$

Solution: $\Delta_f G° = +203.3$ kJ mol^{-1} and $Q = \dfrac{P_H}{P_{H_2}^{1/2}} = \dfrac{2}{2^{1/2}} = \sqrt{2}$ then

$$\Delta_r G = \Delta_r G° + RT \ln Q = +203.3 \frac{kJ}{mol} + \left(8.314 \frac{J}{K \cdot mol}\right)\left(\frac{1 kJ}{1000 J}\right)(298 \text{ K}) \ln\left(\sqrt{2}\right) =$$
$+204.2$ kJ mol^{-1}

The entropy of the product (1 mol) is decreased more than the entropy of the reactant (1/2 mol). Since the product is relatively less favoured, $\Delta_f G°$ is more positive.

Check: The units (kJ mol^{-1}) are correct. The Q is greater than 1, so $\Delta_f G°$ is increased under the new standard conditions.

17.103   **Given:** $K = 3.9 \times 10^5$ at 300 K and $K = 1.2 \times 10^{-1}$ at 500 K **Find:** $\Delta_r H°, \Delta_r S°$
Conceptual Plan: Plot ln K versus 1/T. The slope will be $-\Delta_r H°/R$ and the intercept will be $\Delta_r S°/R$.

Solution: Plot ln K versus $1/T$. Since $\ln K = -\dfrac{\Delta_r H°}{R}\dfrac{1}{T} + \dfrac{\Delta_r S°}{R}$, the negative of the slope will be $-\dfrac{\Delta_r H°}{R}$

and the intercept will be $\dfrac{\Delta_r S°}{R}$. The slope can be determined by measuring $\Delta y/\Delta x$ on the plot or by using functions such as "add trendline" in Excel. Since the slope is +11246 K,

$\Delta_r H° = -\text{slope } R =$

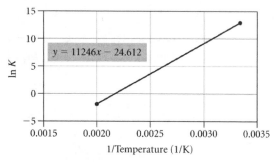

$= -(+11246 \text{ K})\left(8.314\dfrac{J}{K \cdot mol}\right)\left(\dfrac{1 kJ}{1000 J}\right) =$
$= -93.499$ kJ mol$^{-1} = -93$ kJ mol^{-1}
Since the intercept is -24.612 K^{-1},
$\Delta_r S° = \text{intercept } R = \left(\dfrac{-24.612}{K}\right)\left(8.314 \dfrac{J}{K \cdot mol}\right)$
$= -204.62$ J K^{-1} mol$^{-1} = -2.0 \times 10^2$ J K^{-1} mol^{-1}.

Note: This problem can also be solved using the mathematically equivalent equation in Problems 93 and 94.
Check: The units are correct (kJ mol^{-1} and J K^{-1} mol^{-1}). The numbers are typical for reactions. Since the slope is positive, the enthalpy change must be negative. The entropy change is expected to be negative since the number of moles of gas is decreasing.

17.105   **Given:** $\Delta_{vap}H$ table **Find:** $\Delta_{vap}S$ then compare values
Conceptual Plan: °C → K then $\Delta_{vap}H, T$ → $\Delta_{vap}S$. The energies involved in changes of state are

$$K = 273.15 + °C \qquad \Delta_{vap}S = \frac{-\Delta_{vap}H}{T}$$

influenced by the nature of the intermolecular forces present in the substance. Consider the nature of the intermolecular forces in the first four liquids and compare them to the intermolecular forces in water and ethanol.
Solution:

Diethyl ether: $T = 273.15 + 34.6 = 307.8$ K then

$$\Delta_{vap}S = \frac{\Delta_{vap}H}{T} = \frac{26.5 \text{ kJ mol}^{-1}}{307.8 \text{ K}} = 0.0861 \text{ kJ K}^{-1} \text{ mol}^{-1} = 86.1 \text{ J K}^{-1} \text{ mol}^{-1}$$

Acetone: $T = 273.15 + 56.1 = 329.3$ K then

$$\Delta_{vap}S = \frac{\Delta_{vap}H}{T} = \frac{29.1 \text{ kJ mol}^{-1}}{329.3 \text{ K}} = 0.0884 \text{ kJ K}^{-1} \text{ mol}^{-1} = 88.4 \text{ J K}^{-1} \text{ mol}^{-1}$$

Benzene: $T = 273.15 + 79.8 = 353.0$ K then

$$\Delta_{vap}S = \frac{\Delta_{vap}H}{T} = \frac{30.8 \text{ kJ mol}^{-1}}{353.0 \text{ K}} = 0.0873 \text{ kJ K}^{-1} \text{ mol}^{-1} = 87.3 \text{ J K}^{-1} \text{ mol}^{-1}$$

Chloroform: $T = 273.15 + 60.8 = 334.0$ K then

$$\Delta_{vap}S = \frac{\Delta_{vap}H}{T} = \frac{29.4 \text{ kJ mol}^{-1}}{334.0 \text{ K}} = 0.0880 \text{ kJ K}^{-1} \text{ mol}^{-1} = 88.0 \text{ J K}^{-1} \text{ mol}^{-1}$$

Ethanol: $T = 273.15 + 77.8 = 351.0$ K then

$$\Delta_{vap}S = \frac{\Delta_{vap}H}{T} = \frac{38.6 \text{ kJ mol}^{-1}}{351.0 \text{ K}} = 0.110 \text{ kJ K}^{-1} \text{ mol}^{-1} = 110 \text{ J K}^{-1} \text{ mol}^{-1}$$

Water: $T = 273.15 + 100 = 373.15$ K then

$$\Delta_{vap}S = \frac{\Delta_{vap}H}{T} = \frac{40.7 \text{ kJ mol}^{-1}}{373.15 \text{ K}} = 0.109 \text{ kJ K}^{-1} \text{ mol}^{-1} = 109 \text{ J K}^{-1} \text{ mol}^{-1}$$

The first four values are very similar, because they have similar intermolecular forces between molecules (dispersion forces and/or dipole-dipole interactions). The values for ethanol and water are higher because the intermolecular forces between molecules are stronger due to hydrogen bonding. Because of this, more energy is dispersed when these interactions are broken.

17.107 **Given:** NaCl $(s) \rightarrow$ Na$^+$ (aq) + Cl$^-$ (aq); $\Delta_f H°$ and $S°$ data for NaCl (s), Na$^+$ (aq) and Cl$^-$ (aq). **Find:** $\Delta_r G°$, K, and solubility of NaCl (s)

Conceptual Plan: $\Delta_f H° \rightarrow \Delta_r H°$ and $S° \rightarrow \Delta_r S°$ then $\Delta_r H°$, $\Delta_r S° \rightarrow \Delta_r G°$

$\Delta_r H° = \sum n_p \Delta_f H°(\text{products}) - \sum n_r \Delta_f H°(\text{reactants})$ $\Delta_r S° = \sum n_p S°(\text{products}) - \sum n_r S°(\text{reactants})$ $\Delta_r G° = \Delta_r H° - T\Delta_r S°$

then $\Delta_r G°$, R, $T \rightarrow K$. **Finally,** $K = K_{sp} \rightarrow S$. **The expression of the solubility product constant of** $A_m X_n$ **is**

$$\Delta_r G° = -RT \ln K$$

$K_{sp} = [A^{n+}]^m [X^{m-}]^n$. **The molar solubility of a compound,** $A_m X_n$, **can be computed directly from** K_{sp} **by solving for** S **in the expression** $K_{sp} = (mS)^m (nS)^n = m^m n^n S^{m+n}$.

Solution:

Reactant/Product	$\Delta_f H°$ (kJ mol^{-1})
NaCl (s)	–411
Na$^+$ (aq)	–240
Cl$^-$ (aq)	–167

$\Delta_r H° = \sum n_p \Delta_f H°(\text{products}) - \sum n_r \Delta_f H°(\text{reactants})$

$= [1\Delta_f H°(\text{Na}^+(aq))) + 1(\Delta_f H°(\text{Cl}^-(aq)))] - [1(\Delta_f H°(\text{NaCl}(s)))]$

$= [(-240 \text{ kJ mol}^{-1}) + (-167 \text{ kJ mol}^{-1})] - [(-411 \text{ kJ mol}^{-1})]$

$= [-407 \text{ kJ mol}^{-1}] - [-411 \text{ kJ mol}^{-1}]$

$= 4 \text{ kJ mol}^{-1}$

Reactant/Product	$S°$ (J K^{-1} mol^{-1})
NaCl (s)	72
Na$^+$ (aq)	59
Cl$^-$ (aq)	57

$S° = \sum n_p S°(\text{products}) - \sum n_r S°(\text{reactants})$

$= [1(S°(\text{Na}^+(aq))) + 1(S°(\text{Cl}^-(aq)))] - [1(S°(\text{NaCl}(s)))]$

$= [(59 \text{ J K}^{-1} \text{ mol}^{-1}) + (57 \text{ J K}^{-1} \text{ mol}^{-1})] - [(72 \text{ J K}^{-1} \text{ mol}^{-1})]$

$= [116 \text{ J K}^{-1} \text{ mol}^{-1}] - [72 \text{ J K}^{-1} \text{ mol}^{-1}]$

$= 44 \text{ J K}^{-1} \text{ mol}^{-1}$

$\Delta_r G° = \Delta_r H° - T\Delta_r S° = 4 \times 10^3 \text{ J mol}^{-1} - (298 \text{ K})(44 \text{ J K}^{-1} \text{ mol}^{-1}) \rightarrow$

$\Delta_r G° = 4 \times 10^3 \text{ J mol}^{-1} - 13.112 \times 10^3 \text{ J mol}^{-1} = -9.112 \times 10^3 \text{ J mol}^{-1} = -9 \text{ kJ mol}^{-1}$

$\Delta_r G° = -RT \ln K$ rearranges to $\ln K = -\dfrac{\Delta_r G°}{RT}$ then $K = e^{-\frac{\Delta_r G°}{RT}} = e^{\frac{-9.112 \times 10^3 \, \text{J mol}^{-1}}{(8.314 \, \text{J mol}^{-1} \text{K}^{-1})(298 \, \text{K})}} \rightarrow$

$K = e^{3.6778} = 39 = K_{sp}$. For NaCl, $A = Na^+$, $m = 1$, $X = Cl^-$, and $n = 1$ so $K_{sp} = S^2$.
Rearrange to solve for S. $S = \sqrt{39} = 6 \text{ mol L}^{-1}$.

Conceptual Problems

17.109 (c) The spontaneity of a reaction says nothing about the speed of a reaction. It only states which direction the reaction will go as it approaches equilibrium.

17.111 (b) has the largest decrease in the number of microstates from the initial to the final state. In (a) there are

initially $\dfrac{9!}{4! \, 4! \, 1!} = 630$ microstates and $\dfrac{9!}{3! \, 3! \, 3!} = 1680$ microstates at the end, so $\Delta_r S > 0$. In (b) there are

initially $\dfrac{9!}{4! \, 2! \, 3!} = 1260$ microstates and $\dfrac{9!}{6! \, 3! \, 0!} = 84$ microstates at the end, so $\Delta_r S < 0$. In (c) there are

initially $\dfrac{9!}{3! \, 4! \, 2!} = 1260$ microstates and $\dfrac{9!}{3! \, 4! \, 2!} = 1260$ microstates at the end, so $\Delta_r S = 0$. Also the final

state in (b) has the least entropy.

17.113 (c) Since the vapour pressure of water at 298 K is 0.03170 bar, as long as the desired pressure (0.010 bar) is less than the equilibrium vapour pressure of water, the reaction will be spontaneous.

18 Electrochemistry

Review Questions

18.1 Electrochemistry uses spontaneous redox reactions to generate electrical energy.

18.3 Oxidation is the loss of electrons and corresponds to an increase in oxidation state. Reduction is the gain of electrons and corresponds to a decrease in oxidation state. Balancing redox reactions can be more complicated than balancing other types of reactions because both the mass (or number of each type of atom) and the charge must be balanced. Redox reactions occurring in aqueous solutions can be balanced by using a special procedure called the half-reaction method of balancing. In this procedure, the overall equation is broken down into two half-reactions: one for oxidation and one for reduction. The half-reactions are balanced individually and then added together so that the number of electrons generated in the oxidation half-reaction is the same as the number of electrons consumed in the reduction half-reaction.

18.5 In all electrochemical cells, the electrode where oxidation occurs is called the anode. In a voltaic cell, the anode is labelled with a negative (–) sign. The anode is negative because the oxidation reaction that occurs at the anode releases electrons. Electrons flow from the anode to the cathode (from negative to positive) through the wires connecting the electrodes.

18.7 A salt bridge is a pathway by which ions can flow between the half-cells, completing an electrical circuit and maintaining electroneutrality, without the solutions in the half-cells totally mixing.

18.9 The standard cell potential E°_{cell} or standard emf is the cell potential under standard conditions (1 mol L^{-1} concentration for reactants in solution and 1 bar pressure for gaseous reactants). The cell potential is a measure of the overall tendency of the redox reaction to occur spontaneously. The more positive the cell potential, the more spontaneous the reaction. A negative cell potential indicates a nonspontaneous reaction.

18.11 Inert electrodes, such as platinum (Pt) or graphite, are used as the anode or cathode (or both) when the reactants and products of one or both of the half-reactions are in the same phase.

18.13 The overall cell potential for any electrochemical cell will always be the difference between the electrode potentials of the cathode and anode, or $E^\circ_{cell} = E^\circ_{cathode} - E^\circ_{anode}$.

18.15 In general, any reduction half-reaction will be spontaneous when paired with the reverse of a half-reaction below it in the table.

18.17 We have seen that a positive standard cell potential (E°_{cell}) corresponds to a spontaneous oxidation–reduction reaction. We also know (from Chapter 17) that the spontaneity of a reaction is determined by the sign of $\Delta_r G^\circ$. Therefore, E°_{cell} and $\Delta_r G^\circ$ must be related. We also know from Section 17.9 that $\Delta_r G^\circ$ for a reaction is related to the equilibrium constant (K) for the reaction. Since E°_{cell} and $\Delta_r G^\circ$ are related, then E°_{cell} and K must also be related. The equation that relates the three quantities is $\Delta_r G^\circ = - RT \ln K = - nFE^\circ_{cell}$.

18.19   The Nernst equation relates concentration and cell potential as follows: $E_{cell} = E°_{cell} - \dfrac{0.0257\ V}{n} \ln Q$, where E_{cell} is the cell potential in V, $E°_{cell}$ is the standard cell potential in V, n is the number of moles of electrons transferred in the redox reaction, and Q is the reaction quotient. Increasing the concentration of the reactants decreases the value of Q and so it increases the cell potential. Increasing the concentration of the products increases the value of Q and so it decreases the cell potential.

18.21   A concentration cell is a voltaic cell in which both half-reactions are the same, but in which a difference in concentration drives the current flow (since the cell potential depends not only on the half-reactions occurring in the cell, but also on the concentrations of the reactants and products in those half-reactions). Therefore, $E_{cell} = E°_{cell} - \dfrac{0.0257\ V}{n} \ln Q$.

18.23   Lead–acid storage batteries consist of six electrochemical cells wired in series, in which each cell produces 2 V for a total of 12 V. Each cell contains a porous lead anode where oxidation occurs according to $Pb\ (s) + HSO_4^-\ (aq) \rightarrow PbSO_4\ (s) + H^+\ (aq) + 2\ e^-$ and a lead(IV) oxide cathode where reduction occurs according to $PbO_2\ (s) + HSO_4^-\ (aq) + 3\ H^+\ (aq) + 2\ e^- \rightarrow PbSO_4\ (s) + 2\ H_2O\ (l)$. As electrical current is drawn from the battery, both the anode and the cathode become coated with $PbSO_4\ (s)$ and the solution becomes depleted of $HSO_4^-\ (aq)$. If the battery is run for a long time without recharging, too much $PbSO_4\ (s)$ develops on the surface of the electrodes and the battery goes dead. The lead–acid storage battery can be recharged, however, by running electrical current through it in reverse. The electrical current, which must come from an external source such as an alternator in a car, causes the preceding reaction to occur in reverse, converting the $PbSO_4\ (s)$ back to $Pb\ (s)$ and $PbO_2\ (s)$, recharging the battery.

18.25   Fuel cells are like batteries, but the reactants must be constantly replenished. Normal batteries lose their ability to generate voltage with use because the reactants become depleted as electrical current is drawn from the battery. In a fuel cell, the reactants—the fuel—constantly flow through the battery, generating electrical current as they undergo a redox reaction.

The most common fuel cell is the hydrogen–oxygen fuel cell. In the cell, hydrogen gas flows past the anode (a screen coated with a platinum catalyst) and undergoes oxidation: $2\ H_2\ (g) + 4\ OH^-\ (aq) \rightarrow 4\ H_2O\ (l) + 4\ e^-$. Oxygen gas flows past the cathode (a similar screen) and undergoes reduction: $O_2\ (g) + 2\ H_2O\ (l) + 4\ e^- \rightarrow 4\ OH^-\ (aq)$. The half-reactions sum to the following overall reaction: $2\ H_2\ (g) + O_2\ (g) \rightarrow 2\ H_2O\ (l)$. Notice that the only product is water.

18.27   Applications of electrolysis include breaking water into hydrogen and oxygen, converting metal oxides to pure metals, production of sodium from molten sodium chloride, and plating metals onto other metals (for example, silver can be plated onto a less expensive metal).

18.29   The anion is oxidized. The cation is reduced to the metal.

18.31   In the electrolysis of aqueous NaCl solutions, two different reduction half-reactions are possible at the cathode: the reduction of Na^+ and the reduction of water.

$2\ Na^+\ (l) + 2\ e^- \rightarrow 2\ Na\ (s)$ $E° = -2.71\ V$

$2\ H_2O\ (l) + 2\ e^- \rightarrow H_2\ (g) + 2\ OH^-\ (aq)$ $E° = -0.41\ V\ ([OH^-] = 10^{-7}\ mol\ L^{-1})$

The half-reaction that occurs most easily (the one with the more positive electrode potential) will be the one that actually occurs.

18.33   We can determine the number of moles of electrons that have flowed in a given electrolysis cell by measuring the total charge that has flowed through the cell, which in turn depends on the magnitude of current and the time that the current has run. Since 1 ampere = 1 C s^{-1}, if we multiply the amount of current (in A) flowing through the cell by the time (in s) that the current flowed, we can find the total charge that passed through the cell in that time: current (C s^{-1}) × time (s) = charge (C). The relationship between charge and the number of moles of electrons is given by Faraday's constant, which corresponds to the charge in coulombs of 1 mol of electrons, so $F = 96\ 485$ C mol^{-1}. These relationships can be used to solve problems involving the stoichiometry of electrolytic cells.

18.35   Moisture must be present for many corrosion reactions to occur. The presence of water is necessary because water is a reactant in many oxidation reactions (such as $4\ Fe^{2+}\ (aq) + O_2\ (g) + (4 + 2n)\ H_2O\ (l) \rightarrow 2\ Fe_2O_3 \cdot n\ H_2O\ (s) + 8\ H^+\ (aq)$), and also because charge (either electrons or ions) must be free to flow between the anodic and cathodic regions.

Additional electrolytes promote more corrosion. The presence of an electrolyte (such as sodium chloride) on the surface of iron promotes rusting because it enhances current flow. This is why cars rust so quickly in cold climates where roads are salted, or in areas directly adjacent to beaches where salt-water mist is present.

The presence of acids promotes corrosion. Since H^+ ions are involved as a reactant in the reduction of oxygen, lower pH enhances the cathodic reaction and leads to faster corrosion.

Problems by Topic

Balancing Redox Reactions

18.37   **Conceptual Plan:** Separate the overall reaction into two half-reactions: one for oxidation and one for reduction. $\rightarrow$ Balance each half-reaction with respect to mass in the following order: 1) balance all elements other than H and O, 2) balance O by adding H_2O, and 3) balance H by adding H^+. $\rightarrow$ Balance each half-reaction with respect to charge by adding electrons. (The sum of the charges on both sides of the equation should be made equal by adding electrons as necessary.) $\rightarrow$ Make the number of electrons in both half-reactions equal by multiplying one or both half-reactions by a small whole number. $\rightarrow$ Add the two half-reactions together, cancelling electrons and other species as necessary. $\rightarrow$ Verify that the reaction is balanced both with respect to mass and with respect to charge.
Solution:

(a)   Separate: $K\ (s) \rightarrow K^+\ (aq)$ and $Cr^{3+}\ (aq) \rightarrow Cr\ (s)$

         Balance elements: $K\ (s) \rightarrow K^+\ (aq)$ and $Cr^{3+}\ (aq) \rightarrow Cr\ (s)$

         Add electrons: $K\ (s) \rightarrow K^+\ (aq) + e^-$ and $Cr^{3+}\ (aq) + 3\ e^- \rightarrow Cr\ (s)$

         Equalize electrons: $3\ K\ (s) \rightarrow 3\ K^+\ (aq) + 3\ e^-$ and $Cr^{3+}\ (aq) + 3\ e^- \rightarrow Cr\ (s)$

         Add half-reactions: $3\ K\ (s) + Cr^{3+}\ (aq) + \cancel{3\ e^-} \rightarrow 3\ K^+\ (aq) + \cancel{3\ e^-} + Cr\ (s)$

         Cancel electrons: $3\ K\ (s) + Cr^{3+}\ (aq) \rightarrow 3\ K^+\ (aq) + Cr\ (s)$

         Check: Reactants   Products

                                      3 K atoms   3 K atoms

                                      1 Cr atom   1 Cr atom

                                      +3 charge   +3 charge

(b)   Separate: $Al\ (s) \rightarrow Al^{3+}\ (aq)$ and $Fe^{2+}\ (aq) \rightarrow Fe\ (s)$

         Balance elements: $Al\ (s) \rightarrow Al^{3+}\ (aq)$ and $Fe^{2+}\ (aq) \rightarrow Fe\ (s)$

         Add electrons: $Al\ (s) \rightarrow Al^{3+}\ (aq) + 3\ e^-$ and $Fe^{2+}\ (aq) + 2\ e^- \rightarrow Fe\ (s)$

         Equalize electrons: $2\ Al\ (s) \rightarrow 2\ Al^{3+}\ (aq) + 6\ e^-$ and $3\ Fe^{2+}\ (aq) + 6\ e^- \rightarrow 3\ Fe\ (s)$

         Add half-reactions: $2\ Al\ (s) + 3\ Fe^{2+}\ (aq) + \cancel{6\ e^-} \rightarrow 2\ Al^{3+}\ (aq) + \cancel{6\ e^-} + 3\ Fe\ (s)$

         Cancel electrons: $2\ Al\ (s) + 3\ Fe^{2+}\ (aq) \rightarrow 2\ Al^{3+}\ (aq) + 3\ Fe\ (s)$

         Check: Reactants   Products

                                      2 Al atoms   2 Al atoms

                                      3 Fe atoms   3 Fe atoms

                                      +6 charge   +6 charge

(c)   Separate: $BrO_3^-\ (aq) \rightarrow Br^-\ (aq)$ and $N_2H_4\ (g) \rightarrow N_2\ (g)$

         Balance non H & O elements: $BrO_3^-\ (aq) \rightarrow Br^-\ (aq)$ and $N_2H_4\ (g) \rightarrow N_2\ (g)$

         Balance O with H_2O: $BrO_3^-\ (aq) \rightarrow Br^-\ (aq) + 3\ H_2O\ (l)$ and $N_2H_4\ (g) \rightarrow N_2\ (g)$

         Balance H with H^+: $BrO_3^-\ (aq) + 6\ H^+\ (aq) \rightarrow Br^-\ (aq) + 3\ H_2O\ (l)$ and $N_2H_4\ (g) \rightarrow N_2\ (g) + 4\ H^+\ (aq)$

         Add electrons:

         $BrO_3^-\ (aq) + 6\ H^+\ (aq) + 6\ e^- \rightarrow Br^-\ (aq) + 3\ H_2O\ (l)$ and $N_2H_4\ (g) \rightarrow N_2\ (g) + 4\ H^+\ (aq) + 4\ e^-$

         Equalize electrons:

         $2\ BrO_3^-\ (aq) + 12\ H^+\ (aq) + 12\ e^- \rightarrow 2\ Br^-\ (aq) + 6\ H_2O\ (l)$ and $3\ N_2H_4\ (g) \rightarrow 3\ N_2\ (g) + 12\ H^+\ (aq) + 12\ e^-$

         Add half-reactions: $2\ BrO_3^-\ (aq) + \cancel{12\ H^+\ (aq)} + 3\ N_2H_4\ (g) + \cancel{12\ e^-} \rightarrow 2\ Br^-\ (aq) + 6\ H_2O\ (l) + 3\ N_2\ (g)$
                                                                                            $+ \cancel{12\ H^+\ (aq)} + \cancel{12\ e^-}$

Cancel electrons & others:	$2 BrO_3^- (aq) + 3 N_2H_4 (g) \rightarrow 2 Br^- (aq) + 6 H_2O (l) + 3 N_2 (g)$	
Check:	Reactants	Products
	2 Br atoms	2 Br atoms
	6 O atoms	6 O atoms
	12 H atoms	12 H atoms
	6 N atoms	6 N atoms
	–2 charge	–2 charge

18.39   **Conceptual Plan: Separate the overall reaction into two half-reactions: one for oxidation and one for reduction. → Balance each half-reaction with respect to mass in the following order: 1) balance all elements other than H and O, 2) balance O by adding H_2O, and 3) balance H by adding H^+. → Balance each half-reaction with respect to charge by adding electrons. (The sum of the charges on both sides of the equation should be made equal by adding electrons as necessary.) → Make the number of electrons in both half-reactions equal by multiplying one or both half-reactions by a small whole number. → Add the two half-reactions together, cancelling electrons and other species as necessary. → Verify that the reaction is balanced both with respect to mass and with respect to charge.**
Solution:

(a)   Separate: $PbO_2 (s) \rightarrow Pb^{2+} (aq)$ and $I^- (aq) \rightarrow I_2 (s)$
    Balance non H & O elements: $PbO_2 (s) \rightarrow Pb^{2+} (aq)$ and $2 I^- (aq) \rightarrow I_2 (s)$
    Balance O with H_2O: $PbO_2 (s) \rightarrow Pb^{2+} (aq) + 2 H_2O (l)$ and $2 I^- (aq) \rightarrow I_2 (s)$
    Balance H with H^+: $PbO_2 (s) + 4 H^+ (aq) \rightarrow Pb^{2+} (aq) + 2 H_2O (l)$ and $2 I^- (aq) \rightarrow I_2 (s)$
    Add electrons: $PbO_2 (s) + 4 H^+ (aq) + 2 e^- \rightarrow Pb^{2+} (aq) + 2 H_2O (l)$ and $2 I^- (aq) \rightarrow I_2 (s) + 2 e^-$
    Equalize electrons: $PbO_2 (s) + 4 H^+ (aq) + 2 e^- \rightarrow Pb^{2+} (aq) + 2 H_2O (l)$ and $2 I^- (aq) \rightarrow I_2 (s) + 2 e^-$
    Add half-reactions: $PbO_2 (s) + 4 H^+ (aq) + 2e^- + 2 I^- (aq) \rightarrow Pb^{2+} (aq) + 2 H_2O (l) + I_2 (s) + 2e^-$
    Cancel electrons & others: $PbO_2 (s) + 4 H^+ (aq) + 2 I^- (aq) \rightarrow Pb^{2+} (aq) + 2 H_2O (l) + I_2 (s)$

Check:	Reactants	Products
	1 Pb atom	1 Pb atom
	2 O atoms	2 O atoms
	4 H atoms	4 H atoms
	2 I atoms	2 I atoms
	+2 charge	+2 charge

(b)   Separate: $MnO_4^- (aq) \rightarrow Mn^{2+} (aq)$ and $SO_3^{2-} (aq) \rightarrow SO_4^{2-} (aq)$
    Balance non H & O elements: $MnO_4^- (aq) \rightarrow Mn^{2+} (aq)$ and $SO_3^{2-} (aq) \rightarrow SO_4^{2-} (aq)$
    Balance O with H_2O: $MnO_4^- (aq) \rightarrow Mn^{2+} (aq) + 4 H_2O (l)$ and $SO_3^{2-} (aq) + H_2O (l) \rightarrow SO_4^{2-} (aq)$
    Balance H with H^+:
        $MnO_4^- (aq) + 8 H^+ (aq) \rightarrow Mn^{2+} (aq) + 4 H_2O (l)$ and $SO_3^{2-} (aq) + H_2O (l) \rightarrow SO_4^{2-} (aq) + 2 H^+ (aq)$
    Add electrons: $MnO_4^- (aq) + 8 H^+ (aq) + 5 e^- \rightarrow Mn^{2+} (aq) + 4 H_2O (l)$ and
                                 $SO_3^{2-} (aq) + H_2O (l) \rightarrow SO_4^{2-} (aq) + 2 H^+ (aq) + 2 e^-$
    Equalize electrons: $2 MnO_4^- (aq) + 16 H^+ (aq) + 10 e^- \rightarrow 2 Mn^{2+} (aq) + 8 H_2O (l)$ and
                         $5 SO_3^{2-} (aq) + 5 H_2O (l) \rightarrow 5 SO_4^{2-} (aq) + 10 H^+ (aq) + 10 e^-$
    Add half-reactions: $2 MnO_4^- (aq) + 6\ \cancel{16}\ H^+ (aq) + \cancel{10 e^-} + 5 SO_3^{2-} (aq) + 5\ \cancel{H_2O (l)} \rightarrow$
                               $2 Mn^{2+} (aq) + 3\ \cancel{8}\ H_2O (l) + 5 SO_4^{2-} (aq) + \cancel{10 H^+} (aq) + \cancel{10 e^-}$
    Cancel electrons: $2 MnO_4^- (aq) + 6 H^+ (aq) + 5 SO_3^{2-} (aq) \rightarrow 2 Mn^{2+} (aq) + 3 H_2O (l) + 5 SO_4^{2-} (aq)$

Check:	Reactants	Products
	2 Mn atoms	2 Mn atoms
	23 O atoms	23 O atoms
	6 H atoms	6 H atoms
	5 S atoms	5 S atoms
	–6 charge	–6 charge

(c)   Separate: $S_2O_3^{2-} (aq) \rightarrow SO_4^{2-} (aq)$ and $Cl_2 (g) \rightarrow Cl^- (aq)$
    Balance non H & O elements: $S_2O_3^{2-} (aq) \rightarrow 2 SO_4^{2-} (aq)$ and $Cl_2 (g) \rightarrow 2 Cl^- (aq)$
    Balance O with H_2O: $S_2O_3^{2-} (aq) + 5 H_2O (l) \rightarrow 2 SO_4^{2-} (aq)$ and $Cl_2 (g) \rightarrow 2 Cl^- (aq)$
    Balance H with H^+: $S_2O_3^{2-} (aq) + 5 H_2O (l) \rightarrow 2 SO_4^{2-} (aq) + 10 H^+ (aq)$ and $Cl_2 (g) \rightarrow 2 Cl^- (aq)$

Add electrons:
$$S_2O_3^{2-}(aq) + 5\,H_2O\,(l) \rightarrow 2\,SO_4^{2-}(aq) + 10\,H^+(aq) + 8\,e^- \text{ and } Cl_2\,(g) + 2\,e^- \rightarrow 2\,Cl^-(aq)$$
Equalize electrons:
$$S_2O_3^{2-}(aq) + 5\,H_2O\,(l) \rightarrow 2\,SO_4^{2-}(aq) + 10\,H^+(aq) + 8\,e^- \text{ and } 4\,Cl_2\,(g) + 8\,e^- \rightarrow 8\,Cl^-(aq)$$
Add half-reactions:
$$S_2O_3^{2-}(aq) + 5\,H_2O\,(l) + 4\,Cl_2\,(g) + \cancel{8\,e^-} \rightarrow 2\,SO_4^{2-}(aq) + 10\,H^+(aq) + \cancel{8\,e^-} + 8\,Cl^-(aq)$$
Cancel electrons: $S_2O_3^{2-}(aq) + 5\,H_2O\,(l) + 4\,Cl_2\,(g) \rightarrow 2\,SO_4^{2-}(aq) + 10\,H^+(aq) + 8\,Cl^-(aq)$

Check:

Reactants	Products
2 S atoms	2 S atoms
8 O atoms	8 O atoms
10 H atoms	10 H atoms
8 Cl atoms	8 Cl atoms
–2 charge	–2 charge

18.41   **Conceptual Plan: Separate the overall reaction into two half-reactions: one for oxidation and one for reduction.** → **Balance each half-reaction with respect to mass in the following order: 1) balance all elements other than H and O, 2) balance O by adding H_2O, 3) balance H by adding H^+, and 4) neutralize H^+ by adding enough OH^- to neutralize each H^+. Add the same number of OH^- ions to each side of the equation.** → **Balance each half-reaction with respect to charge by adding electrons. (The sum of the charges on both sides of the equation should be made equal by adding electrons as necessary.)** → **Make the number of electrons in both half-reactions equal by multiplying one or both half-reactions by a small whole number.** → **Add the two half-reactions together, cancelling electrons and other species as necessary.** → **Verify that the reaction is balanced both with respect to mass and with respect to charge.** **Solution:**

(a)   Separate: $ClO_2\,(aq) \rightarrow ClO_2^-\,(aq)$ and $H_2O_2\,(aq) \rightarrow O_2\,(g)$
Balance non H & O elements: $ClO_2\,(aq) \rightarrow ClO_2^-\,(aq)$ and $H_2O_2\,(aq) \rightarrow O_2\,(g)$
Balance O with H_2O: $ClO_2\,(aq) \rightarrow ClO_2^-\,(aq)$ and $H_2O_2\,(aq) \rightarrow O_2\,(g)$
Balance H with H^+: $ClO_2\,(aq) \rightarrow ClO_2^-\,(aq)$ and $H_2O_2\,(aq) \rightarrow O_2\,(g) + 2\,H^+\,(aq)$
Neutralize H^+ with OH^-:
$$ClO_2\,(aq) \rightarrow ClO_2^-\,(aq) \text{ and } H_2O_2\,(aq) + 2\,OH^-\,(aq) \rightarrow O_2\,(g) + \underbrace{2\,H^+\,(aq) + 2\,OH^-\,(aq)}_{2\,H_2O\,(l)}$$

Add electrons: $ClO_2\,(aq) + e^- \rightarrow ClO_2^-\,(aq)$ and $H_2O_2\,(aq) + 2\,OH^-\,(aq) \rightarrow O_2\,(g) + 2\,H_2O\,(l) + 2\,e^-$
Equalize electrons:
$$2\,ClO_2\,(aq) + 2\,e^- \rightarrow 2\,ClO_2^-\,(aq) \text{ and } H_2O_2\,(aq) + 2\,OH^-\,(aq) \rightarrow O_2\,(g) + 2\,H_2O\,(l) + 2\,e^-$$
Add half-reactions:
$$2\,ClO_2\,(aq) + \cancel{2\,e^-} + H_2O_2\,(aq) + 2\,OH^-\,(aq) \rightarrow 2\,ClO_2^-\,(aq) + O_2\,(g) + 2\,H_2O\,(l) + \cancel{2\,e^-}$$
Cancel electrons: $2\,ClO_2\,(aq) + H_2O_2\,(aq) + 2\,OH^-\,(aq) \rightarrow 2\,ClO_2^-\,(aq) + O_2\,(g) + 2\,H_2O\,(l)$

Check:

Reactants	Products
2 Cl atoms	2 Cl atoms
8 O atoms	8 O atoms
4 H atoms	4 H atoms
–2 charge	–2 charge

(b)   Separate: $MnO_4^-\,(aq) \rightarrow MnO_2\,(s)$ and $Al\,(s) \rightarrow Al(OH)_4^-\,(aq)$
Balance non H & O elements: $MnO_4^-\,(aq) \rightarrow MnO_2\,(s)$ and $Al\,(s) \rightarrow Al(OH)_4^-\,(aq)$
Balance O with H_2O: $MnO_4^-\,(aq) \rightarrow MnO_2\,(s) + 2\,H_2O\,(l)$ and $Al\,(s) + 4\,H_2O\,(l) \rightarrow Al(OH)_4^-\,(aq)$
Balance H with H^+:
$MnO_4^-\,(aq) + 4\,H^+\,(aq) \rightarrow MnO_2\,(s) + 2\,H_2O\,(l)$ and $Al\,(s) + 4\,H_2O\,(l) \rightarrow Al(OH)_4^-\,(aq) + 4\,H^+\,(aq)$
Neutralize H^+ with OH^-: $MnO_4^-\,(aq) + \underbrace{4\,H^+\,(aq) + 4\,OH^-\,(aq)}_{2\,4\,H_2O\,(l)} \rightarrow MnO_2\,(s) + 2\,\cancel{H_2O\,(l)} + 4\,OH^-\,(aq)$

and $Al\,(s) + 4\,\cancel{H_2O\,(l)} + 4\,OH^-\,(aq) \rightarrow Al(OH)_4^-\,(aq) + \underbrace{4\,H^+\,(aq) + 4\,OH^-\,(aq)}_{4\,H_2O\,(l)}$

Add electrons: $MnO_4^-\,(aq) + 2\,H_2O\,(l) + 3\,e^- \rightarrow MnO_2\,(s) + 4\,OH^-\,(aq)$ and
$$Al\,(s) + 4\,OH^-\,(aq) \rightarrow Al(OH)_4^-\,(aq) + 3\,e^-$$
Equalize electrons: $MnO_4^-\,(aq) + 2\,H_2O\,(l) + 3\,e^- \rightarrow MnO_2\,(s) + 4\,OH^-\,(aq)$ and
$$Al\,(s) + 4\,OH^-\,(aq) \rightarrow Al(OH)_4^-\,(aq) + 3\,e^-$$

Add half-reactions:
$MnO_4^- (aq) + 2 H_2O (l) + \cancel{3 e^-} + Al (s) + \cancel{4 OH^- (aq)} \rightarrow MnO_2 (s) + \cancel{4 OH^- (aq)} + Al(OH)_4^- (aq) + \cancel{3 e^-}$
Cancel electrons: $MnO_4^- (aq) + 2 H_2O (l) + Al (s) \rightarrow MnO_2 (s) + Al(OH)_4^- (aq)$
Check: <u>Reactants</u>   <u>Products</u>
                                 1 Mn atom   1 Mn atom
                                 6 O atoms   6 O atoms
                                 4 H atoms   4 H atoms
                                 1 Al atom   1 Al atom
                                 −1 charge   −1 charge

(c)   Separate: $Cl_2 (g) \rightarrow Cl^- (aq)$ and $Cl_2 (g) \rightarrow ClO^- (aq)$
       Balance non H & O elements: $Cl_2 (g) \rightarrow 2 Cl^- (aq)$ and $Cl_2 (g) \rightarrow 2 ClO^- (aq)$
       Balance O with H_2O: $Cl_2 (g) \rightarrow 2 Cl^- (aq)$ and $Cl_2 (g) + 2 H_2O (l) \rightarrow 2 ClO^- (aq)$
       Balance H with H^+: $Cl_2 (g) \rightarrow 2 Cl^- (aq)$ and $Cl_2 (g) + 2 H_2O (l) \rightarrow 2 ClO^- (aq) + 4 H^+ (aq)$
       Neutralize H^+ with OH^-:
       $Cl_2 (g) \rightarrow 2 Cl^- (aq)$ and $Cl_2 (g) + \cancel{2 H_2O (l)} + 4 OH^- (aq) \rightarrow 2 ClO^- (aq) + \underline{4 H^+ (aq) + 4 OH^- (aq)}$
                                                                                              $\overset{2}{\cancel{4}} H_2O (l)$

       Add electrons: $Cl_2 (g) + 2 e^- \rightarrow 2 Cl^- (aq)$ and $Cl_2 (g) + 4 OH^- (aq) \rightarrow 2 ClO^- (aq) + 2 H_2O (l) + 2 e^-$
       Equalize electrons: $Cl_2 (g) + 2 e^- \rightarrow 2 Cl^- (aq)$ and $Cl_2 (g) + 4 OH^- (aq) \rightarrow 2 ClO^- (aq) + 2 H_2O (l) + 2 e^-$
       Add half-reactions: $Cl_2 (g) + \cancel{2 e^-} + Cl_2 (g) + 4 OH^- (aq) \rightarrow 2 Cl^- (aq) + 2 ClO^- (aq) + 2 H_2O (l) + \cancel{2 e^-}$
       Cancel electrons: $2 Cl_2 (g) + 4 OH^- (aq) \rightarrow 2 Cl^- (aq) + 2 ClO^- (aq) + 2 H_2O (l)$
       Simplify: $Cl_2 (g) + 2 OH^- (aq) \rightarrow Cl^- (aq) + ClO^- (aq) + H_2O (l)$
       Check: <u>Reactants</u>   <u>Products</u>
                                    2 Cl atoms   2 Cl atoms
                                    2 O atoms   2 O atoms
                                    2 H atoms   2 H atoms
                                    −2 charge   −2 charge

Voltaic Cells, Standard Cell Potentials, and Direction of Spontaneity

18.43   **Given:** voltaic cell overall redox reaction
         Find: sketch voltaic cell, labelling anode, cathode, all species, and direction of electron flow
         Conceptual Plan: Separate the overall reaction into two half-cell reactions and add electrons as needed to balance reactions. Put the anode reaction on the left (oxidation = electrons as product) and the cathode reaction on the right (reduction = electrons as reactant). Electrons flow from anode to cathode.
         Solution:

(a) $2 Ag^+ (aq) + Pb (s) \rightarrow 2 Ag (s) + Pb^{2+} (aq)$ separates to $2 Ag^+ (aq) \rightarrow$
       $2 Ag (s)$ and $Pb (s) \rightarrow Pb^{2+} (aq)$ then add electrons to balance to get the
       cathode reaction: $2 Ag^+ (aq) + 2 e^- \rightarrow 2 Ag (s)$ and the anode reaction:
       $Pb (s) \rightarrow Pb^{2+} (aq) + 2 e^-$.

       Since we have Pb (s) as the reactant for the oxidation, it will be our
       anode. Since we have Ag (s) as the product for the reduction, it will be
       our cathode. Simplify the cathode reaction, dividing all terms by 2.

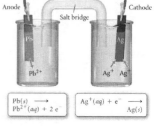

(b) $2 ClO_2 (g) + 2 I^- (aq) \rightarrow 2 ClO_2^- (aq) + I_2 (s)$ separates to $2 ClO_2 (g)$
       $\rightarrow 2 ClO_2^- (aq)$ and $2 I^- (aq) \rightarrow I_2 (s)$ then add electrons to balance
       to get the cathode reaction: $2 ClO_2 (g) + 2 e^- \rightarrow 2 ClO_2^- (aq)$ and the
       anode reaction: $2 I^- (aq) \rightarrow I_2 (s) + 2 e^-$.

       Since we have $I^- (aq)$ as the reactant for the oxidation, we will need
       to use Pt as our anode. Since we have $ClO_2^- (aq)$ as the product for
       the reduction, we will need to use Pt as our cathode. Since $ClO_2 (g)$
       is our reactant for the reduction, we need to use an electrode assem-
       bly like that used for a SHE. Simplify the cathode reaction, dividing
       all terms by 2.

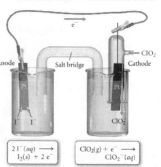

(c) $O_2 (g) + 4 H^+ (aq) + 2 Zn (s) \rightarrow 2 H_2O (l) + 2 Zn^{2+} (aq)$ separates to $O_2 (g) + 4 H^+ (aq) \rightarrow 2 H_2O (l)$ and $2 Zn (s) \rightarrow 2 Zn^{2+} (aq)$ then add electrons to balance to get the cathode reaction: $O_2 (g) + 4 H^+ (aq) + 4 e^- \rightarrow 2 H_2O (l)$ and the anode reaction: $2 Zn (s) \rightarrow 2 Zn^{2+} (aq) + 4 e^-$.

Since we have Zn (s) as the reactant for the oxidation, it will be our anode. Since we have H_2O (l) as the product for the reduction, we will need to use Pt as our cathode. Since O_2 (g) is our reactant for the reduction, we need to use an electrode assembly like the one that is used for a SHE. Simplify the anode reaction, dividing all terms by 2.

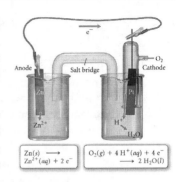

18.45 **Given:** overall reactions from Problem 43 **Find:** E°_{cell}
Conceptual Plan: Look up half-reactions from the solution of Problem 43 in Table 18.1. Calculate the standard cell potential by subtracting the electrode potential of the anode from the electrode potential of the cathode: $E^\circ_{cell} = E^\circ_{cathode} - E^\circ_{anode}$.
Solution:

(a) $Ag^+ (aq) + e^- \rightarrow Ag (s)$ $E^\circ = 0.80$ V $= E^\circ_{cathode}$ and Pb (s) $\rightarrow Pb^{2+} (aq) + 2 e^-$ $E^\circ = -0.13$ V $= E^\circ_{anode}$. Then $E^\circ_{cell} = E^\circ_{cathode} - E^\circ_{anode} = 0.80$ V $- (-0.13$ V$) = 0.93$ V.

(b) $ClO_2 (g) + e^- \rightarrow ClO_2^- (aq)$ $E^\circ = 0.95$ V $= E^\circ_{cathode}$ and $2 I^- (aq) \rightarrow I_2 (s) + 2 e^-$ $E^\circ = +0.54$ V $= E^\circ_{anode}$. Then $E^\circ_{cell} = E^\circ_{cathode} - E^\circ_{anode} = 0.95$ V $- 0.54$ V $= 0.41$ V.

(c) $O_2 (g) + 4 H^+ (aq) + 4 e^- \rightarrow 2 H_2O (l)$ $E^\circ = 1.23$ V and Zn (s) $\rightarrow Zn^{2+} (aq) + 2 e^-$ $E^\circ = -0.76$ V $= E^\circ_{anode}$. Then $E^\circ_{cell} = E^\circ_{cathode} - E^\circ_{anode} = 1.23$ V $- (-0.76$ V$) = 1.99$ V.

Check: The units (V) are correct. All of the voltages are positive, which is consistent with a voltaic cell.

18.47 **Given:** voltaic cell drawing
Find: (a) determine electron flow direction, anode, and cathode; (b) write balanced overall reaction and calculate E°_{cell}; (c) label electrodes as + and –; and (d) directions of anions and cations from salt bridge
Conceptual Plan: Look at each half-cell and write a reduction reaction by using electrode and solution composition and adding electrons to balance. Look up half-reactions and standard electrode potentials in Table 18.1. Since this is a voltaic cell, the cell potentials must be assigned to give a positive E°_{cell}. Calculate the standard cell potential by subtracting the electrode potential of the anode from the electrode potential of the cathode: $E^\circ_{cell} = E^\circ_{cathode} - E^\circ_{anode}$, choosing the electrode assignments to give a positive E°_{cell}.

(a) **Label the electrode where the oxidation occurs as the anode. Label the electrode where the reduction occurs as the cathode. Electrons flow from anode to cathode.**

(b) **Take two half-cell reactions and multiply the reactions as necessary to equalize the number of electrons transferred. Add the two half-cell reactions and cancel electrons and any other species.**

(c) **Label anode as (–) and cathode as (+).**

(d) **Cations will flow from the salt bridge toward the cathode and the anions will flow from the salt bridge toward the anode.**
Solution:
left side: $Fe^{3+} (aq) \rightarrow Fe (s)$ and right side: $Cr^{3+} (aq) \rightarrow Cr (s)$ add electrons to balance $Fe^{3+} (aq) + 3 e^- \rightarrow Fe (s)$ and right side: $Cr^{3+} (aq) + 3 e^- \rightarrow Cr (s)$. Look up cell standard electrode potentials: $Fe^{3+} (aq) + 3 e^- \rightarrow Fe (s)$ $E^\circ = -0.036$ V and $Cr^{3+} (aq) + 3 e^- \rightarrow Cr (s)$ $E^\circ = -0.73$ V. In order to get a positive cell potential, the second reaction is the oxidation reaction (anode). $E^\circ_{cell} = E^\circ_{cathode} - E^\circ_{anode} = -0.036$ V $- (-0.73$ V$) = 0.69$ V. (a, c, and d)

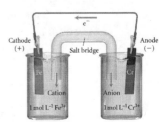

(b) Add two half-reactions with the second reaction reversed.
$Fe^{3+} (aq) + 3 e^- + Cr (s) \rightarrow Fe (s) + Cr^{3+} (aq) + 3 e^-$.
Cancel electrons to get: $Fe^{3+} (aq) + Cr (s) \rightarrow Fe (s) + Cr^{3+} (aq)$.

Check: All atoms and charge are balanced. The units (V) are correct. The cell potential is positive, which is consistent with a voltaic cell.

18.49   **Given:** overall reactions from Problem 43   **Find:** line notation
Conceptual Plan: Use the solution from Problem 43. Write the oxidation half-reaction components on the left and the reduction on the right. A double vertical line (ǁ), indicating the salt bridge, separates the two half-reactions. Substances in different phases are separated by a single vertical line (ǀ), which represents the boundary between the phases. For some redox reactions, the reactants and products of one or both of the half-reactions may be in the same phase. In these cases, the reactants and products are simply separated from each other with a comma in the line diagram. Such cells use an inert electrode, such as platinum (Pt) or graphite, as the anode or cathode (or both).
Solution:

(a)   Reduction reaction: $Ag^+ (aq) + e^- \rightarrow Ag (s)$ and the oxidation reaction: $Pb (s) \rightarrow Pb^{2+} (aq) + 2 e^-$ so
       $Pb (s) \,|\, Pb^{2+} (aq) \,\|\, Ag^+ (aq) \,|\, Ag (s)$

(b)   Reduction reaction: $ClO_2 (g) + e^- \rightarrow ClO_2^- (aq)$ and the oxidation reaction: $2\, I^- (aq) \rightarrow I_2 (s) + 2 e^-$ so
       $Pt (s) \,|\, I^- (aq) \,|\, I_2 (s) \,\|\, ClO_2 (g) \,|\, ClO_2^- (aq) \,|\, Pt (s)$

(c)   Reduction reaction: $O_2 (g) + 4\, H^+ (aq) + 4 e^- \rightarrow 2\, H_2O (l)$ and the oxidation reaction: $Zn (s) \rightarrow Zn^{2+}$
       $(aq) + 2 e^-$ so $Zn (s) \,|\, Zn^{2+} (aq) \,\|\, O_2 (g) \,|\, H^+ (aq), H_2O (l) \,|\, Pt (s)$

18.51   **Given:** $Sn (s) \,|\, Sn^{2+} (aq) \,\|\, NO_3^- (aq), H^+ (aq), H_2O (l) \,|\, NO (g) \,|\, Pt (s)$
Find: sketch voltaic cell, labelling anode, cathode, all species, direction of electron flow, and E°_{cell}
Conceptual Plan: Separate overall reaction into two half-cell reactions knowing that the oxidation half-reaction components are on the left and the reduction half-reaction components are on the right. Add electrons as needed to balance reactions. Multiply the half-reactions by the appropriate factors to have an equal number of electrons transferred. Add the half-cell reactions and cancel electrons. Put the anode reaction on the left (oxidation = electrons as product) and the cathode reaction on the right (reduction = electrons as reactant). Electrons flow from anode to cathode. Look up half-reactions in Table 18.1. Calculate the standard cell potential by subtracting the electrode potential of the anode from the electrode potential of the cathode: $E^\circ_{cell} = E^\circ_{cathode} - E^\circ_{anode}$.
Solution: Oxidation reaction (anode): $Sn (s) \rightarrow Sn^{2+} (aq) + 2 e^-$ $E^\circ = -0.14$ V
and reduction reaction (cathode): $NO_3^- (aq) + 4\, H^+ (aq) + 3 e^- \rightarrow NO (g) +$
$2\, H_2O (l)$ $E^\circ = 0.96$ V. $E^\circ_{cell} = E^\circ_{cathode} - E^\circ_{anode} = 0.96$ V $- (-0.14$ V$) =$
1.10 V. Multiply first reaction by 3 and the second reaction by 2 so that 6 electrons are transferred. $3\, Sn (s) \rightarrow 3\, Sn^{2+} (aq) + 6 e^-$ and $2\, NO_3^- (aq) + 8\, H^+ (aq)$
$+ 6 e^- \rightarrow 2\, NO (g) + 4\, H_2O (l)$. Add the two half-reactions and cancel electrons $3\, Sn (s) + 2\, NO_3^- (aq) + 8\, H^+ (aq) + \cancel{6 e^-} \rightarrow 3\, Sn^{2+} (aq) + \cancel{6 e^-} + 2\, NO (g)$
$+ 4\, H_2O (l)$. So balanced reaction is $3\, Sn (s) + 2\, NO_3^- (aq) + 8\, H^+ (aq) \rightarrow$
$3\, Sn^{2+} (aq) + 2\, NO (g) + 4\, H_2O (l)$.

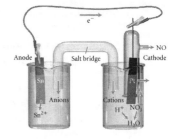

Check: All atoms and charge are balanced. The units (V) are correct. The cell potential is positive, which is consistent with a voltaic cell.

18.53   **Given:** overall reactions   **Find:** spontaneity in forward direction
Conceptual Plan: Separate the overall reaction into two half-cell reactions and add electrons as needed to balance reactions. Look up half-reactions in Table 18.1. Calculate the standard cell potential by subtracting the electrode potential of the anode from the electrode potential of the cathode: $E^\circ_{cell} = E^\circ_{cathode} - E^\circ_{anode}$. If $E^\circ_{cell} > 0$ the reaction is spontaneous in the forward direction.
Solution:

(a) $Ni (s) + Zn^{2+} (aq) \rightarrow Ni^{2+} (aq) + Zn (s)$ separates to $Ni (s) \rightarrow Ni^{2+} (aq)$ and $Zn^{2+} (aq) \rightarrow Zn (s)$ add electrons $Ni (s) \rightarrow Ni^{2+} (aq) + 2 e^-$ and $Zn^{2+} (aq) + 2 e^- \rightarrow Zn (s)$. Look up electrode potentials. Ni is oxidized so $E^\circ = -0.23$ V $= E^\circ_{anode}$. Zn^{2+} is reduced so $E^\circ = -0.76$ V $= E^\circ_{cathode}$. Then $E^\circ_{cell} = E^\circ_{cathode} - E^\circ_{anode} = -0.76$ V $- (-0.23$ V$) = 0.53$ V and so the reaction is nonspontaneous.

(b) $Ni (s) + Pb^{2+} (aq) \rightarrow Ni^{2+} (aq) + Pb (s)$ separates to $Ni (s) \rightarrow Ni^{2+} (aq)$ and $Pb^{2+} (aq) \rightarrow Pb (s)$ add electrons $Ni (s) \rightarrow Ni^{2+} (aq) + 2 e^-$ and $Pb^{2+} (aq) + 2 e^- \rightarrow Pb (s)$. Look up electrode potentials. Ni is oxidized so $E^\circ = -0.23$ V $= E^\circ_{anode}$. Pb^{2+} is reduced so $E^\circ = -0.13$ V $= E^\circ_{cathode}$. Then $E^\circ_{cell} = E^\circ_{cathode} - E^\circ_{anode} = -0.13$ V $- (-0.23$ V$) = 0.10$ V and so the reaction is spontaneous.

(c)   Al (*s*) + 3 Ag$^+$ (*aq*) → Al^{3+} (*aq*) + 3 Ag (*s*) separates to Al (*s*) → Al^{3+} (*aq*) and 3 Ag$^+$ (*aq*) → 3 Ag (*s*) add electrons Al (*s*) → Al^{3+} (*aq*) + 3 e$^-$ and 3 Ag$^+$ (*aq*) + 3 e$^-$ → 3 Ag (*s*). Simplify the Ag reaction to Ag$^+$ (*aq*) + e$^-$ → Ag (*s*). Look up electrode potentials. Al is oxidized so $E° = -1.66$ V $= E°_{anode}$. Ag$^+$ is reduced so $E° = 0.80$ V $= E°_{cathode}$. Then $E°_{cell} = E°_{cathode} - E°_{anode} = 0.80$ V $- (-1.66$ V$) = 2.46$ V and so the reaction is spontaneous.

(d)   Pb (*s*) + Mn^{2+} (*aq*) → Pb^{2+} (*aq*) + Mn (*s*) separates to Pb (*s*) → Pb^{2+} (*aq*) and Mn^{2+} (*aq*) → Mn (*s*) add electrons Pb (*s*) → Pb^{2+} (*aq*) + 2 e$^-$ and Mn^{2+} (*aq*) + 2 e$^-$ → Mn (*s*). Look up electrode potentials. Pb is oxidized so $E° = -0.13$ V $= E°_{anode}$. Mn^{2+} is reduced so $E° = -1.18$ V $= E°_{cathode}$. Then $E°_{cell} = E°_{cathode} - E°_{anode} = -1.18$ V $- (-0.13$ V$) = -1.05$ V and so the reaction is nonspontaneous.

Check: The units (V) are correct. If the voltage is positive, the reaction is spontaneous. If the voltage is negative, the reaction is nonspontaneous.

18.55   In order for a metal to be able to reduce an ion, it must be below it in Table 18.1 (need positive $E°_{cell} = E°_{cathode} - E°_{anode}$). So we need a metal that is below Mn^{2+} but above Mg^{2+}. Aluminum is the only one in the table that meets these criteria.

18.57   In general, metals whose reduction half-reactions lie below the reduction of H$^+$ to H$_2$ in Table 18.1 will dissolve in acids, while metals above it will not. (a) Al and (c) Pb meet this criterion. To write the balanced redox reactions, pair the oxidation of the metal with the reduction of H$^+$ to H$_2$ (2 H$^+$ (*aq*) + 2 e$^-$ → H$_2$ (*g*)). For Al, Al (*s*) → Al^{3+} (*aq*) + 3 e$^-$. In order to balance the number of electrons transferred we need to multiply the Al reaction by 2 and the H$^+$ reaction by 3. So, 2 Al (*s*) → 2 Al^{3+} (*aq*) + 6 e$^-$ and 6 H$^+$ (*aq*) + 6 e$^-$ → 3 H$_2$ (*g*). Adding the two reactions: 2 Al (*s*) + 6 H$^+$ (*aq*) + 6̶e̶$^-$ → 2 Al^{3+} (*aq*) + 6̶e̶$^-$ + 3 H$_2$ (*g*). Simplify to 2 Al (*s*) + 6 H$^+$(*aq*) → 2 Al^{3+} (*aq*) + 3 H$_2$ (*g*). For Pb, Pb (*s*) → Pb^{2+} (*aq*) + 2 e$^-$. Since each reaction involves 2 electrons we can add the two reactions. Pb (*s*) + 2 H$^+$ (*aq*) + 2̶e̶$^-$ → Pb^{2+} (*aq*) + 2̶e̶$^-$ + H$_2$ (*g*). Simplify to Pb (*s*) + 2 H$^+$ (*aq*) → Pb^{2+} (*aq*) + H$_2$ (*g*).

18.59   Nitric acid (HNO$_3$) oxidizes metals through the following reduction half-reaction: NO$_3^-$ (*aq*) + 4 H$^+$ (*aq*) + 3 e$^-$ → NO (*g*) + 2 H$_2$O (*l*) $E° = 0.96$ V. Since this half-reaction is above the reduction of H$^+$ in Table 18.1, HNO$_3$ can oxidize metals (such as copper, for example) that cannot be oxidized by HCl. (a) Cu, which is below nitric acid in the table, will be oxidized, but (b) Au, which is above nitric acid in the table (which has an electrode potential of 1.50 V), will not be oxidized. To write the balanced redox reactions, pair the oxidation of the metal with the reduction of nitric acid (NO$_3^-$ (*aq*) + 4 H$^+$ (*aq*) + 3 e$^-$ → NO (*g*) + 2 H$_2$O (*l*)). For Cu, Cu (*s*) → Cu^{2+} (*aq*) + 2 e$^-$. In order to balance the number of electrons transferred we need to multiply the Cu reaction by 3 and the nitric acid reaction by 2. So, 3 Cu (*s*) → 3 Cu^{2+} (*aq*) + 6 e$^-$ and 2 NO$_3^-$ (*aq*) + 8 H$^+$ (*aq*) + 6 e$^-$ → 2 NO (*g*) + 4 H$_2$O (*l*). Adding the two reactions: 3 Cu (*s*) + 2 NO$_3^-$ (*aq*) + 8 H$^+$ (*aq*) + 6̶e̶$^-$ → 3 Cu^{2+} (*aq*) + 6̶e̶$^-$ + 2 NO (*g*) + 4 H$_2$O (*l*). Simplify to 3 Cu (*s*) + 2 NO$_3^-$ (*aq*) + 8 H$^+$ (*aq*) → 3 Cu^{2+} (*aq*) + 2 NO (*g*) + 4 H$_2$O (*l*).

18.61   **Given:** overall reactions   **Find:** $E°_{cell}$ and spontaneity in forward direction
Conceptual Plan: Separate the overall reaction into two half-cell reactions and add electrons as needed to balance reactions. Look up half-reactions in Table 18.1. Calculate the standard cell potential by subtracting the electrode potential of the anode from the electrode potential of the cathode: $E°_{cell} = E°_{cathode} - E°_{anode}$. If $E°_{cell} > 0$ the reaction is spontaneous in the forward direction.
Solution:

(a)   2 Cu (*s*) + Mn^{2+} (*aq*) → 2 Cu$^+$ (*aq*) + Mn (*s*) separates to 2 Cu (*s*) → 2 Cu$^+$ (*aq*) and Mn^{2+} (*aq*) → Mn (*s*) add electrons 2 Cu (*s*) → 2 Cu$^+$ (*aq*) + 2 e$^-$ and Mn^{2+} (*aq*) + 2 e$^-$ → Mn (*s*). Simplify the Cu reaction to: Cu (*s*) → Cu$^+$ (*aq*) + e$^-$. Look up electrode potentials. Cu is oxidized so $E° = 0.52$ V $= E°_{anode}$. Mn^{2+} is reduced so $E° = -1.18$ V $= E°_{cathode}$. Then $E°_{cell} = E°_{cathode} - E°_{anode} = -1.18$ V $- 0.52$ V $= -1.70$ V and so the reaction is nonspontaneous.

(b)   MnO$_2$ (*s*) + 4 H$^+$(*aq*) + Zn (*s*) → Mn^{2+} (*aq*) + 2 H$_2$O (*l*) + Zn^{2+} (*aq*) separates to MnO$_2$ (*s*) + 4 H$^+$ (*aq*) → Mn^{2+} (*aq*) + 2 H$_2$O (*l*) and Zn (*s*) → Zn^{2+} (*aq*) add electrons MnO$_2$ (*s*) + 4 H$^+$ (*aq*) + 2 e$^-$ → Mn^{2+} (*aq*) + 2 H$_2$O (*l*) and Zn (*s*) → Zn^{2+} (*aq*) + 2 e$^-$. Look up electrode potentials. Zn is oxidized so $E° = -0.76$ V $= E°_{anode}$. Mn is reduced so $E° = 1.21$ V $= E°_{cathode}$. Then $E°_{cell} = E°_{cathode} - E°_{anode} = 1.21$ V $- (-0.76$ V$) = 1.97$ V and so the reaction is spontaneous.

(c) Cl_2 (g) + 2 F$^-$ (aq) → 2 Cl$^-$ (aq) + F$_2$ (g) separates to Cl_2 (g) → 2 Cl$^-$ (aq) and 2 F$^-$ (aq) → F$_2$ (g) add
electrons Cl_2 (g) + 2 e$^-$ → 2 Cl$^-$ (aq) and 2 F$^-$ (aq) → F$_2$ (g) + 2 e$^-$. Look up electrode potentials. F$^-$ is
oxidized so $E° = 2.87$ V $= E°_{anode}$. Cl is reduced so $E° = 1.36$ V $= E°_{cathode}$. Then $E°_{cell} = E°_{cathode} - E°_{anode}$
$= 1.36$ V $- 2.87$ V $= -1.51$ V and so the reaction is nonspontaneous.

Check: The units (V) are correct. If the voltage is positive, the reaction is spontaneous.

18.63   (a)   Pb^{2+}. The strongest oxidizing agent is the one with the reduction reaction that is closest to the top of
Table 18.1 (most positive, least negative electrode potential).

Cell Potential, Gibbs Energy, and the Equilibrium Constant

18.65   **Given:** overall reactions   **Find:** $\Delta_r G°$ and spontaneity in forward direction
**Conceptual Plan: Separate the overall reaction into two half-cell reactions and add electrons as needed
to balance reactions. Look up half-reactions in Table 18.1. Calculate the standard cell potential by sub-
tracting the electrode potential of the anode from the electrode potential of the cathode: $E°_{cell} = E°_{cathode} -
E°_{anode}$, then calculate $\Delta_r G°$ using $\Delta_r G° = -nFE°_{cell}$.**
Solution:

(a)   Pb^{2+} (aq) + Mg (s) → Pb (s) + Mg^{2+} (aq) separates to Pb^{2+} (aq) → Pb (s) and Mg (s) → Mg^{2+} (aq). Add
electrons. Pb^{2+} (aq) + 2 e$^-$ → Pb (s) and Mg (s) → Mg^{2+} (aq) + 2 e$^-$. Look up electrode potentials. Mg
is oxidized so $E° = -2.37$ V $= E°_{anode}$. Pb^{2+} is reduced so $E° = -0.13$ V $= E°_{cathode}$. Then $E°_{cell}$
$= E°_{cathode} - E°_{anode} = -0.13$ V $- (-2.37$ V) $= 2.24$ V. $n = 2$ so $\Delta_r G° = -nFE°_{cell}$

$= -2 \times \dfrac{96\ 485\ C}{mol} \times 2.24$ V $= -2 \times 96\ 485\ \dfrac{C}{mol} \times 2.24\ \dfrac{J}{C} = -4.32 \times 10^5$ J mol$^{-1} = -432$ kJ mol^{-1}.

(b)   Br$_2$ (l) + 2 Cl$^-$ (aq) → 2 Br$^-$ (aq) + Cl$_2$ (g) separates to Br$_2$ (g) → 2 Br$^-$ (aq) and 2 Cl$^-$ (aq) → Cl$_2$ (g).
Add electrons. Br$_2$ (g) + 2 e$^-$ → 2 Br$^-$ (aq) and 2 Cl$^-$ (aq) → Cl$_2$ (g) + 2 e$^-$. Look up cell potentials.
Cl is oxidized so $E° = 1.36$ V $= E°_{anode}$. Br is reduced so $E° = 1.09$ V $= E°_{cathode}$. Then $E°_{cell} = E°_{cathode}$
$- E°_{anode} = 1.09$ V $- 1.36$ V $= -0.27$ V. $n = 2$ so $\Delta_r G° = -nFE°_{cell}$

$= -2 \times \dfrac{96\ 485\ C}{mol} \times -0.27$ V $= -2 \times 96\ 485\ \dfrac{C}{mol} \times -0.27\ \dfrac{J}{C} = 5.2 \times 10^4$ J mol$^{-1} = 52$ kJ mol^{-1}.

(c) MnO_2 (s) + 4 H$^+$(aq) + Cu (s) → Mn^{2+} (aq) + 2 H$_2$O (l) + Cu^{2+} (aq) separates to MnO_2 (s) + 4 H$^+$(aq)
→ Mn^{2+} (aq) + 2 H$_2$O (l) and Cu (s) → Cu^{2+} (aq). Add electrons. MnO_2 (s) + 4 H$^+$(aq) + 2 e$^-$ →
Mn^{2+} (aq) + 2 H$_2$O (l) and Cu (s) → Cu^{2+} (aq) + 2 e$^-$. Look up cell potentials. Cu is oxidized so $E°$
$= 0.34$ V $= E°_{anode}$. Mn is reduced so $E° = 1.21$ V $= E°_{cathode}$. Then $E°_{cell} = E°_{cathode} - E°_{anode}$

$= 1.21$ V $- 0.34$ V $= 0.87$ V. $n = 2$ so $\Delta_r G° = -nFE°_{cell} = -2 \times \dfrac{96\ 485\ C}{mol} \times 0.87$ V $=$

$-2 \times 96\ 485\ \dfrac{C}{mol} \times 0.87\ \dfrac{J}{C} = -1.6788 \times 10^5$ J mol$^{-1} = -1.7 \times 10^2$ kJ mol^{-1}.

Check: The units (kJ mol^{-1}) are correct. If the voltage is positive, the reaction is spontaneous and the free
energy change is negative.

18.67   **Given:** overall reactions from Problem 65   **Find:** K
Conceptual Plan: °C → K then $\Delta_r G°, T$ → K

$\qquad\qquad\qquad$ K = 273.15 + °C $\qquad\qquad$ $\Delta_r G° = -RT \ln K$

Solution: $T = 273.15 + 25$ °C $= 298$ K then

(a) $\Delta_r G° = -RT \ln K$. Rearrange to solve for K.

$$K = e^{\frac{-\Delta_r G°}{RT}} = e^{\dfrac{-(-432\ \text{kJ mol}^{-1}) \times \frac{1000\ \text{J}}{1\ \text{kJ}}}{\left(8.314\ \frac{\text{J}}{\text{K} \cdot \text{mol}}\right)(298\ \text{K})}} = e^{174.364} = 5.31 \times 10^{75}.$$

(b) $\Delta_r G° = -RT \ln K$. Rearrange to solve for K.

$$K = e^{\frac{-\Delta_r G°}{RT}} = e^{\dfrac{-52\ \text{kJ mol}^{-1} \times \frac{1000\ \text{J}}{1\ \text{kJ}}}{\left(8.314\ \frac{\text{J}}{\text{K} \cdot \text{mol}}\right)(298\ \text{K})}} = e^{-20.988} = 7.7 \times 10^{-10}.$$

(c) $\Delta_r G° = -RT \ln K$. Rearrange to solve for K.

$$K = e^{\frac{-\Delta_r G°}{RT}} = e^{\dfrac{-(-170 \ \cancel{kJ \ mol^{-1}}) \times \dfrac{1000 \ \cancel{J}}{1 \ \cancel{kJ}}}{\left(8.314 \dfrac{\cancel{J}}{\cancel{K \cdot mol}}\right)(298 \ \cancel{K})}} = e^{68.6156} = 6.3 \times 10^{29}.$$

Check: The units (none) are correct. If the voltage is positive, the reaction is spontaneous and the Gibbs energy change is negative and the equilibrium constant is large.

18.69 **Given:** $Ni^{2+} (aq) + Cd (s) \rightarrow$ **Find:** K

Conceptual Plan: Write two half-cell reactions and add electrons as needed to balance the reactions. Look up half-reactions in Table 18.1. Calculate the standard cell potential by subtracting the electrode potential of the anode from the electrode potential of the cathode: $E°_{cell} = E°_{cathode} - E°_{anode}$, **then** °C → K **then** $E°_{cell}, n, T \rightarrow K$.

$K = 273.15 + °C$ $\quad \Delta_r G° = -RT \ln K = -nFE°_{cell}$

Solution: $Ni^{2+} (aq) + 2 e^- \rightarrow Ni (s)$ and $Cd (s) \rightarrow Cd^{2+} (aq) + 2 e^-$. Look up electrode potentials. Cd is oxidized so $E° = -0.40 \ V = E°_{anode}$. Ni^{2+} is reduced so $E° = -0.23 \ V = E°_{cathode}$. Then $E°_{cell} = E°_{cathode} - E°_{anode} = -0.23 \ V - (-0.40 \ V) = 0.17 \ V$. The overall reaction is $Ni^{2+} (aq) + Cd (s) \rightarrow Ni (s) + Cd^{2+} (aq)$. $n = 2$ and $T = 273.15 + 25$ °C = 298 K then $\Delta_r G° = -RT \ln K = -nFE°_{cell}$. Rearrange to solve for K.

$$K = e^{\frac{nFE°_{cell}}{RT}} = e^{\dfrac{2 \times 96 \ 485 \ \cancel{C} \times 0.17 \ \dfrac{\cancel{J}}{\cancel{C}}}{\cancel{mol}}} = e^{13.241} = 5.6 \times 10^5.$$

Check: The units (none) are correct. If the voltage is positive, the reaction is spontaneous and the equilibrium constant is large.

18.71 **Given:** $n = 2$ and $K = 25$ **Find:** $\Delta_r G°$ and $E°_{cell}$

Conceptual Plan: $K, T \rightarrow \Delta_r G°$ **and** $\Delta_r G°, n \rightarrow E°_{cell}$

$\Delta_r G° = -RT \ln K$ $\qquad\qquad \Delta_r G° = -nFE°_{cell}$

Solution: $\Delta_r G° = -RT \ln K = -\left(8.314 \dfrac{J}{K \cdot mol}\right)(298 \ K) \ln 25 = -7.97500 \times 10^3 \ J \ mol^{-1} = -8.0 \ kJ \ mol^{-1}$ and

$\Delta_r G° = -nFE°_{cell}$. Rearrange to solve for $E°_{cell}$.

$$E°_{cell} = \frac{\Delta_r G°}{-nF} = \frac{-7.97500 \times 10^3 \ J \ \cancel{mol^{-1}}}{-2 \times \dfrac{96 \ 485 \ C}{\cancel{mol}}} = 0.041 \ \frac{J}{C} = 0.041 \ V.$$

Check: The units ($kJ \ mol^{-1}$ and V) are correct. If $K > 1$ then the voltage is positive, the Gibbs energy change is negative.

Nonstandard Conditions and the Nernst Equation

18.73 **Given:** $Sn^{2+} (aq) + Mn (s) \rightarrow Sn (s) + Mn^{2+} (aq)$

Find: (a) $E°_{cell}$; (b) E_{cell} when $[Sn^{2+}] = 0.0100 \ mol \ L^{-1}$; $[Mn^{2+}] = 2.00 \ mol \ L^{-1}$; and (c) E_{cell} when $[Sn^{2+}] = 2.00 \ mol \ L^{-1}$; $[Mn^{2+}] = 0.0100 \ mol \ L^{-1}$

Conceptual Plan: (a) Separate the overall reaction into two half-cell reactions and add electrons as needed to balance the reactions. Look up half-reactions in Table 18.1. Calculate the standard cell potential by subtracting the electrode potential of the anode from the electrode potential of the cathode: $E°_{cell} = E°_{cathode} - E°_{anode}$. **(b) and (c)** $E°_{cell}, [Sn^{2+}], [Mn^{2+}], n \rightarrow E_{cell}$

$$E_{cell} = E°_{cell} - \frac{0.0257 \ V}{n} \ln Q \quad \text{where} \quad Q = \frac{[Mn^{2+}]}{[Sn^{2+}]}$$

Solution:

(a)   Separate the overall reaction: Sn^{2+} (aq) → Sn (s) and Mn (s) → Mn^{2+} (aq). Add electrons Sn^{2+} (aq) + 2 e^- → Sn (s) and Mn (s) → Mn^{2+} (aq) + 2 e^-. Look up electrode potentials. Mn is oxidized so $E° = -1.18$ V = $E°_{anode}$. Sn^{2+} is reduced so $E° = -0.14$ V = $E°_{cathode}$. Then $E°_{cell} = E°_{cathode} - E°_{anode} = -0.14$ V $- (-1.18$ V$) = 1.04$ V.

(b) $Q = \dfrac{[Mn^{2+}]}{[Sn^{2+}]} = \dfrac{2.00 \; \overline{mol\,L}^{-1}}{0.0100 \; \overline{mol\,L}^{-1}} = 200.$ and $n = 2$ then

$E_{cell} = E°_{cell} - \dfrac{0.0257 \text{ V}}{n} \ln Q = 1.04 \text{ V} - \dfrac{0.0257 \text{ V}}{2} \ln (200) = 0.97$ V

(c) $Q = \dfrac{[Mn^{2+}]}{[Sn^{2+}]} = \dfrac{0.0100 \; \overline{mol\,L}^{-1}}{2.00 \; \overline{mol\,L}^{-1}} = 0.00500$ and $n = 2$ then

$E_{cell} = E°_{cell} - \dfrac{0.0257 \text{ V}}{n} \ln Q = 1.04 \text{ V} - \dfrac{0.0257 \text{ V}}{2} \ln (0.00500) = 1.11$ V

Check: The units (V, V, and V) are correct. The Sn^{2+} reduction reaction is above the Mn^{2+} reduction reaction, so the standard cell potential will be positive. Having more products than reactants reduces the cell potential. Having more reactants than products raises the cell potential.

18.75   **Given:** Pb (s) → Pb^{2+} $(aq, 0.10$ mol $L^{-1})$ + 2 e^- and MnO_4^- $(aq, 1.50$ mol $L^{-1})$ + 4 H^+ $(aq, 2.0$ mol $L^{-1})$ + 3 e^- → MnO_2 (s) + 2 H_2O (l) **Find:** E_{cell}
Conceptual Plan: Look up half-reactions in Table 18.1. Calculate the standard cell potential by subtracting the electrode potential of the anode from the electrode potential of the cathode: $E°_{cell} = E°_{cathode} - E°_{anode}$. **Equalize the number of electrons transferred by multiplying the first reaction by 3 and the second reaction by 2. Add the two half-cell reactions and cancel the electrons.**
Then $E°_{cell}$, $[Pb^{2+}]$, $[MnO_4^-]$, $[H^+]$, n → E_{cell}

$$E_{cell} = E°_{cell} - \dfrac{0.0257 \text{ V}}{n} \ln Q \text{ where } Q = \dfrac{[Pb^{2+}]^3}{[MnO_4^-]^2[H^+]^8}$$

Solution: Pb is oxidized so $E° = -0.13$ V = $E°_{anode}$. Mn is reduced so $E° = 1.68$ V = $E°_{cathode}$. Then $E°_{cell} = E°_{cathode} - E°_{anode} = 1.68$ V $- (-0.13$ V$) = 1.81$ V. Equalize the electrons: 3 Pb (s) → 3 Pb^{2+} (aq) + 6 e^- and 2 MnO_4^- (aq) + 8 H^+ (aq) + 6 e^- → 2 MnO_2 (s) + 4 H_2O (l). Add the two reactions: 3 Pb (s) + 2 MnO_4^- (aq) + 8 H^+ (aq) + $\cancel{6\,e^-}$ → 3 Pb^{2+} (aq) + $\cancel{6\,e^-}$ + 2 MnO_2 (s) + 4 H_2O (l). Cancel the electrons: 3 Pb (s) + 2 MnO_4^- (aq) + 8 H^+ (aq) → 3 Pb^{2+} (aq) + 2 MnO_2 (s) + 4 H_2O (l). So $n = 6$ and $Q = \dfrac{[Pb^{2+}]^3}{[MnO_4^-]^2[H^+]^8} = \dfrac{(0.10)^3}{(1.50)^2(2.0)^8}$

$= 1.\underline{7}361 \times 10^{-6}$ then $E_{cell} = E°_{cell} - \dfrac{0.0257 \text{ V}}{n} \ln Q = 1.81 \text{ V} - \dfrac{0.0257 \text{ V}}{6} \ln 1.7361 \times 10^{-6} = 1.87$ V.

Check: The units (V) are correct. The MnO_4^- reduction reaction is above the Pb^{2+} reduction reaction, so the standard cell potential will be positive. Having more reactants than products raises the cell potential.

18.77   **Given:** Zn/Zn^{2+} and Ni/Ni^{2+} half-cells in voltaic cell; initially $[Ni^{2+}] = 1.50$ mol L^{-1}, and $[Zn^{2+}] = 0.100$ mol L^{-1}
Find: (a) initial E_{cell}; (b) E_{cell} when $[Ni^{2+}] = 0.500$ mol L^{-1}; and (c) $[Ni^{2+}]$ and $[Zn^{2+}]$ when $E_{cell} = 0.45$ V
Conceptual Plan:

(a)   **Write two half-cell reactions and add electrons as needed to balance reactions. Look up half-reactions in Table 18.1. Calculate the standard cell potential by subtracting the electrode potential of the anode from the electrode potential of the cathode:** $E°_{cell} = E°_{cathode} - E°_{anode}$. **Choose the direction of the half-cell reactions so that** $E°_{cell} > 0$. **Add two half-cell reactions and cancel electrons to generate overall reaction. Define Q based on overall reaction. Then** $E°_{cell}$, $[Ni^{2+}]$, $[Zn^{2+}]$, n → E_{cell}

$$E_{cell} = E°_{cell} - \dfrac{0.0257 \text{ V}}{n} \ln Q$$

(b)   **When** $[Ni^{2+}] = 0.500$ mol L^{-1}, **then** $[Zn^{2+}] = 1.100$ mol L^{-1} **(since the stoichiometric coefficients for** Ni^{2+}: Zn^{2+} **are 1:1, and the** $[Ni^{2+}]$ **drops by 1.00 mol** L^{-1}, **the other concentration must rise by 1.00 mol** L^{-1}). **Then** $E°_{cell}$, $[Ni^{2+}]$, $[Zn^{2+}]$, n → E_{cell}

$$E_{cell} = E°_{cell} - \dfrac{0.0257 \text{ V}}{n} \ln Q$$

(c) $E°_{cell}, E_{cell}, n \rightarrow [Zn^{2+}]/[Ni^{2+}] \rightarrow [Ni^{2+}], [Zn^{2+}]$

$$E_{cell} = E°_{cell} - \frac{0.0257 \text{ V}}{n} \ln Q \quad [Ni^{2+}] + [Zn^{2+}] = 1.50 \text{ mol L}^{-1} + 0.100 \text{ mol L}^{-1} = 1.60 \text{ mol L}^{-1}$$

Solution:

(a) $Zn^{2+} (aq) + 2 e^- \rightarrow Zn (s)$ and $Ni^{2+} (aq) + 2 e^- \rightarrow Ni (s)$. Look up electrode potentials. For Zn, $E° = -0.76$ V. For Ni, $E° = -0.23$ V. In order to get a positive $E°_{cell}$ Zn is oxidized so $E° = -0.76$ V $= E°_{anode}$. Ni^{2+} is reduced so $E° = -0.23$ V $= E°_{cathode}$. Then $E°_{cell} = E°_{cathode} - E°_{anode} = -0.23$ V $- (-0.76$ V$) = 0.53$ V. Adding the two half-cell reactions: $Zn (s) + Ni^{2+} (aq) + \cancel{2 e^-} \rightarrow Zn^{2+} (aq) + \cancel{2 e^-} + Ni (s)$. The overall reaction is $Zn (s) + Ni^{2+} (aq) \rightarrow Zn^{2+} (aq) + Ni (s)$. Then $Q = \dfrac{[Zn^{2+}]}{[Ni^{2+}]} = \dfrac{0.100}{1.50} = 0.0666667$ and $n = 2$

then $E_{cell} = E°_{cell} - \dfrac{0.0257 \text{ V}}{n} \ln Q = 0.53$ V $- \dfrac{0.0257 \text{ V}}{2} \ln 0.0666667 = 0.56$ V.

(b) $Q = \dfrac{[Zn^{2+}]}{[Ni^{2+}]} = \dfrac{1.100}{0.500} = 2.20$ then

$E_{cell} = E°_{cell} - \dfrac{0.0257 \text{ V}}{n} \ln Q = 0.53$ V $- \dfrac{0.0257 \text{ V}}{2} \ln 2.20 = 0.52$ V.

(c) $E_{cell} = E°_{cell} - \dfrac{0.0257 \text{ V}}{n} \ln Q$ so 0.45 V $= 0.53$ V $- \dfrac{0.0257 \text{ V}}{2} \ln Q \rightarrow 0.08 \cancel{V} = \dfrac{0.0257 \cancel{V}}{2} \ln Q \rightarrow$

$\ln Q = 6.22568 \rightarrow Q = e^{6.22568} = 505.57$ then $Q = 505.57 = \dfrac{[Zn^{2+}]}{1.60 \text{ mol L}^{-1} - [Zn^{2+}]}$ solving for $[Zn^{2+}]$

$(505.57)(1.60 \text{ mol L}^{-1} - [Zn^{2+}]) = [Zn^{2+}] \rightarrow [Zn^{2+}] = \dfrac{808.912 \text{ mol L}^{-1}}{506.57} = 1.59684 \text{ mol L}^{-1}$

$= 1.60 \text{ mol L}^{-1}$ then $[Ni^{2+}] = 1.60 \text{ mol L}^{-1} - 1.59684 \text{ mol L}^{-1} = 0.003 \text{ mol L}^{-1}$.

Check: The units (V, V, and mol L^{-1}) are correct. The standard cell potential is positive and since there are more reactants than products this raises the cell potential. As the reaction proceeds, reactants are converted to products so the cell potential drops for parts (b) and (c).

18.79 **Given:** Cd (s) + Fe^{2+} (aq) $\rightarrow$ Cd^{2+} (aq) + Fe (s) **Find:** [Cd^{2+}]/[Fe^{2+}] ratio above which reaction is spontaneous **Conceptual Plan: Write two half-cell reactions and add electrons as needed to balance reactions. Look up half-reactions in Table 18.1. Calculate the standard cell potential by subtracting the electrode potential of the anode from the electrode potential of the cathode:** $E°_{cell} = E°_{cathode} - E°_{anode}$. **Add two half-cell reactions and cancel electrons to generate overall reaction.**
Then, set $E_{cell} = 0$ (the point between a spontaneous and nonspontaneous reaction) and $E°_{cell}, n, E_{cell} \rightarrow Q$ which is equal to [Cd^{2+}]/[Fe^{2+}].

$$E_{cell} = E°_{cell} - \frac{0.0257 \text{ V}}{n} \ln Q \qquad Q = \frac{[Cd^{2+}]}{[Fe^{2+}]}$$

Solution: Cd (s) $\rightarrow$ Cd^{2+} (aq) + 2 e$^-$ and Fe^{2+} (aq) + 2 e$^-$ $\rightarrow$ Fe (s). Look up electrode potentials. For Fe, $E° = -0.45$ V. For Cd, $E° = -0.40$ V (from Appendix II.D). Fe^{2+} is reduced so $E° = -0.45$ V $= E°_{cathode}$. Cd is oxidized so $E° = -0.40$ V $= E°_{anode}$. Then $E°_{cell} = E°_{cathode} - E°_{anode} = -0.45$ V $- (-0.40$ V$) = -0.05$ V. Adding the half-cell reactions: Cd (s) + Fe^{2+} (aq) + $\cancel{2 e^-}$ $\rightarrow$ Cd^{2+} (aq) + Fe (s) + $\cancel{2 e^-}$. $Q = \dfrac{[Cd^{2+}]}{[Fe^{2+}]}$ and $n = 2$.

$E_{cell} = E°_{cell} - \dfrac{0.0257 \text{ V}}{n} \ln Q \rightarrow 0.0 = -0.05 - \dfrac{0.0257 \text{ V}}{n} \ln Q \rightarrow 0.05 = -\dfrac{0.0257 \text{ V}}{n} \ln Q \rightarrow$

$\ln Q = -3.891 \rightarrow Q = e^{-3.891} = 0.0204 = \dfrac{[Cd^{2+}]}{[Fe^{2+}]}$

Check: The units (none) are correct. The reaction is nonspontaneous under standard conditions. If the [Cd^{2+}]/[Fe^{2+}] ratio is less than 0.0204 then E_{cell} will be greater than zero and the reaction will be spontaneous.

18.81   **Given:** Zn/Zn^{2+} concentration cell, with $[Zn^{2+}] = 2.0$ mol L^{-1} in one half-cell and $[Zn^{2+}] = 1.0 \times 10^{-3}$ mol L^{-1} in other half-cell
Find: sketch a voltaic cell, labelling the anode, the cathode, the reactions at electrodes, all species, and the direction of electron flow
Conceptual Plan: In a concentration cell, the half-cell with the higher concentration is always the half-cell where the reduction takes place (contains the cathode). The two half-cell reactions are the same, only reversed. Put anode reaction on the left (oxidation = electrons as product) and cathode reaction on the right (reduction = electrons as reactant). Electrons flow from anode to cathode.
Solution:

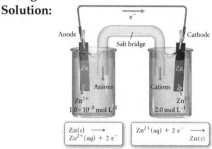

Check: The figure looks similar to the right side of Figure 18.12.

18.83   **Given:** Sn/Sn^{2+} concentration cell with $E_{cell} = 0.10$ V **Find:** ratio of $[Sn^{2+}]$ in two half-cells
Conceptual Plan: Determine n, then E°_{cell}, E_{cell}, $n \rightarrow Q$ = ratio of $[Sn^{2+}]$ in two half-cells.

$$E_{cell} = E^{\circ}_{cell} - \frac{0.0257 \text{ V}}{n} \ln Q$$

Solution: Since Sn^{2+} $(aq) + 2 e^- \rightarrow Sn$ (s), $n = 2$. In a concentration cell, $E^{\circ}_{cell} = 0$ V. So

$$E_{cell} = E^{\circ}_{cell} - \frac{0.0257 \text{ V}}{n} \ln Q \text{ so } 0.10 \text{ V} = 0.00 \text{ V} - \frac{0.0257 \text{ V}}{2} \ln Q \rightarrow 0.10 \text{ V} = -\frac{0.0257 \text{ V}}{2} \ln Q \rightarrow$$

$$\ln Q = -7.7821 \rightarrow Q = e^{-7.7821} = 4.2 \times 10^{-4} = \frac{[Sn^{2+}](ox)}{[Sn^{2+}](red)}.$$

Check: The units (none) are correct. Since the concentration in the reduction reaction half-cell is always greater than the concentration in the oxidation half-cell in a voltaic concentration cell, the Q or ratio of two cells is less than 1.

Batteries, Fuel Cells, and Corrosion

18.85   **Given:** alkaline battery **Find:** optimum mass ratio of Zn to MnO_2
Conceptual Plan: Look up alkaline battery reactions. Use stoichiometry to get mole ratio. Then

Zn $(s) + 2 OH^-$ $(aq) \rightarrow Zn(OH)_2$ $(s) + 2 e^-$ $\frac{1 \text{ mol Zn}}{2 \text{ mol } MnO_2}$

$2 MnO_2$ $(s) + 2 H_2O$ $(l) + 2 e^- \rightarrow 2 MnO(OH)$ $(s) + 2 OH^-$ (aq).

mol Zn $\rightarrow$ g Zn then mol MnO_2 $\rightarrow$ g MnO_2.

$\frac{65.41 \text{ g Zn}}{1 \text{ mol Zn}}$ $\frac{1 \text{ mol } MnO_2}{86.94 \text{ g } MnO_2}$

Solution: $\frac{1 \text{ mol Zn}}{2 \text{ mol } MnO_2} \times \frac{65.41 \text{ g Zn}}{1 \text{ mol Zn}} \times \frac{1 \text{ mol } MnO_2}{86.94 \text{ g } MnO_2} = 0.3762 \frac{\text{g Zn}}{\text{g } MnO_2}$.

Check: The units (mass ratio) are correct. Since more moles of MnO_2 are needed and the molar mass is larger, the ratio is less than 1.

18.87   **Given:** CH_4 $(g) + 2 O_2$ $(g) \rightarrow CO_2$ $(g) + 2 H_2O$ (g) **Find:** E°_{cell}
Conceptual Plan: $\Delta_r G^{\circ} = \sum n_p \Delta_f G^{\circ}(\text{products}) - \sum n_r \Delta_f G^{\circ}(\text{reactants})$ and determine n then

$\Delta_r G^{\circ}, n \rightarrow E^{\circ}_{cell}$

$\Delta_r G^{\circ} = -nFE^{\circ}_{cell}$

Solution:

Reactant/Product	$\Delta_f G^{\circ}(kJ \text{ mol}^{-1}$ from Appendix IIB)
CH_4 (g)	-50.5
O_2 (g)	0.0
CO_2 (g)	-394.4
H_2O (g)	-228.6

Be sure to pull data for the correct formula and phase.

$$\Delta_r G° = \sum n_p \Delta_f G°(\text{products}) - \sum n_r \Delta_f G°(\text{reactants})$$
$$= [1(\Delta_f G°(CO_2\,(g))) + 2(\Delta_f G°(H_2O\,(g)))] - [1(\Delta_f G°(CH_4\,(g))) + 2(\Delta_f G°(O_2\,(g)))]$$
$$= [1(-394.4\text{ kJ mol}^{-1}) + 2(-228.6\text{ kJ mol}^{-1})] - [1(-50.5\text{ kJ mol}^{-1}) + 2(0.0\text{ kJ mol}^{-1})]$$
$$= [-851.6\text{ kJ mol}^{-1}] - [-50.5\text{ kJ mol}^{-1}]$$
$$= -801.1\text{ kJ mol}^{-1} = -8.011 \times 10^5\text{ J mol}^{-1}$$

Also, since one C atom goes from an oxidation state of -4 to $+4$ and 4 O atoms are going from 0 to -2, then $n = 8$ and $\Delta_r G° = -nFE°_{\text{cell}}$. Rearrange to solve for $E°_{\text{cell}}$.

$$E°_{\text{cell}} = \frac{\Delta_r G°}{-nF} = \frac{-8.011 \times 10^5\text{ J mol}^{-1}}{-8 \times \dfrac{96\,485\text{ C}}{\text{mol}}} = 1.038\text{ J C}^{-1} = 1.038\text{ V}.$$

Check: The units (V) are correct. The cell voltage is positive, which is consistent with a spontaneous reaction.

18.89   When iron corrodes or rusts, it oxidizes to Fe^{2+}. In order for a metal to be able to protect iron, it must be more easily oxidized than iron or be below it in Table 18.1. (a) Zn and (c) Mn meet this criterion.

Electrolytic Cells and Electrolysis

18.91   **Given:** electrolytic cell sketch
Find: (a) label the anode and cathode and indicate half-reactions, (b) indicate direction of electron flow, and (c) label battery terminals and calculate minimum voltage to drive the reaction
Conceptual Plan: (a) Write two half-cell reactions and add electrons as needed to balance reactions. Look up half-reactions in Table 18.1. Calculate the standard cell potential by subtracting the electrode potential of the anode from the electrode potential of the cathode: $E°_{\text{cell}} = E°_{\text{cathode}} - E°_{\text{anode}}$. Choose the direction of the half-cell reactions so that $E°_{\text{cell}} < 0$. (b) Electrons flow from anode to cathode. (c) Each half-cell reaction moves forward, so direction of the concentration changes can be determined.
Solution:

(a) $Ni^{2+}\,(aq) + 2\,e^- \rightarrow Ni\,(s)$ and $Cd^{2+}\,(aq) + 2\,e^- \rightarrow Cd\,(s)$. Look up electrode potentials. For Ni, $E° = -0.23$ V. For Cd, $E° = -0.40$ V. In order to get a negative cell potential, Ni is oxidized so $E° = -0.23\text{ V} = E°_{\text{anode}}$. Cd^{2+} is reduced so $E° = -0.23\text{ V} = E°_{\text{cathode}}$. Then $E°_{\text{cell}} = E°_{\text{cathode}} - E°_{\text{anode}}$ $= -0.40\text{ V} - (-0.23\text{ V}) = -0.17$ V. Since oxidation occurs at the anode, the Ni is the anode and the reaction is $Ni\,(s) \rightarrow Ni^{2+}\,(aq) + 2\,e^-$. Since reduction takes place at the cathode, Cd is the cathode and the reaction is $Cd^{2+}\,(aq) + 2\,e^- \rightarrow Cd\,(s)$.

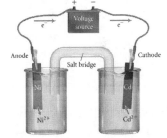

(c)   Since reduction is occurring at the cathode, the battery terminal closest to the cathode is the negative terminal. Since the cell potential from part (a) is $= -0.17$ V, a minimum of 0.17 V must be applied by the battery.
Check: The reaction is nonspontaneous, since the reduction of Ni^{2+} is above Cd^{2+}. Electrons still flow from the anode to the cathode. The reaction can be made spontaneous with the application of electrical energy.

18.93   **Given:** electrolysis of molten KBr   **Find:** write half-reactions
Conceptual Plan: Write two half-cell reactions, taking the cation and the anion to their elemental forms at high temperatures and adding electrons as needed to balance reactions.
Solution: KBr breaks apart to K^+ and Br^-. $K^+\,(l) + e^- \rightarrow K\,(l)$ and $2\,Br^-\,(l) \rightarrow Br_2\,(g) + 2\,e^-$.
Check: The cation is reduced and the anion is oxidized. Mass and charge are balanced in the reactions.

18.95   **Given:** electrolysis of mixture of molten KBr and molten LiBr   **Find:** write half-reactions
Conceptual Plan: Write two half-cell reactions, taking the cation and the anion to their elemental forms at high temperatures and adding electrons as needed to balance reactions. Look up cation electrode potentials to see which one generates the more spontaneous reaction.

Solution: KBr breaks apart to K^+ and Br^-. K^+ (l) + $e^- \rightarrow$ K (l) and 2 Br^- (l) $\rightarrow$ Br_2 (g) + 2 e^-. LiBr breaks apart to Li^+ and Br^-. Li^+ (l) + $e^- \rightarrow$ Li (l) and 2 Br^- (l) $\rightarrow$ Br_2 (g) + 2 e^-. The anions are the same so the anode reaction is 2 Br^- (l) $\rightarrow$ Br_2 (g) + 2 e^-. Looking up the cation electrode potentials, for K^+ $E° = -2.92$ V and for Li^+ $E° = -3.04$ V. Since the electrode potential is more positive for K^+, the reaction at the cathode is K^+ (l) + $e^- \rightarrow$ K (l). **Check:** The cation is reduced and the anion is oxidized. Mass and charge are balanced in the reactions. The cation that is higher in Table 18.1 will be the reaction at the cathode.

18.97   **Given:** electrolysis of aqueous solutions   **Find:** write half-reactions
Conceptual Plan: Write two half-cell reactions, taking the cation and the anion to their elemental forms at standard conditions and adding electrons as needed to balance reactions. Look up electrode potentials and compare to the electrode potentials for the electrolysis of water to see which one generates the more spontaneous reaction.
Solution: The hydrolysis of water reactions are, at a neutral pH, O_2 (g) + 4 H^+ (aq) + 2 $e^- \rightarrow$ 2 H_2O (l) where $E° = 0.82$ V; and when $[OH^-] = 10^{-7}$ mol L^{-1} 2 H_2O (l) + 2 $e^- \rightarrow$ H_2 (g) + OH^- (aq) where $E° = -0.41$ V.

(a)   NaBr breaks apart to Na^+ and Br^-. Na^+ (aq) + $e^- \rightarrow$ Na (s) and 2 Br^- (aq) $\rightarrow$ Br_2 (l) + 2 e^-. Looking up the half-cell potentials, for Na^+ $E°_{cathode} = E° = -2.71$ V and for Br^- $E°_{anode} = E° = 1.09$ V. Since 0.82 V is less positive than $E°_{anode} = 1.09$ V, the oxidation reaction will be 2 H_2O (l) $\rightarrow$ O_2 (g) + 4 H^+ (aq) + 4 e^- at the anode. Since -0.41 V is more positive than -2.71 V, the reduction reaction will be 2 H_2O (l) + 2 $e^- \rightarrow$ H_2 (g) + OH^- (aq) at the cathode.

(b) PbI_2 breaks apart to Pb^{2+} and I^-. Pb^{2+} (aq) + 2 $e^- \rightarrow$ Pb (s) and 2 I^- (aq) $\rightarrow$ I_2 (s) + 2 e^-. Looking up the half-cell potentials, for Pb^{2+} $E°_{cathode} = E° = -0.13$ V and for I^- $E°_{anode} = E° = 0.54$ V. Since $E°_{anode} = 0.54$ V is less positive than 0.82 V, the oxidation reaction will be 2 I^- (aq) $\rightarrow$ I_2 (s) + 2 e^- at the anode. Since -0.13 V is more positive than -0.41 V, the reduction reaction will be Pb^{2+} (aq) + 2 $e^- \rightarrow$ Pb (s) at the cathode.

(c) Na_2SO_4 breaks apart to Na^+ and SO_4^{2-}. Na^+ (aq) + $e^- \rightarrow$ Na (s) and SO_4^{2-} (aq) + 4 H^+ (aq) + 2 $e^- \rightarrow$ H_2SO_3 (aq) + H_2O (l). Notice that both of these are reductions. Since S is in such a high oxidation state (+6) it cannot be oxidized. Looking up the half-cell potentials, for Na^+ $E°_{cathode} = E° = -2.71$ V and for SO_4^{2-} $E°_{cathode} = E° = 0.20$ V. Since sodium sulfate solutions are neutral and not acidic, even though 0.20 V is more positive than -0.41 V and -2.71 V, the reduction reaction will not be SO_4^{2-} (aq) + 4 H^+ (aq) + 2 $e^- \rightarrow$ H_2SO_3 (aq) + H_2O (l) at the cathode, which only occurs in acidic solutions. Thus, the reduction reaction will be 2 H_2O (l) + 2 $e^- \rightarrow$ H_2 (g) + 2OH^- (aq). Since only one oxidation reaction is possible, the oxidation reaction will be 2 H_2O (l) $\rightarrow$ O_2 (g) + 4 H^+ (aq) + 4 e^- at the anode.
Check: The most positive reactions are the reactions that will occur.

18.99   **Given:** electrolysis cell to electroplate Cu onto a metal surface
Find: draw a cell and label the anode and cathode and write half-reactions
Conceptual Plan: Write two half-cell reactions and add electrons as needed to balance reactions. The cathode reaction will be the reduction of Cu^{2+} to the metal. The anode will be the reverse reaction.
Solution:

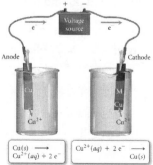

Check: The metal to be plated is the cathode, since metal ions are converted to Cu (s) on the surface of the metal.

18.101   **Given:** Cu electroplating of 325 mg Cu at a current of 5.6 A; Cu^{2+} (aq) + 2 $e^- \rightarrow$ Cu (s)   **Find:** time
Conceptual Plan: mg Cu $\rightarrow$ g Cu $\rightarrow$ mol Cu $\rightarrow$ mol $e^- \rightarrow$ C $\rightarrow$ s

$$\frac{1\,g}{1000\,mg} \quad \frac{1\,mol\,Cu}{63.55\,g\,Cu} \quad \frac{2\,mol\,e^-}{1\,mol\,Cu} \quad \frac{96\,485\,C}{1\,mol\,e^-} \quad \frac{1\,s}{5.6\,C}$$

Solution: $325 \, \overline{mg \, Cu} \times \dfrac{1 \, \overline{g \, Cu}}{1000 \, \overline{mg \, Cu}} \times \dfrac{1 \, \overline{mol \, Cu}}{63.55 \, \overline{g \, Cu}} \times \dfrac{2 \, \overline{mol \, e^-}}{1 \, \overline{mol \, Cu}} \times \dfrac{96 \, 485 \, \overline{C}}{1 \, \overline{mol \, e^-}} \times \dfrac{1 \, s}{5.6 \, \overline{C}} = 180 \, s.$

Check: The units (s) are correct. Since far less than a mole of Cu is electroplated, the time is short.

18.103   **Given:** Na electrolysis, 1.0 kg in one hour   **Find:** current

Conceptual Plan: $Na^+ \, (l) + e^- \rightarrow Na \, (l) \quad \dfrac{kg \, Na}{h} \rightarrow \dfrac{g \, Na}{h} \rightarrow \dfrac{mol \, Na}{h} \rightarrow \dfrac{mol \, e^-}{h} \rightarrow \dfrac{C}{h} \rightarrow \dfrac{C}{min} \rightarrow \dfrac{C}{s}$

$\dfrac{1000 \, g}{1 \, kg} \quad \dfrac{1 \, mol \, Na}{22.99 \, g \, Na} \quad \dfrac{1 \, mol \, e^-}{1 \, mol \, Na} \quad \dfrac{96 \, 485 \, C}{1 mol \, e^-} \quad \dfrac{1 \, h}{60 \, min} \quad \dfrac{1 \, min}{60 \, s}$

Solution:

$\dfrac{1.0 \, \overline{kg \, Na}}{1 \, h} \times \dfrac{1000 \, \overline{g \, Na}}{1 \, \overline{kg \, Na}} \times \dfrac{1 \, \overline{mol \, Na}}{22.99 \, \overline{g \, Na}} \times \dfrac{1 \, \overline{mol \, e^-}}{1 \, \overline{mol \, Na}} \times \dfrac{96 \, 485 \, C}{1 \, \overline{mol \, e^-}} \times \dfrac{1 \, \overline{h}}{60 \, \overline{min}} \times \dfrac{1 \, \overline{min}}{60 \, s} = 1.2 \times 10^3 \, \dfrac{C}{s} = 1.2 \times 10^3 \, A$

Check: The units (A) are correct. Since the amount per hour is so large we expect a very large current.

Cumulative Problems

18.105   **Given:** $MnO_4^- \, (aq) + Zn \, (s) \rightarrow Mn^{2+} \, (aq) + Zn^{2+} \, (aq)$, 0.500 mol L^{-1} $KMnO_4$ and 2.85 g Zn
Find: balanced equation and volume $KMnO_4$ solution
Conceptual Plan: Separate the overall reaction into two half-reactions: one for oxidation and one for reduction. $\rightarrow$ Balance each half-reaction with respect to mass in the following order: 1) balance all elements other than H and O, 2) balance O by adding H_2O, and 3) balance H by adding H^+. $\rightarrow$ Balance each half-reaction with respect to charge by adding electrons. (The sum of the charges on both sides of the equation should be made equal by adding electrons as necessary.) $\rightarrow$ Make the number of electrons in both half-reactions equal by multiplying one or both half-reactions by a small whole number. $\rightarrow$ Add the two half-reactions together, cancelling electrons and other species as necessary. $\rightarrow$ Verify that the reaction is balanced both with respect to mass and with respect to charge. Then
g Zn $\rightarrow$ mol Zn $\rightarrow$ mol MnO_4^- $\rightarrow$ L MnO_4^- $\rightarrow$ mL MnO_4^-.

$\dfrac{1 \, mol \, Zn}{65.41 \, g \, Zn} \quad \dfrac{2 \, mol \, MnO_4^-}{5 \, mol \, Zn} \quad \dfrac{1 \, L \, MnO_4^-}{0.500 \, mol \, MnO_4^-} \quad \dfrac{1000 \, mL \, MnO_4^-}{1 \, L \, MnO_4^-}$

Solution:

Separate: $MnO_4^- \, (aq) \rightarrow \, Mn^{2+} \, (aq)$ and $Zn \, (s) \rightarrow Zn^{2+} \, (aq)$
Balance non H & O elements: $MnO_4^- \, (aq) \rightarrow \, Mn^{2+} \, (aq)$ and $Zn \, (s) \rightarrow Zn^{2+} \, (aq)$
Balance O with H_2O: $MnO_4^- \, (aq) \rightarrow \, Mn^{2+} \, (aq) + 4 \, H_2O \, (l)$ and $Zn \, (s) \rightarrow Zn^{2+} \, (aq)$
Balance H with H^+: $MnO_4^- \, (aq) + 8 \, H^+ \, (aq) \rightarrow Mn^{2+} \, (aq) + 4 \, H_2O \, (l)$ and $Zn \, (s) \rightarrow Zn^{2+} \, (aq)$
Add electrons: $MnO_4^- \, (aq) + 8 \, H^+ \, (aq) + 5 \, e^- \rightarrow Mn^{2+} \, (aq) + 4 \, H_2O \, (l)$ and $Zn \, (s) \rightarrow Zn^{2+} \, (aq) + 2 \, e^-$
Equalize electrons:
   $2 \, MnO_4^- \, (aq) + 16 \, H^+ \, (aq) + 10 \, e^- \rightarrow 2 \, Mn^{2+} \, (aq) + 8 \, H_2O \, (l)$ and $5 \, Zn \, (s) \rightarrow 5 \, Zn^{2+} \, (aq) + 10 \, e^-$
Add half-reactions:
   $2 \, MnO_4^- \, (aq) + 16 \, H^+ \, (aq) + \cancel{10 \, e^-} + 5 \, Zn \, (s) \rightarrow 2 \, Mn^{2+} \, (aq) + 8 \, H_2O \, (l) + 5 \, Zn^{2+} \, (aq) + \cancel{10 \, e^-}$
Cancel electrons: $2 \, MnO_4^- \, (aq) + 16 \, H^+ \, (aq) + 5 \, Zn \, (s) \rightarrow 2 \, Mn^{2+} \, (aq) + 8 \, H_2O \, (l) + 5 \, Zn^{2+} \, (aq)$

$2.85 \, \overline{g \, Zn} \times \dfrac{1 \, \overline{mol \, Zn}}{65.41 \, \overline{g \, Zn}} \times \dfrac{2 \, \overline{mol \, MnO_4^-}}{5 \, \overline{mol \, Zn}} \times \dfrac{1 \, \overline{L \, MnO_4^-}}{0.500 \, \overline{mol \, MnO_4^-}} \times \dfrac{1000 \, mL \, MnO_4^-}{1 \, \overline{L \, MnO_4^-}} = 34.9 \, mL \, MnO_4^-$

= 34.9 mL $KMnO_4$.

Check:

Reactants	Products
2 Mn atoms	2 Mn atoms
8 O atoms	8 O atoms
16 H atoms	16 H atoms
5 Zn atoms	5 Zn atoms
+14 charge	+14 charge

The units (mL) are correct. Since far less than a mole of zinc is used, less than a mole of permanganate is consumed, so the volume is less than a litre.

18.107   **Given:** beaker with Al strip and Cu^{2+} ions   **Find:** draw sketch after Al is submerged for a few minutes
Conceptual Plan: Write two half-cell reactions and add electrons as needed to balance reactions. Look up half-reactions in Table 18.1. Calculate the standard cell potential by subtracting the electrode potential of the anode from the electrode potential of the cathode: $E°_{cell} = E°_{cathode} - E°_{anode}$. If $E°_{cell} > 0$ the reaction is spontaneous in the forward direction and Al will dissolve and Cu will deposit.

Solution: Al (s) → Al^{3+} (aq) and Cu^{2+} (aq) → Cu (s) add electrons Al (s) → Al^{3+} (aq) + 3 e$^-$ and Cu^{2+} (aq) + 2 e$^-$ → Cu (s). Look up electrode potentials. Al is oxidized so $E^\circ_{anode} = E^\circ = -1.66$ V Cu^{2+} is reduced so $E^\circ_{cathode} = E^\circ = 0.34$ V. Then $E^\circ_{cell} = E^\circ_{cathode} - E^\circ_{anode} = 0.34$ V $-$ (-1.66 V) $= 2.00$ V and so the reaction is spontaneous. Al will dissolve to generate Al^{3+} (aq) and Cu (s) will deposit.

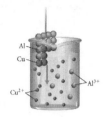

Check: The units (V) are correct. If the voltage is positive, the reaction is spontaneous so Al will dissolve and Cu will deposit.

18.109   **Given:** (a) 2.15 g Al; (b) 4.85 g Cu; and (c) 2.42 g Ag in 3.5 mol L^{-1} HI

Find: if metal dissolves, write a balanced reaction and the minimum amount of HI needed to dissolve the metal

Conceptual Plan: In general, metals whose reduction half-reactions lie below the reduction of H$^+$ to H$_2$ in Table 18.1 will dissolve in acids, while metals above it will not. Stop here if the metal does not dissolve. To write the balanced redox reactions, pair the oxidation of the metal with the reduction of H$^+$ to H$_2$ (2 H$^+$(aq) + 2 e$^-$ → H$_2$(g)). Balance the number of electrons transferred. Add the two reactions. Cancel electrons. Then g metal → mol metal → mol H$^+$ → L HI → mL HI

$$ \text{molar mass} \quad \frac{x \text{ mol H}^+}{y \text{ mol metal}} \quad \frac{1 \text{ L HI}}{3.5 \text{ mol HI}} \quad \frac{1000 \text{ mL HI}}{1 \text{ L HI}} $$

Solution:

(a)   Al meets this criterion. For Al, Al (s) → Al^{3+} (aq) + 3 e$^-$. We need to multiply the Al reaction by 2 and the H$^+$ reaction by 3. So, 2 Al (s) → 2 Al^{3+} (aq) + 6 e$^-$ and 6 H$^+$ (aq) + 6 e$^-$ → 3 H$_2$ (g). Add the half-reactions together: 2 Al (s) + 6 H$^+$ (aq) + $\overline{6e^-}$ → 2 Al^{3+} (aq) + $\overline{6e^-}$ + 3 H$_2$ (g). Simplify to 2 Al (s) + 6 H$^+$ (aq) → 2 Al^{3+} (aq) + 3 H$_2$ (g). Then

$$ 2.15 \text{ g Al} \times \frac{1 \text{ mol Al}}{26.98 \text{ g Al}} \times \frac{6 \text{ mol H}^+}{2 \text{ mol Al}} \times \frac{1 \text{ mol HI}}{1 \text{ mol H}^+} \times \frac{1 \text{ L HI}}{3.5 \text{ mol HI}} \times \frac{1000 \text{ mL HI}}{1 \text{ L HI}} = 68.3 \text{ mL HI.} $$

(b)   Cu does not meet this criterion, so it will not dissolve in HI.

(c)   Ag does not meet this criterion, so it will not dissolve in HI.

Check: Only metals with negative electrode potentials will dissolve. The volume of acid needed is fairly small since the amount of metal is much less than 1 mole and the concentration of acid is high.

18.111   **Given:** Pt (s) | H$_2$ $(g, 1$ bar$)$ | H$^+$ $(aq, ?$ mol L$^{-1})$ || Cu^{2+} $(aq, 1.0$ mol L$^{-1})$ | Cu (s), $E_{cell} = 355$ mV   **Find:** pH

Conceptual Plan: Write half-reactions from line notation. Look up half-reactions in Table 18.1. Calculate the standard cell potential by subtracting the electrode potential of the anode from the electrode potential of the cathode: $E^\circ_{cell} = E^\circ_{cathode} - E^\circ_{anode}$. Add the two half-cell reactions and cancel the electrons. Then mV → V then E°_{cell}, E_{cell}, P_{H_2}, [Cu^{2+}], n → [H$^+$] → pH.

$$ \frac{1 \text{ V}}{1000 \text{ mV}} \qquad\qquad E_{cell} = E^\circ_{cell} - \frac{0.0257 \text{ V}}{n} \ln Q \quad \text{pH} = -\log [\text{H}^+] $$

Solution: The half-reactions are H$_2$ (g) → 2 H$^+$(aq) + 2 e$^-$ and Cu^{2+} (aq) + 2 e$^-$ → Cu (s). H is oxidized so $E^\circ = 0.00$ V $= E^\circ_{anode}$. Cu is reduced so $E^\circ = 0.34$ V $= E^\circ_{cathode}$. Then $E^\circ_{cell} = E^\circ_{cathode} - E^\circ_{anode} = 0.34$ V $- 0.00$ V $= 0.34$ V. Add the two reactions: H$_2$ (g) + Cu^{2+} (aq) + $\overline{2e^-}$ → 2 H$^+$ (aq) + $\overline{2e^-}$ + Cu (s).

Cancel the electrons: H$_2$ (g) + Cu^{2+} (aq) → 2 H$^+$ (aq) + Cu (s). Then $355 \text{ mV} \times \dfrac{1 \text{ V}}{1000 \text{ mV}} = 0.355$ V. So $n = 2$

and $Q = \dfrac{[\text{H}^+]^2}{P_{H_2}[\text{Cu}^{2+}]} = \dfrac{(x)^2}{(1)(1.0)} = x^2$ then $E_{cell} = E^\circ_{cell} - \dfrac{0.0257 \text{ V}}{n} \ln Q$ substitute in values and solve for x.

0.355 V $= 0.34$ V $- \dfrac{0.0257 \text{ V}}{2} \ln x^2$ → 0.015 V $= -\dfrac{0.0257 \text{ V}}{2} \ln x^2$ → $-1.1673 = \ln x^2$ →

$x^2 = e^{-1.1673} = 0.31135$ → $x = 0.55786$ then pH $= -\log [\text{H}^+] = -\log [0.55786] = 0.25347 = 0.3$.

Check: The units (none) are correct. The pH is acidic, which is consistent with dissolving a metal in acid.

18.113   You should be wary of the battery because the most a pairing of half-cell reactions can generate is 5 to 6 V, not 24 V.

18.115   **Given:** Mg oxidation and Cu^{2+} reduction; initially [Mg^{2+}] = 1.0 x 10^{-4} mol L^{-1} and [Cu^{2+}] = 1.5 mol L^{-1} in 1.0 L half-cells   **Find:** (a) initial E_{cell}; (b) E_{cell} after 5.0 A for 8.0 h; and (c) how long can battery deliver 5.0 A

Conceptual Plan:

(a) Write the two half-cell reactions and add electrons as needed to balance reactions. Look up half-reactions in Table 18.1. Calculate the standard cell potential by subtracting the electrode potential of the anode from the electrode potential of the cathode: $E°_{cell} = E°_{cathode} - E°_{anode}$. Add the two half-cell reactions, cancel electrons, and determine n. Then $E°_{cell}, [Mg^{2+}], [Cu^{2+}], n \rightarrow E_{cell}$.

$$E_{cell} = E°_{cell} - \frac{0.0257 \text{ V}}{n} \ln Q$$

(b) $h \rightarrow \min \rightarrow s \rightarrow C \rightarrow \text{mol } e^- \rightarrow \text{mol Cu reduced} \rightarrow [Cu^{2+}]$ and

$$\frac{60 \text{ min}}{1 \text{ h}} \quad \frac{60 \text{ s}}{1 \text{ min}} \quad \frac{5.0 \text{ C}}{1 \text{ s}} \quad \frac{1 \text{ mol } e^-}{96\,485 \text{ C}} \quad \frac{1 \text{ mol Cu}^{2+}}{2 \text{ mol } e^-} \text{ since } V = 1.0 \text{ L} \quad [Cu^{2+}] = [Cu^{2+}] - \frac{\text{mol Cu}^{2+} \text{ reduced}}{1.0 \text{ L}}$$

$\text{mol Cu reduced} \rightarrow \text{mol Mg oxidized} \rightarrow [Mg^{2+}]$

$$\frac{1 \text{ mol Mg oxidized}}{1 \text{ mol Cu}^{2+} \text{reduced}} \text{ since } V = 1.0 \text{ L} \quad [Mg^{2+}] = [Mg^{2+}] + \frac{\text{mol Mg oxidized}}{1.0 \text{ L}}$$

(c) $[Cu^{2+}] \rightarrow \text{mol } e^- \rightarrow C \rightarrow s \rightarrow \min \rightarrow h$

$$\frac{1 \text{ mol } e^-}{2 \text{ mol Cu}^{2+}} \quad \frac{96\,485 \text{ C}}{1 \text{ mol } e^-} \quad \frac{1 \text{ s}}{5.0 \text{ C}} \quad \frac{1 \text{ min}}{60 \text{ s}} \quad \frac{1 \text{ h}}{60 \text{ min}}$$

Solution:

(a) Write half-reactions and add electrons: $Cu^{2+}(aq) + 2 e^- \rightarrow Cu(s)$ and $Mg(s) \rightarrow Mg^{2+}(aq) + 2 e^-$. Look up electrode potentials. Mg is oxidized so $E° = -2.37 \text{ V} = E°_{anode}$. Cu^{2+} is reduced so $E° = 0.34 \text{ V} = E°_{cathode}$. Then $E°_{cell} = E°_{cathode} - E°_{anode} = 0.34 \text{ V} - (-2.37 \text{ V}) = 2.71 \text{ V}$. Add the two half-cell reactions: $Cu^{2+}(aq) + 2e^- + Mg(s) \rightarrow Cu(s) + Mg^{2+}(aq) + 2e^-$. Simplify to $Cu^{2+}(aq) + Mg(s) \rightarrow Cu(s) + Mg^{2+}(aq)$. So $Q = \frac{[Mg^{2+}]}{[Cu^{2+}]} = \frac{1.0 \times 10^{-4}}{1.5} = 6.6667 \times 10^{-5}$ and $n = 2$ then

$$E_{cell} = E°_{cell} - \frac{0.0257 \text{ V}}{n} \ln Q = 2.71 \text{ V} - \frac{0.0257 \text{ V}}{2} \ln 6.6667 \times 10^{-5} = 2.83356 \text{ V} = 2.83 \text{ V}.$$

(b) $8.0 \text{ h} \times \frac{60 \text{ min}}{1 \text{ h}} \times \frac{60 \text{ s}}{1 \text{ min}} \times \frac{5.0 \text{ C}}{1 \text{ s}} \times \frac{1 \text{ mol } e^-}{96\,485 \text{ C}} \times \frac{1 \text{ mol Cu}^{2+}}{2 \text{ mol } e^-} = 0.74623 \text{ mol Cu}^{2+}$ and

$$[Cu^{2+}] = [Cu^{2+}] - \frac{\text{mol Cu}^{2+} \text{ reduced}}{1.0 \text{ L}} = 1.5 \text{ mol L}^{-1} - \frac{0.74623 \text{ mol Cu}^{2+}}{1.0 \text{ L}} = 0.75377 \text{ mol L}^{-1} \text{ Cu}^{2+} \text{ and}$$

$$0.74623 \text{ mol Cu}^{2+} \times \frac{1 \text{ mol Mg oxidized}}{1 \text{ mol Cu}^{2+} \text{reduced}} = 0.74623 \text{ mol Mg oxidized and}$$

$$[Mg^{2+}] = [Mg^{2+}] + \frac{\text{mol Mg oxidized}}{1.0 \text{ L}} = 1.0 \times 10^{-4} \text{ mol L}^{-1} + \frac{0.74623 \text{ mol Mg oxidized}}{1.0 \text{ L}}$$

$$= 0.74633 \text{ mol L}^{-1} \text{ Mg}^{2+}$$

$$Q = \frac{[Mg^{2+}]}{[Cu^{2+}]} = \frac{0.74633}{0.75377} = 0.99013 \text{ and } n = 2 \text{ then}$$

$$E_{cell} = E°_{cell} - \frac{0.0257 \text{ V}}{n} \ln Q = 2.71 \text{ V} - \frac{0.0257 \text{ V}}{2} \ln 0.99013 = 2.71013 \text{ V} = 2.71 \text{ V}.$$

(c) In 1.0 L there are initially 1.5 moles of Cu^{2+}. So

$$1.5 \text{ mol Cu}^{2+} \times \frac{2 \text{ mol } e^-}{1 \text{ mol Cu}^{2+}} \times \frac{96\,485 \text{ C}}{1 \text{ mol } e^-} \times \frac{1 \text{ s}}{5.0 \text{ C}} \times \frac{1 \text{ min}}{60 \text{ s}} \times \frac{1 \text{ h}}{60 \text{ min}} = 16 \text{ h}$$

Check: The units (V, V, and h) are correct. The Cu^{2+} reduction reaction is above the Mg^{2+} reduction reaction, so the standard cell potential will be positive. Having more reactants than products increases the cell potential. As the reaction proceeds the potential drops. The concentrations drop by $\frac{1}{2}$ in 8 hours (part (b)), so it is all consumed in 16 hours.

18.117 **Given:** water electrolysis at 7.8 A; $H_2(g)$: $V = 25.0 \text{ L}, P = 25.0 \text{ atm}; T = 25 \text{ °C}$ **Find:** time
Conceptual Plan: °C $\rightarrow$ K then $V, P, T \rightarrow n$ then write half-reactions

$$K = °C + 273.15 \qquad PV = nRT$$

$\text{mol } H_2 \rightarrow \text{mol } e^- \rightarrow C \rightarrow s \rightarrow \min \rightarrow h$

$$\frac{2 \text{ mol } e^-}{1 \text{ mol } H_2} \quad \frac{96\,485 \text{ C}}{1 \text{ mol } e^-} \quad \frac{1 \text{ s}}{7.8 \text{ C}} \quad \frac{1 \text{ min}}{60 \text{ s}} \quad \frac{1 \text{ h}}{60 \text{ min}}$$

Solution: $T = 25\,°C + 273.15 = 298$ K, then $PV = nRT$. Rearrange to solve for n.

$$n = \frac{PV}{RT} = \frac{25.0 \text{ atm} \times 25.0 \text{ L}}{0.08206 \dfrac{\text{L} \cdot \text{atm}}{\text{mol} \cdot \text{K}} \times 298 \text{ K}} = 25.5583 \text{ mol } H_2.$$ The hydrolysis of water reactions are

$2\,H_2O\,(l) \rightarrow O_2\,(g) + 4\,H^+\,(aq) + 4\,e^-$ and $2\,H_2O\,(l) + 2\,e^- \rightarrow H_2\,(g) + OH^-\,(aq)$.

$25.5583 \text{ mol } H_2 \times \dfrac{2 \text{ mol } e^-}{1 \text{ mol } H_2} \times \dfrac{96\,485 \text{ C}}{1 \text{ mol } e^-} \times \dfrac{1 \text{ s}}{7.8 \text{ C}} \times \dfrac{1 \text{ min}}{60 \text{ s}} \times \dfrac{1 \text{ h}}{60 \text{ min}} = 176 \text{ h}.$

Check: The units (h) are correct. Since we have 25 L of gas at 25 atm (= 25.33 bar) and 25 °C we expect ~25 moles of gas (remember 1 mole of gas at STP = 22.7 L). A very long time is expected since we have so many moles of gas to generate.

18.119 **Given:** $Cu\,(s)\,|\,CuI\,(s)\,|\,I^-\,(aq,\,1.0 \text{ mol } L^{-1})\,||\,Cu^+\,(aq,\,1.0 \text{ mol } L^{-1})\,|\,Cu\,(s)$, $K_{sp}\,(CuI) = 1.1 \times 10^{-12}$ **Find:** E_{cell}
Conceptual Plan: Write half-reactions from line notation. Since this is a concentration cell $E^°_{cell} = 0.00$ V.
Then K_{sp}, $[I^-] \rightarrow [Cu^+](ox)$ then $E^°_{cell}$, $[Cu^+](ox)$, $[Cu^+](red)$, $n \rightarrow E_{cell}$.

$$K_{sp} = [Cu^+]\,[I^-] \qquad\qquad E_{cell} = E^°_{cell} - \frac{0.0257 \text{ V}}{n} \ln Q$$

Solution: The half-reactions are $Cu\,(s) \rightarrow Cu^+\,(aq) + e^-$ and $Cu^+\,(aq) + e^- \rightarrow Cu\,(s)$. Since this is a concentration cell $E^°_{cell} = 0.00$ V and $n = 1$. Since $K_{sp} = [Cu^+]\,[I^-]$, rearrange to solve for $[Cu^+](ox)$.

$$[Cu^+]\,(ox) = \frac{K_{sp}}{[I^-]} = \frac{1.1 \times 10^{-12}}{1.0} = 1.1 \times 10^{-12} \text{ mol } L^{-1} \text{ then}$$

$$Q = \frac{[Cu^+](ox)}{[Cu^+](red)} = \frac{1.1 \times 10^{-12}}{1.0} = 1.1 \times 10^{-12} \text{ then}$$

$$E_{cell} = E^°_{cell} - \frac{0.0257 \text{ V}}{n} \ln Q = 0.00 \text{ V} - \frac{0.0257 \text{ V}}{1} \ln (1.1 \times 10^{-12}) = 0.71 \text{ V}.$$

Check: The units (V) are correct. Since $[Cu^+](ox)$ is so low and $[Cu^+](red)$ is high, the Q is very small so the voltage increase compared to the standard value is significant.

18.121 **Given:** (a) disproportionation of $Mn^{2+}\,(aq)$ to $Mn\,(s)$ and $MnO_2\,(s)$; and (b) disproportionation of $MnO_2\,(s)$ to $Mn^{2+}\,(aq)$ and $MnO_4^-\,(s)$ in acidic solution **Find:** $\Delta_r G°$ and K
Conceptual Plan: Separate the overall reaction into two half-reactions: one for oxidation and one for reduction. $\rightarrow$ Balance each half-reaction with respect to mass in the following order: 1) balance all elements other than H and O, 2) balance O by adding H_2O, and 3) balance H by adding H^+. $\rightarrow$ Balance each half-reaction with respect to charge by adding electrons. (The sum of the charges on both sides of the equation should be made equal by adding electrons as necessary.) $\rightarrow$ Make the number of electrons in both half-reactions equal by multiplying one or both half-reactions by a small whole number. $\rightarrow$ Add the two half-reactions together, cancelling electrons and other species as necessary. $\rightarrow$ Verify that the reaction is balanced both with respect to mass and with respect to charge. Look up half-reactions in Table 18.1. Calculate the standard cell potential by subtracting the electrode potential of the anode from the electrode potential of the cathode: $E^°_{cell} = E^°_{cathode} - E^°_{anode}$.
Then calculate $\Delta_r G°$ using $\Delta_r G° = -nFE^°_{cell}$. Finally °C $\rightarrow$ K then $\Delta_r G°$, $T \rightarrow K$.

$$K = 273.15 + °C \qquad\qquad \Delta_r G° = -RT \ln K$$

Solution:

(a) Separate: $\qquad\qquad\qquad\qquad Mn^{2+}\,(aq) \rightarrow MnO_2\,(s) \qquad$ and $\qquad\qquad Mn^{2+}\,(aq) \rightarrow Mn\,(s)$

Balance non H & O elements: $Mn^{2+}\,(aq) \rightarrow MnO_2\,(s) \qquad$ and $\qquad\qquad Mn^{2+}\,(aq) \rightarrow Mn\,(s)$

Balance O with H_2O: $Mn^{2+}\,(aq) + 2\,H_2O\,(l) \rightarrow MnO_2\,(s) \qquad$ and $\qquad Mn^{2+}\,(aq) \rightarrow Mn\,(s)$

Balance H with H^+: $Mn^{2+}\,(aq) + 2\,H_2O\,(l) \rightarrow MnO_2\,(s) + 4\,H^+\,(aq)$ and $\quad Mn^{2+}\,(aq) \rightarrow Mn\,(s)$

Add electrons: $Mn^{2+}\,(aq) + 2\,H_2O\,(l) \rightarrow MnO_2\,(s) + 4\,H^+\,(aq) + 2\,e^-$ and $Mn^{2+}\,(aq) + 2\,e^- \rightarrow Mn\,(s)$

Equalize electrons: $Mn^{2+}\,(aq) + 2\,H_2O\,(l) \rightarrow MnO_2\,(s) + 4\,H^+\,(aq) + 2\,e^-$ and $Mn^{2+}\,(aq) + 2\,e^- \rightarrow Mn\,(s)$

Add half-reactions: $Mn^{2+}\,(aq) + 2\,H_2O\,(l) + Mn^{2+}\,(aq) + \cancel{2\,e^-} \rightarrow MnO_2\,(s) + 4\,H^+\,(aq) + \cancel{2\,e^-} + Mn\,(s)$

Cancel electrons: $2\,Mn^{2+}\,(aq) + 2\,H_2O\,(l) \rightarrow MnO_2\,(s) + 4\,H^+\,(aq) + Mn\,(s)$

Look up electrode potentials. Mn is oxidized in the first half-cell reaction so $E^°_{anode} = E° = 1.21$ V. Mn is reduced in the second half-cell reaction so $E^°_{cathode} = E° = -1.18$ V. Then $E^°_{cell} = E^°_{cathode} - E^°_{anode}$ $= -1.18$ V $- 1.21$ V $= -2.39$ V. $n = 2$ so

$$\Delta_r G° = -nFE°_{cell} = -2 \times \frac{96\ 485\ C}{mol} \times -2.39\ V = -2 \times 96\ 485\ \frac{C}{mol} \times -2.39\ \frac{J}{C} =$$

$4.61198 \times 10^5\ J\ mol^{-1} = 461\ kJ\ mol^{-1}$ and $T = 273.15 + 25\ °C = 298\ K$ then
$\Delta_r G° = -RT \ln K$. Rearrange to solve for K.

$$K = e^{\frac{-\Delta_r G°}{RT}} = e^{\frac{-4.61198 \times 10^5\ J\ mol^{-1}}{\left(8.314\ \frac{J}{K \cdot mol}\right)(298\ K)}} = e^{-186.149} = 1.4 \times 10^{-81}$$

Check:

Reactants	Products
2 Mn atoms	2 Mn atoms
2 O atoms	2 O atoms
4 H atoms	4 H atoms
+4 charge	+4 charge

The units (kJ mol^{-1} and none) are correct. If the voltage is negative, the reaction is nonspontaneous and the Gibbs energy change is very positive and the equilibrium constant is extremely small.

(b)   Separate: $MnO_2\ (s) \rightarrow Mn^{2+}\ (aq)$ and $MnO_2\ (s) \rightarrow MnO_4^-\ (aq)$
Balance non H & O elements: $MnO_2\ (s) \rightarrow Mn^{2+}\ (aq)$ and $MnO_2\ (s) \rightarrow MnO_4^-\ (aq)$
Balance O with H_2O: $MnO_2\ (s) \rightarrow Mn^{2+}\ (aq) + 2\ H_2O\ (l)$ and $MnO_2\ (s) + 2\ H_2O\ (l) \rightarrow MnO_4^-\ (aq)$
Balance H with H^+:
$MnO_2\ (s) + 4\ H^+\ (aq) \rightarrow Mn^{2+}\ (aq) + 2\ H_2O\ (l)$ and $MnO_2\ (s) + 2\ H_2O\ (l) \rightarrow MnO_4^-\ (aq) + 4\ H^+\ (aq)$
Add electrons: $MnO_2\ (s) + 4\ H^+(aq) + 2\ e^- \rightarrow Mn^{2+}\ (aq) + 2\ H_2O\ (l)$ and $MnO_2\ (s) + 2\ H_2O\ (l) \rightarrow$
$$MnO_4^-\ (aq) + 4\ H^+\ (aq) + 3e^-$$
Equalize electrons: $3\ MnO_2\ (s) + 12\ H^+\ (aq) + 6\ e^- \rightarrow 3\ Mn^{2+}\ (aq) + 6\ H_2O\ (l)$ and
$$2\ MnO_2\ (s) + 4\ H_2O\ (l) \rightarrow 2\ MnO_4^-\ (aq) + 8\ H^+\ (aq) + 6\ e^-$$
Add half-reactions: $3\ MnO_2\ (s) + \cancel{4}\ \cancel{12}\ H^+(aq) + \cancel{6e^-} + 2\ MnO_2\ (s) + \cancel{4}\ H_2O\ (l) \rightarrow$
$$3\ Mn^{2+}\ (aq) + 2\ \cancel{6}\ H_2O\ (l) + 2\ MnO_4^-\ (aq) + \cancel{8}\ H^+(aq) + \cancel{6e^-}$$
Cancel electrons & species: $5\ MnO_2\ (s) + 4\ H^+\ (aq) \rightarrow 3\ Mn^{2+}\ (aq) + 2\ H_2O\ (l) + 2\ MnO_4^-\ (aq)$
Look up electrode potentials. Mn is reduced in the first half-cell reaction so $E°_{cathode} = E° = 1.21\ V$. Mn is oxidized in the second half-cell reaction so $E°_{anode} = E° = 1.68\ V$. Then $E°_{cell} = E°_{cathode} - E°_{anode}$
$= 1.21\ V - 1.68\ V = -0.47\ V$. $n = 6$ so

$$\Delta_r G° = -nFE°_{cell} = -6 \times \frac{96\ 485\ C}{mol} \times -0.47\ V = -6 \times 96\ 485\ \frac{C}{mol} \times -0.47\ \frac{J}{C}$$

$= 2.7209 \times 10^5\ J\ mol^{-1} = 270\ kJ\ mol^{-1} = 2.7 \times 10^2\ kJ\ mol^{-1}$. $T = 273.15 + 25\ °C = 298\ K$

then $\Delta_r G° = -RT \ln K$.

Rearrange to solve for K. $K = e^{\frac{-\Delta_r G°}{RT}} = e^{\frac{-2.7209 \times 10^5\ J\ mol^{-1}}{\left(8.314\ \frac{J}{K \cdot mol}\right)(298\ K)}} = e^{-109.82} = 2.0 \times 10^{-48}$

Check:

Reactants	Products
5 Mn atoms	5 Mn atoms
10 O atoms	10 O atoms
4 H atoms	4 H atoms
+4 charge	+4 charge

The units (kJ mol^{-1} and none) are correct. If the voltage is negative, the reaction is nonspontaneous, the free energy change is very positive, and the equilibrium constant is extremely small. The voltage is less than in part (a), so the free energy change is not as large and the equilibrium constant is not as small.

18.123   **Given:** metal, M, 50.9 g mol^{-1}, 1.20 g of metal reduced in 23.6 minutes at 6.42 A from molten chloride
Find: empirical formula of chloride
Conceptual Plan: min $\rightarrow$ s $\rightarrow$ C $\rightarrow$ mol e$^-$ and g M $\rightarrow$ mol M then mol e$^-$, mol M $\rightarrow$ charge $\rightarrow$ MCl$_x$

$$\frac{60\ s}{1\ min} \quad \frac{6.42\ C}{1\ s} \quad \frac{1\ mol\ e^-}{96\ 485\ C} \qquad \frac{1\ mol\ M}{50.9\ g\ M} \qquad\qquad \frac{1\ mol\ e^-}{1\ mol\ M}$$

Solution: $23.6 \text{ min} \times \dfrac{60 \text{ s}}{1 \text{ min}} \times \dfrac{6.42 \text{ C}}{1 \text{ s}} \times \dfrac{1 \text{ mol e}^-}{96\,485 \text{ C}} = 0.0942190 \text{ mol e}^-$ and

$1.20 \text{ g M} \times \dfrac{1 \text{ mol M}}{50.9 \text{ g M}} = 0.0235756 \text{ mol M}$ then $\dfrac{0.0942190 \text{ mol e}^-}{0.0235756 \text{ mol M}} = 3.99646 \dfrac{\text{e}^-}{\text{M}}$

so the empirical formula is MCl_4.

Check: The units (none) are correct. The result was an integer within the error of the measurements. The formula is typical for a metal salt. It could be vanadium, which has a +4 oxidation state.

18.125   **Given:** 0.535 g impure Sn; dissolve to form Sn^{2+} and titrate with 0.0344 L of 0.0448 mol L^{-1} NO_3^- to generate NO
       Find: percent by mass Sn
       Conceptual Plan: use balanced reaction from Problem 40(c) then
       $\mathbf{L \rightarrow mol\ NO_3^- \rightarrow mol\ Sn \rightarrow g\ Sn \rightarrow percent\ by\ mass\ Sn}$

$M = \dfrac{\text{mol}}{\text{L}} \qquad \dfrac{3 \text{ mol Sn}}{2 \text{ mol NO}_3^-} \quad \dfrac{118.71 \text{ g Sn}}{1 \text{ mol Sn}} \qquad \text{percent by mass Sn} = \dfrac{\text{g Sn}}{\text{g sample}} \times 100\%$

       Solution: $2 \text{ NO}_3^- \ (aq) + 8 \text{ H}^+ \ (aq) + 3 \text{ Sn}^{2+} \ (aq) \rightarrow 2 \text{ NO } (g) + 4 \text{ H}_2\text{O } (l) + 3 \text{ Sn}^{4+} \ (aq)$

$0.0344 \text{ L} \times \dfrac{0.0448 \text{ mol NO}_3^-}{1 \text{ L}} \times \dfrac{3 \text{ mol Sn}}{2 \text{ mol NO}_3^-} \times \dfrac{118.71 \text{ g Sn}}{1 \text{ mol Sn}} = 0.2744195 \text{ g Sn}$ then

percent by mass Sn $= \dfrac{\text{g Sn}}{\text{g sample}} \times 100\% = \dfrac{0.2744195 \text{ g Sn}}{0.535 \text{ g sample}} \times 100\% = 51.3\%$ by mass Sn.

       Check: The units (% by mass) are correct. The result was a number less than 100%.

18.127   **Given:** 1.25 L of a 0.552 mol L^{-1} HBr solution, convert H^+ to H_2 (g) for 73 minutes at 11.32 A   **Find:** pH
       Conceptual Plan: min $\rightarrow$ s $\rightarrow$ C $\rightarrow$ mol e$^-$ $\rightarrow$ mol H$^+$ consumed and L, mol L^{-1} $\rightarrow$ mol H$^+$ initially then

$\dfrac{60 \text{ s}}{1 \text{ min}} \quad \dfrac{11.32 \text{ C}}{1 \text{ s}} \quad \dfrac{1 \text{ mol e}^-}{96\,485 \text{ C}} \quad \dfrac{2 \text{ mol H}^+}{2 \text{ mol e}^-} \qquad\qquad M = \dfrac{\text{mol}}{\text{L}}$

       mol H$^+$ initially, mol H$^+$ consumed $\rightarrow$ mol H$^+$ remaining then mol H$^+$ remaining, L $\rightarrow$ [H$^+$] $\rightarrow$ pH

mol H$^+$ initially – mol H$^+$ consumed = mol H$^+$ remaining $\qquad\qquad M = \dfrac{\text{mol}}{\text{L}} \quad$ pH $= -\log$ [H$^+$]

       Solution: $2 \text{ H}^+ \ (aq) + 2 \text{ e}^- \rightarrow \text{H}_2 \ (g)$

$73 \text{ min} \times \dfrac{60 \text{ s}}{1 \text{ min}} \times \dfrac{11.32 \text{ C}}{1 \text{ s}} \times \dfrac{1 \text{ mol e}^-}{96\,485 \text{ C}} \times \dfrac{2 \text{ mol H}^+}{2 \text{ mol e}^-} = 0.513879 \text{ mol H}^+$ consumed and

$1.25 \text{ L H}^+ \times \dfrac{0.552 \text{ mol H}^+}{1 \text{ L H}^+} = 0.690 \text{ mol H}^+$ initially then mol H$^+$ initially – mol H$^+$ consumed =

mol H$^+$ remaining $= 0.690$ mol H$^+$ initially $- 0.513879$ mol H$^+$ consumed $= 0.17612$ mol H$^+$ remaining

then $[\text{H}^+] = \dfrac{0.17612 \text{ mol H}^+}{1.25 \text{ L}} = 0.140897 \text{ mol L}^{-1}$ H$^+$ then pH $= -\log$ [H$^+$] $= -\log 0.140897 = 0.85$.

       Check: The units (none) are correct. The result is a pH higher than the initial pH ($-\log (0.552) = 0.258$), as is expected.

18.129   **Given:** MnO_2/Mn^{2+} electrode at pH 10.24   **Find:** $[Mn^{2+}]$ to get half-cell potential = 0.00 V
       Conceptual Plan: pH $\rightarrow$ [H$^+$] then

pH $= -\log$ [H$^+$]

       Write half-cell reactions and look up half-reactions in Table 18.1. Define Q based on half-cell reaction.
       Then $E^\circ_{\text{half-cell}}$, n, [H$^+$] $\rightarrow$ [Mn^{2+}].

$E_{\text{half-cell}} = E^\circ_{\text{half-cell}} - \dfrac{0.0257 \text{ V}}{n} \ln Q$

       Solution: Since pH $= -\log$ [H$^+$] so [H$^+$] $= 10^{-\text{pH}} = 10^{-10.24} = 5.75440 \times 10^{-11}$ mol L^{-1}

$MnO_2 \ (s) + 4 \text{ H}^+(aq) + 2 \text{ e}^- \rightarrow \text{Mn}^{2+} \ (aq) + 2 \text{ H}_2\text{O } (l) \quad E^\circ_{\text{half-cell}} = 1.21 \text{ V}, n = 2, \text{ and } Q = \dfrac{[\text{Mn}^{2+}]}{[\text{H}^+]^4}$.

$E_{\text{half-cell}} = E^\circ_{\text{half-cell}} - \dfrac{0.0257 \text{ V}}{n} \ln Q$ so $0.00 \text{ V} = 1.21 \text{ V} - \dfrac{0.0257 \text{ V}}{2} \ln \dfrac{[\text{Mn}^{2+}]}{(5.75440 \times 10^{-11})^4} \rightarrow$

$1.21 \text{ V} = \dfrac{0.0257 \text{ V}}{2} \ln \dfrac{[\text{Mn}^{2+}]}{(5.75440 \times 10^{-11})^4} \rightarrow 94.1634 = \ln \dfrac{[\text{Mn}^{2+}]}{(5.75440 \times 10^{-11})^4} \rightarrow$

$\dfrac{[\text{Mn}^{2+}]}{(5.75440 \times 10^{-11})^4} = e^{94.1634} = 7.84594 \times 10^{40} \rightarrow [\text{Mn}^{2+}] = 0.857662 \text{ mol L}^{-1} = 0.86 \text{ mol L}^{-1} \text{ Mn}^{2+}$

Check: The units (mol L^{-1}) are correct. The standard half-cell potential is very large and positive. Most of the shift towards 0.00 V is due to the fourth-order dependence in [H$^+$] at a high pH, so the [Mn^{2+}] is close to 1 mol L^{-1}. So the concentration is reasonable.

Challenge Problems

18.131   **Given:** hydrogen–oxygen fuel cell; 1.2 x 10^3 kWh of electricity/month   **Find:** V of H$_2$ (g) at STP/month
Conceptual Plan: Write half-reactions. Look up half-reactions at pH 7. The reaction on the left is the oxidation. Calculate the standard cell potential by subtracting the electrode potential of the anode from the electrode potential of the cathode: $E°_{cell} = E°_{cathode} - E°_{anode}$. Add the two half-cell reactions and cancel the electrons. Then kWh $\rightarrow$ J $\rightarrow$ C $\rightarrow$ mol e$^-$ $\rightarrow$ mol H$_2$ $\rightarrow$ V.

$$\frac{3.60 \times 10^6 \text{ J}}{1 \text{ kWh}} \quad \frac{1 \text{ C}}{1.23 \text{ J}} \quad \frac{1 \text{ mol e}^-}{96\,485 \text{ C}} \quad \frac{2 \text{ mol H}_2}{4 \text{ mol e}^-} \quad \text{at STP} \quad \frac{22.7 \text{ L}}{1 \text{ mol H}_2}$$

Solution: 2 H$_2$ (g) + 4 OH$^-$ (aq) $\rightarrow$ 4 H$_2$O (l) + 4 e$^-$ where $E°$ = $-$ 0.83 V = $E°_{anode}$; and O$_2$ (g) + 2 H$_2$O (l) + 4 e$^-$ $\rightarrow$ 4 OH$^-$ (aq) where $E°$ = 0.40 V = $E°_{cathode}$. $E°_{cell} = E°_{cathode} - E°_{anode}$ = 0.40 V $-$ ($-$ 0.83 V) = 1.23 V = 1.23 J C^{-1} and n = 4. Net reaction is 2 H$_2$ (g) + O$_2$ (g) $\rightarrow$ 2 H$_2$O (l). Then

$$1.2 \times 10^3 \text{ kWh} \times \frac{3.60 \times 10^6 \text{ J}}{1 \text{ kWh}} \times \frac{1 \text{ C}}{1.23 \text{ J}} \times \frac{1 \text{ mol e}^-}{96\,485 \text{ C}} \times \frac{2 \text{ mol H}_2}{4 \text{ mol e}^-} \times \frac{22.7 \text{ L}}{1 \text{ mol H}_2} = 4.1 \times 10^5 \text{ L}.$$

Check: The units (L) are correct. A large volume is expected since we are trying to generate a large amount of electricity.

18.133   **Given:** Au^{3+}/Au electroplating; surface area = 49.8 cm^2, Au thickness = 1.00 x 10^{-3} cm, density = 19.3 g cm^{-3}; at 3.25 A   **Find:** time
Conceptual Plan: Write the half-cell reaction and add electrons as needed to balance reactions. Then surface area, thickness $\rightarrow$ V $\rightarrow$ g Au $\rightarrow$ mol Au $\rightarrow$ mol e$^-$ $\rightarrow$ C $\rightarrow$ s.

$$V = \text{surface area} \times \text{thickness} \quad \frac{19.3 \text{ g Au}}{1 \text{ cm}^3 \text{ Au}} \quad \frac{1 \text{ mol Au}}{196.97 \text{ g Au}} \quad \frac{3 \text{ mol e}^-}{1 \text{ mol Au}} \quad \frac{96\,485 \text{ C}}{1 \text{ mol e}^-} \quad \frac{1 \text{ s}}{3.25 \text{ C}}$$

Solution: Write the half-reaction and add electrons: Au^{3+} (aq) + 3 e$^-$ $\rightarrow$ Au (s).
V = surface area x thickness = (49.8 cm^2)(1.00 x 10^{-3} cm) = 0.0498 cm^3 then

$$0.0498 \text{ cm}^3 \text{ Au} \times \frac{19.3 \text{ g Au}}{1 \text{ cm}^3 \text{ Au}} \times \frac{1 \text{ mol Au}}{196.97 \text{ g Au}} \times \frac{3 \text{ mol e}^-}{1 \text{ mol Au}} \times \frac{96\,485 \text{ C}}{1 \text{ mol e}^-} \times \frac{1 \text{ s}}{3.25 \text{ C}} = 435 \text{ s}.$$

Check: The units (s) are correct. Since the layer is so thin there is far less than a mole of gold, so the time is not very long. In order to be an economical process, it must be fairly quick.

18.135   **Given:** C$_2$O$_4^{2-}$ $\rightarrow$ CO$_2$ and MnO$_4^-$ (aq) $\rightarrow$ Mn^{2+} (aq); 50.1 mL of MnO$_4^-$ to titrate 0.339 g Na$_2$C$_2$O$_4$; and 4.62 g U sample titrated by 32.3 mL MnO$_4^-$; and UO^{2+} $\rightarrow$ UO$_2^{2+}$ **Find:** percent U in sample
Conceptual Plan: Separate the overall reaction into two half-reactions: one for oxidation and one for reduction. $\rightarrow$ Balance each half-reaction with respect to mass in the following order: 1) balance all elements other than H and O, 2) balance O by adding H$_2$O, and 3) balance H by adding H$^+$. $\rightarrow$ Balance each half-reaction with respect to charge by adding electrons. (The sum of the charges on both sides of the equation should be made equal by adding electrons as necessary.) $\rightarrow$ Make the number of electrons in both half-reactions equal by multiplying one or both half-reactions by a small whole number. $\rightarrow$ Add the two half-reactions together, cancelling electrons and other species as necessary. $\rightarrow$ Verify that the reaction is balanced both with respect to mass and with respect to charge. Then mL MnO$_4^-$ $\rightarrow$ L MnO$_4^-$ and g Na$_2$C$_2$O$_4$ $\rightarrow$ mol Na$_2$C$_2$O$_4$ $\rightarrow$ mol MnO$_4^-$ then

$$\frac{1 \text{ L MnO}_4^-}{1000 \text{ mL MnO}_4^-} \qquad \frac{1 \text{ mol Na}_2\text{C}_2\text{O}_4}{134.00 \text{ g Na}_2\text{C}_2\text{O}_4} \qquad \frac{2 \text{ mol MnO}_4^-}{5 \text{ mol Na}_2\text{C}_2\text{O}_4}$$

L MnO$_4^-$ $\rightarrow$ mol MnO$_4^-$ $\rightarrow$ mol L^{-1} MnO$_4^-$ then write U half-reactions and balance as above.

$$\frac{1 \text{ L MnO}_4^-}{0.500 \text{ mol MnO}_4^-} \qquad M = \frac{\text{mol MnO}_4^-}{\text{L}}$$

Make the number of electrons in both half-reactions equal by multiplying one or both half-reactions by a small whole number. $\rightarrow$ Add the two half-reactions together, cancelling electrons and other species as necessary. $\rightarrow$ Verify that the reaction is balanced both with respect to mass and with respect to charge. Then mL MnO$_4^-$ $\rightarrow$ mol L^{-1} MnO$_4^-$ $\rightarrow$ mol MnO$_4^-$ $\rightarrow$ mol U $\rightarrow$ g U then g U, g sample $\rightarrow$ % U.

$$M = \frac{\text{mol MnO}_4^-}{\text{L}} \qquad \frac{5 \text{ mol U}}{2 \text{ mol MnO}_4^-} \qquad \frac{238.03 \text{ g U}}{1 \text{ mol U}} \qquad \text{percent U} = \frac{\text{g U}}{\text{g sample}} \times 100\%$$

Solution:

Separate: $MnO_4^- (aq) \rightarrow Mn^{2+} (aq)$ and $C_2O_4^{2-} (aq) \rightarrow CO_2 (g)$

Balance non H & O elements: $MnO_4^- (aq) \rightarrow Mn^{2+} (aq)$ and $C_2O_4^{2-} (aq) \rightarrow 2\,CO_2 (g)$

Balance O with H_2O: $MnO_4^- (aq) \rightarrow Mn^{2+} (aq) + 4\,H_2O (l)$ and $C_2O_4^{2-} (aq) \rightarrow 2\,CO_2 (g)$

Balance H with H^+: $MnO_4^- (aq) + 8\,H^+ (aq) \rightarrow Mn^{2+} (aq) + 4\,H_2O (l)$ and $C_2O_4^{2-} (aq) \rightarrow 2\,CO_2 (g)$

Add electrons: $MnO_4^- (aq) + 8\,H^+ (aq) + 5\,e^- \rightarrow Mn^{2+} (aq) + 4\,H_2O (l)$ and $C_2O_4^{2-} (aq) \rightarrow 2\,CO_2 (g) + 2\,e^-$

Equalize electrons:

   $2\,MnO_4^- (aq) + 16\,H^+ (aq) + 10\,e^- \rightarrow 2\,Mn^{2+} (aq) + 8\,H_2O (l)$ and $5\,C_2O_4^{2-} (aq) \rightarrow 10\,CO_2 (g) + 10\,e^-$

Add half-reactions:

   $2\,MnO_4^- (aq) + 16\,H^+ (aq) + \cancel{10\,e^-} + 5\,C_2O_4^{2-} (aq) \rightarrow 2\,Mn^{2+} (aq) + 8\,H_2O (l) + 10\,CO_2 (g) + \cancel{10\,e^-}$

Cancel electrons: $2\,MnO_4^- (aq) + 16\,H^+ (aq) + 5\,C_2O_4^{2-} (aq) \rightarrow 2\,Mn^{2+} (aq) + 8\,H_2O (l) + 10\,CO_2 (g)$

then $50.1\ \cancel{mL\ MnO_4^-} \times \dfrac{1\ L\ MnO_4^-}{1000\ \cancel{mL\ MnO_4^-}} = 0.0501\ L\ MnO_4^-$

$0.39\ \cancel{g\ Na_2C_2O_4} \times \dfrac{1\ \cancel{mol\ Na_2C_2O_4}}{134.00\ \cancel{g\ Na_2C_2O_4}} \times \dfrac{2\ mol\ MnO_4^-}{5\ \cancel{mol\ Na_2C_2O_4}} = 0.0010119403\ mol\ MnO_4^-$

$M = \dfrac{0.0010119403\ mol\ MnO_4^-}{0.0501\ L} = 0.020198409\ mol\ L^{-1}\ MnO_4^-$

Separate: $MnO_4^- (aq) \rightarrow Mn^{2+} (aq)$ and $UO^{2+} (aq) \rightarrow UO_2^{2+} (aq)$

Balance non H & O elements: $MnO_4^- (aq) \rightarrow Mn^{2+} (aq)$ and $UO^{2+} (aq) \rightarrow UO_2^{2+} (aq)$

Balance O with H_2O: $MnO_4^- (aq) \rightarrow Mn^{2+} (aq) + 4\,H_2O (l)$ and $UO^{2+} (aq) + H_2O (l) \rightarrow UO_2^{2+} (aq)$

Balance H with H^+:

   $MnO_4^- (aq) + 8\,H^+ (aq) \rightarrow Mn^{2+} (aq) + 4\,H_2O (l)$ and $UO^{2+} (aq) + H_2O (l) \rightarrow UO_2^{2+} (aq) + 2\,H^+ (aq)$

Add electrons: $MnO_4^- (aq) + 8\,H^+ (aq) + 5\,e^- \rightarrow Mn^{2+} (aq) + 4\,H_2O (l)$ and

                             $UO^{2+} (aq) + H_2O (l) \rightarrow UO_2^{2+} (aq) + 2\,H^+ (aq) + 2\,e^-$

Equalize electrons: $2\,MnO_4^- (aq) + 16\,H^+ (aq) + 10\,e^- \rightarrow 2\,Mn^{2+} (aq) + 8\,H_2O (l)$ and

                        $5\,UO^{2+} (aq) + 5\,H_2O (l) \rightarrow 5\,UO_2^{2+} (aq) + 10\,H^+ (aq) + 10\,e^-$

Add half-reactions: $2\,MnO_4^- (aq) + 6\ \cancel{16}\ H^+ (aq) + \cancel{10\,e^-} + 5\,UO^{2+} (aq) + \cancel{5\,H_2O (l)} \rightarrow$

                      $2\,Mn^{2+} (aq) + 3\ \cancel{8}\ H_2O (l) + 5\,UO_2^{2+} (aq) + \cancel{10\,H^+ (aq)} + \cancel{10\,e^-}$

Cancel electrons & species:

           $2\,MnO_4^- (aq) + 6\,H^+ (aq) + 5\,UO^{2+} (aq) \rightarrow 2\,Mn^{2+} (aq) + 3\,H_2O (l) + 5\,UO_2^{2+} (aq)$

$32.5\ \cancel{mL\ MnO_4^-} \times \dfrac{0.020198409\ \cancel{mol\ MnO_4^-}}{1000\ \cancel{mL\ MnO_4^-}} \times \dfrac{5\ \cancel{mol\ U}}{2\ \cancel{mol\ MnO_4^-}} \times \dfrac{238.03\ g\ U}{1\ \cancel{mol\ U}} = 0.39063597\ g\ U$ then

$percent\ U = \dfrac{g\ U}{g\ sample} \times 100\% = \dfrac{0.39063597\ g\ U}{4.62\ g\ sample} \times 100\% = 8.46\%.$

Check: first reaction

Reactants	Products
2 Mn atoms	2 Mn atoms
28 O atoms	28 O atoms
16 H atoms	16 H atoms
10 C atoms	10 C atoms
+4 charge	+4 charge

         second reaction

Reactants	Products
2 Mn atoms	2 Mn atoms
13 O atoms	13 O atoms
6 H atoms	6 H atoms
5 U atoms	5 U atoms
+14 charge	+14 charge

The reactions are balanced. The units (%) are correct. The percentage is between 0 and 100%.

18.137   The overall cell reaction for the first cell is $2 Cu^+(aq) \rightarrow Cu^{2+}(aq) + Cu (s)$. The overall cell reaction for the second cell is the same but the half-reactions that compose it are different from the first cell. The biggest difference in $E°$ is because $n = 1$ for the first cell and $n = 2$ for the second cell. Since $\Delta_r G° = -nFE°_{cell}$ for the first cell

$$\Delta_r G° = -1 \times \frac{96\ 485\ C}{mol} \times 0.364\ V = -1 \times 96\ 485\ \frac{C}{mol} \times 0.364\ \frac{J}{C} = -35.1\ kJ\ mol^{-1}\ and\ for\ the$$

second cell

$$\Delta_r G° = -2 \times \frac{96\ 485\ C}{mol} \times 0.182\ V = -2 \times 96\ 485\ \frac{C}{mol} \times 0.182\ \frac{J}{C} = -35.1\ kJ\ mol^{-1}.\ Thus\ \Delta_r G°\ is$$

the same.

Conceptual Problems

18.139   (a)   Look for anion reductions that are in between the electrode potentials of Cl_2 and Br_2. The only one that meets this criterion is the dichromate ion.

19 Radioactivity and Nuclear Chemistry

Review Questions

19.1 Radioactivity is the emission of subatomic particles or high-energy electromagnetic radiation by the nuclei of certain atoms. Radioactivity was discovered in 1896 by a French scientist named Antoine-Henri Becquerel (1852–1908). Becquerel placed crystals—composed of potassium uranyl sulfate, a compound known to phosphoresce—on top of a photographic plate wrapped in black cloth. The photographic plate showed a dark exposure spot where the crystals had been. Becquerel, Marie Curie, and Pierre Curie received the Nobel Prize for the discovery of radioactivity.

19.3 A is the mass number (number of protons + neutrons), Z is the atomic number (number of protons), and X is the chemical symbol of the element.

19.5 An alpha particle has the same symbol as a helium nucleus, ^4_2He. When an element emits an alpha particle, the number of protons in its nucleus decreases by two and the mass number decreases by four, transforming it into a different element.

19.7 Gamma rays are high-energy (short-wavelength) photons and have a symbol of $^0_0\gamma$. A gamma ray has no charge and no mass. When a gamma-ray photon is emitted from a radioactive atom, it does not change the mass number or the atomic number of the element. Gamma rays, however, are usually emitted in conjunction with other types of radiation.

19.9 Electron capture occurs when a nucleus assimilates an electron from an inner orbital of its electron cloud. Like positron emission, the net effect of electron capture is the conversion of a proton into a neutron: $^1_1\text{p} + ^{\ 0}_{-1}\text{e} \rightarrow ^1_0\text{n}$. When an atom undergoes electron capture, its atomic number decreases by one because it has one less proton, and its mass number is unchanged.

19.11 For the lighter elements, the N/Z ratio of stable isotopes is about one (equal numbers of neutrons and protons). However, beyond about $Z = 20$, the N/Z ratio of stable nuclei begins to get larger (reaching about 1.5). Above $Z = 83$, stable nuclei do not exist.

19.13 (a) Film-badge dosimeters consist of photographic film held in a small case that is pinned to clothing and are standard for most people working with or near radioactive substances. These badges are collected and processed (or developed) regularly as a way to monitor a person's exposure. The more exposed the film has become in a given period of time, the more radioactivity the person has been exposed to.

(b) A Geiger-Müller counter (commonly referred to as a Geiger counter) is an instrument that can detect radioactivity instantaneously. Particles emitted by radioactive nuclei pass through an argon-filled chamber. The energetic particles create a trail of ionized argon atoms. An applied high voltage between a wire within the chamber and the chamber itself causes these newly formed ions to produce an electrical signal that can be detected on a meter or turned into an audible click. Each click corresponds to a radioactive particle passing through the argon gas chamber. This clicking is the stereotypical sound most people associate with a radiation detector.

(c)   A scintillation counter is another instrument that can detect radioactivity instantaneously. In this device, the radioactive emissions pass through a material (such as NaI or CsI) that emits ultraviolet or visible light in response to excitation by energetic particles. The radioactivity excites the atoms to a higher energy state. The atoms release this energy as light, which is then detected and turned into an electrical signal that can be read on a meter.

19.15   Radiocarbon dating, a technique devised in 1949 by Willard Libby at the University of Chicago, is used by archeologists, geologists, anthropologists, and other scientists to estimate the ages of fossils and artifacts. Carbon-14 is constantly formed in the upper atmosphere by the neutron bombardment of nitrogen and then decays back to nitrogen by beta emission with a half-life of 5730 years. The continuous formation of carbon-14 in the atmosphere and its continuous decay back to nitrogen-14 produces a nearly constant equilibrium amount of atmospheric carbon-14, which is oxidized to carbon dioxide and incorporated into plants by photosynthesis. The C-14 then makes its way up the food chain and ultimately into all living organisms. As a result, all living plants, animals, and humans contain the same ratio of carbon-14 to carbon-12 (^{14}C : ^{12}C) as is found in the atmosphere. When a living organism dies, however, it stops incorporating new carbon-14 into its tissues. The ^{14}C : ^{12}C ratio then decreases with a half-life of 5730 years. The accuracy of carbon-14 dating can be checked against objects whose ages are known from historical sources.

In order to make C-14 dating more accurate, scientists have studied the carbon-14 content of western bristlecone pine trees, which can live up to 5000 years. The tree trunk contains growth rings corresponding to each year of the tree's life, and the wood laid down in each ring incorporates carbon derived from the carbon dioxide in the atmosphere at that time. The rings thus provide a record of the historical atmospheric carbon-14 content and allow for corrections to carbon-14 concentrations due to atmospheric changes.

The maximum age that can be estimated from carbon-14 dating is about 50 000 years—beyond that, the amount of carbon-14 becomes too low to measure accurately.

19.17   Nuclear fission is the splitting of an atom into smaller products. The process emits enormous amounts of energy. Three researchers in Germany—Lise Meitner (1878–1968), Fritz Strassmann (1902–1980), and Otto Hahn (1879–1968), repeating uranium bombardment experiments by Fermi, performed careful chemical analysis of the products. The nucleus of the neutron-bombarded uranium atom is split into barium, krypton, and other smaller products. A nuclear equation for a fission reaction, showing how uranium breaks apart into the daughter nuclides, is $^{235}_{92}$U + $^{1}_{0}$n → $^{140}_{56}$Ba + $^{93}_{36}$Kr + 3 $^{1}_{0}$n + energy. The process produces three neutrons, which have the potential to initiate fission in three other U-235 atoms. Scientists quickly realized that a sample rich in U-235 could undergo a chain reaction in which neutrons produced by the fission of one uranium nucleus would induce fission in other uranium nuclei. The result would be a self-amplifying reaction capable of producing an enormous amount of energy—an atomic bomb. However, to make a bomb, a critical mass of U-235—enough U-235 to produce a self-sustaining reaction—would be necessary. Since an enormous amount of energy is produced, it can be used to produce steam to drive turbines (as shown in Figure 19.11).

19.19   The advantages of using fission to generate electricity are 1) a typical nuclear power plant generates enough electricity for a city of about 1 million people and uses about 50 kg of fuel per day as opposed to a coal-burning power plant using about 2 000 000 kg of fuel to generate the same amount of electricity); and 2) a nuclear power plant generates no air pollution and no greenhouse gases. (Coal-burning power plants also emit carbon dioxide, a greenhouse gas.) The disadvantages are 1) the danger of nuclear accidents, such as overheating and the release of radiation, and 2) waste disposal, since the products of the reaction are radioactive and have long half-lives.

19.21   This difference in mass between the products and the reactants is known as the mass defect. The energy corresponding to the mass defect, obtained by substituting the mass defect into the equation $E = mc^2$, is known as the nuclear binding energy, the amount of energy that would be required to break apart the nucleus into its component nucleons. The nuclear binding energy per nucleon peaks at a mass number of 60. The significance of this is that the nuclides with mass numbers of about 60 are among the most stable.

19.23   An extremely high temperature is required for fusion to occur. To date, no material can withstand these temperatures.

19.25   In a single-stage linear accelerator, a charged particle such as a proton is accelerated in an evacuated tube. The accelerating force is provided by a potential difference between the ends of the tube. In multistage linear accelerators, such as the Stanford Linear Accelerator (SLAC) at Stanford University (Figure 19.15), a series of tubes of increasing length are connected to a source of alternating voltage, as shown in Figure 19.15. The voltage alternates in such a way that, as a positively charged particle leaves a particular tube, that tube becomes positively charged, repelling the particle to the next tube. At the same time, the tube the particle is now approaching becomes negatively charged, pulling the particle toward it. This continues throughout the linear accelerator, allowing the particle to be accelerated to velocities up to 90% of the speed of light. Linear accelerators can be used to conduct nuclear transmutations, making nuclides that don't normally exist in nature.

19.27   The energy associated with radioactivity can ionize molecules. When radiation ionizes important molecules in living cells, problems can develop. The ingestion of radioactive materials, especially alpha and beta emitters, is particularly dangerous because the radioactivity is then inside the body and can do even more damage. The effects of radiation can be divided into three different types: acute radiation damage, increased cancer risk, and genetic effects.

19.29   The biological effectiveness factor, or RBE, (for relative biological effectiveness), was used to correct the dosage (in rads) for the type of radiation. Now the absorbed dose in Gray (Gy) is multiplied by a radiation weighting factor (W_R) to obtain the equivalent dose in sievert (Sv). The equivalent dose for alpha radiation, for example, is much higher than for gamma radiation.

Radioactive Decay and Nuclide Stability

19.31   **Conceptual Plan: Begin with the symbol for a parent nuclide on the left side of the equation and the symbol for a particle on the right side (except for electron capture).** $\rightarrow$ **Equalize the sum of the mass numbers and the sum of the atomic numbers on both sides of the equation by writing the appropriate mass number and atomic number for the unknown daughter nuclide.** $\rightarrow$ **Using the periodic table, deduce the identity of the unknown daughter nuclide from the atomic number and write its symbol.**
Solution:

(a)   U-234 (alpha decay) $^{234}_{92}\text{U} \rightarrow {}^{?}_{?}? + {}^{4}_{2}\text{He}$ then $^{234}_{92}\text{U} \rightarrow {}^{230}_{90}? + {}^{4}_{2}\text{He}$ then $^{234}_{92}\text{U} \rightarrow {}^{230}_{90}\text{Th} + {}^{4}_{2}\text{He}$

(b)   Th-230 (alpha decay) $^{230}_{90}\text{Th} \rightarrow {}^{?}_{?}? + {}^{4}_{2}\text{He}$ then $^{230}_{90}\text{Th} \rightarrow {}^{226}_{88}? + {}^{4}_{2}\text{He}$ then $^{230}_{90}\text{Th} \rightarrow {}^{226}_{88}\text{Ra} + {}^{4}_{2}\text{He}$

(c)   Pb-214 (beta decay) $^{214}_{82}\text{Pb} \rightarrow {}^{?}_{?}? + {}^{0}_{-1}\text{e}$ then $^{214}_{82}\text{Pb} \rightarrow {}^{214}_{83}? + {}^{0}_{-1}\text{e}$ then $^{214}_{82}\text{Pb} \rightarrow {}^{214}_{83}\text{Bi} + {}^{0}_{-1}\text{e}$

(d)   N-13 (positron emission) $^{13}_{7}\text{N} \rightarrow {}^{?}_{?}? + {}^{0}_{+1}\text{e}$ then $^{13}_{7}\text{N} \rightarrow {}^{13}_{6}? + {}^{0}_{+1}\text{e}$ then $^{13}_{7}\text{N} \rightarrow {}^{13}_{6}\text{C} + {}^{0}_{+1}\text{e}$

(e)   Cr-51 (electron capture) $^{51}_{24}\text{Cr} + {}^{0}_{-1}\text{e} \rightarrow {}^{?}_{?}?$ then $^{51}_{24}\text{Cr} + {}^{0}_{-1}\text{e} \rightarrow {}^{51}_{23}?$ then $^{51}_{24}\text{Cr} + {}^{0}_{-1}\text{e} \rightarrow {}^{51}_{23}\text{V}$
Check: (a) 234 = 230 + 4, 92 = 90 + 2, and thorium is atomic number 90. (b) 230 = 226 + 4, 90 = 88 + 2, and radium is atomic number 88. (c) 214 = 214 + 0, 82 = 83 − 1, and bismuth is atomic number 83. (d) 13 = 13 + 0, 7 = 6 + 1, and carbon is atomic number 6. (e) 51 + 0 = 51, 24 − 1 = 23, and vanadium is atomic number 23.

19.33   **Given:** Th-232 decay series: α, β, β, α **Find:** balanced decay reactions
Conceptual Plan: Begin with the symbol for a parent nuclide on the left side of the equation and the symbol for a particle on the right side (except for electron capture). $\rightarrow$ **Equalize the sum of the mass numbers and the sum of the atomic numbers on both sides of the equation by writing the appropriate mass number and atomic number for the unknown daughter nuclide.** $\rightarrow$ **Using the periodic table, deduce the identity of the unknown daughter nuclide from the atomic number and write its symbol.** $\rightarrow$ **Use the product of this reaction to write the next reaction.**
Solution:
Th-232 (alpha decay) $^{232}_{90}\text{Th} \rightarrow {}^{?}_{?}? + {}^{4}_{2}\text{He}$ then $^{232}_{90}\text{Th} \rightarrow {}^{228}_{88}? + {}^{4}_{2}\text{He}$ then $^{232}_{90}\text{Th} \rightarrow {}^{228}_{88}\text{Ra} + {}^{4}_{2}\text{He}$
Ra-228 (beta decay) $^{228}_{88}\text{Ra} \rightarrow {}^{?}_{?}? + {}^{0}_{-1}\text{e}$ then $^{228}_{88}\text{Ra} \rightarrow {}^{228}_{89}? + {}^{0}_{-1}\text{e}$ then $^{228}_{88}\text{Ra} \rightarrow {}^{228}_{89}\text{Ac} + {}^{0}_{-1}\text{e}$
Ac-228 (beta decay) $^{228}_{89}\text{Ac} \rightarrow {}^{?}_{?}? + {}^{0}_{-1}\text{e}$ then $^{228}_{89}\text{Ac} \rightarrow {}^{228}_{90}? + {}^{0}_{-1}\text{e}$ then $^{228}_{89}\text{Ac} \rightarrow {}^{228}_{90}\text{Th} + {}^{0}_{-1}\text{e}$
Th-228 (alpha decay) $^{228}_{90}\text{Th} \rightarrow {}^{?}_{?}? + {}^{4}_{2}\text{He}$ then $^{228}_{90}\text{Th} \rightarrow {}^{224}_{88}? + {}^{4}_{2}\text{He}$ then $^{228}_{90}\text{Th} \rightarrow {}^{224}_{88}\text{Ra} + {}^{4}_{2}\text{He}$

Thus the decay series is: $^{232}_{90}\text{Th} \rightarrow ^{228}_{88}\text{Ra} + ^{4}_{2}\text{He}$, $^{228}_{88}\text{Ra} \rightarrow ^{228}_{89}\text{Ac} + ^{0}_{-1}\text{e}$, $^{228}_{89}\text{Ac} \rightarrow ^{228}_{90}\text{Th} + ^{0}_{-1}\text{e}$, $^{228}_{90}\text{Th} \rightarrow ^{224}_{88}\text{Ra} + ^{4}_{2}\text{He}$.

Check: 232 = 228 + 4, 90 = 88 + 2, and radium is atomic number 88. 228 = 228 + 0, 88 = 89 − 1, and actinium is atomic number 89. 228 = 228 + 0, 89 = 90 − 1, and thorium is atomic number 90. 228 = 224 + 4, 90 = 88 + 2, and radium is atomic number 88.

19.35   **Conceptual Plan: Equalize the sum of the mass numbers and the sum of the atomic numbers on both sides of the equation by writing the appropriate mass number and atomic number for the unknown species. → Using the periodic table and the list of particles, deduce the identity of the unknown species from the atomic number and write its symbol.**
Solution:

(a) $^{?}_{?}? \rightarrow ^{217}_{85}\text{At} + ^{4}_{2}\text{He}$ becomes $^{221}_{87}? \rightarrow ^{217}_{85}\text{At} + ^{4}_{2}\text{He}$ then $^{221}_{87}\text{Fr} \rightarrow ^{217}_{85}\text{At} + ^{4}_{2}\text{He}$

(b) $^{241}_{94}\text{Pu} \rightarrow ^{241}_{95}\text{Am} + ^{?}_{?}?$ becomes $^{241}_{94}\text{Pu} \rightarrow ^{241}_{95}\text{Am} + ^{0}_{-1}?$ then $^{241}_{94}\text{Pu} \rightarrow ^{241}_{95}\text{Am} + ^{0}_{-1}\text{e}$

(c) $^{19}_{11}\text{Na} \rightarrow ^{19}_{10}\text{Ne} + ^{?}_{?}?$ becomes $^{19}_{11}\text{Na} \rightarrow ^{19}_{10}\text{Ne} + ^{0}_{1}?$ then $^{19}_{11}\text{Na} \rightarrow ^{19}_{10}\text{Ne} + ^{0}_{+1}\text{e}$

(d) $^{75}_{34}\text{Se} + ^{?}_{?}? \rightarrow ^{75}_{33}\text{As}$ becomes $^{75}_{34}\text{Se} + ^{0}_{-1}? \rightarrow ^{75}_{33}\text{As}$ then $^{75}_{34}\text{Se} + ^{0}_{-1}\text{e} \rightarrow ^{75}_{33}\text{As}$

Check: (a) 221 = 217 + 4, 87 = 85 + 2, and francium is atomic number 87. (b) 241 = 241 + 0, 94 = 95 − 1, and the particle is a beta particle. (c) 19 = 19 + 0, 11 = 10 + 1, and the particle is a positron. (d) 75 = 75 + 0, 34 − 1 = 33, and the particle is an electron.

19.37   (a)   Mg-26: $N = 14$, $Z = 12$, stable, N/Z ratio is close to 1, acceptable for low Z atoms

(b)   Ne-25: $N = 13$, $Z = 10$, not stable, N/Z ratio much too high for low Z atom

(c)   Co-51: $N = 24$, $Z = 27$, not stable, N/Z ratio is less than 1, much too low

(d)   Te-124: $N = 72$, $Z = 52$, stable, N/Z ratio is acceptable for this Z

19.39   Sc, V, and Mn, each have odd numbers of protons. Atoms with an odd number of protons typically have fewer stable isotopes than those with an even number of protons.

19.41   (a)   Mo-109, $N = 67$, $Z = 42$, $N/Z = 1.6$, beta decay, since N/Z is too high

(b)   Ru-90, $N = 46$, $Z = 44$, $N/Z = 1.0$, positron emission, since N/Z is too low

(c)   P-27, $N = 12$, $Z = 15$, $N/Z = 0.8$, positron emission, since N/Z is too low

(d)   Rn-196, $N = 110$, $Z = 86$, $N/Z = 1.3$, positron emission, since N/Z is too low

19.43   (a)   Cs-125, $N/Z = 70/55 = 1.3$; Cs-113, $N/Z = 58/55 = 1.1$; Cs-125 will have the longer half-life, since it is closer to the proper N/Z

(b)   Fe-70, $N/Z = 44/26 = 1.7$; Fe-62, $N/Z = 36/26 = 1.4$; Fe-62 will have the longer half-life, since it is closer to the proper N/Z

The Kinetics of Radioactive Decay and Radiometric Dating

19.45   **Given:** U-235, $t_{1/2}$ for radioactive decay = 703 million years   **Find:** t to 10.0% of initial amount
Conceptual Plan: Radioactive decay implies first-order kinetics, $t_{1/2} \rightarrow k$ then

$$t_{1/2} = \frac{0.693}{k}$$

$m_{\text{U-235 0}}$, $m_{\text{U-235 t}}$, $k \rightarrow t$

$$\ln N_t = -kt + \ln N_0$$

Solution: $t_{1/2} = \dfrac{0.693}{k}$ rearrange to solve for k. $k = \dfrac{0.693}{t_{1/2}} = \dfrac{0.693}{703 \times 10^6 \text{ y}} = 9.857752 \times 10^{-10} \text{ y}^{-1}$. Since

$\ln m_{U\text{-}235\,t} = -kt + \ln m_{U\text{-}235\,0}$ rearrange to solve for t

$$t = -\frac{1}{k}\ln\frac{m_{U\text{-}235\,t}}{m_{U\text{-}235\,0}} = -\frac{1}{9.857752 \times 10^{-10}\,\text{y}^{-1}}\ln\frac{10.0\%}{100.0\%} = 2.34 \times 10^9\,\text{y}.$$

Check: The units (y) are correct. The time is just over three half-lives, when 1/8 of the original amount will be left.

19.47   **Given:** $t_{1/2}$ for isotope decay = 3.8 days; 1.55 g isotope initially **Find:** mass of isotope after 5.5 days
Conceptual Plan: Radioactive decay implies first-order kinetics, $t_{1/2} \rightarrow k$ then

$$t_{1/2} = \frac{0.693}{k}$$

$m_{\text{isotope }0},\, t,\, k \rightarrow m_{\text{isotope }t}$
$\ln N_t = -kt + \ln N_0$

Solution: $t_{1/2} = \dfrac{0.693}{k}$ rearrange to solve for k. $k = \dfrac{0.693}{t_{1/2}} = \dfrac{0.693}{3.8\,\text{days}} = 0.18237\,\text{day}^{-1}$. Since

$\ln N_t = -kt + \ln N_0 = -(0.18237\,\text{day}^{-1})(5.5\,\text{days}) + \ln(1.55\,\text{g}) = -0.56478 \rightarrow N_t = e^{-0.56478} = 0.57\,\text{g}.$

Check: The units (g) are correct. The amount is consistent with a time between one and two half-lives.

19.49   **Given:** F-18 initial decay rate = 1.5×10^5 Bq, $t_{1/2}$ for F-18 = 1.83 h **Find:** t to decay rate of 2.5×10^3 Bq
Conceptual Plan: Radioactive decay implies first-order kinetics, $t_{1/2} \rightarrow k$ then $\text{Rate}_0,\,\text{Rate}_t,\,k \rightarrow t$

$$t_{1/2} = \frac{0.693}{k} \qquad \ln\frac{\text{Rate}_t}{\text{Rate}_0} = -kt$$

Solution: $t_{1/2} = \dfrac{0.693}{k}$ rearrange to solve for k. $k = \dfrac{0.693}{t_{1/2}} = \dfrac{0.693}{1.83\,\text{h}} = 0.378689\,\text{h}^{-1}$. Since

$\ln\dfrac{\text{Rate}_t}{\text{Rate}_0} = -kt$ rearrange to solve for t

$$t = -\frac{1}{k}\ln\frac{\text{Rate}_t}{\text{Rate}_0} = -\frac{1}{0.378689\,\text{h}^{-1}}\ln\frac{2.5 \times 10^3\,\text{Bq}}{1.5 \times 10^5\,\text{Bq}} = 10.8\,\text{h}.$$

Check: The units (h) are correct. The time is between five and six half-lives and the rate is just over $1/2^6$ of the initial rate.

19.51   **Given:** boat analysis, C-14/C-12 = 72.5% of living organism **Find:** t
Other: $t_{1/2}$ for decay of C-14 = 5730 years
Conceptual Plan: Radioactive decay implies first-order kinetics, $t_{1/2} \rightarrow k$ then 72.5 % of $m_{\text{C-14}\,0},\, k \rightarrow t$

$$t_{1/2} = \frac{0.693}{k} \qquad \ln N_t = -kt + \ln N_0$$

Solution: $t_{1/2} = \dfrac{0.693}{k}$ rearrange to solve for k. $k = \dfrac{0.693}{t_{1/2}} = \dfrac{0.693}{5730\,\text{y}} = 1.20942 \times 10^{-4}\,\text{y}^{-1}$ then

$m_{\text{C-14}\,t} = 0.725\,m_{\text{C-14}\,0}$. Since $\ln m_{\text{C-14}\,t} = -kt + \ln m_{\text{C-14}\,0}$ rearrange to solve for t.

$$t = -\frac{1}{k}\ln\frac{m_{\text{C-14}\,t}}{m_{\text{C-14}\,0}} = -\frac{1}{1.20942 \times 10^{-4}\,\text{y}^{-1}}\ln\frac{0.725\,m_{\text{C-14}\,0}}{m_{\text{C-14}\,0}} = 2.66 \times 10^3\,\text{y}.$$

Check: The units (y) are correct. The time to 72.5% decay is consistent with a time less than one half-life.

19.53   **Given:** skull analysis, C-14 decay rate = $2.55 \times 10^{-1}\,\text{s}^{-1}\,\text{g}^{-1}$ in living organisms and $1.4 \times 10^{-2}\,\text{s}^{-1}\,\text{g}^{-1}$ in skull
Find: t **Other:** $t_{1/2}$ for decay of C-14 = 5730 years
Conceptual Plan: Radioactive decay implies first-order kinetics, $t_{1/2} \rightarrow k$ then $\text{Rate}_0,\,\text{Rate}_t,\,k \rightarrow t$

$$t_{1/2} = \frac{0.693}{k} \qquad \ln\frac{\text{Rate}_t}{\text{Rate}_0} = -kt$$

Solution: $t_{1/2} = \dfrac{0.693}{k}$ rearrange to solve for k. $k = \dfrac{0.693}{t_{1/2}} = \dfrac{0.693}{5730\,\text{y}} = 1.20942 \times 10^{-4}\,\text{y}^{-1}$

Since $\ln\dfrac{\text{Rate}_t}{\text{Rate}_0} = -kt$, rearrange to solve for t.

$$t = -\frac{1}{k}\ln\frac{\text{Rate}_t}{\text{Rate}_0} = -\frac{1}{1.20942 \times 10^{-4}\,\text{y}^{-1}}\ln\frac{1.4 \times 10^{-2}\,\text{s}^{-1}\,\text{g}^{-1}}{2.55 \times 10^{-1}\,\text{s}^{-1}\,\text{g}^{-1}} = 2.40 \times 10^4\,\text{y}.$$

Check: The units (y) are correct. The rate is 6% of initial value and the time is consistent with a time just more than four half-lives.

19.55 **Given:** rock analysis, $m_{U\text{-}238} = 1.00$ g; $m_{Pb\text{-}206} = 0.438$ g, no Pb-206 initially **Find:** age of rock
Other: $t_{1/2}$ for decay of U-238 to Pb-206 = 4.5 x 10^9 years
Conceptual Plan: Radioactive decay implies first-order kinetics, $t_{1/2}$ $\rightarrow$ k **then**

$$t_{1/2} = \frac{0.693}{k}$$

g Pb-206 $\rightarrow$ mol Pb-206 $\rightarrow$ mol U-238 $\rightarrow$ g U-238 then $m_{U\text{-}238\ 0},\ m_{U\text{-}238\ t},\ k \rightarrow t$

$$\frac{1\ \text{mol Pb-206}}{206\ \text{g Pb-206}} \qquad \frac{1\ \text{mol U-238}}{1\ \text{mol Pb-206}} \qquad \frac{238\ \text{g U-238}}{1\ \text{mol U-238}}$$

$$\ln N_t = -k\,t + \ln N_0$$

Solution: $t_{1/2} = \dfrac{0.693}{k}$ rearrange to solve for k. $k = \dfrac{0.693}{t_{1/2}} = \dfrac{0.693}{4.5 \times 10^9\ \text{y}} = 1.54 \times 10^{-10}\ \text{y}^{-1}$ then

$$0.438\ \cancel{\text{g Pb-206}} \times \frac{1\ \cancel{\text{mol Pb-206}}}{206\ \cancel{\text{g Pb-206}}} \times \frac{1\ \cancel{\text{mol U-238}}}{1\ \cancel{\text{mol Pb-206}}} \times \frac{238\ \text{g U-238}}{1\ \cancel{\text{mol U-238}}} = 0.506039\ \text{g U-238. Since}$$

$\ln \dfrac{m_{U\text{-}238\ t}}{m_{U\text{-}238\ 0}} = -k\,t$, rearrange to solve for t.

$$t = -\frac{1}{k} \ln \frac{m_{U\text{-}238\ t}}{m_{U\text{-}238\ 0}} = -\frac{1}{1.54 \times 10^{-10}\ \text{y}^{-1}} \ln \frac{1.00\ \cancel{\text{g U-238}}}{(1.00 + 0.506039)\cancel{\text{g U-238}}} = 2.7 \times 10^9\ \text{y.}$$

Check: The units (y) are correct. The amount of Pb-206 is less than half of the initial U-238 amount and time is less than one half-life.

Fission, Fusion, and Transmutation

19.57 **Given:** U-235 fission induced by neutrons to Xe-144 and Sr-90 **Find:** number of neutrons produced
Conceptual Plan: Write the species given on the appropriate side of the equation. $\rightarrow$ **Equalize the sum of the mass numbers and the sum of the atomic numbers on both sides of the equation by writing the stoichiometric coefficient in front of the desired species.**
Solution: $^{235}_{92}\text{U} + ^{1}_{0}\text{n} \rightarrow ^{144}_{54}\text{Xe} + ^{90}_{38}\text{Sr} + ?\,^{1}_{0}\text{n}$ becomes $^{235}_{92}\text{U} + ^{1}_{0}\text{n} \rightarrow ^{144}_{54}\text{Xe} + ^{90}_{38}\text{Sr} + 2\,^{1}_{0}\text{n}$ so two neutrons are produced.
Check: 235 + 1 = 144 + 90 + 2, 92 + 0 = 54 + 38 + 0, and no other particle is necessary to balance the equation.

19.59 **Given:** fusion of two H-2 atoms to form He-3 and one neutron **Find:** balanced equation
Conceptual Plan: Write the species given on the appropriate side of the equation. $\rightarrow$ **Equalize the sum of the mass numbers and the sum of the atomic numbers on both sides of the equation by writing the stoichiometric coefficient in front of the desired species.**
Solution: $2\,^{2}_{1}\text{H} \rightarrow ^{3}_{2}\text{He} + ^{1}_{0}\text{n.}$
Check: 2(2) = 3 + 1, 2(1) = 2 + 0, and no other particle is necessary to balance the equation.

19.61 **Given:** U-238 bombarded by neutrons to form U-239, which undergoes two beta decays to form Pu-239
Find: balanced equations
Conceptual Plan: Write the species given on the appropriate side of the equation. $\rightarrow$ **Equalize the sum of the mass numbers and the sum of the atomic numbers on both sides of the equation by writing the stoichiometric coefficient in front of the desired species.** $\rightarrow$ **Use the product of this reaction to write the next reaction until the process is complete.**
Solution: $^{238}_{92}\text{U} + ?\,^{1}_{0}\text{n} \rightarrow ^{239}_{92}\text{U}$ becomes $^{238}_{92}\text{U} + ^{1}_{0}\text{n} \rightarrow ^{239}_{92}\text{U}$ then
beta decay $^{239}_{92}\text{U} \rightarrow ^{239}_{?}? + ^{0}_{-1}\text{e}$ becomes $^{239}_{92}\text{U} \rightarrow ^{239}_{93}? + ^{0}_{-1}\text{e}$ then $^{239}_{92}\text{U} \rightarrow ^{239}_{93}\text{Np} + ^{0}_{-1}\text{e}$ then
beta decay $^{239}_{93}\text{Np} \rightarrow ^{239}_{?}? + ^{0}_{-1}\text{e}$ becomes $^{239}_{93}\text{Np} \rightarrow ^{239}_{94}? + ^{0}_{-1}\text{e}$ then $^{239}_{93}\text{Np} \rightarrow ^{239}_{94}\text{Pu} + ^{0}_{-1}\text{e.}$
The entire process is $^{238}_{92}\text{U} + ^{1}_{0}\text{n} \rightarrow ^{239}_{92}\text{U}, ^{239}_{92}\text{U} \rightarrow ^{239}_{93}\text{Np} + ^{0}_{-1}\text{e}, ^{239}_{93}\text{Np} \rightarrow ^{239}_{94}\text{Pu} + ^{0}_{-1}\text{e.}$
Check: 238 + 1 = 239, 92 + 0 = 92, and no other particle is necessary to balance the equation. 239 = 239 + 0, 92 = 93 − 1, and neptunium is atomic number 93. 239 = 239 + 0, 93 = 94 − 1, and plutonium is atomic number 94.

19.63 **Given:** Rf-257 synthesized by bombarding Cf-249 with C-12 **Find:** balanced equation
Conceptual Plan: Write the species given on the appropriate side of the equation. $\rightarrow$ **Equalize the sum of the mass numbers and the sum of the atomic numbers on both sides of the equation by writing the stoichiometric coefficient in front of the desired species.** $\rightarrow$ **Use the product of this reaction to write the next reaction until the process is complete.**
Solution: $^{249}_{98}\text{Cf} + ^{12}_{6}\text{C} \rightarrow ^{257}_{?}\text{Rf} + ?\,^{?}_{?}?$ becomes $^{249}_{98}\text{Cf} + ^{12}_{6}\text{C} \rightarrow ^{257}_{104}\text{Rf} + 4\,^{1}_{0}\text{n.}$

Check: 249 + 12 = 257 + 4, 98 + 6 = 104 + 0, and rutherfordium is atomic number 104, four neutrons are needed to balance the equation.

Energetics of Nuclear Reactions, Mass Defect, and Nuclear Binding Energy

19.65   **Given:** 1.0 g of matter converted to energy **Find:** energy

Conceptual Plan: g $\rightarrow$ kg $\rightarrow$ E

$$\frac{1 \text{ kg}}{1000 \text{ g}} \qquad E = m c^2$$

Solution: $1.0 \text{ g} \times \dfrac{1 \text{ kg}}{1000 \text{ g}} = 0.0010 \text{ kg}$ then $E = m c^2 = (0.0010 \text{ kg})\left(2.9979 \times 10^8 \dfrac{\text{m}}{\text{s}}\right)^2 = 9.0 \times 10^{13} \text{ J}$

Check: The units (J) are correct. The magnitude of the answer makes physical sense because we are converting a large number of atoms to energy.

19.67   **Given:** (a) O-16 = 15.994915 amu; (b) Ni-58 = 57.935346 amu; and (c) Xe-129 = 128.904780 amu

Find: mass defect and nuclear binding energy per nucleon

Conceptual Plan: $_Z^A$X, isotope mass $\rightarrow$ mass defect $\rightarrow$ nuclear binding energy per nucleon

$$\text{mass defect} = Z(\text{mass } _1^1\text{H}) + (A - Z)(\text{mass } _0^1\text{n}) - \text{mass of isotope} \qquad \frac{931.5 \text{ MeV}}{(1 \text{ amu})(A \text{ nucleons})}$$

Solution: mass defect $= Z(\text{mass } _1^1\text{H}) + (A - Z)(\text{mass } _0^1\text{n}) - \text{mass of isotope.}$

(a)   O-16 mass defect $= 8(1.00783 \text{ amu}) + (16 - 8)(1.00866 \text{ amu}) - 15.994915 \text{ amu}$

$= 0.1370055 \text{ amu} = 0.13701 \text{ amu}$ and $0.1370055 \text{ amu} \times \dfrac{931.5 \text{ MeV}}{(1 \text{ amu})(16 \text{ nucleons})} = 7.976 \dfrac{\text{MeV}}{\text{nucleon}}.$

(b)   Ni-58 mass defect $= 28(1.00783 \text{ amu}) + (58 - 28)(1.00866 \text{ amu}) - 57.935346 \text{ amu}$

$= 0.543694 \text{ amu} = 0.54369 \text{ amu}$ and $0.543694 \text{ amu} \times \dfrac{931.5 \text{ MeV}}{(1 \text{ amu})(58 \text{ nucleons})} = 8.732 \dfrac{\text{MeV}}{\text{nucleon}}.$

(c)   Xe-129 mass defect $= 54(1.00783 \text{ amu}) + (129 - 54)(1.00866 \text{ amu}) - 128.904780 \text{ amu}$

$= 1.16754 \text{ amu}$ and $1.16754 \text{ amu} \times \dfrac{931.5 \text{ MeV}}{(1 \text{ amu}) (129 \text{ nucleons})} = 8.431 \dfrac{\text{MeV}}{\text{nucleon}}.$

Check: The units (amu and MeV/nucleon) are correct. The mass defect increases with an increasing number of nucleons, but the MeV/nucleon does not change by as much (on a relative basis).

19.69   **Given:** $_{92}^{235}\text{U} + _0^1\text{n} \rightarrow _{54}^{144}\text{Xe} + _{38}^{90}\text{Sr} + 2 _0^1\text{n}$, U-235 = 235.043922 amu, Xe-144 = 143.9385 amu, and Sr-90 = 89.907738 amu **Find:** energy per g of U-235

Conceptual Plan: mass of products & reactants $\rightarrow$ mass defect $\rightarrow$ mass defect / g of U-235 then

$$\text{mass defect} = \sum\text{mass of reactants} - \sum\text{mass of products} \qquad \frac{\text{mass defect}}{235.043922 \text{ g U-235}}$$

g $\rightarrow$ kg $\rightarrow$ E

$$\frac{1 \text{ kg}}{1000 \text{ g}} \qquad E = m c^2$$

Solution: mass defect $= \sum$mass of reactants $- \sum$mass of products; notice that we can cancel a neutron from each side to get: $_{92}^{235}\text{U} \rightarrow _{54}^{144}\text{Xe} + _{38}^{90}\text{Sr} + _0^1\text{n}$ and

mass defect $= 235.043922 \text{ g} - (143.9385 \text{ g} + 89.907738 \text{ g} + 1.00866 \text{ g}) = 0.189024 \text{ g}$

then $\dfrac{0.189024 \text{ g}}{235.043922 \text{ g U-235}} \times \dfrac{1 \text{ kg}}{1000 \text{ g}} = 8.04207 \times 10^{-7} \dfrac{\text{kg}}{\text{g U-235}}$ then

$E = m c^2 = \left(8.04207 \times 10^{-7} \dfrac{\text{kg}}{\text{g U-235}}\right)\left(2.9979 \times 10^8 \dfrac{\text{m}}{\text{s}}\right)^2 = 7.228 \times 10^{10} \dfrac{\text{J}}{\text{g U-235}}.$

Check: The units (J) are correct. A large amount of energy is expected per gram of fuel in a nuclear reactor.

19.71   **Given:** $2 _1^2\text{H} \rightarrow _2^3\text{He} + _0^1\text{n}$, H-2 = 2.014102 amu, and He-3 = 3.016029 amu **Find:** energy per g reactant

Conceptual Plan: mass of products & reactants $\rightarrow$ mass defect $\rightarrow$ mass defect / g of H-2 then

$$\text{mass defect} = \sum\text{mass of reactants} - \sum\text{mass of products} \qquad \frac{\text{mass defect}}{2(2.014102 \text{ g H-2})}$$

g $\rightarrow$ kg $\rightarrow$ E

$$\frac{1 \text{ kg}}{1000 \text{ g}} \qquad E = m c^2$$

Solution: mass defect $= \sum$ mass of reactants $- \sum$ mass of products and

mass defect $= 2(2.014102 \text{ g}) - (3.016029 \text{ g} + 1.00866 \text{ g}) = 0.003515 \text{ g}$

then $\dfrac{0.003515 \text{ g}}{2(2.014102 \text{ g H-2})} \times \dfrac{1 \text{ kg}}{1000 \text{ g}} = 8.72597 \times 10^{-7} \dfrac{\text{kg}}{\text{g H-2}}$ then

$E = m c^2 = \left(8.72597 \times 10^{-7} \dfrac{\text{kg}}{\text{g H-2}}\right)\left(2.9979 \times 10^8 \dfrac{\text{m}}{\text{s}}\right)^2 = 7.84 \times 10^{10} \dfrac{\text{J}}{\text{g H-2}}.$

Check: The units (J) are correct. A large amount of energy is expected per gram of fuel in a fusion reaction.

Effects and Applications of Radioactivity

19.73   **Given:** 75 kg human exposed to 0.328 Gy and falling from chair   **Find:** energy absorbed in each case
Conceptual Plan: Gy, kg $\rightarrow$ J and assume $d = 0.50$ m chair height then mass, $d \rightarrow$ J

$$1 \text{ Gy} = \dfrac{1 \text{ J}}{1 \text{ kg body tissue}} \qquad\qquad E = F \cdot d = m g d$$

Solution: $0.328 \text{ Gy} = 0.328 \dfrac{1 \text{ J}}{1 \text{ kg body tissue}} \times 75 \text{ kg} = 25 \text{ J}$ and

$E = F \cdot d = m g d = 75 \text{ kg} \times 9.8 \dfrac{\text{m}}{\text{s}^2} \times 0.50 \text{ m} = 370 \text{ kg} \dfrac{\text{m}^2}{\text{s}^2} = 370 \text{ J}.$

Check: The units (J and J) are correct. Allowable radiation exposures are low, since the radiation is very ionizing and, thus, damaging to tissue. Falling may have more energy, but it is not ionizing.

19.75   **Given:** $t_{1/2}$ for F-18 $= 1.83$ h, 65% of F-18 makes it to the hospital travelling at 60.0 km h^{-1}
Find: distance between hospital and cyclotron
Conceptual Plan: $t_{1/2} \rightarrow k$ then $m_{\text{F-18 }0}, m_{\text{F-18 }t}, k \rightarrow t$ then h $\rightarrow$ km

$$t_{1/2} = \dfrac{0.693}{k} \qquad \ln \dfrac{m_{\text{F-18 }t}}{m_{\text{F-18 }0}} = -kt \qquad \dfrac{60.0 \text{ km}}{1 \text{ h}}$$

Solution: $t_{1/2} = \dfrac{0.693}{k}$ rearrange to solve for k. $k = \dfrac{0.693}{t_{1/2}} = \dfrac{0.693}{1.83 \text{ h}} = 0.378689 \text{ h}^{-1}.$ Since

$\ln \dfrac{m_{\text{F-18 }t}}{m_{\text{F-18 }0}} = -kt$ rearrange to solve for t

$t = -\dfrac{1}{k} \ln \dfrac{m_{\text{F-18 }t}}{m_{\text{F-18 }0}} = -\dfrac{1}{0.378689 \text{ h}^{-1}} \ln \dfrac{0.65 \, \overline{m_{\text{F-18 }0}}}{\overline{m_{\text{F-18 }0}}} = 1.1376 \text{ h}.$ Then

$1.1376 \text{ h} \times \dfrac{60.0 \text{ km}}{1 \text{ h}} = 68 \text{ km}.$

Check: The units (km) are correct. The time is less than one half-life, so the distance is less than 1.83 times the speed of travel.

Cumulative Problems

19.77   **Given:** incomplete reactions   **Find:** balanced reaction and energy (in J mol^{-1} reactant)
Conceptual Plan: Equalize the sum of the mass numbers and the sum of the atomic numbers on both sides of the equation by writing the appropriate mass number and atomic number for the unknown species. $\rightarrow$ Using the periodic table and the list of particles, deduce the identity of the unknown species from the atomic number and write its symbol. then
mass of products & reactants $\rightarrow$ mass defect in g $\rightarrow$ mass defect in kg $\rightarrow$ E

$$\text{mass defect} = \sum \text{mass of reactants} - \sum \text{mass of products} \qquad \dfrac{1 \text{ kg}}{1000 \text{ g}} \qquad E = m c^2$$

Solution:

(a) $^{?}_{?}? + {}^{9}_{4}\text{Be} \rightarrow {}^{6}_{3}\text{Li} + {}^{4}_{2}\text{He}$ becomes ${}^{1}_{1}? + {}^{9}_{4}\text{Be} \rightarrow {}^{6}_{3}\text{Li} + {}^{4}_{2}\text{He}$ then ${}^{1}_{1}\text{H} + {}^{9}_{4}\text{Be} \rightarrow {}^{6}_{3}\text{Li} + {}^{4}_{2}\text{He}$

mass defect $= \sum$ mass of reactants $- \sum$ mass of products and

mass defect $= (1.00783 \text{ g} + 9.012182 \text{ g}) - (6.015122 \text{ g} + 4.002603 \text{ g}) = 0.002287 \text{ g}$

then $\dfrac{0.002287 \text{ g}}{2 \text{ mol reactants}} \times \dfrac{1 \text{ kg}}{1000 \text{ g}} = 1.1435 \times 10^{-6} \dfrac{\text{kg}}{\text{mol reactants}}$ then

$E = m c^2 = \left(1.1435 \times 10^{-6} \dfrac{\text{kg}}{\text{mol reactants}}\right)\left(2.9979 \times 10^8 \dfrac{\text{m}}{\text{s}}\right)^2 = 1.03 \times 10^{11} \dfrac{\text{J}}{\text{mol reactants}}.$

Check: $1 + 9 = 6 + 4$, $1 + 4 = 3 + 2$. The units (J) are correct.

(b) $^{209}_{83}Bi + ^{64}_{28}Ni \rightarrow ^{272}_{111}Rg + ^{?}_{?}$ becomes $^{209}_{83}Bi + ^{64}_{28}Ni \rightarrow ^{272}_{111}Rg + ^{1}_{0}$? then $^{209}_{83}Bi + ^{64}_{28}Ni \rightarrow ^{272}_{111}Rg + ^{1}_{0}n$

mass defect = $(208.980384 \text{ g} + 63.927969 \text{ g}) - (272.1535 \text{ g} + 1.00866 \text{ g}) = -0.253807 \text{ g}$

(Note: Since this is negative, energy must be put in.)

then $\dfrac{0.253807 \text{ g}}{2 \text{ mol reactants}} \times \dfrac{1 \text{ kg}}{1000 \text{ g}} = 1.269035 \times 10^{-4} \dfrac{\text{kg}}{\text{mol reactants}}$ then

$E = m c^2 = \left(1.269035 \times 10^{-4} \dfrac{\text{kg}}{\text{mol reactants}}\right)\left(2.9979 \times 10^8 \dfrac{\text{m}}{\text{s}}\right)^2 = 1.141 \times 10^{13} \dfrac{\text{J}}{\text{mol reactants}}$

Check: $209 + 64 = 272 + 1$, $83 + 28 = 111 + 0$. The units (J) are correct.

(c) $^{179}_{74}W + ^{?}_{?} \rightarrow ^{179}_{73}Ta$ becomes $^{179}_{74}W + ^{0}_{-1}? \rightarrow ^{179}_{73}Ta$ then $^{179}_{74}W + ^{0}_{-1}e \rightarrow ^{179}_{73}Ta$

mass defect = $(178.94707 \text{ g} + 0.00055 \text{ g}) - 178.94593 \text{ g} = 0.00169 \text{ g}$ then

$\dfrac{0.00169 \text{ g}}{2 \text{ mol reactants}} \times \dfrac{1 \text{ kg}}{1000 \text{ g}} = 8.45 \times 10^{-7} \dfrac{\text{kg}}{\text{mol reactants}}$ then

$E = m c^2 = \left(8.45 \times 10^{-7} \dfrac{\text{kg}}{\text{mol reactants}}\right)\left(2.9979 \times 10^8 \dfrac{\text{m}}{\text{s}}\right)^2 = 7.59 \times 10^{10} \dfrac{\text{J}}{\text{mol reactants}}$

Check: $179 + 0 = 179$, $74 - 1 = 73$. The units (J) are correct.

19.79 **Given:** (a) Ru-114, (b) Ra-216, (c) Zn-58, and (d) Ne-31 **Find:** Write a nuclear equation for the most likely decay. **Conceptual Plan: Referring to the valley of stability graph in Figure 19.5, decide on the most likely decay mode depending on N/Z (too high = beta decay, too low = positron emission). → Write the symbol for the parent nuclide on the left side of the equation and the symbol for a particle on the right side. → Equalize the sum of the mass numbers and the sum of the atomic numbers on both sides of the equation by writing the appropriate mass number and atomic number for the unknown daughter nuclide. → Using the periodic table, deduce the identity of the unknown daughter nuclide from the atomic number and write its symbol.**
Solution:

(a) Ru-114 ($N/Z = 1.59$) will undergo beta decay $^{114}_{44}Ru \rightarrow ^{?}_{?} + ^{0}_{-1}e$ then $^{114}_{44}Ru \rightarrow ^{114}_{45}? + ^{0}_{-1}e$ then
$^{114}_{44}Ru \rightarrow ^{114}_{45}Rh + ^{0}_{-1}e$

(b) Ra-216 ($N/Z = 1.45$) will undergo positron emission $^{216}_{88}Ra \rightarrow ^{?}_{?} + ^{0}_{+1}e$ then $^{216}_{88}Ra \rightarrow ^{216}_{87}? + ^{0}_{+1}e$ then
$^{216}_{88}Ra \rightarrow ^{216}_{87}Fr + ^{0}_{+1}e$

(c) Zn-58 ($N/Z = 0.93$) will undergo positron emission $^{58}_{30}Zn \rightarrow ^{?}_{?} + ^{0}_{+1}e$ then $^{58}_{30}Zn \rightarrow ^{58}_{29}? + ^{0}_{+1}e$ then
$^{58}_{30}Zn \rightarrow ^{58}_{29}Cu + ^{0}_{+1}e$

(d) Ne-31 ($N/Z = 2.10$) will undergo beta decay $^{31}_{10}Ne \rightarrow ^{?}_{?} + ^{0}_{-1}e$ then $^{31}_{10}Ne \rightarrow ^{31}_{11}? + ^{0}_{-1}e$ then
$^{31}_{10}Ne \rightarrow ^{31}_{11}Na + ^{0}_{-1}e$
Check: (a) $114 = 114 + 0$, $44 = 45 - 1$, and rhodium is atomic number 45. (b) $216 = 216 + 0$, $88 = 87 + 1$, and francium is atomic number 87. (c) $58 = 58 + 0$, $30 = 29 + 1$, and copper is atomic number 29. (d) $31 = 31 + 0$, $10 = 11 - 1$, and sodium is atomic number 11.

19.81 **Given:** Bi-210, $t_{1/2} = 5.0$ days, 1.2 g Bi-210, 209.984105 amu, 5.5% absorbed
Find: beta emissions in 13.5 days and dose (in Bq)
Conceptual Plan: $t_{1/2} \rightarrow k$ then $m_{\text{Bi-210 } 0}, t, k \rightarrow m_{\text{Bi-210 } t}$ then

$t_{1/2} = \dfrac{0.693}{k}$ $\ln N_t = -k t + \ln N_0$

$g_0, g_t \rightarrow$ g decayed $\rightarrow$ mol decayed $\rightarrow$ beta decays then day $\rightarrow$ h $\rightarrow$ min $\rightarrow$ s then

$g_0 - g_t = $ g decayed $\dfrac{1 \text{ mol Bi-210}}{209.984105 \text{ g Bi-210}}$ $\dfrac{6.022 \times 10^{23} \text{ beta decays}}{1 \text{ mol Bi-210}}$ $\dfrac{1 \text{ day}}{24 \text{ h}}$ $\dfrac{60 \text{ min}}{1 \text{ h}}$ $\dfrac{60 \text{ s}}{1 \text{ min}}$

beta decays, s $\rightarrow$ beta decays / s $\rightarrow$ Bq available $\rightarrow$ Bq absorbed

take ratio $\dfrac{1 \text{ Bq}}{\dfrac{1 \text{ decay}}{s}}$ $\dfrac{5.5 \text{ Bq absorbed}}{100 \text{ Bq emitted}}$

Solution: $t_{1/2} = \dfrac{0.693}{k}$ rearrange to solve for k. $k = \dfrac{0.693}{t_{1/2}} = \dfrac{0.693}{5.0 \text{ days}} = 0.1386 \text{ day}^{-1}$. Since

$\ln m_{\text{Bi-210 } t} = -kt + \ln m_{\text{Bi-210 } 0} = -(0.1386 \text{ day}^{-1})(13.5 \text{ days}) + \ln(1.2 \text{ g}) = -1.6888 \rightarrow$

$m_{\text{Bi-210 } t} = e^{-1.6888} = 0.18475 \text{ g}$. Then $g_0 - g_t = \text{g decayed} = 1.2 \text{ g} - 0.18475 \text{ g} = 1.0153 \text{ g Bi-210}$

then $1.0153 \text{ g Bi-210} \times \dfrac{1 \text{ mol Bi-210}}{209.984105 \text{ g Bi-210}} \times \dfrac{6.022 \times 10^{23} \text{ beta decays}}{1 \text{ mol Bi-210}} = 2.9116 \times 10^{21}$ beta decays

$= 2.9 \times 10^{21}$ beta decays then $13.5 \text{ days} \times \dfrac{24 \text{ h}}{1 \text{ day}} \times \dfrac{60 \text{ min}}{1 \text{ h}} \times \dfrac{60 \text{ s}}{1 \text{ min}} = 1.1664 \times 10^6 \text{ s}$ then

$\dfrac{2.9116 \times 10^{21} \text{ beta decays}}{1.1664 \times 10^6 \text{ s}} \times \dfrac{1 \text{ Bq}}{1 \dfrac{\text{decay}}{\text{s}}} = 2.4962 \times 10^{15} \text{ Bq emitted} \times \dfrac{5.5 \text{ Bq absorbed}}{100 \text{ Bq emitted}} = 1.4 \times 10^{14} \text{ Bq.}$

Check: The units (decays and Bq) are correct. The amount that decays is large since the time is over three half-lives and we have a relatively large amount of the isotope. Since the decay is large, the dosage is large.

19.83   **Given:** Ra-226 (226.025402 amu) decays to Rn-224, $t_{1/2} = 1.6 \times 10^3$ y, 25.0 g Ra-226, $T = 25.0 \,°\text{C}$, $P = 1.0$ atm
Find: V of Rn-224 gas produced in 5.0 days
Conceptual Plan: day $\rightarrow$ **y then** $t_{1/2}$ $\rightarrow$ **k then** $m_{\text{Ra-226 } 0}$, t, k $\rightarrow$ $m_{\text{Ra-226 } t}$

$$\dfrac{1 \text{ y}}{365.24 \text{ days}} \qquad t_{1/2} = \dfrac{0.693}{k} \qquad \ln N_t = -kt + \ln N_0$$

then g_0, g_t $\rightarrow$ **g decayed** $\rightarrow$ **mol decayed** $\rightarrow$ **mol Rn-224 formed then** $°\text{C}$ $\rightarrow$ **K then then** P, n, T $\rightarrow$ V

$$g_0 - g_t = \text{g decayed} \quad \dfrac{1 \text{ mol Ra-226}}{226.025402 \text{ g Ra-226}} \quad \dfrac{1 \text{ mol Rn-224}}{1 \text{ mol Ra-226}} \qquad K = °\text{C} + 273.15 \qquad PV = nRT$$

Solution: $5.0 \text{ days} \times \dfrac{1 \text{ y}}{365.24 \text{ days}} = 0.013690 \text{ y}$ then $t_{1/2} = \dfrac{0.693}{k}$ rearrange to solve for k.

$k = \dfrac{0.693}{t_{1/2}} = \dfrac{0.693}{1.6 \times 10^3 \text{ y}} = 4.33125 \times 10^{-4} \text{ y}^{-1}$. Since

$\ln m_{\text{Ra-226 } t} = -kt + \ln m_{\text{Ra-226 } 0} = -(4.33125 \times 10^{-4} \text{ y}^{-1})(0.013690 \text{ y}) + \ln(25.0 \text{ g}) = 3.21887$

$\rightarrow m_{\text{Ra-226 } t} = e^{3.21887} = 24.9999 \text{ g}$. Then

$mg_0 - mg_t = \text{mg decayed} = 25.0 \text{ g} - 24.9999 \text{ g} = 0.000148 \text{ g Ra-226}$ then

$0.000148 \text{ g Ra-226} \times \dfrac{1 \text{ mol Ra-226}}{226.025402 \text{ g Ra-226}} \times \dfrac{1 \text{ mol Rn-224}}{1 \text{ mol Ra-226}} = 6.5582 \times 10^{-7} \text{ mol Rn-224}$ then

and $T = 25.0 \,°\text{C} + 273.15 = 298.2 \text{ K}$, then $PV = nRT$ Rearrange to solve for V.

$V = \dfrac{nRT}{P} = \dfrac{6.5582 \times 10^{-7} \text{ mol} \times 0.08206 \dfrac{\text{L} \cdot \text{atm}}{\text{mol} \cdot \text{K}} \times 298.2 \text{ K}}{1.0 \text{ atm}} = 1.6048 \times 10^{-5} \text{ L} = 1.6 \times 10^{-5} \text{ L}$. Two

significant figures are reported as requested in the problem.
Check: The units (L) are correct. The amount of gas is small since the time is so small compared to the half-life.

19.85   **Given:** $^0_{+1}e + {}^0_{-1}e \rightarrow 2 {}^0_0\gamma$ **Find:** energy (in kJ mol^{-1})
Conceptual Plan:
mass of products & reactants $\rightarrow$ **mass defect (g)** $\rightarrow$ **kg** $\rightarrow$ **kg mol^{-1}** $\rightarrow$ E **(J mol^{-1})** $\rightarrow$ E **(kJ mol^{-1})**

$$\text{mass defect} = \textstyle\sum \text{mass of reactants} - \textstyle\sum \text{mass of products} \quad \dfrac{1 \text{ kg}}{1000 \text{ g}} \quad 2 \text{ mol} \quad E = mc^2 \quad \dfrac{1 \text{ kJ}}{1000 \text{ J}}$$

Solution: mass defect $= \sum \text{mass of reactants} - \sum \text{mass of products} = (0.00055 \text{ g} + 0.00055 \text{ g}) - 0 \text{ g}$

$= 0.00110 \text{ g}$ then $\dfrac{0.00110 \text{ g}}{2 \text{ mol}} \times \dfrac{1 \text{ kg}}{1000 \text{ g}} = 5.50 \times 10^{-7} \text{ kg mol}^{-1}$ then

$E = mc^2 = \left(5.50 \times 10^{-7} \dfrac{\text{kg}}{\text{mol}}\right)\left(2.9979 \times 10^8 \dfrac{\text{m}}{\text{s}}\right)^2 = 4.94307 \times 10^{10} \dfrac{\text{J}}{\text{mol}} \times \dfrac{1 \text{ kJ}}{1000 \text{ J}} = 4.94 \times 10^7 \text{ kJ mol}^{-1}$.

Check: The units (kJ mol^{-1}) are correct. A large amount of energy is expected per mole of mass lost. The photon is in the gamma ray region of the electromagnetic spectrum.

19.87   **Given:** $^3\text{He} = 3.016030$ amu   **Find:** nuclear binding energy per atom
Conceptual Plan: $^A_Z X$, **isotope mass** $\rightarrow$ **mass defect** $\rightarrow$ **nuclear binding energy per nucleon**

$$\text{mass defect} = Z(\text{mass } ^1_1\text{H}) + (A - Z)(\text{mass } ^1_0\text{n}) - \text{mass of isotope} \qquad \dfrac{931.5 \text{ MeV}}{1 \text{ amu}}$$

Solution: mass defect $= Z(\text{mass }{}_1^1\text{H}) + (A - Z)(\text{mass }{}_0^1\text{n}) - \text{mass of isotope.}$

He-3 mass defect $= 2(1.00783 \text{ amu}) + (3 - 2)(1.00866 \text{ amu}) - 3.016030 \text{ amu} = 0.00829 \text{ amu}$

and $0.00829 \text{ amu} \times \dfrac{931.5 \text{ MeV}}{1 \text{ amu}} = 7.72 \text{ MeV.}$

Check: The units (MeV) are correct. The number of nucleons is small, so the MeV is not that large.

19.89　**Given:** ^{247}Es and five neutrons made by bombarding ^{238}U　**Find:** identity of bombarding particle

Conceptual Plan: Begin with the symbols for the nuclides given. → **Equalize the sum of the mass numbers and the sum of the atomic numbers on both sides of the equation by writing the appropriate mass number and atomic number for the unknown bombarding particle.** → **Using the periodic table, deduce the identity of the unknown nuclide from the atomic number and write its symbol.**

Solution:

${}^{238}_{92}\text{U} + {}^{?}_{?}? \rightarrow {}^{247}_{99}\text{Es} + 5\,{}^{1}_{0}\text{n}$ then ${}^{238}_{92}\text{U} + {}^{14}_{7}? \rightarrow {}^{247}_{99}\text{Es} + 5\,{}^{1}_{0}\text{n}$ then ${}^{238}_{92}\text{U} + {}^{14}_{7}\text{N} \rightarrow {}^{247}_{99}\text{Es} + 5\,{}^{1}_{0}\text{n}$

Check: $238 + 14 = 247 + 5(1)$, $92 + 7 = 99 + 5(0)$, and nitrogen is atomic number 7.

19.91　**Given:** $t_{1/2}$ for decay of ^{238}U $= 4.5 \times 10^9$ years, 1.6 g rock, 29 Bq, all radioactivity from U-238

Find: percent by mass ^{238}U in rock

Conceptual Plan: $t_{1/2} \rightarrow k$ and s $\rightarrow$ min $\rightarrow$ h $\rightarrow$ day $\rightarrow$ y then Rate, $k \rightarrow N \rightarrow$ mol ^{238}U $\rightarrow$ g ^{238}U

$$t_{1/2} = \frac{0.693}{k} \quad \cdot \quad \frac{1 \text{ min}}{60 \text{ s}} \quad \frac{1 \text{ h}}{60 \text{ min}} \quad \frac{1 \text{ day}}{24 \text{ h}} \quad \frac{1 \text{ y}}{365.24 \text{ days}} \qquad \text{Rate} = k\,N \quad \frac{1 \text{ mol decays}}{6.022 \times 10^{23} \text{ decays}} \quad \frac{238 \text{ g }{}^{238}\text{U}}{1 \text{ mol }{}^{238}\text{U}}$$

then g ^{238}U, g rock $\rightarrow$ percent by mass ^{238}U

$$\text{percent by mass }{}^{238}\text{U} = \frac{\text{g }{}^{238}\text{U}}{\text{g rock}} \times 100\%$$

Solution: $t_{1/2} = \dfrac{0.693}{k}$ rearrange to solve for k. $k = \dfrac{0.693}{t_{1/2}} = \dfrac{0.693}{4.5 \times 10^9 \text{ y}} = 1.54 \times 10^{-10} \text{ y}^{-1}$ and

$1 \text{ s} \times \dfrac{1 \text{ min}}{60 \text{ s}} \times \dfrac{1 \text{ h}}{60 \text{ min}} \times \dfrac{1 \text{ day}}{24 \text{ h}} \times \dfrac{1 \text{ y}}{365.24 \text{ days}} = 3.16889554 \times 10^{-8} \text{ y}$. Rate $= k\,N$. Rearrange to

solve for N.

$$N = \frac{\text{Rate}}{k} = \frac{29\,\dfrac{\text{decays}}{3.16889554 \times 10^{-8} \text{ y}}}{1.54 \times 10^{-10} \text{ y}^{-1}} = 5.9425 \times 10^{18} \text{ decays then}$$

$$5.9425 \times 10^{18} \text{ decays} \times \frac{1 \text{ mol decays}}{6.022 \times 10^{23} \text{ decays}} \times \frac{238 \text{ g }{}^{238}\text{U}}{1 \text{ mol }{}^{238}\text{U}} = 2.3486 \times 10^{-3} \text{ g }{}^{238}\text{U then}$$

$$\text{percent by mass }{}^{238}\text{U} = \frac{\text{g }{}^{238}\text{U}}{\text{g rock}} \times 100\% = \frac{2.3486 \times 10^{-3}\text{g }{}^{238}\text{U}}{1.6 \text{ g rock}} \times 100\% = 0.15\%.$$

Check: The units (%) are correct. The mass percent is low because the dis/s is low.

19.93　**Given:** $V = 1.50$ L, $P = 745$ mmHg, $T = 25.0$ °C, 3.55% Ra-220 by volume, $t_{1/2} = 55.6$ s

Find: number of alpha particles emitted in 5.00 min

Conceptual Plan: mmHg → **atm and °C** → **K then** $P, V, T \rightarrow n_{\text{Total}} \rightarrow n_{\text{Ra-220}}$ **and min** → **s**

$$\frac{1 \text{ atm}}{760 \text{ mmHg}} \qquad K = °C + 273.15 \qquad PV = nRT \qquad \frac{3.55 \text{ Ra-220 particles}}{100 \text{ gas particles}} \qquad \frac{60 \text{ s}}{1 \text{ min}}$$

then $t_{1/2} \rightarrow k$ then $n_{\text{Ra-220 0}}, t, k \rightarrow n_{\text{Ra-220 }t} \rightarrow$ number of particles remaining → particles emitted

$$t_{1/2} = \frac{0.693}{k} \qquad \ln N_t = -k\,t + \ln N_0 \qquad \frac{6.022 \times 10^{23} \text{ particles}}{1 \text{ mol}}$$

Solution: $745 \text{ mmHg} \times \dfrac{1 \text{ atm}}{760 \text{ mmHg}} = 0.9802632 \text{ atm}$ and $T = 25.0$ °C $+ 273.15 = 298.2$ K, then

$PV = nRT$ Rearrange to solve for n.

$$n = \frac{PV}{RT} = \frac{0.9802632 \text{ atm} \times 1.50 \text{ L}}{0.08206\,\dfrac{\text{L} \cdot \text{atm}}{\text{mol} \cdot \text{K}} \times 298.2 \text{ K}} = 0.06008897 \text{ mol gas particles}$$

then $0.06008897 \text{ mol gas particles} \times \dfrac{3.55 \text{ mol Ra-220 particles}}{100 \text{ mol gas particles}} = 0.002133158 \text{ mol Ra-220 particles}$

$$5.00 \text{ min} \times \frac{60 \text{ s}}{1 \text{ min}} = 300. \text{ s then } t_{1/2} = \frac{0.693}{k} \text{ and rearrange to solve for } k.$$

$$k = \frac{0.693}{t_{1/2}} = \frac{0.693}{55.6 \text{ s}} = 0.01246403 \text{ s}^{-1}. \text{ Since}$$

$$\ln m_{\text{Ra-220 } t} = -kt + \ln m_{\text{Ra-220 } 0} = -(0.01246403 \text{ s}^{-1})(300. \text{ s}) + \ln (0.002133158 \text{ mol})$$
$$= -9.889361 \rightarrow$$

$$m_{\text{Ra-220 } t} = e^{-9.889361} = 5.071136 \times 10^{-5} \text{ mol alpha particles remaining.}$$

The number of alpha particles emitted would be the difference between this and the initial number of moles.

$$0.002133158 \text{ mol} - 0.00005071136 \text{ mol} = 0.002082446 \text{ mol}$$

$$0.002082446 \text{ mol} \times \frac{6.022 \times 10^{23} \text{ particles}}{1 \text{ mol}} = 1.254062 \times 10^{21} \text{ particles} = 1.25 \times 10^{21} \text{ particles.}$$

Check: The units (particles) are correct. The amount of particles is far less than a mole, since we have far less than a mole of gas.

19.95 **Given:** ${}^{0}_{+1}e + {}^{0}_{-1}e \rightarrow 2{}^{0}_{0}\gamma$ **Find:** wavelength of gamma ray photons

Conceptual Plan:

mass of products & reactants $\rightarrow$ mass defect (g) $\rightarrow$ kg $\rightarrow$ kg mol^{-1} $\rightarrow$ E (J mol^{-1})

$$\text{mass defect} = \sum \text{mass of reactants} - \sum \text{mass of products} \quad \frac{1 \text{ kg}}{1000 \text{ g}} \quad 2 \text{ mol} \quad E = mc^2$$

This energy is for 2 moles of γ, so E (J/2 mol γ) $\rightarrow$ E (J/ γ photon) $\rightarrow$ λ.

$$\frac{1 \text{ mol photons}}{6.022 \times 10^{23} \text{ photons}} \quad E = \frac{hc}{\lambda}$$

Solution: mass defect $= \sum$ mass of reactants $- \sum$ mass of products $= (0.00055 \text{ g} + 0.00055 \text{ g}) - 0 \text{ g}$

$$= 0.00110 \text{ g then } \frac{0.00110 \text{ g}}{2 \text{ mol}} \times \frac{1 \text{ kg}}{1000 \text{ g}} = 5.50 \times 10^{-7} \frac{\text{kg}}{\text{mol}} \text{ then}$$

$$E = mc^2 = \left(5.50 \times 10^{-7} \frac{\text{kg}}{\text{mol}}\right)\left(2.9979 \times 10^8 \frac{\text{m}}{\text{s}}\right)^2 = 4.94307 \times 10^{10} \frac{\text{J}}{\text{mol}}$$

$$E = 4.94307 \times 10^{10} \frac{\text{J}}{\text{mol } \gamma} \times \frac{1 \text{ mol } \gamma}{6.022 \times 10^{23} \gamma \text{ photons}} = 8.20836 \times 10^{-14} \frac{\text{J}}{\gamma \text{ photons}}. \text{ Then } E = \frac{hc}{\lambda}. \text{ Rearrange}$$

to solve for λ. $\lambda = \dfrac{hc}{E} = \dfrac{(6.626 \times 10^{-34} \text{ J} \cdot \text{s})\left(2.9979 \times 10^8 \dfrac{\text{m}}{\text{s}}\right)}{8.20836 \times 10^{-14} \dfrac{\text{J}}{\gamma \text{ photons}}} = 2.42 \times 10^{-12} \text{ m} = 2.42 \text{ pm.}$

Check: The units (m or pm) are correct. A large amount of energy is expected per mole of mass lost. The photon is in the gamma ray region of the electromagnetic spectrum.

19.97 **Given:** ${}^{2}_{1}H + {}^{2}_{1}H \rightarrow {}^{3}_{2}He + {}^{1}_{0}n$ releases 3.3 MeV; ${}^{2}_{1}H + {}^{2}_{1}H \rightarrow {}^{3}_{1}H + {}^{1}_{1}p$ releases 4.0 MeV

Find: the energy change for ${}^{3}_{2}He + {}^{1}_{0}n \rightarrow {}^{3}_{1}H + {}^{1}_{1}p$ and explain why this can happen at a much lower temperature

Conceptual Plan: Use Hess's law to calculate the energy change, and give the two reactions.

Solution:

$${}^{3}_{2}He + {}^{1}_{0}n \rightarrow {}^{2}_{1}H + {}^{2}_{1}H \quad \Delta E = \quad 3.3 \text{ MeV}$$
$${}^{2}_{1}H + {}^{2}_{1}H \rightarrow {}^{3}_{1}H + {}^{1}_{1}p \quad \Delta E = -4.0 \text{ MeV}$$
$$\overline{{}^{3}_{2}He + {}^{1}_{0}n \rightarrow {}^{3}_{1}H + {}^{1}_{1}p \quad \Delta E = -0.7 \text{ MeV}}$$

The energy change is much less and there is no coulombic barrier for collision with a neutron, so the process can occur at lower temperatures.

Check: The units (MeV) are correct. Since one reaction releases energy and one requires energy, the resulting energy change is much smaller in magnitude.

Challenge Problems

19.99 (a) **Given:** 72 500 kg Al (*s*) and 10 Al (*s*) + 6 NH_4ClO_4 (*s*) → 4 Al_2O_3 (*s*) + 2 $AlCl_3$ (*s*) + 12 H_2O (*g*) + 3 N_2 (*g*) and 608 000 kg O_2 (*g*) that reacts with hydrogen to form gaseous water
Find: energy generated ($\Delta_r H°$)
Conceptual Plan: Write a balanced reaction for O_2 (*g*) then

$\Delta_r H° = \sum n_p \Delta_f H°(\text{products}) - \sum n_r \Delta_f H°(\text{reactants})$ **then**

kg → g → mol → energy then add the results from the two reactions.

$\frac{1000\ g}{1\ kg}$ molar mass $\Delta_r H°$

Solution:

Reactant/Product	$\Delta_f H°$(kJ mol^{-1} from Appendix IIB)
Al (*s*)	0.0
NH_4ClO_4 (*s*)	− 295
Al_2O_3 (*s*)	− 1675.7
$AlCl_3$ (*s*)	− 704.2
H_2O (*g*)	− 241.8
N_2 (*g*)	0.0

Be sure to pull data for the correct formula and phase.

$\Delta_r H° = \sum n_p \Delta_f H°(\text{products}) - \sum n_r \Delta_f H°(\text{reactants})$

$= [4(\Delta_f H°(Al_2O_3\ (s))) + 2(\Delta_f H°(AlCl_3\ (s))) + 12(\Delta_f H°(H_2O\ (g))) + 3(\Delta_f H°(N_2\ (g)))]$

$\qquad\qquad\qquad\qquad\qquad\qquad\qquad\quad - [10(\Delta_f H°(Al\ (s))) + 6(\Delta_f H°(NH_4ClO_4\ (s)))]$

$= [4(-1675.7\ kJ) + 2(-704.2\ kJ) + 12(-241.8\ kJ) + 3(0.0\ kJ)] - [10(0.0\ kJ) + 6(-295\ kJ)]$

$= [-11012.8\ kJ] - [-1770.\ kJ]$

$= -9242.8\ kJ$

then 72 500 $\cancel{kg\ Al}$ × $\frac{1000\ \cancel{g\ Al}}{1\ \cancel{kg\ Al}}$ × $\frac{1\ \cancel{mol\ Al}}{26.98\ \cancel{g\ Al}}$ × $\frac{9242.8\ kJ}{10\ \cancel{mol\ Al}}$ = 2.483703 × 10^9 kJ.

balanced reaction: H_2 (*g*) + $\frac{1}{2} O_2$ (*g*) → H_2O (*g*) $\Delta_r H° = \Delta_f H°(H_2O\ (g)) = -241.8$ kJ mol^{-1} then

608 000 $\cancel{kg\ O_2}$ × $\frac{1000\ \cancel{g\ O_2}}{1\ \cancel{kg\ O_2}}$ × $\frac{1\ \cancel{mol\ O_2}}{32.00\ \cancel{g\ O_2}}$ × $\frac{241.8\ kJ}{0.5\ \cancel{mol\ O_2}}$ = 9.1884 × 10^9 kJ. So the total is

2.483703 × 10^9 kJ + 9.1884 × 10^9 kJ = 1.1672103 × 10^{10} kJ = 1.167 × 10^{10} kJ.
Check: The units (kJ) are correct. The answer is very large because the reactions are very exothermic and the weight of reactants is so large.

(b) **Given:** ^1_1H + $^{-1}_{-1}p$ + $^0_{+1}e$ → $^0_0\gamma$ **Find:** mass of antimatter to give same energy as part (a)
Conceptual Plan: Since the reaction is an annihilation reaction, no matter will be left, so the mass of antimatter is the same as the mass of the hydrogen. so kJ → J → kg → g

$\frac{1000\ J}{1\ kJ}$ $E = mc^2$ $\frac{1000\ g}{1\ kg}$

Solution: 1.1672103 × 10^{10} $\cancel{kJ}$ × $\frac{1000\ J}{1\ \cancel{kJ}}$ = 1.1672103 × 10^{13} J. Since $E = mc^2$, rearrange to solve for *m*.

$m = \dfrac{E}{c^2} = \dfrac{1.1672103 \times 10^{13}\ kg\ \frac{m^2}{s^2}}{\left(2.9979 \times 10^8\ \frac{m}{s}\right)^2}$ = 1.299 × 10^{-4} $\cancel{kg}$ × $\frac{1000\ g}{1\ \cancel{kg}}$ = 0.1299 g total matter, 0.649 g each

of matter and antimatter.
Check: The units (g) are correct. A small mass is expected since nuclear reactions generate a large amount of energy.

19.101 The information needed to answer this problem can be searched for on the internet. A good search term would be "natural decay chains" or "natural radioactive decay of U-235." From that search it is possible to determine the following: $^{235}_{92}U$ → $^{207}_{82}Pb$ and $^{232}_{90}Th$ → $^{208}_{82}Pb$. Examples of these decay series can be found online, and from them it is possible to determine that $^{235}_{92}U \rightarrow \, ^{207}_{82}Pb$ occurs through 7 α decays. Or, since the difference in the mass numbers is 28 and each α decay causes a loss of two neutrons and two protons (for a total mass of 4), then $28 \div 4 = 7$.

By similar reasoning: $^{232}_{90}Th \rightarrow \, ^{208}_{82}Pb$ occurs through 6 α decays. (Since the difference in the mass numbers is 24 and each α decay causes a loss of two neutrons and two protons (for a total mass of 4) then $24 \div 4 = 6$.)

19.103 **Given:** $H^{38}_{17}Cl\,(g) \rightarrow \, ^{38}_{18}Ar\,(g) + \, ^{0}_{-1}e + 1/2\,H_2\,(g)$, 0.40 mol $H^{38}_{17}Cl\,(g)$; $V = 6.24$ L, $P = 1650$ mmHg, $t_{1/2} = 80.0$ min **Find:** T

Conceptual Plan: Since $t = 2\,t_{1/2}$ then $N_{\text{Cl-38}\,t} = \frac{1}{4}\,N_{\text{Cl-38}\,0} \rightarrow n_{\text{gas}\,t}$ then mmHg $\rightarrow$ atm and

$$n_{\text{gas}\,t} = 3/2\,n_{HCl\,0} - 1/2\,n_{HCl\,t} \qquad \frac{1\text{ atm}}{760\text{ mmHg}}$$

$P, V, n_{\text{gas}\,t} \rightarrow T$

$$PV = nRT$$

Solution: Since $t = 2\,t_{1/2}$ then $N_{\text{Cl-38}\,t} = \frac{1}{4}\,N_{\text{Cl-38}\,0} = \frac{1}{4}\,(0.40\text{ mol}) = 0.10$ mol. As the HCl disintegrates, it produces argon gas, beta particles, and hydrogen gas, with a ratio of three particles produced (2 Ar, 1 H_2) for every 2 HCl molecules that decay. There were initially 0.40 mole of undisintegrated gas, and now there are 0.10 mole HCl remaining. So the total number of gas particles now in the container is

$n_{\text{gas}\,t} = 3/2\,n_{HCl\,0} - 1/2\,n_{HCl\,t} = 3/2(0.40\text{ mol}) - 1/2\,(0.10\text{ mol}) = 0.55$ mol gas then $PV = nRT$. Rearrange

to solve for T. $T = \dfrac{PV}{nR} = \dfrac{1650\text{ mmHg} \times \dfrac{1\text{ atm}}{760\text{ mmHg}} \times 6.24\text{ L}}{0.55\text{ mol} \times 0.08206\,\dfrac{\text{L}\cdot\text{atm}}{\text{mol}\cdot\text{K}}} = 300.17\text{ K} = 3.0 \times 10^2\text{ K}$

Check: The units (K) are correct. The temperature is reasonable considering the volume of a gas at STP and most of the initial 0.40 mol has decomposed.

Conceptual Problems

19.105 **Given:** $^{21}_{9}F \rightarrow \, ^{?}_{?}? + \, ^{0}_{-1}e$ **Find:** missing nucleus

Conceptual Plan: Write the species given on the appropriate side of the equation. $\rightarrow$ Equalize the sum of the mass numbers and the sum of the atomic numbers on both sides of the equation by writing the stoichiometric coefficient in front of the desired species.

Solution: $^{21}_{9}F \rightarrow \, ^{?}_{?}? + \, ^{0}_{-1}e$ becomes $^{21}_{9}F \rightarrow \, ^{21}_{10}Ne + \, ^{0}_{-1}e$.

Check: $21 = 21 + 0$, and $9 = 10 + -1$. Neon is atomic number 10 and no other species are needed to balance the equation.

19.107 Nuclide A is more dangerous because the half-life is shorter (18.5 days) and so it decays faster.

20 Organic Chemistry I: Structures

Review Questions

20.1   Organic chemistry is the study of compounds containing carbon combined with one or more of the elements hydrogen, nitrogen, oxygen, and sulfur, including their properties and their reactions.

20.3   Carbon is unique in its ability to form four covalent bonds, its ability to form double and triple bonds, and its tendency to catenate (that is, to form chains).

20.5   (a)   When carbon forms four single bonds the hybridization is sp^3 and the geometry is tetrahedral.

　　　　(b)   When carbon forms two single bonds and one double bond the hybridization is sp^2 and the geometry is trigonal planar.

　　　　(c)   When carbon forms one single bond and one triple bond the hybridization is sp and the geometry is linear.

20.7   Hydrocarbons can be classified into four different types: alkanes, alkenes, alkynes, and aromatic hydrocarbons. Their generic formulas are C_nH_{2n+2}, C_nH_{2n}, C_nH_{2n-2}, and formulas containing a benzene ring, respectively, where n = the number of carbon atoms.

20.9   The structure of benzene, C_6H_6, is a six-member ring where three pi bonds are delocalized on all six of the C—C bonds that form the ring. Benzene rings are represented as one or both of the Kekulé structures,

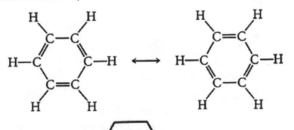

in a shorthand notation, or as a ball-and-stick diagram with molecular

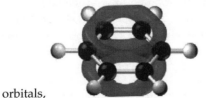

orbitals,

20.11   A functional group is a characteristic atom or group of atoms that is inserted into a hydrocarbon. Examples of functional groups are alcohols (—OH), halogens (—X, where X = F, Cl, Br, or I), and carboxylic acids (—COOH).

20.13   Amines are organic compounds that contain nitrogen. One or more of the hydrogen atoms on an ammonia molecule are replaced by a hydrocarbon group. The simplest amines have the following general structural formula of RNH_2, where R represents a hydrocarbon group. This would be a primary amine. If there are two R groups, R_2NH or $RR'NH$, this would be a secondary amine. If all three hydrogen atoms are replaced by different alkyl groups to give a formula of $RR'R''N$ this is called a tertiary amine. For C_3H_9N the following structures are possible:

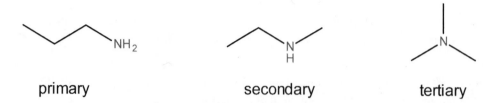

primary   secondary   tertiary

20.15   The generic structure for ethers has the formula of ROR', where R and R' represent hydrocarbon groups. The two hydrocarbon groups are linked through an oxygen atom. R and R' may be the same group or different groups. The structures of two ethers with formula $C_4H_{10}O$ are $CH_3CH_2OCH_2CH_3$ and $CH_3CH_2\,CH_2OCH_3$.

20.17   The generic structure of an acyl group is

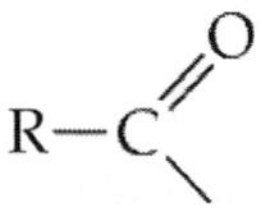

$$R-C\overset{\displaystyle O}{\underset{\displaystyle \diagdown}{\diagup\!\!\!\parallel}}$$

where R is an alkyl group. The acyl group can be attached to a variety of atoms except H or C. Several possibilities are shown in Table 20.5 on page 880 of the textbook.

20.19   Important resonance structures of the carboxylate anion are:

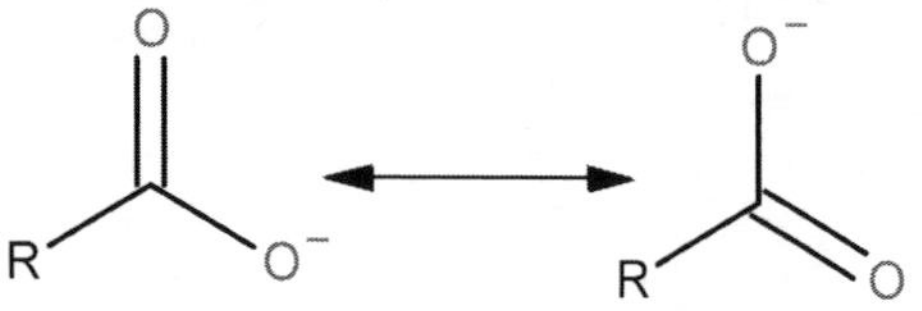

20.21   Functional group isomerism is where two or more molecules have the same molecular formula but the structures either have different functional groups or the same functional group is located in a different position in the molecule. For example, ethanol and dimethyl ether have the same molecular formula but different functional groups, whereas propan-1-ol and propan-2-ol have the same functional group in different locations.

20.23   Conformational isomers are a subclass of stereoisomers and they are the result of bond rotations. Conformational isomers can be interconverted simply by rotating around single bonds without breaking any bonds. The two main classes of conformational isomers are eclipsed and staggered conformations. (See Figure 20.4, page 882 for examples.) Staggered conformers have the C—H bonds on different carbons as far apart from each other as possible with a dihedral angle of 60°. Eclipsed conformers have the C—H bonds on different carbons aligned with each other with a dihedral angle of 0°.

20.25   *Cis–trans* isomerism in alkenes involves having the major groups in an alkene on the same (*cis*) or opposite (*trans*) side of the double bond. They cannot interconvert without breaking the π bond and are considered configurational isomers. *Cis–trans* isomers are a type of stereoisomer known as diastereomers. They have completely different physical properties (MP, BP, density, etc.) from each other.

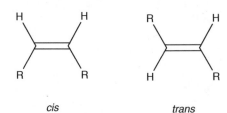

cis   *trans*

20.27   Objects such as hands, feet, and curve-bladed hockey sticks are chiral objects. They are considered "handed," that is, one is the mirror image of the other, but they are not superimposable. You cannot replace one with its mirror image. Molecules exhibit chirality when at least one carbon in the molecule is attached to four different substituents or groups. (A methyl group and an ethyl group are different even though they can both be considered alkyl groups.) Enantiomers are a pair of mirror image molecules that cannot be superimposed or twisted in any way in three dimensions to become the mirror image.

20.29   Some of the physical and chemical properties of enantiomers are indistinguishable from one another. Typically the melting points, boiling points, and densities will be the same for either enantiomer. However, enantiomers differ from each other in the direction in which they rotate the plane of polarized light and their chemical behaviour in a chiral environment. An example of the latter would be a compound such as adrenaline, where one enantiomer is a cardiac stimulant and the other is not.

20.31   The index of hydrogen deficiency (IHD) indicates the difference between a saturated compound (no rings or double/triple bonds) and the compound under observation in terms of hydrogen count. Typically, a calculation is made based on the molecular formula C_nH_{2n+2} to determine the number of hydrogen atoms in a saturated alkane with n carbon atoms. Then the number of hydrogen atoms in the compound of interest is subtracted from the first value and the result is divided by two to obtain the IHD. Adjustments are made for the presence of nitrogen (one additional hydrogen in the parent formula for each nitrogen present) and halogen atoms (treated as hydrogen in the count). A ring or a double bond has an IHD count of one and a triple bond has an IHD count of two. Thus the IHD gives an indication of how many rings and double or triple bonds are possible in the compound of interest based on its molecular formula. A molecule with an IHD of four might contain a ring and three double bonds or two triple bonds or any other combination that adds to four.

20.33   A ^{13}C NMR spectrum can identify the number of unique types of carbon atoms in a molecule and provide information about the chemical environment of the atoms. Symmetry in the molecule will typically reduce the number of carbon signals in the spectrum.

Hydrocarbons

20.35   Assuming there are no rings in each of the following and only one multiple bond, then:

     (a) C_5H_{12} is an alkane. It is identical to the parent compound C_5H_{12}.

     (b) C_3H_6 is an alkene. It has two less hydrogens than the parent compound C_3H_8.

     (c) C_7H_{12} is an alkyne. It has four less hydrogens than the parent compound C_7H_{16}.

     (d) $C_{11}H_{22}$ is an alkene. It has two less hydrogens than the parent compound $C_{11}H_{24}$.

20.37   (a) $CH_3-C \equiv C-CH_3$ sp^3 sp sp sp^3

         (b)

             sp^3 at top, sp^2 at the four remaining ring positions

         (c) $(CH_3)_2-CH-CH=CH_2$ sp^3 sp^3 sp^2 sp^2

         (d) $CH_3-CH=CH_2$ sp^3 sp^2 sp^2

20.39   (a)

[structure: two anthracene-type resonance structures connected by a double-headed arrow]

  (b)

[structure: two pyrene-type resonance structures connected by a double-headed arrow]

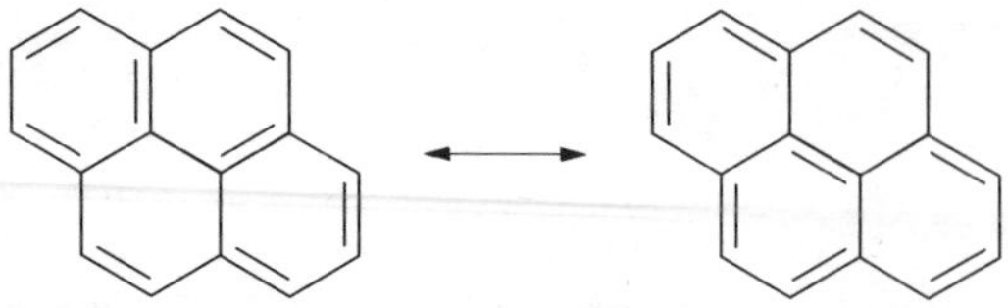

Functional Groups

20.41   (a) NH_2—CH_3 all sp^3

  (b)

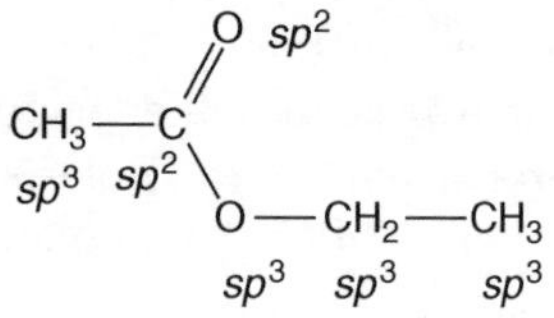

[structure:
$$CH_3—C \begin{matrix} \nearrow O \; sp^2 \\ \searrow O—CH_2—CH_3 \end{matrix}$$
sp^3 sp^2 below CH_3—C; sp^3 sp^3 sp^3 below O—CH_2—CH_3]

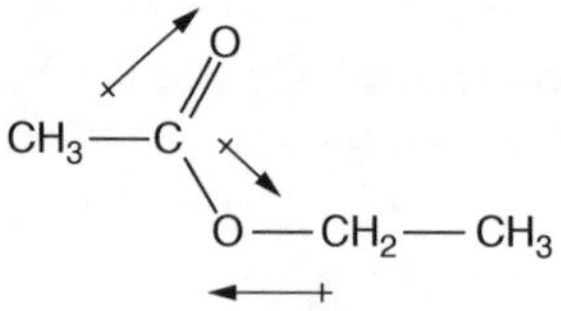

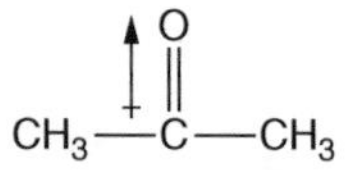

  (c)

[structure:
$$CH_3—\overset{\overset{O\;sp^2}{\|}}{C}—CH_3$$
sp^3 sp^2 sp^3]

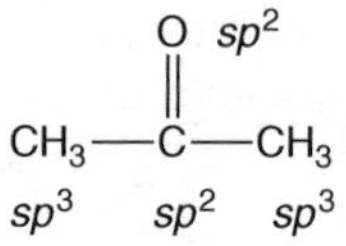

  (d)

[structure:
$$CH_3—CH_2—C \begin{matrix} \nearrow O \; sp^2 \\ \searrow Cl \; sp^3 \end{matrix}$$
sp^3 sp^3 sp^2]

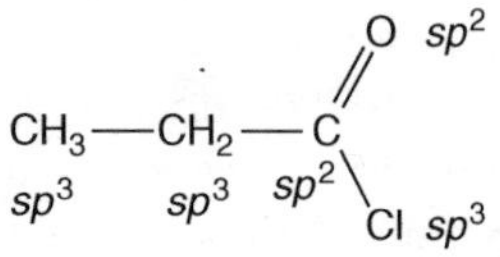

20.43   Dipoles between heteroatoms and hydrogen are not shown such as occurs in methanamine in part (a).

  (a)   [dipole arrow] NH_2—CH_3 (b) [structure of CH_3—C with O and O—CH_2—CH_3 with dipole arrows]

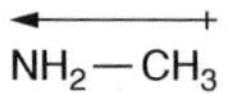

  (c) [structure of CH_3—C($=O$)—CH_3 with dipole arrow]   (d) [structure of CH_3—CH_2—C with O and Cl with dipole arrows]

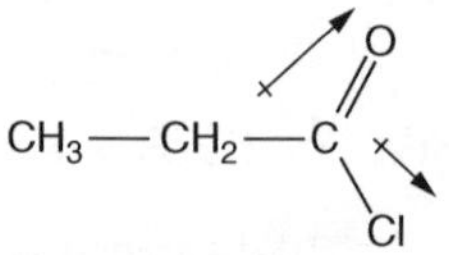

20.45 $CH_3CH_2CH_3 < CH_3COCH_3 < CH_3CHOHCH_3$ These are due to differing intermolecular forces. Propane has only dispersion forces, propanone has those plus dipole–dipole interactions and thus a higher boiling point, and propan-2-ol has all of the intermolecular forces of the previous two plus hydrogen bonding and so has the highest boiling point of the three. Note: propanone written this way is a bit tricky because the $C{=}O$ is not shown explicitly. It is implied because the C before the O has no hydrogens attached to it and thus would need a double bond with oxygen in order to have four bonds.

Constitutional Isomerism

20.47 $CH_2{=}CH—CH_2—CH_2—CH_2—CH_3$, $CH_3—CH{=}CH—CH_2—CH_2—CH_3$, and $CH_3—CH_2—CH{=}CH—CH_2—CH_3$ are the only structural isomers. Remember that *cis–trans* isomerism generates geometric isomers, not structural isomers.

20.49   The nine constitutional isomers of heptane are:

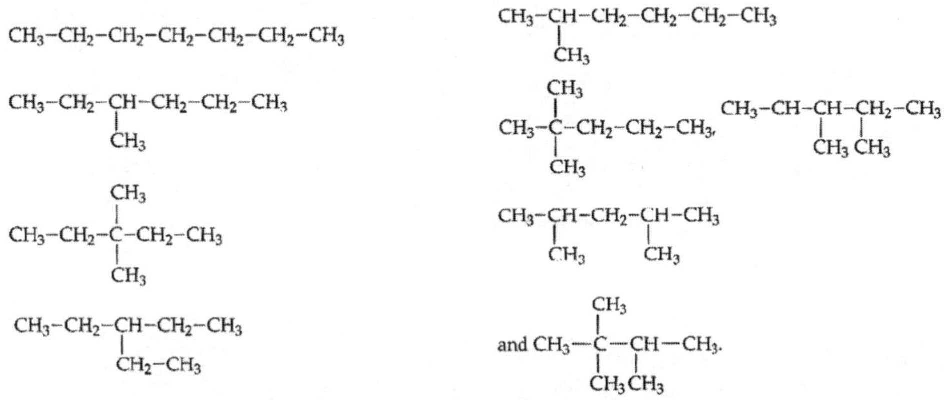

CH₃–CH₂–CH₂–CH₂–CH₂–CH₂–CH₃

$$CH_3-\overset{\displaystyle |}{\underset{\displaystyle CH_3}{CH}}-CH_2-CH_2-CH_2-CH_3$$

$$CH_3-CH_2-\overset{\displaystyle |}{\underset{\displaystyle CH_3}{CH}}-CH_2-CH_2-CH_3$$

$$CH_3-\overset{\displaystyle CH_3}{\underset{\displaystyle CH_3}{\overset{\displaystyle |}{\underset{\displaystyle |}{C}}}}-CH_2-CH_2-CH_3,$$

$$CH_3-\overset{\displaystyle CH_3}{\underset{\displaystyle CH_3}{\overset{\displaystyle |}{\underset{\displaystyle |}{C}}}}-CH_2-CH_3$$

$$CH_3-\overset{\displaystyle |}{\underset{\displaystyle CH_3}{CH}}-\overset{\displaystyle |}{\underset{\displaystyle CH_3}{CH}}-CH_2-CH_3$$

$$CH_3-CH_2-\overset{\displaystyle |}{\underset{\displaystyle CH_2-CH_3}{CH}}-CH_2-CH_3$$

$$CH_3-\overset{\displaystyle |}{\underset{\displaystyle CH_3}{CH}}-CH_2-\overset{\displaystyle |}{\underset{\displaystyle CH_3}{CH}}-CH_3$$

$$and\ CH_3-\overset{\displaystyle CH_3}{\underset{\displaystyle CH_3}{\overset{\displaystyle |}{\underset{\displaystyle |}{C}}}}-\overset{\displaystyle |}{\underset{\displaystyle CH_3}{CH}}-CH_3.$$

20.51   (a)   No, these molecules have different molecular formulae.
         (b)   Yes, these molecules have the same molecular formulae but different structures.
         (c)   Yes, these molecules have the same molecular formulae but different structures.

20.53   These molecules are cyclic and therefore have a ring but no double bond in order to fit the molecular formula C_6H_{12}. Any five of the following would fit the requirements.

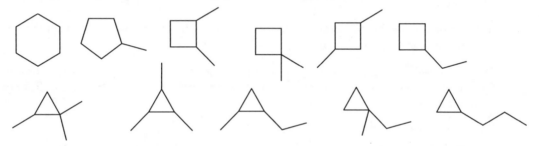

20.55   These molecules have two fewer hydrogens than the parent (or saturated) compound. They contain either a ring or a double bond. Any three of the following would fit the requirements. There are many other possibilities than the ones shown below.

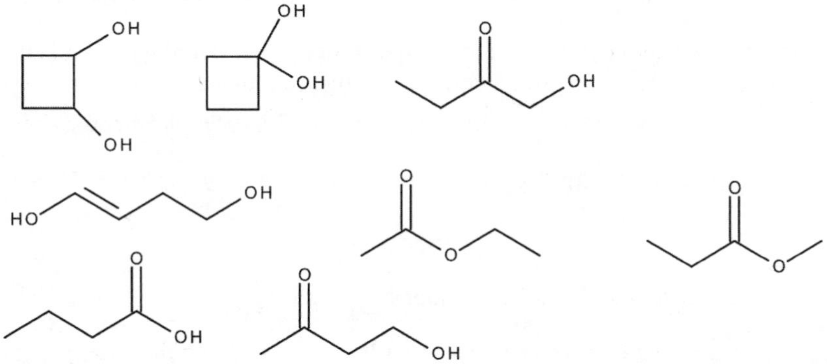

Conformational Isomerism

20.57   Newman projections for ohloroethane

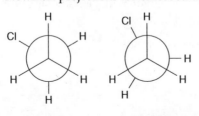

Staggered   Eclipsed

20.59   Newman projections for 1-chloropropane

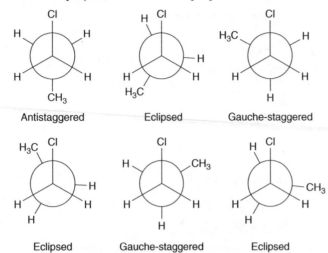

Antistaggered	Eclipsed	Gauche-staggered

Eclipsed	Gauche-staggered	Eclipsed

Configurational Isomerism

20.61   (a)   Since both CH_3 groups are on the same side of the double bond this molecule has a *cis* or *Z* configuration.

(b)   In this molecule the highest priority groups (CH_3 and Cl) are on opposite sides of the double bond and thus the configuration is *trans* or *E*.

(c)   This molecule is a little more complex than the previous two, so a diagram may be useful. The configuration is Z. Once there are more than two groups attached to the double bond, *cis* is not typically used.

On the left hand side of the double bond, Cl has priority over the CH3

On the right hand side of the double bond, the ethyl group has priority over the H

(d)   Using the same logic as in (c) above but with the groups shifted around in the molecule the configuration is *E*. Once there are more than two groups attached to the double bond, *trans* is not typically used.

On the left hand side of the double bond, CH3 has priority over the H

On the right hand side of the double bond, Cl has priority over the ethyl group

20.63   (a)   They are enantiomers, because they are mirror images of each other.

(b)   They are the same, because you can get the second molecule by rotating the first molecule counter-clockwise about the C—H bond.

(c)   They are enantiomers, because they are mirror images of each other.

20.65   (a)   They are the same, because the central carbon has only three different substituents and by rotation about the vertical C—CH_3 bond you can get the second molecule.

(b)   They are enantiomers, because they are mirror images of each other.

(c)   They are the same, because you can get the second molecule by rotating the first molecule counter-clockwise about the C—H bond.

20.67   (a)   This molecule has no chirality centre and therefore cannot be assigned an *R* or *S* configuration.

(b)   The *R* or *S* configuration can best be determined by assigning priorities to each group, then building a model and manipulating it to put the lowest priority group at the back. Failing that, mentally turn the model so that the lowest priority group goes into the page as shown below.

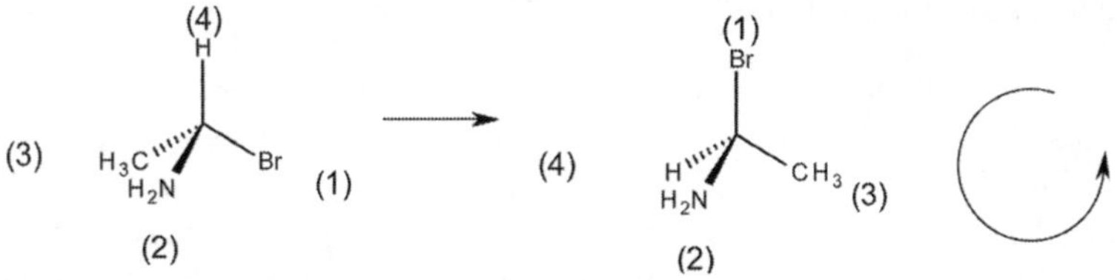

The molecule shown has an *S* configuration. Its mirror image, shown on the right of the question in the book, has an *R* configuration.

(c)   Since both molecules are the same only one needs to be evaluated. The configuration for both structures is *S*.

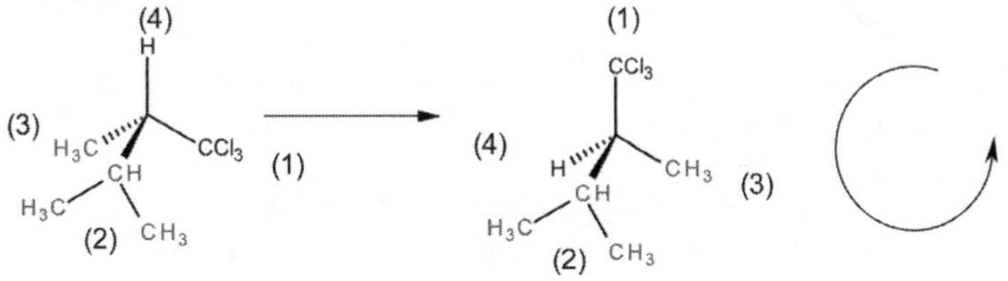

20.69   (a)   *S*, since the carbonyl group has first priority followed by the CH_2OH, then the methyl group, and finally the hydrogen.

(b)   *R*, since all the groups have a CH_2 attached to the chirality centre so go out to the next atom on the substituent to determine priority. (See diagram below.) The next step is to twist the molecule so that the lowest priority group is pointing into the paper.

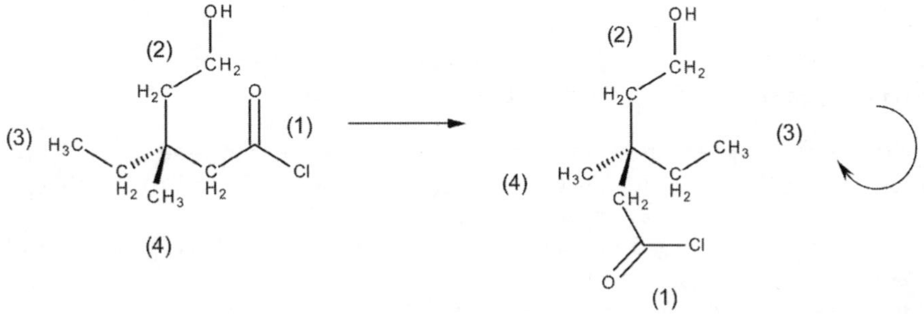

(c)   *S*, since the carbonyl group has first priority followed by the $CH=CH_2$, then the ethyl group, and finally the hydrogen. Then rotate the molecule clockwise along the carbon–carbonyl bond and follow the priorities.

(d)   *R*, since I has highest priority followed by Br and then the methyl group, with the hydrogen being lowest priority.

Structure Determination

20.71   (a)   IHD = 3; the parent formula for a compound with four carbons is C_4H_{10}. The presence of oxygen does not change the number of hydrogens in the parent formula. There are six missing hydrogen atoms, which when divided by two gives the IHD of three. This means there could be any combination of rings, double bonds, and triple bonds to add to three. (Keep in mind that IHD = one per ring, one per double bond, and two per triple bond.)

(b)   IHD = 3; the parent formula for a compound with four carbons is C_4H_{10}. The presence of oxygen does not change the number of hydrogens in the parent formula. There are six missing hydrogen atoms, which when divided by two gives the IHD of three. This means there could be any combination of rings, double bonds, and triple bonds to add to three. (Keep in mind that IHD = one per ring, one per double bond, and two per triple bond.)

(c)   IHD = 4; the parent formula for a compound with five carbons is C_5H_{12}. The presence of oxygen does not change the number of hydrogens in the parent formula. There are eight missing hydrogen atoms, which when divided by two gives the IHD of four. This means there could be any combination of rings, double bonds, and triple bonds to add to four. (Keep in mind that IHD = one per ring, one per double bond, and two per triple bond.) Typically, an IHD of four or higher suggests the presence of a benzene ring in the compound.

(d)   IHD = 6; the parent formula for a compound with six carbons is C_6H_{14}. The presence of oxygen does not change the number of hydrogens in the parent formula. The presence of nitrogen requires two additional hydrogen atoms in the parent formula, so it becomes C_6H_{16}. There are 12 missing hydrogen atoms, which when divided by two gives the IHD of six. This means there could be any combination of rings, double bonds, and triple bonds to add to six. (Keep in mind that IHD = one per ring, one per double bond, and two per triple bond.) Typically, an IHD of four or higher suggests the presence of a benzene ring in the compound.

20.73   (a)   IHD = 1; the parent formula for a compound with four carbons is C_4H_{10}. The presence of oxygen does not change the number of hydrogens in the parent formula. There are two missing hydrogen atoms, which when divided by two gives the IHD of one, thus a ring or a double bond may be found in the molecule. This most likely suggests that a carboxylic acid or ester could be present or a combination of a ketone or aldehyde group with an alcohol or ether group.

(b)   IHD = 0; the parent formula for a compound with three carbons is C_3H_8. The presence of oxygen does not change the number of hydrogens in the parent formula. There is no deficiency of hydrogens, thus no rings, double bonds, or triple bonds. This suggests an alcohol or an ether group must be present.

20.75   (a)   The frequency ranges of strong absorptions in the IR spectrum of an amine are 3100–3500 cm^{-1} for N—H (medium) and 2850–3300 cm^{-1} for C—H.

(b)   The frequency ranges of strong absorptions in the IR spectrum of a carboxylic acid are 3200–3500 cm^{-1} for O—H, 2850–3300 cm^{-1} for C—H, 1630–1800 cm^{-1} for C=O, and 1050–1250 cm^{-1} for C—O.

20.77   (a)   The number of different sets of chemically equivalent carbon atoms in the molecule shown below is three.

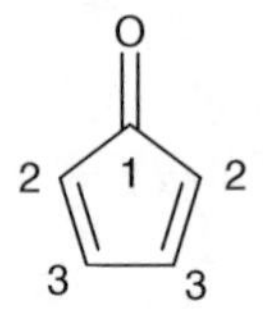

(b)   The number of different sets of chemically equivalent carbon atoms in 2-methylhexane is six.

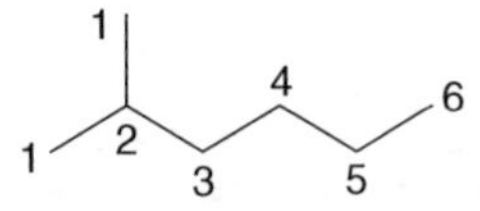

Cumulative Problems

20.79   There is no resonance structure for part (c).

(a)

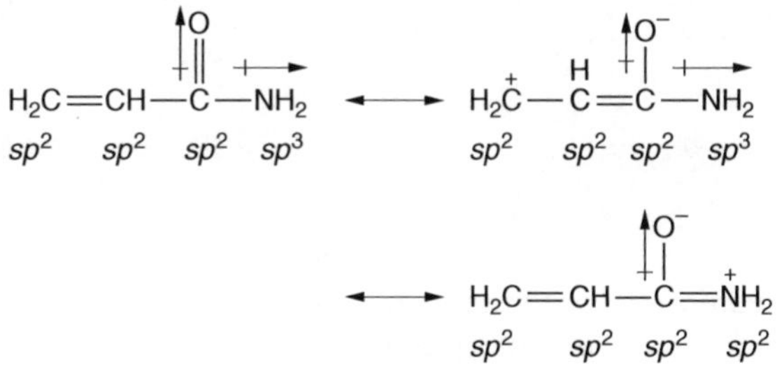

(b)

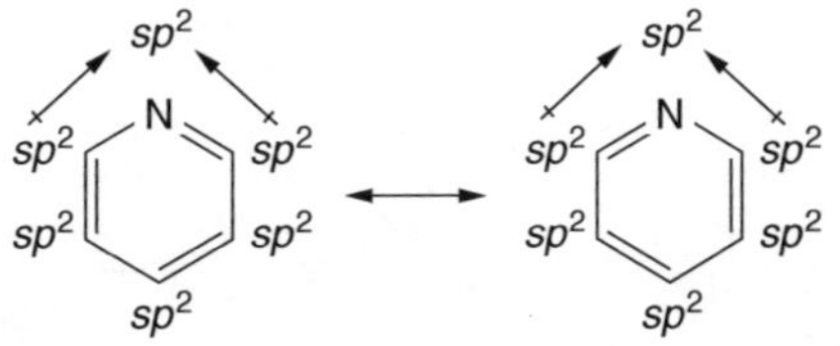

(c)

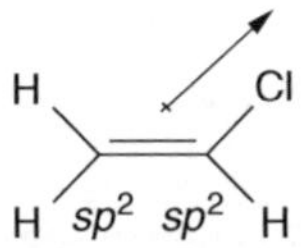

20.81   (a)   Here are some example answers that are different from the Answers appendix.

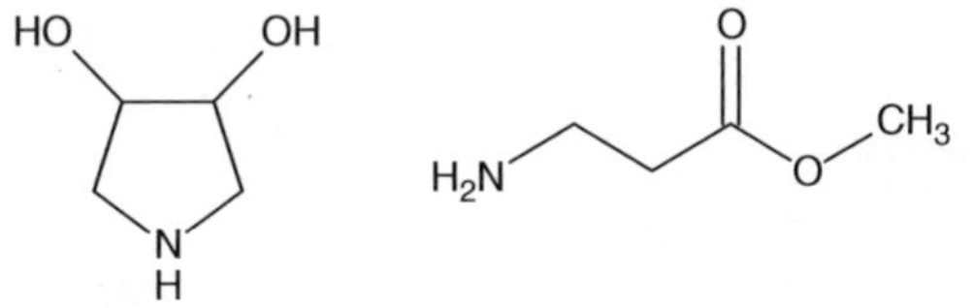

(b)   Here are some example answers that are different from the Answers appendix.

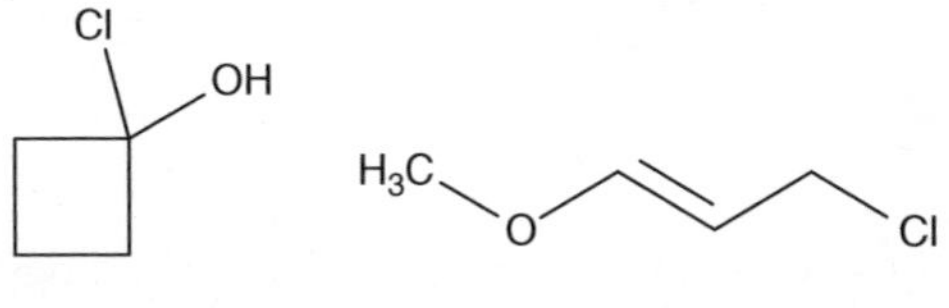

(c)   Here are some example answers that are different from the Answers appendix.

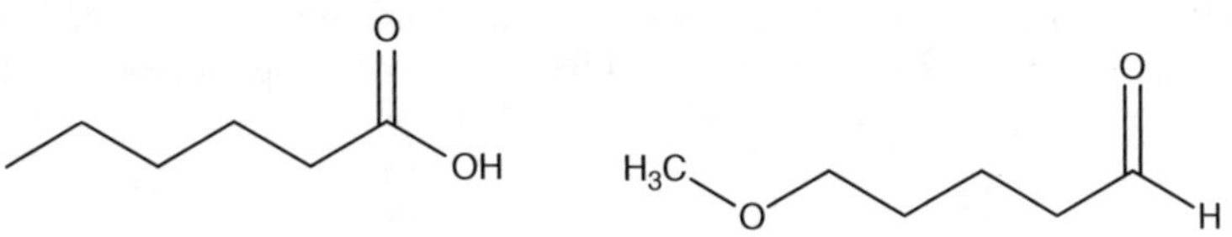

20.83   Structures b and c do not have a chirality centre. Structure a displays stereoisomerism. All are shown below:

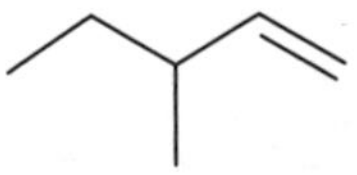

3-methylpent-1-ene 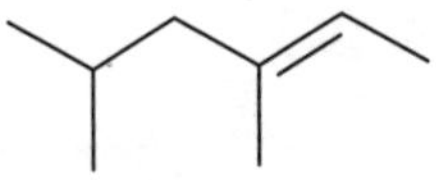   3,5-dimethylhex-2-ene 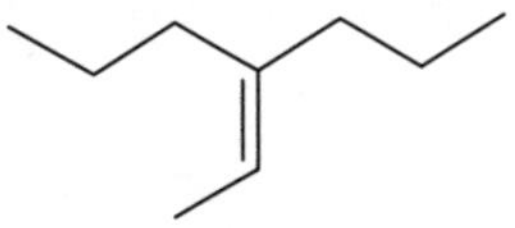   3-propylhex-2-ene

20.85   Seven alcohols with formula C_4H_8O are shown below. Several others are possible.

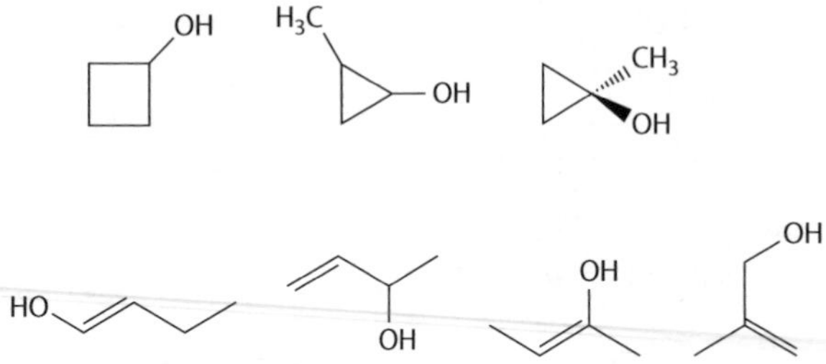

20.87   (a)   IHD = 1; the parent formula for a compound with three carbons is C_3H_8. The presence of oxygen does not change the number of hydrogens in the parent formula. There are two missing hydrogen atoms, which when divided by two gives the IHD of one. This means there could be a ring or a double bond.

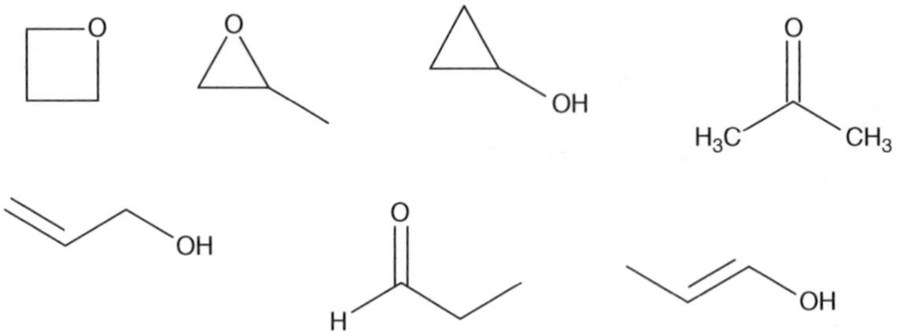

                 (b)   IHD = 1; the parent formula for a compound with five carbons is C_5H_{12}. The presence of oxygen does not change the number of hydrogens in the parent formula. There are two missing hydrogen atoms, which when divided by two gives the IHD of one. This means there could be a ring or a double bond. There are many possibilities for potential structures.

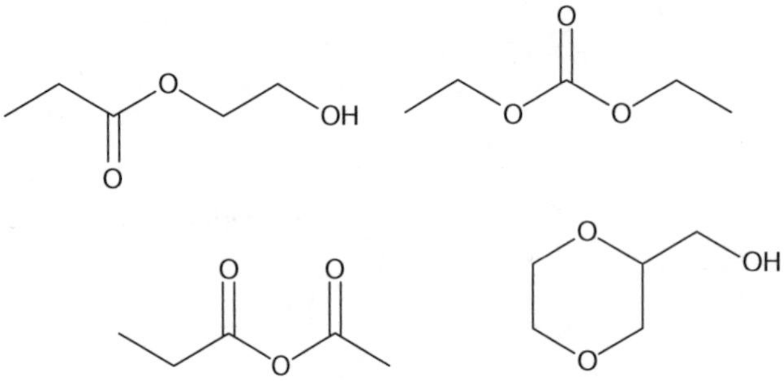

                 (c)   IHD = 4; the parent formula for a compound with six carbons is C_6H_{14}. The halogen atoms are considered to be equivalent to hydrogen atoms, so they are added to the number of hydrogens to bring the number to six in the parent formula. There are eight missing hydrogen atoms, which when divided by two gives the IHD of four. This means there could be any combination of rings, double bonds, and triple bonds to add to four. (Keep in mind that IHD = one per ring, one per double bond, and two per triple bond.) Typically, an IHD of four or higher suggests the presence of a benzene ring in the compound.

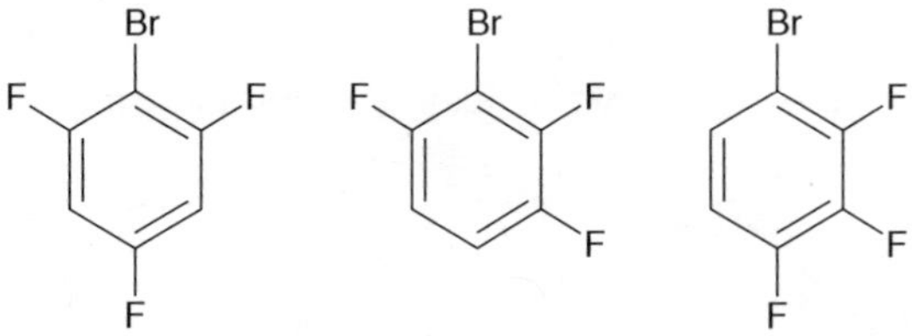

20.89   (a)   The strong absorptions in the IR spectrum are at 2850–3300 cm^{-1} for C—H, 3200–3500 cm^{-1} for O—H, and 1050–1250 cm^{-1} for C—O. There are six absorptions in the ^{13}C NMR spectrum.

(b)   The strong absorptions in the IR spectrum are at 2850–3300 cm^{-1} for C—H and 1630–1800 cm^{-1} for C=O. There are three absorptions in the ^{13}C NMR spectrum.

Challenge Problems

20.91   The chirality centres are indicated below with numbers 1 – 5. The double bonds are labelled a – c.

Centre **1** is *S* with OH as priority 1, the carbon going toward bond **b** as priority 2, the carbon going toward bond **a** as priority 3, and the H (not shown) as priority 4.

Centre **2** is *R* with the carbon of bond **c** as priority 1, carbon **3** as priority 2, carbon **4** as priority 3, and the H (not shown) as priority 4.

Centre **3** is *R* with carbon **2** as priority 1, carbon **4** as priority 2, the unlabelled carbon above 3 as priority 3, and the CH$_3$ (shown as a solid wedge) as priority 4.

Centre **4** is *R* with carbon **3** as priority 1, the solid wedge as priority 2, the CH$_2$ below carbon **4** as priority 3, and the H (not shown) as priority 4.

Centre **5** is *S* with the solid wedge as priority 1, the CH$_2$ to the right of carbon **5** as priority 2, the dashed wedge as priority 3, and the H (not shown) as priority 4.

Bond **a** has no possible *cis–trans* or *E/Z* isomerism because one end is a CH$_2$ and thus both atoms coming from the double bond are identical.

Bond **b** is *Z*. The left-hand carbon of the double bond is attached to a CH$_2$ attached to one C (low priority) and a C attached to 3 C's (high priority). The right-hand carbon is attached to an H (low priority) and a C (high priority). Since the high-priority groups are both on the bottom of the double bond (same side) the configuration is *Z*.

Bond **c** is *E*. The left-hand carbon is attached to an H (low priority) and a C (high priority). The right-hand carbon of the double bond is attached to a CH$_2$ attached to one C (low priority) and a C attached to 2 C's (high priority). Since the high-priority groups are above and below the double bond (opposite sides) the configuration is *E*.

20.93   There are eight sets of chemically equivalent carbon atoms in indigo, as indicated below:

20.95   The molecular formula of C$_3$H$_8$O gives an IHD = 0, meaning no rings, no double bonds, and no triple bonds. The IR shows a strong absorption at 3100 cm^{-1}, which is consistent with an O—H group. There are three signals in the ^{13}C NMR, suggesting that each carbon in the molecule is unique. This leads to the identity of propan-1-ol.

20.97   The molecular formula of C$_4$H$_{10}$O gives an IHD = 0. There is no deficiency of hydrogens, thus no rings, double bonds, or triple bonds. The ^{13}C NMR shows only two absorptions, meaning there are only two sets of chemically equivalent carbon atoms. This suggests symmetry in the compound. Finally, the IR shows no O—H absorption, suggesting an ether. The compound is ethoxyethane, commonly known as diethyl ether.

20.99   The molecular formula C$_8$H$_8$ has an IHD = 5. There are no double bonds or triple bonds, thus the hydrogen deficiency is due solely to the presence of rings. The single absorption in the ^{13}C NMR means there is only one set of chemically equivalent carbon atoms. The hint states that the compound is known as cubane.

Drawing a cube and then analyzing it shows five rings and massive symmetry resulting in all carbons being chemically equivalent.

Conceptual Problems

20.101   Structures b and d are chiral since they each have one carbon atom with four different groups attached.

20.103   There are four sets of chemically equivalent carbon atoms.

21 Organic Chemistry II: Reactions

21.1 An inductive effect results from bond polarization due to adjacent, electronegative atoms. When an electronegative atom is nearby it induces a dipole. The dipole, in turn, polarizes the nearby C—H bond making the molecule more acidic.

When a hydrogen atom is removed from a molecule a conjugate base with a negative charge results. If the charge can be delocalized or distributed through the molecule, the conjugate base is said to be resonance stabilized. This causes the original molecule to be more acidic than a molecule that cannot resonance stabilize its conjugate base.

21.3 The acid or base reagent chosen should be just strong enough to take a reaction to completion while minimizing the cost and safety risk.

21.5 Hydrocarbon combustion reactions involve hydrocarbons being burned in oxygen to produce carbon dioxide and water. The carbon atoms are oxidized in the process. For example:

$$C_3H_8 + 5\,O_2 \rightarrow 3\,CO_2 + 4\,H_2O$$

21.7 The products of the oxidation of primary alcohols are aldehydes or carboxylic acids. The products of the oxidation of secondary alcohols are ketones. Reagents used to accomplish this are listed in Table 21.2 on page 918 of the textbook. A common oxidizing reagent is Jones reagent, which is an aqueous solution of potassium dichromate and sulfuric acid.

21.9 A nucleophilic substitution reaction is a reaction where a molecule or ion (known as a nucleophile) donates a lone pair of electrons to a carbon atom (known as an electrophile) that is in a polar bond with another atom or group of atoms (known as the leaving group) causing that group to leave. An example of such a reaction is given below:

$$\begin{array}{cccc} HO^- & + & CH_3CH_2Br \rightarrow & CH_3CH_2OH + Br^- \\ \text{Nucleophile} & & \text{substrate} & \text{product} \qquad \text{leaving group} \end{array}$$

21.11 A nucleophile is a molecule or ion capable of donating a lone pair of electrons to an electrophile. Some good nucleophiles are OH^-, CN^-, and RS^-. Others can be found in Table 21.3 on page 924 of the textbook.

21.13 In an S_N1 mechanism the leaving group leaves and the electrophilic carbon becomes a carbocation. The nucleophile attacks the carbocation, which is planar, from either side of the plane forming a racemic mixture. In an S_N2 mechanism the nucleophile approaches the electrophilic carbon from the side of the molecule opposite to the leaving group. During the transition state the leaving group gradually pulls away from the electrophile. The alkyl groups attached to the electrophilic carbon gradually move away from the nucleophile and toward the space previously occupied by the leaving group causing an inversion of configuration.

21.15 Zaitsev's rule says that if more than one alkene is produced in a reaction, the major product (the one produced in the largest amount) is the most substituted alkene. In the example below the left-hand product is the most substituted and thus the major product.

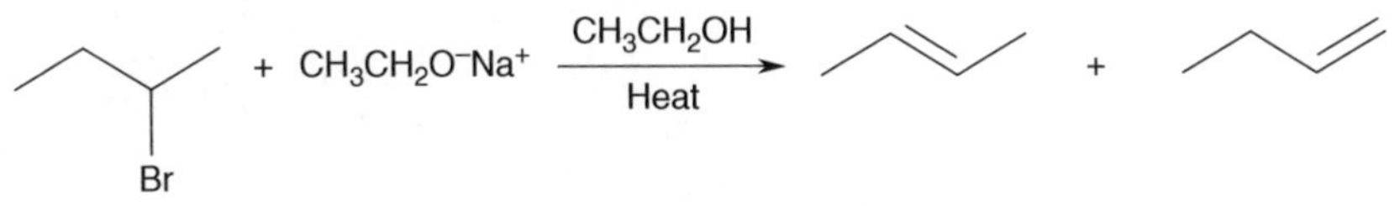

21.17   An oxonium ion is formed when the —OH group on a molecule is protonated to form —OH_2^+. It is important because the OH group by itself is not a good leaving group. but when protonated to form the oxonium ion it becomes a very good leaving group.

21.19   Elimination reactions and electrophilic addition reactions are mechanistically similar in that both reactions involve an electrophile forming a new bond with a nucleophile by accepting a pair of electrons.

21.21   Nucleophilic addition to aldehydes and ketones occurs by having the nucleophile attack the carbon of the carbonyl group that is electrophilic. This causes the π bond to break, leaving a single bond between carbon and oxygen and a negative charge on oxygen. Finally, the oxygen reacts with a hydrogen atom to form the OH group.

21.23   A Grignard reaction is the reaction between an aldehyde or ketone and a Grignard reagent. A Grignard reagent has the general formula RMgX (X = I, Br, Cl) and is made by reacting RX with magnesium metal in an anhydrous ether solvent (anhydrous means without water). A Grignard reaction is an important way of attaching carbon atoms to each other. The carbon atom attached to the magnesium in the Grignard reagent holds a partial negative charge and thus acts at the nucleophile, while the carbon atom of the carbonyl group in the aldehyde or ketone holds a partial positive charge and acts as the electrophile.

21.25   Acyl groups consist of a carbonyl group attached to a good leaving group, such as a halogen or an alkoxy group. When an acyl group is attacked by a nucleophile, a substitution of the nucleophile for the leaving group occurs. Since some leaving groups are better than others, a more reactive acyl group can be converted into a less reactive acyl group, but the opposite does not occur easily. Interconversions of acyl groups are shown in Table 21.5 on page 935 of the textbook.

21.27   A polymer is a long, chain-like molecule composed of repeating units called monomers. A monomer is the repeating unit. A monomer can be a simple molecule like ethene or ethan-1,2-diol, or it can be a very complex molecule with several different functional groups.

21.29   Two well-known examples of step-growth polymers are polyesters and nylon. Kevlar is also a step-growth polymer. Two well-known examples of addition polymers are polyethylene and polyvinylchloride (PVC).

Problems by Topic

Organic Acids and Bases

21.31   The Lewis structures of the conjugate bases are as follows:

(a)

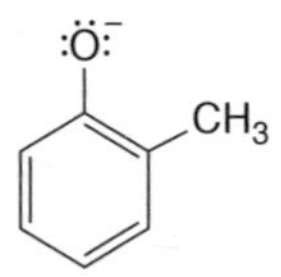

(b)

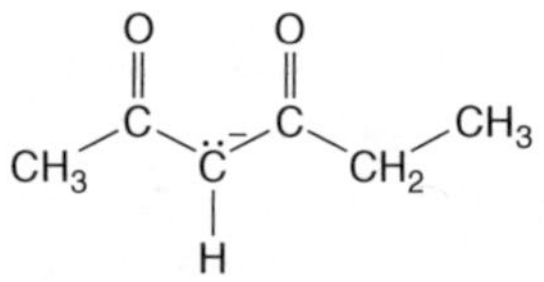

(c) $CH_3CH_2NH_2$

(d) $CH_3CH_2CO_2^-$

21.33 The mechanisms for the reactions with sulfuric acid are as follows:

(a)

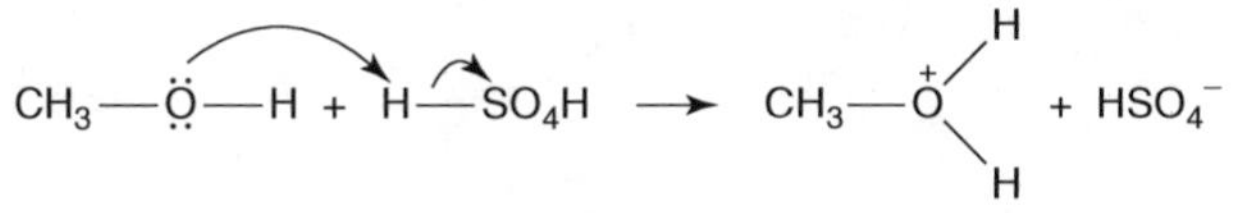

$$CH_3-\overset{..}{O}-H + H-SO_4H \longrightarrow CH_3-\overset{+}{\overset{H}{\underset{H}{O}}} + HSO_4^-$$

(b)

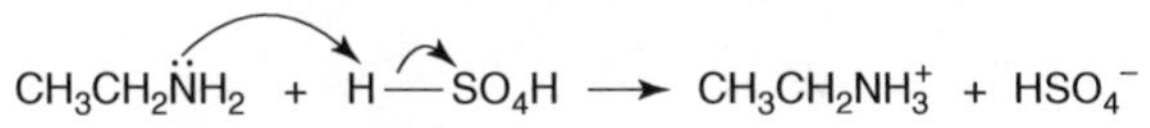

$$CH_3CH_2\overset{..}{N}H_2 + H-SO_4H \longrightarrow CH_3CH_2NH_3^+ + HSO_4^-$$

(c)

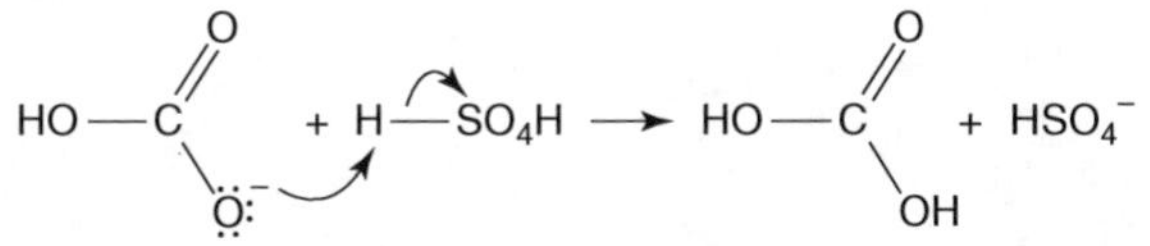

$$HO-\overset{O}{\overset{\|}{C}}\underset{\overset{..}{O}:^-}{} + H-SO_4H \longrightarrow HO-\overset{O}{\overset{\|}{C}}_{OH} + HSO_4^-$$

(d)

$$CH_3-\overset{..}{O}:^- + H-SO_4H \longrightarrow CH_3-OH + HSO_4^-$$

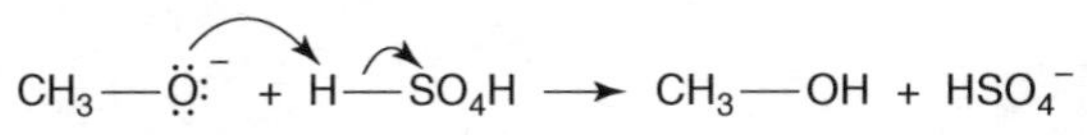

21.35 (a) A strong base is needed, so $NaNH_2$ would be best.

(b) Any base will work, so NH_3, $NaOH$, etc.

(c) Any acid will work, so HCl is a good idea.

21.37 The resonance structures of the conjugate bases are as follows:

(a)

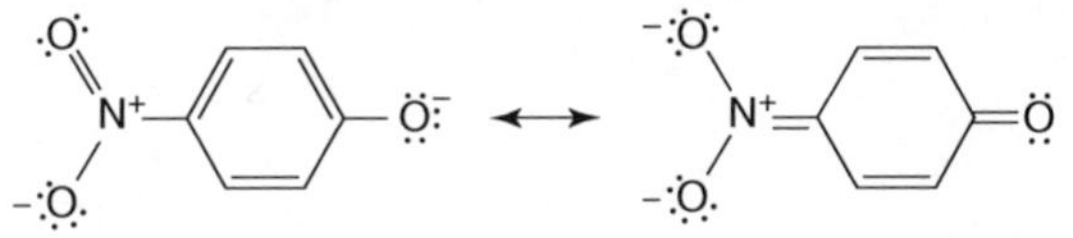

(b)

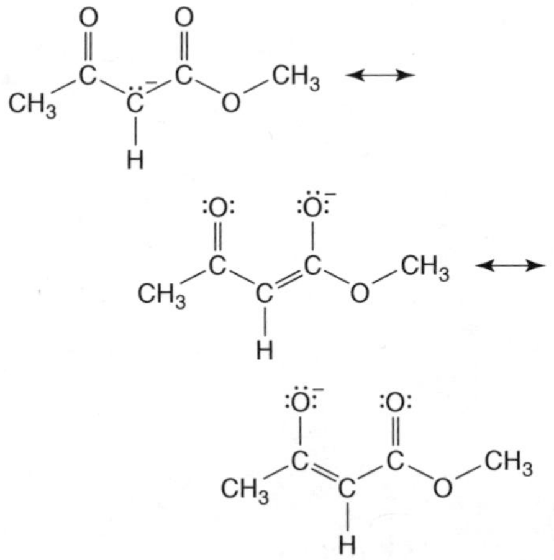

Oxidation and Reduction

21.39 The rules for calculating oxidation states for carbon atoms in organic molecules are given on page 916 of the textbook. Using those rules, the following oxidation states are assigned:

(a) The CH_3— carbon is assigned –1 for each bond to hydrogen and 0 for the bond to carbon.

The $C{=}O$ carbon is assigned +1 for each bond to oxygen and –1 for the bond to hydrogen.

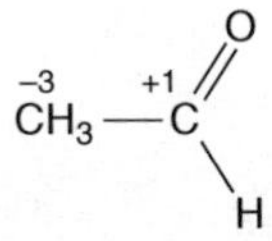

$$\overset{-3}{CH_3}-\overset{+1}{C}\overset{O}{\underset{H}{\diagup}}$$

(b)   The CH_3— carbon is assigned –1 for each bond to hydrogen and 0 for the bond to carbon.

The $C\equiv$carbon is only attached to carbon and so is assigned 0.

$$\overset{-3}{CH_3}-\overset{0}{C}\equiv\overset{0}{C}-\overset{-3}{CH_3}$$

(c)   Each of these carbons is assigned +1 for the Cl and –1 for the hydrogen.

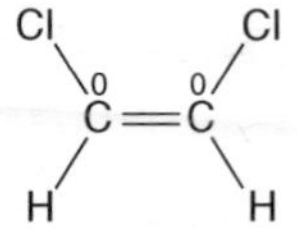

21.41   (a) $CH_3CH_2CH_3 + 5\,O_2 \rightarrow 3\,CO_2 + 4\,H_2O$

(b) $H_2C{=}CHCH_2CH_3 + 6\,O_2 \rightarrow 4\,CO_2 + 4\,H_2O$

(c) $2\,HC{\equiv}CH + 5\,O_2 \rightarrow 4\,CO_2 + 2\,H_2O$

21.43   (a)

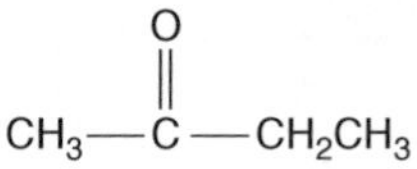

(b) $CH_3CH_2CH_2CH_2CH_3$

(c)

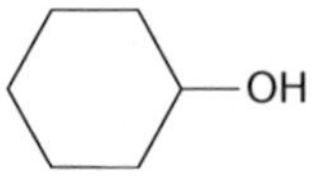

(d) $CH_3CH_2CH_2NO_2$

21.45   (a) $K_2Cr_2O_7, H_2SO_4$ (b) $H_2, Pd/C$

Nucleophilic Substitution Reactions

21.47   (a)

(b) $CH_3CH_2CHCH_3$ + NaI $\longrightarrow$ $CH_3CH_2CHCH_3$ + NaBr
                | |
                Br   I

(c) $(CH_3CH_2)_2NH$ + $ClCH_2CH_2OH$ $\xrightarrow{\text{NaOH}}$

$(CH_3CH_2)_2N{-}CH_2CH_2OH$ + H_2O + NaCl

21.49   (a) S_N1— a tertiary substrate is being attacked by a weak nucleophile.

(b) S_N2— a primary substrate is being attacked by a strong nucleophile.

21.51   (a)

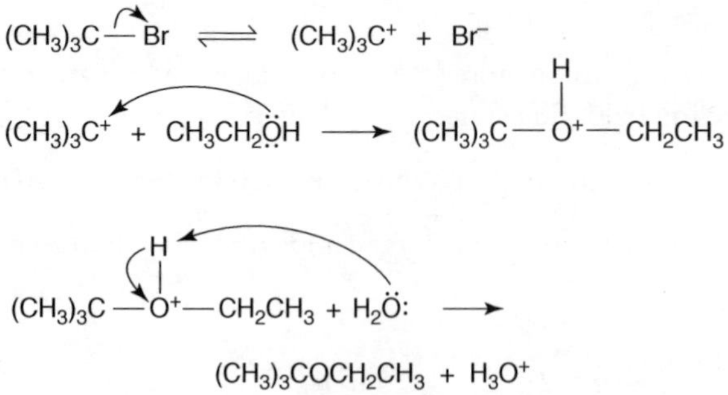

(b)

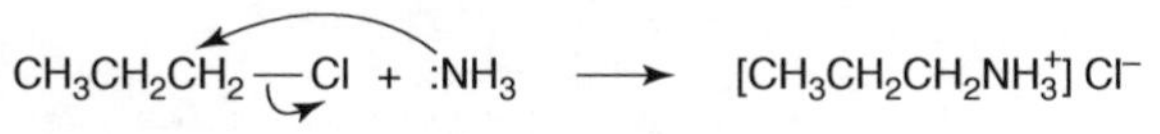

$$CH_3CH_2CH_2 - Cl + :NH_3 \longrightarrow [CH_3CH_2CH_2NH_3^+] \, Cl^-$$

21.53   (a)   inversion

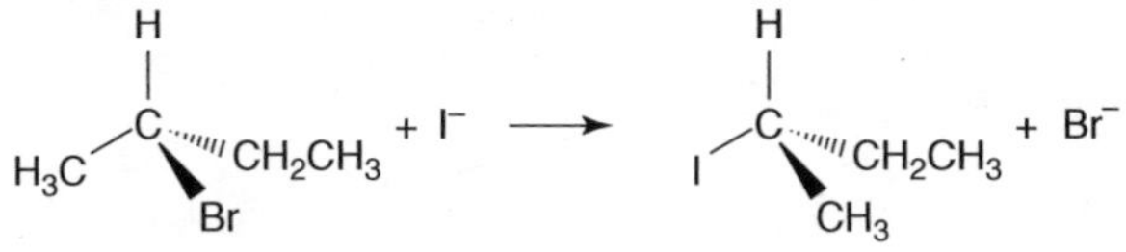

(b)   inversion

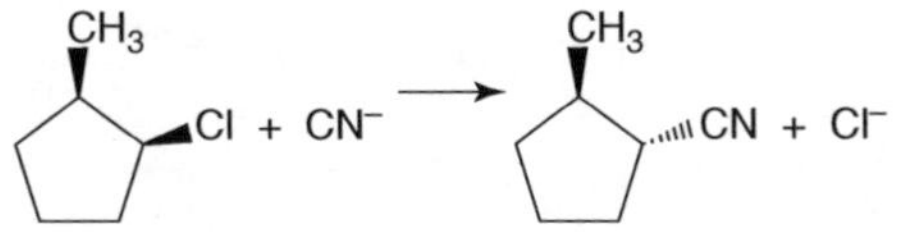

(c)   racemization

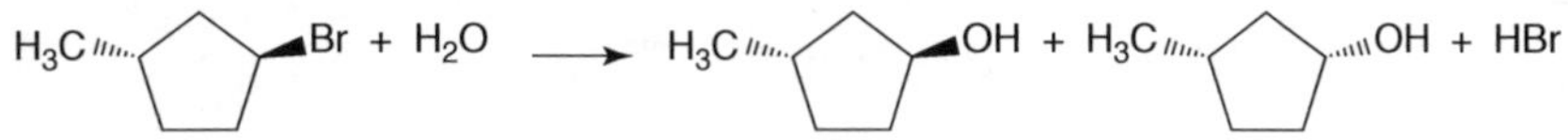

Elimination Reactions

21.55   (a)

$$CH_3CH_2CH_2CH_2CH_2OH \xrightarrow[\text{Heat}]{H_2SO_4} CH_3CH_2CH_2CH=CH_2 + H_2O$$

(b)

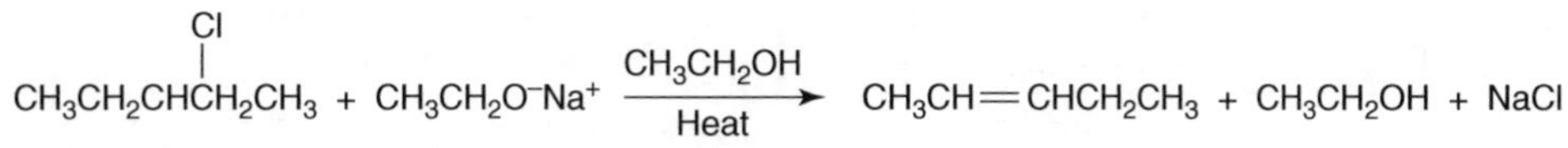

(c)

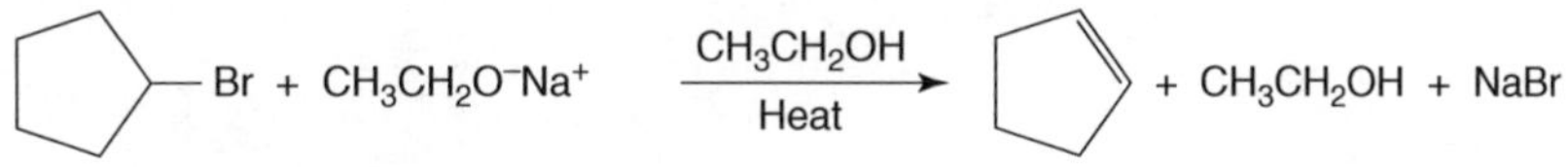

(d)

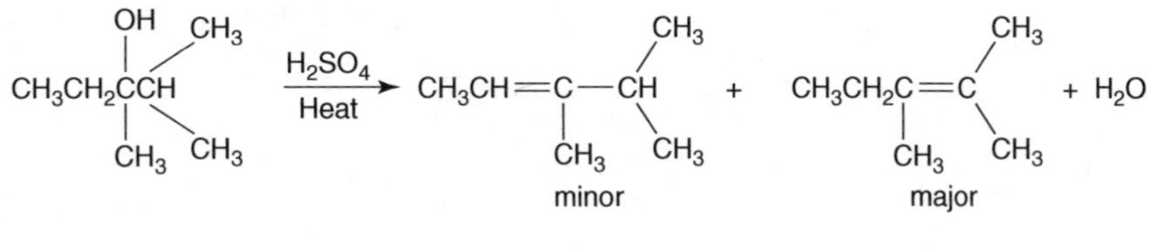

21.57   (a)

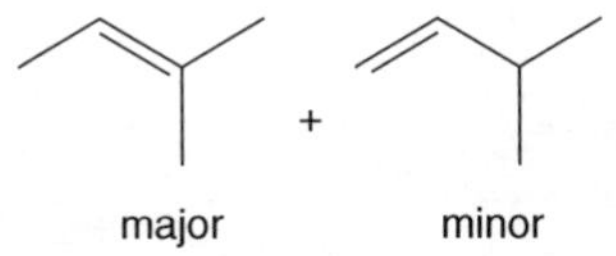

major   minor

(b)

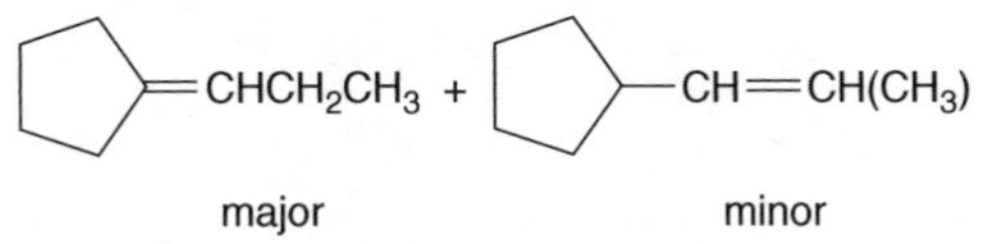

major   minor

(c)

major   minor

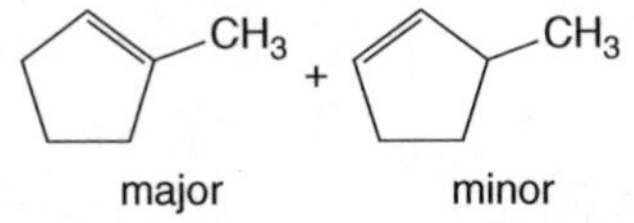

21.59   (a)   E2—secondary substrate with strong base

(b)   E1—tertiary substrate with weak base

21.61   (a)

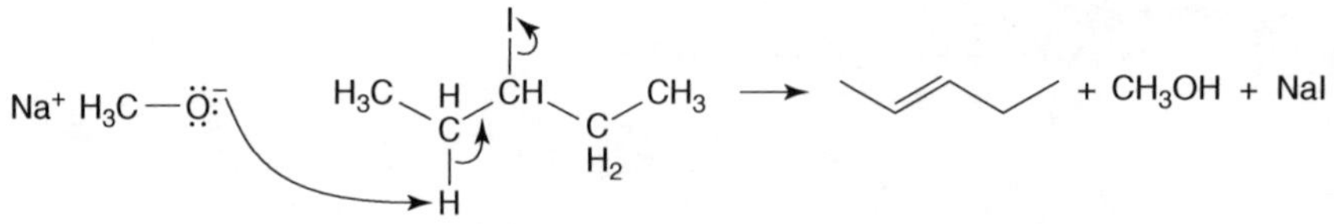

Na⁺ H₃C—Ö:⁻   H₃C, H CH—C—CH₃   ⟶   ⟍⟍⟋⟍ + CH₃OH + NaI

(b)

⟍Cl ⇌ ⟍⁺ + Cl⁻

⟍⁺—CH + HÖCH₃ ⟶ ⟍C=⟋ + H₂O⁺CH₃

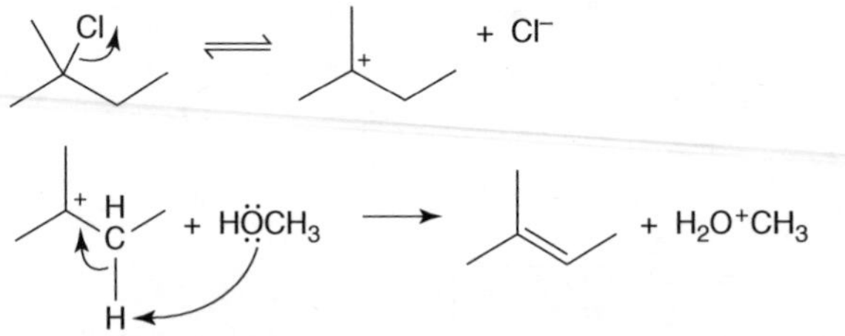

H₂O⁺CH₃ + Cl⁻ ⟶ HOCH₃ + HCl

Electrophilic Additions to Alkenes

21.63   (a)

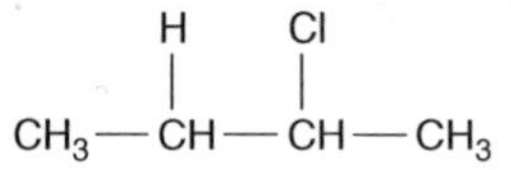

$$CH_3-\underset{\underset{H}{|}}{CH}-\underset{\underset{Cl}{|}}{CH}-CH_3$$

(b)

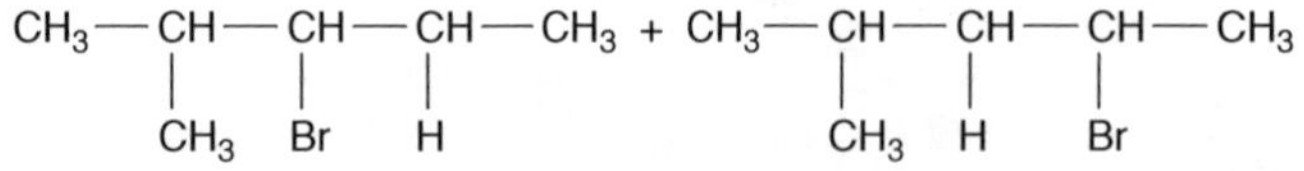

$$CH_3-CH-\underset{\underset{CH_3}{|}}{CH}-\underset{\underset{Br}{|}}{CH}-\underset{\underset{H}{|}}{CH}-CH_3 + CH_3-\underset{\underset{CH_3}{|}}{CH}-\underset{\underset{H}{|}}{CH}-\underset{\underset{Br}{|}}{CH}-CH_3$$

(c)

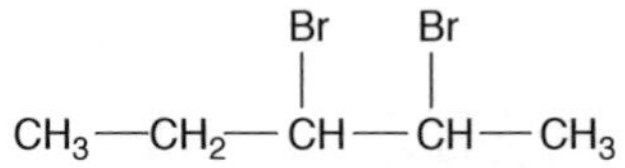

$$CH_3-CH_2-\underset{\underset{Br}{|}}{CH}-\underset{\underset{Br}{|}}{CH}-CH_3$$

(d)

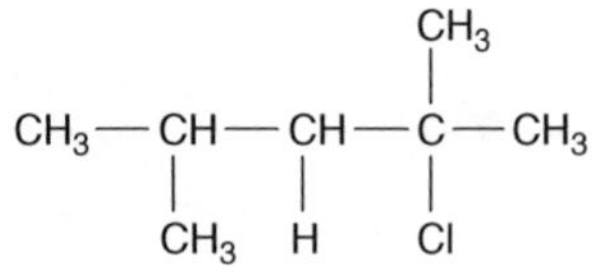

$$CH_3-\underset{\underset{CH_3}{|}}{CH}-\underset{\underset{H}{|}}{CH}-\underset{\underset{Cl}{|}}{\overset{\overset{CH_3}{|}}{C}}-CH_3$$

21.65   (a)

$$CH_3-\underset{\underset{CH_3}{|}}{CH}-CH=CH_2 + H_2 \xrightarrow{Pd/C} CH_3-\underset{\underset{CH_3}{|}}{CH}-CH_2-CH_3$$

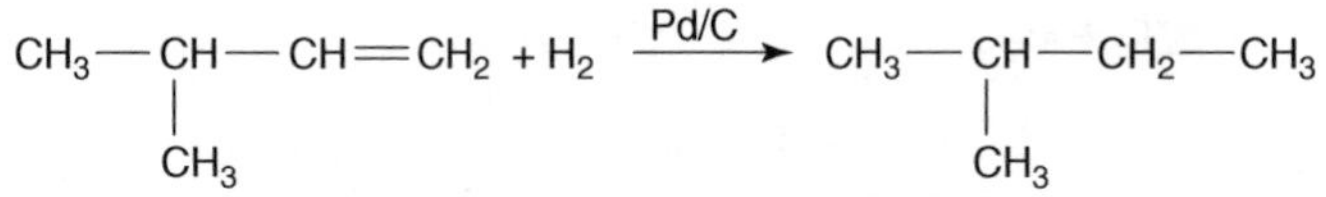

(b)

$$CH_2=CH-CH_3 + H_2 \xrightarrow{Pd/C} CH_3-CH_2-CH_3$$

21.67   (a)

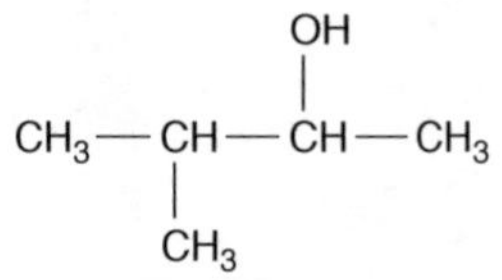

$$CH_3-\underset{\underset{CH_3}{|}}{CH}-\underset{\overset{\overset{OH}{|}}{}}{CH}-CH_3$$

(b)

(cyclohexane oxide / epoxide structure)

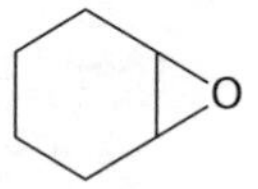

(c)

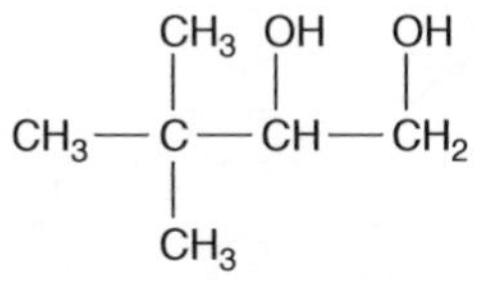

$$CH_3-\underset{\underset{CH_3}{|}}{\overset{\overset{CH_3}{|}}{C}}-\underset{\underset{}{\overset{OH}{|}}}{CH}-\underset{\underset{}{\overset{OH}{|}}}{CH_2}$$

21.69   (a)   This requires an acid-catalyzed addition of water to a double bond. Use H^+, H_2O.

(b)   This requires an addition of HCl to the double bond.

(c)   This is a hydrogenation reaction, so use H_2 and the Pd/C catalyst.

(d)   Addition of two bromine atoms to a double bond requires the use of Br_2.

Nucleophilic Additions to Aldehydes and Ketones

21.71   (a)

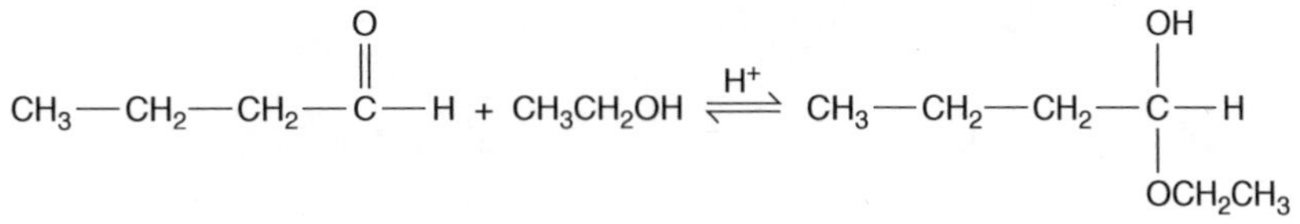

$$CH_3-CH_2-CH_2-\overset{\overset{O}{\|}}{C}-H + CH_3CH_2OH \underset{}{\overset{H^+}{\rightleftharpoons}} CH_3-CH_2-CH_2-\underset{\underset{OCH_2CH_3}{|}}{\overset{\overset{OH}{|}}{C}}-H$$

(b)

$$CH_3-CH_2-\overset{\overset{O}{\|}}{C}-CH_3 + CH_3-\underset{}{\overset{\overset{OH}{|}}{CH}}-CH_3 \underset{}{\overset{H^+}{\rightleftharpoons}} CH_3-CH_2-\underset{\underset{O-CH(CH_3)_2}{|}}{\overset{\overset{OH}{|}}{C}}-CH_3$$

(c)

cyclopentyl$-\overset{\overset{O}{\|}}{C}-H$ + CH_3OH $\overset{H^+}{\rightleftharpoons}$ cyclopentyl$-\underset{\underset{OCH_3}{|}}{\overset{\overset{OH}{|}}{C}}-H$

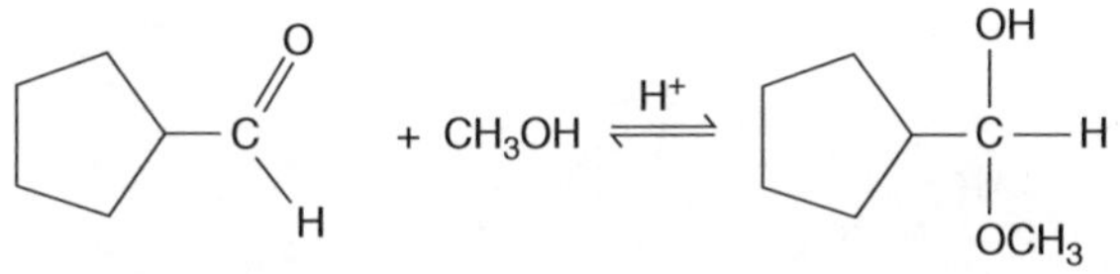

21.73   (a)

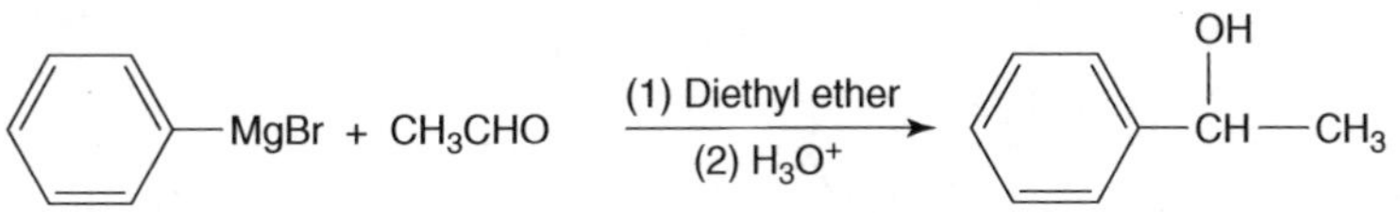

phenyl$-MgBr$ + CH_3CHO $\xrightarrow[\text{(2) } H_3O^+]{\text{(1) Diethyl ether}}$ phenyl$-\underset{}{\overset{\overset{OH}{|}}{CH}}-CH_3$

(b)

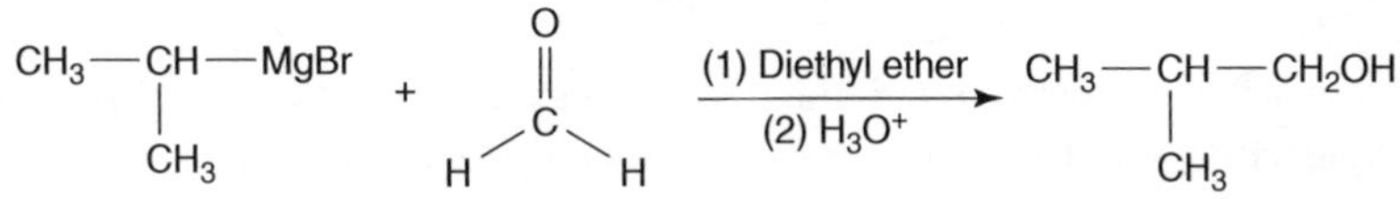

$CH_3-\underset{\underset{CH_3}{|}}{CH}-MgBr$ + $\overset{\overset{O}{\|}}{\underset{H \quad H}{C}}$ $\xrightarrow[\text{(2) } H_3O^+]{\text{(1) Diethyl ether}}$ $CH_3-\underset{\underset{CH_3}{|}}{CH}-CH_2OH$

(c)

CH_3MgI + $CH_3CH_2\overset{\overset{O}{\|}}{C}CH_2CH_3$ $\xrightarrow[\text{(2) } H_3O^+]{\text{(1) Diethyl ether}}$ $CH_3CH_2\underset{\underset{CH_3}{|}}{\overset{\overset{OH}{|}}{C}}CH_2CH_3$

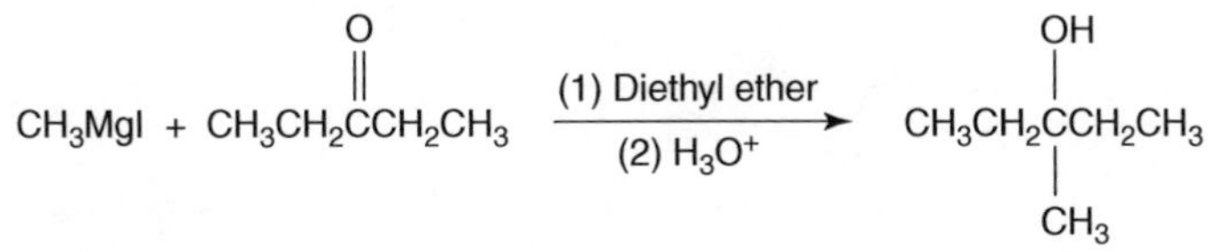

21.75   (a)

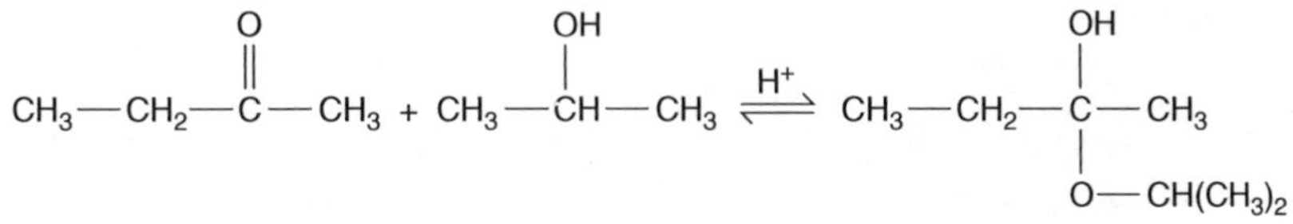

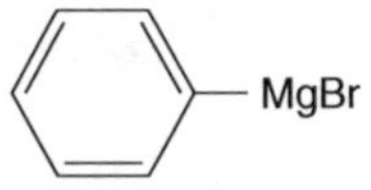

phenyl$-MgBr$

(b)

cyclohexyl$-MgBr$

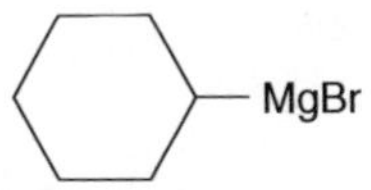

Nucleophilic Substitutions of Acyl Compounds

21.77   (a)

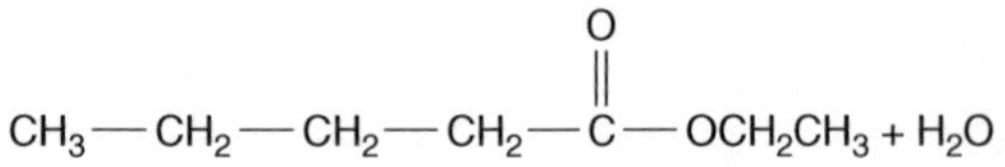

$$CH_3-CH_2-CH_2-CH_2-\overset{\displaystyle O}{\overset{\|}{C}}-OCH_2CH_3 + H_2O$$

(b)

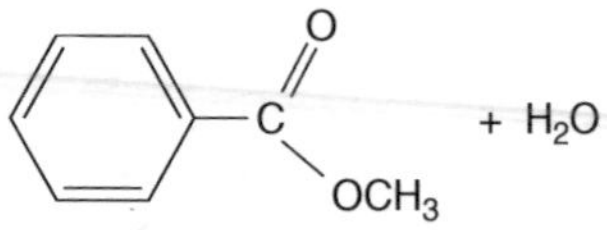

21.79   (a)

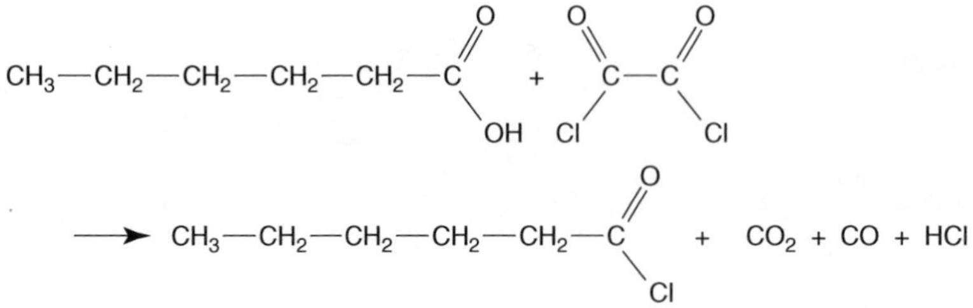

(b)

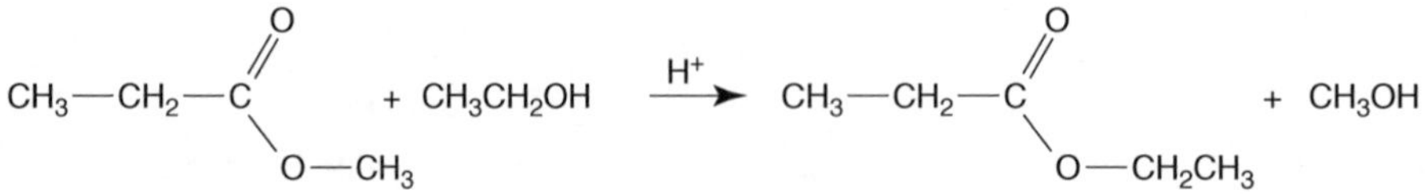

(c)

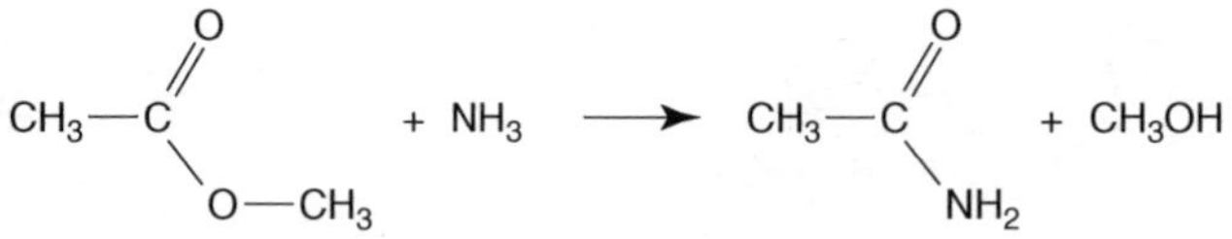

(d)

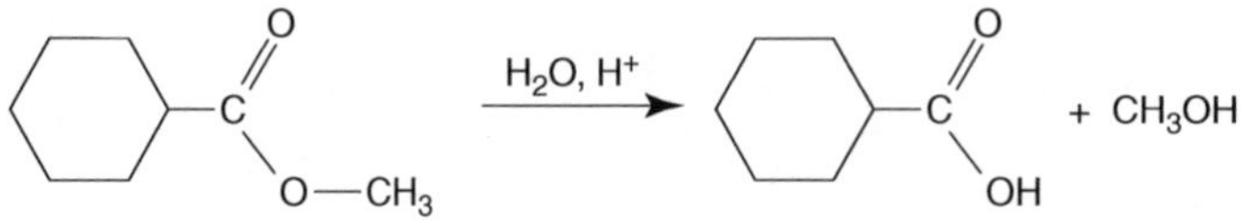

21.81   (a)   Keep in mind that when there are functional groups at each end of the molecule, and if they are four or five atoms apart, they will form five- or six-membered rings.

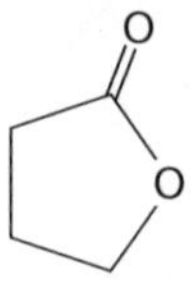

(b)

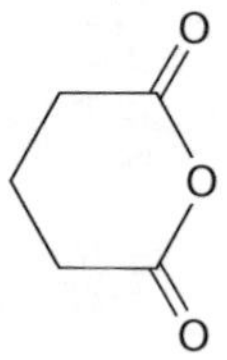

21.83   (a)   When looking at the reactant and product, look for what has changed. In this case the Cl has been replaced by an O_2CCH_3 group. The best reactant to use to do this would be NaO_2CCH_3.

       (b)   In order to convert a carboxylic acid to an amide it is best to convert first to an acyl halide, which is more reactive, and then convert to the amide. So for step 1 use $SOCl_2$ or $(COCl)_2$ and then use $HN(CH_3)_2$. Also remember that the conversion to an amide requires two equivalents of the amine.

Electrophilic Aromatic Substitutions

21.85   (a)

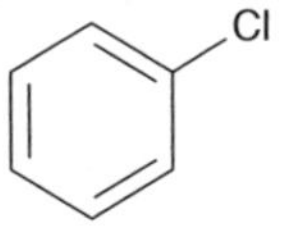

       (b)

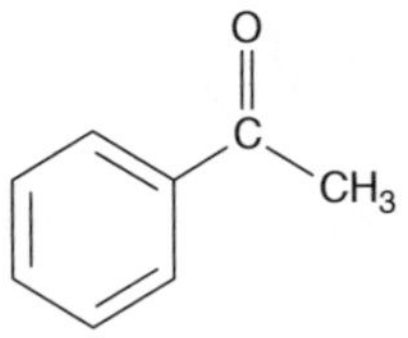

       (c)

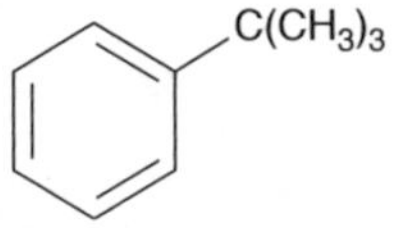

21.87   (a)

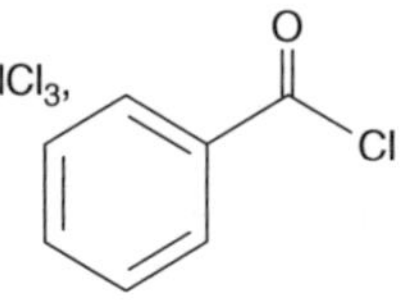

       (b) $AlCl_3$,

       (c) Cl_2, $FeCl_3$

Polymerization

21.89   Teflon, a polymer of tetrafluoroethene

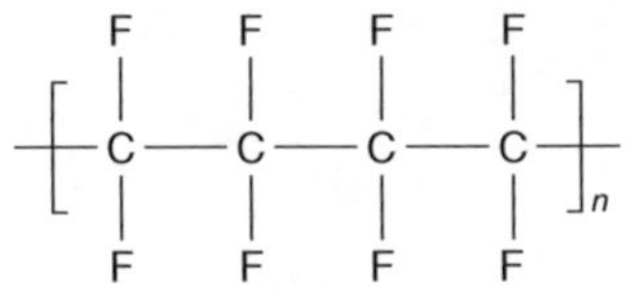

21.91   The dimer of terephthalic acid and ethylene glycol

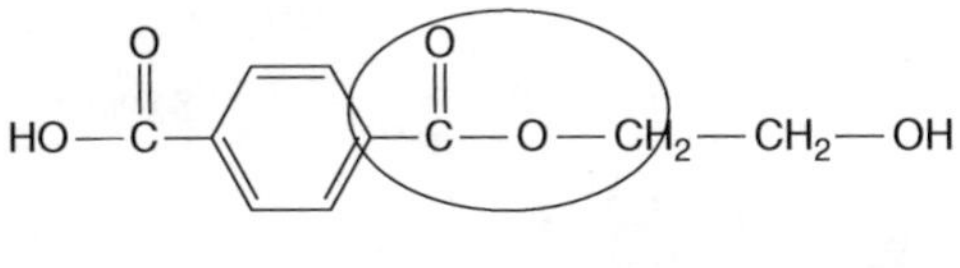

21.93   (a)

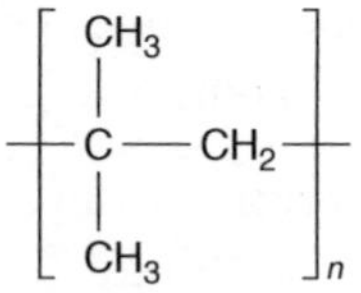

     (b)

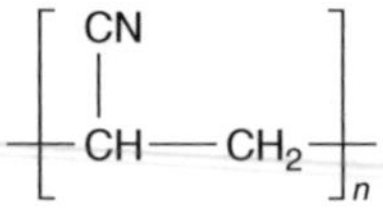

Cumulative Problems

21.95   (a)   acid–base

     (b)   nucleophilic substitution

     (c)   nucleophilic addition

     (d)   nucleophilic substitution

21.97   (a)   racemic mixture

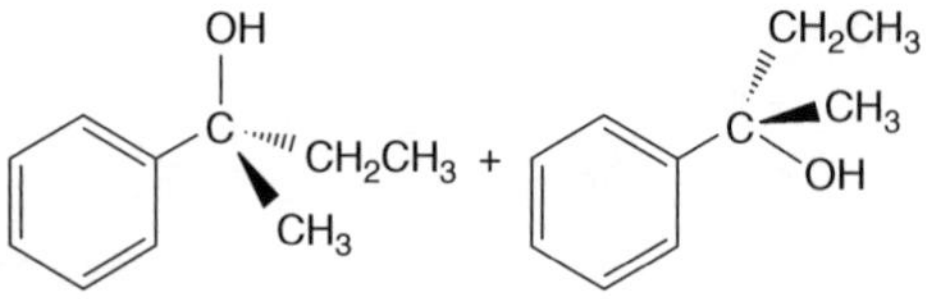

     (b)   *R* enantiomer

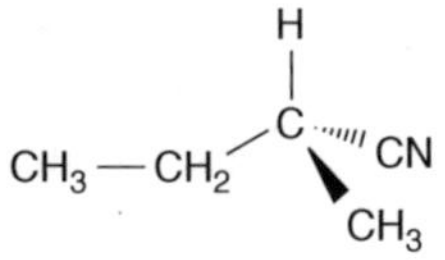

21.99   (a)

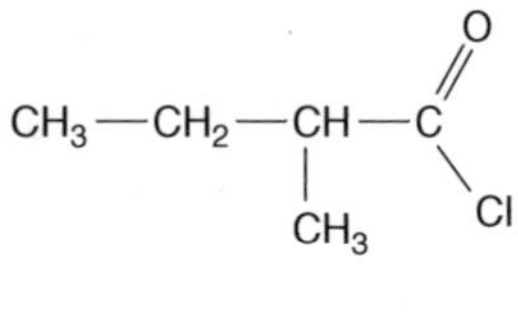

     (b)

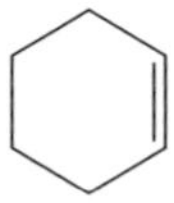

     (c)

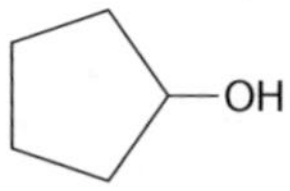

     (d)

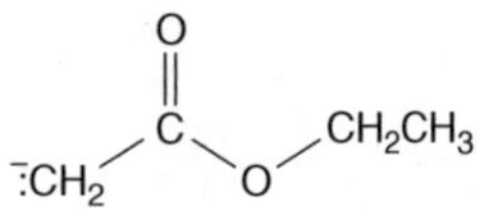

21.101   (a)

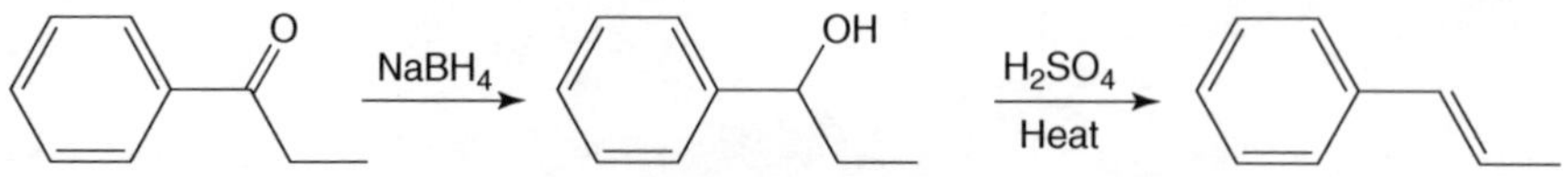

(b)

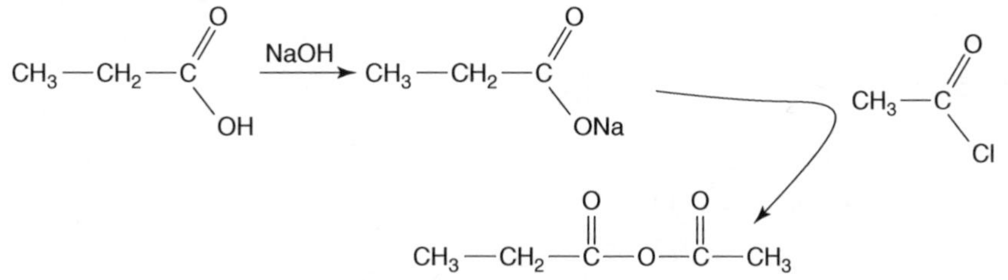

21.103 **Given:** 15.5 kg but-2-ene **Find:** grams H_2 gas required to completely react
Balanced chemical equation: $CH_3CH=CHCH_3 + H_2 \rightarrow CH_3CH_2CH_2CH_3$
Conceptual Plan: 15.5 kg $\rightarrow$ g but-2-ene $\rightarrow$ mol but-2-ene $\rightarrow$ mol H_2 $\rightarrow$ g H_2

$$\frac{10^3\,g}{1\,kg} \qquad \frac{1\,mol}{56.12\,g} \qquad \frac{1\,mol\,but\text{-}2\text{-}ene}{1\,mol\,H_2} \qquad \frac{2.016\,g\,H_2}{1\,mol\,H_2}$$

Solution: $15.5 \text{ kg but-2-ene } \times \dfrac{10^3\,g}{1\,kg} \times \dfrac{1\,mol}{56.12\,g} \times \dfrac{1\,mol\,H_2}{1\,mol\,but\text{-}2\text{-}ene} \times \dfrac{2.016\,g\,H_2}{1\,mol\,H_2} = 558\,g$

21.105 (a) **Given:** 1.2 kg acetyl chloride (CH_3COCl) **Find:** kg acetic acid (CH_3COOH)
Balanced chemical equation: $CH_3COOH + SOCl_2 \rightarrow CH_3COCl + HCl + SO_2$ *or* $CH_3COOH + (COCl)_2 \rightarrow CH_3COCl + HCl + CO_2 + CO$
Conceptual Plan: 1.2 kg CH_3COCl $\rightarrow$ g CH_3COCl $\rightarrow$ mol CH_3COCl $\rightarrow$ mol CH_3COOH $\rightarrow$

$$\frac{10^3\,g}{1\,kg} \qquad \frac{1\,mol\,CH_3COCl}{78.5\,g\,CH_3COCl} \qquad \frac{1\,mol\,CH_3COCl}{1\,mol\,CH_3COOH} \qquad \frac{60.06\,g\,CH_3COOH}{1\,mol\,CH_3COOH}$$

g CH_3COOH $\rightarrow$ kg CH_3COOH

$$\frac{1\,kg}{10^3\,g}$$

Solution:

$$1.2 \text{ kg } CH_3COCl \times \frac{10^3\,g}{1\,kg} \times \frac{1\,mol}{78.5\,g} \times \frac{1\,mol\,CH_3COOH}{1\,mol\,CH_3COCl} \times \frac{60.06\,g\,CH_3COOH}{1\,mol\,CH_3COOH} \times \frac{1\,kg}{10^3\,g} = 0.92\,kg$$

(b) **Given:** 1.2 kg acetyl chloride (CH_3COCl) **Find:** kg HCl, SO_2, CO_2, and CO
Balanced chemical equation: $CH_3COOH + SOCl_2 \rightarrow CH_3COCl + HCl + SO_2$ *or* $CH_3COOH + (COCl)_2 \rightarrow CH_3COCl + HCl + CO_2 + CO$
Conceptual Plan: 1.2 kg CH_3COCl $\rightarrow$ g CH_3COCl $\rightarrow$ mol CH_3COCl $\rightarrow$ mol HCl, SO_2, CO_2, or

$$\frac{10^3\,g}{1\,kg} \qquad \frac{1\,mol\,CH_3COCl}{78.5\,g\,CH_3COCl} \qquad \frac{1\,mol\,CH_3COCl}{1\,mol\,by\text{-}product}$$

CO $\rightarrow$ g HCl, SO_2, CO_2, or CO $\rightarrow$ kg HCl, SO_2, CO_2, or CO

molar mass of by-product $\qquad \dfrac{1\,kg}{10^3\,g}$

Solution: $1.2 \text{ kg } CH_3COCl \times \dfrac{10^3\,g}{1\,kg} \times \dfrac{1\,mol}{78.5\,g} = 15.2866 \text{ mol } CH_3COCl$. Since the mole-to-mole ratio

for acetyl chloride to each by-product is 1:1, then moles of CH_3COCl = mol HCl = mol SO_2 = mol CO_2 = mol CO. Thus, kg of each by-product is obtained as follows:

$$15.2866 \text{ mol HCl} \times \frac{36.46\,g}{1\,mol} \times \frac{1\,kg}{10^3\,g} = 0.56\,kg\,HCl$$

$$15.2866 \text{ mol } SO_2 \times \frac{60.07\,g}{1\,mol} \times \frac{1\,kg}{10^3\,g} = 0.98\,kg\,SO_2$$

$$15.2866 \text{ mol } CO_2 \times \frac{44.01\,g}{1\,mol} \times \frac{1\,kg}{10^3\,g} = 0.67\,kg\,CO_2$$

$$15.2866 \text{ mol CO} \times \frac{28.01\,g}{1\,mol} \times \frac{1\,kg}{10^3\,g} = 0.43\,kg\,CO$$

Challenge Problems

21.107   A possible mechanism:

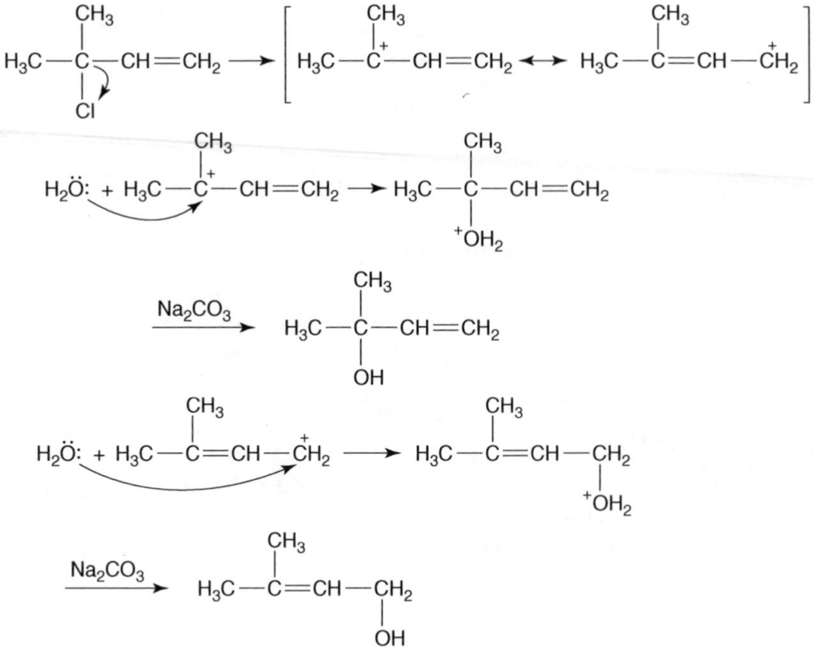

21.109   The alcohol is oxidized to a carboxylic acid by the addition of $K_2Cr_2O_7$ and H_2SO_4. Then ethanol and an acid catalyst such as dilute sulfuric acid are used to convert the carboxylic acid to an ester as shown below.

21.111   (a)

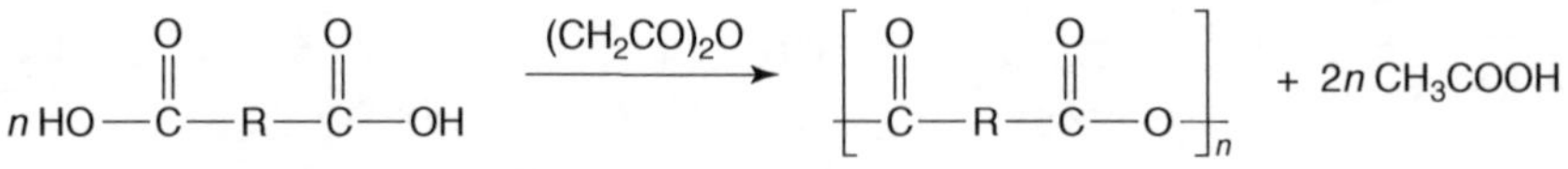

(b)

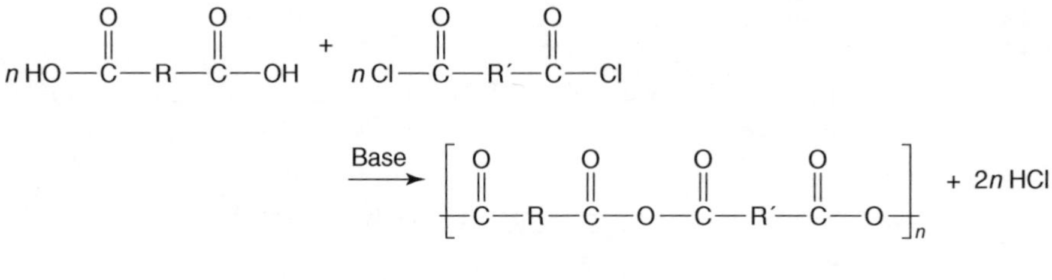

Conceptual Problems

21.113   Excess ammonia is added to react with the HCl that is produced during the reaction and neutralize it.

21.115   This is an oxidation–reduction reaction. Lithium is oxidized from 0 to +1 and carbon is reduced from +1 to −1 during the reaction.

22 Biochemistry

Review Questions

22.1   Biochemistry is that area at the interface between chemistry and biology that strives to understand living organisms at the molecular level. It is the study of the chemistry occurring in living organisms. To help diabetics, Frederick Sanger discovered the detailed chemical structure of human insulin. This allowed the synthesis of insulin. This was further enhanced by biotechnology advances, particularly by Genentech, that allowed researchers to insert the human gene for insulin into the DNA of bacterial cells. This new way to manufacture human insulin revolutionized the treatment of diabetes since human insulin is now readily available.

22.3   A fatty acid is a carboxylic acid with a long hydrocarbon tail. The general structure for a fatty acid is as follows:

where R represents a hydrocarbon chain containing 3 to 19 carbon atoms.

22.5   Triglycerides are triesters composed of glycerol with three fatty acids attached. The general structure of a triglyceride is as follows:

22.7   Phospholipids have the same basic structure as triglycerides, except that one of the fatty acid groups is replaced with a phosphate group. Unlike a fatty acid, which is nonpolar, the phosphate group is polar. The phospholipid molecule has a polar region and a nonpolar region. The polar part of the molecule is hydrophilic while the nonpolar part is hydrophobic.

Glycolipids have similar structures and properties. The nonpolar section of a glycolipid is composed of a fatty acid chain and a hydrocarbon chain. However, the polar section is a sugar molecule.

The structure of phospholipids and glycolipids makes them ideal components of cell membranes, where the polar parts can interact with the aqueous environments inside and outside the cell and the nonpolar parts interact with each other, forming a double-layered structure called a lipid bilayer. Lipid bilayers encapsulate cells and many cellular structures.

22.9   Carbohydrates have the general formula $(CH_2O)_n$. Structurally, carbohydrates are polyhydroxy aldehydes or ketones. Carbohydrates are responsible for short-term storage of energy in living organisms, and they make up the main structural components of plants.

22.11   Simple carbohydrates are the simple sugars, monosaccharides and disaccharides. Polysaccharides, which are long, chainlike molecules composed of many monosaccharide units bonded together, are complex carbohydrates.

22.13   Proteins are the workhorse molecules in living organisms and are involved in virtually all facets of cell structure and function. Most of the chemical reactions that occur in living organisms are enabled by enzymes, proteins that act as catalysts in biochemical reactions. Proteins are also the structural elements of muscle, skin, and cartilage. Proteins transport oxygen in the blood, act as antibodies to fight disease, and function as hormones to regulate metabolic processes.

22.15   The R groups, or side chains, differ chemically from one amino acid to another. When amino acids are strung together to make a protein, the chemical properties of the R groups determine the structure and properties of the protein.

22.17

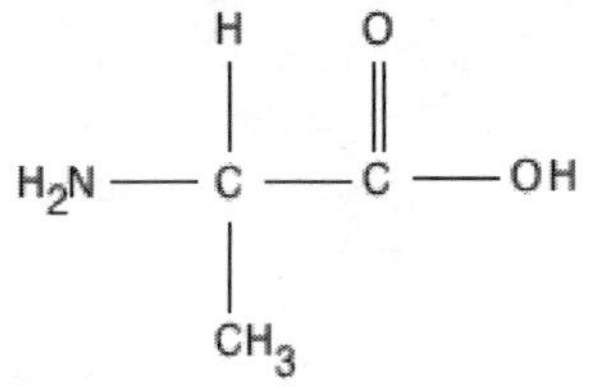

Alanine (Ala)

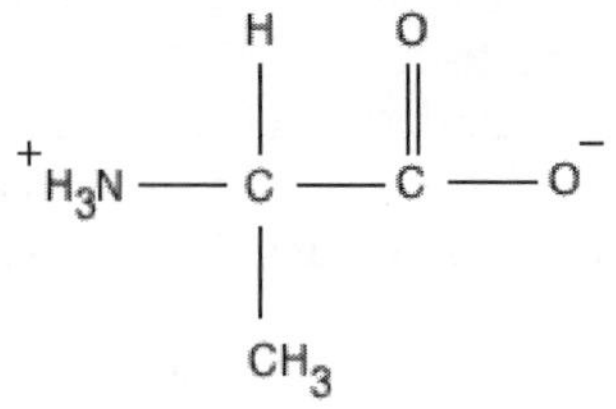

22.19   The 10 essential amino acids are phenylalanine, tryptophan, isoleucine, histidine, lysine, valine, threonine, methionine, arginine, and leucine. These amino acids are called essential amino acids because they can not be synthesized in the body. They must come from food and in the proportions that match the needs of protein synthesis.

22.21   The primary structure of a protein is the amino acid sequence.

The secondary structure refers to the repeating patterns in the arrangement of protein chains such as α-helices and β-sheets.

The tertiary structure refers to the large-scale twists and folds found in globular proteins but not fibrous proteins.

The quaternary structure refers to the arrangement of subunits in proteins that have more than one polypeptide chain.

22.23   In the α-helix structure, the amino acid chain is wrapped into a tight coil in which the side chains extend outward from the coil. The structure is maintained by hydrogen bonding interaction between NH and CO groups along the peptide backbone of the protein.

In the β-pleated sheet, the chain is extended and forms a zigzag pattern. The peptide backbones of neighbouring chains interact with one another through hydrogen bonding to form zigzag-shaped sheets.

22.25   Nucleic acids are polymers. The individual units composing nucleic acids are called nucleotides. Each nucleotide has three parts: a sugar, a base, and a phosphate group, which serves as a link between sugars.

22.27   A codon is a sequence of three bases that codes for one amino acid.

A gene is a sequence of codons within a DNA molecule that codes for a single protein.

Genes are contained in structures within cells called chromosomes. There are 46 chromosomes in the nuclei of human cells.

22.29   When a cell is about to divide, the DNA unwinds and the hydrogen bonds joining the complementary bases break, forming two daughter strands. With the help of the enzyme DNA polymerase, a complement to each daughter strand with the correct complementary bases in the correct sequence is formed. The hydrogen bonds between the strands then re-form, resulting in two complete copies of the original DNA, one for each daughter cell.

Problems by Topic

Lipids

22.31 (a)   No. It is an alkane chain.

(b)   No. It is an amino acid.

(c)   Yes. It is a saturated fatty acid.

(d)   Yes. It is a steroid, cholesterol.

22.33 (a)   Yes. It is a saturated fatty acid.

(b)   No. It is an alkane.

(c)   No. It is an ether.

(d)   Yes. It is a monounsaturated fatty acid.

22.35

$$H_2C-OH$$
$$HO-CH \qquad + \quad 3\left[HOOC(CH_2)_6\left(CH_2CH=CH\right)_2(CH_2)_4CH_3\right]$$
$$H_2C-OH$$

$$\longrightarrow$$

$$H_2C-O-\overset{O}{\overset{\|}{C}}-(CH_2)_6\left(CH_2CH=CH\right)_2(CH_2)_4CH_3$$

$$HC-O-\overset{O}{\overset{\|}{C}}-(CH_2)_6\left(CH_2CH=CH\right)_2(CH_2)_4CH_3 \quad + \quad 3\ H_2O$$

$$H_2C-O-\overset{O}{\overset{\|}{C}}-(CH_2)_6\left(CH_2CH=CH\right)_2(CH_2)_4CH_3$$

The double bonds in the linoleic acid would most likely make this triglyceride liquid at room temperature.

Carbohydrates

22.37 (a)   Yes, it is a carbohydrate; it is a monosaccharide.

(b)   No, it is not a carbohydrate; it is a steroid: β-estradiol.

(c)   Yes, it is a carbohydrate; it is a disaccharide.

(d)   No, it is not a carbohydrate; it is a peptide.

22.39   (a)   The C—O double bond was on a terminal carbon prior to ring formation, so it is an aldose. There are six carbon atoms, so it is a hexose.

(b)   The C—O double bond is on a terminal carbon, so it is an aldose. There are five carbon atoms, so it is a pentose.

(c)   The C—O double bond is NOT on a terminal carbon, so it is a ketose. There are four carbon atoms, so it is a tetrose.

(d)   The C—O double bond was on a terminal carbon prior to ring formation, so it is an aldose. There are four carbon atoms, so it is a tetrose.

22.41   (a)   Five of the six carbon atoms have four different substituents attached; therefore, there are five chiral centres.

The best way to see the stereochemistry is to build the model. Some of the decisions can be deceiving unless you can see this molecule in three dimensions. It is particularly difficult in cyclic compounds to try to visualize the stereochemistry mentally.

The substituents around carbon 1 are prioritized according to the Cahn-Ingold-Prelog rules covered in Section 20.7. The etheric oxygen is first priority, followed by the CH group to the left, then the CH_2OH group above, and the fourth priority is the hydrogen atom. Assuming the hydrogen atom is at the back then the rotation from priority 1 to 2 to 3 is clockwise and thus this is an R configuration.

With carbon 2 the etheric oxygen has first priority, followed by the OH group below, then the carbon 3 group, and the fourth priority is the hydrogen atom. If you can visualize twisting the molecule so that the hydrogen atom is away from you then the rotation from priority 1 to 2 to 3 is counterclockwise and thus this is an S configuration.

With carbon 3 the OH group has first priority, followed by the carbon 2 group, then the carbon 4 group, and the fourth priority is the hydrogen atom. If you can visualize twisting the molecule so that the hydrogen atom is away from you then the rotation from priority 1 to 2 to 3 is clockwise and thus this is an R configuration.

For carbon 4 the OH is first priority, followed by carbon 3 (it is attached to a C with an OH coming off it) then carbon 5 (it is attached to a C with a CH_2OH), and the fourth priority is the hydrogen atom. Viewed from above so that the hydrogen atom is at the bottom then the rotation from priority 1 to 2 to 3 is counterclockwise and thus this is an S configuration.

For carbon 5 the OH group again has first priority, followed by carbon 1 (attached to H, C, and O-C), then carbon 4 (attached to H, C, and O-H), and the fourth priority is the hydrogen atom. If you can visualize viewing the molecule from the opposite side of the ring, the hydrogen atom is away from you and the rotation from priority 1 to 2 to 3 is clockwise and this is an R configuration.

(b) Three of the five carbon atoms have four different substituents attached; therefore, there are three chiral centres.

The best way to see the stereochemistry is to build the model. Some of the decisions can be deceiving unless you can see this molecule in three dimensions.

The substituents around carbon 1 are prioritized according to the Cahn-Ingold-Prelog rules covered in Section 20.7. The OH group is first priority, followed by the aldehyde group above, then carbon 2 and the rest of the molecule below, and the fourth priority is the hydrogen atom. Since the hydrogen atom is horizontal then it is projected toward you.

What can you do if the lowest priority group is not toward the back?

1.   You can build a model of the compound and rotate it so that the low priority group is away from you.

2.   You can mentally rotate the molecule putting the hydrogen in the proper orientation.

3.   You can switch the hydrogen with the aldehyde thus putting the low priority group at the back. The configuration of the altered structure would be *S*, the opposite of the original configuration in the original structure.

Anyone of these methods should lead you to an *R* configuration at carbon 1.

The reasoning process for carbon 2 and 3 is identical where in each case the carbon above in the drawing has higher priority than the carbon below.

(c) Only one of the four carbon atoms has four different substituents attached; therefore, there is only one chiral centre.

The best way to see the stereochemistry is to build the model. Some of the decisions can be deceiving unless you can see this molecule in three dimensions.

The substituents around carbon 1 are prioritized according to the Cahn-Ingold-Prelog rules covered in Section 20.7. The OH group is first priority, followed by the keto group above, then the CH₂OH below, and the fourth priority is the hydrogen atom. There is still the problem of the hydrogen atom being horizontal and thus pointed forward, so you will need build the molecule or invert it mentally to see the correct configuration.

(d)   Three of the four carbon atoms have four different substituents attached; therefore, there are three chiral centres.

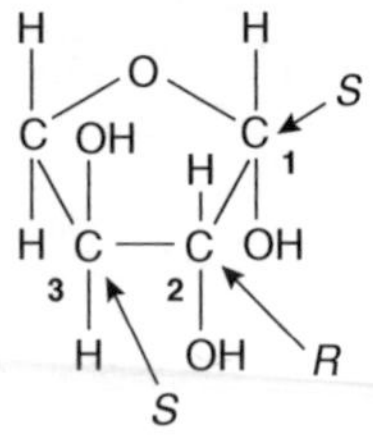

The best way to see the stereochemistry is to build the model. Some of the decisions can be deceiving unless you can see this molecule in three dimensions. It is particularly difficult in cyclic compounds to try to visualize the stereochemistry mentally.

The reasoning here is very similar to part (a) above.

The substituents around carbon 1 are prioritized according to the Cahn-Ingold-Prelog rules covered in Section 20.7. The etheric oxygen is first priority, followed by the OH group below, then the carbon 2 group, and the fourth priority is the hydrogen atom. Assuming the hydrogen atom is at the back (or looking at the molecule from below) the rotation from priority 1 to 2 to 3 is counterclockwise and thus this is an *S* configuration.

The substituents around carbon 2 are prioritized with the OH group as first priority, followed by carbon 1, then carbon 3, and the fourth priority is the hydrogen atom. Assuming the hydrogen atom is at the back (or looking at the molecule from below) the rotation from priority 1 to 2 to 3 is clockwise and thus this is an *R* configuration.

The substituents around carbon 3 are prioritized with the OH group as first priority, followed by carbon 2, then the CH$_2$ group, and the fourth priority is the hydrogen atom. Assuming the hydrogen atom is at the back (or looking at the molecule from above) the rotation from priority 1 to 2 to 3 is counterclockwise and thus this is an *S* configuration.

22.43   Glucose

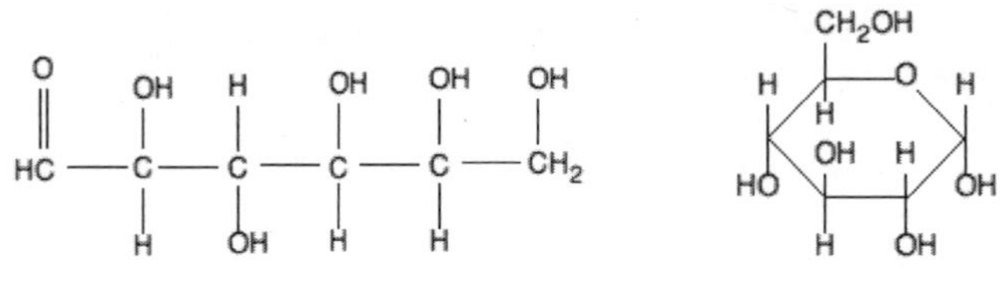

22.45   Hydrolysis is the addition of a water molecule across the glycosidic linkage to make monosaccharides.

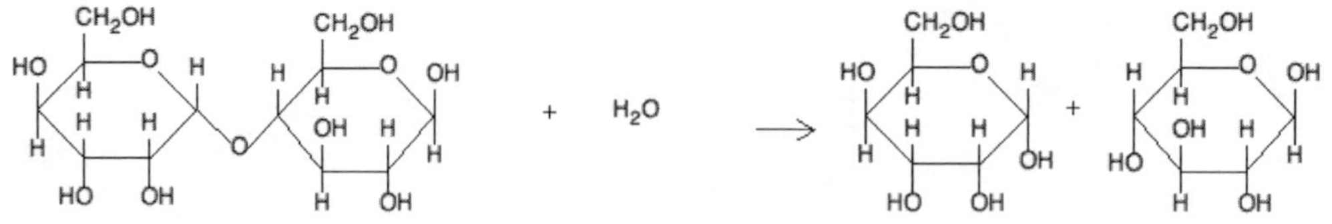

22.47

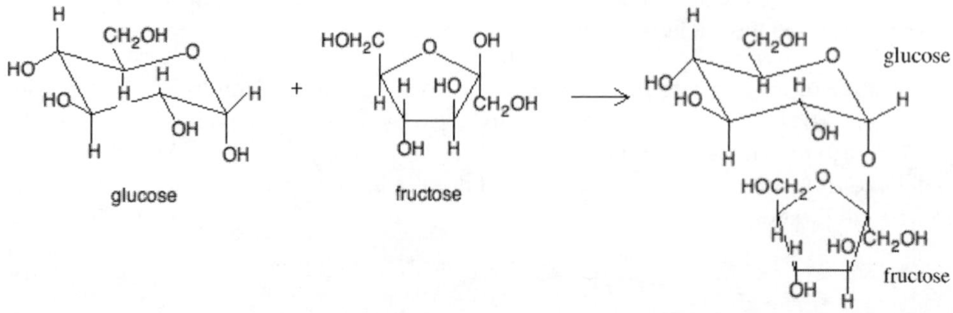

Amino Acids and Proteins

22.49   (a)   Thr = Threonine

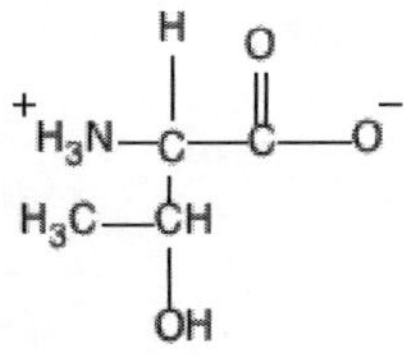

(b)   Ala = Alanine

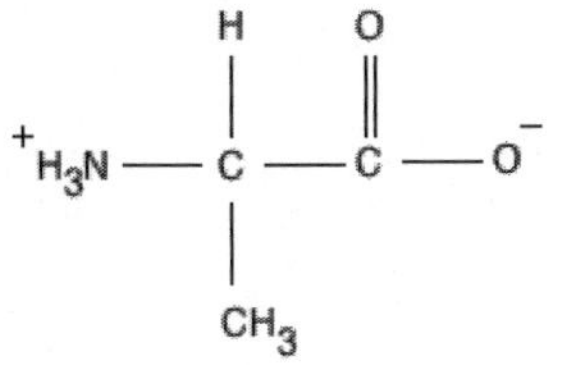

(c)   Leu = Leucine

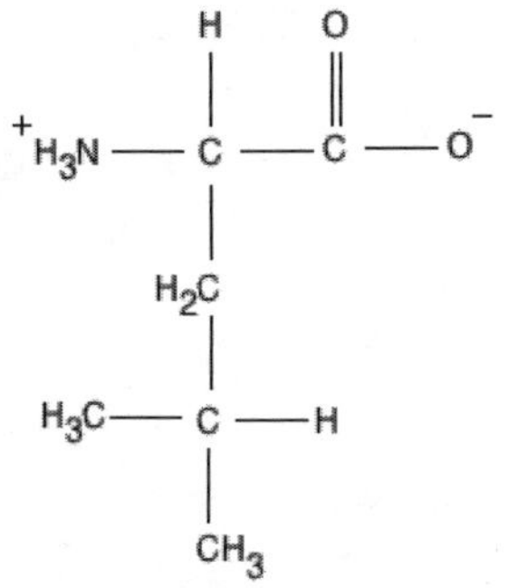

(d)   Lys = Lysine

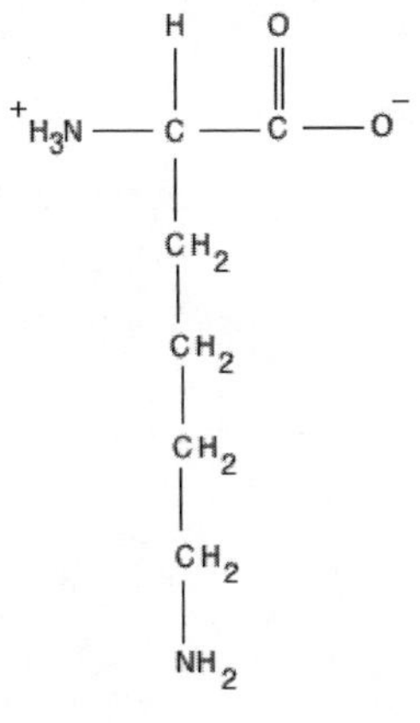

22.51   L – Alanine   D – Alanine

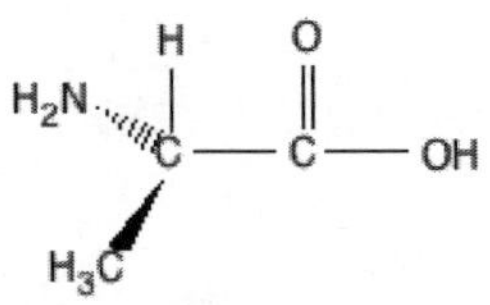

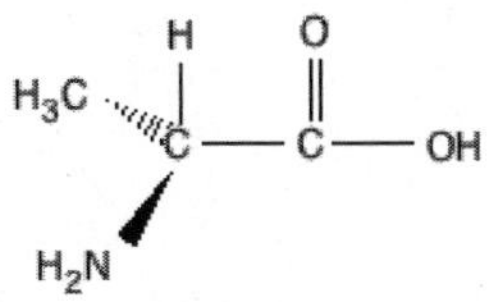

22.53   Because the N-terminal end and the C-terminal end are specific in a peptide, six tripeptides can be made from the three amino acids: serine, glycine, and cysteine.

Ser – Gly – Cys   Ser – Cys – Gly   Gly – Cys – Ser   Gly – Ser – Cys

Cys – Ser – Gly   Cys – Gly – Ser

22.55   Peptide bonds are formed when the carboxylic end of one amino acid reacts with the amine end of another amino acid.

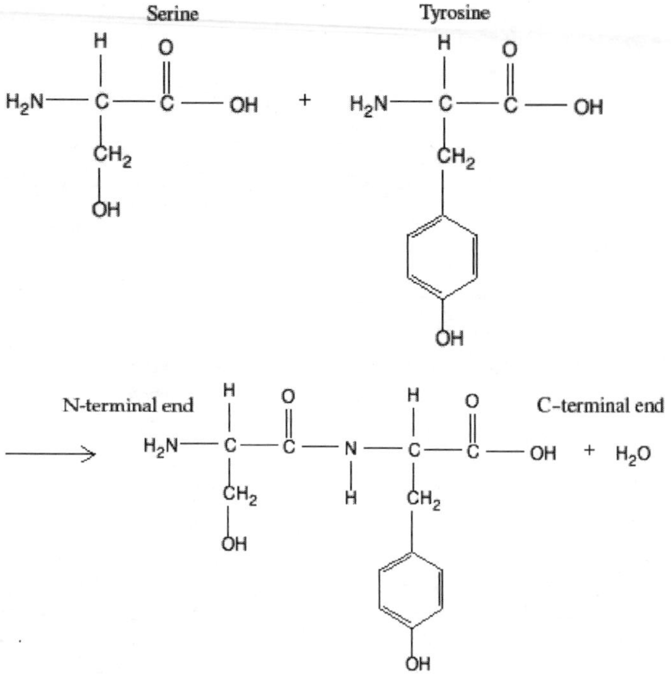

22.57   Peptide bonds are formed when the carboxylic end of one amino acid reacts with the amine end of another amino acid.

(a)   Gln – Met – Cys

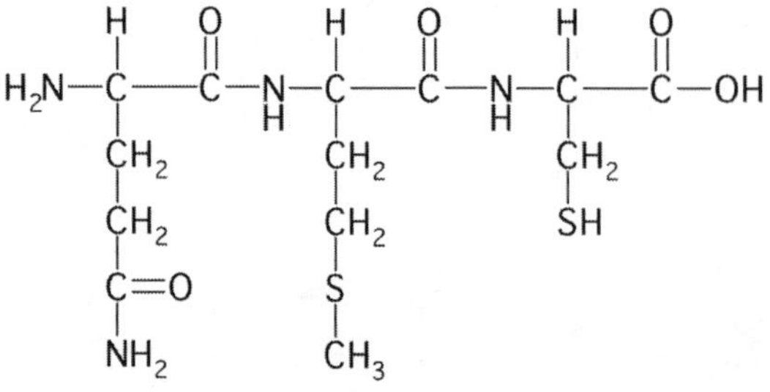

(b)   Ser – Leu – Cys

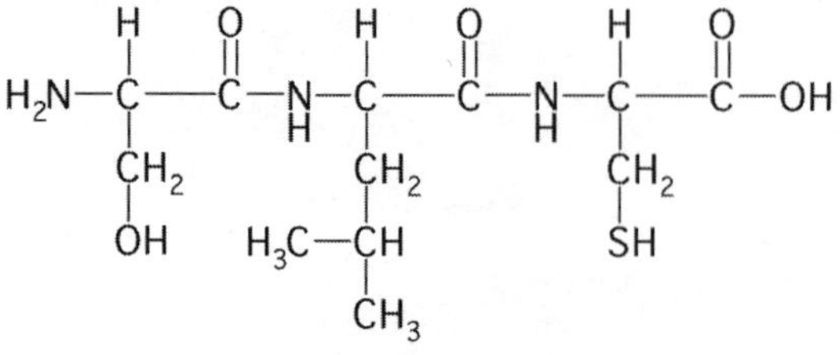

(c)   Cys – Leu – Ser

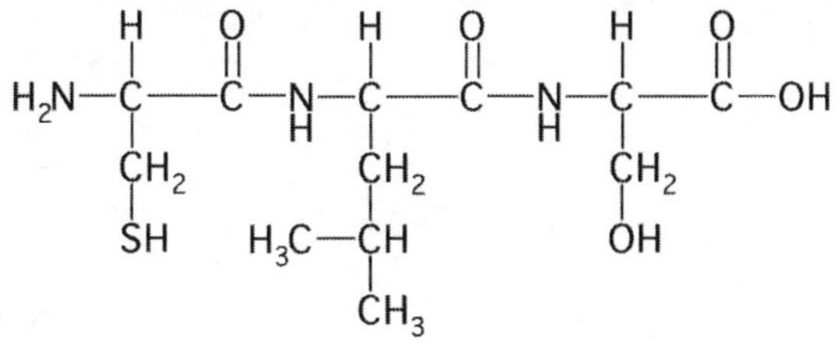

22.59   This would be a tertiary structure. Tertiary structure refers to the large-scale twists and folds of globular proteins. These are maintained by interactions between the R groups of amino acids that are separated by long distances in the chain sequence.

22.61   This would be a primary structure. Primary structure is simply the amino acid sequence. It is maintained by the peptide bonds that hold amino acids together.

Nucleic Acids

22.63   (a)   Yes, it is a nucleotide and the base is A, adenine.

          (b)   No, it is not a nucleotide; it is the base A, adenine.

          (c)   Yes, it is a nucleotide, and the base is T, thymine.

          (d)   No, it is not a nucleotide; it is the amino acid methionine.

22.65   The two purine bases are:
          Adenine   Guanine

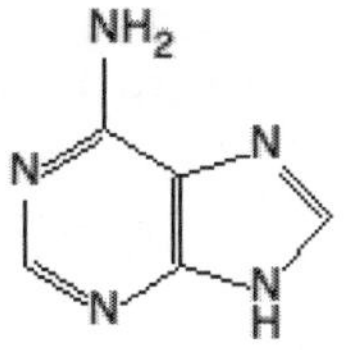

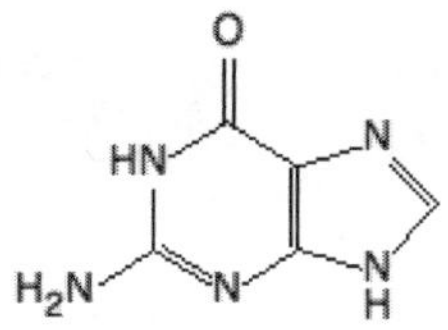

22.67   The bases pair in the specific arrangement: Adenine always pairs with thymine and guanine always pairs with cytosine.
          The sequence
          T G T A C G C
          would have the complementary sequence

          A C A T G C G

22.69   Every amino acid has a specific codon that is composed of three nucleotides. So, 154 amino acids would need 154 codons and 462 nucleotides.

Cumulative Problems

22.71   (a)   Peptide bonds link amino acids to form proteins.

          (b)   A glycosidic linkage is the connection between sugar molecules to form carbohydrates.

          (c)   An ester linkage forms between the glycol molecule and a fatty acid to form lipids.

22.73   A codon is a sequence of three nucleotides with their associated bases. A nucleotide is a combination of a sugar group, a phosphate group, and a base. A codon codes for a specific amino acid. A gene is a sequence of codons that codes for a specific protein.

22.75   Draw the Lewis structure for alanine:

     Determine the VSEPR geometry:

         N has three bonding pairs and one lone pair, which is trigonal pyramidal molecular geometry.

         C_1 has four bonding pairs of electrons, which gives tetrahedral molecular geometry.

         C_2 has three bonding pairs of electrons, which gives trigonal planar molecular geometry.

         C_3 has four bonding pairs of electrons, which gives tetrahedral molecular geometry.

         O has two bonding pairs of electrons, and two lone pairs, which gives bent molecular geometry.

22.77   Amino acids that are most likely to be involved in hydrophobic interactions would be ones that have a non-polar R group. These would be alanine, valine, leucine, isoleucine, and phenylalanine.

           Alanine   Valine   Leucine

           Isoleucine   Phenylalanine

22.79　The reagents added break up the polypeptide but do not rearrange it. Therefore, by comparing the fragments from the two reagents we can deduce the structure of the polypeptide.

Reagent 1:　　　Ala – Leu – Phe – Gly – Asn – Lys　Trp – Glu – Cys　Gly – Arg

Reagent 2:　　　Gly – Arg – Ala – Leu – Phe　Gly – Asn – Lys – Trp　Glu – Cys

So the sequence is:　Gly – Arg – Ala – Leu – Phe – Gly – Asn – Lys – Trp – Glu – Cys

22.81

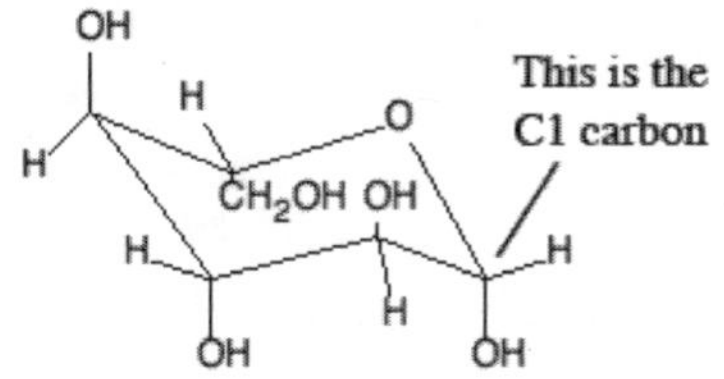

α form　　　　　　　　　　β form

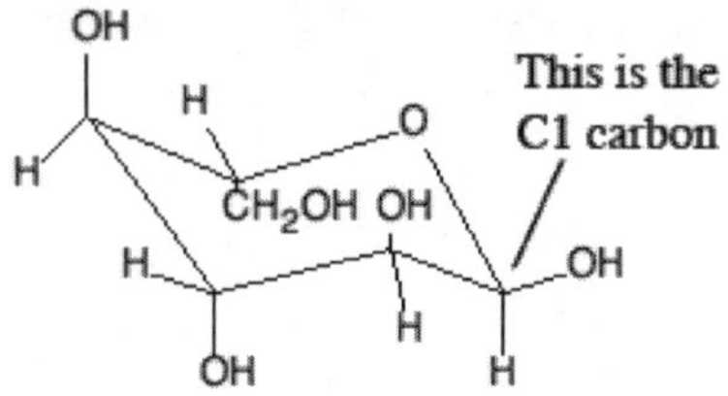

22.83　From the Gibbs–Helmholtz equation: $\Delta G = \Delta H - T\Delta S$ when ΔG is negative, the process is spontaneous. At high temperature, the ΔS term (which is positive) will dominate and ΔG will be negative and the DNA strand will be disrupted. At low temperature, the enthalpy of formation of the hydrogen bonds between the base pairs is a negative term and will dominate and cause ΔG to be negative and thus the DNA strand will form.

22.85

(a) L-alanine　(b) L-cysteine　(c) L-serine　(d) L-aspartic acid

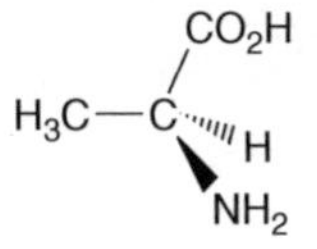

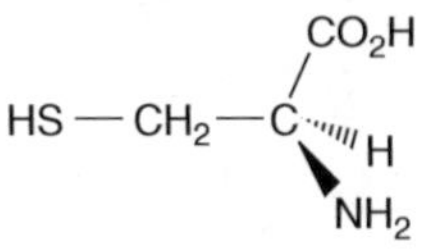

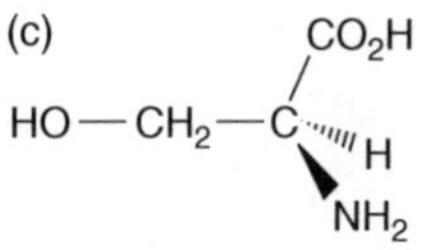

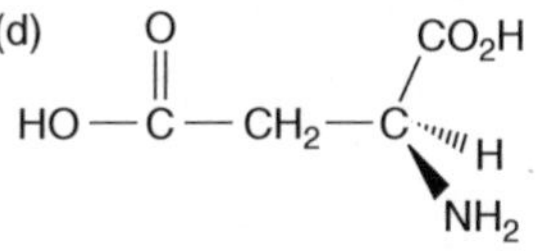

Challenge Problems

22.87　The DNA chain forms with a phosphate linkage between the C_5 carbon on one sugar and the C_3 carbon on the next sugar. When the fake thymine is introduced into the cell, DNA replication cannot occur because the N chain is attached at the C_3 position instead of the —OH group and this will keep future phosphate linkages from forming between the sugars and stop the replication.

22.89　First rearrange the Michaelis–Menten equation to the form of a straight line: $y = mx + b$.

$$V_0 = \frac{V_{max}[\text{glucose}]}{K_t + [\text{glucose}]} \qquad \frac{1}{V_0} = \frac{K_t + [\text{glucose}]}{V_{max}[\text{glucose}]} \qquad \frac{1}{V_0} = \frac{K_t}{V_{max}[\text{glucose}]} + \frac{[\text{glucose}]}{V_{max}[\text{glucose}]}$$

$$\frac{1}{V_0} = \frac{K_t}{V_{max}[\text{glucose}]} + \frac{1}{V_{max}} \qquad \text{So: } y = \frac{1}{V_0}; \ x = \frac{1}{[\text{glucose}]}; \ m = \frac{K_t}{V_{max}}; \ b = \frac{1}{V_{max}}$$

[glucose] mM	V_0 μM min^{-1}	1/[glucose] L mmol^{-1}	$1/V_0$ min μM^{-1}
0.5	12	2.0	0.083
1.0	19	1.0	0.053
2.0	27	0.50	0.037
3.0	32	0.33	0.031
4.0	35	0.25	0.029

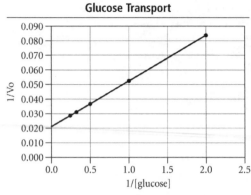

Glucose Transport

$$y = 0.021 \text{ min } \mu M^{-1} = \frac{1}{V_{max}}; \; m = 0.0353 \text{ min mmol}^{-1} = \frac{K_t}{V_{max}}; \text{ So } V_{max} = 47.6 \; \mu M \text{ min}^{-1} \text{ and } K_t = 1.68 \text{ mmol}$$

22.91   At pH = 2: $H_3N^+CH_2COO^- + H^+ \rightleftharpoons H_3N^+CH_2COOH$ $pK_a = 2.3$

$$pH = pK_a + \log\frac{[A^-]}{[HA]} \qquad 2.0 = 2.3 + \log\frac{[A^-]}{[HA]} \qquad \frac{[A^-]}{[HA]} = 0.5$$

At pH = 10: $H_3N^+CH_2COO^- \rightleftharpoons H_2NCH_2COO^- + H^+$ $pK_a = 9.6$

$$pH = pK_a + \log\frac{[A^-]}{[HA]} \qquad 10 = 9.6 + \log\frac{[A^-]}{[HA]} \qquad \frac{[A^-]}{[HA]} = 2.5$$

The glycine is neutral when $[H_3N^+CH_2COOH] = [H_2NCH_2COO^-]$

$H_3N^+CH_2COOH \rightleftharpoons \cancel{H_3N^+CH_2COO^-} + H^+$ $pK_a = 2.3$

$\cancel{H_3N^+CH_2COO^-} \rightleftharpoons H_2NCH_2COO^- + H^+$ $pK_a = 9.6$

$H_3N^+CH_2COOH \rightleftharpoons H_2NCH_2COO^- + 2H^+$ $pK_a = 11.9$

$$2pH = pK_a + \log\frac{[A^-]}{[HA]} \quad \text{but we have said that } [A^-] = [HA]$$

so: $2pH = pK_a = 11.9$ and $pH = 5.95 = 6$

Conceptual Problems

22.93   A three-base codon codes for a single amino acid. With only three bases there would be 27 (3 x 3 x 3) different three-base arrangements, so potentially this would allow for all the amino acids needed. However, nature usually allows for a built-in redundancy and so most amino acids have multiple codons. In addition, some codons are used as stop codons, so the actual system of four bases allowing for 64 three-base arrangements provides the necessary redundancy.

23 Chemistry of the Nonmetals

Review Questions

23.1 Boron nitride contains BN units that are isoelectronic with carbon in the sense that each BN unit contains eight valence electrons, or four per atom (just like carbon). Also the size and electronegativity of the carbon atom is almost equal to the average of a boron atom and nitrogen atom. Therefore, BN forms a number of structures that are similar to those formed by carbon, including nanotubes.

23.3 The metallic character of the main-group elements increases going down each column because of the increasing size of the atoms and decreasing electronegativity.

23.5 Silica melts when heated above 1500 °C. After melting, if cooled quickly, silica does not crystallize back into the quartz structure. Instead, the Si atoms and O atoms form a randomly ordered or amorphous structure called a glass. A slow cooling will result in the crystalline quartz structure.

23.7 (a) Orthosilicates (or nesosilicates) are minerals in which silicon bonds to oxygen in tetrahedral SiO_4^{4-} polyatomic anions (four electrons are gained, satisfying the octet rule for the oxygen atoms) that are isolated in the structure (not bonded to other tetrahedrons). The minerals require cations that have a total charge of 4+ to neutralize the negative charge.

(b) Amphiboles are minerals with double silicate chains. The repeating unit in the crystal is $Si_4O_{11}^{6-}$. Half of the tetrahedrons are bonded by two of the four corner O atoms, and half of the tetrahedrons are bonded by three of the four corners, bonding the two chains together. The bonding within the double chains is very strong, but the bonding between the double chains is not as strong, often resulting in fibrous-type minerals such as asbestos.

(c) Pyroxenes (or inosilicates) are minerals in which many of the silica tetrahedrons are bonded together forming chains. The formula unit for these chains is the SiO_3^{2-} unit, and the repeating unit in the structure is two formula units ($Si_2O_6^{4-}$). Two of the oxygen atoms are bonded to two silicon atoms (and thus to two other tetrahedrons) on two of the four corners of each tetrahedron. The silicate chains are held together by ionic bonding to metal cations that lie between the chains.

(d) Pyrosilicates (or sorosilicates) are minerals in which the silicate tetrahedrons can also form structures in which two tetrahedrons share one corner forming a disilicate ion, which has the formula $Si_2O_7^{6-}$. This group requires cations that balance the 6– charge on $Si_2O_7^{6-}$.

(e) Feldspars are a common aluminosilicate in which SiO_2 units become AlO_2^- upon substitution of aluminum. The negative charge is balanced by a positive counterion. This leads to a covalent network of $AlSi_3O_8^-$ or $Al_2Si_2O_8^{2-}$ units.

23.9 Boron tends to form electron-deficient compounds (compounds in which boron lacks an octet) because it has only three valence electrons. Examples of these compounds are boron halides, such as BF_3 and BCl_3.

23.11   Solid carbon dioxide is referred to as dry ice because at 1 atmosphere it goes directly from a solid to a gas (sublimes) without going through a liquid or wet phase.

23.13   About 21% of Earth's atmosphere is composed of O_2.

23.15   Earth's early atmosphere was reducing (instead of oxidizing) and contained hydrogen, methane, ammonia, and carbon dioxide. About 2.7 billion years ago, cyanobacteria (blue-green algae) began to convert the carbon dioxide and water to oxygen by photosynthesis.

Problems by Topic

Silicates: The Most Abundant Matter in Earth's Crust

23.17   (a)   +4. In SiO_2, (Si ox state) + 2(O ox state) = 0. Since O ox state = –2, Si ox state = – 2(–2) = +4.

          (b)   +4. In SiO_4^{4-}, (Si ox state) + 4(O ox state) = – 4. Since O ox state = –2, Si ox state = – 4 – 4(–2) = +4.

          (c)   +4. In $Si_2O_7^{6-}$, 2(Si ox state) + 7(O ox state) = – 6. Since O ox state = –2, Si ox state = $\frac{1}{2}$ (– 6 – 7(–2)) = +4.

23.19   Three SiO_4^{4-} units have a total charge of – 12. In trying to combine Ca^{2+} and Al^{3+} to get a total charge of + 12, the only possible combination is to use three Ca^{2+} and two Al^{3+} ions. The formula unit is $Ca_3Al_2(SiO_4)_3$.

23.21   Since OH has a –1 charge, Al has a +3 charge, and Si_2O_5 has a –2 charge, 2(Al ox state) + 1(Si_2O_5 charge) + x(OH^- charge) = 0, so 2(+3) + 1(–2) + x(–1) = 0 and x = 4.

23.23   In Table 23.2, SiO_4 has a – 4 charge and it belongs to the class of orthosilicates, where the silicate tetrahedra stand alone, not linked to each other. The – 4 charge balances with a common oxidation state of Zr of +4.

23.25   Ca has a +2 charge, Mg has a +2 charge, Fe commonly has a charge of +2 or +3, and OH has a charge of – 1. So far the charge balance is 2(+2) + 4(+2) + 1(+2 or +3) + (Si_7AlO_{22} charge) + 2(–1) = 0 or Si_7AlO_{22} charge = – 12 or – 13. Looking at Table 23.2 and recalling that one AlO_2^- unit replaces one SiO_2 unit, $Si_4O_{11}^{6-}$ units are the best match. If we double the unit and replace one-eighth of the Sis with Al, the new unit will be Si_7AlO_{22} and the charge will be 2(– 6) +1(–1) = –13. The charge on Fe will be +3 and the class is amphibole, with a double chain structure.

Boron and Its Remarkable Structures

23.27   **Given:** $Na_2[B_4O_5(OH)_4] \cdot 3 H_2O$ = kernite, 1.0×10^3 kg kernite-bearing ore, 0.98% by mass kernite, 65% B recovery **Find:** g boron recovered
          Conceptual Plan: kg ore → g ore → g kernite → g B possible → g B recovered

$$\frac{1000\ g}{1\ kg} \qquad \frac{0.98\ g\ kernite}{100\ g\ ore} \qquad \frac{4(10.81)\ g\ B}{291.3\ g\ kernite} \qquad \frac{65\ g\ B\ recovered}{100\ g\ B}$$

          Solution:

$$1.0 \times 10^3\ \cancel{kg\ ore} \times \frac{1000\ \cancel{g\ ore}}{1\ \cancel{kg\ ore}} \times \frac{0.98\ \cancel{g\ kernite}}{100\ \cancel{g\ ore}} \times \frac{4(10.81)\ \cancel{g\ B}}{291.3\ \cancel{g\ kernite}} \times \frac{65\ g\ B\ recovered}{100\ \cancel{g\ B}} = 950\ g\ B\ recovered$$

          Check: The units (g) are correct. The magnitude of the answer makes physical sense because there is very little mineral in the ore, a low recovery, and little B in the ore.

23.29   The bond angles are different in BCl_3 versus NCl_3 because B has three valence electrons and N has five valence electrons. The boron compound does not obey the octet rule: B has sp^2 hybridization and a trigonal planar geometry. The nitrogen compound does obey the octet rule, has a lone pair of electrons, sp^3 hybridization, and a trigonal pyramidal geometry (based on a tetrahedral geometry).

23.31   (a)   Looking at Figure 23.11, $B_6H_6^{2-}$ has six vertices and eight faces since it has an octahedral shape.

          (b) $B_{12}H_{12}^{2-}$ has the formula of a *closo*-borane ($B_nH_n^{2-}$). It has 12 vertices and 20 faces since it has an icosohedral shape.

23.33   *Closo*-boranes have the formula $B_nH_n^{2-}$ and form fully closed polyhedra with triangular sides. Each of the vertices in the polyhedra is a boron atom with an attached hydrogen atom. *Nido*-boranes, named from the Latin word for *net*, have the formula B_nH_{n+4}. They consist of a cage of boron atoms missing one corner. *Arachno*-boranes, named from the Greek word for *web*, have the formula B_nH_{n+6}. They consist of a cage of boron atoms that is missing two or three corners.

Carbon, Carbides, and Carbonates

23.35   Graphite is a good lubricant because the structure has strong covalent bonds within the sheets of the structure, but weak interactions between the sheets that allow the sheets to easily slide over one another. The diamond structure consists of carbon atoms connected to four other carbon atoms at the corners of a tetrahedron. This bonding extends throughout three dimensions, making giant molecules described as network covalent solids. There are no weak interactions in the diamond structure.

23.37   Regular charcoal is in large chunks that still resemble the wood from which it is made. Activated charcoal is treated with steam to break up the chunks into a finely divided powder with a high surface area.

23.39   Ionic carbides are composed of carbon and low-electronegativity metals such as the alkali metals and alkaline earth metals. Most of the ionic carbides contain the dicarbide ion, C_2^{2-}, commonly called the acetylide ion. Covalent carbides are composed of carbon and low-electronegativity nonmetals or metalloids. The most important covalent carbide is silicon carbide (SiC), a very hard material.

23.41   (a)   As the pressure is reduced, the solid will be converted directly to a gas.

         (b)   As the temperature is reduced, the gas will be converted to a liquid and then to a solid.

         (c)   As the temperature is increased, the solid will be converted directly to a gas.

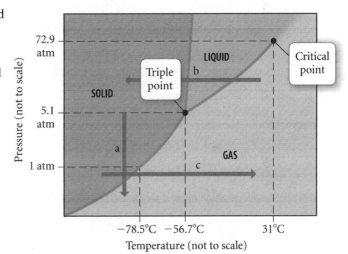

23.43   (a)   The reaction will be similar to that of iron oxide and carbon monoxide: $CO\ (g) + CuO\ (s) \xrightarrow{\text{heat}} CO_2\ (g) + Cu\ (s)$. Note that the oxidation state of carbon increases by two and the oxidation state of Cu decreases by two.

         (b)   This reaction is discussed in Section 23.5, $SiO_2\ (s) + 3\ C\ (s) \xrightarrow{\text{heat}} SiC\ (s) + 2\ CO\ (g)$.

23.45   (a)   +2. In CO, (C ox state) + (O ox state) = 0. Since O ox state = –2, C ox state = +2.

         (b)   +4. In CO_2, (C ox state) + 2(O ox state) = 0. Since O ox state = –2, C ox state = –2(–2) = +4.

         (c)   +4/3. In C_3O_2, 3(C ox state) + 2(O ox state) = 0. Since O ox state = –2, C ox state = 1/3(–2(–2)) = +4/3.

Nitrogen and Phosphorus: Essential Elements for Life

23.47   Even though there is a tremendous amount of N_2 gas in the atmosphere, the strong triple bond in elemental nitrogen renders it unusable by plants. In order to be used as fertilizer, elemental nitrogen has to be fixed, which means that it has to be converted into a nitrogen-containing compound like NH_3.

23.49   White phosphorus consists of P_4 molecules in a tetrahedral shape, with the phosphorus atoms at the corners of the tetrahedron as shown in Figure 23.19. The bond angles between the three P atoms on any one face of the tetrahedron are small (60°) and strained, making the P_4 molecule unstable and reactive. When heated to about 300 °C in the absence of air, white phosphorus slightly changes its structure to a different allotrope called red phosphorus, which is amorphous. The general structure of red phosphorus is similar to that of white phosphorus, except that one of the bonds between two phosphorus atoms in the tetrahedron is broken, as shown in Figure 23.20. These two phosphorus atoms then link to other phosphorus atoms making chains that can vary in structure. The red phosphorus structure is more stable because there is less strain when the linkage is changed.

23.51 **Given:** saltpeter (KNO_3) and Chile saltpeter ($NaNO_3$) **Find:** mass percent N in each mineral
Conceptual Plan: mineral formula → mass percent nitrogen

$$\text{mass percent nitrogen} = \frac{14.01 \text{ g N}}{\text{formula weight of mineral}} \times 100\%$$

Solution: For KNO_3:

$$\text{mass percent nitrogen} = \frac{14.01 \text{ g N}}{\text{formula weight of mineral}} \times 100\% = \frac{14.01 \text{ g}}{101.11 \text{ g}} \times 100\% = 13.86\%$$

and for $NaNO_3$:

$$\text{mass percent nitrogen} = \frac{14.01 \text{ g N}}{\text{formula weight of mineral}} \times 100\% = \frac{14.01 \text{ g}}{85.00 \text{ g}} \times 100\% = 16.48\%.$$

Check: The units (%) are correct. The relative magnitudes of the answers make physical sense because K is heavier than Na.

23.53 **Given:** decomposition of hydrogen azide (HN_3) to its elements
Find: stability at room temperature, stability at any temperature
Conceptual Plan: Write the reaction. Evaluate $\Delta_r G°$ then determine if $\Delta_r G > 0$ at any T.

$$\Delta G = \Delta_r H - T\Delta_r S$$

Solution: HN_3 (g) → 3/2 N_2 (g) + 1/2 H_2 (g), at 25 °C $\Delta_r G° = -\Delta_f G°(HN_3 (g)) = -1422$ kJ mol^{-1} so the decomposition is spontaneous at room temperature. $\Delta_r H° = -\Delta_f H°(HN_3 (g)) = -1447$ kJ mol^{-1}, and $\Delta_r S° > 0$ since the decomposition generates more moles of gas. Since $\Delta_r G = \Delta_r H - T\Delta_r S$ we see that both the enthalpy and the entropy term favour decomposition, and so $\Delta_r G$ is always negative and hydrogen azide is unstable at all temperatures.
Check: Azides are used as explosives, so it is not surprising that they are unstable.

23.55 (a) This reaction is a decomposition reaction, NH_4NO_3 (aq) $\xrightarrow{\text{heat}}$ N_2O (g) + 2 H_2O (l).

(b) This reaction is discussed in Section 23.6, 3 NO_2 (g) + H_2O (l) → 2 HNO_3 (l) + NO (g).

(c) This reaction is discussed in Section 23.6, 2 PCl_3 (l) + O_2 (g) → 2 $POCl_3$ (l).

23.57 For N_3^-: 3(N ox state) = −1, so N ox state = −1/3.
For $N_2H_5^+$: 2(N ox state) + 5(H ox state) = +1. Since H ox state = +1, N ox state = $\frac{1}{2}$ (1 − 5(+1)) = −2.
For NO_3^-: 1(N ox state) + 3(O ox state) = −1. Since O ox state = −2, N ox state = −1 − 3(−2) = +5.
For NH_4^+: 1(N ox state) + 4(H ox state) = +1. Since H ox state = +1, N ox state = +1 − 4(+1) = −3.
For NO_2^-: 1(N ox state) + 2(O ox state) = −1. Since O ox state = −2, N ox state = −1 − 2(−2) = +3.
So $NO_3^- > NO_2^- > N_3^- > N_2H_5^+ > NH_4^+$.

23.59 P has five valence electrons and Cl has seven valence electrons and so PCl_3 has 5 + 3(7) = 26 valence electrons and PCl_5 has 5 + 5(7) = 40 valence electrons. Since the electronegativity of P is less than the electronegativity of Cl, the P is in the middle. So the Lewis structures are:

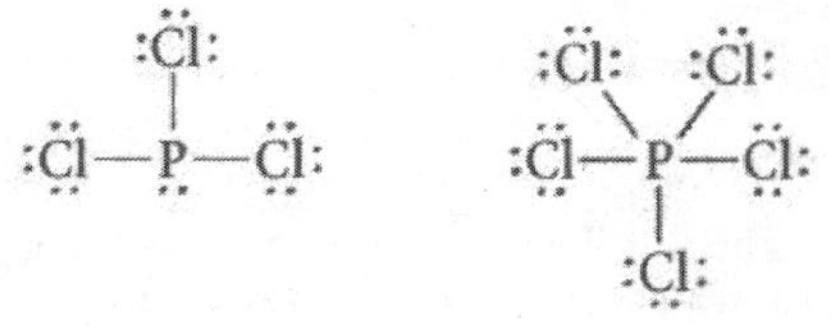

Notice that the PCl_5 has an expanded octet, which is allowed since P is in the third row of the periodic table and Cl is a fairly small atom. Since the PCl_3 has four electron groups surrounding the P atom, the electron geometry is tetrahedral. Since there is one lone pair the molecular geometry is trigonal pyramidal. Since the PCl_5 has five electron groups surrounding the P atom (and no lone pairs), the molecular geometry is trigonal bipyramidal.

23.61   **Given:** urea $(CO(NH_2)_2)$ reacts with water to produce 23 g ammonium carbonate   **Find:** g urea needed

    Conceptual Plan: Write a balanced equation.

$$g\ (NH_4)_2CO_3 \rightarrow mol\ (NH_4)_2CO_3 \rightarrow mol\ CO(NH_2)_2 \rightarrow g\ CO(NH_2)_2$$

$$\frac{1\ mol\ (NH_4)_2CO_3}{96.09\ g\ (NH_4)_2CO_3} \quad \frac{1\ mol\ CO(NH_2)_2}{1\ mol\ (NH_4)_2CO_3} \quad \frac{60.06\ g\ CO(NH_2)_2}{1\ mol\ CO(NH_2)_2}$$

    Solution: $CO(NH_2)_2\ (aq) + 2\ H_2O\ (l) \rightarrow (NH_4)_2CO_3\ (aq)$ then

$$23\ \overline{g\ (NH_4)_2CO_3} \times \frac{1\ \overline{mol\ (NH_4)_2CO_3}}{96.09\ \overline{g\ (NH_4)_2CO_3}} \times \frac{1\ \overline{mol\ CO(NH_2)_2}}{1\ \overline{mol\ (NH_4)_2CO_3}} \times \frac{60.06\ g\ CO(NH_2)_2}{1\ \overline{mol\ CO(NH_2)_2}} = 14\ g\ CO(NH_2)_2$$

    Check: The units (g) are correct. The magnitude of the answer (14) makes physical sense because we are generating 23 g of $(NH_4)_2CO_3$. Since we are adding water to the urea, the amount of urea must be less than 23 g.

23.63   Tetraphosphorus hexaoxide, $P_4O_6\ (s)$, forms when the amount of oxygen is limited, and tetraphosphorus decaoxide, $P_4O_{10}\ (s)$, is formed when greater amounts of oxygen are available.

Oxygen

23.65   The major commercial production method of elemental oxygen is the fractionation of air. Air is cooled until its components liquefy. Then the air is warmed, and components such as N_2 and Ar are separated, leaving oxygen behind.

23.67   In oxides the oxidation state of O is –2, in peroxides it is –1, and in superoxides it is $-\frac{1}{2}$. Alkali metals and alkaline earth metals have only two possible oxidation states: 0 and +1 for the alkali metals and +2 for alkaline earth metals.

    (a) LiO_2 is a superoxide, since 1(Li ox state) + 2(O ox state) = 0 and O ox state $= -\frac{1}{2}(+1) = -1/2$.

    (b)   CaO is an oxide, since 1(Ca ox state) + 1(O ox state) = 0 and O ox state $= -1(+2) = -2$.

    (c) K_2O_2 is a peroxide, since 2(K ox state) + 2(O ox state) = 0 and O ox state $= -\frac{1}{2}(2(+1)) = -1$.

Sulfur: A Dangerous but Useful Element

23.69   Initially, liquid sulfur becomes less viscous when heated because the S_8 rings have greater thermal energy, which overcomes intermolecular forces. Above 150 °C the rings break and the broken rings entangle one another, causing greater viscosity. Above 180 °C the intermolecular forces weaken and the solution becomes less viscous.

23.71   **Given:** 1.0 L of 5.00×10^{-5} mol L^{-1} $Na_2S\ (aq)$ **Find:** maximum g of metal sulfide that can dissolve

    Other: $K_{sp}\ (PbS) = 9.04 \times 10^{-29}$, $K_{sp}\ (ZnS) = 2 \times 10^{-25}$

    Conceptual Plan: M $Na_2S \rightarrow$ M $S^{2-} \rightarrow$ M metal sulfide $\rightarrow$ mol metal sulfide $\rightarrow$ g metal sulfide

$$Na_2S\ (s) \rightarrow 2\ Na^+(aq) + S^{2-}\ (aq)\ ICE\ Table \qquad M = \frac{mol}{L} \qquad \mathcal{M}$$

    Solution: Since 1 S^{2-} ion is generated for each Na_2S, $[S^{2-}] = 5.00 \times 10^{-5}$ mol L^{-1} Na_2S.

    (a)

$PbS\ (s) \rightleftharpoons$	$Pb^{2+}\ (aq)$	$+\ S^{2-}\ (aq)$
Initial	0.00	5.00×10^{-5}
Change	S	S
Equil	S	$5.00 \times 10^{-5} + S$

$$K_{sp}\ (PbS) = [Pb^{2+}]\ [S^{2-}] = 9.04 \times 10^{-29} = S\ (5.00 \times 10^{-5} + S)$$

    Since $S \ll 5.00 \times 10^{-5}$, $9.04 \times 10^{-29} = S\ (5.00 \times 10^{-5})$, and $S = 1.81 \times 10^{-24}$ mol L^{-1}. (Note that the assumption that S was very small was good.) Since there is 1.0 L of solution, we can dissolve at most 1.8×10^{-24} moles of PbS then $1.8 \times 10^{-24}\ \overline{mol\ PbS} \times \dfrac{239.3\ g\ PbS}{1\ \overline{mol\ PbS}} = 4.3 \times 10^{-22}$ g PbS.

(b)

$$ZnS\ (s) \rightleftharpoons Zn^{2+}\ (aq) + S^{2-}\ (aq)$$

Initial	0.00	5.00×10^{-5}
Change	S	S
Equil	S	$5.00 \times 10^{-5} + S$

$K_{sp}\ (ZnS) = [Zn^{2+}]\ [S^{2-}] = 2 \times 10^{-25} = S\ (5.00 \times 10^{-5} + S)$

Since $S << 5.00 \times 10^{-5}$, $2 \times 10^{-25} = S\ (5.00 \times 10^{-5})$, and $S = 4 \times 10^{-21}$ mol L^{-1}. (Note that the assumption that S was very small was good.) Since there is 1.0 L of solution, we can dissolve at most 4×10^{-21} moles of ZnS then

4×10^{-21} mol ZnS $\times \dfrac{97.45\ g\ ZnS}{1\ mol\ ZnS} = 4 \times 10^{-19}$ g ZnS.

Check: The units (g) are correct. The magnitude of the answer makes physical sense because the solubility constants are so small. The amount of PbS that can dissolve is less than the amount of ZnS because the solubility constant is much smaller.

23.73 **Given:** iron pyrite (FeS$_2$) roasted generating S$_2$ (g), 5.5 kg iron pyrite **Find:** balanced reaction and $V\ S_2$ at STP
Conceptual Plan: Write the reaction then kg FeS$_2 \rightarrow$ g FeS$_2 \rightarrow$ mol FeS$_2 \rightarrow$ mol S$_2 \rightarrow V\ S_2$.

$$\dfrac{1000\ g}{1\ kg} \qquad \dfrac{1\ mol\ FeS_2}{119.99\ g\ FeS_2} \qquad \dfrac{1\ mol\ S_2}{2\ mol\ FeS_2} \qquad \dfrac{22.70\ L\ S_2}{1\ mol\ S_2}$$

Solution: $2\ FeS_2\ (s) \xrightarrow{heat} 2\ FeS\ (s) + S_2\ (g)$, then

5.5 kg FeS$_2 \times \dfrac{1000\ g\ FeS_2}{1\ kg\ FeS_2} \times \dfrac{1\ mol\ FeS_2}{119.99\ g\ FeS_2} \times \dfrac{1\ mol\ S_2}{2\ mol\ FeS_2} \times \dfrac{22.70\ L\ S_2}{1\ mol\ S_2} = 520$ L S$_2$

Check: The units (L) are correct. The magnitude of the answer makes physical sense because there is much more than a mole of iron pyrite, so the volume of gas is many times 23 L.

Halogens

23.75 $3\ Cl_2\ (g) + CS_2\ (g) \xrightarrow{catalyst} S_2Cl_2\ (s) + CCl_4\ (g)$. Cl is being reduced and S is being oxidized.

Cumulative Problems

23.77 **Given:** lignite coal 1 mol%S and bituminous coal 5 mol%S, 1.00×10^2 kg coal
Find: g H$_2$SO$_4$ produced
Conceptual Plan: Table 23.3 composition $\rightarrow \mathcal{M}$ then

$$\mathcal{M} = \dfrac{(mol\%C)(12.01\ g\ mol^{-1}) + (mol\%H)(1.008\ g\ mol^{-1}) + (mol\%O)(16.00\ g\ mol^{-1}) + (mol\%S)(32.07\ g\ mol^{-1})}{100\%}$$

kg coal $\rightarrow$ g coal $\rightarrow$ mol coal $\rightarrow$ mol S $\rightarrow$ mol H$_2$SO$_4 \rightarrow$ g H$_2$SO$_4$

$$\dfrac{1000\ g}{1\ kg} \qquad \mathcal{M} \qquad \dfrac{1\ or\ 5\ mol\ S}{100\ mol\ coal} \quad \dfrac{1\ mol\ H_2SO_4}{1\ mol\ S} \qquad \dfrac{98.07\ g\ H_2SO_4}{1\ mol\ H_2SO_4}$$

Solution: Lignite:

$\mathcal{M} = \dfrac{(mol\%C)(12.01\ g\ mol^{-1}) + (mol\%H)(1.008\ g\ mol^{-1}) + (mol\%O)(16.00\ g\ mol^{-1}) + (mol\%S)(32.07\ g\ mol^{-1})}{100\%}$

$= \dfrac{(71\ mol\%C)(12.01\ g\ mol^{-1}) + (4\ mol\%H)(1.008\ g\ mol^{-1}) + (23\ mol\%O)(16.00\ g\ mol^{-1}) + (1\ mol\%S)(32.07\ g\ mol^{-1})}{100\%}$

$= 12.56812$ g mol^{-1}

1.00×10^2 kg coal $\times \dfrac{1000\ g\ coal}{1\ kg\ coal} \times \dfrac{1\ mol\ coal}{12.56812\ g\ coal} \times \dfrac{1\ mol\ S}{100\ mol\ coal} \times \dfrac{1\ mol\ H_2SO_4}{1\ mol\ S} \times \dfrac{98.09\ g\ H_2SO_4}{1\ mol\ H_2SO_4}$

$= 7.805 \times 10^3$ g H$_2$SO$_4 = 8$ kg H$_2$SO$_4$

Bituminous:

$\mathcal{M} = \dfrac{(mol\%C)(12.01\ g\ mol^{-1}) + (mol\%H)(1.008\ g\ mol^{-1}) + (mol\%O)(16.00\ g\ mol^{-1}) + (mol\%S)(32.07\ g\ mol^{-1})}{100\%}$

$= \dfrac{(80\ mol\%C)(12.01\ g\ mol^{-1}) + (6\ mol\%H)(1.008\ g\ mol^{-1}) + (8\ mol\%O)(16.00\ g\ mol^{-1}) + (5\ mol\%S)(32.07\ g\ mol^{-1})}{100\%}$

$= 12.55198$ g mol^{-1}

$$1.00 \times 10^2 \text{ kg coal} \times \frac{1000 \text{ g coal}}{1 \text{ kg coal}} \times \frac{1 \text{ mol coal}}{12.55198 \text{ g coal}} \times \frac{5 \text{ mol S}}{100 \text{ mol coal}} \times \frac{1 \text{ mol H}_2\text{SO}_4}{1 \text{ mol S}} \times \frac{98.09 \text{ g H}_2\text{SO}_4}{1 \text{ mol H}_2\text{SO}_4}$$

$$= 3.9074 \times 10^4 \text{ g H}_2\text{SO}_4 = 40 \text{ kg H}_2\text{SO}_4$$

Check: The units (kg and kg) are correct. The magnitude of the answer makes physical sense because sulfuric acid is heavier than sulfur and it more than balances out the sulfur content in the coal. Bituminous coal has a higher percentage of S than lignite coal.

23.79   The strength of an acid is determined by the strength of the bond of the H to the rest of the molecule—the weaker the bond, the stronger the acid. Since Cl is more electronegative than I, it pulls density away from the O more than I does, and so the O cannot interact with the H as strongly.

23.81   **Given:** HCl versus X = (a) Cl_2, (b) HF, and (c) HI **Find:** ratio of effusion rates HCl / X
Conceptual Plan: $\mathcal{M}(\text{HCl})$, $\mathcal{M}(\text{X}) \rightarrow$ **Rate (HCl) / Rate (X)**

$$\frac{\text{Rate (HCl)}}{\text{Rate (X)}} = \sqrt{\frac{\mathcal{M}(\text{X})}{\mathcal{M}(\text{HCl})}}$$

Solution: HCl: $\mathcal{M} = \dfrac{36.46 \text{ g}}{1 \text{ mol}} \times \dfrac{1 \text{ kg}}{1000 \text{ g}} = 0.03646 \text{ kg mol}^{-1}$

(a) Cl_2: $\mathcal{M} = \dfrac{70.90 \text{ g}}{1 \text{ mol}} \times \dfrac{1 \text{ kg}}{1000 \text{ g}} = 0.07090 \text{ kg mol}^{-1}$,

$$\frac{\text{Rate (HCl)}}{\text{Rate (Cl}_2)} = \sqrt{\frac{\mathcal{M}(\text{Cl}_2)}{\mathcal{M}(\text{HCl})}} = \sqrt{\frac{0.07090 \text{ kg mol}^{-1}}{0.03646 \text{ kg mol}^{-1}}} = 1.394.$$

(b)   HF: $\mathcal{M} = \dfrac{20.01 \text{ g}}{1 \text{ mol}} \times \dfrac{1 \text{ kg}}{1000 \text{ g}} = 0.02001 \text{ kg mol}^{-1}$,

$$\frac{\text{Rate (HCl)}}{\text{Rate (HF)}} = \sqrt{\frac{\mathcal{M}(\text{HF})}{\mathcal{M}(\text{HCl})}} = \sqrt{\frac{0.02001 \text{ kg mol}^{-1}}{0.03646 \text{ kg mol}^{-1}}} = 0.7408.$$

(c)   HI: $\mathcal{M} = \dfrac{127.91 \text{ g}}{1 \text{ mol}} \times \dfrac{1 \text{ kg}}{1000 \text{ g}} = 0.12791 \text{ kg mol}^{-1}$,

$$\frac{\text{Rate (HCl)}}{\text{Rate (HI)}} = \sqrt{\frac{\mathcal{M}(\text{HI})}{\mathcal{M}(\text{HCl})}} = \sqrt{\frac{0.12791 \text{ kg mol}^{-1}}{0.03646 \text{ kg mol}^{-1}}} = 1.873.$$

Check: The units (none) are correct. The magnitudes of the answers make sense; the heavier molecules have the lower effusion rate (because they move slower).

23.83   Sodium peroxide is Na_2O_2, so the reaction is $4 \text{ Na}_2\text{O}_2 (s) + 3 \text{ Fe} (s) \rightarrow 4 \text{ Na}_2\text{O} (s) + \text{Fe}_3\text{O}_4 (s)$. Note that the oxidation state of O is decreasing from –1 to –2, needing eight electrons and the oxidation state of Fe is increasing from 0 to + 8/3, generating eight moles of electrons for three moles of Fe.

23.85   **Given:** O_2^+, O_2, O_2^-, O_2^{2-} and MO Theory **Find:** explain bond lengths and state, which are diamagnetic
Conceptual Plan: Use the diagram from Chapter 10 and fill it with the appropriate number of electrons to determine bond order and note if they are diamagnetic.
Solution:
O_2^+ has 11 valence electrons (6 for each oxygen atom minus 1 for the positive charge) in $n = 2$ shell and so its

MO configuration is $\sigma_{2s}^2, \sigma_{2s}^{*2}, \sigma_{2p}^2, \pi_{2p}^4, \pi_{2p}^{*1}$, the bond order $= \dfrac{\text{bonding electrons} - \text{antibonding electrons}}{2}$

$= \dfrac{8 - 3}{2} = +2.5$ and it is paramagnetic (unpaired electron).

O_2 has 12 valence electrons (6 for each oxygen atom) in $n = 2$ shell and so its MO configuration is $\sigma_{2s}^2, \sigma_{2s}^{*2},$

$\sigma_{2p}^2, \pi_{2p}^4, \pi_{2p}^{*2}$, the bond order $= \dfrac{\text{bonding electrons} - \text{antibonding electrons}}{2} = \dfrac{8 - 4}{2} = +2$ and it is diamagnetic.

O_2^- has 13 valence electrons (6 for each oxygen atom plus 1 for the negative charge) in $n = 2$ shell and so its

MO configuration is $\sigma_{2s}^2, \sigma_{2s}^{*2}, \sigma_{2p}^2, \pi_{2p}^4, \pi_{2p}^{*3}$, the bond order $= \dfrac{\text{bonding electrons} - \text{antibonding electrons}}{2}$

$= \dfrac{8 - 5}{2} = +1.5$ and it is paramagnetic (unpaired electron).

O_2^{2-} has 14 valence electrons (6 for each oxygen atom plus 2 for the 2- charge) in $n = 2$ shell and so its MO

configuration is $\sigma_{2s}^2, \sigma_{2s}^{*2}, \sigma_{2p}^2, \pi_{2p}^4, \pi_{2p}^{*4}$, the bond order $= \dfrac{\text{bonding electrons} - \text{antibonding electrons}}{2}$

$= \dfrac{8 - 6}{2} = +1$ and it is diamagnetic (all paired electrons).

The bond order is decreasing because the electrons are being added to an antibonding orbital. As expected, the higher the bond order, the shorter the bond.

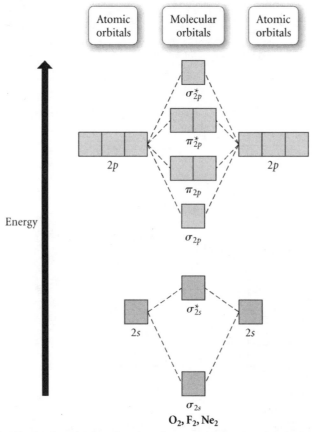

O_2, F_2, Ne_2

Check: The higher the bond order, the more electron orbital overlap and the shorter and stronger the bond. Molecular oxygen is paramagnetic and because of the number of π_{2p} and π_{2p}^* orbitals, many configurations are paramagnetic.

23.87 **Given:** 1.0 mol C; C(diamond) $(s) \rightarrow$ C (g) **Find:** $\Delta_r H^\circ$
Conceptual Plan: Consider the structure of diamond in Figure 23.14 to determine the number of bonds on each C atom. Write the reaction. Then $\Delta_r H^\circ = \sum n_p \Delta_f H^\circ \text{(products)} - \sum n_r \Delta_f H^\circ \text{(reactants)}$ and using C—C bond energy in Table 9.1 calculate the energy of breaking the number of moles of bonds calculated earlier in this problem.
Solution: Since each carbon in the diamond structure has four bonds and there are two carbons involved in each bond, a total of 2.0 moles of C—C bonds are broken to generate 1.0 moles of C (g).
C(diamond) $(s) \rightarrow$ C (g)

Reactant/Product	$\Delta_f H^\circ$ (kJ mol^{-1} from Appendix IIB)
C (s)	1.88
C (g)	716.7

Be sure to pull data for the correct formula and phase.

$$\Delta_r H° = \sum n_p \Delta_f H°(\text{products}) - \sum n_r \Delta_f H°(\text{reactants})$$
$$= [1(\Delta_f H°(\text{C }(g)))] - [1(\Delta_f H°(\text{C(diamond) }(s)))]$$
$$= [1(716.7 \text{ kJ})] - [1(1.88 \text{ kJ})]$$
$$= 714.8 \text{ kJ mol}^{-1}$$

Since the C—C bond energy in Table 9.1 is 347 kJ mol^{-1}, 2.0 ~~mol C≡C bonds~~ $\times \dfrac{347 \text{ kJ}}{1 ~~\text{mol C≡C bond}~~}$

= 690 kJ. The C—C bond strength in Table 9.1 is an average bond strength for a wide variety of structures. This value, calculated from the bond energy, is lower than the heat of the reaction calculated above because it doesn't include van der Waals attractions between C atoms not directly bonded to each other.

23.89 **Given:** $SO_2 (g) + H_2O (l) \rightarrow H_2SO_3 (aq)$; generation of 1 mol L^{-1} SO$_2$ (aq) **Find:** $\Delta_r H°$
Conceptual Plan: Write the reaction. Then $\Delta_r H° = \sum n_p \Delta_f H°(\text{products}) - \sum n_r \Delta_f H°(\text{reactants})$.
Solution: $SO_2 (g) + H_2O (l) \rightarrow H_2SO_3 (aq)$ Assume that the reaction goes to completion.

Reactant/Product	$\Delta_f H°$(kJ mol^{-1} from Appendix IIB)
H$_2$SO$_3$ (aq)	− 633
SO$_2$ (g)	− 296.8
H$_2$O (l)	− 285.8

Be sure to pull data for the correct formula and phase.
$$\Delta_r H° = \sum n_p \Delta_f H°(\text{products}) - \sum n_r \Delta_f H°(\text{reactants})$$
$$= [1(\Delta_f H°(\text{H}_2\text{SO}_3 (aq)))] - [1(\Delta_f H°(\text{SO}_2 (g))) + 1(\Delta_f H°(\text{H}_2\text{O} (l)))]$$
$$= [1(-633 \text{ kJ})] - [1(-296.8 \text{ kJ}) + 1(-285.8 \text{ kJ})]$$
$$= [-633 \text{ kJ}] - [-582.6 \text{ kJ}]$$
$$= -50 \text{ kJ}$$

Check: The units (kJ) are correct. The magnitude of the answer (–50 kJ) makes sense because all of the heats of formation are negative and so most of the heats cancel each other out.

Challenge Problems

23.91 **Given:** iron oxides + CO (g) → Fe (s) + CO$_2$ (g), where (a) Fe$_3$O$_4$, (b) FeO, and (c) Fe$_2$O$_3$ **Find:** $\Delta_r H°$
Conceptual Plan: Write the reaction. Then $\Delta_r H° = \sum n_p \Delta_f H°(\text{products}) - \sum n_r \Delta_f H°(\text{reactants})$.
Solution: (a) $Fe_3O_4 (s) + 4 CO (g) \rightarrow 3 Fe (s) + 4 CO_2 (g)$

Reactant/Product	$\Delta_f H°$(kJ mol^{-1} from Appendix IIB)
Fe$_3$O$_4$ (s)	− 1118.4
CO (g)	− 110.5
Fe (s)	0.0
CO$_2$ (g)	− 393.5

Be sure to pull data for the correct formula and phase.
$$\Delta_r H° = \sum n_p \Delta_f H°(\text{products}) - \sum n_r \Delta_f H°(\text{reactants})$$
$$= [3(\Delta_f H°(\text{Fe} (s))) + 4(\Delta_f H°(\text{CO}_2 (g)))] - [1(\Delta_f H°(\text{Fe}_3\text{O}_4 (s))) + 4(\Delta_f H°(\text{CO} (g)))]$$
$$= [3(0.0 \text{ kJ}) + 4(-393.5 \text{ kJ})] - [1(-1118.4 \text{ kJ}) + 4(-110.5 \text{ kJ})]$$
$$= [-1574.0 \text{ kJ}] - [-1560.4 \text{ kJ}]$$
$$= -13.6 \text{ kJ}$$

(b) $FeO (s) + CO (g) \rightarrow Fe (s) + CO_2 (g)$

Reactant/Product	$\Delta_f H°$(kJ mol^{-1} from Appendix IIB)
FeO (s)	− 272.0
CO (g)	− 110.5
Fe (s)	0.0
CO$_2$ (g)	− 393.5

Be sure to pull data for the correct formula and phase.

$$\Delta_r H° = \sum n_p \Delta_f H°(\text{products}) - \sum n_r \Delta_f H°(\text{reactants})$$
$$= [1(\Delta_f H°(\text{Fe} (s))) + 1(\Delta_f H°(CO_2 (g)))] - [1(\Delta_f H°(\text{FeO} (s))) + 1(\Delta_f H°(CO (g)))]$$
$$= [1(0.0 \text{ kJ}) + 1(-393.5 \text{ kJ})] - [1(-272.0 \text{ kJ}) + 1(-110.5 \text{ kJ})]$$
$$= [-393.5 \text{ kJ}] - [-382.5 \text{ kJ}]$$
$$= -11.0 \text{ kJ}$$

(c) $Fe_2O_3 (s) + 3 CO (g) \rightarrow 2 Fe (s) + 3 CO_2 (g)$

Reactant/Product	$\Delta_f H°$(kJ mol^{-1} from Appendix IIB)
$Fe_2O_3 (s)$	− 824.2
$CO (g)$	− 110.5
$Fe (s)$	0.0
$CO_2 (g)$	− 393.5

Be sure to pull data for the correct formula and phase.

$$\Delta_r H° = \sum n_p \Delta_f H°(\text{products}) - \sum n_r \Delta_f H°(\text{reactants})$$
$$= [2(\Delta_f H°(\text{Fe} (s))) + 3(\Delta_f H°(CO_2 (g)))] - [1(\Delta_f H°(Fe_2O_3 (s))) + 3(\Delta_f H°(CO (g)))]$$
$$= [2(0.0 \text{ kJ}) + 3(-393.5 \text{ kJ})] - [1(-824.2 \text{ kJ}) + 3(-110.5 \text{ kJ})]$$
$$= [-1180.5 \text{ kJ}] - [-1155.7 \text{ kJ}]$$
$$= -24.8 \text{ kJ}.$$

Fe_2O_3 is the most exothermic because it has the highest oxidation state and therefore oxidizes the most CO per mole of Fe.

Check: The units (kJ) are correct. The answers are negative, which means that the reactions are exothermic.

23.93   (a)   This is a linear molecule. Each C has four valence electrons and each O has six valence electrons, so C_3O_2 has 3(4) + 2(6) = 24 valence electrons. All of the bonds are double bonds so the Lewis structure is $\ddot{O}\!=\!C\!=\!C\!=\!C\!=\!\ddot{O}$

(b)   Since each carbon has two electron groups and needs to make two pi bonds, the hybridization is *sp*.

(c) $\ddot{O}\!=\!C\!=\!C\!=\!C\!=\!\ddot{O} + 2 H\!-\!\ddot{O}\!-\!H \rightarrow$ H−O−C(=O)−C(H)(H)−C(=O)−O−H. The reaction involves breaking 2 C=C bonds and 2 O—H bonds, then making 2 C—H bonds, 2 C—C bonds, and 2 C—O bonds. The number of C=O bonds broken and created are equal, so they can be disregarded. Four O—H bonds are broken and two formed, so two of the bonds may be cancelled out on the reactants side, and all may be cancelled out on the products side. Thus, using values from Table 9.1,

$$\Delta_r H° = \sum \Delta H (\text{bonds broken}) - \sum \Delta H (\text{bonds formed})$$
$$= [2(611 \text{ kJ}) + 2(464 \text{ kJ})] + [-2(414 \text{ kJ}) - 2(347 \text{ kJ}) - 2(360 \text{ kJ})] = [2150 \text{ kJ}] + [-2242 \text{ kJ}]$$
$$= -92 \text{ kJ}$$

23.95   (a)   Since the overall reaction is the sum of the two reactions, K_b for the overall reaction will be the product of the two individual K_bs, so $K_b = K_{b_1} \cdot K_{b_2} = (8.5 \times 10^{-7})(8.9 \times 10^{-16}) = 7.6 \times 10^{-22}$.

(b) $K_{a_1} = K_w / K_{b_1} = (1.0 \times 10^{-14})/(8.5 \times 10^{-7}) = 1.2 \times 10^{-8}$.

(c)   **Given:** pH = 8.5, 0.012 mol N_2H_4 in 1.0 L **Find:** $[N_2H_4]$, $[N_2H_5^+]$, and $[N_2H_6^{2+}]$
Other: $K_{b_1} = 8.5 \times 10^{-7}$, $K_{b_2} = 8.9 \times 10^{-16}$
Conceptual Plan: pH $\rightarrow$ pOH $\rightarrow$ [OH$^-$] and mol N_2H_4, L $\rightarrow$ mol L^{-1} N_2H_4 then
$$\text{pH + pOH = 14} \quad \text{pOH} = -\log[\text{OH}^-] \qquad M = \frac{\text{mol}}{\text{L}}$$
[OH$^-$], $[N_2H_4]_0$ $\rightarrow$ $[N_2H_4]$, $[N_2H_5^+]$ and [OH$^-$], $[N_2H_4]_0$ $\rightarrow$ $[N_2H_5^+]$, $[N_2H_6^{2+}]$
          ICE Table   *ICE Table*

Solution: pH + pOH = 14 so pOH = 14 − pH = 14.0 − 8.5 = 5.5 then $[OH^-] = 10^{-pOH} = 10^{-5.5}$ = 3.16 x 10^{-6}. There are 0.012 mol N_2H_4 in 1.0 L so $[N_2H_4]_0$ = 0.012 mol L^{-1}. Set up first ICE Table.

$$N_2H_4\ (aq)\ +\ H_2O\ (l)\ \rightleftharpoons\ N_2H_5^+(aq)\ +\ OH^-(aq)$$

	N_2H_4		$N_2H_5^+$	OH^-
Initial	0.0012		0.00	3.16 x 10^{-6}
Change	−x		x	
Equil	0.0012 − x		x	3.16 x 10^{-6}

Since the solution is buffered, [OH⁻] will be unchanged.

$$K_{b_1} = \frac{[N_2H_5^+][OH^-]}{[N_2H_4]} = \frac{(x)(3.16 \times 10^{-6})}{0.012 - x} = 8.5 \times 10^{-7}.\ \text{Solve for } x.$$

$(x)(3.16 \times 10^{-6}) = 8.5 \times 10^{-7}(0.012 - x) \rightarrow$
$x\ (3.16 \times 10^{-6} + 8.5 \times 10^{-7}) = 1.02 \times 10^{-8} \rightarrow x = 0.0025$ so $[N_2H_4]$ = 0.012 mol L^{-1} − 0.0025 mol L^{-1} = 0.010 mol L^{-1} and $[N_2H_5^+]$ = 0.0025 mol L^{-1}. Then set up second ICE Chart.

$$N_2H_5^+\ (aq)\ +\ H_2O\ (l)\ \rightleftharpoons\ N_2H_6^{2+}(aq)\ +\ OH^-(aq)$$

	$N_2H_5^+$		$N_2H_6^{2+}$	OH^-
Initial	0.0025		0.00	3.16 x 10^{-6}
Change	−x		x	
Equil	0.0025 − x		x	3.16 x 10^{-6}

Since the solution is buffered, [OH⁻] will be unchanged.

$$K_{b_2} = \frac{[N_2H_6^{2+}][OH^-]}{[N_2H_5^+]} = \frac{(x)(3.16 \times 10^{-6})}{0.0025 - x} = 8.9 \times 10^{-16}\ \text{Since } x \ll 0.0025\ \text{then}$$

$\dfrac{(x)(3.16 \times 10^{-6})}{0.0025} = 8.9 \times 10^{-16}$ and $x = 7.0 \times 10^{-13}$ mol $L^{-1} = [N_2H_6^{2+}]$. (Note that the assumption that x was very small was good.)

Check: The units (mol L^{-1}) are correct. The magnitude of the answer makes physical sense because only a portion of the hydrazine dissociates and the product concentrations get smaller and smaller.

23.97   The acid is H−O−N = N−O−H and the base is [H−N−N⁺=O ↔ H−N−N⁺−O⁻ with H, O⁻ and H, O]. The acid is weaker than nitrous acid because of electron donation by resonance in contributing structures such as H−N⁺=O ↔ H−N⁺−O⁻ (with O⁻ and O) stabilize nitrous acid. $H_2N_2O_2$ is a weaker acid than nitrous acid because it has fewer O atoms per N atom. The base is weaker than ammonia because of electron withdrawal by the electronegative nitro group.

Conceptual Problems

23.99   The triple bond in nitrogen is much stronger than the double bond in oxygen, so it is much harder to break. This makes it less likely that the bond in nitrogen will be broken.

23.101   Sodium dihydrogen phosphate (NaH_2PO_4) can act as a weak base or a weak acid. A buffer can be made by mixing it with either Na_2HPO_4 or with Na_3PO_4, depending on the desired pH of the buffer solution.

23.103   F is extremely small and highly electronegative, so there is a huge driving force to fill the octet by adding an electron, giving a −1 oxidation state. Other halogens have access to the d orbitals, which allows for more hybridization and oxidation state options.

23.105 SO_3 cannot be a reducing agent, because the oxidation state of S is + 6, the highest possible oxidation state for S. Reducing agents need to be able to be oxidized. SO_2 can be a reducing agent or an oxidizing agent, because the oxidation state of S is + 4.

24 Metals and Metallurgy

Review Questions

24.1   The source of vanadium in some crude oil is the very animals from which the oil was formed. It appears that some extinct animals used vanadium for oxygen transport.

24.3   Even though over 2% of the Earth's mass is nickel, most of this is in the Earth's core, and because the core is so far from the surface, it is not accessible.

24.5   The mineral is the phase that contains the desired element(s) and the gangue is the undesired material. These are generally separated by physical methods.

24.7   Sodium cyanide has been traditionally used to leach gold by forming a soluble gold complex ($Au(CN)_2^-$). The problem with this process is that cyanide is very toxic and this process has often resulted in the contamination of streams and rivers. New alternatives, such as using thiosulfate ions ($S_2O_3^-$), are being investigated to replace it.

24.9   The body-centred cubic unit cell consists of a cube with one atom at each corner and one atom in the very centre of the cube. In the body-centred unit cell, the atoms do not touch along each edge of the cube, but rather touch along the diagonal line that runs from one corner, through the middle of the cube, to the opposite corner. The body-centred unit cell contains two atoms per unit cell because the centre atom is not shared with any other neighbouring cells. The coordination number of the body-centred cubic unit cell is eight, and the packing efficiency is 68%. The face-centred cubic unit cell is characterized by a cube with one atom at each corner and one atom in the centre of each cube face. In the face-centred unit cell (like the body-centred unit cell), the atoms do not touch along each edge of the cube. Instead, the atoms touch along the face diagonal. The face-centred unit cell contains four atoms per unit cell because the centre atoms on each of the six faces are shared between two unit cells. So there are $\frac{1}{2}$ x 6 = 3 face-centred atoms plus $\frac{1}{8}$ x 8 = 1 corner atom for a total of four atoms per unit cell. The coordination number of the face-centred cubic unit cell is 12 and its packing efficiency is 74%. In the face-centred structure, any one atom strongly interacts with more atoms than in either the simple cubic unit cell or the body-centred cubic unit cell.

24.11   Copper was one of the first metals used because it can be found in nature in its elemental form.

24.13   Bronze is an alloy of copper and tin. Brass is an alloy of copper and zinc.

Problems by Topic

The General Properties and Natural Distribution of Metals

24.15   Metals are opaque, are good conductors of heat and electricity, and are ductile and malleable, meaning that they can be drawn into wires and flattened into sheets.

24.17   Aluminum, iron, calcium, magnesium, sodium, and potassium are all over 1% of the Earth's crust, as shown in Figure 23.2.

24.19   Hematite (Fe_2O_3) and magnetite (Fe_3O_4) are important mineral sources of iron. Cinnabar (HgS) is an important mineral source of mercury. Vanadinite [$Pb_5(VO_4)_3Cl$] and carnotite [$K_2(UO_2)_2(VO_4)_2 \cdot 3H_2O$] are important mineral sources of vanadium. Columbite [$Fe(NbO_3)_2$] is an important mineral source of niobium.

Metallurgical Processes

24.21 $MgCO_3\ (s)\ \xrightarrow{\text{heat}}\ MgO\ (s) + CO_2\ (g)$ and $Mg(OH)_2\ (s)\ \xrightarrow{\text{heat}}\ MgO\ (s) + H_2O\ (g)$.

24.23   A flux is a material that will react with the gangue to form a substance with a low melting point. MgO is the flux in this reaction.

24.25   Hydrometallurgy is used to separate metals from ores by selectively dissolving the metal in a solution, filtering out impurities, and then reducing the metal to its elemental form.

24.27   The Bayer process is a hydrometallurgical process by which Al_2O_3 is selectively dissolved, leaving other oxides as solids. The soluble form of aluminum is $Al(OH)_4^-$.

24.29   Sponge powdered iron contains many small holes in the iron particles due to escaping of oxygen when the iron is reduced. Water-atomized powdered iron has much more smooth and dense particles as the powder is formed from molten iron.

Metal Structures and Alloys

24.31   (a)   When one-half of the V atoms are replaced by Cr atoms, the composition will be 50% Cr by moles and 50% V by moles. To get percent by mass assume 100 moles of alloy, so

$$\text{percent by mass Cr} = \frac{(\text{mol\% Cr})(52.00\ \text{g mol}^{-1})}{(\text{mol\% Cr})(52.00\ \text{g mol}^{-1}) + (\text{mol\% V})(50.94\ \text{g mol}^{-1})} \times 100\%$$

$$= \frac{(50\ \text{mol})(52.00\ \text{g mol}^{-1})}{(50\ \text{mol})(52.00\ \text{g mol}^{-1}) + (50\ \text{mol})(50.94\ \text{g mol}^{-1})} \times 100\% = 50.5\%\ \text{Cr by mass}$$

and percent by mass V = 100.0% − 50.5% = 49.5% V.

(b)   When one-fourth of the V atoms are replaced by Fe atoms, the composition will be 25% Fe by moles and 75% V by moles. To get percent by mass assume 100 moles of alloy, so

$$\text{percent by mass Fe} = \frac{(\text{mol\% Fe})(55.85\ \text{g mol}^{-1})}{(\text{mol\% Fe})(55.85\ \text{g mol}^{-1}) + (\text{mol\% V})(50.94\ \text{g mol}^{-1})} \times 100\%$$

$$= \frac{(25\ \text{mol})(55.85\ \text{g mol}^{-1})}{(25\ \text{mol})(55.85\ \text{g mol}^{-1}) + (75\ \text{mol})(50.94\ \text{g mol}^{-1})} \times 100\% = 26.8\%\ \text{Fe by mass}$$

and percent by mass V = 100.0% − 26.8% = 73.2% V.

(c)   When one-fourth of the V atoms are replaced by Cr atoms and one-fourth of the V atoms are replaced by Fe atoms, the composition will be 25% Cr by moles, 25% Fe by moles, and 50% V by moles. To get percent by mass assume 100 moles of alloy, so

percent by mass Cr

$$= \frac{(\text{mol\% Cr})(52.00\ \text{g mol}^{-1})}{(\text{mol\% Cr})(52.00\ \text{g mol}^{-1}) + (\text{mol\% Fe})(55.85\ \text{g mol}^{-1}) + (\text{mol\% V})(50.94\ \text{g mol}^{-1})} \times 100\%$$

$$= \frac{(25\ \text{mol})(52.00\ \text{g mol}^{-1})}{(25\ \text{mol})(52.00\ \text{g mol}^{-1}) + (25\ \text{mol})(55.85\ \text{g mol}^{-1}) + (50\ \text{mol})(50.94\ \text{g mol}^{-1})} \times 100\%$$

$$= 24.8\%\ \text{Cr by mass},$$

percent by mass Fe

$$= \frac{(\text{mol\% Fe})(55.85\ \text{g mol}^{-1})}{(\text{mol\% Cr})(52.00\ \text{g mol}^{-1}) + (\text{mol\% Fe})(55.85\ \text{g mol}^{-1}) + (\text{mol\% V})(50.94\ \text{g mol}^{-1})} \times 100\%$$

$$= \frac{(25 \; \text{mol})(55.85 \; \text{g mol}^{-1})}{(25 \; \text{mol})(52.00 \; \text{g mol}^{-1}) + (25 \; \text{mol})(55.85 \; \text{g mol}^{-1}) + (50 \; \text{mol})(50.94 \; \text{g mol}^{-1})} \times 100\%$$

= 26.6% Fe by mass
and percent by mass V = 100.0% − (24.8% + 26.6%) = 48.6% V.

24.33   Cr and Fe both form body-centred cubic structures. In addition, they are very close together in the periodic table (atomic numbers 24 and 26, respectively), so their respective atomic radii are probably close enough to form an alloy.

24.35   This phase diagram indicates that the solid and liquid phases are completely miscible. The composition is determined by determining the x-axis value at the point.
A: solid with 20% Cr and 100% − 20% = 80% Fe.
B: liquid with 50% Cr and 100% − 50% = 50% Fe.

24.37   This phase diagram indicates that the solid and liquid phases are not completely miscible. Single phases only exist between the pure component and the red line. The composition will be a mixture of the two structures. The composition of the two phases is determined by moving to the left and right until reaching the red lines. The x-axis value is the composition of that structure. According to the lever rule, the phase that is closer to the point is the dominant phase.
A: solid with 20% Co and 100% − 20% = 80% Cu overall composition. One phase will be the copper structure with ∼ 4% Co, and the other phase will be the Co structure with ∼ 7% Cu. According to the lever rule there will be more of the Cu structure, since point A is closer to the Cu structure phase boundary line.
B: solid single phase with Co structure and composition of 90% Co and 100% − 90% = 10% Cu.

24.39   Since C (77 pm) is much smaller than Fe (126 pm), it will fill interstitial holes. Since Mn (130 pm) and Si (118 pm) are close to the same size as Fe, they will substitute for Fe in the lattice.

24.41   (a)   Since there are the same number of octahedral holes as there are metal atoms in a closest packed structure and half are filled with N, the formula is Mo_2N.

         (b)   Since there are twice as many tetrahedral holes as there are metal atoms, and all of the tetrahedral holes are occupied, the formula is CrH_2.

Sources, Properties, and Products of Some of the 3d Transition Metals

24.43   (a)   Zn, since sphalerite is ZnS.

         (b)   Cu, since malachite is $Cu_2(OH)_2CO_3$.

         (c)   Mn, since hausmannite is Mn_3O_4.

24.45   **Given:** calcination of rhodochrosite ($MnCO_3$) **Find:** heat of reaction
Conceptual Plan: Write the reaction. Then $\Delta_r H° = \sum n_p \Delta_f H°\textbf{(products)} - \sum n_r \Delta_f H°\textbf{(reactants)}.$
Solution: $MnCO_3 (s) + \frac{1}{2} O_2 (g) \xrightarrow{\text{heat}} MnO_2 (s) + CO_2 (g)$

Reactant/Product	$\Delta_f H°$(kJ mol^{-1} from Appendix IIB)
$MnCO_3 (s)$	−894.1
$O_2 (g)$	0.0
$MnO_2 (s)$	−520.0
$CO_2 (g)$	−393.5

Be sure to pull data for the correct formula and phase.

$\Delta_r H° = \sum n_p \Delta_f H°\text{(products)} - \sum n_r \Delta_f H°\text{(reactants)}$

$= [1(\Delta_f H°(MnO_2 (s))) + 1(\Delta_f H°(CO_2 (g)))] - [1(\Delta_f H°(MnCO_3 (s))) + 1/2(\Delta_f H°(O_2 (g)))]$

$= [1(−520.0 \; \text{kJ}) + 1(−393.5 \; \text{kJ})] - [1(−894.1 \; \text{kJ}) + 1/2(0.0 \; \text{kJ})]$

$= [−913.5 \; \text{kJ}] - [−894.1 \; \text{kJ}]$

$= −19.4 \; \text{kJ}$

Check: The units (kJ) are correct. The answer is negative, which means that the reaction is exothermic.

24.47   When Cr is added to steel it reacts with oxygen in steel to prevent it from rusting. A Cr steel alloy would be used in any situation where a steel might be easily oxidized, such as when it comes in contact with water.

24.49   Rutile = TiO_2: The composition will be 33.3% Ti by moles and 66.7% O by moles. To get percent by mass assume 100 moles of atoms, so

percent by mass Ti $= \dfrac{(\text{mol\% Ti})(47.87 \text{ g mol}^{-1})}{(\text{mol\% Ti})(47.87 \text{ g mol}^{-1}) + (\text{mol\% O})(16.00 \text{ g mol}^{-1})}$ x 100%

$= \dfrac{(33.3 \text{ mol})(47.87 \text{ g mol}^{-1})}{(33.3 \text{ mol})(47.87 \text{ g mol}^{-1}) + (66.7 \text{ mol})(16.00 \text{ g mol}^{-1})}$ x 100% = 59.9% Ti by mass.

Ilmenite = $FeTiO_3$: The composition will be 20.0% Ti by moles, 20.0% Fe by moles, and 60.0% O by moles. To get percent by mass assume 100 moles of atoms, so
percent by mass Ti

$= \dfrac{(\text{mol\% Ti})(47.87 \text{ g mol}^{-1})}{(\text{mol\% Ti})(47.87 \text{ g mol}^{-1}) + (\text{mol\% Fe})(55.85 \text{ g mol}^{-1}) + (\text{mol\% O})(16.00 \text{ g mol}^{-1})}$ x 100%

$= \dfrac{(20.0 \text{ mol})(47.87 \text{ g mol}^{-1})}{(20.0 \text{ mol})(47.87 \text{ g mol}^{-1}) + (20.0 \text{ mol})(55.85 \text{ g mol}^{-1}) + (60.0 \text{ mol})(16.00 \text{ g mol}^{-1})}$ x 100%

= 31.6% Ti by mass.

24.51   Titanium must be arc-melted in an inert atmosphere because the high temperature and flow of electrons would cause the metal to oxidize in a normal atmosphere.

24.53 TiO_2 is the most important industrial product of titanium and is often used as a pigment in white paint.

24.55   The Bayer process is a hydrometallurgical process used to separate the bauxite ($Al_2O_3 \cdot n\ H_2O$) from the iron and silicon oxide with which it is usually found. In this process, the bauxite is digested with a hot, concentrated, aqueous NaOH solution under high pressure. The basic aluminum solution is separated from the oxide solids, and then the aluminum oxide is precipitated out of the solution by neutralizing it. Calcination of the precipitate at temperatures greater than 1000 °C yields anhydrous alumina (Al_2O_3). Electrolysis is then used to reduce the aluminum to metal.

24.57   Carbaloy steel contains cobalt and tungsten.

Cumulative Problems

24.59   **Given:** ilmenite, 2.0×10^4 kg of ore, 0.051% by mass ilmenite, 87% Fe recovery and 63% Ti recovery
         Find: g Fe and Ti recovered
         Conceptual Plan: ilmenite = $FeTiO_3$ kg ore $\to$ g ore $\to$ g ilmenite $\to$ g Ti possible $\to$ g Ti recovered
         $\dfrac{1000 \text{ g}}{1 \text{ kg}} \quad \dfrac{0.051 \text{ g ilmenite}}{100 \text{ g ore}} \quad \dfrac{1(47.87) \text{ g Ti}}{151.72 \text{ g ilmenite}} \quad \dfrac{63 \text{ g Ti recovered}}{100 \text{ g Ti}}$

and g ilmenite $\to$ g Fe possible $\to$ g Fe recovered
$\dfrac{1(55.85) \text{ g Fe}}{151.72 \text{ g ilmenite}} \quad \dfrac{87 \text{ g Fe recovered}}{100 \text{ g Fe}}$

Solution: $2.0 \times 10^4 \text{ kg ore} \times \dfrac{1000 \text{ g ore}}{1 \text{ kg ore}} \times \dfrac{0.051 \text{ g ilmenite}}{100 \text{ g ore}} = 1.02 \times 10^4$ g ilmenite then

$1.02 \times 10^4 \text{ g ilmenite} \times \dfrac{1(47.87) \text{ g Ti}}{151.72 \text{ g ilmenite}} \times \dfrac{63 \text{ g Ti recovered}}{100 \text{ g Ti}} = 2.0 \times 10^3$ g Ti recovered = 2.0 kg Ti recovered

and $1.02 \times 10^4 \text{ g ilmenite} \times \dfrac{1(55.85) \text{ g Fe}}{151.72 \text{ g ilmenite}} \times \dfrac{87 \text{ g Fe recovered}}{100 \text{ g Fe}}$

= 3.3×10^3 g Fe recovered = 3.3 kg Fe recovered.

Check: The units (g) are correct. The magnitudes of the answers make physical sense because there is very little mineral in the ore. The amount of Fe recovered is higher than Ti recovered because the atomic weight of Fe and the percent recovery of Fe are both higher than Ti.

24.61   Four atoms surround a tetrahedral hole and six atoms surround an octahedral hole. The octahedral hole is larger because it is surrounded by a greater number of atoms.

24.63   Manganese has one more *d* electron orbital available for bonding than chromium.

24.65   Ferromagnetic atoms, like paramagnetic atoms, have unpaired electrons. However, in ferromagnetic atoms, these electrons align with their spin oriented in the same direction, resulting in a permanent magnetic field.

24.67   The nuclear charge of the last three is relatively high because of the lanthanide series in which the $4f$ subshell falls between them and the other six metals of the group.

Challenge Problems

24.69   **Given:** cylinder, $h = 5.62$ cm after pressing, $r = 4.00$ cm; d (before pressing) = 2.41 g mL^{-1}, d (after pressing) = 6.85 g mL^{-1}, d (solid iron) = 7.78 g mL^{-1}
Find: (a) original height, (b) theoretical height if $d = d$ (solid iron), and (c) % voids in component

Conceptual Plan: (a) Since $d = \dfrac{m}{V}$, $V = \pi\, r^2\, h$, **and the mass of iron is constant, this means that** $d \propto \dfrac{1}{h}$.
So d **(before pressing),** d **(after pressing),** h **(after pressing)** $\rightarrow$ h **(before pressing)**
$$\frac{d_1}{d_2} = \frac{h_2}{h_1}$$

(b) d **(solid iron),** d **(after pressing),** h **(after pressing)** $\rightarrow$ h **(solid iron)**
$$\frac{d_1}{d_2} = \frac{h_2}{h_1}$$

(c)   **Assume** d **(air) = 0, so** d **(solid iron),** d **(after pressing)** $\rightarrow$ **% voids**
$$\% \text{ voids} = \frac{d_{\text{after pressing}} - d_{\text{solid iron}}}{d_{\text{after pressing}}} \times 100\%$$

Solution: (a) $\dfrac{d_1}{d_2} = \dfrac{h_2}{h_1}$ Rearrange to solve for h_2. $h_2 = \dfrac{d_1 h_1}{d_2} = \dfrac{6.85 \ \text{g mL}^{-1} \times 5.62 \ \text{cm}}{2.41 \ \text{g mL}^{-1}} = 16.0$ cm.

(b) $\dfrac{d_1}{d_2} = \dfrac{h_2}{h_1}$ Rearrange to solve for h_2. $h_2 = \dfrac{d_1 h_1}{d_2} = \dfrac{6.85 \ \text{g mL}^{-1} \times 5.62 \ \text{cm}}{7.78 \ \text{g mL}^{-1}} = 4.95$ cm.

(c) $\% \text{ voids} = \dfrac{d_{\text{solid iron}} - d_{\text{after pressing}}}{d_{\text{after pressing}}} \times 100\% = \dfrac{7.78 \ \text{g mL}^{-1} - 6.85 \ \text{g mL}^{-1}}{6.85 \ \text{g mL}^{-1}} \times 100\% = 14\%$

Check: The units (cm, cm, and %) are correct. The higher the density, the smaller the height, so the answer for (a) is greater than 5.62 cm and the answer for (b) is smaller than 5.62 cm. Since the density of the pressed component is close to the density of solid iron, the volume of voids is low.

24.71   Since there are the same number of octahedral holes as there are metal atoms in a closest packed structure and twice as many tetrahedral holes as there are metal atoms there are a total of three holes for each metal atom and the formula would be LaH_3. Since the formula is $LaH_{2.76}$, the percentage of holes filled is $(2.76/3) \times 100\% = 92.0\%$ filled.

24.73   Using the data in Appendix II and $K_f\ ([Cu(CN)_2]^-) = 1.0 \times 10^{24}$:

#1	$[Ag(CN)_2]^-\ (aq) \rightleftharpoons Ag^+(aq) + 2CN^-(aq)$		$K_1 = 1/K_f = 1/\ 1.0 \times 10^{21} = 1.0 \times 10^{-21}$
#2	$Ag^+(aq) + e^- \rightleftharpoons Ag\ (s)$		$E^\circ = 0.80$ V $= E^\circ_{\text{cathode}}$
#3	$Cu\ (s) \rightleftharpoons Cu^+(aq) + e^-$		$E^\circ = 0.52$ V $= E^\circ_{\text{anode}}$
#4	$Cu^+(aq) + 2CN^-(aq) \rightleftharpoons [Cu(CN)_2]^-\ (aq)$		$K_f = 1.0 \times 10^{24}$

$\overline{[Ag(CN)_2]^-\ (aq) + Cu\ (s) \rightleftharpoons [Cu(CN)_2]^-\ (aq)\ +\ Ag\ (s)}$

If we add reactions #2 and #3 we get that $E^\circ_{\text{cell}} = E^\circ_{\text{cathode}} - E^\circ_{\text{anode}} = 0.80$ V $- 0.52$ V $= 0.28$ V and $n = 1$ so

$\Delta_r G^\circ = -n\, F\, E^\circ_{\text{cell}} = -1\ \text{mol e}^- \times \dfrac{96\ 485\ \text{C}}{\text{mol e}^-} \times 0.28\ \text{V} = -96\ 485\ \text{C} \times 0.28\ \dfrac{\text{J}}{\text{C}} = -2.70158 \times 10^4\ \text{J}$

$= -27.0158\ \text{kJ}$

and $T = 298$ K then $\Delta_r G^\circ = -R\, T \ln K$. Rearrange to solve for K.

$$K_{2+3} = e^{\frac{-\Delta_r G^\circ}{RT}} = e^{\frac{-(-2.70158 \times 10^4 \text{ J})}{\left(8.314\frac{\text{J}}{\text{K} \cdot \text{mol}}\right)(298 \text{ K})}} = e^{10.9742} = 5.43989 \times 10^4$$

The overall reaction is now the sum of the four reactions, the overall reaction $K = K_1 \times K_{2+3} \times K_f =$ $(1.0 \times 10^{-21}) \times (5.43989 \times 10^4) \times (1.0 \times 10^{24}) = \underline{5}.43989 \times 10^7 = 5.4 \times 10^7$.

24.75   First, roast to form the oxide.
$$4 \text{ CoAsS } (s) + 9 \text{ O}_2 (g) \rightarrow 4 \text{ CoO } (s) + 4 \text{ SO}_2 (g) + \text{As}_4\text{O}_6 (s)$$
Then reduce the oxide with coke.
$$\text{CoO } (s) + \text{C } (s) \rightarrow \text{Co } (s) + \text{CO } (g)$$
The oxides of arsenic are relatively volatile and can be separated. But they are poisonous. In addition, SO_2 and CO are also poisonous.

Conceptual Problems

24.77   Gold and silver are found in their elemental forms because of their low reactivity. Sodium and calcium are Group 1 and Group 2 metals, respectively, and are highly reactive as they readily lose their valence electrons to obtain octets.

25 Transition Metals and Coordination Compounds

Review Questions

25.1   A transition metal atom forms an ion by losing the ns^2 (valence shell) electrons first.

25.3   The +2 oxidation state is common because most of the transition metals have two electrons occupying the ns orbitals. These electrons are lost first by the metal.

25.5   A ligand can be considered a Lewis base because it donates a pair of electrons. The transition metal ion would be a Lewis acid because it accepts the pair of electrons.

25.7   *Cis–trans* isomerism occurs in square planar complexes of the general formula MA_2B_2 or octahedral complexes of the general formula MA_4B_2.

25.9   Because of the spatial arrangement of the ligands, the normally degenerate d orbitals are split in energy. The difference between these split d orbitals is the crystal field splitting energy. The magnitude of the splitting depends on the particular complex. In strong-field complexes the splitting is large, and in weak-field complexes the splitting is small. The magnitude of the crystal field splitting depends in large part on the ligands attached to the central metal ion.

25.11 Zn^{2+} has a filled d subshell, while Cu^{2+} has nine d electrons. Since Zn^{2+} has this filled d subshell, the colour of the compounds will be white. Cu^{2+} has an incomplete d subshell, so different ligands will cause a different crystal field splitting and the compounds will have colour.

25.13   Almost all tetrahedral complexes are high-spin because of reduced ligand–metal interactions. The d orbitals in a tetrahedral complex are interacting with only four ligands, as opposed to six in the octahedral complex, so the value of Δ is generally smaller.

Problems by Topic

Properties of Transition Metals

25.15   Identify the noble gas that precedes the element and put it in square brackets.
         Determine the outer principal quantum level for the s orbital. Subtract one to obtain the quantum level for the d orbital. If the element is in the third or fourth transition series, include $(n - 2)f$ electrons in the configuration.
         Count across the row to see how many electrons are in the neutral atom.
         For an ion, remove the required number of electrons, first from the s and then from the d orbitals.

(a)   Ni; Ni^{2+}
         The noble gas that precedes Ni is Ar. Ni is in the fourth period so the orbitals we use are $4s$ and $3d$ and Ni has 10 more electrons than Ar.
         Ni $[Ar]4s^2 3d^8$
         Ni will lose electrons from the $4s$ and then from the $3d$.
         Ni^{2+} $[Ar]4s^0 3d^8$

(b)   Mn; Mn^{4+}
The noble gas that precedes Mn is Ar. Mn is in the fourth period so the orbitals we use are $4s$ and $3d$ and Mn has seven more electrons than Ar.
Mn $[Ar]4s^23d^5$
Mn will lose electrons from the $4s$ and then from the $3d$.
Mn^{4+} $[Ar]4s^03d^3$

(c)   Y; Y^+
The noble gas that precedes Y is Kr. Y is in the fifth period so the orbitals we use are $5s$ and $4d$ and Y has three more electrons than Kr.
Y $[Kr]5s^24d^1$
Y will lose electrons from the $5s$ and then from the $4d$.
Y^+ $[Kr]5s^14d^1$

(d)   Ta; Ta^{2+}
The noble gas that precedes Ta is Xe. Ta is in the sixth period so the orbitals we use are $6s$, $5d$, and $4f$ and Ta has 19 more electrons than Xe.
Ta $[Xe]6s^24f^{14}5d^3$
Ta will lose electrons from the $6s$ and then from the $5d$.
Ta^{2+} $[Xe]6s^04f^{14}5d^3$

25.17   (a)   V   Highest oxidation state = +5. V = $[Ar]4s^23d^3$. Since V is to the left of Mn, it can lose all of the $4s$ and $3d$ electrons, so the highest oxidation state is +5.

(b)   Re   Highest oxidation state = +7. Re = $[Xe]6s^24f^{14}5d^5$. Re can lose all of the $6s$ and $5d$ electrons, so the highest oxidation state is +7.

(c)   Pd   Highest oxidation state = +4. Pd = $[Kr]4d^{10}$. Pd can lose four electrons from the $4d$ orbitals, so the highest oxidation state is +4.

Coordination Compounds

25.19   (a) $[Cr(H_2O)_6]^{3+}$ H_2O is neutral, so Cr has an oxidation state of +3. There are six H_2O molecules attached to each Cr, so the coordination number is 6.

(b) $[Co(NH_3)_3Cl_3]^-$ NH_3 is neutral and Cl has charge of –1. The sum of the oxidation state of Co and the charge of chloride ion = 1–. $x + (3(-1)) = -1$, $x = +2$, therefore the oxidation state of Co is +2. The three NH_3 molecules and the three Cl^- ions are bound directly to the Co atom, therefore the coordination number is 6.

(c) $[Cu(CN)_4]^{2-}$ CN has a charge of –1. The sum of the oxidation state of Cu and the charge of the cyanide ion = 2–. $x + (4(-1)) = 2-$, $x = +2$, therefore, the oxidation state of Cu is +2. The four cyanide ions are directly bound to the Cu atom, therefore, the coordination number is 4.

(d) $[Ag(NH_3)_2]^+$ NH_3 is neutral, so Ag has an oxidation number of +1. There are two NH_3 molecules attached to each Ag atom, so the coordination number is 2.

25.21   (a) $[Cr(H_2O)_6]^{3+}$ is hexaaquachromium(III) ion.
$[Cr(H_2O)_6]^{3+}$ is a complex cation.
Name the ligand: H_2O is aqua.
Name the metal ion: Cr^{3+} is chromium(III).
Name the complex ion by adding the prefixes to indicate the number of each ligand, followed by the name of each ligand and the name of the metal ion: hexaaquachromium(III) ion.

(b) $[Cu(CN)_4]^{2-}$ is tetracyanocuprate(II) ion.
$[Cu(CN)_4]^{2-}$ is a complex anion.
Name the ligand: CN^- is cyano.
Name the metal ion: Cu^{2+} is cuprate(II) because the complex is an anion.
Name the complex ion by adding the prefix to indicate the number of each ligand, followed by the name of each ligand and the name of the metal ion: tetracyanocuprate(II) ion.

(c) $[Fe(NH_3)_5Br]SO_4$ is pentaamminebromoiron(III) sulfate.
        $[Fe(NH_3)_5Br]^{2+}$ is a complex cation, $SO_4{}^{2-}$ is sulfate.
        Name the ligands in alphabetical order: NH_3 is ammine, Br^- is bromo.
        Name the metal cation: Fe^{3+} is iron(III).
        Name the complex ion by adding prefixes to indicate the number of each ligand, followed by the name of the ligand and the name of the metal ion: pentaamminebromoiron(III).
        Name the compound by writing the name of the cation before the anion. The only space is between the ion names: pentaamminebromoiron(III) sulfate.

(d) $[Co(H_2O)_4(NH_3)(OH)]Cl_2$ is amminetetraaquahydroxocobalt(III) chloride.
        $[Co(H_2O)_4(NH_3)(OH)]^{2+}$ is a complex cation, Cl^- is chloride.
        Name the ligands in alphabetical order: NH_3 is ammine, H_2O is aqua, OH^- is hydroxo.
        Name the metal cation: Co^{3+} is cobalt(III).
        Name the complex ion by adding prefixes to indicate the number of each ligand, followed by the name of the ligand and the metal ion: amminetetraaquahydroxocobalt(III).
        Name the compound by writing the name of the cation before the anion. The only space is between the ion names: amminetetraaquahydroxocobalt(III) chloride.

25.23   (a)   Hexamminechromium(III) is a complex ion with Cr^{3+} metal ion and six NH_3 ligands. $[Cr(NH_3)_6]^{3+}$

        (b)   Potassium hexacyanoferrate(III) is a compound with three K^+ cations and a complex anion with Fe^{3+} metal ion and six CN^- ligands. $K_3[Fe(CN)_6]$

        (c)   Ethylenediaminedithiocyanatocopper(II) is a compound with a Cu^{2+} metal ion, an ethylenediamine ligand, and two SCN^- ligands. $[Cu(en)(SCN)_2]$

        (d)   Tetraaquaplatinum(II) hexachloroplatinate(IV) is a complex compound with a complex cation that contains a Pt^{2+} metal ion, four H_2O ligands, and a complex anion that contains a Pt^{4+} metal ion and six Cl^- ligands. $[Pt(H_2O)_4][PtCl_6]$

25.25   (a) $[Co(NH_3)_3(CN)_3]$ is triamminetricyanocobalt(III).

        (b)   Since ethylenediamine is a bidentate ligand, you need three to have a coordination number of 6. $[Cr(en)_3]^{3+}$ is tris(ethylenediamine)chromium(III) ion.

Structure and Isomerism

25.27   In linkage isomers, the ligand coordinates to the metal in different ways.

pentaamminenitromanganese(III) ion   pentaamminenitritomanganese(III) ion

25.29   Coordination isomers occur when a coordinated ligand exchanges places with the uncoordinated counterion.
        $[Fe(H_2O)_5Cl]Cl \cdot H_2O$ pentaaquachloroiron(II) chloride monohydrate
        $[Fe(H_2O)_4Cl_2] \cdot 2H_2O$ tetraaquadichloroiron(II) dihydrate

25.31   Stereoisomers result when the ligands bonded to the metal have a different spatial arrangement.

        (a)   No, an octahedral complex has to have at least two different ligands to exhibit stereoisomerism.

        (b)   Yes, there will be *cis–trans* isomers.

(c)   Yes, there will be *fac–mer* isomers.

(d)   No, a square planar complex has to have at least two different ligands to exhibit stereoisomerism.

(e)   Yes, there will be *cis–trans* isomers.

25.33   (a)   Square planar [NiWXYZ]$^{2+}$ would have three geometric isomers.

(b)   Tetrahedral [ZnWXYZ]$^{2+}$ would have two enantiomeric stereoisomers.

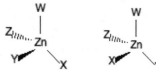

25.35   (a)   [Cr(CO)$_3$(NH$_3$)$_3$]$^{3+}$ has a coordination number of 6 and is octahedral. There will be *fac* and *mer* isomers and no optical isomers because rotation of the mirror images are superimposable upon each other.

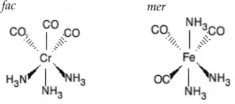

(b)   [Pd(CO)$_2$(H$_2$O)Cl]$^+$ has a coordination number of 4, and is a d^8 complex so it is square planar. There will be *cis* and *trans* isomers. There will be no optical isomers because rotation of the mirror images are superimposable upon each other.

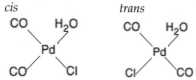

25.37   [Cr(NH$_3$)$_2$(ox)$_2$]$^-$ has a coordination number of 6 and is octahedral. There will be *cis* and *trans* isomers. The *cis* isomer has a mirror image that is nonsuperimposable.

trans   *cis*

Bonding in Coordination Compounds

25.39   (a)   Zn^{2+} d^{10} (b) Fe^{3+} d^5 high-spin   low-spin

(c) V^{3+} d^2 (d) Co^{2+} d^7 high-spin

25.41   **Given:** $[CrCl_6]^{3-}$ $\lambda = 735$ nm absorbance maximum   **Find:** crystal field energy
Conceptual Plan: $\lambda \rightarrow \Delta$ (J) $\rightarrow$ J ion^{-1} $\rightarrow$ kJ mol^{-1}

$$\Delta = \frac{hc}{\lambda} \quad \frac{6.022 \times 10^{23} \text{ ions}}{1 \text{ mol}} \quad \frac{1 \text{ kJ}}{1000 \text{ J}}$$

Solution: $\dfrac{\left(6.626 \times 10^{-34} \text{ J} \cdot \text{s}\right)\left(3.00 \times 10^8 \dfrac{\text{m}}{\text{s}}\right)}{(735 \text{ nm})\left(\dfrac{1 \times 10^{-9} \text{ m}}{1 \text{ nm}}\right)} = 2.704 \times 10^{-19} \text{ J ion}^{-1}$

$2.704 \times 10^{-19} \dfrac{\text{J}}{\text{ion}} \times \dfrac{6.022 \times 10^{23} \text{ ions}}{1 \text{ mol}} \times \dfrac{1 \text{ kJ}}{1000 \text{ J}} = 163 \text{ kJ mol}^{-1}$

Check: Cl is a weak-field ligand and would be expected to have a relatively small Δ, which is consistent with a value of 163 kJ mol^{-1}.

25.43   The crystal field ligand strength would be $CN^- > NH_3 > F^-$. The smaller the wavelength, the larger the energy and the greater the crystal field splitting that would be observed. So $[Co(CN)_6]^{3-}$ would have a smaller wavelength than $[Co(NH_3)_6]^{3+}$, which would have a smaller wavelength than $[CoF_6]^{3-}$.
So: $[Co(CN)_6]^{3-} = 290$ nm, which absorbs in the UV and would have a colourless solution.
    $[Co(NH_3)_6]^{3+} = 440$ nm, which absorbs in the blue and would have an orange solution.
    $[CoF_6]^{3-} = 770$ nm, which absorbs in the red and would have a green solution.

25.45 Mn^{2+} is d^5 and there are five unpaired electrons, so the crystal field splitting energy, Δ, is small compared to the energy to pair the electrons. Therefore, NH_3 induces a weak field with Mn^{2+}.

25.47   (a) $[RhCl_6]^{3-}$ Rh^{3+} d^6 Cl^- is a weak-field ligand, so the value of Δ will be small. This gives four unpaired electrons.

    (b) $[Co(OH)_6]^{4-}$ Co^{2+} d^7 OH^- is a weak-field ligand, so the value of Δ will be small. This gives three unpaired electrons.

    (c)   *cis*-$[Fe(en)(NO_2)_2]^+$ Fe^{3+} d^5 en and NO_2^- are strong-field ligands, so the value of Δ will be large. This gives one unpaired electron.

25.49 $[CoCl_4]^{2-}$ Co^{2+} is d^7, Cl^- is a weak-field ligand, so the value of Δ will be small and there will be three unpaired electrons. The crystal field splitting for a tetrahedral structure is as follows:

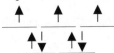

Applications of Coordination Compounds

25.51   Hemoglobin, cytochrome c, and chlorophyll all contain a porphyrin ligand.

25.53   Oxyhemoglobin is low-spin and a red colour. Since it is low-spin, the crystal field splitting energy must be large. The red colour means that the complex absorbs in the green region (~500 nm), which also indicates a large crystal field splitting energy, therefore, O_2 must be a strong-field ligand.

Deoxyhemoglobin is high-spin and a blue colour. Since it is high-spin, the crystal field splitting energy must be small. The blue colour means that the complex absorbs in the orange region (~600 nm), which also indicates a small crystal field splitting energy. Both of these are consistent with H_2O as a weak-field ligand.

Cumulative Problems

25.55   (a)   Cr $[Ar]4s^1 3d^5$ (b)   Cu $[Ar]4s^1 3d^{10}$
              Cr^+ $[Ar]4s^0 3d^5$ Cu^+ $[Ar]4s^0 3d^{10}$
              Cr^{2+} $[Ar]4s^0 3d^4$ Cu^{2+} $[Ar]4s^0 3d^9$
              Cr^{3+} $[Ar]4s^0 3d^3$

25.57   (a)

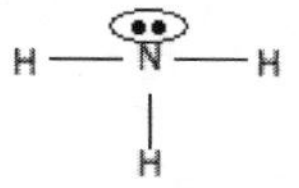

$$H - N - H$$
$$|$$
$$H$$

(b)

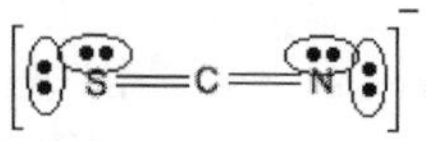

$$\left[:S = C = N: \right]^-$$ ligand can bond from either end.

(c)

$$\overset{O}{\underset{H \quad H}{}}$$

25.59   An octahedral complex has six ligands.
        $MA_2B_2C_2$ will have *cis–trans* isomers: all *cis*; A *trans*, B,C *cis*; B *trans*, A,C *cis*; C *trans*, A,B *cis*; all *trans*
        MAB_2C_3 will have *fac–mer* isomers
        MA_2B_3C will have *fac–mer* isomers
        MAB_3C_2 will have *fac–mer* isomers
        MA_3B_2C will have *fac–mer* isomers
        MA_2BC_3 will have *fac–mer* isomers
        MA_3BC_2 will have *fac–mer* isomers
        $MABC_4$ will have AB *cis–trans isomers*
        MAB_4C will have AC *cis–trans isomers*
        MA_4BC will have BC *cis–trans isomers*

25.61 $[Fe(ox)_3]^{3-}$ Fe^{3+} d^5 coordination number = 6, octahedral, structure has a nonsuperimposable mirror image.

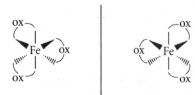

25.63 $[Mn(CN)_6]^{3-}$ Mn^{3+} d^4 has a coordination number of 6 and is octahedral. CN^- is a strong-field ligand and will cause a large crystal field splitting energy so the ion is low-spin.

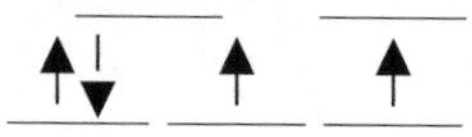

The ion will be paramagnetic with two unpaired electrons.

25.65   There are five stereoisomers, one of which is chiral.

1.   2. 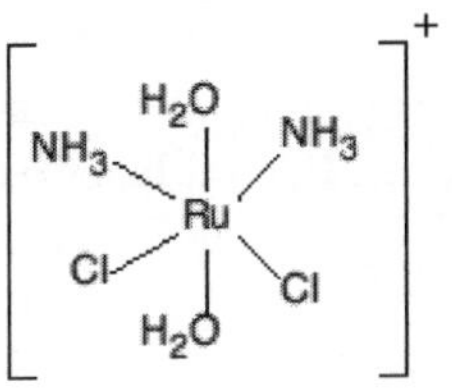   3.

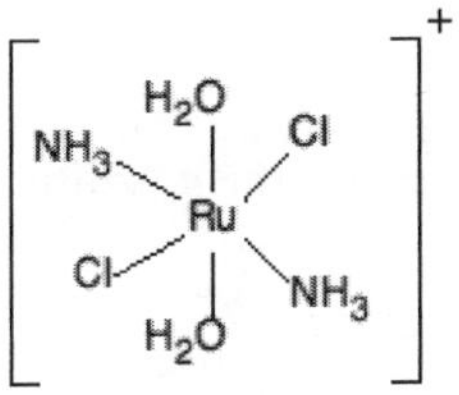

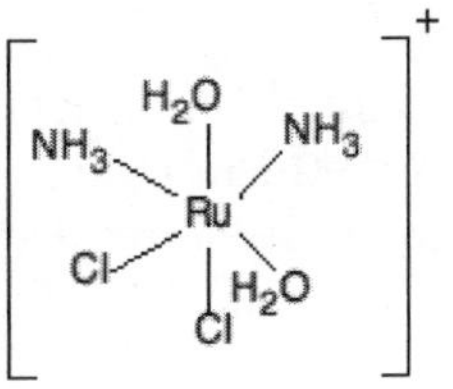

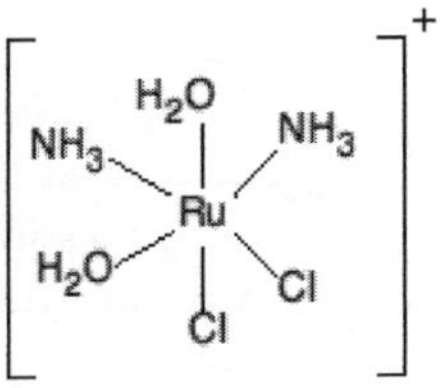

chiral

4.   5.

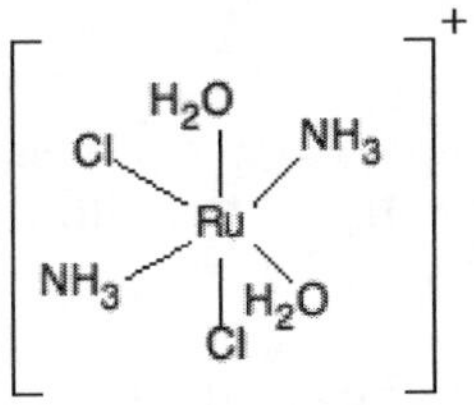

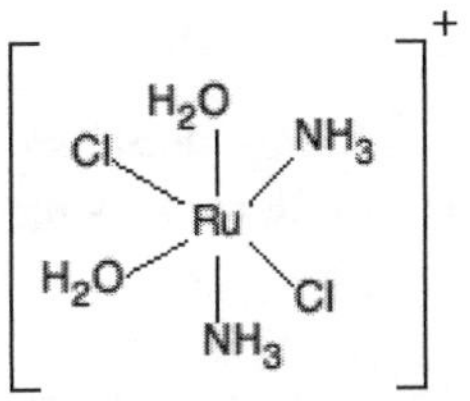

Challenge Problems

25.67   **Given:** 46.7% Pt, 17.0% Cl, 14.8% P, 17.2% C, 4.34% H; **Find:** formula, structures, and names for both compounds
Conceptual Plan: % composition $\rightarrow$ pseudoformula $\rightarrow$ formula

$$n = \frac{g}{molar\ mass} \qquad \text{divide by smallest}$$

Solution: $46.7\ \text{g Pt} \times \dfrac{1\ \text{mol Pt}}{195.08\ \text{g Pt}} = 0.23936\ \text{mol Pt}$ $17.0\ \text{g Cl} \times \dfrac{1\ \text{mol Cl}}{35.45\ \text{g Cl}} = 0.47955\ \text{mol Cl}$

$14.8\ \text{g P} \times \dfrac{1\ \text{mol P}}{30.97\ \text{g P}} = 0.47788\ \text{mol P}$ $17.2\ \text{g C} \times \dfrac{1\ \text{mol C}}{12.01\ \text{g C}} = 1.4321\ \text{mol C}$

$4.34\ \text{g H} \times \dfrac{1\ \text{mol H}}{1.008\ \text{g H}} = 4.3056\ \text{mol H}$

$Pt_{0.23936}Cl_{0.47955}P_{0.47788}C_{1.4321}H_{4.3056}$

$Pt_{\frac{0.23936}{0.23936}}Cl_{\frac{0.47955}{0.23936}}P_{\frac{0.47788}{0.23936}}C_{\frac{1.4321}{0.23936}}H_{\frac{4.3056}{0.23936}}$

$PtCl_2P_2C_6H_{18}$

$[Pt(P(CH_3)_3)_2Cl_2]$

cis-dichlorobis(trimethylphosphine)platinum(II)   *trans*-dichlorobis(trimethylphosphine)platinum(II)

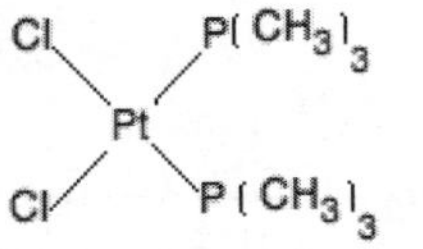

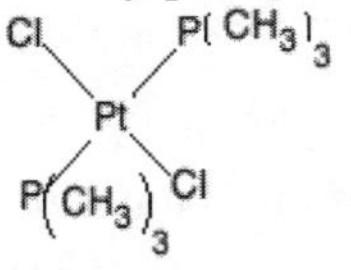

25.69

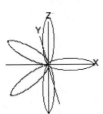

          The trigonal bipyramidal complex ion has lobes along the *x*-axis and between the
x- and *y*-axes and along the *z*-axis. So, the ligands will interact most strongly with z^2 orbital and then with
the $x^2 - y^2$ and the *xy* orbitals and will not interact with the *xz* or the *yz* orbitals. So the crystal field splitting
would look like the following:

$$\overline{}\, z^2$$
$$\overline{}\, x^2 - y^2 \qquad \overline{}\, xy$$
$$\overline{}\, xz \qquad \overline{}\, yz$$

25.71 (a) **Given:** $K_{sp}(NiS) = 3 \times 10^{-16}$ **Find:** solubility in water
Conceptual Plan: Write the reaction, prepare an ICE table, substitute into the equilibrium expression, and solve for S (molar solubility).
Solution: $NiS(s) \rightleftharpoons Ni^{2+}(aq) + S^{2-}(aq)$

I	0.0	0.0
C	S	S
E	S	S

$K_{sp} = [Ni^{2+}][S^{2-}] \quad 3 \times 10^{-16} = S^2$
$S = 1.7 \times 10^{-8} = 2 \times 10^{-8} \text{ mol L}^{-1}$

(b) **Given:** $K_{sp}(NiS) = 3 \times 10^{-16}$ $K_f [Ni(NH_3)_6]^{2+} = 2.0 \times 10^8$ **Find:** solubility in 3.0 mol L^{-1} NH$_3$
Conceptual Plan: Sum the reaction, prepare an ICE table, substitute into the equilibrium expression, and solve for S (molar solubility).
Solution:

Reaction 1: $\qquad\qquad\qquad NiS(s) \rightleftharpoons Ni^{2+}(aq) + S^{2-}(aq) \qquad K_{sp}(NiS) = 3 \times 10^{-16}$
Reaction 2: $Ni^{2+}(aq) + 6\,NH_3(aq) \rightleftharpoons Ni(NH_3)_6{}^{2+}(aq) \qquad K_f = 2.0 \times 10^8$

Reaction 3: $NiS(s) + 6\,NH_3(aq) \rightleftharpoons Ni(NH_3)_6{}^{2+}(aq) + S^{2-}(aq) \quad K = K_{sp}\,K_f = 6.0 \times 10^{-8}$

I	3.0 M	0.0	0.0
C	$-6S$	S	S
E	$3.0 - 6S$	S	S

$K = \dfrac{[Ni(NH_3)_6{}^{2+}][S^2]}{[NH_3]^6} \quad 6.0 \times 10^{-8} = \dfrac{(S)(S)}{(3.0 - 6S)^6}$

Assume S is small compared to 3.0.
$S^2 = 4.37 \times 10^{-5}$
$S = 6.6 \times 10^{-3} \text{ mol L}^{-1}$

(c) NiS is more soluble in ammonia because the formation of the $[Ni(NH_3)_6]^{2+}$ complex ion is highly favourable. The formation removes Ni^{2+} ion from the solution, causing more of the NiS to dissolve.

25.73 If the complexes exhibit lability, there will be exchange of H$_2$O with the halide and some of the halide will be in solution. So, prepare complexes with two different halides (e.g. Cl$^-$ and Br$^-$) so that you have $[MCl_6]^{3-}$ and $[MBr_6]^{3-}$. Place both complexes in the same aqueous solution. If the complexes exhibit lability, then a mixed complex containing both Cl$^-$ and Br$^-$ ligands, $[MCl_xBr_y]^{3-}$, will be formed since Cl$^-$ and Br$^-$ would both be in solution when the ligands were exchanged with H$_2$O. If this mixed complex does not form, then the $[MX_6]^{3-}$ complex does not exhibit lability.

25.75 **Given:** 0.10 mol L^{-1} NaI, Cd(OH)$_2$(s) $K_{sp} = 7.2 \times 10^{-15}$; Cd(I)$_4{}^{2-}$(aq) $K_f = 2 \times 10^6$ **Find:** pH
Conceptual Plan: Combine the solubility product reaction of Cd(OH)$_2$(s) and the formation reaction of Cd(I)$_4{}^{2-}$ and determine the K for the new reaction. Prepare an ICE table and solve for S (molar solubility). Then determine the [OH$^-$], pOH, and pH.
Solution: $\quad Cd(OH)_2(s) \rightleftharpoons Cd^{2+}(aq) + 2\,OH^-(aq) \qquad K_{sp} = 7.2 \times 10^{-15}$
$\qquad\qquad Cd^{2+}(aq) + 4\,I^-(aq) \rightleftharpoons Cd\,I_4{}^{2-}(aq) \qquad K_f = 2 \times 10^6$

$Cd(OH)_2(s) + 4\,I^-(aq) \rightleftharpoons Cd\,I_4{}^{2-}(aq) + 2\,OH^-(aq) \qquad K = 1.44 \times 10^{-8}$

I	0.10 M	0	0
C	$-4S$	S	$2S$
E	$0.10 - 4S$	S	$2S$

$K = 1.44 \times 10^{-8} = \dfrac{[Cd\,I_4{}^{2-}][OH^-]^2}{[I^-]^4} = \dfrac{(S)(2S)^2}{(0.10 - 4S)^4} \qquad$ Assume $S \ll 0.10$.

$1.44 \times 10^{-8} = \dfrac{4S^3}{(0.10)^4}$

$S = 7.11 \times 10^{-5}$; $[OH^-] = 2S = 2(7.11 \times 10^{-5}) = 1.42 \times 10^{-4}$
$pOH = -\log(1.42 \times 10^{-4}) = 3.85 = 3.9 \quad pH = 14.0 - 3.9 = 10.1$

Check: The answer makes sense because the presence of I^- drives the equilibrium for dissociation of $Cd(OH)_2$ to the right, greatly increasing the concentration of OH^- ions.

Conceptual Problems

25.77   M with ligand A forms a green solution. This means that the solution is absorbing red, which has a long wavelength, lower energy, and small Δ.

M with ligand B forms a violet solution. This means that the solution is absorbing yellow, which has a shorter wavelength and higher energy. This would have a larger Δ.

So, ligand B results in the larger Δ.